AMERICAN CONSTITUTIONAL LAW

Rocco J. Tresolini

Late of Lehigh University

Martin Shapiro

University of California, Irvine

AMERICAN CONSTITUTIONAL LAW

THIRD EDITION

THE MACMILLAN COMPANY

COLLIER-MACMILLAN LIMITED   *LONDON*

This book is dedicated to

Spencer D. Parratt,

who taught us the important things.

THE MACMILLAN COMPANY
866 Third Avenue, New York, New York 10022

COLLIER-MACMILLAN CANADA, LTD., Toronto, Ontario

PRINTED IN THE UNITED STATES OF AMERICA

Preface to the Third Edition

PROFESSOR TRESOLINI'S untimely death occurred just as he was beginning work on the third edition of *American Constitutional Law*. He was a distinguished representative of a school of thought somewhat different from my own; the subject matter of constitutional law is one about which reasonable men necessarily differ on nearly every specific issue and perhaps even more on which emphasis and balance of materials are most desirable. In undertaking the task of revision, I have entertained a very strong presumption of correctness for Professor Tresolini's work—the sort of presumption with which students of the Supreme Court are all familiar. Accordingly, not only do the general conception, format, and range of the book remain basically unchanged, but what Professor Tresolini wrote earlier remains unaltered at almost every point. In a few places, however, most notably in the section on interest groups in Chapter 3, I have taken the liberty of adopting compromise language of the sort that probably would have emerged had I enjoyed the good fortune of real collaboration.

The major task of revision, then, has been one of addition: of bringing the book up to date with the rapid development of constitutional law that has occurred under the Warren Court. Twenty-one new cases have been included, unfortunately and inevitably at the cost of some older ones. No essential case has disappeared, however, and great care has been taken to cover the losses by additional comments in the text and by editing the new cases to include discussions of the older ones now omitted.

There are a few major changes in organization. Chapters 7 and 8 of the second edition have been combined because their basic thrust was always the constitutional relationship between Congress and the President rather than the independent powers of each. The treatment of Congressional investigations is now concentrated in Chapter 15, where the later investigation cases such as *Watkins* and *Barenblatt* always appeared. The chapter on freedom of speech has been considerably expanded. A chapter on the right of privacy has been added. Its place, last in the book, in part symbolizes its status as the newest constitutional right. But it also forces the student to review much of the material presented earlier in the book, for the privacy theme runs through many areas of constitutional law.

It remains to make some general comments about courses in constitutional law—or more properly the history of constitutional doctrine. In another place I have indicated my discontent with such courses.[1] Particularly where they are the sole or single required course in law for political science majors, they raise very serious problems. That Professor Tresolini appreciated these problems is, I think, indicated by his inclusion of Chapter 3 as well as a chapter on the administrative process. Indeed, a small irony of his death is that a revisor's deference has probably made the third edition of this book more conservative than it would have been had he lived. My own view is that where a single or required course on law is taught, it should be either a course on the Supreme Court, comparable in scope, method, and approach to those on Congress and the Presidency, or a general course on the judicial or lawmaking process. I would be less than frank if I did not admit now that my coauthorship of this book was undertaken with the long-run intention of shifting its emphasis even further away from a concern for the historical evolution of constitutional doctrine and further toward a concern for the contemporary political role of the Supreme Court, in both the constitutional and nonconstitutional spheres.

In the meantime, and particularly where they are offered alongside courses more oriented to political science, conventional constitutional law courses have a major redeeming virtue—a virtue that should keep them in the catalog longer than many a currently stylish social science title. The necessarily positivistic emphasis of political science, and its concentration on power, interest, conflict, and compromise, is readily vulgarized by undergraduates so that they come to see politics as a cynical struggle for power and a game of "pressure" and "deals." The study of constitutional law presents students with real, and sometimes great, men sincerely confronting the problem of shaping the good life in the good society, and offering reasoned justifications of what they do aimed at persuading other men of good faith of the rightness and

---

[1] *Law and Politics in the Supreme Court* (New York: The Free Press, 1964), pp. 1–6.

justice of their decisions. Thus, it provides an important antidote to cynicism, and an important reminder that much of politics really does consist of men seeking just solutions by reasoning together. In this sense the constitutional law course can be good political science and even better liberal humanistic education.

M. S.

Preface to the Second Edition

THE basic ideas and patterns of the first edition have been followed in this revised and enlarged edition. However, this is more than a mere plate-saving revision. In addition to a thorough updating of the book, a number of important changes in both content and organization have been made which are designed to make the book more useful to both students and teachers. These changes have stemmed largely from my own experience in teaching the first edition and that of a number of colleagues in various institutions throughout the country. The most important changes may be listed as follows:

1. *Elimination and Addition of Cases.* Twelve cases from the first edition have been dropped for a variety of reasons. Some have been superseded by more important recent cases; some contributed little to the student's over-all understanding of American constitutional law; others have been removed simply to make room for some more recent cases in new and emerging areas of constitutional law. At the same time 36 additional cases have been added to bring the total number to well over 100. This has been done for several reasons. First of all, a number of historically significant cases which were only summarized or briefly noted in the first edition have been added because experience has shown that these important cases can be better understood if students have access to the edited opinions. Hence, such great cases as *Cohens* v. *Virginia, Luther* v. *Borden, Dred Scott* v. *Sandford,* and a number

of others are reproduced in this new edition. At the same time the most important recent cases involving such issues as reapportionment, school prayers and Bible reading, Sunday closing laws, and sit-ins have been added. The addition of these cases makes the book much more suitable for two-semester courses in constitutional law; yet the book remains small enough for use in one-semester courses.

2. *More Emphasis on the Political Nature of the Court's Work.* A new introductory chapter (3) has been added to bring to the students' attention some of the most valuable recent insights and findings of the public law fraternity. Such topics as factors in the selection of Supreme Court justices, "influences" on the Court, interest-group activity, and the impact of judicial decisions discussed in Chapter 3 are designed to supplement the more *formal* materials in Chapters 1 and 2. Also, a number of the introductory essays have been reorganized and rewritten to emphasize this where appropriate.

Since constitutional law is essentially a product of constitutional and political conflicts, it is important for the student to see that conflict mirrored in the opinions. Hence, as in the first edition, this book is rich in concurring and dissenting opinions.

3. *Reorganization of the Book.* The book is now divided into three rather than two parts, with a changed order of some chapters. This arrangement better describes what the Court is actually doing and makes possible a better grouping of relevant materials. The materials from several chapters previously standing alone have been incorporated into other chapters. To make them more teachable in the light of newer materials the internal organization of a number of chapters has also been changed.

4. *Miscellaneous Changes.* A number of other changes and additions have been made. Ten new biographical sketches, including those of all the present members of the Court, have been added to Appendix II. *All* new bibliographical materials appear in the footnotes or in the selected reading list, Appendix III. Finally, no stone has been left unturned in the effort to continue to make this a truly teachable book.

In this revision I have, of course, relied heavily on the work of a number of scholars in the field of constitutional law. However, an author has an obligation to do more than bring together the work of others. He himself must try to make some contribution to the field. In the years since the first edition of this book I have been engaged in studying the lives and times of a number of Supreme Court justices and in attempting to analyze some of their most important opinions. Several papers and a small book [*Justice and the Supreme Court* (Philadelphia: J. B. Lippincott, 1963)] have grown out of this work. I hope that the experience has helped enrich this revised edition.

A NOTE OF THANKS

Most important, I wish to express my gratitude to all of those who adopted the book for without them there would be no second edition. Many users of the book as well as others have given encouragement or shared with me their experiences with the first edition. I am particularly grateful to the fol-lowing: Robert Anderson, Utica College; Henry J. Abraham, University of Pennsylvania; Paul C. Bartholomew, University of Notre Dame; Major Julian Bradbury, United States Air Force Academy; the late John Cotton Brown, Cornell College; Robert G. Dixon, Jr., George Washington School of Law; Charles P. Edwards, previously of Westminster College, now with the Depart-ment of State; Donald W. Flaherty, Dickinson College; J. Cullen Ganey, Chief Judge, United States District Court, Eastern District of Pennsylvania; Franz B. Gross, Pennsylvania Military College; D. Joy Humes, Wells College; Father William O'Brien, Georgetown University; John Owens, University of California, Davis; Spencer D. Parratt and Michael O. Sawyer, Syracuse Uni-versity; Richard W. Taylor, Coe College; Robert G. Thompson, San Fran-cisco State College; John C. Vanderzell, Franklin and Marshall College.

A special note of thanks is due Professor Alton D. Kidd of Allegheny College who has shared with me his insights on the work of the Court gained during his periodic stays in Washington as an assistant to Senator Wayne Morse. Special thanks are due also to Professors C. Peter Magrath of Brown University and Lawrence Parkus of Bowdoin College, who suggested a num-ber of changes. Most of their suggestions have been followed in this new edition. Professors John W. Hopkirk and William M. Rolofson of Pennsyl-vania Military College have contributed more than they realize to this revised edition. Over the past several years, Dr. O. B. Conaway, Jr., Dean, Graduate School of Public Affairs, State University of New York, has provided en-couragement and help in various ways.

Grateful acknowledgments are due several of my colleagues at Lehigh: Dr. Glenn J. Christensen, Provost and Vice-President; Dr. Lawrence H. Gipson, Pulitzer prize-winning historian; Dr. George D. Harmon; Professor Ernst B. Schulz; Dean W. Ross Yates. Miss Sandra K. Snellmen typed a number of drafts of the manuscript with her usual skill and patience. Librar-ians at the Biddle Law Library, University of Pennsylvania, Lehigh Univer-sity, and the Library of Congress were always helpful. Two grants from the American Philosophical Society enabled me to thoroughly investigate some aspects of constitutional law which have indirectly enriched this work.

Finally, I am indebted to Robert J. Patterson and David H. Tiffany of The Macmillan Company for their long-standing faith in this work.

R. J. T.

Preface to the
First Edition

THIS book is designed primarily for use by undergraduate and graduate students of American constitutional law. Teachers of American government and American history also may find the materials useful for collateral reading assignments in areas which require more adequate treatment than is normally found in standard textbooks in these fields. Moreover, it is hoped that the book may prove helpful to the nonspecialist who seeks to know more about how the American constitutional system operates.

For two major reasons, no attempt has been made to satisfy the needs of the student in professional law schools. In the first place, the writer claims no competence in determining course requirements for such students. Secondly, the constitutional law course in the majority of American law schools must, of necessity, deal with numerous technical matters which are of little or no utility to the average undergraduate student. The same course in the undergraduate liberal arts curriculum is more broadly conceived and is concerned principally with the important and unique role of the Supreme Court as a policy-making body in the American governmental system. The law school approach may be easily discerned by a perusal of the leading textbooks used by these schools. Although they vary somewhat in emphasis and content, most of these textbooks contain a great number of cases with extended notes of a highly technical nature. Although suitable for law school students, such books do not necessarily provide the undergraduate student with the insight needed to understand the operation of the Supreme Court as a policy-making body. As a matter of fact, the reading of a large number of cases with extended notes may result in confusion rather than enlightenment. It has been this writer's experience and that of a goodly number of his colleagues that a restricted number of carefully selected cases (with concurring and dissenting opinions when needed to point up basic conflicts and problems faced by the Court) is most likely to enhance student understanding of the federal government as it functions within constitutional limitations.

The problem of classification and the selection of cases to be included has been a difficult one, and this writer makes no claim to having found a perfect solution. Enough cases have been included to give the instructor some opportunity for selection. Many of the traditional cases of historical significance requisite for a mature understanding of fundamental doctrines and of the evolution of basic constitutional principles are, of course, included. The writer is also firmly convinced that a comprehension of the major contemporary constitutional problems is essential if the citizen is to deal effectively with the principal issues faced by modern democratic societies now and in future years. To this end the liberal arts course in constitutional law should make a major contribution. Therefore, recent judicial decisions which throw light upon the outstanding constitutional controversies and problems of our time, and which seem to have enduring qualities, have been utilized generously and classified in categories which help to reveal their contemporaneous nature. Civil rights cases have been emphasized particularly, because so much of the important work of the Supreme Court in recent years has been in this area.

The teaching of constitutional law during the past several years has led the writer to certain conclusions concerning content and method of such a course. These conclusions need to be noted briefly in order to justify to both the instructor and student what are considered to be certain unique features of this book.

1. It seems to be assumed by the great majority of writers in this field that the student understands a great deal more about American government than he really does. Even if the student has already completed the average undergraduate course in American government, he has, with few exceptions, either forgotten or missed some important basic concepts which are required for an understanding of the constitutional system. Also, the student usually has a poor grasp of the broad outlines of American constitutional history. As a result, the reading of a large number of Supreme Court decisions, standing by themselves, has little value.

I have tried in this book to provide coordination and historical perspective through the use of introductory essays for each chapter and additional commentary, where necessary, before each case. In addition, Chapters 1 and 2 are designed to provide the student with a broad general review of the historical development and nature of the American constitutional system and to give him specific data relating to such matters as federal court structure and jurisdiction, actual operation of the Supreme Court, methods, and source materials in American constitutional law. These and other materials in Chapters 1 and 2 should make for better understanding of the actual functions of the Court and more intelligent reading of the cases. Although many outstanding essays could have been incorporated for use as introductory materials, the writer has prepared each introductory essay and commentary for the sake of continuity and similarity of style. Of course, I have relied heavily on the well-known scholars in this field in the preparation of these materials.

2. Most writers in this field also assume, wrongly, that liberal arts students are familiar with technical legal terms and that they know how to find the law. Unhappily, most undergraduate students have never been taught these things. To overcome this difficulty, technical legal terms are explained fully when they are first used in the book. In addition, Chapter 2 contains the basic materials on how to find the law.

3. I know of no book designed for the liberal arts course in constitutional law which provides the student with a brief general description of the lives of individual justices. Although it is extremely difficult to know exactly how judges arrive at their decisions, it stands to reason that such matters as the social and economic philosophy of a justice and his personal likes and dislikes play important roles in the shaping of his decisions. Felix Frankfurter stated the problem some years before he himself was appointed to the Court:

> But the words of the Constitution on which . . . solution [of problems facing the Supreme Court] is based are so unrestrained by their intrinsic meaning, or by their history, or by tradition, or by prior decisions, that they leave the individual justice free, if indeed they do not compel him, to gather meaning not from reading the Constitution but from reading life.[1]

It would be impossible for any person—even a Supreme Court justice—to divorce himself completely from his background. As the late Justice Cardozo pointed out, "There is in each of us a stream of tendency, whether you choose to call it philosophy or not, which gives coherence and direction to thought and action. Judges cannot escape that current any more than other mortals. All their lives, forces which they do not recognize and cannot name, have been tugging at them—inherited instincts, traditional beliefs, acquired convictions; and the resultant is an outlook on life, a conception of social needs, a sense in James's phrase of "the total push and pressure of the cosmos,' which, when reasons are nicely balanced, must determine where choice shall fall."[2]

Because many Supreme Court decisions can be explained only by reference to the social and economic predilections of individual justices and of segments of the society of which they were a part, it is important for students to know something about them. Certainly, a student will better understand Justice McReynolds' decisions if he knows something about that jurist's personal attitude toward Franklin D. Roosevelt and the New Deal. Or, an appreciation

[1] Felix Frankfurter and James M. Landis, *The Business of the Supreme Court* (New York: Macmillan, 1928), p. 310.

[2] Benjamin N. Cardozo, *The Nature of the Judicial Process* (New Haven: Yale University Press, 1921), p. 12.

of Justice Frankfurter's basic judicial philosophy will aid the student in better understanding why Frankfurter felt impelled to disagree with his liberal colleagues in *West Virginia* v. *Barnette.*

While in the process of reading cases, students should have easy access to brief statements concerning the important views of individual judges. Such summaries, although not entirely adequate, should help in the comprehension of some of the twists and turns in the reasoning process of the justices. For this reason I have included a brief biographical sketch of each justice who has rendered a majority, concurring, or dissenting opinion reproduced in this book, with some of his basic views on important constitutional questions and his political orientation (Appendix II). Of course, these sketches can only summarize the most salient aspects of a justice's life and thought. But they are important in emphasizing the human side of the law and in revealing how the personal element affects decisions of the Court. In addition, it is hoped that these brief sketches will stimulate students to read more comprehensive biographical materials.

In the biographical notes, most attention has been given to those justices who have been of greatest influence in the history of the Court and to those whose opinions appear most frequently in the text. It is suggested that students form the habit of consulting the pertinent biographical sketches as they read the opinions reproduced in the book. The introductory essays and commentaries also contain relevant materials on individual justices. A chronological listing of all Supreme Court justices is also found in Appendix II.

4. Another unique aspect of this book is the inclusion of Chapter 19, "Civil Liberties and the Administrative Process." The materials in Chapter 19 are essential for understanding current changes in the social and economic life of America and corresponding changes in constitutional philosophy. During the twentieth century, governmental powers have become increasingly centralized in the national government, and within the national government itself there has been an enormous expansion of executive powers to meet the exigencies of an industrial civilization. In this process, the Supreme Court has had to adjust the constitutional system to meet the demands of modern government and still maintain the substance and form of democratic government. This has been a difficult task indeed. In the future, much of our constitutional law undoubtedly will be understood only if the administrative process is given proper attention, since the problems created by the continued expansion of governmental activities will become increasingly complex.

The materials of Chapter 19 may be classified under administrative as well as constitutional law, for these two areas of concentration overlap or supplement one another to some degree. Professor James Hart, a well-known authority in administrative law, has noted that "administrative and constitutional law bear to each other the relation of overlapping but nonconcentric circles."[3] He illustrates this point as follows:

[3] James Hart, *An Introduction to Administrative Law* (New York: Appleton-Century-Crofts, 1950), p. 13.

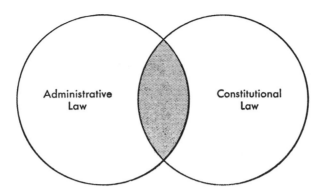

In short, there are a number of important topics that may be appropriately classified under both fields. Many of these topics cannot be ignored by a student of constitutional law, since it is largely through materials classified in both areas that the student can discern the changing role of the American state. And unfortunately, very few undergraduate institutions offer a course in administrative law, so that an added responsibility devolves on teachers of constitutional law.

The decision to expand the coverage of constitutional law has necessitated curtailing some material in other sections which has declined in significance. However, through careful choice of cases, tighter editing of these cases, and the use of somewhat more detailed introductory essays and commentaries where needed, all essential materials found in the traditional categories have been retained. Of course, it would be impossible to deal with the administrative process in its entirety within the confines of one chapter of any book. No attempt has been made to do this. Instead, the introductory essay and case materials found in Chapter 19 are designed to acquaint the student with some of the chief constitutional problems posed by the rise of administrative agencies, particularly in the area of civil rights.

5. Finally, every attempt has been made to make this a truly teachable book. Some variations from the traditional categories or changes in organization have been prompted by the author's personal experiences and discussions with students and colleagues. In most instances, the facts of each case, together with how the case got to the Supreme Court, are outlined clearly before the opinion is reproduced. The facts have not been summarized only when they are stated succinctly in a particular decision or when it was felt that a fuller appreciation and understanding of the case could be acquired by a reading of the statement of facts exactly as it appears in the opinion. Each of the parties to the case has been identified clearly when necessary to avoid confusion. A list of carefully selected readings is found in Appendix III. This bibliography is not intended to be comprehensive, but includes only those readily accessible books which seem to be most worthwhile for liberal-arts students. All of the footnotes in the text have been fully documented, so that students

who wish to dig deeper into a particular subject may have readily available references to use as a starting point.

A NOTE OF THANKS

Without the support and encouragement of many persons and groups, completion of this book would have been impossible. I owe a real debt to Dr. Spencer D. Parratt, Professor of Political Science at the Maxwell Graduate School of Syracuse University, to whom this book is gratefully dedicated. As a warm and enthusiastic teacher of public law, Professor Parratt provided much of my inspiration for further excursions in the field. I am also indebted to Dr. Louis F. Hackemann, former professor of classics, who many years ago encouraged me to pursue my academic interests.

During the early stages of preparation, a number of criticisms and suggestions made by Professor David Fellman, of the University of Wisconsin, and Professor Jay C. Heinlein, of the University of Cincinnati, saved the writer from many errors. Early discussions concerning various aspects of the book with Dr. Thomas E. Joyner, now of the New York State Division of Housing, also proved helpful. The writer was fortunate indeed in having had the completed manuscript read with care and attention by Dr. John C. Leek, of the University of Oklahoma. His scholarly criticisms and suggestions have greatly improved the book. Mr. Roger J. Howley of The Macmillan Company has given me constant help and cooperation at every stage of the book's preparation. His lively interest has been a continual source of encouragement.

Many of my Lehigh University colleagues have given me valuable assistance in various ways. I have profited greatly from discussions about the book with Professors Ernst B. Schulz, W. Ross Yates, and Finn B. Jensen. Dr. George D. Harmon generously consented to every request for aid over a period of years. Dr. Glenn J. Christensen, Dean of the College of Arts and Science, encouraged the completion of the project in many ways. Mr. William J. Morrissey, a former student and now a practicing attorney, helped greatly in the selection and editing of the cases. All the typing was done by Miss Mary J. Silvoy with extraordinary skill and sense of dedication. The Lehigh University Institute of Research provided grants for the preparation of several papers in public law which have been utilized in various ways in connection with this book. Mr. John V. Pieski, another former student, was of great help with various technical details during the final stages of preparation.

Two grants from the Social Science Research Council have contributed indirectly to the enrichment of this work. A grant under the Council's Undergraduate Research Stipend Program in 1953–54 enabled the writer and others to initiate a comprehensive study in criminal procedures and to spend a considerable amount of time investigating this phase of American constitutional law at the Biddle Law Library of the University of Pennsylvania. In the summer of 1956, the writer learned to make more intelligent and more systematic use of legal materials and legal concepts as a participant in the Council's Institute in Law and Social Relations, held at Harvard Law School.

Finally, I must express my gratitude to my wife, Virginia Krohn Tresolini, for helping to create an atmosphere which made concentrated work possible and for her characteristic forbearance during my lengthy absorption in this project.

R. J. T.

Contents

5   The Federal System   117

INTRODUCTION

6   Powers of Congress and the President   143

INTRODUCTION

PART II   ECONOMIC REGULATION IN A FEDERAL SYSTEM

7   The Contract Clause   183

INTRODUCTION

8   The States and the Commerce Power   203

INTRODUCTION

PART III   POLITICAL AND
              CIVIL RIGHTS

16 War and the Constitution   555

17 Race Discrimination and Equal Protection of Laws   585

18 Criminal Procedure   655

19   Civil Liberties and the Administrative Process   733

INTRODUCTION

20   Privacy   755

INTRODUCTION

APPENDIXES

Table of Cases

[Titles in italic capitals and figures in underscored italic type refer to opinions reprinted in the volume. Italic capital and lower case type is used for cases cited or discussed in the essays and opinions.]

I
Institutional Aspects

". . . . But the provisions of the Constitution are not mathematical formulas having their essence in their form; they are organic living institutions transplanted from English soil. Their significance is vital, not formal; it is to be gathered not simply by taking the words and a dictionary, but by considering their origin and the line of their growth."

Oliver Wendell Holmes
In *Gompers* v. *United States,*
233 U.S. 604, 610 (1914).

1
The American Constitutional System

From 1789 to the Present

The concept of a written constitution is one of the unique contributions that the United States has made to the art of government. The American Constitution, which has been in effect since 1789, is the oldest written national constitution now in use. Its long life seems even more remarkable when we consider the changes that have taken place in the United States since the Constitutional Convention of 1787.

The fifty-five delegates who attended the Philadelphia Convention came from twelve states (Rhode Island did not send a delegation) clustered along the eastern seaboard. Each of these states was extremely jealous of its powers, and as a group they were unwilling to relinquish their powers to a central government. What was then the United States encompassed an area of about 350,000 square miles, a large portion of which was Indian country where settlers needed armed protection. To the north of this cluster of states was British Canada; to the west was Spanish territory; and the south was bounded by Spanish Florida. The total population of the United States in 1789 numbered about four million whites. The great majority of these people were of British stock living in rural areas or small towns. Approximately 75 per cent of them were farmers, while the rest were small craftsmen, tradesmen, merchants, professional men, or seamen. The delegates to the Constitutional Convention went to Philadelphia on horseback or by stagecoach; extremely poor roads made travel risky, slow, and uncomfortable; there were no automobiles or trains; radio, television, and the telephone were still many generations away.

The role of the American state has changed drastically in the 175 years since the adoption of the Constitution. The early American conception of government, while including the notion of government support for business, particularly in the realms of finance and communication, rested heavily on the belief that government should impose as few restrictions as possible on society. There was general agreement that the function of government was to maintain law and order and to protect life, liberty, and property from both internal and external threats. The individual was to be left free to follow his own interests, in competition with other individuals. This emphasis on individual freedom was largely negative in nature. Among other things, it signified freedom from arbitrary arrest and imprisonment, freedom from executive tyranny, freedom from taxation without representation, and freedom of speech, worship, and association.

The doctrine of individualism was particularly suited to eighteenth- and nineteenth-century America. Everywhere there was room for expansion. The frontier, with its virtually free land, beckoned to the adventuresome and energetic. Great new areas were being opened for exploration and colonization. New inventions and discoveries created new jobs and new tools for the conquest of natural resources and the creation of new wealth. By the beginning of the twentieth century, however, this epoch was rapidly coming to an end as the result of the industrial revolution, the growth in population, the rise of giant industrial corporations, and numerous other factors.

The phenomenal changes that have occurred in America since 1789 could not possibly have been foreseen by the framers of the Constitution. The population has multiplied more than forty times. The simple agrarian society of 1789 has been transformed into an intricate and complex industrial one whose power and influence extend to every corner of the world. The majority of the people now dwell in urban areas and perform tasks in manufacturing, commerce, and transportation which were unknown to the Americans of 1787. Modern means of communication and transportation have knit together closely the various areas of the nation. A flood of immigrants has altered drastically the original racial composition of the country. In this transformation, the United States suffered through a terrible civil war that almost wrecked the union of states. Its power was decisively felt in two world wars during the twentieth century. Since 1939, the United States has been the leader in the development of nuclear weapons.

As Americans moved from rural areas to large urban centers, and mass production, with its early unregulated competition, replaced the artisan, a change took place in the economic life of the country that resulted in a corresponding change in the attitude toward government. In the highly industrialized society the individual became less and less self-sufficient. As the opportunity to contract on even terms with employers was curtailed and as social and economic problems became more complex, Americans began to look to the government for help. National crises engendered by two world wars and the serious economic depressions of the 1930s further stimulated the expansion of governmental services. Today, increasing numbers of Americans look upon government as the positive promoter of the people's general welfare. Both major political parties are now committed to programs involving social security, the maintenance of minimum health standards, minimum wages, unemployment insurance, and countless other services.

> The net effect has been a shift in political, economic, and social philosophies from individualism towards socialism, from acceptance of an economic system operating in response to the profit motive to belief in one in which government planning and direction is to play an increased role, from a social philosophy which admitted the duty of government to intervene in the distribution of income to a limited extent to one urging government to interpose for that purpose on an ever-increasing scale, and from a political and constitutional theory of rather restricted federal activity to one in which the federal government was assigned the major role in realizing the social objectives explicit or implicit in the new approaches to our social and economic problems.[1]

Survival of the Constitution

While these tremendous changes have been taking place, the American constitutional framework has remained essentially the same as in 1789. For some time, many people believed that the Constitution had survived so many drastic changes principally because the framers, who were looked upon as "an assembly of demigods" endowed with exceptionally perceptive powers, had created an original instrument of government. So august an Englishman as William Gladstone called the American Constitution "the most wonderful work ever struck off at a given time by the brain and purpose of man." Another Englishman, however, in a classic study of American government, arrived at a more realistic appraisal when he noted that "the American Constitution is no exception to the rule that everything which has power to win the obedience and respect of men must have its roots deep in the past and that the more slowly every institution has grown, so much the more enduring it is likely to prove. There is little in the Constitution that is absolutely new. There is much that is as old as Magna Carta."[2]

The labors and experiences of many generations of men molded the work of the Constitutional Convention. In referring to the Convention, one writer stated that it is essential to know what was done and said and thought on the

[1] Henry Rottschaeffer, "The Constitution and a Planned Economy," *Michigan Law Review*, Vol. 38 (1940), pp. 1133–34.

[2] James Bryce, *The American Commonwealth* (New York: Macmillan, 1910), Vol. I, p. 28.

eventful occasion. But such behavior stemmed from the stream of the things that had gone before."[3] This fact does not detract from the reputation of the framers, for they were a group of highly gifted and politically capable men who, of necessity, relied heavily on many previous ideas, principles, and practices of government. The men who wrote the Constitution were familiar with the operation of English and western European governments. They were also familiar with such outstanding English documents as the Magna Carta (1215), Petition of Rights of 1628, and Bill of Rights (1689), which represented important milestones in the growth of English political institutions. They were well versed in the chief political writings of the period and were influenced most profoundly by John Locke's *Two Treatises on Government,* Montesquieu's *Spirit of the Laws,* and William Blackstone's *Commentaries on the Laws of England.* In addition, the records and experiences of the colonial governments, of the Continental Congress, of the Articles of Confederation, and of the early state governments under their respective constitutions were important sources of many of the ideas and principles of government that were incorporated in the Constitution.

If the Constitution is not, then, an original, sacrosanct document, how has it been able to survive the multiple transformations noted above? The reason is simply that it is a flexible, dynamic document that has been greatly changed and expanded through judicial interpretation, legislative enactments, and custom and usage, and, to a lesser degree, by the formal process of amendment provided for in the document itself. This has been possible because important provisions of the Constitution are so vague and nebulous that room is left for growth and modification within its framework. For example, the Constitution says that Congress shall have power "to regulate Commerce with foreign nations, and among the several States, and with Indian tribes." But commerce is not specially defined. Nor does the Constitution state what actually constitutes commerce "with foreign nations" or "among the several states." Each generation interprets these phrases in its own way. Another outstanding example is the phrase "due process of law," which, as will be seen, has quite a different meaning today from what it had seventy-five years ago.

The late Charles A. Beard, a well-known historian and political scientist, referred to the Constitution as a "living thing" because it contained so many vague words and phrases that needed to be interpreted by human beings. Professor Beard listed the following expressions, among others, as being vague and indefinite: general welfare, necessary and proper, full faith and credit, republican form of government, unreasonable searches and seizures, impartial jury, cruel and unusual punishments, powers not delegated to the United States by the Constitution, and privileges and immunities.

> Each of these words or phrases covers some core of reality and justice on which a general consensus can be reached. But around the core is a huge shadow

[3] Conyers Read (ed.), *The Constitution Reconsidered* (New York: Columbia University Press, 1938), p. xiv.

in which the good and wise can wander indefinitely without ever coming to any agreement respecting the command made by the "law." Ever since the Constitution was framed, or particular amendments were added, dispute has raged among men of strong minds and pure hearts over the meaning of these cloud-covered words and phrases. . . . Now, these vague words and phrases must be interpreted by men and women who have occasion to use them, as members of government and as citizens urging policies on government. The words and phrases cannot rise out of the Constitution and interpret themselves. Some human being, with all the parts and passions of such a creature, must undertake the task of giving them meaning in subsidiary laws and practices.[4]

Thus, the "great generalities of the Constitution have a content and a significance that vary from age to age."[5]

The ambiguous terms of the Constitution have made possible changes in interpretation to meet the demands of the times. In this process, the President and Congress, as well as the Supreme Court, have played a vital role, because each may interpret provisions of the Constitution. The Supreme Court has loomed particularly large in this process, however, because it has been thought to have "final" authority to interpret the provisions of the Constitution. Actually, there have been numerous instances in our constitutional history when Supreme Court opinions have been "overturned" or reversed either by the Court itself or in some other manner. For example, three amendments to the Constitution—the Eleventh, Thirteenth, and Sixteenth—were designed to repudiate specific Supreme Court decisions. The Eleventh Amendment reversed the decision in *Chisholm* v. *Georgia,* 2 Dall. 419 (1793), which had held that an individual could sue a state in the federal courts without the consent of the state. In the famous Dred Scott case,[6] the majority of the Court held that the Missouri Compromise, which was designed to ban slavery in the territories, was unconstitutional. Eight years later slavery was abolished throughout the United States by the Thirteenth Amendment, and the first sentence of the Fourteenth Amendment (1868) overturned the rule of citizenship declared by the Court in the Dred Scott case. The Sixteenth Amendment was ratified fewer than twenty years after the Supreme Court had decided[7] that an income tax could not be levied by Congress without apportioning it among the states according to population. Numerous instances of Supreme Court reversals of its own previous decisions could be cited. An outstanding example involved the question of child labor. In the famous case of *Hammer* v. *Dagenhart,* 247 U.S. 251 (1918), the Supreme Court held that Congress could not exclude from interstate commerce the goods manufactured by child labor. In 1941 a markedly changed Court specifically overruled[8] the Hammer case, so that

---

[4] Charles A. Beard, "The Living Constitution," *The Annals,* Vol. 185 (May 1936), pp. 30–31.

[5] Benjamin N. Cardozo, *The Nature of the Judicial Process* (New Haven: Yale University Press, 1921), p. 17.

[6] *Dred Scott* v. *Sanford,* 19 How. 393 (1857).

[7] *Pollock* v. *Farmers' Loan and Trust Co.,* 158 U.S. 601 (1895).

[8] *U.S.* v. *Darby,* 312 U.S. 100 (1941).

today an individual cannot hire children in the production of goods intended for shipment in interstate commerce. On other occasions both Congress and the President have initiated attempts to limit the powers of the Court.

Despite the fact that Supreme Court decisions are not final in the true sense of the word, it would be a mistake to underestimate the contribution of the Court in interpreting the Constitution. In large measure, the survival of the Constitution has been made possible by the Supreme Court's constant interpretation and reinterpretation to meet changing American social, economic, and political conditions. Many judges and legal scholars have noted that the ambiguous words and phrases of the Constitution are "empty vessels" into which a Supreme Court justice can pour almost anything he desires. In a way, the Supreme Court operates as a permanent constitutional convention. "It continues the work of the Convention of 1787 by adapting through interpretation the great charter of government, and thus its duties become political, in the highest sense of the word, as well as judicial."[9] In short, as one writer has put it, "the Supreme Court makes the Constitution march."[10] Thus, the Supreme Court has played a vital role in providing stability and permanence to the American system of government under the Constitution. But just what is the American Constitution and what are its important features?

The Constitution and Constitutional Law

THE CONSTITUTION

The majority of well-known students of American government agrees that the term *constitution* cannot be defined precisely. But for practical purposes, the Constitution of the United States can be referred to as the document that went into effect in 1789 as it has been amended and interpreted to the present time. To date, twenty-four amendments have been added. The first ten amendments are generally considered part of the original document, because they were approved in the first session of Congress and subsequently ratified, in 1791, by the legislatures of three-fourths of the states.

The American Constitution, which is composed of an introductory part known as the Preamble, the seven articles, and the twenty-four amendments, has three major objectives:

1. It establishes the framework or structure of government.
2. It delegates or assigns the powers to the government.
3. It restrains the exercise of these powers by governmental officials in order that certain individual rights can be preserved.

[9] James M. Beck, *The Constitution of the United States* (New York: George H. Doran, 1924), p. 221.

[10] Frederick M. Davenport, *The Bacon Lectures on the Constitution of the United States* (Boston: Boston University Heffernan Press, 1939), p. 347.

The Constitution thus serves a dual function in that it *both grants and limits powers*. The constitutional founders saw the need for establishing what was regarded in 1789 as a strong central government, but their previous political experience and knowledge had convinced them that they could not place unqualified trust in government officials. A brief perusal of some of the fundamental principles around which the Constitutional provisions are built will indicate, in part, this conflict of ideologies.

Popular Sovereignty and Limited Government

The theory of popular sovereignty and limited government, which is perhaps the most significant concept underlying the American constitutional system, evolved along a slow and tortuous path. From the time of Magna Carta in 1215, when King John was forced to make certain concessions to the noblemen and clergy, the idea was gradually developed that governmental power flows *from* the people. Thus, the Preamble of the Constitution states that "We the people of the United States . . . do ordain and establish this Constitution for the United States of America."

This theory of popular sovereignty was indeed a revolutionary one in an age when monarchy and sovereignty were widely viewed as synonymous. This is not to say that the Constitution initially established a political system that was democratic by present-day standards. Many persons, including those without adequate property holdings, women, and numerous Negroes, were not qualified to vote. Senators were not elected directly by the people, and even the provision for an Electoral College reflects a certain suspicion of direct popular political expression on the part of the framers of the Constitution. But although complete democracy was not established in 1789, a sound foundation was laid for the future development of more democratic government.

In short, the American constitutional system rests on the firm conviction that governmental affairs must be conducted in accordance with the consent of the people. Americans are assumed to be capable of self-government; there is no legal limit to the power of the people. We have a limited government in the sense that government officials possess *only* such powers as have been conferred on them by the electorate.

Separation of Powers and Checks and Balances

As a further safeguard against possible tyrannical rule, the Constitution set up three institutionally distinct and theoretically equal organs of central government: legislative, executive, and judicial. These three organs were tied together in a dynamic relationship of cooperation and conflict by a system of checks and balances that, in various ways, provided for each of the three branches of government to have some check on the other two.

The rhetoric of separation of powers has always been important in political theory and in the evolution of the American constitutional system. Long before the American Revolution, many political theorists, including John Locke and Montesquieu, had incorporated this idea into their writings. The theme of divided authority runs throughout the whole body of American constitutional law. Many cases involving the meaning of the principle have been decided by the Supreme Court. A large number of cases in various chapters of this book that are classified under other subject headings are concerned with the meaning of this doctrine. As one writer puts it, "The development of the doctrine of the separation of powers in England and in this country was not worked out in the study, but in contests with the king on the field of battle, in the legislative chambers, and in the courts of law."[11]

In theory, the principle of separation of powers means simply that the powers of government are divided among the legislative, executive, and judicial branches, and that the powers of a particular branch can be exercised only by an officer of that branch.

Of course, modern governments cannot function properly unless there is some overlapping of functions among the branches of government. In practice, a complete separation of executive, legislative, and judicial powers has never prevailed in the United States. The framers of the Constitution, who had relied principally on the writings of Montesquieu for their conceptions of the principle of separation of powers, did not believe that *absolute* separation was possible or desirable. In *The Federalist,* No. 47, James Madison stated that Montesquieu did not favor a strict or absolute separation of powers. He noted:

> In saying, "There can be no liberty where the legislative and executive powers are united in the same person, or body of magistrates," or, if the power of judging be not separated from the legislative and executive powers," he [Montesquieu] did not mean that these departments ought to have no *partial agency* in, or no *control* over, the acts of each other. His meaning, as his own words import, and still more conclusively as illustrated by the example in his eye, can amount to no more than this, that where the *whole* power of one department is exercised by the same hands which possess the *whole* power of another department, the fundamental principles of a free constitution are subverted.[12]

Justice Holmes supported Madison's observation when he stated that "it does not seem to need argument to show that, however we may disguise it by veiling words, we do not and cannot carry out the distinction between legislative and executive action with mathematical precision and divide the branches into watertight compartments, were it ever so desirable to do so, which I am far from believing that it is, or that the Constitution requires."[13] In short, the practical needs of governments do not conform to the strict theoretical definition of separation of powers.

---

[11] Arthur T. Vanderbilt, *The Doctrine of the Separation of Powers and its Present-Day Significance* (Lincoln: University of Nebraska Press, 1953), p. 143.

[12] *The Federalist,* No. 47 (Modern Library Ed.; New York: Random House, n.d.), pp. 314–15.

[13] Dissenting opinion in *Springer* v. *Government of Philippine Islands,* 277 U.S. 189 (1928).

Perhaps the greatest confusion has arisen because it might seem at first glance that the constitutional separation of powers prescribes that the legislature possess all law-making power, the executive all administrative power, and the judiciary all power to decide individual cases under the law. In fact, while the Constitution gives each branch certain distinct authorities, each branch is assigned some law-making, some administrative, and some judicial tasks.

The practical experiences of the American colonists had made them fearful of the concentration of power in despotic hands. As Madison noted in *The Federalist,* No. 47, "The accumulation of all powers, legislative, executive and judiciary, in the same hands, whether of one, a few, or many, and whether hereditary, self-appointed, or elective, may justly be pronounced as the very definition of tyranny." The framers of the Constitution believed that the principle of separation of powers would help to prevent the rise of tyrannical governments by making it impossible for a single group of persons to exercise too much power. Nevertheless, the principle is neither mentioned specifically in the Constitution nor explicitly adopted. Rather, it is implied from the structure of the Constitution itself, in which Article I is devoted to Congress, Article II to the President, and Article III to the federal courts.

Although the principle of separation of powers as embodied in the federal Constitution applies only to the national government, the majority of the state constitutions provide for separation by express provisions or by implication.[14] The classic example of an express provision is that written into the Massachusetts Constitution of 1780, which provides as follows:

> In the government of this Commonwealth the legislative department shall never exercise the executive and the judicial powers, or either of them: the executive shall never exercise the legislative and judicial powers, or either of them: the judicial shall never exercise the legislative and executive powers, or either of them: to the end it may be a government of laws and not of men.

Despite their attachment to the principle of separation of powers, the framers of the Constitution did not view it as an absolute doctrine. Although the three departments were made separate and distinct, a system of constitutional checks and balances was devised that permits some blending of powers. A number of these provisions are noted in *Ex Parte Grossman,* 267 U.S. 87 (1925), as follows:

> By affirmative action through the veto power, the Executive and one more than one-third of either House may defeat all legislation. One half of the House and two-thirds of the Senate may impeach and remove the members of the Judiciary. The Executive can reprieve or pardon all offenses after their commission, either before trial, during trial, or after trial, by individuals, or by classes, conditionally or absolutely, and this without modification or regulation by Congress. . . .

[14] Malcolm P. Sharp, "The Classical American Doctrine of Separation of Powers," *University of Chicago Law Review,* Vol. 2 (1935), p. 385.

Negatively, one House of Congress can withhold all appropriations and stop the operations of government. The Senate can hold up all appointments, confirmation of which either the Constitution or a statute requires, and thus deprive the President of the necesssary agents with which he is to take care that the laws be faithfully executed.

The difficulties of classifying all the functions of government into three neat pidgeon holes and the necessity for the commingling of powers among the three branches of government are demonstrated well by the development and uses of contempt powers. The word *contempt* was used originally in England to denote an act committed in violation of an order or writ of the king or of any of his subordinate officers. Any such disobedience might result in an offender's quick or summary punishment without the use of any formal procedural safeguards. Despite the fact that the roots of the contempt power are found in the English executive, the courts have ruled on many occasions that the power is exclusively "inherent" in the judiciary. They have ruled that the contempt power is needed to enable courts to carry on their proceedings in an effective manner. Orderly administration of justice requires that those who persist in disturbing or slowing down judicial proceedings be punished without undue delay. On numerous occasions, the Supreme Court has ruled that summary conviction and punishment by judicial officers is consistent with the guaranties of due process of law. However, the doctrine that the contempt power is exclusively inherent in the judiciary has been weakened by the fact that legislative bodies have been allowed to use this "judicial" power. Neither the Senate nor the House of Representatives possesses express powers under the Constitution to punish for contempt except for disorderly conduct or failure to attend sessions on the part of members.[15] However, in a number of cases, Congress has been recognized to possess implied summary contempt powers under limited circumstances in order to insure the effectiveness of its legislative authority. In addition, a number of states have conferred contempt powers on administrative agencies by express constitutional provisions or by statute. Thus, a power that is supposedly judicial can be exercised by legislative officers and state executive officers as well.[16]

American political practice, too, has greatly modified the principle of a strict separation of powers. One or another branch of the federal government may dominate at a particular time. For example, during the Reconstruction days which followed the Civil War, Congress was able to dominate the executive. On the other hand, Franklin D. Roosevelt's personality and his own political philosophy, together with unprecedented crises, enabled him to dominate Congress, at least for a short time, with relative ease.

[15] Article I, Section 5, Clauses 1, 2.

[16] Much of the material in this paragraph is based on R. J. Tresolini, "The Use of Summary Contempt Powers by Administrative Agencies," *Dickinson Law Review*, Vol. 54 (1950), p. 395.

Federalism

As already noted, the Preamble states that the people established the Constitution. However, the formation of the American union was made possible by the states themselves, acting as sovereign units, rather than by the action of the whole people of the United States. The original states, being very jealous of their powers, were extremely reluctant to create a strong national government. In the light of this and other considerations, the American constitutional system was based on a division of power between the federal government and the states. This was accomplished by enumerating the powers of the national government in the body of the Constitution and leaving unspecified, residual powers to the states. This principle was theoretically ensured by the Tenth Amendment, ratified in 1791, which provided that "The powers not delegated to the United States by the Constitution, nor prohibited by it to the states, are reserved to the States respectively, or to the people." Chapter 5 deals with some of the major constitutional problems raised by the division of powers between the national and state governments.

The Rule of Law

The classic formulation of the rule of law was set forth by A. V. Dicey, who was the foremost scholar of English constitutional law during the latter part of the nineteenth century. As will be seen, particularly in the discussion of the administrative process in Chapter 20, Dicey's rigid statement of the rule of law no longer fits the facts of modern government in either England or the United States. Nevertheless, because his theory has been influential in the development of certain aspects of American constitutional law, the most salient features of his rule must be noted. According to Dicey, the rule of law had three distinct meanings, two of which are pertinent to this discussion.

1. No man is punishable or can be lawfully made to suffer in body or goods except for a distinct breach of law established in the ordinary legal manner before the ordinary courts of the land. . . .
2. . . . No man is above the law. . . . Every man . . . is subject to the ordinary law of the realm.[17]

The clearest expression of the rule of law in United States history is found in Article XXX of the Massachusetts Constitution of 1780, which established the separation-of-powers doctrine "to the end that it may be a government of laws and not of men." Although not specifically stated in the federal Constitution, the same idea is implicit in that document. Of course, the phrases "government of laws" and "government of men" have meaning only in a relative sense, because men ultimately must make and administer the laws. Yet,

[17] Albert V. Dicey, *Introduction to the Study of the Constitution* (London: Macmillan, 1939), pp. 188–95. The first edition of Dicey's book was published in 1885.

the idea behind the doctrine is clear. It means that the system of laws under which we live must be applied equally to each citizen and that no person may be subject to the arbitrary decisions of government officers. Federal governmental action must be based on law—that is, it must not conflict with the Constitution and statutes passed by Congress, which constitute an expression of the people's sovereign will. "The difference, then, between a government of laws and a government of men (to the extent that these phrases have any real meaning) is not a difference in kind but a difference of degree only. It is nevertheless a difference of high and important degree; for it bespeaks a difference in spirit; and in government, as in most other human institutions, the spirit is often the essence."[18]

CONSTITUTIONAL LAW

As in the case of the term *constitution,* constitutional law cannot be precisely defined. In its broadest sense, the term *constitutional law* designates that branch of jurisprudence dealing with the formation, construction, and interpretation of constitutions. Because the fundamental law in the United States is the written Constitution, interpretations of that document by the President, Congress, court decisions, and rulings of public officials, as well as governmental habits and customs, constitute a part of our constitutional law. However, the decisions of the courts, and especially the Supreme Court, are the principal sources of information relating to the meaning and interpretation of the Constitution. Not all court decisions are concerned with constitutional interpretation, but those cases which are from the chief source of our constitutional law. This fact led the late Professor E. S. Corwin, one of the best-known students of the Constitution, to remark, "As employed in this country, Constitutional Law signifies a body of rules resulting from the interpretation by a high court of a written constitutional instrument in the course of disposing of cases in which the validity, in relation to the constitutional instrument, of some act of governmental power, State or National, has been challenged."[19]

Periods of Constitutional Development

A broad survey of the American constitutional system discloses five major periods of development. These periods are by no means precise, nor would other writers necessarily agree with the particular breakdown of periods that follows. Nevertheless, this outline does provide us with markers or boundaries that should make it easier to discern major shifts in policy or outstanding social, economic, and political issues. In addition, this brief survey should provide the student with a background against which the cases can be read

[18] Howard L. McBain, *The Living Constitution* (New York: Macmillan, 1927), pp. 5–6.
[19] Edward S. Corwin (ed.), *The Constitution of the United States of America* (Washington: Legislative Reference Service, Library of Congress, 1953), p. ix.

more meaningfully. Much of the material appearing in the remaining pages of this chapter is more fully developed in various other portions of the text.

THE MARSHALL ERA (1789–1835)

During this early period, the legislature was regarded as the most important branch of the national government. Most Americans firmly believed that legislatures were best suited to represent the people and their interests. Their long and difficult experience in the Colonies and their knowledge of English and Continental history had made them extremely fearful of strong executives.

At first, Americans showed very little interest in the work of the Supreme Court. After the ratification of the Constitution, the state courts still handled most legal matters. The Supreme Court had no cases to decide during the first three years of its existence. The Court's lack of prestige is indicated by the fact that many outstanding persons declined appointments to the highest judicial tribunal in the land. The chief justiceship was refused by Patrick Henry and Alexander Hamilton. John Jay, the first Chief Justice, resigned the post to serve as governor of New York. He refused a second appointment in 1800. Other justices either resigned from the Court or declined appointments in favor of state judicial positions. Unlike the executive and legislative branches, Supreme Court sessions were held in such places as basement apartments and Capitol committee rooms. It was not until 1935 that an elaborate building was provided for sessions of the Court.

Gradually, however, the Supreme Court gained in power and prestige. John Marshall, the fourth chief justice, who served in that post from 1801 to 1835, was responsible for the growing influence of the judiciary. He was without question the dominant justice of this period, if not of our entire history. Marshall took over the leadership of the Court during its formative period and was thus presented with the unique opportunity of directing the major lines of American constitutional development. He was more than equal to the occasion. In addition to his wide political experience, he was endowed with a fertile mind, cleverness, imagination, and courage. These great talents were used to establish clearly the supremacy of the national government.

Marshall's creed was enunciated in a number of his great decisions, such as *McCulloch* v. *Maryland* and *Gibbons* v. *Ogden,* which are considered in other portions of this book. Professor Corwin has summarized Marshall's major principles of constitutional construction as follows:[20]

1. Since the American Constitution is derived from the American people, it must be interpreted so as to secure to them the fullest benefit of its provisions. This idea is implicit in the "necessary and proper" clause of the Constitution, which provides that, in addition to its enumerated powers, Congress may make "all laws which shall be necessary and proper for carrying into execu-

---

[20] Edward S. Corwin, *The Twilight of the Supreme Court* (New Haven: Yale University Press, 1934), p. 7. See also, by the same author, *The Bacon Lestures on the Constitution of the United States* (Boston: Boston University Heffernan Press, 1939), p. 414.

tion the foregoing powers, and all other powers vested by this Constitution in the government of the United States, or in any department thereof."

2. The existence of the states did not limit the powers of the national government. This, according to Marshall, was implicit in the "supremacy" clause, which provides that "This Constitution, and the laws of the United States which shall be made in pursuance thereof; and all treaties made, or which shall be made, under the authority of the United States, shall be the supreme law of the land; and the judges in every state shall be bound thereby, anything in the Constitution or laws of any state to the contrary notwithstanding."

3. The Supreme Court is ultimately responsible for the interpretation of the Constitution in the interest of national supremacy. The decisions of the Supreme Court are therefore binding on the states. This principle of judicial review of legislation was enunciated in *Marbury* v. *Madison*.

4. The Constitution was designed to serve the American people for many generations. To this end, the Supreme Court must interpret the Constitution to meet the changing needs of the people in order that the Constitution may survive.

Marshall's constitutional creed has been extremely influential in the development of American constitutional law. He looms so large that one sometimes fails to realize that there were other justices sitting with Marshall.[21]

Not until many years after John Marshall's death were his contributions to American constitutional law fully understood and appreciated. During his tenure on the Court, only a few opinions attracted a great deal of public attention. The majority of the early cases involved disputes between private individuals that did not demand the consideration of important constitutional issues. Civil liberties cases, which today attract wide public attention, were almost nonexistent. However, by the end of this period it became clear that a civil rights issue—the slavery controversy—would become important. But the slavery controversy was actually part of the problem of states' rights versus federal centralization, which was the chief constitutional issue before the country.

Marshall's nationalistic interpretation of the Constitution had helped establish the federal government. He had used what power and prestige the Court had in supporting the nationalism of Hamilton. Marshall's influence on the constitutional system could never be erased. But the Jeffersonian theory of states' rights was still far from dead.

THE TANEY COURT (1836–1864)

Like John Marshall, Roger B. Taney (pronounced *Tawney*), who was chief justice from 1836 to 1864, was a man of wide political experience and great ability. Although he had once been a strong Federalist, Taney was an ardent

---

[21] Joseph Story and William Johnson were outstanding figures on the Court during this period. A distinguished biography of Johnson has thrown new light on the operation of the Marshall Court, Donald G. Morgan, *Justice William Johnson, the First Dissenter* (Columbia: University of South Carolina Press, 1954).

supporter of Andrew Jackson, who had been elected to the presidency in 1828 and 1832. The Jacksonians, who represented the newer agrarian and pioneer elements in American politics, were suspicious of centralized powers. Although aware of the virtues of a union of states, they sought to reassert the rights of the states and local government units. Thus, Jackson, in his Second Inaugural Address, noted his readiness "to exercise my constitutional powers in arresting measures which may directly or indirectly encroach upon the rights of the States or tend to consolidate all political power in the General Government."[22]

To say that Taney became the spokesman for the Jacksonians would be to exaggerate, for the Supreme Court after 1835 did not break completely with the Marshall Court. Taney did reassert some state powers, but the principle of national supremacy was not destroyed. The Taney Court also reflected the new democratic era to some extent, because it was more concerned with the rights of ordinary people as against private property interests.

The most dramatic decision of this period was the Dred Scott case, which represented an unfortunate attempt by the Supreme Court to resolve the slavery issue. This case is also of importance because it extended the power of the Supreme Court:

> The majority here attempted to transform the guarantees of civil liberties contained in the first eight amendments into positive protections to the rights of property in slaves. In arguing that the guarantees of these amendments restrict the discretionary power of Congress, Taney was making the first judicial assertion of a general supervisory jurisdiction over Congress. The Missouri Compromise Act was, furthermore, the first Congressional act of any general consequence which the court held invalid. Temporarily the prestige of the Court suffered from the effects of the decision, but as we look back over the history of the review of Congressional legislation, it is apparent that, in a long-run sense, the case was a critical victory in the campaign for judicial control.[23]

The issue of states' rights versus federal centralization was finally settled on the battlefields of the Civil War. The Confederacy, the central core of states'-rights sentiment, was destroyed. In terms of American constitutional development, the North's victory was decisive, because it made secession impossible and guaranteed the future of "an indestructible Union."

THE RISE OF JUDICIAL POWER (1865–1898)

The verdict of the Civil War laid the foundation for the development of a cohesive national government. Although problems of federal versus states' rights persist to this day, the period of federation really ended with the Civil War; the period of rapid national growth was about to begin. The American

---

[22] James D. Richardson, *Messages and Papers of the Presidents,* Vol. III (March 4, 1833), p. 4.

[23] Benjamin F. Wright, *The Growth of American Constitutional Law* (Boston: Houghton Mifflin, 1942), pp. 76–77.

scene changed drastically during this period: the nation's railroad system was greatly expanded, giant industrial corporations doing business on a national scale came into being, and the factory system accelerated the growth of large urban centers.

In this vast transformation, with business operating largely without governmental restraint, some groups were bound to suffer. Farmers began to demand that the railroads be regulated; the abuses of the new industrial system brought vehement outcries from the ranks of labor. More and more, these and other groups turned to the national government for help in the solution of new problems. Thus, this period witnessed a definite trend toward centralization of powers in the national government. The establishment of the Interstate Commerce Commission in 1887 to deal with certain abuses of the railroads and the Sherman Anti-Trust Act of 1890 to deal with the monopoly problem were simply the first of the now tremendous number of federal laws regulating many areas of activity.

In the years after the Civil War, the Supreme Court became more active and federal judicial powers were greatly enlarged. During the tenure of Salmon P. Chase alone (1864–1873), the Supreme Court declared ten acts of Congress unconstitutional. It will be recalled that only two acts of Congress were held void (*Marbury* v. *Madison* and the Dred Scott case) in the previous seventy-four year history of the Court. Throughout this period, many state as well as federal laws were held invalid.

The increased activity of the Supreme Court dismayed large elements of the American population, because the legislation struck down was usually designed to aid such groups as farmers and laborers, who had been badly hurt by the new industrial development. The Court chose to ignore many popular demands. Instead, it became an effective censor of state and federal legislation which was thought to interfere with private property. This it did by interpreting such vague constitutional phrases as due process of law, direct taxes, and interstate commerce according to the justices' own conservative economic predilections. At the same time, the Court was in the process of narrowly defining the provisions of the Fourteenth and Fifteenth Amendments, which were designed to guarantee basic civil rights to the newly freed Negro. By the end of this period, the Court's restricted interpretation of these amendments had made it impossible to use them effectively against racial discrimination.

Throughout the later years of this period public attention was focused on the Supreme Court rather than on Congress. To many people, the Court had become an instrument for the maintenance of the property rights of the rich and the preservation of a laissez-faire economy. To others it was a bulwark against insidious legislative encroachments upon individual rights and the "American way of life." Rightly or wrongly, by 1898 the Court had enunciated doctrines that made it an important determiner of American life and legislation. In succeeding years it would apply these doctrines with an often heavy hand.

THE RISE OF EXECUTIVE POWER (1898–1937)

In governmental affairs, the most persistent trend of the twentieth century has been the growth in the power and prestige of the executive branch in virtually every country. In the United States, neither the early fear of executive powers nor the separation-of-powers doctrine has prevented the rise of the executive branch to a position of predominant leadership in the affairs of state.

Many factors have been responsible for the phenomenal growth of executive powers in America. The social and economic changes brought about by industrialization required the intervention of the national government in a multitude of new areas. Because neither the courts nor Congress could regulate these areas adequately, these new functions came to be performed by the executive branch, largely through newly created administrative officers and bodies.[24] The powers of the executive branch were further expanded during crises of wars and depressions, which had to be fought on a national scale. The personal attitudes of "strong" presidents such as Theodore Roosevelt, Woodrow Wilson, and Franklin D. Roosevelt also resulted in increased power and prestige of the executive branch. This growth of executive powers went hand in hand with the gradual centralization of more powers in the federal government.

During this period, the Supreme Court continued to invalidate social and economic legislation demanded by large segments of the American people. "Until 1937, Supreme Court decisions, in now advancing, now receding waves, used due-process clauses and other constitutional provisions to hold back the expansion of state and federal regulatory powers."[25] The period came to a dramatic end in the struggle between Franklin D. Roosevelt and the Court. Roosevelt had won the presidency over Hoover in a Democratic party landslide which also swept overwhelming Democratic majorities into both houses of Congress. The central election issue was the question of how to reduce the effects of the severe economic depression that had begun with the stock-market collapse of 1929. Roosevelt had promised to take bold steps to deal with the Depression. To this end, his administration launched the New Deal program on taking office in 1933. This program consisted of a large number of revolutionary measures designed to solve the most pressing economic problems. It was this nationwide recovery program, whose constitutionality was soon to be passed on by the Supreme Court, that precipitated the dramatic struggle with the President.

When the New Deal statutes came before the Supreme Court, that body was divided almost equally between conservative and liberal justices. It was almost

---

[24] This development is covered in more detail in Chapter 19. The growth of executive powers from English origins is outlined in the writer's "The Development of Administrative Law," *University of Pittsburgh Law Review*, Vol. 12 (1951), pp. 362–80.

[25] Carl B. Swisher, *American Constitutional Development* (Boston: Houghton Mifflin, 1943), p. 1019.

a foregone conclusion that the four conservative members—James Mc-Reynolds, Pierce Butler, George Sutherland, and Willis Van Devanter—would vote against the New Deal measures. Each of these justices was thoroughly committed to the philosophy of laissez faire and limited federal power. Justice Louis D. Brandeis, Harlan F. Stone, and Benjamin N. Cardozo were the liberals who were sympathetic to the New Deal program. Chief Justice Hughes and Owen J. Roberts, the other two members of the Court, could not be classified with either group. They held the balance of power. As it turned out, Roberts and Hughes were usually found in the conservative camp.

The first New Deal law did not come before the Court until 1935, but within the next sixteen months decisions were rendered in ten major cases involving New Deal measures. The Court invalidated eight out of the ten measures and thereby destroyed the heart of the Roosevelt program. During the sixteen month period, the Court struck down in succession Section 9(c) of the National Industrial Recovery Act, the NRA itself, the Railroad Pension Act, the Farm Mortgage Law, the Agricultural Adjustment Act, the AAA amendments, the Bituminous Coal Act, and the Municipal Bankruptcy Act. Once these laws were declared to be unconstitutional, ". . . the basic cleavage between judicial oligarchy and popular power could no longer be concealed or circumvented. In one short term the Court had woven a tight constitutional web to bind political power at all levels. . . . By the spring of 1936 it looked as if the Court had wrecked the New Deal on the shoals and rocks of unconstitutionality."[26] It was clear that the fate of the New Deal would ultimately have to be decided by the American people in the election of 1936.

The Roosevelt administration's overwhelming victory in 1936 put the electorate's stamp of approval on the New Deal. With 60 per cent of the voters behind him, the President felt that the time had come for an assault on the Court majority, which was so hostile to his program. Early in 1937, Congress was presented with Roosevelt's famous court-packing bill, which was designed to make sweeping changes in the federal judiciary. The bill provided for the voluntary retirement of Supreme Court justices at the age of seventy. For each member of the Court who reached the age limit but failed to retire, the President would appoint an additional justice. The maximum number of Court justices was fixed at fifteen. According to the President, the Court plan had two chief purposes, as follows: "By bringing into the judicial system a steady and continuing stream of new and younger blood, I hope, first, to make the administration of all Federal justice speedier and therefore less costly; secondly, to bring to the decision of social and economic problems younger men who have had personal experience and contact with modern facts and circumstances under which average men have to live and work. This plan will save our National Constitution from hardening of the judicial arteries."[27]

[26] Alpheus T. Mason, *The Supreme Court: Vehicle of Revealed Truth or Power Group, 1930–1937* (Boston: Boston University Press, 1953), pp. 36–37.
[27] Senate *Reports,* 75th Cong., 1st sess., Doc. No. 711, pp. 41–45.

Although Congress failed to approve the Court-packing bill, the attempted reorganization resulted in a liberalized court. Roosevelt "had lost the battle but won the war," largely because of a change in the temper of the Court itself. During the 168 days in which Congress was considering the President's bill, the Court made the famous "switch in time which saved nine" by abandoning its opposition to the New Deal. This was made possible by a change in the previous views of Chief Justice Hughes and Justice Roberts, who may have been influenced by both the election of 1936 and the fear that continued opposition to social change would eventually wreck the Supreme Court. (Hughes denied that these considerations accounted for his change of judicial views.) By the spring of 1937, the Court had dramatically reversed itself in a series of decisions upholding a minimum-wage statute of the state of Washington, the amended Railway Labor Act of 1934, the Farm Mortgage Act of 1935, the National Labor Relations Act of 1935, and the Social Security Act of 1935. With the return of economic policy making to the people and their legislatures, a new era began in American constitutional development.

THE NEW ERA (1937–PRESENT)

Since 1937, Supreme Court decisions have followed two main lines: In the first place, the Court's constitutional decisions have not been concerned greatly with the protection of property rights and the maintenance of a laissez-faire system. Extensive federal regulation of many new areas has now become an accepted and permanent part of American life. Both major political parties are committed to programs that involve the expansion of national powers. The retreat of the Court from its 1936 position concerning the New Deal is indicated by the fact that from 1936 to 1955 only three minor pieces of federal legislation were held unconstitutional.[28]

---

[28] In *Tot* v. *United States,* 319 U.S. 463 (1943), the Court held that a section of the Federal Firearms Act, which established a presumption of guilt based on a prior conviction and present possession of a firearm, violated due process under the Fifth Amendment. In *United States* v. *Lovett,* 328 U.S. 303 (1946), a rider attached to an appropriations bill providing that three government employees were not to be paid their salaries was held to constitute a bill of attainder forbidden by the Constitution. A minor provision of the Food and Drug Act was invalidated in *United States* v. *Cardiff,* 344 U.S. 174 (1952). Since 1955, however, the tempo has changed with the Court overturning some piece of federal legislation on the average of almost once a year. *United States ex rel. Toth* v. *Quarles,* 350 U.S. 11 (1955) (section of Uniform Code of Military Justice); *Reid* v. *Covert,* 354 U.S. 1 (1957) (section of U.C.M.J.) *Trop* v. *Dulles,* 356 U.S. 86 (1958) (section of Nationality Act of 1940); *Kinsella* v. *Singleton,* 361 U.S. 234 (1960) (section of U.C.M.J.); *Kennedy* v. *Mendoza-Martinez,* 372 U.S. 144 (1963) (section of Nationality Act); *Schneider* v. *Rusk,* 377 U.S. 163 (1964) (section of the Immigration and Nationality Act of 1964); *Aptheker* v. *Sec. of State,* 378 U.S. 500 (1964) (section of the Subversive Activities Control Act); *Lamont* v. *Postmaster General,* 381 U.S. 301 (1965) (section of the Postal Service Act of 1962); *United States* v. *Brown,* 381 U.S. 437 (1965) (section of the Labor Management and Reporting Act of 1959); *Albertson* v. *Subversive Activities Control Board,* 382 U.S. 70 (1965) (section of Subversive Ac-

The second major trend in Supreme Court decisions since 1937 has been the increased Court protection afforded to civil liberties. While in the process of relegating economic and property rights to a subordinate constitutional position, the Court was involved in the creation and development of elaborate new protections of personal rights. Although the Court has allowed great inroads to be made on both property and personal rights during periods of national emergency, the main body of civil liberties has been preserved. During World War II, for example, the unfortunate compulsory evacuation of American citizens of Japanese ancestry from the West Coast and the complete military suppression of civil government in Hawaii were the only instances of serious infringement of individual liberty. This is not to say that each Court of the new era since 1937 has been consistently on the side of civil rights. Nevertheless, a long-term general change is easily discernible in the Court's attitude on matters involving civil liberties.

The new judicial attitude had its roots in a few opinions involving interpretation of World War I legislation dealing with espionage and subversion. Later, under the guiding hand of Charles Evans Hughes, who was chief justice from 1930 to 1941, the Court began a spirited defense of the letter and spirit of the Bill of Rights. From 1941 to 1946, under Chief Justice Harlan Stone, the Court continued to defend personal rights. When Fred M. Vinson became chief justice in 1946, the general expectation was that the Supreme Court would continue the defense of civil liberties. However, despite the bitter dissents of its more liberal members, the Vinson Court was reluctant to give strong support to civil liberties. Decisions unfavorable to the protection of civil rights were rendered by the Vinson Court in the majority of such cases that it considered.[29] The Chief Justice himself, and Justices Tom Clark, Stanley Reed, Sherman Minton, and usually Harold Burton and Felix Frankfurter, refused to intervene in civil liberties cases. The irony was that many of these justices, with the exception of Reed, were appointed to the bench by President Truman, who had evidenced deep concern for the protection of individual rights.

Under the leadership of Earl Warren, who succeeded Vinson as Chief Justice in 1953, the Supreme Court again seemed determined to protect personal freedoms. Writing late in 1955, a well-known political observer remarked that the Supreme Court is now conveying the idea that it is remarkably united on preserving the rights of the individual, whether he be a Negro waiting for a train, or going to school, or a civil servant robbed of his pride and means of

---

tivities Control Act); *Afroyim,* v. *Rusk,* 387 U.S. 253 (1967) (section of Nationality Act). *Lamont* marks the first time the Supreme Court declared a federal statute unconstitutional under the freedom of speech provisions of the First Amendment; and *Aptheker* creates a constitutional right to travel "closely related to rights of free speech and association."

[29] C. Herman Pritchett, *Civil Liberties and the Vinson Court* (Chicago: University of Chicago Press, 1954).

livelihood by unidentified accusers, or a business man denied the right to travel freely about the world. . . . The Chief Justice of the United States has taken the lead in reasserting the constitutional liberties of the people. . . . After years of unparalleled aggression by the executive and legislative branches against the rights of the individual, the judiciary has stepped in to balance the scales."[30] The Warren Court's determination to preserve civil rights has been indicated by the public statements of the Chief Justice himself as well as by the court decisions. Some two years after his appointment as Chief Justice, Warren noted that the "pursuit of justice is not the vain pursuit of a remote abstraction; it is a continuing direction of our daily conduct. Thus, it is that when the generation of 1980 receives from us the Bill of Rights, the document will not have exactly the same meaning it had when we received it from our fathers. We will pass on a better Bill of Rights or a worse one, tarnished by neglect or burnished by growing use. If these rights are real, they need constant and imaginative application to new situations."[31]

As will be seen more clearly in the chapters that follow, the Warren Court, with few exceptions, has consistently defended individual freedoms. In the period from 1953 to 1962, the justices were often divided into two blocks. The acknowledged leader of the civil libertarians was Justice Black, ably supported by Justices Brennan, Douglas, and the Chief Justice himself. These "judicial activists" believe that the Court must play a positive role in the protection of individual liberties. They sought to promote social welfare and to protect American freedom from erosion by partisan legislative bodies and executive officers. Justice Black and his supporters thus viewed the Court as the ultimate guardian of constitutional rights. Justice Felix Frankfurter headed another bloc on the Court that advocated a policy of "judicial self-restraint." He and his supporters believed that the primary responsibility for governing lies with the people and their duly elected officers. They felt that the Court must take a back seat to legislative bodies lest the freedom of the people to govern themselves be hampered by "judicial legislation." In short, Justice Frankfurter was wary of judicial attempts to impose Justice on the community; to deprive it of the wisdom that comes from self-inflicted wounds and the strength that grows with the burden of responsibility."[32] Justice Frankfurter was usually supported by Justice Harlan, who seems to have become the new leader of the "self-restraint" bloc, and Justices Stewart, Whittaker, and Clark. Yet on several occasions one or more of these justices voted with the

---

[30] James Reston, *The New York Times* (Dec. 5, 1955).

[31] Earl Warren, "The Law and the Future," *Fortune* (November 1955), p. 230.

[32] Wallace Mendelson, *Justices Black and Frankfurter: Conflict on the Court* (Chicago: University of Chicago Press, 1961), p. 131. The philosophy of the judicial activists is well delineated in a series of lectures by Justices Black, Brennan, Douglas, and Chief Justice Warren in Edmond Cahn (ed.), *The Great Rights* (New York: Macmillan, 1963). See also Irving Dillard (ed.), *One Man's Stand for Freedom: Mr. Justice Black and the Bill of Rights* (New York: Knopf, 1963); Charles L. Black, Jr., *The People and the Court* (New York: Macmillan, 1960); and Martin Shapiro, *Freedom of Speech, The Supreme Court and Judicial Review* (Englewood Cliffs, N.J.: Prentice-Hall, 1966).

civil libertarians. Justices Frankfurter and Whittaker retired in 1962 to be replaced by President Kennedy's appointees, Justices Goldberg and White. President Johnson appointed Justices Abe Fortas and Thurgood Marshall to the seats previously held by Justices Goldberg and Clark. During this period, the patterns of alliance have not always been so clear, with the judicial self-restraint block sometimes reduced to Justice Harlan alone or in company with one other justice, and on other occasions Justice Black opposing the civil libertarians when he has felt that overzealous pursuit of political rights endangered the rule of the law that guarantees those rights. The unanticipated resignation of Justice Fortas, together with the retirement of Chief Justice Warren, foreshadowed a major change in the personnel of the Court presided over by the new Chief Justice, Warren Burger. In any event, in our time the Supreme Court will, in all probability, continue to give practical meaning to our highest ideals and to remind us of our fundamental freedoms.

During the period under review, the growth in the power of the executive branch continued unabated. In fact, America's participation in World War II required an even greater concentration of power in the executive branch of the government. The intervention of the national government into many areas of activity continued after the cessation of hostilities because of sustained industrial expansion, popular demand for increasing social and economic services, the Korean and Vietnamese conflicts, and the explosion of our urban problems. The growth in executive powers was accompanied necessarily by a continuation of the trend toward centralization of governmental powers at the national level. Concern over the curtailment of state authority prompted the appointment, in 1953, of a presidential commission to study the role of the national government in relation to the states and their political subdivisions. The commission's report summarized well the trend toward the growth of national powers:

> The almost continuous presence of a crisis, either economic or military, has accounted for vast expansions of national activities. Many of these programs have been of an emergency nature; a great many others, however, have lastingly influenced the division of governmental responsibilities between the National Government and the States. . . . War and economic crisis have not been the only major causes of the growing pressure for national action. Equally insistent pressures have been brought about by intensified industrialization and population shifts from rural to urban areas; new advances in transportation and communications; and, flowing from these developments, greatly accelerated mobility of people and interchange of ideas. These changes have been reflected in part in a growing governmental concern with the economic and social welfare of the individual. And many individuals who once looked no further than their city hall or State capitol now turn toward Washington when problems arise. *We are doing as a Nation many things that we once did as individuals, as local communities, or as states.*[33]

[33] *Report* of the Commission on Intergovernmental Relations (June 1955), p. 1. Italics supplied.

In the years ahead, the powers of the executive branch are likely to grow. At the same time, the trend toward increasing national authority will probably continue. Thus, much of American constitutional law will continue to revolve around problems associated with the growth of executive powers, federal versus state authority, and civil rights. How these problems are resolved, and how the American people respond to the tasks of world leadership and the maintenance of world peace, will determine to a large extent the future course of American constitutional development.

2
The Federal Courts and the Law

Our federal system of government makes necessary two separate systems of law—that of the states and that of the national government. Thus, two separate and distinct sets of courts exist side by side in the United States. This dual court system is one of the most confusing aspects of American law. The state courts decide the majority of both civil and criminal cases. Yet each of the state courts has very little or no connection with the federal courts.

One might well ask why the framers of the Constitution decided to create an independent federal judiciary when they could have authorized the existing state courts to apply federal law whenever necessary. There were many objections to this scheme.

It would have meant placing the authority of the federal government under the supervision and, to a large extent, the control of many independent judicial bodies. If different interpretations of the Constitution and laws were adopted by the different state courts, the effectiveness of the federal government would be much impaired, if, indeed, it were not destroyed. The states, moreover, were exceedingly jealous of their own authority and viewed with suspicion the establishment of a national government. On the other hand, there were many positive reasons for the establishment of a national judiciary. Besides the necessity for a uniform construction of federal law in all parts of the country, there had to be impartial forums for the adjudication of such questions as the disposition of federal property, disputes between the various states, controversies between citizens of different states, and other similar matters. Very wisely, the Constitutional Convention of 1787 adopted the plan of a federal judiciary. Had they not done so, it is doubtful if the government they established would have survived.[1]

Jurisdiction of Federal Courts

Under our dual court system, the duties and jurisdiction of each system must be defined as precisely as possible. Article III of the Constitution defines specifically the jurisdiction of the federal courts. Under the Tenth Amendment, all other cases are tried in the state courts.

The cases and controversies that are subject to federal jurisdiction fall into two distinct classes: first, those that depend on the nature of the subject matter; secondly, those that depend on the nature of the parties involved without regard to subject matter. Article III enumerates nine types of cases or controversies that can be brought to the federal courts for decision:

Nature of the Subject Matter

1. All cases arising under the Constitution, federal laws, and treaties.
2. Admiralty and maritime cases. (Although there are numerous cases dealing with maritime contracts, damage actions, etc., they are of relatively little importance in the study of constitutional law. Such cases are usually of more interest to students of international law.)

Nature of the Parties

3. Cases affecting ambassadors, other public ministers, and consuls.
4. Controversies to which the United States is a party.
5. Controversies between two or more states.
6. Controversies between a state and citizens of another state.
7. Controversies between citizens of different states. These are known as diversity of citizenship cases.
8. Controversies between citizens of the same state claiming lands under grants of different states.
9. Controversies between a state, or citizens of a state, and a foreign government or its citizens or subjects. (This clause has been limited by judicial decisions and the Eleventh Amendment, which deprived the federal courts of jurisdiction in suits brought against a state by citizens of another state or by citizens of a foreign state.)

A case or controversy must fall within one of the classes listed here in order to be brought before a federal court. However, this does not mean that the federal courts alone may take jurisdiction in each instance. Congress may provide that some cases in the categories listed here may be tried by state as well

---

[1] Clarence N. Callender, *American Courts: Their Organization and Procedure* (New York: McGraw-Hill, 1927), pp. 36–37.

as federal courts. An important area of such concurrent jurisdiction is suits between citizens of different states when the sum of $10,000 or more is involved. On the other hand, Congress has given the federal courts exclusive jurisdiction over some matters. For example, federal courts *must* decide disputes involving suits against ambassadors and foreign consuls; bankruptcy, copyright, and admiralty cases; all cases involving federal criminal laws.

Organization of Federal Courts

The Constitution has very little to say about the organization of federal courts. Section 1 of Article III provides that the "judicial power of the United States shall be vested in one Supreme Court, and in such inferior courts as the Congress may from time to time ordain and establish." Thus, the only court provided for in the Constitution is one Supreme Court, with Congress given the responsibility for the creation of other federal courts. Neither does the Constitution say anything regarding the number of judges deemed necessary for the Supreme Court or any inferior courts which may be created by Congress. Beginning with the First Judiciary Act of 1789, Congress has enacted various laws that supplement Article III and account for the present structure and organization of the federal courts. The First Judiciary Act is of particular importance because it proved to be basic to the development of the present federal court organization. The act has been said to have three claims to greatness:

1. It set up a federal court organization which lasted almost unchanged for nearly one-hundred years.
2. A section of the Act empowering the Supreme Court to supervise the state courts was one of the "most important nationalizing influences" during our early history.
3. Most important, the tradition of a system of federal courts operating throughout the nation was firmly established.[2]

DISTRICT COURTS

At the bottom of the federal court system are the United States District Courts. They are courts of original jurisdiction; in other words, all cases and controversies involving federal questions, with the exception of the few disputes that start in the Supreme Court or specialized legislative courts, are tried first in the district courts. The fifty states, together with the District of Columbia and Puerto Rico, are divided into some ninety districts, with a court in each district. The number of courts varies from time to time, as Congress may create additional ones when the need arises. There is at least one federal district court in each of the states. In the larger and more heavily populated

---

[2] Felix Frankfurter and James M. Landis, *The Business of the Supreme Court* (New York: Macmillan, 1928), p. 4.

states, where there is a greater volume of work, there are more district courts. For example, New York and Texas each have four.

The majority of cases in the district courts are heard by one judge. In some instances, such as when an injunction is sought to restrain the enforcement of a federal or state law that is said to be unconstitutional, a panel of three judges must decide the issue. Two or more judges may hear cases simultaneously in different places within the same district when the number of cases is large.

The federal district courts dispose of most federal cases. In recent years, their work has increased tremendously because of the development of a large body of federal criminal law and the increasing number of civil cases filed each year. Between 1940 and 1955, the number of civil cases alone increased by 55 per cent. This increase has resulted in long delays in the administration of justice simply because the rise in the number of district judges has not kept pace with the increased workload.

Like other federal judges, district judges (with the exception of those in Puerto Rico, who serve for terms of eight years) are appointed for life by the President, with the advice and consent of the Senate, and may be removed only by impeachment for misconduct.

Because the district courts are original trial courts having jurisdiction over both criminal and civil cases involving federal law, they are the only federal courts that normally use a jury. Some of the most dramatic and spectacular cases of recent years were originally tried in district courts. In 1951, a federal jury in New York City found Julius and Ethel Rosenberg guilty of atomic espionage. The death sentence subsequently imposed by a district judge stirred worldwide interest and resulted in numerous public controversies involving political as well as legal questions. In another sensational trial before a district court, the jury found that eleven leaders of the Communist party were guilty of conspiring to organize a political party in order to teach and advocate the overthrow of the American system of government by force and violence. The convictions were upheld by the Supreme Court in *Dennis* v. *United States,* which is fully considered in Chapter 15. Because of their duty to enforce the reapportionment and antidiscrimination decisions of the Supreme Court, in recent years the district courts have frequently been at the center of bitter political struggles.

COURTS OF APPEALS

Above the district courts are the Courts of Appeals. Prior to 1948, these courts were called the Circuit Courts of Appeals. They were created in 1891 to relieve the Supreme Court of some of its appellate work. As the name suggests, these courts have only appellate jurisdiction. They hear appeals from the district courts and from important independent regulatory commissions. They are courts of final appeal in the majority of cases, because only a few of the cases they consider are carried to the Supreme Court for decision.

The territory of the United States is divided into ten numbered areas known as circuits, and in each of these areas there is a Court of Appeals. In addition, the District of Columbia comprises an unnumbered circuit with its own Court of Appeals, which is concerned principally with the large volume of litigation arising from the work of numerous federal administrative agencies in Washington. The numbered circuits encompass much larger areas. The Court of Appeals for the First Circuit, for example, disposes of cases from Maine, Massachusetts, New Hampshire, Puerto Rico, and Rhode Island; the Tenth Circuit includes Colorado, Kansas, New Mexico, Oklahoma, Utah, and Wyoming. Each of the eleven Courts of Appeals has from three to nine judges, depending on the volume of judicial work. A panel of three judges usually reviews cases, with the judge who is senior in service acting as presiding officer. Until 1891, each Supreme Court justice was required to "ride the circuit"; that is, to hold court in his assigned circuit as well as to perform his duties as a member of the highest court. Although Supreme Court justices no longer ride the circuit, each of the justices is still assigned to particular circuits in a supervisory capacity.

SUPREME COURT

The Supreme Court of the United States is at the top of the federal court system. It consists of a chief justice and eight associate justices. Any six justices are necessary to constitute a quorum. The number of justices on the Court at a given time is set by Congress. From time to time the number has varied. The Court began with a chief justice and five associate justices. In 1801, the total number was reduced to five; in 1802, the number was six again; seven in 1807; nine in 1837; and ten in 1863. In 1866, the number was fixed at seven by Congress, but the Court had not got down to that figure before Congress raised it again, in 1869, to nine. That number has remained unchanged since that date.

The Supreme Court has both original and appellate jurisdiction. Article III, Section 2, states as follows: "In all cases affecting ambassadors, other public ministers, and consuls, and those in which a State shall be party, the Supreme Court shall have original jurisdiction. In all other cases before mentioned, the Supreme Court shall have appellate jurisdiction, both as to law and fact, with such exceptions, and under such regulations, as the Congress shall make." However, for all practical purposes, the Supreme Court is principally an appellate court, because the cases in which it has original jurisdiction are not numerous: criminal cases involving such personnel are nonexistent because of diplomatic immunity; nor is the constitutional grant of original jurisdiction necessarily an exclusive one, because Congress may authorize other federal courts to exercise concurrent jurisdiction. Cases are appealed to the Supreme Court from the state courts, *directly* from the district courts in some instances, from the Courts of Appeals, and occasionally from legislative courts such as the Court of Military Appeals. Courts are termed *legislative* rather than *constitutional* courts because Congress has established them under authority implied from constitutional provisions other than Article III. Because judges of legislative courts are not governed by Article III, they need not be appointed for life or good behavior nor removed by impeachment. The Court of Claims was included in the legislative court category until 1953, when Congress declared it to be a Court established under Article III. Similarly, Congress changed the United States Customs Court and the United States Court of Customs and Patent Appeals to constitutional courts in 1956 and 1958, respectively.

At present the Supreme Court disposes of about 3,800 cases annually. Written opinions are handed down in about 125 of these cases each year.[3] A careful preliminary scrutiny of each case is made by the Court before it is placed on the calendar for argument. In recent years, this sifting process has enabled the Court to dispose, without argument, of many cases coming from both the federal and state courts.

How Cases Are Appealed to the Supreme Court

Cases must be appealed to the Supreme Court in accordance with the procedure established by Congress. At present, cases reach the Supreme Court by three principle methods: (1) by appeal; (2) by writ of certiorari; (3) by certification. The writ of error was utilized in some of the older cases in much the same way as appeal, but it was abolished for federal court usage in 1928. Relief which could be obtained in federal courts by the writ of error is now obtainable generally by appeal.

APPEAL

In broad terms the word *appeal* denotes any method used to bring a case to a higher court for review. In the more technical sense used here, it refers to the method of review, which is a matter of right of one of the parties to an action. In other words, the higher court *must* hear the case when it is brought by appeal. The Supreme Court *must* review cases from state courts in two instances: (1) where the validity of a treaty or statute of the United States is questioned and the state court has held it *invalid;* (2) where the validity of a state law has been questioned on the ground that it contravenes the Constitution, treaties, or laws of the United States and the state court *sustains* its validity.

The Supreme Court may review by appeal decisions of the Courts of Appeals when a federal statute is held unconstitutional in a suit to which the United States is a party or when a state statute is held to be invalid as repugnant to the Constitution, treaties, or laws of the United States. Although the majority of district court decisions are reviewed only by a court of appeals, some cases may be carried, on *appeal,* from a district court directly to the

---

[3] These figures are based on surveys of the work of the Supreme Court published each November in the *Harvard Law Review*.

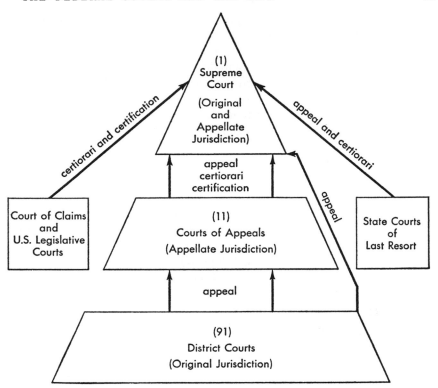

Federal Court Structure and Flow of Cases to the Supreme Court.

Supreme Court. Such direct appeals are allowed because some questions raised in the district court are of such importance that they need to be settled by the district court are of such importance that they need to be settled by the Supreme Court as quickly as possible. Direct appeals are allowed in the following situations: (1) where the district court has held an act of Congress unconstitutional; (2) where the district court has ruled against the United States in a criminal case; (3) where either a one-judge or three-judge district court has rendered a judgment in a suit brought by the United States to enforce the antitrust laws, the Interstate Commerce Act, and some provisions of the Federal Communications Act; (4) where a three-judge district court grants or denies an injunction in suits setting aside orders of the Interstate Commerce Commission and in suits to restrain the enforcement of state or federal statutes on the grounds of unconstitutionality.

Although review by appeal is important, the right of a litigant to carry his case to the Supreme Court has been extremely limited. In 1925, Congress gave the Supreme Court almost complete power to decide what cases it would hear by allowing the Court to grant or deny petitions for writs of certiorari as it saw fit. In addition, the Supreme Court will review a case on appeal only if the justices feel that a substantial federal question has been raised. Thus, the

Court exercises discretion even in appeals cases. For example, during one term of the Court, thirty-seven out of the fifty appeals dismissed were refused a hearing "for want of a substantial federal question. Since the court must pass judgment on the question of substantiality, its so-called compulsory jurisdiction has a strong element of discretion in it. The only difference between a dismissal of an appeal for lack of a substantial federal question and a denial of a petition for certiorari is that in the latter case no reason is ordinarily given, whereas in the former the Court must at least assert the absence, in its judgment, of a substantial issue."[4]

WRIT OF CERTIORARI

Persons who have been adversely affected by the decision of a lower court can petition for a writ of certiorari. This writ can be defined as an order to the lower court to send the entire record of the case to the higher court for review. It is granted by the Supreme Court when four justices feel that the issues raised are of sufficient public importance to merit consideration. Petitions for writs of certiorari are filed in accordance with prescribed forms, the petitioner stating why he feels the Court should grant the writ. The opposing party also may file a brief outlining the reasons why the case should not be reviewed by the Court on certiorari.[5] According to the Revised Rules of the Supreme Court, "a review on writ of certiorari is not a matter of right, but of sound judicial discretion, and will be granted only where there are special important reasons therefor." The Supreme Court may review on certiorari decisions of state courts when a federal question is involved and there exists no right of appeal, decisions of the Courts of Appeals, and decisions of some of the legislative courts. Only a few (less than 15 per cent) of the total number of petitions for writs of certiorari filed each year are granted by the Court.

CERTIFICATION

This is a seldom-used method of appeal whereby a lower court requests that the Supreme Court answer certain questions of law so that a correct decision may be made. The Supreme Court may answer the questions, after which the lower court may reach a decision in light of the answers provided; or, in instances when a Court of Appeals has certified questions, the entire record of the case may be ordered up for decision by the Supreme Court itself. This method of appeal is not within the control of the litigants, because only the lower court may determine whether or not clarifications on points of law are required. Only the Courts of Appeals and the Court of Claims may certify questions to the Supreme Court for review.

[4] David Fellman, "Constitutional Law in 1951–1952," *American Political Science Review,* Vol. 47 (March 1953), p. 127.

[5] Sample forms used in connection with petitions for certiorari, appeals, certification, and other writs are reproduced in Robert L. Stern and Eugene Gressman, *Supreme Court Practice* (Washington, D.C.: Bureau of National Affairs, Inc., 1954), pp. 381–434.

How the Supreme Court Decides Cases

The Supreme Court's annual term runs from the first Monday in October to the following June. After adjournment, special sessions may be called by the chief justice to consider questions of exceptional importance and urgency. For example, a special session was called in the summer of 1942 to deal with the case of German saboteurs. During the first week of the term the Court usually disposes of work that has accumulated over the summer months. After that the Court divides its time between the hearing of cases and recesses. The general pattern is for the Court to hear oral argument for two weeks and then to recess for two weeks to study cases and write opinions. Many cases are disposed of in *per curiam* opinions, which are simply brief announcements, without full explanation, of the decision reached by the Court itself, rather than through the written opinion of one of its members.[6] A *per curiam* opinion may state simply that "the appeal is dismissed for want of a substantial federal question." The method of disposing cases by full opinion has remained substantially the same over a number of years. The procedure followed may be outlined briefly as follows:

1. Cases filed in the Supreme Court are first placed on one of three dockets. The most important of these is the *Appellate Docket,* which consists of cases from the lower courts for review. The few cases in which the original jurisdiction of the Court is invoked are placed on the *Original Docket.* The *Miscellaneous Docket,* which was created in 1945, is comprised of a wide variety of petitions, including a large number coming from prisoners who seek to challenge the legality of their convictions.[7] Applications for the extraordinary writs, such as mandamus and habeas corpus, are also placed on the *Miscellaneous Docket.*

2. The party bringing the action before the Supreme Court must file a brief, usually within forty-five days after the case has been placed on the docket. Thirty days later an answering brief must be filed by the other contending party. When the case comes before the Court on a writ of certiorari, the party bringing the action is called the *petitioner,* with the answering party known as the *respondent.* In appeal cases, the *appellant* brings the action, with the other party being referred to as the *appellee.* Forty copies of the brief must be filed with the clerk of the Supreme Court by counsel for each party. The brief, which is filed in accordance with prescribed form, generally states the issues of the case, the questions presented, actions of the lower courts, and all necessary legal arguments with the citation of cases and statutes relied on. A brief may also be filed by a person who is not a party to the case but acts as *amicus*

---

[6] An evaluation of the Court's *per curiam* practice is found in a Note, *Harvard Law Review,* Vol. 69 (1956), pp. 707–25.

[7] Edwin McElwain, "The Business of the Supreme Court as conducted by Chief Justice Hughes," *Harvard Law Review,* Vol. 63 (1949), pp. 20–24.

curiae, or friend of the court. For example, the Solicitor General of the United States may file a brief as a friend of the court if a case involves issues of direct interest or concern to the federal government.

3. All the briefs filed are studied by each of the justices with the aid of their respective law clerks. The decision as to whether or not oral arguments need to be heard is made after the briefs and other pertinent materials have been analyzed thoroughly. The maximum time allowed for oral argument is usually one hour for each of the contending parties. During the oral presentation, the justices may ask questions or request additional data on pertinent points of the case. Many Supreme Court justices have noted the importance of the oral argument. Chief Justice Hughes remarked that "it is a great saving of time of the court, in the examination of extended records and briefs, to obtain the grasp of the case that is made possible by oral discussion and to be able more quickly to separate the wheat from the chaff."[8]

4. After all the written and oral arguments have been presented, the justices meet in conference to vote on the case. These conferences are held each Friday morning while the Court is sitting. All the discussions are private, with only the members of the Court allowed in the conference room. What actually takes place at the conference can be determined only by the few comments that the justices themselves have made. However, the conference procedure is known not to vary greatly from year to year. Justice Stone described the work of the conference as follows:

On the day before the conference each judge receives a list of cases which will be taken up at the conference, and the order in which they will be considered. This list actually includes every case which is ready for final disposition, including the cases argued the day before the conference and all pending motions and applications for certiorari.

At conference each case is presented for discussion by the Chief Justice, usually by a brief statement of the facts, the questions of law involved, and with such suggestions for their disposition as he may think appropriate. No cases have been assigned to any particular judge in advance of the conference. Each justice is prepared to discuss the case at length and to give his views as to the proper solution of the questions presented. In Mr. Justice Holmes' pungent phrase, each must be ready to "recite" on the case. Each judge is requested by the Chief Justice, in the order of seniority, to give his views and the conclusions which he has reached. The discussion is of the freest character and at the end, after full opportunity has been given for each member of the Court to be heard and for the asking and answering of questions, the vote is taken and recorded in the reverse order of the discussion, the youngest, in point of service, voting first.

On the same evening, after the conclusion of the conference, each member of the Court receives at his home a memorandum from the Chief Justice advising him of the assignment of cases for opinions. Opinions are written for the most

[8] Charles E. Hughes, *The Supreme Court of the United States* (New York: Garden City Publishing Co., 1936), p. 58.

part in recess, and as they are written they are printed and circulated among the justices, who make suggestions for their correction and revision. At the next succeeding conference these suggestions are brought before the full conference and accepted or rejected as the case may be. On the following Monday the opinion is announced by the writer as the opinion of the Court.[9]

In addition to the majority decision of the Court, separate concurring and dissenting opinions may be written, although concurrence or dissent may be expressed without written opinion. Any justice is free to write a separate opinion if he is not satisfied with the majority decision. A *concurring opinion* is one that agrees with the Court's decision but disagrees with the reasoning by which the decision was reached. *Dissenting opinions* may be written when one or more of the justices disagrees with the decision of the Court as well as with the reasoning used in reaching the decision. Important concurring and dissenting opinions are useful for the student of government, as they may help clarify the majority opinion of the Court and reveal the important political, social, and economic conflicts involved in the case. The dissenting opinion "provides an argument opposing that of the majority which may be seized upon by lawyers and urged in succeeding cases with some hope of success. It calls attention to defects in the position of the majority forcing a rethinking and perhaps strengthening of that position. It further calls the majority to the bar of public opinion and enlightened legal opinion."[10] However, dissenting opinions may obscure as well as clarify the basic issues.

> The technique of the dissenter often is to exaggerate the holding of the Court beyond the meaning of the majority and then to blast away at the excess. . . . Then, too, dissenters frequently force the majority to take positions more extreme than was originally intended. The classic example is the Dred Scott case, in which Chief Justice Taney's extreme statements were absent in his original draft and were inserted only after Mr. Justice McLean, then a more than passive candidate for the presidency, raised the issue in dissent. The *right of dissent* is a valuable one. Wisely used on well-chosen occasions, it has been of great service to the profession and to the law. . . . The tradition of great dissents built around such names as Holmes, Brandeis, Cardozo, and Stone is not due to the frequency or multiplicity of their dissents, but to their quality and the importance of the few cases in which they carried their disagreement beyond the conference table. Also, quite contrary to the popular notion, relatively few of all dissents recorded in the Supreme Court have later become law, although some of these are of great importance.[11]

[9] Harlan F. Stone, "Fifty Years' Work of the United States Supreme Court," *American Bar Association Journal,* Vol. 14 (August–September 1928), p. 436.

[10] Loren P. Beth, "Justice Harlan and the Uses of Dissent," *American Political Science Review,* Vol. 49 (December 1955), p. 1104.

[11] Robert H. Jackson, *The Supreme Court in the American System of Government* (Cambridge: Harvard University Press, 1955), pp. 18–19.

Sometimes Supreme Court opinions contain materials that are not pertinent to the basic issues of the case. In other words, in the course of rendering an opinion, a justice may wander away from the major points of the case and make remarks that are not essential to the reasoning or decision. In legal terminology such remarks are known as *obiter dicta,* meaning that which was put in by the way or incidentally. Although obiter dicta do not establish principles of law, they may provide insights into a justice's personal views or indicate the development of particular judicial trends.

Source Materials in Constitutional Law

Supreme Court opinions are available in three separate editions.

United States Reports (cited as U.S.). This is the official edition of Supreme Court cases, which is published by the federal government. Usually the opinions of each term of the Court can be incorporated in two or three volumes of the *Reports.* Until 1875, the reports of Supreme Court decisions were cited by the name of the reporter as follows:

1789–1800	Dallas (Dall.)	4 volumes
1801–1815	Cranch (Cr.)	9 volumes
1816–1827	Wheaton (Wheat.)	12 volumes
1828–1842	Peters (Pet.)	16 volumes
1843–1860	Howard (How.)	24 volumes
1861–1862	Black (Bl.)	2 volumes
1863–1874	Wallace (Wall.)	23 volumes
1875–1882	Otto	17 volumes

The total number of volumes cited by the name of the reporter is 107. After 1882, and beginning with Volume 108, the official reports are cited by number only.

United States Supreme Court Reports, Lawyers' Edition (cited as L. Ed.). This edition is privately published by the Lawyers' Cooperative Publishing Company. Both the *Lawyers' Edition* and the *Supreme Court Reporter,* listed subsequently, contain more detailed headnotes than the official *United States Reports.* The headnotes, which appear at the beginning of the opinion, are designed to summarize the legal contents of the case. Those that appear in the two privately published editions are prepared by editorial staffs to assist lawyers in quickly obtaining comprehensive summaries of the case law in a particular subject matter. The *Lawyers' Edition* of the Supreme Court Reports also carries excerpts from the briefs of counsel and annotations of important cases. At the 1966 term of the Court, the *Lawyers' Edition* began a second series beginning again at Volume 1 (cited as L. Ed 2d).

Supreme Court Reporter (cited as Sup. Ct.). This edition, which is similar to the *Lawyers' Edition,* is published by West Publishing Company. It contains only those Supreme Court cases decided since 1882.

In citing cases, the volume number comes first, followed by the abbreviated title of the report in which the case appears and the page number, with the date in parentheses at the end. For example, the complete citation for the case of *Lochner* v. *New York,* decided in 1905, is 198 U.S. 45; 25 Sup. Ct. 539; 49 L. Ed. 937 (1905). This means that the full text of the Lochner case may be found in Volume 198 of the *United States Reports* at page 45, or in Volume 25 of the *Supreme Court Reporter* at page 539, or in Volume 49 of the *Lawyers' Edition* at page 937. The citation for *Marbury* v. *Madison* is 1 Cranch 137; 2 L. Ed. 60 (1803). The case can therefore be found in Volume 1 of *Cranch* at page 137 or in Volume 2 of the *Lawyers' Edition* at page 60.

One need not wait until the bound volumes appear to read the full text of a Supreme Court case. Decisions of great public significance are often reproduced in full by some leading newspapers, such as *The New York Times.* Also, the federal government publishes each decision in pamphlet or advance-sheet form as *Preliminary Prints.* These advance sheets appear about five to eight weeks after the decision is rendered. The two private publishers also issue advance sheets, which appear much earlier than those of the federal government. Complete opinions are available most rapidly in the *United States Law Week,* published by the Bureau of National Affairs, and in the *Supreme Court Bulletin,* published by Commerce Clearing House.

Decisions of the lower federal courts to 1924 are found in the *Federal Reporter,* which went to Volume 300, and are cited as Fed. or F. After 1924, the cases were collected in a second series known as *Federal Reporter, second series,* and cited as Fed. (2d) or F. 2d. Since 1932, the decisions of the district courts have been published separately in *Federal Supplement,* cited as F. Supp. or F.S.

Decisions rendered by the highest state courts are published in separate volumes by each state or by a commercial publisher. In addition, a regional reporting system combines the decisions of several state courts in one publication. For example, the *Atlantic Reporter* carries decisions of Connecticut, Delaware, Maine, Maryland, New Hampshire, New Jersey, Pennsylvania, Rhode Island, and Vermont since 1885. The *Southern Reporter* contains decisions of the states of Alabama, Florida, Louisiana, and Mississippi since 1887. The Northeastern, Northwestern, Pacific, Southeastern, and Southwestern *Reports* contain the state cases of their respective areas. In citing state cases, the same practice is followed of giving the volume number first, the abbreviated title of the report in which the case appears, and the page number. For example, the complete citation for the Massachusetts case of *Furbush* v. *Connolly* is 318 Mass. 511, 62 N.E. 2d., 595 (1945). This means that this case, which was decided in 1945, may be found in Volume 318 of the *Massachusetts Reports* at page 511 or in Volume 62 of the *Northeastern Reporter,* second series, at page 595.

How to Read Supreme Court Cases

The title of each case is taken from the names of the two parties to the controversy. The name that appears first is the party that is bringing the action, or the *plaintiff*. The *defendant* is the other party, against whom the action is taken. He must answer the charges brought by the plaintiff. Each of the parties may be referred to as indicated in the following hypothetical case:

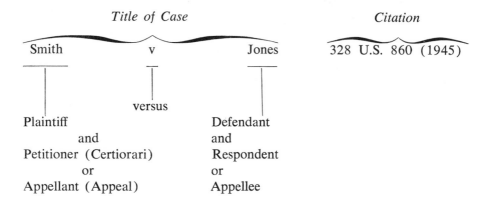

Title of Case			*Citation*
Smith	v	Jones	328 U.S. 860 (1945)
	versus		
Plaintiff		Defendant	
and		and	
Petitioner (Certiorari)		Respondent	
or		or	
Appellant (Appeal)		Appellee	

A few of the cases in this volume have been presented in full and therefore appear exactly as they were decided by the Court. However, the majority of them have been edited to eliminate technical legal matters and side issues which are of little use to the student of constitutional law.

There is no one best way to read and analyze these cases. How this is done depends largely on each individual's habits and methods of study. Nevertheless, an understanding of the decision, especially during the early stages, can best be acquired by following a prescribed pattern or outline that helps to bring out the essential issues of each case. The student should read the case in its entirety at least once before attempting to use the following outline:

1. *Title and Citation.*
2. *Fact of the Case.* Here the student should make a short statement concerning the circumstances that brought about the case or controversy. The statement of facts sometimes appears in concise form at the beginning of an opinion. In other instances, the facts are found scattered throughout the case. On some occasions, the best recital of the facts is found in a dissenting opinion. Students usually obtain a better grasp of the case if the identity of the parties to the action is clearly established and if the holdings of the lower courts, if any, are understood clearly.
3. *Legal Question or Questions.* The question presented is revealed by the statement of facts, which should indicate the nature of the conflict of interests which the Court must resolve. The legal question is many times

concisely stated by the Court. For example, in *Coyle* v. *Smith,* 221 U.S. 599 (1911), the Court stated that "the only question for review by us is whether the provision of the enabling act was a valid limitation upon the power of the state after its admission, which overrides any subsequent legislation repugnant thereto."

4. *Holding.* This is the Court's answer to the question or questions presented.

5. *Opinion.* The opinion refers to the chain of legal reasoning that led the Court to its holding. The Court's line of reasoning should be outlined point by point, because an understanding of the entire case will depend largely on how well the Court's reasoning process is followed.

6. *Separate Opinion or Opinions.* Both concurring and dissenting opinions should be carefully analyzed to show major points of conflict with the majority opinion.

7. *Comment and Evaluation.* Here the student should personally evaluate the importance of the case, show its relationship, if any, with other cases studied, and indicate its place in the whole stream of American constitutional law. This is also the place to criticize or praise the opinions or make any other comment that seems significant to the student.

3
The Justices of the Supreme Court

The life of a Supreme Court justice is a lonely, somewhat monastic one. Moreover, the work is exacting and isolated from the mainstream of day-to-day *partisan* political activity. The terrible demands on a Supreme Court justice were brought home clearly in 1962, with Justice Charles E. Whittaker's statement that he was retiring because of the "great volume and continuous stresses" of the work which had brought him to the "point of physical exhaustion."[1] The late Learned Hand, widely regarded as one of the most distinguished federal court judges of his time, despite the fact that he was never elevated to the Supreme Court, remarked, shortly before his death at the age of eighty-nine, that as a judge for fifty-two years he had spent a "lifetime of utter drudgery, shoveling smoke." In a recent article, the Solicitor General of the United States, who is in charge of all government litigation before the Supreme Court, wrote that the problems with which the justices deal "are so difficult, the number and variety of cases are so overwhelming, the implications are so far-reaching that one sits humbled by the demands upon them."[2]

Yet, for a number of reasons, a seat on a federal court, particularly the Supreme Court, is a highly coveted one. A Supreme Court justice enjoys a

[1] As quoted in *The New York Times* (April 1, 1962), p. 10E.

[2] Archibald Cox, "The Nature of Supreme Court Litigation," *Journal of the American Judicature Society,* Vol. 45 (October 1961), p. 96.

great deal of prestige; probably only the office of the President is more highly regarded by the American people. The justices of the highest court have the challenging opportunity to grapple with the most significant problems which confront the nation. Chief Justice Warren once remarked that he was happy to have traded the life of politics for a more cloistered life on the Court. "I found it was very satisfying," he said, "to have time to dig into original sources and indulge in contemplation—an opportunity that had been denied to me for a great many years. As I go along, the interest of doing this is increasing so that I could not imagine going back to the other life."[3]

Selection of Supreme Court Justices

The Constitution provides for the appointment of Supreme Court justices by the President by and with the advice and consent of the Senate. They serve for life "during good behavior" and may be removed by impeachment only. No member of the Court has ever been removed by the impeachment process, although Samuel Chase, who served on the Court from 1796 to 1811, was impeached by the House of Representatives but acquitted by the Senate.

Unlike the offices of President, senator, and representative, the qualifications necessary for appointment to the Court are not stipulated by the Constitution. Theoretically, the President could appoint anyone to the Court, so long as that person could take the oath required of all government officials to support the Constitution. In practice, however, there are certain informal requirements that must be met. All the justices, for example, have been lawyers, and despite the silence of the Constitution, this requirement will undoubtedly be maintained.

In the final analysis, only the President *really* knows why he chooses a particular person for the Court, and he may have considered so many factors that even he could not single out the determining one, so that all of the speculation and "inside information" relating to judicial appointments may well be erroneous. Nevertheless, a number of key factors considered in the selection of a justice can be isolated. They may be listed as follows:

POLITICAL CONSIDERATIONS

Party membership and activity have always been of utmost importance in the selection of justices. Rare indeed are the instances when a President has appointed a man to the Supreme Court who is not a member of his own political party. This has been true from the beginning of the Court's history, when President Washington named ardent Federalists to the Court, to the present time. For example, when President Eisenhower named Governor Warren of California to be the fourteenth Chief Justice of the United States

---

[3] Quoted by Anthony Lewis, *The New York Times* (October 18, 1959), p. 1.

in 1953, it was the first appointment by a Republican president in over twenty years. At that time all the members of the Court were Democrats, except Associate Justice Harold H. Burton, who was a Republican senator from Ohio when he was named to the bench by President Truman. Burton's appointment to the Court can be explained, in part, by the fact that he was a close friend of the President and had worked ably with him on a special committee investigating defense production when both men were members of the Senate.

There have been similarly sound explanations for each of the other eleven times that a President has named a chief justice or justice from outside his own party. President Hoover, for example, was all but forced to name Justice Cardozo, a New York Democrat, to replace Justice Holmes, because he was so obviously the outstanding man for the post. Moreover, Hoover was urged to name Cardozo by powerful members of the bar, United States senators, and other leading public figures. Two major reasons have been advanced to explain why President Eisenhower named Justice Brennan, a Roman Catholic and New Jersey Democrat, to the Court. Some observers felt that since the appointment came on the eve of the 1956 presidential election, Eisenhower was making a bid for votes from members of Brennan's party and faith in the Eastern states. Others have discounted this theory and argued that the basic reason for Brennan's appointment was the strong support he received from key Republicans and bar association leaders who were trying to persuade the President that broad judicial experience should be a prime qualification for appointment to the Court.[4] Brennan had ten years' experience as a state judge and was serving on the Supreme Court of New Jersey when appointed.

In making Supreme Court appointments the President is, of course, interested in much more than the mere party label of a candidate. What he wants is to place men on the Court who actively share his views on the important social, political, and economic issues of the day. In brief, he wants a man who supports the policies and progam of his administration. Nowhere has this been better demonstrated than in the letter President Theodore Roosevelt wrote to Senator Henry Cabot Lodge of Massachusetts when he was considering elevating Justice Holmes to the Supreme Court to replace Justice Gray. The President wrote as follows:

> In the ordinary and low sense which we attach to the words "partisan" and "politician," a judge of the Supreme Court should be neither. But in the higher sense, in the proper sense, he is not in my judgment fitted for the position unless he is a party man, a constructive statesman, constantly keeping in mind his adherence to the principles and policies under which this nation has been built up and in accordance with which it must go on; and keeping in mind also his relations with his fellow statesmen who in other branches of the government are striving in cooperation with him to advance the ends of government.
>
> *Now I should like to know that Judge Holmes was in entire sympathy with*

[4] Philip Yeager and John Stark, "The Supreme Court in Transition," *The New York Times Magazine* (March 10, 1957), p. 13.

*our views, that is with your views and mine and Judge Gray's . . . before I
would feel justified in appointing him.* Judge Gray has been one of the most
valuable members of the Court. I should hold myself as guilty of an irreparable
wrong to the nation if I should put in his place any man who was not absolutely
sane and sound on the great national policies for which we stand in public life.[5]

Holmes did receive the appointment but later bitterly disappointed the
President when he wrote the "promonopoly" dissenting opinion in a close
(5 to 4) case,[6] an opinion that went against the heart of Roosevelt's antitrust
program. After that, relations between Holmes and the President were always
strained. Holmes later wrote that his dissenting opinion broke up his "incipi-
ent friendship" with the President, who viewed it as a "political departure (or,
I suspect, more truly, couldn't forgive anyone who stands in his way). We
talked freely later but it never was the same after that, and if he had not been
restrained by his friends, I am told that he would have made a fool of himself
and would have excluded me from the White House."[7]

The Holmes appointment demonstrates clearly that no matter how careful
he may be, a President cannot be certain that the justices he chooses will perform as expected. Chief Justice John Marshall fervently carried on the principles of the Federalists just as President John Adams thought he would, and
Chief Justice Taney did not completely disappoint his good friend President
Jackson. On the other hand, Justice McReynolds, chosen by the liberal President Wilson, became one of the most wrathful, hard-bitten conservatives ever
to sit on the Court, while much to the surprise of many of his Republican
supporters, Justice Brennan quickly joined the libertarian bloc on the Warren
Court.[8]

Nevertheless, every President will continue to name men to the Court who
appear to share his basic political views. In fact, a President often appoints
men to the highest bench simply as a reward for helping him obtain the nomination and win the election or for other valuable services to the party. For
example, as head of the Kentucky delegation to the Republican National Convention in 1876, John Marshall Harlan took the entire delegation into the
Rutherford B. Hayes camp at the crucial moment. As a result, Hayes won the
nomination and subsequently became President after a bitter, hotly debated
contest. Undoubtedly this was one of the factors leading to Harlan's appointment to the Court. There are many other examples: Hugo Black was an ardent
New Dealer who vigorously supported Franklin D. Roosevelt's program in the
Senate before becoming the President's first appointee to the Supreme Court

---

[5] Henry Cabot Lodge, *Selections from the Correspondence of Theodore Roosevelt and
Henry Cabot Lodge, 1894–1918* (New York: Scribner, 1925), Vol. I, pp. 517–19. (Emphasis supplied.)

[6] *Northern Securities Co.* v. *United States,* 193 U.S. 197 (1904).

[7] *Holmes–Pollock Letters,* (Cambridge: Harvard University Press, 1941), Vol. II,
pp. 63–64.

[8] An excellent case study of the whole appointment process is found in David Danelski, *A Supreme Court Justice Is Appointed* (New York: Random House, 1964).

in 1937. Earl Warren was named Chief Justice in 1953 after giving considerable help to the Eisenhower campaign in the Western states. Both Byron R. White and Arthur J. Goldberg, President Kennedy's two appointees to the Court, had actively campaigned in his behalf in the presidential election of 1960.

In discussing political considerations, the role of the Senate must be kept in mind. The hearings before the Senate Judiciary Committee, which first considers the qualifications of a prospective justice, indicate clearly that partisan politics play an important part in the confirmation of a Supreme Court justice.[9] The nomination of Louis D. Brandeis was opposed by many lawyers and public officers because of his alleged "radical position" on important social and economic issues. As chairman of the Senate Judiciary Committee, Senator George Norris opposed the appointment of Charles Evans Hughes to the chief-justiceship because of Hughes' close association with powerful private corporations and financial interests. Some Southern senators objected to the nomination of John Marshall Harlan in 1954 because his grandfather was the only justice to dissent from the opinion in *Plessy* v. *Ferguson,* 163 U.S. 573 (1896), upholding the "separate but equal" doctrine of racial segregation. Although only one man has been rejected by the Senate in recent years (Judge John J. Parker, in 1930, because of supposed anti-Negro and antilabor feelings), the power is still there, and most Presidents have been reluctant to risk a contest with the Senate by nominating "politically unacceptable" men for the Court.

PERSONAL FRIENDSHIP

The role of personal friendship in Supreme Court appointments is extremely difficult to measure because so many other factors (usually of a political nature) may also be present. Nevertheless, in some instances, it has been of crucial importance. President Taft, for example, believed firmly that younger men should be on the Court, but he nominated sixty-five-year-old Horace H. Lurton in 1909, principally because they had become close friends while sitting together as federal circuit court judges.[10] President Wilson was willing to risk a serious fight with the Senate to name his personal friend, Louis D. Brandeis, to the Court in 1916. Personal friendship was an important factor in each of President Truman's four Supreme Court appointments (Chief Justice Fred M. Vinson, Justices Harold H. Burton, Tom C. Clark, and Sherman Minton).

RELIGIOUS AND ETHNIC AFFILIATION

Again, the religious factor is ordinarily related to other considerations and difficult to assess. However, the policy of giving broad representation to the

---

[9] For a detailed discussion, see Henry J. Abraham and Edward M. Goldberg, "A Note on the Appointment of Justices of the Supreme Court of the United States," *American Bar Association Journal,* Vol. 20 (February 1960), p. 152.

[10] Daniel S. McHargue, "President Taft's Appointments to the Court," *Journal of Politics,* Vol. 12 (1950), p. 478.

nation's religious denominations has been an important factor in some cases. In recent years there has usually been one Catholic and one Jewish member on the Court. This has been the result in some measure of pressures from the minority denominations for representation and of the desire of the President to obtain their political support. Some observers felt that one motive in President Kennedy's choice of Arthur J. Goldberg to replace Justice Frankfurter in 1962 was the desire to maintain the modern practice (since 1916) of having at least one Jewish member on the Court, a practice continued by the appointment of Justice Fortas to replace Justice Goldberg. On the other hand, President Taft named Edward D. White to the chief justiceship in 1910, principally because he shared his constitutional views and not simply because he was a Catholic. Similarly, as we have seen, Justice Cardozo's superb qualifications, rather than the fact that he was Jewish, accounted for his appointment to the Court. The appointment of Justice Thurgood Marshall undoubtedly begins a new tradition of Negro representation. President Nixon, however, has announced that he will not follow the customs of ethnic and geographic representation.

GEOGRAPHICAL AND SECTIONAL CONSIDERATIONS

During the first century of the Republic, when Supreme Court justices were required to ride the circuit, geographical and sectional considerations were of controlling importance, because it was deemed essential that the justice come from the circuit he was to serve. Thus, Samuel F. Miller was named to the Court in 1862 by President Lincoln in part because a new circuit arrangement maneuvered through Congress by Miller and his supporters created a place for him.[11] Miller was nominated to the Court only one day after Lincoln approved the reorganization of the circuits.

With the end of regular circuit duties for Supreme Court justices at the turn of the century, geographical considerations became less important. However, presidents do generally try to maintain a geographical balance on the Court. For example, the appointment of Justice Wiley B. Rutledge in 1943 was influenced by the fact that he "had geography"; that is, he was a Midwesterner who was needed on the Court to help maintain some semblance of sectional balance. The appointment of Justice Cardozo in 1932 demonstrates that geographical considerations can be disregarded when other factors are involved. Two New Yorkers—Chief Justice Hughes and Justice Stone—were already on the Court when Cardozo, also from New York, was nominated.

PRIOR JUDICIAL EXPERIENCE

Although, on the whole, prior judicial experience is of minor importance in Supreme Court appointments, it sometimes is a crucial factor. In part because

[11] Charles Fairman, *Mr. Justice Miller and the Supreme Court, 1862–1890* (Cambridge: Harvard University Press, 1939), pp. 40–50.

of the pressure of the organized bar and of some senators and representatives, President Eisenhower showed a marked preference for experienced men. After the initial appointment of Chief Justice Warren, Eisenhower's four other nominees all had served on the bench—Justices Harlan, Brennan, Whittaker, and Stewart. From time to time bills have been introduced in Congress that would require five or even ten years' service as a judge for a Supreme Court nominee. None of these bills has been enacted, largely because most students of the Court agree with retired Justice Frankfurter that "the correlation between prior judicial experience and fitness for the Supreme Court is zero. The significance of the greatest among the Justices who had such experience, Holmes and Cardozo, derived not from that judicial experience but from the fact that they were Holmes and Cardozo. They were thinkers, and more particularly, legal philosophers."[12]

Prior judicial experience is not essential because of the peculiar nature of the Court's work. The Supreme Court is not the usual type of law court; it is concerned principally with resolving major questions of public law—that is, questions arising out of broad, fundamental issues of public policy.[13] Throughout our history, almost every major political issue before the country has ultimately reached the Supreme Court in the guise of private litigation. What is required for the resolution of these issues is political judgment of the highest order, rather than technical judicial proficiency in private law. Hence, judicial experience, although perhaps helpful, is not essential for success on the Court; in fact, if it had been a prerequisite in the past, most of the greatest Supreme Court justices, such as Marshall, Story, Taney, Miller, Hughes (first appointment), and Brandeis, would have never reached the highest bench. It is interesting to note, however, that three recent appointees, Justices Goldberg, Fortas, and Marshall, although lacking extended prior judicial experience, had previously had long and very successful records as practicing attorneys representing important clients before the Supreme and other courts. Chief Justice Burger had previously served on a Federal Court of Appeals, but his appointment to that post had been a reward for political services.

MISCELLANEOUS FACTORS

Many other factors, such as age, distinguished service in high federal office, preeminence at the bar, and even chance, or as Justice Frankfurter has said, the "caprices of fortune," sometimes play an important part in Supreme Court appointments. For a variety of reasons, two of the most distinguished lower court judges in recent American history—Learned Hand of the second federal circuit and Arthur Vanderbilt of New Jersey—never reached the highest bench.

[12] Felix Frankfurter, "The Supreme Court in the Mirror of Justices," *University of Pennsylvania Law Review,* Vol. 105 (1957), p. 781.
[13] Rocco J. Tresolini, "In Defense of the Supreme Court," *Social Science,* Vol. 36 (January 1961), pp. 38–39.

That the "caprices of fortune" may well be decisive is aptly demonstrated by President Grant's nomination of Morrison R. Waite to the chief justiceship in 1874.[14] Waite was by no means Grant's first choice. The President had first offered the job to one of his closest political allies, Senator Roscoe Conkling of New York, a well-known, unscrupulous, machine politician, who declined because he had other unfulfilled political ambitions. Grant then reportedly offered the position to two other senators, but both declined. Grant's Secretary of State, Hamilton Fish, also declined the appointment. The next nominee was seventy-year-old Caleb Cushing of Massachusetts, who was widely known as a "political prostitute" who "never allowed principle or conscience to stand in the way of gain." The hue and cry raised against Cushing forced Grant to withdraw the nomination. Grant then named his Attorney General, George H. Williams, who had been maneuvering for the post by trying to persuade the President that it would be unwise to promote any of the sitting justices, to the top position. But Williams was an unfit candidate with a doubtful reputation and a scheming wife who had used her influence to obtain immunity from prosecution for various persons in return for payments of $30,000. Opposition to Williams' nomination was so strong that Grant finally withdrew his name. Grant then turned to Waite in hopes that his very obscurity would assure his confirmation. An Ohioan later remarked that "it was the queerest appointment that was ever made during Grant's two terms. Everybody was surprised and none more so than men from our own state, where he lived." Waite was confirmed by the Senate without difficulty, but his appointment aroused little enthusiasm. "The general reaction was that, while better Chief Justices could have been found, the country was lucky to get one who was at least an honest man and a competent lawyer. The Senate hastened to confirm the nomination for fear Grant might change his mind and do worse."

A close perusal of the biographical sketches in Appendix II will help reveal, among other things, the many disparate considerations that influence the selection of justices. Remember too that, although the President is alone responsible for his judicial appointments, he receives suggestions from many sources. The Attorney General of the United States is most influential in this regard. He screens candidates, maintains liaison with members of Congress and others interested in pushing a particular candidate, and most important, makes recommendations to the President. The various bar associations are also extremely influential. In recent years the American Bar Association has played an increasingly important role through its Committee on the Federal Judiciary, which reports on the professional qualifications of candidates seriously con-

---

[14] Most of the materials in this paragraph are drawn from the *Morrison R. Waite Papers,* Manuscript Division, Library of Congress, and appeared in Rocco J. Tresolini, "Chief Justice Morrison R. Waite and the Public Interest," *Northwest Ohio Quarterly: A Journal of History and Civilization,* Vol. 34 (Summer 1962), pp. 124–37. This is also related in a distinguished new biography of Waite. See C. Peter Magrath, *Morrison R. Waite: The Triumph of Character* (New York: Macmillan, 1963), Ch. 1.

sidered for appointment to the Supreme Court.[15] A negative report from this committee practically eliminates a candidate from further consideration.

The justices themselves have no official role in the selection of their associates, but there have been times when their influence has been felt. Justice Miller, for example, though he failed, used all the means at his disposal to secure an appointment for his brother-in-law. Chief Justice Taft used his influence unashamedly with the President and other key figures to secure appointments for the men he wanted. He was instrumental in the selection of both Justices Butler and Sanford. Moreover, Taft was "completely successful in keeping out men who he thought would misinterpret the Constitution or increase dissension within the Court."[16] When considering a successor to Chief Justice Hughes in 1941, President Roosevelt followed the advice of both Hughes and Justice Frankfurter in elevating Justice Stone to the center chair.

Role of the Chief Justice

The chief justiceship of the United States is undoubtedly the most powerful judicial office in the world. In terms of prestige, the Chief Justice ranks next to the President. Yet, by custom and tradition, the Chief Justice reigns; he does not rule. The extent of his influence depends on his ability and personality. In deciding cases he has but one vote. Nevertheless, he occupies a central position because of his special administrative duties in connection with the daily work of the Court. The Chief Justice can exert great influence in carrying out three specific functions.

PRESIDING OFFICER

As presiding officer, the Chief Justice sets the "tone and tempo of all its proceedings. If the Chief is systematic and industrious in his habits, the Court will meet on time and keep abreast of its work. The attitude of the Chief Justice is invariably reflected in the work of the other judges and in the conduct of counsel who appear before the court."[17]

MODERATOR OF COURT CONFERENCES

Perhaps the Chief Justice's greatest opportunity for leadership comes in his role as the moderator of the Court conferences where the cases are discussed and judgments rendered. A strong chief can influence the decision in many

[15] For an extended discussion, see John R. Schmidhauser, *The Supreme Court: Its Politics, Personalities and Procedures* (New York: Holt, Rinehart and Winston, 1960), Ch. 2.

[16] Walter F. Murphy, "In His Own Image: Mr. Chief Justice Taft and Supreme Court Appointments," *The Supreme Court Review* (1961), p. 188.

[17] Merlo J. Pusey, "Chief Protector of the Constitution," *The New York Times Magazine* (September 20, 1953), p. 13.

cases, because he is the discussion leader and has the first opportunity to state his conclusions in the conference, even though he is the last to vote. Chief Justice Hughes was able to dominate the Court because of his ability to conduct business in an efficient, kindly manner.

> In Court and in conference he struck the pitch, as it were, for the orchestra. He guided discussion by opening up the lines for it to travel, focusing on essentials, evoking candid exchange on subtle and complex issues, and avoiding redundant talk. He never checked free debate, but the atmosphere which he created, the moral authority which he exerted, inhibited irrelevance, repetition and fruitless discussion. He was a master of timing: he knew when discussion should be deferred and when brought to an issue. He also showed uncommon resourcefulness in drawing elements of agreement out of differences and thereby narrowing, if not always escaping, conflicts. He knew when a case was over; he had no lingering afterthoughts born of a feeling of defeat, and thereby avoided the fostering of cleavages. Intellectual issues were dealt with by him as such. As a result, differences in opinion did not arouse personal sensitiveness.[18]

ASSIGNMENT OF OPINION

The Chief Justice assigns the writing of the Court's opinion, provided he is among the majority. If he is not with the majority, the senior justice on the majority side assigns the opinion. In discharging this function, Chief Justice Hughes was "like a general deploying his army. His governing consideration was what was best for the Court as to the particular case in the particular situation. That meant disregard of self but not of the importance of the chief justiceship as a symbol. For there are occasions when an opinion should carry the extra weight which pronouncement by the Chief Justice gives. Selection of the Court's voice also calls for resourcefulness, so that the Court should not be denied the persuasiveness of a particular justice. . . . The grounds for assignment may not always be obvious to the outsider. Indeed, they are not always so to the members of the Court; the reasons normally remain within the breast of the Chief Justice. But these involve, if the duty is wisely discharged, perhaps the most delicate judgment demanded of the Chief Justice."[19]

Of course, not all of the chief justices have had the capacity for inspired leadership. Some of the great leaders on the Court never reached the higher post. Men such as Joseph Story, Oliver Wendell Holmes, Louis D. Brandeis, Stephen J. Field, and Joseph P. Bradley made much greater contributions than some chief justices. Chief Justice Hughes made this point well when he said that "Marshall's pre-eminence was due to the fact that he was John

---

[18] Felix Frankfurter, "The Administrative Side of Chief Justice Hughes," *Harvard Law Review,* Vol. 63 (1949), p. 3.

[19] *Ibid.,* pp. 3, 4. The conference leadership and opinion assignment powers of the chief justice are examined by David Danelski in "The Influence of the Chief Justice in the Decisional Process," in Walter F. Murphy and C. Herman Pritchett (eds.), *Courts, Judges, and Politics* (New York: Random House, 1961).

Marshall, not simply that he was Chief Justice."[20] But whether chief justice or associate justice, the job of one who renders opinions in our nation's highest tribunal calls for the ". . . faculties that are demanded of the historian and the philosopher and the prophet. The last demand upon him—to make some forecast of the consequences of his action—is perhaps the heaviest. To pierce the curtain of the future, to give shape and visage to mysteries still in the womb of time, is the gift of imagination."[21]

"Influences" on the Justices

In the *Preface* to the first edition of this book, we stressed the fact that "the social and economic philosophy of a justice and his personal likes and dislikes play important roles in the shaping of his decisions," and hence that the careful reading of the biographical sketches of individual justices in Appendix II would increase the student's understanding of how the personal element may sometimes affect decisions of the Court. Perhaps even more important in indicating the impact of judicial attitudes on judicial opinions than biographical studies are those borrowing the techniques of social psychology, the leading example of which is Glendon Schubert's, *The Judicial Mind* (Evanston, Ill.: Northwestern University Press, 1965). In addition, it is well to remember that the aphorism "no man is an island" is as applicable to Supreme Court justices as it is to men in other walks of life. Professor Paul A. Freund of the Harvard Law School has aptly written that "the law is not made by judge alone but by 'Judge and Company.' "[22] Other individuals and groups "influence" the law that judges make in various and sometimes surprising ways. However, the student must be careful not to construe the word *influence* in terms of crude threats, bribes, or string pulling. The major mode of lobbying in all political life is to seek to persuade public officials by means of calm and reasoned argumentation that the policy desired is in the public interest and will contribute to the public good. The influence spoken of here is the influence of logic and reason, such as "a well-reasoned and ably written brief, be it by one of the litigants or a brief *amicus curiae;* a persuasive oral argument on behalf of an issue at bar; a timely, thoughtful, and convincing book, monograph, speech, or law review article on the general or specific issue; a strategically timed use of a bona fide case,"[23] or an appeal to widely held sentiments of political and social justice. The influences on the justices may be classified as follows:

[20] Charles E. Hughes, The Supreme Court of the United States (New York: Columbia University Press, 1928), p. 58.

[21] Felix Frankfurter, "The Job of a Supreme Court Justice," *The New York Times Magazine* (November 28, 1954), p. 14.

[22] Paul A. Freund, *The Supreme Court of the United States, Its Business, Purposes and Performance* (Cleveland: World, 1961), p. 146.

[23] Henry J. Abraham, *The Judicial Process* (New York: Oxford University Press, 1962), p. 205. See also Loren P. Beth, *Politics, the Constitution and the Supreme Court* (Evanston, Ill.: Harper & Row, 1962), p. 67.

LAWYERS AND THE LEGAL PROFESSION

An obvious but important fact is that Supreme Court justices, "however broad and varied their past experience, are lawyers. With each other they share, to a large degree, a common background of legal knowledge and craftsmanship."[24] After elevation to the Supreme Court, many of the justices' closest ties continue to be with other lawyers. Chief Justice Taft and Justice Sutherland, for example, continued as important leaders in various activities of the American Bar Association after appointment to the Court. The resignation of Chief Justice Warren from the American Bar Association in 1959 because of that organization's anticipated criticism of the Court represented a "dramatic exception to a normally close relationship."[25] Thus, in varying degrees the justices continue to share the values of the legal profession, which in many subtle and sometimes subconscious ways help shape their judicial opinions.

At the same time a justice is deeply affected by the traditions and institutional ethos of the Court itself. Justice Frankfurter once remarked that the "judicial process demands that a judge move within the framework of relevant legal rules and the covenanted modes of thought for ascertaining them. . . . *There is a good deal of shallow talk that the judicial robe does not change the man within. It does.*"[26]

More directly, the justices often borrow heavily from the briefs and arguments of counsel in the preparation of their opinions. Many of Daniel Webster's arguments, for example, found their way into the opinions of Chief Justice Marshall. In discussing his argument before Marshall and the Court in *Gibbons* v. *Ogden* (Chapter 8), Webster said: "I think I never experienced more intellectual pleasure than in arguing that novel question to a great man who could appreciate it, and take it in; and he did take it in, as a baby takes in its mother's milk."[27] After the decision Webster observed that Marshall's opinion ". . . was little else than a recital of my argument. The Chief Justice told me that he had little to do but to repeat that argument, as that covered the whole ground."[28] John Archibald Campbell's forceful oral argument calling for economic freedom from governmental controls in the *Slaughterhouse Cases* (Chapter 11) failed to carry the Court but greatly influenced Justice Fields' dissenting opinion which was soon to carry the day. Relying heavily on Fields' opinion, subsequent court majorities transformed the due process clause of the Fourteenth Amendment into a powerful instrument with which to preserve laissez-faire economics and the property rights of the rich. Another famous example of a lawyer's deep influence on the Court is the successful develop-

---

[24] Thomas H. Eliot, "The Teaching of Law in the Undergraduate Program," paper delivered at the annual meeting of the American Political Science Association, Washington, D.C. (September 12, 1959).

[25] Schmidhauser, *op. cit.,* p. 66.

[26] *Public Utilities Commission* v. *Pollack,* 343 U.S. 466–67 (1959). (Italics supplied.)

[27] Charles Warren, *The Supreme Court in United States History,* Vol. 2 (Boston: Little, Brown, 1922), p. 63.

[28] *Ibid.,* pp. 70–71.

ment of the "Brandeis brief" by Louis D. Brandeis before he was named to the Court. As noted more fully in Chapter 12, Brandeis relied on facts and statistics as well as legal arguments to show that women needed protection from excessive hours of labor.

Lawyers also affect decisions of the Court in more subtle ways. The influence of great teachers of law such as Felix Frankfurter, who taught at the Harvard Law School for twenty-five years, is difficult to measure; yet certainly such teachers help shape the law. Increasingly, articles appearing in law reviews and other legal journals that are often closely examined by the justices may be influential in the formulation of legal doctrine.[29] Many times the law clerks (two for each justice; three for the Chief Justice), who are among the most able and intelligent of the recent law school graduates, serve as an important funnel for ideas between the justices and the law schools. Finally, the influences discussed in the next two classifications are brought about largely by men who are lawyers.

ADMINISTRATIVE OFFICERS AND LOWER COURT JUDGES

As noted in Chapter 19, the growth in the power of administrative officers in the twentieth century posed some serious problems for the Supreme Court. However, as administrative agencies became more firmly established and their powers more clearly defined, many aspects of the administrative process were insulated from the possibility of judicial review. Today, even when review does occur, the Court is generally very reluctant to overrule decisions of administrative officers.[30] The justices usually defer to the decisions of well-established agencies and respected administrative officers. Professor Freund has wondered, for example, if the decision in *Korematsu* v. *United States* (Chapter 16) "would have been the same had the final administrative determination been made by someone whose judgment was less deeply respected than Secretary [of War] Stimson's."[31]

The deference shown by the Supreme Court to certain lower courts or individual justices may greatly influence the decisions. A classic example is Chief Justice Vinson's opinion in *Dennis* v. *United States* (Chapter 15), where he relied heavily on the court of appeals' decision written by Judge Hand. Vinson quoted extensively from Hand's opinion and adopted his rule of decision with the comment that "As articulated by Chief Judge Hand, it is as succinct and inclusive as any other we might devise at this time. It takes into consideration those factors which we deem relevant, and relates their significances. More we cannot expect from words."

---

[29] Chester A. Newland, "Legal Periodicals and the United States Supreme Court," *Midwest Journal of Political Science,* Vol. 3 (February 1959), p. 58.

[30] Peter Woll, *Administrative Law: The Informal Process* (Berkeley and Los Angeles: University of California Press, 1963), p. 164. For a critique of modern bureaucracy by a former member of the Federal Trade Commission, see Lowell Mason, *The Language of Dissent* (Cleveland and New York: World, 1959).

[31] Freund, *op. cit.,* pp. 146–47.

Decisions of respected courts, such as the New York Court of Appeals, with a good record of protecting individual rights are often followed by the Supreme Court with little question. Judge Henry W. Edgerton of the federal Court of Appeals for the District of Columbia was widely respected for his careful and lucid opinions on civil liberties, and they were consistently followed by the Court; "the record of support of these opinions at the hands of the Supreme Court is most impressive evidence of Edgerton's stature as a judge."[32] Finally "one may speculate whether the decision in *Betts* v. *Brady* [overruled in *Gideon* v. *Wainwright* (see Chapter 18)], holding the appointment of counsel for indigent criminal defendants in state courts not to be an invariable constitutional requirement, would have been the same had the opinion of the court below been written by someone less highly esteemed than Chief Judge Bond of Maryland, who is referred to by name in Mr. Justice Robert's opinion no fewer than fifteen times."[33]

ORGANIZED INTEREST GROUPS

Organized interest groups may attempt to influence decisions of the Supreme Court principally by sponsoring and promoting test cases and by entering cases as *amici curiae*. Such attempts may be difficult to discern, because by all outward appearances a particular case may appear to be simply a contest between two private litigants. However, the two parties in the case may be sponsored and supported by conflicting interest groups who are seeking broader objectives.

> Organizations support legal action because individuals lack the necessary time, money, and skill. With no delays a case takes an average of four years to pass through two courts to the Supreme Court of the United States. A series of cases on related questions affecting the permanent interest of a group may extend over two decades or more. The constant attention that litigation demands, especially when new arguments are being advanced, makes the employment of regular counsel economical. This may be supplemented by a legal staff of some size and by volunteer lawyers of distinction. Parties also pay court costs and meet the expense of printing the record and briefs. Organizations are better able to provide the continuity demanded in litigation than individuals. Some individuals do maintain responsibility for their own cases even at the Supreme Court level, but this is difficult under modern conditions.[34]

In the early 1900s the National Consumers League, organized to improve

---

[32] Eleanor Bontecou (ed.), *Freedom in the Balance: Opinions of Judge Henry W. Edgerton Relating to Civil Liberties* (Ithaca, N.Y.: Cornell University Press, 1960), p. 14.

[33] Freund, *loc. cit.,* p. 146.

[34] Clement E. Vose, "Litigation as a Form of Pressure Group Activity," *The Annals of the American Academy of Political and Social Science,* Vol. 319 (September 1958), p. 22.

the lot of women and children in industry, hired Louis D. Brandeis and other sympathetic lawyers to defend labor legislation from attacks in the courts. This was the group that sponsored the "Brandeis brief," which later became so influential in subsequent Supreme Court decisions.[35] In 1934, conservative business bitterly opposed to the New Deal organized the American Liberty League, which filed reports and prepared briefs in key cases arguing that important New Deal statutes were unconstitutional. The American Civil Liberties Union, long dedicated to the protection of American freedoms, has influenced the course of litigation by filing briefs and providing counsel for defendants claiming a denial of constitutional rights.

The two most recent and best examples of interest-group activity are provided by the zealous members of a minority sect known as Jehovah's Witnesses (discussed fully in Chapter 14) and by the National Association for the Advancement of Colored People (NAACP). To obtain a maximum of what they considered their religious freedom, the Jehovah's Witnesses went into court with a vengeance. Beginning in 1938, they brought more than fifty *bona fide* test cases to the Supreme Court by supporting members who had violated a local ordinance or state statute. The Witnesses won all but a handful of these cases and thereby curbed every major attempt to limit their activities. As is often the case with other interest groups, the Jehovah's Witnesses concentrated on litigation for their victories because of their ". . . total helplessness in any other area. Their numbers and hence their political weight were negligible. Further impairing any appeal to the legislature or public opinion was the Witnesses' extreme unpopularity. Their offensive literature, their aggressive missionary methods, their doubtful patriotism, and their inability to advance the most reasonable argument without dragging in the iniquities of the Catholic Church, all tended to convince a large segment of the population that any Witness misfortunes were all deserved."[36]

The NAACP played a key role in preparing the way for the *Public School Segregation Cases* (Chapter 17) and in improving generally the legal status of the Negroes. Since the end of World War II the NAACP has won more than 50 cases in the Supreme Court in its attempt to secure racial equality before the law for the 21 million American Negroes. "By presenting test cases to the Supreme Court, the NAACP has won successive gains protecting the right of Negroes in voting, housing, transportation, education, and service on juries. Each effort has followed the development of new theories of legal interpretation and required the preparation of specific actions in the courts to challenge existing precedent. The NAACP Legal Defense Fund has accomplished

[35] Clement E. Vose, "The National Consumers League and the Brandeis Brief," *Midwest Journal of Political Science* (1957), p. 267. The major tactics of business groups attempting to influence the Court are discussed by Nathan Hakman, in "Business Influence in the Judicial Process," *Western Business Review*, Vol. 1 (1957), p. 124.

[36] David R. Manwaring, *Render Unto Caesar: The Flag Salute Controversy* (Chicago: University of Chicago Press, 1962), pp. 33–34.

these two tasks through the cooperation of associated and allied groups."[37] That the road for the NAACP has been a long and hard one is demonstrated by its painstaking efforts to outlaw restrictive covenants. The organization brought cases to the courts for over thirty years and spent $100,000 before winning a signal victory in the Supreme Court in the 1948 case of *Shelley* v. *Kraemer*[38] (Chapter 17). And that victory probably would not have been possible without changed social and political circumstances and the support of numerous other groups. Eighteen organizations filed briefs as *amici curiae* supporting the NAACP position in the Shelley case. These included such diverse groups as the American Jewish Congress, American Federation of Labor, Human Relations Commission of the Protestant Council of New York City, American Civil Liberties Union, and American Association for the United Nations.[39]

The Supreme Court, therefore, is sometimes a good mirror, as Justice Frankfurter once noted, of the struggles of dominant forces outside the Court. Yet a word of caution is in order when discussing the influence of interest groups. In constitutional cases, the Supreme Court is of course "aware of competing interests, and often can decide the case only by giving preference to one or the other, but not all the interests are represented by organizations or are even discernible as 'groups' in any significant sense. . . ."[40] Relatively few cases are brought to the Supreme Court by organized groups themselves.[41] Typically a particular class of persons or economic interests is represented in court by a single litigant who may not consciously be trying to defend anyone's interests but his own. Thus, the railroad seeking to free itself from a state regulation by appeal to the Supreme Court under the commerce clause, or a felon seeking to have a conviction based on wiretapping reversed by asserting a constitutional right to privacy, may have neither asked for nor received help from the Association of American Railroads or an association of American criminals, but by litigating they may aid the cause of railroads and criminals in general. Even more significant, the criminal may be protecting the rights of all those honest men interested in preserving themselves from the threat of a technologically advanced police state, and considerations of those interests may weigh far more heavily with the Court than the interests of the immediate litigants.

Thus, naive pressure-group conceptions do not adequately describe the subtle intersection of political and social interests with the Supreme Court. Nor should crude analogies, which fail to take into account differing political styles

[37] Vose, "Litigation as a Form of Pressure Group Activity," *op. cit.*, p. 24.

[38] Clement E. Vose, *Caucasians Only: The Supreme Court, the NAACP, and the Restrictive Covenant Cases* (Berkeley and Los Angeles: University of California Press, 1959), p. 213.

[39] *Ibid.*, pp. 193–97.

[40] Eliot, *op. cit.*

[41] See Nathan Hakman, "Lobbying the Supreme Court—An Appraisal of Political Science Folklore," *Fordham Law Review*, Vol. 35 (October 1966).

and role demands, be drawn between interest-group activities in the legislative and executive spheres and those in the judicial. To say that both courts and interests are part of politics is not to say that judges respond to interest claims in exactly the same ways congressmen and administrators do.

Impact of the Court's Decisions

One fact to bear in mind is that once the Supreme Court has made a decision, it can do little else. Congress may enact laws to enforce the decision, the President may send in armed forces or use his extensive political powers in more subtle ways to support the Court's holding, but the Court itself can do little or nothing, for it has no pressure groups, no devoted clientele, no army to enforce its decisions. What happens, then, after the justices render a decision in a particular case? Does everyone affected immediately feel bound by the Court ruling? Do others defy the Court by simply ignoring or attempting to evade the decision? Depending on the case, any or all of these things may happen. There may be a whole range of responses to a particular Supreme Court decision, for the impact upon the nation as a whole is by no means uniform. "However well established may be the Court's role as the expounder of the constitutional document, the impact of a decision will depend on many individuals and circumstances far beyond the confines of the Court."[42] In general, the Supreme Court is most effective in securing compliance with its decisions when it has clearly "enunciated well-publicized broad general principles"[43] and when resistance from lower courts, other government officials, and the public is at a minimum. Yet, throughout our history there have always been those who refused to be bound by the justices' decisions and found ways of circumventing them by simply ignoring them, by formal amendment to the Constitution (Eleventh, Thirteenth, and Sixteenth, as noted in Chapter 1), by pressures on Congress, by evasion and delays in compliance, and even by force.[44] There are many recent examples.

The decisions concerning released time programs of religious education (*McCollum* v. *Board of Education* and *Zorach* v. *Clauson,* Chapter 14) were widely ignored or evaded. In the *McCollum* case the Court held 8 to 1 that the use of public school buildings for released time programs violated the separation of church and state clause of the First Amendment. Yet,

---

[42] Frank J. Sorauf, "*Zorach* v. *Clauson:* The Impact of a Supreme Court Decision," *American Political Science Review,* Vol. 53 (September 1959), p. 777.

[43] John P. Frank, *Marble Palace* (New York: Knopf, 1958), p. 22.

[44] Jack W. Peltason, *Federal Courts in the Political Process* (New York: Random House, 1955), pp. 55–64. See also Samuel Krislov, "The Perimeters of Power, Patterns of Compliance and Opposition to Supreme Court Decisions," paper delivered at the annual meeting of the American Political Science Association, New York (September 6, 1963).

It is no secret that after the *McCollum* decision, and despite it, many communities continued to hold released time classes in public school buildings. The most conservative estimate places noncompliance at 15 per cent of the programs, and other estimates run up to 40 to 50 per cent in some states. Five years later in the *Zorach* case the Court reaffirmed the *McCollum* ruling but offered the localities a clearly constitutional alternative: religious education off school premises. Have local religious and educational groups met the Court half-way and given up released time in the school room? The answer is "no—not entirely." In 1956 a knowledgeable authority on school law wrote that "school systems in virtually every state violate in some way the legal principle concerning religious instruction in the public schools." Some of the violations are unwitting, he wrote, but knowing violators include "some persons holding responsible church or school positions."[45]

Thus the "evidence of noncompliance with the Zorach ruling indicates the limited effectiveness of the Court in maintaining constitutional uniformity within the federal system. Especially in religiously homogeneous communities, where there are no dissident elements strong enough to protest or begin court action, the *McCollum* and *Zorach* rules are evaded and ignored."[46]

The most recent school prayer cases (*Engel* v. *Vitale, Abington School District* v. *Schempp, Murray* v. *Curlett,* Chapter 14) resulted in widespread verbal resistance and noncompliance. A storm of protest greeted the Court's decision in *Engel* v. *Vitale,* which held that a nondenominational prayer written by the New York Board of Regents for use in the public schools was unconstitutional. In fact, few decisions in American history have aroused such public anguish. The furor was so great that the Columbia Broadcasting Company took the unprecedented step of presenting a two-hour television program, entitled "Storm over the Supreme Court," explaining the role of the Court in American history and exploring the issues of the school prayer decision.[47] Although the *Engel* decision had many supporters, it was loudly condemned by newspapers, politicians, many Roman Catholics, a good proportion of Protestants, the American Legion, and even former Presidents Hoover and Eisenhower. For example, Representative George W. Andrews, a Democrat from Alabama who had previously attacked the *School Segregation Cases* in bitter language, remarked that "they (the justices) put the Negroes in the schools and now they've driven God out."[48] Cardinal Spellman said: "I am shocked and frightened that the Supreme Court has declared unconstitutional a simple and voluntary declaration of belief in God by public school children.

[45] Sorauf, *op. cit.,* pp. 785–86. See also Gordon Patric, "The Impact of a Court Decision: Aftermath of the McCollum Case," *Journal of Public Law,* Vol. 6 (Fall 1957), p. 455.

[46] *Ibid.,* p. 791.

[47] Presented in two parts on February 20 and March 13, 1963. Transcripts of the program may be obtained from CBS News, 51 W. 52nd St., New York, N.Y.

[48] *The New York Times* (June 26, 1962), p. 16.

The decision strikes at the very heart of the Godly tradition in which America's children have for so long been raised."[49] Evangelist Billy Graham called the decision "another step toward secularism in the United States. . . . The framers of our constitution meant we were to have freedom of religion, not freedom from religion."[50] *Engel* v. *Vitale* was deplored and damned on the floor of Congress, where several proposals for a constitutional amendment nullifying the decision were introduced. At its annual meeting, the Governors' Conference adopted a resolution, with only the governor of New York abstaining, condemning the decision and calling for a constitutional amendment which would allow the use of voluntary prayers in public classrooms.

Given this response to the *Engel* decision, many commentators demanded that the ruling be ignored. Gradually, however, the realization grew that many of the more extreme statements had been made by politicians and others who had never bothered to read the Court's opinion! Calmer voices prevailed and the furor died down.

When the Court outlawed Bible reading and the recitation of the Lord's Prayer in public schools a year later (*Abington School District* v. *Schempp, Murray* v. *Curlett*), the reaction was less violent. This was the result in part of the fact that the Court wrote a more careful series of opinions. In his long majority opinion Justice Clark attempted to set at rest some of the public fears brought on by *Engel* v. *Vitale*. Explanatory concurring opinions by Justices Brennan and Goldberg also helped obtain acceptance of the decision. Moreover, many religious groups had anticipated the decision and had quietly urged acceptance. Nevertheless, there were still those who refused to comply. Three months after the decision, Arkansas, Alabama, and Delaware still required Bible reading or the recitation of the Lord's Prayer in public schools. State officials in South Carolina, Florida, and Texas were giving local authorities discretion in deciding what to do, generally with the understanding that religious observances were not required.[51] In Pennsylvania ten of the state's 2,500 school districts voted to continue Bible reading despite the Supreme Court decision. The Pennsylvania Attorney General announced that the state did not plan to institute legal action against school districts refusing to comply with the Court's ruling.

The greatest resistance by far in recent years has been to the Court's segregation cases. Ten years after the 1954 *School Segregation Cases,* only about 10 per cent of the South's Negro students were attending integrated classes. One writer has noted that the failure to obey the Court in this area "constitutes the most disgraceful act of mass contempt in the history of the nation."[52]

[49] *Ibid.,* p. 17.
[50] *Idem.*
[51] *Ibid.* (September 8, 1963), p. 9E.
[52] Edward Bennett Williams, *One Man's Freedom* (New York: Atheneum, 1962), p. 300. Two major studies of school district compliance with the Supreme Court's religious decisions have appeared recently. Richard Johnson, *The Dynamics of Compliance:*

Some of the many problems which prevent the translation of printed decisions into living law in this area are examined in Chapter 17. Here we need only point out that in some areas resistance has been so great that local groups have been willing to abandon public education completely rather than to comply with the Court's order to integrate the schools.

While the compliance battle rages in the South, a series of new problems are likely to share the spotlight for at least the next decade. Many Northern school districts are unlkely to end de facto segregation without some judicial prodding. The Supreme Court's reapportionment decisions (see Chapter 4) create major compliance problems for the state legislatures and the state and federal courts charged with their implementation. The actual impact on police practices of the Court's decisions on the rights of accused persons (see Chapter 18) remains very much in doubt.[53]

Perhaps the most interesting of all impact problems has been the response of Congress to the Court's controversial decisions in the subversion, religion, apportionment, and criminal procedure areas. Shifting coalitions, frequently consisting of Southern and Northern conservatives, have proposed a series of statutes and constitutional amendments, some designed to reverse specific Supreme Court rulings and others to deprive the Court of certain areas of its jurisdiction. Even though the Court's congressional opponents have enjoyed relatively little success, they have come close enough, often enough, to make their efforts a major concern to friends of the Court.[54]

In 1968, as part of an omnibus crime bill that provided badly needed federal aid to local police and gun control provisions, and in the context of the wave of emotion following Senator Kennedy's assassination, the opponents of the Court managed to get through Congress the "reversal" of three Supreme Court decisions. The legislation provided that (1) federal trial courts might find confessions voluntary and admissible as evidence even if the suspect had not been warned of his right to remain silent; (2) federal officers might hold suspects up to six hours (longer in some cases) before arraignment without rendering confessions made during this period inadmissible; and (3) that identifications made at police lineups where the accused was not represented by counsel are admissible at a subsequent trial. None of these legislative provisions apply to state courts or police procedures, and the constitutionality of each was seriously in doubt at the time of passage. It is unlikely that they will actually reverse Supreme Court doctrines on the admissibility of confessions.

Supreme Court Decision-Making from a New Perspective (Evanston, Ill.: Northwestern University Press, 1968); and William K. Muir, Jr., *Prayer in the Public Schools* (Chicago: University of Chicago Press, 1968).

[53] See "Interrogations in New Haven: The Impact of Miranda," *Yale Law Journal,* Vol. 49 (July 1967) p. 1519.

[54] The earlier phases of this story may be followed in Water Murphy, *Congress and the Court* (Chicago: University of Chicago Press, 1962); C. Herman Pritchett, *Congress Versus the Supreme Court* (Minneapolis: University of Minnesota Press, 1961); and Harry P. Stumpf, "Congressional Responses To Supreme Court Rulings," *Journal of Public Law,* Vol. 14 (1966).

The Constitution and Supreme Court Cases

The time for preliminaries is over, and we turn now to the cases themselves. As these are read, keep in mind that the Constitution of the United States contains fewer than 8,000 words and can be read in half an hour.

> As a document the written Constitution is in many ways a superb piece of work. It is short, tense and comprehensive. It outlines a practical system of national government that the first Congress and President found understandable and workable. By the breadth of its terminology and by its provisions for amendments, it makes it possible for Congress and the people to adopt it in practice to changing needs, ideas and conditions as the occasion arises.[55]

Yet a careful reading of the Constitution and its amendments will not provide one with an understanding of American constitutional law, simply because the Constitution is hardly more than an outline. "Constitutions can only map out the terrain roughly, leaving much to be filled in."[56] To understand the American constitutional system, one must study the leading decisions of the Supreme Court, which interprets the Constitution, for much of the "filling in" is done by that Court. Nevertheless, the cases should not be studied until after several careful readings of the Constitution, reproduced in Appendix I.

The Constitution is a "directing channel through which the stream of national existence may safely pass."[57] That document still has meaning for our time, because the Supreme Court continually pours new wine into the old bottles. In carrying out this crucial task of applying the great principles of the Constitution to the specific problems of our times, the Court must, in the long run, rely on the good will and faith of an *informed* people if it is to survive.

[55] William Anderson, "The Intention of the Framers: A Note on Constitutional Interpretation," *American Political Science Review,* Vol. 49 (June 1955), p. 346.

[56] Judge Learned Hand, in an address quoted in Irving Dillard (ed.), *The Spirit of Liberty* (New York: Knopf, 1952), p. 176.

[57] Homer Cummings, "The American Constitutional Method," an address delivered before the Association of the Bar of New York City, December 18, 1935, published by U.S. Government Printing Office (1937).

4
The Courts and Judicial Review

As is the idea of a written constitution, the concept of judicial review is a unique American contribution to the art and practice of government. Judicial review may be defined as the power possessed by American courts to declare that legislative and executive actions are null and void if they violate the written constitution. Three branches of judicial review may be distinguished, as follows:

1. *"National" Judicial Review.* The power of all American courts from the lowest to the highest to pass upon the validity of acts of Congress under the Constitution.
2. *"Federal" Judicial Review.* The power and duty of all courts to abide by the supremacy clause of the Constitution (Article VI) in construing state constitutional provisions and statutes in conflict with the federal Constitution and laws and treaties of the United States.
3. *"State" Judicial Review.* The power of state courts to review laws of the state legislatures under the respective state constitutions.[1]

The power of judicial review is usually associated with the Supreme Court, because it renders *final* judgments in cases involving the interpretation of the

[1] Edward S. Corwin, "Judicial Review," *Encyclopedia of the Social Sciences,* Vol. 8, (1932), p. 457.

federal constitution. Cases involving only state constitutional issues are finally determined by the highest state courts.

The concept of judicial review rests upon an

> extraordinarily simple foundation. Stripped to its essence, it is almost too plain for stating. The Constitution is the supreme law. It was ordained by the people, the ultimate source of all political authority. It confers limited powers on the national government. These limitations derive partly from the mere fact that these powers are enumerated—the government cannot exercise powers not granted to it—and partly from certain express prohibitions upon its powers or upon the manner of their exercise. If the government consciously or unconsciously oversteps these limitations there must be some authority competent to hold it in control, to thwart its unconstitutional attempt, and thus to vindicate and preserve inviolate the will of the people as expressed in the Constitution. This power the courts exercise. This is the beginning and the end of the theory of judicial review.[2]

The great prestige of the Supreme Court stems largely from the fact that it has final authority in the interpretation of the Constitution. In the exercise of this duty the Supreme Court acts as a superlegislature of great political powers. In the minds of the American people, the Court has been identified almost exclusively with the function of judicial review. "The people have seemed to feel that the Supreme Court, whatever its defects, is still the most detached, dispassionate, and trustworthy custodian that our system affords for the translation of abstract into concrete constitutional commands."[3]

Much has been written regarding the question as to whether or not the framers of the Constitution intended that the Supreme Court exercise the power of judicial review. A noted historian concluded many years ago that the majority of the leading delegates to the Philadelphia Convention of 1787 favored judicial review.[4] Professor Corwin later arrived at a similar conclusion.[5] In *The Federalist,* No. 78, Alexander Hamilton expressed clearly the necessity for judicial review in a constitutional system:

> The interpretation of the laws is the proper and peculiar province of the courts. A constitution is, in fact, and must be regarded by the judges, as a fundamental law. It therefore belongs to them to ascertain its meaning, as well as the meaning of any particular act proceeding from the legislative body. If there should happen to be an irreconcilable variance between the two, that which has

---

[2] Howard L. McBain, "Some Aspects of Judicial Review," *Bacon Lectures on the Constitution of the United States* (Boston University Heffernan Press, 1939), pp. 376–77.

[3] *Op. cit.,* p. 23.

[4] Charles A. Beard, *The Supreme Court and the Constitution* (New York: Macmillan, 1912), p. 118.

[5] Edward S. Corwin, *The Doctrine of Judicial Review* (Princeton, N.J.: Princeton University Press, 1914); see also by the same author, "The Constitution as Instrument and as Symbol," *American Political Science Review,* Vol. 30 (December 1936), p. 1078.

the superior obligation and validity ought, of course, to be preferred to the statute, the intention of the people to the intention of their agents.

Nevertheless, judicial review was *not* expressly granted by the Constitution. It was first asserted by Chief Justice Marshall in the famous case of *Marbury* v. *Madison* (1803). The Supreme Court had exercised the power of judicial review in earlier cases that sustained federal and state laws, but for the first time in *Marbury* v. *Madison* an act of Congress was invalidated.[6] A major state law was first held void by the Court as a violation of a provision of the Constitution in 1810.[7]

Since the decision in *Marbury* v. *Madison,* the Supreme Court has declared only some 85 acts of Congress unconstitutional. As the arbiter between the state and federal legal systems, however, the Court has declared void many more state statutes involving federal questions. Judicial review of state statutes has been extremely significant in the maintenance of the federal system. Justice Holmes once declared that he did "not think the United States would come to an end if we lost our power to declare an act of Congress void. I do think the Union would be imperiled if we could not make that declaration as to the laws of the several states."[8] And Chief Justice Hughes noted that "far more important to the development of the country than the decisions holding acts of Congress to be invalid, have been those in which the authority of Congress has been sustained and adequate national power to meet the necessities of a growing country has been found to exist within constitutional limitations."[9]

Limitations on Judicial Review

The practice of judicial review has survived and prospered largely because of the support that the Supreme Court has received from the American people and because of numerous limitations that the Court has imposed on itself. Originally the weakest of the three branches of the federal government, the Supreme Court has grown in power and prestige by wise use of its great power of judicial review. Conflicts with the legislative and executive branches have been minimized by its self-imposed limitations. "In short, judicial self-restraint and judicial power seem to be the opposite sides of the same coin: it has been

[6] *Marbury* v. *Madison* was actually the second case in which a law of Congress was declared unconstitutional. In 1794, the Court held an act of Congress void in *U.S.* v. *Yale Todd,* but the decision was simply reported in a note in a much later case, *U.S.* v. *Ferreira,* 13 How. 40 (1851). Authorities disagree on the case of Yale Todd; some hold that to say that an act of Congress was held unconstitutional in that case is inaccurate.

[7] *Fletcher* v. *Peck,* 6 Cr. 87 (1810).

[8] Oliver W. Holmes, "Law and the Court," *Collected Legal Papers* (New York: Harcourt, Brace, 1920), p. 295.

[9] Charles E. Hughes, *The Supreme Court of the United States* (New York: Columbia University Press, 1928), pp. 96–97.

by judicious application of the former that the latter has been maintained. A tradition beginning with Marshall's coup in *Marbury* v. *Madison* . . . suggests that the Court's power has been maintained by a wise refusal to employ it in unequal combat."[10] In addition to its refusal to render decisions on constitutional questions unless absolutely necessary in order to decide a case, the Court has placed the following limitations on itself.

CASE OR CONTROVERSY

The Supreme Court will exercise the power of judicial review only if an actual case or controversy is presented—litigation involving a real conflict of rights and interests between contending parties. The Court, therefore, cannot take the initiative in declaring laws unconstitutional. "It has no self-starting capacity and must await the action of some litigant so aggrieved as to have a justiciable case. Also, its pronouncement must await the decision in the lower courts. Often it is years after a statute is put on the books and begins to take effect before a decision on a constitutional question can be heard by the Supreme Court."[11] Of course, what constitutes a real case or controversy must be decided by the Court, and on some occasions it has ignored this limitation by rendering decisions in test cases. The Court also has refused to give advisory opinions and to decide moot cases. (A moot case is one that has ceased to have practical importance during the course of a trial or pending an appeal.)

POLITICAL QUESTIONS

The Supreme Court will not decide "political questions," because they must be resolved by the executive or legislature, which together constitute the political branches of the government. The term *political question* cannot be defined precisely, because the Court may expand or contract the definition as it sees fit. In other words, a political question is whatever the Supreme Court says it is. Nevertheless, certain questions are clearly political. They are discussed fully subsequently.

STARE DECISIS (TO STAND BY THE DECISIONS)

The rule of *stare decisis,* or precedent, theoretically limits the Supreme Court, because this means that previous decisions of the Court are binding on it in cases involving exactly the same issue. Although *stare decisis* is generally applicable to all American courts, including the Supreme Court, when they are dealing with statutes and common law, it has not even in theory been strictly applicable in the sphere of judicial review because of the duty of every judge to render "correct" constitutional decisions no matter what the errors of his predecessors. The Court has refused to follow precedent in many in-

---

[10] John P. Roche, "Judicial Self-Restraint," *American Political Science Review,* Vol. 49 (September 1955), p. 722.

[11] Robert H. Jackson, *The Supreme Court in the American System of Government* (Cambridge: Harvard University Press, 1955), p. 24.

stances; in addition, the Court has at times expressly overruled previous decisions.

AVOIDING THE CONSTITUTIONAL ISSUE

The Court will not pass on a constitutional question, although properly presented by the record, if there is also present some other ground on which the case may be disposed of. This rule has found some varied application. Thus, if a case can be decided on either of two grounds, one involving a constitutional question, the other a question of statutory construction or general law, the Court will decide only the latter. . . . Appeals from the highest court of a state challenging its decision of a question under the Federal Constitution are frequently dismissed because the judgment can be sustained on an independent state ground.[13]

PRESUMPTION OF CONSTITUTIONALITY

Justice Washington once wrote, "It is but a decent respect due to the wisdom, integrity and patriotism of the legislative body, by which any law is passed, to presume in favor of its validity, . . ."[14] The justices will normally presume that a statute is constitutional unless the opposite is clearly demonstrated. But the presumption of constitutionality is entertained by the Court much more strongly in some areas than others, and it has openly declared its particular suspicion of statutes based on racial classifications and broadly drawn, sweeping statutes that impinge upon speech and association.[15]

STANDING

An individual has standing to challenge the constitutionality of a law only if his personal rights are directly affected by the operation of the statute. To have standing, one must show "not only that the statute is invalid, but that he [party invoking judicial power] has sustained or is immediately in danger of sustaining some direct injury as the result of its enforcement, and not merely that he suffers in some indefinite way in common with people generally."[16] "The Court will not pass upon the validity of a statute upon complaint of one who fails to show that he is injured by its operation."[17]

But injury alone is not enough. To have standing, a legal right must be violated. In *Alabama Power Co.* v. *Ickes,* 302 U.S. 464 (1938), the Supreme Court noted that "where, although there is damage, there is no violation of a right no action can be maintained." And in *Tennessee Electric Power Co.* v. *TVA,* 306 U.S. 118 (1939), the Court held that governmental action which threatens to injure an individual cannot be challenged "unless the right in-

---

[13] Justice Brandeis concurring in *Ashwander* v. *Tennessee Valley Authority,* 297 U.S. 288, 346 (1936).

[14] Justice B. Washington in *Ogden* v. *Saunders,* 12 Wheat. 213 (1827).

[15] See *Korematsu* v. *United States,* 323 U.S. 214, 216 (1944); Shapiro, *op. cit.* Chs. II and IV.

[16] *Frothingham* v. *Mellon,* 262 U.S. 447, 488 (1923).

[17] Justice Brandeis, *Ashwander* v. *TVA.*

vaded is a legal right—one of property, one arising out of contract, one protected against tortious invasion, or one founded on a statute which confers a privilege."

Although many states allow any taxpayer standing to challenge the legality of any state expenditure, tax payers' suits have not been permitted in federal courts. The Supreme Court has now opened the door just slightly at least for challenges resting on specific guarantees of the Bill of Rights and directed at congressional expenditures under its Article I taxing and spending power. [*Flast* v. *Cohen,* 392 U.S. 83 (1968).]

MISCELLANEOUS LIMITATIONS

There are a number of other limitations that the Supreme Court has imposed upon itself in the exercise of its power of judicial review. The Court has often noted that certain parts of a statute may be constitutional while others are unconstitutional. In such instances, the justices will allow the valid parts of the law to stand undisturbed and reject only the unconstitutional parts if the valid portions are so separate and independent that they can stand alone. Whether or not the parts of a statute are separable must be finally determined by the Court. In *Carter* v. *Carter Coal Co.,* 298 U.S. 238 (1936), it held that the price-fixing provisions of the Guffey Coal Act were inseparable from the labor provisions, even though Congress had specifically provided for the separation of the two parts.

In recent years, the Court has been extremely reluctant to interfere with the holdings of both state and federal administrative officers. The justices have felt that, in many areas where expert technical knowledge is required, they should not substitute their judgment for that of the administrator. Of course, judicial self-restraint is also evidenced by the fact that the Court, as noted in Chapter 2, has almost complete control of its business and grants certiorari in only a small percentage of cases.

It should be emphasized that the self-imposed limitations noted here are by no means always followed or adhered to. Neither is it to be implied that restraints cannot be the result of other forces. The comparatively recent practice, for example, of enacting detailed legislation to resolve many problems that were once almost completely in the hands of the courts has certainly reduced the area of judicial discretion. Nevertheless, the most significant curtailments of the power of judicial review have come from the Court itself. Its rules of self-limitation have helped make judicial review sporadic, because, under them, the Court "has avoided passing upon a large part of all the constitutional questions pressed upon it for decision."[18] On other occasions the operation of one or more of these rules has delayed a decision on a constitutional question for many years. The Dred Scott case, for example, held void a law that had been enacted thirty-seven years before. The Court did not rule on the important Smith Act of 1940 until 1951.[19]

[18] Justice Brandeis, *Ashwander* v. *TVA.*
[19] *Dennis* v. *United States,* 341 U.S. 494 (1951).

Background of *Marbury* v. *Madison*

In *Marbury* v. *Madison,* Chief Justice Marshall took a court of law and "made it into an organ of government."[20] To understand fully Marshall's decision, one must know something of the historical setting in which it was decided.

John Marshall was an ardent Federalist who had seen his party, under the leadership of John Adams, barely win the presidency in 1796. Major opposition to Federalist policies came from the Republican party, led by Jefferson. The Federalists, in accordance with the views of Hamilton, favored a strong national government and keenly distrusted the people's capacity for self-government. The Jeffersonians, on the other hand, were extremely suspicious of centralized national authority and had greater faith in the masses.

In the summer of 1798, the Adams administration pushed through Congress the drastic Alien and Sedition Acts, which were designed principally to curtail the vigorous and allegedly intemperate criticisms leveled against Federalist officeholders by the Jeffersonians. The Alien and Sedition Acts were actually composed of four separate measures. Three measures, known as the Alien Acts, dealt with the problems presented by "radical" foreigners, who were largely supporters of Jefferson, whereas the Sedition Act was specifically designed to subdue criticism of the administration by the Republican "rabble." Vigorous enforcement of the Sedition Act by Federalist judges enraged the Republicans; their resentment found expression in the Virginia and Kentucky Resolutions of 1798 (written by Madison and Jefferson), which declared that the Alien and Sedition Acts were unconstitutional and that the states should assert their rights over Congress. These resolutions were bitterly debated as part of the presidential campaign of 1800, and the unpopularity of the Alien and Sedition Acts undoubtedly contributed to the downfall of the Federalists. In the election of 1800, Jefferson and the Republican party won a decisive victory.

But the Federalists were not to be denied. They tried to maintain their influence by finding positions for loyal Federalists in the period between the election of 1800 and the inauguration of Jefferson on March 4, 1801. In January, 1801, President Adams named his Secretary of State, John Marshall, to be Chief Justice of the United States. The "lame duck" Congress passed the Judiciary Act of 1801, which created a number of new judgeships in the lower courts. The act also provided that the next vacancy on the Supreme Court should not be filled, thereby reducing the membership of the Court from six to five justices and making impossible an appointment by the new Republican president. Another law of the "lame duck" Congress empowered President Adams to appoint forty-two new justices of the peace for the District of Columbia. Loyal Federalists, of course, were appointed. But the time

[20] Charles P. Curtis, Jr., *Lions Under the Throne* (Boston: Houghton Mifflin, 1947), p. ix.

was short and some of the commissions of office for the District of Columbia were not signed by President Adams until midnight on March 3, 1801. As a result, a number of commissions were in the office of John Marshall, the outgoing Secretary of State, awaiting delivery when Jefferson became President. Jefferson ordered his new Secretary of State, James Madison, not to deliver some of the commissions to the "midnight appointees." Thus the stage was set for the case of *Marbury* v. *Madison*.

William Marbury was one of the midnight appointees whose commissions as justices of the peace for the District of Columbia had not been delivered. He and three other appointees petitioned the Supreme Court for a writ of mandamus to compel Secretary of State Madison to deliver the commissions (A mandamus is an ancient common law writ that originated in England. In this country it is granted by American courts in the name of the state to compel a corporation, officer or inferior court to perform a particular duty required by law. The violation of a writ of mandamus constitutes a contempt of the court which issued it.) In December 1801, Chief Justice Marshall requested that Madison show cause (give any possible lawful reasons) why the writ of mandamus should not be issued. Madison ignored the request. The prevalent opinion was that Marshall would order Madison to deliver the commissions and thereby precipitate a struggle between the Court and the executive branch. But Marshall did no such thing. Although he scolded Madison for his failure to deliver the commissions, he held that Madison could not be compelled to act, because the statute cited by Marbury and the three other appointees was unconstitutional. They had relied on Section 13 of the Judiciary Act of 1789, which stated that the Supreme Court could issue writs of mandamus in "cases warranted by the principles and usages of law, to any courts appointed, or persons holding office, under the authority of the United States." Marshall reasoned that this act enlarged the original jurisdiction of the Supreme Court beyond that stipulated in Article III of the Constitution. Under Article III, original jurisdiction was conferred on the Supreme Court in only two types of cases, those "affecting ambassadors, other public ministers and consuls, and those in which a state shall be party." Marbury's suit did not fall into either of these categories and therefore, by the provisions of Article III, could not be brought initially to the Supreme Court. Because there was a contradiction between the law of Congress and the Constitution, the Supreme Court had a clear duty to maintain the higher law of the Constitution and declare the legislative act null and void. Thus, Marshall established the power of the Supreme Court to declare acts of Congress unconstitutional.

REASONS FOR MARSHALL'S DECISION

Marshall actually went out of his way to declare Section 13 of the Judiciary Act void, for he might easily have avoided the issue of constitutionality in a number of ways. For example, the Court simply could have refused to hear the case, because it had no jurisdiction under Article III. Such an action would have left Marbury free to bring his case in the proper court and would have avoided a conflict between Article III and the Judiciary Act. But *Marshall did not wish to avoid the issue of constitutionality.* His decision was largely political. When *Marbury* v. *Madison* came before the Court, the judiciary was under severe attack. In 1802, The Republican Congress had repealed the Judiciary Act of 1801. This action removed the new Federalist judges from the bench and added a new justice to the Supreme Court. Another law passed during the same year provided that the Court should hold one, rather than two, sessions a year. The effect of this law was to cause a lapse of almost a full year in the Court's sessions. The Republican Congress also debated the possibility of using the impeachment process to remove Federalist judges for alleged misconduct in office. In *Marbury* v. *Madison,* Marshall saw an opportunity to avoid a collision with his arch enemy, Jefferson, and at the same time strike a blow for the judiciary. He "was aware of a rising opposition to the theory of judicial control over legislation, and he no doubt concluded that the wavering opinions on federal judicial supremacy needed to be replaced by a positive and unmistakable assertion of authority."[21] And how could Jefferson and his followers effectively object, for, by refusing to order Madison to deliver the commissions, Marshall had decided in favor of the Republicans!

It is almost inconceivable that a decision that "has proved to be one of those very special occurrences that mark an epoch in the life of the republic"[22] should emerge out of such a trivial set of circumstances. William Marbury was an obscure gentleman. The office of justice of the peace is a relatively insignificant one. And yet just such seemingly unimportant private litigations are the vehicles through which fundamental constitutional issues are ultimately determined in the United States.

Although *Marbury* v. *Madison* established the practice of judicial review, no statute of Congress was held invalid again until the Dred Scott case in 1857. There the Court held that the Missouri Compromise Act of 1820, which excluded slavery from the territories, was unconstitutional. The Dred Scott case represented "an important enlargement of the scope of judicial review over the doctrine of *Marbury* v. *Madison.* Marshall's early decision had held that the Court could refuse to enforce laws purporting to change its own jurisdiction when the Court believed those laws to be invalid. In the Dred Scott case, Taney and his colleagues go much further. They hold that the judgment of Congress as to the scope of one of its own legislative powers, this time a power in no way concerning the Court, is wrong and that the act so passed is unconstitutional. The Court, in other words, takes on the task of determining whether Congress has exercised powers which the Constitution has not delegated to it."[23]

[21] Charles C. Haines, *The American Doctrine of Judicial Supremacy* (New York: Macmillan, 1914), p. 170.

[22] Edmond Cahn (ed.), *Supreme Court and Supreme Law* (Bloomington: Indiana University Press, 1954), p. 25.

[23] Robert E. Cushman, *The Role of the Supreme Court in a Democratic Nation* (Urbana: University of Illinois Press, 1938), p. 30.

OPPOSITION TO MARSHALL'S DECISION

The decision in *Marbury* v. *Madison* is not classified among Marshall's great masterpieces. His reasoning is persuasive and impressive, but it can be refuted. The most effective answer to Marshall's argument was given in a dissenting opinion written by Judge Gibson of the Supreme Court of Pennsylvania in the relatively unimportant case of *Eakin* v. *Raub,* decided in 1825. *Eakin* v. *Raub* cannot be analyzed in conformity with the outline suggested in Chapter 2, but Judge Gibson's arguments in opposition to the doctrine of judicial review can be extracted easily.[24]

Political Questions and *Baker* v. *Carr*

As one writer has said, the doctrine of political questions is a ". . . magical formula which has the practical result of relieving a Court of the necessity of thinking further about a particular problem. It is a device for transferring the responsibility for decision of questions to another branch of the government; and it may sometimes operate to leave a problem in mid-air so that no branch decides it."[25] A number of questions have been termed *political* by the courts. These include questions arising out of the conduct of foreign relations and some questions relating to the amending process of the Constitution, as noted subsequently in *Coleman* v. *Miller.* Since the case of *Luther* v. *Borden* (Chapter 4), the Supreme Court has held consistently that what constitutes a "republican form of government" is a political question. For a long time questions involving the reapportionment of districts for congressional representation were deemed political by some of the justices. The crucial case for many years was *Colegrove* v. *Green* [351 U.S. 536 (1946)]. Only seven justices voted in *Colegrove.* Justice Frankfurter wrote the opinion of the Court, joined by Justices Reed and Burton. He ruled that districting was a political question beyond the reach of the courts. Justices Black, Douglas, and Murphy dissented. arguing that the Court should declare the state apportionment statute in question unconstitutional. Justice Rutledge, the crucial seventh vote to break the 3 to 3 tie, argued that the Court did have the power to intervene, but should exercise its discretion not to do so in this particular case. (Colegrove had asked for an injunction—that is, a court order—forbidding state officials from holding an election under the old apportionment

---

[24] Twenty years later, Judge Gibson stated that he no longer subscribed to the views announced in his dissenting opinion for two reasons: "First, because a recently held state constitutional convention (Pennsylvania), by its silence on the subject, had sanctioned the right of the court to deal with the acts of the legislature; and, next, 'from the experience of the necessity of the case.'" Robert von Moschzisker, *Judicial Review of Legislation* (Washington, D.C.: National Association for Constitutional Government, 1923), p. 91.

[25] John P. Frank, "Political Questions," in Edmond Cahn (ed.), *Supreme Court and Supreme Law* (Bloomington: Indiana University Press, 1954), p. 37.

law. An injunction is an "equitable remedy." Its historical origin is not in the common law, but in the equity courts of England. Such courts had "equitable discretion" to refuse a remedy when it would do more harm than good. Modern courts inherit this discretion when dealing with equitable remedies.) Thus, counting Justice Rutledge's vote one way, there is a 4 to 3 majority in *Colegrove* not to intervene. Counting it the other way, there is a 4 to 3 vote that the Court does have the power to intervene when it wants to.

In the case of *Gomillion* v. *Lightfoot* (Chapter 17), the Court seemed to weaken the *Colegrove* rule, for it held unconstitutional an Alabama state law redefining the boundaries of the city of Tuskegee so as to exclude nearly all the Negro voters without removing a single white voter. Although the *Gomillion* case was concerned chiefly with racial discrimination rather than with reapportionment, it has been viewed as a steppingstone for the reexamination of *Colegrove* v. *Green*. This occurred in the now famous case of *Baker* v. *Carr* (Chapter 4), where the federal courts were held to have jurisdiction to scrutinize the fairness of legislative apportionments under the Fourteenth Amendment and to take steps to assure that serious inequities are wiped out. However, the Supreme Court did not give any guidance on the critical question of what constitutes a "fair" apportionment.

 Baker v. *Carr* is a landmark decision in American constitutional law. In fact, many observers agree that it is the Court's most important decision since *Marbury* v. *Madison*. This may be so, because the *Baker* ruling will deeply affect the governmental power structure by shifting legislative power from rural areas, and to a certain extent from central cities, to suburbs. Thus *Baker* v. *Carr* "is not only an obviously important case. It is a critically different kind of case *because it calls upon the courts to sit in judgment on the possession and distribution of political power*. In the context of more than a century and half of judicial review this is something distinctly new in the function of constitutional interpretation and application."[26] The *Baker* case "rests on a principle of judicial necessity to act to preserve the very essence of the democratic process. . . . It was, and remains, a very large step in the direction of close judicial scrutiny of the politics of the people. As 'an eminently realistic body of men,' it is difficult to suppose that the Court was uninfluenced by the fact of exhaustion of non-judicial modes of relief over a period of several decades."[27]

Unlike most Supreme Court decisions, *Baker* v. *Carr* had an almost immediate impact. In fact, never before, after an assertion of expanded jurisdiction by the Court, has there been such a flurry of widespread political and judicial activity. Almost within hours of the decision, litigation was begun in state and federal courts challenging the existing schemes of legislative repre-

[26] Robert G. Dixon, Jr., "Reapportionment and Political Rejuvenation: A Devil's Advocate View," paper delivered at meeting of American Society for Legal History, Williamsburg, Va. (March 23, 1963).

[27] Robert G. Dixon, Jr., "Legislative Apportionment and the Federal Constitution," *Law and Contemporary Problems*, Vol. 27 (Summer 1962), p. 384.

sentation. At one time or another, nearly every state has been involved in litigation and more than half of them have had apportionment arrangements of one sort or another overturned by the courts. In many states both regular and special sessions of the legislature are in the process of changing present arrangements. In Georgia, for example, the legislature acted under pressure to modify the *county unit* system to provide fewer inequities in party primaries. The Georgia county unit scheme assigned to each county electoral votes that went to the candidate receiving the highest popular votes. It was designed principally to disfranchise the urban Negro population. Relying heavily on *Baker* v. *Carr,* a federal district court held that Georgia's revised county unit system violated the equal protection clause of the Fourteenth Amendment. In *Gray* v. *Sanders,* 372 U.S. 368 (1963), the Supreme Court agreed with the lower Court. Moreover, the highest Court further held that the equal protection clause of the Fourteenth Amendment requires that every voter be equal to every other voter in the state when he casts his ballot in a statewide election. Speaking for the Court over the lone dissent of Justice Harlan, Justice Douglas stated as follows:

> Georgia gives every qualified voter one vote in a state-wide election; but in counting those votes she employs the county unit system which in end result weights the rural vote more heavily than the urban vote and weights some small rural counties heavier than other larger rural counties. . . . How can one person be given twice or 10 times the voting power of another person in a state-wide election merely because he lives in a rural area or because he lives in the smallest rural county? Once the geographical unit for which a representative is chosen is designated, all who participate in the election are to have an equal vote. . . . The conception of political equality . . . can mean only one thing —one person, one vote.[28]

These decisions culminated in the Court's landmark opinion in *Wesberry* v. *Sanders* (Chapter 4), where it was held that, under Article I, Section 2, of the Constitution, congressional districts within each state must be roughly equal in population. Thus, for the first time since *Baker* v. *Carr,* the Court imposed a definitive yardstick on the makeup of political districts. Before delivering his stinging dissent in the case, Justice Harlan remarked from the bench as follows: "I consider this occasion certainly the most solemn since I have been on this Court. And I think one would have to search the pages of

[28] There has been a veritable flood of materials on *Baker* v. *Carr* and its aftermath. The following are among the most useful commentaries: Paul T. David and Ralph Eisenberg, *State Legislative Redistricting, Major Issues in the Wake of Judicial Decision* (Chicago: Public Administration Service, 1962); Malcolm E. Jewell (ed.), *The Politics of Reapportionment* (New York: Atherton Press, 1962); Phil C. Neal, "*Baker* v. *Carr*: Politics in Search of Law," *Supreme Court Review* (1962); pp. 252–327; "Symposium on the Electoral Process," 2 parts, *Law and Contemporary Problems,* Vol. 27 (Spring and Summer, 1962), and Gordon E. Baker, *The Reapportionment Revolution* (New York: Random House, 1966).

history to find a case whose importance equals what we have decided to-day."[29]

In Georgia, where the Wesberry case had originated, the reaction was unbelievably swift. Four days after the decision, the state legislature, in a wild and tumultuous session, divided the heavily populated Atlanta district in two, each with its own congressman, and redrew the lines of other districts to provide units of near-equal size in terms of population. In June 1964, the Court followed the basic principle of the *Wesberry* case and held, in *Reynolds* v. *Sims,* 377 U.S. 533 (1964), that the Equal Protection clause requires that districts in *both* houses of a state legislature must also be substantially equal in population.

The Court is now struggling with the problem of local elections, such as those to school boards. Although it is sticking close to one man–one vote, it promises to provide some flexibility in this area. (*Avery* v. *Midland County,* 390 U.S. 474 (1968).

The Court has also directly intervened in the seating of legislators. It declared the Georgia legislature's refusal to seat an elected candidate because of statements he had made a violation of freedom of speech guarantees. *Bond* v. *Floyd,* 385 U.S. 116 (1966). The Court also held that the power of Congress to determine the qualifications of its members extended only to those qualifications (age, citizenship, place of residence) specifically provided in the Constitution and not to the prospective member's past behavior. However, the Court carefully preserved Congress' power to expel members as specified in Article I, Section 5.

Changing the Constitution

As noted in Chapter 1, the federal Constitution has been changed greatly by judicial rulings, legislative enactments, executive actions, and customs and usages, as well as by the formal process of amendment. In fact, the formal method of change provided by Article V of the Constitution has proved to be less important than the informal methods. But the constitutional framers could not foresee this, and, in any event, the political theory on which the American constitutional system was based made some means of formal amendment absolutely necessary. "The people were sovereign: it followed that they could make a constitution. Corollary to this, of course, they could revise and amend the document which they had adopted."[30]

Article V divides the procedure for formal amendment into two parts: *proposal and ratification.* Amendments may be proposed in two ways: (1) by two-thirds vote of both houses of Congress; (2) by national constitutional

---

[29] *The New York Times* (Feburary 18, 1964), p. 1.

[30] Lester B. Orfield, *The Amending of the Federal Constitution* (Ann Arbor: University of Michigan Press, 1942), p. 1.

conventions called by Congress upon application of two-thirds of the state legislatures. All of the twenty-four amendments have been proposed by Congress. Amendments may be ratified by two methods, too: (1) by the legislatures of three-fourths of the states; and (2) by special conventions in three-fourths of the states. All of the amendments, with the exception of the Twenty-first, which repealed the Eighteenth, or Prohibition, Amendment, have been ratified by state legislatures. Congress has sole power to determine which method of ratification is to be used.[31]

Given the large volume of proposed constitutional amendments, many of them directly or indirectly aimed at the Supreme Court,[32] and the approval of many state legislatures of a call for a constitutional convention, the role of the Court in the amending process is of some contemporary significance. A number of questions pertaining to the amending process have had to be answered by the Supreme Court. In the first case involving the procedure for amending the Constitution, the Court held that the President's approval is not required for a proposed amendment.[33] Much later, the Court held that the two-thirds vote required for proposing amendments is a "vote of two-thirds of the members present—assuming the presence of a quorum, and not a vote of two-thirds of the entire membership, present and absent."[34]

The Court has rendered a number of decisions on the procedure for ratification. In *Hawke* v. *Smith,* 253 U.S. 221 (1920), it held that the state of Ohio could not provide for the ratification of the Eighteenth Amendment by popular referendum, because such a procedure altered the plain language of Article V, which provides for ratification by state "legislatures" rather than by direct action of the people. The Court noted that the power to ratify a proposed amendment "has its source in the Federal Constitution. The act of ratification by the state derives its authority from the Federal Constitution, to which the state and its people have alike assented. . . . Any other view might lead to endless confusion in the manner of ratification of Federal amendments." Despite the decision in *Hawke* v. *Smith,* ratification of an amendment by specially chosen conventions in the states seems to bring about the same result as a referendum vote, if our experience with the ratification of the Twenty-first Amendment provides any lessons. In that instance, the state ratifying conventions did not act as deliberative assemblies. They simply recorded the vote of the people.

Article V does not stipulate any time limit for the ratification of amendments. When the Eighteenth Amendment was proposed, Congress, for the first time, provided that ratification was to be completed within seven years.

---

[31] *United States* v. *Sprague,* 282 U.S. 716 (1931).

[32] One of the best discussions of the proposal for amending Article V is found in Charles L. Black, Jr., "The Proposed Amendment of Article V: A Threatened Disaster," *Yale Law Journal,* Vol. 72 (1963), pp. 957–66.

[33] *Hollingsworth* v. *Virginia,* 3 Dall. 378 (1798).

[34] National Prohibition Cases, 253 U.S. 350 (1920). Neither is the Governor's approval required in the ratification process.

In *Dillon* v. *Gloss,* 256 U.S. 368 (1921), the Supreme Court held that Congress had the power to impose a time limitation because Article V clearly implied that the "ratification must be within some reasonable time after the proposal." The Court felt that seven years was a reasonable limit. Congress also set a time limit of seven years for the ratification of the Twentieth, Twenty-first, and Twenty-second Amendments. Each of these was ratified long before the seven-year period expired.

Until 1939, when *Coleman* v. *Miller* [307 U.S. 433 (1939)] was decided, the general assumption was that all the steps in the amending process were justiciable. But in the Coleman case, the Court held that *some* steps in the amending process were political questions that had to be resolved by Congress. Whether the decision of *Coleman* v. *Miller* means that the Supreme Court will not take jurisdiction in any case involving the amending process remains to be seen. In this connection, it is important to note the concurring opinion, in which four justices reasoned that Congress has *exclusive* control over the amending process. "The process itself is 'political' in its entirety, from submission until an amendment becomes part of the Constitution, and is not subject to judicial guidance, control, or interference at any point."

Federal Courts and State Law

Article III of the Constitution provides that the federal judicial power shall extend to controversies between citizens of different states. Thus, for example, if Smith, a citizen of Pennsylvania, wrecks his automobile in a collision on an Indiana highway with Jones, a citizen of Indiana, Smith may sue Jones in a federal district court rather than in an Indiana state court if the amount involved is $10,000 or more. Smith, thereby, does not suffer from any disadvantages that might result from suing in Jones's home state. Before the federal courts, both Smith and Jones stand equally regardless of their state citizenship. But a federal court is then faced with the question of what law to apply. Should it apply the law of Indiana or Pennsylvania? Or is there some federal common law that may be applied?

Section 34 of the Judiciary Act of 1789 provided that "the laws of the several states, except where the Constitution, treaties, or statutes of the United States otherwise require or provide, shall be regarded as rules of decision in trials at common law, in the courts of the United States, in cases where they apply." But in *Swift* v. *Tyson,* 16 Pet. 1 (1842), the Supreme Court ruled that the federal courts could disregard state court decisions in diversity of citizenship cases involving matters of general jurisprudence and commercial law. In delivering the opinion of the Court in *Swift* v. *Tyson,* Justice Story construed the word *laws* in Section 34 of the Judiciary Act of 1789 to mean "enactments promulgated by the legislative authority" of the state only. Therefore, decisions of state courts were not binding on the federal courts, and the latter were left free to apply and expand their own common law in many fields.

"An important practical justification of Story's decision was the belief that the federal courts, headed by the Supreme Court, would bring about a uniform interpretation of the common law, which otherwise would be applied differently in different localities with great confusion as the result. The expected order was not achieved. The states continued to interpret the common law in their own way, while the federal courts added to the confusion by building up one more interpretation. Individual justices had protested from time to time against the further expansion of the rule in *Swift* v. *Tyson*."[35] Finally, in *Erie Railroad Co.* v. *Tompkins,* the Supreme Court overruled *Swift* v. *Tyson* and, thereby, reversed a ninety-six-year-old precedent. Since the Erie Railroad decision in 1938, the federal courts have followed decisions of state courts in diversity cases. However "the law growing out of *Erie Railroad Co.* v. *Tompkins* pertains only to litigation in the federal courts by virtue of the diversity of citizenship of the parties and involving state-created rights. Where an action is in the federal court on some other jurisdictional basis or involves rights created or protected by federal law, federal facts or policies, the doctrine of *Erie Railroad Co.* v. *Tompkins* does not apply."[36]

The *Erie Railroad* case is only one of many Supreme Court decisions that are concerned with procedural problems of various kinds.[37] Although limitations of space preclude the inclusion of other cases, this does not mean that problems of procedure are unimportant. Virtually all societies have a sense of procedure, and the forms of judicial procedure used provide clues to the nature of a particular society. "It is procedure that spells much of the difference between rule by law and rule by whim or caprice. Steadfast adherence to strict procedural safeguards is our main assurance that there will be equal justice under law."[38]

WILLIAM MARBURY v. JAMES MADISON
SECRETARY OF STATE OF THE UNITED STATES,
1 Cranch 137; 2 L. Ed. 60 (1803)

MR. JUSTICE MARSHALL delivered the opinion of the Court:

At the last term, on the affidavits then read and filed with the clerk, a rule was granted in this case, requiring the Secretary of State to show cause why a mandamus should not issue, directing him to deliver to William Marbury his commission as a justice of the peace for the county of Washington, in the District of Columbia.

No cause has been shown, and the

---

[35] Carl B. Swisher, *American Constitutional Development* (New York: Houghton Mifflin, 1943), p. 977.

[36] Herbert F. Goodrich, *Handbook of the Conflict of Laws* (St. Paul, Minn.: West Publishing Co., 1949), pp. 44–45.

[37] David Fellman, "Ten Years of the Supreme Court: 1937–1947; Federalism," *American Political Science Review,* Vol. 41 (December 1947), p. 1149–53.

[38] Justice Douglas concurring in *Joint Anti-Fascist Committee* v. *McGrath,* 341 U.S. 23 (1951).

present motion is for a mandamus. The peculiar delicacy of this case, the novelty of some of its circumstances, and the real difficulty attending the points which occur in it, require a complete exposition of the principles on which the opinion to be given by the court is founded.

These principles have been, on the side of the applicant, very ably argued at the bar. In rendering the opinion of the court, there will be some departure in form, though not in substance, from the points stated in that argument.

In the order in which the court has viewed this subject, the following questions have been considered and decided.

1. Has the applicant a right to the commission he demands?

2. If he has a right, and that right has been violated, do the laws of his country afford him a remedy?

3. If they do afford him a remedy, is it a *mandamus* issuing from this court?

. . . It is . . . the opinion of the court,

1. That, by signing the commission of Mr. Marbury, the President of the United States appointed him a justice of peace, for the county of Washington in the District of Columbia; and that the seal of the United States, affixed thereto by the Secretary of State, is conclusive testimony of the verity of the signature, and of the completion of the appointment; and that the appointment conferred on him a legal right to the office for the space of five years.

2. That, having this legal title to the office, he has a consequent right to the commission; a refusal to deliver which, is a plain violation of that right, for which the laws of this country afford him a remedy.

It remains to be enquired whether,

3. He is entitled to the remedy for which he applies. This depends on,

1. The nature of the writ applied for and,

2. The power of this court.

. . . This, then, is a plain case for a mandamus, either to deliver the commission, or a copy of it from the record; and it only remains to be enquired, whether it can issue from this court.

The act to establish the judicial courts of the United States authorizes the Supreme Court "to issue writs of mandamus in cases warranted by the principles and usages of law, to any courts appointed, or persons holding office, under the authority of the United States."

The Secretary of State, being a person holding an office under the authority of the United States, is precisely within the letter of the description, and if this court is not authorized to issue a writ of mandamus to such an officer, it must be because the law is unconstitutional, and therefore absolutely incapable of conferring the authority, and assigning the duties which its words purport to confer and assign.

The Constitution vests the whole judicial power of the United States in one supreme court, and such inferior courts as Congress shall, from time to time, ordain and establish. This power is expressly extended to all cases arising under the laws of the United States; and, consequently, in some form, may be exercised over the present case; because the right claimed is given by a law of the United States.

In the distribution of this power it is declared that "the Supreme Court shall have original jurisdiction in all cases affecting ambassadors, other public ministers and consuls, and those in which a state shall be a party. In all other cases, the Supreme Court shall have appellate jurisdiction."

It has been insisted, at the bar, that, as the original grant of jurisdiction to the supreme and inferior courts, is general, and the clause assigning original jurisdiction to the Supreme Court contains no negative or restrictive words, the power remains to the legislature to assign original jurisdiction to that court in other cases than those specified in the article which has been recited; provided those cases belong to the judicial power of the United States.

If it had been intended to leave it in the discretion of the legislature to apportion the judicial power between the supreme and inferior courts according to the will of that body, it would certainly have been useless to have proceeded further than to have defined the judicial power, and the tribunals in which it should be vested. The subsequent part of the section is mere surplusage, is entirely without meaning, if such is to be the construction. If Congress remains at liberty to give this court appellate jurisdiction, where the Constitution has declared their jurisdiction shall be original; and original jurisdiction where the Constitution has declared it shall be appellate, the distribution of jurisdiction made in the Constitution is form without substance.

Affirmative words are often, in their operation, negative of other objects than those affirmed; and in this case, a negative or exclusive sense must be given to them, or they have no operation at all.

It cannot be presumed that any clause in the Constitution is intended to be without effect; and, therefore, such a construction is inadmissible unless the words require it.

. . . To enable this court, then to issue a mandamus, it must be shown to be an exercise of appellate jurisdiction, or to be necessary to enable them to exercise appellate jurisdiction.

It has been stated at the bar that the appellate jurisdiction may be exercised in a variety of forms, and that, if it be the will of the legislature that a mandamus should be used for that purpose, that will must be obeyed. This is true, yet the jurisdiction must be appellate, not original.

It is the essential criterion of appellate jurisdiction that it revises and corrects the proceedings in a cause already instituted, and does not create that cause. Although, therefore, a mandamus may be directed to courts, yet to issue such a writ to an officer for the delivery of a paper is in effect the same as to sustain an original action for that paper, and, therefore, seems not to belong to appellate, but to original jurisdiction. Neither is it necessary, in such a case as this, to enable the court to exercise its appellate jurisdiction.

The authority, therefore, given to the Supreme Court by the act establishing the judicial courts of the United States, to issue writs of mandamus to public officers, appears not to be warranted by the Constitution; and it becomes necessary to inquire whether a jurisdiction so conferred can be exercised.

The question, whether an act repugnant to the Constitution can become the law of the land, is a question deeply interesting to the United States; but, happily, not of an intricacy proportioned to its interest. It seems only necessary to recognize certain principles, supposed to have been long and well established, to decide it.

That the people have an original right to establish, for their future government, such principles as, in their opinion, shall most conduce to their own happiness is the basis on which the whole American fabric had been erected. The exercise of this original right is a very great exertion; nor can it, nor ought it, to be frequently repeated. The principles, therefore, so established, are deemed fundamental.

And as the authority from which they proceed is supreme, and can seldom act, they are designed to be permanent.

This original and supreme will organizes the government, and assigns to different departments their respective powers. It may either stop here, or establish certain limits not to be transcended by those departments.

The government of the United States is of the latter description. The powers of the legislature are defined and limited; and that those limits may not be mistaken, or forgotten, the Constitution is written. To what purpose are powers limited, and to what purpose is that limitation committed to writing, if these limits may, at any time, be passed by those intended to be restrained? The distinction between a government with limited and unlimited powers is abolished if those limits do not confine the persons on whom they are imposed, and if acts prohibited and acts allowed are of equal obligation. It is a proposition too plain to be contested, that the Constitution controls any legislative act repugnant to it; or, that the legislature may alter the Constitution by an ordinary act.

Between these alternatives there is no middle ground. The Constitution is either a superior paramount law, unchangeable by ordinary means, or it is on a level with ordinary legislative acts, and, like other acts, is alterable when the legislature shall please to alter it.

If the former part of the alternative be true, then a legislative act contrary to the Constitution is not law: if the latter part be true, then written constitutions are absurd attempts on the part of the people to limit a power in its own nature illimitable.

Certainly all those who have framed written constitutions contemplate them as forming the fundamental and paramount law of the nation, and consequently, the theory of every such government must be, that an act of the legislature, repugnant to the constitution, is void.

This theory is essentially attached to a written constitution, and is, consequently, to be considered by this court as one of the fundamental principles of our society. It is not therefore to be lost sight of in the further consideration of this subject.

If an act of the legislature, repugnant to the Constitution, is void, does it, notwithstanding its invalidity, bind the courts, and oblige them to give it effect? Or, in other words, though it be not law, does it constitute a rule as operative as if it was a law? This would be to overthrow in fact what was established in theory; and would seem, at first view, an absurdity too gross to be insisted on. It shall, however, receive a more attentive consideration.

It is emphatically the province and duty of the judicial department to say what the law is. Those who apply the rule to particular cases must, of necessity, expound and interpret that rule. If two laws conflict with each other, the courts must decide on the operation of each.

So if a law be in opposition to the Constitution; if both the law and the Constitution apply to a particular case, so that the court must either decide that case conformably to the law, disregarding the Constitution; or conformably to the Constitution, disregarding the law; the court must determine which of these conflicting rules governs the case. This is of the very essence of judicial duty.

If, then, the courts are to regard the Constitution, and the Constitution is superior to any ordinary act of the legislature, the Constitution, and not such ordinary act, must govern the case to which they both apply.

Those, then, who controvert the principle that the Constitution is to be considered, in court, as a paramount law, are reduced to the necessity of maintaining that courts must close their eyes on the Constitution, and see only the law.

This doctrine would subvert the very foundation of all written constitutions. It would declare that an act which, according to the principles and theory of our government, is entirely void, is yet, in practice, completely obligatory. It would declare that if the legislature shall do what is expressly forbidden, such act, notwithstanding the express prohibition, is in reality effectual. It would be giving to the legislature a practical and real omnipotence, with the same breath which professes to restrict their powers within narrow limits. It is prescribing limits and declaring that those limits may be passed at pleasure.

That it thus reduces to nothing what we have deemed the greatest improvement on political institutions—a written constitution—would of itself be sufficient, in America, where written constitutions have been viewed with so much reverence, for rejecting the construction. But the peculiar expressions of the Constitution of the United States furnish additional arguments in favor of its rejection.

The judicial power of the United States is extended to all cases arising under the Constitution.

Could it be the intention of those who gave this power to say that, in using it, the Constitution should not be looked into? That a case arising under the Constitution should be decided without examining the instrument under which it rises?

This is too extravagant to be maintained.

In some cases then, the Constitution must be looked into by the judges. And if they can open it at all, what part of it are they forbidden to read or to obey?

There are many other parts of the Constitution which serve to illustrate this subject.

It is declared that "no tax or duty shall be laid on articles exported from any state." Suppose a duty on the export of cotton, of tobacco, or of flour; and a suit instituted to recover it. Ought judgment to be rendered in such a case? Ought the judges to close their eyes on the Constitution, and see only the law?

The Constitution declares that "no bill of attainder or ex post facto law shall be passed."

If, however, such a bill should be passed and a person should be prosecuted under it; must the court condemn to death those victims whom the Constitution endeavours to preserve?

"No person," says the Constitution, "shall be convicted of treason unless on the testimony of two witnesses to the same overt act, or on confession in open court."

Here the language of the Constitution is addressed especially to the courts. It prescribes, directly for them, a rule of evidence not to be departed from. If the legislature should change that rule, and declare *one* witness, or a confession *out* of court, sufficient for conviction, must the constitutional principle yield to the legislative act?

From these, and many other selections which might be made, it is apparent that the framers of the Constitution contemplated that instrument as a rule for the government of *courts,* as well as of the legislature.

Why otherwise does it direct the judges to take an oath to support it? This oath certainly applies in an especial manner to their conduct in their official character. How immoral to impose it on them, if they were to be used as the instruments, and the knowing instruments, for violating what they swear to support!

The oath of office, too, imposed by the legislature, is completely demonstrative of the legislative opinion on this subject. It is in these words: "I do solemnly swear that I will administer justice without respect to persons, and do equal right to the poor and to the rich; and that I will faithfully and impartially discharge all the duties incumbent on me as _____, according to the best of my abilities and understanding agreeably to the *Constitution* and laws of the United States."

Why does a judge swear to discharge his duties agreeably to the Constitution of the United States, if that Constitution forms no rule for his government? If it is closed upon him, and cannot be inspected by him?

If such be the real state of things, this is worse than solemn mockery. To prescribe, or to take this oath, becomes equally a crime.

It is also not entirely unworthy of observation that, in declaring what shall be the *supreme* law of the land, the *Constitution* itself is first mentioned; and not the laws of the United States generally, but those only which shall be made in *pursuance* of the Constitution, have that rank.

Thus, the particular phraseology of the Constitution of the United States confirms and strengthens the principle, supposed to be essential to all written constitutions, that a law repugnant to the Constitution is void; and that *courts,* as well as other departments, are bound by that instrument.

The rule must be discharged.

EAKIN *v.* RAUB
12 Sergeant and Rawle (Pa. Supreme Court) 330 (1825)

JUDGE GIBSON:

I am aware that a right to declare all unconstitutional acts void . . . is generally held as a professional dogma; but I apprehend rather as a matter of faith than of reason. I admit that I once embraced the same doctrine, but without examination, and I shall therefore state the arguments that impelled me to abandon it, with great respect for those by whom it is still maintained. But I may premise, that it is not a little remarkable that, although the right in question has all along been claimed by the judiciary, no judge has ventured to discuss it, except Chief Justice Marshall, and if the argument of a jurist so distinguished for the strength of his ratiocinative powers be found inconclusive, it may fairly be set down to the

weakness of the position which he attempts to defend. . . .

The ordinary and essential powers of the judiciary do not extend to the annulling of an act of the legislature. . . .

The Constitution and the right of the legislature to pass the act, may be in collision. But is that a legitimate subject for judicial determination? If it be. the judiciary must be a peculiar organ, to revise the proceedings of the legislature, and to correct its mistakes; and in what part of the Constitution are we to look for this proud pre-eminence? Viewing the matter in the opposite direction, what would be thought of an act of assembly in which it should be declared that the Supreme Court had, in a particular case, put a wrong construction on the Constitution of the

United States, and that the judgment should therefore be reversed? It would doubtless be thought a usurpation of judicial power. But it is by no means clear that to declare a law void which has been enacted according to the forms prescribed in the Constitution is not a usurpation of legislative power. . . .

But it has been said to be emphatically the business of the judiciary to ascertain and pronounce what the law is; and that this necessarily involves a consideration of the Constitution. It does so; but how far? If the judiciary will inquire into anything besides the form of enactment, where shall it stop? There must be some point of limitation to such an inquiry; for no one will pretend that a judge would be justifiable in calling for the election returns, or scrutinizing the qualifications for those who composed the legislature. . . .

Everyone knows how seldom men think exactly alike on ordinary subjects; and a government constructed on the principle of assent by all its parts would be inadequate to the most simple operations. The notion of a complication of counter-checks has been carried to an extent in theory of which the framers of the Constitution never dreamt. When the entire sovereignty was separated into its elementary parts, and distributed to the appropriate branches, all things incident to the exercise of its powers were committed to each branch exclusively. The negative which each part of the legislature may exercise, in regard to the acts of the other, was thought sufficient to prevent material infractions of the restraints which were put on the power of the whole; for, had it been intended to interpose the judiciary as an additional barrier, the matter would surely not have been left in doubt. The judges would not have been left to stand on the insecure and evershifting ground of public opinion as to constructive powers; they would have been placed

on the impregnable ground of an express grant. . . .

[W]hat I have in view in this inquiry, is the supposed right of the judiciary to interfere in cases where the Constitution is to be carried into effect through the instrumentality of the legislature, and where that organ must necessarily first decide on the constitutionality of its own act. The oath to support the Constitution is not peculiar to the judges, but is taken indiscriminately by every officer of the government, and is designed rather as a test of the political principles of the man, than to bind the officer in the discharge of his duty: otherwise it is difficult to determine what operation it is to have in the case of a recorder of deeds, for instance, who, in the execution of his office, has nothing to do with the Constitution. But granting it to relate to the official conduct of the judge, as well as every other officer, and not to his political principles, still it must be understood in reference to supporting the Constitution *only as far as that may be involved in his official duty;* and consequently, if his official duty does not comprehend an inquiry into the authority of the legislature, neither does his oath.

But do not the judges do a positive act in violation of the Constitution when they give effect to an unconstitutional law? Not if the law has been passed according to the forms established in the Constitution. The fallacy of the question is in supposing that the judiciary adopts the acts of the legislature as its own; whereas the enactment of a law and the interpretation of it are not concurrent acts, and as the judiciary is not required to concur in the enactment, neither is it in the breach of the Constitution which may be the consequence of the enactment. The fault is imputable to the legislature, and on it the responsibility exclusively rests. . . .

LUTHER v. BORDEN
7 How. 1; 12 L. Ed. 581 (1849)

[*This case grew out of an extremely unusual set of circumstances. In 1841, the Constitution of Rhode Island, which was essentially the original Colonial charter of 1663 with a few minor adaptations, still strictly limited the right to vote. Although universal manhood suffrage had been generally adopted by the other states, property ownership was still a requirement for voting in Rhode Island. All attempts to broaden the franchise were defeated. In 1841, agitation for a new constitution increased. Under the leadership of a young lawyer, Thomas W. Dorr, mass meetings were held throughout the state, a constitutional convention was called, and a new constitution establishing adult manhood suffrage was written. Dorr was elected Governor under the new constitution, and he immediately tried to put the new government into operation. However, the regular government refused to recognize the new constitution and took steps to put down the "insurrection." It declared martial law, called out the state militia, and appealed to President Tyler for aid. Although no federal forces were used, the "Dorr Rebellion" was crushed. Dorr himself was captured, tried for treason, and sentenced to life imprisonment. He was later pardoned, and in 1842 the charter government yielded to popular pressures and drafted a new constitution that provided for wider electoral rights.*

Nevertheless, many of Dorr's supporters felt that the courts might hold that the new government was the rightful one, because it had the support of a majority of the people. Thus, an unimportant civil controversy between Luther and Borden was pushed to the Supreme Court. Luther, a follower of Dorr, was arrested in his home for insurrection by Borden and others, who were members of the state militia acting under orders of the charter government. Luther moved to Massachusetts in order to bring the case before the federal courts on the basis of diversity of citizenship. He sued Borden for illegal trespass on the grounds that the charter governments' declaration of martial law was void because the Dorr government, supported by the majority of the people, was the rightful government. The courts were thus invited to determine which of the two governments was the lawful government of the state. A federal circuit court ruled in Borden's favor. Luther then brought the case to the Supreme Court on a writ of error.]

MR. CHIEF JUSTICE TANEY delivered the opinion of the Court:

The fourth section of the fourth article of the Constitution of the United States provides that the United States shall guarantee to every State in the Union a republican form of government, and shall protect each of them against invasion; and on the application of the legislature or of the executive (when the legislature cannot be convened) against domestic violence.

Under this article of the Constitution it rests with Congress to decide what government is the established one in a State. For as the United States guarantee to each State a republican government, Congress must necessarily decide what government is established in the State before it can determine whether it is republican or not. And when the senators and representatives of a State are admitted into the councils of the Union, the authority of the government under which they are appointed, as well as its republican character, is recognized by the proper constitutional authority. And its decision is binding on every other department of the government, and could not be questioned in a judicial tribunal. It is true that the contest in this case did not last long enough to bring the matter to this issue; and as no senators or representatives were elected under the authority of the government of which Mr. Dorr was the head, Congress was not called upon to decide the controversy. Yet the right to decide is placed there, and not in the courts.

So, too, as relates to the clause in the above-mentioned article of the Constitution, providing for cases of domestic violence. It rested with Congress, too, to determine upon the means proper to be adopted to fulfill this guarantee. They might, if they had deemed it most advisible to do so, have placed it in the power of a court to decide when the contingency had happened which required the federal government to interfere. But Congress thought otherwise, and no doubt wisely; and by the act of February 28, 1795, provided, that, "in case of an insurrection in any State against the government thereof, it shall be lawful for the President of the United States, on application of the legislature of such State or of the executive (when the legislature cannot be convened), to call forth such number of the militia of any other State or States, as may be applied for, as he may judge sufficient to suppress such insurrection."

By this act, the power of deciding whether the exigency had arisen upon which the government of the United States is bound to interfere, is given to the President. He is to act upon the application of the legislature or of the executive, and consequently he must determine what body of men constitute the legislature, and who is the governor, before he can act. The fact that both

parties claim the right to the government cannot alter the case, for both cannot be entitled to it. If there is an armed conflict, like the one of which we are speaking, it is a case of domestic violence, and one of the parties must be in insurrection against the lawful government. And the President must, of necessity, decide which is the government, and which party is unlawfully arrayed against it, before he can perform the duty imposed upon him by the act of Congress.

After the President has acted and called out the militia, is a Circuit Court of the United States authorized to inquire whether his decision was right? Could the court, while the parties were actually contending in arms for the possession of the government, call witnesses before it and inquire which party represented a majority of the people? If it could, then it would become the duty of the court (provided it came to the conclusion that the President had decided incorrectly) to discharge those who were arrested or detained by the troops in the service of the United States or the government which the President was endeavoring to maintain. If the judicial power extends so far, the guarantee contained in the Constitution of the United States is a guarantee of anarchy, and not of order. Yet if this right does not reside in the courts when the conflict is raging, if the judicial power is at that time bound to follow the decision of the political, it must be equally bound when the contest is over. It cannot, when peace is restored, punish as offenses and crimes the acts which it before recognized, and was bound to recognize, as lawful.

It is true that in this case the militia were not called out by the President. But upon the application of the governor under the charter government, the President recognized him as the executive power of the State, and took measures to call out the militia to support his authority if it should be found necessary for the general government to interfere; and it is admitted in the argument, that it was the knowledge of this decision that put an end to the armed opposition to the charter government, and prevented any further efforts to establish by force the proposed constitution. The interference of the President, therefore, by announcing his determination, was as effectual as if the militia had been assembled under his orders. And it should be equally authoritative. For certainly no court of the United States, with a knowledge of this decision, would have been justified in recognizing the opposing party as the lawful government; or in treating as wrongdoers or insurgents the officers of the government which the President had recognized, and was prepared to support by an armed force. In the case of foreign nations, the government acknowledged by the President is always recognized in the courts of justice. And this principle has been applied by the act of Congress to the sovereign States of the Union.

It is said that this power in the President is dangerous to liberty, and may be abused. All power may be abused if placed in unworthy hands. But it would be difficult, we think, to point out any other hands in which this power would be more safe, and at the same time equally effectual. When citizens of the same State are in arms against each other, and the constituted authorities unable to execute the laws, the interposition of the United States must be prompt, or it is of little value. The ordinary course of proceedings in courts of justice would be utterly unfit for the crisis. And the elevated office of the President, chosen as he is by the people of the United States, and the high responsibility he could not fail to feel when acting in a case of so much moment, appear to furnish as strong safeguards against a wilful abuse of power as human prudence and foresight could well provide. At all events, it is conferred upon him by the Constitution and laws of the United States, and must therefore be respected and enforced in its judicial tribunals. . . .

Undoubtedly, if the President in exercising this power shall fall into error, or invade the rights of the people of the State, it would be in the power of Congress to apply the proper remedy. But the courts must administer the law as they find it. . . .

Much of the argument on the part of the plaintiff turned upon political rights and political questions, upon which the court has been urged to express an opinion. We decline doing so. The high power has been conferred on this court of passing judgment upon the acts of the State sovereignties, and of the legislative and executive branches of the federal government, and of determining whether they are beyond the limits of power marked out for them respectively by the Constitution of the United States. This tribunal, therefore, should be the last to overstep the boundaries which limit its own jurisdiction. And while it should always be ready to meet any question confided to it by the Constitution, it is equally its duty not to pass beyond its appropriate sphere of action, and to take care not to involve itself in discussions which properly belong to other forums. No one, we believe, has ever doubted the proposition, that, according to the institutions of this country, the sovereignty in every State resides in the people of the State, and that they may alter and change their form of government at their own pleasure. But whether they have changed it or not by abolishing an old government, and establishing a new one in its place, is a question to be settled by the political power. And when that power has decided, the courts are bound to take notice of its decision, and to follow it.

The judgment of the Circuit Court must therefore be

Affirmed.

[MR. JUSTICE WOODBURY wrote a dissenting opinion.]

BAKER *v.* CARR
369 U.S. 186; 82 Sup. Ct. 691; 7 L. Ed. 2d 633 (1962)

[*The General Assembly of Tennessee consists of a Senate of thirty-three members and a House of Representatives of ninety-nine members. The Constitution of Tennessee provides that representation in the legislature shall be based on the number of qualified voters residing in each county. It also provides for an apportionment of the legislators every ten years to be determined according to the federal census. In 1901, the state legislature reapportioned representation on the basis of the 1900 federal census, but despite the constitutional requirement, no subsequent reapportionment was made up to the time of* Baker v. Carr. *In the meantime, the population of Tennessee increased by 75 per cent, and many people moved from rural to urban areas. These changes resulted in extreme disparities in the number of voters in each voting district. For example, Moore County, with 2,340 voters, elected one representative, whereas Shelby County, with 312,245 voters, elected only seven. In some senatorial districts there were only 30,000 voters, whereas others had as many as 130,000. As a result of such disparities, voters in districts having only 40 per cent of the voting population could elect sixty-three of the ninety-nine representatives, and 37 per cent of the voters could elect twenty of the thirty-three members of the Senate. All attempts to reapportion in accordance with the state constitution had failed.*

In 1959, Baker and other qualified voters of Tennessee brought suit against Carr, the Tennessee Secretary of State, and other public officials, alleging deprivation of federal constitutional rights. The plaintiffs argued that the state's system of apportionment was "utterly arbitrary," thereby denying them equal protection of the laws under the Fourteenth Amendment "by virtue of debasement of their votes." A federal district court, relying on Colegrove v. Green, *dismissed the complaint in 1960. The case then went to the Supreme Court on appeal.*]

MR. JUSTICE BRENNAN delivered the opinion of the Court:

I

. . . The District Court's Opinion and Order of Dismissal

Because we deal with this case on appeal from an order of dismissal granted on appellees' motions, precise identification of the issues presently confronting us demands clear exposition of

the grounds upon which the District Court rested in dismissing the case. The dismissal order recited that the court sustained the appellees' grounds "(1) that the Court lacks jurisdiction of the subject matter, and (2) that the complaint fails to state a claim upon which relief can be granted. . . ."

The District Court's dismissal order . . . rested . . . upon lack of subject-matter jurisdiction and lack of justifiable cause of action without attempting to distinguish between these grounds. . . .

The court proceeded to explain its action as turning on the case's presenting a "question of the distribution of political strength for legislative purposes." For,

"from a review of [numerous Supreme Court] . . . decisions there can be no doubt that the federal rule, as enunciated and applied by the Supreme Court, is that the federal courts, whether from a lack of jurisdiction or from the inappropriateness of the subject matter for judicial consideration, will not intervene in cases of this type to compel legislative reapportionment. . . ."

The court went on to express doubts as to the feasibility of the various possible remedies sought by the plaintiffs. . . . Then it made clear that its dismissal reflected a view not of doubt that violation of constitutional rights was alleged, but of a court's impotence to correct that violation:

"With the plaintiff's argument that the legislature of Tennessee is guilty of a clear violation of the state constitution and of the rights of the plaintiffs the Court entirely agrees. It also agrees that the evil is a serious one which should be corrected without further delay. But even so the remedy in this situation clearly does not lie with the courts. It has long been recognized and is accepted doctrine that there are indeed some rights guaranteed by the Constitution for the violation of which the courts cannot give redress. . . ."

In light of the District Court's treatment of the case, we hold today only (a) that the court possessed jurisdiction of the subject matter; (b) that a justiciable cause of action is stated upon which appellants would be entitled to appropriate relief; and (c) because appellees raise the issue before this Court, that the appellants have standing to challenge the Tennessee apportionment statutes. Beyond noting that we have no cause at this stage to doubt the District Court will be able to fashion relief if violations of constitutional rights are found, it is improper now to consider what remedy would be most appropriate if appellants prevail at the trial.

II

Jurisdiction of the Subject Matter

The District Court was uncertain whether our cases withholding federal judicial relief rested upon a lack of federal jurisdiction or upon the inappropriateness of the subject matter for judicial consideration—what we have designated "nonjusticiability." The distinction between the two grounds is significant. In the instance of nonjusticiability, consideration of the cause is not wholly and immediately foreclosed; rather, the Court's inquiry necessarily proceeds to the point of deciding whether the duty asserted can be judicially identified and its breach judicially determined, and whether protection for the right asserted can be judicially molded. In the instance of lack of jurisdiction the cause either does not "arise under" the Federal Constitution, laws or treaties (or fall within one of the other enumerated categories of Art. III, 2), or is not a "case or controversy" within the meaning of that section; or the cause is not one described by any jurisdictional statute. Our conclusion . . . that this cause presents no nonjusticiable "political question" settles the only possible doubt that it is a case or controversy. Under the present heading of "Jurisdiction of the Subject Matter" we hold only that the matter set forth in the complaint does arise under the Constitution. . . .

An unbroken line of our precedents sustains the federal courts' jurisdiction of the subject matter of federal constitutional claims of this nature. The first cases involved the redistricting of States for the purpose of electing Representatives to the Federal Congress. . . . When the Minnesota Supreme Court affirmed the dismissal of a suit to enjoin the Secretary of State of Minnesota from acting under Minnesota redistricting legislation, we reviewed the constitutional merits of the legislation and reversed the State Supreme Court. *Smiley* v. *Holm,* 285 U.S. 355. . . . When a three-judge District Court . . . permanently enjoined officers of the State of Mississippi from conducting an election of Representatives under a Mississippi redistricting act, we reviewed the federal questions on the merits and reversed the District Court. *Wood* v. *Broom,* 287 U.S. 1. . . .

The appellees refer to *Colegrove* v. *Green* . . . as authority that the District Court lacked jurisdiction of the subject matter. Appellees misconceive the holding of that case. The holding was precisely contrary to their reading of it. Seven members of the Court participated in the decision. Unlike many other cases in this field which have assumed without discussion that there was jurisdiction, all three opinions filed in *Colegrove* discussed the question. Two of the opinions expressing the views of four of the Justices, a majority, flatly held that there was jurisdiction of the subject matter. Mr. Justice Black, joined by Mr. Justice Douglas and Mr. Justice Murphy, stated: "It is my judgment that the District Court had jurisdiction. . . ." Mr. Justice Rutledge, writing separately, expressed agreement with this conclusion. . . . Indeed, it is even questionable that the opinion of Mr. Justice Frankfurter, joined by Justices Reed and Burton, doubted jurisdiction of the subject matter. . . .

Several subsequent cases similar to *Colegrove* have been decided by the Court in summary per curiam statements. None was dismissed for want of jurisdiction of the subject. . . .

Two cases decided with opinions after *Colegrove* likewise plainly imply that the subject matter of this suit is within District Court jurisdiction. In *MacDougall* v. *Green,* 335 U.S. 281, the District Court dismissed for want of jurisdiction . . . a suit to enjoin enforcement of the requirement that nominees for state-wide elections be supported by a petition signed by a minimum number of persons from at least fifty of the State's 102 counties. This Court's disagreement with that action is clear since the Court affirmed the judgment after a review of the merits and concluded that the particular claim there was without merit. In *South* v. *Peters,* 339 U.S. 276, we affirmed the dismissal of an attack on the Georgia "county unit" system but founded our action on a ground that plainly would not have been reached if the lower court lacked jurisdiction of the subject matter. . . . The express words of our holding were that "federal courts consistently refuse to exercise their equity powers in cases posing political issues arising from a state's geographical distribution of electoral strength among its political subdivisions. . . ."

We hold that the District Court has jurisdiction of the subject matter of the federal constitutional claim asserted in the complaint.

III
Standing

A federal court cannot "pronounce any statute, either of a State or of the United States, void, because irreconcilable with the Constitution, except as it is called upon to adjudge the legal rights of litigants in actual controversies. . . ." Have the appellants alleged such a personal stake in the outcome of the controversy as to assure that concrete adverseness which sharpens the presentation of issues upon which the court so largely depends for illumination of difficult constitutional questions? This is the gist of the question of standing. It is, of course, a question of federal law. . . .

We hold that the appellants do have standing to maintain this suit. Our decisions plainly support this conclusion. Many of the cases have assumed rather than articulated the premise in deciding the merits of similar claims. And *Colegrove* v. *Green* . . . squarely held that voters who allege facts showing disadvantage to themselves as individuals have standing to sue. A number of cases decided after *Colegrove* recognized the standing of the voters there involved to bring those actions.

These appellants seek relief in order to protect or vindicate an interest of their own, and of those similarly situated. Their constitutional claim is, in substance, that the 1901 statute constitutes arbitrary and capricious state action, offensive to the Fourteenth Amendment in its irrational disregard of the standard of apportionment prescribed by the State's Constitution or of any standard, effecting a gross disproportion of representation to voting population. The injury which appellants assert is that this classification disfavors the voters in the counties in which they reside, placing them in a position of constitutionally unjustifiable inequality vis-a-vis voters in irrationally favored counties. . . .

It would not be necessary to decide whether appellants' allegations of impairment of their votes by the 1901 apportionment will, ultimately, entitle them to any relief, in order to hold that they have standing to seek it. If such impairment does produce a legally cognizable injury, they are among those who have sustained it. They are asserting "a plain, direct and adequate interest in maintaining the effectiveness of their votes," . . . not merely a claim of "the right, possessed by every citizen, to require that the Government be administered according to law. . . ."

IV
Justiciability

In holding that the subject matter of this suit was not justiciable, the District Court relied on *Colegrove* v. *Green* . . . and subsequent per curiam cases. . . . We understand the District Court to have read the cited cases as compelling the conclusion that since the appellants sought to have a legislative apportionment held unconstitutional, their suit presented a "political question" and was therefor nonjusticiable. We hold that this challenge to an apportionment presents no nonjusticiable "political question." The cited cases do not hold the contrary.

Of course the mere fact that the suit seeks protection of a political right does not mean it presents a political question. Such an objection "is little more than a play upon words. . . ." Rather, it is argued that apportionment cases, whatever the actual wording of the complaint, can involve no federal constitutional right except one resting on the guaranty of a republican form of government, and that complaints based on that clause have been held to present political questions which are nonjusticiable.

We hold that the claim pleaded here neither rests upon nor implicates the Guaranty Clause and that its justiciability is therefore not foreclosed by our decisions of cases involving that clause. The District Court misinterpreted *Colegrove* v. *Green* and other decisions of this Court on which it relied. Appellants' claim that they are being denied equal protection is justiciable, and if "discrimination is sufficiently shown, the right to relief under the equal protection clause is not diminished by the fact that the discrimination relates to political rights." *Snowden* v. *Hughes,* 321 U.S. 1. . . . To show why we reject the argument based on the Guaranty Clause . . . we deem it necessary first to consider the contours of the "political question" doctrine.

Our discussion . . . requires review of a number of "political question" cases, in order to expose the attributes of the doctrine. . . . That review reveals that in the Guaranty Clause cases and in the other "political question" cases, it is the relationship between the judiciary and the coordinate branches of the Federal Government, and not the federal judiciary's relationship to the States, which gives rise to the "political question. . . ."

The nonjusticiability of a political question is primarily a function of the separation of powers. Much confusion results from the capacity of the "political question" label to obscure the need for case-by-case inquiry. Deciding whether a matter has in any measure been committed by the Constitution to another branch of government, or whether the action of that branch exceeds whatever authority has been committed, is itself a delicate exercise in constitutional interpretation, and is a responsibility of this Court as ultimate interpreter of the Constitution. . . .

Prominent on the surface of any case held to involve a political question is found a textually demonstrable constitutional commitment of the issue to a coordinate political department; or a lack of judicially discoverable and manageable standards for resolving it; or the impossibility of deciding without an initial policy determination of a kind clearly for nonjudicial discretion; or the impossibility of a court's undertaking independent resolution without expressing lack of the respect due coordinate branches of government; or an unusual need for unquestioning adherence to a political decision already made; or the potentiality of embarassment from multifarious pronouncements by various departments on one question.

Unless one of these formulations is inextricable from the case at bar, there should be no dismissal for nonjusticiability on the ground of a political question's presence. The doctrine of which we treat is one of "political questions," not one of "political cases." The courts cannot reject as "no law suit" a bona fide controversy as to whether some action denominated "political" exceeds constitutional authority. . . .

But it is argued that this case shares the characteristics of decisions that constitute a category not yet considered, cases concerning the Constitution's guaranty, in Art. IV, Section 4, of a republican form of government. . . . [*The Court then discusses, at great length,* Luther v. Borden *and numerous other cases holding that the republican guaranty provision is judicially unenforceable.*]

We conclude . . . that the nonjusticiability of claims resting on the Guaranty Clause which arises from their embodiment of questions that were thought "political," can have no bearing upon the justiciability of the equal protection claim presented in this case. . . . [W]e emphasize that it is the involvement in Guaranty Clause claims of the elements thought to define "political questions," and no other feature, which could render them nonjusticiable. Specifically, we have said that such claims are not held nonjusticiable because they touch matters of state governmental organization. . . .

[O]nly last Term, in *Gomillion* v. *Lightfoot* . . . we applied the Fifteenth Amendment to strike down a redrafting of municipal boundaries which effected a discriminatory impairment of voting rights, in the face of what a majority of the Court of Appeals thought to be a sweeping commitment to state legislatures of the power to draw and redraw such boundaries. . . .

We conclude that the complaint's allegations of a denial of equal protection present a justiciable constitutional cause of action upon which appellants are entitled to a trial and a decision. The right asserted is within the reach of judicial protection under the Fourteenth Amendment.

The judgment of the District Court is reversed and the cause is remanded for further proceedings consistent with this opinion.

Reversed and remanded.

MR. JUSTICE WHITTAKER did not participate in the decision of this case.

MR. JUSTICE DOUGLAS, concurring:

While I join the opinion of the Court and, like the Court, do not reach the merits, a word of explanation is necessary. I put to one side the problems of "political" questions involving the distribution of power between this Court, the Congress, and the Chief Executive. We have here a phase of the recurring problem of the relation of the federal courts to state agencies. More particularly, the question is the extent to which a State may weight one person's vote more heavily than it does another's. . . .

The traditional test under the Equal Protection Clause has been whether a State has made "an invidious discrimination," as it does when it selects "a particular race or nationality for oppressive treatment. . . ." Universal equality is not the test; there is room for weighting. As we stated in *Williamson* v. *Lee Optical Co.,* 348 U.S. 483.

. . . "The prohibition of the Equal Protection Clause goes no further than the invidious discrimination."

I agree with my Brother Clark that if the allegations in the complaint can be sustained a case for relief is established. We are told that a single vote in Moore County, Tennessee, is worth 19 votes in Hamilton County, that one vote in Stewart or in Chester County is worth nearly eight times a single vote in Shelby or Knox County. The opportunity to prove that an "invidious discrimination" exists should therefore be given the appellants. . . .

With the exceptions of *Colegrove* v. *Green,* . . . *South* v. *Peters,* . . . and the decisions they spawned, the Court has never thought that protection of voting rights was beyond judicial cognizance. Today's treatment of those cases removes the only impediment to judicial cognizance of the claims stated in the present complaint.

The justiciability of the present claims being established, any relief accorded can be fashioned in the light of well-known principles of equity.

MR. JUSTICE CLARK, concurring:

. . . The Court holds that the appellants have alleged a cause of action. However, it refuses to award relief here —although the facts are undisputed— and fails to give the District Court any guidance whatever. One dissenting opinion, bursting with words that go through so much and conclude with so little, contemns the majority action as "a massive repudiation of the experience of our whole past." Another describes the complaint as merely asserting conclusory allegations that Tennessee's apportionment is "incorrect," "arbitrary," "obsolete," and "unconstitutional." I believe it can be shown that this case is distinguishable from earlier cases dealing with the distribution of political power by a State, that a patent violation of the Equal Protection Clause of the United States Constitution has been shown, and that an appropriate remedy may be formulated.

I

I take the law of the case from *Mac-Dougall* v. *Green* . . . which involved an attack under the Equal Protection Clause upon an Illinois election statute. The Court decided that case on its merits without hindrance from the "political question" doctrine. Although the statute under attack was upheld, it is clear that the Court based its decision upon the determination that the statute represented a rational state policy. It stated:

"It would be strange indeed, and doctrinaire, for this Court, applying such broad constitutional concepts as due process and equal protection of the laws, to deny a State the power to assure a proper diffusion of political initiative as between its thinly populated counties and those having concentrated masses, in view of the fact that the latter have practical opportunities for exerting their political weight at the polls not available to the former. . . ."

The other cases upon which my Brethren dwell are all distinguishable or inapposite. The widely heralded case of *Colegrove* v. *Green* . . . was one not only in which the Court was bobtailed but in which there was no majority opinion. Indeed, even the "political question" point in Mr. Justice Frankfurter's opinion was no more than an alternative ground. Moreover, the appellants did not present an equal protection argument. While it has served as a Mother Hubbard to most of the subsequent cases, I feel it was in that respect illcast and for all of these reasons put it to one side. Likewise, I do not consider the Guaranty Clause cases based on Art. I, Section 4, of the Con-

stitution, because it is not invoked here and it involves different criteria, as the Courts' opinion indicates. . . . Finally, the Georgia county unit system cases, such as *South* v. *Peters,* . . . reflect the viewpoint of MacDougall, i.e., to refrain from intervening where there is some rational policy behind the State's system.

II

The controlling facts cannot be disputed. It appears from the record that 37 per cent of the voters of Tennessee elect 20 of the 33 Senators while 40 per cent of the voters elect 63 of the 99 members of the House. But this might not on its fact be an "invidious discrimination," . . . for a "statutory discrimination will not be set aside if any state of facts reasonably may be conceived to justify it." *McGowan* v. *Maryland,* 366 U.S. 420, 426 (1961).

It is true that the apportionment policy incorporated in Tennessee's Constitution, i.e., state-wide numerical equality of representation with certain minor qualifications, is a rational one. On a county-by-county comparison a districting plan based thereon naturally will have disparities in representation due to the qualifications. But this to my mind does not raise constitutional problems, for the over-all policy is reasonable. However, the root of the trouble is not in Tennessee's Constitution, for admittedly its policy has not been followed. The discrimination lies in the action of Tennessee's Assembly in allocating legislative seats to counties or districts created by it. Try as one may, Tennessee's apportionment just cannot be made to fit the pattern cut by its Constitution. This was the finding of the District Court. The policy of the Constitution referred to by the dissenters, therefore, is of no relevance here. We must examine what the Assembly has done. The frequency and magnitude of the inequalities in the present districting admit of no policy whatever; . . . [t]he apportionment picture in Tennessee is a topsy-turvical maze of gigantic proportions. . . . Tennessee's apportionment is a crazy quilt without rational basis. . . .

No one—except the dissenters advocating the Harlan "adjusted 'total representation'" formula—contends that mathematical equality among voters is required by the Equal Protection Clause. But certainly there must be some rational design to a State's districting. The discrimination here does not fit any pattern—as I have said, it is but a crazy quilt. My Brother Harlan contends that other proposed apportionment plans contain disparities. Instead of chasing those rabbits he should first pause long enough to meet appellants' proof of discrimination by showing that in fact the present plan follows a rational policy. Not being able to do this, he merely counters with such generalities as "classic legislative judgment," no "significant discrepancy," and "de minimis departures." I submit that even a casual glance at the present apportionment picture shows these conclusions to be entirely fanciful. If present representation has a policy at all, it is to maintain the status quo of invidious discrimination at any cost. . . .

III

Although I find the Tennessee apportionment statute offends the Equal Protection Clause, I would not consider intervention by this Court into so delicate a field if there were any other relief available to the people of Tennessee. But the majority of the people of Tennessee have no "practical opportunities for exerting their political weight at the polls" to correct the existing "invidious discrimination." Tennessee has no initiative and referendum. I have searched diligently for other "practical opportunities" present under the law. I find none other than through the federal courts. The majority of the voters have been caught up in a legislative strait jacket. Tennessee has an "informed, civically militant electorate" and "an aroused popular conscience," but it does not sear the "conscience of the people's representatives." This is because the legislative policy has riveted the present seats in the Assembly to their respective constituencies, and by the votes of their incumbents a reapportionment of any kind is prevented. The people have been rebuffed at the hands of the Assembly; they have tried the constitutional convention route, but since the call must originate in the Assembly it, too, has been fruitless. They have tried Tennessee courts with the same result, and Governors have fought the tide only to flounder. It is said that there is recourse in Congress and perhaps that may be, but from a practical standpoint this is without substance. To date Congress has never undertaken such a task in any State. We therefore must conclude that the people of Tennessee are stymied and without judicial intervention will be saddled with the present discrimination in the affairs of their state government.

IV

Finally, we must consider if there are any appropriate modes of effective judicial relief. The federal courts are, of course, not forums for political debates, nor should they resolve themselves into state constitutional conventions or legislative assemblies. Nor should their jurisdiction be exercised in the hope that such a declaration, as is made today, may have the direct effect of bringing on legislative action and relieving the courts of the problem of fashioning relief. To my mind this would be nothing less than blackjacking the Assembly into reapportioning the State. If judicial competence were lacking to fashion an effective decree, I would dismiss this appeal. However . . . I see no such difficulty in the position of this case. One plan might be to start with the existing assembly districts, consolidate some of them, and award the seats thus released to those counties suffering the most egregious discrimination. Other possibilities are present and might be more effective. But the plan here suggested would at least release the strangle hold now on the Assembly and permit it to redistrict itself. . . .

In view of the detailed study that the Court has given this problem, it is unfortunate that a decision is not reached on the merits. The majority appears to hold, at least sub silentio, that an invidious discrimination is present, but it remands to the three-judge court for it to make what is certain to be that formal determination. . . . [N]ot being able to muster a court to dispose of the case on the merits, I concur in the opinion of the majority and acquiesce in the decison to remand. . . .

As John Rutledge (later Chief Justice) said 175 years ago in the course of the Constitutional Convention, a chief function of the Court is to secure the national rights. Its decision today supports the proposition for which our forebears fought and many died, namely that "to be fully conformable to the principle of right, the form of government must be representative." That is the keystone upon which our government was founded and lacking which no republic can survive. It is well for this Court to practice self-restraint and discipline in constitutional adjudication, but never in its history have those principles received sanction where the national rights of so many have been so clearly infringed for so long a time. National respect for the courts is more enhanced through the forthright enforcement of those rights rather than by rendering them nugatory through the interposition of subterfuges. In my view the ultimate decision today is in the greatest tradition of this Court.

MR. JUSTICE STEWART, concurring:

The separate writings of my dissenting and concurring Brothers stray so far from the subject of today's decision as to convey, I think, a distressingly inaccurate impression of what the Court decides. For that reason, I think it appropriate, in joining the opinion of the Court, to emphasize in a few words what the opinion does and does not say. . . .

The complaint in this case asserts that Tennessee's system of apportionment is utterly arbitrary—without any possible justification in rationality. The District Court did not reach the merits of that claim, and this Court quite properly expresses no view on the subject. Contrary to the suggestion of my Brother Harlan, the Court does not say or imply that "state legislatures must be so structured as to reflect with approximate equality the voice of every voter. . . ." The Court does not say or imply that there is anything in the Federal Constitution "to prevent a State, acting not irrationally, from choosing any electoral legislative structure it thinks best suited to the interests, temper, and custom of its people. . . ." And contrary to the suggestion of my Brother Douglas, the Court most assuredly does not decide the question, "May a State weight the vote of one county or one district more heavily than it weights the vote in another?" . . .

My Brother Clark has made a convincing prima facie showing that Tennessee's system of apportionment is in fact utterly arbitrary—without any possible justification in rationality. My Brother Harlan has, with imagination and ingenuity, hypothesized possibly rational bases for Tennessee's system. But the merits of this case are not before us now. The defendants have not yet had an opportunity to be heard in defense of the State's system of apportionment; indeed, they have not yet even filed an answer to the complaint. As in other cases, the proper place for the trial is in the trial court, not here.

MR. JUSTICE FRANKFURTER, whom MR. JUSTICE HARLAN joins, dissenting:

The Court today reverses a uniform course of decision established by a dozen cases, including one by which the very claim now sustained was unanimously rejected only five years ago. The impressive body of rulings thus cast aside reflected the equally uniform course of our political history regarding the relationship between population and legislative representation—a wholly different matter from denial of the franchise to individuals because of race, color, religion or sex. Such a massive repudiation of the experience of our whole past in asserting destructively novel judicial power demands a detailed analysis of the role of this Court in our constitutional scheme. Disregard of inherent limits in the effective exercise of the Court's "judicial Power" not only presages the futility of judicial intervention in the essentially political conflict of forces by which the relation between population and representation has time out of mind been and now is determined. It may well impair the Court's position as the ultimate organ of "the supreme Law of the Land" in that vast range of legal problems, often strongly entangled in popular feeling, on which this Court must pronounce. The Court's authority—possessed neither of the purse nor the sword—ultimately rests on sustained public confidence in its moral sanction. Such feeling must be nourished by the Court's complete detachment, in fact as in appearance, from political entanglements and by abstention from injecting itself into the clash of political forces in political settlements.

A hypothetical claim resting on abstract assumptions is now for the first time made the basis for affording illusory relief for a particular evil even though it foreshadows deeper and more pervasive difficulties in consequence. The claim is hypothetical and the assumptions are abstract because the Court does not vouchsafe the lower courts—state and federal—guide-lines for formulating specific, definite, wholly unprecedented remedies for the inevitable litigations that today's umbrageous disposition is bound to stimulate in connection with politically motivated reapportionments in so many States. In such a setting, to promulgate jurisdiction in the abstract is meaningless. It is devoid of reality as "a brooding omnipresence in the sky" for it conveys no intimation what relief, if any, a District Court is capable of affording that would not invite legislatures to play ducks and drakes with the judiciary. For this Court to direct the District Court to enforce a claim to which the Court has over the years consistently found itself required to deny legal enforcement and at the same time to find it necessary to withhold any guidance to the lower court how to enforce this turnabout, new legal claim, manifests an odd—indeed an esoteric—conception of judicial propriety. One of the Court's supporting opinions, as elucidated by commentary, unwittingly affords a disheartening preview of the mathematical quagmire (apart from divers judicially inappropriate and elusive determinants), into which this Court today catapults the lower courts of the country without so much as adumbrating the basis for a legal calculus as a means of extrication. Even assuming the indispensable intellectual disinterestedness on the part of judges in such matters, they do not have accepted legal standards or criteria or even reliable analogies to draw upon for making judicial judgments. To charge courts with the task of accommodating the incommensurable factors of policy that underlie these mathematical puzzles is to attribute, however flatteringly, omnicompetence to judges. The Framers of the Constitution persistently rejected a proposal that embodied this assumption and Thomas Jefferson never entertained it.

Recent legislation, creating a district appropriately described as "an atrocity of ingenuity," is not unique. Considering the gross inequality among legislative electoral units within almost every State, the Court naturally shrinks from asserting that in districting at least substantial equality is a constitutional requirement enforceable by courts. Room continues to be allowed for weighting. This of course implies that geography, economics, urban-rural conflict, and all the other non-legal factors which have throughout our history entered into political districting are to some extent not to be ruled out in the undefined vista now opened up by review in the federal courts of state reapportionments. To some extent—aye, there's the rub. In effect, today's decision empowers the courts of the country to devise what should constitute the proper composition of the legislatures of the 50 States. If state courts should for one reason or another find themselves unable to discharge this task, the duty of doing so is put on the federal courts or on this Court, if State views do not satisfy this Court's notion of what is proper districting.

We were soothingly told at the bar of this Court that we need not worry about the kind of remedy a court could effectively fashion once the abstract constitutional right to have courts pass on a state-wide system of electoral districting is recognized as a matter of judicial rhetoric, because legislatures would heed the Court's admonition. This is not only an euphoric hope. It implies a sorry confession of judicial impotence in place of a frank acknowledgment that there is not under our Constitution a judicial remedy for every political mischief, for every undesirable exercise of legislative power. The Framers carefully and with deliberate forethought refused so to enthrone the judiciary. In this situation, as in other of like nature, appeal for relief does not belong here. Appeal must be to an informed, civically militant electorate. In a democratic society like ours, relief must come through an aroused popular conscience that sears the conscience of the people's representatives. In any event there is nothing judicially more unseemly nor more self-defeating than for this Court to make in terrorem pronouncements, to indulge in merely empty rhetoric, sounding a word of promise to the ear, sure to be disappointing to the hope. . . .

I

In sustaining appellants' claim, based on the Fourteenth Amendment, that the District Court may entertain this suit, this Court's uniform course of decision over the years is overruled or disregarded. Explicitly it begins with *Colegrove* v. *Green* . . . but its roots run deep in the Court's historic adjudicatory process.

Colegrove held that a federal court should not entertain an action for declaratory and injunctive relief to adjudicate the constitutionality, under the Equal Protection Clause and other federal constitutional and statutory provisions, of a state statute establishing the respective districts for the State's election of Representatives to the Congress. Two opinions were written by the four Justices who composed the majority of the seven sitting members of the Court. Both opinions joining in the result in *Colegrove* v. *Green* agreed that considerations were controlling which dictated denial of jurisdiction though not in the strict sense of want of power. While the two opinions show a divergence of view regarding some of these considerations, there are important points of concurrence. Both opinions demonstrate a predominant concern, first, with avoiding federal judicial involvement; second, with respect to the difficulty—in view of the nature of the problems of apportionment and its history in this country—of drawing on or devising judicial standards for judgment, as opposed to legislative determinations, of the part which mere numerical equality among voters should play as a criterion for the allocation of political power; and, third, with problems of finding appropriate modes of relief—particularly, the problem of resolving the essentially political issue of the relative merits of at-large elections and elections held in districts of unequal population. . . .

II

The *Colegrove* doctrine, in the form in which repeated decisions have settled it, was not an innovation. It represents long judicial thought and experience. From its earliest opinions this Court has consistently recognized a class of controversies which do not lend themselves to judicial standards and judicial remedies. To classify the various instances as "political questions" is rather a form of stating this conclusion than revealing of analysis. Some of the cases so labelled have no relevance here. But from others emerge unifying considerations that are compelling. . . . [*Justice Frankfurter then reviews numerous cases involving "political questions" under the following headings: war and foreign affairs, structure and organization of state political institutions, Negro disfranchisement, and abstract questions of political power.*]

The influence of these converging considerations—the caution not to undertake decision where standards meet for judicial judgment are lacking, the reluctance to interfere with matters of state government in the absence of an unquestionable and effectively enforceable mandate, the unwillingness to make courts arbiters of the broad issues of political organization historically committed to other institutions and for whose adjustment the judicial process is ill-adapted—has been decisive of the settled line of cases, reaching back more than a century, which holds that Art. IV, Section 4, of the Constitution, guaranteeing to the States "a Republican Form of Government," is not enforceable through the courts. . . .

III

The present case involves all of the elements that have made the Guarantee Clause cases non-judiciable. It is, in effect, a Guarantee Clause claim masquerading under a different label. But it cannot make the case more fit for judicial action that appellants invoke the Fourteenth Amendment rather than Art. IV, Section 4, where, in fact, the gist of their complaint is the same—unless it can be found that the Fourteenth Amendment speaks with greater particularity to their situation. . . .

What, then, is this question of legislative apportionment? Appellants invoke the right to vote and to have their votes counted. But they are permitted to vote and their votes are counted. They go to the polls, they cast their ballots, they send their representatives to the state councils. Their complaint is simply that the representatives are not sufficiently numerous or powerful—in short, that Tennessee has adopted a basis of representation with which they are dissatisfied. Talk of "debasement" or "dilution" is circular talk. One cannot speak of "debasement" or "dilution" of the value of a vote until there is first defined a standard of reference as to what a vote should be worth. What is actually asked of the Court in this case is to choose among competing bases of representation—ultimately, really among competing theories of political philosophy—in order to establish an appropriate frame of government for the State of Tennessee and thereby for all the states of the Union.

In such a matter, abstract analogies which ignore the facts of history deal in unrealities; they betray reason. This is not a case in which a State has, through a device however oblique and sophisticated, denied Negroes or Jews or red-headed persons a vote, or given them only a third or a sixth of a vote. That was *Gomillion* v. *Lightfoot*. . . . What Tennessee illustrates is an old and still widespread method of representation—representation by local geographical division, only in part respective of population—in preference to others, others, forsooth, more appealing. Appellants contest this choice and seek to make this Court the arbiter of the disagreement. They would make the Equal Protection Clause the charter of adjudication, asserting that the equality which it guarantees comports, if not the assurance of equal weight to every voter's vote, at least the basic conception that representation ought to be proportionate to population, a standard by reference to which the reasonableness of apportionment plans may be judged.

To find such a political conception legally enforceable in the broad and unspecific guarantee of equal protection is to rewrite the Constitution. . . . Certainly, "equal protection" is no more secure a foundation for judicial judgment of the permissibility of varying forms of representative government than

is "Republican Form." Indeed since "equal protection of the laws" can only mean an equality of persons standing in the same relation to whatever governmental action is challenged, the determination whether treatment is equal presupposses a determination concerning the nature of the relationship. This, with respect to apportionment, means an inquiry into the theoretic base of representation in an acceptably republican state. For a court could not determine the equal-protection issue without in fact first determining the Republican-Form issue, simply because what is reasonable for equal protection purposes will depend upon what frame of government, basically, is allowed. To divorce "equal protection" from "Republican Form" is to talk about half a question.

The notion that representation proportioned to the geographic spread of population is so universally accepted as a necessary element of equality between man and man that it must be taken to be the standard of a political equality preserved by the Fourteenth Amendment—that it is, in appellants' words "the basic principle of representative government"—is, to put it bluntly, not true. However desirable and however desired by some among the great political thinkers and framers of our government, it has never been generally practiced, today or in the past. It was not the English system, it was not the colonial system, it was not the system chosen for the national government by the Constitution, it was not the system exclusively or even predominantly practiced by the States today. Unless judges, the judges of this Court, are to make their private views of political wisdom the measure of the Constitution—views which in all honesty cannot but give the appearance, if not reflect the reality, of involvement with the business of partisan politics so inescapably a part of apportionment controversies—the

Fourteenth Amendment, "itself a historical product," . . . provides no guide for judicial oversight of the representation problem. . . . [*Justice Frankfurter then deals at length with representation and apportionment practices in Great Britain, the Colonies and the Union, and the states at the time of the ratification of the Fourteenth Amendment and contemporary times.*]

Manifestly, the Equal Protection Clause supplies no clearer guide for judicial examination of apportionment methods than would the Guarantee Clause itself. Apportionment, by its character, is a subject of extraordinary complexity, involving—even after the fundamental theoretical issues concerning what is to be represented in a representative legislature have been fought out or compromised—considerations of geography, demography, electoral convenience, economic and social cohesions or divergencies among particular local groups, communications, the practical effects of political institutions like the lobby and the city machine, ancient traditions and ties of settled usage respect for proven incumbents of long experience and senior status, mathematical mechanics, censuses compiling relevant data, and a host of others. Legislative responses throughout the country to the apportionment demands of the 1960 Census have glaringly confirmed that these are not factors that lend themselves to evaluations of a nature that are the staple of judicial determinations or for which judges are equipped to adjudicate by legal training or experience or native wit. And this is the more so true because in every strand of this complicated, intricate web of values meet the contending forces of partisan politics. The practical significance of apportionment is that the next election results may differ because of it. Apportionment battles are overwhelmingly party or intra-party con-

tests. It will add a virulent source of friction and tension in federal-state relations to embroil the federal judiciary in them.

Appellants, however, contend that the federal courts may provide the standard which the Fourteenth Amendment lacks by reference to the provisions of the constitution of Tennessee. The argument is that although the same or greater disparities of electoral strength may be suffered to exist immune from federal judicial review in States where they result from apportionment legislation consistent with state constitutions, the Tennessee legislature may not abridge the rights which, on its face, its own constitution appears to give, without by that act denying equal protection of the laws. It is said that the law of Tennessee, as expressed by the words of its written constitution, has made the basic choice among policies in favor of representation proportioned to population, and that it is no longer open to the State to allot its voting power on other principles.

This reasoning does not bear analysis. Like claims invoking state constitutional requirement have been rejected here and for good reason. It is settled that whatever federal consequences may derive from a discrimination worked by a state statute must be the same as if the same discrimination were written into the State's fundamental law. . . . Appellants complain of a practice which, by their own allegations, has been the law of Tennessee for sixty years. They allege that the apportionment act of 1901 created unequal districts when passed and still maintains unequal districts. They allege that the Legislature has since 1901 purposefully retained unequal districts. And the Supreme Court of Tennessee has refused to invalidate the law establishing these unequal districts. . . . Tennessee's law and its policy respecting apportionment are what sixty years of practice show them to be, not what appellants cull from the unenforced and, according to its own judiciary, unenforceable words of its Constitution. . . .

In all of the apportionment cases which have come before the Court, a consideration which has been weighty in determining their non-judiciability has been the difficulty or impossibility of devising effective judicial remedies in this class of case. An injunction restraining a general election unless the legislature reapportions would paralyze the critical centers of a State's political system and threaten political dislocation whose consequences are not foreseeable. A declaration devoid of implied compulsion of injunctive or other relief would be an idle threat. Surely a Federal District Court could not itself remap the State: the same complexities which impede effective judicial review of apportionment a fortiori make impossible a court's consideration of these imponderables as an original matter. And the choice of elections at large as opposed to elections by district, however unequal the districts, is a matter of sweeping political judgment having enormous political implications, the nature and reach of which are certainly beyond the informed understanding of, and capacity for appraisal by, courts. . . .

Although the District Court had jurisdiction in the very restricted sense of power to determine whether it could adjudicate the claim, the case is of that class of political controversy which, by the nature of its subject, is unfit for federal judicial action. The judgment of the District Court, in dismissing the complaint for failure to state a claim on which relief can be granted, should therefore be affirmed.

Dissenting opinion of MR. JUSTICE HARLAN, whom MR. JUSTICE FRANKFURTER joins:

The dissenting opinion of Mr. Justice Frankfurter, in which I join, demonstrates the abrupt departure the majority makes from judicial history by putting the federal courts into this area of state concerns—an area which, in this instance, the Tennessee state courts themselves have refused to enter. . . .

It is at once essential to recognize this case for what it is. The issue here relates not to a method of state electoral apportionment by which seats in the federal House of Representatives are allocated, but solely to the right of a State to fix the basis of representation in its own legislature. Until it is first decided to what extent that right is limited by the Federal Constitution, and whether what Tennessee has done or failed to do in this instance runs afoul of any such limitation, we need not reach the issues of justiciability" or "political question" or any of the other considerations which in such cases as *Colegrove* v. *Green* . . . led the Court to decline to adjudicate a challenge to a state apportionment affecting seats in the federal House of Representatives, in the absence of a controlling Act of Congress. . . .

The appellants' claim in this case ultimately rests entirely on the Equal Protection Clause of the Fourteenth Amendment. It is asserted that Tennessee has violated the Equal Protection Clause by maintaining in effect a system of apportionment that grossly favors in legislative representation the rural sections of the State as against its urban communities. Stripped to its essentials the complaint purports to set forth three constitutional claims of varying breadth:

(1) The Equal Protection Clause requires that each vote cast in state legislative elections be given approximately equal weight.

(2) Short of this, the existing apportionment of state legislators is so unreasonable as to amount to an arbi-

trary and capricious act of classification on the part of the Tennessee Legislature, which is offensive to the Equal Protection Clause.

(3) In any event, the existing apportionment is rendered invalid under the Fourteenth Amendment because it flies in the face of the Tennessee Constitution. . . .

I

I can find nothing in the Equal Protection Clause or elsewhere in the Federal Constitution which expressly or impliedly supports the view that state legislatures must be so structured as to reflect with approximate equality the voice of every voter. Not only is that proposition refuted by history, as shown by my Brother Frankfurter, but it strikes deep into the heart of our federal system. Its acceptance would require us to turn our backs on the regard which this Court has always shown for the judgment of state legislatures and courts on matters of basically local concern.

In the last analysis, what lies at the core of this controversy is a difference of opinion as to the function of representative government. It is surely beyond argument that those who have the responsibility for devising a system of representation may permissibly consider that factors other than bare numbers should be taken into account. The existence of the United States Senate is proof enough of that. To consider that we may ignore the Tennessee Legislature's judgment in this instance because that body was the product of an asymmetrical electoral apportionment would in effect be to assume the very conclusion here disputed. Hence we must accept the present form of the Tennessee Legislature as the embodiment of the State's choice, or, more realistically, its compromise, between competing political philosophies. The federal courts have not been empowered by the Equal Protection Clause to judge whether this resolution of the State's internal political conflict is desirable or undesirable, wise or unwise. . . .

[T]here is nothing in the Federal Constitution to prevent a State, acting not irrationally, from choosing any electoral legislative structure it thinks best suited to the interests, temper, and custom of its people. . . .

A State's choice to distribute electoral strength among geographical units, rather than according to a census of population, is certainly no less a rational decision of policy than would be its choice to levy a tax on property rather than a tax on income. Both are legislative judgments entitled to equal respect from this Court.

II

The claim that Tennessee's system of apportionment is so unreasonable as to amount to a capricious classification of voting strength stands up no better under dispassionate analysis.

The Court has said time and again that the Equal Protection Clause does not demand of state enactments either mathematical identity or rigid equality. . . . All that is prohibited is "invidious discrimination" bearing no rational relation to any permissible policy of the State. . . .

What then is the basis for the claim made in this case that the distribution of state senators and representatives is the product of capriciousness or of some constitutionally prohibited policy? It is not that Tennessee has arranged its electoral districts with a deliberate purpose to dilute the voting strength of one race, cf. *Gomillion* v. *Lightfoot*, . . . or that some religious group is intentionally under-represented. Nor is it a charge that the legislature has indulged in sheer caprice by allotting representatives to each county on the basis of a throw of the dice, or of some other determinant bearing no rational relation to the question of apportionment. Rather, the claim is that the State Legislature has unreasonably retained substantially the same allocation of senators and representatives as was established by statue in 1901, refusing to recognize the great shift in the population balance between urban and rural communities that has occurred in the meantime. . . .

A Federal District Court is asked to say that the passage of time has rendered the 1901 apportionment obsolete to the point where its continuance becomes vulnerable under the Fourteenth Amendment. But is not this matter one that involves a classic legislative judgment? Surely it lies within the province of a state legislature to conclude that an existing allocation of senators and representatives constitutes a desirable balance of geographical and demographical representation, or that in the interest of stability of government it would be best to defer for some further time the redistribution of seats in the state legislature.

Indeed, I would hardly think it unconstitutional if a state legislature's expressed reason for establishing or maintaining an electoral imbalance between its rural and urban population were to protect the State's agricultural interests from the sheer weight of numbers of those residing in its cities. . . . These are matters of local policy, on the wisdom of which the federal judiciary is neither permitted nor qualified to sit in judgment. . . .

It is my view that the majority opinion has failed to point to any recognizable constitutional claim alleged in this complaint. Indeed, it is interesting to note that my Brother Stewart is at pains to disclaim for himself, and to point out that the majority opinion does not suggest, that the Federal Constitution requires of the States any particular

kind of electoral apportionment, still less that they must accord to each voter approximately equal voting strength. . . . But that being so, what, may it be asked, is left of this complaint? Surely the bare allegations that the existing Tennessee apportionment is "incorrect," "arbitrary," "obsolete" and "unconstitutional"—amounting to nothing more than legal conclusions—do not themselves save the complaint from dismissal. . . .

From a reading of the majority and concurring opinions one will not find it difficult to catch the premises that underlie this decision. The fact that the appellants have been unable to obtain political redress of their asserted grievances appears to be regarded as a matter which should lead the Court to stretch to find some basis for judicial intervention. While the Equal Protection Clause is invoked, the opinion for the Court notably eschews explaining how, consonant with past decisions, the undisputed facts in this case can be considered to show a violation of that constitutional provision. The majority seems to have accepted the argument, pressed at the bar, that if this Court merely asserts authority in this field, Tennessee and other "malapportioning" States will quickly respond with appropriate political action, so that this Court need not be greatly concerned about the federal courts becoming further involved in these matters. At the same time the majority has wholly failed to reckon with what the future may hold in store if this optimistic prediction is not fulfilled. Thus, what the Court is doing reflects more an adventure in judicial experimentation than a solid piece of constitutional adjudication. . . .

In conclusion, it is appropriate to say that one need not agree, as a citizen, with what Tennessee has done or failed to do, in order to deprecate, as a judge, what the majority is doing today. Those observers of the Court who see it primarily as the last refuge for the correction of all inequality or injustice, no matter what its nature or source, will no doubt applaud this decision and its break with the past. Those who consider that continuing national respect for the Court's authority depends in large measure upon its wise exercise of self-restraint and discipline in constitutional adjudication, will view the decision with deep concern.

I would

Affirm.

WESBERRY *v.* SANDERS
376 U.S. 1; 84 Sup. Ct.; 11 L. Ed. 2d 481 (1964)

[*This important case originated in Atlanta, Georgia, when Wesberry and another qualified voter brought a suit claiming that population disparities in congressional districts deprived them of a right under the Federal Constitution to have their votes for congressmen given the same weight as the votes of other Georgians. The Atlanta congressional district had 823,680 persons as compared with the total population of 272,154 in the smallest district of the state. The average population of the ten Georgia districts was 394,312. Each district elects only one congressman.*

In his suit Wesberry asked that the Georgia districting statute be declared invalid and the Sanders, the Governor of Georgia, and the state Secretary of State be enjoined from conducting elections under it. Wesberry contended that voters in the Atlanta district were deprived of the full benefit of their right to vote in violation of the following:

1. Article I, Section 2 of the Constitution, which provides that "The House of Representatives shall be composed of members chosen every second year by the People of the several states. . . ."

2. The Due Process, Equal Protection, and Privileges and Immunities Clauses of the Fourteenth Amendment.

3. The part of Section 2 of the Fourteenth Amendment providing that "Representatives shall be apportioned among the several States according to their respective numbers. . . ."

In a two-to-one decision, a federal district court dismissed the complaint on the ground that challenges to apportionment of congressional districts raised only "political" questions, which are not justiciable. The district court relied on Justice Frankfurter's opinion in Colegrove v. Green *in reaching its decision. The dissenting district judge relied on* Baker v. Carr. *The case then went to the Supreme Court on appeal.*]

MR. JUSTICE BLACK delivered the opinion of the Court:

. . . *Baker* v. *Carr* . . . considered a challenge to a 1901 Tennessee statute providing for apportionment of State Representatives and Senators under the State's constitution, which called for apportionment among counties or districts "according to the number of qualified voters in each." The complaint there charged that the State's constitutional command to apportion on the basis of the number of qualified voters had not been followed in the

1901 statute and that the districts were so discriminatorily disparate in number of qualified voters that the plaintiffs and persons similarly situated were, "by virtue of the debasement of their votes," denied the equal protection of the laws guaranteed them by the Fourteenth Amendment. The cause there of the alleged "debasement" of votes for state legislators—districts containing widely varying numbers of people—was precisely that which was alleged to debase votes for Congressmen in *Colegrove* v. *Green* . . . and in the present case. The Court in *Baker* pointed out that the opinion of Mr. Justice Frankfurter in *Colegrove,* upon the reasoning of which the majority below leaned heavily in dismissing "for want of equity," was approved by only three of the seven Justices sitting. After full consideration of *Colegrove,* the Court in *Baker* held (1) that the District Court had jurisdiction of the subject matter; (2) that the qualified Tennessee voters there had standing to sue; and (3) that the plaintiffs had stated a justiciable cause of action on which relief could be granted.

The reasons which led to these conclusions in *Baker* are equally persuasive here. . . . Mr. Justice Frankfurter's *Colegrove* opinion contended that Art. I, Section 4, of the Constitution had given Congress "exclusive authority" to protect the right of citizens to vote for Congressmen, but we made it clear in *Baker* that nothing in the language of that article gives support to a construction that would immunize state congressional apportionment laws which debase a citizen's right to vote from the power of courts to protect the constitutional rights of individuals from legislative destruction, a power recognized at least since our decision in *Marbury* v. *Madison.* . . . The right to vote is too important in our free society to be stripped of judicial protection by such an interpretation of Article I. This dis-

missal can no more be justified on the ground of "want of equity" than on the ground of "nonjusticiability." We therefore hold that the District Court erred in dismissing the complaint.

. . . We hold that, construed in its historical context, the command of Art. I, Section 2, that Representatives be chosen "by the People of the several States" means that as nearly as is practicable one man's vote in a congressional election is to be worth as much as another's. This rule is followed automatically, of course, when Representatives are chosen as a group on a statewide basis, as was a widespread practice in the first fifty years of our Nation's history. It would be extraordinary to suggest that in such statewide elections the votes of inhabitants of some parts of a State . . . could be weighed at two or three times the value of the votes of people living in more populous parts of the State. . . . Cf. *Gray* v. *Sanders.* . . . We do not believe that the Framers of the Constitution intended to permit the same vote-diluting discrimination to be accomplished through the device of districts containing widely varied numbers of inhabitants. To say that a vote is worth more in one district than in another would not only run counter to our fundamental ideas of democratic government, it would cast aside the principle of a House of Representatives elected "by the People," a principle tenaciously fought for and established at the Constitutional Convention. The history of the Constitution, particularly that part of it relating to the adoption of Art. I, Section 2, reveals that those who framed the Constitution meant that, no matter what the mechanics of an election, whether statewide or by districts, it was population which was to be the basis of the House of Representatives. . . . [*Justice Black then relies principally on the debates of the Constitutional Convention to show that the framers intended that every man's vote was "to count alike".*]

. . . It would defeat the principle solemnly embodied in the Great Compromise—equal representation in the House of equal numbers of people—for us to hold that, within the States, legislatures may draw the lines of congressional districts in such a way as to give some voters a greater voice in choosing a Congressman than others. The House of Representatives, the [*Constitutional*] Convention agreed, was to represent the people as individuals, and on a basis of complete equality for each voter. The delegates were quite aware of what Madison called the "vicious representation" in Great Britain whereby "rotten boroughs" with few inhabitants were represented in Parliament on or almost on a par with cities of greater population. [*James*] Wilson urged that people must escape the evils of the English system under which one man could send two members to Parliament to represent the borough of Old Sarum while London's million people sent but four. The delegates referred to rotten borough apportionments in some of the state legislatures as the kind of objectionable governmental action that the Constitution should not tolerate in the election of congressional representatives.

Madison in *The Federalist* described the system of division of States into congressional districts, the method which he and others assumed States probably would adopt: "The city of Philadelphia is supposed to contain between fifty and sixty thousand souls. It will therefore form nearly two districts for the choice of Federal Representatives." "[N]umbers," he said, not only are a suitable way to represent wealth but in any event "are the only proper scale of representation." In the state conventions, speakers urging ratification of the Constitution emphasized the theme of equal representation in the House which

had permeated the debates in Philadelphia. Charles Cotesworth Pinckney told the South Carolina Convention, "the House of Representatives will be elected immediately by the people, and represent them and their personal rights individually. . . ." Speakers at the ratifying conventions emphasized that the House of Representatives was meant to be free of the malapportionment then existing in some of the state legislatures —such as those of Connecticut, Rhode Island, and South Carolina—and argued that the power given Congress in Art. I, Section 4, was meant to be used to vindicate the people's right to equality of representation in the House. Congress' power, said John Steele at the North Carolina convention, was not to be used to allow Congress to create rotten boroughs; in answer to another delegate's suggestion that Congress might use its power to favor people living near the seacoast, Steele said that Congress "most probably" would "lay the State off into districts," and if it made laws "inconsistent with the Constitution, independent judges will not uphold them, nor will the people obey them."

Soon after the Constitution was adopted, James Wilson of Pennsylvania, by then as Associate Justice of this Court, gave a series of lectures at Philadelphia in which, drawing on his experience as one of the most active members of the Constitutional Convention, he said:

"[A]ll elections ought to be equal. Elections are equal, when a given number of citizens, in one part of the state, choose as many representatives, as are chosen by the same number of citizens, in any other part of the state. In this manner, the proportion of the representatives and of the constituents will remain invariably the same."

It is in the light of such history that

we must construe Art. I, Section 2, of the Constitution, which, carrying out the ideas of Madison and those of like views, provides that Representatives shall be chosen "by the People of the several States" and shall be "apportioned among the several States . . . according to their respective numbers." It is not surprising that our Court has held that this Article gives persons qualified to vote a constitutional right to vote and to have their votes counted. . . . No right is more precious in a free country than that of having a voice in the election of those who make the laws under which, as good citizens, we must live. Other rights, even the most basic, are illusory if the right to vote is undermined. Our Constitution leaves no room for classification of people in a way that unnecessarily abridges this right. . . .

While it may not be possible to draw congressional districts with mathematical precision, that is no excuse for ignoring our Constitutions' plain objective of making equal representation for equal numbers of people the fundamental goal for the House of Representatives. That is the high standard of justice and common sense which the Founders set for us.

Reversed and remanded

MR. JUSTICE CLARK, concurring in part and dissenting in part.

Unfortunately I can join neither the opinion of the Court nor the dissent of my Brother Harlan. It is true that the opening sentence of Art. I, Section 2, of the Constitution provides that Representatives are to be chosen "by the People of the several States. . . ." However, in my view, Brother Harlan has clearly demonstrated that both the historical background and language preclude a finding that Art. I, Section 2, lays down the *ipse dixit* "one person, one vote" in congressional elections. On the other hand, I agree with the

majority that congressional districting is subject to judicial scrutiny. . . .

MR. JUSTICE HARLAN, dissenting:

I had not expected to witness the day when the Supreme Court of the United States would render a decision which casts grave doubt on the constitutionality of the composition of the House of Representatives. It is not an exaggeration to say that such is the effect of today's decision. The Court's holding that the Constitution requires States to select Representatives either by elections at large or by elections in districts composed "as nearly as is practicable" of equal population places in jeopardy the seats of almost all the members of the present House of Representatives.

In the last congressional election, in 1962, Representatives from forty-two States were elected from congressional districts. In all but five of those States, the difference between the populations of the largest and smallest districts exceeded 100,000 persons. A difference of this magnitude in the size of districts the average population of which in each State is less than 500,000 is presumably not equality among districts "as nearly as is practicable," although the Court does not reveal its definition of that phrase. Thus, today's decision impugns the validity of the election of 398 Representatives from thirty-seven States, leaving a "constitutional" House of thirty-seven members now sitting.

Only a demonstration which could not be avoided would justify this Court in rendering a decision the effect of which, inescapably as I see it, is to declare constitutionally defective the very composition of a coordinate branch of the Federal Government. The Court's opinion not only fails to make such a demonstration. It is unsound logically on its face and demonstrably unsound historically. . . .

Before coming to grips with the reasoning that carries such extraordinary consequences, it is important to have firmly in mind the provisions of Article I of the Constitution which controls this case:

"Section 2. The House of Representatives shall be composed of Members chosen every second Year by the People of the several States, and the Electors in each State shall have the Qualifications requisite for Electors of the most numerous Branch of the State Legislature.

"Representatives and direct Taxes shall be apportioned among the several States which may be included within this Union, according to their respective Numbers, which shall be determined by adding to the whole Number of free Persons, including those bound to Service for a Term of Years, and excluding Indians not taxed, three-fifths of all other Persons. The actual Enumeration shall be made within three Years after the first Meeting of the Congress of the United States, and within every subsequent Term of ten Years, in such Manner as they shall by Law direct. The Number of Representatives shall not exceed one for every thirty Thousand, but each State shall have at Least one Representative. . . .

"Section 4. The Times, Places and Manner of holding Elections for Senators and Representatives, shall be prescribed in each State by the Legislature thereof; but the Congress may at any time by Law make or alter such Regulations, except as to the Places of chusing Senators.

"Section 5. Each House shall be the Judge of the Elections, Returns and Qualifications of its own Members. . . ."

. . . [T]hese constitutional provisions and their "historical context," . . . establish:

1. that congressional Representives

are to be apportioned among the several States largely, but not entirely, according to population;

2. that the States have plenary power to select their allotted Repretatives in accordance with any method of popular election they please, subject only to the supervisory power of Congress; and

3. that the supervisory power of Congress is exclusive.

In short, in the absence of legislation providing for equal districts by the Georgia Legislature or by Congress, these appellants have no right to the judicial relief which they seek. It goes without saying that it is beyond the province of this Court to decide whether equally populated districts is the preferable method for electing Representatives, whether state legislatures would have acted more fairly or wisely had they adopted such a method, or whether Congress has been derelict in not requiring state legislatures to follow that course. Once it is clear that there is no constitutional right at stake, that ends the case. . . .

Disclaiming all reliance on other provisions of the Constitution, in particular those of the Fourteenth Amendment on which the appellants relied below and in this Court, the Court holds that the provision in Art. I, Section 2, for election of Representatives "by the People" means that congressional districts are to be "as nearly as is practicable" equal in population. . . . Stripped of rhetoric and a "historical context," . . . which bears little resemblance to the evidence found in the pages of history . . . the Court's opinion supports its holding only with the bland assertion that "the principle of a House of Representatives elected "by the People' " would be "cast aside" if "a vote is worth more in one district than in another," . . . if congressional districts within a State, each electing a single Representative, are not equal in population. The fact, however, that Georgia's ten Representatives are elected "by the People" of Georgia, just as Representatives from other States are elected "by the People of the several States." This is all that the Constitution requires.

Although the Court finds necessity for its artificial construction of Article I in the undoubted importance of the right to vote, that right is not involved in this case. All of the appellants do vote. The Court's talk about "debasement" and "dilution" of the vote is a model of circular reasoning, in which the premises of the argument feed on the conclusion. Moreover, by focusing exclusively on numbers in disregard of the area and shape of a congressional district as well as party affiliations within the district, the Court deals in abstractions which will be recognized even by the politically unsophisticated to have little relevance to the realities of political life.

In any event, the very sentence of Art. I, Section 2, on which the Court exclusively relies confers the right to vote for Representatives only on those whom the State has found qualified to vote for members of "the most numerous Branch of the State Legislature." . . . So far as Article I is concerned, it is within the State's power to confer that right only on persons of wealth or of a particular sex or, if the State chose, living in specified areas of the State. Were Georgia to find the residents of the Fifth District unqualified to vote for Representatives to the State House of Representatives, they could not vote for Representatives to Congress, according to the express words of Art. I, Section 2. Other provisions of the Constitution would, of course, be relevant, but so far as Art. I, Section 2, is concerned, the disqualification would be within Georgia's power. How can it be,

then that this very same sentence prevents Georgia from apportioning its Representatives as it chooses? The truth is that it does not.

The Court purports to find support for its position in the third paragraph of Art. I, Section 2, which provides for the apportionment of Representatives among the States. The appearance of support in that section derives from the Court's confusion of two issues: direct election of Representatives within the States and the apportionment of Representatives among the States. Those issues are distinct, and were separately treated in the Constitution. The fallacy of the Court's reasoning in this regard is illustrated by its slide, obscured by intervening discussion . . . from the intention of the delegates at the Philadelphia Convention "that in allocating Congressmen the number assigned to each State should be determined solely by the number of the State's inhabitants," . . . to a "principle solemnly embodied in the Great Compromise— equal representation in the House of equal numbers of people,". . . . The delegates did have the former intention and made clear provision for it. Although many, perhaps most, of them also believed generally—but assuredly not in the precise, formalistic way of the majority of the Court—that within the States representation should be based on population, they did not surreptitiously slip their belief into the Constitution in the phrase "by the People," to be discovered 175 years later like a Shakespearian anagram.

Far from supporting the Court, the apportionment of Representatives among the States shows how blindly the Court has marched to its decision. Representatives were to be apportioned among the States on the basis of free population plus three-fifths of the slave population. Since no slave voted, the inclusion of three-fifths of their number in the basis of apportionment gave the favored States respresentation far in excess of their voting population. If, then, slaves were intended to be without representation, Article I did exactly what the Court now says it prohibited: it "weighted" the vote of voters in the slave States. Alternatively, it might have been thought that Representatives elected by free men of a State would speak also for the slaves. But since the slaves added to the representation only of their own State, Representatives from the slave States could have been thought to speak only for the slaves of their own States, indicating both that the Convention believed it possible for a representative elected by one group to speak for another non-voting group and that Representatives were in large degree still thought of as speaking for the whole population of a State.

There is a further basis for demonstrating the hollowness of the Court's assertion that Article I requires "one man's vote in a congressional election . . . to be worth as much as another's." . . . Nothing that the Court does today will disturb the fact that although in 1960 the population of an average congressional district was 410,481, the States of Alaska, Nevada, and Wyoming each have a Representative in Congress, although their respective populations are 226,167, 285,278, and 330,066. In entire disregard of population, Art. I, Section 2, guarantees each of these States and every other State "at Least one Representative." It is whimsical to assert in the face of this guarantee that an absolute principle of "equal representation in the House of equal numbers of people" is "solemnly embodied" in Article I. All that there is is a provision which bases representation in the House, generally but not entirely, on the population of the States. The provision for representation of each State in the House of Representatives is not

a mere exception to the principle framed by the majority; it shows that no such principle is to be found.

Finally in this array of hurdles to its decision which the Court surmounts only by knocking them down in Section 4 of Art. I. . . . The delegates were well aware of the problem of "rotten boroughs,". . . . It cannot be supposed that delegates to the Convention would have labored to establish a principle of equal representation only to bury it, one would have thought beyond discovery, in Section 2, and omit all mention of it from Section 4, which deals explicitly with the conduct of elections. Section 4 states without qualification that the state legislatures shall prescribe regulations for the conduct of elections for Representatives and, equally without qualification, that Congress may make or alter such regulations. There is nothing to indicate any limitation whatsoever on this grant of plenary initial and supervisory power. The Court's holding is, of course, derogatory not only of the power of the state legislatures but also of the power of Congress, both theoretically and as they have actually exercised their power. . . . It freezes upon both, for no reason other than that it seems wise to the majority of the present Court, a particular political theory for the selection of Representatives. . . .

There is dubious propriety in turning to the "historical context" of contitutional provisions which speak so consistently and plainly. But, as one might expect when the Constitution itself is free from ambiguity, the surrounding history makes what is already clear even clearer.

As the Court repeatedly emphasizes, delegates to the Philadelphia Convention frequently expressed their view that representation should be based on population. There were also, however, many statements favoring limited monarchy and property qualifications for suffrage and expressions of disapproval for unrestricted democracy. Such expressions prove as little on one side of this case as they do on the other. Whatever the dominant political philosophy at the Convention, one thing seems clear: it is in the last degree unlikely that most or even many of the delegates would have subscribed to the principle of "one person, one vote,". . . . Moreover, the statements approving population-based representation were focused on the problem of how representation should be apportioned among the States in the House of Representatives. The Great Compromise concerned representation of the States in the Congress. In all of the discussion surrounding the basis of representation of the House and all of the discussion whether Representatives should be elected by the legislatures or the people of the States, there is nothing which suggests even remotely that the delegates had in mind the problem of districting within a State.

The subject of districting within the States is discussed explicitly with reference to the provisions of Art. I, Section 4, which the Court so pointedly neglects. . . . [T]he Convention understood the state legislature to have plenary power over the conduct of elections for Representatives, including the power to district well or badly, subject only to the supervisory power of Congress. How, then, can the Court hold that Art. I, Section 2, prevents the state legislatures from districting as they choose? . . .

Materials supplementary to the debates are as unequivocal. In the ratifying conventions, there was no suggestion that the provisions of Art. I, Section 2, restricted the power of the States to prescribe the conduct of elections conferred on them by Art. I, Section 4. None of the Court's references to the ratification debates supports the view that the provision for election of Representatives "by the People" was intended to have any application to the apportionment of Representatives within the States; in each instance, the cited passage merely repeats what the Constitution itself provides: that Representatives were to be elected by the people of the States. . . . [*Justice Harlan then discusses the debates in several ratifying conventions and pertinent passages from* The Federalist *and concludes that the states, subject only to the control of Congress, could district as they chose.*]

. . . The upshot of all this is that the language of Art. I, Section 2 and 4, the surrounding text, and the relevant history are all in strong and consistent direct contradiction of the Court's holding. The constitutional scheme vests in the States plenary power to regulate the conduct of elections for Representatives, and, in order to protect the Federal Government, provides for congressional supervision of the States' exercise of their power. Within this scheme, the appellants do not have the right which they assert, in the absence of the provision for equal districts by the Georgia Legislature or the Congress. The constitutional right which the Court creates is manufactured out of whole cloth. . . .

The unstated premise of the Court's conclusion quite obviously is that the Congress has not dealt, and the Court believes it will not deal, with the problem of congressional apportionment in accordance with what the Court believes to be sound political principles. Laying aside for the moment the validity of such a consideration as a factor in constitutional interpretation, it becomes relevant to examine the history of congressional action under Art. I, Section 4. This history reveals that the Court is not simply undertaking to exercise a power which the Constitution reserves to the Congress; it is also overruling congressional judgment. . . .

For a period of about fifty years . . . [*1842–1911*] Congress, by repeated legislative act, imposed on the States the requirement that congressional districts be equal in population. (This, of course, is the very requirement which the Court now declares to have been constitutionally required of the States all along without implementing legislation.) Subsequently, after giving express attention to the problem, Congress eliminated that requirement, with the intention of permitting the States to find their own solutions. Since then, despite repeated efforts to obtain congressional action again, Congress has continued to leave the problem and its solution to the States. It cannot be contended, therefore, that the Court's decision today fills a gap left by the Congress. On the contrary, the Court substitutes its own judgment for that of the Congress. . . .

Today's decision has portents for our society and the Court itself which should be recognized. This is not a case in which the Court vindicates the kind of individual rights that are assured by the Due Process Clause of the Fourteenth Amendment, whose "vague contours," . . . of course leave much room for constitutional developments necessitated by changing conditions in a dynamic society. Nor is this a case in which an emergent set of facts requires the Court to frame new principles to protect recognized constitutional rights. The claim for judicial relief in this case strikes at one of the fundamental doctrines of our system of government, the separation of powers. In upholding that claim, the Court attempts to effect reforms in a field which the Constitution, as plainly as can be, has committed exclusively to the political process.

This Court, no less than all other branches of the Government, is bound by the Constitution. The Constitution does not confer on the Court blanket authority to step into every situation where the political branch may be thought to have fallen short. The stability of this institution ultimately depends not only upon its being alert to keep the other branches of government within constitutional bounds but equally upon recognition of the limitations on the Court's own functions in the constitutional system.

What is done today saps the political process. The promise of judicial intervention in matters of this sort cannot but encourage popular inertia in efforts for political reform through the political process, with the inevitable result that the process is itself weakened. By yielding to the demand for a judicial remedy in this instance, the Court in my view does a disservice both to itself and to the broader values of our system of government.

Believing that the complaint fails to disclose a constitutional claim, I would affirm the judgment below dismissing the complaint. . . .

MR. JUSTICE STEWART:

I think it is established that "this Court has power to afford relief in a case of this type as against the objection that the issues are not justiciable," and I cannot subscribe to any possible implication to the contrary which may lurk in Mr. Justice Harlan's dissenting opinion. With this single qualification I join the dissent because I think Mr. Justice Harlan has unanswerably demonstrated that Art. I, Section 2, of the Constitution gives no mandate to this Court or to any court to ordain that congressional districts within each State must be equal in population.

5

The Federal System

As indicated in Chapter 1, the American constitutional system is based on a division of powers between the national government and the states; under our federal system, the powers of the national government are enumerated in the body of the Constitution, whereas those powers not delegated to the national government are reserved to the states or to the people. The Tenth Amendment was designed to make the principle of federalism secure. The survival of this federal system of government, the first to be established among the great nations, has been of great influence, because many newer governments also have problems of integrating subordinate political and ethnic units.

Although the words *federal* or *federation* are not used in the Constitution, the creation of a federal system of government was the natural solution for the thirteen original states.[1] The establishment of a unitary system of government that concentrated all powers in the national government would have been impossible because of the necessity for compromise between the advo-

[1] K. C. Wheare, *Federal Government* (London: Oxford University Press, 1951), p. 1. See also William S. Livingston, *Federalism and Constitutional Change* (Oxford: Clarendon Press, 1956), p. 1, where the author notes that ". . . federal governments and federal constitutions do not grow simply by accident. They arise in response to certain stimuli; a federal system is consciously adopted as a means of solving the problems represented by these stimuli."

cates of states' rights and the supporters of a strong central government. The framers of the Constitution "rejected summarily the advice of those few, like Hamilton, who sought to build a unitary authority, to abolish the States as autonomous units, and to provide for the appointment of governors from the National Capital. They also overruled decisively the considerably greater number who wanted to keep the union a mere confederation."[2] Instead, they created our federal system of government. "Federalism was the means and price of the formation of the Union. It was inevitable, therefore, that its basic concepts should determine much of our history."[3]

In establishing the federal system, the framers of the Constitution used three major devices, as follows:

1. The states were preserved as separate sources of authority and as organs of administration.
2. The states were given important powers in connection with the composition and selection of the national government.
3. The powers of government were distributed between the national government and the states.[4]

Distribution of Powers

POWERS OF THE NATIONAL GOVERNMENT

The national government possesses all those powers that are delegated to it by the Constitution either expressly or by implication. These powers are enumerated principally as powers of Congress in Article I, Section 8. Included among these are the power to tax, borrow and coin money, maintain armies and navies, conduct foreign relations, and regulate interstate and foreign commerce. After the enumeration of powers in Article I, Section 8, the Constitution grants Congress further authority to "make all laws which shall be necessary and proper for carrying into execution the foregoing powers, and all other powers vested by the Constitution in the government of the United States, or in any department or officer thereof." This general grant of implied powers in the "elastic" or "necessary and proper" clause of the Constitution has raised numerous questions as to the actual scope of national authority. In many instances, such questions have been resolved by the Supreme Court.

Despite the fact that the states are supreme in their sphere of activities, the federal Constitution and national laws constitute the supreme law of the land

---

[2] *Report* of the Commission on Intergovernmental Relations (June 1955), p. 10.

[3] Herbert Wechsler, "The Political Safeguards of Federalism: The Role of the States in the Composition and Selection of the National Government," in Arthur W. Macmahon (ed.), *Federalism Mature and Emergent* (Garden City, N.Y.: Doubleday, 1955), p. 97.

[4] *Ibid.*, pp. 97–98.

when conflicts arise from attempts of both jurisdictions to govern the same subject matter. The supremacy of national authority is indicated by Article VI, clause 2, of the Constitution, which provides as follows:

> This Constitution, and the laws of the United States which shall be made in pursuance thereof; and all treaties made, or which shall be made, under the authority of the United States, shall be the supreme law of the land; and the judges in every state shall be bound thereby, any thing in the Constitution or laws of any state to the contrary notwithstanding.

In recent years extensive discussions of the constitutional theories of state and national powers have stemmed from the publication of a massive two-volume work by William W. Crosskey, a professor of law at the University of Chicago.[5] The author argues that the framers of the Constitution did *not* establish a government with powers divided between the states and the federal government. Instead, he maintains that the framers wished to create a unitary state with full powers vested in the national government unrestricted by any concept of states' rights. Furthermore, Crosskey states the framers intended that Congress be supreme with almost unlimited powers to control our entire national life. To date, he has failed to convince the leading students of the Constitution that his view is the correct one. One reviewer of Professor Crosskey's book has this to say:

> Some readers will rejoice over the possibility that his book may strengthen the nationalist case in issues still to be brought before the courts. But most of us will believe the Mississippi was started in the right direction; that the Constitution as we have known it for 165 years, supported and beloved by the great mass of Americans, is the right Constitution.[6]

POWERS OF THE STATES

The state governments possess those powers that are not given to the national government nor prohibited to the states. Because the Constitution deals principally with national powers, the fact that important powers are left to the states is sometimes forgotten. Among others, the states have the power to establish schools and supervise education, regulate intrastate commerce, conduct elections, establish local government units, and borrow money. In addition, a broad and generally undefined *"police power"* enables the states to take action to protect and promote the health, safety, morals, and general welfare of their inhabitants.

---

[5] *Politics and the Constitution in the History of the United States,* 2 vols. (Chicago: University of Chicago Press, 1953).

[6] Allan Nevins, *The New York Times Book Review* (May 31, 1953), p. 7. Another good review is found in the *American Political Science Review,* Vol. 47 (December 1953), pp. 1152–58. See also Stuart G. Brown, *The First Republicans* (Syracuse: Syracuse University Press, 1954), pp. 176–86.

EXCLUSIVE AND CONCURRENT POWERS

The powers of the national and state governments are sometimes exclusive and sometimes concurrent. Most of the powers of the national government are exclusive. For example, the federal government alone has power to make treaties, to coin money, and to govern the District of Columbia. The states also have certain exclusive powers, such as those that relate to wills and domestic relations. When powers are shared by both the states and the national government, they are said to be concurrent. For example, both Congress and the states have the power to tax and borrow money. Both levels of government may take property for public purposes, enact bankruptcy laws, and establish courts. The only example of a constitutional provision expressly granting concurrent powers to both the federal government and the states is found in the Eighteenth Amendment. Section 2 of that Amendment provided that "the Congress and the several states shall have concurrent power to enforce this article by appropriate legislation."

Role of the Supreme Court in the Federal System

Of course, it was impossible for the framers of the Constitution to draw a precise line between the powers of the national government and those of the states. And even if such a line of demarcation could have been drawn at any time during our constitutional history, it would have needed revision from time to time to meet the demands of new and changing conditions. Conflicts between national and state authorities are inevitable in a federal system of government. Such conflicts must be resolved by peaceful means if the union of states is to be maintained as the servant of the American people. The Civil War may be viewed as an example of what happens when the machinery for the peaceful resolution of conflicts between the states and national authority breaks down.

Because the line of division between state and federal powers is vague and indefinite, some branch of government must resolve the inevitable clashes. Actually, the President and Congress, as well as the Supreme Court, play an important role in maintaining a working federalism.

> Conflicts between localism and centralism are by no means resolved wholly by the apparatus of judicial review. It is part of our political theory that each department of the government has responsibility in the first instance for interpreting and applying the Constitution as a limitation on its own action. The President's use of the veto on constitutional grounds, if not overridden by Congress, will foreclose the courts from receiving the question of constitutional law. Congress, moreover, enjoys considerable authority over the jurisdiction of the federal courts, which it can exercise to cut off the appellate jurisdiction of the Supreme Court. . . . The role of the judiciary is limited not only by the re-

sourcefulness of other branches of government but also by the complexes of private power that lie outside the framework of constitutional limitations. Whether we are to enjoy a free national market, as the commerce clause envisaged, depends as much upon the practices of business enterprise as upon the governmental acts of member states. While a state may not by legislative fiat permit its commercial resources to be developed for local enjoyment and forbid their export to other states, the Constitution is silent and neutral on the power of private groups thus to restrict the market. The Constitution reflects an eighteenth-century faith in economic liberalism.[7]

Nevertheless, although much of the shape of the federal system is left to the working of politics, the Supreme Court plays a key role in preserving the balance of power between the states and the federal government. The Court's role as official umpire in disputes between the states and the federal government should be revealed clearly by the cases which follow. However, the issue of federalism also will be encountered in many other topics of constitutional law, such as commerce (Chapters 8 and 9) and fiscal powers of Congress (Chapter 10).

John Marshall's Nationalism

In the case of *McCulloch* v. *Maryland,* the classic statement of the doctrine of implied powers is presented. The decision of John Marshall in this case is probably the most notable and ablest of all the opinions he delivered during his long tenure on the Court. One of Marshall's admirers stated that "in his opinion in this case John Marshall rose to the loftiest heights of judicial statemanship. If his fame rested solely on this one effort, it would be secure."[8] In *McCulloch* v. *Maryland,* Marshall in effect "rewrote the fundamental law of the Nation; or perhaps, it may be more accurate to say that he made a written instrument a living thing, capable of growth, capable of keeping pace with the advancement of the American people and ministering to their changing necessities. This greatest of Marshall's treatises on government may well be entitled the 'Vitality of the Constitution.' "[9]

In the *McCulloch* case, Marshall was faced with a clear-cut issue between state and national powers, because he needed to interpret the meaning of the "necessary and proper" clause of Article I of the Constitution. Actually, his decision in *McCulloch* v. *Maryland* was clearly foreshadowed by an earlier opinion. In *United States* v. *Fisher,* 2 Cranch 358 (1805), Marshall had noted that in construing the "necessary and proper" clause "it would be in-

---

[7] Paul A. Freund, "Umpiring the Federal System," Arthur W. Macmahan (ed.), in *Federalism Mature and Emergent* (Garden City, N.Y.: Doubleday, 1955), pp. 160–61.

[8] Albert J. Beveridge, *The Life of John Marshall* (Boston: Houghton Mifflin, 1919), Vol. 4, p. 282.

[9] *Ibid.,* p. 308.

correct and would produce endless difficulty, if the opinion should be maintained, that no law was authorized which was not indispensably necessary to give effect to a specified power. Congress must possess the choice of means, and must be empowered to use any means which are in fact conducive to the exercise of a power granted by the Constitution." Nevertheless, the classic statement of the doctrine of implied powers is found in *McCulloch* v. *Maryland*.

To comprehend fully Marshall's decision in the *McCulloch* case, an appreciation of the political history of that period is necessary. The first Bank of the United States, proposed by Hamilton with Federalist support, was chartered by Congress in 1791 for a period of twenty years. The bank was established over the bitter protests of Jefferson and Madison, who were opposed to the centralization of financial powers in the federal government. Jefferson and his strict-constructionist followers further argued that because the Constitution did not specifically grant Congress the power to charter a bank, it could not do so. Although the bank was run efficiently, it was never a popular institution. As a consequence, its charter was not renewed in 1811. Instead, the states chartered a number of new banks to take care of the financial needs of the country. But chaos rather than financial stability resulted. "When the restraining and regulating influence of that conservative and ably managed institution [First Bank of the United States] was removed altogether, local banking began a course that ended in a mad carnival of roguery, to the ruin of legitimate business and the impoverishment and bankruptcy of hundreds of thousands of the general public."[10]

President Madison's previous opposition to the bank vanished, and under his leadership the Second Bank of the United States was chartered in 1816 to avert further financial difficulties. But the Second Bank became even more unpopular than its predecessor. It was not managed as efficiently as the First Bank, and as financial difficulties continued, a number of states passed laws or constitutional amendments designed to restrict its activities. One such state was Maryland, where inefficient management of the Baltimore branch of the Second Bank had resulted in heavy losses to a number of investors. The Maryland law, which is explained fully at the beginning of the case, is what Marshall had to deal with in *McCulloch* v. *Maryland*.

Marshall's decision was the signal for a bitter attack on the Supreme Court, principally by the supporters of states' rights. "From his plantation the aging Jefferson called for resistance." For "behind that opinion Jefferson saw lurking the specter of a consolidated government."[11] A number of newspapers throughout the country denounced Marshall and the Court. The Virginia legislature passed a resolution condemning the decision and called for a constitutional amendment that would create a "super-tribunal" over the Supreme

---

[10] *Ibid.,* p. 177.

[11] Donald G. Morgan, *Justice William Johnston, The First Dissenter* (Columbia: University of South Carolina Press, 1954), pp. 110–11.

Court to decide questions involving the "powers of the general and state governments." Ohio, Indiana, Illinois, and Tennessee also passed resolutions attacking Marshall's opinion. Pennsylvania proposed a constitutional amendment that would forbid Congress to establish any bank outside the District of Columbia. But these bitter attacks receded gradually as the nation became concerned increasingly with the dispute over slavery, and five years later, when Ohio attempted to defy the Supreme Court, Marshall reaffirmed the decision of *McCulloch* v. *Maryland.*[12]

In conjunction with *McCulloch* v. *Maryland,* we should consider two other opinions of John Marshall—*Gibbons* v. *Ogden* and *Cohens* v. *Virginia. Gibbons* v. *Ogden* is considered fully in Chapter 8. In *Cohens* v. *Virginia* (Chapter 5) Marshall held that the power of the Supreme Court was superior to that of the state courts whenever federal rights were involved.

Marshall's arguments in *Cohens* v. *Virginia* constitute, to a great extent, a restatement of Justice Story's decision in *Martin* v. *Hunter's Lessee,* 1 Wheat. 304 (1816). But Marshall's statement in *Cohens* v. *Virginia* is much more logical and persuasive. Many years later, the powerful opinion of Chief Justice Taney in *Ableman* v. *Booth,* 21 How. 506 (1859), further enhanced the power of the Supreme Court. In that case it was held that the Wisconsin Supreme Court could not grant a writ of habeas corpus to Booth, an abolitionist editor, who was being held in federal custody for the violation of a federal law. Taney held:

> No state judge or court, after they are judicially informed that the party is imprisoned under the authority of the United States, has any right to interfere with him, or to require him to be brought before them. . . . And no power is more clearly conferred by the Constitution and laws of the United States, than the power of this court [Supreme Court] to decide, ultimately and finally, all cases arising under such Constitution and laws; and for that purpose to bring here for revision . . . the judgment of a state court, where such questions have arisen, and the right claimed under them denied by the highest judicial tribunal in the State.

Like his decision in *McCulloch* v. *Maryland,* Marshall's opinion in *Cohens* v. *Virginia* was roundly denounced by the antinationalist group. Marshall himself was led to remark that his decision in *Cohens* v. *Virginia* "has been assaulted with a degree of virulence transcending what has appeared on any former occasion."[13] But Marshall and his principles endured. In six short years, from 1819 through 1824, Marshall's opinions in *McCulloch* v. *Maryland, Osborn* v. *Bank of the United States, Cohens* v. *Virginia,* and *Gibbons* v. *Ogden* established, for all time, the national character of the United States.

[12] *Osborn* v. *Bank of the United States,* 9 Wheat. 738 (1824).
[13] Letter of John Marshall to Mr. Justice Story, June 15, 1821, reproduced in Erwin C. Surrency (ed.), *The Marshall Reader* (New York: Oceana Publications, 1955), p. 210.

Conflict in Federal and State Activities

McCulloch v. *Maryland* established clearly that the states could not interfere with or place burdens on the federal government. However, it was left to later cases to define what actually constituted interference with federal authority. In the famous case of *In re Neagle,* 135 U.S. 1 (1890), which was a real crime thriller, the Supreme Court ordered that Neagle, a United States deputy marshal, be released from California's custody for killing a man who had threatened and assaulted Justice Stephen J. Field. Neagle had been authorized to guard the justice, who was on circuit duty in California, by a presidential order, which was regarded as federal "law." Because Neagle was acting under the authority of the law of the United States, he was "not liable to answer in the courts of California."

Two other cases in this chapter *Missouri* v. *Holland* and *Pennsylvania* v. *Nelson* provide examples of other conflicts between state and federal authorities which were resolved by the Supreme Court. The Court's decision in *Pennsylvania* v. *Nelson* was criticized severely by some newspapers and by a number of congressmen who viewed the decision as another challenge to the doctrine of "states' rights." Of course, the Court was already under attack in some of the same quarters for its decision in the Public School Segregation Cases (Chapter 17).

McCULLOCH *v.* MARYLAND
4 Wheat. 316; 4 L. Ed. 579 (1819)

[*The Baltimore branch of the Second Bank of the United States was established in 1817. One year later, Maryland enacted a statute requiring that all banks not chartered by the state either pay a tax on each issuance of bank notes or make an annual payment of $15,000 to the state. McCulloch, the cashier of the Baltimore branch of the Second Bank, issued bank notes without complying with the state law. A Maryland county court and the state's highest court sustained the tax law. The bank then carried the case to the Supreme Court on a writ of error.*

The lawyers for both sides in this famous case were the most distinguished of their day. Daniel Webster, William Pinkney, and William Wirt, the Attorney-General of the United States, argued the case for the bank. Maryland was represented by lawyers of equal stature. The Supreme Court heard arguments for nine days, with Pinkney speaking eloquently for three days in behalf of the bank. Marshall delivered the opinion of the Court only three days after the arguments were concluded. In his opinion, Marshall relied heavily on Pinkney's three-day speech.]

MR. CHIEF JUSTICE MARSHALL delivered the opinion of the Court:

In the case now to be determined, the defendant, a sovereign State, denies the obligation of a law enacted by the legislature of the Union, and the plaintiff, on his part, contests the validity of an act which has been passed by the legislature of that State. The constitution of our country, in its most interesting and vital parts, is to be considered; the conflicting powers of the government of the Union and of its members, as marked in that constitution, are to be discussed; and an opinion given, which may essentially influence the great operations of government.

. . . The first question made in the cause is, has Congress power to incorporate a bank?

. . . If any one proposition could command the universal assent of mankind, we might expect it would be this —that the government of the Union, though limited in its powers, is supreme within its sphere of action. This would seem to result necessarily from its nature. It is the government of all; its powers are delegated by all; it represents all, and acts for all. Though any one State may be willing to control its operations, no State is willing to allow others to control them. The nation, on those subjects on which it can act, must necessarily bind its component parts. But this question is not left to mere reason: the people have, in express terms, decided it, by saying, "this Constitution, and the laws of the United States, which shall be made in pursuance thereof, shall be the supreme law of the land," and by requiring that the members of the State legislatures, and the officers of the executive and judicial departments of the States, shall take the oath of fidelity of it.

The government of the United States, then, though limited in its powers, is supreme; and its laws, when made in pursuance of the Constitution, form the supreme law of the land, "any thing in the Constitution or laws of any State to the contrary notwithstanding."

Among the enumerated powers, we do not find that of establishing a bank or creating a corporation. But there is no phrase in the instrument which, like the Articles of Confederation, excludes incidental or implied powers; and which requires that every thing granted shall be expressly and minutely described. Even the Tenth Amendment, which was framed for the purpose of quieting the excessive jealousies which had been excited, omits the word "expressly," and declares only that the powers "not delegated to the United States, nor prohibited to the States, are reserved to the States or to the people"; thus leaving the question, whether the particular power which may become the subject of contest has been delegated to the one government, or prohibited to the other, to depend on a fair construction of the whole instrument. The men who drew and adopted this amendment had experienced the embarassments resulting from the insertion of this word in the Articles of Confederation, and probably omitted it to avoid those embarassments. A constitution, to contain an accurate detail of all the subdivisions of which its great powers will admit, and of all the means by which they may be carried into execution, would partake of the prolixity of a legal code, and could scarcely be embraced by the human mind. It would probably never be understood by the public. Its nature, therefore, requires that only its great outlines should be marked, its important objects designated, and the minor ingredients which compose those objects be deduced from the nature of the objects themselves. That this idea was entertained by the framers of the American Constitution is not only to be inferred from the nature of the instrument, but from the language. Why else were some of the limitations, found in the ninth section of the first article, introduced? It is also, in some degree, warranted by their having omitted to use any restrictive term which might prevent its receiving a fair and just interpretation. In considering this question, then, we must never forget that it is *a constitution* we are expounding.

Although, among the enumerated powers of government, we do not find the word "bank" or "incorporation," we find the great powers to lay and collect taxes; to borrow money; to regulate commerce; to declare and conduct a war; and to raise and support armies and navies. The sword and the purse, all the external relations, and no inconsiderable portion of the industry of the nation, are entrusted to its government. It can never be pretended that these vast powers draw after them others of inferior importance, merely because they are inferior. Such an idea can never be advanced. But it may with great reason be contended that a government, entrusted with such ample powers, on the due execution of which the happiness and prosperity of the nation so vitally depends, must also be entrusted with ample means for their execution. The power being given, it is the interest of the nation to facilitate its execution. It can never be their interest, and cannot be presumed to have been their intention, to clog and embarrass its execution by withholding the most appropriate means. Throughout this vast republic, from the St. Croix to the Gulf of Mexico, from the Atlantic to the Pacific, revenue is to be collected and expended, armies are to be marched and supported. The exigencies of the nation may require that the treasure raised in the north should be transported to the south, *that* raised in the east conveyed to the west, or that this order should be reversed. Is that construction of the Constitution to be preferred which would render these operations difficult, hazardous, and expensive? Can we adopt that construction (unless the words imperiously require it) which would impute to the framers of that instrument, when granting these powers for the public good, the intention of

impeding their exercise by withholding a choice of means? If, indeed, such be the mandate of the Constitution, we have only to obey; but that instrument does not profess to enumerate the means by which the powers it confers may be executed; nor does it prohibit the creation of a corporation, if the existence of such a being be essential to the beneficial exercise of those powers. It is, then, the subject of fair inquiry, how far such means may be employed.

. . . But the Constitution of the United States has not left the right of Congress to employ the necessary means for the execution of the powers conferred on the government to general reasoning. To its enumeration of powers is added that of making "all laws which shall be necessary and proper, for carrying into execution the foregoing powers, and all other powers vested by this Constitution, in the government of the United States, or in any department thereof."

The counsel for the State of Maryland have urged various arguments, to prove that this clause, though in terms a grant of power, is not so in effect; but is really restrictive of the general right, which might otherwise be implied, of selecting means for executing the enumerated powers.

In support of this proposition, they have found it necessary to contend that this clause was inserted for the purpose of conferring on Congress the power of making laws. That, without it, doubts might be entertained whether Congress could exercise its powers in the form of legislation.

But could this be the object for which it was inserted? A government is created by the people, having legislative, executive, and judicial powers. Its legislative powers are vested in a Congress, which is to consist of a Senate and House of Representatives. Each house may determine the rule of its proceedings; and it is declared that every bill which shall have passed both houses shall, before it becomes a law, be presented to the President of the United States. The seventh section describes the course of proceedings, by which a bill shall become a law; and, then, the eighth enumerates the powers of Congress. Could it be necessary to say that a legislature should exercise legislative powers in the shape of legislation? After allowing each house to prescribe its own course of proceeding, after describing the manner in which a bill should become a law, would it have entered into the mind of a single member of the Convention that an express power to make laws was necessary to enable the legislature to make them? That a legislature, endowed with legislative powers, can legislate, is a proposition too self-evident to have been questioned.

But the argument on which most reliance is placed is drawn from the peculiar language of this clause. Congress is not empowered by it to make all laws which may have relation to the powers conferred on the government, but such only as may be *"necessary and proper"* for carrying them into execution. The word *"necessary,"* is considered as controlling the whole sentence, and as limiting the right to pass laws for the execution of the granted powers to such as are indispensable, and without which the power would be nugatory. That it excludes the choice of means, and leaves to Congress, in each case, that only which is most direct and simple.

. . . This clause as construed by the State of Maryland, would abridge, and almost annihilate, this useful and necessary right of the legislature to select its means. That this could not be intended, is, we should think, had it not been already controverted, too apparent for controversy. We think so for the following reasons:

1st. The clause is placed among the powers of Congress, not among the limitations on those powers.

2nd. Its terms purport to enlarge, not to diminish the powers vested in the government. It purports to be an additional power, not a restriction on those already granted. . . . Had the intention been to make this clause restrictive, it would unquestionably have been so in form as well as in effect.

The result of the most careful and attentive consideration bestowed upon this clause is, that if it does not enlarge, it cannot be construed to restrain the powers of Congress, or to impair the right of the legislature to exercise its best judgment in the selection of measures to carry into execution the constitutional powers of the government. If no other motive for its insertion can be suggested, a sufficient one is found in the desire to remove all doubts respecting the right to legislate on that vast mass of incidental powers which must be involved in the Constitution, if that instrument be not a splendid bauble.

We admit, as all must admit, that the powers of the government are limited, and that its limits are not to be transcended. But we think the sound construction of the Constitution must allow to the national legislature that discretion, with respect to the means by which the powers it confers are to be carried into execution, which will enable that body to perform the hight duties assigned to it, in the manner most beneficial to the people. Let the end be legitimate, let it be within the scope of the Constitution, and all means which are appropriate, which are plainly adapted to that end, which are not prohibited, but consist with the letter and spirit of the Constitution, are constitutional.

. . . The choice of means implies a right to choose a national bank in preference to State banks, and Congress alone can make the election.

After the most deliberate consideration, it is the unanimous and decided
opinion of this Court that the act to
incorporate the Bank of the United
States is a law made in pursuance of the
Constitution, and is a part of the
supreme law of the land.

The branches, proceeding from the
same stock, and being conducive to
the complete accomplishment of the object, are equally constitutional. It would
have been unwise to locate them in
the charter, and it would be unnecessarily inconvenient to employ the legislative power in making those subordinate arrangements. The great duties of
the bank are prescribed; those duties
require branches; and the bank itself
may, we think, be safely trusted with
the selection of places where those
branches shall be fixed; reserving always
to the government the right to require
that a branch shall be located where it
may be deemed necessary.

It being the opinion of the Court that
the act incorporating the bank is constitutional; and that the power of establishing a branch in the State of Maryland might be properly exercised by the
bank itself, we proceed to inquire. . . .
Whether the State of Maryland may,
without violating the Constitution, tax
that branch?

That the power of taxation is one of
vital importance; that it is retained by
the States; that it is not abridged by the
grant of a similar power to the government of the Union; that it is to be concurrently exercised by the two governments; are truths which have never been
denied. But such is the paramount character of the Constitution that its capacity
to withdraw any subject from the action
of even this power is admitted. The
States are expressly forbidden to lay any
duties on imports or exports, except
what may be absolutely necessary for
executing their inspection laws. If the
obligation of this prohibition must be

conceded—if it may restrain a State
from the exercise of its taxing power
on imports and exports; the same paramount character would seem to restrain,
as it certainly may restrain a State from
such other exercise of this power as is
in its nature incompatible with, and
repugnant to, the constitutional laws of
the Union.

. . . That the power to tax involves
the power to destroy; that the power
to destroy may defeat and render useless the power to create; that there is a
plain repugnance in conferring on one
government a power to control the
constitutional measures of another,
which other, with respect to those very
measures, is declared to be supreme
over that which exerts the control, are
propositions not to be denied.

. . . If we apply the principle for
which the State of Maryland contends
to the Constitution generally, we shall
find it capable of changing totally the
character of that instrument. We shall
find it capable of arresting all the measures of the government, and of prostrat-
ing it at the foot of the States. The
American people have declared their
Constitution, and the laws made in
pursuance thereof, to be supreme; but
this principle would transfer the supremacy, in fact, to the States.

If the States may tax one instrument
employed by the government in the
execution of its powers, they may tax
any and every other instrument. They
may tax the mail; they may tax the
mint; they may tax patent rights; they
may tax the papers of the custom-house;
they may tax judicial process; they may
tax all the means employed by the
government, to an excess which would
defeat all the ends of government. This
was not intended by the American
people. They did not design to make
their government dependent on the
States.

. . . If the controlling power of the

States be established; if their supremacy as to taxation be acknowledged; what is to restrain their exercising this control in any shape they may please to give it? Their sovereignty is not confined to taxation. That is not the only mode in which it might be displayed. The question is, in truth, a question of supremacy; and, if the right of the States to tax the means employed by the general government be conceded, the declaration that the Constitution, and the laws made in pursuance thereof, shall be the supreme law of the land, is empty and unmeaning declamation.

. . . It has also been insisted that, as the power of taxation in the general and State governments is acknowledged to be concurrent, every argument which would sustain the right of the general government to tax banks chartered by the States, will equally sustain the right of the States to tax banks chartered by the general government.

But the two cases are not on the same reason. The people of all the States have created the general government, and have conferred upon it the general power of taxation. The people of all the States, and the States themselves, are represented in Congress, and, by their representatives, exercise this power. When they tax the chartered institutions of the States, they tax their constituents; and these taxes must be uniform. But, when a State taxes the operations of the government of the United States, it acts upon institutions created, not by their own constituents, but by people over whom they claim no control. It acts upon the measures of a government created by others as well as themselves, for the benefit of others in common with themselves. The difference is that which always exists, and always must exist, between the action of the whole on a part, and the action of a part on the whole—between the laws of a government declared to be supreme, and those of a government which, when in opposition to those laws, is not supreme.

. . . [T]he States have no power, by taxation or otherwise, to retard, impede, burden, or in any manner control, the operations of the constitutional laws enacted by Congress to carry into execution the powers vested in the general government. This is, we think, the unavoidable consequence of that supremacy which the Constitution has declared.

We are unanimously of opinion, that the law passed by the legislature of Maryland imposing a tax on the Bank of the United States is unconstitutional and void. . . .

COHENS v. VIRGINIA
6 Wheat. 264; 5 L. Ed. 257 (1821)

[In 1802, Congress passed a law authorizing the District of Columbia to conduct lotteries. The money raised was to be used for improvements in the city of Washington that could not be brought about with available funds. Accordingly, the city passed an ordinance creating a lottery. The state of Virginia had a law prohibiting the sale of lottery tickets except for lotteries established by that state. P. J. and M. J. Cohen were arrested at their office in Norfolk, Va., for selling tickets for the Washington lottery. The borough court found them guilty and imposed a fine of $100. The case then went to the Supreme Court on a writ of error, because there was no higher state court "which could take cognizance of the case." Virginia did not object to the appeal, because it wished to force the issue of the Supreme Court's authority over state actions. The Court upheld the Cohens' conviction under *the state statute on the ground that the federal statute authorizing a lottery applied only to the Disrict of Columbia. The importance of the case lies not in the holding, however, but rather in Marshall's powerful argument that the Supreme Court had the authority to review the judgment of a state court.]*

MR. CHIEF JUSTICE MARSHALL delivered the opinion of the Court:

The questions presented to the Court . . . are of great magnitude, and may be truly said vitally to affect the Union. They exclude the inquiry whether the constitution and laws of the United States have been violated by the judgment which the plaintiffs in error seek to review; and maintain that, admitting such violation, it is not in the power of the government to apply a corrective. They maintain that the nation does not possess a department capable of restraining peaceably, and by authority of law, any attempts which may be made, by a part, against the legitimate powers of the whole; and that the government is reduced to the alternative of submitting to such attempts, or of resisting them by force. They maintain that the constitution of the United States has provided no tribunal for the final construction of itself, or of the laws or treaties of the nation; but that this power may be exercised in the last resort by the Courts of every State in the Union. That the constitution, laws, and treaties, may receive as many constructions as there are States; and that this is not a mischief, or, if a mischief, is irremediable. . . .

First. The first question to be considered is, whether the jurisdiction of this Court is excluded by the character of the parties, one of them being a State, and the other a citizen of that State?

The second section of the third article of the constitution defines the extent of the judicial power of the United States. Jurisdiction is given to the Courts of the Union in two classes of cases. In the first, their jurisdiction depends on the character of the cause, whoever may be the parties. This class comprehends "all cases in law and equity arising under this constitution, the laws of the United States, and treaties made, or which shall be made, under their authority." This clause extends the jurisdiction of the Court to all the cases described, without making in its terms any exception whatever, and without any regard to the condition of the party. If there be any exception, it is to be implied against the express words of the article.

In the second class, the jurisdiction depends entirely on the character of the parties. In this are comprehended "controversies between two or more States, between a State and citizens of another State, and between a State and foreign States, citizens or subjects." If these be the parties, it is entirely unimportant what may be the subject of controversy. Be it what it may, these parties have a constitutional right to come into the Courts of the Union. . . .

If . . . a case arising under the constitution, or a law, must be one in which a party comes into Court to demand something conferred on him by the constitution or a law, we think the construction too narrow. A case in law or equity consists of the right of the one party, as well as of the other, and may truly be said to arise under the constitution or a law of the United States, whenever its correct decision depends on the construction of either. . . .

The jurisdiction of the Court, then, being extended by the letter of the constitution to all cases arising under it, or under the laws of the United States, it follows that those who would withdraw any cases of this description from that jurisdiction, must sustain the exemption they claim on the spirit and true meaning of the constitution, which spirit and true meaning must be so apparent as to overrule the words which its framers have employed.

The counsel for the defendant in error have undertaken to do this; and have laid down the general proposition, that a sovereign independent State is not suable, except by its own consent.

This general proposition will not be controverted. But its consent is not requisite in each particular case. It may be given in a general law. And if a State has surrendered any portion of its sovereignty, the question whether a liability to suit be a part of this portion, depends on the instrument by which the surrender is made. If, upon a just construction of that instrument, it shall appear that the State has submitted to be sued, then it has parted with this sovereign right of judging in every case on the justice of its own pretensions, and has entrusted that power to a tribunal in whose impartiality it confides.

The American States, as well as the American people, have believed a close and firm Union to be essential to their liberty and to their happiness. They have been taught by experience, that this Union cannot exist without a government for the whole; and they have been taught by the same experience that this government would be a mere shadow, that must disappoint all their hopes, unless invested with large portions of that sovereignty which belongs to independent States. Under the influence of this opinion, and thus instructed by experience, the American people, in the conventions of their respective States, adopted the present constitution.

If it could be doubted, whether from its nature, it were not supreme in all cases where it is empowered to act, that doubt would be removed by the declaration, that "this constitution, and the laws of the United States, which shall be made in pursuance thereof, and all treaties made, or which shall be made, under the authority of the United States, shall be the supreme law of the land; and the judges in every State shall be bound thereby; any thing in the constitution or laws of any State to the contrary notwithstanding."

This is the authoritative language of the American people; and, if gentlemen please, of the American States. It marks, with lines too strong to be mistaken, the characteristic distinction between the government of the Union, and those of the States. The general government, though limited as to its objects, is supreme with respect to those objects. This principle is a part of the constitution; and if there be any who deny its necessity, none can deny its authority.

To this supreme government ample powers are confided; and if it were possible to doubt the great purposes for which they were so confided, the people of the United States have declared, that they are given "in order to form a more perfect union, establish justice, ensure domestic tranquillity, provide for the common defence, promote the general welfare, and secure the blessings of liberty to themselves and their posterity."

With the ample powers confided to this supreme government, for these interesting purposes, are connected many express and important limitations on the sovereignty of the States, which are made for the same purposes. The powers of the Union, on the great subjects of war, peace, and commerce and on many others, are in themselves limitations of the sovereignty of the States; but in addition to these, the sovereignty of the States is surrendered in many instances where the surrender can only operate to the benefit of the people, and where, perhaps, no other power is conferred on Congress than a conservative power to maintain the principles established in the constitution. The maintenance of these principles in their purity, is certainly among the great duties of the government. One of the instruments by which this duty may be peaceably performed, is the judicial department. It is authorized to decide all cases of every description, arising under the constitution or laws of the United States. From this general grant of jurisdiction, no exception is made of those cases in which a State may be a party. When we consider the situation of the government of the Union and of a State, in relation to each other; the nature of our constitution; the subordination of the State governments to that constitution; the great purpose for which jurisdiction over all cases arising under the constitution and laws of the United States, is confided to the judicial department; are we at liberty to insert in this general grant, an exception of those cases in which a State many be a party? Will the spirit of the constitution justify this attempt to control its words? We think it will not. We think a case arising under the constitution or laws of the United States, is cognizable in the Courts of the Union, whoever may be the parties to that case. . . .

One of the express objects, then, for which the judicial department was established, is the decision of controversies between States, and between a State and individuals. The mere circumstance, that a State is a party, gives jurisdiction to the Court. How, then, can it be contended, that the very same instrument, in the very same section, should be so construed, as that this same circumstance should withdraw a case from the jurisdiction of the Court, where the constitution or laws of the United States are supposed to have been violated? The constitution gave to every person having a claim upon a State, a right to submit his case to the Court of the nation. However unimportant his claim might be, however little the community might be interested in its decision, the framers of our constitution thought it necessary for the purposes of justice, to provide a tribunal as superior to influence as possible, in which that claim might be decided. . . .

The mischievous consequences of the construction contended for on the part of Virginia, are also entitled to great consideration. It would prostrate, it has been said, the government and its laws at the feet of every State in the Union. And would not this be its effect? What power of the government could be executed by its own means, in any State disposed to resist its execution by a couse of legislation? The laws must be executed by individuals acting within the several States. If these individuals may be exposed to penalties, and if the Courts of the Union cannot correct the judgments by which these penalties may be enforced, the course of the government may be, at any time, arrested by the will of one of its members. Each member will possess a veto on the will of the whole. . . .

These collisions may take place in times of no extraordinary commotion. But a constitution is framed for ages to come, and is designed to approach immortality as nearly as human institutions can approach it. Its course cannot always be tranquil. It is exposed to storms and tempests, and its framers must be unwise statesmen indeed, if they have not provided it, as far as its nature will permit, with the means of self-preservation from the perils it may be destined to encounter. No government ought to be so defective in its organization, as not to contain within itself the means of securing the execution of its own laws against other dangers than those which occur every day. Courts of justice are the means most usually employed; and it is reasonable to expect that a government should repose on its own Courts, rather than on others. There is certainly nothing in the circumstances under which our constitution was formed; nothing in the history of the times, which would justify the opinion that the confidence reposed in the States was so implicit as to leave in them and their tribunals the power of resisting or defeating, in the form of law, the legitimate measures of the Union. . . .

If jurisdiction depended entirely on the character of the parties, and was not given where the parties have not an original right to come into Court, that part of the second section of the third article, which extends the judicial power to all cases arising under the constitution and laws of the United States, would be mere surplusage. It is to give jurisdiction where the character of the parties would not give it, that this very important part of the clause was inserted. It may be true, that the partiality of the State tribunals, in ordinary controversies between a State and its citizens, was not apprehended, and therefore the judicial power of the Union was not extended to such cases; but this was not the sole nor the greatest object for which this department was created. A more important, a much more interesting object, was the preservation of the constitution and laws of the United States, so far as they can be preserved by judicial authority; and therefore the jurisdiction of the Courts of the Union was expressly extended to all cases arising under that constitution and those laws. If the constitution or laws may be violated by proceedings instituted by a State against its own citizens, and if

that violation may be such as essentially to affect the constitution and the laws, such as to arrest the progress of government in its constitutional course, why should these cases be excepted from that provision which expressly extends the judicial power of the Union to all cases arising under the constitution and laws? . . .

It is most true that this Court will not take jurisdiction if it should not: but it is equally true, that it must take jurisdiction if it should. The judiciary cannot, as the legislature may, avoid a measure because it approaches the confines of the constitution. We cannot pass it by because it is doubtful. With whatever doubts, with whatever difficulties, a case may be attended, we must decide it, if it be brought before us. We have no more right to decline the exercise of jurisdiction which is given, than to usurp that which is not given. The one or the other would be treason to the constitution. Questions may occur which we would gladly avoid; but we cannot avoid them. All we can do is, to exercise our best judgment, and conscientiously to perform our duty. In doing this, on the present occasion, we find this tribunal invested with appellate jurisdiction in all cases arising under the constitution and laws of the United States. We find no exception to this grant and we cannot insert one. . . .

This leads to a consideration of the Eleventh Amendment.

It is in these words: "The judicial power of the United States shall not be construed to extend to any suit in law or equity commenced or prosecuted against one of the United States, by citizens of another State, or by citizens or subjects of any foreign State."

It is a part of our history, that, at the adoption of the constitution, all the States were greatly indebted; and the apprehension that these debts might be prosecuted in the federal Courts, formed a very serious objection to that instrument. Suits were instituted; and the Court maintained its jurisdiction. The alarm was general; and, to quiet the apprehensions that were so extensively entertained, this amendment was proposed in Congress, and adopted by the State legislatures. That its motive was not to maintain the sovereignty of a State from the degradation supposed to attend a compulsory appearance before the tribunal of the nation, may be inferred from the terms of the amendment. It does not comprehend controversies between two or more States, or between a State and a foreign State. The jurisdiction of the Court still extends to these cases: and in these a State may still be sued. We must ascribe the amendment, then, to some other cause than the dignity of a State. There is no difficulty in finding this cause. Those who were inhibited from commencing a suit against a State, or from prosecuting one which might be commenced before the adoption of the amendment, were persons who might probably be its creditors. There was not much reason to fear that foreign or sister States would be creditors to any considerable amount, and there was reason to retain the jurisdiction of the Court in those cases, because it might be essential to the preservation of peace. The amendment, therefore, extended to suits commenced or prosecuted by individuals, but not to those brought by States. . . .

A general interest might well be felt in leaving to a State the full power of consulting its convenience in the adjustment of its debts, or of other claims upon it; but no interest could be felt in so changing the relations between the whole and its parts, as to strip the government of the means of protecting, by the instrumentality of its Courts, the constitution and laws from active violation. . . .

Under the judiciary act, the effect of a writ of error is simply to bring the record into Court, and submit the judgment of the inferior tribunal to re-examination. It does not in any manner act upon the parties; it acts only on the record. It removes the record into the supervising tribunal. Where, then, a State obtains a judgment against an individual, and the Court, rendering such judgment, overrules a defense set up under the constitution of laws of the United States, the transfer of this record into the Supreme Court, for the sole purpose of inquiring whether the judgment violates the constitution or laws of the United States, can, with no propriety, we think, be denominated a suit commenced or prosecuted against the state whose judgment is so far re-examined. Nothing is demanded from the State. No claim against it of any description is asserted or prosecuted. The party is not to be restored to the possession of any thing. Essentially, it is an appeal on a single point; and the defendant who appeals from a judgment rendered against him is never said to commence or prosecute a suit against the plaintiff who has obtained the judgment. . . .

It is, then, the opinion of the Court, that the defendant who removes a judgment rendered against him by a State Court into this Court, for the purpose of re-examining the question, whether that judgment be in violation of the constitution or laws of the United States, does not commence or prosecute a suit against the States. . . .

Second. The second objection to the jurisdiction of the Court is, that its appellate power cannot be exercised, in any case, over the judgment of a State Court.

This objection is sustained chiefly by

arguments drawn from the supposed total separation of the judiciary of a State from that of the Union, and their entire independence of each other. The argument considers the federal judiciary as completely foreign to that of a State; and as being no more connected with it in any respect whatever, than the Court of a foreign State. If this hypothesis be just, the argument founded on it is equally so; but if the hypothesis be not supported by the constitution, the argument fails with it.

This hypothesis is not founded on any words in the constitution, which might seem to countenance it, but on the unreasonableness of giving a contrary construction to words which seem to require it; and on the incompatibility of the application of the appellate jurisdiction to the judgments of State Courts, with that constitutional relation which subsists between the government of the Union and the governments of those States which compose it.

Let this unreasonableness, this total incompatibility, be examined.

That the United States form, for many, and for most important purposes, a single nation, has not yet been denied. In war, we are one people. In making peace, we are one people. In all commercial regulations, we are one and the same people. In many other respects, the American people are one; and the government which is alone capable of controlling and managing their interests in all these respects, is the government of the Union. It is their government, and in that character they have no other. America has chosen to be, in many respects, and to many purposes, a nation; and for all these purposes, her government is complete; to all these objects, it is competent. The people have declared, that in the exercise of all powers given for these objects, it is supreme. It can, then, in effecting these objects, legitimately control all individuals or governments within the American territory. The constitution and laws of a State, so far as they are repugnant to the constitution and laws of the United States, are absolutely void. These States are constituent parts of the United States. They are members of one great empire—for some purposes sovereign, for some purposes subordinate.

In a government so constituted, is it unreasonable that the judicial power should be competent to give efficacy to the constitutional laws of the legislature? That department can decide on the validity of the constitution or law of a State, if it be repugnant to the constitution or to a law of the United States. It is unreasonable that it should also be empowered to decide on the judgment of a State tribunal enforcing such unconstitutional law? It is so very unreasonable as to furnish a justification for controlling the words of the constitution?

We think it is not. We think that in a government acknowledgedly supreme, with respect to objects of vital interest to the nation, there is nothing inconsistent with sound reason, nothing incompatible with the nature of government, in making all its departments supreme, so far as respects those objects, and so far as is necessary to their attainment. The exercise of the appellate power over those judgments of the State tribunals which may contravene the constitution or laws of the United States, is, we believe, essential to the attainment of those objects.

The propriety of entrusting the construction of the constitution, and laws made in pursuance thereof, to the judiciary of the Union, has not, we believe, as yet, been drawn into question. It seems to be a corollary from this political axiom, that the federal Courts should either possess exclusive jurisdiction in such cases, or a power to revise the judgment rendered in them, by the State tribunals. If the federal and State Courts have concurrent jurisdiction in all cases arising under the constitution, laws, and treaties of the United States; and if a case of this description brought in a State Court cannot be removed before judgment, nor revised after judgment, then the construction of the constitution, laws, and treaties of the United States, is not confided particularly to their judicial department, but is confided equally to that department and to the State Courts, however they may be constituted. "Thirteen independent Courts," says a very celebrated statesman (and we have now more than twenty such Courts), "of final jurisdiction over the same causes, arising upon the same laws, is a hydra in government, from which nothing but contradiction and confusion can proceed."

Dismissing the unpleasant suggestion that any motives which may not be fairly avowed, or which ought not to exist, can ever influence a State or its Courts, the necessity of uniformity, as well as correctness in expounding the constitution and laws of the United States, would itself suggest the propriety of vesting in some single tribunal the power of deciding, in the last resort, all cases in which they are involved.

We are not restrained, then, by the political relations between the general and State governments, from construing the words of the constitution, defining the judicial power, in their true sense. We are not bound to construe them more restrictively than they naturally import.

They give to the Supreme Court appellate jurisdiction in all cases arising under the constitution, laws, and treaties of the United States. The words are broad enough to comprehend all cases

of this description, in whatever Court they may be decided. . . .

The framers of the constitution would naturally examine the state of things existing at the time; and their work sufficiently attests that they did so. All acknowledge that they convened for the purpose of strengthening the confederation by enlarging the powers of the government, and by giving efficacy to those which it before possessed, but could not exercise. They inform us themselves, in the instrument they presented to the American public, that one of its objects was to form a more perfect union. Under such circumstances, we certainly should not expect to find, in that instrument, a diminution of the powers of the actual government. . . .

This opinion has been already drawn out to too great a length to admit of entering into a particular consideration of the various forms in which the counsel who made this point has, with much ingenuity, presented his argument to the Court. The argument in all its forms is essentially the same. It is founded, not on the words of the constitution, but on its spirit, a spirit extracted, not from the words of the instrument, but from his view of the nature of our Union, and of the great fundamental principles on which the fabric stands.

To this argument, in all its forms, the same answer may be given. Let the nature and objects of our Union be considered; let the great fundamental principles, on which the fabric stands, be examined; and we think the result must be, that there is nothing so extravagantly absurd in giving to the Court of the nation the power of revising the decisions of local tribunals on questions which affect the nation, as to require that words which import this power should be restricted by a forced construction. . . .

MISSOURI *v.* HOLLAND, UNITED STATES GAME WARDEN
252 U.S. 346; 40 Sup. Ct. 382; 64 L. Ed. 641 (1920)

[*The state of Missouri appealed from the holding of a federal district court that dismissed a bill in equity. The facts are outlined in the opinion.*]

MR. JUSTICE HOLMES delivered the opinion of the Court:

This is a bill in equity, brought by the state of Missouri to prevent a game warden of the United States from attempting to enforce the Migratory Bird Treaty Act of July 3, 1918, . . . and the regulations made by the Secretary of Agriculture in pursuance of the same. The ground of the bill is that the statute is an unconstitutional interference with the rights reserved to the states by the Tenth Amendment, and that the acts of the defendant, done and threatened under that authority, invade the sovereign right of the state and contravene its will manifested in statutes. . . .

On December 8, 1916, a treaty between the United States and Great Britain was proclaimed by the President. It recited that many species of birds in the annual migrations traversed many parts of the United States and of Canada, that they were of great value as a source of food and in destroying insects injurious to vegetation, but were in danger of extermination through lack of adequate protection. It therefore provided for specified closed seasons and protection in other forms, and agreed that the two powers would take or propose to their lawmaking bodies the necessary measures for carrying the treaty out. . . . The above-mentioned Act of July 3, 1918, . . . prohibited the killing, capturing, or selling of any of the migratory birds included in the terms of the treaty except as permitted by regulations compatible with those terms, to be made by the Secretary of Agriculture. . . . [A]s we have said, the question raised is the general one whether the treaty and statute are void as an interference with the rights reserved to the states.

To answer this question, it is not enough to refer to the Tenth Amendment, reserving the powers not delegated to the United States, because by Article II, §2, the power to make treaties is delegated expressly, and by Article VI, treaties made under the authority of the United States, along with the Constitution and laws of the United States, made in pursuance thereof, are declared the supreme law of the land. If the treaty is valid, there can be no dispute about the validity of the statute under Article I, §8, as a necessary and proper means to execute the powers of the government. The language of the Constitution as to the supremacy of treaties being general, the question before us is narrowed to an inquiry into the ground upon which the present supposed exception is placed.

It is said that a treaty cannot be valid if it infringes the Constitution; that there are limits, therefore, to the treaty-making power; and that one such limit is that what an act of Congress could not do unaided, in derogation of the powers reserved to the states, a treaty cannot do. An earlier act of Congress that attempted by itself, and not in pursuance of a treaty, to regulate the killing of migratory birds within the states, had been held bad in the district court. *United States* v. *Shauver,* 213 Fed. 154; *United States* v. *McCullagh,* 221 Fed. 288. Those decisions were supported by arguments that migratory birds were owned by the states in their sovereign capacity, for the benefit of their people, and that under cases like *Geer* v. *Connecticut,* 161 U.S. 519, this control was one that Congress had no power to displace. The same argument is supposed to apply now with equal force.

Whether the two cases cited were decided rightly or not, they cannot be accepted as a test of the treaty power. Acts of Congress are the supreme law of the land only when made in pursuance of the Constitution, while treaties are declared to be so when made under the authority of the United States. It is open to question whether the authority of the United States means more than the formal acts prescribed to make the convention. We do not mean to imply that there are no qualifications to the treaty-making power; but they must be ascertained in a different way. It is obvious that there may be matters of the sharpest exigency for the national well-being that an act of Congress could not deal with, but that a treaty followed by such an act could, and it is not lightly to be assumed that, in matters requiring national action, "a power which must belong to and somewhere reside in every civilized government" is not to be found. . . . We are not yet discussing the particular case before us, but only are considering the validity of the test proposed. With regard to that, we may add that when we are dealing with words that also are a constituent act, like the Constitution of the United States, we must realize that they have called into life a being the development of which could not have been foreseen completely by the most gifted of its begetters. It was enough for them to realize or to hope that they had created an organism; it has taken a century and has cost their successors much sweat and blood to prove that they

created a nation. The case before us must be considered in the light of our whole experience, and not merely in that of what was said a hundred years ago. The treaty in question does not contravene any prohibitory words to be found in the Constitution. The only question is whether it is forbidden by some invisible radiation from the general terms of the Tenth Amendment. We must consider what this country has become in deciding what that amendment has reserved.

The state, as we have intimated, founds its claim of exclusive authority upon an assertion of title to migratory birds—an assertion that is embodied in statute. No doubt it is true that, as between a state and its inhabitants, the state may regulate the killing and sale of such birds, but it does not follow that its authority is exclusive of paramount powers. To put the claim of the state upon title is to lean upon a slender reed. Wild birds are not in the possession of anyone; and possession is the beginning of ownership. The whole foundation of the state's rights is the presence within their jurisdiction of birds that yesterday had not arrived, tomorrow may be in another state, and in a week a thousand miles away. If we are to be accurate, we cannot put the case of the state upon higher ground than that the treaty deals with creatures that for the moment are within the state borders, that it must be carried out by officers of the United States within the same territory, and that, but for the treaty, the state would be free to regulate this subject itself.

As most of the laws of the United States are carried out within the states, and as many of them deal with matters which, in the silence of such laws, the state might regulate, such general grounds are not enough to support Missouri's claim. Valid treaties, of course, "are as binding within the territorial limits of the states, as they are effective throughout the dominion of the United States. . . ." No doubt the great body of private relations usually falls within the control of the state, but a treaty may override its power. . . .

Here a national interest of very nearly the first magnitude is involved. It can be protected only by national action in concert with that of another power. The subject matter is only transitorily within the state, and has no permanent habitat therein. But for the treaty and the statute, there soon might be no birds for any powers to deal with. We see nothing in the Constitution that compels the government to sit by while a food supply is cut off and the protectors of our forests and of our crops are destroyed. It is not sufficient to rely upon the states. The reliance is vain, and were it otherwise, the question is whether the United States is forbidden to act. We are of opinion that the treaty and statute must be upheld. . . .

MR. JUSTICE VAN DEVANTER and MR. JUSTICE PITNEY dissent.

PENNSYLVANIA v. NELSON
350 U.S. 497; 76 Sup. Ct. 477; 100 L. Ed. 640 (1955)

[*Steve Nelson, an acknowledged Communist party leader in Pennsylvania, was convicted on charges of violating the state's sedition law. He was fined and sentenced to imprisonment for twenty years. Before his conviction in Pennsylvania, Nelson had been sentenced to a five-year term by a federal court for violation of the Smith Act of 1940. The federal case was being appealed to the Supreme Court during the period that the state was acting against Nelson. The Supreme Court of Pennsylvania reversed the state conviction on the grounds that the Smith Act superseded state legislation in the field of sedition. Pennsylvania then brought the case to the Supreme Court on a writ of certiorari. That decision is reproduced here. Nelson also challenged his conviction under the Smith Act in the federal court on the ground that the testimony of one of the government's informants was unreliable. In 1956, the Supreme Court upheld Nelson's contention and ordered that he and his codefendants be given a new trial.*]

MR. CHIEF JUSTICE WARREN delivered the opinion of the Court:

It should be said at the outset that the decision in this case does not affect the right of States to enforce their sedition laws at times when the Federal Government has not occupied the field and is not protecting the entire country from seditious conduct. . . .

Where, as in the instant case, Congress has not stated specifically whether a federal statute has occupied a field in which the States are otherwise free to legislate, different criteria have furnished touchstones for decision. . . .

In this case, we think that each of several tests of supersession is met. *First,* "the scheme of federal regulation [is] so pervasive as to make reasonable the inference that Congress left no room for the States to supplement it. . . ." The Congress determined in 1940 that it was necessary for it to reenter the field of antisubversive legislation, which had been abandoned by it in 1921. In that year, it enacted the Smith Act, which proscribes advocacy of the overthrow of any government— federal, state, or local—by force and violence and organization of and knowing membership in a group which so advocates. Conspiracy to commit any of these acts is punishable under the general criminal conspiracy provisions. . . . The Internal Security Act of 1950 is aimed more directly at Communist organizations: It distinguishes between "Communist-action organization" and "Communist front organizations," requiring such organizations to register and to file annual reports with the Attorney General giving complete details as to their officers and funds. Members of Communist-action organizations who have not been registered by their organization must register as individuals. Failure to register . . . is punishable by a fine of not more than $10,000 for an offending organization and by a fine of not more than $10,000 or imprisonment for not more than five years or both for an individual offender—each day of failure to register constituting a separate offense. And the Act imposes certain sanctions upon both "action" and "front" organizations and their members. The Communist Control Act of 1954 declares "that the Communist party of the United States, although purportedly a political party, is in fact an instrumentality of a conspiracy to overthrow the Government of the United States" and that "its role as the agency of a hostile foreign power renders its existence a clear, present, and continuing danger to the security of the United States." It also contains a legislative finding that the Communist party is a "Communist-action organization" within the meaning of the Internal Security Act of 1950 and provides that "knowing" members of the Communist party are "subject to all provisions and penalties" of the Act. It furthermore sets up a new classification of "Communist-infiltrated organizations" and provides for the imposition of sanctions against them.

We examine these Acts only to determine the congressional plan. Looking to all of them in the aggregate, the conclusion is inescapable that Congress has intended to occupy the field of sedition. Taken as a whole, they evince a congressional plan which makes it reasonable to determine that no room has been left for the States to supplement it. Therefore, a state sedition statute is superseded regardless of whether it purports to supplement the federal law. . . .

Second, the federal statutes "touch a field in which the federal interest is so dominant that the federal system [must] be assumed to preclude enforcement of state laws on the same subject. . . ." Congress has devised an all-embracing program for resistance to the various forms of totalitarian aggression. Our external defenses have been strengthened, and a plan to protect against internal subversion has been made by it. It has appropriated vast sums, not only for our own protection, but also to strengthen freedom throughout the world. It has charged the Federal Bureau of Investigation and the Central Intelligence Agency with responsibility for intelligence concerning Communist seditious activities against our Government, and has denominated such activities as part of a world conspiracy. It accordingly proscribed sedition against all government in the nation . . . national, state, and local. Congress declared that these steps were taken "to provide for the common defense, to preserve the sovereignty of the United States as an independent nation, and to guarantee to each State a republican form of government. . . ." Congress having thus treated seditious conduct as a matter of vital national concern, it is in no sense a local enforcement problem. . . .

Third, enforcement of state sedition acts presents a serious danger of conflict with the administration of the federal program. Since 1939, in order to avoid a hampering of uniform enforcement of its program by sporadic local prosecutions, the Federal Government has urged local authorities not to intervene in such matters, but to turn over to the federal authorities immediately and unevaluated all information concerning subversive activities. . . .

Moreover, the Pennsylvania Statute presents a peculiar danger of interference with the federal program. For, as the court below observed:

"Unlike the Smith Act, which can be administered only by federal officers acting in their official capacities, indictment for sedition under the Pennsylvania statute can be initiated upon an information made by a private individual. The opportunity thus present for the indulgence of personal spite and hatred or for furthering some selfish advantage or ambition need only be mentioned to be appreciated. Defense of the Nation by law, no less than by arms, should be a public and not a private undertaking. It is important that punitive sanctions for sedition *against the United States* be such as having been promulgated by the central governmental authority and administered under the supervision and review of that authority's judiciary. If that be done, sedition will be detected and punished, no less, wherever it may be found, and the right of the individual to speak freely and without fear, even in criticism of the government, will at the same time be protected."

. . . [F]orty-two States plus Alaska and Hawaii have statutes which in some form prohibit advocacy of the violent overthrow of established government. These statutes are entitled anti-sedition statutes, criminal anarchy laws, criminal syndicalist laws, etc. Although all of them are primarily directed against the overthrow of the United States Government, they are in no sense uniform. And our attention has not been called to any case where the prosecution has been successfully directed against an attempt to destroy state or local government. Some of these Acts are studiously drawn and purport to protect fundamental rights by appropriate definitions, standards of proof and orderly procedures in keeping with the avowed congressional purpose "to protect freedom from those who would destroy it, without infringing upon the freedom of all our people." Others are vague and are almost wholly without such safeguards. Some even purport to punish mere membership in subversive organizations, which the federal statutes do not punish where federal registration requirements have been fulfilled. . . .

Since we find that Congress has occupied the field to the exclusion of parallel state legislation, that the dominant interest of the Federal Government precludes state intervention, and that administration of state Acts would conflict with the operation of the federal plan, we are convinced that the decision of the Supreme Court of Pennsylvania is unassailable. . . .

The judgment of the Supreme Court of Pennsylvania is

Affirmed.

MR. JUSTICE REED, with whom MR. JUSTICE BURTON, and MR. JUSTICE MINTON join, dissenting:

. . . Congress has not, in any of its statutes relating to sedition, specifically barred the exercise of state power to punish the same Acts under state law. And, we read the majority opinion to assume for this case that, absent federal legislation, there is no constitutional bar to punishment of sedition against the United States by both a State and the Nation. The majority limits to the federal courts the power to try charges of sedition against the Federal Government.

. . . [T]his Court should not void state legislation without a clear mandate from Congress.

We cannot agree that the federal criminal sanctions against sedition directed at the United States are of such a pervasive character as to indicate an intention to void state action. . . .

We are citizens of the United States and of the State wherein we reside and are dependent upon the strength of both to preserve our rights and liberties. Both may enact criminal statutes for mutual protection unless Congress has otherwise provided. . . .

. . . The Smith Act appear in Title 18 of the United States Code, which Title codifies the federal criminal laws. Section 3231 of that Title provides:

"[N]othing in this title shall be held to take away or impair the jurisdiction of the courts of the several states under the laws thereof."

That declaration springs from the federal character of our Nation. It recognizes the fact that maintenance of order and fairness rests primarily with the States. The section was first enacted in 1825 and has appeared successively in the federal criminal laws since that time. This Court has interpreted the section to mean that States may provide concurrent legislation in the absence of explicit congressional intent to the contrary. . . . The majority's position in this case cannot be reconciled with that clear authorization of Congress.

. . . We would reverse the judgment of the Supreme Court of Pennsylvania.

6

Powers of Congress and the President

The framers of the Constitution relied principally on Congress to carry on the work of the newly established federal government. This is indicated by the fact that they vested the principal powers of the new government in the Congress. That the constitutional framers should place a great deal of faith in the national legislature was almost inevitable. As a result of their experiences under the Articles of Confederation, they did not wish to create an inadequate and weak legislative body; at the same time, they still had vivid recollections of the tyranny of the British Crown. In vesting important powers in Congress, they sought to steer a middle course between executive tyranny and weak government.

Delegation of Legislative Powers

Although Congress has several nonlegislative functions, such as those pertaining to the amending process, impeachment proceedings, and investigations, its most important power is that of enacting laws. Because Article I of the Constitution provides that all legislative powers are to be vested in Congress, essential legislative functions cannot be abdicated or transferred to other branches or levels of government. There is no explicit provision in the Constitution that prohibits the delegation of legislative power, but three related ideas have been relied upon as bases for this interdiction. These ideas may be classified as follows:

1. *Principle of Separation of Powers.* The rule against delegation of legislative powers is based largely on this principle. Since the Constitution vests legislative powers in Congress, a delegation of such powers to the other branches would be a violation of the separation-of-powers doctrine. As the Supreme Court noted in *Hampton and Co.* v. *United States,* 276 U.S. 394 (1928), "in carrying out that constitutional division into three branches, it is a breach of the National fundamental law if Congress gives up its legislative power and transfers it to the President, or to the Judicial branch, or if by law it attempts to invest itself or its members with either executive power or judicial power."

2. *The Common-Law Maxim "Delegata Potestas Non Potest Delegari"* (meaning simply that delegated power cannot be delegated). The theory here is that since Congress is serving as a legal agent of the people, it cannot delegate away any of its functions. Actually, this doctrine, "insofar as it is asserted to be a principle of constitutional law, is built upon the thinnest of implications, or is the product of the unwritten super-constitution."[1] Nevertheless, the maxim has been invoked in a number of cases as an additional support for the rule against delegation of legislative powers.

3. *Concept of Due Process of Law.* Under the concept of due process of law, Congress cannot delegate regulatory powers to private individuals. A person affected by the action of private individuals acting under powers delegated by Congress would be said to be denied due process of law. In addition, a person is deprived of liberty or property without due process of law when his rights have been "adversely affected by exercise of unrestrained legislative discretion in the hands of an administrative officer or agency."[2]

Despite the sources of the rule against delegation of legislative powers noted here, one can see that the doctrine does not rest upon a clear-cut constitutional principle. For a long time, the Supreme Court was very liberal in its interpretation of the rule. In the early case of *Wayman* v. *Southard,* 10 Wheat. 1 (1825), the Court held that Congress could delegate to the federal courts the power to regulate their own proceedings. In so doing, the courts were

[1] P. W. Duff and H. E. Whiteside, "Delegata Potestas Non Potest Delegari: A Maxim of American Constitutional Law," *Cornell Law Quarterly,* Vol. 14 (1929), p. 196. The article is reprinted in *Selected Essays on Constitutional Law* (Chicago: Foundation Press, 1938), Vol. 4, pp. 291–316.

[2] Robert Cushman, "The Constitutional Status of the Independent Regulatory Commission," *Cornell Law Quarterly,* Vol. 24 (1938), pp. 32–33.

simply "filling in the details" of a statute. In rendering the opinion of the Court, Chief Justice Marshall stated:

> Congress may certainly delegate to others, powers which the legislature may rightfully exercise itself. . . . The line has not been exactly drawn which separates those important subjects, which must be entirely regulated by the legislature itself, from those of less interest, in which a general provision may be made, and power given to those who are to act under such general provisions to fill up the details.

In another early case,[3] the Supreme Court upheld a statute that authorized the President to revive an embargo act if he found that certain conditions existed. In the important case of *Field* v. *Clark,* 143 U.S. 649 (1892), the Court upheld an act that authorized the President to suspend the operation of existing tariff provisions if he found that foreign governments imposed duties on American products that he deemed unequal and unreasonable. The Court stated that the act did not ". . . invest the President with the power of legislation. Legislative power was exercised when Congress declared that the suspension should take effect upon a named contingency (contingent legislation). What the President was required to do was simply in execution of the act of Congress. It was not the making of law. He was the mere agent of the law-making department to ascertain and declare the event upon which its expressed will was to take effect."

In these and other cases the Supreme Court upheld specific delegations, even though it repeated the rule that Congress could not delegate legislative powers. The delegations were justified on the bases that another department could fill in the details of a statute or that Congress may legislate contingently. In many instances, the Court termed the delegations quasi-legislative or administrative, thus avoiding the constitutional problem. Actually, the Court could do little but uphold the broad delegations of power. For as time went on, the increased complexity of industrial America and the increasing social and economic demands upon government forced Congress to delegate more and more powers. As the functions of government expanded, it became apparent that they had to be administered by well-trained individuals. By its very nature, Congress could not administer the new functions adequately. Congressmen are not chosen because of any specific technical skills, and the complicated problems which arise may, in many instances, be solved only by the application of specialized skills and information. Furthermore, Congress does not have time to concern itself with technical matters. The judiciary could not be called upon to administer the new functions, as the courts have confined themselves strictly to problems that are almost purely judicial in nature. Moreover, the courts can only act when an actual case or controversy exists. Therefore, the new functions came to be performed by the President and numerous administrative bodies.

[3] *Brig Aurora* v. *United States,* 7 Cr. 382 (1813).

By the time the New Deal government came to power, Congress apparently could delegate its powers whenever it thought necessary with little, if any, fear of judicial disapproval.[4] In numerous cases the Supreme Court had developed a vague rule that provided that delegations were constitutional when Congress established a standard to guide the action. A delegation without standards, or one that gave an "unfettered" discretion to executive officers, would be unconstitutional. Nevertheless, up to 1935, the Court had never invalidated a statute on the basis that legislative powers were unconstitutionally delegated to the executive.

But in 1935, in the case of *Panama Refining Co.* v. *Ryan,* 293 U.S. 388, the Supreme Court for the first time held that a statute (National Industrial Recovery Act of 1933) contained an unconstitutional grant of legislative powers to the president. The NIRA was one of the most ambitious of the New Deal efforts to end the depression and restore prosperity. To that end it was designed to shorten working hours, raise wages, and increase employment. The National Recovery Administration (NRA), which the act created, was to work with industry in setting up codes in a joint battle against the depression. The states, of course, also enacted legislation designed to help restore prosperity. A number of the oil-producing states had passed laws restricting the production of oil during 1933 and 1934 in an effort to raise prices. In the Panama Refining case, the Supreme Court invalidated the section of the NIRA that gave the President power to prevent the movement in interstate commerce of "hot oil"—oil produced or taken from storage in violation of the limits set by state laws. Only Justice Cardozo dissented in the hot oil case. He maintained that the discretionary power granted to the President was not "unconfined and vagrant. It is canalized within banks that keep it from overflowing."

Four months after the decision in the Panama Refining case, the Supreme Court held that the whole NIRA was unconstitutional in *Schechter* v. *United States* (p. 153). On the question of the unconstitutional delegation of legislative powers, the *Schechter* case followed substantially the reasoning in the hot oil case. But perhaps an even more important ground for the invalidation of the entire NIRA in the *Schechter* case related to the Court's interpretation of the power of Congress to regulate interstate commerce. That portion of the decision dealing with interstate commerce should be viewed in conjunction with the cases in Chapter 9.

In only one other case—*Carter* v. *Carter Coal Co.,* 298 U.S. 238 (1936) —has the Supreme Court held that there has been an unconstitutional delegation of legislative power. In the *Carter* case, the Court invalidated the labor provisions of the Bituminous Coal Act of 1935 on the ground that they delegated legislative authority to fix maximum hours and minimum wages to a private rather than an official governmental agency. The Court noted that this

---

[4] Edward S. Corwin, *The Twilight of the Supreme Court* (New Haven: Yale Univeristy Press, 1934), p. 145.

constituted legislative delegation "in its most noxious form; for it is not even delegation to an official or an official body, presumptively disinterested, but to private persons whose interests may be and often are adverse to the interests of others in the same business." Since the decision in the *Carter* case, the Supreme Court has upheld every delegation that has come before it. In *Yakus* v. *United States,* which dealt with World War II price control powers granted the Office of Price Administration (OPA), and numerous other cases since 1936, the Court has upheld many delegations that prescribe few, if any, basic standards to guide the administrator. For example, in *Lichter* v. *United States,* 334 U.S. 742 (1948), the Court said that "it is not necessary that Congress supply administrative officials with a specific formula for their guidance in a field where flexibility and the adaptation of the Congressional policy to infinitely variable conditions constitute the essence of the program."

Why then were delegations held unconstitutional during the early New Deal period? In part, this can be explained by the fact that much of the New Deal legislation was drawn up hastily and was, therefore, poorly drafted. In addition, the scope of the delegation involved in the *Schechter* case was very great. It constituted, without doubt, the most sweeping congressional delegation in American history. The decisions may be explained also in terms of the opposition to the New Deal by some of the conservative members of the Court, even though in some instances even the liberal justices voted to invalidate important New Deal measures. The nondelegation doctrine was an easily available weapon that could be used to kill legislation inconsistent with a judge's conception of a laissez-faire system.

> [The *Schechter* and *Panama* cases] remain as a warning to Congress not to go too far too fast. But "too far" seems to mean simply that the lawmakers must not try to regulate all business at once, while "too fast" indicates only that some apparent, although not necessarily real, limitations on administrative discretion must be found in the statute. If these conclusions are correct they raise the question as to whether the doctrine that delegated powers may not be redelegated has any significance in modern constitutional law. Never literally true, it appears that the maxim is no longer even substantially accurate. Practical necessity seems the only limitation left as far as delegability is concerned. It is not true, as long as the *Schechter* and *Panama* cases are not overruled, that there are no limitations whatever, but such limitations as remain are determined by the rule of reason rather than the doctrine of non-delegability.[5]

Furthermore, where international rather than domestic relations are concerned, the Supreme Court has refused to place restrictions upon congressional delegations of broad discretionary powers to the President. In *United States* v. *Curtiss-Wright Export Corp.* (Chapter 6), the Court noted that in the maintenance of our international relations, Congress must "accord to the President a degree of discretion and freedom from statutory restriction which

[5] Charles B. Nutting, "Congressional Delegations Since the Schechter Case," *Mississippi Law Journal,* Vol. 14 (1942), pp. 366–67.

would not be admissible were domestic affairs alone involved." The reasons for this distinction between delegations of power in domestic affairs and power over foreign relations are outlined in the case.

The Presidency

In the twentieth century, the vital role of the President in both national and international affairs can hardly be exaggerated. The office of the President is undoubtedly the most important single post in the world. "A modern President of the United States is not merely the executive of history's greatest democracy, he literally holds in his hands the fate of the civilized world."[6] The burdens of the office have become so great that former President Truman was led to remark: "No one man can really fill the presidency. It is an executive job that is almost fantastic. No absolute monarch has ever had such decisions to make or the responsibilities that the President of the United States has."

The vast powers now exercised by modern presidents could not have been envisioned by the framers of the Constitution. In fact, the framers were not quite sure how the executive branch should be set up. The fear of executive tyranny, coupled with a strong faith in legislative bodies, made some of the framers reluctant to confer important powers upon a single executive. On the other hand, experience with a weak, headless government under the Articles of Confederation led others to demand a strong executive. The framers thereby faced the difficult task of providing for an executive branch that could deal effectively with national problems but that, at the same time, was not so strong that it would overwhelm the other two branches. This they tried to do in Article II of the Constitution, which deals with the executive branch.

The language of Article II is very vague and indefinite when compared with Articles I and III, which define the authority of the other branches of government. Article II loosely provides that the executive power is vested in the President and that he shall take care that the laws be faithfully executed. Of course, the President was given other more specific powers under Article II. He was made commander-in-chief of the Army and Navy. He was empowered to appoint numerous officers, to grant pardons and reprieves, to make treaties, to receive ambassadors and ministers, and to perform certain important duties in connection with Congress. Nevertheless, the Constitution does not define precisely the boundaries of executive power. Although Article II provides the base for the present-day power of the President, the scope of his authority

---

[6] Cabell Phillips, "The Crushing Burden of the Presidency," *The New York Times Magazine* (October 2, 1955), p. 11. See also Sidney Hyman, "When He Enters the Oval Room," *The New York Times Magazine* (January 22, 1961), p. 5. For an exhaustive review of the powers of the President, see Vol. 2 of Bernard Schwartz, *A Commentary on the Constitution of the United States* (New York: Macmillan, 1963).

is much larger than is indicated by the rudimentary constitutional provisions. In short, the modern Presidency is largely the product of practical political experience.

The vagueness of the Constitution virtually "invited men of will, courage, and program to build a Presidential tradition,"[7] and opened the door to the emergence of three conceptions of the nature and scope of presidential power. These may be enumerated as follows:

1. The *stewardship theory* was advanced by Theodore Roosevelt in 1913. He maintained that the President is simply the "steward of the people," who therefore is under the duty to do "anything that the needs of the nation demanded unless such action was forbidden by the Constitution and the laws."[8]

2. The *constitutional theory* was set forth in 1916 by ex-President Taft, who was extremely critical of the stewardship theory. Taft maintained that the President could exercise only those powers given to him by specific clauses of the Constitution.[9] Later, however, when Taft was Chief Justice, he indicated greater sympathy for the stewardship theory in his decisions in *Myers* v. *United States,* 272 U.S. 52 (1926). Taft's early position "may have been tinged by a sense of personal frustration. In 1916, he could look back on almost four years of administration by Woodrow Wilson—four years which he probably believed would have been the second Taft Administration had not Theodore Roosevelt bolted the regular Republican organization."[10]

3. The *prerogative theory* was advanced by F. D. Roosevelt in 1942, when he recommended to Congress that certain price-control legislation be repealed. He went on to say that "in the event that the Congress should fail to act and act adequately, I shall accept the responsibility, and I will act," F. D. Roosevelt thus went beyond the stewardship theory during World War II, when most people recognized that the President needed broad powers to cope with new emergency situations.

At this point in history, the exponents of the broad view of presidential powers clearly have won the day. But even in the twentieth century, the scope of this power depends to a large degree on the qualities of the President himself. Furthermore, the President is limited, first of all, by various provisions of the Constitution. For example, he must share the general power to govern

---

[7] James W. Hurst, *The Growth of American Law: The Law Makers* (Boston: Little, Brown, 1950), p. 384.

[8] Theodore Roosevelt, *An Autobiography,* (New York: Macmillan, 1913), pp. 388–89.

[9] W. H. Taft, *Our Chief Magistrate and His Powers* (New York: Columbia University Press, 1916), p. 139.

[10] Louis Brownlow, *The President and the Presidency* (Chicago: Public Administration Service, 1949), p. 6.

with the other two branches of government. He shares the treaty-making power with the Senate. The Twenty-second Amendment establishes a flat ban on a third term. The President's powers are also restricted by specific actions of Congress and the courts, by his own or the opposing political party, and by public opinion.

The courts are the least reliable restraint upon the powers of the President. In fact, the Supreme Court has done more to expand than to contract presidential powers. For example, in the case of *In re Neagle,* which is discussed in Chapter 5, the Court attributed powers to the President that were not specifically granted by statute or expressly mentioned in the Constitution. In numerous other instances, the Court has supported the strong actions of various Presidents. Although on some occasions the Court has proved to be an important restraint upon presidential powers, in the long run "the Court can be expected to go on rationalizing most pretensions of most Presidents."[11] This is particularly so in periods of emergency, when the Court has been reluctant to interfere with the President in the absence of *extreme* abuses of authority.

Presidential Powers in Internal Affairs

The student of constitutional law must remember that numerous executive practices, rather than Supreme Court decisions, have established the real traditions of presidential power. Nevertheless, there are a number of important cases dealing with the scope of executive powers in both internal and foreign affairs. Some of the most important of these are noted subsequently. Others, such as *Ex Parte Milligan,* are discussed in other chapters.

In *Mississippi* v. *Johnson* (Chapter 6), the Supreme Court clearly stated that the judiciary could not control the acts of the President. This case was decided in the midst of the struggle between President Johnson and Congress over the reconstruction of the South. Johnson favored a policy of moderation, whereas the Radical Republicans in Congress wished to impose strict military control over the defeated rebellious states. The Reconstruction Acts at issue in *Mississippi* v. *Johnson* were designed to place the Southern states under military rule. By its decision in the case, the Court avoided a serious clash with Congress.

The President's immunity from judicial control under the doctrine of *Mississippi* v. *Johnson* does not extend to his subordinate executive officers. The President's subordinates may be enjoined from carrying out a threatened illegal act or be compelled to perform a legal duty by a writ of mandamus. This lack of immunity on the part of the President's subordinates is demonstrated by the Steel Seizure case, *Youngstown Sheet and Tube Co.* v. *Sawyer* (p. 161).

[11] Clinton Rossiter, *The American Presidency* (New York: Harcourt, Brace, 1960), p. 59.

APPOINTMENT AND REMOVAL OF OFFICERS

The President exerts a great deal of influence over internal affairs through his power to appoint and remove public officers. Article II of the Constitution provides that the President shall nominate and, by and with the advice and consent of the Senate, appoint ambassadors, public ministers, consuls, judges of the Supreme Court, and other officers of the United States whose appointments are not otherwise provided by law. Article II also declares that Congress may vest the appointment of inferior officers in the President alone, in the courts of law, or in the heads of departments. The Constitution does not define the term *inferior officers,* so Congress actually decides who shall fall in this category.

The Constitution does not, however, provide for the removal of federal executive officers except through the cumbersome, seldom-used impeachment process. Important questions concerning the President's removal power are thereby left unanswered by the Constitution. Not until 1926, in the celebrated case of *Myers* v. *United States* (p. 168), was the Supreme Court finally forced to resolve important questions concerning the President's removal powers.

The Myers decision resulted in considerable controversy because of two important propositions laid down by the Court, as follows:

1. The power to remove an executive officer of the United States who has been appointed by the President by and with the advice and consent of the Senate belongs to the *President alone* under the Constitution.
2. Because the President may remove executive officers, a necessary corollary is that *all such officers may be removed at his discretion.* "The result of this ruling is to deny to Congress, which alone has power under the Constitution to create officers, any right to determine their tenure as against the removal power" of the President.[12]

The Myers decision thus appeared to give the President unlimited power to remove all officers, with the exception of federal judges, in whose appointment he had participated. But the broad dictum of the case was limited considerably in *Humphrey's Executor* v. *United States* (p. 174). Since that decision, the President may continue to remove purely executive officers at will, but officers exercising quasijudicial and quasilegislative powers are protected by congressional limitations on the President's removal power. But because no precise definition of a purely executive officer can be given, the courts must decide in each individual case how a federal officer is to be classified. In 1941, for example, the Supreme Court denied certiorari in *Morgan* v. *United States,* 312 U.S. 701, after a lower federal court had approved President Roosevelt's removal of the chairman of the Tennessee Valley Authority. The lower court had held that the Humphrey case did not apply because the TVA

---

[12] Edward S. Corwin, *The President's Removal Power Under the Constitution* (New York: National Municipal League, 1927), p. vi.

"exercises predominately an executive or administrative function." It should not be "aligned with the Federal Trade Commission, the Interstate Commerce Commission or other administrative bodies mainly exercising clearly quasi-legislative or quasi-judicial functions—it is predominantly an administrative arm of the executive department." Nevertheless, the Humphrey case placed important restrictions upon the President's removal powers during a turbulent period in the relationship between President F. D. Roosevelt and the Court.

In *Weiner* v. *United States,* 357 U.S. 349 (1958), the Court reasserted the Humphrey's rule prohibiting Presidential removal from quasijudicial agencies even when Congress had said nothing about removal one way or the other.

PRESIDENT'S POWER TO SEIZE PRIVATE PROPERTY

Like the *Myers* decision, the Steel Seizure case aroused great public interest, largely because of its important implications concerning the boundaries of presidential powers. The seven separate opinions of the case total 128 pages in the *Reports* and contain a great deal of important data on the powers of the Chief Executive. The case demonstrates well that executive powers, even during an alleged emergency, may still be subject to judicial control. The decision constitutes a dramatic vindication of American constitutional government.

Control over Foreign Affairs

The conduct of foreign affairs is primarily the responsibility of the President and his subordinates in the Department of State. Of course, the President's authority in foreign relations is shared with Congress, particularly the Senate. Through its power to appropriate money, Congress exercises important controls over foreign affairs. The President has authority to ratify treaties only after receiving the concurrence of two-thirds of the Senate. His power to appoint diplomats and consuls is subject to ratification by a Senate majority. Nevertheless, the President's position in foreign relations is "paramount, if not indeed dominant." The "growth of presidential authority in this area seems to have been almost inevitable. Constitution, laws, custom, the practice of other nations, and the logic of history have combined to place the President in a dominant position."[13] That Congress may delegate vast powers to the President in the field of foreign affairs is indicated clearly by *United States* v. *Curtiss-Wright Export Corp.* (p. 177). Indeed, in resolutions connected with the Korean and Vietnamese wars, Congress delegated much of its power to declare war to the President, although serious doubts have been raised as to the constitutionality of these congressional actions.

The President has freed himself from the Senate in some instances by using executive agreements rather than treaties to make international arrangements.

[13] Rossiter, *op. cit.,* p. 26.

Such agreements do not require the approval of the Senate, but the Supreme Court ruled in *United States* v. *Belmont,* 301 U.S. 324 (1937), that they have the same legal effect as formal treaties. The principle of the *Belmont* case was confirmed in *United States* v. *Pink,* 315 U.S. 203 (1942).

A. L. A. SCHECHTER POULTRY CORP. *et al.* v. UNITED STATES
295 U.S. 495; 55 Sup. Ct. 837; 79 L. Ed. 1570 (1935)

MR. CHIEF JUSTICE HUGHES delivered the opinion of the Court:

Petitioners . . . were convicted in the District Court of the United States for the Eastern District of New York on eighteen counts of an indictment charging violations of what is known as the "Live Poultry Code," and on an additional count for conspiracy to commit such violations. . . . (T)he defendants contended (1) that the Code had been adopted pursuant to an unconstitutional delegation by Congress of legislative power; (2) that it attempted to regulate intrastate transactions which lay outside the authority of Congress; and (3) that in certain provisions it was repugnant to the due process clause of the Fifth Amendment. . . .

New York City is the largest live-poultry market in the United States. Ninety-six per cent of the live poultry there marketed comes from other States. Three-fourths of this amount arrives by rail and is consigned to commission men or receivers. . . . The commission men transact by far the greater part of the business on a commission basis, representing the shippers as agents, and remitting to them the proceeds of sale, less commissions, freight, and handling charges. Otherwise, they buy for their own account. They sell to slaughterhouse operators who are also called market-men.

The defendants are slaughterhouse operators of the latter class. A. L. A. Schechter Poultry Corporation and Schechter Live Poultry Market are corporations conducting wholesale poultry slaughterhouse markets in Brooklyn, New York City. . . . They buy the poultry for slaughter and resale. After the poultry is trucked to their slaughterhouse markets in Brooklyn, it is there sold, usually within twenty-four hours, to retail poultry dealers and butchers who sell directly to consumers. . . . Defendants do not sell poultry in interstate commerce.

The "Live Poultry Code" was promulgated under §3 of the National Industrial Recovery Act. That section . . . authorizes the President to approve "codes of fair competition."

. . . The "Live Poultry Code" was approved by the President on April 13, 1934. . . .

. . . The Code is established as "a code of fair competition for the live-poultry industry of the metropolitan area in and about the City of New York."

. . . The Code fixes the number of hours for work-days. It provides that no employee, with certain exceptions, shall be permitted to work in excess of forty (40) hours in any one week, and that no employee, save as stated, "shall be paid in any pay period less than at the rate of fifty (50) cents per hour." The article containing "general labor provisions" prohibits the employment of any person under sixteen years of age, and declares that employees shall have the right of "collective bargaining," and freedom of choice with respect to labor organizations, in the terms of §7(a) of the Act. The minimum number of employees who shall be employed by slaughterhouse operators is fixed, the number being graduated according to the average volume of weekly sales. . . .

The seventh article, containing "trade practice provisions," prohibits various practices which are said to constitute "unfair methods of competition. . . ."

The President approved the Code by an executive order. . . .

Of the eighteen counts of the indictment upon which the defendants were convicted, aside from the count for conspiracy, two counts charged violation of the minimum-wage and maximum-hour provisions of the Code, and ten counts were for violation of the requirement (found in the "trade practice provisions") of "straight killing." This requirement was really one of "straight" selling. The term "straight killing" was defined in the Code as "the practice of requiring persons purchasing poultry for resale to accept the run of any half coop, coop, or coops, as purchased by slaughterhouse operators, except for culls." The charges in the ten counts, respectively, were that the defendants in selling to retail dealers and butchers had permitted "selections of individual chickens taken from particular coops and half coops."

Of the other six counts, one charged the sale to a butcher of an unfit chicken; two counts charged the making of sales without having the poultry inspected or approved in accordance with regulations or ordinances of the City of New York; two counts charged the making of false reports or the failure to make reports relating to the range of daily prices and volume of sales for certain periods; and the remaining count was for sales to slaughterers or dealers who were without licenses required by the ordinances and regulations of the city of New York.

First. Two preliminary points are stressed by the Government with respect to the appropriate approach to the important questions presented. We are told that the provision of the statute authorizing the adoption of codes must be viewed in the light of the grave national crisis with which Congress was confronted. Undoubtedly, the conditions to which power is addressed are always to be considered when the exercise of power is challenged. Extraordinary conditions may call for extraordinary remedies. But the argument necessarily stops short of an attempt to justify action which lies outside the sphere of constitutional authority. Extraordinary conditions do not create or enlarge constitutional power. The Constitution established a national government with powers deemed to be adequate, as they have proved to be both in war and peace, but these powers of the national government are limited by the constitutional grants. Those who act under these grants are not at liberty to transcend the imposed limits because they believe that more or different power is necessary. Such assertions of extraconstitutional authority were anticipated and precluded by the explicit terms of the Tenth Amendment—"The powers not delegated to the United States by the Constitution, nor prohibited by it to the States, are reserved to the States respectively, or to the people. . . ."

Second. The Question of the Delegation of Legislative Power. . . . The Constitution provides that "All legislative powers herein granted shall be vested in a Congress of the United States, which shall consist of a Senate and House of Representatives." Art. I, §1. And the Congress is authorized "To make all laws which shall be necessary and proper for carrying into execution" its general powers. Art. I, §8, par. 18. The Congress is not permitted to abdicate or to transfer to others the essential legislative functions with which it is thus vested. We have repeatedly recognized the necessity of adapting legislation to complex conditions involving a host of details with which the national legislature cannot deal directly. We pointed out in the *Panama Company* case that the Constitution has never been regarded as denying to Congress the necessary resources of flexibility and practicality, which will enable it to perform its function in laying down policies and establishing standards, while leaving to selected instrumentalities the making of subordinate rules within prescribed limits and the determination of facts to which the policy as declared by the legislature is to apply. But we said that the constant recognition of the necessity and validity of such provisions, and the wide range of administrative authority which has been developed by means of them, cannot be allowed to obscure the limitations of the authority to delegate, if our constitutional system is to be maintained. . . .

Accordingly, we look to the statute to see whether Congress has overstepped these limitations—whether Congress in authorizing "codes of fair competition" has itself established the standards of legal obligation, thus performing its essential legislative function, or, by the failure to enact such standards, has attempted to transfer that function to others. . . .

What is meant by "fair competition" as the term is used in the Act? Does it refer to a category established in the law, and is the authority to make codes limited accordingly? Or is it used as a convenient designation for whatever set of laws the formulators of a code for a particular trade or industry may propose and the President may approve (subject to certain restrictions), or the President may himself prescribe, as

being wise and beneficent provisions for the government of the trade or industry in order to accomplish the broad purpose of rehabilitation, correction, and expansion which are stated in the first section of Title I?

The Act does not define "fair competition. . . ."

The Government urges that the codes will "consist of rules of competition deemed fair for each industry by representative members of that industry— by the persons most vitally concerned and most familiar with its problems." Instances are cited in which Congress has availed itself of such assistance; as, e.g., in the exercise of its authority over the public domain, with respect to the recognition of local customs or rules of miners as to mining claims, or, in matters of a more or less technical nature, as in designating the standard height of drawbars. But would it be seriously contended that Congress could delegate its legislative authority to trade or industrial associations or groups so as to empower them to enact the laws they deem to be wise and beneficent for the rehabilitation and expansion of their trade or industries? Could trade or industrial associations or groups be constituted legislative bodies for that purpose because such associations or groups be constituted legislative bodies for that purpose because such associations or groups are familiar with the problems of their enterprises? And, could an effort of that sort be made valid by such a preface of generalities as to permissible aims as we find in Section 1 of Title I? The answer is obvious. Such a delegation of legislative power is unknown to our law and is utterly inconsistent with the constitutional prerogatives and duties of Congress.

The question, then, turns upon the authority which §3 of the Recovery Act vests in the President to approve or prescribe. If the codes have standing as penal statutes, this must be due to the effect of the executive action. But Congress cannot delegate legislative power to the President to exercise an unfettered discretion to make whatever laws he thinks may be needed or advisable for the rehabilitation and expansion of trade or industry. . . .

. . . Secton 3 of the Recovery Act is without precedent. It supplies no standards for any trade, industry, or activity. It does not undertake to prescribe rules of conduct to be applied to particular states of fact determined by appropriate administrative procedure. Instead of prescribing rules of conduct, it authorizes the making of codes to prescribe them. For that legislative undertaking, §3 sets up no standards, aside from the statement of the general aims of rehabilitation, correction, and expansion described in Section 1. In view of the scope of that broad declaration, and of the nature of the few restrictions that are imposed, the discretion of the President in approving or prescribing codes, and thus enacting laws for the government of trade and industry throughout the country, is virtually unfettered. We think that the code-making authority thus conferred is an unconstitutional delegation of legislative power.

Third. The Question of the Application of the Provisions of the Live Poultry Code to Intrastate Transactions. Although the validity of the codes (apart from the question of delegation) rests upon the commerce clause of the Constitution, §3(a) is not in terms limited to interstate and foreign commerce. From the generality of its terms, and from the argument of the Government at the bar, it would appear that §3(a) was designed to authorize codes without that limitation. But under §3(f) penalties are confined to violations of a code provision "in any transaction in or affecting interstate or foreign commerce." This aspect of the case presents the question whether the particular provisions of the Live Poultry Code, which the defendants were convicted for violating and for having conspired to violate, were within the regulating power of Congress.

These provisions relate to the hours and wages of those employed by defendants in their slaughterhouses in Brooklyn and to the sales there made to retail dealers and butchers.

(1) Were these transactions *"in"* interstate commerce? Much is made of the fact that almost all the poultry coming to New York is sent there from other States. But the code provisions, as here applied, do not concern the transportation of the poultry from other States to New York, or the transactions of the commission men or others to whom it is consigned, or the sales made by such consignees to defendants. When defendants had made their purchases, whether at the West Washington Market in New York City or at the railroad terminals serving the City, or elsewhere, the poultry was trucked to their slaughterhouses in Brooklyn for local disposition. The interstate transactions in relation to that poultry then ended. Defendants held the poultry at their slaughterhouse markets for slaughter and local sale to retail dealers and butchers, who in turn sold directly to consumers. Neither the slaughtering nor the sales by defendants were transactions in interstate commerce. . . .

The undisputed facts thus afford no warrant for the argument that the poultry handled by defendants at their slaughterhouse markets was in a *"current"* or *"flow"* of interstate commerce and was thus subject to congressional regulation. The mere fact that there may be a constant flow of commodities into a State does not mean that the flow continues after the property has arrived and has become commingled with the mass of property within the State and is there held solely for local disposition and use. So far as the poultry here in question is concerned, the flow in interstate commerce had ceased. The poultry had come to a permanent rest within the State. It was not held, used, or sold by defendants in relation to any further transactions in interstate commerce and was not destined for transportation to other States. Hence, decisions which deal with a stream of interstate commerce—where goods come to rest within a State temporarily and are later to go forward in interstate commerce—and with the regulations of transactions involved in that practical continuity of movement, are not applicable here. . . .

(2) Did the defendants' transactions directly *"affect"* interstate commerce so as to be subject to federal regulation? The power of Congress extends not only to the regulation of transactions which are part of interstate commerce, but to the protection of that commerce from injury. It matters not that the injury may be due to the conduct of those engaged in intrastate operations. Thus, Congress may protect the safety of those employed in interstate transportation "no matter what may be the source of the dangers which threaten it. . . ." We said in *Second Employers' Liability Cases,* 223 U.S. 1, 51, that it is the "effect upon interstate commerce," not "the source of the injury," which is "the criterion of congressional power. . . ."

. . . Defendants have been convicted, not upon direct charges of injury to interstate commerce or of interference with persons engaged in that commerce, but of violations of certain provisions of the Live Poultry Code and of conspiracy to commit these violations. Interstate commerce is brought in only upon the charge that violations of these provisions—as to hours and wages of employees and local sales—*"affected"* interstate commerce.

In determining how far the federal government may go in controlling intrastate transactions upon the ground that they "affect" interstate commerce, there is a necessary and well-established distinction between direct and indirect effects. The precise line can be drawn only as individual cases arise, but the distinction is clear in principle. Direct effects are illustrated by the railroad cases, . . . as e.g., the effect of failure to use prescribed safety appliances on railroads which are the highways of both interstate and intrastate commerce, injury to an employee engaged in interstate transportation by the negligence of an employee engaged in an intrastate movement, the fixing of rates for intrastate transportation which unjustly discriminate against interstate commerce. But where the effect of intrastate transactions upon interstate commerce is merely indirect, such transactions remain within the domain of state power. If the commerce clause were construed to reach all enterprises and transactions which could be said to have an indirect effect upon interstate commerce, the federal authority would embrace practically all the activities of the people, and the authority of the State over its domestic concerns would exist only by sufferance of the federal government. Indeed, on such a theory, even the development of the State's commercial facilities would be subject to federal control. . . .

. . . [T]he distinction between direct and indirect efforts of intrastate transactions upon interstate commerce must be recognized as a fundamental one, essential to the maintenance of our constitutional system. Otherwise, as we have said, there would be virtually no limit to the federal power and for all practical purposes we should have a completely centralized government. We must consider the provisions here in question in the light of this distinction.

The question of chief importance relates to the provisions of the Code as to the hours and wages of those employed in defendants' slaughterhouse markets. It is plain that these requirements are imposed in order to govern the details of defendants' management of their local business. The persons employed in slaughtering and selling in local trade are not employed in interstate commerce. Their hours and wages have no direct relation to interstate commerce.

. . . The apparent implication is that the federal authority under the commerce clause should be deemed to extend to the establishment of rules to govern wages and hours in intrastate trade and industry generally throughout the country, thus overriding the authority of the States to deal with domestic problems arising from labor conditions in their internal commerce.

It is not the province of the Court to consider the economic advantages or disadvantages of such a centralized system. It is sufficient to say that the Federal Constitution does not provide for it. Our growth and development have called for wide use of the commerce power of the federal government in its control over the expanded activities of interstate commerce, and in protecting that commerce from burdens, interferences, and conspiracies to restrain and monopolize it. But the authority of the federal government may not be pushed to such an extreme as to destroy the distinction, which the commerce clause itself establishes, between commerce "among the several States" and the internal concerns of a State. The same answer must be made to the contention that is based upon the serious economic situation which led to the passage of the Recovery Act—the fall in prices, the decline in wages and employment, and the curtailment of the market for commodities. Stress is laid upon the great importance of maintaining wage distributions which would provide the necessary stimulus in starting "the cumulative forces making for expanding commercial activity." Without in any way disparaging this motive, it is enough to say that the recuperative efforts of the federal government must be made in a manner consistent with the authority granted by the Constitution.

We are of the opinion that the attempt through the provisions of the Code to fix the hours and wages of employees of defendants in their intrastate business was not a valid exercise of federal power.

The other violations for which defendants were convicted related to the making of local sales. Ten counts, for violation of the provision as to "straight killing," were for permitting customers to make "selections of individual chickens taken from particular coops and half coops." Whether or not this practice is good or bad for the local trade, its effect, if any, upon interstate commerce was only indirect. The same may be said of violations of the Code by intrastate transactions consisting of the sale "of an unfit chicken" and of sales which were not in accord with the ordinances of the City of New York. The requirement of reports as to prices and volumes of defendants' sales was incident to the effort to control their intrastate business.

In view of these conclusions, we find it unnecessary to discuss other questions which have been raised as to the validity of certain provisions of the Code under the due process clause of the Fifth Amendment.

On both the grounds we have discussed, the attempted delegation of legislative power, and the attempted regulation of intrastate transactions which affect interstate commerce only indirectly, we hold the code provisions here in question to be invalid and that the judgment of conviction must be reversed. . . .

MR. JUSTICE CARDOZO, concurring: [MR. JUSTICE STONE joined in this opinion.]

The delegated power of legislation which has found expression in this code is not canalized within banks that keep it from overflowing. It is unconfined and vagrant, if I may borrow my own words in an earlier opinion. . . .

. . . Here, in the case before us, is an attempted delegation not confined to any single act nor to any class or group of acts identified or described by reference to a standard. Here in effect is a roving commission to inquire into evils and upon discovery correct them.

I have said that there is no standard, definite or even approximate, to which legislation must conform. Let me make my meaning more precise. If codes of fair competition are codes eliminating "unfair" methods of competition ascertained upon inquiry to prevail in one industry or another, there is no unlawful delegation of legislative functions when the President is directed to inquire into such practices and denounce them when discovered. For many years a like power has been committed to the Federal Trade Commission with the approval of this court in a long series of decisions. . . . Delegation in such circumstances is born of the necessities of the occasion. The industries of the country are too many and diverse to make it possible for Congress, in respect of matters such as these, to legislate directly with adequate appreciation of varying conditions. Nor is the substance of the power changed because the President may act at the instance of trade or industrial associations having special knowledge of the facts. Their

function is strictly advisory; it is the *imprimatur* of the President that begets the quality of law. . . .

But there is another conception of codes of fair competition, their significance and function, which leads to very different consequences, though it is one that is struggling now for recognition and acceptance. By this other conception a code is not to be restricted to the elimination of business practices that would be characterized by general acceptation as oppressive or unfair. It is to include whatever ordinances may be desirable or helpful for the well-being or prosperity of the industry affected. In that view, the function of its adoption is not merely negative, but positive; the planning of improvements as well as the extirpation of abuses. What is fair, as thus conceived, is not something to be contrasted with what is unfair or fraudulent or tricky. The extension becomes as wide as the field of industrial regulation. If that conception shall prevail, anything that Congress may do within the limits of the commerce clause for the betterment of business may be done by the President upon the recommendation of a trade association by calling it a code. This is delegation running riot. No such plenitude of power is susceptible of transfer. . . .

But there is another objection, far-reaching and incurable, aside from any defect of unlawful delegation.

If this code had been adopted by Congress itself, and not by the President on the advice of an industrial association, it would even then be void unless authority to adopt it is included in the grant of power "to regulate commerce with foreign nations and among the several states. . . ."

I find no authority in that grant for the regulation of wages and hours of labor in the intrastate transactions that make up the defendants' business. . . .

MISSISSIPPI *v.* JOHNSON
4 Wall. 475; 18 L. Ed. 437 (1867)

THE CHIEF JUSTICE [CHASE] delivered the opinion of the Court:

A motion was made, some days since, in behalf of the State of Mississippi, for leave to file a bill in the name of the State, praying this court perpetually to enjoin and restrain Andrew Johnson, President of the United States, and E. O. C. Ord, General commanding in the District of Mississippi and Arkansas, from executing, or in any manner carrying out, certain acts of Congress therein named.

The acts referred to are those of March 2d and March 23d, 1867, commonly known as the Reconstruction Acts.

The Attorney-General objected to the leave asked for, upon the ground that no bill which makes a President a defendant, and seeks an injunction against him to restrain the performance of his duties as President, should be allowed to be filed in this court. . . .

The single point which requires consideration is this: Can the President be restrained by injunction from carrying into effect an act of Congress alleged to be unconstitutional?

It is assumed by the counsel for the State of Mississippi that the President, in the execution of the Reconstruction Acts, is required to perform a mere ministerial duty. In this assumption there is, we think, a confounding of the terms ministerial and executive, which are by no means equivalent in import.

A ministerial duty, the performance of which may, in proper cases, be required of the head of a department, by judicial process, is one in respect to which nothing is left to discretion. It is a simple, definite duty, arising under conditions admitted or proved to exist, and imposed by law.

The case of *Marbury* v. *Madison* . . . furnishes an illustration. A citizen had been nominated, confirmed, and appointed a justice of the peace for the District of Columbia, and his commission had been made out, signed, and sealed. Nothing remained to be done except delivery, and the duty of delivery was imposed by law on the Secretary of State. It was held that the performance of this duty might be enforced by *mandamus* issuing from a court having jurisdiction. . . .

Very different is the duty of the President in the exercise of the power to see that the laws are faithfully executed, and among these laws the acts named in the bill. By the first of these acts he is required to assign generals to command in the several military districts, and to detail sufficient military force to enable such officers to discharge their duties under the law. By the supplementary act, other duties are imposed on the several commanding generals, and these duties must necessarily be performed under the supervision of the President as commander-in-chief. The duty thus imposed on the President is in no just sense ministerial. It is purely executive and political.

An attempt on the part of the judicial department of the government to enforce the performance of such duties by the President might be justly characterized, in the language of Chief Justice Marshall, as "an absurd and excessive extravagance."

It is true that in the instance before us the interpositon of the court is not sought to enforce action by the Executive under constitutional legislation, but to restrain such action under legislation alleged to be unconstitutional. But we are unable to perceive that this circumstance takes the case out of the general principles which forbid judicial interference with the exercise of Executive discretion.

It was admitted in the argument that the application now made to us is without a precedent; and this is of much weight against it.

Had it been supposed at the bar that this court would, in any case, interpose by injunction to prevent the execution of an unconstitutional act of Congress, it can hardly be doubted that applications with that object would have been heretofore addressed to it. . . .

The fact that no such application was ever before made in any case indicates the general judgment of the profession that no such application should be entertained.

It will hardly be contended that Congress [the Courts?] can interpose, in any case, to restrain the enactment of an unconstitutional law; and yet how can the right to judicial interposition to prevent such an enactment, when the purpose is evident and the execution of that purpose certain, be distinguished, in principle, from the right to such interposition against the execution of such a law by the President?

The Congress is the legislative department of the government; the President is the executive department. Neither can be restrained in its action by the judicial department; though the acts of both, when performed, are, in proper cases, subject to its cognizance.

The impropriety of such interference will be clearly seen upon consideration of its possible consequences.

Suppose the bill filed and the injunction prayed for [be] allowed. If the President refuse obedience, it is needless to observe that the court is without power to enforce its process. If, on the other hand, the President complies with the order of the court and refuses to execute the acts of Congress, is it not clear that a collision may occur between the executive and legislative departments of the government? May not the House of Representatives impeach the President for such refusal? And in that case could this court interfere, in behalf of the President, thus endangered by compliance with its mandate, and restrain by injunction the Senate of the United States from sitting as a court of impeachment? Would the strange spectacle be offered to the public world of an attempt by this court to arrest proceedings in that court?

These questions answer themselves. . . .

It has been suggested that the bill contains a prayer that, if the relief sought cannot be had against Andrew Johnson as President, it may be granted against Andrew Johnson as a citizen of Tennessee. But it is plain that relief as against the execution of an act of Congress by Andrew Johnson, is relief against its execution by the President. A bill praying an injunction against the execution of an act of Congress by the incumbent of the presidential office cannot be received, whether it describes him as President or as a citizen of a State.

The motion for leave to file the bill is, therefore,

Denied.

YOUNGSTOWN SHEET & TUBE CO. *et al. v.* SAWYER
343 U.S. 579; 72 Sup. Ct. 863; 96 L. Ed. 1153 (1952)

[*This case, which is popularly known as the Steel Seizure case, was the climax of a long dispute between the steel companies and their employees over terms of new collective-bargaining agreements. In December 1951, the United Steelworkers of America, CIO, served notice that a strike would be called on December 31, 1951. The Federal Mediation and Conciliation Service intervened immediately but failed to negotiate a settlement. The President then referred the dispute to the Federal Wage Stabilization Board, which also failed to bring about an agreement. On April 4, 1952, the Union announced that a nationwide strike would begin on April 9. A few hours before the strike deadline, President Truman issued an executive order authorizing Sawyer, the Secretary of Commerce, to seize and continue operation of the steel mills. The President's order was not based on any statutory authority. He directed the seizure because the proposed strike would have seriously jeopardized national defense. (At this time American troops were fighting in Korea.) The Secretary of Commerce issued the appropriate orders taking possession of the steel mills for the United States. President Truman reported the seizure to Congress in two separate messages, but Congress took no action. The steel companies complied with the seizure order under protest and sought an injunction restraining Sawyer from a federal district court. On April 30, the district court issued a preliminary injunction restraining the Secretary of Commerce from "continuing the seizure and possession of the plants." On the same day the court of appeals stayed the district court's injunction. Because the dispute raised issues of vital national importance, the Supreme Court acted promptly; it granted certiorari on May 3, and heard argument on May 12. The decision was handed down on June 2, 1952.]*

MR. JUSTICE BLACK delivered the opinion of the Court:

We are asked to decide whether the President was acting within his constitutional power when he issued an order directing the Secretary of Commerce to take possession of and operate most of the nation's steel mills. The mill owners argue that the President's order amounts to lawmaking, a legislative function which the Constitution has expressly confided to the Congress and not to the President. The Government's position is that the order was made on findings of the President that his action was necessary to avert a national catastrophe which would inevitably result from a stoppage of steel production, and that in meeting this grave emergency the President was acting within the aggregate of his constitutional powers as the nation's Chief Executive and the Commander-in-Chief of the Armed Forces of the United States. . . .

The President's power, if any, to issue the order must stem either from an act of Congress or from the Constitution itself. There is no statute that expressly authorizes the President to take possession of property as he did here. Nor is there any act of Congress to which our attention has been directed from which such a power can fairly be implied. Indeed, we do not understand the Government to rely on statutory authorization for this seizure. There are two statutes which do authorize the President to take both personal and real property under certain conditions. (The Selective Service Act of 1948 and the Defense Production Act of 1950.) However, the Government admits that these conditions were not met and that the President's order was not rooted in either of the statutes. The Government refers to the seizure provisions of one of these statutes . . . as "much too cumbersome, involved, and time-consuming for the crisis which was at hand."

Moreover, the use of the seizure technique to solve labor disputes in order to prevent work stoppages was not only unauthorized by any congressional enactment; prior to this controversy, Congress had refused to adopt that method of settling labor disputes. When the Taft-Hartley Act was under consideration in 1947. Congress rejected an amendment which would have authorized such governmental seizures in cases of emergency. Apparently it was thought that the technique of seizure, like that of compulsory arbitration, would interfere with the process of collective bargaining. Consequently, the plan Congress adopted in that Act did not provide for seizure under any circumstances. Instead, the plan sought to bring about settlements by use of the customary devices of mediation, conciliation, investigation by boards of inquiry, and public reports. In some instances temporary injunctions were authorized to provide cooling-off periods. All this failing, unions were left free to strike after a secret vote by employees as to whether they wished to accept their employers' final settlement offer.

It is clear that if the President had authority to issue the order he did, it must be found in some provision of the Constitution. And it is not claimed that express constitutional language grants this power to the President. The contention is that presidential power should be implied from the aggregate of his powers under the Constitution. Particular reliance is placed on provisions in Article II which say that "The executive Power shall be vested in a President . . ."; that "he shall take Care that the Laws be faithfully executed"; and that he "shall be Commander-in-Chief of the Army and Navy of the United States."

The order cannot properly be sustained as an exercise of the President's military power as Commander-in-Chief of the Armed Forces. The Government attempts to do so by citing a number of cases upholding broad powers in military commanders engaged in day-to-day fighting in a theater of war. Such cases need not concern us here. Even though "theater of war" be an expanding concept, we cannot with faithfulness to our constitutional system hold that the Commander-in-Chief of the Armed Forces has the ultimate power as such to take possession of private property in order to keep labor disputes from stopping production. This is a job for the nation's lawmakers, not for its military authorities.

Nor can the seizure order be sustained because of the several constitutional provisions that grant executive power to the President. In the framework of our Constitution, the President's power to see that the laws are faithfully executed refutes the idea that he is to be a lawmaker. The Constitution limits his functions in the lawmaking process to the recommending of laws he thinks wise and the vetoing of laws he thinks bad. And the Constitution is neither silent nor equivocal about who shall make laws which the President is to execute. The first section of the first article says that "All legislative Powers herein granted shall be vested in a Congress of the United States. . . ."

The President's order does not direct that a congressional policy be executed in a manner prescribed by Congress—it directs that a presidential policy be executed in a manner prescribed by the President. The preamble of the order itself, like that of many statutes, sets out reasons why the President believes certain policies should be adopted, proclaims these policies as rules of conduct to be followed, and again like a statute, authorizes a government official to promulgate additional rules and regulations consistent with the policy proclaimed and needed to carry that policy into execution. The power of Congress to adopt such public policies as those proclaimed by the order is beyond question. It can authorize the taking of private property for public use. It can make laws regulating the relationships between employers and employees, prescribing rules designed to settle labor disputes, and fixing wages and working conditions in certain fields of our economy. The Constitution does not subject this lawmaking power of Congress to presidential or military supervision or control.

It is said that other Presidents without congressional authority have taken possession of private business enterprises in order to settle labor disputes. But even if this be true, Congress has not thereby lost its exclusive constitutional authority to make laws necessary and proper to carry out the powers vested by the Constitution "in the Government of the United States, or any Department or Officer thereof."

The Founders of this nation entrusted the lawmaking power to the Congress alone in both good and bad times. It would do no good to recall the historical events, the fears of power and the hopes for freedom that lay behind their choice. Such a review would but confirm our holding that this seizure order cannot stand.

The judgement of the District Court is

Affirmed.

MR. JUSTICE FRANKFURTER, concurring:

Although the considerations relevant to the legal enforcement of the principle of separation of powers seem to me more complicated and flexible than may appear from what Mr. Justice Black has written, I join his opinion because I thoroughly agree with the application of the principle to the circumstances of this case. . . .

The issue before us can be met, and therefore should be, without attempting to define the President's powers comprehensively. I shall not attempt to delineate what belongs to him by virtue of his office beyond the power even of Congress to contract; what authority belongs to him until Congress acts; what kind of problems may be dealt with either by the Congress or by the President or by both . . .; what power must be exercised by the Congress and cannot be delegated to the President. It is as unprofitable to lump together in an undiscriminating hotch-potch past presidential actions claimed to be derived from occupancy of the office as it is to conjure up hypothetical future cases. The judiciary may, as this case proves, have to intervene in determining where authority lies as between the democratic forces in our scheme of government. But in doing so we should be wary and humble. Such is the teaching of this Court's role in the history of the country.

It is in this mood and with this perspective that the issue before the Court must be approached. We must therefore put to one side consideration of what powers the President would have had if there had been no legislation whatever bearing on the authority asserted by the seizure, or if the seizure had been only for a short, explicitly temporary period, to be terminated automatically unless Congressional approval were given. These and other questions, like or unlike, are not now here. I would exceed my authority were I to say anything about them.

The question before the Court comes in this setting. Congress has frequently —at least sixteen times since 1916— specifically provided for executive seizure of production, transportation, communications, or storage facilities. In every case it has qualified this grant of power with limitations and safeguards. This body of enactments . . . demonstrates that Congress deemed seizure so drastic a power as to require that it be carefully circumscribed whenever the President was vested with this extraordinary authority. The power to seize has uniformly been given only for a limited period or for a defined emergency, or has been repealed after a short period. Its exercise has been restricted to particular circumstances such as "time of war or when war is imminent," "the needs of public safety" or of "national security or defense," or "urgent and impending need." The period of governmental operation has been limited, as, for instance, to "sixty days after the restoration of productive efficiency." Seizure statutes usually make executive action dependent on detailed conditions: for example, (a) failure or refusal of the owner of a plant to meet governmental supply needs or (b) failure of voluntary negotiations with the owner for the use of a plant necessary for great public ends. Congress often has specified the particular executive agency which should seize or operate the plants or whose judgment would appropriately test the need for seizure. Congress also has not left to implication that just compensation be paid; it has usually legislated in detail regarding enforcement of this litigation-breeding general requirement. . . .

Congress in 1947 was again called upon to consider whether governmental seizure should be used to avoid serious industrial shutdowns. Congress decided against conferring such power generally and in advance, without special Congressional enactment to meet each particular need. Under the urgency of telephone and coal strikes in the winter of 1946, Congress addressed itself to the problems raised by "national emergency" strikes and lockouts. The termination of wartime seizure powers on December 31, 1946, brought these matters to the attention of Congress with vivid impact. A proposal that the President be given powers to seize plants to avert a shutdown where the "health or safety" of the nation was endangered, was thoroughly canvassed by Congress and rejected. No room for doubt remains that the proponents as well as the opponents of the bill which became the Labor Management Relations Act of 1947 clearly understood that as a result of that legislation the only recourse for preventing a shutdown in any basic industry, after failure of mediation, was Congress. Authorization for seizure as an available remedy for potential dangers was unequivocally put aside. . . .

In adopting the provisions which it did, by the Labor Management Relations Act of 1947, for dealing with a "national emergency" arising out of a breakdown in peaceful industrial relations, Congress was very familiar with governmental seizure as a protective measure. On a balance of considerations, Congress chose not to lodge this power in the President. It chose not to make available in advance a remedy to which both industry and labor were fiercely hostile. In deciding that authority to seize should be given to the President only after full consideration of the particular situation should show such legislation to be necessary, Congress presumably acted on experience with similar industrial conflicts in the past. It evidently assumed that industrial shutdowns in basic industries are not instances of spontaneous generation, and that danger warnings are sufficiently plain before the event to give ample opportunity to start the legislative process into action.

In any event, nothing can be plainer than that Congress made a conscious choice of policy in a field full of perplexity and peculiarly within legislative responsibility for choice. In formulating legislation for dealing with industrial conflicts, Congress could not more clearly and emphatically have withheld authority than it did in 1947. . . .

By the Labor Management Relations Act of 1947, Congress said to the President, "You may not seize. Please report to us and ask for seizure power if you think it is needed in a specific situation. . . ." But it is now claimed that the President has seizure power by virtue of the Defense Production Act of 1950 and its Amendments. And the claim is based on the occurence of new events—Korea and the need for stabilization, etc.—although it was well known that seizure power was withheld by the Act of 1947, and although the President, whose specific requests for other authority were in the main granted by Congress, never suggested that in view of the new events he needed the power of seizure which Congress in its judgment had decided to withhold from him. . . .

MR. JUSTICE JACKSON, concurring:

The actual art of governing under our Constitution does not and cannot conform to judicial definitions of the power of any of its branches based on isolated clauses or even single Articles torn from context. While the Constitution diffuses power the better to secure liberty, it also contemplates that practice will integrate the dispersed powers into a workable government. It enjoins upon its branches separateness but interdependence, autonomy but reciprocity. Presidential powers are not fixed but fluctuate, depending upon their disjunction or conjunction with those of Congress. We may well begin by a somewhat over-simplified grouping of practical situations in which a President may doubt, or others may challenge, his powers, and by distinguishing roughly the legal consequences of this factor of relativity.

1. When the President acts pursuant to an express or implied authorization of Congress, his authority is at its maximum, for it includes all that he possesses in his own right plus all that Congress can delegate. In these circumstances, and in these only, may he be said (for what it may be worth) to personify the federal sovereignty. If his act is held unconstitutional under these circumstances, it usually means that the Federal Government as an undivided whole lacks power. A seizure executed by the President pursuant to an Act of Congress would be supported by the strongest of presumptions and the widest latitude of judicial interpretation, and the burden of persuasion would rest heavily upon any who might attack it.

2. When the President acts in absence of either a congressional grant or denial of authority, he can only rely upon his own independent powers, but there is a zone of twilight in which he and Congress may have concurrent authority, or in which its distribution is uncertain. Therefore, congressional inertia, indifference or quiescence may sometimes, at least as a practical matter, enable, if not invite, measures on independent presidential responsibility. In this area, any actual test of power is likely to depend on the imperatives of events and contemporary imponderables rather than on abstract theories of law.

3. When the President takes measures incompatible with the expressed or implied will of Congress, his power is at its lowest ebb, for then he can rely only upon his own constitutional powers minus any constitutional powers of Congress over the matter. Courts can sustain exclusive presidential control in such a case only by disabling the Congress from acting upon the subject. Presidential claim to a power at once so conclusive and preclusive must be scrutinized with caution, for what is at stake

is the equilibrium established by our constitutional system.

Into which of these classifications does this executive seizure of the steel industry fit? It is eliminated from the first by admission, for it is conceded that no congressional authorization exists for this seizure. That takes away also the support of the many precedents and declarations which were made in relation, and must be confined, to this category.

Can it then be defended under flexible tests available to the second category? It seems clearly eliminated from that class because Congress has not left seizure of private property an open field but has covered it by three statutory policies inconsistent with this seizure. In cases where the purpose is to supply needs of the Government itself, two courses are provided: one, seizure of a plant which fails to comply with obligatory orders placed by the Government; another, condemnation of facilities, including temporary use under the power of eminent domain. The third is applicable where it is the general economy of the country that is to be protected rather than exclusive governmental interests. None of these were invoked. In choosing a different and inconsistent way of his own, the President cannot claim that it is necessitated or invited by failure of Congress to legislate upon the occasions, grounds, and methods for seizure of industrial properties.

This leaves the current seizure to be justified only by the severe tests under the third grouping, where it can be supported only by any remainder of executive power after substraction of such powers as Congress may have over the subject. In short, we can sustain the President only by holding that seizure of such strike-bound industries is within his domain and beyond control

of Congress. Thus, this Court's first review of such seizures occurs under circumstances which leave presidential power most vulnerable to attack and in the least favorable of possible constitutional postures. . . .

MR. JUSTICE BURTON, concurring:

The controlling fact here is that Congress, within its constitutionally delegated power, has prescribed for the President specific procedures, exclusive of seizure, for his use in meeting the present type of emergency. Congress has reserved to itself the right to determine where and when to authorize the seizure of property in meeting such an emergency. Under these circumstances, the President's order of April 8 invaded the jurisdiction of Congress. It violated the essence of the principle of the separation of governmental powers. Accordingly, the injunction against its effectiveness should be sustained.

MR. JUSTICE CLARK, concurring:

I conclude that where Congress has laid down specific procedures to deal with the type of crisis confronting the President, he must follow those procedures in meeting the crisis; but that in the absence of such action by Congress, the President's independent power to act depends upon the gravity of the situation confronting the nation, I cannot sustain the seizure in question because here . . . Congress had prescribed methods to be followed by the President in meeting the emergency at hand. . . .

[MR. JUSTICE DOUGLAS also wrote a concurring opinion.]

MR. CHIEF JUSTICE VINSON, with whom MR. JUSTICE REED and MR. JUSTICE MINTON join, dissenting:

. . . Focusing now on the situation confronting the President on the night of April 8, 1952, we cannot but conclude that the President was performing his duty under the Constitution to "take Care that the Laws be faithfully executed"—a duty described by President Benjamin Harrison as "the central idea of the office."

The President reported to Congress the morning after the seizure that he acted because a work stoppage in steel production would immediately imperil the safety of the nation by preventing execution of the legislative programs for procurement of military equipment. And, while a shutdown could be averted by granting the price concessions requested by plaintiffs, granting such concessions would disrupt the price stabilization program also enacted by Congress. Rather than fail to execute either legislative program, the President acted to execute both.

Much of the argument in this case has been directed at straw men. We do not now have before us the case of a President acting solely on the basis of his own notions of the public welfare. Nor is there any question of unlimited executive power in this case. The President himself closed the door to any such claim when he sent his Message to Congress stating his purpose to abide by any action of Congress, whether approving or disapproving his seizure action. Here, the President immediately made sure that Congress was fully informed of the temporary action he had taken only to preserve the legislative programs from destruction until Congress could act.

The absence of a specific statute authorizing seizure of the steel mills as a mode of executing the laws—both the military procurement program and the anti-inflation program—has not until today been thought to prevent the President from executing the laws. Unlike an administrative commission confined to the enforcement of the statute under which is was created, or the head of a department when administering a particular statute, the President is a constitutional officer charged with taking care that a "mass of legislation" be executed. Flexibility as to mode of execution to meet critical situations is a matter of practical necessity. . . .

As the District Judge stated, this is no time for "timorous" judicial action. But neither is this a time for timorous executive action. Faced with the duty of executing the defense programs which Congress had enacted and the disastrous effects that any stoppage in steel production would have on these programs, the President acted to preserve those programs by seizing the steel mills. There is no question that the possession was other than temporary in character and subject to congressional direction—either approving, disapproving, or regulating the manner in which the mills were to be administered and returned to the owners. The President immediately informed Congress of his action and clearly stated his intention to abide by the legislative will. No basis for claims of arbitrary action, unlimited powers, or dictatorial usurpation of congressional power appears from the facts of this case. On the contrary, judicial, legislative, and executive precedents throughout our history demonstrate that in this case the President acted in full conformity with his duties under the Constitution. Accordingly, we would reverse the order of the District Court.

MYERS v. UNITED STATES
272 U.S. 52; 47 Sup. Ct. 21; 71 L. Ed. 160 (1926)

[*In 1917, Frank S. Myers was appointed postmaster of Portland, Oregon, for a term of four years by President Wilson. About three years later, Myers was re-*

moved from the politically sensitive office by the President without the consent of the Senate. The 1876 statute under which Myers was appointed, and which was still in force, provided that postmasters could be removed by the President only "with the advice and consent of the Senate." Wilson made a recess appointment to fill Myers' post, but the Senate never confirmed it. In the meantime, Myers protested his removal and refused to pursue any other occupation. When the four-year period for which he had been appointed expired, he sued in the United States Court of Claims for the salary due him; this amounted to $8,838.71. The Court of Claims ruled against Myers, holding that he had lost his right of action because of the delay in suing. While the case was still being litigated, Myers died. His widow then brought the case to the Supreme Court on appeal.

An interesting sidelight to this case is that both Justices Brandeis and Mc-Reynolds (as well as Holmes) dissented sharply from the opinion of Chief Justice Taft, who, as President, had named both men to the Court.]

MR. CHIEF JUSTICE TAFT delivered the opinion of the Court:

This case presents the question whether under the Constitution the President has the exclusive power of removing executive officers of the United States whom he has appointed by and with the advice and consent of the Senate. . . .

The question where the power of removal of executive officers appointed by the President by and with the advice and consent of the Senate was vested, was presented early in the first session of the First Congress. There is no express provision respecting removals in the Constitution, except as Section 4 of Article 2 . . . provides for removal from office by impeachment. The subject was not discussed in the Constitution Convention. . . .

In the House of Representatives of the First Congress, on Tuesday, May 18, 1789, Mr. Madison moved in the Committee of the Whole that there should be established three executive departments, one of Foreign Affairs, another of the Treasury, and a third of War, at the head of each of which there should be a Secretary to be appointed by the President by and with the advice and consent of the Senate, and to be removable by the President. The committee agreed to the establishment

of a Department of Foreign Affairs, but a discussion ensued as to making the Secretary removable by the President. . . . "The question was now taken and carried, by a considerable majority, in favor of declaring the power of removal to be in the President. . . ."

Mr. Madison and his associates in the discussion in the House dwelt at length upon the necessity there was for construing Article 2 to give the President the sole power of removal in his responsibility for the conduct of the executive branch, and enforced this by emphasizing his duty expressly declared in the third section of the Article to "take care that the laws be faithfully executed. . . ."

The vesting of the executive power in the President was essentially a grant of the power to execute the laws. But the President alone and unaided could not execute the laws. He must execute them by the assistance of subordinates. This view has since been repeatedly affirmed by this court. . . . As he is specifically to take care that they be faithfully executed, the reasonable implication, even in the absence of express words, was that as part of his executive power he should select those who were to act for him under his direction in the execution of the laws. The further implication must be, in the absence of any express limitation respecting removals, that as his selection of administrative officers is essential to the execution of the laws by him, so must be his power of removing those for whom he can not continue to be responsible. . . . It was urged that the natural meaning of the term "executive power" granted the President included the appointment and removal of executive subordinates. If such appointments and removals were not in exercise of the executive power, what were they? They certainly were not the exercise of legislative or judicial power in government as usually understood. . . .

It was pointed out in this great debate [of 1789] that the power of removal, though equally essential to the executive power, is different in its nature from that of appointment. . . . A veto by the Senate—a part of the legislative branch of the government—upon removals is a much greater limitation upon the executive branch and a much more serious blending of the legislative with the executive than a rejection of a proposed appointment. It is not to be implied. The rejection of a nominee of the President for a particular office does not greatly embarrass him in the conscientious discharge of his high duties in the selection of those who are to aid him, because the President usually has an ample field from which to select for office, according to his preference, competent and capable men. The Senate has full power to reject newly-proposed appointees whenever the President shall remove the incumbents. Such a check enables the Senate to prevent the filling of offices with bad or incompetent men or with those against whom there is tenable objection.

The power to prevent the removal of an officer who has served under the President is different from the authority to consent to or reject his appointment. When a nomination is made, it may be presumed that the Senate is, or may become, as well advised as to the fitness of the nominee as the President, but in the nature of things the defects in ability or intelligence or loyalty in the administration of the laws of one who has served as an officer under the President, are facts as to which the President, or his trusted subordinates, must be better informed than the Senate, and the power to remove him may, therefore, be regarded as confined for very sound and practical reasons, to the governmental authority which has administrative control. The power of removal is incident to the power of appointment, not to the power of advising and consenting to appointment, and when the grant of the executive power is enforced by the express mandate to take care that the laws be faithfully executed, it emphasizes the necessity for including within the executive power as conferred the exclusive power of removal. . . .

A reference of the whole power of removal to general legislation by Congress is quite out of keeping with the plan of government devised by the framers of the Constitution. It could never have been intended to leave to Congress unlimited discretion to vary fundamentally the operation of the great independent executive branch of government and thus most seriously to weaken it. It would be a delegation by the Convention to Congress of the function of defining the primary boundaries of another of the three great divisions of government. The inclusion of removals of executive officers in the executive power vested in the President by Article 2 according to its usual definition, and the implication of his power of removal of such officers from the provision of Section 2 expressly recognizing in him the power of their appointment, are a much more natural and appropriate source of the removing power.

It is reasonable to suppose also that

had it been intended to give to Congress power to regulate or control removals in the manner suggested, it would have been included among the specifically enumerated legislative powers in Article 1, or in the specified limitations on the executive power in Article 2. The difference between the grant of legislative power under Article 1 to Congress which is limited to powers therein enumerated, and the more general grant of the executive power to the President under Article 2, is significant. The fact that the executive power is given in general terms strengthened by specific terms where emphasis is appropriate, and limited by direct expressions where limitation is needed, and that no express limit is placed on the power of removal by the executive is a convincing indication that none was intended. . . .

We come now to consider an argument advanced and strongly pressed on behalf of the complainant, that this case concerns only the removal of a postmaster, that a postmaster is an inferior officer, that such an office was not included within the legislative decision of 1789, which related only to superior officers to be appointed by the President by and with the advice and consent of the Senate. . . .

The power to remove inferior executive officers, like that to remove superior executive officers, is an incident of the power to appoint them, and is in its nature an executive power. The authority of Congress given by the excepting clause to vest the appointment of such inferior officers in the heads of departments carries with it authority incidentally to invest the heads of departments with power to remove. It has been the practice of Congress to do so and this court has recognized that power. The court also has recognized . . . that Congress in committing the appointment of such inferior officers to the heads of departments may prescribe incidental regulations controlling and restricting the latter in the exercise of the power of removal. But the court never has held, nor reasonably could hold, although it is argued to the contrary on behalf of the appellant, that the excepting clause enables Congress to draw to itself, or to either branch of it, the power to remove or the right to participate in the exercise of that power. To do this would be to go beyond the words and implications of that clause and to infringe the constitutional principle of the separation of governmental powers.

Assuming then the power of Congress to regulate removals as incidental to the exercise of its constitutional power to vest appointments of inferior officers in the heads of departments, certainly so long as Congress does not exercise that power, the power of removal must remain where the Constitution places it, with the President, as part of the executive power, in accordance with the legislative decision of 1789 which we have been considering. . . .

For the reasons given, we must therefore hold that the provision of the law of 1876 by which the unrestricted power of removal of first-class postmasters is denied to the President is in violation of the Constitution and invalid. This leads to an affirmance of the judgment of the Court of Claims. . . .

Judgment

Affirmed.

MR. JUSTICE HOLMES, dissenting:

My brothers McReynolds and Brandeis have discussed the question before us with exhaustive research and I say a few words merely to emphasize my agreement with their conclusion.

The arguments drawn from the executive power of the President, and from his duty to appoint officers of the United States (when Congress does not vest the appointment elsewhere), to take care that the laws be faithfully executed, and to commission all officers of the

United States, seem to me spiders' webs inadequate to control the dominant facts.

We have to deal with an office that owes its existence to Congress and that Congress may abolish tomorrow. Its duration and the pay attached to it while it lasts depend on Congress alone. Congress alone confers on the President the power to appoint to it and at any time may transfer the power to other hands. With such power over its own creation, I have no more trouble in believing that Congress has power to prescribe a term of life for it free from any interference than I have in accepting the undoubted power of Congress to decree its end. I have equally little trouble in accepting its power to prolong the tenure of an incumbent until Congress or the Senate shall have assented to his removal. The duty of the President to see that the laws be executed is a duty that does not go beyond the laws or require him to achieve more than Congress sees fit to leave within his power.

The separate opinion of MR. JUSTICE MC REYNOLDS:

. . . The long struggle for civil service reform and the legislation designed to insure some security of official tenure ought not to be forgotten. Again and again Congress has enacted statutes prescribing restrictions on removals and by approving them many Presidents have affirmed its power therein. . . .

Nothing short of language clear beyond serious disputation should be held to clothe the President with authority wholly beyond congressional control arbitrarily to dismiss every officer whom he appoints except a few judges. There are no such words in the Constitution, and the asserted inference conflicts with the heretofore accepted theory that this government is one of carefully enumerated powers under an intelligible character. . . .

If the phrase "executive power" in-

folds the one now claimed many others heretofore totally unsuspected may lie there awaiting future supposed necessity; and no human intelligence can define the field of the President's permissible activities. "A masked battery of constructive powers would complete the destruction of liberty. . . ."

Congress has long and vigorously asserted its right to restrict removals and there has been no common executive practice based upon a contrary view. The President has often removed, and it is admitted that he may remove, with either the express or implied assent of Congress; but the present theory is that he may override the declared will of that body. This goes far beyond any practice heretofore approved or followed; it conflicts with the history of the Constitution, with the ordinary rules of interpretation, and with the construction approved by Congress since the beginning and emphatically sanctioned by this court. To adopt it would be revolutionary. . . .

In any rational search for answers to the questions arising upon this record, it is important not to forget—

That this is a government of limited powers definitely enumerated and granted by a written Constitution.

That the Constitution must be interpreted by attributing to its words the meaning which they bore at the time of its adoption and in view of commonly-accepted canons of construction, its history, early and long-continued practices under it, and relevant opinions of this court.

That the Constitution endows Congress with plenary powers "to establish post offices and post roads."

That, exercising this power during the years from 1789 to 1836, Congress provided for postmasters and vested the power to appoint and remove all of them at pleasure in the Postmaster General.

That the Constitution contains no words which specifically grant to the President power to remove duly appointed officers. And it is definitely settled that he cannot remove those whom he has not appointed—certainly they can be removed only as Congress may permit.

That postmasters are inferior officers within the meaning of Art. 2, Section 2, of the Constitution.

That from its first session to the last one Congress has often asserted its right to restrict the President's power to remove inferior officers, although appointed by him with the consent of the Senate.

That many Presidents have approved statutes limiting the power of the executive to remove, and that from the beginning such limitations have been respected in practice.

That this court, as early as 1803, in an opinion never overruled and rendered in a case where it was necessary to decide the question, positively declared that the President had no power to remove at will an inferior officer appointed with consent of the Senate to serve for a definite term fixed by an Act of Congress.

That the power of Congress to restrict removals by the President was recognized by this court as late as 1903. . . .

That the proceedings in the Constitutional Convention of 1787, the political history of the times, contemporaneous opinion, common canons of construction, the action of Congress from the beginning and opinions of this court, all oppose the theory that by vesting "the executive power" in the President the Constitution gave him an illimitable right to remove inferior officers. . . .

MR. JUSTICE BRANDEIS, dissenting:

The separation of the powers of government did not make each branch completely autonomous. It left each in some measure, dependent upon the others, as it left to each power to exercise, in some respects, functions in their nature executive, legislative and judicial. Obviously the President cannot secure full execution of the laws, if Congress denies to him adequate means of doing so. Full execution may be defeated because Congress declines to create offices indispensable for that purpose. Or, because Congress having created the office, declines to make the indispensable appropriation. Or, because Congress having both created the office and made the appropriation, prevents, by restrictions which it imposes, the appointment of officials who in quality and character are indispensable to the efficient execution of the law. If, in any such way, adequate means are denied to the President, the fault will lie with Congress. The President performs his full constitutional duty, if, with the means and instruments provided by Congress and within the limitations prescribed by it, he uses his best endeavors to secure the faithful execution of the laws enacted. . . .

Checks and balances were established in order that this should be "a government of laws and not of men. . . ." [A]n uncontrollable power of removal in the Chief Executive "is a doctrine not to be learned in American governments. . . ." The doctrine of the separation of powers was adopted by the Convention of 1787 not to promote efficiency but to preclude the exercise of arbitrary power. The purpose was not to avoid friction, but, by means of the inevitable friction incident to the distribution of the governmental powers among three departments, to save the people from autocracy. In order to prevent arbitrary executive action, the Constitution provided in terms that presidential appointments be made with the consent of the Senate, unless Congress should otherwise provide; and this clause was construed by Alexander Hamilton in *The Federalist,* No. 77, as requiring like consent to removals. Limiting further executive prerogatives customary in monarchies, the Constitution empowered Congress to vest the appointment of inferior officers, "as we think proper, in the President alone, in the Courts of Law, or in the Heads of Departments." Nothing in support of the claim of uncontrollable power can be inferred from the silence of the Convention of 1787 on the subject of re-

moval. For the outstanding fact remains that every specific proposal to confer such uncontrollable power upon the President was rejected. In America, as in England, the conviction prevailed then that the people must look to representative assemblies for the protection of their liberties. And protection of the individual, even if he be an official, from the arbitrary or capricious exercise of power was then believed to be an essential of free government.

HUMPHREY'S EXECUTOR *v.* UNITED STATES
295 U.S. 602; 55 Sup. Ct. 869; 79 L. Ed. 1611 (1935)

[*In 1931, William E. Humphrey was nominated by President Hoover to succeed himself as a member of the Federal Trade Commission. Upon Senate confirmation, Humphrey was appointed to the commission for a seven-year term. His term was to expire in 1938. However, in 1933, President Roosevelt asked Humphrey to resign so that he could be replaced by a commissioner whose views concerning business regulation were in harmony with those of the President and his new administration. After some correspondence with the President, Humphrey refused to resign. In October 1933, the President removed him from his office. Humphrey insisted that he could not be removed and continued to perform the duties of his office without compensation. When Humphrey died, his executor (Rathbun) sued in the Court of Claims to recover the Commissioner's salary from the time the President attempted to remove him from office to the time of his death in 1934. The Court of Claims certified two questions relating to the removal power of the President to the Supreme Court for decision.*]

MR. JUSTICE SUTHERLAND delivered the opinion of the Court:

. . . [T]he following questions are certified:

"1. Do the provisions of section 1 of the Federal Trade Commission Act, stating that 'any commissioner may be removed by the President for inefficiency, neglect of duty, or malfeasance in office,' restrict or limit the power of the President to remove a commissioner except upon one or more of the causes named?"

"If the foregoing question is answered in the affirmative, then—

"2. If the power of the President to remove a commissioner is restricted or

limited as shown by the foregoing interrogatory and the answer made thereto, is such a restriction or limitation valid under the Constitution of the United States?" . . .

First. The question first to be considered is whether, by the provisions of §1 of the Federal Trade Commission Act already quoted, the President's power is limited to removal for the specific causes enumerated therein. . . .

The statute fixes a term of office, in accordance with many precedents. The first commissioners appointed are to continue in office for terms of three, four, five, six, and seven years, respectively; and their successors are to be appointed for a term of seven years—any commissioner being subject to removal by the President for inefficiency, neglect of duty, or malfeasance in office. The words of the act are definite and unambiguous.

The government says the phrase "continue in office" is of no legal significance and, moreover, applies only to the first commissioners. We think it has significance. It may be that, literally, its application is restricted as suggested; but it, nevertheless, lends support to a view contrary to that of the government as to the meaning of the entire requirement in respect of tenure; for it is not easy to suppose that Congress intended to secure the first commissioners against removal except for the causes specified and deny like security to their successors. Putting this phrase aside, however, the fixing of a definite term subject to removal for cause, unless there be some countervailing provision or circumstance indicating the contrary, which here we are unable to find, is enough to establish the legislative intent that the term is not to be curtailed in the absence of such cause. But if the intention of Congress that no removal should be made during the specified term except for one or more of the enumerated causes were not clear upon the face of the statute, as we think it is, it would be made clear by a consideration of the character of the commission and the legislative history which accompanied and preceded the passage of the act.

The commission is to be nonpartisan; and it must, from the very nature of its duties, act with entire impartiality. It is charged with the enforcement of no policy except the policy of the law. Its duties are neither political nor executive, but predominantly quasi-judicial and quasi-legislative. Like the Interstate Commerce Commission, its members are called upon to exercise the trained judgment of a body of experts "appointed by law and informed by experience. . . ."

The legislative reports in both houses of Congress clearly reflect the view that a fixed term was necessary to the effective and fair administration of the law. . . .

The debates in both houses demonstrate that the prevailing view was that the commission was not to be "subject to anybody in the government but . . . only to the people of the United States"; free from "political domination or control" or the "probability or possibility of such a thing"; to be "separate and apart from any existing department of the government—not subject to the orders of the President. . . ."

Thus, the language of the act, the legislative reports, and the general purposes of the legislation as reflected by the debates, all combine to demonstrate the Congressional intent to create a body of experts who shall gain experience by length of service—a body which shall be independent of executive authority, *except in its selection,* and free to exercise its judgment without the leave or hindrance of any other official or any department of the government. To the accomplishment of these purposes, it is clear that Congress was of opinion that length and certainty of tenure would vitally contribute. And to hold that, nevertheless, the members of the commission continue in office at the mere will of the President, might be to thwart, in large measure, the very ends which Congress sought to realize by definitely fixing the term of office.

We conclude that the intent of the act is to limit the executive power of removal to the causes enumerated, the existence of none of which is claimed here; and we pass to the second question.

Second. To support its contention that the removal provision of §1, as we have just construed it, is an unconstitutional interference with the executive power of the President, the government's chief reliance is *Myers* v. *United States*. . . .

The office of a postmaster is so essentially unlike the office now involved that the decision in the *Myers* case cannot be accepted as controlling our decision here. A postmaster is an executive officer restricted to the performance of executive functions. He is charged with no duty at all related to either the legislative or judicial power. The actual decision in the *Myers* case finds support in the theory that such an officer is merely one of the units in the executive department and, hence, inherently subject to the exclusive and illimitable power of removal by the Chief Executive, whose subordinate and aid he is. Putting aside *dicta,* which may be followed if sufficiently persuasive but which are not controlling, the necessary reach of the decision goes far enough to include all purely executive officers. It goes no farther;—much less does it include an officer who occupies no place in the executive department and who exercises no part of the executive power vested by the Constitution in the President.

The Federal Trade Commission is an administrative body created by Congress to carry into effect legislative policies embodied in the statute in accordance with the legislative standard therein prescribed, and to perform other specified duties as a legislative or as a judicial aid. Such a body cannot in any proper sense be characterized as an arm or an eye of the executive. Its duties are performed without executive leave and, in the contemplation of the statute, must be free from executive control. In administering the provisions of the statute in respect of "unfair methods of competition"—that is to say, in filling in and administering the details embodied by that general standard—the commis-

sion acts in part quasi-legislatively and in part quasi-judicially. In making investigations and reports thereon for the information of Congress under §6, in aid of the legislative power, it acts as a legislative agency. Under §7, which authorizes the commission to act as a master in chancery under rules prescribed by the court, it acts as an agency of the judiciary. To the extent that it exercises any executive function —as distinguished from executive power in the constitutional sense—it does so in the discharge and effectuation of its quasi-legislative or quasi-judicial powers, or as an agency of the legislative or judicial departments of the government.

If Congress is without authority to prescribe causes for removal of members of the trade commission and limit executive power of removal accordingly, that power at once becomes practically all-inclusive in respect of civil officers with the exception of the judiciary provided for by the Constitution. The Solicitor General, at the bar, apparently recognizing this to be true, with commendable candor, agreed that his view in respect of the removability of members of the Federal Trade Commission necessitated a like view in respect to the Interstate Commerce Commission and the Court of Claims. We are thus confronted with the serious question whether not only the members of these quasi-legislative and quasi-judicial bodies, but the judges of the legislative Court of Claims, exercising judicial power . . . , continue in office only at the pleasure of the President.

We think it plain under the Constitution that illimitable power of removal is not possessed by the President in respect of officers of the character of those just named. The authority of Congress, in creating quasi-legislative or quasi-judicial agencies, to require them to act in discharge of their duties independently of executive control cannot well be doubted; and that authority includes, as an appropriate incident, power to fix the period during which they shall continue in office, and to forbid their removal except for cause in the meantime. For it is quite evident that one who holds his office only during the pleasure of another, cannot be depended upon to maintain an attitude of independence against the latter's will.

The fundamental necessity of maintaining each of the three general departments of government entirely free from the control or coercive influence, direct or indirect, of either of the others, has often been stressed and is hardly open to serious question. So much is implied in the very fact of the separation of the powers of these departments by the Constitution; and in the rule which recognizes their essential coequality. The sound application of a principle that makes one master in his own house precludes him from imposing his control in the house of another who is master there. . . .

The power of removal here claimed for the President falls within this principle, since its coercive influence threatens the independence of a commission, which is not only wholly disconnected from the executive department, but which, as already fully appears, was created by Congress as a means of carrying into operation legislative and judicial powers, and as an agency of the legislative and judicial departments. . . .

The result of what we now have said is this: Whether the power of the President to remove an officer shall prevail over the authority of Congress to condition the power by fixing a definite term and precluding a removal except for cause, will depend upon the character of the office; the *Myers* decision, affirming the power of the President alone to make the removal, is confined to purely executive officers; and as to officers of the kind here under consideration, we hold that no removal can be made during the prescribed term for which the officer is appointed, except for one or more of the causes named in the applicable statute:

To the extent that, between the decision in the *Myers* case, which sustains the unrestrictable power of the President to remove purely executive officers, and our present decision that such power does not extend to an office such as that here involved, there shall remain a field of doubt, we leave such cases as may fall within it for future consideration and determination as they may arise.

In accordance with the foregoing, the questions submitted are answered.

Question No. 1, Yes.
Question No. 2, Yes.

UNITED STATES *v.* CURTISS-WRIGHT EXPORT CORP. *et al.*
299 U.S. 304; 57 Sup. Ct. 216; 81 L. Ed. 255 (1936)

[A Joint Resolution of Congress approved on May 28, 1934, empowered the President to prohibit the sale of arms and munitions to Bolivia and Paraguay, who were then at war, if in his judgment such an action might restore peace. On the same day, President F. D. Roosevelt issued a proclamation forbidding the sale of war materials to both countries. Violation of the presidential proclamation constituted a crime punishable by fine or imprisonment, or both. The Curtiss-Wright Corporation was charged with having conspired to sell fifteen machine guns to Bolivia in violation of the President's order. The company demurred to the indictment on the ground that the joint resolution's delegation of power to

*the President was invalid. After the District Court of New York sustained the
demurrer, the United States appealed directly to the Supreme Court.*]

MR. JUSTICE SUTHERLAND delivered the opinion of the Court:

. . . *First.* It is contended that by the Joint Resolution, the going into effect and continued operation of the resolution was conditioned (a) upon the President's judgment as to its beneficial effect upon the re-establishment of peace between the countries engaged in armed conflict in the Chaco; (b) upon the making of a proclamation, which was left to his unfettered discretion, thus constituting an attempted substitution of the President's will for that of Congress; (c) upon the making of a proclamation putting an end to the operation of the resolution, which again was left to the President's unfettered discretion; and (d) further, that the extent of its operation in particular cases was subject to limitation and exception by the President, controlled by no standard. In each of these particulars, appellees urge that Congress abdicated its essential functions and delegated them to the Executive.

Whether, if the Joint Resolution had related solely to internal affairs it would be open to the challenge that it constituted an unlawful delegation of legislative power to the Executive, we find it unnecessary to determine. The whole aim of the resolution is to affect a situation entirely external to the United States, and falling within the category of foreign affairs. The determination which we are called to make, therefore, is whether the Joint Resolution, as applied to that situation, is vulnerable to attack under the rule that forbids a delegation of the law-making power. In other words, assuming (but not deciding) that the challenged delegation, if it were confined to internal affairs, would be invalid, may it nevertheless be sustained on the ground that its ex-

clusive aim to afford a remedy for a hurtful condition within foreign territory?

It will contribute to the elucidation of the question if we first consider the differences between the powers of the federal government in respect of foreign or external affairs and those in respect of domestic or internal affairs. That there are differences between them, and that these differences are fundamental, may not be doubted.

The two classes of powers are different, both in respect of their origin and their nature. The broad statement that the federal government can exercise no powers except those specifically enumerated in the constitution, and such implied powers as are necessary and proper to carry into effect the enumerated powers, is categorically true only in respect of our internal affairs. In that field, the primary purpose of the Constitution was to carve from the general mass of legislative powers *then possessed by the states* such portions as it was thought desirable to vest in the federal government, leaving those not included in the enumeration still in the states. . . . That this doctrine applies only to powers which the states had, is self-evident. And since the states severally never possessed international powers, such powers could not have been carved from the mass of state powers but obviously were transmitted to the United States from some other source. During the colonial period, those powers were possessed exclusively by and were entirely under the control of the Crown. By the Declaration of Independence, "the Representatives of the United States of America" declared the United (not the several) Colonies to be free and independent states, and as such to have "full Power to levy

War, conclude Peace, contract Alliances, establish Commerce and to do all other Acts and Things which Independent States may of right do."

As a result of the separation from Great Britain by the colonies acting as a unit, the powers of external sovereignty passed from the Crown not to the colonies severally, but to the colonies in their collective and corporate capacity as the United States of America. Even before the Declaration, the colonies were a unit in foreign affairs, acting through a common agency—namely the Continental Congress, composed of delegates from the thirteen colonies. That agency exercised the powers of war and peace, raised an army, created a navy, and finally adopted the Declaration of Independence. Rulers come and go; governments end and forms of government change; but sovereignty survives. A political society cannot endure without a supreme will somewhere. Sovereignty is never held in suspense. When, therefore, the external sovereignty of Great Britain in respect of the colonies ceased, it immediately passed to the Union. . . . That fact was given practical application almost at once. The treaty of peace, made on September 23, 1783, was concluded between his Britannic Majesty and the "United States of America. . . ."

The Union existed before the Constitution, which was ordained and established among other things to form "a more perfect Union. . . ."

It results that the investment of the federal government with the powers of external sovereignty did not depend upon the affirmative grants of the Constitution. The powers to declare and wage war, to conclude peace, to make treaties, to maintain diplomatic relations with other sovereignties, if they had never been mentioned in the Constitution, would have vested in the federal government as necessary concomi-

tants of nationality. . . . As a member of the family of nations, the right and power of the United States in that field are equal to the right and power of the other members of the international family. Otherwise, the United States is not completely sovereign. . . .

Not only, as we have shown, is the federal power over external affairs in origin and essential character different from that over internal affairs, but participation in the exercise of the power is significantly limited. In this vast external realm, with its important, complicated, delicate and manifold problems, the President alone has the power to speak or listen as a representative of the nation. He *makes* treaties with the advice and consent of the Senate; but he alone negotiates. Into the field of negotiation the Senate cannot intrude; and Congress itself is powerless to invade it. As Marshall said . . . , "The President is the sole organ of the nation in its external relations, and its sole representative with foreign nations. . . ."

It is important to bear in mind that we are here dealing not alone with an authority vested in the President by an exertion of legislative power, but with such an authority plus the very delicate, plenary and exclusive power of the President as the sole organ of the federal government in the field of international relations—a power which does not require as a basis for its exercise an act of Congress, but which, of course, like every other government power, must be exercised in subordination to the applicable provisions of the Constitution. It is quite apparent that if, in the maintenance of our international relations, embarrassment—perhaps serious embarrassment—is to be avoided and success for our aims achieved, congressional legislation which is to be made effective through negotiation and inquiry within the international field must often accord to the President a degree of discretion and freedom from statutory restriction which would not be admissible were domestic affairs alone involved. Moreover, he, not Congress, has the better opportunity of knowing the conditions which prevail in foreign countries, and especially is this true in time of war. He has his confidential sources of information. He has his agents in the form of diplomatic, consular, and other officials. Secrecy in respect of information gathered by them may be highly necessary, and the premature disclosure of it productive of harmful results. Indeed, so clearly is this true that the first President refused to accede to a request to lay before the House of Representative the instructions, correspondence, and documents relating to the negotiation of the Jay Treaty—a refusal the wisdom of which was recognized by the House itself and has never since been doubted. . . .

In the light of the foregoing observations, it is evident that this court should not be in haste to apply a general rule which will have the effect of condemning legislation like that under review as constituting an unlawful delegation of legislative power. The principles which justify such legislation find overwhelming support in the unbroken legislative practice which has prevailed almost from the inception of the national government to the present day. . . .

Practically every volume of the United States contains one or more acts or joint resolutions of Congress authorizing action by the President in respect of subjects affecting foreign relations, which either leave the exercise of the power to his unrestricted judgment, or provide a standard far more general than that which has always been considered requisite with regard to domestic affairs. . . .

The results of holding that the joint resolution here under attack is void and unenforceable as constituting an unlawful delegation of legislative power would be to stamp this multitude of comparable acts and resolutions as likewise invalid. And while this court may not, and should not, hesitate to declare acts of Congress, however many times repeated, to be unconstitutional if beyond all rational doubt it finds them to be so, an impressive array of legislation such as we have just set forth, enacted by nearly every Congress from the beginning of our national existence to the present day, must be given unusual weight in the process of reaching a correct determination of the problem. A legislative practice such as we have here, evidenced not by only occasional instances, but marked by the movement of a steady stream for a century and a half of time, goes a long way in the direction of proving the presence of unassailable ground for the constitutionality of the practice, to be found in the origin and history of the power involved, or in its nature, or in both combined.

. . . [B]oth upon principle and in accordance with precedent, we conclude there is sufficient warrant for the broad discretion vested in the President to determine whether the enforcement of the statute will have a beneficial effect upon the re-establishment of peace in the affected countries; whether he shall make proclamation to bring the resolution into operation; whether and when the resolution shall cease to operate and to make proclamation accordingly; and to prescribe limitations and exceptions to which the enforcement of the resolution shall be subject. . . .

Reversed.

MR. JUSTICE MCREYNOLDS does not agree. He is of opinion that the court below reached the right conclusion and its judgment ought to be affirmed.

MR. JUSTICE STONE took no part in the consideration or decision of this case.

II
Economic Regulation in a Federal System

"Our Constitution is not a strait-jacket. It is a living organism. As such it is capable of growth—of expansion and of adaptation to new conditions. Growth implies changes, political, economic and social. Growth which is significant manifests itself rather in intellectual and moral conceptions than in material things. Because our Constitution possesses the capacity of adaptation, it has endured as the fundamental law of an ever-developing people."

Unpublished passage in Justice Brandeis' original dissenting opinion in *United States* v. *Moreland*, 258 U.S. 433 (1922). Quoted in Alexander M. Bickel, *The Least Dangerous Branch* (New York and Indianapolis: Bobbs-Merrill, 1962), p. 107.

7
The Contract Clause

The Constitution (Article I, Section 10) declares that no state shall pass any law impairing the obligation of contracts. In the early case of *Sturges* v. *Crowninshield,* 4 Wheat. 122 (1819), Chief Justice Marshall defined the key terms of the contract clause:

> A contract is an agreement in which a party undertakes to do, or not to do, a particular thing. The law binds him to perform his undertaking, and this is, of course, the obligation of his contract. In the case at bar, the defendant has given his promissory note to pay the plaintiff a sum of money on or before a certain day. The contract binds him to pay that sum on that day; and this is its obligation. Any law which releases a part of this obligation, must, in the literal sense of the word, impair it. Much more must a law impair it which makes it totally invalid and entirely discharges it.

The contract clause and the monetary provisions of Article I, Section 10, were designed to protect the creditor classes. Under the Articles of Confederation, the states had passed numerous laws that interfered with the vested property rights of creditors. As indicated in *Home Building and Loan Assoc.* v. *Blaisdell* (p. 196), the contract clause was framed for the specific purpose of preventing state legislation for the relief of debtors, particularly in times of financial emergencies. Thus, the clause would help "to provide adequate safeguards for property and contracts against state legislative power." This was "one of the most important objects of the framers, if indeed it was not the most important."[1]

Expansion of the Contract Clause

The contract clause constitutes a limitation on the states *alone*. There is no corresponding restriction upon the federal government, but the due process clause of the Fifth Amendment provides some protection against arbitrary interference with contracts from this level. Also, the framers obviously intended that the contract clause prohibit the states from interfering only with contracts between *individuals*. But Chief Justice Marshall, in a number of historic opinions, expanded the meaning of the contract clause far beyond the original intention of the framers.

The Supreme Court first interpreted the contract clause in *Fletcher* v. *Peck,* 6 Cr. 87 (1810), where a state statute was held void under the Constitution for the first time. The case had its origin in a Georgia statute in 1795 that granted more than 35 million acres of rich territory to four land companies. The passage of the bill was secured by wholesale bribery and unbelievable corruption. In fact, the whole affair was the "most resounding scandal of the generation."[2] Popular indignation forced the next session of the Georgia legislature to revoke the grant on the ground that it had been secured by fraud. Meanwhile, however, some of the land had been purchased by innocent third parties in New England and other parts of the country. These buyers contested the validity of the rescinding act on the ground that the original grant was a contract that could not be impaired. In an opinion written by Chief Justice Marshall, the Court agreed unanimously with the purchasers and held that the Georgia rescinding act violated the contract clause when the land in question had passed into the hands of innocent third parties. Marshall thus expanded the meaning of the clause by making it applicable to transactions to which the state itself was a party. The contract clause now could be applied to public as well as private contracts.

Marshall extended the contract clause still further in the famous case of *Dartmouth College* v. *Woodward,* by holding that a corporate charter is a contract protected against infringement by state legislatures. Although the case involved an educational rather than an industrial institution, it was of tremendous importance to the economic development of the nation, because it gave assurance to business corporations that they would be protected from legislative interference. The decision was announced at a time when numer-

---

[1] Edward S. Corwin, *John Marshall and the Constitution* (New Haven: Yale University Press, 1919), p. 147.

[2] *Ibid.,* p. 152. The full story is told in C. Peter Magrath, *Yazoo: Law and Politics in the New Republic* (Providence: Brown University Press, 1966).

ous corporations ". . . were springing up in response to the necessity for larger and more constant business units and because of the convenience and profit of such organizations. Marshall's opinion was a tremendous stimulant to this natural economic tendency. It reassured investors in corporate securities and gave confidence and steadiness to the business world. America could not have been developed so rapidly and solidly without the power which the law as announced by Marshall gave to industrial organization."[3]

Marshall's decisions in the contract-clause cases reveal his strong nationalism and, in particular, his extreme conservatism. In fact, "no group of his cases so well illustrates his conservatism. By employing a far broader conception of contract than had been prevalent in 1787, and by combining this conception with the principles of eighteenth-century natural law, he was able to make of the contract clause a mighty instrument for the protection of the rights of private property."[4]

Modification of Marshall's Contract Doctrines

Subsequent decisions of the Court modified considerably the hard doctrines of Marshall's contract-clause cases. His attempt to extend the clause to protect *all past and future* contracts from state laws which might impair them met with defeat in *Ogden* v. *Saunders,* 12 Wheat. 213 (1827), because he could not carry the majority of the Court with him. For the first and only time in his entire judicial career, Marshall dissented on a question of constitutional law. With the decision in *Ogden* v. *Saunders,* further expansion of the contract clause as a curb on state legislation came to an end. If the case had come before the Court a few years earlier, Marshall "might have had his way and made the obligation of contract as inclusive as the later interpretation of liberty of contract under the due process clause. But by 1827 a majority of the Court was unwilling to go so far, and the first great restriction upon the scope of the clause was set forth over the stout opposition of the Chief Justice."[5]

Marshall's doctrines were limited further by the Taney Court, principally in the famous case of *Charles River Bridge Co.* v. *Warren* (p. 191). In that case, Chief Justice Taney held that although charter contracts were to be honored, the terms of such contracts were to be strictly construed. In short, a contract was to be limited to the actual provisions of the charter. Nothing was to be implied. Taney noted that "the continued existence of a government would be of no great value, if by implications and presumptions, it was disarmed of the powers necessary to accomplish the ends of its creation; and

[3] Albert J. Beveridge, *The Life of John Marshall* (Boston: Houghton Mifflin, 1919), Vol. 4, p. 276.

[4] Benjamin F. Wright, *The Contract Clause of the Constitution* (Cambridge: Harvard University Press, 1938), p. 28.

[5] *Ibid.,* p. 52

the functions it was designed to perform, transferred to the hands of privileged corporations."

Although Marshall's contract concepts were modified by the Taney Court, they were not abandoned. The contract clause continued to be invoked for the defense of property rights in a great number of cases until 1890. In fact, the clause reached its highest point of importance during the great industrial era following the Civil War. But after 1890, the contract clause as an instrument for the protection of private rights declined in significance. This decline was due principally to the expansion of the due process clause of the Fourteenth Amendment as an even more important vehicle for the protection of vested economic interests.

> The displacement of the contract clause by due process of law is but an incident in the continuous development of an idea. The former clause had become too circumscribed by judicially created or permitted limitations, and its place was gradually taken by another clause where the absence of restrictive precedent allowed freer pay to judicial discretion. [But] the decline of the contract clause after 1890 canot be taken as an indication that old-style conceptual individualism based on contract was dead. The battle was to be fought with a newer and a more deadly weapon. The contract clause was to become merely a technical provision to be applied to varying situations in the light of well-established precedents. In terms of specific cases its application did not, on that account, become less important. But it ceased to be the vehicle which conveyed new bodies of ideas into the law of the Constitution.[6]

The most important contract case of recent years is *Home Building and Loan Assoc.* v. *Blaisdell,* where the Court allowed the state's police power to make certain inroads on contract rights, even though the contract clause was designed by the framers to prevent just such state laws as the one at issue in the *Blaisdell* case. The Minnesota Mortgage Moratorium Act discussed in the case was enacted to meet an acute problem resulting from the economic depression that began in 1929. There was widespread popular demand in Minnesota as well as in other states for some kind of mortgage relief. The Minnesota bill was passed by both houses of the state legislature without a dissenting vote.

THE TRUSTEES OF DARTMOUTH COLLEGE *v.* WOODWARD

[*Dartmouth College was granted a charter by the English Crown in 1769. The charter created a board of trustees of twelve members who were empowered to govern the affairs of the new college. The founder and first president of the college died in 1779, whereupon his son, John Wheelock, became president. However, Wheelock was removed from the presidency by the board of trustees after numerous unpleasant conflicts that attracted statewide attention. The two political parties in the state were also drawn into the controversy, the Federalists supporting*

---

[6] *Ibid.,* p. 258.

the trustees while the Republicans sided with Wheelock. In 1816, the Republican majority in the state legislature enacted three laws that amended the original charter and provided for a new governing body for the institution, whose name was changed to Dartmouth University. The old trustees refused to be governed by the new law and continued to run the college with the support of loyal members of the faculty and the majority of the student body. The new "state" trustees appointed by the Governor "removed" the old trustees and reelected Wheelock to the presidency.

The old board of trustees contended that the 1816 legislation impaired the obligation of contract contained in the original charter of 1769 and brought an action in the state courts to recover possession of the college charter, records, seal, and accounts from Woodward, the secretary of the new board. (Woodward had been secretary and treasurer of the original college, but he had sided with the Wheelock faction in the dispute.) The state courts ruled against the college. The old trustees then took the case to the Supreme Court on a writ of error, and Daniel Webster argued with "emotional eloquence" in behalf of the college from which he had graduated.]

The opinion of the Court was delivered by MR. CHIEF JUSTICE MARSHALL:

. . . It can require no argument to prove that the circumstances of this case constitute a contract. An application is made to the Crown for a charter to incorporate a religious and literary institution. In the application, it is stated that large contributions have been made for the object, which will be conferred on the corporation, as soon as it shall be created. The charter is granted, and on its faith the property is conveyed. Surely in this transaction every ingredient of a complete and legitimate contract is to be found.

The points for consideration are,

1. Is this contract protected by the Constitution of the United States?

2. Is it impaired by the acts under which the defendant holds?

1. On the first point it has been argued, that the word "contract," in its broadest sense, would comprehend the political relations between the government and its citizens, would extend to offices held within a State for State purposes, and to many of those laws concerning civil institutions which must change with circumstances, and be modified by ordinary legislation; which deeply concern the public, and which, to preserve good government, the public judgment must control. That even marriage is a contract, and its obligations are affected by the laws respecting divorces. That the clause in the Constitution, if construed in its greatest latitude, would prohibit these laws. Taken in its broad unlimited sense, the clause would be an unprofitable and vexatious interference with the internal concerns of a State, would unnecessarily and unwisely embarrass its legislation, and render immutable those civil institutions which are established for purposes of internal government, and which, to subserve those purposes, ought to vary with varying circumstances. That as the framers of the Constitution could never have intended to insert in that instrument a provision so unnecessary, so mischievous, and so repugnant to its general spirit, the term *"contract"* must be understood in a more limited sense. That it must be understood as intended to guard against a power of at least doubtful utility, the abuse of which had been extensively felt; and to restrain the legislature in future from violating the right to property. That anterior to

the formation of the Constitution, a course of legislation had prevailed in many, if not in all, of the States, which weakened the confidence of man in man, and embarrassed all transactions between individuals, by dispensing with a faithful performance of engagements. To correct this mischief, by restraining the power which produced it, the State legislatures were forbidden "to pass any law impairing the obligation of contracts," that is, of contracts respecting property, under which some individual could claim a right to something beneficial to himself; and that since the clause in the Constitution must in construction receive some limitation, it may be confined, and ought to be confined, to cases of this description; to cases within the mischief it was intended to remedy.

The general correctness of these observations cannot be controverted. That the framers of the Constitution did not intend to restrain the States in the regulation of their civil institutions, adopted for internal government, and that the instrument they have given us is not to be so construed, may be admitted. The provision of the Constitution never has been understood to embrace other contracts than those which respect property, or some object of value, and confer rights which may be asserted in a court of justice. It never has been understood to restrict the general right of the legislature to legislate on the subject of divorces. Those acts enable some tribunal, not to impair a marriage contract, but to liberate one of the parties because it has been broken by the other. When any State legislature shall pass an act annulling all marriage contracts, or allowing either party to annul it without the consent of the other, it will be time enough to inquire whether such an act be constitutional.

The parties in this case differ less on general principles, less on the true con-

struction of the Constitution in the abstract, than on the application of those principles to this case, and on the true construction of the charter of 1769. This is the point on which the case essentially depends. If the act of incorporation be a grant of political power, if it create a civil institution to be employed in the administration of the government, or if the funds of the college be public property, or if the State of New Hampshire, as a government, be alone interested in its transactions, the subject is one in which the legislature of the State may act according to its own judgment, unrestrained by any limitation of its power imposed by the Constitution of the United States.

But if this be a private eleemosynary institution, endowed with a capacity to take property for objects unconnected with government, whose funds are bestowed by individuals on the faith of the charter; if the donors have stipulated for the future disposition and management of those funds in the manner prescribed by themselves; there may be more difficulty in the case, although neither the persons who have made these stipulations, nor those for whose benefit they were made, should be parties to the cause. Those who are no longer interested in the property may yet retain such an interest in the preservation of their own arrangements as to have a right to insist that those arrangements shall be held sacred. Or, if they have themselves disappeared, it becomes a subject of serious and anxious inquiry, whether those whom they have legally empowered to represent them forever, may not assert all the rights which they possessed while in being; whether, if they be without personal representatives who may feel injured by a violation of the compact, the trustees be not so completely their representatives in the eye of the law as to stand in their place, not only as respects the government of the college, but also as respect the maintenance of the college charter.

It becomes then the duty of the Court most seriously to examine this charter, and to ascertain its true character.

. . . A corporation is an artificial being, invisible, intangible, and existing only in contemplation of law. Being the mere creature of law, it possesses only those properties which the charter of its creation confers upon it, either expressly, or as incidental to its very existence. These are such as are supposed best calculated to effect the object for which it was created. Among the most important are immortality, and, if the expression may be allowed, individuality; properties, by which a perpetual succession of many persons are considered as the same, and may act as a single individual. They enable a corporation to manage its own affairs, and to hold property without the perplexing intricacies, the hazardous and endless necessity, of perpetual conveyances for the purpose of transmitting it from hand to hand. It is chiefly for the purpose of clothing bodies of men, in succession, with these qualities and capacities, that corporations were invented, and are in use. By these means, a perpetual succession of individuals are capable of acting for the promotion of the particular object, like one immortal being. . . .

The objects for which a corporation is created are universally such as the government wishes to promote. They are deemed beneficial to the country; and this benefit constitutes the consideration, and, in most cases, the sole consideration of the grant. In most eleemosynary institutions, the object would be difficult, perhaps unattainable, without the aid of a charter of incorporation. Charitable, or public-spirited individuals, desirous of making permanent appropriations for charitable or other useful purposes, find it impossible to effect their design securely, and certainly, without an incorporating act. They apply to the government, state their beneficent object, and offer to advance the money necessary for its accomplishment, provided the government will confer on the instrument which is to execute their designs the capacity to execute them. . . .

[I]t appears, that Dartmouth College is an eleemosynary institution, incorporated for the purpose of perpetuating the application of the bounty of the donors, to the specified objects of that bounty; that its trustees or governors were originally named by the founder, and invested with the power of perpetuating themselves; that they are not public officers, nor is it a civil institution, participating in the administration of government; but a charity school, or a seminary of education, incorporated for the preservation of its property, and the perpetual application of that property to the objects of its creation. . . .

This is plainly a contract to which the donors, the trustees, and the Crown (to whose rights and obligations New Hampshire succeeds) were the original parties. It is a contract made on a valuable consideration. It is a contract for the security and disposition of property. It is a contract, on the faith of which, real and personal estate has been conveyed to the corporation. It is then a contract within the letter of the Constitution, and within its spirit also, unless the fact that the property is invested by the donors in trustees for the promotion of religion and education, for the benefit of persons who are perpetually changing, though the objects remain the same, shall create a particular exception, taking this case out of the prohibition contained in the Constitution.

It is more than possible, that the preservation of rights of this description was not particularly in the view of the framers of the Constitution, when the clause under consideration was introduced into that instrument. It is probable, that interferences of more frequent recurrence, to which the temptation was stronger, and of which the mischief was more extensive, constituted the great motive for imposing this restriction on the State legislatures. But although a particular and a rare case may not, in itself, be of sufficient magnitude to induce a rule, yet it must be governed by the rule, when established, unless some plain and strong reason for excluding it can be given. It is not enough to say, that this particular case was not in the mind of the Convention, when the article was framed, nor of the American people, when it was adopted. It is necessary to go farther, and to say that, had this particular case been suggested, the language would have been so varied as to exclude it, or it would have been made a special exception. The case being within the words of the rule, must be within its operation likewise, unless there be something in the literal construction so obviously absurd, or mischievous, or repugnant to the general spirit of the instrument, as to justify those who expound the Constitution in making it an exception. . . .

The opinion of the Court, after mature deliberation, is that this is a contract, the obligation of which cannot be impaired without violating the Constitution of the United States. This opinion appears to us to be equally supported by reason, and by the former decisions of this Court.

2. We next proceed to the inquiry, whether its obligation has been impaired by those acts of the legislature of New Hampshire, to which the special verdict refers.

From the review of this charter which has been taken, it appears that the whole power of governing the college, of appointing and removing tutors, of fixing their salaries, of directing the course of study to be pursued by the students, and of filling up vacancies created in their own body, was vested in the trustees. On the part of the Crown it was expressly stipulated that this corporation, thus constituted, should continue forever; and that the number of trustees should forever consist of twelve, and no more. By this contract the Crown was bound, and could have made no violent alteration in its essential terms, without impairing its obligation.

By the Revolution, the duties, as well as the powers, of government devolved on the people of New Hampshire. It is admitted that among the latter was comprehended the transcendent power of parliament, as well as that of the executive department. It is too clear to require the support of argument, that all contracts and rights respecting property remained unchanged by the revolution. The obligations then, which were created by the charter to Dartmouth College, were the same in the new, that they had been in the old government. The power of the government was also the same. A repeal of this charter at any time prior to the adoption of the present constitution of the United States would have been an extraordinary and unprecedented act of power, but one which could have been contested only by the restrictions upon the legislature to be found in the constitution of the State. But the Constitution of the United States has imposed this additional limitation, that the legislature of a State shall pass no act "impairing the obligation of contracts."

It has already stated, that the act "to amend the charter, and enlarge and improve the corporation of Dartmouth College," increases the number of trustees to twenty-one, gives the appointment of the additional members to the executive of the State, and creates a board of overseers, to consist of twenty-five persons, of whom twenty-one are also appointed by the executive of New Hampshire, who have power to inspect and control the most important acts of the trustees.

On the effect of this law, two opinions cannot be entertained. Between acting directly, and acting through the agency of trustees and overseers, no essential difference is perceived. The whole power of governing the college is transferred from trustees appointed according to the will of the founder, expressed in the charter, to the executive of New Hampshire. The management and application of the funds of this eleemosynary institution, which are placed by the donors in the hands of trustees named in the charter, and empowered to perpetuate themselves, are placed by this act under the control of the government of the State. The will of the State is substituted for the will of the donors in every essential operation of the college. This is not an immaterial change. The founders of the college contracted, not merely for the perpetual application of the funds which they gave, to the objects for which those funds were given; they contracted also, to secure that application by the constitution of the corporation. They contracted for a system which should, as far as human foresight can provide, retain forever the government of the literary institution they had formed, in the hands of persons approved by themselves. This system is totally changed. The charter of 1769 exists no longer. It is reorganized; and reorganized in such a manner as to convert a literary institution, moulded according to the will of its founders, and placed under the control of private literary men, into a machine entirely subservient to the will of government. This may be for the advantage of literature in general; but it is not according to the will of the donors, and is subversive of that contract, on the faith of which their property was given. . . .

It results from this opinion, that the acts of the legislature of New Hampshire, which are stated in the special verdict found in this cause, are repugnant to the Constitution of the United States; and that the judgment on this special verdict ought to have been for the plaintiffs. The judgment of the State Court must, therefore, be

Reversed.

[MR. JUSTICE WASHINGTON and MR. JUSTICE STORY delivered separate concurring opinions. MR. JUSTICE DUVALL dissented.]

CHARLES RIVER BRIDGE CO. *v.* WARREN BRIDGE CO.
11 Pet. 420; 9 L. Ed. 773 (1837)

[*To overcome the inconvenience of transportation by ferries, the Massachusetts legislature, in 1785, granted the Charles River Bridge Company a charter to construct a bridge between Charleston and Boston with the power to collect tolls for forty years (later extended to seventy years). This franchise replaced an exclusive ferry right granted to Harvard College in 1650; provision was made for compensating Harvard for the impairment of its ferry franchise. The Charles River Bridge was built at considerable financial risk, but it proved to be an extremely profitable venture. However, the management of the bridge monopoly became involved in party politics, and in 1828 the state legislature authorized the Warren Bridge Company to construct another bridge very close to the old one. On the*

*Boston side the bridges were to be 825 feet apart, whereas on the Charleston side
the distance between them was to be only 264 feet. No tolls were to be charged
on the new bridge as soon as its construction had been paid for or at the end of
a maximum period of six years. The Charles River Bridge Company sought an
injunction to prevent the erection of the Warren bridge and then, after the bridge
was built, for general relief, contending that the legislature, in authorizing the
new bridge, violated the contract clause of the Constitution. The Massachusetts
supreme court rejected the plaintiff company's bill for an injunction and other
relief. The case then went to the Supreme Court on a writ of error.]*

MR. CHIEF JUSTICE TANEY delivered the
opinion of the Court:

The questions involved in this case
are of the gravest character, and the
court has given to them the most anxious and deliberate consideration. The
value of the right claimed by the plaintiffs is large in amount; and many persons may no doubt be seriously affected
in their pecuniary interests by any decision which the court may pronounce;
and the questions which have been
raised as to the power of the several
states, in relation to the corporations
they have chartered, are pregnant with
important consequences; not only to
the individuals who are concerned in
the corporate franchises, but to the
communities in which they exist. . . .

The plaintiffs in error insist, mainly
upon two grounds: First. That by virtue
of the grant of 1650, Harvard College
was entitled, in perpetuity, to the right
of keeping a ferry between Charleston
and Boston; that this right was exclusive; and that the legislature had not the
power to establish another ferry on the
same line of travel, because it would
infringe the rights of the college; and
that these rights, upon the erection of
the bridge in the place of the ferry,
under the charter of 1785, were transferred to, and became vested in "the
proprietors of the Charles River bridge";
and that under, and by virtue of this
transfer of the ferry right, the rights of
the bridge company were as exclusive
in that line of travel, as the rights of the
ferry. Second. That independently of

the ferry right, the acts of the legislature of Massachusetts of 1785, and
1792, by their true construction, necessarily implied that the legislature would
not authorize another bridge, and especially a free one, by the side of this,
and placed in the same line of travel,
whereby the franchise granted to "the
proprietors of the Charles River bridge"
should be rendered of no value; and the
plaintiffs in error contend, that the grant
of the ferry to the college, and of the
charter to the proprietors of the bridge,
are both contracts on the part of the
state; and that the law authorizing the
erection of the Warren bridge in 1828,
impairs the obligation of one or both of
these contracts. . . .

But upon what ground can the plaintiffs in error contend that the ferry
rights of the college have been transferred to the proprietors of the bridge?
If they have been thus transferred, it
must be by some mode of transfer
known to the law; and the evidence relied on to prove it, can be pointed out
in the record. How was it transferred?
It is not suggested that there ever was,
in point of fact, a deed of conveyance
executed by the college to the bridge
company. Is there any evidence in the
record from which such a conveyance
may, upon legal principle, be presumed? The testimony before the court,
so far from laying the foundation for
such a presumption, repels it in the
most positive terms. The petition to the
legislature, in 1785, on which the charter was granted, does not suggest an

assignment, nor any agreement or consent on the part of the college; and the petitioners do not appear to have regarded the wishes of that institution, as by any means necessary to ensure their success. They place their application entirely on considerations of public interest and public convenience, and the superior advantages of a communication across Charles River by a bridge, instead of a ferry. . . .

This brings us to the act of the legislature of Massachusetts, of 1785, by which the plaintiffs were incorporated by the name of "The Proprietors of the Charles River Bridge"; and it is here, and in the law of 1792, prolonging their charter, that we must look for the extent and nature of the franchise conferred upon the plaintiffs.

Much has been said in the argument of the principles of construction by which this law is to be expounded, and what undertakings, on the part of the state may be implied. The court think there can be no serious difficulty on that head. It is the grant of certain franchises by the public to a private corporation, and in a matter where the public interest is concerned. The rule of construction in such cases is well settled, both in England, and by the decisions of our tribunals. . . . "[T]he rule of construction in all such cases, is now fully established to be this—that any ambiguity in the terms of the contract, must operate against the adventurers, and in favor of the public, and the plaintiffs can claim nothing that is not clearly given them by the act. . . .

[T]he object and end of all government is to promote the happiness and prosperity of the community by which it is established; and it can never be assumed, that the government intended to diminish its power of accomplishing the end for which it was created. And in a country like ours, free, active, and enterprising, continually advancing in numbers and wealth; new channels of communication are daily found necessary, both for travel and trade; and are essential to the comfort, convenience, and prosperity of the people. A state ought never to be presumed to surrender this power, because, like the taxing power, the whole community have an interest in preserving it undiminished. And when a corporation alleges, that a state has surrendered for seventy years, its power of improvement and public accommodation, in a great and important line of travel, along which a vast number of its citizens must daily pass; the community have a right to insist . . . "that its abandonment ought not to be presumed, in a case, in which the deliberate purpose of the state to abandon it does not appear." The continued existence of a government would be of no great value, if by implications and presumptions, it was disarmed of the powers necessary to accomplish the ends of its creation; and the functions it was designed to perform, transferred to the hands of privileged corporations. . . . No one will question that the interests of the great body of the people of the state, would, in this instance, be affected by the surrender of this great line of travel to a single corporation, with the right to exact toll, and exclude competition for seventy years. While the rights of private property are sacredly guarded, we must not forget that the community also have rights, and that the happiness and well-being of every citizen depends on their faithful preservation.

Adopting the rule of construction above stated as the settled one, we proceed to apply it to the charter of 1785, to the proprietors of the Charles River bridge. This act of incorporation is in the usual form, and the privileges such as are commonly given to corporations of that kind. It confers on them the ordinary faculties of a corporation, for the purpose of building the bridge; and establishes certain rates of toll, which the company are authorized to take. This is the whole grant. There is no exclusive privilege given to them over the waters of Charles River, above or below their bridge. No right to erect another bridge themselves, nor to prevent other persons from erecting one. No engagement from the state, that another shall not be erected; and no undertaking not to sanction competition, nor to make improvements that may diminish the amount of its income. Upon all these subjects the charter is silent; and nothing is said in it about a line of travel, so much insisted on in the argument, in which they are to have exclusive privileges. No words are used, from which an intention to grant any of these rights can be inferred. If the plaintiff is entitled to them, it must be implied, simply, from the nature of the grant; and cannot be inferred, from the words by which the grant is made.

The relative position of the Warren bridge has already been described. It does not interrupt the passage over the Charles River bridge, nor make the way to it or from it less convenient. None of the faculties or franchises granted to that corporation, have been revoked by the legislature; and its right to take the tolls granted by the charter remains unaltered. In short, all the franchises and rights of property enumerated in the charter, and there mentioned to have been granted to it, remain unimpaired. But its income is destroyed by the Warren bridge; which, being free, draws off the passengers and property which would have gone over it, and renders their franchise of no value. This is the gist of the complaint. For it is not pretended, that the erection of the Warren bridge would have done them any injury, or in any degree affected their right of property; if it had not dimin-

ished the amount of their tolls. In order then to entitle themselves to relief, it is necessary to show, that the legislature contracted not to do the act of which they complain; and that they impaired, or in other words violated that contract by the erection of the Warren bridge.

The inquiry then is, does the charter contain such a contract on the part of the state? Is there any such stipulation to be found in that instrument? It must be admitted on all hands, that there is none—no words that even relate to another bridge, or to the diminution of their tolls, or to the line of travel. If a contract on that subject can be gathered from the charter, it must be by implication; and cannot be found in the words used. Can such an agreement be implied? The rule of construction before stated is an answer to the question. In charters of this description, no rights are taken from the public, or given to the corporation, beyond those which the words of the charter, by their natural and proper construction, purport to convey. There are no words which import such a contract as the plaintiffs in error contend for, and none can be implied. . . .

Indeed, the practice and usage of almost every state in the Union, old enough to have commenced the work of internal improvement, is opposed to the doctrine contended for on the part of the plaintiffs in error. Turnpike roads have been made in succession, on the same line of travel; the later ones interfering materially with the profits of the first. These corporations have, in some instances, been utterly ruined by the introduction of newer and better modes of transportation, and travelling. In some cases, rail roads have rendered the turnpike roads on the same line of travel so entirely useless, that the franchise of the turnpike corporation is not worth preserving.

Yet in none of these cases have the corporations supposed that their privileges were invaded, or any contract violated on the part of the state. Amid the multitude of cases which have occurred, and have been daily occurring for the last forty or fifty years, this is the first instance in which such an implied contract has been contended for, and this court called upon to infer it from an ordinary act of incorporation, containing nothing more than the usual stipulations and provisions to be found in every such law. The absence of any such controversy, when there must have been so many occasions to give rise to it, proves that neither states, nor individuals, nor corporations, ever imagined that such a contract could be implied from such charters. It shows that the men who voted for these laws, never imagined that they were forming such a contract; and if we maintain that they have made it, we must create it by a legal fiction, in opposition to the truth of the fact, and the obvious intention of the party. We cannot deal thus with the rights reserved to the states; and by legal intendments and mere technical reasoning, take away from them any portion of that power over their own internal police and improvement, which is so necessary to their well-being and prosperity. . . .

The judgment of the supreme judicial court of the commonwealth of Massachusetts, dismissing the plaintiffs' bill, must, therefore, be affirmed, with costs.

[MR. JUSTICE MC LEAN wrote an opinion urging that the bill be dismissed for lack of jurisdiction. He believed, however, that the plaintiffs' claim had merit.]

MR. JUSTICE STORY, dissenting:

. . . I maintain, that, upon the principles of common reason and legal interpretation, the present grant carries with it a necessary implication that the legislature shall do no act to destroy or essentially to impair the franchise; that (as one of the learned judges of the state court expressed it), there is an implied agreement of the state to grant the undisturbed use of the bridge and its tolls, so far as respects any acts of its own, or of any persons acting under its authority. In other words, the state, impliedly, contracts not to resume its grants, or to do any act to the prejudice or destruction of its grant. I maintain, that there is no authority or principle established in relation to the construction of crown grants, or legislative grants; which does not concede and justify this doctrine. Where the thing is given, the incidents, without which it cannot be enjoyed, are also given. . . . I maintain that a different doctrine is utterly repugnant to all the principles of the common law, applicable to all franchises of a like nature; and that we must overturn some of the best securities of the rights of property, before it can be established. . . . I maintain, that under the principles of the common law, there exists no more right in the legislature of Massachusetts, to erect the Warren bridge, to the ruin of the franchise of the Charles River bridge, than exists to transfer the latter to the former, or to authorize the former to demolish the latter. If the legislature does not mean in its grant to give any exclusive rights, let it say so, expressly; directly; and in terms admitting of no misconstruction. . . .

My judgment is formed upon the terms of the grant, its nature and objects, its design and duties; and, in its interpretation, I seek for no new principles, but I apply such as are as old as the very rudiments of the common law.

. . .

Upon the whole, my judgment is, that the act of the legislature of Massachusetts granting the charter of Warren bridge, is an act impairing the obligation of the prior contract and grant to the proprietors of Charles River bridge; and, by the constitution of the United States, it is therefore utterly void. I am for reversing the decree of the state

court (dismissing the bill); and for remanding the cause to the state court for further proceedings, as to law and justice shall appertain.

[MR. JUSTICE THOMPSON concurred in this opinion.]

HOME BUILDING AND LOAN ASSOCIATION v. BLAISDELL
290 U.S. 398; 54 Sup. Ct. 231; 78 L. Ed. 413 (1934)

[Blaisdell and his wife owned some property in Minneapolis that they had mortgaged to the Home Building and Loan Association, the appellant. The loan company foreclosed the mortgage by reason of appellees' default. Blaisdell and his wife then sought to extend the date of redemption under the terms of the Minnesota Mortgage Moratorium Act, which had been passed in 1933. That law provided procedures for temporarily extending the time for the redemption of real property from foreclosures and sale during the emergency produced by the economic depression. Upon Blaisdell's application, a county court extended the period of redemption from May 2, 1933, to May 1, 1935. The county court granted the extension on condition that the appellees pay a certain amount each month through the extended period to cover taxes, insurance, interest, and mortgage indebtedness. The Supreme Court of Minnesota affirmed the judgment and upheld the statute. The loan company then appealed to the Supreme Court, contending that the Minnesota law violated the contract clause and the due process and equal protection clauses of the Fourteenth Amendment.]

MR. CHIEF JUSTICE HUGHES delivered the opinion of the Court:
. . . The state court upheld the statute as an emergency measure. Although conceding that the obligations of the mortgage contract were impaired, the court decided that what it thus described as an impairment was, notwithstanding the contract clause of the Federal Constitution, within the police power of the State as that power was called into exercise by the public economic emergency which the legislature had found to exist. Attention is thus directed to the preamble and first section of the statute, which described the existing emergency in terms that were deemed to justify the temporary relief which the statute affords. The state court, declaring that it could not say

that this legislative finding was without basis, supplemented that finding by its own statement of conditions of which it took judicial notice. The court said:
"In addition to the weight to be given the determination of the legislature that an economic emergency exists which demands relief, the court must take notice of other considerations. The members of the legislature come from every community of the state and from all the walks of life. They are familiar with conditions generally in every calling, occupation, profession, and business in the state. Not only they, but the courts must be guided by what is common knowledge. It is common knowledge that in the last few years land values have shrunk enormously. Loans made a few years ago upon the basis of

the then going values cannot possibly be replaced on the basis of present values. We all know that when this law was enacted the large financial companies, which had made it their business to invest in mortgages, had ceased to do so. No bank would directly or indirectly loan on real estate mortgages. Life-insurance companies, large investors in such mortgages, had even declared a moratorium as to the loan provisions of their policy contracts. The President had closed banks temporarily. The Congress, in addition to many extraordinary measures looking to the relief of the economic emergency, had passed an act to supply funds whereby mortgagors may be able within a reasonable time to refinance their mortgages or redeem from sales where the redemption has not expired. With this knowledge the court cannot well hold that the legislature had no basis in fact for the conclusion that an economic emergency existed which called for the exercise of the police power to grant relief."

In determining whether the provision for this temporary and conditional relief exceeds the power of the State by reason of the clause in the Federal Constitution prohibiting impairment of the obligations of contracts, we must consider the relation of emergency to constitutional power, the historical setting of the contract clause, the development of the jurisprudence of this Court in the construction of that clause, and the principles of construction which we may consider to be established.

Emergency does not create power. Emergency does not increase granted power or remove or diminish the restrictions imposed upon power granted or reserved. The Constitution was adopted in a period of grave emergency. Its grants of power to the Federal Government and its limitations of the power of the States were determined in the light of emergency and they are not altered by emergency. What power was thus granted and what limitations were thus imposed are questions which have always been, and always will be, the subject of close examination under our constitutional system.

While emergency does not create power, emergency may furnish the occasion for the exercise of power. . . . The constitutional question presented in the light of an emergency is whether the power possessed embraces the particular exercise of it in response to particular conditions. Thus, the war power of the Federal Government is not created by the emergency of war, but it is a power given to meet that emergency. It is a power to wage war successfully, and thus it permits the harnessing of the entire energies of the people in a supreme cooperative effort to preserve the nation. But even the war power does not remove constitutional limitations safeguarding essential liberties. When the provisions of the Constitution, in grant or restriction, are specific, so particularized as not to admit of construction, no question is presented. Thus, emergency would not permit a State to have more than two Senators in the Congress, or permit the election of President by a general popular vote without regard to the number of electors to which the States are respectively entitled, or permit the States to "coin money" or to "make anything but gold and silver coin a tender in payment of debts." But where constitutional grants and limitations of power are set forth in general clauses, which afford a broad outline, the process of construction is essential to fill in the details. That is true of the contract clause. . . .

In the construction of the contract clause, the debates in the Constitutional Convention are of little aid. But the reasons which led to the adoption of that clause, and of the other prohibitions of Section 10 of Article I, are not left in doubt and have frequently been described with eloquent emphasis. The widespread distress following the Revolutionary period, and the plight of debtors, had called forth in the States an ignoble array of legislative schemes for the defeat of creditors and the invasion of contractual obligations. Legislative interferences had been so numerous and extreme that the confidence essential to prosperous trade had been undermined and the utter destruction of credit was threatened. . . .

But full recognition of the occasion and general purpose of the clause does not suffice to fix its precise scope. Nor does an examination of the details of prior legislation in the States yield criteria which can be considered controlling. To ascertain the scope of the constitutional prohibition we examine the course of judicial decisions in its application. These put it beyond question that the prohibition is not an absolute one and is not to be read with literal exactness like a mathematical formula. . . .

The inescapable problems of construction have been: What is a contract? What are the obligations of contracts? What constitutes impairment of these obligations? What residuum of power is there still in the States in relation to the operation of contracts, to protect the vital interests of the community? Questions of this character, "of no small nicety and intricacy, have vexed the legislative halls, as well as the judicial tribunals, with an uncounted variety and frequency of litigation and speculation."

. . . Not only is the constitutional provision qualified by the measure of control which the State retains over remedial processes, but the State also continues to possess authority to safeguard the vital interests of its people.

It does not matter that legislation appropriate to that end "has the result of modifying or abrogating contracts already in effect." . . . Not only are existing laws read into contracts in order to fix obligations as between the parties, but the reservation of essential attributes of sovereign power is also read into contracts as a postulate of the legal order. The policy of protecting contracts against impairment presupposes the maintenance of a government by virtue of which contractual relations are worth while—a government which retains adequate authority to secure the peace and good order of society. This principle of harmonizing the constitutional prohibition with the necessary residuum of state power has had progressive recognition in the decisions of this Court. . . .

The legislature cannot "bargain away the public health or the public morals." Thus, the constitutional provision against the impairment of contracts was held not to be violated by an amendment of the state constitution which put an end to a lottery theretofore authorized by the legislature. *Stone* v. *Mississippi,* 101 U.S. 814. . . . The lottery was a valid enterprise when established under express state authority, but the legislature in the public interest could put a stop to it. A similar rule has been applied to the control by the State of the sale of intoxicating liquors. . . . The States retain adequate power to protect the public health against the maintenance of nuisances despite insistence upon existing contracts. . . . Legislation to protect the public safety comes within the same category of reserved power. . . . This principle has had recent and noteworthy application to the regulation of the use of public highways by common carriers and "contract carriers," where the assertion of interference with existing contract rights has been without avail. . . .

The argument is pressed that in the cases we have cited the obligation of contracts was affected only incidentally. This argument proceeds upon a misconception. The question is not whether the legislative action affects contracts incidentally, or directly or indirectly, but whether the legislation is addressed to a legitimate end and the measures taken are reasonable and appropriate to that end. Another argument, which comes more closely to the point, is that the state power may be addressed directly to the prevention of the enforcement of contracts only when these are of a sort which the legislature in its discretion may denounce as being in themselves hostile to public morals, or public health, safety, or welfare, or where the prohibition is merely of injurious practices; that interference with the enforcement of other and valid contracts according to appropriate legal procedure, although the interference is temporary and for a public purpose, is not permissible. This is but to contend that in the latter case the end is not legitimate in the view that it cannot be reconciled with a fair interpretation of the constitutional provision.

Undoubtedly, whatever is reserved of state power must be consistent with the fair intent of the constitutional limitation of that power. The reserved power cannot be construed so as to destroy the limitation, nor is the limitation to be construed to destroy the reserved power in its essential aspects. They must be construed in harmony with each other. This principle precludes a construction which would permit the State to adopt as its policy the repudiation of debts or the destruction of contracts or the denial of means to enforce them. But it does not follow that conditions may not arise in which a temporary restraint of enforcement may be consistent with the spirit and purpose of the constitutional provision

and thus be found to be within the range of the reserved power of the State to protect the vital interests of the community. It cannot be maintained that the constitutional prohibition should be so construed as to prevent limited and temporary interpositions with respect to the enforcement of contracts if made necessary by a great public calamity such as fire, flood, or earthquake. . . . The reservation of state power appropriate to such extraordinary conditions may be deemed to be as much a part of all contracts, as is the reservation of state power to protect the public interest in the other situations to which we have referred. And if state power exists to give temporary relief from the enforcement of contracts in the presence of disasters due to physical causes such as fire, flood, or earthquake, that power cannot be said to be nonexistent when the urgent public need demanding such relief is produced by other and economic causes. . . .

It is manifest . . . that there has been a growing appreciation of public needs and of the necessity of finding ground for a rational compromise between individual rights and public welfare. The settlement and consequent contraction of the public domain, the pressure of a constantly increasing density of population, the interrelation of the activities of our people and the complexity of our economic interests, have inevitably led to an increased use of the organization of society in order to protect the very bases of individual opportunity. Where, in earlier days, it was thought that only the concerns of individuals or of classes were involved, and that those of the State itself were touched only remotely, it has later been found that the fundamental interests of the State are directly affected; and that the question is no longer merely that of one party to a contract as against another, but of the use of reasonable means to safeguard the economic structure upon which the good of all depends.

It is no answer to say that this public need was not apprehended a century ago, or to insist that what the provision of the Constitution meant to the vision of that day it must mean to the vision of our time. If by the statement that what the Constitution meant at the time of its adoption it means today, it is intended to say that the great clauses of the Constitution must be confined to the interpretation which the framers, with the conditions and outlook of their time, would have placed upon them, the statement carries its own refutation. It was to guard against such a narrow conception that Chief Justice Marshall uttered the memorable warning—"We must never forget that it is a *constitution* we are expounding" (*McCulloch* v. *Maryland* . . .)—"a constitution intended to endure for ages to come, and consequently, to be adapted to the various *crises* of human affairs." . . . When we are dealing with the words of the Constitution, said this Court in *Missouri* v. *Holland,* "we must realize that they have called into life a being the development of which could not have been foreseen completely by the most gifted of its begetters. . . . The case before us must be consdered in the light of our whole experience and not merely in that of what was said a hundred years ago."

Nor is it helpful to attempt to draw a fine distinction between the intended meaning of the words of the Constitution and their intended application. When we consider the contract clause and the decisions which have expounded it in harmony with the essential reserved power of the States to protect the security of their peoples, we find no warrant for the conclusion that the clause has been warped by these decisions from its proper significance or that the founders of our Government would have interpreted the clause differently had they had occasion to assume that responsibility in the conditions of the later day. The vast body of law which has been developed was unknown to the fathers, but it is believed to have preserved the essential content and the spirit of the Constitution. With a growing recognition of public needs and the relation of individual right to public security, the court has sought to prevent the perversion of the clause through its use as an instrument to throttle the capacity of the States to protect their fundamental interests. This development is a growth from the seeds which the fathers planted. . . .

Applying the criteria established by our decision we conclude:

1. An emergency existed in Minnesota which furnished a proper occasion for the exercise of the reserved power of the State to protect the vital interests of the community. The declarations of the existence of this emergency by the legislature and by the Supreme Court of Minnesota cannot be regarded as a subterfuge or as lacking in adequate basis. . . .

2. The legislation was addressed to a legitimate end, that is, the legislation was not for the mere advantage of particular individuals but for the protection of a basic interest of society.

3. In view of the nature of the contracts in question—mortgages of unquestionable validity—the relief afforded and justified by the emergency, in order not to contravene the constitutional provision, could only be of a character appropriate to that emergency and could be granted only upon reasonable conditions.

4. The conditions upon which the period of redemption is extended do not appear to be unreasonable. . . .

5. The legislation is temporary in operation. It is limited to the exigency which called it forth. . . .

We are of the opinion that the Minnesota statute as here applied does not violate the contract clause of the Federal Constitution. Whether the legislation is wise or unwise as a matter of policy is a question with which we are not concerned.

What has been said on that point is also applicable to the contention presented under the due process clause. . . .

Nor do we think that the statute denies to the appellant the equal protection of the laws. The classification which the statute makes cannot be said to be an arbitrary one. . . .

Judgment

Affirmed.

MR. JUSTICE SUTHERLAND, dissenting:

Few questions of greater moment than that just decided have been submitted for judicial inquiry during this generation. He simply closes his eyes to the necessary implications of the decision who fails to see in it the potentiality of future gradual but ever-advancing encroachments upon the sanctity of private and public contracts. The effect of the Minnesota legislation, though serious enough in itself, is of trivial significance compared with the far more serious and dangerous inroads upon the limitations of the Constitution which are almost certain to ensue as a consequence naturally following any step beyond the boundaries fixed by that instrument. And those of us who are thus apprehensive of the effect of this decision would, in a matter so important, be neglectful of our duty should we fail to spread upon the permanent records of the court the reasons which move us to the opposite view.

A provision of the Constitution, it is hardly necessary to say, does not admit of two distinctly opposite interpretations. It does not mean one thing at one time and an entirely different thing at another time. If the contract impairment clause, when framed and adopted, meant that the terms of a contract for the payment of money could not be altered . . . by a state statute enacted for the relief of hardly pressed debtors to the end and with the effect of postponing payment or enforcement during and because of an economic or financial emergency, it is but to state the obvious to say that it means the same now. . . .

The Minnesota statute either impairs the obligation of contracts or it does not. If it does not, the occasion to which it relates becomes immaterial, since then the passage of the statute is the exercise of a normal, unrestricted, state power and requires no special occasion to render it effective. If it does, the emergency no more furnishes a proper occasion for its exercise than if the emergency were nonexistent. And so, while, in form, the suggested distinction seems to put us forward in a straight line, in reality it simply carries us back in a circle, like bewildered travelers lost in a wood, to the point where we parted company with the view of the state court. . . .

. . . The phrase, "obligation of a contract," in the constitutional sense imports a legal duty to perform the specified obligation of *that* contract, not to substitute and perform, against the will of one of the parties, a different, albeit equally valuable, obligation. And a state, under the contract impairment clause, has no more power to accomplish such a substitution than has one of the parties to the contract against the will of the other. It cannot do so either by acting directly upon the contract, or by bringing about the result under the guise of a statute in form acting only upon the remedy. If it could, the efficacy of the constitutional restriction would, in large measure, be made to disappear. . . .

I am authorized to say that MR. JUSTICE VAN DEVANTER, MR. JUSTICE MC REYN-OLDS and MR. JUSTICE BUTLER concur in this opinion.

8

The States
and the Commerce Power

Congress did not have the power to regulate interstate and foreign commerce under the Articles of Confederation. As a result, each state attempted to protect local business at the expense of the other states through the erection of a number of trade barriers. The need for more centralized control over commerce soon became one of the "moving purposes" that brought about the Constitutional Convention in 1787. After a number of conflicting views had been compromised at the Convention, the power to regulate commerce was vested in Congress. Article I, Section 8, of the Constitution provides that Congress "shall have power . . . to regulate commerce with foreign nations and among the several states and with Indian tribes." In this brief provision the framers sought to prevent the states from interfering with the regulation of commerce across state lines. They hoped to eliminate "barriers to interstate and foreign trade which the several states had erected for the purpose of collecting toll from business originating in other states or in foreign countries and for the purpose of reserving local business opportunities for the benefit of local businessmen. The commerce clause was one of a number of clauses in the Constitution by which the framers sought to remove local fetters from business and to keep them removed."[1]

[1] Carl B. Swisher, *The Growth of Constitutional Power in the United States* (Chicago: University of Chicago Press, 1945), p. 79.

The constitutional meaning of the commerce clause has been developed and expanded by a great number of statutory enactments and through judicial interpretation. As a result, the clause has become one of the most important grants of authority in the Constitution. Justice Stone once said that the "commerce clause and the wise interpretation of it, perhaps more than any other contributing element, have united to bind the several states into a nation."[2] The importance of the commerce clause can hardly be exaggerated, for no provision of the Constitution "has been more vitally involved in the development of our national economic life and in the transitions through which our constitutional system has passed."[3] Largely through the use of the commerce power, the national government today regulates almost every conceivable aspect of American life. Of course, other powers of the federal government, such as the powers to tax, to spend for the public welfare, and to establish post offices and post roads, and the war power, have been used to expand national authority. Yet, the commerce power is used most frequently and continues to expand to immense and fascinating proportions.

The commerce clause has a two-fold rather than a single effect:

1. It is the source of the most important powers exercised by the federal government in times of peace.
2. With the exception of the Fourteenth Amendment, the commerce clause is the most important limitation on the powers of the states.[4]

In other words, as Justice William O. Douglas has noted, the commerce clause "has a negative as well as a positive aspect. The clause not only serves to augment federal authority. By its own force it also cuts down the power of a constituent state in its exercise of what normally would be a part of its residual police power." Of course, "both the positive and negative aspects of the commerce clause have grave importance."[5]

But the Constitution does not define specific spheres of state and national authority over interstate commerce. Thus, by default, the Supreme Court is given the power to decide finally what the states and the federal government may or may not do with respect to interstate commerce. In this process the Court again becomes the referee between the claims of national and local authorities. In choosing between competing interests, the Court thereby involves itself irrevocably in the formulation of fundamental policy in an extremely important area.

[2] Harlan F. Stone, "Fifty Years Work of the United States Supreme Court," *American Bar Association Journal,* Vol. 14 (Aug.–Sept. 1928), p. 430.

[3] George L. Haskins, "Marshall and the Commerce Clause of the Constitution," in W. Melville Jones (ed.), *Chief Justice John Marshall* (Ithaca, N.Y.: Cornell University Press, 1956), p. 145.

[4] Edward S. Corwin (ed.), *The Constitution of the United States of America, Analysis and Interpretation* (Washington, D.C.: Government Printing Office, 1953), p. 118.

[5] William O. Douglas, *We the Judges* (Garden City, N.Y.: Doubleday, 1956), p. 222.

The first case under the commerce clause to reach the Supreme Court was *Gibbons* v. *Ogden,* which involved an unpopular steamboat monopoly in New York. This first great case involved the negative rather than the positive aspects of the commerce clause. In *Gibbons* v. *Ogden,* John Marshall held simply that a state regulation affecting commerce is invalid when it is in conflict with a law of Congress. In this last of his major decisions, Marshall defined commerce and described the federal commerce power "with a breadth never yet exceeded." His broad view of the commerce power permeates the entire opinion. It made possible the development of commerce under federal, rather than state, control.

Unlike Marshall's other great decisions, the opinion in *Gibbons* v. *Ogden* was greeted with acclaim, which must have indeed warmed Marshall's aging heart. He had at last delivered a popular opinion, largely because he had ruled against a monopoly. The public was so satisfied that "they were, for the most part, quiescent as to Marshall's assertion of nationalism in this particular case."[6] And there were important practical effects of *Gibbons* v. *Ogden.*

Steamboat navigation of American waters increased suddenly at an incredible rate. The opening of the Hudson River and Long Island Sound to the free passage of steamboats gave immediate impetus to the growth of New York as a commercial center, while New England manufacturing was given new life because the transportation of anthracite coal became cheap and easy. From a less immediate standpoint, *Gibbons* v. *Ogden* was the needed guarantee that interstate rail, telephone and telegraph, oil and gas pipe lines might be built across state lines without the threat of local interference from state action. In short, Marshall's opinion was . . . the "emancipation proclamation of American commerce."[7]

In *Gibbons* v. *Ogden* the Supreme Court did not answer the question as to whether or not the states had concurrent power over interstate commerce. The concurring opinion of Justice William Johnson, Jefferson's first appointee to the Supreme Court, is surprising in that he maintained that Congress had exclusive power over interstate commerce. In that opinion, which ranks as one of Johnson's best, "he was defending before the public his extreme assertion of national power."[8] But although Marshall was inclined to agree with Johnson's view, he was unwilling to hold specifically that the federal power over interstate commerce was exclusive.

Marshall was presented with an opportunity to explain his position more fully in *Willson* v. *Blackbird Creek Marsh Co.,* 2 Pet. 245 (1829). In that case he upheld a Delaware statute, enacted under the state's police power, that authorized the building of a dam across a small but navigable waterway. The

[6] Albert J. Beveridge, *The Life of John Marshall* (Boston: Houghton Mifflin, 1919), p. 446.

[7] Haskins, *op. cit.,* pp. 152–53.

[8] Donald G. Morgan, *Justice William Johnson, The First Dissenter* (Columbia: University of South Carolina Press, 1954), p. 205.

dam had been erected in order to drain marshes for the protection of health and the enhancement of property values, but it had been broken by Willson's vessel, sailing under a federal coasting license. Marshall pointed out that Delaware could regulate in this instance, because Congress had not attempted to deal with the local matter involved. Speaking for the Court, he asserted: "We do not think that the Act empowering the Blackbird Creek Marsh Company to place a dam across the creek, can, under all the circumstances of the case, be considered as repugnant to the power to regulate commerce in its dormant state, or as being in conflict with any law passed on the subject." But Marshall did not attempt to provide any further explanation of this statement. His decision "plainly implies that the Delaware statute falls outside the ban of the 'dormant' commerce clause, because it is not a regulation of commerce, but of 'police.' State regulations of commerce were one thing; state exercise of the police power quite another. But Marshall hardly furnished us a litmus-paper test for distinguishing one from the other. He gave us only intimations."[9]

In the absence of a coherently expressed doctrine, the Court continued to be plagued with problems involving the validity of state laws affecting foreign or interstate commerce. The cases decided during much of the Taney era did not clarify the state of the law. Instead, the Court vacillated in a confused and muddled way on the extent to which the commerce clause limited regulations of interstate commerce by the state legislatures.[10] Finally, in the classic case of *Cooley* v. *Board of Wardens,* the Supreme Court fashioned a new formula that combined both the exclusive and concurrent doctrines. In short, the Court held that the commerce power is exclusive with respect to some matters and concurrent with respect to others. But although the principle of the *Cooley* case is still important, it is extremely difficult to apply, because there are so many possible regulations of commerce. Hence, the majority opinion of Justice Curtis in the *Cooley* case does not constitute a precise, automatic rule for deciding cases. It did turn the attention of the Court away from an analysis of the commerce power to the *subject* upon which the power operated. But in each case the Court must now face the difficult question as to whether a particular subject of commercial regulation requires uniform and national control or whether it is so local in character that a state may regulate.

Limitations on the Powers of the States

Decisions of the Supreme Court have made clear the doctrine that the "purpose of the commerce clause was not to preclude all state regulation of commerce crossing state lines but to prevent discrimination and the erection of

[9] Felix Frankfurter, *The Commerce Clause Under Marshall, Taney and Waite* (Chapel Hill: University of North Carolina Press, 1937), pp. 29–30.

[10] *Mayor of New York* v. *Miln,* 11 Pet. 102 (1837); *License Cases,* 5 How. 504 (1847); *Passenger Cases,* 7 How. 283 (1849).

barriers or obstacles to the free flow of commerce, interstate or foreign."[11] Actually, the states have passed very little legislation that is designed principally for the purpose of regulating interstate commerce. But much state legislation concerning local matters happens to affect persons or transactions in interstate commerce, and many such acts have been challenged on the ground that they place unconstitutional burdens on interstate commerce.

The states sometimes burden commerce primarily in the exercise of the following two powers:

Police Powers of the States. In enacting legislation for the protection of the health, safety, and welfare of its inhabitants, a state may sometimes impose burdens upon or affect interstate commerce. In general, such a state law is valid only if it does not conflict with a law of Congress and if it does not impose an *unreasonable* burden on interstate commerce. Thus, a state police regulation is valid if it has only an indirect or incidental effect upon interstate commerce.

Power of the States to Tax. State tax laws sometimes have an important impact on interstate commerce.

> In imposing taxes for state purposes a state is not exercising any power which the Constitution has conferred upon Congress. It is only when the tax operates to regulate commerce between the states or with foreign nations to an extent which infringes the authority conferred upon Congress, that the tax can be said to exceed constitutional limitations. Forms of state taxation whose tendency is to prohibit the commerce or place it at a disadvantage as compared with or in competition with intrastate commerce, and any state tax which discriminates against the commerce, are familiar examples of the exercise of state taxing power in an unconstitutional manner, because of its obvious regulatory effect upon commerce between the states. But it was not the purpose of the commerce clause to relieve those engaged in interstate commerce of their just share of state tax burdens, merely because an incidental or consequential effect of the tax is an increase in the cost of doing the business. Not all state taxation is to be condemned because, in some manner, it has an effect upon commerce between the states, and there are many forms of tax whose burdens, when distributed through the play of economic forces, affect interstate commerce which nevertheless fall short of the regulation of the commerce which the Constitution leaves to Congress.[12]

It is impossible to formulate a precise rule by which the Supreme Court may determine whether the police or taxing powers of a state have been exercised in such a way as to burden interstate commerce. Each case must be decided in the light of its own particular facts. Nevertheless, it is true that, with the steady growth of interstate commerce, particularly since 1890, the commerce clause has been used with increasing frequency to invalidate state regulatory and tax measures.

[11] Justice Stone dissenting in *Di Santo* v. *Pennsylvania,* 273 U.S. 34 (1927).
[12] *McGoldrick* v. *Berwind-White Coal Mining Co.,* 309 U.S. 33 (1940).

That the task of the Court in resolving the conflict between federal and state authorities remains a difficult one is apparent in the majority and minority opinions in *Southern Pacific Company* v. *Arizona* (p. 220). Justice Black's vigorous dissenting opinion in this case is of particular importance, as it indicates his position on what the role of the Supreme Court should be in the determination of policy in this area. In addition, it reveals Justice Black's well-known attachment to the Taney principle that the commerce clause, per se, does not limit the powers of the state. *Edwards* v. *California,* is concerned also with the conflict between state police power and interstate commerce, but the unique facts of the case led four members of the Court to base the decision on grounds other than commerce. The position of the four justices is revealed clearly in Justice Jackson's concurring opinion.

Many decisions involving complex and technical rules have been rendered that are concerned with the limitations imposed by the commerce clause upon the states' power to tax. In the early case of *Brown* v. *Maryland,* 12 Wheat. 419 (1827), Chief Justice Marshall held that a state license tax upon goods imported from abroad and still in their original packages was void because it was in conflict with the powers of Congress under the commerce clause. The Maryland tax also was said to violate the express clause of the Constitution (Art. I, Section 10), which prohibits the states from taxing imports and exports without the consent of Congress. Marshall further noted that "we suppose the principles laid down in this case to apply equally to importations from a sister state." However, not until 1890, in the case of *Leisy* v. *Hardin,* 135 U.S. 100, was the original-package doctrine applied to interstate commerce. But the doctrine, which means simply that goods imported from abroad or from another state are not subject to state regulations until they are sold in the original package or until the package is broken, is only a rough rule of thumb that cannot be applied precisely. As Justice Cardozo asserted in *Baldwin* v. *Seelig,* 294 U.S. 511 (1935), "the test of the 'original package' is not inflexible and final for the transactions of interstate commerce. In brief, the test of the original package is not an ultimate principle. It is an illustration of a principle. It marks a convenient boundary and one sufficiently precise save in exceptional conditions. What is ultimate is the principle that one state in its dealings with another may not place itself in a position of economic isolation. Formulas and catchwords are subordinate to this overmastering requirement."

Perhaps far more important than the original-package doctrine was Marshall's dictum in *Brown* v. *Maryland* that the commerce clause placed broad limitations upon the states' powers of taxation.[13]

---

[13] The original-package doctrine is not applied in regard to the states' police powers, which may affect interstate commerce; but it has *no* application to the states' power to tax goods in interstate commerce. However, in the field of foreign commerce the doctrine has never lost its vitality. It is still applied by the courts to prevent the states from taxing imports from abroad or from prohibiting imports from foreign countries under the states' police powers.

He all but held that the commerce clause impliedly prohibits *all* taxation of interstate commerce. This doctrine of Marshall's runs like a red thread throughout the cases dealing with state taxation, and the underlying principle to which the Court has sought to give effect is that the states have no power to withhold, or unduly to burden, the privilege of engaging in interstate commerce. At the same time, it has been recognized that the power of the states to tax in order to maintain their governments must not be unduly curtailed and that interstate commerce must pay its way. Hence there has arisen in the field of taxation the same problem of accommodating state and national interests with which Marshall was concerned in the Ogden and Blackbird cases, and the Court has repeatedly recognized the relevance of those cases to the problem of state taxation.[14]

Many vexing issues indeed have been presented to the Court by the attempts of the states to tax one or more incidents of interstate commerce. In general, "despite mechanical or artificial distinctions sometimes taken between the taxes deemed permissible and those condemned, the decisions appear to be predicated on a practical judgment as to the likelihood of the tax being used to place interstate commerce at a competitive disadvantage."[15]

The issues have become quite complex, particularly in relation to state taxes based on gross receipts of interstate corporations operating within their boundaries and property taxes directed at equipment like jet aircraft that are sometimes in one state and sometimes in another. Most of the issues are canvassed in such cases as *Northwestern States Portland Cement Co.* v. *Minnesota,* 358 U.S. 450 (1959); *General Motors Corp.* v. *Washington,* 377 U.S. 436 (1964); and *Central R.R.* v. *Pennsylvania,* 370 U.S. 607 (1962).

GIBBONS *v.* OGDEN
9 Wheat 1; 6 L. Ed. 23 (1824)

[*Robert Livingston*[16] *and Robert Fulton were pioneers in the development of a practical steamboat. In 1807, their vessel made a successful trip from New York to Albany. The next year the New York State legislature granted the two men an exclusive thirty-year franchise to operate steamboats on New York waters. Under the terms of the monopoly, no person was to be allowed to navigate New York waters without first securing a license from Fulton and Livingston. Any unlicensed vessel found on New York waters was to be forfeited to them. Steamboat navigation developed very rapidly after 1808, and the New York monopoly became extremely unpopular. A number of states passed retaliatory measures: Connecticut,*

---

[14] Haskins, *op. cit.,* p. 162.

[15] Justice Stone, in a note in *McGoldrick* v. *Berwind-White Coal Mining Co.,* 309 U.S. 33 (1940).

[16] Livingston's important role in pioneering the steamboat and his scramble for the New York monopoly, as well as his other public activities, are discussed fully in George Dangerfield, *Chancellor Robert R. Livingston of New York, 1746–1813* (New York: Harcourt, Brace, 1960).

for example, prohibited vessels licensed by Fulton and Livingston from entering the state's waters; other states made exclusive grants similar to the New York monopoly. Thus, when the case of Gibbons v. Ogden first arose, the states were engaged in bitter commercial warfare.

Ogden, who had been licensed by Fulton and Livingston, operated boats from New York to New Jersey. Gibbons also operated boats between the two states in direct competition with Ogden under a coasting license obtained from the federal government. Ogden began a suit to enjoin Gibbons from continuing in the interstate business. A decision written by Chancellor James Kent, perhaps the outstanding jurist of his day, sustained the steamboat monopoly and granted Ogden an injunction. The highest state court affirmed. Gibbons then appealed to the Supreme Court.]

MR. CHIEF JUSTICE MARSHALL delivered the opinion of the Court:

The appellant contends that this decree is erroneous, because the laws which purport to give the exclusive privilege it sustains, are repugnant to the Constitution and laws of the United States.

They are said to be repugnant—

1st. To that clause in the Constitution which authorizes Congress to regulate commerce.

2d. To that which authorizes Congress to promote the progress of science and useful arts. . . .

As preliminary to the very able discussions of the Constitution which we have heard from the bar, and as having some influence on its construction, reference has been made to the political situation of these States, anterior to its formation. It has been said, that they were sovereign, were completely independent, and were connected with each other only by a league. This is true. But, when these allied sovereigns converted their league into a government, when they converted their Congress of Ambassadors, deputed to deliberate on their common concerns, and to recommend measures of general utility, into a Legislature, empowered to enact laws on the most interesting subjects, the whole character in which the States appear underwent a change, the extent of which must be determined by a fair consideration of the instrument by which that change was effected.

This instrument contains an enumeration of powers expressly granted by the people to their government. It has been said that these powers ought to be construed strictly. But why ought they to be so construed? Is there one sentence in the Constitution which gives countenance to this rule? In the last of the enumerated powers, that which grants, expressly, the means for carrying all others into execution, Congress is authorized "to make all laws which shall be necessary and proper" for the purpose. But this limitation on the means which may be used is not extended to the powers which are conferred; nor is there one sentence in the Constitution, which has been pointed out by the gentlemen of the bar, or which we have been able to discern that prescribes this rule. We do not, therefore, think ourselves justified in adopting it. What do gentlemen mean by a strict construction? If they contend only against that enlarged construction which would extend words beyond their natural and obvious import, we might question the application of the term, but should not controvert the principle. If they contend for that narrow construction which, in support of some theory not to be found in the Constitution, would deny to the government those powers which the words of the grant, as usually understood, import, and which are consistent with the general views and objects of the instrument; for that narrow construction, which would cripple the government, and render it unequal to the objects for which it is declared to be instituted, and to which the powers given, as fairly understood, render it competent; then we cannot perceive the propriety of this strict construction, nor adopt it as the rule by which the Constitution is to be expounded. As men whose intentions require no concealment generally employ the words which most directly and aptly express the ideas they intend to convey, the enlightened patriots who framed our Constitution, and the people who adopted it, must be understood to have employed words in their natural sense, and to have intended what they have said. If, from the imperfection of human language, there should be serious doubts respecting the extent of any given power, it is a well settled rule that the objects for which it was given, especially when those objects are expressed in the instrument itself, should have great influence in the construction. We know of no reason for excluding this rule from the present case. The grant does not convey power which might be beneficial to the grantor, if retained by himself, or which can enure solely to the benefit of the grantee; but is an investment of power for the general advantage, in the hands of agents selected for that purpose; which power can never be exercised by the people themselves, but must be placed in the hands of agents, or lie dormant. We know of no rule for construing the extent of such powers, other than is given by the language of the instrument which confers them, taken in connexion with the purposes for which they were conferred.

The words are, "Congress shall have power to regulate commerce with foreign nations, and among the several States, and with the Indian tribes."

The subject to be regulated is commerce; and our Constitution being, as was aptly said at the bar, one of enumeration and not of definition, to ascertain the extent of the power it becomes necessary to settle the meaning of the word. The counsel for the appellee would limit it to traffic, to buying and selling, or the interchange of commodities, and do not admit that it comprehends navigation. This would restrict a general term, applicable to many objects, to one of its significations. Commerce, undoubtedly, is traffic, but it is something more; it is intercourse. It describes the commercial intercourse between nations, and parts of nations, in all its branches, and is regulated by prescribing rules for carrying on that intercourse. The mind can scarcely conceive a system for regulating commerce between nations which shall exclude all laws concerning navigation, which shall be silent on the admission of the vessels of one nation into the ports of the other, and be confined to prescribing rules for the conduct of individuals in the actual employment of buying and selling, or of barter.

If commerce does not include navigation, the government of the Union has no direct power over that subject, and can make no law prescribing what shall constitute American vessels, or requiring that they shall be navigated by American seamen. Yet this power has been exercised from the commencement of the government, has been understood by all to be a commercial regulation. All America understands, and has uniformly understood, the word "commerce" to comprehend navigation. It was so understood, and must have been so understood, when the Constitution was framed. The power over commerce, including navigation, was one of the primary objects for which the people of

America adopted their government, and must have been contemplated in forming it. The convention must have used the word in that sense, because all have understood it in that sense; and the attempt to restrict it comes too late.

. . . The word used in the Constitution, then, comprehends, and has been always understood to comprehend, navigation within its meaning; and a power to regulate navigation is as expressly granted as if that term had been added to the word "commerce."

To what commerce does this power extend? The Constitution informs us, to commerce "with the foreign nations, and among the several States, and with the Indian tribes."

It has, we believe, been universally admitted, that these words comprehend every species of commercial intercourse between the United States and foreign nations. No sort of trade can be carried on between this country and any other, to which this power does not extend. It has been truly said that commerce, as the word is used in the Constitution, is a unit, every part of which is indicated by the term.

If this be the admitted meaning of the word in its application to foreign nations, it must carry the same meaning throughout the sentence, and remain a unit, unless there be some plain intelligible cause which alters it.

The subject to which the power is next applied is to commerce "among the several States." The word "among" means intermingled with. A thing which is among others, is intermingled with them. Commerce among the States cannot stop at the external boundary line of each State, but may be introduced into the interior.

It is not intended to say that these words comprehend that commerce which is completely internal, which is carried on between man and man in a State, or between different parts of the same State, and which does not extend to or affect other States. Such a power would be inconvenient, and is certainly unnecessary.

Comprehensive as the word "among" is, it may very properly be restricted to that commerce which concerns more States than one. . . . The completely internal commerce of a State, then, may be considered as reserved for the State itself.

But, in regulating commerce with foreign nations, the power of Congress does not stop at the jurisdictional lines of the several States. It would be a very useless power if it could not pass those lines. The commerce of the United States with foreign nations is that of the whole United States. Every district has a right to participate in it. The deep streams which penetrate our country in every direction pass through the interior of almost every State in the Union, and furnish the means of exerting this right. If Congress has the power to regulate it, that power must be exercised whenever the subject exists. If it exists within the States, if a foreign voyage may commence or terminate at a port within a State, then the power of Congress may be exercised within a State.

This principle is, if possible, still more clear when applied to commerce "among the several States." They either join each other, in which case they are separated by a mathematical line, or they are remote from each other, in which case other States lie between them. What is commerce "among" them; and how is it to be conducted? Can a trading expedition between two adjoining States commence and terminate outside of each? And if the trading intercourse be between two States remote from each other, must it not commence in one, terminate in the other, and probably pass through a third? Commerce among the States must, of necessity, be commerce with the States. In the regulation of trade with the Indian tribes, the action of the law, especially when the Constitution was made, was chiefly within a State. The power of Congress, then, whatever it may be, must be exercised within the territorial jurisdiction of the several States.

. . . We are now arrived at the inquiry—What is this power?

It is the power to regulate; that is, to prescribe the rule by which commerce is to be governed. This power, like all others vested in Congress, is complete in itself, may be exercised to its utmost extent, and acknowledges no limitations other than are prescribed in the Constitution. These are expressed in plain terms, and do not affect the questions which arise in this case, or which have been discussed at the bar. If, as has always been understood, the sovereignty of Congress, though limited to specified objects, is plenary as to those objects, the power over commerce with foreign nations, and among the several States, is vested in Congress as absolutely as it would be in a single government, having in its constitution the same restrictions on the exercise of the power as are found in the Constitution of the United States. . . .

The power of Congress, then, comprehends navigation within the limits of every State in the Union; so far as that navigation may be, in any manner, connected with "commerce with foreign nations, or among the several States, or with the Indian tribes." It may, of consequence, pass the jurisdictional line of New York, and act upon the very waters to which the prohibition now under consideration applies.

But it has been urged with great earnestness that, although the power of Congress to regulate commerce with foreign nations, and among the several States, be co-extensive with the subject itself, and have no other limits than are prescribed in the Constitution, yet the States may severally exercise the same power within their respective jurisdictions. In support of this argument, it is said that they possessed it as an inseparable attribute of sovereignty before the formation of the Constitution, and still retain it, except so far as they have surrendered it by that instrument; that this principle results from the nature of the government, and is secured by the Tenth Amendment; that an affirmative grant of power is not exclusive, unless in its own nature it be such that the continued exercise of it by the former possessor is inconsistent with the grant, and that this is not of that description.

The appellant, conceding these postulates, except the last, contends that full power to regulate a particular subject implies the whole power, and leaves no residuum; that a grant of the whole is incompatible with the existence of a right in another to any part of it.

Both parties have appealed to the Constitution, to legislative acts, and judicial decisions; and have drawn arguments from all these sources to support and illustrate the proposition they respectively maintain.

. . . In discussing the question, whether this power is still in the States, in the case under consideration, we may dismiss from it the inquiry, whether it is surrendered by the mere grant to Congress, or is retained until Congress shall exercise the power. We may dismiss that inquiry, because it has been exercised, and the regulations which Congress deemed it proper to make are now in full operation. The sole question is, can a State regulate commerce with foreign nations and among the States, while Congress is regulating it?

. . . The act passed in 1803, prohibiting the importation of slaves into any State which shall itself prohibit their importation, implies, it is said, an admission that the States possessed the power to exclude or admit them; from which it is inferred, that they possess the same power with respect to other articles.

If this inference were correct; if this power was exercised, not under any particular clause in the Constitution, but in virtue of a general right over the subject of commerce, to exist as long as the Constitution itself, it might now be exercised. Any State might now import African slaves into its own territory. But it is obvious that the power of the States over this subject, previous to the year 1808, constitutes an exception to the power of Congress to regulate commerce, and the exception is expressed in such words as to manifest clearly the intention to continue the pre-existing right of the States to admit or exclude, for a limited period. The words are, "the migration or importation of such persons as any of the States, now existing, *shall* think proper to admit, shall not be prohibited by the Congress prior to the year 1808." The whole object of the exception is to preserve the power to those States which might be disposed to exercise it; and its language seems to the Court to convey this idea unequivocally. The possession of this particular power, then, during the time limited in the Constitution, cannot be admitted to prove the possession of any other similar power.

It has been said, that the act of August 7, 1789, acknowledges a concurrent power in the States to regulate the conduct of pilots, and hence is inferred an admission of their concurrent right with Congress to regulate commerce with foreign nations, and amongst the States. But this inference is not, we think, justified by the fact.

Although Congress cannot enable a State to legislate, Congress may adopt the provisions of a State on any subject. When the government of the Union was brought into existence, it found a system for the regulation of its pilots in full force in every State. The act which has been mentioned adopts this system and gives it the same validity as if its provisions had been specially made by Congress. But the act, it may be said, is prospective also, and the adoption of laws to be made in future, presupposes the right in the maker to legislate on the subject.

The act unquestionably manifests an intention to leave this subject entirely to the States, until Congress should think proper to interpose; but the very enactment of such a law indicates an opinion that it was necessary; that the existing system would not be applicable to the new state of things unless expressly applied to it by Congress.

. . . These acts were cited at the bar for the purpose of showing an opinion in Congress, that the States possess, concurrently with the Legislature of the Union, the power to regulate commerce with foreign nations and among the States. Upon reviewing them, we think they do not establish the proposition they were intended to prove. They show the opinion, that the States retain powers enabling them to pass the laws to which allusion has been made, not that those laws proceed from the particular power which has been delegated to Congress.

It has been contended by the counsel for the appellant that, as the word "to regulate" implies in its nature full power over the thing to be regulated, it excludes, necessarily, the action of all others that would perform the same operation on the same thing. That regulation is designed for the entire result, applying to those parts which remain as they were, as well as to those which are altered. It produces a uniform whole, which is as much disturbed and deranged by changing what the regulating power designs to leave untouched, as that on which it has operated.

There is great force in this argument, and the Court is not satisfied that it has been refuted.

Since, however, in exercising the power of regulating their own purely internal affairs, whether of trading or police, the States may sometimes enact laws, the validity of which depends on their interfering with, and being contrary to, an act of Congress passed in pursuance of the Constitution, the Court will enter upon the inquiry, whether the laws of New York, as expounded by the highest tribunal of that State, have, in their application to this case, come into collision with an act of Congress, and deprived a citizen of a right to which that act entitles him. Should this collision exist, it will be immaterial whether those laws were passed in virtue of a concurrent power "to regulate commerce with foreign nations and among the several States" or in virtue of a power to regulate their domestic trade and police. In one case and the other, the acts of New York must yield to the law of Congress; and the decision sustaining the privilege they confer, against a right given by a law of the Union, must be erroneous.

This opinion has been frequently expressed in this Court, and is founded as well on the nature of the government as on the words of the Constitution. In argument, however, it has been contended that if a law passed by a State, in the exercise of its acknowledged sovereignty, comes into conflict with a law passed by Congress in pursuance of the Constitution, they affect the subject, and each other, like equal opposing powers.

But the framers of our Constitution foresaw this state of things, and provided for it by declaring the supremacy not only of itself, but of the laws made

in pursuance of it. The nullity of any act inconsistent with the Constitution is produced by the declaration that the Constitution is the supreme law. The appropriate application of that part of the clause which confers the same supremacy on laws and treaties, is to such acts of the State Legislatures as do not transcend their powers, but, though enacted in the execution of acknowledged State powers, interfere with or are contrary to the laws of Congress, made in pursuance of the Constitution, or some treaty made under the authority of the United States. In every such case, the act of Congress, or the treaty, is supreme; and the law of the State, though enacted in the exercise of powers not controverted, must yield to it.

. . . The questions, . . . whether the conveyance of passengers be a part of the coasting trade, and whether a vessel can be protected in that occupation by a coasting license, are not, and cannot be, raised in this case. The real and sole question seems to be whether a steam machine, in actual use, deprives a vessel of the privileges conferred by a license.

In considering this question, the first idea which presents itself is, that the laws of Congress for the regulation of commerce do not look to the principle by which vessels are moved. That subject is left entirely to individual discretion; and, in that vast and complex system of legislative enactment concerning it, which embraces everything that the Legislature thought it necessary to notice, there is not, we believe, one word respecting the peculiar principle by which vessels are propelled through the water, except what may be found in a single act granting a particular privilege to steam boats. With this exception, every act, either prescribing duties or granting privileges, applies to every vessel, whether navigated by the instrumentality of wind or fire, of sails or machinery. The whole weight of proof, then, is thrown upon him who would introduce a distinction to which the words of the law give no countenance.

If a real difference could be admitted to exist between vessels carrying passengers and others, it has already been observed that there is no fact in this case which can bring up that question. And, if the occupation of steam boats be a matter of such general notoriety that the Court may be presumed to know it, although not specially informed by the record, then we deny that the transportation of passengers is their exclusive occupation. It is a matter of general history, that in our western waters their principal employment is the transportation of merchandise; and all know that in the waters of the Atlantic they are frequently so employed.

But all inquiry into this subject seems to the Court to be put completely at rest by the act already mentioned, entitled, "An act for the enrolling and licensing of steam boats."

This act authorizes a steam boat employed, or intended to be employed, only in a river or bay of the United States, owned wholly or in part by an alien, resident within the United States, to be enrolled and licensed as if the same belonged to a citizen of the United States.

This act demonstrates the opinion of Congress that steam boats may be enrolled and licensed in common with vessels using sails. They are, of course, entitled to the same privileges, and can no more be restrained from navigating waters, and entering ports which are free to such vessels, than if they were wafted on their voyage by winds instead of being propelled by the agency of fire. The one element may be as legitimately used as the other for every commercial purpose authorized by the law of the Union; and the act of a State inhibiting the use of either to any vessel having a license under the act of Congress comes, we think, in direct collision with that act.

As this decides the cause, it is unnecessary to enter in an examination of that part of the Constitution which empowers Congress to promote the progress of science and the useful arts.

Reversed.

[MR. JUSTICE JOHNSON concurred on the ground that the power of Congress over interstate commerce was intended to be exclusive and that the licensing act did not affect the case.]

COOLEY *v.* BOARD OF WARDENS OF THE PORT OF PHILADELPHIA　12 How. 299; 13 L. Ed. 996 (1852)

[*In 1803, the Pennsylvania legislature enacted a statute that set up various rules regarding pilotage in the port of Philadelphia. A particular section of the law required vessels to receive pilots for entering or leaving the port. A fine of half the pilotage fee was levied against any vessel that did not use a pilot. Cooley violated the law by refusing to pay the fines on two of his vessels, neither of which had employed a pilot. In a suit to recover the fees, judgments were rendered against Cooley in the state courts. Cooley then brought the cases to the Supreme Court on writs of error.*]

MR. JUSTICE CURTIS delivered the opinion of the Court:

We think this particular regulation concerning half-pilotage fees is an appropriate part of a general system of regulations of this subject. Testing it by the practice of commercial States and countries legislating on this subject, we find it has usually been deemed necessary to make similar provisions. Numerous laws of this kind are cited in the learned argument of the counsel for the defendant in error; and their fitness, as a part of a system of pilotage, in many places, may be inferred from their existence in so many different States and countries. . . .

It remains to consider the objection that it is repugnant to the third clause of the eighth section of the first article. "The Congress shall have power to regulate commerce with foreign nations and among the several States, and with the Indian tribes."

That the power to regulate includes the regulation of navigation, we consider settled. And when we look to the nature of the service performed by pilots, to the relations which that service and its compensations bear to navigation between the several States, and between the ports of the United States and foreign countries, we are brought to the conclusion that the regulation of the qualifications of pilots, of the modes and times of offering and rendering their services, of the responsibilities which shall rest upon them, of the powers they shall possess, of the compensation they may demand, and of the penalties by which their rights and duties may be enforced, do constitute regulations of navigation, and consequently of commerce, within the just meaning of this clause of the Constitution.

The power to regulate navigation is the power to prescribe rules in conformity with which navigation must be carried on. It extends to the persons who conduct it, as well as to the instruments used. Accordingly, the first Congress assembled under the Constitution passed laws requiring the masters of ships and vessels of the United States to be citizens of the United States, and established many rules for the government and regulation of officers and seamen. . . . These have been from time to time added to and changed, and we are not aware that their validity has been questioned.

Now, a pilot, so far as respects the navigation of the vessel in that part of the voyage which is his pilotage-ground, is the temporary master charged with the safety of the vessel and cargo, and of the lives of those on board, and intrusted with the command of the crew. He is not only one of the persons engaged in navigation, but he occupies a most important and responsible place among those thus engaged. And if Congress has power to regulate the seamen who assist the pilot in the management of the vessel, a power never denied, we can perceive no valid reason why the pilot should be beyond the reach of the same power. It is true that, according to the usages of modern commerce on the ocean, the pilot is on board only during a part of the voyage between ports of different States, or between ports of the United States and foreign countries; but if he is on board for such a purpose and during so much of the voyage as to be engaged in navigation, the power to regulate navigation extends to him while thus engaged, as clearly as it would if he were to remain on board throughout the whole passage, from port to port. For it is a power which extends to every part of the voyage, and may regulate those who conduct or assist in conducting navigation in one part of a voyage as much as in another part, or during the whole voyage.

Nor should it be lost sight of that this subject of the regulation of pilots and pilotage has an intimate connection with, and an important relation to, the general subject of commerce with foreign nations and among the several States, over which it was one main object of the Constitution to create a national control. Conflicts between the laws of neighboring States and discriminations favorable or adverse to commerce with particular foreign nations might be created by State laws regulating pilotage, deeply affecting that equality of commercial rights, and that freedom from State interference, which those who formed the Constitution were so anxious to secure, and which the experience of more than half a century has taught us to value so highly.

. . . And a majority of the Court are of opinion, that a regulation of pilots is a regulation of commerce within the grant to Congress of the commercial power, contained in the third clause of the eighth section of the first article of the Constitution.

It becomes necessary, therefore, to consider whether this law of Pennsylvania, being a regulation of commerce, is valid.

The act of Congress of the 7th of August, 1789, Sect. 4, is as follows:

"That all pilots in the bays, inlets, rivers, harbors, and ports of the United States shall continue to be regulated in conformity with the existing laws of the States, respectively, wherein such pilots may be, or with such laws as the States may respectively hereafter enact for the purpose, until further legislative provision shall be made by Congress."

. . . If the States were divested of the power to legislate on this subject by the grant of the commercial power to Congress, it is plain this act could not confer upon them power thus to legislate. If the Constitution excluded the States from making any law regulating commerce, certainly Congress cannot regrant, or in any manner reconvey to the States that power. . . . [W]e are brought directly and unavoidably to the consideration of the question, whether the grant of the commercial power to Congress did *per se* deprive the States

of all power to regulate pilots. This question has never been decided by this Court, nor in our judgment, has any case depending upon all the considerations which must govern this one come before this Court. The grant of commercial power to Congress does not contain any terms which expressly exclude the States from exercising an authority over its subject matter. If they are excluded, it must be because the nature of the power thus granted to Congress requires that a similar authority should not exist in the States. If it were conceded on the one side, that the nature of this power, like that to legislate for the District of Columbia, is absolutely and totally repugnant to the existence of similar power in the States, probably no one would deny that the grant of the power to Congress as effectually and perfectly excludes the States from all future legislation on the subject as if express words had been used to exclude them. And on the other hand, if it were admitted that the existence of this power in Congress, like the power of taxation, is compatible with the existence of a similar power in the States, then it would be in conformity with the contemporary exposition of the Constitution (*Federalist*, No. 32) and with the judicial construction given from time to time by this Court, after the most deliberate consideration, to hold that the mere grant of such a power to Congress did not imply a prohibition on the States to exercise the same power; that it is not the mere existence of such a power, but its exercise by Congress, which may be incompatible with the exercise of the same power by the States, and that the States may legislate in the absence of congressional regulations. . . .

The diversities of opinion, therefore, which have existed on this subject, have arisen from the different views taken of the nature of this power. But when the nature of a power like this is spoken of, when it is said that the nature of the power requires that it should be exercised exclusively by Congress, it must be intended to refer to the subjects of that power, and to say they are of such a nature as to require exclusive legislation by Congress. Now the power to regulate commerce embraces a vast field, containing not only many, but exceedingly various subjects, quite unlike in their nature; some imperatively demanding a single uniform rule, operating equally on the commerce of the United States in every port, and some, like the subject now in question, as imperatively demanding that diversity, which alone can meet the local necessities of navigation.

Either absolutely to affirm or deny that the nature of this power requires exclusive legislation by Congress is to lose sight of the nature of the subjects of this power, and to assert concerning all of them what is really applicable but to a part. Whatever subjects of this power are in their nature national, or admit only of one uniform system or plan of regulation, may justly be said to be of such a nature as to require exclusive legislation by Congress. That this cannot be affirmed of laws for the regulation of pilots and pilotage is plain. The act of 1789 contains a clear and authoritative declaration by the first Congress, that the nature of this subject is such that, until Congress should find it necessary to exert its power, it should be left to the legislation of the States; that it is local and not national; that it is likely to be the best provided for, not by one system, or plan of regulations, but by as many as the legislative discretion of the several States should deem applicable to the local peculiarities of the ports within their limits.

Viewed in this light, so much of this act of 1789 as declares that pilots shall continue to be regulated "by such laws as the States may respectively hereafter enact for that purpose," instead of being held to be inoperative as an attempt to confer on the States a power to legislate, of which the Constitution had deprived them, is allowed an appropriate and important signification. It manifests the understanding of Congress, at the outset of the government, that the nature of this subject is not such as to require its exclusive legislation. The practice of the States, and of the national government, has been in conformity with this declaration from the origin of the national government to this time; and the nature of the subject when examined is such as to leave no doubt of the superior fitness and propriety, not to say the absolute necessity, of different systems of regulation, drawn from local knowledge and experience, and conformed to local wants. How then can we say, that by the mere grant of power to regulate commerce, the States are deprived of all the power to legislate on this subject, because from the nature of the power the legislation of Congress must be exclusive. This would be to affirm that the nature of the power is in any case something different from the nature of the subject to which, in such case, the power extends, and that the nature of the power necessarily demands, in all cases, exclusive legislation by Congress, while the nature of one of the subjects of that power not only does not require such exclusive legislation, but may be best provided for by many different systems enacted by the States in conformity with the circumstances of the ports within their limits. In construing an instrument designed for the formation of a government, and in determining the extent of one of its important grants of power to legislate, we can make no such distinction between the nature of the power and the nature of the subject on which that power was intended practically to operate, nor consider the grant more extensive by affirming of the power, what is not true of its subject now in question.

It is the opinion of a majority of the Court that the mere grant to Congress of the power to regulate commerce did not deprive the States of power to regulate pilots, and that although Congress has legislated on this subject, its legislation manifests an intention, with a single exception, not to regulate this subject, but to leave its regulation to the several States. To these precise questions, which are all we are called on to decide, this opinion must be understood to be confined. It does not extend to the question what other subjects, under the commercial power, are within the exclusive control of Congress, or may be regulated by the States in the absence of all congressional legislation; nor to the general question how far any regulation of a subject by Congress may be deemed to operate as an exclusion of all legislation by the States upon the same subject. We decide the precise questions before us, upon what we deem sound principles, applicable to this particular subject in the state in which the legislation of Congress has left it. We go no further.

. . . We are of opinion that this State law . . . is therefore valid, and the judgment of the Supreme Court of Pennsylvania in each case must be

Affirmed.

[MR. JUSTICE MC LEAN and MR. JUSTICE WAYNE dissented. MR. JUSTICE DANIEL wrote a separate opinion concurring with the judgment of the Court, but differed in reasoning on the basis that the control of pilotage was an "original and inherent" state power not "subject to the sanction of the federal government."]

SOUTHERN PACIFIC CO. *v.* ARIZONA
325 U.S. 761; 65 Sup. Ct. 1515; 89 L. Ed. 1915 (1945)

[*The Arizona Train Limit Law of 1912 made it unlawful for any person or corporation to operate within the state a railroad train with more than fourteen passenger cars or more than seventy freight cars. The law was a safety measure designed to avoid accidents resulting from the "slack action" of individual cars on long trains. Slack action is defined as the amount of free movement of one car before it transmits its motion to an adjoining coupled car. A fine was to be paid for each violation of the law. In 1940, Arizona tried to collect penalties from the Southern Pacific Company for violations of the law. The company admitted the violations but contended that the act was unconstitutional. The trial court rendered a judgment for the company, but the state supreme court reversed the judgment and upheld the constitutionality of the law. The company then brought the case to the Supreme Court on appeal.*]

MR. CHIEF JUSTICE STONE delivered the opinion of the Court:

. . . The questions for decision are whether Congress has, by legislative enactment, restricted the power of the states to regulate the length of interstate trains as a safety measure and, if not, whether the statute contravenes the commerce clause of the Federal Constitution. . . .

Congress, in enacting legislation within its constitutional authority over interstate commerce, will not be deemed to have intended to strike down a state statute designed to protect the health and safety of the public unless its purpose to do so is clearly manifested. . . . or unless the state law, in terms or in its practical administration, conflicts with the Act of Congress, or plainly and palpably infringes its policy. . . .

Congress, although asked to do so, has declined to pass legislation specifically limiting trains to seventy cars. We are therefore brought to appellant's principal contention, that the state statute contravenes the commerce clause of the Federal Constitution.

Although the commerce clause conferred on the national government power to regulate commerce, its possession of the power does not exclude all state power of regulation. Ever since *Willson* v. *Blackbird Creek Marsh Co.,* 2 Pet, 245, and *Cooley* v. *Board of Wardens,* 12 How. 299, it has been recognized that, in the absence of conflicting legislation by Congress, there is a residuum of power in the state to make laws governing matters of local concern which nevertheless in some measure affect interstate commerce or even, to some extent, regulate it. . . . Thus the states may regulate matters which, because of their number and diversity, may never be adequately dealt with by Congress. . . . When the regulation of matters of local concern is local in character and effect, and its impact on the national commerce does not seriously interfere with its operation, and the consequent incentive to deal with them nationally is slight, such regulation has been generally held to be within state authority. . . .

But ever since *Gibbons* v. *Ogden* . . . the states have not been deemed to have authority to impede substantially the free flow of commerce from state to state, or to regulate those phases of the national commerce which, because of the need of national uniformity, demand that their regulation, if any, be prescribed by a single authority. . . .

Whether or not this long-recognized distribution of power between the national and the state governments is predicated upon the implications of the commerce clause itself . . . or upon the presumed intention of Congress, where Congress has not spoken. . . . the result is the same.

In the application of these principles some enactments may be found to be plainly within and others plainly without state power. But between these extremes lies the infinite variety of cases in which regulation of local matters may also operate as a regulation of commerce, in which reconciliation of the conflicting claims of state and national power is to be attained only by some appraisal and accommodation of the competing demands of the state and national interests involved. . . .

For a hundred years it has been accepted constitutional doctrine that the commerce clause, without the aid of Congressional legislation, thus affords some protection from state legislation inimical to the national commerce, and that in such cases, where Congress has not acted, this Court, and not the state legislature, is under the commerce clause the final arbiter of the competing demands of state and national interests. . . .

Congress has undoubted power to redefine the distribution of power over interstate commerce. It may either permit the states to regulate the commerce in a manner which would otherwise not be permissible, . . . or exclude state regulation even of matters of peculiarly local concern which nevertheless affect interstate commerce. . . .

But in general Congress has left it to the courts to formulate the rules thus interpreting the commerce clause in its application, doubtless because it has appreciated the destructive consequences to the commerce of the nation if their protection were withdrawn, . . . and has been aware that in their application state laws will not be invalidated without the support of relevant factual material which will "afford a sure basis" for an informed judgment. . . . Meanwhile, Congress has accommodated its legislation, as have the states, to these rules as an established feature of our constitutional system. There has thus been left to the states wide scope for the regulation of matters of local state concern, even though it in some measure affects the commerce, provided it does not materially restrict the free flow of commerce across state lines, or interfere with it in matters with respect to which uniformity of regulation is of predominant national concern.

Hence the matters for ultimate determination here are the nature and extent of the burden which the state regulation of interstate trains, adopted as a safety measure, imposes on interstate commerce, and whether the relative weights of the state and national interests involved are such as to make inapplicable the rule, generally observed, that the free flow of interstate commerce and its freedom from local restraints in matters requiring uniformity of regulation are interests safeguarded by the commerce clause from state interference. . . .

The findings show that the operation of long trains, that is, trains of more than fourteen passenger and more than seventy freight cars, is standard practice over the main lines of the railroads of the United States, and that, if the length of trains is to be regulated at all, national uniformity in the regulation adopted, such as only Congress can prescribe, is practically indispensable to the operation of an efficient and economical national railway system. On many railroads passenger trains of more than fourteen cars and freight trains of more than seventy cars are operated, and on some systems freight trains are

run ranging from 125 to 160 cars in length. Outside of Arizona, where the length of trains is not restricted, appellant runs a substantial proportion of long trains. . . .

The record shows a definite relationship between operating costs and the length of trains, the increase in length resulting in a reduction of operating costs per car. The additional cost of operation of trains complying with the Train Limit Law in Arizona amounts for the two railroads traversing that state to about $1,000,000 a year. The reduction in train lengths also impedes efficient operation. More locomotives and more manpower are required; the necessary conversion and reconversion of train lengths at terminals, and the delay caused by breaking up and remaking long trains upon entering and leaving the state in order to comply with the law, delays the traffic and diminishes its volume moved in a given time, especially when traffic is heavy. . . .

The unchallenged findings leave no doubt that the Arizona Train Limit Law imposes a serious burden on the interstate commerce conducted by appellant. It materially impedes the movement of appellant's interstate trains through that state and interposes a substantial obstruction to the national policy proclaimed by Congress, to promote adequate, economical, and efficient railway transportation service. . . . Enforcement of the law in Arizona, while train lengths remain unregulated or are regulated by varying standards in other states, must inevitably result in an impairment of uniformity of efficient railroad operation because the railroads are subjected to regulation which is not uniform in its application. Compliance with a state statute limiting train lengths requires interstate trains of a length lawful in other states to be broken up and reconstituted as they enter each state according as it may impose varying limitations upon train lengths. The alternative is for the carrier to conform to the lowest train limit restriction of any of the states through which its trains pass, whose laws thus control the carriers' operations both within and without the regulating state. . . .

If one state may regulate train lengths, so may all the others, and they need not prescribe the same maximum limitation. The practical effect of such regulation is to control train operations beyond the boundaries of the state exacting it because of the necessity of breaking up and reassembling long trains at the nearest terminal points before entering and after leaving the regulating state. The serious impediment to the free flow of commerce by the local regulation of train lengths and the practical necessity that such regulation, if any, must be prescribed by a single body having a nationwide authority are apparent.

The trial court found that the Arizona law had no reasonable relation to safety, and made train operation more dangerous. Examination of the evidence and the detailed findings makes it clear that this conclusion was rested on facts found which indicate that such increased danger of accident and personal injury as may result from the greater length of trains is more than offset by the increase in the number of accidents resulting from the larger number of trains when train lengths are reduced. In considering the effect of the statute as a safety measure, therefore, the factor of controlling significance for present purposes is not whether there is basis for the conclusion of the Arizona Supreme Court that the increase in length of trains beyond the statutory maximum has an adverse effect upon safety of operation. The decisive question is whether in the circumstances the total effect of the law as a safety measure in reducing accidents and casualties is so slight or problematical as not to outweigh the national interest in keeping interstate commerce free from interferences which seriously impede it and subject it to local regulation which does not have a uniform effect on the interstate train journey which it interrupts. . . .

We think, as the trial court found, that the Arizona Train Limit Law, viewed as a safety measure, affords at most slight and dubious advantage, if any, over unregulated train lengths. . . . Its undoubted effect on the commerce is the regulation, without securing uniformity, of the length of trains operated in interstate commerce, which lack is itself a primary cause of preventing the free flow of commerce by delaying it and by substantially increasing its cost and impairing its efficiency. In these respects the case differs from those where a state, by regulatory measures affecting the commerce, has removed or reduced safety hazards without substantial interference with the interstate movement of trains. . . .

The principle that, without controlling Congressional action, a state may not regulate interstate commerce so as substantially to affect its flow or deprive it of needed uniformity in its regulation is not to be avoided by "simply invoking the convenient apologetics of the police power."

. . . [W]e conclude that the state does go too far. Its regulation of train lengths, admittedly obstructive to interstate train operation, and having a seriously adverse effect on transportation efficiency and economy, passes beyond what is plainly essential for safety since it does not appear that it will lessen rather than increase the danger of accident. Its attempted regulation of the operation of interstate trains cannot establish nationwide control such as is essential to the maintenance of an efficient transportation system, which Congress alone can prescribe. The state interest cannot be preserved at the expense of the national interest by an enactment which regulates interstate train lengths without securing such control, which is a matter of national concern. To this the interest of the state here asserted is subordinate.

Appellees especially rely on the full train-crew cases, *Chicago, R.I. & P.R. Co.* v. *Arkansas* (219 U.S. 453) . . . and also on *South Carolina Highway Dept.* v. *Barnwell Bros.* (303 U.S. 177) . . . as supporting the state's authority to regulate the length of interstate trains. While the full train-crew laws undoubtedly placed an added financial burden on the railroads in order to serve a local interest, they did not obstruct interstate transportation or seriously impede it. They had no effects outside the state beyond those of picking up and setting down the extra employees at the state boundaries; they involved no wasted use of facilities or serious impairment of transportation efficiency, which are among the factors of controlling weight here. In sustaining those laws the Court considered the restriction a minimal burden on the commerce comparable to the law requiring the licensing of engineers as a safeguard against those of reckless and intemperate habits, sustained in *Smith* v. *Alabama,* 124 U.S. 465, or those afflicted with color blindness, upheld in *Nashville, C. & St. L. R. Co.* v. *Alabama,* 128 U.S. 96, and other similar regulations. . . .

South Carolina Highway Dept. v. *Barnwell Bros. supra,* was concerned with the power of the state to regulate the weight and width of motor cars passing interstate over its highways, a legislative field over which the state has a far more extensive control than over interstate railroads. In that case . . .

we were at pains to point out that there are few subjects of state regulation affecting interstate commerce which are so peculiarly of local concern as is the use of the state's highways. Unlike the railroads local highways are built, owned, and maintained by the state or its municipal subdivisions. The state is responsible for their safe and economical administration. Regulations affecting the safety of their use must be applied alike to intrastate and interstate traffic. The fact that they affect alike shippers in interstate and intrastate commerce in great numbers, within as well as without the state, is a safeguard against regulatory abuses. Their regulation is akin to quarantine measures, game laws, and like local regulations of rivers, harbors, piers, and docks, with respect to which the state has exceptional scope for the exercise of its regulatory power, and which, Congress not acting, have been sustained even though they materially interfere with interstate commerce. . . .

The contrast between the present regulation and the full train-crew laws in point of their effects on the commerce, and the like contrast with the highway safety regulations, in point of the nature of the subject of regulation and the state's interest in it, illustrate and emphasize the considerations which enter into a determination of the relative weights of state and national interests where state regulation affecting interstate commerce is attempted. Here examination of all the relevant factors makes it plain that the state interest is outweighed by the interest of the nation in an adequate, economical, and efficient railway transportation service, which must prevail.

Reversed.

MR. JUSTICE RUTLEDGE concurs in the result.

MR. JUSTICE BLACK, dissenting:

In *Hennington* v. *Georgia,* 163 U.S.

299, 304, a case which involved the power of a state to regulate interstate traffic, this Court said, "The whole theory of our government, federal and state, is hostile to the idea that questions of legislative authority may depend . . . upon opinions of judges as to the wisdom or want of wisdom in the enactment of laws under powers clearly conferred upon the legislature." What the Court decides today is that it is unwise governmental policy to regulate the length of trains. I am therefore constrained to note my dissent. . . .

. . . [T]he determination of whether it is in the interest of society for the length of trains to be governmentally regulated is a matter of public policy. Someone must fix that policy—either the Congress, or the state, or the courts. A century and a half of constitutional history and government admonishes this Court to leave that choice to the elected legislative representatives of the people themselves, where it properly belong both on democratic principles and the requirements of efficient government.

I think that legislatures, to the exclusion of courts, have the constitutional power to enact laws limiting train lengths for the purpose of reducing injuries brought about by "slack movements." Their power is not less because a requirement of short trains might increase grade-crossing accidents. This latter fact raises an entirely different element of danger which is itself subject to legislative regulation. For legislatures may, if necessary, require railroads to take appropriate steps to reduce the likelihood of injuries at grade crossings. . . . And the fact that grade-crossing improvements may be expensive is no sufficient reason to say that an unconstitutional "burden" is put upon a railroad even though it be an interstate road. . . .

There have been many sharp divisions of this Court concerning its authority, in the absence of congressional enactment, to invalidate state laws as violating the Commerce Clause. . . . That discussion need not be renewed here, because even the broadest exponents of judicial power in this field have not heretofore expressed doubt as to a state's power, absent a paramount congressional declaration, to regulate interstate trains in the interest of safety. For as early as 1913, this Court, speaking through Mr. Justice Hughes, later Chief Justice, referred to "the settled principle that, in the absence of legislation by Congress, the states are not denied the exercise of their power to secure safety in the physical operation of railroad trains within their territory, even though such trains are used in interstate commerce. That has been the law since the beginning of railroad transportation." *Atlantic Coast Line R. Co.* v. *Georgia,* 234 U.S. 280, 291. Until today, the oft-repeated principles of that case have never been repudiated in whole or in part. . . .

This record in its entirety leaves me with no doubt whatever that many employees have been seriously injured and killed in the past, and that many more are likely to be so in the future, because of "slack movement" in trains. Everyday knowledge, as well as direct evidence presented at the various hearings, substantiates the report of the Senate Committee that the danger from slack movement is greater in long trains than in short trains. It may be that offsetting dangers are possible in the operation of short trains. The balancing of these probabilities, however, is not in my judgment a matter for judicial determination, but one which calls for legislative consideration. Representatives elected by the people to make their laws, rather than judges appointed to interpret those laws, can best determine the policies which govern the people. That at least is the basic principle on which our democratic society rests. I

would affirm the judgment of the Supreme Court of Arizona.

[MR. JUSTICE DOUGLAS also wrote a dissenting opinion.]

EDWARDS v. CALIFORNIA
314 U.S. 160; 62 Sup. Ct. 164; 86 L. Ed. 119 (1941)

[*Edwards, who was a citizen of the United States and a resident of Marysville, California, went to Texas in 1939 to bring his wife's brother, Frank Duncan, to Marysville. Duncan was an American citizen and a resident of Texas. When Edwards arrived in Texas, he learned that Duncan had last been employed by the Works Progress Administration. He thus was aware of the fact that Duncan was and continued to be an indigent person throughout the case. The two men went to California in Edwards' car. Duncan had about $20 when he left Texas, but by the time he reached Marysville it had all been spent. Duncan lived with Edwards' family for approximately ten days until he received financial help from the Farm Security Administration.*

A complaint was filed against Edwards under Section 2615 of the Welfare and Institutions Code of California, which provided as follows: "Every person, firm or corporation or officer or agent thereof that brings or assists in bringing into the State any indigent person who is not a resident of the State, knowing him to be an indigent person, is guilty of a misdemeanor." Edwards was convicted of violating the law. He was sentenced to six months' imprisonment in the county jail, and sentence was suspended. The Superior Court of Yuba County, California, affirmed the conviction, holding the statute constitutional as a valid exercise of the state's police power. Edwards then brought an appeal to the Supreme Court requesting that the judgment of the Superior Court be reversed.]

MR. JUSTICE BRYNES delivered the opinion of the Court:

. . . Article I, §8 of the Constitution delegates to the Congress the authority to regulate interstate commerce. And it is settled beyond question that the transportation of persons is "commerce," within the meaning of that provision. It is nevertheless true, that the States are not wholly precluded from exercising their police power in matters of local concern even though they may thereby affect interstate commerce. . . . The issue presented in this case, therefore, is whether the prohibition embodied in §2615 against the "bringing" or transportation of indigent persons into California is within the police power of that State. We think that it is not, and hold

that it is an unconstitutional barrier to interstate commerce.

The grave and perplexing social and economic dislocation which this statute reflects is a matter of common knowledge and concern. We are not unmindful of it. We appreciate that the spectacle of large segments of our population constantly on the move has given rise to urgent demands upon the ingenuity of government. . . . The State asserts that the huge influx of migrants into California in recent years has resulted in problems of health, morals, and especially finance, the proportions of which are staggering. It is not for us to say that this is not true. We have repeatedly and recently affirmed, and we now reaffirm, that we do not conceive it our function to pass upon "the wisdom, need, or appropriateness" of the legislative efforts of the States to solve such difficulties. . . .

But this does not mean that there are no boundaries to the permissible area of State legislative activity. There are. And none is more certain than the prohibition against attempts on the part of any single State to isolate itself from difficulties common to all of them by restraining the transportation of persons and property across its borders. It is frequently the case that a State might gain a momentary respite from the pressure of events by the simple expedient of shutting its gates to the outside world. But, in the words of Mr. Justice Cardozo: "The Constitution was framed under the dominion of a political philosophy less parochial in range. It was framed upon the theory that the peoples of the several States must sink or swim together, and that in the long run prosperity and salvation are in union and not division." *Baldwin* v. *Seelig,* 294 U.S. 511, 523.

It is difficult to conceive of a statute more squarely in conflict with this theory than the Section challenged here. Its express purpose and inevitable effect is to prohibit the transportation of indigent persons across the California border. The burden upon interstate commerce is intended and immediate; it is the plain and sole function of the statute. Moreover, the indigent nonresidents who are the real victims of the statute are deprived of the opportunity to exert political pressure upon the California legislature in order to obtain a change in policy. . . . We think this statute must fail under any known test of the validity of State interference with interstate commerce.

It is urged, however, that the concept which underlies §2615 enjoys a firm basis in English and American history. This is the notion that each community should care for its own indigent, that relief is solely the responsibility of local government. Of this it must first be said that we are not now called upon to determine anything other than the propriety of an attempt by a State to prohibit the transportation of indigent nonresidents into its territory. The nature and extent of its obligation to afford relief to newcomers is not here involved. We do, however, suggest that the theory of the Elizabethan poor laws no longer fits the facts. Recent years, and particularly the past decade, have been marked by a growing recognition that in an industrial society the task of providing assistance to the needy has ceased to be local in character. The duty to share the burden, if not wholly to assume it, has been recognized not only by State governments, but by the Federal government as well. The changed attitude is reflected in the Social Security laws under which the Federal and State governments cooperate for the care of the aged, the blind, and dependent children. . . . It is reflected in the works programs under which work is furnished the unemployed, with the States supplying approximately 25 per cent and the Federal government approximately 75 per cent of the cost. . . . It is further reflected in the Farm Security laws, under which the entire cost of the relief provisions is borne by the Federal government. . . .

Indeed, the record in this very case illustrates the inadequate basis in fact for the theory that relief is presently a local matter. Before leaving Texas, Duncan had received assistance from the Works Progress Administration. After arriving in California he was aided by the Farm Security Administration, which, as we have said, is wholly financed by the Federal government. This is not to say that our judgment would be different if Duncan had received relief from local agencies in

Texas and California. Nor is it to suggest that the financial burden of assistance to indigent persons does not continue to fall heavily upon local and State governments. It is only to illustrate that in not inconsiderable measure the relief of the needy has become the common responsibility and concern of the whole nation.

What has been said with respect to financing relief is not without its bearing upon the regulation of the transportation of indigent persons. For the social phenomenon of large-scale interstate migration is as certainly a matter of national concern as the provision of assistance to those who have found a permanent or temporary abode. Moreover, and unlike the relief problem, this phenomenon does not admit to diverse treatment by the several States. The prohibition against transporting indigent nonresidents into one State is an open invitation of retaliatory measures, and the burdens upon the transportation of such persons become cumulative. Moreover, it would be a virtual impossibility for migrants and those who transport them to acquaint themselves with the peculiar rules of admission of many States. "The Court has repeatedly declared that the grant (the commerce clause) established the immunity of interstate commerce from the control of the States respecting all those subjects embraced within the grant which are of such a nature as to demand that, if regulated at all, their regulation must be prescribed by a single authority." . . . We are of the opinion that the transportation of indigent persons from State to State clearly falls within this class of subjects. The scope of Congressional power to deal with this problem we are not now called upon to decide.

There remains to be noticed only the contention that the limitation upon State power to interfere with the interstate transportation of persons is subject to an exception in the case of "paupers." It is true that support for this contention may be found in early decisions of this Court, In *City of New York* v. *Miln,* 11 Pet. 102, . . . it was said that it is "as competent and as necessary for a State to provide precautionary measures against the moral pestilence of paupers, vagabonds, and possibly convicts, as it is to guard against the physical pestilence, which may arise from unsound and infectious articles imported. . . ." This language has been casually repeated in numerous later cases up to the turn of the century. . . . In none of these cases, however, was the power of a State to exclude "paupers" actually involved.

Whether an able-bodied but unemployed person like Duncan is a "pauper" within the historical meaning of the term is open to considerable doubt. . . . But assuming that the term is applicable to him and to persons similarly situated, we do not consider ourselves bound by the language referred to. *City of New York* v. *Miln* was decided in 1837. Whatever may have been the notion then prevailing, we do not think that it will now be seriously contended that because a person is without employment and without funds he constitutes a "moral pestilence." Poverty and immorality are not synonymous.

We are of the opinion that §2615 is not a valid exercise of the police power of California; that it imposes an unconstitutional burden upon interstate commerce, and that the conviction under it cannot be sustained. In the view we have taken, it is unnecessary to decide whether the Section is repugnant to other provisions of the Constitution.

Reversed.

MR. JUSTICE JACKSON concurring:

I concur in the result reached by the Court, and I agree that the grounds of its decision are permissible ones under applicable authorities. But the migrations of a human being, of whom it is charged that he possesses nothing that can be sold and has no wherewithal to buy, do not fit easily into my notions as to what is commerce. To hold that the measure of his rights is the commerce clause is likely to result eventually either in distorting the commercial law or in denaturing human rights. I turn, therefore, away from principles by which commerce is regulated to that clause of the Constitution by virtue of which Duncan is a citizen of the United States and which forbids any State to abridge his privileges or immunities as such.

This clause was adopted to make United States citizenship the dominant and paramount allegiance among us. The return which the law had long associated with allegiance was protection. The power of citizenship as a shield against oppression was widely known from the example of Paul's Roman citizenship, which sent the centurion scurrying to his higher-ups with the message: "Take heed what thou doest: for this man is a Roman." I suppose none of us doubts that the hope of imparting to American citizenship some of this vitality was the purpose of declaring in the Fourteenth Amendment: "All persons born or naturalized in the United States, and subject to the jurisdiction thereof, are citizens of the United States and of the State wherein they reside. No State shall make or enforce any law which shall abridge the privileges or immunities of citizens of the United States. . . ."

But the hope proclaimed in such generality soon shriveled in the process of judicial interpretation. For nearly three-quarters of a century this Court rejected every plea to the privileges and immunities clause. . . .

While instances of valid "privileges or immunities" must be but few, I am convinced that this is one. I do not ignore or belittle the difficulties of what has been characterized by this Court as an "almost forgotten" clause. But the difficulty of the task does not excuse us from giving these general and abstract words whatever of specific content and concreteness they will bear as we mark out their application, case by case. That is the method of the common law, and it has been the method of this Court with other no less general statements in our fundamental law. This Court has not been timorous about giving concrete meaning to such obscure and vagrant phrases as "due process," "general welfare," "equal protection," or even "commerce among the several States." But it has always hesitated to give any real meaning to the privileges and immunities clause lest it improvidently give too much.

This Court should, however, hold squarely that it is, a privilege of citizenship of the United States, protected from state abridgment, to enter any state of the Union, either for temporary sojourn or for the establishment of permanent residence therein and for gaining resultant citizenship thereof. If national citizenship means less than this, it means nothing.

The language of the Fourteenth Amendment declaring two kinds of citizenship is discriminating. It is: "All persons born or naturalized in the United States, and subject to the jurisdiction thereof, are citizens of the United States and of the State wherein they reside." While it thus establishes national citizenship from the mere circumstances of birth within the territory and jurisdiction of the United States, birth within a state does not establish citizenship thereof. State citizenship is ephemeral. It results only from residence and is gained or lost therewith. That choice of residence was subject to local approval is contrary to the inescapable implications of the westward movement of our civilization.

Even as to an alien who had "been admitted to the United States under the Federal law," this Court, through Mr. Justice Hughes, declared that "He was thus admitted with the privilege of entering and abiding in the United States, and hence of entering and abiding in any State in the Union. . . ." Why we should hesitate to hold that federal citizenship implies rights to enter and abide in any state of the Union at least equal to those possessed by aliens passes my understanding. The world is even more upside down than I had supposed it to be, if California must accept aliens in deference to their federal privileges but is free to turn back citizens of the United States unless we treat them as subjects of commerce.

The right of the citizen to migrate from state to state which, I agree with Mr. Justice Douglas, is shown by our precedents to be one of national citizenship, is not, however, an unlimited one. In addition to being subject to all constitutional limitations imposed by the federal government, such citizen is subject to some control by state governments. He may not, if a fugitive from justice, claim freedom to migrate unmolested, nor may he endanger others by carrying contagion about. These causes, and perhaps others that do not occur to me now, warrant any public authority in stopping a man where it finds him and arresting his progress across a state line quite as much as from place to place within the state.

It is here that we meet the real crux of this case. Does "indigence" as defined by the application of the California statute constitute a basis for restricting the freedom of a citizen, as crime or contagion warrants its restriction? We should say now, and in no uncertain terms, that a man's mere property status, without more, cannot be used by a state to test, qualify, or limit his rights as a citizen of the United States. "Indigence" in itself is neither a source of rights or a basis for denying them. The mere state of being without funds is a neutral fact—constitutionally an irrelevance, like race, creed, or color. I agree with what I understand to be the holding of the Court that cases which may indicate the contrary are overruled.

Any measure which would divide our citizenry on the basis of property into one class free to move from state to state and another class that is poverty-bound to the place where it has suffered misfortune is not only at war with the habit and custom by which our country has expanded, but is also a short-sighted blow at the security of property itself. Property can have no more dangerous, even if unwitting, enemy than one who would make its possession a pretext for unequal or exclusive civil rights. Where those rights are derived from national citizenship no state may impose such a test, and whether the Congress could do so we are not called upon to inquire.

I think California had no right to make the condition of Duncan's purse, with no evidence of violation by him of any law or social policy which caused it, the basis of excluding him or of punishing one who extended him aid.

If I doubted whether his federal citizenship alone were enough to open the gates of California to Duncan, my doubt would disappear on consideration of the obligations of such citizenship. Duncan owes a duty to render military service, and this Court has said that this duty is the result of his citizenship. Mr. Chief Justice White declared in the *Selective Draft Law Cases,* 245 U.S. 366, . . . "It may not be doubted that the very conception of a just government and its duty to the citizen includes the reciprocal obligation of the citizen to render military service in case of need and the right to compel it." A contention that a citizen's duty to render military service is suspended by "indigence" would meet with little favor. Rich or penniless, Duncan's citizenship under the Constitution pledges his strength to the defense of California as a part of the United States, and his right to migrate to any part of the land he must defend is someting she must respect under the same instrument. Unless this Court is willing to say that citizenship of the United States means at least this much to the citizen, then our heritage of constitutional privileges and immunities is only a promise to the ear to be broken to the hope, a teasing illusion like a munificent bequest in a pauper's will.

[MR. JUSTICE DOUGLAS also wrote a concurring opinion, in which MR. JUSTICE BLACK and MR. JUSTICE MURPHY joined. Justice Douglas agreed with Justice Jaskson in maintaining that the right to move freely from state to state was an incident of national citizenship protected by the privileges and immunities clause of the Fourteenth Amendment.]

9
Congress and the Commerce Power

Despite Marshall's early broad interpretation of the federal government's commerce power in *Gibbons* v. *Ogden,* the development of the commerce clause as a grant of *positive* powers to Congress had no substantial development until the beginning of the twentieth century. Throughout the nineteenth century, decisions of the Supreme Court under the commerce clause dealt ". . . almost entirely with the permissibility of state activity which it was claimed discriminated against or burdened interstate commerce. During this period there was perhaps little occasion for the affimative exercise of the commerce power, and the *influence of the clause on American life and law was a negative one,* resulting almost wholly from its operation as a restraint upon the powers of the states."[1] But as the nation grew and an industrial society emerged, particularly after the Civil War, more and more "local" commercial matters required a uniform system of national legislation. For example, a unanimous decision of the Supreme Court in the 1869 case of *Paul* v. *Virginia,* 8 Wall. 168, declared that a Virginia state statute did not offend the commerce clause because "issuing a policy of insurance is not a transaction of commerce." Seventy-five years later the Court held in *United States* v. *South-Eastern Underwriters' Assoc.,* 322 U.S. 533 (1944), that the business of in-

---

[1] *Wickard* v. *Filburn,* 317 U.S. 111 (1942). Italics supplied.

surance is within the federal commerce power and, therefore, is subject to regulation under the Sherman Anti-Trust Act of 1890. In rendering the majority opinion, Justice Black remarked that no "commercial enterprise of any kind which conducts its activities across state lines" can be wholly beyond the commerce power of Congress. "We cannot make an exception of the business of insurance."

Perhaps nowhere is the change from local to national regulation better demonstrated than in the case of the railroads. In 1877, in a group of cases known as the Granger cases, the Supreme Court held that the states could fix minimum and maximum railroad and other rates in the absence of congressional legislation.[2] But only nine years later the Court felt compelled to repudiate its views in the Granger cases: in *Wabash, St. Louis and Pacific Railroad Co.* v. *Illinois,* 118 U.S. 557 (1886), the Court held that an Illinois statute, which imposed a penalty for lower rates on long hauls that extended beyond the borders of the state, was in conflict with the commerce clause even though Congress had not legislated in this field. "Here was a matter that demanded single unified control. The interests of interstate movement could not be left to the individual policies of the states."[3] But if the states could not regulate, and Congress had not done so, how were railroad rates to be controlled? The answer came a few months after the *Wabash* case when Congress created the Interstate Commerce Commission (ICC) to fill the resulting gap. With the enactment of the Interstate Commerce Act of 1887, the commerce clause ". . . began to exert positive influence in American law and life. This first important federal resort to the commerce power was followed in 1890 by the Sherman Anti-Trust Act and, thereafter, mainly after 1903, by many others. These statutes ushered in new phases of adjudication, which required the Court to approach the interpretation of the commerce clause in the light of an actual exercise by Congress of its power thereunder."[4]

The early congressional attempts to control interstate commerce, as indicated by the Interstate Commerce and Sherman Acts, were resisted strenuously by the business community, which was wedded to the laissez-faire concept. The industrial and business interests of the country relied heavily on a narrow construction of the commerce clause as well as on the due process clause of the Fourteenth Amendment as constitutional weapons to resist governmental control. The commerce clause, however, had been the sole constitutional basis for the Sherman Act, which was intended to prevent combinations and conspiracies in restraint of trade among the states. When the

---

[2] The first and most celebrated of the Granger cases was *Munn* v. *Illinois,* 94 U.S. 113 (1877), which is considered fully in Chapter 11. The Granger movement, which was influential particularly in the 1870s, was organized and led by Western farmers who wished to curtail the abuses of the railroads. Their efforts resulted in the enactment of remedial legislation in a number of states. Some of this legislation was upheld in the Granger cases.

[3] Felix Frankfurter, *The Commerce Clause Under Marshall, Taney and Waite* (Chapel Hill: University of North Carolina Press, 1937), p. 100.

[4] *Wickard* v. *Filburn.*

Court first dealt with the Sherman Act, in *United States* v. *E. C. Knight Co.,* (p. 238), it allowed "but little scope to the power of Congress."[5] For in the *Knight* case the Court, dominated by the laissez-faire philosophy, held that the Sherman Act could not be applied to a virtual monopoly of the sugar industry because the manufacture of sugar was not in interstate commerce. In delivering the opinion, Chief Justice Fuller indicated clearly the Court's suspicion of any national legislation under the commerce clause that threatened the independence of the states and the nation's laissez-faire economic system. For all practical purposes, the Sugar Trust case virtually set aside the Sherman Act; Justice Harlan, who was the lone dissenter in the case, remarked that "while the opinion of the Court does not declare the act of 1890 to be unconstitutional, it defeats the main object for which it was passed." During the same term the Court delivered two other extremely conservative opinions[6] that brought storms of protest from large segments of the American people, who were now convinced that the judiciary had become the reactionary defender of entrenched economic interests.

"Even while important opinions in this line of restrictive authority were being written, however, other cases called forth broader interpretations of the commerce clause destined to supersede the earlier ones, and to bring about a return to the principles first enunciated by Chief Justice Marshall in *Gibbons* v. *Ogden*."[7] In *Swift and Co.* v. *United States,* 196 U.S. 375 (1905), the Court held that a combination of meat packers was an illegal monopoly under the Sherman Act on the ground that its activities were transactions in interstate commerce. Speaking for a unanimous Court, Justice Holmes stated the "commerce among the states is not a technical legal conception, but a practical one, drawn from the course of business. When cattle are sent for sale from a place in one state, with the expectation that they will end their transit, after purchase, in another, and when in effect they do so, with only the interruption necessary to find a purchaser at the stockyards, and when this is a typical, constantly recurring course, the current thus existing is a current of commerce among the states, and the purchase of the cattle is a part and incident of such commerce."[8]

---

[5] *Ibid.*

[6] In *Pollock* v. *Farmers' Loan and Trust Co.,* 158 U.S. 601 (1895), the Court held that taxes on income derived from land or personal property were direct taxes and therefore unconstitutional because they had not been properly levied. This case was overruled by the Sixteenth Amendment, ratified in 1913 (see Chapter 10). In the case of *In re Debs,* 158 U.S. 564 (1895), the Court upheld a sweeping antilabor injunction issued in connection with the famous Pullman strike in Chicago during the summer of 1894.

[7] *Wickard* v. *Filburn.*

[8] Other prior cases also restricted the authority of the Knight case. In *Addyston Pipe and Steel Co.* v. *United States,* 175 U.S. 211 (1899), the Court held that a combination in the manufacture and sale of cast-iron pipe violated the Sherman Act. This was the first successful application of the Sherman Act to an industrial combination. In *Northern Securities Co.* v. *United States,* 193 U.S. 197 (1904), the Court held that the acquisi-

In some later cases the Court continued to demonstrate its readiness to construe the commerce clause broadly. In the well-known Shreveport case [*Houston E. and W. Railroad Co.* v. *United States,* 234 U.S. 342 (1914)], the Court upheld the power of the ICC to fix intrastate railroad rates because of their effect on interstate commerce. Local or intrastate commerce could be regulated by the federal government in this situation because of its "close and substantial relation" to interstate commerce. And in the case of *Stafford* v. *Wallace,* 258 U.S. 495 (1922), the Court upheld, with only one dissenting vote, the Packers and Stockyards Act of 1921, which was designed to bring the activities of commission men and livestock dealers under federal control. In sustaining the statute, Chief Justice Taft relied heavily on the *Swift* decision and noted that the ". . . application of the commerce clause of the Constitution in the *Swift* case was the result of the natural development of interstate commerce under modern conditions. It was the inevitable recognition of the great central fact that such streams of commerce from one part of the country to another which are ever-flowing are in their very essence the commerce among the states and with foreign nations which historically it was one of the chief purposes of the Constitution to bring under national protection and control."

Federal Police Powers

In a series of cases during the same period, the Court began to sustain the use of the commerce clause as a basis for the exercise of federal police powers. Theoretically, the power to legislate in the interest of the health, morals, safety, and the general welfare of the community is reserved to the states under the Tenth Amendment, because the Constitution does not grant such power to Congress. However, Congress has used some of its delegated powers, such as its commerce, taxing, and postal powers, to legislate for purely social and economic ends. In 1903, in the case of *Champion* v. *Ames,* 188 U.S. 321 (1903), the Court for the first time sustained a federal act based on the commerce clause that prohibited the interstate shipment of lottery tickets. Thus, the doctrine that Congress was empowered to exclude dangerous or evil objects from interstate commerce received judicial blessing. Shortly after the decision in the Lottery case, Congress proceeded to enact a number of statutes that barred objectionable articles from interstate commerce or that forbade the use of interstate commerce facilities for immoral or criminal activities. The cases upholding these statutes are noted in *Hammer* v. *Dagenhart* (p. 243).

The Supreme Court's restrictive interpretation of the commerce clause appeared again in *Hammer* v. *Dagenhart.* In that case, the Court held that Congress could not prohibit from interstate commerce goods produced with the

---

tion by a holding company of the stock of competing railroads was a violation of the Sherman Act.

aid of children. The classic dissent of Justice Holmes in *Hammer* v. *Dagenhart* was used twenty-five years later by Justice Stone to overrule the majority opinion [*United States* v. *Darby* (p. 247)]. In the *Hammer* case the Court relied heavily on its decision in the Sugar Trust case.

Thus, when the Court was confronted with the constitutionality of the New Deal legislation under the commerce clause, two lines of precedent were available. The Court could construe the federal commerce power narrowly, as was done in *United States* v. *E. C. Knight Co.* and in *Hammer* v. *Dagenhart*. Or, the Court could take a broad view of the commerce power, in line with the decisions in such cases as *Gibbons* v. *Ogden, Swift and Co.* v. *United States* and *Stafford* v. *Wallace*.

The Expanding National Commerce Power

We noted in Chapter 1 that by the spring of 1936 the Supreme Court had all but wrecked the New Deal. In the process of invalidating a number of key New Deal measures, the Court majority had opposed vigorously any expansion of the federal commerce power. In fact, the Court seemed determined, in the *Schechter* case (Chapter 6), to maintain the distinction between commerce and manufacturing as enunciated in the Sugar Trust case and *Hammer* v. *Dagenhart*. And in *Carter* v. *Carter Coal Co.,* 298 U.S. 238 (1936), which held void the Bituminous Coal Conservation Act of 1935 (Guffey Act), the Court emphasized that Congress could not regulate the relations between employers and workmen in the coal industry because such relations did not affect interstate commerce directly. Justice Sutherland's vigorous defense of states' rights in the majority opinion in the *Carter* case appeared to doom the New Deal's efforts to control various aspects of industrial activity.[9]

Yet, less than a year later, on April 12, 1937, the Supreme Court ruled that the *Schechter* and *Carter* precedents were "inapplicable" and upheld the National Labor Relations Act (Wagner Act) in a series of five separate cases. In the first and most important of these cases [*National Labor Relations Board* v. *Jones and Laughlin Steel Corp.* (p. 250)], the Court significantly gave the federal interstate commerce power its maximum sweep. The "*Jones and Laughlin* case is the great modern case on the scope of federal power over interstate commerce. Other cases involving much smaller businesses were decided the same day with the same result. The way was open for general control of business by the federal government if the people so wished. The panoramic

---

[9] During this same period, the case of *Kentucky Whip and Collar Co.* v. *Illinois Central R.R. Co.,* 299 U.S. 334 (1937), was also decided. Here the Court subscribed to a broader view of the commerce clause, as it refused to apply cases that had been most restrictive in the interpretation of the commerce power. The restrictive interpretation was also weakened by *Whitfield* v. *Ohio,* 297 U.S. 431 (1936). This case sustained the Hawes-Cooper Act of 1929, which provided that convict-made goods would be subject to the laws of the state on their arrival therein.

view of the *Jones and Laughlin* case emerges: the United States consists no longer of fifty separate economic entities. Economically we are one nation, and accordingly, in economic matters we stand or fall together. The Great Depression taught us this, and the Court of the Nine Old Men confirmed it."[10] Two facts must be noted about the Wagner Act cases: (1) The cases were decided by the same justices who had invalidated the key New Deal measures; this was made possible when Justice Roberts abandoned the conservatives and voted with the liberal group. (2) The decisions came at a time when the Roosevelt court-packing proposal was being hotly debated, so that the President's proposed court reform now seemed unnecessary.

Shortly after the decision in the *Jones and Laughlin* case, the Court upheld the Social Security Act in *Steward Machine Co.* v. *Davis,* which is discussed in the following chapter. The New Deal experiment was now sanctioned by a majority of the Court's members. "Thus, the Court, with no change of its Justices, had ridden out of the storm and when it closed the books for the term (1936–37) it had rewritten the law of the Constitution."[11] Since 1937, the federal commerce power has continued to expand.

The breadth of federal powers under the commerce clause today is illustrated well in cases dealing with agriculture. In *Mulford* v. *Smith,* 307 U.S. 38 (1939), the Court upheld the Agricultural Adjustment Act of 1938 as it pertained to the fixing of marketing quotas for flue-cured tobacco. The act was based on the commerce clause. In the extreme case of *Wickard* v. *Filburn* (p. 255) the Court went a step further. The unanimous opinion of the Court in the *Filburn* case represents one of the broadest holdings to date under the commerce clause.[12] That case has recently been reaffirmed in *McClung* v. *Katzenbach,* 379 U.S. 294 (1964), upholding the constitutionality, under the commerce clause, of the Civil Rights Act of 1964 as applied to restaurants that have no interstate customers but receive substantial amounts of their foodstuffs from other states. It may well be that today "the federal commerce power is as broad as the economic needs of the nation,"[13] and indeed must be broad enough to go far beyond purely economic needs.

UNITED STATES *v.* E. C. KNIGHT CO.
156 U.S. 1; 15 Sup. Ct. 249; 39 L. Ed. 325 (1895)

[*In 1892, the American Sugar Refining Company, a New Jersey corporation that controlled a majority of the sugar refining companies in the United States, ob-*

---

[10] Jere Williams, *The Supreme Court Speaks* (Austin: University of Texas Press, 1956), p. 295.

[11] Robert H. Jackson, *The Struggle for Judicial Supremacy* (New York: Knopf, 1941), p. 235.

[12] In recent years, the Court has interpreted the commerce clause very broadly in a number of other cases, such as *United States* v. *Sullivan,* 332 U.S. 689 (1948) and *Lorain Journal Co.* v. *United States,* 342 U.S. 143 (1951).

[13] *American Power and Light Co.* v. *Securities and Exchange Commission,* 329 U.S. 90 (1946).

tained nearly complete control of the manufacture and distribution of refined sugar by purchasing the stock of the E. C. Knight Company and three other Philadelphia refineries. The government brought suit under the newly enacted Sherman Anti-Trust Act of 1890 to break up the contract on the ground that it constituted a "combination . . . in restraint of trade and commerce among the several states." The lower federal courts held that the facts did not show a contract, combination, or conspiracy to restrain or monopolize trade or commerce. The United States then brought the case to the Supreme Court on appeal.]

MR. CHIEF JUSTICE FULLER, after stating the case, delivered the opinion of the Court:

. . . The fundamental question is, whether conceding that the existence of a monopoly in manufacture is established by the evidence, that monopoly can be directly suppressed under the act of Congress in the mode attempted by this bill.

It cannot be denied that the power of a State to protect the lives, health, and property of its citizens, and to preserve good order and the public morals, "the power to govern men and things within the limits of its dominion," is a power originally and always belonging to the States, not surrendered by them to the general government, nor directly restrained by the Constitution of the United States, and essentially exclusive. The relief of the citizens of each State from the burden of monopoly and the evils resulting from the restraint of trade among such citizens was left with the States to deal with, and this court has recognized their possession of that power even to the extent of holding that an employment or business carried on by private individuals, when it becomes a matter of such public interest and importance as to create a common charge or burden upon the citizen; in other words, when it becomes a practical monopoly, to which the citizen is compelled to resort and by means of which a tribute can be exacted from the community, is subject to regulation by state legislative power. On the other hand, the power of Congress to regulate commerce among the several States is also exclusive. The Constitution does not provide that interstate commerce shall be free, but, by the grant of this exclusive power to regulate it, it was left free except as Congress might impose restraints. Therefore it has been determined that the failure of Congress to exercise this exclusive power in any case is an expression of its will that the subject shall be free from restrictions or impositions upon it by the several States, and if a law passed by a State in the exercise of its acknowledged powers comes into conflict with that will, the Congress and the State cannot occupy the position of equal opposing sovereignties, because the Constitution declares its supremacy and that of the laws passed to pursuance thereof; and that which is not supreme must yield to that which is supreme. "Commerce, undoubtedly, is traffic," said Chief Justice Marshall, "but it is something more; it is intercourse. It describes the commercial intercourse between nations and parts of nations in all its branches, and is regulated by prescribing rules for carrying on that intercourse." That which belongs to commerce is within the jurisdiction of the United States, but that which does not belong to commerce is within the jurisdiction of the police power of the State. . . .

The argument is that the power to control the manufacture of refined sugar is a monopoly over a necessary of life, to the enjoyment of which by a large part of the population of the United States interstate commerce is indispensable, and that, therefore, the general government in the exercise of the power to regulate commerce may repress such monopoly directly and set aside the instruments which have created it. But this argument cannot be confined to necessaries of life merely, and must include all articles of general consumption. Doubtless the power to control the manufacture of a given thing involves in a certain sense the control of its disposition, but this is a secondary and not the primary sense; and although the exercise of that power may result in bringing the operation of commerce into play, it does not control it, and affects it only incidentally and indirectly. Commerce succeeds to manufacture, and is not a part of it. The power to regulate commerce is the power to prescribe the rule by which commerce shall be governed, and is a power independent of the power to suppress monopoly. But it may operate in repression of monopoly whenever that comes within the rules by which commerce is governed or whenever the transaction is itself a monopoly of commerce.

It is vital that the independence of the commercial power and of the police power, and the delimitation between them, however sometimes perplexing, should always be recognized and observed, for while the one furnishes the strongest bond of union, the other is essential to the preservation of the autonomy of the States as required by our dual form of government; and acknowledged evils, however grave and urgent they may appear to be, had better be borne, than the risk be run, in the effort to suppress them, of more serious consequences by resort to expedients of even doubtful constitutionality.

It will be perceived how far-reaching the proposition is that the power of dealing with a monopoly directly may be exercised by the general government whenever interstate or international commerce may be ultimately affected. The regulation of commerce applies to the subjects of commerce and not to matters of internal police. Contracts to buy, sell, or exchange goods to be transported among the several States, the transportation and its instrumentalities, and articles bought, sold, or exchanged for the purposes of such transit among the States, or put in the way of transit, may be regulated, but this is because they form part of interstate trade or commerce. The fact that an article is manufactured for export to another State does not of itself make it an article of interstate commerce, and the intent of the manufacturer does not determine the time when the article or product passes from the control of the State and belongs to commerce. . . .

Contracts, combinations, or conspiracies to control domestic enterprise in manufacture, agriculture, mining, production in all its forms, or to raise or lower prices or wages, might unquestionably tend to restrain external as well as domestic trade, but the restraint would be an indirect result, however inevitable and whatever its extent, and such result would not necessarily determine the object of the contract, combination, or conspiracy.

Again, all the authorities agree that in order to vitiate a contract or combination it is not essential that its result should be a complete monopoly; it is sufficient if it really tends to that end and to deprive the public of the advantages which flow from free competition. Slight reflection will show that if the national power extends to all contracts and combinations in manufacture, agriculture, mining, and other productive industries, whose ultimate result may affect external commerce, comparatively little of business operations and affairs would be left for state control.

It was in the light of well-settled principles that the act of July 2, 1890, was framed. Congress did not attempt thereby to assert the power to deal with monopoly directly as such; or to limit and restrict the rights of corporations created by the States or the citizens of the States in the acquisition, control, or disposition of property; or to regulate or prescribe the price or prices at which such property or the products thereof should be sold; or to make criminal the acts of persons in the acquisition and control of property which the States of their residence or creation sanctioned or permitted. Aside from the provisions applicable where Congress might exercise municipal power, what the law struck at was combinations, contracts, and conspiracies to monopolize trade and commerce among the several States or with foreign nations; but the contracts and acts of the defendants related exclusively to the acquisition of the Philadelphia refineries and the business of sugar refining in Pennsylvania, and bore no direct relation to commerce between the States or with foreign nations. The object was manifestly private gain in the manufacture of the commodity, but not through the control of interstate or foreign commerce. It is true that the bill alleged that the products of these refineries were sold and distributed among the several States, and that all the companies were engaged in trade or commerce with the several States and with foreign nations; but this was no more than to say that trade and commerce served manufacture to fulfill its function. . . . There was nothing in the proofs to indicate any intention to put a restraint upon trade or commerce, and the fact, as we have seen, that

trade or commerce might be indirectly affected was not enough to entitle complainants to a decree. . . .

Decree affirmed.

MR. JUSTICE HARLAN, dissenting:

. . . In its consideration of the important constitutional question presented, this court assumes on the record before us that the result of the transactions disclosed by the pleadings and proof was the creation of a monopoly in the manufacture of a necessary of life. If this combination, so far as its operations necessarily or directly affect interstate commerce, cannot be restrained or suppressed under some power granted to Congress, it will be cause for regret that the patriotic statesmen who framed the Constitution did not forsee the necessity of investing the national government with power to deal with gigantic monopolies holding in their grasp, and injuriously controlling in their own interest, the entire trade among the States in food products that are essential to the comfort of every household in the land. . . .

What is commerce among the States? The decisions of this court fully answer the question. "Commerce, undoubtedly, is traffic, but it is something more: it is intercourse." It does not embrace the completely interior traffic of the respective States—that which is "carried on between man and man in a State, or between different parts of the same State and which does not extend to or affect other States"—but it does embrace "every species of commercial intercourse" between the United States and foreign nations and among the States, and, therefore, it includes such traffic or trade, buying, selling, and interchange of commodities, as directly affects or necessarily involves the interests of the People of the United States. "Commerce, as the word is used in the Constitution, is a unit," and "cannot stop at the external boundary line of each State, but may be introduced into the interior." "The genius and character of the whole government seem to be, that its action is to be applied to all the external concerns of the nation, and to those internal concerns which affect the States generally."

These principles were announced in *Gibbons* v. *Ogden*, and have often been approved. . . .

In the light of these principles, determining as well the scope of the power to regulate commerce among the States as the nature of such commerce, we are to inquire whether the act of Congress July 2, 1890, . . . entitled "An act to protect trade and commerce against unlawful restraints and monopolies," . . . is repugnant to the Constitution. . . .

It would seem to be indisputable that no combination of corporations or individuals can, of right, impose unlawful restraints upon interstate trade, whether upon transportation or upon such interstate intercourse and traffic as precede transportation, any more than it can, of right, impose unreasonable restraints upon the completely internal traffic of a State. The supposition cannot be indulged that this general proposition will be disputed. If it be true that a combination of corporations or individuals may, so far as the power of Congress is concerned, subject interstate trade, in any of its stages, to unlawful restraints, the conclusion is inevitable that the Constitution has failed to accomplish one primary object of the Union, which was to place commerce among the States under the control of the common government of all the people, and thereby relieve or protect it against burdens or restrictions imposed, by whatever authority, for the benefit of particular localities or special interests . . .

The power of Congress covers and protects the absolute freedom of such intercourse and trade among the States as may or must succeed manufacture and precede transportation from place of purchase. This would seem to be conceded; for, the court in the present case expressly declare that "contracts to buy, sell, or exchange goods to be transported among the several States, the transportation and its instrumentalities, and articles bought, sold, or exchanged for the purpose of such transit among the States, or put in the way of transit, may be regulated, but this is because they form part of interstate trade or commerce." Here is a direct admission —one which the settled doctrines of this court justify—that contracts to buy and the purchasing of goods to be transported from one State to another, and transportation, with its instrumentalities, are all parts of interstate trade or commerce. Each part of such trade is then under the protection of Congress. And yet, by the opinion and judgment in this case, if I do not misapprehend them. Congress is without power to protect the commercial intercourse that such purchasing necessarily involves against the restraints and burdens arising from the existence of combinations that meet purchasers, from whatever State they come, with the threat—for it is nothing more or less than a threat—that they shall not purchase what they desire to purchase, except at the prices fixed by such combinations. A citizen of Missouri has the right to go in person, or send orders, to Pennsylvania and New Jersey for the purpose of purchasing refined sugar. But of what value is that right if he is confronted in those States by a vast combination which absolutely controls the price of that article by reason of its having acquired all the sugar refineries in the United States in order that they may fix prices in their own interest exclusively?

In my judgment, the citizens of the several States composing the Union are entitled, of right, to buy goods in the State where they are manufactured, or in any other State, without being confronted by an illegal combination whose business extends throughout the whole country, which by the law everywhere is an enemy to the public interests, and which prevents such buying, except at prices arbitrarily fixed by it. I insist that the free course of trade among the States cannot coexist with such combinations. When I speak of trade I mean the buying and selling of articles of every kind that are recognized articles of interstate commerce. Whatever improperly obstructs the free course of interstate intercourse and trade, as involved in the buying and selling of articles to be carried from one State to another, may be reached by Congress, under its authority to regulate commerce among the States. The exercise of that authority so as to make trade among the States, in all recognized articles of commerce, absolutely free from unreasonable or illegal restrictions imposed by combinations, is justified by an express grant of power to Congress and would redound to the welfare of the whole country. I am unable to perceve that any such result would imperil the autonomy of the States, especially as that result cannot be attained through the action of any one State. . . .

To the general government has been committed the control of commercial intercourse among the States, to the end that it may be free at all times from any restraints except such as Congress may impose or permit for the benefit of the whole country. The common government of all the people is the only one that can adequately deal with a matter which directly and injuriously affects the entire commerce of the country, which concerns equally all the people of the Union, and which, it must be confessed, cannot be adequately controlled by any one State. Its authority should not be so weakened by construction that it cannot reach and eradicate evils that, beyond all question, tend to defeat an object which that government is entitled, by the Constitution, to accomplish. . . .

I dissent from the opinion and judgment of the court.

HAMMER v. DAGENHART
247 U.S. 251; 38 Sup. Ct. 529; 62 L. Ed. 1101 (1918)

[*In 1916, Congress passed a law providing that goods produced by child labor should be excluded from shipment in interstate or foreign commerce. Dagenhart, the father of two children who were employed in a North Carolina cotton mill, brought suit in a district court to enjoin Hammer, United States District Attorney, from enforcing the act against his children. The district court granted Dagenhart the injunction, holding that the law was unconstitutional. Hammer then appealed to the Supreme Court.*]

MR. JUSTICE DAY delivered the opinion of the Court:

. . . The attack upon the act rests upon three propositions:

First. It is not a regulation of interstate and foreign commerce.

Second. It contravenes the Tenth Amendment to the Constitution.

Third. It conflicts with the Fifth Amendment to the Constitution.

The controlling question for decision is: Is it within the authority of Congress in regulating commerce among the states to prohibit the transportation in interstate commerce of manufactured goods, the product of a factory in which, within thirty days prior to their removal therefrom, children under the age of fourteen have been employed or permitted to work, or children between the ages of fourteen and sixteen years have been employed or permitted to work more than eight hours in any day, or more than six days in any week, or after the hour of 7 o'clock P.M. or before the hour of 6 o'clock A.M.?

The power essential to the passage of this act, the government contends, is found in the commerce clause of the Constitution, which authorizes Congress to regulate commerce with foreign nations and among the states.

In *Gibbons* v. *Ogden* . . . Chief Justice Marshall, speaking for this court, and defining the extent and nature of the commerce power, said: "It is the power to regulate—that is, to prescribe the rule by which commerce is to be governed." In other words, the power is one to control the means by which commerce is carried on, which is directly the contrary of the assumed right to forbid commerce from moving and thus destroy it as to particular commodities. But it is insisted that adjudged cases in this court establish the doctrine that the power to regulate given to Congress incidentally includes the authority to prohibit the movement of ordinary commodities, and therefore that the subject is not open for discussion. The cases demonstrate the contrary. They rest upon the character of the particular subjects dealt with and the fact that the scope of governmental authority, state or national, possesed over them, is such that the authority to prohibit is, as to them, but the exertion of the power to regulate.

The first of these cases is *Champion* v. *Ames,* 188 U.S. 321, the so-called

effect to keep the channels of commerce free from use in the transportation of tickets used in the promotion of lottery schemes. In *Hipolite Egg Co.* v. *United States,* 220 U.S. 45, this court sustained the power of Congress to pass the Pure Food and Drugs Act, which prohibited the introduction into the states by means of interstate commerce of impure foods and drugs. In *Hoke* v. *United States,* 227 U.S. 308, this court sustained the constitutionality of the so-called "White Slave Traffic Act," whereby transportation of a woman in interstate commerce for the purpose of prostitution was forbidden. . . .

In *Caminetti* v. *United States,* 242 U.S. 470, we held that Congress might prohibit the transportation of women in interstate commerce for the purposes of debauchery and kindred purposes. In *Clark Distilling Co.* v. *Western Maryland R. Co.,* 242 U.S. 311, the power of Congress over the transportation of intoxicating liquors was sustained. . . .

In each of these instances the use of interstate transportation was necessary to the accomplishment of harmful results. In other words, although the power over interstate transportation was to regulate, that could only be accomplished by prohibiting the use of the facilities of interstate commerce to effect the evil intended.

This element is wanting in the present case. The thing intended to be accomplished by this statute is the denial of the facilities of interstate commerce to those manufacturers in the states who employ children within the prohibited ages. The act in its effect does not regulate transportation among the states, but aims to standardize the ages at which children may be employed in mining and manufacturing within the states. The goods shipped are of themselves harmless. The act permits them to be freely shipped after thirty days from the time of their removal from the factory. When offered for shipment, and before transportation begins, the labor of their production is over, and the mere fact that they were intended for interstate commerce transportation does not make their production subject to Federal control under the commerce power.

Commerce "consists of intercourse and traffic . . . and includes the transportation of persons and property, as well as the purchase, sale, and exchange of commodities." The making of goods and the mining of coal are not commerce, nor does the fact that these things are to be afterwards shipped, or used in interstate commerce, make their production a part thereof. . . .

Over interstate transportation, or its incidents, the regulatory power of Congress is ample, but the production of articles intended for interstate commerce is a matter of local regulation. . . .

The grant of power to Congress over the subject of interstate commerce was to enable it to regulate such commerce, and not to give it authority to control the states in their exercise of the police power over local trade and manufacture.

The grant of authority over a purely Federal matter was not intended to destroy the local power always existing and carefully reserved to the states in the Tenth Amendment to the Constitution. . . .

That there should be limitations upon the right to employ children in mines and factories in the interest of their own and the public welfare, all will admit. That such employment is generally deemed to require regulation is shown by the fact that the brief of counsel states that every state in the Union has a law upon the subject, limiting the right to thus employ children. In North Carolina, the state wherein is located the factory in which the employment was had in the present

case, no child under twelve years of age is permitted to work.

It may be desirable that such laws be uniform, but our Federal government is one of enumerated powers. . . .

In interpreting the Constitution it must never be forgotten that the nation is made up of states, to which are intrusted the powers of local government. And to them and to the people the powers not expressly delegated to the national government are reserved. . . . To sustain this statute would not be, in our judgment, a recognition of the lawful exertion of congressional authority over interstate commerce, but would sanction an invasion by the Federal power of the control of a matter purely local in its character, and over which no authority has been delegated to Congress in conferring the power to regulate commerce among the states.

We have neither authority nor disposition to question the motives of Congress in enacting this legislation. The purposes intended must be attained consistently with constitutional limitations upon the exercise of authority, Federal and state, to the end that each may continue to discharge, harmoniously with the other, the duties intrusted to it by the Constitution.

In our view the necessary effect of this act is, by means of a prohibition against the movement in interstate commerce of ordinary commercial commodities, to regulate the hours of labor of children in factories and mines within the states—a purely state authority. Thus the act in a twofold sense is repugnant to the Constitution. It not only transcends the authority delegated to Congress over commerce, but also exerts a power as to a purely local matter to which the Federal authority does not extend. The far-reaching result of upholding the act cannot be more plainly indicated than by pointing out that if Congress can thus regulate matters intrusted to local authority by prohibition of the movement of commodities in interstate commerce, all freedom of commerce will be at an end, and the power of the states over local matters may be eliminated, and thus our system of government be practically destroyed.

. . . We hold that this law exceeds the constitutional authority of Congress. It follows that the decree of the District Court must be

Affirmed.

MR. JUSTICE HOLMES, dissenting:

. . . [T]he statute in question is within the power expressly given to Congress, if considered only as to its immediate effects, and . . . if invalid it is so only upon some collateral ground. The statute confines itself to prohibiting the carriage of certain goods in interstate or foreign commerce. Congress is given power to regulate such commerce in unqualified terms. It would not be argued today that the power to regulate does not include the power to prohibit. Regulation means the prohibition of something, and when interstate commerce is the matter to be regulated I cannot doubt that the regulations may prohibit any part of such commerce that Congress sees fit to forbid. At all events it is established by the *Lottery Case* and others that have followed it that a law is not beyond the regulative power of Congress merely because it prohibits certain transportation out-and-out. . . .

The question, then, is narrowed to whether the exercise of its otherwise constitutional power by Congress can be pronounced unconstitutional because of its possible reaction upon the conduct of the states in a matter upon which I have admitted that they are free from direct control. I should have thought that that matter had been disposed of so fully as to leave no room for doubt. I should have thought that the most

conspicuous decisions of this court had made it clear that the power to regulate commerce and other constitutional powers could not be cut down or qualified by the fact that it might interfere with the carrying out of the domestic policy of any state.

. . . It does not matter whether the supposed evil precedes or follows the transportation. It is enough that, in the opinion of Congress, the transportation encourages the evil. . . .

The notion that prohibition is any less prohibition when applied to things now thought evil I do not understand. But if there is any matter upon which civilized countries have agreed—far more unanimously than they have with regard to intoxicants and some other matters over which this country is now emotionally aroused—it is the evil of premature and excessive child labor. I should have thought that if we were to introduce our own moral conceptions where, in my opinion, they do not belong, this was pre-eminently a case for upholding the exercise of all its powers by the United States.

But I had thought that the propriety of the exercise of a power admitted to exist in some cases was for the consideration of Congress alone, and that this court always had disavowed the right to intrude its judgment upon questions of policy or morals. It is not for this court to pronounce when prohibition is necessary to regulation if it ever may be necessary—to say that it is permissible as against strong dring, but not as against the product of ruined lives.

The act does not meddle with anything belonging to the states. They may regulate their internal affairs and their domestic commerce as they like. But when they seek to send their products across the state line they are no longer within their rights. If there were no Constitution and no Congress their power to cross the line would depend upon their neighbors. Under the Constitution such commerce belongs not to the states, but to Congress to regulate. It may carry out its views of public policy whatever indirect effect they may have upon the activities of the states. Instead of being encountered by a prohibitive tariff at her boundaries, the state encounters the public policy of the United States, which it is for Congress to express. The public policy of the United States is shaped with a view to the benefit of the nation as a whole. If, as has been the case within the memory of men still living, a state should take a different view of the propriety of sustaining a lottery from that which generally prevails, I cannot believe that the fact would require a different decision from that reached in *Champion* v. *Ames*. Yet in that case it would be said with quite as much force as in this that Congress was attempting to intermeddle with the state's domestic affairs. The national welfare as understood by Congress may require a different attitude within its sphere from that of some self-seeking state. It seems to me entirely constitutional for Congress to enforce its understanding by all the means at its command.

MR. JUSTICE MCKENNA, MR. JUSTICE BRANDEIS, and MR. JUSTICE CLARKE concur in this opinion.

UNITED STATES *v.* DARBY
312 U.S. 100; 61 Sup. Ct. 451; 85 L. Ed. 609 (1941)

[*Darby manufactured lumber for shipment in interstate commerce. He was indicted for violation of various sections of the Fair Labor Standards Act of 1938, which fixed minimum wages and maximum hours for employees engaged in producing goods for shipment in interstate commerce. A district court quashed the indictment, holding that the regulation of wages and hours of employment of persons engaged in the manufacture of goods for possible shipment in interstate commerce was not within the commerce power of Congress. The United States appealed directly to the Supreme Court.*]

MR. JUSTICE STONE delivered the opinion of the Court:

The two principal questions raised by the record in this case are, *first,* whether Congress has constitutional power to prohibit the shipment in interstate commerce of lumber manufactured by employees whose wages are less than a prescribed minimum or whose weekly hours of labor at that wage are greater than a prescribed maximum, and, *second,* whether it has power to prohibit the employment of workmen in the production of goods "for interstate commerce" at other than prescribed wages and hours. . . .

The indictment charges that appellee is engaged, in the State of Georgia, in the business of acquiring raw materials, which he manufactures into finished lumber with the intent, when manufactured, to ship it in interstate commerce to customers outside the state, and that he does in fact so ship a large part of the lumber so produced. There are numerous counts charging appellee with the shipment in interstate commerce from Georgia to point outside the state of lumber in the production of which, for interstate commerce, appellee has employed workmen at less than the prescribed minimum wage or more than the prescribed maximum hours without payment to them of any wage for overtime. . . .

The case comes here on assignments

by the Government that the district court erred in so far as it held that Congress was without constitutional power to penalize the acts set forth in the indictment, and appellee seeks to sustain the decision below on the grounds that the prohibition by Congress of those Acts is unauthorized by the Commerce Clause and is prohibited by the Fifth Amendment. . . . [W]e . . . confine our decision to the validity and construction of the statute. . . .

While manufacture is not of itself interstate commerce, the shipment of manufactured goods interstate is such commerce and the prohibition of such shipment by Congress is indubitably a regulation of the commerce. The power to regulate commerce is the power "to prescribe the rule by which commerce is governed." *Gibbons* v. *Ogden* . . . It extends not only to those regulations which aid, foster, and protect the commerce, but embraces those which prohibit it. . . . It is conceded that the power of Congress to prohibit transportation in interstate commerce includes noxious articles, *Lottery Case,* . . . stolen articles, *Brooks* v. *United States,* . . . kidnaped persons, *Gooch* v. *United States,* . . . and articles such as intoxicating liquor or convict-made goods, traffic in which is forbidden or restricted by the laws of the state of destination. *Kentucky Whip & Collar Co.* v. *Illinois Central R. Co.* . . .

But it is said that the present prohibition falls within the scope of none of these categories; that while the prohibition is nominally a regulation of the commerce its motive or purpose is regulation of wages and hours of persons engaged in manufacture, the control of which has been reserved to the states and upon which Georgia and some of the states of destination have placed no restriction; that the effect of the present statute is not to exclude the proscribed articles from interstate commerce in aid of state regulation as in *Kentucky Whip & Collar Co.* v. *Illinois Central R. Co.* . . . but instead, under the guise of a regulation of interstate commerce, it undertakes to regulate wages and hours within the state contrary to the policy of the state which has elected to leave them unregulated. . . .

The motive and purpose of the present regulation are plainly to make effective the Congressional conception of public policy that interstate commerce should not be made the instrument of competition in the distribution of goods produced under substandard labor conditions, which competition is injurious to the commerce and to the states from and to which the commerce flows. The motive and purpose of a regulation of interstate commerce are matters for the legislative judgment, upon the exercise of which the Constitution places no restriction and over which the courts are given no control. . . . Whatever their motive and purpose, regulations of commerce which do not infringe some constitutional prohibition are within the plenary power conferred on Congress by the Commerce Clause. Subject only to that limitation, presently to be considered, we conclude that the prohibition of the shipment interstate of goods produced under the forbidden substandard labor conditions is within the constitutional authority of Congress.

In the more than a century which has elapsed since the decision of *Gibbons* v. *Ogden,* these principles of constitutional interpretation have been so long and repeatedly recognized by this Court as applicable to the Commerce Clause, that there would be little occasion for repeating them now were it not for the decision of this Court twenty-two years ago in *Hammer* v. *Dagenhart.* . . . In that case it was held by a bare majority of the Court, over the powerful and now classic dissent of Mr. Justice Holmes setting forth the fundamental issues involved, that Congress was without power to exclude the products of child labor from interstate commerce. The reasoning and conclusion of the Court's opinion there cannot be reconciled with the conclusion which we have reached, that the power of Congress under the Commerce Clause is plenary to exclude any article from interstate commerce subject only to the specific prohibitions of the Constitution.

Hammer v. *Dagenhart* has not been followed. The distinction on which the decision was rested that Congressional power to prohibit interstate commerce is limited to articles which in themselves have some harmful or deleterious property—a distinction which was novel when made and unsupported by any provision of the Constitution—has long since been abandoned. . . .

The conclusion is inescapable that *Hammer* v. *Dagenhart* was a departure from the principles which have prevailed in the interpretation of the Commerce Clause both before and since the decision and that such vitality, as a precedent, as it then had has long since been exhausted. It should be and now is overruled.

Validity of the Wage and Hour Requirements. Section 15(a) (2) and §§6 and 7 require employers to conform to the wage and hour provisions with respect to all employees engaged in the production of goods for interstate commerce. As appellee's employees are not alleged to be "engaged in interstate commerce" the validity of the prohibition turns on the question whether the employment, under other than the prescribed labor standards, of employees engaged in the production of goods for interstate commerce is so related to the commerce and so affects it as to be within the reach of the power of Congress to regulate it. . . .

Congress, having by the present Act adopted the policy of excluding from interstate commerce all goods produced for the commerce which do not conform to the specified labor standards, it may choose the means reasonably adapted to the attainment of the permitted end, even though they involve control of intrastate activities. Such legislation has often been sustained with respect to powers, other than the commerce power granted to the national government, when the means chosen, although not themselves within the granted power, were nevertheless deemed appropriate aids to the accomplishment of some purpose within an admitted power of the national government. . . . A familiar like exercise of power is the regulation of intrastate transactions which are so commingled with or related to interstate commerce that all must be regulated if the interstate commerce is to be effectively controlled. . . . Similarly Congress may require inspection and preventive treatment of all cattle in a disease-infected area in order to prevent shipment in interstate commerce of some of the cattle without the treatment. . . . It may prohibit the removal, at destination, of labels required by the Pure Food & Drug Acts to be affixed to articles transported in interstate commerce. . . .

The Sherman Act and the National Labor Relations Act are familiar examples of the exertion of the commerce power to prohibit or control activities wholly intrastate because of their effect on interstate commerce. . . .

The means adopted by §15(a) (2) for the protection of interstate commerce by the suppression of the production of the condemned goods for interstate commerce is so related to the commerce and so affects it as to be within the reach of the commerce power. . . . Congress, to attain its objective in the suppression of nation-wide competition in interstate commerce by goods produced under substandard labor conditions, has made no distinction as the volume or amount of shipments in the commerce or of production for commerce by any particular shipper or producer. It recognized that in present-day industry, competition by a small part may affect the whole and that the total effect of the competition of many small producers may be great. . . .

So far as *Carter* v. *Carter Coal Co.* . . . is inconsistent with this conclusion, its doctrine is limited in principle by the decisions under the Sherman Act and the National Labor Relations Act, which we have cited and which we follow. . . .

Our conclusion is unaffected by the Tenth Amendment which provides: "The powers not delegated to the United States by the Constitution, nor prohibited by it to the States, are reserved to the States respectively, or to the people." The amendment states but a truism that all is retained which has not been surrendered. There is nothing in the history of its adoption to suggest that it was more than declaratory of the relationship between the national and state governments as it had been established by the Constitution before the amendment or that its purpose was other than to allay fears that the new national government might seek to exercise powers not granted, and that the states might not be able to exercise fully their reserved powers. . . .

Validity of the Wage and Hour Provisions Under the Fifth Amendment. Both provisions are minimum-wage requirements compelling the payment of a minimum standard wage with a prescribed increased wage for overtime. . . . Since our decision in *West Coast Hotel Co.* v. *Parrish*, . . . it is no longer open to question that the fixing of a minimum wage is within the legislative power and that the bare fact of its exercise is not a denial of due process under the Fifth more than under the Fourteenth Amendment. Nor is it any longer open to question that it is within the legislative power to fix maximum hours. . . .

The Act is sufficiently definite to meet constitutional demands. One who employs persons, without conforming to the prescribed wage and hour conditions, to work on goods which he ships or expects to ship across state lines, is warned that he may be subject to the criminal penalities of the Act. No more is required. . . .

Reversed.

NATIONAL LABOR RELATIONS BOARD *v.* JONES AND LAUGHLIN STEEL CORPORATION
301 U.S. 1; 57 Sup. Ct. 615; 81 L. Ed. 893 (1937)

[*The National Labor Relations Act of 1935 was designed to reduce the number of labor disputes that burdened interstate and foreign commerce. The motivation behind the act was the granting of the right of collective bargaining. The act forbids a number of unfair labor practices. The National Labor Relations Board was empowered to issue cease and desist orders against companies that engaged in any unfair practice prohibited by the act. In the instant case, the Jones and Laughlin Steel Corporation had discharged ten employees because of their labor union activities. After a proper hearing, the board ordered that the employees be reinstated. Upon the company's refusal to comply with the order, the board petitioned the circuit court of appeals to enforce the order in accordance with the act. The Court refused to enforce the board's action, stating that it "lay beyond the range of federal power." The Supreme Court granted certiorari.*]

MR. CHIEF JUSTICE HUGHES delivered the opinion of the Court:

. . . The facts as to the nature and scope of the business of the Jones & Laughlin Steel Corporation have been found by the Labor Board. . . . The Labor Board has found: The corporation is organized under the laws of Pennsylvania and has its principal office at Pittsburgh. It is engaged in the business of manufacturing iron and steel in plants situated in Pittsburgh and nearby Aliquippa, Pennsylvania. It manufactures and distributes a widely diversified line of steel and pig iron, being the fourth largest producer of steel in the United States. With its subsidiaries—nineteen in number—it is a completely integrated enterprise, owning and operating ore, coal, and limestone properties, lake and river transportation facilities and terminal railroads located at its manufacturing plants. It owns or controls mines in Michigan and Minnesota. It operates four ore steamships on the Great Lakes used in the transportation of ore to its factories. It owns coal mines in Pennsylvania. It operates towboats and steam barges used in carrying coal to its factories. It owns limestone properties in various places in Pennsylvania and West Virginia. It owns the Monongahela connecting railroad, which connects the plants of the Pittsburgh works and forms an interconnection with the Pennsylvania, New York Central, and Baltimore and Ohio Railroad systems. It owns the Aliquippa and Southern Railroad Company, which connects the Aliquippa works with the Pittsburgh and Lake Erie, part of the New York Central system. Much of its product is shipped to its warehouses in Chicago, Detroit, Cincinnati, and Memphis—to the last two places by means of its own barges and transportation equipment. In Long Island City, New York, and in New Orleans it operates structural-steel fabricating shops in connection with the warehousing of semifinished materials sent from its works. Through one of its wholly-owned subsidiaries it owns, leases, and operates stores, warehouses, and yards for the distribution of equipment and supplies for drilling and operating oil and gas mills and for pipe lines, refineries, and pumping stations. It has sales offices in twenty cities in the United States and a wholly-owned subsidiary which is devoted exclusively to distributing its product in Canada. Approximately 75 per cent of its product is shipped out of Pennsylvania.

Summarizing these operations, the Labor Board concluded that the works in Pittsburgh and Aliquippa "might be likened to the heart of a self-contained, highly integrated body. They draw in the raw materials from Michigan, Minnesota, West Virginia, Pennsylvania in part through arteries and by means controlled by the respondent; they transform the materials and then pump them out of all parts of the nation through the vast mechanism which the respondent has elaborated. . . ."

The Scope of the Act. The Act is challenged in its entirety as an attempt to regulate all industry, thus invading the reserved powers of the State over their local concerns. It is asserted that the references in the Act to interstate and foreign commerce are colorable at best; that the Act is not a true regulation of such commerce or of matters which directly affect it but on the contrary has the fundamental object of placing under the compulsory supervision of the Federal government all industrial labor relations within the nation. The argument seeks support in the broad words of the preamble (Section 1) and in the sweep of the provisions of the Act, and it is further insisted that its legislative history shows an essential universal purpose in the light of which its scope cannot be limited by either construction or by the application of the separability clause.

If this conception of terms, intent, and consequent inseparability were sound, the Act would necessarily fall by reason of the limitation upon the Federal power which inheres in the constitutional grant, as well as because of the explicit reservation of the Tenth Amendment. *A.L.A. Schechter Poultry Corp.* v. *United States.* . . . The authority of the Federal government may not be pushed to such an extreme as to destroy the distinction, which the commerce clause itself establishes, between commerce "among the several States" and the internal concerns of a State. That distinction between what is national and what is local in the activities of commerce is vital to the maintenance of our Federal system. . . .

We think it clear that the National Labor Relations Act may be construed so as to operate within the sphere of constitutional authority. The jurisdiction conferred upon the Board, and invoked in this instance, is found in §10(a), which provides:

"Sec. 10(a), The Board is empowered, as hereinafter provided, to prevent any person from engaging in any unfair labor practice (listed in §8) affecting commerce."

The critical words of this provision, prescribing the limits of the Board's authority in dealing with the labor practices, are "affecting commerce. . . ."

There can be no question that the commerce thus contemplated by the Act (aside from that within a Territory or the District of Columbia) is interstate and foreign commerce in the constitutional sense. The Act also defines the term "affecting commerce" §2(7):

"The term 'affecting commerce' means in commerce, or burdening or obstructing commerce or the free flow of commerce, or having led or tending to lead to a labor dispute burdening or obstructing commerce or the free flow of commerce."

This definition is one of exclusion as well as inclusion. The grant of authority to the Board does not purport to extend to the relationship between all industrial employees and employers. Its terms do not impose collective bargaining upon all industry regardless of effects upon interstate or foreign commerce. It purports to reach only what may be deemed to burden or obstruct that commerce and, thus qualified, it must be construed as contemplating the exercise of control within constitutional bounds. It is a familiar principle that acts which directly burden or obstruct interstate or foreign commerce, or its free flow, are within the reach of the congressional power. Acts having that effect are not rendered immune because they grow out of labor disputes. . . . It is the effect upon commerce, not the source of the injury, which is the criterion. . . . Whether or not particular action does affect commerce in such a close and intimate fashion as to be subject to Federal control, and hence to lie within the authority conferred upon the Board, is left by the statute to be determined as individual cases arise. We are thus to inquire whether in the instant case the constitutional boundary has been passed. . . .

The Application of the Act to Employees Engaged in Production—The

Principle Involved. Respondent says that whatever may be said of employees engaged in interstate commerce, the industrial relations and activities in the manufacturing department of respondent's enterprise are not subject to Federal regulation. The argument rests upon the proposition that manufacturing in itself is not commerce. . . .

The various parts of respondent's enterprise are described (by the government) as interdependent and as thus involving "a great movement of iron ore, coal, and limestone along well-defined paths to the steel mills, thence through them, and thence in the form of steel products into the consuming centers of the country—a definite and well-understood course of business." It is urged that these activities constitute a "stream" or "flow" of commerce, of which the Aliquippa manufacturing plant is the focal point, and that industrial strife at that point would cripple the entire movement. . . .

We do not find it necessary to determine whether these features of defendant's business dispose of the asserted analogy to the "stream of commerce" cases. The instances in which that metaphor has been used are but particular, and not exclusive, illustrations of the protective power which the Government invokes in support of the present Act. The congressional authority to protect interstate commerce from burdens and obstructions is not limited to transactions which can be deemed to be an essential part of a "flow" of interstate or foreign commerce. Burdens and obstructions may be due to injurious action springing from other sources. The fundamental principle is that the power to regulate commerce is the power to enact "all appropriate legislation" for "its protection and advancement" . . .; to adopt measures "to promote its growth and insure its safety" . . .; "to

foster, protect, control, and restrain. . . ." That power is plenary and may be exerted to protect interstate commerce "no matter what the source of the dangers which threaten it. . . ." Although activities may be intrastate in character when separately considered, if they have such a close and substantial relation to interstate commerce that their control is essential or appropriate to protect that commerce from burdens and obstructions. Congress cannot be denied the power to exercise that control. . . . Undoubtedly the scope of this power must be considered in the light of our dual system of government and may not be extended so as to embrace effects upon interstate commerce so indirect and remote that to embrace them, in view of our complex society, would effectually obliterate the distinction between what is national and what is local and create a completely centralized government. . . . The question is necessarily one of degree. . . .

[T]he fact that the employees here concerned were engaged in production is not determinative. The question remains as to the effect upon interstate commerce of the labor practice involved. In the *A. L. A. Schechter Poultry Corp. Case,* . . . we found that the effect there was so remote as to be beyond the Federal power. To find "immediacy or directness" there was to find it "almost everywhere," a result inconsistent with the maintenance of our Federal system. In the *Carter Case,* . . . the Court was of the opinion that the provisions of the statute relating to production were invalid upon several grounds—that there was improper delegation of legislative power, and that the requirements not only went beyond any sustainable measure of protection of interstate commerce but were also inconsistent with due process. These cases are not controlling here. . . .

Effects of the Unfair Labor Practice

in Respondent's Enterprise. Giving full weight to respondents contention with respect to a break in the complete continuity of the "stream of commerce" by reason of respondent's manufacturing operations, the fact remains that the stoppage of those operations by industrial strife would have a most serious effect upon interstate commerce. In view of respondent's far-flung activities, it is idle to say that the effect would be indirect or remote. It is obvious that it would be immediate and might be catastrophic. We are asked to shut our eyes to the plainest facts of our national life and to deal with the question of direct and indirect effects in an intellectual vacuum. Because there may be but indirect and remote effects upon interstate commerce in connection with a host of local enterprises throughout the country, it does not follow that other industrial activities do not have such a close and intimate relation to interstate commerce as to make the presence of industrial strife a matter of the most urgent national concern. When industries organize themselves on a national scale, making their relation to interstate commerce the dominant factor in their activities, how can it be maintained that their industrial labor relations constitute a forbidden field into which Congress may not enter when it is necessary to protect interstate commerce from the paralyzing consequences of industrial war? We have often said that interstate commerce itself is a practical conception. It is equally true that interferences with that commerce must be appraised by a judgment that does not ignore actual experience.

Experience has abundantly demonstrated that the recognition of the right of employees to self-organization and to have representatives of their own choosing for the purpose of collective bargaining is often an essential condition of industrial peace. Refusal to confer and negotiate has been one of the most prolific causes of strife. . . .

It is not necessary again to detail the facts to respondent's enterprise. Instead of being beyond the pale, we think that it presents in a most striking way the close and intimate relation which a manufacturing industry may have to interstate commerce, and we have no doubt that Congress had constitutional authority to safeguard the right of respondent's employees to self-organization and freedom in the choice of representatives for collective bargaining. . . .

Our conclusion is that the order of the Board was within its competency and that the Act is valid as here applied. The judgment of the Circuit Court of Appeals is reversed and the cause is remanded for further proceedings in conformity with this opinion.

Reversed.

MR. JUSTICE | MC REYNOLDS delivered the following dissenting opinion:

MR. JUSTICE VAN DEVANTER, MR. JUSTICE SUTHERLAND, MR. JUSTICE BUTLER and I are unable to agree with the decisions just announced. . . .

The Court, as we think, departs from well-established principles followed in *A. L. A. Schechter Poultry Corp.* v. *United States* . . . and *Carter* v. *Carter Coal Co.* . . . Upon the authority of these decisions . . . the power of Congress under the commerce clause does not extend to relations between employers and their employees engaged in manufacture, and therefore the Act conferred upon the National Relations Board no authority in respect of matters covered by the questioned orders. . . . No decision of judicial opinion to the contrary has been cited, and we find none. . . .

WICKARD, SECRETARY OF AGRICULTURE, et al. v. FILBURN
317 U.S. 111; 63 Sup. Ct. 82; 87 L. Ed. 122 (1942)

[*Filburn, the appellee, owned and operated a small farm in Ohio. Under the terms of the Agricutural Adjustment Act of 1938, which was designed to stabilize agricultural production, Filburn was given a wheat acreage quota of 11.1 acres for his 1941 crop. But he sowed twenty-three acres of wheat, claiming that the excess wheat was produced for use on his own farm rather than for shipment in interstate commerce. He refused to pay the penalty of $117.11 for producing the extra wheat and brought an action to enjoin the Secretary of Agriculture and others from enforcing the penalty. The proclamation of national quotas had been made by the Secretary as stipulated by the Agricultural Adjustment Act. A three-judge district court issued the injunction on grounds that did not involve the major constitutional issue. The Secretary of Agriculture and others then appealed to the Supreme Court. The portions of the opinion printed here deal only with the major constitutional issue presented to the Court.*]

MR. JUSTICE JACKSON delivered the opinion of the Court:

It is urged that under the commerce clause of the Constitution, Article I, §8, clause 3, Congress does not possess the power it has in this instance sought to exercise. The question would merit little consideration since our decision in *United States* v. *Darby* . . . sustaining the federal power to regulate production of goods for commerce, except for the fact that this Act extends federal regulation to production not intended in any part for commerce but wholly for consumption on the farm. The Act includes a definition of "market" and its derivatives, so that as related to wheat, in addition to its conventional meaning, it also means to dispose of "by feeding (in any form) to poultry or livestock which, or the products of which, are sold, bartered, or exchanged, or to be so disposed of." Hence, marketing quotas not only embrace all that may be sold without penalty but also what may be consumed on the premises. Wheat produced on excess acreage is designated as "available for marketing" as so defined, and the penalty is imposed thereon. Penalties do not depend upon whether any part of the wheat, either within or without the quota, is sold or intended to be sold. The sum of this is that the Federal Government fixes a quota including all that the farmer may harvest for sale or for his own farm needs, and declares that wheat produced on excess acreage may neither be disposed of nor used except upon payment of the penalty, or except it is stored as required by the Act or delivered to the Secretary of Agriculture.

Appellee says that this is a regulation of production and consumption of wheat. Such activities are, he urges, beyond the reach of Congressional power under the commerce clause, since they are local in character, and their effects upon interstate commerce are at most "indirect." In answer the Government argues that the statute regulates neither production nor consumption, but only marketing; and, in the alternative, that if the Act does go beyond the regulation of marketing it is sustainable as a "necessary and proper" implementation of the power of Congress over interstate commerce.

The Government's concern lest the Act be held to be a regulation of production or consumption, rather than of marketing, is attributable to a few dicta and decisions of this Court which might be understood to lay it down that activities such as "production," "manufacturing," and "mining" are strictly "local" and, except in special circumstances which are not present here, cannot be regulated under the commerce power because their effects upon interstate commerce are, as matter of law, only "indirect." Even today, when this power has been held to have great latitude, there is no decision of this Court that such activities may be regulated where no part of the product is intended for interstate commerce or intermingled with the subjects thereof. We believe that a review of the course of decision under the commerce clause will make plain, however, that questions of the power of Congress are not to be decided by reference to any formula which would give controlling force to nomenclature such as "production" and "indirect" and foreclose consideration of the actual effects of the activity in question upon interstate commerce.

At the beginning Chief Justice Marshall described the federal commerce power with a breadth never yet exceeded. *Gibbons* v. *Ogden*. . . . He made emphatic the embracing and penetrating nature of this power by warning that effective restraints on its exercise must proceed from political rather than from judicial processes.

. . . Once an economic measure of the reach of the power granted to Congress in the commerce clause is accepted, questions of federal power cannot be decided simply by finding the activity in question to be "production," nor can consideration of its economic effects be forclosed by calling them "indirect." The present Chief Justice has said in summary of the present state of the law: "The commerce power is not confined in its exercise to the regulation of commerce among the states. It extends to those

activities intrastate which so affect interstate commerce, or the exertion of the power of Congress over it, as to make regulation of them appropriate means to the attainment of a legitimate end, the effective execution of the granted power to regulate interstate commerce. . . . The power of Congress over interstate commerce is plenary and complete in itself, may be exercised to its utmost extent, and acknowledges no limitations other than are prescribed in the Constitution. . . . It follows that no form of state activity can constitutionally thwart the regulatory power granted by the commerce clause to Congress. Hence the reach of that power extends to those intrastate activities which in a substantial way interfere with or obstruct the exercise of the granted power." *United States* v. *Wrightwood Dairy Co.,* 315 U.S. 110. . . .

Whether the subject of the regulation in question was "production," "consumption," or "marketing" is, therefore, not material for purposes of deciding the question of federal power before us. That an activity of a local character may help in a doubtful case to determine whether Congress intended to reach it. The same consideration might help in determining whether in the absence of congressional action it would be permissible for the state to exert its power on the subject matter, even though in so doing it to some degree affected interstate commerce. But even if appellee's activity be local and though it may not be regarded as commerce, it may still, whatever its nature, be reached by Congress if it exerts a substantial economic effect on interstate commerce, and this irrespective of whether such effect is what might at some earlier time have been defined as "direct" or "indirect."

. . . The maintenance by government regulation of a price for wheat undoubtedly can be accomplished as effectively by sustaining or increasing the demand as by limiting the supply. The effect of the statute before us is to restrict the amount which may be produced for market and the extent as well to which one may forestall resort to the market by producing to meet his own needs. That appellee's own contribution to the demand for wheat may be trivial by itself is not enough to remove him from the scope of federal regulation where, as here, his contribution, taken together with that of many others similarly situated, is far from trivial. . . .

It is well established by decision of this Court that the power to regulate commerce includes the power to regulate the prices at which commodities in that commerce are dealt in and practices affecting such prices. One of the primary purposes of the Act in question was to increase the market price of wheat, and to that end to limit the volume thereof that could affect the market. It can hardly be denied that a factor of such volume and variability as home-consumed wheat would have a substantial influence on price and market conditions. This may arise because being in marketable condition such wheat overhangs the market and, if induced by rising prices, tends to flow into the market and check price increases. But if we assume that it is never marketed, it supplies a need of the man who grew it which would

otherwise be reflected by purchases in the open market. Home-grown wheat in this sense competes with wheat in commerce. The stimulation of commerce is a use of the regulatory function quite as definitely as prohibitions or restrictions thereon. This record leaves us in no doubt that Congress may properly have considered that wheat consumed on the farm where grown, if wholly outside the scheme of regulation, would have a substantial effect in defeating and obstructing its purpose to stimulate trade therein at increased prices.

It is said, however, that this Act, forcing some farmers into the market to buy what they could provide for themselves, is an unfair promotion of the markets and prices of specializing wheat growers. It is of the essence of regulation that it lays a restraining hand on the self-interest of the regulated and that advantages from the regulation commonly fall to others. The conflicts of economic interest between the regulated and those who advantage by it are wisely left under our system to resolution by the Congress under its more flexible and responsible legislative process. Such conflicts rarely lend themselves to judicial determination. And with the wisdom, workability, or fairness of the plan of regulation we have nothing to do. . . .

Reversed.

10
Taxation and Fiscal Powers of Congress

The power to tax is, of course, essential for the maintenance of any governmental system. One of the most serious weaknesses of the Articles of Confederation was that Congress could not levy and collect taxes. Consequently, not surprisingly the power to tax is the first to be enumerated in Article I of the Constitution. This first paragraph grants broad powers to Congress to "lay and collect taxes, duties, imposts and excises, to pay the debts and provide for the common defence and general welfare of the United States." There are only a few essential constitutional limitations on this sweeping grant of power to Congress. These may be enumerated as follows:

1. *Duties, imposts, and excises must be levied uniformly throughout the United States* (Art. I, Sect. 8, cl. 1). This restriction does not require that all articles be taxed uniformly, but simply that the categories and rates of such taxes be the same throughout the country. In *Florida* v. *Mellon,* 273 U.S. 12 (1927), the Supreme Court noted that the Constitution requires that a tax law shall be uniform only "in the sense that by its provisions the rule of liability shall be the same in all parts of the United States."

2. *Direct taxes must be apportioned among the states according to population* (Art. I, Sect. 2, cl. 3; Art. I, Sect. 9, cl. 4). Direct taxes (with the

exception of income taxes) have seldom been used in the United States. The question of whether the income tax was a direct or indirect tax was once the subject of serious controversy. In 1861, an income tax law was upheld by the Supreme Court in a unanimous decision in *Springer* v. *United States,* 102 U.S. 586 (1881). This statute expired in 1872, but in 1894 another, somewhat different, income tax law was passed. In *Pollock* v. *Farmers' Loan and Trust Co.,* the Court ruled that taxes on income derived from land or personal property were direct and therefore unconstitutional because they were not apportioned among the states according to population. The effect of the *Pollock* case was overcome by the Sixteenth Amendment, which empowers Congress to levy and collect taxes on incomes "from whatever source derived, without apportionment among the several states, and without regard to any census or enumeration."

3. *No tax or duty may be levied on articles exported from any state* (Art. I, Sect. 9, cl. 5). This limitation was added to appease the Southern states, who were afraid that their exports of cotton and other goods would be subject to discrimination.

The taxing power of Congress is also subject to other implied limitations found in parts of the Constitution that are not directly connected with taxation. For example, important restrictions flow from the due process clause of the Fifth Amendment and from the very existence of a federal form of government. Such limitations have been developed principally by interpretation of various constitutional clauses by the Supreme Court. The most important of these restrictions are examined in more detail in the discussion of the cases below.

In addition to the taxing power, the Constitution grants Congress the power to coin money and regulate its values (Art. I, Sect. 8, cl. 5) and to borrow money on the credit of the United States (Art. I, Sect. 8, cl. 2). These fiscal powers of Congress have been used not only to raise and spend money but also to regulate social and economic conditions and to control the ups and downs in the business cycle.

Intergovernmental Tax Immunity

The power of Congress to tax is concurrent with that of the state governments. The "entire field of taxation remains open to each of the governments, national and state." The "burden of taxation of each sovereign may fall on the same persons, natural and artificial, the same property, privilege, or activity."[1] But the Constitution is silent about whether or not the states and the

---

[1] Owen J. Roberts, *The Court and the Constitution* (Cambridge: Harvard University Press, 1951), p. 3.

national government may tax the instrumentalities of one another. Hence, this question had to be settled by the Supreme Court.

It will be recalled from Chapter 5 that in *McCulloch* v. *Maryland* the Court held that the agencies and instrumentalities of the federal government could not be taxed by the states. Chief Justice Marshall's famous phrase in that case, "the power to tax involves the power to destroy," was the basis for establishing federal immunity from state taxation. The principle announced in *McCulloch* v. *Maryland* was broadened in *Dobbins* v. *Commissioners of Erie County,* 16 Pet. 435 (1842), where the Court held federal salaries immune from state taxation. Finally, in 1870, the Court expanded the immunity doctrine by making it applicable to federal taxation of state instrumentalities in the case of *Collector* v. *Day,* 11 Wall. 113 (1871). In that case, the Court relied on both the *McCulloch* and *Dobbins* decisions in holding that the salary of a state judge was exempt from federal taxation. Thus, "some fifty years after the Court established the immunity of federal instrumentalities from state taxation (in *McCulloch* v. *Maryland*), the immunity was made reciprocal in *Collector* v. *Day,* on the theory that 'the exception rests upon necessary implication, and is upheld by the great law of self-preservation.' "[2]

The doctrine of tax immunity enunciated in *McCulloch* v. *Maryland* had "its origin in political necessity. In a real sense, Marshall's formulation of the immunity doctrine was part of his larger struggle against state's rights."[3] In one sense, *Collector* v. *Day* was in conflict with portions of *McCulloch* v. *Maryland* and other important decisions establishing the principle of federal supremacy. For the clear implication of *Collector* v. *Day* was that the national government and the states are equal. But, as Justice Stone indicated in a later case, the state immunity from national taxation recognized in *Collector* v. *Day* was "narrowly limited to a state judicial officer engaged in the performance of a function which pertained to state governments at the time the Constitution was adopted."[4] Another important fact to remember about this case is that it was decided during the Reconstruction period, when the Court "was engaged in endeavoring to stem the tendency in Congress toward extreme centralization at the expense of state rights."[5]

The doctrine of *Collector* v. *Day* was never applied widely after the Reconstruction era. And in recent years the area of the states' immunity from federal taxation has been reduced greatly. In fact, the whole doctrine of intergovernmental tax immunity has undergone considerable modification. Changes

[2] David Fellman, "Ten Years of the Supreme Court: 1937–1947, Federalism," *American Political Science Review,* Vol. 41, (1947), p. 1157.

[3] Samuel J. Konefsky, *Chief Justice Stone and the Supreme Court* (New York: Macmillan, 1945), p. 42.

[4] *Helvering* v. *Gerhardt,* 304 U.S. 405 (1938). In this case the Court overruled an earlier decision [*Brush* v. *Commissioner of Internal Revenue,* 300 U.S. 352 (1937)], and held that the salaries of officers of the New York Port Authority were not immune from federal income taxation.

[5] John M. Mathews, *The American Constitutional System,* (New York: McGraw-Hill, 1940), p. 259.

first appeared in *South Carolina* v. *United States,* 199 U.S. 437 (1905). South Carolina had taken over the business of dispensing liquor. But when the federal government attempted to collect the national excise tax on liquor dealers, the state claimed immunity under the doctrine of *Collector* v. *Day.* In holding that South Carolina was required to pay the tax, the Supreme Court drew a distinction between state functions that were strictly governmental and those that were business or proprietary in nature. Governmental functions were said to be immune from taxation, but when a state enters an ordinary business, such as the liquor business, as South Carolina had done, no immunity existed.

The *South Carolina* case imposed upon the Court the difficult task of determining in specific cases when a particular function was or was not a governmental one. That this is extremely difficult to do is demonstrated by numerous decisions. For example, in *Brush* v. *Commissioner of Internal Revenue* the Court held that because a waterworks is a governmental function, the salary of an employee of the Bureau of Water Supply in New York City was immune from federal income taxation. But in *Allen* v. *Regents of University of Georgia,* 304 U.S. 439 (1938), the Court held that receipts from state university contests were liable to federal taxation because such contests are proprietary rather than governmental in nature. Of the *Brush* and *Allen* cases, it has been well said that "it would be interesting to see whether a Byzantine theologian could discover any genuine distinction between the two cases."[6] Thus, as Justice Jackson once remarked, "it is easy to see that the line between the taxable and the immune has been drawn with an unsteady hand."[7]

From time to time various members of the Court protested against the illogical distinction between governmental and business activities and called for a complete reexamination of the entire tax-immunity doctrine. Justice Stone took the lead in this development; he wrote the majority opinions in *Helvering* v. *Gerhardt* and *Graves* v. *New York* ex rel. *O'Keefe* (p. 272), which modified considerably the doctrine of intergovernmental tax immunity.

In the case of *New York* v. *United States,* 326 U.S. 572 (1946), the Court held that the sale of mineral waters by the state of New York constituted a business function that was subject to a federal tax. The case is important principally because some of the justices were willing to reject the traditional distinction between governmental and business activities as a basis for applying the doctrine of tax immunity. Although no new general rule was framed in the *New York* case, the Court will undoubtedly continue to search for more realistic criteria. To this end, Chief Justice Stone, who was joined by Justices Reed, Murphy, and Burton in his concurring opinion in *New York* v. *United States,* repeated what he had said in an earlier case as follows:

> Taxation by either the state or the federal government affects in some measure the cost of operation of the other. But neither government may destroy the

[6] Fellman, *op. cit.,* p. 1158.
[7] *United States* v. *Allegheny County,* 322 U.S. 174 (1944).

other nor curtail in any substantial manner the exercise of its powers. Hence the limitation upon the taxing power of each, so far as it affects the other, must receive a practical construction which permits both to function with the minimum of interference each with the other; and that limitation cannot be so varied or extended as seriously to impair either the taxing power of the government imposing the tax or the appropriate exercise of the functions of the government affected by it.

Purposes of Taxation: Revenue and Regulation

Taxes are usually levied for the obvious purpose of raising money. But taxation is also an inevitable form of regulation. In the words of Justice Stone, "every tax is in some measure regulatory. To some extent it interposes an economic impediment to the activity taxed as compared with others not taxed."[8] Thus, the taxing power "becomes an instrument available to government for accomplishing objectives other than raising revenue."[9]

When tax laws are designed to produce income for the support of governmental activities, no constitutional questions are raised. Furthermore, the Supreme Court has generally sanctioned tax laws that are primarily regulatory or even destructive in nature when such laws are used to aid Congress in exercising some other power, such as the regulation of commerce or the control of the currency. In short, "regulatory or destructive taxation may properly be used as a means of doing anything falling within the delegated powers of Congress."[10] In 1866, for example, Congress levied an annual tax of 10 per cent on state bank notes. The purpose of the law was not revenue but rather to drive the state notes out of existence, thereby giving to the newly established national banks a monopoly on bank note circulation. The tax was upheld by the Supreme Court in *Veazie Bank* v. *Fenno,* 8 Wall. 533 (1869), on the ground that Congress could have achieved the same result by directly prohibiting the issuance of state bank notes under its power to regulate the currency.

On some occasions, however, Congress has used its taxing power to regulate matters that are *outside* the scope of any of its delegated powers. Such legislation raises much more difficult constitutional questions. In some early cases, the Supreme Court refused to look into the motives of Congress and sustained a number of regulatory or destructive tax laws. In *McCray* v. *United States,* 195 U.S. 27 (1904), the Court upheld an act which levied a ¼-cent per pound tax on uncolored oleomargarine and a tax of ten cents per pound on oleomargarine colored yellow to resemble butter. The tax, which had been

[8] *Sonzinsky* v. *United States,* 300 U.S. 506 (1937).

[9] Roy Blough, *The Federal Taxing Process* (Englewood Cliffs, N.J.: Prentice-Hall, 1952), p. 410.

[10] Robert Cushman, "Social and Economic Control Through Taxation," *Minnesota Law Review,* Vol. 18 (1934), p. 759. Reprinted in *Selected Essays of Constitutional Law,* Vol. 3, (1938), p. 543.

supported vigorously by dairy farmers, was designed chiefly to discourage the consumption of oleomargarine in favor of butter. Justice White, in delivering the majority opinion, quoted from a previous decision of Chief Justice Fuller, stating that "the Act before us is on its face an act for levying taxes, and although it may operate in so doing to prevent deception in the sale of oleomargarine as and for butter, its primary object must be assumed to be the raising of revenue." Not until 1950 did the concerted efforts of margarine manufacturers, urban consumers, and others result in the repeal of all federal oleomargarine taxes, over the vigorous opposition of the dairy interests. Shortly after the *McCray* decision, when Congress was also in the process of expanding its federal police powers under the commerce clause (Chapter 9), the taxing power was used to regulate the manufacture of white-phosphorous matches and narcotics. The match tax was never challenged in the courts, but the narcotics law was upheld in a 5-to-4 decision in *United States* v. *Doremus,* 249 U.S. 86 (1919).

In spite of these decisions, the Court announced a different doctrine in 1922 in the case of *Bailey* v. *Drexel Furniture Co.,* which declared the second Child Labor Law unconstitutional.[11] In *Hammer* v. *Dagenhart* (Chapter 9), the Court had invalidated the Child Labor Law of 1916 because the commerce power had been abused. The second Child Labor Law sought to accomplish the same objectives as the 1916 law by using the taxing power of Congress as the basis for regulation. But again the attempt to regulate child labor failed. The tax at issue in the *Bailey* case was declared to be a penalty rather than a true tax. In addition, the Court regarded the regulation of child labor as a function reserved to the states. The *Bailey* case thus established an important limitation on the congressional use of the taxing power for police power purposes.

Purposes of Taxation and the New Deal

Since the *Bailey* and *McCray* decisions were largely irreconcilable, the Court, after 1922, had two lines of reasoning that it could follow in dealing with tax statutes. The Court soon proceeded to make use of both precedents. For example, the doctrine of the *McCray* case was followed in *Magnano Co.* v. *Hamilton,* 292 U.S. 40 (1934), where the Court upheld a state statute that taxed all butter substitutes in the state so heavily that the articles were destroyed. In the *Magnano* case the Court refused to examine the motives behind the tax. On the other hand, the Court followed the *Bailey* case in *United States* v. *Constantine,* 296 U.S. 287 (1935). In that case a special federal excise tax of $1,000 on retail liquor dealers who violated state laws was held

[11] On the same day the *Bailey* decision was rendered, the Court held void the Future Trading Act of 1921, which imposed a heavy tax on the sale of grain for future delivery. *Hill* v. *Wallace,* 259 U.S. 44 (1922). The act was invalidated on the authority of the *Bailey* case.

to be a penalty rather than a tax and thereby encroached upon the police powers of the state.

By the time the New Deal statutes came before the Court, the two possible lines of reasoning had been established clearly. The Court's use of the two available precedents to 1935 has been well summarized as follows:

> When it [the Supreme Court] wishes to uphold the statute, it utilizes the doctrine of the *McCray* and *Magnano* cases, which may be called the doctrine of judicial obtuseness, and refuses to see or know about the tax anything that does not appear in the language of the act. If, however, the act pushes too far and impinges upon interests that the Court feels are entitled to protection, it falls back upon the doctrine of the child-labor tax case [Bailey], takes judicial notice of the palpable legislative intention to destroy rather than to raise money, and declares the act void on the ground that it is not a tax at all but a regulation.[12]

We have already stated that in 1935 and 1936 the Supreme Court was in the process of invalidating important New Deal measures. In 1935, the Court struck down the first of the major New Deal programs (the NIRA) in *Schechter Poultry Corp.* v. *United States.* In January 1936, the Court held unconstitutional the second major New Deal measure, the Agricultural Adjustment Act of 1933, in *United States* v. *Butler.* That case should be read with the following points in mind: (1) The Court followed the narrow construction of the federal taxing power as announced in the *Bailey* and *Constantine* cases. (2) For the first time, the Court interpreted the general welfare clause of the Constitution. In so doing, the Court reviewed the leading views concerning the intent and scope of that clause. Although the Court endorsed Hamilton's version of the general welfare clause, it applied Madison's conception of the clause to the case at hand. (3) In holding that the spending power of Congress was limited by the Tenth Amendment, the Court reasserted the doctrine of "dual federalism," which had been employed in many previous taxation and commerce cases. The doctrine of dual federalism had its roots in the concept of nation-state equality as opposed to national supremacy. It meant simply that the Tenth Amendment limited the delegated powers of Congress. The concept of dual federalism was expressly overruled in *United States* v. *Darby* (Chapter 9). (4) Justice Stone 's scorching and impassioned dissenting opinion deserves careful scrutiny, as it reveals some of the fundamental differences between the liberal and conservative justices during this period.

The decision in the *Butler* case undermined the Roosevelt farm program and raised serious doubts about the constitutionality of other important New Deal measures. Yet only sixteen months later the *Butler* decision was narrowed greatly in *Steward Machine Co.* v. *Davis,* which upheld the unemploy-

---

[12] Robert Cushman, "Constitutional Law in 1933–34," *American Political Science Review,* Vol. 29 (Febuary 1935), p. 51.

ment compensation provisions of the Social Security Act of 1935. On the same day the Court sustained the old-age pension phase of the Social Security program in *Helvering* v. *Davis,* 301 U.S. 619 (1937). In these cases the Court returned to a broader interpretation of the federal taxing power.

It is difficult to reconcile the *Butler* and *Steward Machine Company* decisions, for the dual federalism doctrine could have been used to invalidate the Social Security Act as well as the AAA. But the Court majority was now ready to accept the New Deal. The Social Security Act cases mark the turn of the tide in the Court's attitude toward New Deal legislation. Since 1937, the expansion of national power under the commerce clause has opened the way for federal tax levies whose purpose is primarily regulation rather than revenue. This is revealed clearly in cases such as *Wickard* v. *Filburn,* discussed in Chapter 9.

The language of more recent cases shows that the Supreme Court will allow wide use of the federal taxing power for the promotion of almost any general welfare program. In *United States* v. *Sanchez,* 340 U.S. 42 (1950), the Court sustained a federal regulatory tax on sales of marijuana. Speaking for the Court, Justice Clark stated as follows:

> It is beyond serious question that a tax does not cease to be valid merely because it regulates, discourages, or even definitely deters the activities taxed. The principle applies even though the revenue obtained is obviously negligible, or the revenue purpose of the tax may be secondary. Nor does a tax statute necessarily fall because it touches on activities which Congress might not otherwise regulate. The tax in question is a legitimate exercise of the taxing power despite its collateral regulatory purpose and effect.

Again, in *United States* v. *Kahriger,* 345 U.S. 22 (1953), the Court upheld a 1951 federal occupational tax on gambling that was designed to regulate as well as to produce revenue. In *Marchetti* v. *United States,* 390 U.S. 39 (1968), the Supreme Court overruled Kahriger on self-incrimination grounds but continued to approve the broad theory of taxation on which it had rested.

POLLOCK v. FARMERS' LOAN AND TRUST CO.
158 U.S. 601; 15 Sup. Ct. 673; 39 L. Ed. 1108 (1895)

[In 1894, a Democratic Congress passed an income tax law that imposed a tax of 2 per cent on incomes above $4,000. Incomes from (1) real estate, (2) stocks, bonds, and other securities, (3) state and municipal bonds, and (4) wages, salaries, and professional earnings were subject to the tax. The law was widely supported by the Populist party, the South, and a scattering of agricultural states. Most opposition came from both Republicans and Democrats in the industrial states, where most of the tax would be collected. The law was tested before the Supreme Court in a most unorthodox way. The ordinary way to test the validity of a tax law is to pay the tax and then sue the government to get it back. But business leaders, who bitterly denounced the law as socialistic, wished to avoid

any delay. A New York lawyer, therefore, arranged to have Charles Pollock, a Boston stockholder of the Farmers' Loan and Trust Company, demand that his company refuse to pay the tax. Pollock filed a bill in a federal circuit court to enjoin the trust company from paying the income tax.

On April 8, 1895, the Court, with Justice Howell E. Jackson absent because of illness, declared the law invalid only insofar as it was applied to income from real estate and state and municipal bonds. The Court was divided on the other questions presented. Within a month, however, a rehearing was granted and the decision below rendered.]

MR. CHIEF JUSTICE FULLER delivered the opinion of the Court:

. . . [T]he Constitution divided Federal taxation into two great classes, the class of direct taxes, and the class of duties, imposts, and excises; and prescribed two rules which qualified the grant of power as to each class.

The power to lay direct taxes apportioned among the several States in proportion to their representation in the popular branch of Congress, a representation based on population as ascertained by the census, was plenary and absolute; but to lay direct taxes without apportionment was forbidden. The power to lay duties, imposts, and excises was subject to the qualification that the imposition must be uniform throughout the United States.

Our previous decision was confined to the consideration of the validity of the tax on the income from real estate, and on the income from municipal bonds. The question thus limited was whether such taxation was direct or not, in the meaning of the Constitution; and the court went no farther, as to the tax on the income from real estate, than to hold that it fell within the same class as the source whence the income was derived, that is, that a tax upon the realty and a tax upon the receipts therefrom were alike direct; while as to the income from municipal bonds, that could not be taxed because of want of power to tax the source, and no reference was made to the nature of the tax as being direct or indirect.

We are now permitted to broaden the field of inquiry, and to determine to which of the two great classes a tax upon a person's entire income, whether derived from rents, or products, or otherwise, of real estate, or from bonds, stocks, or other forms of personal property, belongs; and we are unable to conclude that the enforced subtraction from the yield of all the owner's real or personal property, in the manner prescribed, is so different from a tax upon the property itself, that it is not a direct, but an indirect tax, in the meaning of the Constitution. . . .

We know of no reason for holding otherwise than that the words "direct taxes," on the one hand, and "duties, imposts and excises," on the other, were used in the Constitution in their natural and obvious sense. Nor, in arriving at what those terms embrace, do we perceive any ground for enlarging them beyond, or narrowing them within, their natural and obvious import at the time the Constitution was framed and ratified. . . .

In the light of the struggle in the convention as to whether or not the new Nation should be empowered to levy taxes directly on the individual until after the States had failed to respond to requisitions—a struggle which did not terminate until the amendment to the effect, proposed by Massachusetts and concurred in by South Carolina, New Hampshire, New York, and Rhode Island, had been rejected—it would seem beyond reasonable question that direct taxation, taking the place as it did of requisitions, was purposely restrained to apportionment according to representation, in order that the former system as to ratio might be retained, while the mode of collection was changed. . . .

The reasons for the clauses of the Constitution in respect of direct taxation are not far to seek. The States, respectively, possessed plenary powers of taxation. They could tax the property of their citizens in such manner and to such extent as they saw fit; they had unrestricted powers to impose duties or imposts on imports from abroad, and excises on manufactures, consumable commodities, or otherwise. They gave up the great sources of revenue derived from commerce; they retained the concurrent power of levying excises, and duties covering anything other than excises; but in respect of them the range of taxation was narrowed by the power granted over interstate commerce, and by the danger of being put at disadvantage in dealing with excises on manufactures. They retained the power of direct taxation, and to that they looked as their chief resource; but even in respect of that, they granted the concurrent power, and if the tax were placed by both governments on the same subject, the claim of the United States had preference. Therefore, they did not grant the power of direct taxation without regard to their own condition and resources as States; but they granted the power of apportioned direct taxation, a power just as efficacious to serve the needs of the general government, but securing to the States the opportunity to pay the amount apportioned, and to recoup from their own citizens in the most feasible way, and in harmony with their systems of local self-government. If, in the changes of wealth and population in particular States, apportionment produced inequality, it was an inequality stipulated for, just as the equal representation of the States, however small, in the Senate, was stipulated for. The Constitution ordains affirmatively that each State shall have two members of that body, and negatively that no State shall by amendment be deprived of its equal suffrage in the Senate without its consent. The Constitution ordains affirmatively that representatives and direct taxes shall be apportioned among the several States according to numbers, and negatively that no direct tax shall be laid unless in proportion to the enumeration. . . .

It is said that a tax on the whole income of property is not a direct tax in the meaning of the Constitution, but a duty, and, as a duty, leviable without apportionment, whether direct or indirect. We do not think so. Direct taxation was not restricted in one breath, and the restriction blown to the winds in another. . . .

Thus we find Mr. Hamilton, while writing to induce the adoption of the Constitution, first, dividing the power of taxation into external and internal, putting into the former the power of imposing duties on imported articles and into the latter all remaining powers; and, second, dividing the latter into direct and indirect, putting into the latter, duties and excises on articles of consumption.

It seems to us to inevitably follow that in Mr. Hamilton's judgment at that time all internal taxes, except duties and excises on articles of consumption, fell into the category of direct taxes. . . .

He gives, . . . it appears to us, a definition which covers the question before us. A tax upon one's whole income is a tax upon the annual receipts from his whole property, and as such falls within the same class as a tax upon that property, and is a direct tax, in the meaning of the Constitution. And Mr. Hamilton in his report on the public credit, in referring to contracts with citizens of a foreign country, said: "This principle, which seems critically correct, would exempt as well the income as the capital of the property. It protects the use, as effectually as the thing. What, in fact, is property, but a fiction, without the beneficial use of it? In many cases, indeed, the income or annuity is the property itself."

. . . The Constitution prohibits any direct tax, unless in proportion to numbers as ascertained by the census; and, in the light of the circumstances to which we have referred, is it not an evasion of the prohibition to hold that a general unapportioned tax, imposed upon all property owners as a body for or in respect of their property, is not direct, in the meaning of the Constitution, because confined to the income therefrom?

Whatever the speculative views of political economists or revenue reformers may be, can it be properly held that the Constitution, taken in its plain and obvious sense, and with due regard to the circumstances attending the formation of the government, authorizes a general unapportioned tax on the products of the farm and the rents of real estate, although imposed merely because of ownership and with no possible means of escape from payment, as belonging to a totally different class from that which includes the property from whence the income proceeds?

There can be but one answer, unless the constitutional restriction is to be treated as utterly illusory and futile, and the object of its framers defeated. We find it impossible to hold that a fundamental requisition, deemed so important as to be enforced by two provisions, one affirmative and one negative, can be refined away by forced distinctions between that which gives value to property, and the property itself.

Nor can we perceive any ground why the same reasoning does not apply to capital in personality held for the purpose of income or ordinarily yielding income, and to the income therefrom. All the real estate of the country, and all its invested personal property, are open to the direct operation of the taxing power if an apportionment be made according to the Constitution. The Constitution does not say that no direct tax shall be laid by apportionment on any other property than land; on the contrary, it forbids all unapportioned direct taxes; and we know of no warrant for excepting personal property from the exercise of the power, or any reason why an apportioned direct tax cannot be laid and assessed. . . .

The stress of the argument is thrown, however, on the assertion that an income tax is not a property tax at all; that it is not a real estate tax, or a crop tax, or a bond tax; that it is an assessment upon the taxpayer on account of his money-spending power as shown by his revenue for the year preceding the assessment; that rents received, crops harvested, interest collected, have lost all connection with their origin, and although once not taxable have become transmuted in their new form into taxable subject-matter; in other words, that income is taxable irrespective of the source from whence it is derived. . . .

We have unanimously held in this case that, so far as this law operates on the receipts from municipal bonds, it cannot be sustained, because it is a tax on the power of the States, and on their instrumentalities to borrow money, and consequently repugnant to the Constitution. But if, as contended, the interest when received has become merely money in the recipient's pocket, and taxable as such without reference to the source from which it came, the question is immaterial whether it could have been originally taxed at all or not. This was admitted by the Attorney General with characteristic candor; and it follows that, if the revenue derived from municipal bonds cannot be taxed because the source cannot be, the same rule applies to revenue from any other source not subject to the tax; and the lack of power to levy any but an apportioned tax on real and personal property equally exists as to the revenue therefrom.

Admitting that this act taxes the income of property irrespective of its source, still we cannot doubt that such a tax is necessarily a direct tax in the meaning of the Constitution. . . .

Our conclusions may, therefore, be summed up as follows:

First. We adhere to the opinion already announced, that, taxes on real estate being indisputably direct taxes, taxes on the rents or income of real estate are equally direct taxes.

Second. We are of opinion that taxes on personal property, or on the income of personal property, are likewise direct taxes.

Third. The tax imposed by sections 27 to 37, inclusive, of the act of 1894, so far as it falls on the income of real estate and of personal property, being a direct tax within the meaning of the Constitution, and, therefore, unconstitutional and void because not apportioned according to representation, all those sections, constituting one entire scheme of taxation, are necessarily invalid.

The decrees herein before entered in this court will be vacated; the decrees below will be reversed, and the cases remanded, with instructions to grant the relief prayer.

MR. JUSTICE HARLAN dissenting:

. . . In my judgment a tax on income derived from real property ought not to be, and until now has never been, regarded by any court as a direct tax on such property within the mean-

ing of the Constitution. As the great mass of lands in most of the States do not bring any rents, and as incomes from rents vary in the different States, such a tax cannot possibly be apportioned among the States on the basis merely of numbers with any approach to equality of right among taxpayers, any more than a tax on carriages or other personal property could be so apportioned. And, in view of former adjudications, beginning with the *Hylton* case and ending with the *Springer* case, a decision now that a tax on income from real property can be laid and collected only by apportioning the same among the States, on the basis of numbers, may, not improperly, be regarded as a judicial revolution, that may sow the seeds of hate and distrust among the people of different sections of our common country. . . .

In determining whether a tax on income from rents is a direct tax, within the meaning of the Constitution, the inquiry is not whether it may in some way indirectly affect the land or the land owner, but whether it is a direct tax on the thing taxed, the land. The circumstance that such a tax may possibly have the effect to diminish the value of the use of the land is neither decisive of the question nor important. While a tax on the land itself, whether at a fixed rate applicable to all lands without regard to their value, or by the acre or according to their market value, might be deemed a direct tax within the meaning of the Constitution as interpreted in the *Hylton* case, a duty on rents is a duty on something distinct and entirely separate from, although issuing out of, the land. . . .

In my judgment—to say nothing of the disregard of the former adjudications of this court, and of the settled practice of the government—this decision may well excite the gravest apprehensions. It strikes at the very foundations of national authority, in that it denies to the general government a power which is, or may become, vital to the very existence and preservation of the Union in a national emergency, such as that of war with a great commercial nation, during which the collection of all duties upon imports will cease or be materially diminished. It tends to re-establish that condition of helplessness in which Congress found itself during the period of the Articles of Confederation, when it was without authority by laws operating directly upon individuals, to lay and collect, through its own agents, taxes sufficient to pay the debts and defray the expenses of government, but was dependent, in all such matters, upon the good will of the States, and their promptness in meeting requisitions made upon them by Congress.

Why do I say that the decision just rendered impairs or menaces the national authority? The reason is so apparent that it need only be stated. In its practical operation this decision withdraws from national taxation not only all incomes derived from real estate, but tangible personal property, "invested personal property, bonds, stocks, investments of all kinds," and the income that may be derived from such property. This results from the fact that by the decision of the court, all such personal property and all incomes from real estate and personal property, are placed beyond national taxation otherwise than by apportionment among the States on the basis simply of population. No such apportionment can possibly be made without doing gross injustice to the many for the benefit of the favored few in particular States. Any attempt upon the part of Congress to apportion among the States, upon the basis simply of

their population, taxation of personal property or of incomes, would tend to arouse such indignation among the freemen of America that it would never be repeated. When, therefore, this court adjudges, as it does now adjudge, that Congress cannot impose a duty or tax upon personal property, or upon income arising either from rents of real estate or from personal property, including invested personal property, bonds, stocks, and investments of all kinds, except by apportioning the sum to be so raised among the States according to population, it practically decides that, without an amendment of the Constitution—two-thirds of both Houses of Congress and three-fourths of the States concurring—such property and incomes can never be made to contribute to the support of the national government. . . .

I cannot assent to an interpretation of the Constitution that impairs and cripples the just powers of the National Government in the essential matter of taxation, and at the same time discriminates against the greater part of the people of our country.

The practical effect of the decision today is to give to certain kinds of property a position of favoritism and advantage inconsistent with the fundamental principles of our social organization, and to invest them with power and influence that may be perilous to that portion of the American people upon whom rests the larger part of the burdens of the government, and who ought not to be subjected to the dominion of aggregated wealth any more than the property of the country should be at the mercy of the lawless.

I dissent from the opinion and judgment of the court.

[JUSTICES BROWN, JACKSON, and WHITE also delivered separate dissenting opinions.]

GRAVES v. N.Y. ex rel. O'KEEFE
306 U.S. 466; 59 Sup. Ct. 595; 83 L. Ed. 927 (1939)

[*O'Keefe, a resident of New York, was an attorney for the Home Owners' Loan Corporation, a federal agency. He contended that Graves and others who constituted the New York State Tax Commission could not subject his salary to state taxation because he was an employee of the HOLC. His argument was that employees of the federal. government are not liable for payment of state income taxes. Two New York State courts agreed with O'Keefe, holding that his salary could not be taxed. The Supreme Court granted certiorari. Ex. rel. in the title of the case is an abbrveiation for the Latin term* ex relatione, *meaning at the information of or by the relation. It is used to show that the complaining party has an interest which under existing legal procedure can be brought only by the attorney general or some other designated state officer.*]

MR. JUSTICE STONE delivered the opinion of the Court:

We are asked to decide whether the imposition by the State of New York of an income tax on the salary of an employee of the Home Owners' Loan Corporation places an unconstitutional burden upon the federal government. . . .

For the purposes of this case we may assume that the creation of the Home Owners' Loan Corporation was a constitutional exercise of the powers of the federal government. . . . As that government derives its authority wholly from powers delegated to it by the Constitution, its every action within its constitutional power is governmental action, and since Congress is made the sole judge of what powers within the constitutional grant are to be exercised, all activities of government constitutionally authorized by Congress must stand on a parity with respect to their constitutional immunity from taxation. . . . And when the national government lawfully acts through a corporation which it owns and controls, those activities are governmental functions entitled to whatever tax immunity attaches to those functions when carried on by the government itself through its departments. . . .

The single question with which we are now concerned is whether the tax laid by the state upon the salary of respondent, employed by a corporate instrumentality of the federal government, imposes an unconstitutional burden upon that government. The theory of the tax immunity of either government, state or national, and its instrumentalities, from taxation by the other, has been rested upon an implied limitation on the taxing power of each, such as to forestall undue interference, through the exercise of that power, with the governmental activities of the other. That the two types of immunity may not, in all respects, stand on a parity has been recognized from the beginning, *McCulloch* v. *Maryland,* . . . and possible differences in application, deriving from differences in the source, nature, and extent of the immunity of the governments and their agencies, were pointed out and discussed by this Court in detail during the last term. *Helvering* v. *Gerhardt* (304 U.S. 405, 412–413, 416). . . .

So far as now relevant, those differences have been thought to be traceable to the fact that the federal government is one of delegated powers in the exercise of which Congress is supreme; so that every agency which Congress can constitutionally create is a governmental agency. And since the power to create the agency includes the implied power to do whatever is needful or appropriate, if not expressly prohibited, to protect the agency, there has been attributed to Congress some scope, the limits of which it is not now necessary to define, for granting or withholding immunity of federal agencies from state taxation. . . .

Congress has declared in §4 of the Act that the Home Owners' Loan Corporation is an instrumentality of the United States and that its bonds are exempt, as to principal and interest, from federal and state taxation, except surtaxes, estate, inheritance, and gift taxes. The corporation itself, "including its franchise, its capital, reserves and surplus, and its loans and income" is likewise exempted from taxation; its real property is subject to tax to the same extent as other real property. But Congress has given no intimation of any purpose either to grant or withhold immunity from state taxation of the salary of the corporation's employees, and the Congressional intention is not to be gathered from the statute by implication. . . .

It is true that the silence of Congress, when it has authority to speak, may sometimes give rise to an implication as to the Congressional purpose. The nature and extent of that implication depend upon the nature of the Congressional power and the effect of its exercise. But there is little scope for the application of that doctrine to the tax immunity of governmental instrumentalities. The constitutional immunity of either government from taxation by other, where Congress is silent, has its source in an implied restriction upon the powers of the taxing government. So far as the implication rests upon the purpose to avoid interference with the functions of the taxed government or the imposition upon it of the economic burden of the tax, it is plain that there is no basis for implying a purpose of Congress to exempt the federal government or its agencies from tax burdens which are unsubstantial or which courts are unable to discern. Silence of Congress implies immunity no more than does the silence of the Constitution. It follows that when exemption from state taxation is claimed on the ground that the federal government is burdened by the tax, and Congress has disclosed no intention with respect to the claimed immunity, it is in order to consider the nature and effect of the alleged burden, and if it appears that there is no ground for implying a constitutional immunity, there is equally a want of any ground for assuming any purpose on the part of Congress to create an immunity.

The present tax is a nondiscriminatory tax on income applied to salaries at a specified rate. It is not in form or substance a tax upon the Home Owners' Loan Corporation or its property or income, nor is it paid by the corporation or the government from their funds. It is measured by income which becomes the property of the taxpayer when received as compensation for his services; and the tax laid upon the privilege of receiving it is paid from his private funds and not from the funds of the government, either directly or indirectly. The theory, which once won a qualified approval, that a tax on income is legally or economically a tax on its source, is no longer tenable . . . , and the only possible basis for implying a constitutional immunity from state income tax of the salary of an employee of the national government or of a governmental agency is that the economic burden of the tax is in some way passed on so as to impose a burden on the national government tantamount to an interference by one government with the other in the performance of its functions. . . .

Assuming, as we do, that the Home Owners' Loan Corporation is clothed with the same immunity from state taxation as the government itself, we cannot say that the present tax on the income of its employees lays any unconstitutional burden upon it. All the reasons for refusing to imply a constitutional prohibition of federal income taxation of salaries of state employees, stated at length in the *Gerhardt* case, are of equal force when immunity is claimed from state income tax on salaries paid by the national government or its agencies. In this respect we perceive no basis for a difference in result whether the taxed income be salary or some other form of compensation, or whether the taxpayer be an employee or an officer of either a state or the national government, or of its instrumentalities. In no case is there basis for the asumption that any such tangible or certain economic burden is imposed on the government concerned as would justify a court's declaring that the taxpayer is clothed with the implied constitutional tax immunity of the government by which he is employed. That assumption, made in *Collector* v. *Day* . . . and in *New York ex rel. Rogers* v. *Graves,* . . . is contrary to the reasoning and to the conclusions reached in the *Gerhardt* case. . . . [Other cases were also cited.] In their light the assumption can no longer be made. *Collector* v. *Day* . . . and *New York ex rel. Rogers* v. *Graves* . . . are overruled so far as they recognize an implied constitutional immunity from income taxation of the salaries of officers or employees of the national or a state government or their instrumentalities.

So much of the burden of a nondiscriminatory general tax upon the incomes of employees of a government, state or national, as may be passed on economically to that government, through the effect of the tax on the price level of labor or materials, is but the normal incident of the organization within the same territory of two governments, each possessing the taxing power. The burden, so far as it can be said to exist or to affect the government in any indirect or incidental way, is one which the Constitution presupposes, and hence it cannot rightly be deemed to be within an implied restriction upon the taxing power of the national and state governments which the Constitution has expressly granted to one and has confirmed to the other. The immunity is not one to be implied from the Constitution, because if allowed it would impose to an inadmissible extent a restriction on the taxing power which the Constitution has reserved to the state governments.

Reversed.

MR. CHIEF JUSTICE HUGHES concurs in the result.

[MR. JUSTICE FRANKFURTER wrote a separate concurring opinion. MR. JUSTICE BUTLER, with MR. JUSTICE MCREYNOLDS concurring, wrote a dissenting opinion.]

BAILEY *v.* DREXEL FURNITURE COMPANY
(CHILD LABOR TAX CASE)
259 U.S. 20; 42 Sup. Ct. 449; 66 L. Ed. 817 (1922)

[*The Child Labor Tax Law, which was part of the Revenue Act of 1919, imposed a 10 per cent tax on the annual net profits of mines and quarries that employed children under sixteen years of age. Mill and factory owners who employed chil-*

dren under the age of fourteen or who permitted children between fourteen and sixteen to work more than an eight-hour day or more than a six-day week also were subject to the 10 per cent penalty. During the taxable year 1919, the Drexel Furniture Company employed a boy under fourteen years of age; it was ordered to pay a tax of some $6,000, which represented 10 per cent of its net profits for the year. The company paid the tax under protest and sued to recover the money on the ground that the law was unconstitutional. A federal district court upheld the company. Bailey, who was the United States Collector of Internal Revenue for the North Carolina district in which the company was located, then brought the case to the Supreme Court on a writ of error.]

MR. CHIEF JUSTICE TAFT delivered the opinion of the court:

This case presents the question of the constitutional validity of the Child Labor Tax Law. . . .

The law is attacked on the ground that it is a regulation of the employment of child labor in the states—an exclusively state function under the Federal Constitution and within the reservations of the Tenth Amendment. It is defended on the ground that it is a mere excise tax, levied by the Congress of the United States under its broad power of taxation conferred by §8, Article I, of the Federal Constitution. We must construe the law and interpret the intent and meaning of Congress from the language of the act. The words are given their ordinary meaning unless the context shows that they are differently used. Does this law impose a tax with only that incidental restraint and regulation which a tax must inevitably involve? Or does it regulate by the use of the so-called tax as a penalty? If a tax, it is clearly an excise. If it were an excise on a commodity or other thing of value, we might not be permitted, under previous decisions of this court, to infer solely from its heavy burden that the act intends a prohibition instead of a tax. But this act is more. It provides a heavy exaction for a departure from a detailed and specified course of conduct in business. That course of business is that employers shall employ in mines and quarries, children of an age greater than sixteen years; in mills and factories, children of an age greater than fourteen years; and shall prevent children of less than sixteen years in mills and factories from working more than eight hours a day or six days in the week. If an employer departs from this prescribed course of business, he is to pay to the government one tenth of his entire net income in the business for a full year. The amount is not to be proportioned in any degree to the extent or frequency of the departures, but is to be paid by the employer in full measure whether he employs 500 children for a year, or employs only one for a day. Moreover, if he does not know the child is within the named age limit, he is not to pay; that is to say, it is only where he knowingly departs from the prescribed course that payment is to be exacted. *Scienters* are associated with penalties, not with taxes. The employer's factory is to be subject to inspection at any time not only by the taxing officers of the Treasury, the Department normally charged with the collection of taxes, but also by the Secretary of Labor and his subordinates, whose normal function is the advancement and protection of the welfare of the workers. In the light of these features of the act, a court must be blind not to see that the so-called tax is imposed to stop the employment of children within the age limits prescribed. Its prohibitory and regulatory effect and purpose are palpable. All others can see and understand this. How can we properly shut our minds to it?

It is the high duty and function of this court in cases regularly brought to its bar to decline to recognize or enforce seeming laws of Congress, dealing with subjects not intrusted to Congress but left or committed by the supreme law of the land to the control of the states. We cannot avoid the duty, even though it requires us to refuse to give effect to legislation designed to promote the highest good. The good sought in unconstitutional legislation is an insidious feature because it leads citizens and legislators of good purpose to promote it without thought of the serious breach it will make in the ark of our covenant, or the harm which will come from breaking down recognized standards. In the maintenance of local self-government, on the one hand, and the national power, on the other, our country has been able to endure and prosper for near a century and a half.

Out of a proper respect for the acts of a coordinate branch of the government, this court has gone far to sustain taxing acts as such, even though there has been ground for suspecting, from the weight of the tax, it was intended to destroy its subject. But in the act before us, the presumption of validity cannot prevail, because the proof of the contrary is found on the very face of its provisions. Grant the validity of this law, and all that Congress would need to do hereafter, in seeking to take over to its control any one of the great number of subjects of public interest, jurisdiction of which the states have never parted with, and which are reserved to them by the Tenth Amendment, would be to enact a detailed measure of complete regulation of the subject and enforce it by a so-called tax upon departures from it. To give such magic to the word "tax" would be to break down all constitutional limitation of the powers of Congress and completely wipe out the sovereignty of the states.

The difference between a tax and a penalty is sometimes difficult to define, and yet the consequences of the distinction in the required method of their collection often are important. Where the sovereign enacting the law has power to impose both tax and penalty, the difference between revenue production and mere regulation may be immaterial; but not so when one sovereign can impose a tax only, and the power of regulation rests in another. Taxes are occasionally imposed in the discretion of the legislature on proper subjects with the primary motive of obtaining revenue from them, and with the incidental motive of discouraging them by making their continuance onerous. They do not lose their character as taxes because of the incidental motive. But there comes a time in the extension of the penalizing features of the so-called tax when it loses its character as such and becomes a mere penalty, with the characteristics of regulation and punishment. Such is the case of the law before us. Although Congress does not invalidate the contract of employment, or expressly declare that the employment within the mentioned ages is illegal, it does exhibit its intent practically to achieve the latter result by adopting the criteria of wrongdoing, and imposing its principal consequence on those who transgress its standard.

The case before us cannot be distinguished from that of *Hammer* v. *Dagenhart*. . . . Congress there enacted a law to prohibit transportation in interstate commerce of goods made at a factory in which there was employment of children within the same ages and for the same number of hours a day and days in a week as are penalized by the act in this case. This court held the law in that case to be void. It said:

"In our view the necessary effect of this act is, by means of a prohibition against the movement in interstate commerce of ordinary commercial commodities, to regulate the hours of labor of children in factories and mines within the states—a purely state authority."

In the case at the bar, Congress, in the name of a tax which, on the face of the act, is a penalty, seeks to do the same thing, and the effort must be equally futile. . . .

For the reasons given, we must hold the Child Labor Tax Law invalid, and the judgment of the District Court is

Affirmed.

[MR. JUSTICE CLARK *wrote a dissenting opinion.*]

UNITED STATES *v.* BUTLER
297 U.S. 1; 56 Sup. Ct. 312; 80 L. Ed. 477 (1936)

[*One of the most important pieces of New Deal legislation was the Agricultural Adjustment Act of 1933. This law was designed to increase the price of agricultural products, and thereby the farmers' purchasing power, by reducing the production of basic agricultural commodities. Provision was made for benefit payments to those farmers who reduced the production of cotton, tobacco, wheat, and other items. The money for the payments was to be raised by levying a tax on the processors of agricultural commodities, such as meat packers and textile manufacturers. Butler, receiver for a Massachusetts cotton corporation, protested the payment of the processing tax on cotton. The district court held that the taxes were valid and ordered them paid. The circuit court of appeals reversed the order. The United States appealed to the Supreme Court.*]

MR. JUSTICE ROBERTS delivered the opinion of the Court:

. . . At the outset the United States contends that the respondents have no standing to question the validity of the tax. The position is that the act is merely a revenue measure levying an excise upon the activity of processing cotton—a proper subject for the imposition of such a tax—the proceeds of which go into the federal treasury and thus become available for appropriation for any purpose. . . . The Government in substance and effect asks us to separate the Agricultural Adjustment Act into two statutes, the one levying an excise on processors of certain commodities, the other appropriating the public moneys independently of the first. . . . [W]e think the legislation now before us is not susceptible of such separation and treatment.

The tax can only be sustained by ignoring the avowed purpose and operation of the act, and holding it a measure merely laying an excise upon processors to raise revenue for the support of government. Beyond cavil the sole object of the legislation is to restore the purchasing power of agricultural products to a parity with that prevailing in an earlier day; to take money from the processor and bestow it upon farmers who will reduce their acreage for the accomplishment of the proposed end, and meanwhile to aid these farmers during the period required to bring the prices of their crops to the desired level.

The tax plays an indispensable part

in the plan of regulation. As stated by the Agricultural Adjustment Administrator, it is "the heart of the law. . . ." A tax automatically goes into effect for a commodity when the Secretary of Agriculture determines that rental or benefit payments are to be made for reduction of production of that commodity. The tax is to cease when rental or benefit payments cease. . . .

It is inaccurate and misleading to speak of the exaction from processors prescribed by the challenged act as a tax, or to say that as a tax it is subject to no infirmity. A tax, in the general understanding of the term, and as used in the Constitution, signifies an exaction for the support of the Government. The word has never been thought to connote the expropriation of money from one group for the benefit of another. We may concede that the latter sort of imposition is constitutional when imposed to effectuate regulation of a matter in which both groups are interested and in respect of which there is a power of legislative regulation. But manifestly no justification for it can be found unless as an integral part of such regulation. The exaction cannot be wrested out of its setting, denominated an excise for raising revenue, and legalized by ignoring its purpose as a mere instrumentality for bringing about a desired end. To do this would be to shut our eyes to what all others than we can see and understand. . . .

We conclude that the act is one regulating agricultural production; that the tax is a mere incident of such regulation and that the respondents have standing to challenge the legality of the exaction.

. . . The Government asserts that even if the respondents may question the propriety of the appropriation embodied in the statute, their attack must fail because Article I, §8, of the Constitution authorizes the contemplated

expenditure of the funds raised by the tax. This contention presents the great and the controlling question in the case. We approach its decision with a sense of our grave responsibility to render judgment in accordance with the principles established for the governance of all three branches of the Government.

There should be no misunderstanding as to the function of this court in such a case. It is sometimes said that the court assumes a power to overrule or control the action of the people's representatives. This is a misconception. The Constitution is the supreme law of the land ordained and established by the people. All legislation must conform to the principles it lays down. When an act of Congress is appropriately challenged in the courts as not conforming to the constitutional mandate, the judicial branch of the Government has only one duty—to lay the article of the Constitution which is invoked beside the statute which is challenged and to decide whether the latter squares with the former. All the court does, or can do, is to announce its considered judgment upon the question. The only power it has, if such it may be called, is the power of judgment. This court neither approves nor condemns any legislative policy. Its delicate and difficult office is to ascertain and declare whether the legislation is in accordance with, or in contravention of, the provisions of the Constitution; and, having done that, its duty ends. . . .

Article I, §8, of the Constitution vests sundry powers in the Congress. But two of its clauses have no bearing upon the validity of the statute under review.

The third clause endows the Congress with power "to regulate Commerce . . . among the several States." Despite a reference in its first section to a burden upon, and an obstruction of the normal currents of commerce, the act under review does not purport to regulate transactions in interstate or foreign commerce. Its stated purpose is the control of agricultural production, a purely local activity, in an effort to raise the prices paid the farmer. Indeed, the Government does not attempt to uphold the validity of the act on the basis of the commerce clause, which, for the purpose of the present case, may be put aside as irrelevant.

The clause thought to authorize the legislation—the first—confers upon the Congress power "to lay and collect Taxes, Duties, Imposts and Excises, to pay the Debts and provide for the common Defence and general Welfare of the United States. . . ." It is not contended that this provision grants power to regulate agricultural production upon the theory that such legislation would promote the general welfare. The Government concedes that the phrase "to provide for the general welfare" qualifies the power "to lay and collect taxes." The view that the clause grants power to provide for the general welfare, independently of the taxing power, has never been authoritatively accepted. Mr. Justice Story points out that if it were adopted "it is obvious that under color of the generality of the words, to 'provide for the common defense and general welfare,' the government of the United States is, in reality, a government of general and unlimited powers, notwithstanding the subsequent enumeration of specific powers." The true construction undoubtedly is that the only thing granted is the power to tax for the purpose of providing funds for payment of the nation's debts and making provision for the general welfare.

Nevertheless the Government asserts that warrant is found in this clause for the adoption of the Agricultural Adjustment Act. The argument is that Congress may appropriate and authorize the spending of moneys for the "general welfare"; that the phrase should be liberally construed to cover anything conducive to national welfare; that decision as to what will promote such welfare rests with Congress alone, and the courts may not review its determination; and finally that the appropriation under attack was in fact for the general welfare of the United States. . . .

Since the foundation of the Nation sharp differences of opinion have persisted as to the true interpretation of the phrase. Madison asserted it amounted to no more than a reference to the other powers enumerated in the subsequent clauses of the same section; that, as the United States is a government of limited and enumerated powers, the grant of power to tax and spend for the general national welfare must be confined to the enumerated legislative fields committed to the Congress. In this view the phrase is mere tautology, for taxation and appropriation are or may be necessary incidents of the exercise of any of the enumerated legislative powers. Hamilton, on the other hand, maintained the clause confers a power separate and distinct from those later enumerated, is not restricted in meaning by the grant of them, and Congress consequently has a substantive power to tax and to appropriate, limited only by the requirement that it shall be exercised to provide for the general welfare of the United States. Each contention has had the support of those whose views are entitled to weight. This court has noticed the question, but has never found it necessary to decide which is the true construction. Mr. Justice Story, in his Commentaries, espouses the Hamiltonian position. . . . Study . . . leads us to conclude that the reading advocated by Mr. Justice Story is the correct one. While, therefore, the power to tax is not unlimited, its confines are set in the clause which confers it, and not in those of §8 which bestow and define the legislative powers of the Congress. It results that the power of Congress to authorize expenditure of public moneys for public purposes is not limited by the direct grants of legislative power found in the Constitution.

But the adoption of the broader construction leaves the power to spend subject to limitations.

. . . Story says that if the tax be not proposed for the common defense or general welfare, but for other objects wholly extraneous, it would be wholly indefensible upon constitutional principles. And he makes it clear that the powers of taxation and appropriation extend only to matters of national, as distinguished from local welfare.

. . . We are not now required to ascertain the scope of the phrase "general welfare of the United States" or to determine whether an appropriation in aid of agriculture falls within it. Wholly apart from that question, another principle embedded in our Constitution prohibits the enforcement of the Agricultural Adjustment Act. The act invades the reserved rights of the states. It is a statutory plan to regulate and control agricultural production, a matter beyond the powers delegated to the federal government. The tax, the appropriation of the funds raised, and the direction for their disbursement, are but parts of the plan. They are but means to an unconstitutional end.

From the accepted doctrine that the United States is a government of delegated powers, it follows that those not expressly granted, or reasonably to be implied from such as are conferred, are reserved to the states or to the people. To forestall any suggestion to the contrary, the Tenth Amendment was adopted. The same proposition, otherwise stated, is that powers not granted are prohibited. None to regulate agricultural production is given, and therefore legislation by Congress for that purpose is forbidden.

. . . If the taxing power may not be used as the instrument to enforce a regulation of matters of state concern with respect to which the Congress has no authority to interfere, may it, as in the present case, be employed to raise the money necessary to purchase a compliance which the Congress is powerless to command? The Government asserts that whatever might be said against the validity of the plan if compulsory, it is constitutionally sound because the end is accomplished by voluntary cooperation. There are two sufficient answers to the contention. The regulation is not in fact voluntary. The farmer, of course, may refuse to comply, but the price of such refusal is the loss of benefits. The amount offered is intended to be sufficient to exert pressure on him to agree to the proposed regulation. The power to confer or withhold unlimited benefits is the power to coerce or destroy. If the cotton grower elects not to accept the benefits, he will receive less for his crops; those who receive payments will be able to undersell him. The result may well be financial ruin. . . . It is clear that the Department of Agriculture has properly described the plan as one to keep a non-cooperating minority in line. This is coercion by economic pressure. The asserted power of choice is illusory.

. . . But if the plan were one for purely voluntary cooperation it would stand no better so far as federal power is concerned. At best it is a scheme for purchasing with federal funds submission to federal regulation of a subject reserved to the states. . . .

Congress has no power to enforce its commands on the farmer to the ends sought by the Agricultural Adjustment Act. It must follow that it may not indirectly accomplish those ends by taxing and spending to purchase compliance. The Constitution and the entire plan of our government negative any such use of the power to tax and to spend as the act undertakes to authorize. It does not help to declare that local conditions throughout the nation have created a situation of national concern; for this is but to say that whenever there is a widespread similarity of local conditions, Congress may ignore constitutional limitations upon its own powers and usurp those reserved to the states. If, in lieu of compulsory regulation of subjects within the states' reserved jurisdiction, which is prohibited, the Congress could invoke the taxing and spending power as a means to accomplish the same end, clause 1 of §8 of Article I would become the instrument for total subversion of the governmental powers reserved to the individual states.

If the act before us is a proper exercise of the federal taxing power, evidently the regulation of all industry throughout the United States may be accomplished by similar exercises of the same power. . . .

Since. . . there was no power in the Congress to impose the contested exaction, . . . the judgment is

Affirmed.

MR. JUSTICE STONE, dissenting:

. . . 1. The power of courts to declare a statute unconstitutional is subject to two guiding principles of decision which ought never to be absent from judicial consciousness. One is that courts are concerned only with the power to enact statutes, not with their wisdom. The other is that while unconstitutional exercise of power by the executive and legislative branches of the government is subject to judicial restraint, the only check upon our own exercise of power is our own sense of self-restraint. For the removal of unwise

laws from the statute books appeal lies not to the courts but to the ballot and to the processes of democratic government.

2. The constitutional power of Congress to levy an excise tax upon the processing of agricultural products is not questioned. The present levy is held invalid, not for any want of power in Congress to lay such a tax to defray public expenditures, including those for the general welfare, but because the use to which its proceeds are put is disapproved.

3. As the present depressed state of agriculture is nationwide in its extent and effects, there is no basis for saying that the expenditure of public money in aid of farmers is not within the specifically granted power of Congress to levy taxes to "provide for the . . . general welfare." The opinion of the Court does not declare otherwise.

. . . It is with these preliminary and hardly controverted matters in mind that we should direct our attention to the pivot on which the decision of the Court is made to turn. It is that a levy unquestionably within the taxing power of Congress may be treated as invalid because it is a step in a plan to regulate agricultural production and is thus a forbidden infringement of state power. . . .

Of the assertion that the payments to farmers are coercive, it is enough to say that no such contention is pressed by the taxpayer, and no such consequences were to be anticipated or appear to have resulted from the administration of the Act. The suggestion of coercion finds no support in the record or in any data showing the actual operation of the Act. Threat of loss, not hope of gain, is the essence of economic coercion. . . .

It is upon the contention that the state power is infringed by purchased regulation of agricultural production that chief reliance is placed. It is insisted that, while the Constitution gives to Congress, in specific and unambiguous terms, the power to tax and spend, the power is subject to limitations which do not find their origin in any express provision of the Constitution and to which other expressly delegated powers are not subject.

. . . The spending power of Congress is in addition to the legislative power and not subordinate to it. This independent grant of the power of the purse, and its very nature, involving in its exercise the duty to insure expenditure within the granted power, presuppose freedom of selection among diverse ends and aims, and the capacity to impose such conditions as will render the choice effective. It is a contradiction in terms to say that there is power to spend for the national welfare, while rejecting any power to impose conditions reasonably adapted to the attainment of the end which alone would justify the expenditure.

. . . That the governmental power of the purse is a great one is not now for the first time announced. Every student of the history of government and economics is aware of its magnitude and of its existence in every civilized government. Both were well understood by the framers of the Constitution when they sanctioned the grant of the spending power to the federal government, and both were recognized by Hamilton and Story, whose view of the spending power as standing on a parity with the other powers specifically granted, have hitherto been generally accepted.

The suggestion that it must now be curtailed by judicial fiat because it may be abused by unwise use hardly rises to the dignity of argument. So may judicial power be abused. . . .

A tortured construction of the Constitution is not to be justified by recourse to extreme examples of reckless congressional spending which might occur if courts could not prevent—expenditures which, even if they could be thought to effect any national purpose, would be possible only by action of a leglislature lost to all sense of public responsibility. Such suppositions are addressed to the mind accustomed to believe that it is the business of courts to sit in judgment on the wisdom of legislative action. Courts are not the only agency of government that must be assumed to have capacity to govern. Congress and the courts both unhappily may falter or be mistaken in the performance of their constitutional duty. But interpretation of our great charter of government which proceeds on any assumption that the responsibility for the preservation of our institutions is the exclusive concern of any one of the three branches of government, or that it alone can save them from destruction is far more likely, in the long run, "to obliterate the constituent members" of "an indestructible union of indestructible states" than the frank recognition that language, even of a constitution, may mean what it says: that the power to tax and spend includes the power to relieve a nationwide economic maladjustment by conditional gifts of money.

MR. JUSTICE BRANDEIS and MR. JUSTICE CARDOZO join in this opinion.

STEWARD MACHINE CO. *v.* DAVIS
301 U.S. 548; 57 Sup. Ct. 883; 81 L. Ed. 1279 (1937)

[*The Steward Machine Company, an Alabama corporation, paid a federal excise tax as required under provisions of the Social Security Act of 1935, which are discussed in the subsequent case. The company sued in a federal district court to recover the payment, asserting that the Social Security Act was unconstitutional. The district court dismissed the complaint, thereby rendering a judgment favorable to Davis, who was a collector of internal revenue. The Court of Appeals for the Fifth Circuit affirmed the judgment. The Supreme Court granted certiorari.]*

MR. JUSTICE CARDOZO delivered the opinion of the Court:

The validity of the tax imposed by the Social Security Act on employers of eight or more is here to be determined. . . .

The Social Security Act (Act of August 14, 1935 . . .) is divided into eleven separate titles, of which only Titles IX and III are so related to this case as to stand in need of summary.

The caption of Title IX is "Tax on Employers of Eight or More." Every employer (with stated exceptions) is to pay for each calendar year "an excise tax, with respect to having individuals in his employ," the tax to be measured by prescribed percentages of the total wages payable by the employer during the calendar year with respect to such employment. . . . One is not, however, an "employer" within the meaning of the act unless he employs eight persons or more. . . . The tax begins with the year 1936, and is payable for the first time on January 31, 1937. During the calendar year 1936 the rate is to be one per cent, during 1937 two per cent, and three per cent thereafter. The proceeds, when collected, go into the Treasury of the United States like internal-revenue collections generally. . . . They are not earmarked in any way. In certain circumstances, however, credits are allowable. . . . If the taxpayer has made contributions to an unemployment fund under a state law, he may credit such contributions against the federal tax, provided, however, that the total credit allowed to any taxpayer shall not exceed 90 per centum of the tax against which it is credited, and provided also that the state law shall

have been certified to the Secretary of the Treasury by the Social Security Board as satisfying certain minimum criteria. . . . Some of the conditions thus attached to the allowance of a credit are designed to give assurance that the state unemployment compensation law shall be one in substance as well as name. Others are designed to give assurance that the contributions shall be protected against loss after payment to the state. To this last end there are provisions that before a state law shall have the approval of the Board it must direct that the contributions to the state fund be paid over immediately to the Secretary of the Treasury to the credit of the "Unemployment Trust Fund." . . . [T]he Fund is to be held by the Secretary of the Treasury, who is to invest in government securities any portion not required in his judgment to meet current withdrawals. He is authorized and directed to pay out of the Fund to any competent state agency such sums as it may duly requisition from the amount standing to its credit. . . .

Title III, which is also challenged as invalid, has the caption "Grants to States for Unemployment Compensation Administration." Under this title, certain sums of money are "authorized to be appropriated" for the purpose of assisting the states in the administration of their unemployment compensation laws. . . . No present appropriation is made to the extent of a single dollar. All that the title does is to authorize future appropriations. . . . The appropriations when made were not specifically out of the proceeds of the employment tax, but out of any moneys in the Treasury. Other sections of the title prescribe the method by which the payments are to be made to the state . . . and also certain conditions to be established to the satisfaction of the Social Security Board before certifying the propriety of a payment to the Secretary of the Treasury. . . . They are designed to give assurance to the Federal Government that the moneys granted by it will not be expended for purposes alien to the grant, and will be used in the administration of genuine unemployment compensation laws.

The assault on the statute proceeds on an extended front. Its assailants take the ground that the tax is not an excise; that it is not uniform throughout the United States as excises are required to be; that its exceptions are so many and arbitrary as to violate the Fifth Amendment; that its purpose was not revenue, but an unlawful invasion of the reserved powers of the states; and that the states in submitting to it have yielded to coercion and have abandoned governmental functions which they are not permitted to surrender.

The objections will be considered seriatim with such further explanation as may be necessary to make their meaning clear.

First. The tax, which is described in the statute as an excise, is laid with uniformity throughout the United States as a duty, an impost, or an excise upon the relation of employment.

1. We are told that the relation of employment is one so essential to the pursuit of happiness that it may not be burdened with a tax. Appeal is made to history. From the precedents of colonial days we are supplied with illustrations of excises common in the colonies. They are said to have been bound up with the enjoyment of particular commodities. Appeal is also made to principle or the analysis of concepts. An excise, we are told, imports a tax upon a privilege; employment, it is said, is a right, not a privilege, from which it follows that employment is not subject to an excise. Neither the one appeal nor the other leads to the desired goal.

As to the argument from history: Doubtless there were many excises in the colonial days and later that were associated, more or less intimately, with the enjoyment or the use of property. This would not prove, even if no others were then known, that the forms then accepted were not subject to enlargement. . . . But in truth other exercises *were* known, and known since early times. . . . Our colonial forbears knew more about ways of taxing than some of their descendants seem to be willing to concede.

The historical prop failing, the prop or fancied prop of principle remains. We learn that employment for lawful gain is a "natural" or "inherent" or "inalienable" right, and not a "privilege" at all. But natural rights, so called, are as much subject to taxation as rights of less importance. An excise is not limited to vocations or activities that may be prohibited altogether. It is not limited to those that are the outcome of a franchise. It extends to vocations or activities pursued as of common right. What the individual does in the operation of a business is amenable to taxation just as much as what he owns, at all events if the classification is not tyrannical or arbitrary. . . .

The subject matter of taxation open to the power of the Congress is as comprehensive as that open to the power of the states, though the method of apportionment may at times be different. . . . The statute books of the states are strewn with illustrations of taxes laid on occupations pursued of common right. We find no basis for a holding that the power in that regard which belongs by accepted practice to the legislatures of the states, has been denied by the Constitution to the Congress of the nation.

2. The tax being an excise, its imposition must conform to the canon of uniformity. There has been no departure from this requirement. According to the settled doctrine the uniformity exacted is geographical, not intrinsic. . . .

Second. The excise is not invalid under the provisions of the Fifth Amendment by force of its exemptions.

The statute does not apply, as we have seen, to employers of less than eight. It does not apply to agricultural labor, or domestic service in a private home, or to some other classes of less importance. Petitioner contends that the effect of these restrictions is an arbitrary discrimination vitiating the tax.

The Fifth Amendment unlike the Fourteenth has no equal protection clause. . . . But even the states, though subject to such a clause, are not confined to a formula of rigid uniformity in framing measures of taxation. . . . They may tax some kinds of property at one rate, and others at another, and exempt others altogether. . . . They may lay an excise on the operations of a particular kind of business, and exempt some other kind of business closely akin thereto. . . . If this latitude of judgment is lawful for the states, it is lawful, *a fortiori,* in legislation by the Congress, which is subject to restraints less narrow and confining. . . .

The classifications and exemptions directed by the statute now in controversy have support in considerations of policy and practical convenience that cannot be condemned as arbitrary. The classifications and exemptions would therefore be upheld if they had been adopted by a state and the provisions of the Fourteenth Amendment were invoked to annul them. . . . The act of Congress is therefore valid, so far at least

as its system of exemptions is concerned, and this though we assume that discrimination, if gross enough, is equivalent to confiscation and subject under the Fifth Amendment to challenge and annulment.

Third. The excise is not void as involving the coercion of the States in contravention of the Tenth Amendment or of restrictions implicit in our federal form of government.

The proceeds of the excise when collected are paid into the Treasury at Washington, and thereafter are subject to appropriation like public moneys generally. . . . No presumption can be indulged that they will be misapplied or wasted. Even if they were collected in the hope or expectation that some other and collateral good would be furthered as an incident, that, without more, would not make the act invalid. . . . This indeed is hardly questioned. The case for the petitioner is built on the contention that here an ulterior aim is wrought into the very structure of the act, and what is even more important, that the aim is not only ulterior but essentially unlawful. In particular, the 90 per cent credit is relied upon as supporting that conclusion. But before the statute succumbs to an assault upon these lines, two propositions must be made out by the assailant. . . . There must be a showing in the first place that separated from the credit the revenue provisions are incapable of standing by themselves. There must be a showing in the second place that the tax and the credit in combination are weapons of coercion, destroying or impairing the autonomy of the states. The truth of each proposition being essential to the success of the assault, we pass for convenience to a consideration of the second, without pausing to inquire whether there has been a demonstration of the first.

To draw the line intelligently between

duress and inducement there is need to remind ourselves of facts as to the problem of unemployment that are now matters of common knowledge. . . . During the years 1929 to 1936, when the country was passing through a cyclical depression, the number of the unemployed mounted to unprecedented heights. Often the average was more than 10 million; at times a peak was attained of 16 million or more. Disaster to the breadwinner meant disaster to dependents. Accordingly the roll of the unemployed, itself formidable enough, was only a partial roll of the destitute or needy. The fact developed quickly that the states were unable to give the requisite relief. The problem had become national in area and dimensions. There was need of help from the nation if the people were not to starve. It is too late today for the argument to be heard with tolerance that in a crisis so extreme the use of the moneys of the nation to relieve the unemployed and their dependents is a use for any purpose narrower than the promotion of the general welfare. . . .

In the presence of this urgent need for some remedial expedient, the question is to be answered whether the expedient adopted has overleapt the bounds of power. The assailants of the statute say that its dominant end and aim is to drive the state legislatures under the whip of economic pressure into the enactment of unemployment compensation laws at the bidding of the central government. Supporters of the statute say that its operation is not constraint, but the creation of a larger freedom, the states and the nation joining in a cooperative endeavor to avert a common evil. Before Congress acted, unemployment compensation insurance was still, for the most part, a project and no more. . . .

The Social Security Act is an attempt to find a method by which all these public agencies may work together to a common end. Every dollar of the new taxes will continue in all likelihood to be used and needed by the nation as long as states are unwilling, whether through timidity or for other motives, to do what can be done at home. At least the inference is permissible that Congress so believed, though retaining undiminished freedom to spend the money as it pleased. On the other hand fulfillment of the home duty will be lightened and encouraged by crediting the taxpayer upon his account with the Treasury of the nation to the extent that his contributions under the laws of the locality have simplified or diminished the problem of relief and the probable demand upon the resources of the fisc [Treasury]. Duplicated taxes, or burdens that approach them, are recognized hardships that government, state or national, may properly avoid. . . . If Congress believed that the general welfare would better be promoted by relief through local units than by the system then in vogue, the cooperating localities ought not in all fairness to pay a second time.

Who then is coerced through the operation of this statute? Not the taxpayer. He pays in fulfillment of the mandate of the local legislature. Not the state. Even now she does not offer a suggestion that in passing the unemployment law she was affected by duress. . . . For all that appears she is satisfied with her choice, and would be sorely disappointed if it were now to be annulled. The difficulty with the petitioner's contention is that it confuses motive with coercion. "Every tax is in some measure regulatory. To some extent it interposes an economic impediment to the activity taxed as compared with others not taxed." . . . In like manner every rebate from a tax when conditioned upon conduct is in some measure a temptation. But to hold that motive or temptation is equivalent to coercion is to plunge the law in endless difficulties. The outcome of such a doctrine is the acceptance of a philosophical determinism by which choice becomes impossible. Till now the law has been guided by a robust common sense which assumes the freedom of the will as a working hypothesis in the solution of its problems. The wisdom of the hypothesis has illustration in this case. Nothing in the case suggests the exertion of a power akin to undue influence, if we assume that such a concept can ever be applied with fitness to the relations between state and nation. Even on that assumption the location of the point at which pressure turns into compulsion, and ceases to be inducement, would be a question of degree—at times, perhaps, of fact. The point had not been reached when Alabama made her choice. We cannot say that she was acting, not of her unfettered will, but under the strain of a persuasion equivalent to undue influence, when she chose to have relief administered under laws of her own making, by agents of her own selection, instead of under federal laws, administered by federal officers, with all the ensuing evils, at least to many minds, of federal patronage and power. There would be a strange irony, indeed, if her choice were now to be annulled on the basis of an assumed duress in the enactment of a statute which her courts have accepted as a true expression of her will. . . . We think the choice must stand. . . .

United States v. *Butler* . . . is cited by petitioner as a decision to the contrary. There a tax was imposed on processors of farm products, the proceeds to be paid to farmers who would reduce their acreage and crops under agreements with the Secretary of Agriculture, the plan of the act being to increase the prices of certain farm products by decreasing the quantities produced. The court held (1) that the so-called tax was not a true one . . . , the proceeds being earmarked for the benefit of farmers complying with the prescribed conditions, (2) that there was an attempt to regulate production without the consent of the state in which production was affected, and (3) that the payments to farmers were coupled with coercive contracts, . . . unlawful in their aim and oppressive in their consequences. The decision was by a divided court, a minority taking the view that the objections were untenable. None of them is applicable to the situation here developed.

(a) The proceeds of the tax in controversy are not earmarked for a special group.

(b) The unemployment compensation law which is a condition of the credit has had the approval of the state and could not be a law without it.

(c) The condition is not linked to an irrevocable agreement, for the state at its pleasure may repeal its unemployment law, . . . terminate the credit, and place itself where it was before the credit was accepted.

(d) The condition is not directed to the attainment of an unlawful end, but to an end, the relief of unemployment, for which nation and state may lawfully cooperate.

Fourth. The statute does not call for a surrender by the states of powers essential to their quasi-sovereign existence.

Argument to the contrary has its source in two sections of the act. One section . . . defines the minimum criteria to which a state compensation system is required to conform if it is to be accepted by the Board as the basis for a credit. The other section . . . rounds out the requirement with complementary rights and duties. Not all the criteria or their incidents are challenged as unlawful. We will speak of them first generally, and then more specifically in so far as they are questioned.

A credit to taxpayers for payments made to a state under a state unemployment law will be manifestly futile in the absence of some assurance that the law leading to the credit is in truth what it professes to be. An unemployment law framed in such a way that the unemployed who look to it will be deprived of reasonable protection is one in name and nothing more. What is basic and essential may be assured by suitable conditions. The terms embodied in these sections are directed to that end. A wide range of judgment is given to the several states as to the particular type of statute to be spread upon their books. For anything to the contrary in the provisions of this act they may use the pooled unemployment form, which is in effect with variations in Alabama, California, Michigan, New York, and elsewhere. They may establish a system of merit ratings applicable at once or to go into effect later on the basis of subsequent experience. . . . They may provide for employee contributions as in Alabama and California, or put the entire burden upon the employer as in New York. They may choose a system of unemployment reserve accounts by which an employer is permitted after his reserve has accumulated to contribute at a reduced rate or even not at all. This is the system which had its origin in Wisconsin. What they may not do, if they would earn the credit, is to depart from those standards which in the judgment of Congress are to be ranked as fundamental. Even if opinion may differ as to the fundamental quality of one or more of the conditions, the difference will not avail to vitiate the statute. In determining essentials Congress must have the benefit of a fair margin of

discretion. One cannot say with reason that this margin has been exceeded, or that the basic standards have been determined in any arbitrary fashion. In the event that some particular condition shall be found to be too uncertain to be capable of enforcement, it may be severed from the others, and what is left will still be valid.

We are to keep in mind steadily that the conditions to be approved by the Board as the basis for a credit are not provisions of a contract, but terms of a statute, which may be altered or repealed. . . . The state does not bind itself to keep the law in force. It does not even bind itself that the moneys paid into the federal fund will be kept there indefinitely or for any stated time. On the contrary, the Secretary of the Treasury will honor a requisition for the whole or any part of the deposit in the fund whenever one is made by the appropriate officials. The only consequence of the repeal or excessive amendment of the statute, or the expenditure of the money, when requisitioned, for other than compensation uses or administrative expenses, is that approval of the law will end, and with it the allowance of a credit, upon notice to the state agency and an opportunity for hearing. . . .

These basic considerations are in truth a solvent of the problem. Subjected to their test, the several objections on the score of abdication are found to be unreal.

Thus, the argument is made that by force of an agreement the moneys when withdrawn must be "paid through public employment offices in the State or through such other agencies as the Board may approve." . . . But in truth there is no agreement as to the method of disbursement. There is only a condition which the state is free at pleasure to disregard or to fulfill. Moreover, approval is not requisite if public employment offices are made the disbursing instruments. Approval is to be a check upon resort to "other agencies" that may, perchance, be irresponsible. A state looking for a credit must give assurance that her system has been organized upon a base of rationality.

There is argument again that the moneys when withdrawn are to be devoted to specific uses, the relief of unemployment, and that by agreement for such payment the quasi-sovereign position of the state has been impaired, if not abandoned. But again there is confusion between promise and condition. Alabama is still free, without breach of an agreement, to change her system over night. No officer or agency of the national Government can force a compensation law upon her or keep it in existence. No officer or agency of that Government, either by suit or other means, can supervise or control the application of the payments.

Finally and chiefly, abdication is supposed to follow from §904 of the statute and the parts of §903 that are complementary thereto. . . . By these the Secretary of the Treasury is authorized and directed to receive and hold in the Unemployment Trust Fund all moneys deposited therein by a state agency for a state unemployment fund and to invest in obligations of the United States such portion of the Fund as is not in his judgment required to meet current withdrawals. We are told that Alabama in consenting to that deposit has renounced the plenitude of power inherent in her statehood.

The same pervasive misconception is in evidence again. All that the state has done is to say in effect through the enactment of a statute that her agents shall be authorized to deposit the unemployment tax receipts in the Treasury at Washington. . . . The statute may be repealed. . . . The consent may be revoked. The deposits may be withdrawn. The moment the state commission gives notice to the depositary that it would like the moneys backs, the Treasurer will return them. To find state destruction there is to find it almost anywhere. With nearly as much reason one might say that a state abdicates its functions when it places the state moneys on deposit in a national bank. . . .

The inference of abdication thus dissolves in thinnest air when the deposit is conceived of as dependent upon a statutory consent, and not upon a contract effective to create a duty. By this we do not intimate that the conclusion would be different if a contract were discovered. Even sovereigns may contract without derogating from their sovereignty. . . . The states are at liberty, upon obtaining the consent of Congress, to make agreements with one another. . . . We find no room for doubt that they may do the like with Congress if the essence of their statehood is maintained without impairment. Alabama is seeking and obtaining a credit of many millions in favor of her citizens out of the Treasury of the nation. Nowhere in our scheme of government—in the limitations express or implied of our federal constitution—do we find that she is prohibited from assenting to conditions that will assure a fair and just requital for benefits received. . . .

The judgment is

Affirmed.

[MR. JUSTICE MC REYNOLDS, MR. JUS-TICE SUTHERLAND, MR. JUSTICE VAN DEVANTER, and MR. JUSTICE BUTLER dissented.]

11

The Fourteenth Amendment
and Economic Regulation

The Thirteenth, Fourteenth, and Fifteenth Amendments, which were adopted at the close of the Civil War, were designed to protect the newly won freedom of the Negro. The Thirteenth Amendment prohibited slavery and involuntary servitude except as a punishment for crime. The Fourteenth Amendment defined citizenship; provided that no state was to abridge the privileges and immunities of citizens of the United States; forbade states to deprive persons of life, liberty, or property without due process of law; and forbade the states to deny anyone the equal protection of the laws. The Fourteenth Amendment also provided for a method of reduced representation in Congress as a punishment for states that denied the right to vote to adult male citizens. The Fifteenth Amendment stated that the right to vote could not be denied on the ground of race, color, or previous condition of servitude.

The Fourteenth Amendment emerged gradually as the most important of the Reconstruction amendments. In fact, this amendment has been the subject of more Supreme Court cases than *any* other provision of the Constitution. Much of the Court's present authority is based on its vague phrases.

Early Judicial Construction of the Fourteenth Amendment

The Fourteenth Amendment was ratified in 1868 and was first interpreted by the Supreme Court in the *Slaughterhouse* cases (p. 302). Interestingly enough, the *Slaughterhouse* cases had nothing to do with the rights of Negroes, but despite the fact that the Court's narrow interpretation of privileges and immunities, due process, and equal protection "dwarfed and dulled" the civil rights protections intended by its framers, the decision constitutes a landmark in American constitutional law. The three key phrases of the amendment are, of course, extremely vague and ambiguous. There is much evidence to indicate that the authors of the Fourteenth Amendment used these vague terms deliberately to insure its approval. Certainly the Amendment's supporters sought to "define United States citizenship authoritatively, to make the restrictions of the first eight amendments applicable to the states, and to render the constitutionality of the Civil Rights Bill (1866) free from doubt. A fear on the part of the reconstructionists that an amendment badly phrased to show these specific objects would not prove acceptable, led to the use of vague and ambiguous phrases which, it was hoped, would accomplish the desired ends without too clearly indicating the purpose."[1]

But soon the Supreme Court was faced with the task of giving some meaning to the Fourteenth Amendment. In the *Slaughterhouse* cases each of these phrases was interpreted very narrowly. What the Court said of each of these clauses had a great effect on the course of constitutional law.

PRIVILEGES AND IMMUNITIES

The Court's narrow construction of the privileges and immunities clause practically obliterated it from the Fourteenth Amendment. Since the *Slaughterhouse* cases, the Court's interpretation of privileges and immunities has not changed substantially, despite the fact that in some recent cases a number of justices seemed willing to enlarge the scope of this clause as an effective check on state action. For example, in *Colgate* v. *Harvey,* 296 U.S. 404 (1935), the Court held that a Vermont income tax law, which exempted interest accrued from money loaned inside the state but taxed income from loans outside the state, violated the privileges and immunities clause as well as the equal protection clause of the Fourteenth Amendment. The majority opinion, written by Justice Sutherland, differed sharply from the doctrine of the *Slaughterhouse* cases by holding that interstate business activity was one of the privileges and immunities of citizens of the United States that could be protected against state action. Justice Stone, with the concurrence of Justices Brandeis and Cardozo, wrote a sharp dissenting opinion. He noted that "since the adoption of the Fourteenth Amendment at least forty-four cases have

[1] Ray A. Brown, "Due Process of Law, Police Power and the Supreme Court," *Columbia Law Review,* Vol. 13 (1913), p. 294; reprinted in *Selected Essays on Constitutional Law, op. cit.,* Vol. 2, p. 97.

been brought to this Court in which state statutes have been assailed as infringements of the privileges and immunities clause. Until today, none has held that state legislation infringed that clause." Later, Justice Stone observed that the Court's use of the privileges and immunities clause in *Colgate* v. *Harvey* was a "rather shocking extension of judicial power, with little to warrant it."[2] Justice Sutherland's opinion may be explained largely by the desire of the more conservative anti-New Deal judges to use the discarded privileges and immunities clause as a weapon against effective governmental action. But Justice Stone's dissenting opinion was to prevail. In 1940, *Colgate* v. *Harvey* was expressly overruled in *Madden* v. *Kentucky,* 309 U.S. 83.

In *Hague* v. *Committee for Industrial Organization,* 307 U.S. 496 (1939), two justices (Roberts and Black) took the position that the rights of citizens to assemble and discuss their rights under the National Labor Relations Act was one of the privileges and immunities of citizens of the United States under the Fourteenth Amendment. Justice Stone again resisted the attempt to vitalize privileges and immunities. He argued that neither freedom of speech nor assembly was a privilege of United States citizens. Instead, these rights were secured without regard to citizenship by the due process clause of the Fourteenth Amendment.

Other attempts have been made since 1940 to broaden the scope of privileges and immunities. We have already seen that in *Edwards* v. *California* (Chapter 8), four justices preferred to base their condemnation of the California "Anti-Okie Law" on privileges and immunities rather than the commerce clause. Again, in *Oyama* v. *California,* 332 U.S. 633 (1948), the Court agreed with the contention of petitioners that the California Alien Land Law deprived Oyama of the "equal protection of California's laws and of his privileges as an American citizen." However, the Court did not enlarge upon this single statement. For the present, the privileges and immunities clause remains the "almost forgotten" clause of the Fourteenth Amendment.

DUE PROCESS OF LAW AND EQUAL PROTECTION

A careful reading of the *Slaughterhouse* cases will disclose that both the due process and equal protection clauses were given very little attention and casually dismissed by Justice Miller. But, unlike its holding with respect to privileges and immunities, the Court's interpretation of due process and equal protection has been set aside completely. In fact, the dissenting opinions in the *Slaughterhouse* cases are more significant than the majority holding in terms of later developments. The dissenting opinions of both Justice Bradley and Swayne in the *Slaughterhouse* cases were based on the due process and equal protection clauses rather than privileges and immunities. Note that the vehement dissent of Justice Field is based on privileges and immunities; however, his dissenting opinion in *Munn* v. *Illinois* is grounded on the due process

[2] Alpheus T. Mason, *Harlan Fiske Stone: Pillar of the Law* (New York: Viking, 1956), p. 399.

clause. In the short period between the two cases Justice Field evidently found that the due process clause would serve as a more reliable tool for the protection of liberty and property.

Munn v. Illinois

The opinion of the Court in *Munn* v. *Illinois* constitutes another important expression of the doctrine of judicial noninterference during this period. *Munn* v. *Illinois* was the most important case in a series known as the Granger cases, so named because they were concerned with laws initiated by an organization of farmers known as the Patrons of Husbandry, or the Grange.[3] Founded in 1867, the Grange, at first, was primarily a social organization designed to promote fellowship among the fiercely individualistic American farmers. But the abuses of the railroads and other corporate groups had, by the early 1870s, transformed the Grangers into a militant, political action group.

The farmers had much to be unhappy about. The deflation following the Civil War had left them heavily indebted, because the value of the dollar had gone up while the demand for farm products had declined. The farmers were almost completely dependent on the railroads to ship their products to market, and the railroads took advantage of the situation by charging all the traffic would bear. In addition, grain elevators were more often than not controlled by railroad managers, who charged outrageous prices for the storage of surplus grain. In short, the farmer was at the mercy of unscrupulous railroad men.

To fight the entrenched power of the railroads the farmers went into politics with a vengeance. Granger writers and orators inflamed public opinion against the "rapacious exploiters." Soon the Grangers elected a number of their own leaders to state governorships. They captured state legislatures in Illinois, Minnesota, Ohio, Michigan, Iowa, and other states and proceeded to press for laws curbing the railroads. Before long a number of states had passed laws setting maximum rates for carrying and storing grain. Illinois had taken the lead in this respect. In 1870, the newly adopted Illinois constitution directed the state legislature to pass laws regulating the storage of grain. The following year the Granger-controlled legislature passed a law that made all grain elevators in cities of 100,000 inhabitants or more *public* elevators. The same law fixed the charges for storage in the elevators much lower than the then-existing rate. In addition, each operator of a grain elevator was required to obtain a license from a county court before transacting any business. Out of this legislation arose the *Munn* case.

In upholding the Illinois statute, Chief Justice Waite remarked, in an often quoted statement, that "for protection against abuses by legislatures the peo-

[3] These materials are drawn from Rocco J. Tresolini, "Chief Justice Morrison R. Waite and the Public Interest," *loc. cit.*

ple must resort to the polls, not to the courts." Waite's holding was supported by the Court for nearly a decade, but by 1890 the justices began to view the Fourteenth Amendment as an important tool for the protection of private property and vested interests. As noted subsequently, this change in constitutional interpretation resulted in part from the pressures of the business community on the Court. Shocked by Waite's majority opinion, the business interests applauded Field's dissenting opinion and leveled a storm of criticism at the decision.

The change in the judicial construction of the Fourteenth Amendment was made possible by the Court's refusal to define authoritatively the due process and equal protection clauses. In *Davidson* v. *New Orleans,* 96 U.S. 97 (1878), the Court noted the difficulties in attempting to define due process of law and asserted that its meaning would have to evolve "by the gradual process of inclusion and exclusion, as the cases presented for decision shall require." Neither has it been possible to distinguish clearly between the protections afforded by the due process clause and those based on equal protection. Obviously, however, the two clauses overlap. "In many cases, laws which have been held invalid as denying due process of law might also have been so held as denying equal protection of the laws, or *vice versa,* and, in fact, in not a few cases the courts have referred to both prohibitions leaving it uncertain which prohibition was deemed the most pertinent and potent in the premises."[4]

Although both the due process and equal protection clauses were destined to grow, the development of due process as a constitutional deterrent to governmental action clearly overshadowed the equal protection clause until 1937. After that date, the use of due process as a substantive protection for private property rights was minimized, and the Court began to view the protection of individual liberties as one of its chief functions. In the protection of personal rights the Supreme Court has utilized increasingly the equal protection clause. The tremendous growth of that clause since 1937 is discussed in Chapter 17.

The Rise of Substantive Due Process

Since the *Slaughterhouse* cases, "the history of the Fourteenth Amendment has been, in the main, the history of the Supreme Court's interpretation of the 'due process' clause."[5] In American constitutional law, "no doctrine has enjoyed greater prestige than 'due process.' The account of its coming up in the world is among the most dramatic of stories. It bustles with color and conflict, with surprise and paradox. A novelist who made ideas his characters would not—for fear of provoking disbelief—have dared to allow his imagina-

---

[4] Westel W. Willoughby, *The Constitutional Law of the United States* (New York: Baker, Voorhis and Co., 1929), Vol. 3, p. 1929.

[5] Edward S. Corwin, *Liberty Against Government* (Baton Rouge: Louisiana State University Press, 1948), p. 127.

tion to contrive such a series of events. Yet beneath the curious rhetoric of case and coincidence, of confused citation and vagrant judgment, the logic of events was always in command of a doctrine headed for parts unknown."[6]

In the 1880s there were powerful forces at work that sought to break down the restricted meaning given to the Fourteenth Amendment in the *Slaughterhouse* cases and *Munn* v. *Illinois*. The United States was in the midst of a great industrial revolution. The legal system of the country was soon to be affected by big industry, big finance, the continued growth in population clustered largely in emerging urban centers, and the increased interdependence of activities. The new American corporate interests wanted to expand and grow without fear of governmental intervention. These powerful interests, which were represented by brilliant lawyers strongly committed to the laissez-faire doctrine, sought to forge the due process clause of the Fourteenth Amendment into a powerful tool for the protection of private property and vested interests against "unreasonable" social legislation. Of course, a number of difficulties first had to be overcome.

Due process had never been defined precisely, but it was associated generally with procedural rights. "The generation that fought the Civil War usually identified due process with common-law procedure."[7] It believed that due process was designed principally to provide persons accused of crime with the right to counsel, protection against arrest without a warrant, and other procedural safeguards that are discussed in Chapter 18. The framers of the Fourteenth Amendment, too, thought that due process of law had "the customary meaning recognized by the courts," which was unquestionably procedural.[8]

However, even before the Civil War, the guarantee of due process of law had been used to protect vested property interests. We saw in Chapter 7 that the doctrine of vested rights had been associated closely with the contract clause. Also, in a series of New York State cases before the Civil War, due process of law was held to guarantee *substantive* as well as *procedural* rights. The most important of these cases was *Wynehamer* v. *New York,* 13 N.Y. 378 (1856), where a state law regulating the manufacture of liquor was held invalid on the ground that it violated the due process clause in the state constitution. The state court noted that this clause was to be viewed as a general restriction on the power of the state legislature to interfere with private property.

The Supreme Court also began to accept the doctrine that due process of law could be used to protect substantive as well as procedural rights against

---

[6] Walton H. Hamilton, "The Path of Due Process of Law," in Congress Read (ed.), *The Constitution Reconsidered* (New York: Columbia University Press, 1938), p. 167.

[7] Charles M. Hough, "Due Process of Law—Today," *Harvard Law Review,* Vol. 32 (1918–19), p. 224.

[8] Joseph B. James, *The Framing of the Fourteenth Amendment* (Urbana: University of Illinois Press, 1956), pp. 86–87.

legislative action.[9] The Court's revolutionary shift from a narrow to a broader conception of due process was gradual but unmistakable. In 1886, the Supreme Court held that corporations were persons within the meaning of the equal protection clause and were therefore entitled to the protection of the Fourteenth Amendment.[10] The Court based this holding on an argument advanced in a previous case by Roscoe Conkling, an influential New York lawyer who had played an important role in the drafting of the Fourteenth Amendment. Conkling maintained that he and members of the drafting committee had "conspired" to use the word *person* instead of *citizen* in the Amendment in order to extend its protection to corporations. Although later historical research indicated clearly that Conkling's "conspiracy" argument was largely fraudulent, it did have some effect on the Supreme Court. In numerous subsequent decisions the Court repeated the assertion that the word *person* in the Fourteenth Amendment included corporations. Of course, many important factors other than Conkling's so-called conspiracy argument contributed to a broader judicial conception of the Fourteenth Amendment. Nevertheless, Conkling's argument "sounded the death knell of the narrow 'Negro-race theory' of the Fourteenth Amendment" indicated in the *Slaughterhouse* cases and *Munn* v. *Illinois.* By so doing, the Court "cleared the way for the modern development of due process of law and the corresponding expansion of the Court's discretionary powers over social and economic legislation."[11]

The decisive case came in 1890. In *Chicago, Milwaukee and St. Paul R.R. Co.* v. *Minnesota,* 134 U.S. 418, the Court held that a Minnesota statute, which delegated the regulation of rates to a commission, could be reviewed under the due process clause of the Fourteenth Amendment. In holding the statute void, the Court stated as follows: "The question of reasonableness of a rate of charge for transportation by a railroad company, involving as it does the element of reasonableness both as regards the company and as regards the public, *is eminently a question for judicial investigation, requiring due process of law for its determination.*" (Italics supplied.) The Court thus converted the due process clause into a positive, judicially enforced restriction over state legislation. Justice Field's dissenting views in the earlier cases had won the day. After 1890, the Supreme Court was to become the "perpetual censor" of state legislation under the Fourteenth Amendment and federal laws under the Fifth Amendment. The victory of due process over the states' police power was discernible clearly in *Lochner* v. *New York,* despite the famous dissent of Justice Holmes. "Even a casual examination of this new judicial attitude will indicate how thoroughgoing a revolution it wrought in

[9] *Hepburn* v. *Griswold,* 8 Wall. 603 (1870); *Davidson* v. *New Orleans,* 96 U.S. 97 (1878).

[10] *Santa Clara County* v. *Southern Pacific R.R. Co.,* 118 U.S. 394 (1886).

[11] Howard J. Graham, "The 'Conspiracy Theory' of the Fourteenth Amendment," *Harvard Law Review,* Vol. 47 (1937–38), p. 372.

our constitutional law. This new doctrine involved two things. First, it imposed upon the courts a new duty, the duty of applying to social legislation the limitations of due process of law and equal protection of the law. Secondly, this duty made it necessary for the courts to determine just how the guaranties of due process and equal protection of the law could be used as yardsticks for measuring the validity of social legislation."[12]

During this period when the Fourteenth Amendment was used with increasing frequency to protect economic rights, the Court interpreted the scope of procedural protections afforded by the Amendment rather narrowly. In a series of decisions, the Court held that the right of indictment by a grand jury, the right to trial by jury in both civil and criminal cases, and the right to be free from self-incrimination were *not* required in *state* judicial proceedings by the Fourteenth Amendment.[13] Each of these procedural safeguards is discussed in greater detail in Chapter 19.

REASONS FOR THE JUDICIAL REVOLUTION IN SUBSTANTIVE DUE PROCESS

In attempting to explain how the judicial attitude toward the Fourteenth Amendment changed so drastically, we must remember that the records of the Supreme Court ". . . reflect only in a series of passing shadows their tumultuous vitality. And the history of due process is far more than the judicial record it has left."[14] A number of important factors contributed to the judicial revolution. Conkling's conspiracy argument and the dissenting opinions in the *Slaughterhouse* and *Munn* cases were of some influence. But there were two other factors that perhaps were of greater importance.

1. The Supreme Court was undoubtedly influenced by the prevailing economic philosophy of laissez faire. This philosophy was supported vigorously by many Americans, particularly by the large corporate interests.

> Due process was fashioned from the most respectable ideological stuff of the later nineteenth century. The ideas out of which it was shaped were in full accord with the dominant thought of the age. In philosophy it was individualism, in government laissez faire, in economics the natural law of supply and demand, in law the freedom of contract. An impact that had been irresistible elsewhere should surely have won its way into constitutional law. Its coming seemed inevitable; the constitutional concept which it made its domicile was a mere matter of doctrinal accident.[15]

[12] Robert E. Cushman, "The Social and Economic Interpretation of the Fourteenth Amendment," *Michigan Law Review*, Vol. 20 (1922), p. 737; reprinted in *Selected Essays on Constitutional Law, op. cit.*, Vol. 2, p. 66.

[13] *Hurtado* v. *California*, 110 U.S. 516 (1884); *Walker* v. *Sauvint*, 92 U.S. 90 (1875); *Maxwell* v. *Dow*, 176 U.S. 581 (1900); *Twining* v. *New Jersey*, 211 U.S. 78 (1908).

[14] Hamilton, *loc. cit.*, p. 188.

[15] *Ibid.*, p. 189. See also Benjamin R. Twiss, *Lawyers and the Constitution* (Princeton, N.J.: Princeton University Press, 1942).

2. Important changes in the personnel of the Court from 1877 to 1890 also helped to bring about the new interpretation of the Fourteenth Amendment. During this period seven justices resigned or died. Of the judges who had decided the *Slaughterhouse* and *Munn* cases, only Justices Bradley and Field remained after the death of Justice Miller in 1890. Each of these justices had written vigorous dissents in the *Slaughterhouse* cases, and Justice Field had dissented in *Munn* v. *Illinois*. The majority of the new Court appointees had been influenced greatly by the propaganda campaign conducted by the American Bar Association in behalf of the laissez-faire doctrine. The Association, which had been founded in 1878, "became a sort of juristic sewing circle for mutual education in the gospel of laissez-faire."[16] That the new justices wished to protect the property interests of the emerging business corporations was not surprising. "By 1890, sturdy individualists of the new monarchism, such as Fuller, Peckham, Brewer, and Field, dominated the Court, and the scope of judicial review was expanded by them so as to delay or prevent American legislatures from dealing with pressing social problems in a manner long approved and practiced by the advanced industrial nations, and demanded by our own altered economic situation."[17]

The Era of Substantive Due Process (1890–1937)

In the period between 1890 and 1937, the Court proceeded to read its own laissez-faire notions into the due process and equal protection clauses of the Fourteenth Amendment. Of course, there were numerous deviations and constant readjustments; but, in general, the Fourteenth Amendment and other constitutional provisions such as the interstate commerce clause were used to strike down state and federal regulatory legislation. Under this new constitutional doctrine, the Court invalidated laws regulating minimum wages and maximum hours in employment, requiring workmen's compensation, regulating various business activities, and fixing prices. The major theme of the new constitutional doctrine was freedom of contract. This is demonstrated well in the *Lochner* case, where the Court defined liberty to include freedom of contract. Thus legislative interference with freedom of contract constituted a deprivation of "liberty" without due process of law. In essence this meant that business interests were free from almost any form of legislative control. The vigorous dissenting opinion of Justice Holmes in the *Lochner* case deserves careful attention, because it was destined to become the majority view of the Court after 1937.

Only three years after the *Lochner* decision, the Court seemed to adopt a much more liberal attitude toward social and economic legislation. In *Muller* v. *Oregon*, 208 U.S. 412 (1908), the Court unanimously sustained

[16] Corwin, *Liberty Against Government, op. cit.*, p. 138.

[17] Alpheus T. Mason, "The Conservative World of Mr. Justice Sutherland, 1883–1910," *American Political Science Review*, Vol. 32 (1938), p. 476.

an Oregon statute that limited the employment of women to ten hours a day in almost any type of industrial establishment. The Court's more liberal attitude toward social and economic legislation resulted, in part, from the influence of the arguments presented by Louis D. Brandeis in defense of the Oregon law. Brandeis, who was then a prominent Boston lawyer, submitted an unusual brief that included only two pages of legal arguments. But over a hundred pages of the brief consisted of American and European facts and statistics designed to show that women needed protection from excessive hours of labor. Brandeis argued that his data, which was obtained from committee reports, commissions on hygiene, inspectors of factories, and various other bureaus, proved that Oregon was justified in reducing a woman's working day for both physiological and social reasons. The majority opinion of the Court, written by Justice Brewer, revealed clearly the influence of what came to be called the Brandeis brief. The Court noted that the legislation and data presented by Brandeis "may not be, technically speaking, authorities, and in them is little or no discussion of the constitutional question presented to us for determination, yet they are significant of a widespread belief that woman's physical structure, and the functions she performs in consequence thereof, justify special legislation restricting or qualifying the conditions under which she should be permitted to toil." Thus the Court approved, for the first time, the revolutionary Brandeis technique of using social and economic facts to determine the reasonableness or unreasonableness of social welfare legislation.

The Brandeis technique was used with success in subsequent cases before the Supreme Court. In *Bunting* v. *Oregon,* 243 U.S. 426 (1917), the Court upheld an Oregon ten-hour law that applied to both men and women, despite a broad statement in the *Muller* case that legislation designed for the protection of women may be sustained "even when like legislation is not necessary for men, and could not be sustained." *Lochner* v. *New York* was not even mentioned in the *Bunting* case. By implication, the *Lochner* case thus appeared to be silently overruled. In *Stettler* v. *O'Hara,* 243 U.S. 629 (1917), the Court divided 4 to 4 and thereby left standing a decision of the Oregon Supreme Court which had upheld the state minimum-wage law. (A decision of a lower court is sustained when there is a tie vote in the Court.)

Despite the apparent liberalism of the *Bunting* and *Stettler* cases, the *Lochner* precedent was far from dead. "Those who had assumed a permanent change in the Court's outlook were to be disappointed. Change in the Court's personnel, and pressure of post-war economic and social views soon reflected themselves in decisions."[18] In the 1923 case of *Adkins* v. *Children's Hospital,* the Court resurrected the *Lochner* precedent to invalidate a minimum-wage law for women and children in the District of Columbia. Justice Brandeis, who had been appointed to the Court in 1916, did not participate in the de-

---

[18] Felix Frankfurter (ed.), *Mr. Justice Holmes* (New York: Coward-McCann, 1931), p. 81.

cision because his daughter was the Secretary of the District Minimum Wage Board, which had been established by the statute to fix minimum wages. But Justice Holmes dissented, and even the conservative Chief Justice (Taft) felt impelled to write a dissenting opinion.

The *Adkins* case was criticized bitterly, but with little practical effect for over a decade. As late as 1936, the Supreme Court held void a New York minimum-wage statute for women and children as a violation of the due process clause of the Fourteenth Amendment by applying the *Adkins* reasoning (*Morehead* v. *New York* ex rel *Tipaldo,* 298 U.S. 587).

The Decline of Substantive Due Process

Despite the *Tipaldo* holding, which was deplored by liberals and conservatives alike, the 1934 case of *Nebbia* v. *New York* was an indication that the Court would soon reject the due process philosophy enunciated in the *Lochner* and *Adkins* decisions. In the *Nebbia* case, the Court abandoned entirely the vague and elusive concept of business affected with the public interest announced in *Munn* v. *Illinois* and appeared reluctant to substitute its judgment for that of state legislators in social and economic policy matters.

The end came in *West Coast Hotel Co.* v. *Parrish,* where the Court expressly overruled the *Adkins* case by a 5-to-4 vote. The reversal of Justice Robert's position in the *Tipaldo* case made the new majority holding possible. Since the *Parrish* decision, the Court has "consciously returned closer and closer to the earlier constitutional principle that states have power to legislate against what are found to be injurious practices in their internal commercial and business affairs, so long as their laws do not run afoul of some specific federal constitutional prohibition, or of some valid federal law. Under this constitutional doctrine the due process clause is no longer to be so broadly construed that the Congress and state legislatures are put in a strait jacket when they attempt to suppress business and industrial conditions which they regard as offensive to the public welfare."[19]Thus, the holdings against which Justices Holmes and Brandeis had for long contended have been rejected by the Court. In the period between 1937 and 1946, the Supreme Court "killed substantive due process almost as dead as the proverbial doornail."[20]

In our time, the importance of the due process clause is to be found in other areas. It is now used primarily to limit legislation affecting individual liberties. The contributions of the due process clause to the protection of human rights, particularly since 1937, are discussed in various chapters of Part III.

[19] *Lincoln Federal Labor Union* v. *Northwestern Iron and Metal Co.,* 335 U.S. 525 (1949).

[20] C. Herman Pritchett, *Civil Liberties and the Vinson Court* (Chicago: University of Chicago Press, 1954), p. 3.

THE *SLAUGHTERHOUSE* CASES
16 Wall. 36; 21 L. Ed. 394 (1873)

[*Three separate cases that grew out of the same set of circumstances are known as the* Slaughterhouse *cases. These cases resulted from a Louisiana statute, enacted in 1869, that granted a monopoly to a slaughterhouse company in New Orleans. The act provided that the slaughtering of all animals in the New Orleans area was to be carried on by a single company for a period of twenty-five years. When the statute was enacted, the Louisiana state legislature was dominated by the Reconstruction, or carpetbag elements, and many legislative officers were under corrupt influences. The legislation had the effect of depriving some 1,000 butchers of work. Some of these butchers sought an injunction against the monopoly in the state courts, contending that they were deprived of the "right to exercise their trade, the business to which they have been trained and on which they depend for the support of themselves and their families." The Supreme Court of Louisiana decided in favor of the slaughterhouse company. The butchers then brought the cases to the Supreme Court on a writ of error.*]

MR. JUSTICE MILLER delivered the opinion of the court:

. . . The plaintiffs in error . . . allege that the statute is a violation of the Constitution of the United States in these several particulars:

That it creates an involuntary servitude forbidden by the thirteenth article of amendment;

That it abridges the privileges and immunities of citizens of the United States;

That it denies to the plaintiffs the equal protection of the laws; and,

That it deprives them of their property without due process of law; contrary to the provisions of the first section of the fourteenth article of amendment.

This court is thus called upon for the first time to give construction to these articles.

. . . [O]n the most casual examination of the language of these amendments [the Thirteenth, Fourteenth, and Fifteenth], no one can fail to be impressed with the one pervading purpose found in them all, lying at the foundation of each, and without which none of them would have been even suggested;

we mean the freedom of the slave race, the security and firm establishment of that freedom, and the protection of the newly-made freeman and citizen from the oppressions of those who had formerly exercised unlimited dominion over him. It is true that only the Fifteenth amendment, in terms, mentions the Negro by speaking of his color and his slavery. But it is just as true that each of the other articles was addressed to the grievances of that race, and designed to remedy them as the Fifteenth.

We do not say that no one else but the Negro can share in this protection. Both the language and spirit of these articles are to have their fair and just weight in any question of construction. Undoubtedly while Negro slavery alone was in the mind of the Congress which proposed the thirteenth article, it forbids any other kind of slavery, now or hereafter. . . .

The first section of the fourteenth article, to which our attention is more specially invited, opens with a definition of citizenship—not only citizenship of the United States, but citizenship of the States. No such definition was previously found in the Constitution, nor had any attempt been made to define it by act of Congress. It had been the occasion of much discussion in the courts, by the executive departments, and in the public journals. It had been said by eminent judges that no man was a citizen of the United States, except as he was a citizen of one of the States composing the Union. Those, therefore, who had been born and resided always in the District of Columbia or in the Territories, though within the United States, were not citizens. Whether this proposition was sound or not had never been judicially decided. But it had been held by this court, in the celebrated *Dred Scott* case, only a few years before the outbreak of the Civil War, that a man of African descent, whether a slave or not, was not and could not be a citizen of a State or of the United States. This decision, while it met the condemnation of some of the ablest statesmen and constitutional lawyers of the country, had never been overruled; and if it was to be accepted as a constitutional limitation of the right of citizenship, then all the Negro race who had recently been made freemen, were still, not only not citizens, but were incapable of becoming so by anything short of an amendment to the Constitution.

To remove this difficulty primarily, and to establish a clear and comprehensive definition of citizenship which should declare what should constitute citizenship of the United States, and also citizenship of a State, the first clause of the first section was framed.

"All persons born or naturalized in the United States, and subject to the jurisdiction thereof, are citizens of the United States and of the State wherein they reside."

The first observation we have to make on this clause is, that it puts at rest both the questions which we stated to have been the subject of differences of opinion. It declares that persons may be citizens of the United States without regard to their citizenship of a particular State, and it overturns the *Dred Scott* decision by making *all persons* born within the United States and subject to its jurisdiction citizens of the United States. That its main purpose was to establish the citizenship of the Negro can admit of no doubt. The phrase, "subject to its jurisdiction," was intended to exclude from its operation children of ministers, consuls, and citizens or subjects of foreign States born within the United States.

The next observation is more important in view of the arguments of counsel in the present case. It is, that the distinction between citizenship of the United States and citizenship of a State is clearly recognized and established. Not only may a man be a citizen of the United States without being a citizen of a State, but an important element is necessary to convert the former into the latter. He must reside within the State to make him a citizen of it, but it is only necessary that he should be born or naturalized in the United States to be a citizen of the Union.

It is quite clear, then, that there is a citizenship of the United States, and a citizenship of a State, which are distinct from each other, and which depend upon different characteristics or circumstances in the individual.

We think this distinction and its explicit recognition in this amendment of great weight in this argument, because the next paragraph of this same section, which is the one mainly relied on by the plaintiffs in error, speaks only of privileges and immunities of citizens of the United States, and does not speak of those of citizens of the several States. The argument, however, in favor of the plaintiffs rests wholly on the assumption that the citizenship is the same, and the privileges and immunities guaranteed by the clause are the same.

The language is, "No State shall make or enforce any law which shall abridge the privileges or immunities of citizens of *the United States*." It is a little remarkable, if this clause was intended as a protection to the citizen of a State against the legislative power of his own State, that the word citizen of the State should be left out when it is so carefully used, and used in contradistinction to citizens of the United States, in the very sentence which precedes it. It is too clear for argument that the change in phraseology was adopted understandingly and with a purpose.

Of the privileges and immunities of the citizen of the United States, and of the privileges and immunities of the citizen of the State, and what they respectively are, we will presently consider; but we wish to state here that it is only the former which are placed by this clause under the protection of the Federal Constitution, and that the latter, whatever they may be, are not intended to have any additional protection by this paragraph of the amendment.

If, then, there is a difference between the privileges and immunities belonging to a citizen of the United States as such, and those belonging to the citizen of the State as such, the latter must rest for their security and protection where they have heretofore rested; for they are not embraced by this paragraph of the amendment.

The first occurrence of the words "privileges and immunities" in our constitutional history, is to be found in the fourth of the articles of the old Confederation.

It declares "that the better to secure and perpetuate mutual friendship and intercourse among the people of the different States in this Union, the free inhabitants of each of these States, paupers, vagabonds, and fugitives from justice excepted, shall be entitled to all the privileges and immunities of free citizens in the several States; and the people of each State shall have free ingress and regress to and from any other State, and shall enjoy therein all the privileges of trade and commerce, subject to the same duties, impositions, and restrictions as the inhabitants thereof respectively."

In the Constitution of the United States, which superseded the Articles of Confederation, the corresponding provision is found in section two of the fourth article, in the following words: "The citizens of each State shall be entitled to all the privileges and immunities of citizens of the several States."

There can be but little question that the purpose of both these provisions is the same, and that the privileges and immunities intended are the same in each. In the article of the Confederation we have some of these specifically mentioned, and enough perhaps to give some general idea of the class of civil rights meant by the phrase. . . .

The constitutional provision there alluded to did not create those rights, which it called privileges and immunities of citizens of the States. It threw around them in that clause no security for the citizen of the State in which they were claimed or exercised. Nor did it profess to control the power of the State governments over the rights of its own citizens.

Its sole purpose was to declare to the several States, that whatever those rights, as you grant or establish them to your own citizens, or as you limit or qualify, or impose restrictions on their exercise, the same, neither more nor less, shall be the measure of the rights of citizens of other States within your jurisdiction.

It would be the vainest show of learning to attempt to prove by citations of authority, that up to the adoption of the recent amendments, no claim or pretence was set up that those rights depended on the Federal government for their existence or protection, beyond the very few express limitations which the Federal Constitution imposed upon the States—such, for instance, as the prohibition against ex post facto laws, bills of attainder, and laws impairing the obligation of contracts. But with the exception of these and a few other restrictions, the entire domain of the privileges and immunities of citizens of the States, as above defined, lay within the constitutional and legislative power of the States, and without that of the Federal government. Was it the purpose of the Fourteenth Amendment, by the simple declaration that no State should make or enforce any law which shall abridge the privileges and immunities of *citizens of the United States,* to transfer the security and protection of all the civil rights which we have mentioned, from the States to the Federal government? And where it is declared that Congress shall have the power to enforce that article, was it intended to bring within the power of Congress the entire domain of civil rights heretofore belonging exclusively to the States?

All this and more must follow, if the proposition of the plaintiffs in error be sound. For not only are these rights subject to the control of Congress whenever in its discretion any of them are supposed to be abridged by State legislation, but that body may also pass laws in advance, limiting and restricting the exercise of legislative power by the States, in their most ordinary and usual functions, as in its judgment it may

think proper on all such subjects. And still further, such a construction followed by the reversal of the judgments of the Supreme Court of Louisiana in these cases, would constitute this court a perpetual censor upon all legislation of the States, on the civil rights of their own citizens, with authority to nullify such as it did not approve as consistent with those rights, as they existed at the time of the adoption of this amendment. The argument we admit is not always the most conclusive which is drawn from the consequences urged against the adoption of a particular construction of an instrument. But when, as in the case before us, these consequences are so serious, so far-reaching and pervading, so great a departure from the structure and spirit of our institutions; when the effect is to fetter and degrade the State governments by subjecting them to the control of Congress, in the exercise of powers heretofore universally conceded to them of the most ordinary and fundamental character; when in fact it radically changes the whole theory of the relations of the State and Federal governments to each other and of both these governments to the people; the argument has a force that is irresistible, in the absence of language which expresses such a purpose too clearly to admit of doubt.

We are convinced that no such results were intended by the Congress which proposed these amendments, nor by the legislatures of the States which ratified them.

Having shown that the privileges and immunities relied on in the argument are those which belong to citizens of the States as such, and that they are left to the State governments for security and protection, and not by this article placed under the special care of the Federal government, we may hold ourselves excused from defining the privileges and immunities of citizens of the United States which no State can abridge, until some case involving those privileges may make it necessary to do so.

But lest it should be said that no such privileges and immunities are to be found if those we have been considering are excluded, we venture to suggest some which owe their existence to the Federal government, its National character, its Constitution, or its laws.

One of these . . . is said to be the right of the citizen of this great country, protected by implied guarantee of its Constitution, "to come to the seat of government to assert any claim he may have upon that government, to transact any business he may have with it, to seek its protection, to share its offices, to engage in administering its functions. He has the right of free access to its seaports, through which all operations of foreign commerce are conducted, to the sub-treasuries, land offices, and courts of justice in the several States." And quoting from the language of Chief Justice Taney . . . it is said "that *for all the great purposes for which the Federal government* was established, we are one people, with one common country, *we are all citizens of the United States;*" . . .

Another privilege of a citizen of the United States is to demand the care and protection of the Federal government over his life, liberty, and property when on the high seas or within the jurisdiction of a foreign government. Of this there can be no doubt, nor that the right depends upon his character as a citizen of the United States. The right to peaceably assemble and petition for redress of grievances, the privilege of the writ of *habeas corpus,* are rights of the citizen guaranteed by the Federal Constitution. The right to use the navigable waters of the United States, however they may penetrate the territory of the several States, all rights secured to our citizens by treaties with foreign nations are dependent upon citizenship of the United States, and not citizenship of a State. One of these privileges is conferred by the very article under consideration. It is that a citizen of the United States can, of his own volition, become a citizen of any State of the Union by a *bona fide* residence therein, with the same rights as other citizens of that State. To these may be added the rights secured by the thirteenth and fifteenth articles of amendment, and by the other clause of the fourteenth, next to be considered.

But it is useless to pursue this branch of the inquiry, since we are of opinion that the rights claimed by these plaintiffs in error, if they have any existence, are not privileges and immunities of citizens of the United States within the meaning of the clause of the Fourteenth Amendment under consideration. . . .

The argument has not been much pressed in these cases that the defendant's charter deprives the plaintiffs of their property without due process of law, or that it denies to them the equal protection of the law. The first of these paragraphs has been in the Constitution since the adoption of the Fifth Amendment, as a restraint upon the Federal power. It is also to be found in some form of expression in the constitutions of nearly all the States, as a restraint upon the power of the States. This law, then, has practically been the same as it now is during the existence of the government, except so far as the present amendment may place the restraining power over the States in this matter in the hands of the Federal government.

We are not without judicial interpretation, therefore, both State and National, of the meaning of this clause. And it is sufficient to say that under no construction of that provision that we have ever seen, or any that we deem admissible, can the restraint imposed by the State of Louisiana upon the exercise of their trade by the butchers of New Orleans be held to be a deprivation of property within the meaning of that provision.

"Nor shall any State deny to any person within its jurisdiction the equal protection of the laws."

In the light of the history of these amendments, and the pervading purpose of them, which we have already discussed, it is not difficult to give a meaning to this clause. The existence of laws in the States where the newly emancipated Negroes resided, which discriminated with gross injustice and hardship against them as a class, was the evil to be remedied by this clause, and by it such laws are forbidden.

If, however, the States did not conform their laws to its requirements, then by the fifth section of the article of amendment Congress was authorized to enforce it by suitable legislation. We doubt very much whether any action of a State not directed by way of discrimination against the Negroes as a class, or on account of their race, will ever be held to come within the purview of this provision. It is so clearly a provision for that race and that emergency, that a strong case would be necessary for its application to any other. But as it is a State that is to be dealt with, and not alone the validity of its laws, we may safely leave that matter until Congress shall have exercised its power, or some case of State oppression, by denial of equal justice in its courts, shall have claimed a decision at our hands. We find no such case in the one before us, and do not deem it necessary to go over the argument again, as it may have relation to this particular clause of the amendment. . . .

The judgments of the Supreme Court of Louisiana in these cases are

Affirmed.

MR. JUSTICE FIELD, dissenting:

. . . The question presented is . . . one of the gravest importance, not merely to the parties here, but to the whole country. It is nothing less than the question whether the recent amendments to the Federal Constitution protect the citizens of the United States against the deprivation of their common rights by State legislation. In my judgment the Fourteenth Amendment does afford such protection, and was so intended by the Congress which framed and the States which adopted it. . . .

The amendment does not attempt to confer any new privileges or immunities upon citizens, or to enumerate or define those already existing. It assumes that there are such privileges and immunities which belong of right to citizens as such, and ordains that they shall not be abridged by State legislation. If this inhibition has no reference to privileges and immunities of this character, but only refers, as held by the majority of the court in their opinion, to such privileges and immunities as were before its adoption specially designated in the Constitution or necessarily implied as belonging to citizens of the United States, it was a vain and idle enactment, which accomplished nothing, and most unnecessarily excited Congress and the people on its passage. With privileges and immunities thus designated or implied, no State could ever have interfered by its laws, and no new constitutional provision was required to inhibit such interference. The supremacy of the Constitution and the laws of the United States always controlled any State legislation of that character. But if the amendment refers to the natural and inalienable rights which belong to all citizens, the inhibition has a profound significance and consequence.

What, then, are the privileges and immunities which are secured against abridgment by State legislation? . . .

The terms, privileges and immunities, are not new in the amendment; they were in the Constitution before the amendment was adopted. They are found in the second section of the fourth article, which declares that "the citizens of each State shall be entitled to all privileges and immunities of citizens in the several States," and they have been the subject of frequent consideration in judicial decisions. In *Corfield* v. *Coryell,* Mr. Justice Washington said he had "no hesitation in confining these expressions to those privileges and immunities which were, in their nature, fundamental; which belong of right to citizens of all free governments, and which have at all times been enjoyed by the citizens of the several States which compose the Union, from the time of their becoming free, independent, and sovereign"; and, in considering what those fundamental privileges were, he said that perhaps it would be more tedious than difficult to enumerate them, but that they might be "all comprehended under the following general heads; protection by the government; the enjoyment of life and liberty, with the right to acquire and possess property of every kind, and to pursue and obtain happiness and safety, subject, nevertheless, to such restraints as the government may justly prescribe for the general good of the whole." This appears to me to be a sound construction of the clause in question. The privileges and immunities designated are those *which of right belong to the citizens of all free governments.* Clearly among these must be placed the right to

pursue a lawful employment in a lawful manner, without other restraint than such as equally affects all persons. . . .

This equality of right, with exemption from all disparaging and partial enactments, in the lawful pursuits of life, throughout the whole country, is the distinguishing privilege of citizens of the United States. To them, everywhere, all pursuits, all professions, all avocations are open without other restrictions than such as are imposed equally upon all others of the same age, sex, and condition. The State may prescribe such regulations for every pursuit and calling of life as will promote the public health, secure the good order and advance the general prosperity of society, but when once prescribed, the pursuit or calling must be free to be followed by every citizen who is within the conditions designated, and will conform to the regulations. This is the fundamental idea upon which our institutions rest, and unless adhered to in the legislation of the country our government will be a republic only in name. The Fourteenth Amendment, in my judgment, makes it essential to the validity of the legislation of every State that this equality of right should be respected. How widely this equality has been departed from, how entirely rejected and trampled upon by the act of Louisiana, I have already shown. And it is to me a matter of profound regret that its validity is recognized by a majority of this court, for by it the right of free labor, one of the most sacred and imprescriptible rights of man, is violated. . . . [G]rants of exclusive privileges, such as is made by the act in question, are opposed to the whole theory of free government, and it requires no aid from any bill of rights to render them void. That only is a free government, in the American sense of the term, under which the inalienable right of every citizen to pursue his happiness is unrestrained, except by just, equal, and impartial laws.

I am authorized by the CHIEF JUSTICE, MR. JUSTICE SWAYNE, and MR. JUSTICE BRADLEY, to state that they concur with me in this dissenting opinion.

[MR. JUSTICE BRADLEY and MR. JUSTICE SWAYNE also wrote separate dissenting opinions.]

MUNN v. ILLINOIS
94 U.S. 113; 24 L. Ed. 77 (1877)

[*Munn was convicted of operating a grain warehouse without a license and of charging higher rates than those established for the storage and handling of grain. Both practices were illegal under an Illinois statute that had been enacted in 1871 after the state constitution of 1870 had empowered the state legislature to regulate the storage of grain. The Illinois Supreme Court affirmed the judgment of a county court that had fined Munn and a partner $100 for the violation. Munn then brought the case to the Supreme Court on a writ of error.*]

MR. CHIEF JUSTICE WAITE delivered the opinion of the court:

The question to be determined in this case is whether the general assembly of Illinois can, under the limitations upon the legislative power of the States imposed by the Constitution of the United States, fix by law the maximum of charges for the storage of grain in warehouses at Chicago and other places in the State having not less than 100,-000 inhabitants, "in which grain is stored in bulk, and in which the grain of different owners is mixed together, or in which grain is stored in such a manner that the identity of different lots or parcels cannot be accurately preserved."

It is claimed that such a law is repugnant—

1. To that part of sect. 8, Art. I, of the Constitution of the United States which confers upon Congress the power "to regulate commerce with foreign nations and among the several States";

2. To that part of sect. 9 of the same article which provides that "no preference shall be given by any regulation of commerce or revenue to the ports of one State over those of another"; and

3. To that part of Amendment Fourteen which ordains that no State shall "deprive any person of life, liberty, or property, without due process of law, nor deny to any person within its jurisdiction the equal protection of the laws."

We will consider the last of these objections first.

Every statute is presumed to be constitutional. The courts ought not to declare one to be unconstitutional, unless it is clearly so. If there is doubt, the expressed will of the legislature should be sustained.

The Constitution contains no definition of the word "deprive," as used in the Fourteenth Amendment. To determine its signification, therefore, it is necessary to ascertain the effect which usage has given it, when employed in the same or a like connection.

While this provision of the amendment is new in the Constitution of the United States, as a limitation upon the powers of the States, it is old as a principle of civilized government. It is found in Magna Carta, and, in substance if not in form, in nearly or quite all the constitutions that have been from time to time adopted by the several States of the Union. By the Fifth Amendment, it was introduced into the Constitution of the United States as a limitation upon the powers of the national government, and by the Fourteenth, as a guaranty against any encroachment upon an acknowledged right of citizenship by the legislatures of the States. . . .

When one becomes a member of society, he necessarily parts with some rights or privileges which, as an individual not affected by his relations to others, he might retain. "A body politic," as aptly defined in the preamble of the Constitution of Massachusetts, "is a social compact by which the whole people covenants with each citizen, and each citizen with the whole people, that all shall be governed by certain laws for the common good." This does not confer power upon the whole people to control rights which are purely and exclusively private, . . . but it does authorize the establishment of laws requiring each citizen to so conduct himself, and so use his own property, as not unnecessarily to injure another. This is the very essence of government. . . . From this source come the police powers, which, as was said by Mr. Chief Justice Taney in the *License Cases,* 5 How. 583, "are nothing more or less than the powers of government inherent in every sovereignty, . . . that is to say, . . . the power to govern men and things." Under these powers the government regulates the conduct of its citizens one towards another, and the manner in which each shall use his own property, when such regulation becomes necessary for the public good. In their exercise it has been customary in England from time

immemorial, and in this country from its first colonization, to regulate ferries, common carriers, hackmen, bakers, millers, wharfingers, innkeepers, etc., and in so doing to fix a maximum of charge to be made for services rendered, accommodations furnished, and articles sold. To this day, statutes are to be found in many of the States upon some or all these subjects; and we think it has never yet been successfully contended that such legislation came within any of the constitutional prohibitions against interference with private property. With the Fifth Amendment in force, Congress, in 1820, conferred power upon the city of Washington "to regulate . . . the rates of wharfage at private wharves, . . . the sweeping of chimneys, and to fix the rates of fees therefor, . . . and the weight and quality of bread" . . . ; and, in 1848, "to make all necessary regulations respecting hackney carriages and the rates of fare of the same, and the rates of hauling by cartmen, wagoners, carmen, and draymen, and rates of commission of auctioneers." . . .

From this it is apparent that, down to the time of the adoption of the Fourteenth Amendment, it was not supposed that statutes regulating the use, or even the price of the use, of private property necessarily deprived an owner of his property without due process of law. Under some circumstances they may, but not under all. The amendment does not change the law in this particular: it simply prevents the States from doing that which will operate as such a deprivation.

This brings us to inquire as to the principles upon which this power of regulation rests, in order that we may determine what is within and what without its operative effect: Looking, then, to the common law, from whence came the right which the Constitution protects, we find that when private property is "affected with a public interest, it ceases to be *juris privati* only." This was said by Lord Chief Justice Hale more than 200 years ago . . . , and has been accepted without objection as an essential element in the law of property ever since. Property does become clothed with a public interest when used in a manner to make it of public consequence, and affect the community at large. When, therefore, one devotes his property to a use in which the public has an interest, he, in effect, grants to the public an interest in that use, and must submit to be controlled by the public for the common good, to the extent of the interest he has thus created. He may withdraw his grant by discontinuing the use; but, so long as he maintains the use, he must submit to the control. . . .

Enough has already been said to show that, when private property is devoted to a public use, it is subject to public regulation. It remains only to ascertain whether the warehouses of these plaintiffs in error, and the business which is carried on there, come within the operation of this principle.

For this purpose we accept as true the statements of fact contained in the elaborate brief of one of the counsel of the plaintiffs in error. From these it appears that "the great producing region of the West and North-west sends its grain by water and rail to Chicago, where the greater part of it is shipped by vessel for transportation to the seaboard by the Great Lakes, and some of it is forwarded by railway to the Eastern ports. . . . Vessels, to some extent, are loaded in the Chicago harbor, and sailed through the St. Lawrence directly to Europe. . . . The quantity (of grain) received in Chicago has made it the greatest grain market in the world. This business has created a demand for means by which the immense quantity of grain can be handled or stored, and these have been found in grain warehouses, which are commonly called elevators, because the grain is elevated from the boat or car, by machinery operated by steam, into bins prepared for its reception, and elevated from the bins, by a like process, into the vessel or car which is to carry it on. . . . In this way the largest traffic between the citizens of the country north and west of Chicago and the citizens of the country lying on the Atlantic coast north of Washington is in grain which passes through the elevators of Chicago. In this way the trade in grain is carried on by the inhabitants of seven or eight of the great States of the West with four or five of the States lying on the seashore, and forms the largest part of interstate commerce in these States. The grain warehouses or elevators in Chicago are immense structures, holding from 300,000 to 1,000,000 bushels at one time, according to size. They are divided into bins of large capacity and great strength. . . . They are located with the river harbor on one side and the railway tracks on the other; and the grain is run through them from car to vessel, or boat to car, as may be demanded in the course of business. It has been found impossible to preserve each owner's grain separate, and this has given rise to a system of inspection and grading, by which the grain of different owners is mixed, and receipts issued for the number of bushels which are negotiable, and redeemable in like kind, upon demand. This mode of conducting the business was inaugurated more than twenty years ago, and has grown to immense proportions. The railways have found it impracticable to own such elevators, and public policy forbids the transaction of such business by the carrier; the ownership has, therefore, been by private individuals, who have embarked their capital and devoted their industry to such business as a private pursuit.

In this connection it must also be borne in mind that, although in 1874 there were in Chicago fourteen warehouses adopted to this particular business, and owned by about thirty persons, nine business firms controlled them, and that the prices charged and received for storage were such "as have been from year to year agreed upon and established by the different elevators or warehouses in the city of Chicago, and which rates have been annually published in one or more newspapers printed in said city, in the month of January in each year, as the established rates for the year then next ensuing such publication." Thus it is apparent that all the elevating facilities through which these vast productions "of seven or eight great States of the West" must pass on the way "to four or five of the States on the sea-shore" may be a "virtual" monopoly.

Under such circumstances it is difficult to see why, if the common carrier, or the miller, or the ferryman, or the innkeeper, or the wharfinger, or the baker, or the cartman, or the hackney-coachman, pursues a public employment and exercises "a sort of public office," these plaintiffs in error do not. They stand, to use again the language of their counsel, in the very "gateway of commerce," and take toll from all who pass. Their business most certainly "tends to a common charge, and is become a thing of public interest and use." Every bushel of grain for its passage "pays a toll, which is a common charge," and, therefore, according to Lord Hale, every such warehouseman "ought to be under public regulation, viz., that he . . . take but a reasonable toll." Certainly, if any business can be clothed "with a public interest,

and cease to be *juris privati* only," this has been. It may not be made so by the operation of the Constitution of Illinois or this statute, but is by the facts.

We also are not permitted to overlook the fact that, for some reason, the people of Illinois, when they revised their Constitution in 1870, saw fit to make it the duty of the general assembly to pass laws "for the protection of producers, shippers, and receivers of grain and produce."

. . . Neither is it a matter of any moment that no precedent can be found for a statute precisely like this. It is conceded that the business is one of recent origin, that its growth has been rapid, and that it is already of great importance. And it must also be conceded that it is a business in which the whole public has a direct and positive interest. It presents, therefore, a case for the application of a long-known and well-established principle in social science, and this statute simply extends the law so as to meet this new development of commercial progress. There is no attempt to compel these owners to grant the public an interest in their property, but to declare their obligations, if they use it in this particular manner. . . .

It is insisted, however, that the owner of property is entitled to a reasonable compensation for its use, even though it be clothed with a public interest, and that what is reasonable is a judicial and not a legislative question.

As has already been shown, the practice has been otherwise. In countries where the common law prevails, it has been customary from time immemorial for the legislature to declare what shall be a reasonable compensation under such circumstances, or, perhaps more properly speaking, to fix a maximum beyond which any charge made would be unreasonable. Undoubtedly, in mere private contracts, relating to matters in which the public has no interest, what is reasonable must be ascertained judicially. But this is because the legislature has no control over such a contract. So, too, in matters which do affect the public interest, and as to which legislative control may be exercised, if there are no statutory regulations upon the subject, the courts must determine what is reasonable. The controlling fact is the power to regulate at all. If that exists, the right to establish the maximum of charge, as one of the means of regulation, is implied. In fact, the common-law rule, which requires the charge to be reasonable, is itself a regulation as to price. Without it the owner could make his rates at will, and compel the public to yield to his terms, or forego the use.

But a mere common-law regulation of trade or business may be changed by statute. A person has no property, no vested interest, in any rule of the common law. . . . Rights of property which have been created by the common law cannot be taken away without due process; but the law itself, as a rule of conduct, may be changed at the will, or even at the whim, of the legislature, unless prevented by constitutional limitations. Indeed, the great office of statutes is to remedy defects in the common law as they are developed, and to adapt it to the changes of time and circumstances. To limit the rate of charge for services rendered in a public employment, or for the use of property in which the public has an interest, is only changing a regulation which existed before. It establishes no new principle in the law, but only gives a new effect to an old one.

We know that this is a power which may be abused; but that is no argument against its existence. For protection against abuses by legislatures the people must resort to the polls, not to the courts.

. . . We come now to consider the effect upon this statute of the power of Congress to regulate commerce.

. . . "It is not everything that affects commerce that amounts to a regulation of it, within the meaning of the Constitution." The warehouses of these plaintiffs in error are situated and their business carried on exclusively within the limits of the State of Illinois. They are used as instruments by those engaged in State as well as those engaged in interstate commerce, but they are no more necessarily a part of commerce itself than the dray or the cart by which, but for them, grain would be transferred from one railroad station to another. Incidentally they may become connected with interstate commerce, but not necessarily so. Their regulation is a thing of domestic concern, and, certainly, until Congress acts in reference to their interstate relations, the State may exercise all the powers of government over them, even though in so doing it may indirectly operate upon commerce outside its immediate jurisdiction. We do not say that a case may not arise in which it will be found that a State, under the form of regulating its own affairs, has encroached upon the exclusive domain of Congress in respect to interstate commerce, but we do say that, upon the facts as they are represented to us in this record, that has not been done.

The remaining objection, to wit, that the statute in its present form is repugnant to sect. 9, Art I, of the Constitution of the United States, because it gives preference to the ports of one State over those of another, may be disposed of by the single remark that this provision operates only as a limitation of the powers of Congress, and in no respect affects the States in the regulation of their domestic affairs.

We conclude, therefore, that the statute in question is not repugnant to

the Constitution of the United States.
. . .

Judgment Affirmed.

MR. JUSTICE FIELD:

I am compelled to dissent from the decision of the court in this case. . . . The principle upon which the opinion of the majority proceeds is, in my judgment, subversive of the rights of private property, heretofore believed to be protected by constitutional guaranties against legislative interference, and is in conflict with the authorities cited in its support. . . .

The question presented . . . is one of the gresatest importance—whether it is within the competency of a State to fix the compensation which an individual may receive for the use of his own property in his private business, and for his services in connection with it.

. . . [I]t would seem from its opinion that the court holds that property loses something of its private character when employed in such a way as to be generally useful. The doctrine declared is that property "becomes clothed with a public interest when used in a manner to make it of public consequence, and affect the community at large"; and from such clothing the right of the legislature is deduced to control the use of the property, and to determine the compensation which the owner may receive for it. When Sir Matthew Hale, and the sages of the law in his day, spoke of property as affected by a public interest, and ceasing from that cause to be *juris privati* solely, that is, ceasing to be held merely in private right, they referred to property dedicated by the owner to public uses, or to property the use of which was granted by the government, or in connection with which special privileges were conferred. Unless the property was thus dedicated, or some right bestowed by the government was held with the property, . . . the property was not affected by any public interest so as to be taken out of the category of property held in private right. But it is not in any such sense that the terms "clothing property with a public interest" are used in this case. From the nature of the business under consideration—the storage of grain—which, in any sense in which the words can be used, is a private business, in which the public are interested only as they are interested in the storage of other products of the soil, or in articles of manufacture, it is clear that the court intended to declare that, whenever one devotes his property to a business which is useful to the public—"affects the community at large"—the legislature can regulate the compensation which the owner may receive for its use, and for his own services in connection with it. . . . The building used by the defendants was for the storage of grain: in such storage, says the court, the public has an interest; therefore the defendants, by devoting the building to that storage, have granted the public an interest in that use, and must submit to have their compensation regulated by the legislature.

If this be sound law, if there be no protection, either in the principles upon which our republican government is founded, or in the prohibitions of the Constitution against such invasion of private rights, all property and all business in the State are held at the mercy of a majority of its legislature. . . . The public is interested in the manufacture of cotton, woolen, and silken fabrics, in the construction of machinery, in the printing and publication of books and periodicals, and in the making of utensils of every variety, useful and ornamental; indeed, there is hardly an enterprise or business engaging the attention and labor of any considerable portion of the community, in which the public has not an interest in the sense in which that term is used by the court in its opinion; and the doctrine which allows the legislature to interfere with and regulate the charges which the owners of property thus employed shall make for its use, that is, the rates at which all these different kinds of business shall be carried on, has never before been asserted, so far as I am aware, by any judicial tribunal in the United States.

The doctrine of the State court, that no one is deprived of his property, within the meaning of the constitutional inhibitions, so long as he retains its title and possession, and the doctrine of this court, that, whenever one's property is used in such a manner as to affect the community at large, it becomes by that fact clothed with a public interest, and ceases to be *juris privati* only, appear to me to destroy, for all useful purposes, the efficacy of the constitutional guaranty. All that is beneficial in property arises from its use, and the fruits of that use; and whatever deprives a person of them deprives him of all that is desirable or valuable in the title and possession. . . .

No State "shall deprive any person of life, liberty, or property without due process of law," says the Fourteenth Amendment to the Constitution. . . .

By the term "liberty," as used in the provision, something more is meant than mere freedom from physical restraint or the bounds of a prison. It means freedom to go where one may choose, and to act in such manner, not inconsistent with the equal rights of others, as his judgment may dictate for the promotion of his happiness; that is, to pursue such callings and avocations as may be most suitable to develop his capacities, and give to them their highest enjoyment.

The same liberal construction which is required for the protection of life and liberty, in all particulars in which life and liberty are of any value, should be applied to the protection of private property. If the legislature of a State, under pretence of providing for the public good, or for any other reason, can determine, against the consent of the owner, the uses to which private property shall be devoted, or the prices which the owner shall receive for its uses, it can deprive him of the property as completely as by a special act for its confiscation or destruction. If, for instance, the owner is prohibited from using his building for the purposes for which it was designed, it is of little consequence that he is permitted to retain the title possession; or, if he is compelled to take as compensation for its use less than the expenses to which he is subjected by its ownership, he is, for all practical purposes, deprived of the property as effectually as if the legislature had ordered his forcible dispossession. If it be admitted that the legislature has any control over the compensation, the extent of that compensation becomes a mere matter of legislative discretion. . .

It is true that the legislation which secures to all protection in their rights, and the equal use and enjoyment of their property, embraces an almost infinite variety of subjects. Whatever affects the peace, good order, morals, and health of the community, comes within its scope; and every one must use and enjoy his property subject to the restrictions which such legislation imposes. What is termed the police power of the State, which, from the language often used respecting it, one would suppose to be an undefined and irresponsible element in government, can only interfere with the conduct of individuals in their intercourse with each other, and in the use of their property, so far as may be required to secure these objects. . . .

There is nothing in the character of the business of the defendants as warehousemen which called for the inter- ference complained of in this case. Their buildings are not nuisances; their occupation of receiving and storing grain infringes upon no rights of others, disturbs no neighborhood, infects not the air, and in no respect prevents others from using and enjoying their property as to them may seem best. The legislation in question is nothing less than a bold assertion of absolute power by the State to control at its discretion the property and business of the citi- zen, and fix the compensation he shall receive. . . . The decision of the court in this case gives unrestrained license to legislative will. . . .

[MR. JUSTICE STRONG concurred in the opinion of MR. JUSTICE FIELD.]

LOCHNER v. NEW YORK
198 U.S. 45; 25 Sup. Ct. 539; 49 L. Ed. 937 (1905)

[*A New York statute known as the Labor Law made it unlawful for an employee in a bakery or confectionery establishment to work more than sixty hours in any one week or an average of over ten hours a day. Lochner, who owned a bakery in Utica, N.Y., was convicted in a county court of requiring one of his employees to work more than sixty hours in one week. His conviction was upheld by the New York appellate courts. Lochner then brought the case to the Supreme Court on a writ of error.*]

MR. JUSTICE PECKHAM delivered the opinion of the Court:

. . . The statute necessarily inter- feres with the right of contract between the employer and employees, concern- ing the number of hours in which the latter may labor in the bakery of the employer. The general right to make a contract in relation to his business is part of the liberty of the individual protected by the Fourteenth Amend- ment of the Federal Constitution. . . . Under the provision no State can de- prive any person of life, liberty, or property without due process of law. The right to purchase or to sell labor is part of the liberty protected by this amendment, unless there are circum- stances which exclude the right. There are, however, certain powers, existing in the sovereignty of each State in the Union, somewhat vaguely termed police powers, the exact description and limita- tion of which have not been attempted by the courts. Those powers, broadly stated and without, at present, any attempt at a more specific limitation, relate to the safety, health, morals, and general welfare of the public. Both property and liberty are held on such reasonable conditions as may be im- posed by the governing power of the State in the exercise of those powers, and with such conditions the Fourteenth Amendment was not designed to inter- fere. . . .

The State, therefore, has power to prevent the individual from making certain kinds of contracts, and in regard to them the Federal Constitution offers no protection. If the contract be one which the State, in the legitimate exer- cise of its police power, has the right to prohibit, it is not prevented from prohibiting it by the Fourteenth Amend- ment. Contracts in violation of a stat- ute, either of the Federal or State government, or a contract to let one's property for immoral purposes, or to do any other unlawful act, could obtain no protection from the Federal Constitution, as coming under the liberty of person or of free contract. Therefore, when the State, by its legislature, in the assumed exercise of its police powers, has passed an act which seriously limits the right to labor or the right of contract in regard to their means of livelihood between persons who are *sui juris* (both employer and employee), it becomes of great importance to determine which shall prevail—the right of the individual to labor for such time as he may choose, or the right of the State to prevent the individual from laboring or from entering into any contract to labor, beyond a certain time prescribed by the State.

It must, of course, be conceded that there is a limit to the valid exercise of the police power by the State. There is no dispute concerning this general proposition. Otherwise the Fourteenth Amendment would have no efficacy and the legislatures of the States would have unbounded power, and it would be enough to say that any piece of legislation was enacted to conserve the morals, the health, or the safety of the people; such legislation would be valid, no matter how absolutely without foundation the claim might be. The claim of the police power would be a mere pretext—become another and delusive name for the supreme sovereignty of the State to be exercised free from constitutional restraint. This is not contended for. In every case that comes before this court, therefore, where legislation of this character is concerned and where the protection of the Federal Constitution is sought, the question necessarily arises: Is this a fair, reasonable and appropriate exercise of the police power of the State, or is it an unreasonable, unnecessary and arbitrary interference with the right of the individual to his personal liberty or to enter into those contracts in relation to labor which may seem to him

appropriate or necessary for the support of himself and his family? Of course the liberty of contract relating to labor includes both parties to it. The one has as must right to purchase as the other to sell labor.

This is not a question of substituting the judgment of the court for that of the legislature. If the act be within the power of the State it is valid, although the judgment of the court might be totally opposed to the enactment of such a law. But the question would still remain: Is it within the police power of the State? and that question must be answered by the court.

The question whether this act is valid as a labor law, pure and simple, may be dismissed in a few words. There is no reasonable ground for interfering with the liberty of person or the right of free contract, by determining the hours of labor in the occupation of a baker. There is no contention that bakers as a class are not equal in intelligence and capacity to men in other trades or manual occupations, or that they are not able to assert their rights and care for themselves without the protecting arm of the State, interferring with their independence of judgment and of action. They are in no sense wards of the State. Viewed in the light of a purely labor law, with no reference whatever to the question of health, we think that a law like the one before us involves neither the safety, the morals, nor the welfare of the public, and that the interest of the public is not in the slightest degree affected by such an act. The law must be upheld, if at all, as a law pertaining to the health of the individual engaged in the occupation of a baker. It does not affect any other portion of the public than those who are engaged in that occupation. Clean and wholesome bread does not depend upon whether the baker works but ten hours per day or only sixty hours a week. The limitation of the hours of labor does not come within the police power on that ground.

It is a question of which of two powers or rights shall prevail—the power of the State to legislate or the right of the individual to liberty of person and freedom of contract. The mere assertion that the subject relates though but in a remote degree to the public health does not necessarily render the enactment valid. The act must have a more direct relation, as a means to an end, and the end itself must be appropriate and legitimate, before an act can be held to be valid which interferes with the general right of an individual to be free in his person and in his power to contract in relation to his own labor. . . .

We think the limit of the police power has been reached and passed in this case. There is, in our judgment, no reasonable foundation for holding this to be necessary or appropriate as a health law to safeguard the public health or the health of the individuals who are following the trade of a baker. If this statute be valid, and if, therefore, a proper case is made out in which to deny the right of an individual, *sui juris,* as employer or employee, to make contracts for the labor of the latter under the protection of the provisions of the Federal Constitution, there would seem to be no length to which legislation of this nature might not go. . . .

We think that there can be no fair doubt that the trade of a baker, in and of itself, is not an unhealthy one to that degree which would authorize the legislature to interfere with the right to labor, and with the right of free contract on the part of the individual, either as employer or employee. In looking through statistics regarding all trades and occupations, it may be true that the trade of a baker does not appear to be as healthy as some other

trades, and is also vastly more healthy than still others. To the common understanding the trade of a baker has never been regarded as an unhealthy one. Very likely physicians would not recommend the exercise of that or of any other trade as a remedy for ill health. Some occupations are more healthy than others, but we think there are none which might not come under the power of the legislature to supervise and control the hours of working therein, if the mere fact that the occupation is not absolutely and perfectly healthy is to confer that right upon the legislative department of the Government. It might be safely affirmed that almost all occupations more or less affect the health. There must be more than the mere fact of the possible existence of some small amount of unhealthiness to warrant legislative interference with liberty. It is unfortunately true that labor, even in any department, may possibly carry with it the seeds of unhealthiness. But are we all, on that account, at the mercy of legislative majorities? A printer, a tinsmith, a locksmith, a carpenter, a cabinetmaker, a dry-goods clerk, a bank's, a lawyer's or a physician's clerk, or a clerk in almost any kind of business, would all come under the power of the legislature on this assumption. No trade, no occupation, no mode of earning one's living, could escape this all-pervading power, and the acts of the legislature in limiting the hours of labor in all employments would be valid, although such limitation might seriously cripple the ability of the laborer to support himself and his family.

. . . It is also urged, pursuing the same line of argument, that it is to the interest of the State that its population should be strong and robust, and therefore any legislation which may be said to tend to make people healthy must be valid as health laws, enacted under the police power. If this be a valid argument and a justification for this kind of legislation, it follows that the protection of the Federal Constitution from undue interference with liberty of person and freedom of contract is visionary, wherever the law is sought to be justified as a valid exercise of the police power. Scarcely any law but might find shelter under such assumptions, and conduct, properly so called, as well as contract, would come under the restrictive sway of the legislature. Not only the hours of employees, but the hours of employers, could be regulated, and doctors, lawyers, scientists, all professional men, as well as athletes and artisans, could be forbidden to fatigue their brains and bodies by prolonged hours of exercise, lest the fighting strength of the State be impaired. We mention these extreme cases because the contention is extreme. We do not believe in the soundness of the views which uphold this law. On the contrary, we think that such a law as this, although passed in the assumed exercise of the police power, and as relating to the public health, or the health of the employees named, is not within that power, and is invalid. The act is not, within any fair meaning of the term, a health law, but is an illegal interference with the rights of individuals, both employers and employees, to make contracts regarding labor upon such terms as they may think best, or which they may agree upon with the other parties to such contracts. Statutes of the nature of that under review, limiting the hours in which grown and intelligent men may labor to earn their living, are mere meddlesome interferences with the rights of the individual, and they are not saved from condemnation by the claim that they are passed in the exercise of the police power and upon the subject of the health of the individual whose rights are interfered

with, unless there be some fair ground, reasonable in and of itself, to say that there is material danger to the public health or to the health of the employees, if the hours of labor are not curtailed. . . .

It was further urged . . . that restricting the hours of labor in the case of bakers was valid because it tended to cleanliness on the part of the workers, as a man was more apt to be cleanly when not overworked, and if cleanly then his "output" was also more likely to be so. . . . In our judgment it is not possible in fact to discover the connection between the number of hours a baker may work in the bakery and the healthful quality of the bread made by the workman. The connection, if any exists, is too shadowy and thin to build any argument for the interference of the legislature. If the man works ten hours a day it is all right, but if ten and a half or eleven his health is in danger and his bread may be unhealthful, and, therefore, he shall not be permitted to do it. This, we think, is unreasonable and entirely arbitrary. . . .

. . . It seems to us that the real object and purpose were simply to regulate the hours of labor between the master and his employees (all being men, *sui juris*) in a private business, not dangerous in any degree to morals or in any real and substantial degree to the health of the employees. Under such circumstances the freedom of master and employee to contract with each other in relation to their employment, and in defining the same, cannot be prohibited or interfered with, without violating the Federal Constitution. . . .

Reversed.

MR. JUSTICE HARLAN, with whom MR. JUSTICE WHITE and MR. JUSTICE DAY concurred, dissenting:

. . . I find it impossible, in view of

common experience, to say that there is here no real or substantial relation between the means employed by the State and the end sought to be accomplished by its legislation. . . .

We judicially know that the question of the number of hours during which a workman should continuously labor has been, for a long period, and is yet, a subject of serious consideration among civilized peoples, and by those having special knowledge of the laws of health. Suppose the statute prohibited labor in bakery and confectionery establishments in excess of 18 hours each day. No one, I take it, could dispute the power of the State to enact such a statute. But the statute before us does not embrace extreme or exceptional cases. It may be said to occupy a middle ground in respect to the hours of labor. What is the true ground for the State to take between legitimate protection, by legislation, of the public health and liberty of contract is not a question easily solved, nor one in respect of which there is or can be absolute certainty. There are very few, if any, questions in political economy about which entire certainty may be predicted. . . .

I do not stop to consider whether any particular view of this economic question presents the sounder theory. What the precise facts are it may be difficult to say. It is enough for the determination of this case, and it is enough for this court to know, that the question is one about which there is room for debate and for an honest difference of opinion. There are many reasons of a weighty, substantial character, based upon the experience of mankind, in support of the theory that, all things considered, more than ten hours' steady work each day, from week to week, in a bakery or confectionery establishment, may endanger the health, and shorten the lives of the

workmen, thereby diminishing their physical and mental capacity to serve the State, and to provide for those dependent upon them.

If such reasons exist, that ought to be the end of this case, for the State is not amenable to the judiciary, in respect of its legislative enactments, unless such enactments are plainly, palpably, beyond all question, inconsistent with the Constitution of the United States. . . . Let the State alone in the management of its purely domestic affairs, so long as it does not appear beyond all question that it has violated the Federal Constitution. This view necessarily results from the principle that the health and safety of the people of a State are primarily for the State to guard and protect. . . .

The judgment in my opinion should be affirmed.

MR. JUSTICE HOLMES, dissenting:

. . . This case is decided upon an economic theory which a large part of the country does not entertain. If it were a question whether I agreed with that theory, I should desire to study it further and long before making up my mind. But I do not conceive that to be my duty, because I strongly believe that my agreement or disagreement has nothing to do with the right of a majority to embody their opinions in law. It is settled by various decisions of this court that state constitutions and state laws may regulate life in many ways which we as legislators might think as injudicious or if you like as tyrannical as this, and which equally with this interfere with the liberty to contract. Sunday laws and usury laws are ancient examples. A more modern one is the prohibition of lotteries. The liberty of the citizen to do as he likes so long as he does not interfere with the liberty of others to do the same, which has been a shibboleth for some well-known writers, is interfered with by school laws, by the Post Office, by every state or municipal institution which takes his money for purposes thought desirable, whether he likes it or not. The Fourteenth Amendment does not enact Mr. Herbert Spencer's Social Statics. . . . United States and state statutes and decisions cutting down the liberty to contract by way of combination are familiar to this court. . . . Two years ago we upheld the prohibition of sales of stock on margins or for future delivery in the constitution of California. . . . The decision sustaining an eight-hour law for miners is still recent. . . . Some of these laws embody convictions or prejudices which judges are likely to share. Some may not. But a constitution is not intended to embody a particular economic theory, whether of paternalism and the organic relation of the citizen to the State or of *laissez faire*. It is made for people of fundamentally differing views, and the accident of our finding certain opinions natural and familiar or novel and even shocking ought not to conclude our judgment upon the question whether statutes embodying them conflict with the Constitution of the United States.

General propositions do not decide concrete cases. The decision will depend on a judgment or intuition more subtle than any articulate major premise. But I think that the proposition just stated, if it is accepted, will carry us far toward the end. Every opinion tends to become a law. I think that the word "liberty" in the Fourteenth Amendment is perverted when it is held to prevent the natural outcome of a dominant opinion, unless it can be said that a rational and fair man necessarily would admit that the statute proposed would infringe fundamental principles as they have been understood by the traditions of our people and our law. It does not need research to show that no such sweeping condemnation can be passed upon the statute before us. A reasonable man might think it a proper measure on the score of health. Men whom I certainly could not pronounce unreasonable would uphold it as a first installment of a general regulation of the hours of work. Whether in the latter aspect it would be open to the charge of inequality I think it unnecessary to discuss.

ADKINS *v.* CHILDREN'S HOSPITAL
261 U.S. 525; 43 Sup. Ct. 394; 67 L. Ed. 785 (1923)

[*An Act of Congress of 1918 provided for the creation of a Minimum Wage Board authorized to set up minimum wages for women and children in the District of Columbia. The Children's Hospital, which employed several women at wages lower than those permitted by the Board, obtained an injunction against enforcement of the Act by Adkins and two others who were members of the Wage Board. A second case decided and reported together with the Children's Hospital case raised the same questions. The trial court decrees granting the injunction were affirmed by a federal court of appeals. Adkins and the other Board members then brought an appeal to the Supreme Court.*]

MR. JUSTICE SUTHERLAND delivered the opinion of the Court:

The question presented for determination by these appeals is the constitutionality of the Act of September 19, 1918, providing for the fixing of minimum wages for women and children in the District of Columbia. . . .

The statute now under consideration is attacked upon the ground that it authorizes an unconstitutional interference with the freedom of contract included within the guaranties of the due process clause of the Fifth Amendment. That the right to contract about one's affairs is a part of the liberty of the individual protected by this clause is settled by the decisions of this court, and is no longer open to question. . . . Within this liberty are contracts of employment of labor. In making such contracts, generally speaking, the parties have an equal right to obtain from each other the best terms they can as the result of private bargaining. . . .

There is, of course, no such thing as absolute freedom of contract. It is subject to a great variety of restraints. But freedom of contract is, nevertheless, the general rule and restraint the exception; and the exercise of legislative authority to abridge it can be justified only by the existence of exceptional circumstances. Whether these circumstances exist in the present case constitutes the question to be answered. . . .

The essential characteristics of the statute now under consideration, which differentiate it from the laws fixing hours of labor, will be made to appear as we proceed. It is sufficient now to point out that the latter . . . deal with incidents of the employment having no necessary effect upon the heart of the contract; that is, the amount of wages to be paid and received. A law forbidding work to continue beyond a given number of hours leaves the parties free to contract about wages and thereby equalize whatever additional burdens may be imposed upon the employer as a result of the restrictions as to hours, by an adjustment in respect of the amount of wages. Enough

has been said to show that the authority to fix hours of labor cannot be exercised except in respect of those occupations where work of long-continued duration is detrimental to health. This court has been careful in every case where the question has been raised, to place its decision upon this limited authority of the legislature to regulate hours of labor, and to disclaim any purpose to uphold the legislation as fixing wages, thus recognizing an essential difference between the two. It seems plain that these decisions afford no real support for any form of law establishing minimum wages.

If now, in the light furnished by the foregoing exceptions to the general rule forbidding legislative interference with freedom of contract, we examine and analyze the statute in question, we shall see that it differs from them in every material respect. . . . It is simply and exclusively a price-fixing law, confined to adult women (for we are not now considering the provisions relating to minors), who are legally as capable of contracting for themselves as men. It forbids two parties having lawful capacity—under penalties as to the employer—to freely contract with one another in respect to the price for which one shall render service to the other in a purely private employment where both are willing, perhaps anxious, to agree, even though the consequences may be to oblige one to surrender a desirable engagement, and the other to dispense with the services of a desirable employee. . . .

The standard furnished by the statute for the guidance of the board is so vague as to be impossible of practical application with any reasonable degree of accuracy. What is sufficient to supply the necessary cost of living for a woman worker and maintain her in good health and protect her morals is obviously not a precise or unvarying sum—not even approximately so. The amount will depend upon a variety of circumstances: the individual temperament; habits of thrift, care, ability to buy necessaries intelligently, and whether the woman live alone or with her family. To those who practice economy, a given sum will afford comfort, while to those of contrary habit the same sum will be wholly inadequate. The cooperative economics of the family group are not taken into account, though they constitute an important consideration in estimating the cost of living, for it is obvious that the individual expense will be less in the case of a member of a family than in the case of one living alone. The relation between earnings and morals is not capable of standardization. It cannot be shown that well-paid women safeguard their morals more carefully than those who are poorly paid. Morality rests upon other considerations than wages; and there is, certainly, no such prevalent connection between the two as to justify a broad attempt to adjust the latter with reference to the former. . . .

The law takes account of the necessities of only one party to the contract. It ignores the necessities of the employer by compelling him to pay not less than a certain sum, not only whether the employee is capable of earning it, but irrespective of the ability of his business to sustain the burden, generously leaving him, of course, the privilege of abandoning his business as an alternative for going on at a loss. Within the limits of the minimum sum, he is precluded, under penalty of fine and imprisonment, from adjusting compensation to the differing merits of his employees. It compels him to pay at least the sum fixed in any event, because the employee needs it, but requires no service of equivalent value from the employee. It therefore undertakes to solve but one half of the problem. . . . To the extent that the sum fixed exceeds the fair value of the services rendered, it amounts to a compulsory exaction from the employer for the support of a partially indigent person, for whose condition there rests upon him no peculiar responsibility, and therefore, in effect, arbitrarily shifts to his shoulders a burden which, if it belongs to anybody, belongs to society as a whole.

The feature of this statute which, perhaps more than any other, puts upon it the stamp of invalidity is that it exacts from the employer an arbitrary payment for a purpose and upon a basis having no causal connection with his business, or of the contract, or the work the employee engages to do. The declared basis . . . is not the value of the service rendered, but the extraneous circumstance that the employee needs to get a prescribed sum of money to insure her subsistence, health, and morals. The ethical right of every worker, man or woman, to a living wage, may be conceded. One of the declared and important purposes of trade organizations is to secure it. And with that principle and with every legitimate effort to realize it in fact, no one can quarrel; but the fallacy of the proposed method of attaining it is that it assumes that every employer is bound, at all events to furnish it. The moral requirement, implicit in every contract of employment, viz., that the amount to be paid and the service to be rendered shall bear to each other some relation of just equivalence, is completely ignored. . . . In principle, there can be no difference between the case of selling labor and the case of selling goods. If one goes to the butcher, the baker, or grocer to buy food, he is morally entitled to obtain the worth of his money, but he is not entitled to more. If what he gets is worth what he pays, he is not justified in demanding more simply because he needs more; and the shopkeeper, having dealt fairly and honestly in that transaction, is not concerned in any peculiar sense with the question of his customer's necessities. . . . [A] statute which prescribes payment without regard to any of these things, and solely with relation to circumstances apart from the contract of employment, the business affected by it, and the work done under it, is so clearly the product of a naked, arbitrary exercise of power, that it cannot be allowed to stand under the Constitution of the United States. . . .

It is said that great benefits have resulted from the operation of such statutes, not alone in the District of Columbia, but in the several states where they have been in force. A mass of reports, opinions of special observers and students of the subject, and the like, has been brought before us in support of this statement, all of which we have found interesting but only mildly persuasive. That the earnings of women now are greater than they were formerly, and that conditions affecting women have become better in other respects, may be conceded; but convincing indications of the logical relation of these desirable changes to the law in question are significantly lacking. They may be, and quite probably are, due to other causes. . . .

Finally, it may be said that if, in the interest of the public welfare, the police power may be invoked to justify the fixing of a minimum wage, it may, when the public welfare is thought to require it, be invoked to justify a maximum wage. The power to fix high wages connotes, by like course of reasoning, the power to fix low wages. If, in the face of the guaranties of the Fifth Amendment, this form of legislation shall be legally justified, the field for the operation of the police

power will have been widened to a great and dangerous degree. If, for example, in the opinion of future lawmakers, wages in the building trades shall become so high as to preclude people of ordinary means from building and owning homes, an authority which sustains the minimum wage will be invoked to support a maximum wage for building laborers and artisans, and the same argument which has been here urged to strip the employer of his constitutional liberty of contract in one direction will be utilized to strip the employee of his constitutional liberty of contract in the opposite direction. A wrong decision does not end with itself: it is a precedent, and, with the swing of sentiment, its bad influence may run from one extremity of the arc to the other.

It has been said that legislation of the kind now under review is required in the interest of social justice, for whose ends freedom of contract may lawfully be subjected to restraint. The liberty of the individual to do as he pleases, even in innocent matters, is not absolute. It must frequently yield to the common good, and the line beyond which the power of interference may not be pressed is neither definite nor unalterable, but may be made to move, within limits not well defined, with changing need and circumstance. Any attempt to fix a rigid boundary would be unwise as well as futile. But, nevertheless, there are limits to the power, and when these have been passed, it becomes the plain duty of the courts, in the proper exercise of their authority, to so declare. To sustain the individual freedom of action contemplated by the Constitution is not to strike down the common good, but to exalt it; for surely the good of society as a whole cannot be better served than by the preservation against arbitrary restraint of the liberties of its constituent members.

It follows from what has been said that the act in question passes the limit prescribed by the Constitution, and, accordingly, the decrees of the court below are affirmed. . . .

MR. CHIEF JUSTICE TAFT, dissenting:

. . . The boundary of the police power, beyond which its exercise becomes an invasion of the guaranty of liberty under the Fifth and Fourteenth Amendments to the Constitution, is not easy to mark. Our court has been laboriously engaged in pricking out a line in successive cases. We must be careful, it seems to me, to follow that line as well as we can, and not to depart from it by suggesting a distinction that is formal rather than real.

Legislatures, in limiting freedom of contract between employee and employer by a minimum wage, proceed on the assumption that employees in the class receiving least pay are not upon a full level of equality of choice with their employer, and in their necessitous circumstances are prone to accept pretty much anything that is offered. They are peculiarly subject to the overreaching of the harsh and greedy employer. The evils of the sweating system and of the long hours and low wages which are characteristic of it are well known. Now, I agree that it is a disputable question in the field of political economy how far a statutory requirement of maximum hours or minimum wages may be a useful remedy for these evils, and whether it may not make the case of the oppressed employee worse than it was before. But it is not the function of this court to hold congressional acts invalid simply because they are passed to carry out economic views which the court believes to be unwise or unsound. . . .

The right of the legislature under the Fifth and Fourteenth Amendments to limit the hours of employment on the score of the health of the employee, it seems to me, has been firmly established. . . .

I am authorized to say that MR. JUSTICE SANFORD concurs in this opinion.

MR. JUSTICE HOLMES, dissenting:

The question in this case is the broad one, whether Congress can establish minimum rates of wages for women in the District of Columbia, with due provision for special circumstances; or whether we must say that Congress has no power to meddle with the matter at all. To me, notwithstanding the deference due to the prevailing judgment of the court, the power of Congress seems absolutely free from doubt. The end— to remove conditions leading to ill health, immorality, and the deterioration of the race—no one would deny to be within the scope of constitutional legislation. The means are means that have the approval of Congress, of many states, and of those governments from which we have learned our greatest lessons. When so many intelligent persons, who have studied the matter more than any of us can, have thought that the means are effective and are worth the price, it seems to me impossible to deny that the belief reasonably may be held by reasonable men. If the law encountered no other objection than that the means bore no relation to the end, or that they cost too much, I do not suppose that anyone would venture to say that it was bad. I agree, of course, that a law answering the foregoing requirements might be invalidated by specific provisions of the Constitution. For instance, it might take private property without just compensation. But, in the present instance, the only objection that can be urged is found within the vague contours of the Fifth Amendment, prohibiting the depriving [of] any person of liberty or property without due process of law. To that I turn.

The earlier decisions upon the same words in the Fourteenth Amendment began within our memory, and went no farther than an unpretentious assertion of the liberty to follow the ordinary callings. Later that innocuous generality was expanded into the dogma, Liberty of Contract. Contract is not specially mentioned in the text that we have to construe. It is merely an example of doing what you want to do, embodied in the word "liberty." But pretty much all law consists in forbidding men to do some things that they want to do, and contract is no more exempt from law than other acts. Without enumerating all the restrictive laws that have been upheld, I will mention a few that seem to me to have interfered with liberty of contract quite as seriously and directly as the one before us. Usury laws prohibit contracts by which a man receives more than so much interest for the money that he lends. Statutes of frauds restrict many contracts to certain forms. Some Sunday laws prohibit practically all contracts during one-seventh of our whole life. Insurance rates may be regulated. . . . Finally, women's hours of labor may be fixed. . . . And the principle was extended to men, with the allowance of a limited overtime, to be paid for "at the rate of time and one-half of the regular wage" in *Bunting* v. *Oregon,* 243 U.S. 426.

I confess that I do not understand the principle on which the power to fix a minimum for the wages of women can be denied by those who admit the power to fix a maximum for their hours of work. I fully assent to the proposition that here, as elsewhere, the distinctions of the law are distinctions of degree; but I perceive no difference in the kind or degree of interference with liberty, the only matter with which we have any concern, between the one case and the other. The bargain is equally affected whichever half you regulate. *Muller* v. *Oregon,* I take it, is as good law today as it was in 1908. It will need more than the Nineteenth Amendment to convince me that there are no differences between men and women, or that legislation cannot take those differences into account. I should not hesitate to take them into account if I thought it necessary to sustain this act. . . . But after *Bunting* v. *Oregon* . . . , I had supposed that it was not necessary, and that *Lochner* v. *New York* . . . would be allowed a deserved repose. . . .

I am of opinion that the statute is valid and that the decree should be reversed.

NEBBIA *v.* NEW YORK
291 U.S. 502; 54 Sup. Ct. 505; 78 L. Ed. 940 (1934)

[*In 1933, the New York State legislature passed a law which was designed to help stabilize the state's milk industry, which had been affected adversely by the economic depression of the 1930's. The law provided for the establishment of a Milk Control Board, which was empowered to fix minimum and maximum prices to be charged for milk. The Board fixed the price of milk sold in stores at nine cents a quart. Nebbia, the proprietor of a grocery store in Rochester, N.Y., was convicted of selling two quarts of milk and a loaf of bread for only eighteen cents in violation of the Board's order. His conviction was sustained by the New York Court of Appeals. Nebbia then brought an appeal to the Supreme Court on the grounds that the Milk Control Law and the Board's order contravened the equal protection clause and the due process clause of the Fourteenth Amendment.*]

MR. JUSTICE ROBERTS delivered the opinion of the Court:

. . . *First*. The appellant urges that the order of the Milk Control Board denies him the equal protection of the laws. It is shown that the order requires him, if he purchases his supply from a dealer, to pay eight cents per quart and five cents per pint, and to resell at not less than nine and six, whereas the same dealer may buy his supply from a farmer at lower prices and deliver milk to consumers at ten cents the quart and six cents the pint. We think the contention that the discrimination deprives the appellant of equal protection is not well founded. For aught that appears, the appellant purchased his supply of milk from a farmer as do distributors, or could have procured it from a farmer if he so desired. There is therefore no showing that the order placed him at a disadvantage, or in fact affected him adversely, and this alone is fatal to the claim of denial of equal protection. But if it were shown that the appellant is compelled to buy from a distributor, the difference in the retail price he is required to charge his customers, from that prescribed for sales by distributors, is not on its face arbitrary or unreasonable, for there are obvious distinctions between the two sorts of merchants which may well justify a difference of treatment, if the legislature possess the power to control the prices to be charged for fluid milk. . . .

Second. The more serious question is whether, in the light of the conditions disclosed, the enforcement of [the price regulation] denied the appellant the due process secured to him by the Fourteenth Amendment. . . .

Under our form of government the use of property and the making of contracts are normally matters of private and not of public concern. The general rule is that both shall be free of governmental interference. But neither property rights nor contract rights are absolute; for government cannot exist if the citizen may at will use his property to the detriment of his fellows, or exercise his freedom of contract to work them harm. Equally fundamental with the private right is that of the public to regulate it in the common interest. . . .

The milk industry in New York has been the subject of long-standing and drastic regulation in the public interest. The legislative investigation of 1932 was persuasive of the fact that for this and other reasons unrestricted competition aggravated existing evils, and the normal law of supply and demand was insufficient to correct maladjustments detrimental to the community. The inquiry disclosed destructive and demoralizing competitive conditions and unfair trade practices which resulted in retail price-cutting and reduced the income of the farmer below the cost of production. We do not understand the appellant to deny that in these circumstances the legislature might reasonably consider further regulation and control desirable for protection of the industry and the consuming public. That body believed conditions could be improved by preventing destructive price-cutting by stores which, due to the flood of surplus milk, were able to buy at much lower prices than the larger distributors and to sell without incurring the delivery costs of the latter. In the order of which complaint is made, the Milk Control Board fixed a price of ten cents per quart for sales by a distributor to a consumer, and nine cents by a store to a consumer, thus recognizing the lower costs of the store, and endeavoring to establish a differential which would be just to both. In the light of the facts, the order appears not to be unreasonable or arbitrary, or without relation to the purpose to prevent ruthless competition from destroying the wholesale price structure on which the farmer depends for his livelihood, and the community for an assured supply of milk.

But we are told that because the law essays to control prices it denies due process. Notwithstanding the admitted power to correct existing economic ills by appropriate regulation of business, even though an indirect result may be a restriction of the freedom of contract or a modification of charges for services or the price of commodities, the appellant urges that direct fixation of prices is a type of regulation absolutely forbidden. His position is that the Fourteenth Amendment requires us to hold the challenged statute void for this reason alone. The argument runs that the public control of rates or prices is *per se* unreasonable and unconstitutional, save as applied to business affected with a public interest; that a business so affected is one in which property is devoted to an enterprise of a sort which the public itself might appropriately undertake, or one whose owner relies on a public grant or franchise for the right to conduct the business, or in which he is bound to serve all who apply; in short, such as is commonly called utility; or a business in its nature a monopoly. The milk industry, it is said, possesses none of these characteristics, and, therefore, not being affected with a public interest, its charges may not be controlled by the state. Upon the soundness of this contention the appellants case against the statute depends.

We may as well say at once that the dairy industry is not, in the accepted sense of the phrase, a public utility. We think the appellant is also right in asserting that there is in this case no suggestion of any monopoly or monopolistic practice. It goes without saying that those engaged in the business are in no way dependent upon public grants or franchises for the privilege of conducting their activities. But if, as must be conceded, the industry is subject to regulation in the public interest, what constitutional principle bars the state from correcting existing maladjustments by legislation touching prices? We think there is no such principle. The due process clause makes no mention of sales or of prices any more than it speaks of business or contracts or buildings or other incidents of property. The thought seems nevertheless to have persisted that there is something peculiarly sacrosanct about the price one may charge for what he makes or sells, and that, however able to regulate other elements of manufacture or trade, with incidental effect upon price, the state is incapable of directly controlling the price itself. This view was negatived many years ago. *Munn* v. *Illinois*. . . .

It is clear that there is no closed class or category of business affected with a public interest, and the function of courts in the application of the Fifth and Fourteenth Amendments is to determine in each case whether circumstances vindicate the challenged regulation as a reasonable exertion of governmental authority or condemn it as arbitrary or discriminatory. . . . The phrase "affected with a public interest" can, in the nature of things, mean no more than that an industry, for adequate reason, is subject to control for the public good. In several of the decisions of this court wherein the expressions "affected with a public interest," and "clothed with a public use," have been brought forward as the criteria of the validity of price control, it has been admitted that they are not susceptible of definition and form an unsatisfactory test of the constitutionality of legislation directed at business practices or prices. These decisions must rest, finally, upon the basis that the requirements of due process were not met because the laws were found arbitrary in their operation and effect. But there can be no doubt that upon proper occasion and by appropriate measures the state may regulate a business in any of its aspects, including the prices to be charged for the products or commodities it sells.

So far as the requirement of due process is concerned, and in the absence of other constitutional restriction, a state is free to adopt whatever economic policy may reasonably be deemed to promote public welfare, and to enforce that policy by legislation adapted to its purpose. The courts are without authority either to declare such policy, or, when it is declared by the legislature, to override it. If the laws passed are seen to have a reasonable relation to a proper legislative purpose, and are neither arbitrary nor discriminatory, the requirements of due process are satisfied. . . .

Price control, like any form of regulation, is unconstitutional only if arbitrary, discriminatory, or demonstrably irrelevant to the policy the legislature is free to adopt, and hence an unnecessary and unwarranted interference with individual liberty. . . .

The judgment is

Affirmed.

[MR. JUSTICE MC REYNOLDS dissented in an opinion concurred in by MR. JUSTICE VAN DEVANTER, MR. JUSTICE SUTHERLAND, and MR. JUSTICE BUTLER.]

WEST COAST HOTEL CO. *v.* PARRISH
300 U.S. 379; 57 Sup. Ct. 578; 81 L. Ed. 703 (1937)

[*In 1913, the state of Washington enacted a minimum-wage law for women and minors. Under the terms of the statute, an administrative board known as the Industrial Welfare Commission was authorized to establish minimum wages and conditions of labor for women and minors in the state. Elsie Parrish was employed as a chambermaid by the West Coast Hotel Company. She and her husband brought suit to recover the difference between the wages paid her by the hotel company and the minimum wage fixed by the commission. (The minimum wage for her job was $14.50 for a forty-eight-hour week.) The trial court decided against Mrs. Parrish, but the Supreme Court of Washington reversed the trial court and sustained the statute. The hotel company then brought the case to the Supreme Court on appeal.*]

MR. CHIEF JUSTICE HUGHES delivered the opinion of the Court:

This case presents the question of the constitutional validity of the minimum-wage law of the State of Washington. . . .

The appellant relies upon the decision of this Court in *Adkins* v. *Children's Hospital,* 261 U.S. 525, which held invalid the District of Columbia Minimum Wage Act, which was attacked under the due process clause of the Fifth Amendment. On the argument at bar, counsel for the appellees attempted to distinguish the *Adkins* case upon the ground that the appellee was employed in a hotel and that the business of an innkeeper was affected with a public interest. That effort at distinction is obviously futile, as it appears that in one of the cases ruled by the *Adkins* opinion the employee was a woman employed as an elevator operator in a hotel. . . .

The Supreme Court of Washington has upheld the minimum-wage statute of that State. It has decided that the statute is a reasonable exercise of the police power of the State. In reaching that conclusion the state court has invoked principles long established by this Court in the application of the Fourteenth Amendment. The state court has refused to regard the decision in the *Adkins* case as determinative and has pointed to our decisions both before and since that case as justifying its position. We are of the opinion that this ruling of the state court demands on our part a re-examination of the *Adkins* case. The importance of the question, in which many States having similar laws are concerned, the close division by which the decision in the *Adkins* case was reached, and the economic conditions which have supervened, and in the light of which the reasonableness of the exercise of the protective power of the State must be considered, make it not only appropriate, but we think imperative, that in deciding the present case the subject should receive fresh consideration. . . .

The principle which must control our decision is not in doubt. The constitutional provision invoked is in the due process clause of the Fourteenth Amendment governing the States, as the due process clause invoked in the *Adkins* case governed Congress. In each case the violation alleged by those attacking minimum-wage regulation for women is deprivation of freedom of contract. What is this freedom? The Constitution does not speak of freedom of contract. It speaks of liberty and prohibits the deprivation of liberty without due process of law. In prohibiting that deprivation the Constitution does not recognize an absolute and uncontrollable liberty. Liberty in each of its phases has its history and connotation. But the liberty safeguarded is liberty in a social organization which requires the protection of law against the evils

which menace the health, safety, morals, and welfare of the people. Liberty under the Constitution is thus necessarily subject to the restraints of due process, and regulation which is reasonable in relation to its subject and is adopted in the interests of the community is due process. . . .

This power under the Constitution to restrict freedom of contract has had many illustrations. That it may be exercised in the public interest with respect to contracts between employer and employee is undeniable. . . .

The point that has been strongly stressed that adult employees should be deemed competent to make their own contracts was decisively met nearly forty years ago in *Holden* v. *Hardy,* where we pointed out the inequality in the footing of the parties. We said . . . :

"The legislature has also recognized the fact, which the experience of legislators in many States has corroborated, that the proprietors of these establishments and their operatives do not stand upon an equality, and that their interests are, to a certain extent, conflicting. The former naturally desire to obtain as much labor as possible from their employees, while the latter are often induced by the fear of discharge to conform to regulations which their judgment, fairly exercised, would pronounce to be detrimental to their health or strength. In other words, the proprietors lay down the rules and the laborers are practically constrained to obey them. In such cases self-interest is often an unsafe guide, and the legislature may properly interpose its authority."

And we added that the fact "that both parties are of full age and competent to contract does not necessarily deprive the State of the power to interfere where the parties do not stand upon an equality, or where the public health demands that one party to the contract shall be protected against himself. . . ."

It is manifest that this established principle is peculiarly applicable in relation to the employment of women, in whose protection the State has a special interest. That phase of the subject received elaborate consideration in *Muller* v. *Oregon* (1908), 208 U.S. 412, where the constitutional authority of the State to limit the working hours of women was sustained. . . .

This array of precedents and the principles they applied were thought by the dissenting Justices in the *Adkins* case to demand that the minimum-wage statute be sustained. The validity of the distinction made by the Court between a minimum wage and a maximum of hours in limiting liberty of contract was especially challenged. . . . That challenge persists and is without any satisfactory answer. . . .

The minimum wage to be paid under the Washington statute is fixed after full consideration by representatives of employers, employees, and the public. It may be assumed that the minimum wage is fixed in consideration of the services that are performed in the particular occupations under normal conditions. Provision is made for special licenses at less wages in the case of women who are incapable of full service. The statement of Mr. Justice Holmes in the *Adkins* case is pertinent: "This statute does not compel anybody to pay anything. It simply forbids employment at rates below those fixed as the minimum requirement of health and right living. It is safe to assume that women will not be employed at even the lowest wages allowed unless they earn them, or unless the employer's business can sustain the burden. In short the law in its character and operation is like hundreds of so-called police laws that have been upheld." . . . And Chief Justice Taft forcibly

pointed out the consideration which is basic in a statute of this character: "Legislatures which adopt a requirement of maximum hours or minimum wages may be presumed to believe that when sweating employers are prevented from paying unduly low wages by positive law they will continue their business, abating that part of their profits, which were wrung from the necessities of their employees, and will concede the better terms required by the law; and that while in individual cases hardships may result, the restriction will enure to the benefit of the general class of employees in whose interest the law is passed and so to that of the community at large. . . ."

We think that the views thus expressed are sound and that the decision in the *Adkins* case was a departure from the true application of the principles governing the regulation by the State of the relation of employer and employed. . . .

With full recognition of the earnestness and vigor which characterize the prevailing opinion in the *Adkins* case, we find it impossible to reconcile that ruling with these well-considered declarations. What can be closer to the public interest than the health of women and their protection from unscrupulous and overreaching employers? And if the protection of women is a legitimate end of the exercise of the state power, how can it be said that the requirement of the payment of a minimum wage fairly fixed in order to meet the very necessities of existence is not an admissible means to that end? The legislature of the State was clearly entitled to consider the situation of women in employment, the fact that they are in the class receiving the least pay, that their bargaining power is relatively weak, and that they are the ready victims of those who would take advantage of their necessitous circumstances. The legislature was entitled to adopt measures to reduce the evils of the "sweating system," the exploiting of workers at wages so low as to be insufficient to meet the bare cost of living, thus making their very helplessness the occasion of a most injurious competition. The legislature had the right to consider that its minimum-wage requirements would be an important aid in carrying out its policy of protection. The adoption of similar requirements by many States evidences a deep-seated conviction both as to the presence of the evil and as to the means adapted to check it. Legislative response to that conviction cannot be regarded as arbitrary or capricious, and that is all we have to decide. Even if the wisdom of the policy be regarded as debatable and its effects uncertain, still the legislature is entitled to its judgment.

There is an additional and compelling consideration which recent economic experience has brought into a strong light. The exploitation of a class of workers who are in an unequal position with respect to bargaining power and are thus relatively defenseless against the denial of a living wage is not only detrimental to their health and well-being but casts a direct burden for their support upon the community. What these workers lose in wages the taxpayers are called to pay. The bare cost of living must be met. We may take judicial notice of the unparalleled demands for relief which arose during the recent period of depression and still continue to an alarming extent despite the degree of economic recovery which has been achieved. It is unnecessary to cite official statistics to establish what is of common knowledge through the length and breadth of the land. While in the instant case no factual brief has been presented, there is no reason to doubt that the State of Washington has encountered the same social problem that is present elsewhere. The community is not bound to provide what is in effect a subsidy for unconscionable employers. The community may direct its law-making power to correct the abuse which springs from their selfish disregard of the public interest. The argument that the legislation in question constitutes an arbitrary discrimination, because it does not extend to men, is unavailing. This Court has frequently held that the legislative authority, acting within its proper field, is not bound to extend its regulation to all cases which it might possibly reach. The legislature "is free to recognize degrees of harm and it may confine its restrictions to those classes of cases where the need is deemed to be clearest." If "the law presumably hits the evil where it is most felt, it is not to be overthrown because there are other instances to which it might have been applied." There is no "doctrinaire requirement" that the legislation should be couched in all-embracing terms. . . .

Our conclusion is that the case of *Adkins* v. *Children's Hospital* . . . should be, and it is, overruled. The judgment of the Supreme Court of the State of Washington is

Affirmed.

[MR. JUSTICE SUTHERLAND, joined by MR. JUSTICE VAN DEVANTER, MR. JUSTICE MC REYNOLDS, and MR. JUSTICE BUTLER, dissented.]

III
Political and Civil Rights

"Although freedom cannot be maintained by expositions alone, in the end they furnish the main strength of liberty. A people gets sooner or later as much freedom as it wants. This want is partly created by prophets on or off the bench, but partly by constant discussion from plain citizens like us. The best safeguard against inroads on freedom of speech lies in the ferment in the thoughts of the young and of those who will not let themselves grow old."

Zechariah Chafee, Jr.

From a lecture entitled, "Thirty-five Years with Freedom of Speech," delivered at Columbia University, March 12, 1952.

12
Rights of Citizenship

This is the first of eight chapters dealing with political and civil rights. By way of introduction, we shall make some general observations and then go on to a discussion of the basic concepts of citizenship.

Political rights are those that enable the citizen to participate in and ultimately to control his government. The rights to vote and hold office and to participate generally in the administration of governmental affairs are examples of such rights. The phrase *civil rights* is much more difficult, if not impossible, to define, because it is really "an abbreviation for a whole complex of relationships among individuals and among groups."[1] In general, the term *civil rights* in the United States refers to the various spheres of private or individual freedoms that cannot be taken away by the government. The theory is simply that there are certain individual rights that are so fundamental that governmental interference with them cannot be tolerated. These individual liberties are protected in many ways. Specific laws, customs and traditions, public opinion, and constitutions all play an important role.

[1] The President's Committee on Civil Rights, *To Secure These Rights* (Washington, D.C.: Government Printing Office, 1947), p. 12. For a comprehensive annotated bibliography on American political and civil rights, see Alexander D. Brooks, *Civil Rights and Liberties in the United States* (New York: Civil Liberties Educational Foundation, 1962). This publication also includes an annotated listing of audiovisual materials.

In the United States, constitutional provisions have been the principal guaranties of political and civil rights. Bills of rights were inserted in all of the original state constitutions. Each of the states admitted into the Union after 1789 has included a bill of rights in its state constitution. In 1791, the first ten amendments were added to the federal Constitution in response to popular demand for specific restrictions upon the national government.

It is easy to understand why most Americans wanted specific individual guaranties written into the early constitutions. They "looked to the experience of the past, and, reflecting upon the evils of preceding ages, concluded that the threat of arbitrary, tyrannical government was very serious. It has been said, 'Bill of rights are for the most part reactions against evils of the past rather than promises for the future.' In their commendable concern for safeguarding freedom of religion, free speech, and a free press, our forefathers naturally were impressed by the threats to these rights scattered through the pages of two centuries of English governmental practice."[2]

Political and Civil Rights in the Federal Constitution

In this and subsequent chapters, attention will be focused principally on the various specific guaranties of freedom and liberty secured by the federal Constitution. These guaranties are found in the body of the original Constitution, in the first ten amendments, and in other amendments subsequently adopted. They may be classified as follows:

PROVISIONS IN ORIGINAL CONSTITUTION

The Suspension of the Writ of Habeas Corpus Is Forbidden Except in Cases of Rebellion or Invasion. (Art. I, Sect. 9.) The writ of habeas corpus directs whomever has a person in custody to bring him before a named court so that it may determine if there is just cause for imprisonment. If the judge or court decides that the person is being detained in violation of the laws, he is released at once. Otherwise the prisoner is kept in custody to await regular trial, or he may remain free on bail before the trial if the court so directs. The provision against suspension of the writ of habeas corpus is viewed as basic simply because every form of liberty is impaired if a person may be imprisoned without explanation or redress. "A man in jail cannot go to church or discuss or publish or assemble or enjoy property or go to the polls."[3]

State and Federal Governments Are Forbidden to Pass Any Bill of Attainder or Ex Post Facto Laws. (Art. I, Sects. 9, 10.) These prohibitions were inserted in the Constitution by the ex-Colonists to prevent legislative

[2] Robert K. Carr, *Federal Protection of Civil Rights: Quest for a Sword* (Ithaca, N.Y.: Cornell University Press, 1947), p. 6.

[3] Zechariah Chafee, Jr., *How Human Rights Got into the Constitution* (Boston: Boston University Press, 1952), p. 51.

bodies from repeating the excesses of the English Parliament in punishing persons unjustly for treason and other crimes. A bill of attainder is a legislative act that inflicts punishment without the safeguards of a judicial trial. An ex post facto law is a *retroactive criminal* law that works to the disadvantage of a person accused of crime.

In the early case of *Calder* v. *Bull,* 3 Dall. 386 (1798), ex post facto laws were said to include those that (1) make acts criminal that were innocent when committed; (2) aggravate a crime or make it greater than it was when committed; (3) inflict greater punishment for a crime; or (4) make conviction easier. There have been relatively few cases dealing with ex post facto laws and bills of attainder in our history. A modern version of a bill of attainder was at issue in *United States* v. *Lovett,* 328 U.S. 303 (1946). Lovett and two other federal government employees were found by the House Un-American Activities Committee to have subversive affiliations. Congress thereupon attached a provision to an appropriation bill that stopped salary payments to the three employees and barred them from future employment with the federal government. The Court held that this action constituted a bill of attainder, because it inflicted punishment without judicial trial.

All Crimes Are to Be Tried by a Jury Except in Cases of Impeachment. This provision is given further emphasis by the Sixth Amendment. Treason is defined specifically, and the evidence necessary for convicting a person of treason is prescribed. (Art. III, Sects. 2, 3.)

Citizens of Each State Are Entitled to All the Privileges and Immunities of Citizens in the Several States. This means simply that a state cannot discriminate against citizens of other states in favor of its own. (Art. IV, Sect. 2.)

No Religious Test Can Be Required As a Qualification for Any Public Office Under the United States. (Art. VI, Sect. 2.)

FIRST TEN AMENDMENTS (BILL OF RIGHTS)

The First Amendment. This amendment, which deals with the important substantive rights of speech, press, assembly, and religion, stands largely by itself. These rights are discussed principally in Chapters 13, 14, and 15.

The Second Amendment. This amendment, which is concerned with the right of people to bear arms, and *the Third Amendment,* which deals with the quartering of troops, were for many years little more than historical curiosities. The Second may regain some importance in connection with proposed gun control laws aimed at problems of urban violence, political assassination, and the creation of private paramilitary organizations.

Amendments IV Through VIII. These amendments can be grouped together, as they are designed principally to afford procedural protections in criminal trials. These rights are discussed in Chapter 18.

The Ninth and Tenth Amendments. These amendments have not ordinarily been used as a basis for protection of fundamental rights in spite of the efforts of one writer who has maintained that the Ninth constitutes a fundamental declaration of natural rights designed to protect the individual.[4] Something of his view, however, is to be found in the opinions in *Griswold* v. *Connecticut* (Chapter 20), particularly that of Justice Goldberg.

OTHER AMENDMENTS

The Civil War Amendments (Thirteenth, Fourteenth, and Fifteenth). These amendments, which have been discussed briefly in Chapter 11, provide a number of additional guaranties.

The Nineteenth, or Women's Suffrage, Amendment. This amendment forbids both the national government and the states to abridge the right of United States citizens to vote because of sex.

The Twenty-fourth Amendment. This amendment prohibits the abridgment of voting rights in elections for federal officers through poll taxes or other such taxes. The Supreme Court has now extended this protection to state elections as well, under the equal protection clause. [*Harper* v. *Virginia State Board of Elections,* 383 U.S. 663 (1966).]

Some of the guaranties of the original Constitution restrict both the national and state governments, but the Bill of Rights was designed to serve as a limitation on the federal government *alone,* and not on the states. Of course, the states and local government units, as well as the national government, may threaten individual rights. Nevertheless, prior to the Civil War period, the protection of individual freedoms from state and local encroachment was left entirely in the hands of the states under the doctrine enunciated by Chief Justice Marshall in *Barron* v. *Baltimore,* 7 Pet. 243 (1833). In that case the Supreme Court declared that the Bill of Rights did not place restraints upon state and local governments. Marshall stated that the first ten amendments ". . . demanded security against the apprehended encroachments of the general [national] government, not against those of the local governments. These amendments contain no expression indicating an intention to apply them to the state governments. This Court cannot so apply them." Thus, with the exception of the restrictions in the original Constitution, the states were left free to define, protect, limit, or abolish political and civil rights as they saw fit without interference from the federal courts.

Partial Nationalization of the Bill of Rights

The adoption of the Civil War amendments imposed important new restrictions on the power of the states to interfere with individual liberties. The restraints placed upon the states by the Thirteenth and Fifteenth Amendments are clear. However, with the exception of the opening clause regarding citizenship, the true purpose and meaning of the Fourteenth Amendment has been subject to much controversy. Some judges and legal writers have argued that

[4] Bennett B. Patterson, *The Forgotten Ninth Amendment* (Indianapolis: Bobbs-Merrill, 1955), p. 19.

the Fourteenth Amendment was designed to incorporate the entire Bill of Rights as a restriction upon the powers of the states. They maintain that the framers of the Fourteenth Amendment wished to extend the full protection of the Bill of Rights to all the people of the country. This view of the Fourteenth Amendment has been most vigorously advocated by Justice Black. In a dissenting opinion in 1947, he stated as follows:

> My study of the historical events that culminated in the Fourteenth Amendment, and the expressions of those who opposed its submission and passage, persuades me that one of the chief objects that the provisions of the Amendment's first section, separately, and as a whole, were intended to accomplish was to make the Bill of Rights applicable to the states. With full knowledge of the import of the *Barron* decision, the framers and backers of the Fourteenth Amendment proclaimed its purpose to be to overturn the constitutional rule that case had announced.[5]

There exists equally persuasive evidence that the Fourteenth Amendment was designed to deal only with the rights of Negroes and that it did not incorporate the Bill of Rights as a limitation upon the states. One well-known scholar has gathered impressive evidence designed to prove that Justice Black's reading of history has been inaccurate.[6]

Regardless of the real purpose of the Fourteenth Amendment, no Supreme Court majority has ever held that the *entire* Bill of Rights constitutes a limitation on the states through the Fourteenth Amendment. In the *Slaughter-house Cases* and other subsequent decisions (Chapter 11), the Court held that the privileges and immunities clause did not protect fundamental rights from state interference, even though the privileges and immunities of *national* citizenship were so protected. With this judicial obliteration of privileges and immunities, the battle shifted to the due process clause. As shown in Chapter 11, this clause was used most successfully to protect vested property rights, but it was not used during the same period to protect individual rights against state action. Eventually the Court held that the due process clause of the Fourteenth Amendment did incorporate *some* of the rights enumerated in the first eight amendments. In short, as Justice Frankfurter noted in a concurring opinion in *Adamson* v. *California* (Chapter 18), there has occurred a "selective incorporation of the first eight amendments into the Fourteenth Amendment. Some are in and some are out." The job of the Supreme Court, then, is to decide which guaranties are in and which are out.

The partial transformation of the due process clause as a bar against state violation of individual rights began with the casual statement of Justice Sanford, speaking for the Court in *Gitlow* v. *New York* (Chapter 13). The Court

---

[5] *Adamson* v. *California* (Chapter 18). Professor William W. Crosskey has supported Justice Black's position in *Politics and the Constitution in the History of the United States, op. cit.,* Vol. II, Ch. 31.

[6] Charles Fairman, "Does the Fourteenth Amendment Incorporate the Bill of Rights? The Original Understanding," *Stanford Law Review,* Vol. 2 (1949), p. 5.

refused to invalidate a New York criminal anarchy law as applied in the *Gitlow* case, but Justice Sanford remarked that "we may and do assume that freedom of speech and of the press which are protected by the First Amendment from abridgement by Congress are among the fundamental personal rights and liberties protected by the due process clause of the Fourteenth Amendment." This was a momentous conclusion indeed, for despite a few statements to the contrary by minority justices, the Court had consistently refused to hold that the Fourteenth Amendment imposed any restrictions upon state legislation dealing with freedom of speech and other individual rights.

> This *Gitlow* case, therefore, affords an illuminating example of the manner in which our constitutional law grows; and it is not the only instance in which early dissenting opinions have quietly become, at a later date, the opinion of the Court, without the direct overruling of previous majority decisions. No one who read Judge Sanford's opinion would imagine that, for over fifty years, counsel had, time and again, attempted to get the Court to hold that rights similar to the right of freedom of speech were protected by the Fourteenth Amendment against infringement by State legislation, and that in every instance the Court had declined so to hold. Yet, in this *Gitlow* case, without even mentioning these previous cases, the Court assumes without argument, that this right of free speech is so protected by the Fourteenth Amendment. Thus, by one short sentence, rights, the protection of which have hitherto been supposed to be within the scope of the State Courts alone, are now brought within the scope of Federal protection and of the United States Supreme Court.[7]

Only two years after the *Gitlow* decision the Court held that a Kansas criminal syndicalism act, as applied to the defendant, violated the due process clause of the Fourteenth Amendment [*Fiske* v. *Kansas,* 274 U.S. 380 (1927)]. This constituted the first enforcement through the Fourteenth Amendment of any of the First Amendment freedoms against the states. In the 1931 case of *Near* v. *Minnesota,* 283 U.S. 1 (1931), the Court squarely invalidated a state statute restricting freedom of speech and press on the ground that it deprived persons of liberty without due process of law. Since that time, the term *liberty* in the Fourteenth Amendment has been interpreted broadly enough to include all the freedoms secured by the First Amendment. Today the guaranties of freedom of speech, assembly, press, and religion, and the prohibition against establishment of a state religion are protected against state as well as national infringement by the Fourteenth Amendment. The leading cases extending the First Amendment guaranties against state action are discussed in Chapters 13 and 14.

In addition, the Supreme Court has held that some of the procedural safeguards of the first eight amendments are applicable to the states when such rights are deemed vital to the operation of democratic government. For ex-

[7] Charles Warren, "The New 'Liberty' Under the Fourteenth Amendment," *Harvard Law Review,* p. 431; reprinted in *Selected Essays on Constitutional Law, op. cit.,* Vol. 2, p. 239.

ample, the right to counsel, the right to a public trial, and the right to be free from coerced confessions are protected against state as well as federal action by the Fourteenth Amendment. It was long held that other procedural safeguards, such as the right to indictment by grand jury and the right to be free from self-incrimination, were not protected by the federal courts against state abridgement because they are not "implicit in the concept of ordered liberty." Justice Cardozo stated in *Palko* v. *Connecticut* (Chapter 18), that only those liberties "which lie at the base of all our civil and political institutions" are protected against state action by the Fourteenth Amendment. Of course, it is difficult, if not impossible, to determine which of the safeguards of the Bill of Rights are fundamental or essential and which are not. The problems faced by the Court in this matter are discussed in Chapter 18 in connection with *Palko* v. *Connecticut,* where the Court attempted to distinguish between the essential and nonessential rights.

The partial incorporation of the Bill of Rights into the Fourteenth Amendment as a restriction upon the states has resulted in a great increase in the number of cases involving individual freedoms that have come before the Supreme Court. The remaining materials of Part III are evidence of the increasingly influential role of the Court in enforcing the constitutional guaranties of political and civil rights as more and more of the Bill of Rights is incorporated.

Citizenship

An individual must be a citizen before he can participate fully in self-government, for without citizenship he usually cannot vote, hold public office, or engage in certain professions. In general, citizenship refers to membership in a political community such as a nation or a state.

The Constitution does not define citizenship, although several references are made to it. Neither did the Constitution distinguish clearly between state and national citizenship or define the relationship between the two. As a result, there was much uncertainty and controversy in regard to citizenship before the Civil War. The proponents of a strong national government were unwilling to accept the view of the state's-rights supporters that national citizenship was subordinate to and derive from state citizenship.[8] The states'-rights view was confirmed by the Supreme Court in the *Dred Scott* case, where the primary of state over national citizenship was recognized.

The controversy over state and national citizenship came to an end in 1868, with the adoption of the Fourteenth Amendment, which provides clearly that "all persons born or naturalized in the United States, and subject to the jurisdiction thereof, are citizens of the United States and of the state wherein they reside." The wording of this opening clause of the Fourteenth Amend-

[8] Luella Gettys, *The Law of Citizenship in the United States* (Chicago; University of Chicago Press, 1934), p. 3.

ment makes clear that national citizenship is primary and dominant instead of dependent upon state citizenship. The primacy of national citizenship is indicated further by the next clause of the Amendment, which provides that "no state shall make or enforce any law which shall abridge the privileges or immunities of citizens of the United States." The Fourteenth Amendment thus overruled the Supreme Court's interpretation of citizenship in the *Dred Scott* case.

The opening clause of the Fourteenth Amendment was designed principally to grant both national and state citizenship to the newly freed Negro. Under its terms, citizenship can be acquired by either birth or naturalization. With a few exceptions noted in the *Wong Kim Ark* case [169 U.S. 649 (1898)], *any* person born in the United States is a citizen regardless of his parentage. Thus, the English doctrine of *jus soli* (law of soil or place), by which citizenship is determined by place of birth, is the fundamental rule in the United States. Under the rule of *jus sanguinis* (law of blood), which is used in continental Europe, a person's citizenship is derived from the nationality of his parents regardless of the place of birth. Although the rule of *jus soli* is predominant in the United States, Congress has provided also that persons may be considered natural-born citizens under the doctrine of *jus sanguinis* in certain instances. For example, a child born abroad of American parents is an American citizen at birth under certain specified conditions.

After the adoption of the Fourteenth Amendment, there was some question as to whether a child born in the United States of parents who were citizens or subjects of a foreign state could acquire citizenship by birth. This confusion was caused by Justice Miller's dictum in the *Slaughterhouse Cases* (Chapter 11), where he said that the phrase "subject to the jurisdiction" in the Fourteenth Amendment was designed to exclude from citizenship those children born in the United States of alien parents. This dictum was reversed by the Court in the *Wong Kim Ark* case. The rule laid down in that case has been followed to this day. In fact, the decision was not challenged in the courts until World War II, when an organization known as the "Native Sons of the Golden West" brought a court action to prevent children born in the United States of Japanese parentage from acquiring American citizenship. The lower federal courts refused to reverse the *Wong Kim Ark* doctrine, and in *Regan* v. *King,* 319 U.S. 753 (1943), the Supreme Court decided not to review the case.

NATURALIZATION

American citizenship may also be acquired by naturalization. Under the Constitution (Article I, Section 8, clause 4), Congress has executive power to establish rules governing the acquisition of citizenship by naturalization. *Collective* naturalization occurs when a large group or an entire population acquires citizenship by a treaty or by a single act of Congress. For example, treaties acquiring the territories of Louisiana and Alaska conveyed citizenship to the inhabitants of these areas. The people of Hawaii, Puerto Rico, the

Virgin Islands, and Guam were collectively naturalized by special acts of Congress.

An alien's right to *individual* naturalization is largely a question of statutory rather than constitutional law. The major function of the courts in naturalization cases, therefore, is to construe the intent of Congress. Only a few such cases have reached the highest court. The most important Supreme Court decisions have involved the naturalization of pacifists or conscientious objectors.

Congress had long required that an alien seeking American citizenship must take an oath that he would support and defend the Constitution and laws of the United States against all foreign and domestic enemies. Did this mean that an applicant for naturalization had to be willing to bear arms in defense of the United States? In three cases the Supreme Court answered in the affirmative. In *United States* v. *Schwimmer,* an educated woman pacifist who was fifty years old was denied citizenship because she stated that she was unwilling to fight in defense of the United States. This case is notable also because of an eloquent dissent by Justice Holmes.

Despite the Holmes dissent in the *Schwimmer* case, the Court, in *United States* v. *Macintosh,* 283 U.S. 605 (1931), denied citizenship to a Yale University professor of religion because he refused to promise in advance to bear arms in defense of the United States. Macintosh, who had served as a chaplain in the Canadian Army in World War I, was willing to participate only in a war that he believed to be morally justified. On the same day that the *Macintosh* case was decided, the Court also denied citizenship to a Canadian nurse who refused to swear without qualification that she would take up arms in defense of the United States [*United States* v. *Bland,* 283 U.S. 636 (1931)].[9]

These three cases established the principle that Congress intended to bar from citizenship any alien who refused to bear arms in defense of the United States. But in *Girouard* v. *United States,* 328 U.S. 61 (1946), the *Schwimmer, Macintosh,* and *Bland* decisions were overruled. In the *Girouard* case, the Court granted citizenship to a Seventh Day Adventist who was willing to perform noncombatant duties in the Army but would not promise to bear arms because of his religious convictions. In the majority opinion, Justice Douglas noted with approval Justice Holmes's dissent in the *Schwimmer* case and state that ". . . refusal to bear arms is not necessarily a sign of disloyalty or a lack of attachment to our institutions. One may serve his country faithfully and devotedly, though his religious scruples make it impossible for him to shoulder a rifle. Devotion to one's country can be as real and as enduring among noncombatants as among combatants." Justice Douglas then concluded that the *Schwimmer, Macintosh,* and *Bland* cases no longer stated the correct rule of law. In a *per curiam* decision in the 1949 case of

---

[9] The *Schwimmer* and *Macintosh* cases are explored thoroughly in Rocco J. Tresolini, *Justice and the Supreme Court* (Philadelphia: Lippincott, 1963), Chs. 4 and 5.

Cohnstaedt v. *Immigration and Naturalization Service,* 339 U.S. 901, the Supreme Court granted citizenship to a man who refused to serve in the army in any capacity on the authority of the *Girouard* case. Justice Holmes's *Schwimmer* dissent had finally prevailed.

The intention of Congress was clarified by legislation enacted in 1950 and 1952 that was in accord with the Supreme Court holdings in the *Girouard* and *Cohnstaedt* holdings. The legislation provided that pacifists who base their refusal to bear arms on religious grounds may be naturalized. However, pacifists who are unwilling to fight because of political, sociological, or philosophical reasons are still barred from citizenship.

LOSS OF CITIZENSHIP

In *Perez* v. *Brownell,* 356 U.S. 44 (1958), the Supreme Court, by a 5-to-4 vote, held that under a section of the Nationality Act of 1940, Congress could deprive a person of citizenship for voting in a foreign election on the ground that this was a reasonable exercise of the power of Congress to regulate foreign affairs. In the same day, however, the Court ruled in another 5-to-4 decision [*Trop* v. *Dulles,* 356 U.S. 86 (1958)] that another section of the Nationality Act of 1940, which prescribed loss of citizenship for desertion from the armed forces during wartime, was unconstitutional. Then, in *Kennedy* v. *Mendoza-Martinez,* 372 U.S. 144 (1963), the Court held certain amendments to the Nationality Act "invalid because in them Congress has plainly employed the sanction of deprivation of nationality as a punishment—for the offense of leaving or remaining outside the country to evade military service—without affording the procedural safeguards guaranteed by the Fifth and Sixth Amendments." In *Schneider* v. *Rusk,* 377 U.S. 163 (1964), the Court struck down provisions for the denaturalization of naturalized citizens who subsequently resided in the country of their birth for three years or more. Finally, in *Afroyim* v. *Rusk,* [p. 354] the Court overruled *Perez* v. *Brownell.*

DRED SCOTT *v.* SANFORD
19 How. 393; 15 L. Ed. 691 (1857)

[*Every student of American history is familiar with the bitter controversy brought about by the* Dred Scott *case. The report of the case occupies 240 pages, with all nine justices writing opinions. Yet the case grew out of a simple set of circumstances: Dred Scott was a slightly built, rather sickly Negro slave belonging to Dr. Emerson, a surgeon in the United States Army stationed in Missouri. In 1834, Dr. Emerson was transferred to a military post in Rock Island, Illinois, where slavery was forbidden. He took Dred Scott with him to his new post. In 1836, Scott again moved with Dr. Emerson to Fort Snelling in the territory of Upper Louisiana (now Minnesota), which was north of latitude 36° 30' and, consequently, an area where slavery was forbidden by the terms of the Missouri Compromise of 1820. Dr. Emerson returned to Missouri with his slave in 1838.*

In 1846, Scott brought suit in a Missouri state court to obtain his freedom on the ground of periods of residence in free territory. Scott won the case, but the judgment was reversed by the Missouri Supreme Court. However, abolitionists and other friends of Dred Scott refused to accept defeat. They arranged for a fictitious sale of Scott to John Sandford, a citizen of New York and brother of the widowed Mrs. Emerson, so that jurisdiction could be taken by a federal circuit court in Missouri. The federal court held that Scott and his family were Negro slaves and hence the "lawful property" of Sandford. The case then went to the Supreme Court on a writ of error.]

MR. CHIEF JUSTICE TANEY delivered the opinion of the Court:

. . . There are two leading questions presented by the record:

1. Had the Circuit Court of the United States jurisdiction to hear and determine the case between these parties? And

2. If it had jurisdiction, is the judgment it has given erroneous or not? . . .

The question is simply this: Can a negro, whose ancestors were imported into this country, and sold as slaves, become a member of the political community formed and brought into existence by the Constitution of the United States, and as such become entitled to all the rights, and privileges, and immunities, guaranteed by that instrument to the citizen? One of which rights is the privilege of suing in a court of the United States in the cases specified in the Constitution. . . .

The words "people of the United States" and "citizens" are synonymous terms, and mean the same thing. They both describe the political body who, according to our republican institutions, form the sovereignty, and who hold the power and conduct the Government through their representatives. They are what we familiarly call the "sovereign people," and every citizen is one of this people, and a constituent member of this sovereignty. The question before us is, whether the class of persons described in the plea in abatement compose a portion of this people, and are constituent members of this sovereignty? We think they are not, and that they are not included, and were not intended to be included, under the word "citizens" in the Constitution, and can therefore claim none of the rights and privileges which that instrument provides for and secures to citizens of the United States. On the contrary, they were at that time considered as a subordinate and inferior class of beings, who had been subjugated by the dominant race, and, whether emancipated or not, yet remained subject to their authority, and had no rights or privileges but such as those who held the power and the government might choose to grant them. . . .

In discussing this question, we must not confound the rights of citizenship which a State may confer within its own limits and the rights of citizenship as a member of the Union. It does not by any means follow, because he has all the rights and privileges of a citizen of a State, that he must be a citizen of the United States. He may have all of the rights and privileges of the citizen of a State, and yet not be entitled to the rights and privileges of a citizen in any other State. For, previous to the adoption of the Constitution of the United States, every State had the undoubted right to confer on whomsoever it pleased the character of citizen, and to endow him with all its rights. But this character of course was confined to the boundaries of the State, and gave him no rights or privileges in other States beyond those secured to him by the laws of nations and the comity of States. Nor have the several States surrendered the power of conferring these rights and privileges by adopting the Constitution of the United States. . . .

It is very clear, therefore, that no State can, by any act or law of its own, passed since the adoption of the Constitution, introduce a new member into the political community created by the Constitution of the United States. . . .

It is true, every person, and every class and description of persons, who were at the time of the adoption of the Constitution recognized as citizens in the several States, became also citizens of this new political body; but none other; it was formed by them, and for them and their posterity, but for no one else. And the personal rights and privileges guaranteed to citizens of this new sovereignty were intended to embrace those only who were then members of the several State communities, or who would afterwards by birthright or otherwise become members, according to the provisions of the Constitution and the principles on which it was founded. . . . And it gave to each citizen rights and privileges outside of his State which he did not before possess, and placed him in every other State upon a perfect equality with its own citizens as to rights of person and rights of property; it made him a citizen of the United States.

It becomes necessary, therefore, to determine who were citizens of the several States when the Constitution was adopted. . . .
[*The Chief Justice then refers to statutes of several Northern and border states prohibiting free Negroes from marrying whites, barring them from militia service, and requiring them to carry passes.*]

The legislation of the States therefore shows, in a manner not to be mis-

taken, the inferior and subject condition of that race at the time the Constitution was adopted, and long afterwards, throughout the thirteen States by which that instrument was framed; and it is hardly consistent with the respect due to these States, to suppose that they regarded at that time as fellow-citizens and members of the sovereignty, a class of beings whom they had thus stigmatized; whom, as we are bound, out of respect to the State sovereignties, to assume they had deemed it just and necessary thus to stigmatize, and upon whom they had impressed such deep and enduring marks of inferiority and degradation; or, that when they met in convention to form the Constitution, they looked upon them as a portion of their constituents, or deigned to include them in the provisions so carefully inserted for the security and protection of the liberties and rights of their citizens. It cannot be supposed that they intended to secure to them rights, and privileges, and rank, in the new political body throughout the Union, which every one of them denied within the limits of its own dominion. More especially, it cannot be believed that the large slaveholding States regarded them as included in the word citizens, or would have consented to a Constitution which might compel them to receive them in that character from another State. For if they were so received, and entitled to the privileges and immunities of citizens, it would exempt them from the operation of the special laws and from the police regulations which they considered to be necessary for their own safety. It would give to persons of the negro race, who were recognised as citizens in any one State of the Union, the right to enter every other State whenever they pleased, singly or in companies, without pass or passport, and without obstruction, to sojourn there as long as they pleased, to go where they pleased at every hour of the day or night without molestation, unless they committed some violation of law for which a white man would be punished; and it would give them the full liberty of speech in public and in private upon all subjects upon which its own citizens might speak; to hold public meetings upon political affairs, and to keep and carry arms wherever they went. And all of this would be done in the face of the subject race of the same color, both free and slaves, and inevitably producing discontent and insubordination among them, and endangering the peace and safety of the State. . . .

Undoubtedly, a person may be a citizen, that is, a member of the community who form the sovereignty, although he exercises no share of the political power, and is incapacitated from holding particular offices. Women and minors, who form a part of the political family, cannot vote; and when a property qualification is required to vote or hold a particular office, those who have not the necessary qualification cannot vote or hold the office, yet they are citizens.

So, too, a person may be entitled to vote by the law of the State, who is not a citizen even of the State itself. And in some of the States of the Union foreigners not naturalized are allowed to vote. And the State may give the right to free negroes and mulattoes, but that does not make them citizens of the State, and still less of the United States. And the provision in the Constitution giving privileges and immunities in other States does not apply to them.

Neither does it apply to a person who, being the citizen of a State, migrates to another State. For then he becomes subject to the laws of the State in which he lives, and he is no longer a citizen of the State from which he removed. And the State in which he resides may then, unquestionably, determine his status or condition, and place him among the class of persons who are not recognised as citizens, but belong to an inferior and subject race; and may deny him the privileges and immunities enjoyed by its citizens. . . .

No one, we presume, supposes that any change in public opinion or feeling, in relation to this unfortunate race, in the civilized nations of Europe or in this country, should induce the court to give to the words of the Constitution a more liberal construction in their favor than they were intended to bear when the instrument was framed and adopted. Such an argument would be altogether inadmissible in any tribunal called on to interpret it. If any of its provisions are deemed unjust, there is a mode prescribed in the instrument itself by which it may be amended; but while it remains unaltered, it must be construed now as it was understood at the time of its adoption. It is not only the same in words, but the same in meaning, and delegates the same powers to the Government, and reserves and secures the same rights and privileges to the citizen; and as long as it continues to exist in its present form, it speaks not only in the same words, but with the same meaning and intent with which it spoke when it came from the hands of its framers, and was voted on and adopted by the people of the United States. Any other rule of construction would abrogate the judicial character of this court, and make it the mere reflex of the popular opinion or passion of the day. This court was not created by the Constitution for such purposes. Higher and graver trusts have been confided to it, and it must not falter in the path of duty. . . .

[T]he court is of opinion, that, . . . Dred Scott was not a citizen of Missouri within the meaning of the Constitution of the United States, and not entitled as such to sue in its courts: and, consequently, that the Circuit Court had no jurisdiction of the case. . . .

We proceed, therefore, to inquire whether the facts relied on by the plaintiff entitled him to his freedom. . . .

In considering this part of the controversy, two questions arise: (1.) Was he, together with his family, free in Missouri by reason of the stay in the territory of the United States . . . ? and (2.) If they were not, is Scott himself free by reason of his removal to Rock Island, in the State of Illinois. . . .

We proceed to examine the first question.

The act of Congress [*the Missouri Compromise*] upon which the plaintiff relies, declares that slavery and involuntary servitude, except as a punishment for crime, shall be forever prohibited in all that part of the territory ceded by France, under the name of Louisiana, which lies north of 36°30′ north latitude, and not included within the limits of Missouri. And the difficulty which meets us at the threshold of this part of the inquiry is, whether Congress was authorized to pass this law under any of the powers granted to it by the Constitution; for if the authority is not given by that instrument, it is the duty of this court to declare it void and inoperative, and incapable of conferring freedom upon any one who is held as a slave under the laws of any one of the States.

The counsel for the plaintiff has laid much stress upon that article in the Constitution which confers on Congress the power "to dispose of and make all needful rules and regulations respecting the territory or other property belonging to the United States";

but, in the judgment of the court, that provision has no bearing on the present controversy, and the power there given, whatever it may be, is confined, and was intended to be confined, to the territory which at that time belonged to, or was claimed by, the United States, and was within their boundaries as settled by the treaty with Great Britain, and can have no influence upon a territory afterwards acquired from a foreign Government. It was a special provision for a known and particular territory, and to meet a present emergency, and nothing more. . . .

This brings us to examine by what provision of the Constitution the present Federal Government, under its delegated and restricted powers, is authorized to acquire territory outside of the original limits of the United States, and what powers it may exercise therein over the person or property of a citizen of the United States, while it remains a Territory, and until it shall be admitted as one of the States of the Union.

There is certainly no power given by the Constitution to the Federal Government to establish or maintain colonies bordering on the United States or at a distance, to be ruled and governed at its own pleasure; nor to enlarge its territorial limits in any way, except by the admission of new States. That power is plainly given; and if a new State is admitted, it needs no further legislation by Congress, because the Constitution itself defines the relative rights and powers, and duties of the State, and the citizens of the State, and the Federal Government. But no power is given to acquire a Territory to be held and governed permanently in that character. . . .

[I]t may be safely assumed that citizens of the United States who migrate to a Territory belonging to the people of the United States, cannot be ruled as mere colonists, dependent upon the will of the General Government, and to be governed by any laws it may think proper to impose. The principle upon which our Governments rest, and upon which alone they continue to exist, is the union of States, sovereign and independent within their own limits in their internal and domestic concerns, and bound together as one people by a General Government possessing certain enumerated and restricted powers, delegated to it by the people of the several States, and exercising supreme authority within the scope of the powers granted to it, throughout the dominion of the United States. A power, therefore, in the General Government to obtain and hold colonies and dependent territories, over which they might legislate without restriction, would be inconsistent with its own existence in its present form. Whatever it acquires it acquires for the benefit of the people of the several States who created it. It is their trustee acting for them, and charged with the duty of promoting the interests of the whole people of the Union in the exercise of the powers specifically granted. . . .

. . . The Territory being a part of the United States, the Government and the citizen both enter it under the authority of the Constitution, with their respective rights defined and marked out; and the Federal Government can exercise no power over his person or property, beyond what that instrument confers, nor lawfully deny any right which it has reserved. . . .

Upon these considerations, it is the opinion of the court that the act of Congress which prohibited a citizen from holding and owning property of this kind in the territory of the United States north of the line therein mentioned, is not warranted by the Constitution, and is therefore void; and that

neither Dred Scott himself, nor any of his family, were made free by being carried into this territory: even if they had been carried there by the owner, with the intention of becoming a permanent resident. . . .

But there is another point in the case which depends on State power and State law. And it is contended, on the part of the plaintiff, that he is made free by being taken to Rock Island, in the State of Illinois, independently of his residence in the territory of the United States; and being so made free, he was not again reduced to a state of slavery by being brought back to Missouri.

Our notice of this part of the case will be very brief; for the principle on which it depends was decided in this court, upon much consideration, in the case of *Strader et al.* v. *Graham,* reported in 19th Howard, 82. In that case, the slaves had been taken from Kentucky to Ohio, with the consent of the owner, and afterwards brought back to Kentucky. And this court held that their status or condition, as free or slave, depended upon the laws of Kentucky, when they were brought back into that State, and not of Ohio; and that this court had no jurisdiction to revise the judgment of a State court upon its own laws. . . .

So in this case. As Scott was a slave when taken into the State of Illinois by his owner, and was there held as such, and brought back in that character, his status, as free or slave, depended on the laws of Missouri, and not of Illinois. . . .

Upon the whole, therefore, it is the judgment of this court, that it appears by the record before us that the plaintiff in error is not a citizen of Missouri, in the sense in which that word is used in the Constitution; and that the Circuit Court of the United States, for that reason, had no jurisdiction in the case, and could give no judgment in it. Its judgment for the defendant must, consequently, be reversed, and a mandate issued, directing the suit to be dismissed for want of jurisdiction. . . .

[JUSTICE NELSON delivered an opinion that supported the following decision. JUSTICE GRIER concurred in the opinions of JUSTICES TANEY and NELSON. JUSTICES DANIEL, CAMPBELL, and CATRON delivered concurring opinions. JUSTICE MC LEAN, as well as JUSTICE CURTIS, dissented.]

MR. JUSTICE CURTIS, dissenting:

I dissent from the opinion pronounced by the Chief Justice, and from the judgment which the majority of the court think it proper to render in this case. . . .

To determine whether any free persons, descended from Africans held in slavery, were citizens of the United States under the Confederation, and consequently at the time of the adoption of the Constitution of the United States, it is only necessary to know whether any such persons were citizens of either of the States under the Confederation, at the time of the adoption of the Constitution.

Of this there can be no doubt. At the time of the ratification of the Articles of Confederation, all free native-born inhabitants of the States of New Hampshire, Massachusetts, New York, New Jersey, and North Carolina, though descended from African slaves, were not only citizens of those States, but such of them as had the other necessary qualifications possessed the franchise of electors, on equal terms with other citizens. . . .

I dissent, therefore, from that part of the opinion of the majority of the court, in which it is held that a person of African descent cannot be a citizen of the United States; and I regret I must go further, and dissent both from what I deem their assumption of authority to examine the constitutionality of the act of Congress commonly called the Missouri compromise act, and the grounds and conclusions announced in their opinion.

Having first decided that they were bound to consider the sufficiency of the plea to the jurisdiction of the Circuit Court, and having decided that this plea showed that the Circuit Court had not jurisdiction, and consequently that this is a case to which the judicial power of the United States does not extend, they have gone on to examine the merits of the case as they appeared on the trial before the court and jury, on the issues joined on the pleas in bar, and so have reached the question of the power of Congress to pass the act of 1820. On so grave a subject as this, I feel obliged to say that, in my opinion, such an exertion of judicial power transcends the limits of the authority of the court, as described by its repeated decisions and, as I understand, acknowledged in this opinion of the majority of the court. . . .

Nor, in my judgment, will the position, that a prohibition to bring slaves into a Territory deprives any one of his property without due process of law, bear examination. . . .

UNITED STATES v. SCHWIMMER
279 U.S. 644; 49 Sup. Ct. 448; 73 L. Ed. 889 (1929)

[*Rosika Schwimmer, a well-educated and highly intelligent pacifist, was born in Hungary in 1877. In 1921, she renounced her allegiance to Hungary, left Europe, and settled in Illinois because she felt that the United States was "the nation most*

likely to lead in building a world federation which would end the militarist epoch."
In November of the same year, she declared her intention to become an American
citizen. Upon completion of the five-year residence requirement in September
1926, Mrs. Schwimmer filed her final petition for naturalization. On a preliminary
questionnaire she was asked. "If necessary, are you willing to take up arms in de-
fense of this country?" Her reply was, "I would not take up arms personally." At
the hearing before a federal district court Mrs. Schwimmer was asked to explain
her reply in the preliminary questionnaire. She stated as follows: "I am able to
take the oath of allegiance without any reservations. I am willing to do everything
that an American citizen has to do except fighting. If American women would be
compelled to do that, I would not do that. I am an uncompromising pacifist. . . .
I am not willing to bear arms."

The district court denied Mrs. Schwimmer's application for citizenship on the
ground that she was "not attached to the principles of the Constitution of the
United States" and that she was "unable to take the oath of allegiance prescribed
by the Naturalization Law without a mental reservation."

A federal court of appeals reversed unanimously and ordered that Mrs. Schwim-
mer's application for citizenship be granted. The United States then brought the
case to the Superior Court on a writ of certiorari.]

MR. JUSTICE BUTLER delivered the opinion of the Court:

. . . Except for eligibility to the Presidency, naturalized citizens stand on the same footing as do native-born citizens. All alike owe allegiance to the Government, and the Government owes to them the duty of protection. These are reciprocal obligations and each is a consideration for the other. . . . But aleins can acquire such equality only by naturalization according to the uniform rules prescribed by the Congress. They have no natural right to become citizens, but only that which is by statute conferred upon them. Because of the great value of the privileges conferred by naturalization, the statutes prescribing qualifications and governing procedure for admission are to be construed with definite purpose to favor and support the Government. And, in order to safeguard against admission of those who are unworthy or who for any reason fail to measure up to required standards, the law puts the burden upon every applicant to show by satisfactory evidence that he has the specified qualifications. . . .

Every alien claiming citizenship is given the right to submit his petition and evidence in support of it. And, if the requisite facts are established, he is entitled as of right to admission. On applications for naturalization the court's function is "to receive the testimony, to compare it with the law, and to judge on both law and fact." . . . We quite recently declared that: "Citizenship is a high privilege and when doubts exist concerning a grant of it, generally at least, they should be resolved in favor of the United States and against the claimant." . . . And when, upon a fair consideration of the evidence adduced upon an application for citizenship, doubt remains in the mind of the court as to any essential matter of fact, the United States is entitled to the benefit of such doubt and the application should be denied.

That it is the duty of citizens by force of arms to defend our government against all enemies whenever necessity arises is a fundamental principle of the Constitution.

The common defense was one of the purposes for which the people ordained and established the Constitution. It empowers Congress to provide for such defense, to declare war, to raise and support armies, to maintain a navy, to make rules for the government and regulation of the land and naval forces, to provide for organizing, arming and disciplining the militia, and for calling it forth to execute the laws of the Union, suppress insurrections and repel invasions; it makes the President commander-in-chief of the army and navy and of the militia of the several States when called into the service of the United States; it declares that a well-regulated militia being necessary to the security of a free State, the right of the people to keep and bear arms, shall not be infringed. We need not refer to the numerous statutes that contemplate defense of the United States, its Constitution and laws by armed citizens. This Court, in the *Selective Draft Law Cases*, 245 U.S. 366, speaking through Chief Justice White, said . . . that "the very conception of a just government and its duty to the citizen includes the reciprocal obligation of the citizen to render military service in case of need. . . ."

Whatever tends to lessen the willingness of citizens to discharge their duty to bear arms in the country's defense detracts from the strength and safety of the government. And their opinions and beliefs as well as their behavior indicating a disposition to hinder in the performance of that duty are subjects of inquiry under the statutory provisions governing naturalization and are of vital importance, for if all or a large number of citizens oppose such defense the "good order and happiness" of the United States can not long endure. And it is evident that the views of applicants for naturalization in respect of such matters may not be disregarded. The influence of conscientious objectors against the use of military

tary force in defense of the principles of our government is apt to be more detrimental than their mere refusal to bear arms. The fact that, by reason of sex, age or other cause, they may be unfit to serve does not lessen their purpose or power to influence others. It is clear from her own statements that the declared opinions of respondent as to armed defense by citizens against enemies of the country were directly pertinent to the investigation of her application.

The record shows that respondent strongly desires to become a citizen. She is a linguist, lecturer and writer; she is well educated and accustomed to discuss governments and civic affairs. Her testimony should be considered having regard to her interest and disclosed ability correctly to express herself. Her claim at the hearing that she possessed the required qualifications and was willing to take the oath was much impaired by other parts of her testimony. Taken as a whole it shows that her objection to military service rests on reasons other than mere inability because of her sex and age personally to bear arms. Her expressed willingness to be treated as the government dealt with conscientious objectors who refused to take up arms in the recent war indicates that she deemed herself to belong to that class. The fact that she is an uncompromising pacifist with no sense of nationalism but only a cosmic sense of belonging to the human family justifies belief that she may be opposed to the use of military force as contemplated by our Constitution and laws. And her testimony clearly suggests that she is disposed to exert her power to influence others to such opposition.

A pacifist in the general sense of the word is one who seeks to maintain peace and to abolish war. Such purposes are in harmony with the Constitution and policy of our government. But the word is also used and understood to mean one who refuses or is unwilling for any purpose to bear arms because of conscientious considerations and who is disposed to encourage others in such refusal. And one who is without any sense of nationalism is not well bound or held by the ties of affection to any nation or government. Such persons are liable to be incapable of the attachment for and devotion to the principles of our Constitution that is required of aliens seeking naturalization.

It is shown by official records and everywhere well known that during the recent war there were found among those who described themselves as pacifists and conscientious objectors many citizens—though happily a minute part of all—who were unwilling to bear arms in that crisis and who refused to obey the laws of the United States and the lawful commands of its officers and encouraged such disobedience in others. Local boards found it necessary to issue a great number of noncombatant certificates, and several thousand who were called to camp made claim because of conscience for exemption from any form of military service. Several hundred were convicted and sentenced to imprisonment for offenses involving disobedience, desertion, propaganda and sedition. It is obvious that the acts of such offenders evidence a want of that attachment to the principles of the Constitution of which he applicant is required to give affirmative evidence by the Naturalization Act.

The language used by respondent to describe her attitude in respect of the principles of the Constitution was vague and ambiguous; the burden was upon her to show what she meant and that her pacifism and lack of nationalistic sense did not oppose the principle that

it is a duty of citizenship by force of arms when necessary to defend the country against all enemies, and that her opinions and beliefs would not prevent or impair the true faith and allegiance required by the Act. She failed to do so. The District Court was bound by the law to deny her application.

The decree of the Circuit Court of Appeals is

Reversed.

The decree of the District Court is
Affirmed.

MR. JUSTICE HOLMES:

The applicant seems to be a woman of superior character and intelligence, obviously more than ordinarily desirable as a citizen of the United States. It is agreed that she is qualified for citizenship except so far as the views set forth in a statement of facts "may show that the applicant is not attached to the principles of the Constitution of the United States and well disposed to the good order and happiness of the same, and except in so far as the same may show that she cannot take the oath of allegiance without a mental reservation." The views referred to are an extreme opinion in favor of pacifism and a statement that she would not bear arms to defend the Constitution. So far as the adequacy of her oath is concerned I hardly can see how that is affected by the statement, inasmuch as she is a woman over fifty years of age, and would not be allowed to bear arms if she wanted to. And as to the opinion the whole examination of the applicant shows that she holds none of the now-dreaded creeds but thoroughly believes in organized government and prefers that of the United States to any other in the world. Surely it cannot show lack of attachment to the principles of the Constitution that she thinks that it can be improved. I suppose that most intelligent people think that it might be.

Her particular improvement looking to the abolition of war seems to me not materially different in its bearing on this case from a wish to establish cabinet government as in England, or a single house, or one term of seven years for the President. To touch a more burning question, only a judge mad with partisanship would exclude because the applicant thought that the Eighteenth Amendment should be repealed.

Of course the fear is that if a war came the applicant would exert activities such as were dealt with in *Schenck v. United States,* 249 U.S. 47. But that seems to me unfounded. Her position and motives are wholly different from those of Schenck. She is an optimist and states in strong and, I do not doubt, sincere words her belief that war will disappear and that the impending destiny of mankind is to unite in peaceful leagues. I do not share that optimism nor do I think that a philosophic view of the world would regard war as absurd. But most people who have known it regard it with horror, as a last resort, and even if not yet ready for cosmopolitan efforts, would welcome any practicable combinations that would increase the power on the side of peace. The notion that the appli-

cant's optimistic anticipations would make her a worse citizen is sufficiently answered by her examination which seems to me a better argument for her admission than any that I can offer. Some of her answers might excite popular prejudice, but if there is any principle of the Constitution that more imperatively calls for attachment than any other it is the principle of free thought—not free thought for those who agree with us but freedom for the thought that we hate. I think that we should adhere to that principle with regard to admission into, as well as to life within this country. And recurring to the opinion that bars this applicant's way, I would suggest that the Quakers have done their share to make the country what it is, that many citizens agree with the applicant's belief and that I had not supposed hitherto that we regretted our inability to expel them because they believe more than some of us do in the teachings of the Sermon on the Mount.

MR. JUSTICE BRANDEIS concurs in this opinion.

MR. JUSTICE SANFORD, dissenting:

I agree, in substance, with the views expressed by the Circuit Court of Appeals, and think its decree should be affirmed.

AFROYIM *v.* RUSK
387 U.S. 253; 87 Sup. Ct. 1660; 18 L. Ed. 2d 757 (1967)

MR. JUSTICE BLACK delivered the opinion of the Court:

Petitioner, born in Poland in 1893, emigrated to this country in 1912 and became a naturalized American citizen in 1926. He went to Israel in 1950, and in 1951 he voluntarily voted in an election for the Israeli Knesset, the legislative body of Israel. In 1960, when he applied for renewal of his United States passport, the Department

of State refused to grant it on the sole ground that he had lost his American citizenship by virtue of § 401 (e) of the Nationality Act of 1940 which provides that a United States citizen shall "lose" his citizenship if he votes "in a political election in a foreign state." Petitioner then brought this declaratory judgment action in federal district court alleging that § 401 (e) violates both the Due Process Clause of the Fifth

Amendment and §1, cl. 1, of the Fourteenth Amendment which grants American citizenship to persons like petitioner. Because neither the Fourteenth Amendment nor any other provision of the Constitution expressly grants Congress the power to take away that citizenship once it has been acquired, petitioner contended that the only way he could lose his citizenship was by his own voluntary renunciation of it. Since the Government took the position that §401 (e) empowers it to terminate citizenship without the citizen's voluntary renunciation, petitioner argued that this section is prohibited by the Constitution. The District Court and the Court of Appeals, rejecting this argument, held that Congress has constitutional authority forcibly to take away citizenship for voting in a foreign country based on its implied power to regulate foreign affairs. Consequently, petitioner was held to have lost his American citizenship regardless of his intention not to give it up. This is precisely what this Court held in *Perez* v. *Brownell* [1958].

Petitioner, relying on the same contentions about voluntary renunciation of citizenship which this Court rejected in upholding §401 (e) in *Perez,* urges us to reconsider that case, adopt the view of the minority there, and overrule it. That case, decided by a 5 to 4 vote ten years ago, has been a source of controversy and confusion ever since, as was emphatically recognized in the opinions of all the judges who participated in this case below. Moreover, in the other cases decided with and since *Perez,* this Court has consistently invalidated on a case-by-case basis various other statutory sections providing for involuntary expatriation. It has done so on various grounds and has refused to hold that citizens can be expatriated without their voluntary renunciation of citizenship. These cases, as well as many commentators, have cast great doubt upon the soundness of *Perez.* . . .

The fundamental issue before this Court here, as it was in *Perez,* is whether Congress can consistently with the Fourteenth Amendment enact a law stripping an American of his citizenship which he has never voluntarily renounced or given up. The majority in *Perez* held that Congress could do this because withdrawal of citizenship is "reasonably calculated to effect the end that is within the power of Congress to achieve." That conclusion was reached by this chain of reasoning: Congress has an implied power to deal with foreign affairs as an indispensable attribute of sovereignty; this implied power, plus the Necessary and Proper Clause, empowers Congress to regulate voting by American citizens in foreign elections; involuntary expatriation is within the "ample scope" of "appropriate modes" Congress can adopt to effectuate its general regulatory power. Then, upon summarily concluding that "there is nothing . . . in the Fourteenth Amendment to warrant drawing from it a restriction upon the power otherwise possessed by Congress to withdraw citizenship," the majority specifically rejected the "notion that the power of Congress to terminate citizenship depends upon the citizen's assent."

First we reject the idea expressed in *Perez* that, aside from the Fourteenth Amendment, Congress has any general power, express or implied, to take away an American citizen's citizenship without his assent. This power cannot, as *Perez* indicated, be sustained as an implied attribute of sovereignty possessed by all nations. Other nations are governed by their own constitutions, if any, and we can draw no support from theirs. In our country the people are sovereign and the Government cannot sever its relationship to the people by taking away their citizenship. Our Constitution governs us and we must never forget that our Constitution limits the Government to those powers specifically granted or those that are necessary and proper to carry out the specifically granted ones. The Constitution, of course, grants Congress no express power to strip people of their citizenship, whether in the exercise of the implied power to regulate foreign affairs or in the exercise of any specifically granted power. And even before the adoption of the Fourteenth Amendment, views were expressed in Congress and by the Court that under the Constitution the Government was granted no power, even under its express power to pass a uniform rule of naturalization, to determine what conduct should and should not result in the loss of citizenship. On three occasions, in 1795, 1797, and 1818, Congress considered and rejected proposals to enact laws which would describe certain conduct as resulting in expatriation. . . . In 1795 and 1797, many members of Congress still adhered to the English doctrine of perpetual allegiance and doubted whether a citizen could even voluntarily renounce his citizenship. By 1818, however, almost no one doubted the existence of the right of voluntary expatriation, but several judicial decisions had indicated that the right could not be exercised by the citizen without the consent of the Federal Government in the form of enabling legislation. Therefore, a bill was introduced to provide that a person could voluntarily relinquish his citizenship by declaring such relinquishment in writing before a district court and then departing from the country. The opponents of the bill argued that Congress had no constitutional authority, either express or implied, either under

the Naturalization Clause or the Necessary and Proper Clause, to provide that a certain act would constitute expatriation. . . . The bill was finally defeated. It is in this setting that six years later, in *Osborn* v. *Bank of the United States* [1824], this Court, speaking through Chief Justice Marshall, declared in what appears to be a mature and well-considered dictim that Congress, once a person becomes a citizen, cannot deprive him of that status:

"[The naturalized citizen] becomes a member of the society, possessing all the rights of a native citizen, and standing, in the view of the constitution, on the footing of a native. The constitution does not authorize Congress to enlarge or abridge those rights. The simple power of the national Legislature, is to prescribe a uniform rule of naturalization, and the exercise of this power exhausts it, so far as respects the individual."

Although these legislative and judicial statements may be regarded as inconclusive and must be considered in the historical context in which they were made, any doubt as to whether prior to the passage of the Fourteenth Amendment Congress had the power to deprive a person against his will of citizenship once obtained should have been removed by the unequivocal terms of the Amendment itself. It provides its own constitutional rule in language calculated completely to control the status of citizenship: "All persons born or naturalized in the United States . . . are citizens of the United States . . . ." There is no indication in these words of a fleeting citizenship, good at the moment it is acquired but subject to destruction by the Government at any time. Rather the Amendment can most reasonably be read as defining a citizenship which a citizen keeps unless he voluntarily relinquishes it. Once acquired, this Fourteenth Amendment citizenship was not to be shifted, canceled, or diluted at the will of the Federal Government, the States, or any other governmental unit.

It is true that the chief interest of the people in giving permanence and security to citizenship in the Fourteenth Amendment was the desire to protect Negroes. The *Dred Scott* decision [1857] had shortly before greatly disturbed many people about the status of Negro citizenship. But the Civil Rights Act of 1866 had already attempted to confer citizenship on all persons born or naturalized in the United States. Nevertheless, when the Fourteenth Amendment passed the House without containing any definition of citizenship, the sponsors of the Amendment in the Senate insisted on inserting a constitutional definition and grant of citizenship. They expressed fears that the citizenship so recently conferred on Negroes by the Civil Rights Act could be just as easily taken away from them by subsequent Congresses, and it was to provide an insuperable obstacle against every governmental effort to strip Negroes of their newly acquired citizenship that the first clause was added to the Fourteenth Amendment. Senator Howard, who sponsored the Amendment in the Senate, thus explained the purpose of the clause:

"It settles the great question of citizenship and removes all doubt as to what persons are or are not citizens of the United States. . . . We desired to put this question of citizenship and the rights of citizens . . . under the civil rights bill beyond the legislative power. . . ."

This undeniable purpose of the Fourteenth Amendment to make citizenship of Negroes permanent and secure would be frustrated by holding that the Government can rob a citizen of his citizenship without his consent by simply proceeding to act under an implied general power to regulate foreign affairs or some other power generally granted. Though the framers of the Amendment were not particularly concerned with the problem of expatriation, it seems undeniable from the language they used that they wanted to put citizenship beyond the power of any governmental unit to destroy. In 1868, two years after the Fourteenth Amendment had been adopted, Congress specifically considered the subject of expatriation. . . .

The entire legislative history of the 1868 Act makes it abundantly clear that there was a strong feeling in the Congress that the only way the citizenship it conferred could be lost was by the voluntary renunciation or abandonment by the citizen himself. And this was the unequivocal statement of the Court in the case of *United States* v. *Wong Kim Ark* [1898]. The issues in that case were whether a person born in the United States to Chinese aliens was a citizen of the United States and whether, nevertheless, he could be excluded under the Chinese Exclusion Act. The Court first held that, within the terms of the Fourteenth Amendment, Wong Kim Ark was a citizen of the United States, and then pointed out that though he might "renounce this citizenship, and become a citizen of . . . any other country," he had never done so. The Court then held that Congress could not do anything to abridge or affect his citizenship conferred by the Fourteenth Amendment. Quoting Chief Justice Marshall's well-considered and oft-repeated dictum in *Osborn* to the effect that Congress under the power of naturalization has "a power to confer citizenship, not a power to take it away," the Court said:

"Congress having no power to abridge the rights conferred by the Constitution upon those who have become naturalized citizens by virtue of acts of Congress, a fortiori no act . . . of Congress . . . can affect citizenship acquired as a birthright, by virtue of the Constitution itself. . . . The Fourteenth Amendment, while it leaves the power, where it was before, in Congress, to regulate naturalization, has conferred no authority upon Congress to restrict the effect of birth, declared by the Constitution to constitute a sufficient and complete right to citizenship."

To uphold Congress' power to take away a man's citizenship because he voted in a foreign election in violation of § 401 (e) would be equivalent to holding that Congress has the power to "abridge," "affect," "restrict the effect of," and "take . . . away" citizenship. Because the Fourteenth Amendment prevents Congress from doing any of these things, we agree with the Chief Justice's dissent in the *Perez* case that the Government is without power to rob a citizen of his citizenship under § 401 (e).

Because the legislative history of the Fourteenth Amendment and the expatriation proposals which preceded and followed it, like most other legislative history, contains many statements from which conflicting inferences can be drawn, our holding might be unwarranted if it rested entirely or principally upon that legislative history. But it does not. Our holding we think is the only one that can stand in view of the language and the purpose of the Fourteenth Amendment, and our construction of that Amendment, we believe, comports more nearly than *Perez* with the principles of liberty and equal justice to all that the entire Fourteenth Amendment was adopted to guarantee. Citizenship is no light trifle to be jeop-ardized any moment Congress decides to do so under the name of one of its general or implied grants of power. In some instances, loss of citizenship can mean that a man is left without the protection of citizenship in any country in the world—as a man without a country. Citizenship in this Nation is a part of a cooperative affair. Its citizenry is the country and the country is its citizenry. The very nature of our free government makes it completely incongruous to have a rule of law under which a group of citizens temporarily in office can deprive another group of citizens of their citizenship. We hold that the Fourteenth Amendment was designed to, and does, protect every citizen of this Nation against a congressional forcible destruction of his citizenship, whatever his creed, color, or race. Our holding does no more than to give to this citizen that which is his own, a constitutional right to remain a citizen in a free country unless he voluntarily relinquishes that citizenship.

Perez v. *Brownell* is overruled. The judgment is

Reversed.

[MR. JUSTICE HARLAN, whom JUSTICES CLARK, STEWART, and WHITE joined, dissenting:]

Ten years ago, in *Perez v. Brownell,* the Court upheld the constitutionality of § 401 (e) of the Nationality Act of 1940. The section deprives of his nationality any citizen who has voted in a foreign political election. The Court reasoned that Congress derived from its power to regulate foreign affairs authority to expatriate any citizen who intentionally commits acts which may be prejudicial to the foreign relations of the United States, and which reasonably may be deemed to indicate a dilution of his allegiance to this country. Congress, it was held, could appropriately consider purposeful voting in a foreign political election to be such an act.

The Court today overrules *Perez,* and declares § 401 (e) unconstitutional, by a remarkable process of circumlocution. First, the Court fails almost entirely to dispute the reasoning in *Perez;* it is essentially content with the conclusory and quite unsubstantiated assertion that Congress is without "any general power, express or implied," to expatriate a citizen "without his assent."* Next, the Court embarks upon a lengthy, albeit incomplete, survey of the historical background to the congressional power at stake here, and yet, at the end, concedes that the history is susceptible to "conflicting inferences." The Court acknowledges that its conclusions might not be warranted by that history alone, and disclaims that the decision today relies, even "principally," upon it. Finally, the Court declares that its result is bottomed upon the "language and purpose" of the Citizenship Clause of the Fourteenth Amendment; in explanation, the Court offers only the terms of the clause itself, the contention that any other result would be "completely incongruous," and the essentially arcane observation that the "citizenry is the country and the country is its citizenry."

I can find nothing in this extraordinary series of circumventions which

---

* . . . Whatever the Court's position, it has assumed that voluntariness is here a term of fixed meaning; in fact, of course, it has been employed to describe both a specific intent to renounce citizenship, and the uncoerced commission of an act conclusively deemed by law to be a relinquishment of citizenship. Until the Court indicates with greater precision what it means by "assent," today's opinion will surely cause still greater confusion in this area of the law.

---

permits, still less compels, the imposition of this constitutional constraint upon the authority of Congress. I must respectfully dissent. . . . [T]he Court relies [on] a brief obiter dictum from the lengthy opinion for the Court in *Osborn* v. *Bank of the United States,* written by Mr. Chief Justice Marshall. This use of the dictum is entirely unpersuasive, for its terms and context make quite plain that it cannot have been intended to reach the questions presented here. The central issue before the Court in *Osborn* was the right of the bank to bring its suit for equitable relief in the courts of the United States. In argument, counsel for *Osborn* had asserted that although the bank had been created by the laws of the United States, it did not necessarily follow that any cause involving the bank had arisen under those laws. Counsel urged by analogy that the naturalization of an alien might as readily be said to confer upon the new citizen a right to bring all his actions in the federal courts. Not surprisingly, the Court rejected the analogy, and remarked that an act of naturalization "does not proceed to give, to regulate, or to prescribe his capacities," since the Constitution demands that naturalized citizens must in all respects stand "on the footing of a native." The Court plainly meant no more than that counsel's analogy is broken by Congress' inability to offer naturalized citizens rights or capacities which differ in any particular from those given to a native-born citizen by birth. Mr. Justice Johnson's discussion of the analogy in dissent confirms the Court's purpose. . . .

The most pertinent evidence from this period upon these questions has been entirely overlooked by the Court. Twice in the two years immediately prior to its passage of the Fourteenth Amendment, Congress exercised the very authority which the Court now suggests that it should have recognized was entirely lacking. In each case, a bill was debated and adopted by both Houses which included provisions to expatriate unwilling citizens.

In the spring and summer of 1864, both Houses debated intensively the Wade-Davis bill to provide reconstruction governments for the States which had seceded to form the Confederacy. Among the bill's provisions was § 14, by which "every person who shall hereafter hold or exercise any office . . . in the rebel service . . . is hereby declared not to be a citizen of the United States." . . . The bill was not signed by President Lincoln before the adjournment of Congress, and thus failed to become law, but a subsequent statement issued by Lincoln makes quite plain that he was not troubled by any doubts of the constitutionality of § 14. Passage of the Wade-Davis bill of itself "suffices to destroy the notion that the men who drafted the Fourteenth Amendment felt that citizenship was an 'absolute.' "

Twelve months later, and less than a year before its passage of the Fourteenth Amendment, Congress adopted a second measure which included provisions that permitted the expatriation of unwilling citizens. Section 21 of the Enrollment Act of 1865 provided that deserters from the military service of the United States "shall be deemed and taken to have voluntarily relinquished and forfeited their rights of citizenship and their rights to become citizens; . . . ." The bitterness of war did not cause Congress here to neglect the requirements of the Constitution; for it was urged in both Houses that § 21 as written was ex post facto, and thus was constitutionally impermissible. Significantly, however, it was never suggested in either debate that expatriation without a citizen's consent lay beyond Con-

gress' authority. . . . The pertinent evidence for the period prior to the adoption of the Fourteenth Amendment can therefore be summarized as follows. The Court's conclusion today is supported only by the statements, associated at least in part with a now abandoned view of citizenship, of three individual Congressmen, and by the ambiguous and inapposite dictum from *Osborn*. Inconsistent with the Court's position are statements from individual Congressmen in 1794, and Congress' passage in 1864 and 1865 of legislation which expressly authorized the expatriation of unwilling citizens. It may be that legislation adopted in the heat of war should be discounted in part by its origins, but, even if this is done, it is surely plain that the Court's conclusion is entirely unwarranted by the available historical evidence for the period prior to the passage of the Fourteenth Amendment. The evidence suggests, to the contrary, that Congress in 1865 understood that it had authority, at least in some circumstances, to deprive a citizen of his nationality.

II.

The evidence with which the Court supports its thesis that the Citizenship Clause of the Fourteenth Amendment was intended to lay at rest any doubts of Congress' inability to expatriate without the citizen's consent is no more persuasive. . . . The debate upon the clause was essentially cursory in both Houses, but there are several clear indications of its intended effect. Its sponsors evidently shared the fears of Senators Stewart and Wade that unless citizenship were defined, freedmen might, under the reasoning of the *Dred Scott* decision, be excluded by the courts from the scope of the Amendment. It was agreed that, since the "courts have stumbled on the subject," it would be prudent to remove the "doubt thrown over" it. The clause would essentially overrule *Dred Scott,* and place beyond question the freedmen's right of citizenship because of birth. . . . Nothing in the debates, however, supports the Court's assertion that the clause was intended to deny Congress its authority to expatriate unwilling citizens. The evidence indicates that its draftsmen instead expected the clause only to declare unreservedly to whom citizenship initially adhered. . . .

The narrow, essentially definitional purpose of the Citizenship Clause is reflected in the clear declarations in the debates that the clause would not revise the prevailing incidents of citizenship. . . . Senator Howard, in the first of the statements relied upon, in part, by the Court, said quite unreservedly that "This amendment [the Citizenship Clause] I have offered is simply declaratory of what I regard as the law of the land already, that every person born within the limits of the United States, and subject to their jurisdiction, is . . . a citizen of the United States." . . . It would be extraordinary if these prominent supporters of the Citizenship Clause could have imagined, as the Court's construction of the clause now demands, that the clause was only "declaratory" of the law "where it now is," and yet that it would entirely withdraw a power twice recently exercised by Congress in their presence.

There is, however, even more positive evidence that the Court's construction of the clause is not that intended by its draftsmen. Between the two brief statements from Senator Howard relied upon by the Court, Howard, in response to a question, said the following:

"I take it for granted that after a man becomes a citizen of the United States under the Constitution he cannot cease to be citizen, *except by* expatriation or *the commission of some crime by which his citizenship shall be forfeited.*" (Emphasis added.)

It would be difficult to imagine a more unqualified rejection of the Court's position; Senator Howard, the clause's sponsor, very plainly believed that it would leave unimpaired Congress' power to deprive unwilling citizens of their citizenship. . . .

The Citizenship Clause thus neither denies nor provides to Congress any power of expatriation; its consequences are, for present purposes, exhausted by its declaration of the classes of individuals to whom citizenship initially attaches. Once obtained, citizenship is of course protected from arbitrary withdrawal by the constraints placed around Congress' powers by the Constitution; it is not proper to create from the Citizenship Clause an additional, and entirely unwarranted, restriction upon legislative authority. The construction now placed on the Citizenship Clause rests, in the last analysis, simply on the Court's ipse dixit, evincing little more, it is quite apparent, than the present majority's own distaste for the expatriation power.

I believe that *Perez* was rightly decided, and on its authority would affirm the judgment of the Court of Appeals.

13
Freedom of Speech, Press, and Assembly

Along with freedom of religion, the First Amendment provides for freedom of speech and press. "Liberty of speech and liberty of press are substantially identical. They are freedom to utter words orally and freedom to write, print, and circulate words."[1] But this freedom of expression would be meaningless if people were not permitted to gather in groups to discuss mutual problems and communicate their feelings and opinions to governmental officers. The First Amendment therefore concludes by providing that the people have the right to assemble peaceably and petition the government for redress of grievances.

In the discussion that follows, two major points should be kept in mind:

1. The First Amendment restrictions applied *only* to Congress for many years. Only after the Supreme Court's expansion of the Fourteenth Amendment could the denial of First Amendment freedoms by the states be challenged in the federal courts.
2. Despite the fact that the First Amendment states categorically that Congress shall make *no* law abridging freedom of speech, the Court has never held that an individual is always entitled to say anything he

[1] Charles A. Beard, *The Republic* (New York: Viking, 1943), p. 153.

pleases, anyway he pleases, in any place he pleases, under any circumstances he pleases. Whether one adopts the most "absolute" interpretation of the First Amendment, as Justices Black and Douglas frequently have done, or read almost all meaning out of the amendment, as Justices Frankfurter and Judge Learned Hand sometimes did,[2] the issue is always just how much freedom of speech the Court is willing to read into the amendment.

The literature and court decisions on freedom of speech, press, and assembly are exceedingly vast and complex.[3] Cases dealing with the right to assemble peaceably are discussed under the major freedom of speech and press headings, because these rights are connected closely. "It was not by accident or coincidence that the rights to freedom in speech and press were coupled in a single guarantee with the rights of the people peaceably to assemble and to petition for redress of grievances. *All these, though not identical, are inseparable.* They are cognate rights."[4]

Early Development

The Supreme Court had little opportunity to clarify the free speech and press guaranties of the First Amendment for many years. The first congressional limitation on freedom of speech was made in the Sedition Act of 1798, only seven years after the adoption of the First Amendment. But the Sedition Act never came before the Supreme Court. In fact, no important case involving freedom of speech or press was decided by the Supreme Court prior to World War I. After that war, an important group of cases came before the Court as the result of convictions obtained under the Espionage Act of 1917 and the amendments to that law enacted in 1918 and known as the Sedition Act. These acts penalized many forms of utterances. Under their provisions, over 1,900 people were prosecuted for alleged subversion and criticism against the federal government. Many so-called radical publications were excluded from the mails, and other forms of suppression became commonplace because of the fears engendered by the war with Germany and the Russian Revolution of 1917. "The First Amendment had no hold on people's minds because no live facts or concrete images were then attached to it. Like an empty box with beautiful words on it, the Amendment collapsed under the impact of terror of Prussian battalions and terror of Bolshevik mobs. So the emotions generated

---

[2] See Learned Hand, *The Bill of Rights* (Cambridge: Harvard University Press, 1958).

[3] In general see Martin Shapiro, *Freedom of Speech: The Supreme Court and Judicial Review* (Englewood Cliffs, N.J.: Prentice-Hall, 1966); *Henry Abraham, Freedom and the Court* (London: Oxford University Press, 1967); Thomas I. Emerson, *Toward a General Theory of the First Amendment* (New York: Random House, 1966).

[4] *Thomas* v. *Collins,* 323 U.S. 516 (1944). (Italics supplied.)

by the two simultaneous cataclysms of war and revolution swept unchecked through American prosecutors, judges, jurymen, and legislators."[5]

CLEAR AND PRESENT DANGER

In the face of these developments it was soon evident that cases involving freedom of speech and press would eventually reach the Supreme Court. The first and most influential decision in terms of later developments was *Schenck* v. *United States* (p. 375). In this case Justice Holmes enunciated the famous "clear and present danger" test for determining the boundary between speech that can be protected by the Constitution and speech that can be punished. He stated:

> The question in every case is whether the words used are used in such circumstances and are of such a nature as to create a clear and present danger that they will bring about the substantive evils that Congress has a right to prevent. It is a question of proximity and degree. When a nation is at war many things that might be said in time of peace are such a hindrance to its effort that their utterance will not be endured so long as men fight and that no Court could regard them as protected by any constitutional right.

Despite the unanimous opinion in the *Schenck* case, the full implication of the clear and present danger test was not appreciated immediately by the majority of the Court. The test was used subsequently to justify convictions under the Espionage Act for the publication of twelve newspaper articles attacking the war[6] and for a speech attacking American participation in the war.[7] But the Court refused to follow the Holmes test in order to place limitations upon the government's power to abridge freedom of speech and press. As a result, both Justices Holmes and Brandeis dissented in three subsequent cases because they felt that the words used by the defendants had not created a clear and present danger to the United States.[8]

BAD TENDENCY TEST

"For twenty years it was an uphill fight to get acceptance of the clear and present danger doctrine by a majority of the Court."[9] In the meantime, the Court propounded the "remote possibility," or "bad tendency," test, which was less favorable to freedom of speech and press. That test was formulated in the *Gitlow* case, previously discussed in Chapter 12 in connection with Justice Stanford's dictum declaring that freedom of speech and press are

---

[5] Zechariah Chafee, Jr., *Thirty-five Years with Freedom of Speech* (New York: Roger N. Baldwin, Civil Liberties Foundation, 1952), p. 4.

[6] *Frohwerk* v. *United States,* 249 U.S. 204 (1919).

[7] *Debs* v. *United States,* 249 U.S. 211 (1919).

[8] *Abrams* v. *United States,* 250 U.S. 616 (1919); *Schaefer* v. *United States,* 251 U.S. 466 (1920); *Pierce* v. *United States,* 252 U.S. 239 (1920).

[9] Robert E. Cushman, *Civil Liberties in the United States* (Ithaca, N.Y.: Cornell University Press, 1956), p. 56.

protected against state infringement by the due process clause of the Four-teenth Amendment. Under the bad tendency test, a legislative body may suppress speech that *tends* to injure the government: It does not have to show that the speech or publication will produce a substantive evil such as an armed uprising or other acts of violence, but merely that the revolutionary doctrines are advocated. As noted in the *Gitlow* case, a state "cannot reason-ably be required to defer the adoption of measures for its own peace and safety until the revolutionary utterances lead to actual disturbances of the public peace or imminent and immediate danger of its own destruction; but it may, in the exercise of its judgment, suppress the threatened danger in its incipiency." But, after 1925, the Court could apply either the clear and pres-ent danger or the bad tendency test in cases involving First Amendment freedoms. The difficulty in applying the clear and present danger test is well illustrated by *Whitney* v. *California* (p. 381) where a conviction was sustained on grounds similar to those in the *Gitlow* case. Of particular importance in the *Whitney* case is the concurring opinion of Justice Brandeis, which is un-doubtedly one of the most powerful statements in behalf of freedom of expres-sion ever written in American history. Eventually, after 1937, the clear and present danger doctrine emerged as a more acceptable standard for judging the constitutionality of restrictions on freedom of speech, press, and assembly.

CRITICISM OF THE CLEAR AND PRESENT DANGER TEST

Although the clear and present danger test still retains much of its vitality, it has been criticized severely by Supreme Court judges and scholars in other fields. Justice Frankfurter was a virorous critic of the doctrine. The reasons for his rejection of clear and present danger are outlined in his concurring opinion in *Dennis* v. *United States* (Chapter 15). Chief Justice Hughes, who was devoted to the cause of civil liberties, never found it necessary to use the clear and present danger test. Neither did Chief Justice Stone utilize the Holmes test for rendering important civil rights decisions. Instead, both Justices Hughes and Stone resolved freedom of speech and press problems on due process grounds.

Perhaps the more severe critic of the clear and present danger doctrine—from a quite different point of view—has been the distinguished educator and philosopher, Alexander Meiklejohn. He has criticized the Holmes test as a "peculiarly inept and unsuccessful attempt to formulate an exception to the principle of the freedom of speech."[10] This criticism is premised on Meikle-john's conviction that freedom of speech on public issues is an *absolute* con-cept. He feels that *everyone* should be able to speak freely on public matter. "There are no exceptions—Communists, Socialists, Fascists, Democrats, Republicans, the foolish, the wise, the dangerous, the safe, those who wish to overthrow the state, those who wish to keep it as it is. There is no reason

[10] Alexander Meiklejohn, *Free Speech and Its Relation to Self-Government* (New York: Harper & Row, 1948), p. 50.

to curb freedom of speech in time of danger or in war. Justice Holmes and the doctrine of clear and present danger are simply wrong. The time of danger is exactly the time to show people that you mean what you say."[11]

The distinguished scholar, Professor Zechariah Chafee, Jr., answered this rather idealistic view as follows:

> Even if Holmes had agreed with Mr. Meiklejohn's view of the First Amendment, his insistence on such absolutism would not have persuaded a single colleague, and scores of men would have gone to prison who have been speaking freely for three decades. The true alternative to Holmes's view of the First Amendment was not at all the perfect immunity for public discussion which Mr. Meiklejohn desires. It was no immunity at all in the face of legislation. Any danger, any tendency in speech to produce bad acts, no matter how remote, would suffice to validate a repressive statute, and the only hope for speakers and writers would lie in being tried by liberal jurymen. What would happen to unpopular discussion is plainly shown by the Espionage Act trials in World War I.[12]

Freedom of Speech and Press After 1930

Although the 1920s witnessed a remarkable growth in the forces of tolerance, the trend of Supreme Court decisions was to uphold the authority of the states and the federal government to restrict freedom of speech and press. This was the situation in 1930 when President Hoover named Charles Evans Hughes to replace Chief Justice Taft, who had resigned. "It was a crucial moment in the development of constitutional safeguards for civil liberty when Hughes returned to the bench. Even such basic rights as freedom of speech and press seemed to hang by a slender thread when challenged by state governments. . . . [Under the powerful influence of the new Chief Justice], the pendulum might easily have swung backward or forward. His decision to push it vigorously forward is one of the most significant facts in our recent constitutional history."[13]

In three decisions rendered in 1931, the new Chief Justice revealed clearly his desire to uphold freedom of speech and press against governmental action. "Something new and astonishing had happened. What had been the lonely views of Justices Holmes and Brandeis were becoming the views of the majority of the Supreme Court."[14] The most important of the three decisions

---

[11] Harold Taylor, "Meiklejohn: The Art of Making People Think," *The New York Times Magazine* (May 5, 1957), p. 20. See also Alexander Meiklejohn, "The First Amendment Is Absolute," *The Supreme Court Review* (1961), p. 245.

[12] Zechariah Chafee, Jr., in his review of Meiklejohn's book cited in note 10, *Harvard Law Review,* Vol. 62 (1949), pp. 900–01.

[13] Merlo J. Pusey, *Charles Evans Hughes* (New York: Macmillan, 1951), Vol. 2, pp. 717–18.

[14] Zechariah Chafee, Jr., *Free Speech in the United States* (Cambridge: Harvard University Press, 1942), p. 362.

was *Near* v. *Minnesota,* for it was the Court's first great decision on censorship of publications.[15] In the *Near* case the Court for the first time obliterated *completely* a state law under the guarantee of liberty clause of the Fourteenth Amendment. In the process it delivered a ringing denunciation of prior restraint, that is the suppression of writing by a censor before its publication rather than its subsequent punishment.

PREFERRED-POSITION DOCTRINE

The pattern established by the Hughes Court for the protection of freedom of speech and press was continued and expanded by the new justices appointed by President Roosevelt. After 1937, the Court became reluctant to declare laws regulating social and economic activities unconstitutional, but at the same time it began to strike down legislative encroachments on personal freedoms. The Roosevelt Court, which included such staunch supporters of civil and political rights as Justices Black, Douglas, Murphy, Stone, and Rutledge, reactivated the doctrine of clear and present danger. At the same time some members of the Court developed the corollary preferred-position concept. This doctrine meant simply that laws restricting freedom of speech, press, religion, and assembly were not to be presumed constitutional. This reversed the traditional principle that all laws are presumed valid by the courts until it is proved beyond all reasonable doubt that the Constitution has been violated. Thus, the preferred-position doctrine shifted the burden of proof to those who defended legislation restricting First Amendment freedoms. They had to convince the Court that the restrictive legislation was indispensable or justified by some clear and present danger to the public security.

Justices Murphy and Rutledge were the most vigorous exponents of the preferred-position doctrine. Perhaps the most extreme statement of the doctrine was made by Justice Rutledge in *Thomas* v. *Collins,* previously cited, where the Court held that a state law that required all labor organizers to secure permits before soliciting members for their unions violated the First and Fourteenth Amendments. Justice Rutledge stated as follows in reference to preferential rights:

> This case confronts us again with the duty our system places on this Court to say where the individual's freedom ends and the State's power begins. Choice on that border, now as always delicate, is perhaps more so where the usual presumption supporting legislation is balanced by the preferred place given in our scheme to the great, the indispensable democratic freedoms secured by the

---

[15] The two other decisions are *Stromberg* v. *California,* 283 U.S. 359 (1931), and *United States* v. *Macintosh,* discussed in Chapter 12 in connection with citizenship. Chief Justice Hughes wrote the majority opinion in the *Stromberg* case, which invalidated a state statute prohibiting the display of a red flag as a symbol of opposition to organized government because it was too vague and uncertain. He wrote the dissenting opinion in the *Macintosh* case. Justices Holmes, Brandeis, and Stone joined him in that opinion.

First Amendment. That priority gives these liberties a sanctity and a sanction not permitting dubious intrusions.

For these reasons any attempt to restrict those liberties must be justified by clear public interest, threatened not doubtfully or remotely, but by clear and present danger. The rational connection between the remedy provided and the evil to be curbed, which in other contexts might support legislation against attack on due process grounds, will not suffice. These rights rest on firmer foundation.

For more than a decade after 1937, the Supreme Court continued to strike down governmental restrictions on First Amendment rights. Thus, with the exception of the cases involving the treatment of Japanese-Americans during World War II, the Court emerged as a vigorous protector of individual rights in case after case. Some of these cases, such as *Thomas* v. *Collins,* have already been examined. In addition, the Court brought peaceful picketing in labor disputes under the protection of the First Amendment in *Thornhill* v. *Alabama,* 310 U.S. 88 (1940), and several subsequent decisions. A notable victory for freedom of assembly came in *Hague* v. *Committee for Industrial Organization,* 307 U.S. 496 (1939), where the Court invalidated a Jersey City ordinance that forbade all public assemblies in streets and parks without a permit from the local director of public safety. The Court reasoned that the ordinance did not make ". . . comfort or convenience in the use of streets or parks the standard of official action. It enables the Director of Safety to refuse a permit on his mere opinion that such refusal will prevent riots, disturbances, or disorderly assemblage. It can thus be made the instrument of arbitrary suppression of free expression of views on national affairs, for the prohibition of all speaking will undoubtedly 'prevent' such eventualities. But uncontrolled official suppression of the privilege cannot be made a substitute for the duty to maintain order in connection with the exercise of the right."

In *Bridges* v. *California,* 314 U.S. 252 (1941), the Court reversed convictions for contempt of court imposed on a labor leader and several newspaper editors because they had published critical comments concerning pending litigation involving a labor dispute. The Court reasoned that the publications did not present a clear and present danger to the orderly administration of justice. Therefore, they were within the permissible limits of free discussion. A similar decision was reached in *Pennekamp* v. *Florida,* 328 U.S. 331 (1946).

The Court's use of the clear and present danger test during this period is demonstrated well by the controversial holding in *Terminiello* v. *Chicago* (p. 387). The *Terminiello* case raised fundamental issues concerning the maintenance of public order, but it did not supply a weighty precedent. Cases of this type must be decided on the basis of the *actual* facts (if they can be unravelled by the appellate courts) surrounding the particular speech. In *Feiner* v. *New York,* 340 U.S. 315 (1951), the Court upheld the conviction of a young university student for making remarks on a city street corner that seemed to stir up much less excitement and disorder than that evoked by the *Terminiello* speech.

Feiner marks the beginning of the period when Justice Frankfurter's philosophy of judicial self-restraint dominated the Court. He rejected the preferred-position doctrine after an exhaustive review of its history, because it expressed "a complicated process of constitutional adjudication by a deceptive formula."[16] With the deaths of Justices Murphy and Rutledge in 1949, and their subsequent replacement by Justices Clark and Minton, only Justices Black and Douglas remained as active supporters of the preferred-position doctrine. After 1949, most of the justices preferred to examine restrictive statutes on the basis of reasonableness, with the presumption that all such laws were valid until proven otherwise.

The low point of the Court's concern for freedom of speech comes with *Dennis* v. *United States* (Chapter 15), in which the justices abandoned the clear and present danger rule for something close to the old, bad tendency test, and *Barenblatt* v. *United States* (Chapter 15), in which the Court in effect held that Congress could infringe upon freedom of speech if it had a good reason to.

The Warren Court reversed this tendency in a number of cases dealing with subversion to be discussed and presented in Chapter 15 along with *Dennis* and *Barenblatt*. Both the clear and present danger test and the preferred-position doctrine have reappeared in majority opinions as well as in an inclination to strike down statutes interfering with speech if they are vague or if their purpose could have been achieved by a more narrowly drawn statute that would have avoided infringing on speech rights. In *Lamont* v. *Postmaster General,* 381 U.S. 301 (1965), the Supreme Court for the first time struck down a congressional statute on First Amendment grounds, and it has recently been acutely sensitive to state attempts to penalize dissent.

DEMONSTRATIONS, SIT-INS, AND CIVIL DISOBEDIENCE

At the present time, freedom of speech problems arise most acutely in connection with the civil rights movement and other social protest demonstrations. The Court had little difficulty striking down crude Southern attempts to block sit-ins and other demonstrations through disturbing-the-peace prosecutions. [See *Garner* v. *Louisiana,* 368 U.S. 157 (1961) and *Edwards* v. *South Carolina,* 372 U.S. 229 (1963).] Subsequently, it was able to avoid crucial issues raised by sit-ins as, in a series of cases, it found that new federal and local statutes desegregating public facilities undercut prosecutions that had been begun before the new laws were passed. [See *Bell* v. *Maryland,* 378 U.S. 226 (1964) and *Hamm* v. *Rock Hill,* 379 U.S. 306 (1964).] However, the Court was eventually faced squarely with the major issue of

---

[16] Concurring opinion in *Kovacs* v. *Cooper,* 336 U.S. 77 (1949). Some writers trace the origin of the preferred-position doctrine to a remark made by Justice Stone in *United States* v. *Carolene Products Co.,* 304 U.S. 144 (1938).

whether demonstrators might be barred from state and private property; that is, whether freedom of speech entitled the speaker to trespass and obstruct the normal operations of business and government. In *Cox* v. *Louisiana,* 379 U.S. 536, 559 (1965) the Court upheld a state law forbidding demonstrations near a courthouse, although it managed to find grounds for reversing the convictions of the picketers. In *Adderley* v. *Florida* (p. 392) it holds that the state need not open all its property to demonstrators who may disrupt its lawful operations. And, in *Walker* v. *Birmingham,* 388 U.S. 307 (1967) it confirmed earlier dicta to the effect that the First Amendment did not protect those who deliberately violated valid laws in the course of social protest.

In this whole area, where the right to be protected from trespassers intersects freedom of speech, Justice Black, an ardent defender of the First Amendment, has played a crucial role, with his vote sometimes being decisive in holding against speakers who have violated others' rights to make use of their property. It is best to let him speak for himself.

> Their argument comes down to this: that . . . they had a perfect constitutional right to assemble and remain in the restaurant, over the owner's continuing objections, for the purpose of expressing themselves by language and "demonstrations" bespeaking their hostility to Hooper's refusal to serve Negroes. . . . Unquestionably, petitioners had a constitutional right to express these views wherever they had an unquestioned legal right to be. But there is the rub. . . . The right to freedom of expression is a right to express views—not a right to force other people to supply a platform or a pulpit.
>
> A great purpose of freedom of speech and press is to provide a forum for settlement of acrimonious disputes peaceably, without resort to intimidation, force, or violence. The experience of ages points to the inexorable fact that people are frequently stirred to violence when property which the law recognizes as theirs is forcibly invaded or occupied by others. Trespass laws are born of this experience. . . . The Constitution does not confer upon any group the right to substitute rule by force for rule by law. Force leads to violence, violence to mob conflicts, and these to rule by the strongest groups with control of the most deadly weapons. [Dissenting in *Bell* v. *Maryland,* 378 U.S. 343, 344–46 (1964).]

Food Employees Local 509 v. *Logan Valley Plaza, Inc.* (p. 397) indicates just how complicated the problem can be and that the Court is likely to take a position toward demonstrators somewhat different from what a reading of *Adderley* alone would suggest. The Court has now held that public school students may exercise some measure of freedom of speech on school campuses, but warned that the First Amendment does not protect activities that interfere with instruction [*Tinker* v. *Des Moines Independent Community School District,* 89 S.Ct. 733 (1969)]. It has also dealt with statutes prohibiting desecration of the flag and threatening the life of the President in such a way as to protect extravagant and abusive speech without hampering government's power to curb riotous conduct. [*Street* v. *New York,* 89 S.Ct. 1354 (1969); *Watts* v. *United States,* 89 S.Ct. 1399 (1969).]

It is likely that the Court will now become seriously involved in the problem of campus protests and other disorder, probably applying something like the clear and present danger rule.

THE EXCLUDED AREAS

In the 1940s and early 1950s, several justices, in the course of trying to show that freedom of speech was not absolutely unlimited, rather casually and often in *dicta,* argued that obscene or libelous statements were not protected by the First Amendment. They also added "fighting words" to the excluded categories. (See p. 434.) These holdings paved the way for the Court's decision, in *Roth* v. *United States,* 354 U.S. 476 (1957), that obscene speech was not protected because it was "utterly without redeeming social importance." The test to determine if a given work is obscene was "whether to the average person, applying contemporary community standards, the dominant theme of the material taken as a whole appeals to prurient interest (i.e., material having a tendency to excite lustful thought)."

Since announcing this test, which authorizes the government to engage in thought control, the Court has faced a long series of obscenity decisions, none of which has been particularly logical or enlightening. It has tacitly abandoned the *Roth* test of obscenity for something close to a hard-core pornography standard, although the justices cannot agree on exactly what that standard is. Material with any redeeming social importance is probably not obscene (even though taken as a whole it appeals to prurient interest). Even material without any social importance may not be obscene if it does not go substantially beyond the limits of candor prevalent in the community (even though it excites lustful thoughts). On the other hand, a man may go to jail for acting like a dirty book peddler even if the book peddled turns out not to be dirty. Although the high point of confusion seemed to be *Jacobelis* v. *Ohio,* 378 U.S. 184 (1964), in which no more than two justices could agree on any given test, the Court seems to have topped itself in three obscenity cases decided in 1966: *A Book* v. *Attorney General* (p. 409); *Ginzburg* v. *United States* (p. 404), and *Mishkin* v. *New York,* 383 U.S. 502 (1966). The Court has also held that states may place greater restrictions on materials sold to minors than those sold to adults. [*Ginsberg* v. *New York,* 390 U.S. 629 (1968). *Note:* Do not confuse this case with *Ginzburg* v. *United States.*] and that mere private possession of obscene materials cannot be a crime. [*Stanley* v. *Georgia,* 89 S.Ct. 1243 (1969).]

In *Burstyn* v. *Wilson,* 343 U.S. 495 (1952), the Court reversed a long-standing decision and ruled that motion pictures are within the free speech and free press guarantees of the First and Fourteenth Amendments—but it has since turned out that the justices did not quite mean it. As the Court pointed out long ago in the landmark *Near* decision, prior restraint (censorship that prevents the utterance from occurring rather than attempting to punish the speaker after the speech) is particularly abhorrent to our traditions of liberty. Yet, the Court has now authorized prior restraint of motion pictures, albeit under strict standards designed to insure speech against arbitrary official action, in *Freedman* v. *Maryland* (p. 415). Moreover, motion picture censorship is allegedly aimed at obscene films, and obscenity is still officially excluded from First Amendment protection. So, by and large, the motion picture "speaker" is still not as free to speak as the rest of us.

The other major excluded area is libel. [See *Beauharnais* v. *Illinois,* 343 U.S. 250 (1952), upholding a group libel statute forbidding derogatory statements about racial, religious, or other similar groups.] But in the important case of *The New York Times* v. *Sullivan* (p. 419), certain kinds of libelous speech are held to be protected by the First Amendment. In a series of decisions since *The New York Times* case, the Court has indicated that the decision applies not only to elected officials, but to appointed ones who make governmental policy (although not to the lowest ranges of civil servants), and to figures of public interest, even those who hold no official governmental position. The Court has also indicated that the question of "reckless disregard" may rest on judicial evaluation of whether there was serious deviation from normal news gathering and editorial practices. [See *Rosenblatt* v. *Baer,* 383 U.S. 75 (1966); *Garrison* v. *Louisiana,* 379 U.S. 64 (1964); *Curtis Publishing Co.* v. *Butts,* 388 U.S. 130 (1967); and *Time, Inc.* v. *Hill,* 385 U.S. 374 (1967).]

FREE SPEECH AND THE JUDICIAL PROCESS

The old issue of press coverage and comment on trials raised in the *Bridges* and *Pennekamp* cases mentioned earlier has returned to the Court in *Sheppard* v. *Maxwell,* 384 U.S. 33 (1966) and *Estes* v. *Texas,* 381 U.S. 532 (1965). In these cases the Court reversed the convictions of two famous defendants, Dr. Samuel Sheppard and Billy Sol Estes, because of "disruptive" activities in the courtroom by newsmen (*Sheppard*) and television personnel (*Estes*). The American Bar Association has recently recommended a new set of rules governing release of information to the press by judges and attorneys. These recommendations have been adopted by some courts and vigorously opposed by much of the press so that future litigation is to be expected. On the other hand, the Supreme Court has now recognized that the planning and conducting of litigation is itself a political right protected by the First Amendment. [*NAACP* v. *Alabama* (p. 423).] The decision is interesting because of the Court's frank avowal that litigation is a political activity. *Cox* v. *Louisiana,* discussed earlier, should also be born in mind in connection with the judicial process and freedom of speech as should the problem of the judge's contempt power to punish demonstrators.

THE RIGHT OF ASSOCIATION

The right of association "is central to any serious conception of constitutional democracy. In the big states of modern times the individual cannot function politically with any measure of effectiveness unless he is free to associate with others without hindrance. In fact, most people find much of their identity, in either economic, social, political, professional or confessional terms, in some form of group activity. . . . It follows that government has an obligation to protect the right of association from invasion, and to refrain from making inroads into that right through its own activities."[18] Even though the right of association has long been assumed to be protected by the First Amendment through the due process clause of the Fourteenth Amendment, there were very few cases on the subject until recent years, when associational rights began to be seriously challenged. The challenge has come chiefly from federal statutes dealing with subversive organizations and the attempt of many Southern states to impede the activities of the NAACP, which has spearheaded the drive of the Negro for equal rights. As indicated in Chapter 16, although the Court has not issued a direct First Amendment challenge to the registration and punishment of members of subversive organizations under the provisions of the various federal security statutes, or to the exposure of subversives by legislative investigation, it has very narrowly circumscribed the kind of membership that may be punished, blocked registration by self-incrimination rulings, and severly limited investigating committee inquiry in all areas where subversion is not clearly and directly involved. The Court has blunted the attempts of the Southern states to cripple the NAACP and thereby defended important rights of association. This is revealed clearly by the significant case of *NAACP* v. *Alabama* (p. 423), where the Court stressed the importance of the freedom to associate in holding that Alabama could not compel the disclosure of the membership lists of organizations, such as the NAACP, that were pursuing lawful ends.

Since the decision in *NAACP* v. *Alabama,* the Court has consistently defended freedom of association.[19] In holding void another more recent attempt by Virginia to curb the activities of the NAACP, Justice Brennan concluded that the Constitution "protects expression and association without regard to the race, creed, or political or religious affiliation of the members of the group which invokes its shield, or to the truth, popularity, or social utility of the ideas and beliefs which are offered."[20] In many of these cases the key question is "anonymous" association—the right of individuals to engage in group political activities without having to tell the government what organizations they do or do not belong to. This right to anonymity is also protected by the Court in *Talley* v. *California,* 362 U.S. 60 (1960), where the Court struck down an ordinance prohibiting the distribution of anonymously printed hand bills.

---

[18] David Fellman, *The Constitutional Right of Association* (Chicago: University of Chicago Press, 1963), p. 104.

[19] *Bates* v. *City of Little Rock,* 361 U.S. 516 (1960); *Shelton* v. *Tucker,* 364 U.S. 479 (1960); *Louisiana* ex rel *Gremillion* v. *NAACP,* 366 U.S. 293 (1961).

[20] *NAACP* v. *Button,* 371 U.S. 415 (1963).

SCHENCK *v.* UNITED STATES
249 U.S. 47; 39 Sup. Ct. 247; 63 L. Ed. 470 (1919)

[*Charles T. Schenck, the general secretary of the Socialist party, and another party member were indicted under the Espionage Act of 1917 for sending out, to men called to military service, 15,000 leaflets urging them to resist the draft. The impassioned language of the leaflets is noted in the subsequent opinion. After conviction in a federal district court, the case went to the Supreme Court on a writ of error.*]

MR. JUSTICE HOLMES delivered the opinion of the court.

. . . The defendants . . . set up the First Amendment to the Constitution, forbidding Congress to make any law abridging the freedom of speech or of the press, and, bringing the case here on that ground, have argued some other points also of which we must dispose. . . .

The document in question, upon its first printed side, recited the First section of the Thirteenth Amendment, said that the idea embodied in it was violated by the Conscription Act, and that a conscript is little better than a convict. In impassioned language it intimated that conscription was despotism in its worst form and a monstrous wrong against humanity, in the interest of Wall Street's chosen few. It said: "Do not submit to intimidation"; but in form at least confined itself to peaceful measures, such as a petition for the repeal of the act. The other and later printed side of the sheet was headed, "Assert Your Rights." It stated reasons for alleging that anyone violated the Constitution when he refused to recognize "your right to assert your opposition to the draft," and went on: "If you do not assert and support your rights, you are helping to deny or disparage rights which it is the solemn duty of all citizens and residents of the United States to retain." It described the arguments on the other side as coming from cunning politicians and a mercenary capitalist press, and even silent consent to the Conscription Law as helping to support an infamous conspiracy. It denied the power to send our citizens away to foreign shores to shoot up the people of other lands, and added that words could not express the condemnation such cold-blooded ruthlessness deserves, etc., etc., winding up, "You must do your share to maintain, support, and uphold the rights of the people of this country." Of course the document would not have been sent unless it had been intended to have some effect, and we do not see what effect it could be expected to have upon persons subject to the draft except to influence them to obstruct the carrying of it out. The defendants do not deny that the jury might find against them on this point.

But it is said, suppose that that was the tendency of this circular, it is protected by the First Amendment to the Constitution. Two of the strongest expressions are said to be quoted respectively from well-known public men. It well may be that the prohibition of laws abridging the freedom of speech is not confined to previous restraints, although to prevent them may have been the main purpose. . . . We admit that in many places and in ordinary times the defendants, in saying all that was said in the circular, would have been within their constitutional rights. But the character of every act depends upon the circumstances in which it is done. . . .

The most stringent protection of free speech would not protect a man in falsely shouting fire in a theater, and causing a panic. It does not even protect a man from an injunction against uttering words that may have all the effect of force. . . . The question in every case is whether the words used are used in such circumstances and are of such a nature as to create a clear and present danger that they will bring about the substantive evils that Congress has a right to prevent. It is a question of proximity and degree. When a nation is at war many things that might be said in time of peace are such a hindrance to its effort that their utter-ance will not be endured so long as men fight, and that no court could regard them as protected by any constitutional right. It seems to be admitted that if an actual obstruction of the recruiting service were proved, liability for words that produced the effect might be enforced. The Statute of 1917, in Section 4, punishes conspiracies to obstruct as well as actual obstruction. If the act (speaking, or circulating a paper), its tendency and the intent with which it is done, are the same, we perceive no ground for saying that success alone warrants making the act a crime. . . .

Judgments affirmed.

GITLOW *v.* NEW YORK
268 U.S. 652; 45 Sup. Ct. 629; 69 L. Ed. 1138 (1925)

[Benjamin Gitlow, a member of the leftwing section of the Socialist party, was convicted and sentenced to prison in the Supreme Court of New York for violation of the State's Criminal Anarchy Act of 1902. As noted here, Gitlow was convicted for having published and circulated papers and leaflets advocating the overthrow of the organized government by force, violence, and other unlawful means. His conviction was affirmed by the Appellate Division and by the New York Court of Appeals (the highest state court). Gitlow then brought the case to the Supreme Court on a writ of error.]

MR. JUSTICE SANFORD delivered the opinion of the Court, saying in part:

. . . The contention here is that the statute, by its terms and as applied in this case, is repugnant to the due process clause of the Fourteenth Amendment. Its material provisions are:

"Section 160. Criminal anarchy defined.—Criminal anarchy is the doctrine that organized government should be overthrown by force or violence, or by assassination of the executive head or of any of the executive officials of government, or by any unlawful means. The advocacy of such doctrine either by words of mouth or writing is a felony.

"Section 161. Advocacy of criminal anarchy.—Any person who:

"1. By word of mouth or writing advocates, advises or teaches the duty, necessity or propriety of overthrowing or overturning organized government by force or violence, or by assassination of the executive head or of any of the executive officials of government, or by any unlawful means; or,

"2. Prints, publishes, edits, issues or knowingly circulates, sells, distributes or publicly displays any book, paper, document, or written or printed matter in any form, containing or advocating, advising or teaching the doctrine that organized government should be overthrown by force, violence or any unlawful means . . . ,

"Is guilty of a felony and punishable" by imprisonment or fine, or both.

The indictment was in two counts. The first charged that the defendants had advocated, advised, and taught the duty, necessity, and propriety of overthrowing and overturning organized government by force, violence, and unlawful means, by certain writings therein set forth, entitled, "The Left Wing Manifesto"; the second, that the defendants had printed, published, and knowingly circulated and distributed a certain paper called "The Revolutionary Age," containing the writings set forth in the first count, advocating, advising, and teaching the doctrine that organized government should be overthrown by force, violence, and unlawful means.

. . . It was admitted that the defendant signed a card subscribing to the Manifesto and Program of the Left Wing, which all applicants were required to sign before being admitted to membership; that he went to different parts of the state to speak to branches of the Socialist party about the principles of the Left Wing, and advocated their adoption; and that he was responsible [as business manager] for the Manifesto as it appeared, that "he knew of the publication, in a general way, and he knew of its publication afterwards, and is responsible for its circulation."

There was no evidence of any effect resulting from the publication and circulation of the Manifesto.

No witnesses were offered in behalf of the defendant. . . .

Coupled with a review of the rise of Socialism, it [the Manifesto] condemned the dominant "moderate Socialism" for its recognition of the necessity of the democratic parliamentary state; repudiated its policy of introducing Socialism by legislative measures; and advocated, in plain and unequivocal language, the necessity of accomplishing the "Communist Revolution: by a militant and "revolutionary Socialism," based on "the class struggle" and mobilizing the "power of the proletariat in action," through mass industrial revolts developing into mass political strikes and "revolutionary mass action," for the purpose of conquering and destroying the parliamentary state and establishing in its place, through a "revolutionary dictatorship of the proletariat," the system of Communist Socialism. The then-recent strikes in Seattle and Winnipeg were cited as instances of a development already verging on revolutionary action and suggestive of proletarian dictatorship, in which the strike workers were "trying to usurp the functions of municipal government"; and Revolutionary Socialism, it was urged, must use these mass industrial revolts to broaden the strike, make it general and militant, and develop it into mass political strikes and revolutionary mass action for the annihilation of the parliamentary state.

. . . The sole contention here is, essentially, that, as there was no evidence of any concrete result flowing from the publication of the Manifesto, or of circumstances showing the likelihood of such result, the statute as construed and applied by the trial court penalizes the mere utterance, as such, of "doctrine having no quality of incitement, without regard either to the circumstances of its utterance or to the likelihood of unlawful sequences; and that, as the exercise of the right of free expression with relation to government is only punishable "in circumstances involving likelihood of substantive evil," the statute contravenes the due process clause of the Fourteenth Amendment.

The argument in support of this contention rests primarily upon the following propositions: first, that the "liberty" protected by the Fourteenth Amendment includes the liberty of speech and of the press; and second, that while liberty of expression "is not absolute," it may be restrained "only in circumstances where its exercise bears a causal relation with some substantive evil, consummated, attempted, or likely"; and as the statute "takes no account of circumstances," it unduly restrains this liberty, and is therefore unconstitutional.

The precise question presented, and the only question which we can consider under this writ of error, then, is whether the statute, as construed and applied in this case by the state courts, deprived the defendant of his liberty of expression, in violation of the due process clause of the Fourteenth Amendment.

The statute does not penalize the utterance or publication of abstract "doctrine" or academic discussion having no quality of incitement to any concrete action. It is not aimed against mere historical or philosophical essays. It does not restrain the advocacy of changes in the form of government by constitutional and lawful means. What it prohibits is language advocating, advising, or teaching the overthrow of organized government by unlawful means. These words imply urging to action. Advocacy is defined in the Century Dictionary as: "1. The act of pleading for, supporting, or recommending; active espousal." It is not the abstract "doctrine" of overthrowing organized government by unlawful means which is denounced by the statute, but the advocacy of action for the accomplishment of that purpose. . . .

The Manifesto, plainly, is neither the statement of abstract doctrine nor, as suggested by counsel, mere prediction that industrial disturbances and revolutionary mass strikes will result spontaneously in an inevitable process of evolution in the economic system. It advocates and urges in fervent language mass action which shall progressively foment industrial disturbances, and, through political mass strikes and revolutionary mass action, overthrow and destroy organized parliamentary government. It concludes with a call to action in these words: "The proletariat revolution and the Communist reconstruction of society—the struggle for these—is now indispensable. . . . The Communist International calls the proletariat of the world to the final struggle!" This is not the expression of philosophical abstraction, the mere prediction of future events: it is the language of direct incitement.

The means advocated for bringing about the destruction of organized parliamentary government, namely, mass industrial revolts usurping the functions of municipal government, political mass strikes directed against the parliamentary state, and revolutionary mass action for its final destruction, necessarily imply the use of force and violence, and in their essential nature are inherently unlawful in a constitutional government of law and order. That the jury were warranted in finding that the Manifesto advocated not merely the abstract doctrine of overwhelming organized government by force, violence, and unlawful means, but action to that end, is clear.

For present purposes we may and do assume that freedom of speech and of the press—which are protected by the First Amendment from abridgment by Congress—are among the fundamental personal rights and "liberties" protected by the due process clause of the Fourteenth Amendment from impairment by the states. . . .

It is a fundamental principle, long

established, that freedom of speech and of the press which is secured by the Constitution does not confer an absolute right to speak or publish, without responsibility, whatever one may choose, or an unrestricted and unbridled license that gives immunity for every possible use of language, and prevents the punishment of those who abuse this freedom. . . .

That a state, in the exercise of its police power, may punish those who abuse this freedom by utterances inimical to the public welfare, tending to corrupt public morals, incite to crime, or disturb the public peace, is not open to question. . . .

And, for yet more imperative reasons, a state may punish utterances endangering the foundations of organized government and threatening its overthrow by unlawful means. These imperil its own existence as a constitutional state. Freedom of speech and press, said Story . . . does not protect disturbances of the public peace or the attempt to subvert the government. It does not protect publications or teachings which tend to subvert or imperil the government, or to impede or hinder it in the performance of its governmental duties. . . . It does not protect publications promoting the overthrow of government by force; the punishment of those who publish articles which tend to destroy organized society being essential to the security of freedom and the stability of the state. . . . And a state may penalize utterances which openly advocate the overthrow of the representative and constitutional form of government of the United States and the several states, by violence or other unlawful means. . . . In short, this freedom does not deprive a state of the primary and essential right of self-preservation. . . .

By enacting the present statute the state has determined, through its legislative body, that utterances advocating the overthrow of organized government by force, violence, and unlawful means, are so inimical to the general welfare, and involve such danger of substantive evil, that they may be penalized in the exercise of its police power. That determination must be given great weight. Every presumption is to be indulged in favor of the validity of the statute. . . . That utterances inciting to the overflow of organized government by unlawful means present a sufficient danger of substantive evil to bring their punishment within the range of legislative discretion is clear. Such utterances, by their very nature, involve danger to the public peace and to the security of the state. They threaten breaches of the peace and ultimate revolution. And the immediate danger is none the less real and substantial because the effect of a given utterance cannot be accurately foreseen. The state cannot reasonably be required to measure the danger from every such utterance in the nice balance of a jeweler's scale. A single revolutionary spark may kindle a fire that, smoldering for a time, may burst into a sweeping and destructive conflagration. It cannot be said that the state is acting arbitrarily or unreasonably when, in the exercise of its judgment as to the measures necessary to protect the public peace and safety, it seeks to extinguish the spark without waiting until it has enkindled the flame or blazed into the conflagration. It cannot reasonably be required to defer the adoption of measures for its own peace and safety until the revolutionary utterances lead to actual disturbances of the public peace or imminent and immediate danger of its own destruction; but it may, in the exercise of its judgment, suppress the threatened danger in its incipiency. . . .

We cannot hold that the present statute is an arbitrary or unreasonable

exercise of the police power of the state, unwarrantably infringing the freedom of speech or press; and we must and do sustain its constitutionality.

This being so it may be applied to every utterance—not too trivial to be beneath the notice of the law—which is of such a character and used with such intent and purpose as to bring it within the prohibition of the statute. . . . In other words, when the legislative body has determined generally, in the constitutional exercise of its discretion, that utterances of a certain kind involve such danger of substantive evil that they may be punished, the question whether any specific utterance coming within the prohibited class is likely, in and of itself, to bring about the substantive evil, is not open to consideration. It is sufficient that the statute itself be constitutional, and that the use of the language comes within its prohibition.

It is clear that the question in such cases is entirely different from that involved in those cases where the statute merely prohibits certain acts involving the danger of substantive evil, without any reference to language itself, and it is sought to apply its provisions to language used by the defendant for the purpose of bringing about the prohibited results. There, if it be contended that the statute cannot be applied to the language used by the defendant because of its protection by the freedom of speech or press, it must necessarily be found, as an original question, without any previous determination by the legislative body, whether the specific language used involved such likelihood of bringing about the substantive evil as to deprive it of the constitutional protection. In such cases it has been held that the general provisions of the statute may be constitutionally applied to the specific utterance of the defendant if its natural tendency and probable effect were to bring about the substantive evil which the legislative body might prevent. *Schenck* v. *United States*. . . . *Debs* v. *United States,* 249 U.S. 211. And the general statement in the *Schenck* case that the "question in every case is whether the words are used in such circumstances and are of such a nature as to create a clear and present danger that they will bring about the substantive evils,"—upon which great reliance is placed in the defendant's argument,—was manifestly intended, as shown by the context, to apply only in cases of this class, and has no application to those like the present, where the legislative body itself has previously determined the danger of substantive evil arising from utterances of a specified character. . . .

[T]he judgment of the court of appeals is affirmed.

MR. JUSTICE HOLMES dissented:

Mr. Justice Brandeis and I are of opinion that this judgment should be reversed. The general principle of free speech, it seems to me, must be taken to be included in the Fourteenth Amendment, in view of the scope that has been given to the word "liberty" as there used, although perhaps it may be accepted with a somewhat larger latitude of interpretation than is allowed to Congress by the sweeping language that governs, or ought to govern, the laws of the United States. If I am right, then I think that the criterion sanctioned by the full court in *Schenck* v. *United States* . . . applies: "The question in every case is whether the words used are used in such circumstances and are of such a nature as to create a clear and present danger that they will bring about the substantive evils that [the state] has a right to prevent." It is true that in my opinion this criterion was departed from in *Abrams* v. *United States,* 250 U.S. 616, but the convictions that I expressed in that case are

too deep for it to be possible for me as yet to believe that it and *Schaefer* v. *United States,* 251 U.S. 466, have settled the law. If what I think the correct test is applied, it is manifest that there was no present danger of an attempt to overthrow the government by force on the part of the admittedly small minority who shared the defendant's views. It is said that this Manifesto was more than a theory, that it was an incitement. Every idea is an incitement. It offers itself for belief, and, if believed, it is acted on unless some other belief outweighs it, or some failure of energy stifles the movement at its birth. The only difference between the expression of an opinion and an incitement in the narrower sense is the speaker's enthusiasm for the result. Eloquence may set fire to reason. But whatever may be thought of the redundant discourse before us, it had no chance of starting a present conflagration. If, in the long run, the beliefs expressed in proletarian dictatorship are destined to be accepted by the dominant forces of the community, the only meaning of free speech is that they should be given their chance and have their way.

If the publication of this document had been laid as an attempt to induce an uprising against government at once, and not at some indefinite time in the future, it would have presented a different question. The object would have been one with which the law might deal, subject to the doubt whether there was any danger that the publication could produce any result; or, in other words, whether it was not futile and too remote from possible consequences. But the indictment alleges the publication and nothing more.

WHITNEY v. CALIFORNIA
274 U.S. 357; 47 Sup. Ct. 641; 71 L. Ed. 1095 (1927)

[*Charlotte Anita Whitney, a niece of Justice Stephen Field and a "renegade" member of the conservative and wealthy Field family, sought, in various ways, to promote the welfare of the poor. In 1919, she assisted in organizing the Communist Labor party of California during a convention in Oakland and was elected a member of its state executive committee. The constitution of the party provided that it be affiliated with the Communist Labor party of America and the Communist International of Moscow. Although she testified that she did not want her party to engage in terrorism or violence, Miss Whitney was convicted of a felony in a county court and sentenced to prison under the California Criminal Syndicalism Act of 1919, whose provisions are noted in the subsequent opinion. A state district court of appeals affirmed the conviction. After the state supreme court refused to review the case, it went to the Supreme Court on a writ of error.*

Even though she again lost her case in the Supreme Court, Miss Whitney was later pardoned by the Governor of California, who was reported to have been greatly influenced by Justice Brandeis' eloquent concurring opinion.]

MR. JUSTICE SANFORD delivered the opinion of the court:

. . . The pertinent provisions of the Criminal Syndicalism Act are

"Section 1. The term 'criminal syndicalism' as used in this act is hereby defined as any doctrine or precept advocating, teaching or aiding and abetting the commission of crime, sabotage (which word is hereby defined as meaning wilful and malicious physical damage or injury to physical property), or unlawful acts of force and violence or unlawful methods of terrorism as a means of accomplishing a change in industrial ownership or control, or effecting any political change.

"Section 2. Any person who : . . . (4) Organizes or assists in organizing, or is or knowingly becomes a member of, any organization, society, group or assemblage of persons organized or assembled to advocate, teach or aid and abet criminal syndicalism. . . .

"Is guilty of a felony and punishable by imprisonment."

The first count of the information, on which the conviction was had, charged that on or about November 28, 1919, in Alameda county, the defendant, in violation of the Criminal Syndicalism Act, "did then and there unlawfully, wilfully, wrongfully, deliberately and feloniously organize and assist in organizing, and was, is, and knowingly became a member of an organization, society, group and assemblage of persons organized and assembled to advocate, teach, aid and abet criminal syndicalism. . . ."

1. While it is not denied that the evidence warranted the jury in finding that the defendant became a member of and assisted in organizing the Communist Labor Party of California, and that this was organized to advocate, teach, aid or abet criminal syndicalism as defined by the act, it is urged that the act, as here construed and applied, deprived the defendant of her liberty without due process of law in that it has made her action in attending the Oakland convention unlawful by reason of "a subsequent event brought about against her will, by the agency of others," with no showing of a specific intent on her part to join in the forbidden purpose of the association, and merely because, by reason of a lack of "prophetic" understanding, she failed to foresee the quality that others would give to the

convention. The argument is, in effect, that the character of the state organization could not be forecast when she attended the convention; that she had no purpose of helping to create an instrument of terrorism and violence; that she "took part in formulating and presenting to the convention a resolution which, if adopted, would have committed the new organization to legitimate policy of political reform by the use of the ballot"; that it was not until after the majority of the convention turned out to be "contrary minded, and other less temperate policies prevailed" that the convention could have taken on the character of criminal syndicalism; and that, as this was done over her protest, her mere presence in the convention, however violent the opinions expressed therein, could not thereby become a crime. This contention, while advanced in the form of a constitutional objection to the act, is in effect nothing more than an effort to review the weight of the evidence for the purpose of showing that the defendant did not join and assist in organizing the Communist Labor Party of California with a knowledge of its unlawful character and purpose. This question, which is foreclosed by the verdict of the jury, —sustained by the court of appeal over the specific objection that it was not supported by the evidence,—is one of fact merely which is not open to review in this court, involving as it does no constitutional question whatever. And we may add that the argument entirely disregards the facts that the defendant had previously taken out a membership card in the national party; that the resolution which she supported did not advocate the use of the ballot to the exclusion of violent and unlawful means of bringing about the desired changes in industrial and political conditions; and that, after the constitution of the California party had been adopted, and this resolution had been voted down and the national program accepted, she not only remained in the convention, without protest, until its close, but subsequently manifested her acquiescence by attending as an alternate member of the state executive committee and continuing as a member of the Communist Labor Party.

2. It is clear that the Syndicalism Act is not repugnant to the due process clause by reason of vagueness and uncertainty of definition. . . .

The act, plainly, meets the essential requirement of due process that a penal statute be "sufficiently explicit to inform those who are subject to it what conduct on their part will render them liable to its penalties," and be couched in terms that are not "so vague that men of common intelligence must necessarily guess at its meaning and differ as to its application. . . ."

3. Neither is the Syndicalism Act repugnant to the equal protection clause, on the ground that as its penalties are confined to those who advocate a resort to violent and unlawful methods as a means of changing industrial and political conditions, it arbitrarily discriminates between such persons and those who may advocate a resort to these methods as a means of maintaining such conditions.

It is settled by repeated decisions of this court that the equal protection clause does not take from a state the power to classify in the adoption of police laws, but admits of the exercise of a wide scope of discretion, and avoids what is done only when it is without any reasonable basis and therefore is purely arbitrary; and that one who assails the classification must carry the burden of showing that it does not rest upon any reasonable basis, but is essentially arbitrary. . . .

The Syndicalism Act is not class legislation; it affects all alike, no matter what their business associations or callings, who come within its terms and do the things prohibited. . . . And there is no substantial basis for the contention that the legislature has arbitrarily or unreasonably limited its application to those advocating the use of violent and unlawful methods to effect changes in industrial and political conditions. . . .

4. Nor is the Syndicalism Act as applied in this case repugnant to the due process clause as a restraint of the rights of free speech, assembly, and association.

That the freedom of speech which is secured by the Constitution does not confer an absolute right to speak, without responsibility, whatever one may choose, or an unrestricted and unbridled license giving immunity for every possible use of language and preventing the punishment of those who abuse this freedom; and that a state in the exercise of its police power may punish those who abuse this freedom by utterances inimical to the public welfare, tending to incite to crime, disturb the public peace, or endanger the foundations of organized government and threaten its overthrow by unlawful means, is not open to question. *Gitlow* v. *New York*. . . .

By enacting the provisions of the Syndicalism Act the state has declared, through its legislative body, that to knowingly be or become a member of or assist in organizing an association to advocate, teach or aid and abet the commission of crimes or unlawful acts of force, violence or terrorism as a means of accomplishing industrial or political changes, involves such danger to the public peace and the security of the state, that these acts should be penalized in the exercise of its police power. That determination must be given great weight. Every presumption is to be indulged in favor of the validity of the statute . . . and it may not be declared unconstitutional unless it is an arbitrary or unreasonable attempt to exercise the authority vested in the state in the public interest. . . .

The essence of the offense denounced by the act is the combining with others in an association for the accomplishment of the desired ends through the advocacy and use of criminal and unlawful methods. It partakes of the nature of a criminal conspiracy. . . . That such united and joint action involves even greater danger to the public peace and security than the isolated utterances and acts of individuals, is clear. We cannot hold that, as here applied, the act is an unreasonable or arbitrary exercise of the police power of the state, unwarrantably infringing any right of free speech, assembly or association, or that those persons are protected from punishment by the due process clause who abuse such rights by joining and furthering an organization thus menacing the peace and welfare of the state.

We find no repugnancy in the Syndicalism Act as applied in this case to either the due process or equal protection clause of the Fourteenth Amendment, on any of the grounds upon which its validity has been here challenged. . . .

MR. JUSTICE BRANDEIS, concurring:

. . . The felony which the statute created is a crime very unlike the old felony of conspiracy or the old misdemeanor of unlawful assembly. The mere act of assisting in forming a society for teaching syndicalism, of becoming a member of it, or of assembling with others for that purpose is given the dynamic quality of crime. There is guilt although the society may not contemplate immediate promulgation of the doctrine. Thus the accused is to be punished, not for attempt, incitement or conspiracy, but for a step

in preparation, which, if it threatens the public order at all, does so only remotely. The novelty in the prohibition introduced is that the statute aims, not at the practice of criminal syndicalism, nor even directly at the preaching of it, but at association with those who propose to preach it.

Despite arguments to the contrary which had seemed to me persuasive, it is settled that the due process clause of the Fourteenth Amendment applies to matters of substantive law as well as to matters of procedure. Thus all fundamental rights comprised within the term "liberty" are protected by the Federal Constitution from invasion by the states. The right of free speech, the right to teach, and the right of assembly are, of course, fundamental rights. . . . These may not be denied or abridged. But, although the rights of free speech and assembly are fundamental, they are not in their nature absolute. Their exercise is subject to restriction, if the particular restriction proposed is required in order to protect the state from destruction or from serious injury, political, economic or moral. That the necessity which is essential to a valid restriction does not exist unless speech would produce, or is intended to produce, a clear and imminent danger of some substantive evil which the state constitutionally may seek to prevent has been settled. See *Schenck* v. *United States*. . . .

It is said to be the function of the legislature to determine whether at a particular time and under the particular circumstances the formation of, or assembly with, a society organized to advocate criminal syndicalism constitutes a clear and present danger of substantive evil; and that by enacting the law here in question the legislature of California determined that question in the affirmative. Compare *Gitlow* v. *New York*. . . . The legislature must obviously decide, in the first instance, whether a danger exists which calls for a particular protective measure. But where a statute is valid only in case certain conditions exist, the enactment of the statute cannot alone establish the facts which are essential to its validity. Prohibitory legislation has repeatedly been held invalid, because unnecessary, where the denial of liberty involved was that of engaging in a particular business. The powers of the courts to strike down an offending law are no less when the interest involved are not property rights, but the fundamental personal rights of free speech and assembly.

This court has not yet fixed the standard by which to determine when a danger shall be deemed clear; how remote the danger may be and yet be deemed present; and what degree of evil shall be deemed sufficiently substantial to justify resort to abridgment of free speech and assembly as the means of protection. To reach sound conclusions on these matters, we must bear in mind why a state is, ordinarily, denied the power to prohibit dissemination of social, economic and political doctrine which a vast majority of its citizens believes to be false and fraught with evil consequence.

Those who won our independence believed that the final end of the state was to make men free to develop their faculties; and that in its government the deliberative forces should prevail over the arbitrary. They valued liberty both as an end and as a means. They believed liberty to be the secret of happiness and courage to be the secret of liberty. They believed that freedom to think as you will and to speak as you think are means indispensable to the discovery and spread of political truth; that without free speech and assembly discussion would be futile; that with them, discussion affords ordinarily adequate protection against the dissemination of noxious doctrine; that the greatest menace to freedom is an inert people; that public discussion is a political duty; and that this should be a fundamental principle of the American government. They recognized the risks to which all human institutions are subject. But they knew that order cannot be secured merely through fear of punishment for its infraction; that it is hazardous to discourage thought, hope and imagination; that fear breeds repression; that repression breeds hate; that hate menaces stable government; that the path of safety lies in the opportunity to discuss freely supposed grievances and proposed remedies; and that the fitting remedy for evil counsels is good ones. Believing in the power of reason as applied through public discussion, they eschewed silence coerced by law—the argument of force in its worst form. Recognizing the occasional tyrannies of governing majorities, they amended the Constitution so that free speech and assembly should be guaranteed.

Fear of serious injury cannot alone justify suppression of free speech and assembly. Men feared witches and burned women. It is the function of speech to free men from the bondage of irrational fears. To justify suppression of free speech there must be reasonable ground to fear that serious evil will result if free speech is practiced. There must be reasonable ground to believe that the danger apprehended is imminent. There must be reasonable ground to believe that the evil to be prevented is a serious one. Every denunciation of existing law tends in some measure to increase the probability that there will be violation of it. Condonation of a breach enhances the probability. Expressions of approval add to the probability. Propagation of the criminal state of mind by teaching syndicalism increases it. Advocacy of lawbreaking heightens it still further. But even advocacy of violation, however reprehensible morally, is not a justification for denying free speech where the advocacy falls short of incitement and there is nothing to indicate that the advocacy would be immediately acted on. The wide difference between advocacy and incitement, between preparation and attempt, between assembling and conspiracy, must be borne in mind. In order to support a finding of clear and present danger it must be shown either that immediate serious violence was to be expected or was advocated, or that the past conduct furnished reason to believe that such advocacy was then contemplated.

Those who won our independence by revolution were not cowards. They did not fear political change. They did not exalt order at the cost of liberty. To courageous, self-reliant men, with confidence in the power of free and fearless reasoning applied through the processes of popular government, no danger flowing from speech can be deemed clear and present, unless the incidence of the evil apprehended is so imminent that it may befall before there is opportunity for full discussion. If there be time to expose through discussion the falsehood and fallacies, to avert the evil by the processes of education, the remedy to be applied is more speech, not enforced silence. Only an emergency can justify repression. Such must be the rule if authority is to be reconciled with freedom. Such, in my opinion, is the command of the Constitution. It is, therefore, always open to Americans to challenge a law abridging free speech and assembly by showing that there was no emergency justifying it.

Moreover, even imminent danger cannot justify resort to prohibition of these functions essential to effective democracy, unless the evil apprehended is relatively serious. Prohibition of free speech and assembly is a measure so stringent that it would be inappropriate as the means for averting a relatively trivial harm to society. A police measure may be unconstitutional merely because the remedy, although effective as means of protection, is unduly harsh or oppressive. Thus, a state might, in the exercise of its police power, make any trespass upon the land of another a crime, regardless of the results or of the intent or purpose of the trespasser. It might, also, punish an attempt, a conspiracy, or an incitement to commit the trespass. But it is hardly conceivable that this court would hold constitutional a statute which punished as a felony the mere voluntary assembly with a society formed to teach that pedestrians had the moral right to cross unenclosed, unposted, waste lands and to advocate their doing so, even if there was imminent danger that advocacy would lead to a trespass. The fact that speech is likely to result in some violence or in destruction of property is not enough to justify its suppression. There must be the probability of serious injury to the state. Among freemen, the deterrents ordinarily to be applied to prevent crime are education and punishment for violations of the law, not abridgment of the rights of free speech and assembly. . . .

Whether, in 1919, when Miss Whitney did the things complained of, there was in California such clear and present danger of serious evil, might have been made the important issue in the case. She might have required that the issue be determined either by the court or the jury. She claimed below that the statute as applied to her violated the Federal Constitution; but she did not claim that it was void because there was no clear and present danger of serious evil, nor did she request that the existence of these conditions of a valid measure thus restricting the rights of free speech and assembly be passed upon by the court or a jury. On the other hand, there was evidence on which the court or jury might have found that such danger existed. I am unable to assent to the suggestion in the opinion of the court that assembling with a political party, formed to advocate the desirability of a proletarian revolution by mass action at some date necessarily far in the future, is not a right within the protection of the Fourteenth Amendment. In the present case, however, there was other testimony which tended to establish the existence of a conspiracy, on the part of members of the International Workers of the World, to commit present serious crimes; and likewise to show that such a conspiracy would be furthered by the activity of the society of which Miss Whitney was a member. Under these circumstances the judgment of the state court cannot be disturbed. . . .

MR. JUSTICE HOLMES joins in this opinion.

EDITORS NOTE. The Supreme Court overruled its decision in *Whitney* in 1969. See the discussion of *Branderberg* v. *Ohio* in Chapter 15.

TERMINIELLO *v.* CHICAGO
337 U.S. 1; 69 Sup. Ct. 894; 93 L. Ed. 1131 (1949)

[*Terminiello was convicted of a breach of the peace in Chicago after he had delivered an extremely provocative address under riotous conditions in a city auditorium. The conviction was affirmed by two higher state courts, including the Illinois Supreme Court. Terminiello then brought his case to the Supreme Court on a writ of certiorari. Additional facts are contained in the majority opinion. A more detailed summary of the conditions under which Terminiello gave his speech is provided by* JUSTICE JACKSON'S *vigorous dissenting opinion.*]

MR. JUSTICE DOUGLAS delivered the opinion of the Court.

Petitioner after jury trial was found guilty of disorderly conduct in violation of a city ordinance of Chicago and fined. The case grew out of an address he delivered in an auditorium in Chicago under the auspices of the Christian Veterans of America. The meeting commanded considerable public attention. The auditorium was filled to capacity with over 800 persons present. Others were turned away. Outside of the auditorium a crowd of about 1,000 persons gathered to protest against the meeting. A cordon of policemen was assigned to the meeting to maintain order; but they were not able to prevent several disturbances. The crowd outside was angry and turbulent.

Petitioner in his speech condemned the conduct of the crowd outside and vigorously, if not viciously, criticized various political and racial groups whose activities he denounced as inimical to the nation's welfare.

The trial court charged that "breach of the peace" consists of any "misbehavior which violates the public peace and decorum"; and that the "misbehavior may constitute a breach of the peace if it stirs the public to anger, invites dispute, brings about a condition of unrest, or creates a disturbance, or if it molests the inhabitants in the enjoyment of peace and quiet by arousing alarm." Petitioner did not take exception to that instruction. But he maintained at all times that the ordinance as applied to his conduct violated his right of free speech under the Federal Constitution. . . .

The argument here has been focused on the issue of whether the content of petitioner's speech was composed of derisive, fighting words, which carried it outside the scope of constitutional guaranties. . . . We do not reach that question, for there is a preliminary question that is dispositive of the case.

As we have noted, the statutory words "breach of the peace" were defined in instructions to the jury to include speech which "stirs the public to anger, invites dispute, brings about a condition of unrest, or creates a disturbance. . . ." That construction of the ordinance is a ruling on a question of state law that is as binding on us as though the precise words had been written into the ordinance. . . .

The vitality of civil and political institutions in our society depends on free discussion. . . . [I]t is only through free debate and free exchange of ideas that government remains responsive to the will of the people and peaceful change is effected. The right to speak freely and to promote diversity of ideas and programs is therefore one of the chief distinctions that sets us apart from totalitarian regimes.

Accordingly a function of free speech under our system of government is to invite dispute. It may indeed best serve its high purpose when it induces a condition of unrest, creates dissatisfaction with conditions as they are, or even stirs people to anger. Speech is often provocative and challenging. It may strike at prejudices and preconceptions and have profound unsettling effects as it presses for acceptance of an idea. That is why freedom of speech, though not absolute, . . . is nevertheless protected against censorship or punishment, unless shown likely to produce a clear and present danger of a serious substantive evil that rises far above public inconvenience, annoyance, or unrest. . . . There is no room under

our Constitution for a more restrictive view. For the alternative would lead to standardization of ideas either by legislatures, courts, or dominant political or community groups.

The ordinance as construed by the trial court seriously invaded this province. It permitted conviction of petitioner if his speech stirred people to anger, invited public dispute, or brought about a condition of unrest. A conviction resting on any of those grounds may not stand.

The fact that petitioner took no exception to the instruction is immaterial. No exception to the instructions was taken in *Stromberg* v. *California,* 283 U.S. 359. But a judgment of conviction based on a general verdict under a state statute was set aside in that case, because one part of the statute was unconstitutional. . . .

. . . [T]he gloss which Illinois placed on the ordinance gives it a meaning and application which are conclusive on us. We need not consider whether as construed it is defective in its entirety. As construed and applied it at least contains parts that are unconstitutional. The verdict was a general one; and we do not know on this record but what it may rest on the invalid clauses.

The statute as construed in the charge to the jury was passed on by the Illinois courts and sustained by them over the objection that as so read it violated the Fourteenth Amendment. The fact that the parties did not dispute its construction makes the adjudication no less ripe for our review, as the *Stromberg* decision indicates. We can only take the statute as the state courts read it. From our point of view it is immaterial whether the state law question as to its meaning was controverted or accepted. The pinch of the statute is in its application. It is that question which the petitioner has brought here. To say therefore that the question on this phase of the case is whether the trial judge gave a wrong charge is wholly to misconceive the issue.

But it is said that throughout the appellate proceedings the Illinois courts assumed that the only conduct punishable and punished under the ordinance was conduct constituting "fighting words." That emphasizes, however, the importance of the rule of the *Stromberg* case. Petitioner was not convicted under a statute so narrowly construed. For all anyone knows he was convicted under the parts of the ordinance (as construed) which, for example, make it an offense merely to invite dispute or to bring about a condition of unrest. We cannot avoid that issue by saying that all Illinois did was to measure petitioner's conduct, not the ordinance, against the Constitution. Petitioner raised both points—that his speech was protected by the Constitution; that the inclusion of his speech within the ordinance was a violation of the Constitution. We would, therefore, strain at technicalities to conclude that the constitutionality of the ordinance as construed and applied to petitioner was not before the Illinois courts. The record makes clear that petitioner at all times challenged the constitutionality of the ordinance as construed and applied to him.

Reversed.

[CHIEF JUSTICE VINSON submitted a dissenting opinion that was in substantial agreement with JUSTICE FRANKFURTER'S subsequent point.]

MR. JUSTICE FRANKFURTER, dissenting:

For the first time in the course of the 130 years in which State prosecutions have come here for review, this Court is today reversing a sentence imposed by a State court on a ground that was urged neither here nor below and that was explicitly disclaimed on behalf of the petitioner at the bar of this Court. . . .

Reliance on *Stromberg* v. *California* . . . for what is done today is wholly misplaced. Neither expressly nor by implication has that decision any bearing upon the issue which the Court's opinion in this case raises, namely, whether it is open for this Court to reverse the highest court of a State on a point which was not brought before that court, did not enter into the judgment rendered by that court, and at no stage of the proceedings in this Court was invoked as error by the State court whose reversal is here sought. The *Stromberg* case presented precisely the opposite situation. In that case the claim which here prevailed was a ground of unconstitutionality urged before the California court; upon its rejection by that court it was made the basis of appeal to this Court; it was here urged as the decisive ground for the reversal of the California judgment.

. . . In the *Stromberg* case an error that was properly urged was sustained. In this case a claim that was not urged but was disavowed is transmitted into a claim denied. . . .

MR. JUSTICE JACKSON and MR. JUSTICE BURTON join this dissent.

MR. JUSTICE JACKSON, dissenting:

. . . [T]he local court that tried Terminiello . . . was dealing with a riot and with a speech that provoked a hostile mob and incited a friendly one, and threatened violence between the two. When the trial judge instructed the jury that it might find Terminiello guilty of inducing a breach of the peace if his behavior stirred the public to anger, invited dispute, brought about unrest, created a disturbance or molested peace and quiet by arousing alarm, he was not speaking of these as harmless or abstract conditions. He was addressing his words to the concrete behavior and specific consequences disclosed by the evidence. He was saying to the jury, in effect, that if this particular speech added fuel to the situation already so inflamed as to threaten to get beyond police control, it could be punished as inducing a breach of peace. . . .

Terminiello, advertised as a Catholic Priest, but revealed at the trial to be under suspension by his Bishop, was brought to Chicago from Birmingham, Alabama, to address a gathering that assembled in response to a call signed by Gerald L. K. Smith. . . .

Terminiello's own testimony shows the conditions under which he spoke. . . .

". . . We got there (the meeting place) approximately fifteen or twenty minutes past eight. The car stopped at the front entrance. There was a crowd of three or four hundred congregated there shouting and cursing and picketing. . . .

"When we got there the pickets were not marching; they were body to body and covered the sidewalk completely, some on the steps so that we had to form a flying wedge to get through. Police escorted us to the building, and I noticed four or five others there.

"They called us 'God damned Fascists, Nazis, out to hang the so-and-sos.' When I entered the building I heard the howls of the people outside. . . . There were four or five plain-clothes officers standing at the entrance to the stage and three or four at the entrance to the back door.

"The officers threatened that if they broke the door again they would arrest them, and every time they opened the door a little to look out something was thrown at the officers, including ice-picks and rocks.

"A number of times the door was broken, was partly broken through. There were doors open this way and

they partly opened and the officers looked out two or three times and each time ice-picks, stones, and bottles were thrown at the police at the door. I took my place on the stage, before this I was about ten or fifteen minutes in the body of the hall.

"I saw a number of windows broken by stones or missiles. I saw the back door being forced open, pushed open.

"The front door was broken partly open after the doors were closed. There were about seven people seated on the stage. Smith opened the meeting with prayer, the Pledge of Allegiance to the Flag, and singing of America. There were other speakers who spoke before me and before I spoke I heard things happening in the hall and coming from the outside.

"I saw rocks being thrown through windows and that continued throughout at least the first half of the meeting, probably longer, and again attempts were made to force the front door, rather the front door was forced partly. The howling continued on the outside, cursing could be heard audibly in the hall at times. Police were rushing in and out of the front door protecting the front door, and there was a general commotion, all kinds of noises and violence—all from the outside.

"Between the time the first speaker spoke and I spoke, stones and bricks were thrown in all the time. I started to speak about thirty-five or forty minutes after the meeting started, a little later than nine o'clock. . . ."

The court below, in addition to this recital, heard other evidence, that the crowd reached an estimated number of 1,500. Picket lines obstructed and interfered with access to the building. The crowd constituted "a surging howling mob hurling epithets" at those who would enter and "tried to tear their clothes off." One young woman's coat was torn off and she had to be assisted into the meeting by policemen. Those inside the hall could hear the loud noises and hear those on the outside yell, "Fascists," "Hitlers," and curse words like "damn Fascists." Bricks were thrown through the windowpanes before and during the speaking. About 28 windows were broken. The street was black with people on both sides for at least a block either way; bottles, stink bombs, and brickbats were thrown. Police were unable to control the mob, which kept breaking the windows at the meeting hall, drowning out the speaker's voice at times and breaking in through the back door of the auditorium. About seventeen of the group outside were arrested by the police.

Knowing of this environment, Terminiello made a long speech. . . .

. . . Evidence showed that it stirred the audience not only to cheer and applaud but to expressions of immediate anger, unrest, and alarm. [The stenographic record of the speech, portions of which were quoted by Justice Jackson, was extremely provocative. Terminiello bitterly attacked the Jewish people and others, using abusive language.]

Terminiello, of course, disclaims being a Fascist. Doubtless many of the indoor audience were not consciously such. His speech, however, followed, with fidelity that is more than coincidental, the pattern of European fascist leaders. . . .

I am unable to see that the local authorities have transgressed the Federal Constitution. Illinois imposed no prior censorship or suppression upon Terminiello. On the contrary, its sufferance and protection was all that enabled him to speak. It does not appear that the motive in punishing him is to silence the ideology he expressed as offensive to the State's policy or as untrue, or has any purpose of controlling his thought or its peaceful communication to others. There is no claim that the proceedings against Terminiello are designed to discriminate against him or the faction he represents or the ideas that he bespeaks. There is no indication that the charge against him is a mere pretext to give the semblance of legality to a covert effort to silence him or to prevent his followers or the public from hearing any truth that is in him.

A trial court and jury has found only that in the context of violence and disorder in which it was made, this speech was a provocation to immediate breach of the peace and therefore cannot claim constitutional immunity from punishment. Under the Constitution as it has been understood and applied, at least until most recently, the State was within its powers in taking this action.

Rioting is a substantive evil, which I take it no one will deny that the State and the City have the right and the duty to prevent and punish. Where an offense is induced by speech, the Court has laid down and often reiterated a test of the power of the authorities to deal with the speaking as also an offense. "The question in every case is whether the words *used are used in such circumstances* and are of *such a nature* as to create a *clear and present danger* that they will bring about the substantive evils that Congress (or the State or City) has a right to prevent." . . . No one ventures to contend that the State on the basis of this test, for whatever it may be worth, was not justified in punishing Terminiello. In this case the evidence proves beyond dispute that danger of rioting and violence in response to the speech was clear, present, and immediate. If this Court has not silently abandoned this long-standing test and substituted for the purposes of this case an unexpressed but more stringent test, the action of the State would have to be sustained. . . .

. . . [I]f we maintain a general policy of free speaking, we must recognize that its inevitable consequence will be sporadic local outbreaks of violence, for it is the nature of men to be intolerant of attacks upon institutions, personalities, and ideas for which they really care. In the long run, maintenance of free speech will be more endangered if the population can have no protection from the abuses which lead

to violence. No liberty is made more secure by holding that its abuses are inseparable from its enjoyment. . . .

This Court has gone far toward accepting the doctrine that civil liberty means the removal of all restraints from these crowds and that all local attempts to maintain order are impairments of the liberty of the citizen. The choice is not between order and liberty. It is between liberty with order and anarchy without either. There is danger that, if the Court does not temper its doctrinaire logic with a little practical wisdom, it will convert the constitutional Bill of Rights into a suicide pact.

I would affirm the conviction.

ADDERLEY v. FLORIDA
385 U.S. 39; 87 Sup. Ct. 242; 17 L. Ed. 2d 149 (1967)

MR. JUSTICE BLACK delivered the opinion of the Court:

Petitioners, Harriett Louise Adderley and thirty-one other persons, were convicted by a jury in a joint trial in the County Judge's Court of Leon County, Florida, on a charge of "trespass with a malicious and mischievous intent" upon the premises of the county jail contrary to § 821.18 of the Florida statutes. . . . Petitioners, apparently all students of the Florida A & M University in Tallahassee, had gone from the school to the jail about a mile away, along with many other students, to "demonstrate" at the jail their protests because of arrests of other protesting students the day before, and perhaps to protest more generally against state and local policies and practices of racial segregation, including segregation of the jail. The county sheriff, legal custodian of the jail and jail grounds, tried to persuade the students to leave the jail grounds. When this did not work, he . . . notified them that they

must leave or he would arrest them for trespassing. . . . Some of the students left but others, including petitioners, remained and they were arrested. . . .

I

Petitioners have insisted from the beginning of these cases that they are controlled and must be reversed because of our prior cases of *Edwards* v. *South Carolina* [1963] and *Cox* v. *Louisiana* [1965]. We cannot agree.

The *Edwards* case, like this one, did come up when a number of persons demonstrated on public property against their State's segregation policies. They also sang hymns and danced, as did the demonstrators in this case. But here the analogies to this case end. In Edwards, the demonstrators went to the South Carolina State Capitol grounds to protest. In this case they went to the jail. Traditionally, state capitol grounds are open to the public. Jails, built for security purposes, are not. The demonstrators at the South Carolina Capitol went in through a public driveway and as they entered they were told by state officials there that they had a right as citizens to go through the State House grounds as long as they were peaceful. Here the demonstrators entered the jail grounds through a driveway used only for jail purposes and without warning to or permission from the sheriff. More importantly, South Carolina sought to prosecute its State Capitol demonstrators by charging them with the common-law crime of breach of the peace. This Court in Edwards took pains to point out at length the indefinite, loose, and broad nature of this charge; indeed, this Court pointed out . . . that the South Carolina Supreme Court had itself declared that the "breach of the peace charge" is "not susceptible of exact definition." South Carolina's power to prosecute, it was emphasized . . . , would have been different had it proceeded under a "precise and narrowly drawn regulatory statute evincing a legislative judgment that certain specific conduct be limited or proscribed" such as, for example, "limiting the periods during which the State House grounds were open to the public . . . ." The South Carolina breach-of-the-peace statute was thus struck down as being so broad and all-embracing as to jeopardize speech, press, assembly and petition, under the constitutional doctrine enunciated in *Cantwell* v. *Connecticut* [1940], and followed in many subsequent cases. And it was on this same ground of vagueness that in *Cox* v. *Louisiana* the Louisiana breach-of-the-peace law used to prosecute Cox was invalidated.

The Florida trespass statute under which these petitioners were charged cannot be challenged on this ground. It is aimed at conduct of one limited kind, that is for one person or persons to trespass upon the property of another with a malicious and mischievous intent. There is no lack of notice in this law, nothing to entrap or fool the unwary.

Petitioners seem to argue that the Florida trespass law is void for vagueness because it requires a trespass to be "with a malicious and mischievous intent . . . ." But these words do not broaden the scope of trespass so as to make it cover a multitude of types of conduct as does the common-law breach-of-the-peace charge. On the contrary, these words narrow the scope of the offense. . . . The use of these terms in the statute, instead of contributing to uncertainty and misunderstanding, actually makes its meaning more understandable and clear. . . . Disturbed and upset by the arrest of their schoolmates the day before, a large number of Florida A & M students assembled on the school grounds and decided to march down to the county jail. Some apparently wanted to get themselves put in jail too, along with the students already there. A group of around two hundred marched from the school and arrived at the jail singing and clapping. They went directly to the jail door entrance where they were met by a deputy sheriff, evidently surprised by their arrival. He asked them to move back, claiming they were blocking the entrance to the jail and fearing that they might attempt to enter the jail. They moved back part of the way, where they stood or sat, singing, clapping and dancing, on the jail driveway and on an adjacent grassy area upon the jail premises. This particular jail entrance and driveway were not normally used by the public, but by the sheriff's department for transporting prisoners to and from the courts several blocks away and by commercial concerns for servicing the jail. Even after their partial retreat, the demonstrators continued to block vehicular passage over this driveway up to the entrance of the jail.* Someone called the sheriff who was at the moment apparently conferring with one of the state court judges about incidents connected with prior arrests for demonstrations. When the sheriff returned to the jail, he immediately inquired if all was safe inside the jail and was told it was. He then engaged in a conversation with two of the leaders. He told them that they were trespassing upon jail property and that he would give them 10 minutes to leave or he would arrest them. Neither of the leaders did anything to disperse the crowd, and one of them told the sheriff that they wanted to get arrested. A local minister talked with some of the demonstrators and told them not to enter the jail, because they could not arrest themselves, but just to remain where they were. After about 10 minutes, the sheriff, in a voice loud enough to be heard by all, told the demonstrators that he was the legal custodian of the jail and its premises, that they were trespassing on county property in violation of the law, that they should all leave forthwith or he would arrest them, and that if they at-

* Although some of the petitioners testified that they had no intention of interfering with vehicular traffic to and from the jail entrance and that they noticed no vehicle trying to enter or leave the driveway, the deputy sheriff testified that it would have been impossible for automobiles to drive up to the jail entrance and that one serviceman, finished with his business in the jail, waited inside because the demonstrators were sitting around and leaning against his truck parked outside. The sheriff testified that the time the demonstrators were there, between 9:30 and 10 A.M. Monday morning, was generally a very busy time for using the jail entrance to transport weekend inmates to the courts and for tradesmen to make service calls on the jail.

tempted to resist arrest, he would charge them with that as a separate offense. Some of the group then left. Others, including all petitioners, did not leave. Some of them sat down. In a few minutes, realizing that the remaining demonstrators had no intention of leaving, the sheriff ordered his deputies to surround those remaining on jail premises and placed them, 107 demonstrators, under arrest. The sheriff unequivocally testified that he did not arrest any person other than those who were on the jail premises. Of the three petitioners testifying, two insisted that they were arrested before they had a chance to leave, had they wanted to, and one testified that she did not intend to leave. The sheriff again explicitly testified that he did not arrest any person who was attempting to leave.

Under the foregoing testimony the jury was authorized to find that the State had proven every essential element of the crime, as it was defined by the state court. That interpretation is, of course, binding on us, leaving only the question of whether conviction of the state offense, thus defined, unconstitutionally deprives petitioners of their rights to freedom of speech, press, assembly or petition. We hold it does not. The sheriff, as jail custodian, had power, as the state courts have here held, to direct that this large crowd of people get off the grounds. There is not a shred of evidence in this record that this power was exercised, or that its exercise was sanctioned by the lower courts, because the sheriff objected to what was being sung or said by the demonstrators or because he disagreed with the objectives of their protest. The record reveals that he objected only to their presence on that part of the jail grounds reserved for jail uses. There is no evidence at all that on any other occasion had similarly large groups of the public been permitted to gather on this portion of the jail grounds for any purpose. Nothing in the Constitution of the United States prevents Florida from even-handed enforcement of its general trespass statute against those refusing to obey the sheriff's order to remove themselves from what amounted to the cultilage of the jail-house. The State, no less than a private owner of property, has power to preserve the property under its control for the use to which it is lawfully dedicated. For this reason there is no merit to the petitioners' argument that they had a constitutional right to stay on the property, over the jail custodian's objections, because this "area chosen for the peaceful civil rights demonstration was not only 'reasonable' but also particularly appropriate . . . ." Such an argument has as its major unarticulated premise the assumption that people who want to propagandize protests or views have a constitutional right to do so whenever and however and wherever they please. That concept of constitutional law was vigorously and forthrightfully rejected in two of the cases petitioners rely on, Cox v. Louisiana, supra, at 554–555 and 563–564. We reject it again. The United States Constitution does not forbid a State to control the use of its own property for its own lawful nondiscriminatory purpose.

These judgments are

Affirmed.

MR. JUSTICE DOUGLAS, with whom THE CHIEF JUSTICE, MR. JUSTICE BRENNAN, and MR. JUSTICE FORTAS concur, dissenting:

The First Amendment, applicable to the States by reason of the Fourteenth . . . , provides that "Congress shall make no law respecting . . . the right of the people peaceably to assemble, and to petition the government for a redress of grievances." These rights, along with religion, speech, and press, are preferred rights of the Constitution,

made so by reason of that explicit guarantee and what Edmond Cahn in Confronting Injustice (1966) referred to as "The Firstness of the First Amendment." With all respect, therefore, the Court errs in treating the case as if it were an ordinary trespass case or an ordinary picketing case.

The jailhouse, like an executive mansion, a legislative chamber, a courthouse, or the statehouse itself (*Edwards v. South Carolina*) is one of the seats of government whether it be the Tower of London, the Bastille, or a small county jail. And when it houses political prisoners or those whom many think are unjustly held, it is an obvious center for protest. The right to petition for the redress of grievances has an ancient history and is not limited to writing a letter or sending a telegram to a congressman; it is not confined to appearing before the local city council, or writing letters to the President or Governor or Mayor. . . . Conventional methods of petitioning may be, and often have been, shut off to large groups of our citizens. Legislators may turn deaf ears; formal complaints may be routed endlessly through a bureaucratic maze; courts may let the wheels of justice grind very slowly. Those who do not control television and radio, those who cannot afford to advertise in newspapers or circulate elaborate pamphlets may have only a more limited type of access to public officials. Their methods should not be condemned as tactics of obstruction and harassment as long as the assembly and petition are peaceable, as these were.

There is no question that petitioners had as their purpose a protest against the arrest of Florida A & M students for trying to integrate public theatres. The sheriff's testimony indicates that he well understood the purpose of the rally. The petitioners who testified unequivocally stated that the group was protesting the arrests, and state and local policies of segregation, including segregation of the jail. This testimony was not contradicted or even questioned. The fact that no one gave a formal speech, that no elaborate handbills were distributed, and that the group was not laden with signs would seem to be immaterial. Such methods are not the sine qua non of petitioning for the redress of grievances. The group did sing "freedom" songs. And history shows that a song can be a powerful tool of protest. . . . There was no violence; no threats of violence; no attempted jail break; no storming of a prison; no plan or plot to do anything but protest. The evidence is uncontradicted that the petitioners' conduct did not upset the jailhouse routine; things went on as they normally would. None of the group entered the jail. Indeed, they moved back from the entrance as they were instructed. There was no shoving, no pushing, no disorder or threat of riot. It is said that some of the group blocked part of the driveway leading to the jail entrance. The chief jailer to be sure testified that vehicles would not have been able to use the driveway. Never did the students locate themselves so as to cause interference with persons or vehicles going to or coming from the jail. Indeed, it is undisputed that the sheriff and deputy sheriff, in separate cars, were able to drive up the driveway to the parking places near the entrance and that no one obstructed their path. Further, it is undisputed that the entrance to the jail was not blocked. And wherever the students were requested to move they did so. If there was congestion, the solution was a further request to move to lawns or parking areas, not complete ejection and arrest. The claim is made that a tradesman waited inside the jail because some of the protestants were sitting around and leaning on his truck.

The only evidence supporting such a conclusion is the testimony of a deputy sheriff that the tradesman "came to the door and then did not leave." His remaining is just as consistent with a desire to satisfy his curiosity as it is with a restraint. Finally the fact that some of the protestants may have felt their cause so just that they were willing to be arrested for making their protest outside the jail seems wholly irrelevant. A petition is nonetheless a petition, though its futility may make martyrdom attractive.

We do violence to the First Amendment when we permit this "petition for redress of grievances" to be turned into a trespass action. . . . In the first place the jailhouse grounds were not marked with "No Trespassing!" signs, nor does respondent claim that the public was generally excluded from the grounds. Only the sheriff's fiat transformed lawful conduct into an unlawful trespass. To say that a private owner could have done the same if the rally had taken place on private property is to speak of a different case, as an assembly and a petition for redress of grievances run to government not to private proprietors.

. . . When we allow Florida to construe her "malicious trespass" statute to bar a person from going on property knowing it is not his own and to apply that prohibition to public property, we discard Cox and Edwards. Would the case be any different if, as is common, the demonstration took place outside a building which housed both the jail and the legislative body? I think not.

There may be some public places which are so clearly committed to other purposes that their use for the airing of grievances is anomalous. There may be some instances in which assemblies and petitions for redress of grievances are not consistent with other necessary purposes of public property. A noisy meeting may be out of keeping with the serenity of the statehouse or the quiet of the courthouse. No one, for example, would suggest that the Senate gallery is the proper place for a vociferous protest rally. And, in other cases it may be necessary to adjust the right to petition for redress of grievances to the other interests inhering in the uses to which the public property is normally put. . . . But this is quite different than saying that all public places are off-limits to people with grievances. . . . And it is farther yet from saying that the "custodian" of the public property in his discretion can decide when public places shall be used for the communication of ideas, especially the constitutional right to assemble and petition for redress of grievances. . . . For to place such discretion in any public official, be he the "custodian" of the public property, or the local police commissioner . . . is to place those who assert their First Amendment

rights at his mercy. It gives him the awesome power to decide whose ideas may be expressed and who shall be denied a place to air their claims and petition their government. Such power is out of step with all our decisions prior to today where we have insisted that before a First Amendment right may be curtailed under the guise of a criminal law, any evil that may be collateral to the exercise of the right, must be isolated and defined in a "narrowly drawn" statute . . . lest the power to control excesses of conduct be used to suppress the constitutional right itself. . . .

That tragic consequence happens today when a trespass law is used to bludgeon those who peacefully exercise a First Amendment right to protest to government against one of the most grievous of all modern oppressions which some of our States are inflicting on our citizens. . . .

AMALGAMATED FOOD EMP. U. LOCAL 590 *v.* LOGAN VALLEY PLAZA
89 Sup. Ct. 1179 (1969)

MR. JUSTICE MARSHALL delivered the opinion of the Court:

This case presents the question whether peaceful picketing of a business enterprise located within a shopping center can be enjoined on the ground that it constitutes an unconsented invasion of the property rights of the owners of the land on which the center is situated.

Logan Valley Plaza, Inc. (Logan), one of the two respondents herein, owns a large, newly developed shopping center complex, known as the Logan Valley Mall, located near the City of Altoona, Pennsylvania. The shopping center is situated at the intersection of Plank Road, which is on the east of the center, and Good's Lane,

which is to the south. Plank Road, also known as U.S. Route 220, is a heavily traveled highway along which traffic moves at a fairly high rate of speed. There are five entrance roads into the center, three from Plank Road and two from Good's Lane. Aside from these five entrances, the shopping center is totally separated from the adjoining roads by earthen berms. The berms are 15 feet wide along Good's Lane and 12 feet wide along Plank Road.

At the time of the events in this case, Logan Valley Mall was occupied by two businesses, Weis Markets, Inc. (Weis), the other respondent herein, and Sears, Roebuck and Co. . . . . The Weis property consists of the enclosed supermarket building, an open but covered porch along the front of the building, and an approximately five-foot wide parcel pickup zone that runs 30 to 40 feet along the porch. The porch functions as a sidewalk in front of the building and the pickup zone is used as a temporary parking place for the loading of purchases into customers' cars by Weis employees.

Between the Weis building and the highway berms are extensive macadam parking lots with parking spaces and driveways lined off thereon. These areas, to which Logan retains title, provide common parking facilities for all the businesses in the shopping center. The distance across the parking lots of the Weis store from the entrances on Good's Lane is approximately 350 feet and from the entrances on Plank Road approximately 400 to 500 feet. The entrance on Plank Road furtherest from Weis property is the main entrance to the shopping center as a whole and is regularly used by customers of Weis. The entrance on Plank Road nearest to Weis is almost exclusively used by patrons of the Sears automobile service station into which it leads directly.

On December 8, 1965, Weis opened for business, employing a wholly nonunion staff of employees. A few days after it opened for business, Weis posted a sign on the exterior of its building prohibiting trespassing or soliciting by anyone other than its employees on its porch or parking lot. On December 17, 1965, members of Amalgamated Food Employees Union, Local 590 began picketing Weis. They carried signs stating that the Weis market was nonunion and that its employees were not "receiving union wages or other benefits." The pickets did not include any employees of Weis, but rather were all employees of competitors of Weis. The picketing continued until December 27, during which time the number

of picketers varied between four and thirteen and averaged around six. The picketing was carried out almost entirely in the parcel pickups area and that portion of the parking lot immediately adjacent thereto. Although some congestion of the parcel pickup area occurred, such congestion was sporadic and infrequent. The picketing was peaceful at all times and unaccompanied by either threats or violence.

On December 27, Weis and Logan instituted an action in equity in the Court of Common Pleas of Blair County, and that court immediately issued an *ex parte* order enjoining petitioners from, *inter alia,* "picketing and trespassing upon . . . the [Weis] storeroom, porch and parcel pick-up area . . . [and] the [Logan] parking area and entrances and exits leading to said parking area." The effect of this order was to require that all picketing be carried on along the berms beside the public roads outside the shopping center. . . . After an evidentiary hearing, which resulted in the establishment of the facts set forth above, the Court of Common Pleas continued indefinitely its original *ex parte* injunction without modification.

On appeal the Pennsylvania Supreme Court, with three Justices dissenting, affirmed the issuance of the injunction on the sole ground that petitioners' conduct constituted a trespass on respondents' property.

We start from the premise that peaceful picketing carried on in a location open generally to the public is, absent other factors involving the purpose or manner of the picketing, protected by the First Amendment. *Thornhill* v. *State of Alabama.* . . . To be sure, this Court has noted that picketing involves elements of both speech and conduct, i.e., patrolling, and has indicated that because of this intermingling of protected and unprotected elements, picketing can be subjected to controls that would not be constitutionally permissible in the case of pure speech. Nevertheless, no case decided by this Court can be found to support, the proposition that the nonspeech aspects of peaceful picketing are so great as to render the provisions of the First Amendment inapplicable to it altogether.

The case squarely presents, therefore, the question whether Pennsylvania's generally valid rules against trespass to private property can be applied in these circumstances to bar petitioners from the Weis and Logan premises. It is clear that if the shopping center premises were not privately owned but instead constituted the business area of a municipality, which they to a large extent resemble, petitioners could not be barred from exercising their First Amendment rights there on the sole ground that title to the property was in the municipality. The essence of . . . [the] opinion [in] *Lovell v. City of Griffin* . . . is that streets, sidewalks, parks, and other similar public places are so historically associated with the exercise of First Amendment rights that access to them for the purpose of exercising such rights cannot constitutionally be denied broadly and absolutely. . . .

This Court has also held, in *Marsh v. State of Alabama* . . . that under some circumstances property that is privately owned may, at least for First Amendment purposes, be treated as though it were publicly held. In *Marsh,* the appellant, a Jehovah's Witness, had undertaken to distribute religious literature on a sidewalk in the business district of Chickasaw, Alabama. Chickasaw, a so-called company town, was wholly owned by the Gulf Shipbuilding Corporation. "The property consists of residential buildings, streets, a system of sewers, a sewage disposal plant, and a 'business block' on which business places are situated. . . . [T]he residents use the business block as their regular shopping center. To do so, they now, as they have for many years, make use of a company-owned paved street and sidewalk located alongside the store fronts in order to enter and leave the stores and the post office. Intersecting company-owned roads at each end of the business block lead into a four-lane public highway which runs parallel to the business block at a distance of thirty feet. There is nothing to stop highway traffic from coming onto the business block and upon arrival a traveler may make free use of the facilities available there. In short the town and its shopping district are accessible to and freely used by the public in general and there is nothing to distinquish them from any other town and shopping center except the fact that the title to the property belongs to a private corporation."

The corporation had posted notices in the stores stating that the premises were private property and that no solicitation of any kind without written permission would be permitted. Appellant Marsh was told that she must have a permit to distribute her literature and that a permit would not be granted to her. When she declared that the company rule could not be utilized to prevent her from exercising her constitutional rights under the First Amendment, she was ordered to leave Chickasaw. She refused to do so and was arrested for violating Alabama's criminal trespass statute. In reversing her conviction under the statute, this Court held that the fact that the property from which appellant was sought to be ejected for exercising her First Amendment rights was owned by a private corporation rather than the State was an insufficient basis to justify the infringement on appellant's right to free expression occasioned thereby. Likewise, the fact that appellant Marsh was herself not a resident of the town was not considered material.

The similarities between the business block in *Marsh* and the shopping center in the present case are striking. The perimeter of Logan Valley Mall is a little less than 1.1 miles. Inside the mall were situated, at the time of trial, two substantial commercial enterprises with numerous others soon to follow. Immediately adjacent to the mall are two roads, one of which is a heavily traveled state highway and from both of which lead entrances directly into the mall. Adjoining the buildings in the middle of the mall are sidewalks for the use of pedestrians going to and from their cars and from building to building. In the parking areas, roadways for the use of vehicular traffic entering and leaving the mall are clearly marked out. The general public has unrestricted access to the mall property. The shopping center here is clearly the functional equivalent to the business district of Chickasaw involved in *Marsh*.

It is true that, unlike the corporation in *Marsh* the respondents here do not own the surrounding residential property and do not provide municipal services therefore. . . .

We see no reason why access to a business district in a company town for the purpose of exercising First Amendment rights should be constitutionally required, while access for the same purpose to property functioning as a business district should be limited simply because the property surrounding the "business district" is not under the same ownership. Here the roadways provided for vehicular movement within the mall and the sidewalks leading from building to building are the functional equivalents of the streets and sidewalks of a normal municipal business district. The shopping center premises are open to the public to the same extent as the commercial center of a normal town. So far as can be determined, the main distinction in practice between use by the public of the Logan Valley Mall and of any other business district, were the decisions of the state courts to stand, would be that those members of the general public who sought to use the mall premises in a manner contrary to the wishes of the respondents could be prevented from so doing.

Such a power on the part of respondents would be, of course, part and parcel of the rights traditionally associated with ownership of private property. And it may well be that respondents' ownership of the property here in question gives them various rights, under the laws of Pennsylvania, to limit the use of that property by members of the public in a manner that would not be permissible were the property owned by a municipality. All we decide here is that because the shopping center serves as the community business block "and is freely accessible and open to the people in the area and those passing through," *Marsh* v. *State of Alabama,* 326 U.S., at 508, 66 S.Ct. at 279, the State may not delegate the power, through the use of its trespass laws, wholly to exclude those members of the public wishing to exercise their First Amendment rights on the premises in a manner and for a purpose generally consonant with the use to which the property is actually put.

We do not hold that respondents, and at their behest the State, are without power to make reasonable regulations governing the exercise of First Amendment rights on their property. Certainly their rights to make such regulations are at the very least co-extensive with the powers possessed by States and municipalities, and recognized in many opinions of this Court to control the use of public property. . . . the exercise of First Amendment rights may be regulated where such exercise will unduly interfere with the normal use of the public property by other members of the public with an equal right of access to it. . . . Because the Pennsylvania courts have held that "picketing and trespassing" can be prohibited absolutely on respondents' premises, we have no occasion to consider the extent to which respondents are entitled to limit the location and manner of the picketing or the number of picketers within the mall in order to prevent interference with either access to the market building or vehicular use of the parcel pickup area and parking lot. . . . Respondents seek to defend the injunction they have obtained by characterizing the requirement that picketing be carried on outside the Logan Mall premises as a regulation rather than a suppression of it. Accepting *arguendo* such a characterization, the question remains, under the First Amendment, whether it is a permissible regulation.

Petitioners' picketing was directed solely at one establishment within the shopping center. The berms surrounding the center are from 350 to 500 feet away from the Weis store. All entry onto the mall premises by customers of Weis, so far as appears, is by vehicle from the roads along which the berms run. Thus the placards bearing the message which petitioners seek to communicate to patrons of Weis must be read by those to whom they are directed either at a distance so great as to render them virtually indecipherable —where the Weis customers are already within the mall—or while the prospective reader is moving by car from the roads onto the mall parking areas via the entrance ways cut through the berms. In addition, the pickets are placed in some danger by being forced to walk along heavily traveled roads along which traffic moves constantly at rates of speed varying from moderate to high. Likewise, the task of distributing handbills to persons in moving automobiles is vastly greater (and more hazardous) than it would be were petitioners permitted to pass them out within the mall to pedestrians. Finally, the requirement that the picketing take place outside the shopping center renders it very difficult for petitioners to limit its effect to Weis only.

It is therefore clear that the restraints on picketing and trespassing approved by the Pennsylvania courts here substantially hinder the communication of the ideas which petitioners seek to express to the patrons of Weis. The fact that the nonspeech aspects of petitioners' activity are also rendered less effective is not particularly compelling in light of the absence of any showing, or reliance by the state courts thereon, that the patrolling accompanying the picketing sought to be carried on was significantly interferring with the use to which the mall property was being put by both respondents and the general public. As we observed earlier, the mere fact that speech is accompanied by conduct does not mean that the speech can be suppressed under the guise of prohibiting the conduct. Here it is perfectly clear that a prohibition against trespass on the mall operates to bar all speech within the shopping center to which respondents object. Yet this Court stated many years ago, "[O]ne is not to have the exercise of his liberty of expression in appropriate, places abridged on the plea that it may be exercised in some other place." *Schneider* v. *State of New Jersey.*

The sole justification offered for the substantial interference with the effectiveness of petitioners' exercise of their First Amendment rights to promulgate their views through handbilling and picketing is respondents' claimed absolute right under state law to prohibit any use of their property by others without their consent. However, unlike a situation involving a person's home, no meaningful claim to protection of a right of privacy can be advanced by respondents here. Nor on the facts of the case can any significant claim to protection of the normal business operation of the property be raised. Naked title is essentially all that is at issue.

The economic development of the United States in the last twenty years reinforces our opinion of the correctness of the approach taken in *Marsh*. The large-scale movement of this country's population from the cities to the suburbs has been accompanied by the advent of the suburban shopping center, typically a cluster of individual retail units on a single large privately owned tract. It has been estimated that by the end of 1966 there were between 10,000 and 11,000 shopping centers in the United States and Canada, accounting for approximately 37 per cent of the total retail sales in those two countries.

These figures illustrate the substantial consequences for workers seeking to challenge substandard working conditions, consumers protesting shoddy or overpriced merchandise, and minority groups seeking nondiscriminatory hiring policies that a contrary decision here would have. Business enterprises located in downtown areas would be subject to on-the-spot public criticism for their practices, but businesses situated in the suburbs could largely immunize themselves from similar criticism by creating a *cordon sanitaire* of parking lots around their stores. Neither precedent nor policy compels a result so at variance with the goal of free expression and communication that is the heart of the First Amendment.

. . . We simply repeat what was said in *Marsh* v. *State of Alabama* . . . . "Ownership does not always mean absolute dominion. The more an owner, for his advantage, opens up his property for use by the public in general, the more do his rights become circumscribed by the statutory and constitutional rights of those who use it." Logan Valley Mall is the functional equivalent of a "business block" and for First Amendment purposes must be treated in substantially the same manner.

The judgment of the Supreme Court of Pennsylvania is reversed and the case is remanded for further proceedings not inconsistent with this opinion. It is so ordered.

MR. JUSTICE DOUGLAS *concurred*.

MR. JUSTICE BLACK, dissenting:

While I generally accept the factual background of this case presented in the Court's opinion, I think it is important to focus on just where this picketing, which was enjoined by the state courts, was actually taking place. The following extract is taken from the trial court's "Findings of Fact."

". . . (a) Small groups of men and women wearing placards . . . walked back and forth in front of the Weis supermarket, more particularly *in the pick-up zone* adjacent to the covered porch [emphasis added];

"(b) Occasional picketing as above described has taken place *on the covered porch itself* [emphasis added]";

Anyone familiar with the operations of a modern-day supermarket knows the importance of the so-called "pick-up zone"—an area where the frequently numerous bags of groceries bought in the store can be loaded conveniently into the customers' cars. . . .

It seems clear to me, in light of the customary way that supermarkets now must operate, that pick-up zones are as much a part of these stores as the inside counters where customers select their goods or the check-out and bagging sections where the goods are paid for. I cannot conceive how such a pick-up zone, even by the wildest stretching of *Marsh* v. *State of Alabama,* 326 U.S. 501, 66 Sup. Ct. 276, 90 L. Ed. 265, could ever be considered dedicated to the public or to pickets. The very first section of the injunction issued by the trial court in this case recognizes this fact and is aimed only at protecting this clearly private property from trespass by the pickets. Thus, the order of the court separately enjoins petitioners from:

> "(a) Picketing and trespassing upon the private property of the plaintiff Weis Markets, Inc., Store No. 40, located at Logan Valley Mall, Altoona, Pennsylvania, including as such private property the storeroom, porch and parcel pick-up area."

While there is language in the majority opinion which indicates that the state courts may still regulate picketing on respondent Weis' private property, this is not sufficient. I think that this Court should declare unequivocally that Section (a) of the lower court's injunction is valid under the First Amendment and that petitioners cannot, under the guise of exercising First Amendment rights, trespass on respondent Weis' private property for the purpose of picketing. It would be just as sensible for this Court to allow the pickets to stand on the check-out counters, thus interfering with customers who wish to pay for their goods, as it is to approve picketing in the pick-up zone which interferes with customers' loading of their cars. At the very least, this wholly severable part of the injunction aimed at the pick-up zone should be affirmed by the Court as valid under the First Amendment. And this is in fact the really important part of the injunction since, as the Court's opinion admits, "the picketing was carried out almost entirely in the parcel pickup area and that portion of the parking lot immediately adjacent thereto."

I would go further, however, and hold that the entire injunction is valid. With the exception of the Weis property mentioned above, the land on which this shopping center (composed of only two stores at the time of trial and approximately seventeen now) is located is owned by respondent Logan Valley Plaza, Inc. Logan has improved its property by putting shops and parking spaces thereon for the use of business customers. Now petitioners contend that they can come onto Logan's property for the purpose of picketing and refuse to leave when asked, and that Logan cannot use state trespass laws to keep them out. The majority of this Court affirms petitioners' contentions. But I cannot accept them, for I believe that whether this Court likes it or not the Constitution recognizes and supports the concept of private ownership of property. The Fifth Amendment provides that "no person shall . . . be deprived of life, liberty, or property, without due process of law; nor shall private property be taken for public use, without just compensation." This means to me that there is no right to picket on the private premises of another to try to convert the owner or others to the views of the pickets. It also means, I think, that if this Court is going to arrogate to itself the power to act as the Government's agent to take a part of Weis' property to give to the pickets for their use, the Court should also award Weis just compensation for the property taken.

In affirming petitioners' contentions the majority opinion relies on *Marsh* v. *State of Alabama,* supra, and holds that respondents' property has been transformed to some type of public property. But *Marsh* was never intended to apply to this kind of situation. *Marsh* dealt with the very special situation of a company-owned town, complete with streets, alleys, sewers, stores, residences, and everything else that goes to make a town. . . . I think it is fair to say that the basis on which the *Marsh* decision rested was that the property involved encompassed an area that for all practical purposes had been turned into a town; the area had all the attributes of a town and was indistinguishable from any other town in Alabama. I can find very little resemblance between the shopping center involved in this case and Chickasaw, Alabama. . . .

The majority opinion recognizes the problem with trying to draw too close an analogy with *Marsh,* but faces a dilemma in that *Marsh* is the only possible authority for treating admittedly privately owned property the way the majority does. Thus the majority opinion concedes that "the respondents here do not own the surrounding residential property and do not provide municipal services therefor." But that is not crucial, according to the majority, since the petitioner in *Marsh* was arrested in the business district of Chickasaw. The majority opinion then concludes that since the petitioner in *Marsh* was given access to the business district of a company town, the petitioners in this case should be given access to the shopping center which was functioning as a business district. But I respectfully suggest that this reasoning completely misreads Marsh and begs the question. The question is under what circumstances can private property be treated as though it were public? The answer that *Marsh* gives is when that property has taken on

all the attributes of a town, i.e., "residential buildings, streets, a system of sewers, a sewage disposal plant and a 'business block' on which business places are situated." . . . I can find nothing in *Marsh* which indicates that if one of these features is present, e.g., a business district, this is sufficient for the Court to confiscate a part of an owner's private property and give its use to people who want to picket on it.

In allowing the trespass here, the majority opinion indicates that Weis and Logan invited the public to the shopping center's parking lot. This statement is contrary to common sense. Of course there was an implicit invitation for customers of the adjacent stores to come and use the marked off places for cars. But the whole public was no more wanted there than they would be invited to park free at a pay parking lot. Is a store owner or several of them together less entitled to have a parking lot set aside for customers than other property owners? To hold that store owners are compelled by law to supply picketing areas for pickets to drive store customers away is to create a court-made law wholly disregarding the constitutional basis on which private ownership of property rests in this country. And of course picketing, that is patroling, is not free speech and not protected as such. . . . These pickets do have a constitutional right to speak about Weis' refusal to hire union labor, but they do not have a constitutional right to compel Weis to furnish them a place to do so on his property. . . .

JUSTICES HARLAN and WHITE dissented.

GINZBURG *v.* UNITED STATES
383 U.S. 463; 86 Sup. Ct. 942; 16 L. Ed. 2d 31 (1966)

[Ginzburg and the case following were decided the same day along with Mishkin *v.* New York. *The two cases should be read together as a catalog of the various tests of obscenity held by various justices.]*

MR. JUSTICE BRENNAN delivered the opinion of the Court:

A judge sitting without a jury in the District Court for the Eastern District of Pennsylvania convicted petitioner Ginzburg and three corporations controlled by him upon all 28 counts of an indictment charging violation of the federal obscenity statute. Each count alleged that a resident of the Eastern District received mailed matter, either one of three publications challenged as obscene, or advertising telling how and where the publications might be obtained. The Court of Appeals for the Third Circuit affirmed. We granted certiorari, . . . We affirm. . . .

In the cases in which this Court has decided obscenity questions since *Roth,* it has regarded the materials as sufficient in themselves for the determination of the question. In the present case, however, the prosecution charged the offense in the context of the circumstances of production, sale, and publicity and assumed that, standing alone, the publications themselves might not be obscene. We agree that the question of obscenity may include consideration of the setting in which the publications were presented as an aid to determining the question of obscenity, and assume without deciding that the prosecution could not have succeeded otherwise. . . . We view the publications against a background of commercial exploitation of erotica solely for the sake of their prurient appeal. The record in that regard amply supports the decision of the trial judge that the mailing of all three publications offended the statute.

The three publications were *Eros,* a hard-cover magazine of expensive format; *Liaison,* a bi-weekly newsletter; and *The Housewife's Handbook on Selective Promiscuity* (hereinafter the *Handbook*), a short book. The issue of *Eros* specified in the indictment, Vol. 1, No. 4, contains fifteen articles and photo-essays on the subject of love, sex, and sexual relations. The specified issue of *Liaison*, Vol. 1, No. 1, contains a prefatory "Letter from the Editors" announcing its dedication to "keeping sex an art and preventing it from becoming a science." The remainder of the issue consists of digests of two articles concerning sex and sexual relations which had earlier appeared in professional journals and a report of an interview with a psychotherapist who favors the broadest license in sexual relationships. As the trial judge noted, "[w]hile the treatment is largely superficial, it is presented entirely without restraint of any kind. According to defendants' own expert, it is entirely without literary merit." 224 F. Supp., at 134. The *Handbook* purports to be a sexual autobiography detailing with complete candor the author's sexual experiences from age three to age thirty-six. The text includes, and prefatory and concluding sections of the book elaborate, her views on such subjects as sex education of children, laws regulating private consensual adult sexual practices, and the equality of women in sexual relationships. It was claimed at trial that women would find the book valuable, for example as a marriage manual or as an aid to the sex education of their children.

Besides testimony as to the merit of the material there was abundant evidence to show that each of the accused publications was originated or sold as stock in trade of the sordid business of pandering—"the business of purveying textual or graphic matter openly advertised to appeal to the erotic interest of their customers. . . ."

The "leer of the sensualist" also permeates the advertising for the three publications. The circulars sent for *Eros* and *Liaison* stressed the sexual candor of the respective publications, and openly boasted that the publishers would take full advantage of what they regarded an unrestricted license allowed by law in the expression of sex and sexual matters. The advertising for the *Handbook,* apparently mailed from New York, consisted almost entirely of a reproduction of the introduction of the book, written by one Dr. Albert Ellis. Although he alludes to the book's informational value and its putative therapeutic usefulness, his remarks are preoccupied with the book's sexual imagery. The solicitation was indiscriminate, not limited to those, such as physicians or psychiatrists, who might independently discern the book's therapeutic worth. Inserted in each advertisement was a slip labeled "Guarantee" and reading, "Documentary Books, Inc. unconditionally guarantees full refund on the price of *The Housewife's Handbook on Selective Promiscuity* if the book fails to reach you because of U.S. Post Office censorship interference." Similar slips appeared in the advertising for *Eros* and *Liaison;* they highlighted the gloss petitioners put on the publications, eliminating any doubt what the purchaser was being asked to buy.

This evidence, in our view, was relevant in determining the ultimate question of "obscenity" and, in the context of this record, serves to resolve all ambiguity and doubt. The deliberate representation of petitioners' publications as erotically arousing, for example, stimulated the reader to accept them as prurient; he looks for titillation, not for saving intellectual content. Similarly, such representation would tend to force public confrontation with the potentially offensive aspects of the work; the brazenness of such an appeal heightens the offensiveness of the publications to those who are offended by such material. And the circumstances of presentation and dissemination of material are equally relevant to determining whether social importance claimed for

material in the courtroom was, in the circumstances, pretense or reality— whether it was the basis upon which it was traded in the marketplace or a spurious claim for litigation purposes. Where the purveyor's sole emphasis is on the sexually provocative aspects of his publications, that fact may be decisive in the determination of obscenity. Certainly in a prosecution which, as here, does not necessarily imply suppression of the materials involved, the fact that they originate or are used as a subject of pandering is relevant to the application of the *Roth* test. . . .

We perceive no threat to First Amendment guarantees in thus holding that in close cases evidence of pandering may be probative with respect to the nature of the material in question and thus satisfy the *Roth* test. No weight is ascribed to the fact that petitioners have profited from the sale of publications which we have assumed but do not hold cannot themselves be adjudged obscene in the abstract; to sanction consideration of this fact might indeed induce self-censorship, and offend the frequently stated principle that commercial activity, in itself, is no justification for narrowing the protection of expression secured by the First Amendment. Rather, the fact that each of these publications was created or exploited entirely on the basis of its appeal to prurient interests strengthens the conclusion that the transactions here were sales of illicit merchandise, not sales of constitutionally protected matter. A conviction for mailing obscene publications, but explained in part by the presence of this element, does not necessarily suppress the materials in question, nor chill their proper distribution for a proper use. Nor should it inhibit the enterprise of others seeking through serious endeavor to advance human knowledge or understanding in science, literature, or art. All that will have been determined is that questionable publications are obscene in a context which brands them as obscene as that term is defined in *Roth*—a use inconsistent with any claim to the shelter of the First Amendment. "The nature of the materials is, of course, relevant as an attribute of the defendant's conduct, but the materials are thus placed in context from which they draw color and character. A wholly different result might be reached in a different setting." *Roth* v. *United States*, 354 U.S., at 495, 77 S. Ct. at 1315 (Warren, C. J., concurring).

It is important to stress that this analysis simply elaborates the test by which the obscenity vel non of the material must be judged. Where an exploitation of interests in titillation by pornography is shown with respect to material lending itself to such exploitation through pervasive treatment or description of sexual matters, such evidence may support the determination that the material is obscene even though in other contexts the material would escape such condemnation. . . .

Affirmed.

MR. JUSTICE BLACK, dissenting:

Only one stark fact emerges with clarity out of the confusing welter of opinions and thousands of words written in this and two other cases today. That fact is that Ginzburg, petitioner here, is now finally and authoritatively condemned to serve five years in prison for distributing printed matter about sex which neither Ginzberg nor anyone else could possibly have known to be criminal. . . . I believe the Federal Government is without any power whatever under the Constitution to put any type of burden on speech and expression of ideas of any kind (as distinguished from conduct). . . . I find it difficult to see how talk about sex can be placed under the kind of censorship the Court here approves without subjecting our society to more dangers than we can anticipate at the moment. It was to avoid exactly such dangers that the First Amendment was written and adopted. For myself, I would follow the course which I believe is required by the First Amendment, that is recognize that sex at least as much as any other aspect of life is so much a part of our society that its discussions should not be made a crime.

I would reverse this case.

MR. JUSTICE HARLAN, dissenting:

. . . I believe that under this statute the Federal Government is constitutionally restricted to banning from the mails only "hardcore pornography," . . . Because I do not think it can be maintained that the material in question here falls within that narrow class, I do not believe it can be excluded from the mails. . . . In fact, the Court in the last analysis sustains the convictions on the express assumption that the items held to be obscene are not, viewing them strictly, obscene at all . . . . The First Amendment, in the obscenity area, no longer fully protects material on its face nonobscene, for such material must now also be examined in the light of the defendant's conduct, attitude, motives. This seems to me a mere euphemism for allowing punishment of a person who mails otherwise constitutionally protected material just because a jury or a judge may not find him or his business agreeable. . . .

MR. JUSTICE STEWART, dissenting:

The petitioner has been sentenced to five years in prison for sending through the mail copies of a magazine, a pamphlet, and a book. There was testimony at his trial that these publications possess artistic and social merit. Personally, I have a hard time discerning any. Most of the material strikes me as both vulgar and unedifying. But if the First Amendment means anything, it means that a man cannot be sent to prison merely for distributing publications which offend a judge's esthetic sensibilities, mine or any other's.

Censorship reflects a society's lack of confidence in itself. It is a hallmark of an authoritarian regime. Long ago those who wrote our First Amendment charted a different course. They believed a society can be truly strong only when it is truly free. In the realm of expression they put their faith, for better or for worse, in the enlightened choice of the people, free from the interference of a policeman's intrusive thumb or a judge's heavy hand. So it is that the Constitution protects coarse expression as well as refined and vulgarity no less than elegance. A book worthless to me may convey something of value to my neighbor. In the free society to which our Constitution has committed us, it is for each to choose for himself.

Because such is the mandate of our Constitution, there is room for only the most restricted view of this Court's decision in *Roth* v. *United States* . . . . In that case the Court held that "obscenity is not within the area of constitutionally protected speech or press." . . . The Court there characterized obscenity as that which is "utterly without redeeming social importance," . . . "deals with sex in a manner appealing to prurient interest," . . . and "goes substantially beyond customary limits of candor in description or representation of such matters." . . . In *Manual Enterprises* v. *Day,* . . . I joined Mr. Justice Harlan's opinion adding "patent indecency" as a further essential element of that which is not constitutionally protected.

There does exist a distinct and easily identifiable class of material in which all of these elements coalesce. It is that, and that alone, which I think government may constitutionally suppress, whether by criminal or civil sanctions.

I have referred to such material before as hardcore pornography, without trying further to define it. . . .

The Court today appears to concede that the materials Ginzburg mailed were themselves protected by the First Amendment. But, the Court says, Ginzburg can still be sentenced to five years in prison for mailing them. Why? Because, says the Court, he was guilty of "commercial exploitation," of "pandering," and of "tiltillation." But Ginzburg was not charged with "commercial exploitation"; he was not charged with "pandering"; he was not charged with "titillation." Therefore, to affirm his conviction now on any of those grounds, even if otherwise valid, is to deny him due process of law. But those grounds are *not,* of course, otherwise valid. Neither the statute under which Ginzburg was convicted nor any other federal statute I know of makes "commercial exploitation" or "pandering" or "titillation" a criminal offense. And any criminal law that sought to do so in the terms so elusively defined by the Court would, of course, be unconstitutionally vague and therefore void. . . .

For me, however, there is another aspect of the Court's opinion in this case that is even more regrettable. Today the Court assumes the power to deny Ralph Ginzburg the protection of the First Amendment because it disapproves of his "sordid business." That is a power the Court does not possess. For the First Amendment protects us all with an even hand. . . . In upholding and enforcing the Bill of Rights, this Court has no power to pick or to choose. When we lose sight of that fixed star of constitutional adjudication, we lose our way. For then we forsake a government of law and are left with government by Big Brother.

I dissent.

A BOOK NAMED "JOHN CLELAND'S MEMOIRS OF A WOMAN OF PLEASURE," ET AL., APPELLANTS *v.* ATTORNEY GENERAL OF THE COMMONWEALTH OF MASSACHUSETTS
383 U.S. 413; 86 Sup. Ct. 975; 16 L. Ed. 2d 1 (1966)

MR. JUSTICE BRENNAN announced the judgment of the Court and delivered an opinion in which the CHIEF JUSTICE and MR. JUSTICE FORTAS join:

This is an obscenity case in which *Memoirs of a Woman of Pleasure* (commonly known as *Fanny Hill*), written by John Cleland in about 1750, was adjudged obscene in a proceeding that put on trial the book itself, and not its publisher or distributor. The proceeding was a civil equity suit brought by the Attorney General of Massachusetts . . . . At the hearing before a justice of the Superior Court, which was conducted, under § 28F, "in accordance with the usual course of proceedings in equity," the court received the book in evidence and also, as allowed by the section, heard the testimony of experts and accepted other evidence, such as book reviews, in order to assess the literary, cultural, or educational character of the book. This constituted the entire evidence . . . . The trial justice entered a final decree, which adjudged *Memoirs* obscene . . . . The Massachusetts Supreme Judicial Court affirmed the decree. . . .

We reverse.

. . . We defined obscenity in *Roth* in the following terms: "[W]hether to the average persons, applying contemporary community standards, the dominant theme of the material taken as a whole appeals to prurient interest." . . . Under this definition, as elaborated in subsequent cases, three elements must coalesce: it must be established that (a) the dominant theme of the material taken as a whole appeals to a prurient interest in sex; (b) the material is patently offensive because it affronts contemporary community standards relating to the description or representation of sexual matters; and (c) the material is utterly without redeeming social value.

The Supreme Judicial Court purported to apply the *Roth* definition of obscenity and held all three criteria satisfied. We need not consider the claim that the court erred in concluding that *Memoirs* satisfied the prurient appeal and patent offensiveness criteria; for reversal is required because the court misinterpreted the social value criterion. The court applied the criterion in this passage:

"It remains to consider whether the book can be said to be 'utterly without social importance.' We are mindful that there was expert testimony, much of which was strained, to the effect that Memoirs is a structural novel with literary merit; that the book displays a skill in characterization and a gift for comedy; that it plays a part in the history of the development of the English novel; and that it contains a moral, namely, that sex with love is superior to sex in a brothel. But the fact that the testimony may indicate this book has some minimal literary value does not mean it is of any social importance. We do not interpret the 'social importance' test as requiring that a book which appeals to prurient interest and is patently offensive must be unqualifiedly worthless before it can be deemed obscene." . . .

The Supreme Judicial Court erred in holding that a book need not be "unqualifiedly worthless before it can be

deemed obscene." A book can not be proscribed unless it is found to be *utterly* without redeeming social value. This is so even though the book is found to possess the requisite prurient appeal and to be patently offensive. Each of the three federal constitutional criteria is to be applied independently; the social value of the book can neither be weighed against nor canceled by its prurient appeal or patent offensiveness. Hence, even on the view of the court below that *Memoirs* possessed only a modicum of social value, its judgment must be reversed as being founded on an erroneous interpretation of a federal constitutional standard.

II

It does not necessarily follow from this reversal that a determination that *Memoirs* is obscene in the constitutional sense would be improper under all circumstances. On the premise, which we have no occasion to assess, that *Memoirs* has the requisite prurient appeal and is patently offensive, but has only a minimum of social value, the circumstances of production, sale, and publicity are relevant in determining whether or not the publication and distribution of the book is constitutionally protected. Evidence that the book was commercially exploited for the sake of prurient appeal, to the exclusion of all other values, might justify the conclusion that the book was utterly without redeeming social importance. It is not that in such a setting the social value test is relaxed so as to dispense with the requirement that a book be *utterly* devoid of social value, but rather that, as we elaborate in *Ginzburg* v. *United States*, . . . where the purveyor's sole emphasis is on the sexually provocative aspects of his publications, a court could accept his evaluation at its face value. In this proceeding, however, the courts were asked to judge

the obscenity of *Memoirs* in the abstract, and the declaration of obscenity was neither aided nor limited by a specific set of circumstances of production, sale, and publicity. All possible uses of the book must therefore be considered, and the mere risk that the book might be exploited by panderers because it so pervasively treats sexual matters cannot alter the fact—given the view of the Massachusetts court attributing to *Memoirs* a modicum of literary and historical value—that the book will have redeeming social importance in the hands of those who publish or distribute it on the basis of that value.

Reversed.

MR. JUSTICE BLACK and MR. JUSTICE STEWART concur in the reversal for the reasons stated in their respective dissenting opinions in *Ginzburg* v. *United States* . . . .

MR. JUSTICE DOUGLAS concurring:

. . . The courts of Massachusetts found the book "obscene" and upheld its suppression. This Court reverses, the prevailing opinion having seized upon language in the opinion of the Massachusetts Supreme Judicial Court in which it is candidly admitted that *Fanny Hill* has at least "some minimal literary value." I do not believe that the Court should decide this case on so disingenuous a basis as this. I base my vote to reverse on my view that the First Amendment does not permit the censorship of expression not brigaded with illegal action. . . . The Constitution forbids abridgment of "freedom of speech, or of the press." Censorship is the most notorious form of abridgment. It substitutes majority rule where minority tastes or viewpoints were to be tolerated. . . .

It is true, as the Court observed in *Roth,* that obscenity laws appeared on the books of a handful of States at the time the First Amendment was adopted. But the First Amendment was, until the

adoption of the Fourteenth, a restraint only upon federal power. Moreover, there is an absence of any *federal* cases or laws relative to obscenity in the period immediately after the adoption of the First Amendment. Congress passed no legislation relating to obscenity until the middle of the nineteenth century. Neither reason nor history warrants exclusion of any particular class of expression from the protection of the First Amendment on nothing more than a judgment that it is utterly without merit. We faced the difficult questions the First Amendment poses with regard to libel in *New York Times Co. v. Sullivan,* . . . where we recognized that "libel can claim no talismanic immunity from constitutional limitations." We ought not to permit fictionalized assertions of constitutional history to obscure those questions here. Were the Court to undertake that inquiry, it would be unable, in my opinion, to escape the conclusion that no interest of society with regard to suppression of "obscene" literature could override the First Amendment to justify censorship.

The censor is always quick to justify his function in terms that are protective of society. But the First Amendment, written in terms that are absolute, deprives the State of any power to pass on the value, the propriety, or the morality of a particular expression. . . .

Whatever may be the reach of the power to regulate *conduct,* I stand by my view in *Roth* v. *United States,* supra, that the First Amendment leaves no power in government over *expression of ideas.* . . .

MR. JUSTICE CLARK, dissenting:

It is with regret that I write this dissenting opinion. However, the public should know of the continuous flow of pornographic material reaching this Court and the increasing problem States have in controlling it. *Memoirs of a Woman of Pleasure,* the book involved

here, is typical. I have "stomached" past cases for almost 10 years without much outcry. Though I am not known to be a purist—or a shrinking violet—this book is too much even for me. It is important that the Court has refused to declare it obscene and thus gives it further circulation. . . .

Let me first pinpoint the effect of today's holding in the obscenity field. While there is no majority opinion in this case, there are three Justices who import a new test into that laid down in *Roth* v. *United States,* . . . namely, that "a book cannot be proscribed unless it is found to be utterly without redeeming social value." I agree with my Brother White that such a condition rejects the basic holding of *Roth* and gives the smut artist free rein to carry on his dirty business. My vote in that case—which was the deciding one for the majority opinion—was cast solely because the Court declared the test of obscenity to be: "whether to the average person, applying contemporary community standards, the dominant theme of the material taken as a whole appeals to prurient interest." I understand that test to include only two constitutional requirements: (1) the book must be judged as a whole, not by its parts; and (2) it must be judged in terms of its appeal to the prurient interest of the average person, applying contemporary community standards. Indeed, obscenity was denoted in *Roth* as having *"such slight social value as a step to truth that any benefit that may be derived . . . is clearly outweighed by the social interest in order and morality. . . .*

. . . Moreover, in no subsequent decision of this Court has any "utterly without redeeming social value" test been suggested, much less expounded. My Brother Harlan in *Manual Enterprises, Inc.* v. *Day* . . . made no reference whatever to such a requirement

in *Roth*. Rather he interpreted *Roth* as including a test of "patent offensiveness" besides "prurient appeal." Nor did my Brother Brennan in his concurring opinion in *Manual Enterprises* mention any "utterly without redeeming social value" test. The first reference to such a test was made by my Brother Brennan in *Jacobellis* v. *State of Ohio* . . . seven years after *Roth*. In an opinion joined only by Justice Goldberg, he there wrote: "Recognizing that the test for obscenity enunciated [in *Roth*] is not perfect, we think any substitute would raise equally difficult problems, and we therefore adhere to that standard." Nevertheless, he proceeded to add:

> "We would reiterate, however, our recognition in *Roth* that obscenity is excluded from the constitutional protection only because it is 'utterly without redeeming social importance' . . . ."

This language was then repeated in the converse to announce this *non sequitur:*

> "It follows that material dealing with sex in a manner that advocates ideas . . . or that has literary or scientific or artistic value or any other form of social importance, may not be branded as obscenity and denied the constitutional protection."

Significantly no opinion in *Jacobellis,* other than that of my Brother Brennan, mentioned the "utterly without redeeming social importance" test which he there introduced into our many and varied previous opinions in obscenity cases. Indeed, rather than recognizing the "utterly without social importance" test, The Chief Justice in his dissent in *Jacobellis,* which I joined, specifically stated:

> "In light of the foregoing, I would reiterate my acceptance of the rule of the *Roth* case: *Material is obscene and not constitutionally protected against regulation and proscription* if 'to the average person applying contemporary community standards, the dominant theme of the material taken as a whole appeals to prurient interest.' " (Emphasis added.) At 202, 84 Sup. Ct. at 1685.

The Chief Justice and myself further asserted that the enforcement of this rule should be committed to the state and federal courts whose judgments made pursuant to the *Roth* rule we would accept, limiting our review to a consideration of whether there is "sufficient evidence" in the record to support a finding of obscenity. At 202, 84 Sup. Ct. at 1685.

II

Three members of the majority hold that reversal here is necessary solely because their novel "utterly without redeeming value" test was not properly interpreted or applied by the Supreme Judicial Court of Massachusetts. Massachusetts now has to retry the case although the "Findings of Fact, Rulings of Law and Order for Final Decree" of the trial court specifically held that "this book is 'utterly without social redeeming importance' in the fields of art, literature, science, news or ideas of any social importance and that it is obscene, indecent and impure." . . .

Brother Brennan reverses on the basis of [a] casual statement, despite the specific findings of the trial court. Why, if the statement is erroneous, Brother Brennan does not affirm the holding of the trial court which beyond question is correct, one cannot tell. This course has often been followed in other cases.

In my view evidence of social importance is relevant to the determination of the ultimate question of obscenity.

But social importance does not constitute a separate and distinct constitutional test. Such evidence must be considered together with evidence that the material in question appeals to prurient interest and is patently offensive."

. . . It is, of course, the duty of the judge or the jury to determine the question of obscenity, viewing the book by contemporary community standards. It can accept the appraisal of experts or discount their testimony in the light of the material itself or other relevant testimony. So-called "literary obscenity," i.e., the use of erotic fantasies of the hard-core type clothed in an engaging literary style has no constitutional protection. If a book deals solely with erotic material in a manner calculated to appeal to the prurient interest, it matters not that it may be expressed in beautiful prose. There are obviously dynamic connections between art and sex—the emotional, intellectual, and physical—but where the former is used solely to promote prurient appeal, it cannot claim constitutional immunity.

. . .

MR. JUSTICE HARLAN, dissenting:

The central development that emerges from the aftermath of *Roth* v. *United States* . . . is that no stable approach to the obscenity problem has yet been devised by this Court. Two justices believe that the First and Fourteenth Amendments absolutely protect obscene and nonobscene material alike. Another justice believes that neither the States nor the Federal Government may suppress any material save for "hard-core pornography." *Roth* in 1957 stressed prurience and utter lack of redeeming social importance;[21] as *Roth*

[21] Given my view of the applicable constitutional standards, I find no occasion to consider the place of "redeeming social importance" in the majority opinion in *Roth,* an issue which further divides the present Court.

has been expounded in this case, in *Ginzburg* v. *United States,* . . . in *Mishkin* v. *State of New York* . . . it has undergone significant transformation. The concept of "pandering," emphasized by the separate opinion of the Chief Justice in *Roth,* now emerges as an uncertain gloss or interpretive aid, and the further requisite of "patent offensiveness" has been made explicit as a result of intervening decisions. Given this tangled state of affairs, I feel free to adhere to the principles first set forth in my separate opinion in *Roth,* 354 U.S., at 496, 77 Sup. Ct., at 1315, which I continue to believe represent the soundest constitutional solution to this intractable problem.

My premise is that in the area of obscenity the Constitution does not bind the States and the Federal Government in precisely the same fashion. This approach is plainly consistent with the language of the First and Fourteenth Amendments and, in my opinion, more responsive to the proper functioning of a federal system of government in this area. See my opinion in *Roth,* 354 U.S., at 505–506, 77 Sup. Ct., at 1319–1320. I believe it is also consistent with past decisions of this Court. Although some forty years have passed since the Court first indicated that the Fourteenth Amendment protects "free speech," see *Gitlow* v. *People of State of New York* . . . ; *Fiske* v. *State of Kansas,* . . . the decisions have never declared that every utterance the Federal Government may not reach or every regulatory scheme it may not enact is also beyond the power of the State. The very criteria used in opinions to delimit the protection of free speech—the gravity of the evil being regulated, see *Schneider* v. *State of New Jersey,* how "clear and present" is the danger, *Schenck* v. *United States,* 249 U.S. 47 (Holmes, J.); the magnitude of "such invasion of free speech as is necessary to avoid the danger" . . . may and do depend on the particular context in which power is exercised. When, for example, the Court in *Beauharnais* v. *People of State of Illinois* . . . upheld a criminal group-libel law because of the "social interest in order and morality" . . . it was acknowledging the responsibility and capacity of the States in such public-welfare matters and not committing itself to uphold any similar federal statute applying to such communications as Congress might otherwise regulate under the commerce power. . . .

Federal suppression of allegedly obscene matter should, in my view, be constitutionally limited to that often described as "hard-core pornography." To be sure, that rubric is not a self-executing standard, but it does describe something that most judges and others will "know . . . when [they] see it" (Stewart, J., in *Jacobellis* v. *State of Ohio,* 378 U.S. 184, 197) . . . and that leaves the smallest room for disagreement between those of varying tastes. To me it is plain, for instance, that *Fanny Hill* does not fall within this class and could not be barred from the federal mails. If further articulation is meaningful, I would characterize as "hard-core" that prurient material that is patently offensive or whose indecency is self-demonstrating and I would describe it substantially as does Mr. Justice Stewart's opinion in Ginzburg. The Federal Government may be conceded a limited interest in excluding from the mails such gross pornography, almost universally condemned in this country. But I believe the dangers of national censorship and the existence of primary responsibility at the state level amply justify drawing the line at this point.

State obscenity laws present problems of quite a different order. The varying conditions across the country, the range of views on the need and reasons for curbing obscenity, and the traditions of local self-government in matters of public welfare all favor a far more flexible attitude in defining the bounds for the States. From my standpoint, the Fourteenth Amendment requires of a State only that it apply criteria rationally related to the accepted notion of obscenity and that it reach results not wholly out of step with current American standards. As to criteria, it should be adequate if the court or jury considers such elements as offensiveness, pruriency, social value, and the like. The latitude which I believe the States deserve cautions against any federally imposed formula listing the exclusive ingredients of obscenity and fixing their proportions. . . .

There is plenty of room, I know, for disagreement in this area of constitutional law. Some will think that what I propose may encourage States to go too far in this field. Others will consider that the Court's present course unduly restricts state experimentation with the still elusive problem of obscenity. For myself, I believe it is the part of wisdom for those of us who happen currently to possess the "final word" to leave room for such experimentation, which indeed is the underlying genius of our federal system.

MR. JUSTICE WHITE, dissenting:

In *Roth* v. *United States* . . . the Court held a publication to be obscene if its predominant theme appeals to the prurient interest in a manner exceeding customary limits of candor. Material of this kind, the Court said, is "utterly without redeeming social importance" and is therefore unprotected by the First Amendment.

To say that material within the *Roth* definition of obscenity is nevertheless not obscene if it has some redeeming social value is to reject one of the basic propositions of the *Roth* case—that such material is not protected *because* it is inherently and utterly without social value.

If "social importance" is to be used as the prevailing opinion uses it today, obscene material, however far beyond customary limits of candor, is immune if it has any literary style, if it contains any historical references or language characteristic of a bygone day, or even if it is printed or bound in an interesting way. Well written, especially effective obscenity is protected; the poorly written is vulnerable. And why shouldn't the fact that some people buy and read such material prove its "social value"?

A fortiori, if the predominant theme of the book appeals to the prurient interest as stated in *Roth* but the book nevertheless contains here and there a passage descriptive of character, geography or architecture, the book would not be "obscene" under the social importance test. I had thought that *Roth* counseled the contrary: That the character of the book is fixed by its predominant theme and is not altered by the presence of minor themes of a different nature. The *Roth* Court's em-

phatic reliance on the quotation from *Chaplinsky* v. *State of New Hampshire* . . . means nothing less:

" ' . . . There are certain well-defined and narrowly limited classes of speech, the prevention and punishment of which have never been thought to raise any Constitutional problem. *These include the lewd and obscene. . . . It has been well observed that such utterances are no essential part of any exposition of ideas, and are of such slight social value as a step to truth that any benefit that may be derived from them is clearly outweighed by the social interest in order and morality. . . .'* (Emphasis added.)" 354 U.S., at 485, 77 Sup. Ct., at 1309.

In my view, "social importance" is not an independent test of obscenity but is relevant only to determining the predominant prurient interest of the material, a determination which the court or the jury will make based on the material itself and all the evidence in the case, expert or otherwise.

FREEDMAN *v.* MARYLAND
380 U.S. 51; 85 Sup. Ct. 734; 13 L. Ed. 2d 649 (1965)

MR. JUSTICE BRENNAN delivered the opinion of the Court:

Appellant sought to challenge the constitutionality of the Maryland motion picture censorship statute, and exhibited the film "Revenge at Daybreak" at his Baltimore theatre without first submitting the picture to the State Board of Censors as required by § 2 of the statute. The State concedes that the picture does not violate the statutory standards and would have received a license if properly submitted, but the appellant was convicted of a § 2 violation despite his contention that the

statute in its entirety unconstitutionally impaired freedom of expression. The Court of Appeals of Maryland affirmed.
We reverse.

I

In *Times Film Corp.* v. *City of Chicago* we considered and upheld a requirement of submission of motion pictures in advance of exhibition. The Court of Appeals held, on the authority of that decision, that "the Maryland censorship law must be held to be not void on its face as violative of the freedoms protected against State action by the First and Fourteenth Amendments." This reliance on *Times Film* was misplaced. The only question tendered for decision in that case was "whether a prior restraint was necessarily unconstitutional *under all circumstances.*" . . . The exhibitor's argument that the requirement of submission without more amounted to a constitutionally prohibited prior restraint was interpreted by the Court in *Times Film* as a contention that the "constitutional protection includes complete and absolute freedom to exhibit, at least once, any and every kind of motion picture . . . even if this film contains the basest type of pornography, or incitement to riot, or forceful overthrow of orderly government . . . ." The Court held that on this "narrow" question, the argument stated the principle against prior restraints too broadly; citing a number of our decisions, the Court quoted the statement from *Near* v. *Minnesota* that "the protection even as to previous restraint is not absolutely unlimited." In rejecting the proffered proposition in *Times Film* the Court emphasized, however, that "[i]t is that question alone which we decide," and it would therefore be inaccurate to say that *Times Film* upheld the specific features of the Chicago censorship ordinance.

Unlike the petitioner in *Times Film,* appellant does not argue that § 2 is unconstitutional simply because it may prevent even the first showing of a film whose exhibition may legitimately be the subject of an obscenity prosecution. He presents a question quite distinct from that passed on in *Times Film;* accepting the rule in *Times Film,* he argues that § 2 constitutes an invalid prior restraint because, in the context of the remainder of the statute, it presents a danger of unduly suppressing protected expression. He focuses particularly on the procedure for an initial decision by the censorship board, which, without any judicial participation, effectively bars exhibition of any disapproved film, unless and until the exhibitor undertakes a time-consuming appeal to the Maryland courts and succeeds in having the Board's decision reversed. Under the statute, the exhibitor is required to submit the film to the Board for examination, but no time limit is imposed for completion of Board action, § 17. If the film is disapproved, or any elimination ordered, § 19 provides that "the person submitting such film or view for examination will receive immediate notice of such elimination or disapproval, and if appealed from, such film or view will be promptly reexamined, in the presence of such person, by two or more members of the Board, and the same finally approved or disapproved promptly after such re-examination, with the right of appeal from the decision of the Board to the Baltimore City Court of Baltimore City. There shall be a further right of appeal from the decision of the Baltimore City Court to the Court of Appeals of Maryland, subject generally to the time and manner provided for taking appeal to the Court of Appeals."

Thus there is no statutory provision for judicial participation in the procedure which bars a film, nor even assurance of prompt judicial review. Risk of delay is built into the Maryland procedure, as is borne out by experience; in the only reported case indicating the length of time required to complete an appeal, the initial judicial determination has taken four months and final vindication of the film on appellate review, six months. . . .

In the area of freedom of expression it is well established that one has standing to challenge a statute on the ground that it delegates overly broad licensing discretion to an administrative office, whether or not his conduct could be proscribed by a properly drawn statute, and whether or not he applied for a license. "One who might have had a license for the asking may . . . call into question the whole scheme of licensing when he is prosecuted for failure to procure it." *Thornhill* v. *Alabama* . . . Standing is recognized in such cases because of the ". . . danger of tolerating, in the area of First Amendment freedoms, the existence of a penal statute susceptible of sweeping and improper application." *NAACP* v. *Button* . . . Although we have no occasion to decide whether the vice of overbroadness infects the Maryland statute, we think that appellant's assertion of a similar danger in the Maryland apparatus of censorship—one always fraught with danger and viewed with suspicion—gives him standing to make that challenge. In substance his argument is that, because the apparatus operates in a statutory context in which judicial review may be too little and too late, the Maryland statute lacks sufficient safeguards for confining the censor's action to judicially determined constitutional limits, and therefore contains the same vice as a statute delegating excessive administrative discretion.

II

Although the Court has said that motion pictures are not "necessarily subject to the precise rules governing any other particular method of expression," *Joseph Burstyn, Inc.* v. *Wilson,* it is as true here as of other forms of expression that "[a]ny system of prior restraints of expression comes to this Court bearing a heavy presumption against its constitutional validity." *Bantam Books, Inc.* v. *Sullivan.* ". . . [U]nder the Fourteenth Amendment, a State is not free to adopt whatever procedures it pleases for dealing with obscenity . . . without regard to the possible consequences for constitutionally protected speech." *Marcus* v. *Search Warrant,* The administration of a censorship system for motion pictures presents peculiar dangers to constitutionally protected speech. Unlike a prosecution for obscenity, a censorship proceeding puts the initial burden on the exhibitor or distributor. Because the censor's business is to censor, there inheres the danger that he may well be less responsive than a court—part of an independent branch of government—to the constitutionally protected interests in free expression. And if it is made unduly onerous, by reason of delay or otherwise, to seek judicial review, the censor's determination may in practice be final.

Applying the settled rule of our cases, we hold that a noncriminal process which requires the prior submission of a film to a censor avoids constitutional infirmity only if it takes place under procedural safeguards designed to obviate the dangers of a censorship system. First, the burden of proving that the film is unprotected expression must rest on the censor. As we said in *Speiser* v. *Randall,* "Where the transcendent value of speech is involved, due process certainly requires . . . that the State bear the burden of persuasion to show that the appellants engaged in criminal speech." Second, while the State may require advance submission of all films, in order to proceed effectively to bar all showings of unprotected films, the requirement cannot be administered in a manner which would lend an effect of finality to the censor's determination whether a film constitutes protected expression. The teaching of our cases is that, because only a judicial determination in an adversary proceeding ensures the necessary sensitivity to freedom of expression, only a procedure requiring a judicial determination suffices to impose a valid final restraint. . . . To this end, the exhibitor must be assured, by statute or authoritative judicial construction, that the censor will, within a specified brief period, either issue a license or go to court to restrain showing the film. Any restraint imposed in advance of a final judicial determination on the merits must similarly be limited to preservation of the status quo for the shortest fixed period compatible with sound judicial resolution. Moreover, we are well aware that, even after expiration of a temporary restraint, an administrative refusal to license, signifying the censor's view that the film is unprotected, may have a discouraging effect on the exhibitor. . . . Therefore, the procedure must also assure a prompt final judicial decision, to minimize the deterrent effect of an interim and possibly erroneous denial of a license.

Without these safeguards, it may prove too burdensome to seek review of the censor's determination. Particularly in the case of motion pictures, it may take very little to deter exhibition in a given locality. The exhibitor's stake in any one picture may be insufficient to warrant a protracted and onerous course of litigation. The distributor, on the other hand, may be equally unwilling to accept the burdens and delays of litigation in a particular area when, without such difficulties, he can freely exhibit his film in most of the rest of the country; for we are told that only four States and a handful of municipalities have active censorship laws.

It is readily apparent that the Maryland procedural scheme does not satisfy these criteria. First, once the censor disapproves the film, the exhibitor must assume the burden of instituting judicial proceedings and of persuading the courts that the film is protected expres-

sion. Second, once the Board has acted against a film, exhibition is prohibited pending judicial review, however protracted. Under the statute, appellant could have been convicted if he had shown the film after unsuccessfully seeking a license, even though no court had ever ruled on the obscenity of the film. Third, it is abundantly clear that the Maryland statute provides no assurance of prompt judicial determination. We hold, therefore, that appellant's conviction must be reversed. The Maryland scheme fails to provide adequate safeguards against undue inhibition of protected expression, and this renders the § 2 requirement of prior submission of films to the Board an invalid previous restraint.

III

How or whether Maryland is to incorporate the required procedural safeguards in the statutory scheme is, of course, for the State to decide. But a model is not lacking: In *Kingsley Books, Inc.* v. *Brown,* we upheld a New York injunctive procedure designed to prevent the sale of obscene books. That procedure postpones any restraint against sale until a judicial determination of obscenity following notice and an adversary hearing. The statute provides for a hearing one day after joinder of issue; the judge must hand down his decision within two days after termination of the hearing. . . .

One possible scheme would be to allow the exhibitor or distributor to submit his film early enough to ensure an orderly final disposition of the case before the scheduled exhibition date— far enough in advance so that the exhibitor could safely advertise the opening on a normal basis. Failing such a scheme or sufficiently early submission under such a scheme, the statute would have to require adjudication considerably more prompt than has been the case under the Maryland statute. Otherwise, litigation might be unduly expensive and protracted, or the victorious exhibitor might find the most propitious opportunity for exhibition past. We do not mean to lay down rigid time limits or procedures, but to suggest considerations in drafting legislation to accord with local exhibition practices, and in doing so to avoid the potentially chilling effect of the Maryland statute on protected expression.

Reversed.

MR. JUSTICE DOUGLAS, whom MR. JUSTICE BLACK joined, concurred.

NEW YORK TIMES CO. *v.* SULLIVAN
376 U.S. 255; 84 Sup. Ct. 710; 11 L. Ed. 686 (1964)

MR. JUSTICE BRENNAN delivered the opinion of the Court:

We are required for the first time in this case to determine the extent to which the constitutional protections for speech and press limit a State's power to award damages in a libel action brought by a public official against critics of his official conduct.

Respondent L. B. Sullivan is one of the three elected Commissioners of the City of Montgomery, Alabama. He testified that he was "Commissioner of Public Affairs and the duties are supervision of the Police Department, Fire Department, Department of Cemetery and Department of Scales." He brought this civil libel action against the four individual petitioners, who are Negroes and Alabama clergymen, and against petitioner the New York Times Company, a New York corporation which publishes the New York Times, a daily newspaper. A jury in the Circuit Court of Montgomery County awarded him damages of $500,000, the full amount claimed, against all the petitioners, and the Supreme Court of Alabama affirmed.

Respondent's complaint alleged that he had been libeled by statements in a full-page advertisement that was carried in the New York Times on March 29, 1960. . . .

It is uncontroverted that some of the statements contained in the [advertisement] were not accurate descriptions of events which occurred in Montgomery. . . .

The trial judge submitted the case to the jury under instructions that the statements in the advertisement were "libelous per se." . . . The jury was instructed that, because the statements were libelous per se . . . "falsity and malice are presumed" . . . and the judge charged that "mere negligence or carelessness is not evidence of actual malice or malice in fact, and does not justify an award of exemplary or punitive damages." He refused to charge, however, that the jury must be "convinced" of malice, in the sense of "actual intent" to harm or "gross negligence and recklessness," to make such an award, and he also refused to require that a verdict for respondent differentiate between compensatory and punitive damages. . . .

Under Alabama law as applied in this case . . . once "libel per se" has been established, the defendant has no defense as to stated facts unless he can persuade the jury that they were true in all their particulars. . . . His privilege of "fair comment" for expressions of opinion depends on the truth of the facts upon which the comment is based. . . . Unless he can discharge the burden of proving truth, general damages are presumed, and may be awarded without proof of pecuniary injury. A showing of actual malice is apparently a prerequisite to recovery of punitive damages, and the defendant may in any event forestall these by a retraction meeting the statutory requirements. Good motives and belief in truth do not negate an inference of malice, but are relevant only in mitigation of punitive damages if the jury chooses to accord them weight. . . .

The question before us is whether this rule of liability, as applied to an action brought by a public official against critics of his official conduct, abridges the freedom of speech and of the press that is guaranteed by the First and Fourteenth Amendments.

Respondent relies heavily, as did the Alabama courts, on statements of this Court to the effect that the Constitution does not protect libelous publications. Those statements do not foreclose our inquiry here. None of the cases sustained the use of libel laws to impose sanctions upon expression critical of the official conduct of public officials. The dictum in *Pennekamp* v. *Florida,* 328 U.S. 331 . . . that "when the statements amount to defamation, a judge has such remedy in damages for libel as do other public servants," implied no view as to what remedy might constitutionally be afforded to public officials. In *Beauharnais* v. *Illinois,* 343 U.S. 250 . . . the Court sustained an Illinois criminal libel statute as applied to a publication held to be both defamatory of a racial group and "liable to cause violence and disorder." But the Court was careful to note that it "retains and exercises authority to nullify action which encroaches on freedom of utterance under the guise of punishing libel"; for "public men, are, as it were, public property," and "discussion cannot be denied and the right, as well as the duty, of criticism must not be stifled." In the only previous case that did present the question of constitutional limi-

tations upon the power to award damages for libel of a public official, the Court was equally divided and the question was not decided. *Schenectady Union Pub. Co.* v. *Sweeney,* 316 U.S. 642. . . . In deciding the question now, we are compelled by neither precedent nor policy to give any more weight to the epithet "libel" than we have to other "mere labels" of state law. Like "insurrection," contempt, advocacy of unlawful acts, breach of the peace, obscenity, solicitation of legal business, and the various other formulae for the repression of expression that have been challenged in this Court, libel can claim no talismanic immunity from constitutional limitations. It must be measured by standards that satisfy the First Amendment.

The general proposition that freedom of expression upon public questions is secured by the First Amendment has long been settled by our decisions. The constitutional safeguard, we have said, "was fashioned to assure unfettered interchange of ideas for the bringing about of political and social changes desired by the people." . . . *Roth* v. *United States.* . . . "The maintenance of the opportunity for free political discussion to the end that government may be responsive to the will of the people and that changes may be obtained by lawful means, an opportunity essential to the security of the Republic, is a fundamental principle of our constitutional system." *Stromberg* v. *California,* 283 U.S. 359. . . . "[I]t is a prized American privilege to speak one's mind, although not always with perfect good taste, on all public institutions," *Bridges* v. *California,* 314 U.S. 252, . . . and this opportunity is to be afforded for "vigorous advocacy" no less than "abstract discussion." *N.A.A.C.P.* v. *Button.* The First Amendment, said Judge Learned Hand, "presupposes that right conclusions are more likely to be gathered out of a multitude of tongues, than through any kind of authoritative selection. To many this is, and always will be, folly; but we have staked upon it our all." *United States* v. *Associated Press,* 52 F.Supp. 362, 372 (D.C.S.D.-N.Y.1943). Mr. Justice Brandeis, in his concurring opinion in *Whitney* v. *California* . . . gave the principle its classic formulation. . . .

Thus we consider this case against the background of a profound national commitment to the principle that debate on public issues should be uninhibited, robust, and wide-open, and that it may well include vehement, caustic, and sometimes unpleasantly sharp attacks on government and public officials. See *Terminiello* v. *Chicago.* . . . The present advertisement, as an expression of grievance and protest on one of the major public issues of our time, would seem clearly to qualify for the constitutional protection. The question is whether it forfeits that protection by the falsity of some of its factual statements and by its alleged defamation of respondent.

Authoritative interpretations of the First Amendment guarantees have consistently refused to recognize an exception for any test of truth, whether administered by judges, juries, or administrative officials—and especially not one that puts the burden of proving truth on the speaker. . . .

That erroneous statement is inevitable in free debate, and that it must be protected if the freedoms of expression are to have the "breathing space" that they "need . . . to survive," *N.A.A.C.P.* v. *Button,* was also recognized by the Court of Appeals for the District of Columbia Circuit in *Sweeney* v. *Patterson,* 128 F.2d 457, 458 (1942). Judge Edgerton spoke for a unanimous court which affirmed the dismissal of a

Congressman's libel suit based upon a newspaper article charging him with anti-Semitism in opposing a judicial appointment. He said:

"Cases which impose liability for erroneous reports of the political conduct of officials reflect the obsolete doctrine that the governed must not criticize their governors. . . . The interest of the public here outweighs the interest of appellant or any other individual. The protection of the public requires not merely discussion, but information. Political conduct and views which some respectable people approve, and others condemn, are constantly imputed to Congressmen. Errors of fact, particularly in regard to a man's mental states and processes, are inevitable. . . . Whatever is added to the field of libel is taken from the field of free debate."

Just as factual error affords no warrant for repressing speech that would otherwise be free, the same is true of injury to official reputation. Where judicial officers are involved, this Court has held that concern for the dignity and reputation of the courts does not justify the punishment as criminal contempt of criticism of the judge or his decision. *Bridges* v. *California.* This is true even though the utterance contains "half-truths" and "misinformation." *Pennekamp* v. *Florida*; such repression can be justified, if at all, only by a clear and present danger of the obstruction of justice. . . .

If neither factual error nor defamatory content suffices to remove the constitutional shield from criticism of official conduct, the combination of the two elements is no less inadequate. This is the lesson to be drawn from the great controversy over the Sedition Act of 1798, 1 Stat. 596, which first crystallized a national awareness of the central meaning of the First Amendment. That statute made it a crime, punishable by a $5,000 fine and five years in prison, "if any person shall write, print, utter or publish . . . any false, scandalous and malicious writing or writings against the government of the United States, or either house of the Congress . . . or the President . . . , with the intent to defame . . . or to bring them or either of them, into contempt or disrepute; or to excite against them, or either or any of them, the hatred of the good people of the United States." The Act allowed the defendant the defense of truth, and provided that the jury were to be judges both of the law and the facts. Despite these qualifications, the Act was vigorously condemned as unconstitutional in an attack joined in by Jefferson and Madison. . . .

Although the Sedition Act was never tested in this Court, the attack upon its validity has carried the day in the court of history. Fines levied in its prosecution were repaid by Act of Congress on the ground that it was unconstitutional. . . . Jefferson, as President, pardoned those who had been convicted and sentenced under the Act and remitted their fines, stating: "I discharged every person under punishment or prosecution under the Sedition Law because I considered, and now consider, that law to be a nullity as absolute and palpable as if Congress had ordered us to fall down and worship a golden image." . . .

The state rule of law is not saved by its allowance of the defense of truth. . . . A rule compelling the critic of official conduct to guarantee the truth of all his factual assertions—and to do so on pain of libel judgments virtually unlimited in amount—leads to . . . "self-censorship." Allowance of the defense of truth, with the burden of proving it on the defendant, does not mean that only false speech will be deterred. Even courts accepting this defense as an adequate safeguard have recognized the difficulties of adducing legal proofs that the alleged libel was true in all its factual particulars. . . . Under such a rule, would-be critics of official conduct may be deterred from voicing their criticism, even though it is believed to be true and even though it is in fact true, because of doubt whether it can be proved in court or fear of the expense of having to do so. They tend to make only statements which "steer far wider of the unlawful zone." . . . The rule thus dampens the vigor and limits the variety of public debate. It is inconsistent with the First and Fourteenth Amendments.

The constitutional guarantees require, we think, a federal rule that prohibits a public official from recovering damages for a defamatory falsehood relating to his official conduct unless he proves that the statement was made with "actual malice"—that is, with knowledge that it was false or with reckless disregard of whether it was false or not. . . .

Such a privilege for criticism of official conduct is appropriately analogous to the protection accorded a public official when *he* is sued for libel by a private citizen. In *Barr* v. *Matteo,* 360 U.S. 564 . . . this Court held the utterance of a federal official to be absolutely privileged if made "within the outer perimeter" of his duties. The States accord the same immunity to statements of their highest officers, although some differentiate their lesser officials and qualify the privilege they enjoy. But all hold that all officials are protected unless actual malice can be proved. The reason for the official privilege is said to be that the threat of damage suits would otherwise "inhibit the fearless, vigorous, and effective administration of policies of government" and "dampen the ardor of all but the most resolute, or the most irresponsible, in the unflinching discharge of their duties." . . . Analogous considerations support the privilege for the citizen-critic of government. It is as much his duty to criticize as it is the official's duty to administer. See *Whitney* v. *California* (concurring opinion of Mr. Justice Brandeis). As Madison said, "the censorial power is in the people over the Government, and not in the Government over the people." It would give public servants an unjustified preference over the public they serve, if critics of official conduct did not have a fair equivalent of the immunity granted to the officials themselves.

We conclude that such a privilege is required by the First and Fourteenth Amendments.

We hold today that the Constitution delimits a State's power to award damages for libel in actions brought by public officials against critics of their official conduct. Since this is such an action, the rule requiring proof of actual malice is applicable. While Alabama law apparently requires proof of actual malice for an award of punitive damages, where general damages are concerned malice is "presumed." Such a presumption is inconsistent with the federal rule. "The power to create presumptions is not a means of escape from constitutional restrictions," *Bailey* v. *Alabama,* 219 U.S. 219. . . . Since the trial judge did not instruct the jury to differentiate between general and punitive damages, it may be that the verdict was wholly an award of one or the other. But it is impossible to know, in view of the general verdict returned. Because of this uncertainty, the judgment must be reversed and the case remanded. . . .

JUSTICES BLACK and DOUGLAS concurred.

NATIONAL ASSOCIATION FOR THE ADVANCEMENT OF COLORED PEOPLE *v.* ALABAMA
357 U.S. 449; 78 Sup. Ct. 1163; 2 L. Ed. 2d 1488 (1958)

[*The controversy over the desegregation of public schools and other accommodations resulted in a number of attempts to curb the activities of the NAACP, a nonprofit membership corporation chartered in New York State, which had long sought to improve the lot of the Negro. This significant case arose from the efforts of Alabama to halt the work of the organization.*

Like many other states, Alabama has a statute requiring out-of-state corporations to register and meet certain other requirements before conducting business in the state. The NAACP opened a regional office in Alabama in 1951, but it never complied with the statute, because it considered itself exempt. In 1956, the state Attorney General brought court action to enjoin the NAACP from conducting further activities within the state and to oust it from Alabama. A state circuit court issued an order restraining the Association from engaging in any further activities and forbidding it to take any steps to qualify itself to do business within the state. The Court also ordered that the Association produce its records and papers, including the names and addresses of all of the group's members and agents in Alabama. After a brief delay, the NAACP produced all the records called for by the production order except the membership lists, the disclosure of which it resisted on constitutional grounds. For refusing to submit its membership lists, the organization was held in contempt and fined $100,000. Petitions for certiorari to review the contempt judgment were twice dismissed by the Supreme Court of Alabama. The Supreme Court then granted certiorari.]

MR. JUSTICE HARLAN delivered the opinion of the Court:

. . . The question presented is whether Alabama, consistently with the Due Process Clause of the Fourteenth Amendment, can compel petitioner to reveal to the State's Attorney General the names and addresses of all its Alabama members and agents, without regard to their positions or functions in the Association. . . .

The Association both urges that it is constitutionally entitled to resist official inquiry into its membership lists, and that it may assert, on behalf of its members, a right personal to them to be protected from compelled disclosure by the State of their affiliation with the Association as revealed by the membership lists. We think that petitioner argues more appropriately the rights of its members, and that its nexus with them is sufficient to permit that it act as their representative before this Court. In so concluding, we reject respondent's argument that the Association lacks standing to assert here constitutional rights pertaining to the members, who are not of course parties to the litigation.

To limit the breadth of issues which must be dealt with in particular litigation, this Court has generally insisted that parties rely only on constitutional rights which are personal to themselves. . . . This rule is related to the broader doctrine that constitutional adjudication should where possible be avoided. . . . The principle is not disrespected where constitutional rights of persons who are not immediately before the Court could not be effectively vindicated except through an appropriate representative before the Court. . . .

If petitioner's rank-and-file members are constitutionally entitled to withhold their connection with the Association despite the production order, it is manifest that this right is properly assertable by the Association. To require that it be claimed by the members themselves would result in nullification of the right at the very moment of its assertion. Petitioner is the appropriate party to assert these rights, because it and its members are in every practical sense identical. The Association, which provides in its constitution that "any person who is in accordance with [its] principles and policies . . ." may become a member, is but the medium through which its individual members seek to make more effective the expression of their own views. The reasonable likelihood that the Association itself through diminished financial support and membership may be adversely affected if production is compelled is a further factor pointing towards our holding that petitioner has standing to complain of the production order on behalf of its members. . . .

We thus reach petitioner's claim that the production order in the state litigation trespasses upon fundamental freedoms protected by the Due Process Clause of the Fourteenth Amendment. Petitioner argues that in view of the facts and circumstances shown in the record, the effect of compelled disclosure of the membership lists will be to abridge the rights of its rank-and-file members to engage in lawful association in support of their common beliefs. It contends that governmental action which, although not directly suppressing association, nevertheless carries this consequence, can be justified only upon some overriding valid interest of the State.

Effective advocacy of both public and private points of view, particularly controversial ones, is undeniably enhanced by group association, as this Court has more than once recognized by remarking upon the close nexus between the freedoms of speech and assembly. . . . It is beyond debate that freedom to engage in association for the advancement of beliefs and ideas is an inseparable aspect of the "liberty" assured by the Due Process Clause of the Fourteenth Amendment, which embraces freedom of speech. . . . Of course, it is immaterial whether the beliefs sought to be advanced by association pertain to political, economic, religious or cultural matters, and state action which may have the effect of curtailing the freedom to associate is subject to the closest scrutiny. . . .

It is hardly a novel perception that compelled disclosure of affiliation with groups engaged in advocacy may constitute as effective a restraint on freedom of association as the forms of governmental action in the cases above were thought likely to produce upon the particular constitutional rights there involved. This Court has recognized the vital relationship between freedom to associate and privacy in one's associations. When referring to the varied forms of governmental action which might interfere with freedom of assembly, it said in *American Communications Assn.* v. *Douds* . . . : "A requirement that adherents of particular religious faiths or political parties wear identifying arm-bands, for example, is obviously of this nature." Compelled disclosure of membership in an organization engaged in advocacy of particular beliefs is of the same order. Inviolability of privacy in group association may in many circumstances be indispensable to preservation of freedom of association, particularly where a group espouses dissident beliefs. . . .

We think that the production order, in the respects here drawn in question, must be regarded as entailing the likelihood of a substantial restraint upon the exercise by petitioner's members of their right to freedom of association. Petitioner has made an uncontroverted showing that on past occasions revela-

tion of the identity of its rank-and-file members has exposed these members to economic reprisal, loss of employment, threat of physical coercion, and other manifestations of public hostility. Under these circumstances, we think it apparent that compelled disclosure of petitioner's Alabama membership is likely to affect adversely the ability of petitioner and its members to pursue their collective effort to foster beliefs which they admittedly have the right to advocate, in that it may induce members to withdraw from the Association and dissuade others from joining it because of fear of exposure of their beliefs shown through their associations and of the consequences of this exposure.

It is not sufficient to answer, as the State does here, that whatever repressive effect compulsory disclosure of names of petitioner's members may have upon participation by Alabama citizens in petitioner's activities follows not from state action but from private community pressures. The crucial factor is the interplay of governmental and private action, for it is only after the initial exertion of state power represented by the production order that private action takes hold.

We turn to the final question whether Alabama has demonstrated an interest in obtaining the disclosures it seeks from petitioner which is sufficient to justify the deterrent effect which we have concluded these disclosures may well have on the free exercise by petitioner's members of their constitutionally protected right of association. . . . It is not of moment that the State has here acted solely through its judicial branch, for whether legislative or judicial, it is still the application of state power which we are asked to scrutinize.

It is important to bear in mind that petitioner asserts no right to absolute immunity from state investigation, and no right to disregard Alabama's laws. As shown by its substantial compliance with the production order, petitioner does not deny Alabama's right to obtain from it such information as the State desires concerning the purposes of the Association and its activities within the State. Petitioner has not objected to divulging the identity of its members who are employed by or hold official positions with it. It has urged the rights solely of its ordinary rank-and-file members. This is therefore not analogous to a case involving the interest of a State in protecting its citizens in their dealings with paid solicitors or agents of foreign corporations by requiring identification. . . .

We hold that the immunity from state scrutiny of membership lists which the Association claims on behalf of its members is here so related to the right of the members to pursue their lawful private interest privately and to associate freely with others in so doing as to come within the protection of the Fourteenth Amendment. And we conclude that Alabama has fallen short of showing a controlling justification for the deterrent effect on the free enjoyment of the right to associate which disclosure of membership lists is likely to have. Accordingly, the judgment of civil contempt and the $100,000 fine which resulted from petitioner's refusal to comply with the production order in this respect must fall. . . .

For the reasons stated, the judgment of the Supreme Court of Alabama must be reversed and the case remanded for proceedings not inconsistent with this opinion.

Reversed.

NAACP *v.* BUTTON
371 U.S. 421, 83 Sup. Ct. 328. 9 L. Ed. 2d 405 (1963)

MR. JUSTICE BRENNAN delivered the opinion of the Court.

There is no substantial dispute as to the facts; the dispute centers about the constitutionality under the Fourteenth Amendment of Chapter 33, as construed and applied by the Virginia Supreme Court of Appeals to include NAACP's activities within the statute's ban against "the improper solicitation of any legal or professional business."
. . .

The basic aims and purposes of NAACP are to secure the elimination of all racial barriers which deprive Negro citizens of the privileges and burdens of equal citizenship rights in the United States. To this end the Association engages in extensive educational and lobbying activities. It also devotes much of its funds and energies to an extensive program of assisting certain kinds of litigation on behalf of its declared purposes. For more than ten years, the Virginia Conference has concentrated upon financing litigation aimed at ending racial segregation in the public schools of the Commonwealth.

The Conference ordinarily will finance only cases in which the assisted litigant retains an NAACP staff lawyer to represent him. . . .

In effect, then, the prospective litigant retains not so much a particular attorney as the "firm" of NAACP and Defense Fund lawyers, which has a corporate reputation for expertness in presenting and arguing the difficult questions of law that frequently arise in civil rights litigation. . . .

Statutory regulation of unethical and nonprofessional conduct by attorneys has been in force in Virginia since

1849. These provisions outlaw, *inter alia,* solicitation of legal business in the form of "running" or "capping." Prior to 1956, however, no attempt was made to proscribe under such regulations the activities of the NAACP, which had been carried on openly for many years in substantially the manner described. In 1956, however, the legislature amended, by the addition of Chapter 33, the provisions of the Virginia Code forbidding solicitation of legal business by a "runner" or "capper" to include, in the definition of "runner" or "capper," an agent for an individual or organization which retains a lawyer in connection with an action to which it is not a party and in which it has no pecuniary right or liability. The Virginia Supreme Court of Appeals . . . held that the activities of NAACP, the Virginia Conference, the Defense Fund, and the lawyers furnished by them, fell within, and could constitutionally be proscribed by, the chapter's expanded definition of improper solicitation of legal business. . . . We reverse the judgment of the Virginia Supreme Court of Appeals. We hold that the activities of the NAACP, its affiliates and legal staff shown on this record are modes of expression and association protected by the First and Fourteenth Amendments which Virginia may not prohibit, under its power to regulate the legal profession, as improper solicitation of legal business violative of Chapter 33 and the Canons of Professional Ethics.

We meet at the outset the contention that "solicitation" is wholly outside the area of freedoms protected by the First Amendment. To this contention there are two answers. The first is that a State cannot foreclose the exercise of constitutional rights by mere labels. The second is that abstract discussion is not the only species of communication which the Constitution protects; the First Amendment also protects vigorous advocacy, certainly of lawful ends, against governmental intrusion. . . . In the context of NAACP objectives, litigation is not a technique of resolving private differences; it is a means for achieving the lawful objectives of equality of treatment by all government, federal, state and local, for the members of the Negro community in this country. It is thus a form of political expression. Groups which find themselves unable to achieve their objectives through the ballot frequently turn to the courts.* Just as it was true of the opponents of New Deal legislation during the 1930s, for example, no less is it true of the Negro minority today. And under the conditions of modern government, litigation may well be the sole practicable avenue open to a minority to petition for redress of grievances.

We need not, in order to find constitutional protection for the kind of cooperative, organizational activity disclosed by this record, whereby Negroes seek through lawful means to achieve legitimate political ends, subsume such activity under a narrow, literal conception of freedom of speech, petition or assembly. For there is no longer any doubt that the First and Fourteenth Amendments protect certain forms of orderly group activity. Thus we have

* Murphy, The South Counterattacks: The Anti-NAACP Laws, 12 W.Pol.Q. 371 (1959). See Bentley, The Process of Government: A Study of Social Pressures (1908); Rosenblum, Law as a Political Instrument (1955); Peltason, Federal Courts in the Political Process (1955); Truman, The Governmental Process: Political Interests and Public Opinion (1955); Vose, The National Consumers' League and the Brandeis Brief, 1 Midw.J. of Pol.Sci. 267 (1957); Comment, Private Attorneys-General: Group Action in the Fight for Civil Liberties, 58 Yale L.J. 574 (1949).

affirmed the right "to engage in association for the advancement of beliefs and ideas." *NAACP* v. *Alabama,* ex rel. Patterson. We have deemed privileged, under certain circumstances, the efforts of a union official to organize workers. . . . And we have refused to countenance compelled disclosure of a person's political associations in language closely applicable to the instant case:

> "Our form of government is built on the premise that every citizen shall have the right to engage in political expression and association. This right was enshrined in the First Amendment of the Bill of Rights. Exercise of these basic freedoms in America has traditionally been through the media of political associations. Any interference with the freedom of a party is simultaneously an interference with the freedom of its adherents. All political ideas cannot and should not be channeled into the programs of our two major parties.

History has amply proved the virtue of political activity by minority, dissident groups . . . ." *Sweezy* v. *New Hampshire.* . . .

The NAACP is not a conventional political party; but the litigation it assists, while serving to vindicate the legal rights of members of the American Negro community, at the same time and perhaps more importantly, makes possible the distinctive contribution of a minority group to the ideas and beliefs of our society. For such a group, association for litigation may be the most effective form of political association.

. . . a statute broadly curtailing group activity leading to litigation may easily become a weapon of oppression, however evenhanded its terms appear. Its mere existence could well freeze out of existence all such activity on behalf of the civil rights of Negro citizens. It is apparent, therefore, that Chapter 33 as construed limits First Amendment freedoms. . . .

14
Freedom of Religion

The only reference to religion in the original Constitution is found in Article VI, which prohibits any religious test for *federal* public offices. However, the First Amendment provides in clear and positive terms that Congress cannot pass laws respecting an establishment of religion or prohibiting its free exercise.

The religious freedom clause of the First Amendment was the product of the colonists' bitter memories of established state churches, religious wars, and various forms of religious persecution.

Members of the Constitutional Convention could look back on an era of bloody religious wars in the Western world. For their religious beliefs both men and women had suffered such tortures as being buried or burned alive. Many Protestant groups had matched the intolerance of the Roman Catholic Church from which they had broken away. The New World also had its experiences with persecution. Although many early settlers had come here as religious fugitives, they rarely practiced tolerance in their new homes. When the Declaration of Independence was written there were only two colonies. Pennsylvania and Delaware, in which all Christian sects were socially and politically on equal footing. Catholics and Jews especially were discriminated against; New York excluded both from suffrage. In many colonies there were established churches: Virginia adhered to the Church of England; Massachusetts, New Hampshire, and Connecticut were Congregationalists. This very diversity of state churches, among other things, enabled the new federal government to deny itself an established religion and permitted the First Amendment to carry freedom of worship beyond practices and guaranties which then generally existed in the states.[1]

The First Amendment launched a unique American experiment in the development of religious freedom and the separation of church and state. "The experiment rested upon the principle that government has no power to legislate in the field of religion either by restricting its free exercise or providing for its support."[2] This was a radical departure indeed from the firmly established tradition that the "relationship between man and God was a matter of legitimate concern of political government."[3]

The religious freedom provision of the First Amendment confirmed the feelings of the overwhelming majority of Americans, who looked upon religion as a private, personal matter. This attitude was reflected in Congress, where very few laws dealing with religion were enacted. Thus very few cases testing the meaning of the religion clause of the First Amendment were brought to the Supreme Court. Although there were several cases on *separation* of church and state, the Court, in the first 150 years after the adoption of the First Amendment, decided only one important case dealing principally with *freedom* of religion [*Reynolds* v. *United States,* 98 U.S. 145 (1878)]. Moreover, under the doctrine of *Barron* v. *Baltimore* (discussed in Chapter 12), the First Amendment could be applied as a restriction upon Congress *only* and not to the states. Thus, the states were constitutionally free for many years to deal with religious matters as they saw fit, because the protection of religious liberty was a matter of state rather than federal constitutional law.

State action affecting religion could be challenged in the Supreme Court on constitutional grounds only after the development of the doctrine that the First Amendment restrictions applied to the states through the Fourteenth Amendment. We have already seen that the process of bringing the First Amendment freedoms under the protection of the Fourteenth Amendment did not begin until 1925, with Justice Sanford's remark in *Gitlow* v. *New York*. In the *Gitlow* case, the term *liberty* in the Fourteenth Amendment was expanded to include freedom of speech, and freedom of the press was brought within the protection of the Fourteenth Amendment in the 1931 case of *Near* v. *Minnesota,* 283 U.S. 1 (1931). In 1937, the right to peaceable assembly was added in *De Jonge* v. *Oregon,* 299 U.S. 353. Finally, in 1940, the Supreme Court held, in *Cantwell* v. *Connecticut* (p. 418), that the freedom of religion provision of the First Amendment constituted a restriction upon the states through the Fourteenth Amendment. In 1947, the Court

---

[1] William O. Penrose, *Freedom Is Ourselves* (Newark, Del.: University of Delaware Press, 1952), p. 30.

[2] Leo Pfeffer, *The Liberties of an American* (Boston: Beacon Press, 1956), p. 33.

[3] *Ibid.,* p. 32.

completed the process of incorporating the First Amendment into the "liberty" of the Fourteenth Amendment by holding, in *Everson* v. *Board of Education* (p. 448), that the establishment of religion clause also restricted state action.

As regards religion, the First Amendment contains *two* prohibitions; it forbids laws that prohibit the free exercise of religion as well as laws respecting an establishment of religion. Although in many cases the Supreme Court considers the free exercise and the separation of church and state as parts of the same principles, for purposes of clarity they should be discussed separately. However, a basic paradox in the relation of the two prohibitions to one another should be noted: The case of *Sherbert* v. *Verner,* 374 U.S. 398 (1963), provides a good illustration. A Seventh Day Adventist, in a town whose factories work a Monday through Saturday week, was denied unemployment benefits because she was not available for work on every working day as required by the statute. The Court held that such a denial placed an unconstitutional burden on the free exercise of her religion, which forbade her to work on Saturday—her Sabbath. (Compare this holding with the Sunday law decisions rendered earlier by the Court, p. 480.) But to protect her free exercise, the Court had to carve out a special, religiously based exemption to the state's general unemployment statute—an exemption that resulted in better treatment for those who refuse to work on Saturday for a religious reason than for those who refuse for some other reason. Thus, in order to protect free exercise, the Court has to require establishment at least in the sense of demanding governmental recognition of a particular religious group as enjoying a special exemption from a statute that all others must obey. It is not easy to see how this dilemma can be resolved.

Free Exercise of Religion

As previously noted, very few cases involving infringements of religious freedom came before the Supreme Court until recent years. In fact, almost all of our constitutional law pertaining to the free exercise of religion and separation of church and state has been developed since 1940.

The meaning of the First Amendment in the field of religion was considered for the first time by the Supreme Court in *Reynolds* v. *United States,* decided in 1878. At that time Mormons had a religious duty, when circumstances permitted, to practice polygamy. Reynolds, a Mormon living in the Territory of Utah, had two wives, in conformity with the religious doctrine of his church. However, Congress had enacted a law that made polygamy a crime in the territories of the United States. Reynolds was tried and convicted of violating the federal law. In his appeal to the Supreme Court he maintained that because polygamy was a part of his religious belief, the Act of Congress violated his free exercise of religion under the First Amendment. Nevertheless, the Court upheld the statute in a unanimous opinion and pointed out that the First Amendment did not deprive Congress of the power to punish actions "which were in violation of social duties or subversive of good order." The Court further stated:

> Laws are made for the government of actions, and while they cannot interfere with mere religious belief and opinions, they may with practices. Suppose that one believed that human sacrifices were a necessary part of religious worship, would it be seriously contended that the civil government under which he lived could not interfere to prevent a sacrifice? Or, if a wife religiously believed it was her duty to burn herself upon the funeral pire of her dead husband, would it be beyond the power of the civil government to prevent her carrying her belief into practice? So here, as a law of the organization of society under the exclusive dominion of the United States, it is provided that plural marriages shall not be allowed. Can a man excuse his practices to the contrary because of his religious belief? To permit this would be to make the professed doctrines of religious belief superior to the law of the land, and in effect to permit every citizen to become a law unto himself. Government could exist only in name under such circumstances.

The *Reynolds* decision established clearly that freedom of religion, like other freedoms, is not absolute or unlimited. Actions in the name of religious liberty that violate criminal law, offend public morals, or interfere with the health, welfare, and safety of the community cannot be condoned. The limits of the free exercise of religion are defined ultimately by the Supreme Court.

JEHOVAH'S WITNESSES

In recent years the issue of religious freedom has been raised most often by a small religious sect known as Jehovah's Witnesses. The Witnesses were first organized in 1884, but they attracted little attention in the United States until the 1930s, when they began a vigorous nationwide campaign to spread their religious doctrines and prepare the world for the second coming of the Lord.

The Witnesses believe in a literal interpretation of the Bible and look at modern history as a struggle between Jesus and Satan. Because they believe they are specially chosen agents of God, the witnesses fight with Jesus in his battle to overcome Satan and usher in the new Kingdom. They regard all organized religion as a "racket" and are especially antagonistic to the Roman Catholic Church. Each Witness regards himself as a minister of the gospel who has the duty to proclaim the word of God to anyone who will listen by calling on people in their homes, distributing religious literature, and playing records that often attack bitterly the religious beliefs of others. The Witnesses' conflicts with the law in various communities stemmed largely from their violent attacks on other religious groups and from their sometimes aggressive and intolerant attitude toward prospective converts.[4] They have suffered widespread unpopularity, too, because of their literal interpretation of Chapter 20

---

[4] Hollis W. Barber, "Religious Liberty v. Police Power: Jehovah's Witnesses," *American Political Science Review,* Vol. 41 (1947), p. 227.

of Exodus, which states that "Thou shalt not make unto thee any graven image . . . ; thou shalt not bow down thyself to them nor serve them." The Witnesses look upon the flag as a graven image and refuse to salute it.

Jehovah's Witnesses have fought vigorously every legal attempt to curb their activities. As a result, they have contributed more to the development of a constitutional law concerning First Amendment liberties than any other group in our history. Justice Stone once remarked that the Witnesses "ought to have an endowment in view of the aid which they give in solving the legal problems of civil liberties."[5] At first glance, that such a small religious sect should leave so great a mark on our constitutional law is surprising. The influence of the Witnesses, out of all proportion to their number, can be explained largely by their fanatical devotion to the cause. Many of those who disagree violently with them admit that they have the courage of martyrs. Each Witness, whether rich or poor, has been willing to contribute heavily in both time and money for the advancement of his beliefs. In addition, the Witnesses have a sense of unity and strength that comes from membership in a worldwide organization of some three million devoted believers.

Many of the Supreme Court cases involving Jehovah's Witnesses have been decided under the freedom of speech, press, and assembly guaranties as well as the freedom of religion clause of the First Amendment. The *Chaplinsky* case noted subsequently and the *Barnette* decision (p. 441), are cases in point. This has been possible because the ". . . constitutional restrictions on laws prohibiting the free exercise of religion are the same as those on laws abridging freedom of speech, press, and assembly. Indeed, the first Jehovah's Witnesses cases were decided under the freedom of speech and of press guaranties, without reference to freedom of religion."[6] The clear and present danger test, which was examined fully in the previous chapter, may be applied to all the rights guaranteed by the First Amendment, even though it was formulated originally for deciding freedom of speech cases.

The Witnesses have won the majority of their cases brought to the Supreme Court since 1938. These include *Lovell* v. *City of Griffin,* 303 U.S. 444 (1938), where they won the right to distribute religious handbills without having first to secure a license from a local official. The Court decided also in *Martin* v. *Struthers,* 319 U.S. 141 (1943), that Witnesses cannot be forbidden to knock on doors or ring doorbells in order to give out handbills and literature. In *Cantwell* v. *Connecticut* they won another notable victory.

On the other hand, the Witnesses' claims were denied by the Supreme Court in a few cases. In *Cox* v. *New Hampshire,* 312 U.S. 569 (1941), the Court ruled that Witnesses may be required to secure a permit before holding a parade or procession on public streets. And in *Chaplinsky* v. *New*

---

[5] From a letter written by Justice Stone to Charles E. Hughes; quoted in Alpheus T. Mason, *Harlan Fiske Stone,* Pillar of the Law (New York: Viking Press, 1956), p. 598.

[6] Leo Pfeffer, "The Supreme Court as Protector of Civil Rights: Freedom of Religion," *Annals,* Vol. 275 (May 1951), p. 77.

Hampshire, 315 U.S. 568 (1942), the Court held that a Witness could be punished for a breach of the peace for using "fighting" words in a public place. In this instance, Chaplinsky called the city marshal of a New Hampshire community "a goddamned racketeer" and a "damned Fascist" because of the marshal's interference with his preaching. In delivering the unanimous opinion of the Court, Justice Murphy, who was a staunch supporter of individual liberties, remarked: "There are certain well-defined and narrowly limited classes of speech, the prevention and punishment of which have never been thought to raise any Constitutional problem. These include the lewd and obscene, the profane, the libelous, and the insulting or 'fighting' words—those which by their very utterance inflict injury or tend to incite an immediate breach of the peace."

The conflict between religious liberty and governmental authority was most dramatically presented to the Supreme Court by the refusal of the Witnesses to permit their children to salute the flag. Before 1940, the flag-salute issue had been presented to the Court on three occasions, but the question was dismissed each time. Finally, in *Minersville School District* v. *Gobitis,* 310 U.S. 586 (1940), the Court sustained the constitutionality of a Pennsylvania school board regulation that required school children to salute the flag despite contentions that the compulsory flag salute violated freedom of religion. Because the case was decided during the country's preparation for possible war, "time and circumstances" very likely played an important role in the Court's opinion, which was delivered by Justice Frankfurter. At the time, the decision was handed down there was intense alarm in the United States because the Nazis were sweeping through France and the Low Countries almost without opposition. Only Justice Stone dissented, but his powerful opinion was to prevail shortly.

The *Gobitis* opinion was criticized severely by the overwhelming majority of responsible commentators. But some looked at the Court's approval of the compulsory flag salute as a signal for the use of more repressive measures against the Witnesses. Shortly after the decision, Witnesses were beaten and driven from several communities. Many local school officials enforced the flag-salute requirement with increased vigor. "In several states the lower courts treated recalcitrant Witnesses' children as delinquents and confined them to state reform schools. The Court itself thus became a weapon in the struggle for men's minds."[7]

Several members of the Court were disturbed deeply by the nation's reaction to the *Gobitis* decision. In June 1942, in connection with another case (*Jones* v. *City of Opelika,* 316 U.S. 584), Justices Black, Douglas, and Murphy, who had voted with the majority in the *Gobitis* case, stated jointly that they had become convinced that the *Gobitis* case was "wrongly decided." These three justices and Justices Rutledge and Jackson, who were appointed after the *Gobitis* decision, joined Justice Stone to reverse the *Gobitis* holding

---

[7] Mason, *Harlan Fiske Stone, op. cit.,* p. 533.

in *West Virginia Board of Education* v. *Barnette* (p. 441). Thus, in one of the most dramatic reversals in the Court's history, Justice Stone's lone dissent became the majority opinion only three years later. Justice Jackson relied heavily on the *Gobitis* dissent in writing the eloquent opinion in the *Barnette* case. Justice Frankfurter's dissent in the *Barnette* case is largely a defense of his *Gobitis* opinion and should be read with care because it reveals clearly his philosophy concerning the nature of the judicial function. From time to time that philosophy has had the support of numerous justices.[8]

Separation of Church and State

During most of our history the establishment of religion clause of the First Amendment has provoked few controversies. A few cases were concerned with various aspects of church-state relationships before recent years, but these did not necessitate an interpretation of the establishment clause. For example, in *Pierce* v. *Society of Sisters,* 268 U.S. 510 (1925), the Court invalidated an Oregon law that required all children to attend the public schools and thus, in effect, abolished private schools. The Court rested its opinion on the right of parents to direct the upbringing and education of their children and on the principle that the Oregon law deprived private schools of business and property without due process of law in violation of the Fourteenth Amendment. A case more closely related to the basic issues was that of *Cochran* v. *Louisiana State Board of Education,* 281 U.S. 370 (1930), where the Court upheld a state law that authorized the distribution of free textbooks to children in *both* public and private schools. In the *Cochran* case the Court proceeded on the theory that the textbooks, which had been purchased by the state for free distribution with public funds, were designed to help children rather than private schools.

Not until 1947, in *Everson* v. *Board of Education* (p. 448), was the meaning of the establishment clause spelled out by the Supreme Court. This case drew the Court into sharp and bitter controversy, "where any action it took was bound to be bitterly attacked."[9] The great difficulties faced by the Court in attempting to define the proper relationship between church and state can be perceived by the various opinions of the *Everson* case, as well as by subsequent decisions to be reproduced here.

Current discussions concerning the use of public funds for both public and private schools reveal clearly that the problem will not be resolved easily by the Supreme Court or any other agency of government. There is too much disagreement over fundamental matters. For example, the Roman Catholic Church and other groups have campaigned vigorously for federal aid to

[8] A most detailed analysis of the *Gobitis* and *Barnette* cases is found in David R. Manwaring, *Render Unto Caesar* (Chicago: University of Chicago Press, 1962).

[9] C. Herman Pritchett, *Civil Liberties and the Vinson Court,* (Chicago: University of Chicago Press, 1954), p. 11.

private as well as public schools. The Roman Catholic bishops of the United States have declared on several occasions that private and parochial schools have "full right" to receive government aid. The bishops argue that students of such schools "have the right to benefit from those measures, grants, or aids, which are manifestly designed for the health, safety, and welfare of American youth, irrespective of the school attended."[10] On the other hand, many Protestant groups oppose the use of public funds for the support of private or church-related schools. They argue that those who desire "to maintain private schools in which general education and religious education are brought together in one institution are appropriately free to do so." However, "the full support for such private schools should be provided by those who choose to maintain them. Asking for the support of church schools by tax funds on the grounds that they contribute to the national welfare is not different in principle from asking for the support of churches by tax funds, for churches surely contribute to the national welfare. Such support would in both cases be contrary to the separation of church and state."[11] That the controversy will be a continuing one is indicated by the fact that today more than five million elementary and high school pupils, or one out of every seven, receive their education in parochial or other private schools, Approximately 90 per cent of these students are in Catholic schools.

The controversy over church-state relationship was fanned anew by the case of *Illinois* ex rel. *McCollum* v. *Board of Education* (p. 455), where a released-time program of religious instruction in the Illinois public schools was held unconstitutional. The decision was greeted by a wave of bitter criticism, because many church groups in various states had developed similar released-time programs. In addition, the *McCollum* decision ". . . was announced when the nation was on the threshold or in the early stages of a period of religious revival. Periods of great fear drive men toward religion, and the steadily advancing threat of atomic destruction made the mid-century a period of great fear. Religion, moreover, had become a staunch ally of nationalism, for in the eyes of many the major difference between Americanism and Communism was acceptance or rejection of God. It was thus scarcely surprising that the *McCollum* decision, which in effect held that the public schools must be not only nonsectarian but secular or godless, should evoke a storm of acrimonious criticism." The voices of many who supported the Court's decision "were drowned in the strident chorus of disapproval."[12]

Against this background of acrimonious criticism the Court again con-

[10] From the text of the Roman Catholic bishops' statement on church-related schools, *The New York Times* (November 20, 1955), p. 84.

[11] From the text of a statement issued by the National Council of Churches of Christ, which is the largest organization of Protestant churches in the United States. *U.S. News and World Report* (December 16, 1955), p. 121. Both sides of the controversy are presented ably in a symposium on religion and the state appearing in *Law and Contemporary Problems*, Vol. 14 (1949), pp. 1–159. See also Philip B. Kurland, *Religion and the Law* (Chicago: Aldine Publishing Co., 1962).

[12] Pfeffer, *op. cit.*, p. 44.

sidered the released-time issue in *Zorach* v. *Clauson* (p. 460). As the dissenters pointed out in the *Zorach* case, some will find it difficult to perceive that a *real* distinction exists between the two released-time programs at issue in the *McCollum* and *Zorach* cases. The majority opinion in the *Zorach* case may have been intended principally "to quiet the storm caused by the *McCollum* decision."[13]

In 1968, the Court upheld another state textbook distribution program using the same arguments used in the *Cochran* case (see p. 435) but also emphasizing that the state might aid only secular education in religious schools [*Board of Education* v. *Allen,* 392 U.S. 236 (1968)].

The Court has also stressed the distinction between secular and religious questions in the work of the courts themselves. *Presbyterian Church in the United States* v. *Mary Elizabeth Blue Hull Memorial Presbyterian Church,* 89 Sup. Ct. 601 (1969) involved a Georgia statute requiring that, in the awarding of disputed church property, courts determine whether one of the rival claimants had departed from the true doctrines of the denomination. The Court held this statute unconstitutional because it required a state court to decide a purely religious question.

SCHOOL PRAYERS AND BIBLE READING

The nationwide controversy set off by the decision in *Engel* v. *Vitale* (p. 464) and the reaction to the outlawing of Bible reading and the recitation of the Lord's Prayer in *Abington School District* v. *Schempp* (p. 471) were discussed in Chapter 3. In each case the Court held that the particular religious practice at issue was unconstitutional because it violated the establishment clause of the First Amendment as made applicable to the states by the Fourteenth Amendment. Despite the furor over these cases, the issues involved were not new or novel. As early as the 1870s several states had outlawed Bible reading in the public schools. The problem was presented to the Supreme Court in *Doremus* v. *Board of Education,* 342 U.S. 429 (1952), which challenged Bible reading in the public schools of New Jersey; but the Court refused to decide the issue, instead resorting to the technical ground that the plaintiff lacked standing to maintain the suit.

The Court held in *Epperson* v. *Arkansas,* 89 Sup. Ct. 266 (1968), that the state's statute forbidding the teaching of evolution in the public schools constituted a violation of the establishment clause because that clause ". . . forbids alike the preference of a religious doctrine or the prohibition of theory which is deemed antagonistic to a particular dogma. . . . The state has no legitimate interest in protecting any or all religions from views distasteful to them." In the course of this opinion, the Court repeated its earlier statement that the "study of religions and of the Bible, from a literary and historic view-

---

[13] Pritchett, *op. cit.,* p. 14. For an attempt to construct an acceptable theory of church-state separation relevant to conditions in the United States today, see Loren P. Beth, "Toward a Modern American Theory of Church-State Relations," *Political Science Quarterly,* Vol. 70 (December 1955), p. 573.

point, presented objectively as part of a secular program of education, need not collide with the First Amendment's prohibition . . . " of establishment.

SUNDAY CLOSING CASES

In four cases decided together and known as the *Sunday Closing Cases* (p. 480), the Court was faced with the difficult task of deciding if Sunday "blue laws" violate both the establishment and free exercise of religion clauses of the First Amendment as applied to the states by the Fourteenth Amendment. In deciding that they do not, the Court wrote more than 150 pages of carefully reasoned opinions. The decision reproduced here has been greatly condensed.

RELIGIOUS TEST FOR PUBLIC OFFICIALS

In the unusual case of *Torcaso* v. *Watkins* [367 U.S. 488 (1961)] the Court, by unanimous vote, held that a Maryland religious test for public office constituted an invasion of freedom of belief and religion.

CANTWELL *v.* CONNECTICUT
310 U.S. 296; 60 Sup. Ct. 900; 84 L. Ed. 1213 (1940)

[*Cantwell and his two sons, members of Jehovah's Witnesses, went from house to house in a predominantly Roman Catholic residential district of New Haven, Connecticut, soliciting money and subscriptions for their religious cause. They were charged in five counts with statutory and common law offenses. All of them were convicted on the third count under a state statute that provided that no person could solicit money for alleged religious purposes without first obtaining a certificate of approval from the secretary of the Public Welfare Council. The Cantwells had not obtained the required permit, claiming that their religious activities did not come within the statute. The Cantwells also were convicted on the fifth count, that of inciting others to breach of the peace, because a phonograph record was played that violently attacked Roman Catholicism. The state supreme court affirmed the convictions of all three on the third count but affirmed the conviction of only one of the Cantwells on the fifth count. The Cantwells brought their case to the Supreme Court on appeal. The Court also granted a writ of certiorari to review the breach of peace conviction.*]

MR. JUSTICE ROBERTS delivered the opinion of the Court:

. . . *First*. We hold that the statute, as construed and applied to the appellants, deprives them of their liberty without due process of law in contravention of the Fourteenth Amendment. The fundamental concept of liberty embodied in that Amendment embraces the liberties guaranteed by the First Amendment. The First Amendment declares that Congress shall make no law respecting an establishment of religion or prohibiting the free exercise thereof. The Fourteenth Amendment has rendered the legislatures of the states as incompetent as Congress to enact such laws. The constitutional inhibition of legislation on the subject of religion has a double aspect. On the one hand, it forestalls compulsion by law of the acceptance of any creed or the practice of any form of worship. Freedom of conscience and freedom to adhere to such religious organization or form of worship as the individual may choose cannot be restricted by law. On the other hand, it safeguards the free exercise of the chosen form of religion. Thus the Amendment embraces two concepts—freedom to believe and freedom to act. The first is absolute but, in the nature of things, the second cannot be. Conduct remains subject to regulation for the protection of society. The freedom to act must have appropriate definition to preserve the enforcement of that protection. In every case the power to regulate must be so exercised as not, in attaining a permissible end, unduly to infringe the protected freedom. No one would contest the proposition that a State may not, by statute, wholly deny the right to preach or to disseminate religious views. Plainly such a previous and absolute restraint would violate the terms of the guaranty. It is equally clear that a State may by general and nondiscriminatory legislation regulate the times, the places, and the manner of soliciting upon its streets, and of holding meetings thereon; and may in other respects safeguard the peace, good order, and comfort of the community, without unconstitutionally invading the liberties protected by the Fourteenth Amendment. The appellants are right in their insistence that the Act in question is not such a regulation. If a certificate is procured, solicitation is permitted without restraint, but in the absence of a certificate solicitation is altogether prohibited. . . .

It will be noted . . . that the Act requires an application to the secretary of the public welfare council of the State; that he is empowered to determine whether the cause is a religious one, and that the issue of a certificate depends upon his affirmative action. If he finds that the cause is not that of religion, to solicit for it becomes a crime. He is not to issue a certificate as a matter of course. His decision to issue or refuse it involves appraisal of facts, the exercise of judgment, and the formation of an opinion. He is authorized to withhold his approval if he determines that the cause is not a religious one. Such a censorship of religion as the means of determining its right to survive is a denial of liberty protected by the First Amendment and included in the liberty which is within the protection of the Fourteenth.

The State asserts that if the licensing officer acts arbitrarily, capriciously, or corruptly, his action is subject to judicial correction. Counsel refer to the rule prevailing in Connecticut that the decision of a commission or an administrative official will be reviewed upon a claim that "it works material damage to individual or corporate rights, or invades or threatens such rights, or is so unreasonable as to justify judicial intervention, or is not consonant with justice, or that a legal duty has not been performed." It is suggested that the statute is to be read as requiring the officer to issue a certificate unless the cause in question is clearly not a religious one; and that if he violates his duty his action will be corrected by a court.

To this suggestion there are several sufficient answers. The line between a discretionary and a ministerial act is not always easy to mark, and the statute has not been construed by the state court to impose a mere ministerial duty on the secretary of the welfare council. Upon his decision as to the nature of the cause, the right to solicit depends. Moreover, the availability of a judicial remedy for abuses in the system of licensing still leaves that system one of previous restraint which, in the field of free speech and press, we have held inadmissible. A statute authorizing previous restraint upon the exercise of the guaranteed freedom by judicial decision after trial is as obnoxious to the Constitution as one providing for like restraint by administrative action.

Nothing we have said is intended even remotely to imply that, under the cloak of religion, persons may, with impunity, commit frauds upon the public. Certainly penal laws are available to punish such conduct. Even the exercise of religion may be at some slight inconvenience in order that the State may protect its citizens from injury. Without doubt a State may protect its citizens from fraudulent solicitation by requiring a stranger in the community, before permitting him publicly to solicit funds for any purpose, to establish his identity and his authority to act for the cause which he purports to represent. The State is likewise free to regulate the time and manner of solicitation generally, in the interest of public safety, peace, comfort, or convenience. But to condition the solicitation of aid for the perpetuation of religious views or systems upon a license, the grant of which rests in the exercise of a determination by state authority as to what is a religious cause, is to lay a forbidden burden upon the exercise of liberty protected by the Constitution.

Second. The offense known as breach of the peace embraces a great variety of conduct destroying or menacing public order and tranquility. It includes not only violent acts but acts and words likely to produce violence in others. No one would have the hardihood to suggest that the principle of freedom of speech sanctions incitement to riot or that religious liberty connotes the privilege to exhort others to physical attack upon those belonging to another sect. When clear and present danger of riot, disorder, interference with traffic upon the public streets, or other immediate threat to public safety, peace, or order,

appears, the power of the State to prevent or punish is obvious. Equally obvious is it that a State may not unduly suppress free communication of views, religious or other, under the guise of conserving desirable conditions. Here we have a situation analogous to a conviction under a statute sweeping in a great variety of conduct under a general and indefinite characterization, and leaving to the executive and judicial branches too wide a discretion in its application. . . .

The record played by Cantwell embodies a general attack on all organized religious systems as instruments of Satan and injurious to man; it then singles out the Roman Catholic Church for strictures couched in terms which naturally would offend not only persons of that persuasion, but all others who respect the honestly-held religious faith of their fellows. The hearers were in fact highly offended. One of them said he felt like hitting Cantwell and the other that he was tempted to throw Cantwell off the street. The one who testified he felt like hitting Cantwell said, in answer to the question "Did you do anything else or have any other reaction?" "No, sir, because he said he would take the victrola and he went." The other witness testified that he told Cantwell he had better get off the street before something happened to him, and that was the end of the matter as Cantwell picked up his books and walked up the street.

Cantwell's conduct, in the view of the court below, considered apart from the effect of his communication upon his hearers, did not amount to a breach of the peace. One may, however, be guilty of the offense if he commit acts or make statements likely to provoke violence and disturbance of good order, even though no such eventuality be intended. Decisions to this effect are many, but examination discloses that, in practically all, the provocative language which was held to amount to a breach of the peace consisted of profane, indecent, or abusive remarks directed to the person of the hearer. Resort to epithets or personal abuse is not in any proper sense communication of information or opinion safeguarded by the Constitution, and its punishment as a criminal act would raise no question under that instrument.

We find in the instant case no assault or threatening of bodily harm, no truculent bearing, no intentional discourtesy, no personal abuse. On the contrary, we find only an effort to persuade a willing listener to buy a book or to contribute money in the interest of what Cantwell, however misguided others may think him, conceived to be true religion.

In the realm of religious faith, and in that of political belief, sharp differences arise. In both fields the tenets of one man may seem the rankest error to his neighbor. To persuade others to his own point of view, the pleader, as we know, at times, resorts to exaggeration, to vilification of men who have been, or are, prominent in church or state, and even to false statement. But the people of this nation have ordained in the light of history, that, in spite of the probability of excesses and abuses, these liberties are, in the long view, essential to enlightened opinion and right conduct on the part of the citizens of a democracy.

The essential characteristic of these liberties is, that under their shield many types of life, character, opinion, and belief can develop unmolested and unobstructed. Nowhere is this shield more necessary than in our own country for a people composed of many races and of many creeds. There are limits to the exercises of these liberties. The danger in these times from the coercive activities of those who in the delusion of racial or religious conceit would incite violence and breaches of the peace in order to deprive others of their equal right to the exercise of their liberties, is emphasized by events familiar to all. These and other transgressions of those limits the States appropriately may punish.

Although the contents of the record not unnaturally aroused animosity, we think that, in the absence of a statute narrowly drawn to define and punish specific conduct as constituting a clear and present danger to a substantial interest of the State, the petitioner's communication, considered in the light of the constitutional guaranties, raised no such clear and present menace to public peace and order as to render him liable to conviction of the common-law offense in question.

The judgment affirming the convictions on the third and fifth counts is reversed, and the cause is remanded for further proceedings not inconsistent with this opinion.

Reversed.

WEST VIRGINIA STATE BOARD OF EDUCATION *v.* BARNETTE
319 U.S. 624; 63 Sup. Ct. 1178; 87 L. Ed. 1628 (1943)

[*After the decision in* Minersville School District v. Gobitis, *the West Virginia Board of Education adopted a resolution requiring all public school teachers and pupils to salute the flag. Refusal to salute the flag was made an act of insubordination that was punishable by expulsion. Readmission was possible only if the expelled child agreed to render the salute; meanwhile, the expelled child was considered unlawfully absent and therefore delinquent. His parents or guardians could* *be prosecuted and if convicted could be made subject to a $50 fine and thirty days in jail.*

A number of the Witnesses' children were expelled from various public schools in West Virginia for refusal to salute the flag. State officials threatened to send these children to reformatories and to prosecute their parents for causing delinquency. Barnette and other Witnesses brought suit in a federal district court to enjoin the enforcement of the Board's regulation. They claimed that the Board's regulation, as applied to them, violated their religious freedom and freedom of speech under the First and Fourteenth Amendments. The district court granted the injunction. The Board of Education then brought the case to the Supreme Court by direct appeal.]

MR. JUSTICE JACKSON delivered the opinion of the Court:

. . . The freedom asserted by these appellees does not bring them into collision with rights asserted by any other individual. It is such conflicts which most frequently require intervention of the State to determine where the rights of one end and those of another begin. But the refusal of these persons to participate in the ceremony does not interfere with or deny rights of others to do so. Nor is there any question in this case that their behavior is peaceable and orderly. The sole conflict is between authority and rights of the individual. The State asserts power to condition access to public education on making a prescribed sign and profession and at the same time to coerce attendance by punishing both parent and child. The latter stand on a right of self-determination in matters that touch individual opinion and personal attitude.

As the present Chief Justice said in dissent in the *Gobitis* case, the State may "require teaching by instruction and study of all in our history and in the structure and organization of our government, including the guaranties of civil liberty, which tend to inspire patriotism and love of country." . . . Here, however, we are dealing with a compulsion of students to declare a belief. They are not merely made acquainted with the flag salute so that they may be informed as to what it

is or even what it means. The issue here is whether this slow and easily neglected route to aroused loyalties constitutionally may be short-cut by substituting a compulsory salute and slogan. . . .

There is no doubt that, in connection with the pledges, the flag salute is a form of utterance, Symbolism is a primitive but effective way of communicating ideas. The use of an emblem or flag to symbolize some system, idea, institution, or personality, is a short cut from mind to mind. Causes and nations, political parties, lodges, and ecclesiastical groups seek to knit the loyalty of their followings to a flag or banner, a color or design. The State announces rank, function, and authority through crowns and maces, uniforms and black robes; the church speaks through the Cross, the Crucifix, the altar and shrine, and clerical raiment. Symbols of State often convey political ideas just as religious symbols come to convey theological ones. Associated with many of these symbols are appropriate gestures of acceptance or respect: a salute, a bowed or bared head, a bended knee. A person gets from a symbol the meaning he puts into it, and what is one man's comfort and inspiration is another's jest and scorn.

Over a decade ago Chief Justice Hughes led this Court in holding that the display of a red flag as a symbol of opposition by peaceful and legal means to organize government was protected by the free-speech guaranties of the Constitution. *Stromberg* v. *California,* 283 U.S. 359. Here it is the State that employs a flag as a symbol of adherence to government as presently organized. It requires the individual to communicate by word and sign his acceptance of the political ideas it thus bespeaks. Objection to this form of communication when coerced is an old one, well known to the framers of the Bill of Rights.

It is also to be noted that the compulsory flag salute and pledge requires affirmation of a belief and an attitude of mind. It is not clear whether the regulation contemplates that pupils forego any contrary convictions of their own and become unwilling converts to the prescribed ceremony, or whether it will be acceptable if they simulate assent by words without belief and by a gesture barren of meaning. It is now a commonplace that censorship or suppression of expression of opinion is tolerated by our Constitution only when the expression presents a clear and present danger of action of a kind the State is empowered to prevent and punish. It would seem that involuntary affirmation could be commanded only on even more immediate and urgent grounds than silence. But here the power of compulsion is involked without any allegation that remaining passive during a flag-salute ritual creates a clear and present danger that would justify an effort even to muffle expression. To sustain the compulsory flag salute we are required to say that a Bill of Rights which guards the individual's right to speak his own mind, left it open to public authorities to compel him to utter what is not in his mind.

Whether the First Amendment to the Constitution will permit officials to order observance of ritual of this nature does not depend upon whether as a voluntary exercise we would think it to be good, bad, or merely innocuous. Any credo of nationalism is likely to include what some disapprove or to omit what others think essential, and to give off different overtones as it takes on different accents or interpretations. If official power exists to coerce acceptance of any patriotic creed, what it shall contain cannot be decided by courts, but must be largely discretionary with the ordaining authority, whose power to prescribe would no doubt include power to amend. Hence validity of the asserted power to force an American citizen publicly to profess any statement of belief or to engage in any ceremony of assent to one, presents questions of power that must be considered independently of any idea we may have as to the utility of the ceremony in question.

Nor does the issue as we see it turn on one's possession of particular religious views or the sincerity with which they are held. While religion supplies appellees' motive for enduring the discomforts of making the issue in this case, many citizens who do not share these religious views hold such a compulsory rite to infringe constitutional liberty of the individual. It is not necessary to inquire whether nonconformist beliefs will exempt from the duty to salute unless we first find power to make the salute a legal duty.

The *Gobitis* decision, however, *assumed,* as did the argument in that case and in this, that power exists in the State to impose the flag-salute discipline upon school children in general. The Court only examined and rejected a claim based on religious beliefs of immunity from an unquestioned general rule. The question which underlies the flag-salute controversy is whether such a ceremony so touching matters of opinion and political attitude may be imposed upon the individual by official authority under powers committed to any political organization under our Constitution. We examine rather than assume existence of this power and, against this broader definition of issues in this case, re-examine specific grounds assigned for the *Gobitis* decision.

1. It was said that the flag-salute controversy confronted the Court with "the problem which Lincoln cast in memorable dilemma: 'Must a government of necessity be too *strong* for the liberties of its people, or too *weak* to maintain its own existence?'" and that the answer must be in favor of strength. . . .

We think these issues may be examined free of pressure or restraint growing out of such considerations.

It may be doubted whether Mr. Lincoln would have thought that the strength of government to maintain itself would be impressively vindicated by our confirming power of the State to expel a handful of children from school. Such over-simplification, so handy in political debate, often lacks the precision necessary to postulates of judicial reasoning. If validly applied to this problem, the utterance cited would resolve every issue of power in favor of those in authority and would require us to override every liberty thought to weaken or delay execution of their policies.

Government of limited power need not be anemic government. Assurance that rights are secure tends to diminish fear and jealousy of strong government, and by making us feel safe to live under it makes for its better support. Without promise of a limiting Bill of Rights it is doubtful if our Constitution could have mustered enough strength to enable its ratification. To enforce those rights today is not to choose weak government over strong government. It is only to adhere as a means of strength to individual freedom of mind in pref-

erence to officially disciplined uniformity, for which history indicates a disappointing and disastrous end.

The subject now before us exemplifies this principle. Free public education, if faithful to the ideal of secular instruction and political neutrality, will not be partisan or enemy of any class, creed, party, or faction. If it is to impose any ideological discipline, however, each party or denomination must seek to control, or failing that, to weaken the influence of the educational system. Observance of the limitations of the Constitution will not weaken government in the field appropriate for its exercise.

2. It was also considered in the *Gobitis* case that functions of educational officers in States, counties, and school districts were such that to interfere with their authority "would in effect make us the school board for the country. . . ."

The Fourteenth Amendment, as now applied to the States, protects the citizen against the State itself and all of its creatures—Boards of Education not excepted. These have, of course, important, delicate, and highly discretionary functions, but none that they may not perform within the limits of the Bill of Rights. That they are educating the young for citizenship is reason for scrupulous protection of constitutional freedoms of the individual, if we are not to strangle the free mind at its source and teach youth to discount important principles of our government as mere platitudes.

Such Boards are numerous and their territorial jurisdiction often small. But small and local authority may feel less sense of responsibility to the Constitution, and agencies of publicity may be less vigilant in calling it to account. The action of Congress in making flag observance voluntary and respecting the conscience of the objector in a matter so vital as raising the Army contrasts sharply with these local regulations in matters relatively trivial to the welfare of the nation. . . .

3. The *Gobitis* opinion reasoned that this is a field "where courts possess no marked and certainly no controlling competence," that it is committed to the legislatures as well as the courts to guard cherished liberties and that it is constitutionally appropriate to "fight out the wise use of legislative authority in the forum of public opinion and before legislative assemblies rather than to transfer such a contest to the judicial arena," since all the "effective means of inducing political changes are left free. . . ."

The very purpose of a Bill of Rights was to withdraw certain subjects from the vicissitudes of political controversy, to place them beyond the reach of majorities and officials and to establish them as legal principles to be applied by the courts. One's right to life, liberty, and property, to free speech, a free press, freedom of worship and assembly, and other fundamental rights may not be submitted to vote; they depend on the outcome of no elections.

In weighing arguments of the parties it is important to distinguish between the due process clause of the Fourteenth Amendment as an instrument for transmitting the principles of the First Amendment and those cases in which it is applied for its own sake. The test of legislation which collides with the Fourteenth, because it also collides with the principles of the First, is much more definitive than the test when only the Fourteenth is involved. Much of the vagueness of the due process clause disappears when the specific prohibitions of the First become its standard. The right of a State to regulate, for example, a public utility may well include, so far as the due process test is concerned, power to

impose all of the restrictions which a legislature may have a "'rational basis" for adopting. But freedoms of speech and of press, of assembly, and of worship may not be infringed on such slender grounds. They are susceptible of restriction only to prevent grave and immediate danger to interests which the State may lawfully protect. It is important to note that while it is the Fourteenth Amendment which bears directly upon the State, it is the more specific limiting principles of the First Amendment that finally govern this case.

Nor does our duty to apply the Bill of Rights to assertions of official authority depend upon our possession of marked competence in the field where the invasion of rights occurs. True, the task of translating the majestic generalities of the Bill of Rights, conceived as part of the pattern of liberal government in the eighteenth century, into concrete restraints on officials dealing with the problems of the twentieth century, is one to disturb self-confidence. These principles grew in soil which also produced a philosophy that the individual was the center of society, that his liberty was attainable through mere absence of governmental restraints, and that government should be entrusted with few controls and only the mildest supervision over men's affairs. We must transplant these rights to a soil in which the *laissez-faire* concept or principle of noninterference has withered at least as to economic affairs, and social advancements are increasingly sought through closer integration of society and through expended and strengthened governmental controls. These changed conditions often deprive precedents of reliability and cast us more than we would choose upon our own judgment. But we act in these matters not only by authority of our competence but by force of our commissions. We cannot, because of modest estimates of our competence in such specialties as public education, withhold the judgment that history authenticates as the function of this Court when liberty is infringed.

4. Lastly, and this is the very heart of the *Gobitis* opinion, it reasons that "National unity is the basis of national security," that the authorities have "the right to select appropriate means for its attainment," and hence reaches the conclusion that such compulsory measures toward "national unity" are constitutional. . . . Upon the verity of this assumption depends our answer in this case.

National unity as an end which officials may foster by persuasion and example is not in question. The problem is whether under our Constitution compulsion as here employed is a permissible means for its achievement.

Struggles to coerce uniformity of sentiment in support of some end thought essential to their time and country have been waged by many good as well as by evil men. Nationalism is a relatively recent phenomenon, but at other times and places the ends have been racial or territorial security, support of a dynasty or regime, and particular plans for saving souls. As first and moderate methods to attain unity have failed, those bent on its accomplishment must resort to an ever-increasing severity.

. . . Ultimate futility of such attempts to compel coherence is the lesson of every such effort from the Roman drive to stamp out Christianity as a disturber of its pagan unity, the Inquisition, as a means to religious and dynastic unity, the Siberian exiles as a means to Russian unity, down to the fast-failing efforts of our present totalitarian enemies. Those who begin coercive elimination of dissent soon find themselves exterminating dissenters. Compulsory unification of opinion achieves only the unanimity of the graveyard.

It seems trite but necessary to say that the First Amendment to our Constitution was designed to avoid these ends by avoiding these beginnings. There is no mysticism in the American concept of the State or of the nature or origin of its authority. We set up government by consent of the governed, and the Bill of Rights denies those in power and legal opportunity to coerce that consent. Authority here is to be controlled by public opinion, not public opinion by authority.

The case is made difficult not because the principles of its decision are obscure but because the flag involved is our own. Nevertheless, we apply the limitations of the Constitution with no fear that freedom to be intellectually and spiritually diverse or even contrary will disintegrate the social organization. To believe that patriotism will not flourish if patriotic ceremonies are voluntary and spontaneous instead of a compulsory routine is to make an unflattering estimate of the appeal of our institutions to free minds. We can have intellectual individualism and the rich cultural diversities that we owe to exceptional minds only at the price of occasional eccentricity and abnormal attitudes. When they are so harmless to others or to the State as those we deal with here, the price is not too great. But freedom to differ is not limited to things that do not matter much. That would be a mere shadow of freedom. The test of its substance is the right to differ as to things that touch the heart of the existing order.

If there is any fixed start in our constitutional constellation, it is that no official, high or petty, can prescribe what shall be orthodox in politics, nationalism, religion, or other matters of opinion or force citizens to confess by word or act their faith therein. If there are any circumstances which permit an exception, they do not now occur to us.

We think the action of the local authorities in compelling the flag salute and pledge transcends constitutional limitations on their power and invades the sphere of intellect and spirit which it is the purpose of the First Amendment to our Constitution to reserve from all official control.

The decision of this Court in *Minersville School District* v. *Gobitis* [is] overruled, and the judgment enjoining enforcement of the West Virginia Regulation is

Affirmed.

[MR. JUSTICE BLACK, MR. JUSTICE DOUGLAS, and MR. JUSTICE MURPHY concurred.]

MR. JUSTICE FRANKFURTER, dissenting:

One who belongs to the most vilified and persecuted minority in history is not likely to be insensible to the freedoms guaranteed by our Constitution. Were my purely personal attitude relevant I should wholeheartedly associate myself with the general libertarian views in the Court's opinion, representing as they do the thought and action of a lifetime. But as judges we are neither Jew nor Gentile, neither Catholic nor agnostic. We owe equal attachment to the Constitution and are equally bound by our judicial obligations whether we derive our citizenship from the earliest or the latest immigrants to these shores. As a member of this Court I am not justified in writing my private notions of policy into the Constitution, no matter how deeply I may cherish them or how mischievous I may deem their disregard. The duty of a judge who must decide which of two claims before the Court shall prevail, that of a State to enact and enforce laws within its general competence or that of an individual to refuse obedience because of the demands of his conscience, is not that of the ordinary person. It can never be emphasized too much that one's own opinion about the wisdom or evil of a law should be excluded altogether when one is doing one's duty on the bench. The only opinion of our own even looking in that direction that is material is our opinion whether legislators could in reason have enacted such a law. In the light of all the circumstances, including the history of this question in this Court, it would require more daring than I possess to deny that reasonable legislators could have taken the action which is before us for review. Most unwillingly, therefore, I must differ from my brethren with regard to legislation like this. I cannot bring my mind to believe that the "liberty" secured by the Due Process Clause gives this Court authority to deny to the State of West Virginia the attainment of that which we all recognize as a legitimate legislative end, namely, the promotion of good citizenship, by employment of the means here chosen.

. . . When Mr. Justice Holmes, speaking for this Court, wrote that "it must be remembered that legislatures are ultimate guardians of the liberties and welfare of the people in quite as great a degree as the courts," . . . he went to the very essence of our constitutional system and the democratic conception of our society. He did not mean that for only some phases of civil government this Court was not to supplant and sit in judgment upon the right or wrong of a challenged measure. He was stating the comprehensive judicial duty and role of this Court in our constitutional scheme whenever legislation is sought to be nullified on any ground, namely, that responsibility for legislation lies with legislatures, answerable as they are directly to the people, and this Court's only and very narrow function is to determine whether within the broad grant of authority vested in legislatures they have exercised a judgment for which reasonable justification can be offered.

. . . The reason why from the beginning even the narrow judicial authority to nullify legislation has been viewed with a jealous eye is that it serves to prevent the full play of the democratic process. The fact that it may be an undemocratic aspect of our scheme of government does not call for its rejection or its disuse. But it is the best of reasons, as this Court has frequently recognized, for the greatest caution in its use.

. . . If the function of this Court is to be essentially no different from that of a legislature, if the considerations governing constitutional construction are to be substantially those that underlie legislation, then indeed judges should not have life tenure and they should be made directly responsible to the electorate. . . .

[MR. JUSTICE ROBERTS and MR. JUSTICE REED also dissented.]

EVERSON v. BOARD OF EDUCATION
330 U.S. 1; 67 Sup. Ct. 504; 91 L. Ed. 711 (1947)

[*A New Jersey statute enacted in 1941 authorized school boards to make rules and contracts for the transportation of school children, including those attending nonprofit private and parochial schools. Under this law, a township board of education (Ewing, N.J.) authorized reimbursement to parents of money spent for school transportation expenses to Catholic parochial schools as well as public schools. Everson, who was a taxpayer in the school district, challenged the right of the Board to reimburse parents of parochial school students. A state court agreed with Everson and held that the New Jersey legislature did not have the power to authorize such payments under the state constitution. However, the highest state court (New Jersey Court of Errors and Appeals) reversed the lower court's decision. Everson then brought the case to the Supreme Court on appeal.*]

MR. JUSTICE BLACK delivered the opinion of the Court:

. . . The only contention here is that the state statute and the resolution, in so far as they authorized reimbursement to parents of children attending parochial schools violate the Federal Constitution in these two respects, which to some extent overlap. *First.* They authorize the State to take by taxation the private property of some and bestow it upon others, to be used for their own private purposes. This, it is alleged, violates the due process clause of the Fourteenth Amendment. *Second.* The statute and the resolution forced inhabitants to pay taxes to help support and maintain schools which are dedicated to, and which regularly teach, the Catholic Faith. This is alleged to be a use of state power to support church schools contrary to the prohibition of the First Amendment, which the Fourteenth Amendment made applicable to the states.

. . . [T]he New Jersey legislature has decided that a public purpose will be served by using tax-raised funds to pay the bus fares of all school children, including those who attend parochial schools. The New Jersey Court of Errors and Appeals has reached the same conclusion. The fact that a state law, passed to satisfy a public need, coincides with the personal desires of the individuals most directly affected is certainly an inadequate reason for us to say that a legislature has erroneously appraised the public need. . . .

It is much too late to argue that legislation intended to facilitate the opportunity of children to get a secular education serves no public purpose. . . . The same thing is no less true of legislation to reimburse needy parents, or all parents, for payment of the fares of their children so that they can ride in public buses to and from schools rather than run the risk of traffic and other hazards incident to walking or "hitchhiking." . . . Nor does it follow that a law has a private rather than a public purpose because it provides that tax-raised funds will be paid to reimburse individuals on account of money spent by them in a way which furthers a public program. . . . Subsidies and loans to individuals such as farmers and homeowners, and to privately-owned transportation systems, as well as many other kinds of businesses, have been commonplace practices in our state and national history. . . .

The New Jersey statute is challenged as a "law respecting an establishment of religion." The First Amendment, as made applicable to the states by the Fourteenth . . . commands that a state "shall make no law respecting an establishment of religion, or prohibiting the words of the First Amendment reflected in the minds of early Americans a vivid mental picture of conditions and practices which they fervently wished to stamp out in order to preserve liberty for themselves and for their posterity. Doubtless their goal has not been entirely reached; but so far has the Nation moved toward it that the expression "law respecting an establishment of religion," probably does not so vividly remind present-day Americans of the evils, fears, and political problems that caused that expression to be written into our Bill of Rights. Whether this New Jersey law is one respecting an "establishment of religion" requires an understanding of the meaning of that language, particularly with respect to the imposition of taxes. . . .

The "establishment of religion" clause of the First Amendment means at least this: Neither a state nor the Federal Government can set up a church. Neither can pass laws which aid one religion, aid all religions, or prefer one religion over another. Neither can force nor influence a person to go to or to remain away from church against his will or force him to profess a belief or disbelief in any religion. No person can be punished for entertaining or professing religious beliefs or disbeliefs, for church attendance or non-attendance. No tax in any amount, large or small, can be levied to support any religious activities or institutions, whatever they may be called, or whatever form they may adopt to teach or practice religion. Neither a state nor the Federal Government can, openly or secretly, participate in the affairs of any religious organizations or groups and *vice versa*. In the words of Jefferson, the clause against establishment of religion by law was intended to erect "a wall of separation between church and State. . . ."

Measured by these standards, we cannot say that the First Amendment prohibits New Jersey from spending tax-raised funds to pay the bus fares of parochial-school pupils as a part of a general program under which it pays the fares of pupils attending public and other schools. It is undoubtedly true that children are helped to get to church schools. There is even a possibility that some of the children might not be sent to the church schools if the parents were compelled to pay their children's bus fares out of their own pockets when transportation to a public school would have been paid for by the State. The same possibility exists where the state requires a local transit company to provide reduced fares to school children, including those attending parochial schools, or where a municipally-owned transportation system undertakes to carry all school children free of charge. Moreover, state-paid policemen, detailed to protect children going to and from church schools from the very real hazards of traffic, would serve much the same purpose and accomplish much the same result as state provisions intended to guarantee free transportation of a kind which the state deems to be best for the school children's welfare. And parents might refuse to risk their children to the serious danger of traffic accidents going to and from parochial schools, the approaches to which were not protected by policemen. Similarly, parents might be reluctant to permit their children to attend schools which the state had cut off from such general government services as ordinary police and fire protection, connections for sewage disposal, public highways and sidewalks. Of course, cutting off church schools from these services, so separate and so indisputably marked off from the religious function, would make it far more difficult for the schools to operate. But such is obviously not the purpose of the First Amendment. The Amendment requires the state to be a neutral in its relations with groups of religious believers and nonbelievers; it does not require the state to be their adversary. State power is no more to be used so as to handicap religions than it is to favor them.

This Court has said that parents may, in the discharge of their duty under state compulsory education laws, send their children to a religious rather than a public school if the school meets the secular educational requirements which the state has power to impose. . . . It appears that these parochial schools meet New Jersey's requirements. The State contributes no money to the schools. It does not support them. Its legislation, as applied, does no more than provide a general program to help parents get their children, regardless of their religion, safely and expeditiously to and from accredited schools.

The First Amendment has erected a wall between church and state. That wall must be kept high and impregnable. We could not approve the slightest breach. New Jersey has not breached it here.

Affirmed.

MR. JUSTICE JACKSON, dissenting:

. . . It is of no importance in this situation whether the beneficiary of this expenditure of tax-raised funds is primarily the parochial school and incidentally the pupil, or whether the aid is directly bestowed on the pupil with indirect benefits to the school. The state cannot maintain a Church and it can no more tax its citizens to furnish free carriage to those who attend a Church. The prohibition against establishment of religion cannot be circumvented by a subsidy, bonus, or reimbursement of expense to individuals for receiving religious instruction and indoctrination. . . .

It seems to me that the basic fallacy in the Court's reasoning, which accounts for its failure to apply the principles it avows, is in ignoring the essentially religious test by which beneficiaries of this expenditure are selected. A policeman protects a Catholic, of course—but not because he is a Catholic; it is because he is a man and a member of our society. The fireman protects the Church school—but not because it is a Church school; it is because it is property, part of the assets of our society. Neither the fireman nor the policeman has to ask before he renders aid, "Is this man or building identified with the Catholic Church?" But before these school authorities draw a check to reimburse for a student's fare they must ask just that question, and if the school is a Catholic one they may render aid because it is such, while if it is of any other faith or is run for profit, the help must be withheld. . . .

The Court's holdings is that this taxpayer has no grievance because the state has decided to make the reimbursement a public purpose and therefore we are bound to regard it as such. I agree that this Court has left, and always should leave to each state, great latitude in deciding for itself, in the light of its own conditions, what shall be public purposes in its scheme of things. It may socialize utilities and economic enterprises and make taxpayers' business out of what conventionally had been private business. It may make public business of individual welfare, health, education, entertainment, or security. But it cannot make public business of religious worship or instruction, or of attendance at religious institutions of any character. There is no answer to the proposition, more fully expounded by Mr. Justice Rutledge, that the effect of the religious freedom Amendment to our Constitution was to take every form of propagation of religion out of the realm of things which could directly or indirectly be made public business and thereby be supported in whole or in part at taxpayers' expense. That is a difference which the Constitution sets up between religion and almost every other subject matter of legislation, a difference which goes to the very root of religious freedom and which the

Court is overlooking today. This freedom was first in the Bill of Rights because it was first in the forefathers' minds; it was set forth in absolute terms, and its strength is in rigidity. It was intended not only to keep the states' hands out of religion, but to keep religion's hands off the state, and, above all, to keep bitter religious controversy out of public life by denying to every denomination any advantage from getting control of public policy or the public purse. Those great ends I cannot but think are immeasurably compromised by today's decision. . . .

But we cannot have it both ways. Religious teaching cannot be a private affair when the state seeks to impose regulations which infringe on it indirectly, and a public affair when it comes to taxing citizens of one faith to aid another, or those of no faith to aid all. If these principles seem harsh in prohibiting aid to Catholic education, it must not be forgotten that it is the same Constitution that alone assures Catholics the right to maintain these schools at all when predominant local sentiment would forbid them. . . . Nor should I think that those who have done so well without this aid would want to see this separation between Church and State broken down. If the state may aid these religious schools, it may therefore regulate them. Many groups have sought aid from tax funds only to find that it carried political controls with it. Indeed this Court has declared that "it is hardly lack of due process for the Government to regulate that which it subsidizes. . . ."

But in any event, the great purposes of the Constitution do not depend on the approval or convenience of those they restrain. I cannot read the history of the struggle to separate political from ecclesiastical affairs . . . without a conviction that the Court today is unconsciously giving the clock's hands a backward turn.

MR. JUSTICE FRANKFURTER joins in this opinion.

MR. JUSTICE RUTLEDGE, with whom MR. JUSTICE FRANKFURTER MR. JUSTICE JACKSON, and MR. JUSTICE BURTON agree, dissenting:

This case forces us to determine squarely for the first time what was "an establishment of religion" in the First Amendment's conception; and by that measure to decide whether New Jersey's action violates its command. . . .

Not simply an established church, but any law respecting an establishment of religion is forbidden. The Amendment was broadly but not loosely phrased. It is the compact and exact summation of its author's views formed during his long struggle for religious freedom. In Madison's own words characterizing Jefferson's Bill for Establishing Religious Freedom, the guaranty he put in our national charter, like the bill he piloted through the Virginia Assembly, was "a Model of technical precision, and perspicuous brevity." Madison could not have confused "church" and "religion," or "an established church" and "an establishment of religion."

The Amendment's purpose was not to strike merely at the official establishment of a single sect, creed, or religion, outlawing only a formal relation such as had prevailed in England and some of the colonies. Necessarily it was to uproot all such relationships. But the object was broader than separating church and state in this narrow sense. It was to create a complete and permanent separation of the spheres of religious activity and civil authority by comprehensively forbidding every form of public aid or support for religion. In proof the Amendment's wording and history unite with this Court's consistent utterances whenever attention has been fixed directly upon the question.

[MR. JUSTICE RUTLEDGE follows with the history of the First Amendment, which he states reveals clearly that the Amendment was designed to forbid the use of any public funds to aid or support religious exercises.]

. . . Does New Jersey's action furnish support for religion by use of the taxing power? Certainly it does, if the test remains undiluted as Jefferson and Madison made it, that money taken by taxation from one is not to be used or given to support another's religious training or belief, or indeed one's own. Today as then the furnishing of "contributions of money for the propagation of opinions which he disbelieves" is the forbidden exaction; and the prohibition is absolute for whatever measure brings that consequence and whatever amount may be sought or given to that end.

The funds used here were raised by taxation. The Court does not dispute, nor could it, that their use does in fact give aid and encouragement to religious instruction. It only concludes that this aid is not "support" in law. . . . Here parents pay money to send their children to parochial schools and funds raised by taxation are used to reimburse them. This not only helps the children to get to school and the parents to send them. It aids them in a substantial way to get the very thing which they are sent to the particular school to secure, namely, religous training and teaching. . . .

New Jersey's action therefore exactly fits the type of exaction and the kind of evil at which Madison and Jefferson struck. Under the test they framed it cannot be said that the cost of transportation is no part of the cost of education or of the religious instruction given. That it is a substantial and a necessary element is shown most plainly by the continuing and increasing demand for the state to assume it. . . .

But we are told that the New Jersey statute is valid in its present application because the appropriation is for a public, not a private purpose, namely, the promotion of education, and the majority accept this idea in the conclusion that all we have here is "public welfare legislation." If that is true and the Amendment's force can be thus destroyed, what has been said becomes all the more pertinent. For then there could be no possible objection to more extensive support of religious education by New Jersey.

If the fact alone be determinative that religious schools are engaged in education, thus promoting the general and individual welfare, together with the legislature's decision that the payment of public moneys for their aid makes their work a public function, then I can see no possible basis, except one of dubious legislative policy, for the state's refusal to make full appropriation for support of private, religious schools, just as is done for public instruction. There could not be, on that basis, valid constitutional objection. . . .

We have here then one substantial issue, not two. To say that New Jersey's appropriation and her use of the power of taxation for raising the funds appropriated are not for public purposes but are for private ends, is to say that they are for the support of religion and religious teaching. Conversely, to say that they are for public purposes is to say that they are not for religious ones.

This is precisely for the reason that education which includes religious training and teaching, and its support, have been made matters of private right and function, not public, by the very terms of the First Amendment. That is the effect not only in its guaranty of religion's free exercise, but also in the prohibition of establishments. It was on this basis of the private character of the function of religious education that this Court held parents entitled to send their children to private, religious schools. *Pierce* v. *Society of Sisters.* . . . Now it declares in effect that the appropriation of public funds to defray part of the cost of attending those schools is for a public purpose. If so, I do not understand why the state cannot go farther or why this case approaches the verge of its power.

. . . Our constitutional policy is exactly the opposite. It does not deny the value or the necessity for religious training, teaching or observance. Rather it secures their free exercise. But to that end it does deny that the state can undertake or sustain them in any form or degree. For this reason the sphere of religious activity, as distinguished from the secular intellectual liberties, has been given the twofold protection and, as the state cannot forbid, neither can it perform or aid in performing the religious functon. The dual prohibition makes that function altogether private. It cannot be made a public one by legislative act. . . .

It is not because religious teaching does not promote the public or the individual's welfare, but because neither is furthered when the state promotes religious education, that the Constitution forbids it to do so. Both legislatures and courts are bound by that distinction. In failure to observe it lies the fallacy of the "public function"–"social legislation" argument. . . .

The reasons underlying the Amendment's policy have not vanished with time or diminished in force. Now as when it was adopted the price of religious freedom is double. It is that the church and religion shall live both within and upon that freedom. There cannot be freedom of religion, safeguarded by the state, and intervention by the church or its agencies in the state's domain or dependency on its largesse. . . . The great condition of religious liberty is that it be maintained free from sustenance, as also from other interferences, by the state. . . . Public money devoted to payment of religious costs, educational or other, brings the quest for more. It brings too the struggle of sect against sect for the larger share or for any. Here one by numbers alone will benefit most, there another. That is precisely the history of societies which have had an established religion and dissident groups. The end of such strife cannot be other than to destroy the cherished liberty. The dominating group will achieve the dominant benefit; or all will embroil the state in their dissensions. . . .

No one conscious of religious values can be unsympathetic toward the burden which our constitutional separation puts on parents who desire religious instruction mixed with secular for their children. They pay taxes for others' children's education, at the same time the added cost of instruction for their own. Nor can one happily see benefits denied to children which others receive, because in conscience they or their parents for them desire a different kind of training others do not demand.

But if those feelings should prevail, there would be an end to our historic constitutional policy and command. No more unjust or discriminatory in fact is it to deny attendants at religious schools the cost of their transportation than it is to deny them tuitions, sustenance for their teachers, or any other educational expense which others receive at public cost. Hardship in fact there is, which none can blink. But, for assuring to those who undergo it the greater, the most comprehensive freedom, it is one written by design and firm intent into our basic law.

Of course discrimination in the legal sense does not exist. The child attending the religious school has the same right as any other to attend the public school. But he foregoes exercising it because the same guaranty which assures this freedom forbids the public school or any agency of the state to give or aid him in securing the religious instruction he seeks.

Were he to accept the common school, he would be the first to protest the teaching there of any creed or faith not his own. And it is precisely for the reason that their atmosphere is wholly secular that children are not sent to public schools under the *Pierce* doctrine. But that is a constitutional necessity, because we have staked the very existence of our country on the faith that complete separation between the state and religion is best for the state and best for religion. . . .

Two great drives are constantly in motion to abridge, in the name of education, the complete division of religion and civil authority which our forefathers made. One is to introduce religious education and observances into the public schools. The other, to obtain public funds for the aid and support of various private religious schools. . . . In my opinion both avenues were closed by the Constitution. Neither should be opened by this Court. The matter is not one of quantity, to be measured by the amount of money expended. Now as in Madison's day it is one of principle, to keep separate the separate spheres as the First Amendment drew them; to prevent the first experiment upon our liberties; and to keep the question from becoming entangled in corrosive precedents. We should not be less strict to keep strong and untarnished the one side of the shield of religious freedom than we have been of the other.

The judgment should be reversed.

ILLINOIS ex rel. McCOLLUM *v.* BOARD OF EDUCATION
333 U.S. 203; 68 Sup. Ct. 461; 92 L. Ed. 648 (1948)

[*Mrs. Vashti McCollum, whose child was enrolled in the Champaign, Illinois, public school system, tried to obtain a writ of mandamus to prohibit the use of the local school facilities for religious instruction. She contended that the religious program conducted in the schools violated the First and Fourteenth Amendments. A county court denied her petition for mandamus. On appeal the state supreme court affirmed. Mrs. McCollum then brought the case to the Supreme Court on appeal. The details of the religious instruction program are given in the Court's opinion.*]

MR. JUSTICE BLACK delivered the opinion of the Court:

This case relates to the power of a state to utilize its tax-supported public school system in aid of religious instruction in so far as that power may be restricted by the First and Fourteenth Amendments to the Federal Constitution. . . .

Appellant's petition for mandamus alleged that religious teachers, employed by private religious groups, were permitted to come weekly into the school buildings during the regular hours set apart for secular teaching, and then and there for a period of thirty minutes substitute their religious teaching for the secular education provided under the compulsory education law. . . .

Although there are disputes between the parties as to various inferences that may or may not properly be drawn from the evidence concerning the religious program, the following facts are shown by the record without dispute. In 1940, interested members of the Jewish, Roman Catholic, and a few of the Protestant faiths formed a voluntary association called the Champaign Council on Religious Education. They obtained permission from the Board of Education to offer classes in religious instruction to public-school pupils in grades four to nine inclusive. Classes were made up of pupils whose parents signed printed cards requesting that their children be permitted to attend; they were held weekly, thirty minutes for the lower grades, forty-five minutes for the higher. The council employed the religious teachers at no expense to the school authorities, but the instructors were subject to the approval and supervision of the superintendent of schools. The classes were taught in three separate religious groups by Protestant teachers, Catholic priests, and a Jewish rabbi, although for the past several years there have apparently been no classes instructed in the Jewish religion. Classes were conducted in the regular classrooms of the school building. Students who did not choose to take the religious instruction were not released from public-school duties; they were required to leave their classrooms and go to some other place in the school building for pursuit of the secular studies. On the other hand, students who were released from secular study for the religious instructions were required to be present at the religious classes. Reports of their presence or absence were to be made to their secular teachers.

The foregoing facts, without reference to others that appear in the record, show the use of tax-supported property for religious instruction carried on by separate religious sects. Pupils compelled by law to go to school for secular education are released in part from their legal duty upon the condition that they attend the religious classes. This is beyond all question a utilization of the tax-established and tax-supported public school system to aid religious groups to spread their faith. And it falls squarely under the ban of the First Amendment (made applicable to the States by the Fourteenth) as we interpreted it in *Everson v. Board of Education. . . .*

To hold that a state cannot consistently with the First and Fourteenth Amendments utilize its public school system to aid any or all religious faiths or sects in the dissemination of their doctrines and ideals does not, as counsel urge, manifest a government hostility to religion or religious teachings. A manifestation of such hostility would be at war with our national tradition as embodied in the First Amendment's guaranty of the free exercise of religion. For the First Amendment rests upon the premise that both religion and government can best work to achieve their lofty aims if each is left free from the other within its respective sphere. Or, as we said in the *Everson* case, the First Amendment has erected a wall between Church and State which must be kept high and impregnable.

Here not only are the State's tax-supported public school buildings used for the dissemination of religious doctrines. The State also affords sectarian groups an invaluable aid in that it helps to provide pupils for their religious classes through the use of the State's compulsory public school machinery. This is not separation of Church and State.

The cause is reversed and remanded to the State Supreme Court for proceedings not inconsistent with this opinion.

Reversed and remanded.

MR. JUSTICE RUTLEDGE and MR. JUSTICE BURTON also concurred in the Court's opinion.

MR. JUSTICE FRANKFURTER delivered the following opinion, in which MR. JUSTICE JACKSON, MR. JUSTICE RUTLEDGE, and MR. JUSTICE BURTON join:

We dissented in *Everson* v. *Board of Education . . .* because in our view the constitutional principle requiring separation of Church and State compelled invalidation of the ordinance sustained by the majority. Illinois has here authorized the commingling of sectarian with secular instruction in the public schools. The Constitution of the United States forbids this.

This case in the light of the *Everson* decision, demonstrates anew that the mere formulation of a relevant constitutional principle is the beginning of the solution of a problem, not its answer. This is so because the meaning of a spacious conception like that of the separation of Church from State is unfolded as appeal is made to the principle from case to case. We are all agreed that the First and the Fourteenth Amendments have a secular reach far more penetrating in the conduct of Government than merely to forbid an "established church." But agreement, in the abstract, that the First Amendment was designed to erect a "wall of separation between church and state," does not preclude a clash of views as to what the wall separates. Involved is not only the constitutional principle but the implications of judicial review in its enforcement. Accommodation of legislative freedom and constitutional limitations upon that freedom cannot be achieved by a mere phrase. We cannot illuminatingly apply the "wall-of-separation" metaphor until we have considered the relevant history of religious education in America, the place of the "released-time" movement in that history, and its precise manifestation in the case before us. . . .

The evolution of colonial education, largely in the service of religion, into the public school system of today is the story of changing conceptions regarding the American democratic society, of the functions of State-maintained education in such a society, and of the role therein of the free exercise of religion by the people. The modern public school derived from a philosophy of freedom reflected in the First Amendment. . . . As the momentum for popular education increased and in turn evoked strong claims for State support of religious education, contests not unlike that which in Virginia had produced Madison's Remonstrance appeared in various forms in other States. New York and Massachusetts provide famous chapters in the history that established dissociation of religious teaching from State-maintained schools. In New York, the rise of the common schools led, despite fierce sectarian opposition, to the barring of tax funds to church schools, and later to any school in which sectarian doctrine was taught. In Massachusetts, largely through the efforts of Horace Mann, all sectarian teachings were barred from the common school to save it from being rent by denominational conflict. The upshot of these controversies, often long and fierce, is fairly summarized by saying that long before the Fourteenth Amendment subjected the States to new limitations, the prohibition of furtherance by the State of religious instruction became the guiding principle, in law and feeling, of the American people. . . .

Separation in the field of education, then was not imposed upon unwilling States by force of superior law. In this respect the Fourteenth Amendment merely reflected a principle then dominant in our national life. To the extent that the Constitution thus made it binding upon the States, the basis of the restriction is the whole experience of our people. Zealous watchfulness against fusion of secular and religious activities by Government itself, through any of its instruments but especially through its educational agencies, was the democratic response of the American community to the particular needs of a young and growing nation, unique in the composition of its people. A totally different situation elsewhere, as illustrated for instance by the English provisions for religious education in State-maintained schools, only serves to illustrate that free societies are not cast on one mold. . . . Different institutions evolve from different historic circumstances.

. . . [T]he intrusion of religious instruction into the public school system of Champaign [cannot] be minimized by saying that it absorbs less than an hour a week; in fact, that affords evidence of a design constitutionally objectionable. If it were merely a question of enabling a child to obtain religious instruction with a receptive mind, the 30 or 45 minutes could readily be found on Saturday or Sunday. If that were all, Champaign might have drawn upon the French system, known in its American manifestation as "dismissed time," whereby one school day is shortened to allow all children to go where they please, leaving those who so desire to go to a religious school. The momentum of the whole school atmosphere and school planning is presumably put behind religious instruction, as given in Champaign, precisely in order to secure for the religious instruction such momentum and planning. To speak to "released time" as being only half or three-quarters of an hour is to draw a thread from a fabric. . . .

Separation means separation, not something less. Jefferson's metaphor in describing the relation between Church and State speaks of a "wall of separation," not of a fine line easily overstepped. The public school is at once the symbol of our democracy and the most pervasive means for promoting our common destiny. In no activity of the State is it more vital to keep out divisive forces than in its schools, to avoid confusing, not to say fusing, what the Constitution sought to keep strictly apart. "The great American principle of eternal separation"—Elihu Root's phrase bears repetition—is one of the vital reliances of our Constitutional system for assuring unities among our people stronger than our diversities. It is the Court's duty to enforce this principle in its full integrity. . . .

MR. JUSTICE REED, dissenting:

. . . The phrase "an establishment of religion" may have been intended by Congress to be aimed only at a state church. When the First Amendment was pending in Congress in substantially its present form, "Mr. Madison said, he apprehended the meaning of the words to be, that Congress should not establish a religion, and enforce the legal observation of it by law, nor compel men to worship God in any manner contrary to their conscience." Passing years, however, have brought about acceptance of a broader meaning, although never until today, I believe, has this Court widened its interpretation to any such degree as holding that recognition of the interest of our nation in religion, through the granting, to qualified representatives of the principal faiths, of opportunity to present religion as an optional, extracurricular subject during released school time in public school buildings, was equivalent to an establishment of religion. A reading of the general statements of eminent statesmen of former days, referred to in the opinions in this case and in *Everson* v. *Board of Education,* . . . will show that circumstances such as those in this case were far from the minds of the authors. The words and spirit of those

statements may be wholeheartedly accepted without in the least impugning the judgment of the State of Illinois. . . .

It seems clear to me that the "aid" referred to by the Court in the *Everson* case could not have been those incidental advantages that religious bodies, with other groups similarly situated, obtain as a by-product of organized society. This explains the well-known fact that all churches receive "aid" from government in the form of freedom from taxation. The *Everson* decision itself justified the transportation of children to church schools by New Jersey for safety reasons. It accords with *Cochran* v. *Louisiana State Board of Education,* . . . , where this Court upheld a free textbook statute of Louisiana against a charge that it aided private schools on the ground that books were for the education of the children, not to aid religious schools. Likewise the National School Lunch Act aids all school children attending tax-exempt schools. In *Bradfield* v. *Roberts,* 175 U.S. 291, this Court held proper the payment of money by the Federal Government to build an addition to a hospital, chartered by individuals who were members of a Roman Catholic sisterhood, and operated under the auspices of the Roman Catholic Church. This was done over the objection that it aided the establishment of religion. While obviously in these instances the respective churches, in a certain sense, were aided, this Court has never held that such "aid" was in violation of the First or Fourteenth Amendment. . . .

The practices of the federal government offer many examples of this kind of "aid" by the state to religion. The Congress of the United States has a chaplain for each House who daily invokes divine blessings and guidance for the proceedings. The armed forces have commissioned chaplains from early days. They conduct the public services in accordance with the liturgical requirements of their respective faiths, ashore and afloat, employing for the purpose property belonging to the United States and dedicated to the services of religion. Under the Servicemen's Readjustment Act of 1944, eligible veterans may receive training at government expense for the ministry in denominational schools. The schools of the District of Columbia have opening exercises which "include a reading from the Bible without note or comment, and the Lord's Prayer."

In the United States Naval Academy and the United States Military Academy, schools wholly supported and completely controlled by the federal government, there are a number of religious activities. Chaplains are attached to both schools. Attendance at church services on Sunday is compulsory at both the Military and Naval Academies. At West Point the Protestant services are held in the Cadet Chapel, the Catholic in the Catholic Chapel, and the Jewish in the Old Cadet Chapel; at Annapolis only Protestant services are held on the reservation, midshipmen of other religious persuasions attend the churches of the city of Annapolis. These facts indicate that both schools since their earliest beginnings have maintained and enforced a pattern of participation in formal worship.

With the general statements in the opinions concerning the constitutional requirement that the nation and the states, by virtue of the First and Fourteenth Amendments, may "make no law respecting an establishment of religion," I am in agreement. But, in the light of the meaning given to those words by the precedents, customs, and practices which I have detailed above, I cannot agree with the Court's conclusion that when pupils compelled by law to go to school for secular education are released from school so as to attend the religious classes, churches are unconstitutionally aided. Whatever may be the wisdom of the arrangement as to the use of the school buildings made with the Champaign Council of Religious Education, it is clear to me that past practice shows such cooperation between the schools and a non-ecclesiastical body is not forbidden by the First Amendment. . . . The prohibition of enactments respecting the establishment of religion do not bar every friendly gesture between church and state. It is not an absolute prohibition against every conceivable situation where the two may work together, any more than the other provisions of the First Amendment—free speech, free press—are absolutes. . . . A state is entitled to have great leeway in its legislation when dealing with the important social problems of its population. A definite violation of legislative limits must be established. . . . Devotion to the great principle of religious liberty should not lead us into a rigid interpretation of the constitutional guaranty that conflicts with accepted habits of our people. This is an instance where, for me, the history of past practices is determinative of the meaning of a constitutional clause, not a decorous introduction to the study of its text. The judgment should be affirmed.

ZORACH v. CLAUSON
343 U.S. 306; 72 Sup. Ct. 679; 96 L. Ed. 954 (1952)

[*Zorach and another New York City resident challenged the constitutionality of the City's released-time program, which is described in the Court's opinion. They contended that the program violated the establishment of religion and free exercise of religion clauses of the First Amendment by reason of the Fourteenth Amendment. The highest state court sustained the released-time program. The case was then brought to the Supreme Court on appeal. (Clauson was a member of the New York City Board of Education.)*]

MR. JUSTICE DOUGLAS delivered the opinion of the Court:

New York City has a program which permits its public schools to release students during the school day so that they may leave the school buildings and school grounds and go to religious centers for religious instruction or devotional exercises. A student is released on written request of his parents. Those not released stay in the classrooms. The churches make weekly reports to the schools, sending a list of children who have been released from public school but who have not reported for religious instruction.

This "released-time" program involves neither religious instruction in public-school classrooms nor the expenditure of public funds. All costs, including the application blanks, are paid by the religious organizations. The case is therefore unlike *McCollum* v. *Board of Education*. . . . In that case the classrooms were turned over to religious instructors. We accordingly held that the program violated the First Amendment which (by reason of the Fourteenth Amendment) prohibits the states from establishing religion or prohibiting its free exercise. . . .

[O]ur problem reduces itself to whether New York by this system has either prohibited the "free exercise" of religion or has made a law "respecting an establishment of religion" within the meaning of the First Amendment.

It takes obtuse reasoning to inject any issue of the "free exercise" of religion to the present case. No one is forced to go to the religious classroom and no religious exercise or instruction is brought to the classrooms of the public schools.

A student need not take religious instruction. He is left to his own desires as to the manner or time of his religious devotions, if any.

There is a suggestion that the system involves the use of coercion to get public-school students into religious classrooms. There is no evidence in the record before us that supports that conclusion. The present record indeed tells us that the school authorities are neutral in this regard and do no more than release students whose parents so request. If in fact coercion were used, if it were established that any one or more teachers were using their office to persuade or force students to take the religious instruction, a wholly different case would be presented. Hence we put aside that claim of coercion both as respects the "free exercise" of religion and "an establishment of religion" within the meaning of the First Amendment.

Moreover, apart from that claim of coercion, we do not see how New York by this type of "released-time" program has made a law respecting an establishment of religion within the meaning of the First Amendment. There is much talk of the separation of Church and State in the history of the Bill of Rights and in the decisions clustering around the First Amendment. See *Everson* v. *Board of Education.* . . . There cannot be the slightest doubt that the First Amendment reflects the philosophy that Church and State should be separated. And so far as interference with the "free exercise" of religion and an "establishment" of religion are concerned, the separation must be complete and unequivocal. The First

Amendment within the scope of its coverage permits no exception; the prohibition is absolute. The First Amendment, however, does not say that in every and all respects there shall be a separation of Church and State. Rather, it studiously defines the manner, the specific ways, in which there shall be no concert or union or dependency one on the other. That is the common sense of the matter. Otherwise the state and religion would be aliens to each other—hostile, suspicious, and even unfriendly. Churches could not be required to pay even property taxes. Municipalities would not be permitted to render police or fire protection to religious groups. Policemen who helped parishioners into their places of worship would violate the Constitution. Prayers in our legislative halls; the appeals to the Almighty in the messages of the Chief Executive; the proclamations making Thanksgiving Day a holiday; "so help me God" in our courtroom oaths—these and all other references to the Almighty that run through our laws, our public rituals, our ceremonies would be flouting the First Amendment. A fastidious atheist or agnostic could even object to the supplication with which the Court opens each session: "God save the United States and this Honorable Court."

We would have to press the concept of separation of Church and State to these extremes to condemn the present law on constitutional grounds. . . .

We are a religious people whose institutions presuppose a Supreme Being. We guarantee the freedom to worship as one chooses. We make room for as wide a variety of beliefs and creeds as the spiritual needs of man deem necessary. We sponsor an attitude on the part of government that shows no partiality to any one group and that lets each flourish according to the zeal of its adherents and the appeal of its dogma. When the state encourages

religious instruction or cooperates with religious authorities by adjusting the schedule of public events to sectarian needs, it follows the best of our traditions. For it then respects the religious nature of our people and accommodates the public service to their spiritual needs. To hold that it may not would be to find in the Constitution a requirement that the government show a callous indifference to religious groups. That would be preferring those who believe in no religion over those who do believe. Government may not finance religious groups nor undertake religious instruction nor blend secular and sectarian education nor use secular institutions to force one or some religion on any person. But we find no constitutional requirement which makes it necessary for government to be hostile to religion and to throw its weight against efforts to widen the effective scope of religious influence. The government must be neutral when it comes to competition between sects. It may not thrust any sect on any person. It may not make a religious observance compulsory. It may not coerce anyone to attend church, to observe a religious holiday, or to take religious instruction. But it can close its doors or suspend its operations as to those who want to repair to their religious sanctuary for worship or instruction. No more than that is undertaken here. . . .

In the *McCollum* case the classrooms were used for religious instruction and the force of the public school was used to promote that instruction. Here, as we have said, the public schools do no more than accommodate their schedules to a program of outside religious instruction. We follow the *McCollum* case. But we cannot expand it to cover the present released-time program unless separation of Church and State means that public institutions can make no adjustments of their schedules to accommodate the religious needs of the people. We cannot read into the Bill of Rights such a philosophy of hostility to religion.

Affirmed.

MR. JUSTICE BLACK, dissenting:

. . . I see no significant difference between the invalid Illinois system and that of New York here sustained. Except for the use of the school buildings in Illinois, there is no difference between the systems which I consider even worthy of mention. In the New York program, as in that of Illinois, the school authorities release some of the children on the condition that they attend the religious classes, get reports on whether they attend, and hold the other children in the school building until the religious hour is over. As we attempted to make categorically clear, the *McCollum* decision would have been the same if the religious classes had not been held in the school buildings. . . .

I am aware that our *McCollum* decision on separation of Church and State has been subjected to a most searching examination throughout the country. Probably few opinions from this Court in recent years have attracted more attention or stirred wider debate. Our insistence on "a wall between Church and State which must be kept high and impregnable" has seemed to some a correct exposition of the philosophy and a true interpretation of the language of the First Amendment to which we should strictly adhere. With equal conviction and sincerity, others have thought the *McCollum* decision fundamentally wrong and have pledged continuous warfare against it. . . .

Here the sole question is whether New York can use its compulsory education laws to help religious sects get attendants presumably too unenthusiastic to go unless moved to do so by the pressure of this state machinery.

That this is the plan, purpose, design, and consequence of the New York program cannot be denied. The state thus makes religious sects beneficiaries of its power to compel children to attend secular schools. Any use of such coercive power by the state to help or hinder some religious sects or to prefer all religious sects over nonbelievers or vice versa is just what I think the First Amendment forbids. In considering whether a state has entered this forbidden field the question is not whether it has entered too far but whether it has entered at all. New York is manipulating its compulsory education laws to help religious sects get pupils. This is not separation but combination of Church and State.

The Court's validation of the New York system rests in part on its statement that Americans are "a religious people whose institutions presuppose a Supreme Being." This was at least true when the First Amendment was adopted; and it was just as true when eight Justices of this Court invalidated the released-time system in *McCollum* on the premise that a state can no more "aid all religions" than it can aid one. It was precisely because eighteenth-century Americans were a religious people divided into many fighting sects that we were given the constitutional mandate to keep Church and State completely separate. . . .

Under our system of religious freedom, people have gone to their religious sanctuaries not because they feared the law but because they loved their God. The choice of all has been as free as the choice of those who answered the call to worship moved only by the music of the old Sunday-morning church bells. The spiritual mind of man has thus been free to believe, disbelieve, or doubt, without repression, great or small, by the heavy hand of government. Statutes authorizing such repression have been stricken. Before today, our judicial opinions have refrained from drawing invidious distinctions between those who believe in no religion and those who do believe. The First Amendment has lost much if the religious follower and the atheist are no longer to be judicially regarded as entitled to equal justice under the law.

State help to religion injects political and party prejudices into a holy field. It too often substitutes force for prayer, hate for love, and persecution for persuasion. Government should not be allowed, under cover of the soft euphemism of "cooperation," to steal into the sacred area of religious choice.

MR. JUSTICE FRANKFURTER, dissenting:

. . . The pith of the case is that formalized religious instruction is substituted for other school activity which those who do not participate in the released-time program are compelled to attend. The school system is very much in operation during this kind of released time. If its doors are closed, they are closed upon those students who do not attend the religious instruction, in order to keep them within the school. That is the very thing which raises the constitutional issue. It is not met by disregarding it. Failure to discuss this issue does not take it out of the case.

. . . The deeply divisive controversy aroused by the attempts to secure public-school pupils for sectarian instruction would promptly end if the advocates of such instruction were content to have the school "close its doors or suspend its operations"—that is, dismiss classes in their entirety, without discrimination—instead of seeking to use the public schools as the instrument for securing attendance at denominational classes. The unwillingness of the promoters of this movement to dispense with such use of the public schools betrays a surprising want of

confidence in the inherent power of the various faiths to draw children to outside sectarian classes—an attitude that hardly reflects the faith of the greatest religious spirits.

MR. JUSTICE JACKSON, dissenting:

This released time program is founded upon a use of the State's power of coercion, which, for me, determines its unconstitutionality. Stripped to its essentials, the plan has two stages: first, that the State compel each student to yield a large part of his time for public secular education; and, second, that some of it be "released" to him on condition that he devote it to sectarian religious purposes.

No one suggests that the Constitution would permit the State directly to require this "released" time to be spent "under the control of a duly constituted religious body." This program accomplishes that forbidden result by indirection. If public education were taking so much of the pupil's time as to injure the public or the students' welfare by encroaching upon their religious opportunity, simply shortening everyone's school day would facilitate voluntary and optional attendance at Church classes. But that suggestion is rejected upon the ground that if they are made free many students will not go to the Church. Hence, they must be deprived of freedom for this period, with Church attendance put to them as one of the two permissible ways of using it.

The greater effectiveness of this system over voluntary attendance after school hours is due to the truant officer who, if the youngster fails to go to the Church school, dogs him back to the public schoolroom. Here schooling is more or less suspended during the "released time" so the nonreligious attendants will not forge ahead of the churchgoing absentees. But it serves as a temporary jail for a pupil who will not go to Church. It takes more subtlety of mind than I possess to deny that this is governmental constraint in support of religion. It is as unconstitutional, in my view, when exerted by indirection as when exercised forthrightly.

As one whose children, as a matter of free choice, have been sent to privately supported Church schools, I may challenge the Court's suggestion that opposition to this plan can only be anti-religious, atheistic, or agnostic. My evangelistic brethren confuse an objection to compulsion with an objection to religion. It is possible to hold a faith with enough confidence to believe that what should be rendered to God does not need to be decided and collected by Caesar.

The day that this country ceases to be free for irreligion it will cease to be free for religion—except for the sect that can win political power. The same epithetical jurisprudence used by the Court today to beat down those who oppose pressuring children into some religion can devise as good epithets tomorrow against those who object to pressuring them into a favored religion. And, after all, if we concede to the State power and wisdom to single out "duly constituted religious" bodies as exclusive alternatives for compulsory secular instruction, it would be logical to also uphold the power and wisdom to choose the true faith among those "duly constituted." We start down a rough road when we begin to mix compulsory public education with compulsory godliness.

A number of Justices just short of a majority of the majority that promulgates today's passionate dialectics joined in answering them in *Illinois* ex rel. *McCollum* v. *Board of Education, . . .* The distinction attempted between that case and this is trivial, almost to the point of cynicism, magnifying its nonessential details and disparaging compulsion which was the underlying reason for invalidity. A reading of the Court's opinion in that case along with its opinion in this case will show such difference of overtones and undertones as to make clear that the *McCollum* case has passed like a storm in a teacup. The wall which the Court was professing to erect between Church and State has become even more warped and twisted than I expected. Today's judgment will be more interesting to students of psychology and of the judicial processes than to students of constitutional law.

ENGEL et al. *v.* VITALE
370 U.S. 421; 82 Sup. Ct. 1261; 8 L. Ed. 2d 601 (1962)

[*In November 1951, the New York State Board of Regents, which controls and supervises the state's public school system, proposed a prayer for daily recitation in the public schools. The brief prayer was regarded by the Board of Regents as nonsectarian and read as follows: "Almighty God, we acknowledge our dependence upon Thee, and we beg Thy blessings upon us, our parents, our teachers and our country." The Regents' proposal was by no means mandatory; it was simply a recommendation that local school boards were free to adopt or not as they saw fit, and only about 10 per cent of the local boards did adopt the prayer.*

In 1958, the school board of New Hyde Park, a Long Island suburb of New York City, adopted the Regents' prayer and directed the school district principal to cause the prayer "to be said aloud by each class in the presence of a teacher at the beginning of each school day." Steven Engel, who had two children enrolled in the Hyde Park schools, and a group of other parents in the community brought suit in a state court with the help of the New York chapter of the American Civil Liberties Union. The parents argued that the use of the official prayer "was contrary to the beliefs, religions and religious practices of both themselves and their children" and hence constituted a violation of the First and Fourteenth Amendments. Specifically, Engel and the other parents asked the trial court for a mandamus to compel the school board to discontinue the use of the prayer, but it was denied. The trial court remanded the case to the school board so that measures could be taken, if necessary, to eliminate any possible coercion and "to protect those who objected to reciting the prayer." The trial court decision was affirmed by the Appellate Division. Upon appeal the New York Court of Appeals (New York's highest court) also affirmed by a vote of 5 to 2, holding that the noncompulsory daily recitation of the prayer did not violate the constitutional guaranties concerning freedom of religion. The Supreme Court then granted certiorari.

The respondents are the members of the New Hyde Park school board. William J. Vitale, Jr., was the presiding officer of the board.]

MR. JUSTICE BLACK delivered the opinion of the Court:

. . . We think that by using its public school system to encourage recitation of the Reagents' prayer, the State of New York has adopted a practice wholly inconsistent with the Establishment Clause. There can, of course, be no doubt that New York's program of daily classroom invocation of God's blessings as prescribed in the Regents' prayer is a religious activity. It is a solemn avowal of divine faith and supplication for the blessings of the Almighty. The nature of such a prayer has always been religious, none of the respondents has denied this and the trial court expressly so found:

"The religious nature of prayer was recognized by Jefferson and has been concurred in by theological writers, the United States Supreme Court and State courts and administrative officials, including New York's Commissioner of Education. A committee of the New York Legislature has agreed.

"The Board of Reagents as *amicus curiae,* the respondents and intervenors all concede the religious nature of prayer, but seek to distinguish this prayer because it is based on our spiritual heritage. . . ."

The petitioners contend among other things that the state laws requiring or permitting use of the Regents' prayer must be struck down as a violation of the Establishment Clause because that prayer was composed by governmental officials as a part of a governmental program to further religious beliefs. For this reason, petitioners argue, the State's use of the Regents' prayer in its public school system breaches the constitutional wall of separation between Church and State. We agree with that contention since we think that the constitutional prohibition against laws respecting an establishment of religion must at least mean that in this country it is no part of the business of government to compose official prayers for any group of the American people to recite as a part of a religious program carried on by government.

It is a matter of history that this very practice of establishing governmentally composed prayers for religious services was one of the reasons which caused many of our early colonists to leave England and seek religious freedom in America. The Book of Common Prayer, which was created under governmental direction and which was approved by Acts of Parliament in 1548 and 1549, set out in minute detail the accepted form and content of prayer and other religious ceremonies to be used in the established, tax-supported Church of England. The controversies over the Book and what should be its content repeatedly threatened to disrupt the peace of that country as the accepted forms of prayer in the established church changed with the views of the particular ruler that happened to be in control at the time. Powerful groups representing some of the varying religious views of the people struggled among themselves to impress their particular views upon the Government and obtain amendments of the Book more suitable to their respective notions of how religious services should be conducted in order that the official religious establishment would advance their particular religious beliefs. Other groups, lacking the necessary political power to influence the Government on the matter, decided to leave England and its established church and seek freedom in America from England's governmentally ordained and supported religion.

It is an unfortunate fact of history that when some of the very groups which had most strenuously opposed the established Church of England found themselves sufficiently in control of colonial governments in this country to write their own prayers into law, they passed laws making their own religion the official religion of their respective colonies. Indeed, as late as the time of the Revolutionary War, there were established churches in at least eight of the thirteen former colonies and established religions in at least four of the other five. But the successful Revolution against English po-

litical domination was shortly followed by intense opposition to the practice of establishing religion by law. This opposition crystallized rapidly into an effective political force in Virginia where the minority religious groups such as Presbyterians, Lutherans, Quakers and Baptists had gained such strength that the adherents to the established Episcopal Church were actually a minority themselves. In 1785–1786, those opposed to the established Church, led by James Madison and Thomas Jefferson, who, though themselves not members of any of these dissenting religious groups, opposed all religious establishments by law on grounds of principle, obtained the enactment of the famous "Virginia Bill for Religious Liberty" by which all religious groups were placed on an equal footing so far as the State was concerned. Similar though less far-reaching legislation was being considered and passed in other States.

By the time of the adoption of the Constitution, our history shows that there was a widespread awareness among many Americans of the dangers of a union of Church and State. These people knew, some of them from bitter personal experience, that one of the greatest dangers to the freedom of the individual to worship in his own way lay in the Government's placing its official stamp of approval upon one particular kind of prayer or one particular form of religious services. They knew the anguish, hardship and bitter strife that could come when zealous religious groups struggled with one another to obtain the Government's stamp of approval from each King, Queen, or Protector that came to temporary power. The Constitution was intended to avert a part of this danger by leaving the government of this country in the hands of the people rather than in the hands of any monarch. But this safeguard was not enough. Our Founders were no more willing to let the content of their prayers and their privilege of praying whenever they pleased be influenced by this ballot box than they were to let these vital matters of personal conscience depend upon the succession of monarchs. The First Amendment was added to the Constitution to stand as a guaranty that neither the power nor the prestige of the Federal Government would be used to control, support or influence the kinds of prayer the American people can say —that the people's religions must not be subjected to the pressures of government for change each time a new political administration is elected to office. Under that Amendment's prohibition against governmental establishment of religion, as reinforced by the provisions of the Fourteenth Amendment, government in this country, be it state or federal, is without power to prescribe by law any particular form of prayer which is to be used as an official prayer in carrying on any program of governmentally sponsored religious activity.

There can be no doubt that New York's state prayer program officially establishes the religious beliefs embodied in the Regents' prayer. The respondents' argument to the contrary, which is largely based upon the contention that the Regents' prayer is "non-denominational" and the fact that the program, as modified and approved by state courts, does not require all pupils to recite the prayer but permits those who wish to do so to remain silent or be excused from the room, ignores the essential nature of the program's constitutional defects. Neither the fact that the prayer may be denominationally neutral, nor the fact that its observance on the part of the students is voluntary can serve to free it from the limitations of the Establishment Clause, as it might

from the Free Exercise Clause, of the First Amendment, both of which are operative against the States by virtue of the Fourteenth Amendment. Although these two clauses may in certain instances overlap, they forbid two quite different kinds of governmental encroachment upon religious freedom. The Establishment Clause, unlike the Free Exercise Clause, does not depend upon any showing of direct governmental compulsion and is violated by the enactmen of laws which establish an official religion whether those laws operate directly to coerce non-observing individuals or not. This is not to say, of course, that laws officially prescribing a particular form of religious worship do not involve coercion of such individuals. When the power, prestige and financial support of government is placed behind a particular religious belief, the indirect coercive pressure upon religious minorities to conform to the prevailing officially approved religion is plain. But the purposes underlying the Establishment Clause go much further than that. Its first and most immediate purpose rested on the belief that a union of government and religion tends to destroy government and to degrade religion. The history of governmentally established religion, both in England and in this country, showed that whenever government had allied itself with one particular form of religion, the inevitable result had been that it had incurred the hatred, disrespect and even contempt of those who held contrary beliefs. That same history showed that many people had lost their respect for any religion that had relied upon the support of government to spread its faith. The Establishment Clause thus stands as an expression of principle on the part of the Founders of our Constitution that religion is too personal, too sacred, too holy, to permit its "unhallowed perversion" by a civil magistrate. Another purpose of the Establishment Clause rested upon an awareness of the historical fact that governmentally established religions and religious persecutions go hand in hand. The Founders knew that only a few years after the Book of Common Prayer became the only accepted form of religious services in the established Church of England, an Act of Uniformity was passed to compel all Englishmen to attend those services and to make it a criminal offense to conduct or attend religious gatherings of any other kind—a law which was consistently flouted by dissenting religious groups in England and which contributed to widespread persecutions of people like John Bunyan who persisted in holding "unlawful [religious] meetings . . . to the great disturbance and distraction of the good subjects of this kingdom. . . ." And they knew that similar persecutions had received the sanction of law in several of the colonies in this country soon after the establishment of official religions in those colonies. It was in large part to get completely away from this sort of systematic religious persecution that the Founders brought into being our Nation, our Constitution, and our Bill of Rights with its prohibition against any governmental establishment of religion. The New York laws officially prescribing the Regents' prayer are inconsistent with both the purposes of the Establishment Clause and with the Establishment Clause itself.

It has been argued that to apply the Constitution in such a way as to prohibit state laws respecting an establishment of religious services in public schools is to indicate a hostility toward religion or toward prayer. Nothing, of course, could be more wrong. The history of man is inseparable from the history of religion. And perhaps it is not too much to say that since the beginning of that history many people have devoutly believed that "More things are wrought by prayer than this world dreams of." It was doubtless largely due to men who believed this that there grew up a sentiment that caused men to leave the cross-currents of officially established state religions and religious persecution in Europe and come to this country filled with the hope that they could find a place in which they could pray when they pleased to the God of their faith in the language they chose. And there were men of this same faith in the power of prayer who led the fight for adoption of our Constitution and also for our Bill of Rights with the very guaranties of religious freedom that forbid the sort of governmental activity which New York has attempted here. These men knew that the First Amendment, which tried to put an end to governmental control of religion and of prayer, was not written to destroy either. They knew rather that it was written to quiet well-justified fears which nearly all of them felt arising out of an awareness that governments of the past had shackled men's tongues to make them speak only the religious thoughts that government wanted them to speak and to pray only to the God that government wanted them to pray to. It is neither sacrilegious nor antireligious to say that each separate government in this country should stay out of the business of writing or sanctioning official prayers and leave that purely religious function to the people themselves and to those the people choose to look to for religious guidance.

It is true that New York's establishment of its Regents' prayer as an officially approved religious doctrine of that State does not amount to a total establishment of one particular religious sect to the exclusion of all others—that, indeed, the governmental endorsement of that prayer seems relatively insignificant when compared to the governmental encroachments upon religion which were commonplace 200 years ago. To those who may subscribe to the view that because the Regents' official prayer is so brief and general there can be no danger to religious freedom in its governmental establishment, however, it may be appropriate to say in the words of James Madison, the author of the First Amendment:

"[I]t is proper to take alarm at the first experiment on our liberties. . . . Who does not see that the same authority which can establish Christianity, in exclusion of all other Religions, may establish with the same ease any particular sect of Christians, in exclusion of all other Sects? That the same authority which can force a citizen to contribute three pence only of his property for the support of any one establishment, may force him to conform to any other establishment in all cases whatsoever?"

The judgment of the Court of Appeals of New York is reversed and the cause remanded for further proceedings not inconsistent with this opinion.

Reversed and remanded.

MR. JUSTICE FRANKFURTER took part in the decision of this case.

MR. JUSTICE WHITE took no part in the consideration or decision of this case.

MR. JUSTICE DOUGLAS, concurring:

. . . The point for decision is whether the Government can constitutionally finance a religious exercise. Our system at the federal and state levels is presently honeycombed with such financing. Nevertheless, I think it is an unconstitutional undertaking whatever form it takes. . . .

What New York does on the opening of its public schools is what we do when we open court. Our Marshall has from the beginning announced the convening of the Court and then added "God save the United States and this honorable court." That utterance is supplication, a prayer in which we, the judges, are free to join, but which we need not recite any more than the students need recite the New York prayer.

What New York does on the opening of its public schools is what each House of Congress does at the opening of each day's business. . . .

In New York the teacher who leads in prayer is on the public payroll; and the time she takes seems minuscule as compared with the salaries appropriated by state legislatures and Congress for chaplains to conduct prayers in the legislative halls. Only a bare fraction of the teacher's time is given to reciting this short twenty-two-word prayer, about the same amount of time that our Marshal spends announcing the opening of our sessions and offering a prayer for this Court. Yet for me the principle is the same, no matter how briefly the prayer is said, for in each of the instances given the person praying is a public official on the public payroll, performing a religious exercise in a governmental institution. It is said that the element of coercion is inherent in the giving of this prayer. If that is true here, it is also true of the prayer with which this Court is convened, and with those that open the Congress. Few adults, let alone children, would leave our courtroom or the Senate or the House while those prayers are being given. Every such audience is in a sense a "captive" audience.

At the same time I cannot say that to authorize this prayer is to establish a religion in the strictly historic meaning of those words. A religion is not established in the usual sense merely by letting those who choose to do so say the prayer that the public school teacher leads. Yet once government finances a religious exercise it inserts a divisive influence into our communities. The New York court said that the prayer given does not conform to all of the tenets of the Jewish, Unitarian, and Ethical Culture groups. One of petitioners is an agnostic. . . .

The First Amendment leaves the Government in a position not of hostility to religion but of neutrality. The philosophy is that the atheist or agnostic—the nonbeliever—is entitled to go his own way. The philosophy is that if government interferes in matters spiritual, it will be a divisive force. The First Amendment teaches that a government neutral in the field of religion better serves all religious interests.

My problem today would be uncomplicated but for *Everson* v. *Board of Education,* . . . which allowed taxpayers' money to be used to pay "the bus fares of parochial school pupils as a part of a general program under which" the fares of pupils attending public and other schools were also paid. The *Everson* case seems in retrospect to be out of line with the First Amendment. Its result is appealing, as it allows aid to be given to needy children. Yet by the same token, public funds could be used to satisfy other needs of children in parochial schools—lunches, books, and tuition being obvious examples.

MR. JUSTICE STEWART, dissenting:

. . . The Court does not hold, nor could it, that New York has interfered with the free exercise of anybody's religion. For the state courts have made clear that those who object to reciting the prayer must be entirely free of any compulsion to do so, including any "embarrassments and pressures." . . . But the Court says that in permitting school children to say this simple prayer, the New York authorities have established "an official religion."

With all respect, I think the Court has misapplied a great constitutional principle. I cannot see how an "official religion" is established by letting those who want to say a prayer say it. On the contrary, I think that to deny the wish of these school children to join in reciting this prayer is to deny them the opportunity of sharing in the spiritual heritage of our Nation.

The Court's historical review of the quarrels over the Book of Common Prayer in England throws no light for me on the issue before us in this case. England had then and has now an established church. Equally unenlightening, I think, is the history of the early establishment and later rejection of an official church in our own States. For we deal here not with the establishment of a state church, which would, of course, be constitutionally impermissible, but with whether school children who want to begin their day by joining in prayer must be prohibited from doing so. Moreover, I think that the Court's task, in this as in all areas of constitutional adjudication, is not responsibly aided by the uncritical invocation of metaphors like the "wall of separation," a phrase nowhere to be found in the Constitution. What is relevant to the issue here is not the history of an established church in sixteenth-century England or in eighteenth-century America, but the history of the religious traditions of our people, reflected in countless practices of the institutions and officials of our government.

At the opening of each day's Session of this Court we stand, while one of our officials invokes the protection of God. Since the days of John Marshall our Crier has said, "God save the United States and this Honorable

Court." Both the Senate and the House of Representatives open their daily Sessions with prayer. Each of our Presidents, from George Washington to John F. Kennedy, has upon assuming his Office asked the protection and help of God.

The Court today says that the state and federal governments are without constitutional power to prescribe any particular form of words to be recited by any group of the American people on any subject touching religion. The third stanza of "The Star-Spangled Banner," made our National Anthem by Act of Congress in 1931, contains these verses:

"Blest with victory and peace,
　　may the heav'n rescued land
Praise the Pow'r that hath made
　　and preserved us a nation!
Then conquer we must,
　　when our cause it is just,
And this be our motto,
　　'In God is our Trust.' "

In 1954, Congress added a phrase to the Pledge of Allegiance to the Flag so that it now contains the words "one Nation under God, indivisible, with liberty and justice for all." In 1952, Congress enacted legislation calling upon the President each year to proclaim a National Day of Prayer. Since 1865, the words "In God We Trust" have been impressed on our coins.

Countless similar examples could be listed, but there is no need to belabor the obvious. . . .

I do not believe that this Court, or the Congress, or the President has by the actions and practices I have mentioned established an "official religion" in violation of the Constitution. And I do not believe the State of New York has done so in this case. What each has done has been to recognize and to follow the deeply entrenched and highly cherished spiritual traditions of our Nation—traditions which come down to us from those who almost two-hundred years ago avowed their "firm reliance on the Protection of Divine Providence" when they proclaimed the freedom and independence of this brave new world.

I dissent.

ABINGTON SCHOOL DISTRICT v. SCHEMPP
MURRAY v. CURLETT
374 U.S. 203, 83 Sup. Ct. 1560, 10 L. Ed. 2d 844 (1963)

[*These companion cases deal with Bible reading and the recitation of the Lord's Prayer in the public schools. The* Schempp *case originated in Pennsylvania, where a state law required that "at least ten verses from the Holy Bible shall be read, without comments, at the opening of each public school on each day." The statute further provided that any child could be excused from attending the Bible reading with the written request of his parent or guardian. The Schempp family—husband, wife, and two children, who attended one of the Abington district schools—was Unitarian and brought suit to enjoin the practice of daily Bible readings, contending that it violated their rights under the establishment clause of the First Amendment as applied to the states by the due process clause of the Fourteenth Amendment. A three-judge district court in Pennsylvania found the statute unconstitutional. The case then went to the Supreme Court on appeal.*

The Murray *case originated in Baltimore, Md., where the Board of School*

Commissioners, relying on an appropriate state statute, adopted a rule providing for opening exercises in the Baltimore public schools consisting primarily of the "reading, without comment, of a chapter in the Holy Bible and/or the use of the Lord's Prayer." Mrs. Murray and her son, a student in one of the city schools, were both professed atheists who found the Bible "nauseating, historically inaccurate, replete with the ravings of madmen." They felt that the public schools should "prepare children to face the problems on earth, not to prepare for heaven —which is a delusional dream of the unsophisticated minds of the ill-educated clergy." The Murrays filed for a mandamus to compel Curlett, the President of the Board of School Commissioners, to rescind the rule requiring Bible reading or the recitation of the Lord's Prayer. The trial court ruled against the Murrays. The Maryland Court of Appeals, the state's highest court, affirmed by a close 4 to 3 vote. The case then went to the Supreme Court on certiorari.]

MR. JUSTICE CLARK delivered the opinion of the Court:

Once again we are called upon to consider the scope of the provision of the First Amendment to the United States Constitution which declares that "Congress shall make no law respecting an establishment of religion or prohibiting the free exercise thereof. . . ." These companion cases present the issues in the context of state action requiring that schools begin each day with readings from the Bible. While raising the basic questions under slightly different factual situations, the cases permit of joint treatment. In light of the history of the First Amendment and of our cases interpreting and applying its requirements, we hold that the practices at issue and the laws requiring them are unconstitutional under the Establishment Clause, as applied to the states through the Fourteenth Amendment. . . .

It is true that religion has been closely identified with our history and government. As we said in *Engel* v. *Vitale* . . . "The history of man is inseparable from the history of religion. And . . . since the beginning of that history many people have devoutly believed that 'More things are wrought by prayer than this world dreams of.'" In *Zorach* v. *Clauson* . . . we gave specific recognition to the proposition

that "we are a religious people whose institutions presuppose a Supreme Being." The fact that the Founding Fathers believed devotedly that there was a God and that the unalienable rights of man were rooted in Him is clearly evidenced in their writings, from the Mayflower Compact to the Constitution itself. This background is evidenced today in our public life through the continuance in our oaths of office from the Presidency to the Alderman of the final supplication, "So help me God." Likewise each House of the Congress provides through its Chaplain an opening prayer, and the sessions of this Court are declared open by the crier in a short ceremony, the final phrase of which invokes the grace of God. Again, there are such manifestations in our military forces, where those of our citizens who are under the restrictions of military service wish to engage in voluntary worship. Indeed, only last year an official survey of the country indicated that 64 per cent of our people have church membership . . . while less than three per cent profess no religion whatever. . . . It can be truly said, therefore, that today, as in the beginning, our national life reflects a religious people. . . .

This is not to say, however, that religion has been so identified with our history and government that religious freedom is not likewise as strongly imbedded in our public and private life. Nothing but the most telling of personal experiences in religious persecution suffered by our forebears . . . could have planted our belief in liberty of religious opinion any more deeply in our heritage. It is true that this liberty frequently was not realized by the colonists, but this is readily accountable to their close ties to the Mother Country. However, the views of Madison and Jefferson, preceded by Roger Williams, came to be incorporated not only in the Federal Constitution but likewise in those of most of our States. This freedom to worship was indispensable in a country whose people came from the four quarters of the earth and brought with them a diversity of religious bodies, each with memberships exceeding 50,000, existing among our people, as well as innumerable small groups. . . .

[T]his Court has decisively settled that the First Amendment's mandate that "Congress shall make no law respecting an establishment of religion, or prohibiting the free exercise thereof" has been made wholly applicable to the states by the Fourteenth Amendment. . . . In a series of cases since *Cantwell* the Court has repeatedly reaffirmed that doctrine, and we do so now. . . .

[T]his Court has rejected unequivocally the contention that the establishment clause forbids only governmental preference of one religion over another. Almost twenty years ago in *Everson* . . . the Court said that "neither a state nor the Federal government can set up a church. Neither can pass laws which aid one religion, or prefer one religion over another." . . . Further, Mr. Justice Rutledge, joined by Justices Frankfurter, Jackson and Burton, declared:

"The [First] Amendment's purpose was not to strike merely at the official establishment of a single sect, creed or religion, outlawing only a formal relation such as had prevailed in England and some of the Colonies. Necessarily it was to uproot all such reationships. But the object was broader than separating church and state in this narrow sense. It was to create a complete and permanent separation of the spheres of religious activity and civil authority by comprehensively forbidding every form of public aid or support for religion. . . ."

The same conclusion has been firmly maintained ever since that time . . . and we reaffirm it now.

While none of the parties to either of these cases has questioned these basic conclusions of the Court, both of which have been long established, recognized and consistently reaffirmed, others continue to question their history, logic and efficacy. Such contentions, in the light of the consistent interpretation in cases of this Court, seem entirely untenable and of value only as academic exercises. . . .

[I]n *Engel* v. *Vitale,* only last year, these principles were so universally recognized that the Court without the citation of a single case and over the sole dissent of Mr. Justice Stewart reaffirmed them. The Court found the twenty-two-word prayer used in "New York's program of daily classroom invocation of God's blessings as prescribed in the Regents' prayer . . . [to be] a religious activity." . . . It held that "it is no part of the business of government to compose official prayers for any group of the American people to recite as a part of a religious program carried on by the government. . . . [T]he Court found that the "first and most immediate purpose [of the Establishment Clause] rested on a belief that a union of government and religion tends to destroy government and to degrade religion." . . . When government, the Court said, allies itself with one particular form of religion, the inevitable result is that it incurs "the hatred, disrespect and even contempt of those who held contrary beliefs."

. . . The wholesome "neutrality" of which this Court's cases speak thus stems from a recognition of the teachings of history that powerful sects or groups might bring about a fusion of governmental and religious functions or a concert or dependency of one upon the other to the end that official support of the State or Federal Government would be placed behind the tenets of one or of all orthodoxies. This the Establishment Clause prohibits. And a further reason for neutrality is found in the Free Exercise Clause, which recognizes the value of religious training, teaching and observance and, more particularly, the right of every person to freely choose his own course with reference thereto, free of any compulsion from the state. This the Free Exercise Clause guarantees. Thus . . . the two clauses may overlap. . . . [T]he Establishment Clause has been directly considered by this Court eight times in the past score of years and, with only one Justice dissenting on the point, it has consistently held that the clause withdrew all legislative power respecting religious belief or the expression thereof. The test may be stated as follows: what are the purpose and the primary effect of the enactment? If either is the advancement or inhibition of religion then the enactment exceeds the scope of legislative power as circumscribed by the Constitution. That is to say that to withstand the strictures of the Establishment Clause there must be a secular legislative purpose and a primary effect that neither advances nor inhibits religion. . . . The Free

Exercise Clause, likewise considered many times here, withdraws from legislative power, state and federal, the exertion of any restraint on the free exercise of religion. Its purpose is to secure religious liberty in the individual by prohibiting any invasions thereof by civil authority. Hence it is necessary in a free exercise case for one to show the coercive effect of the enactment as it operates against him in the practice of his religion. The distinction between the two clauses is apparent—a violation of the Free Exercise Clause is predicated on coercion while the Establishment Clause violation need not be so intended.

Applying the Establishment Clause principles to the cases at bar we find that the States are requiring the selection and reading at the opening of the school day of verses from the Holy Bible and the recitation of the Lord's Prayer by the students in unison. These exercises are prescribed as part of the curricular activities of students who are required by law to attend school. They are held in the school buildings under the supervision and with the participation of teachers employed in those schools. None of these factors, other than compulsory school attendance, was present in the program upheld in *Zorach* v. *Clauson*.

The conclusion follows that in both cases the laws require religious exercises and such exercises are being conducted in direct violation of the rights of the appellees and petitioners. Nor are these required exercises mitigated by the fact that individual students may absent themselves upon parental request, for that fact furnishes no defense to a claim of unconstitutionality under the Establishment Clause. . . . Further, it is no defense to urge that the religious practices here may be relatively minor encroachments on the First Amendment. The breach of neutrality that is today a trickling stream may all too soon become a raging torrent and, in the words of Madison, "it is proper to take alarm at the first experiment on our liberties."

. . . It is insisted that unless these religious exercises are permitted a "religion of secularism" is established in the schools. We agree of course that the State may not establish a "religion of secularism" in the sense of affirmatively opposing or showing hostility to religion, thus "preferring those who believe in no religion over those who do believe." . . . We do not agree, however, that this decision in any sense has that effect. In addition, it might well be said that one's education is not complete without a study of comparative religion or the history of religion and its relationship to the advancement of civilization. It certainly may be said that the Bible is worthy of study for its literary and historic qualities. Nothing we have said here indicates that such study of the Bible or of religion, when presented objectively as part of a secular program of education, may not be effected consistent with the First Amendment. But the exercises here do not fall into those categories. They are religious exercises, required by the States in violation of the command of the First Amendment that the Government maintain strict neutrality, neither aiding nor opposing religion.

Finally, we cannot accept that the concept of neutrality, which does not permit a State to require a religious exercise even with the consent of the majority of those affected, collides with the majority's right to free exercise of religion. While the Free Exercise Clause clearly prohibits the use of State action to deny the rights of free exercise to anyone, it has never meant that a majority could use the machinery of the State to practice its beliefs. Such a contention was effectively answered by Mr. Justice Jackson for the Court in *West Virginia Board of Education* v. *Barnette* . . . :

"The very purpose of a Bill of Rights was to withdraw certain subjects from the vicissitudes of political controversy, to place them beyond the reach of majorities and officials and to establish them as legal principles to be applied by the courts. One's right to . . . freedom of worship . . . and other fundamental rights may not be submitted to vote; they depend on the outcome of no elections."

The place of religion in our society is an exalted one, achieved through a long tradition of reliance on the home, the church and the inviolable citadel of the individual heart and mind. We have come to recognize through bitter experience that it is not within the power of government to invade that citadel, whether its purpose or effect be to aid or oppose, to advance or retard. In the relationship between man and religion, the State is firmly committed to a position of neutrality. Though the application of that rule requires interpretation of a delicate sort, the rule itself is clearly and concisely stated in the words of the First Amendment. Applying that rule to the facts of these cases, we affirm the judgment in [the *Schempp* case]. In [*Murray* v. *Curlett*] the judgment is reversed and the cause remanded to the Maryland Court of Appeals for further proceedings consistent with this opinion.

It is so ordered.

MR. JUSTICE DOUGLAS, concurring:

In these cases we have no coercive religious exercise aimed at making the students conform. The prayers announced are not compulsory, though some may think they have that indirect effect because the nonconformist student may be induced to participate for fear of being called an "odd-ball." But that coercion, if it be present, has not been shown; so the vices of the present regimes are different.

The regimes violate the Establishment Clause in two different ways. In each case the State is conducting a religious exercise; and, as the Court holds, that cannot be done without violating the "neutrality" required of the State by the balance of power between individual, church and state that has been struck by the First Amendment. But the Establishment Clause is not limited to precluding the State itself from conducting religious exercises. It also forbids the State to employ its facilities or funds in a way that gives any church, or all churches, greater strength in our society than it would have by relying on its members alone. Thus, the present regimes must fall under that clause for the additional reason that public funds, though small in amount, are being used to promote a religious exercise. Through the mechanism of the State, all of the people are being required to finance a religious exercise that only some of the people want and that violates the sensibilities of others.

The most effective way to establish any institution is to finance it; and this truth is reflected in the appeals by church groups for public funds to finance their religious schools. Financing a church either in its strictly religious activities or in its other activities is equally unconstitutional, as I understand the Establishment Clause. Budgets for one activity may be technically separable from budgets for others. But the institution is an inseparable whole, a living organism, which is strengthened in proselytizing when it is strengthened in any department by contributions from other than its own members.

Such contributions may not be made by the State even in a minor degree

without violating the Establishment Clause. It is not the amount of public funds expended; as this case illustrates, it is the use to which public funds are put that is controlling. For the First Amendment does not say that some forms of establishment are allowed; it says that "no law respecting an establishment of religion" shall be made. What may not be done directly may be done indirectly lest the Establishment Clause become a mockery.

MR. JUSTICE BRENNAN, concurring:

. . . The Court's historic duty to expound the meaning of the Constitution has encountered few issues more intricate or more demanding than that of the relationship between religion and the public schools. . . .

When John Locke ventured in 1689, "I esteem it above all things necessary to distinguish exactly the business of civil government from that of religion and to settle the just bounds that lie between the one and the other," he anticipated the necessity which would be thought by the Framers to require adoption of a First Amendment, but not the difficulty that would be experienced in defining those "just bounds." The fact is that the line which separates the secular from the sectarian in American life is elusive. . . .

I see no escape from the conclusion that the exercises called in question in these two cases violate the constitutional mandate. . . .

The religious nature of the exercises here challenged seems plain. Unless *Engel* v. *Vitale* is to be overruled, or we are to engage in wholly disingenuous distinction, we cannot sustain these practices. Daily recital of the Lord's Prayer and the reading of passages of Scripture are quite as clearly breaches of the command of the Establishment Clause as was the daily use of the rather bland Regents' Prayer in the New York public schools. Indeed,

I would suppose that if anything the Lord's Prayer and the Holy Bible are more clearly sectarian, and the present violations of the First Amendment consequently more serious.

[*In the next twenty-seven pages of his opinion Justice Brennan reviews the long history of Bible reading and daily prayer in the public schools and concludes that "these practices standing by themselves constitute an impermissible breach of the Establishment Clause."*]

. . . These considerations bring me to a final contention of the school officials in these cases: that the invalidation of the exercises at bar permits this Court no alternative but to declare unconstitutional every vestige, however slight, of co-operation or accommodation between religion and government. I cannot accept that contention. While it is not, of course, appropriate for this Court to decide questions not presently before it, I venture to suggest that religious exercises in the public schools present a unique problem. For not every involvement of religion in public life violates the Establishment Clause. Our decision in these cases does not clearly forecast anything about the constitutionality of other types of interdependence between religious and other public institutions. . . .

I think a brief survey of certain of these forms of accommodation will reveal that the First Amendment commands not official hostility toward religion, but only a strict neutrality in matters of religion. Moreover, it may serve to suggest that the scope of our holding today is to be measured by the special circumstances under which these cases have arisen, and by the particular dangers to church and state which religious exercises in the public schools present. . . .

A. The Conflict Between Establishment and Free Exercise.—There are certain practices, conceivably violative of the Establishment Clause, the striking down of which might seriously interfere with certain religious liberties also protected by the First Amendment. Provisions for churches and chaplains at military establishments for those in the armed services may afford one such example. The like provision by state and federal governments for chaplains in penal institutions may afford another example. It is argued that such provisions may be assumed to contravene the Establishment Clause, yet be sustained on constitutional grounds as necessary to secure to the members of the Armed Forces and prisoners those rights of worship guaranteed under the Free Exercise Clause. Since government has deprived such persons of the opportunity to practice their faith at places of their choice, the argument runs, government may, in order to avoid infringing the free exercise guaranties, provide substitutes where it requires such persons to be. Such a principle might support, for example, the constitutionality of draft exemptions for ministers and divinity students . . . ; of the excusal of children from school on their respective religious holidays; and of the allowance by government of temporary use of public buildings by religious organizations when their own churches have become unavailable because of a disaster or emergency.

Such activities and practices seem distinguishable from the sponsorship of daily Bible reading and prayer recital. For one thing, there is no element of coercion present in the appointment of military or prison chaplains; the soldier or convict who declines the opportunities for worship would not ordinarily subject himself to the suspicion or obloquy of his peers. Of special significance to this distinction is the fact that we are here usually dealing with adults, not with impressionable children as in the public schools. Moreover, the school exercises are not designed to provide the pupils with general opportunities for worship denied them by the legal obligation to attend school. The student's compelled presence in school for five days a week in no way renders the regular religious facilities of the community less accessible to him than they are to others. The situation of the school child is therefore plainly unlike that of the isolated soldier or the prisoner. . . .

B. *Establishment and Exercises in Legislative Bodies.*—The saying of invocational prayers in legislative chambers, state or federal, and the appointment of legislative chaplains, might well represent no involvements of the kind prohibited by the Establishment Clause. Legislators, federal and state, are mature adults who may presumably absent themselves from such public and ceremonial exercises without incurring any penalty, direct or indirect. It may also be significant that, at least in the case of the Congress, Art. I, Section 5, of the Constitution makes each House the monitor of the "Rules of its Proceedings" so that it is at least arguable whether such matters present "political questions" the resolution of which is exclusively confided to Congress. . . . Finally, there is the difficult question of who may be heard to challenge such practices. . . .

C. *Non–Devotional Use of the Bible in the Public Schools.*—The holding of the Court today plainly does not foreclose teaching about the Holy Scriptures or about the differences between religious sects in classes in literature or history. Indeed, whether or not the Bible is involved, it would be impossible to teach meaningfully many subjects in the social sciences or the humanities without some mention of religion. To what extent, and at what

points in the curriculum religious materials should be cited, are matters which the courts ought to entrust very largely to the experienced officials who superintend our Nation's public schools. They are experts in such matters, and we are not. . . .

D. *Uniform Tax Exemptions Incidentally Available to Religious Institutions.*—Nothing we hold today questions the propriety of certain tax deductions or exemptions which incidentally benefit churches and religious institutions, along with many secular charities and nonprofit organizations. If religious institutions benefit, it is in spite of rather than because of their religious character. For religious institutions simply share benefits which government makes generally available to educational, charitable, and eleemosynary groups. There is no indication that taxing authorities have used such benefits in any way to subsidize worship or foster belief in God. And as among religious beneficiaries, the tax exemption or deduction can be truly nondiscriminatory, available on equal terms to small as well as large religious bodies, to popular and unpopular sects, and to those organizations which reject as well as those which accept a belief in God.

E. *Religious Considerations in Public Welfare Programs.*—Since government may not support or directly aid religious activities without violating the Establishment Clause, there might be some doubt whether nondiscriminatory programs of governmental aid may constitutionally include individuals who become eligible wholly or partially for religious reasons. For example, it might be suggested that where a State provides unemployment compensation generally to those who are unable to find suitable work, it may not extend such benefits to persons who are unemployed by reason of religious beliefs or practices without thereby establishing the religion to which those persons belong. Therefore, the argument runs, the State may avoid an establishment only by singling out and excluding such persons on the ground that religious beliefs or practices have made them potential beneficiaries. Such a construction would, it seems to me, require government to impose religious discriminations and disabilities, thereby jeopardizing the free exercise of religion, in order to avoid what is thought to constitute an establishment.

The inescapable flaw in the argument, I suggest, is its quite unrealistic view of the aims of the Establishment Clause. The Framers were not concerned with the effects of certain incidental aids to individual worshippers which come about as by-products of general and nondiscriminatory welfare programs. If such benefits serve to make easier or less expensive the practice of a particular creed, or of all religions, it can hardly be said that the purpose of the program is in any way religious, or that the consequence of its nondiscriminatory application is to create the forbidden degree of interdependence between secular and sectarian institutions. I cannot therefore accept the suggestion, which seems to me implicit in the argument outlined here, that every judicial or administrative construction which is designed to prevent a public welfare program from abridging the free exercise of religious beliefs, is for that reason *ipso facto* an establishment of religion.

F. Activities Which, Though Religious in Origin, Have Ceased to Have Religious Meaning.—As we noted in our Sunday Law decisions, nearly every criminal law on the books can be traced to some religious principle or inspiration. But that does not make the present enforcement of the criminal law in any sense an establishment of religion, simply because it accords with widely-held religious principles. . . . This rationale suggests that the use of the motto "In God We Trust" in currency, on documents and public buildings and the like may not offend the clause. It is not that the use of those four words can be dismissed as "de minimis"—for I suspect there would be intense opposition to the abandonment of that motto. The truth is that we have simply interwoven the motto so deeply into the fabric of our civil polity that its present use may well not present that type of involvement which the First Amendment prohibits.

This general principle might also serve to insulate the various patriotic exercises and activities used in the public schools and elsewhere which, whatever may have been their origins, no longer have a religious purpose or meaning. The reference to divinity in the revised pledge of allegiance, for example, may merely recognize the historical fact that our Nation was believed to have been founded "under God." Thus reciting the pledge may be no more of a religious exercise than the reading aloud of Lincoln's Gettysburg Address, which contains an allusion to the same historical fact. . . .

MR. JUSTICE GOLDBERG, with whom MR. JUSTICE HARLAN joins, concurring:

. . . Neither the state nor this Court can or should ignore the significance of the fact that a vast portion of our people believe in and worship God and that many of our legal, political and personal values derive historically from religious teachings. Government must inevitably take cognizance of the existence of religion and, indeed, under certain circumstances the First Amendment may require that it do so. And it seems clear to me from the opinions in the present and past cases that the Court would recognize the propriety of providing military chaplains and of the teaching about religion, as distinguished from the teaching of religion, in the public schools. The examples could readily be multiplied, for both the required and the permissible accommodations between state and church frame the relation as one free of hostility or favor and productive of religious and political harmony, but without undue involvement of one in the concerns or practices of the other. To be sure, the judgment in each case is a delicate one, but it must be made if we are to do loyal service as judges to the ultimate First Amendment objective of religious liberty.

The practices here involved do not fall within any sensible or acceptable concept of compelled or permitted accommodation and involve the state so significantly and directly in the realm of the sectarian as to give rise to those very divisive influences and inhibitions of freedom which both religion clauses of the First Amendment preclude. The state has ordained and has utilized its facilities to engage in unmistakably religious exercises—the devotional reading and recitation of the Holy Bible—in a manner having substantial and significant import and impact. That it has selected, rather than written, a particular devotional liturgy seems to me without constitutional import. The pervasive religiosity and direct governmental involvement inhering in the prescription of prayer and Bible reading in the public schools, during and as part of the curricular day, involving young impressionable children whose school attendance is statutorily compelled, and utilizing the prestige, power, and influence of school administration, staff, and authority, cannot realistically be termed simply accommodation, and must fall within the interdiction of the First Amendment. I find nothing in the opinion of the Court which says more than this. . . .

MR. JUSTICE STEWART, dissenting:

I think the records in the two cases before us are so fundamentally deficient as to make impossible an informed or responsible determination of the constitutional issues presented. Specifically, I cannot agree that on these records we can say that the Establishment Clause has necessarily been violated. But I think there exist serious questions under both that provision and the Free Exercise Clause—insofar as each is imbedded in the Fourteenth Amendment—which require the remand of these cases for the taking of additional evidence. . . .

I would remand both cases for further hearings.

SUNDAY CLOSING CASES
366 U.S. 420; 81 Sup. Ct. 1101; 6 L. Ed. 2d. 393 (1961)

[*The Sunday blue laws of Maryland, Massachusetts, and Pennsylvania were examined by the Supreme Court in four cases decided together and known as the Sunday Closing Cases. In two cases, the Sunday closing laws of Maryland and Pennsylvania were challenged by regular commercial establishments. The two other cases were brought in Massachusetts and Pennsylvania by Jewish merchants who argued that because their religion required that their shops be closed on Saturdays, the Sunday Closing laws limited them to a five-day week. In all the cases the statutes were challenged on the ground that they violated the equal pro-*

tection clause of the Fourteenth Amendment because they contained so many exceptions for certain kinds of commercial activities. The Supreme Court agreed unanimously that equal protection had not been violated because the Fourteenth Amendment permits the states a ". . . wide scope of discretion in enacting laws which affect some groups of citizens differently from others. State legislators are presumed to have acted within their constitutional power despite the fact that, in practice, their laws result in some inequality." The argument on the issue of equal protection is not reproduced here, except for the brief opinion of Justice Stewart, which concisely raises the free exercise, as opposed to the establishment, problem.

The other opinions that follow are from McGowan v. Maryland, *the most important of the four cases. Margaret McGowan and other employees of a large discount department store located on a highway in Maryland were indicted for selling goods on Sunday in violation of the state's Sunday closing laws. The laws prohibited the sale on Sunday of all merchandise except such items as tobacco products, milk, bread, fruits, gasoline, drugs, and newspapers. The employees were convicted in a state court, and each was fined $5 and costs, and the convictions were affirmed by the Maryland Court of Appeals. The case then went to the Supreme Court on appeal.]*

MR. CHIEF JUSTICE WARREN delivered the opinion of the Court:

. . . The . . . questions for decision are whether the Maryland Sunday Closing Laws conflict with the Federal Constitution's provisions for religious liberty. First, appellants contend here that the statutes applicable to Anne Arundel County violate the constitutional guaranty of freedom of religion in that the statutes' effect is to prohibit the free exercise of religion in contravention of the First Amendment, made applicable to the States by the Fourteenth Amendment. But appellants allege only economic injury to themselves; they do not allege any infringement of their own religious freedoms due to Sunday closing. In fact, the record is silent as to what appellants' religious beliefs are. Since the general rule is that "a litigant may only assert his own constitutional rights or immunities," . . . we hold that appellants have no standing to raise this contention. . . .

Secondly, appellants contend that the statutes violate the guaranty of separation of church and state in that the

statutes are laws respecting an establishment of religion contrary to the First Amendment, made applicable to the states by the Fourteenth Amendment. If the purpose of the "establishment" clause was only to insure protection for the "free exercise" of religion, then what we have said above concerning appellant's standing to raise the "free exercise" contention would appear to be true here. However, the writings of Madison, who was the First Amendment's architect, demonstrate that the establishment of a religion was equally feared because of its tendencies to political tyranny and subversion of civil authority. . . . Appellants here concededly have suffered direct economic injury, allegedly due to the imposition on them of the tenets of the Christian religion. We find that, in these circumstances, these appellants have standing to complain that the statutes are laws respecting an establishment of religion.

The essence of appellant's "establishment" argument is that Sunday is the Sabbath day of the predominant Christian sects; that the purpose of the enforced stoppage of labor on that day is to facilitate and encourage church attendance; that the purpose of setting Sunday as a day of universal rest is to induce people with no religion or people with marginal religious beliefs to join the predominant Christian sects; that the purpose of the atmosphere of tranquility created by Sunday closing is to aid the conduct of church services and religious observance of the sacred day. . . . There is no dispute that the original laws which dealt with Sunday labor were motivated by religious forces. But what we must decide is whether present Sunday legislation, having undergone extensive changes from the earliest forms, still retains its religious character.

Sunday Closing Laws go far back into American history, having been brought to the colonies with a background of English legislation dating to the thirteenth century. . . . [C]learly . . . the English Sunday legislation was in aid of the established church.

The American colonial Sunday restrictions arose soon after settlement. Starting in 1650, the Plymouth Colony proscribed servile work, unnecessary travelling, sports, and the sale of alcoholic beverages on the Lord's day and enacted laws concerning church attendance. The Massachusetts Bay Colony and the Connecticut and New Haven Colonies enacted similar prohibitions, some even earlier in the seventeenth century. The religious orientation of the colonial statutes was equally apparent. . . .

But, despite the strongly religious origin of these laws, beginning before the eighteenth century, nonreligious arguments for Sunday closing began to be heard more distinctly and the statutes began to lose some of their totally religious flavor. In the middle 1700s, Blackstone wrote, "[T]he keeping one day in the seven holy, as a time of relaxation and refreshment as well as for public worship, is of admirable service to a state considered merely as a civil institution. It humanizes, by the help of conversation and society, the manners of the lower classes; which would otherwise degenerate into a sordid ferocity and savage selfishness of spirit; it enables the industrious workman to pursue his occupation in the ensuing week with health and cheerfulness." . . . The preamble to a 1679 Rhode Island enactment stated that the reason for the ban on Sunday employment was that "persons being evil minded, have presumed to employ in servile labor, more than necessity requireth, their servants. . . ." With the advent of the First Amendment, the colonial provisions requiring church attendance were soon repealed. . . .

More recently, further secular justifications have been advanced for making Sunday a day of rest, a day when people may recover from the labors of the week just passed and may physically and mentally prepare for the week's work to come. . . .

The proponents of Sunday closing legislation are no longer exclusively representatives of religious interests. Recent New Jersey Sunday legislation was supported by labor groups and trade associations. . . .

Almost every State in our country presently has some type of Sunday regulation and over forty possess a relatively comprehensive system. . . . Some of our States now enforce their Sunday legislation through Departments of Labor. . . . Thus have Sunday laws evolved from the wholly religious sanctions that originally were enacted. . . .

[I]n order to dispose of the case before us, we must consider the standards by which the Maryland statutes are to be measured. . . .

[T]he First Amendment, in its final form, did not simply bar a congressional enactment establishing a church; it forbade all laws respecting an establishment of religion. Thus, this Court has given the Amendment a "broad interpretation" . . . "in the light of its history and the evils it was designed forever to suppress. . . ." It has found that the First and Fourteenth Amendments afford protection against religious establishment far more extensive than merely to forbid a national or state church. . . .

However, it is equally true that the "Establishment" Clause does not ban federal or state regulation of conduct whose reason or effect merely happens to coincide or harmonize with the tenets of some or all religions. In many instances, the Congress or state legislatures conclude that the general welfare of society, wholly apart from any religious considerations, demands such regulation. Thus, for temporal purposes, murder is illegal. And the fact that this agrees with the dictates of the Judaeo-Christian religions while it may disagree with others does not invalidate the regulation. So too with the questions of adultery and polygamy. . . .

In light of the evolution of our Sunday Closing Laws through the centuries, and of their more or less recent emphasis upon secular considerations, it is not difficult to discern that as presently written and administered, most of them, at least, are of a secular rather than of a religious character, and that presently they bear no relationship to establishment of religion as those words are used in the Constitution of the United States.

Throughout this century and longer, both the federal and state governments have oriented their activities very largely toward improvement of the health, safety, recreation and general well-being of our citizens. Numerous laws affecting public health, safety factors in industry, laws affecting public health, safety factors in industry, laws affecting hours and conditions of labor of women and children, week-end diversion at parks and beaches, and cultural activities of various kinds, now point the way toward the good life for all. Sunday Closing Laws, like those before us, have become part and parcel of this great governmental concern wholly apart from their original purposes or connotations. The present purpose and effect of most of them is to provide a uniform day of rest for all citizens; the fact that this day is Sunday, a day of particular significance for the dominant Christian sects, does not bar the State from achieving its secular goals. To say that the States cannot prescribe Sunday as a day of rest for these purposes solely because centuries ago such laws had their genesis in religion would give a constitutional interpretation of hostility to the public welfare rather than one of mere separation of church and State. . . .

But, this does not answer all of appellants' contentions. We are told that the State has other means at its disposal to accomplish its secular purpose, other courses that would not even remotely or incidentally give state aid to religion. . . . It is true that if the State's interest were simply to provide for its citizens a periodic respite from work, a regulation demanding that everyone rest one day in seven, leaving the choice of the day to the individual, would suffice.

However, the State's purpose is not merely to provide a one-day-in-seven work stoppage. In addition to this, the State seeks to set one day apart from all others as a day of rest, repose, recreation and tranquility—a day which all members of the family and community have the opportunity to spend and enjoy together, a day in which there exists relative quiet and disassociation from the everyday intensity of commercial activities, a day in which people may visit friends and relatives who are not available during working days.

Obviously, a state is empowered to determine that a rest-one-day-in-seven statute would not accomplish this purpose; that it would not provide for a general cessation of activity, a special atmosphere of tranquility, a day which all members of the family or friends and relatives might spend together. Furthermore, it seems plain that the problems involved in enforcing such a provision would be exceedingly more difficult than those in enforcing a common-day-of-rest provision.

Moreover, it is common knowledge that the first day of the week has come to have special significance as a rest day in this country. People of all religions and people with no religion regard Sunday as a time for family activity, for visiting friends and relatives, for late-sleeping, for passive and active entertainments, for dining out and the like. . . . Sunday is a day apart from all others. The cause is irrelevant; the fact exists. It would seem unrealistic for enforcement purposes and perhaps detrimental to the general welfare to require a state to choose a common-day-of-rest other than that which most persons would select of their own accord. For these reasons, we hold that the Maryland statutes are not laws respecting an establishment of religion. . . .

Accordingly, the decision is

Affirmed.

MR. JUSTICE DOUGLAS, dissenting [*in all four cases*]:

. . . I do not see how a State can make protesting citizens refrain from doing innocent acts on Sunday because the doing of those acts offends sentiments of their Christian neighbors.

The institutions of our society are founded on the belief that there is an authority higher than the authority of the State; that there is a moral law which the state is powerless to alter; that the individual possesses rights, conferred by the Creator, which government must respect. . . .

[T]hose who fashioned the Constitution decided that if and when God is to be served, His service will not be motivated by coercive measures of government. . . . [T]he First Amendment . . . means, as I understand it, that if a religious leaven is to be worked into the affairs of our people, it is to be done by individuals and groups, not by the government. This necessarily means, first, that the dogma, creed, scruples, or practices of no religious group or sect are to be preferred over those of any others; second, that no one shall be interfered with by government for practicing the religion of his choice; third, that the state may not require anyone to practice a religion or even any religion; and fourth, that the state cannot compel one so to conduct himself as not to offend the religious scruples of another. The idea, as I understand it, was to limit the power of government to act in religious matters . . . , not to limit the freedom of religious men to act religiously nor to restrict the freedom of atheists or agnostics.

The First Amendment commands government to have no interest in theology or ritual; it admonishes government to be interested in allowing religious freedom to flourish—whether the result is to produce Catholics, Jews, or Protestants, or to turn the people toward the path of Buddha, or to end in a predominantly Moslem nation, or to produce in the long run atheists or agnostics. On matters of this kind government must be neutral. This freedom plainly includes freedom from religion with the right to believe, speak, write, publish and advocate antireligious programs. . . . Certainly the "free exercise" clause does not require that everyone embrace the theology of some church or of some faith, or observe the religious practices of any majority or minority sect. The First Amendment by its "establishment" clause prevents, of course, the selection by government of an "official" church. Yet the ban plainly extends farther than that. . . . The "establishment" clause protects citizens also against any law which selects any religious custom, practice, or ritual, puts the force of government behind it, and fines, imprisons, or otherwise penalizes a person for not observing it. The Government plainly could not join forces with one religious group and decree a universal and symbolic circumcision. Nor could it require all children to be baptized or give tax exemptions only to those whose children were baptized.

Could it require a fast from sunrise to sunset throughout the Moslem month of Ramadan? I should think not. Yet how then can it make criminal the doing of other acts, as innocent as eating, during the day that Christians revere?

Sunday is a word heavily overlaid with connotations and traditions deriving from the Christian roots of our civilization that color all judgments concerning it. . . .

The issue of these cases would therefore be in better focus if we imagined that a state legislature, controlled by orthodox Jews and Seventh Day Adventists, passed a law making it a crime to keep a shop open on Saturdays. Would a Baptist, Catholic, Methodist, or Presbyterian be compelled to obey that law or go to jail or pay a fine? Or suppose Moslems grew in political strength here and got a law through a state legislature making it a crime to keep a shop open on Fridays? Would the rest of us have to submit under the fear of criminal sanctions? . . .

The Court picks and chooses language from various decisions to bolster its conclusion that these Sunday Laws in the modern setting are "civil regulations." No matter how much is written, no matter what is said, the parentage of these laws is the Fourth Commandment; and they serve and satisfy the religious predispositions of our Christian communities. After all, the labels a State places on its laws are not binding on us when we are confronted with a constitutional decision. We reach our own conclusion as to the character, effect, and practical operation of the regulation in determining its constitutionality. . . .

It seems to me plain that by these laws the States compel one, under sanction of law, to refrain from work or recreation on Sunday because of the majority's religious views about that day. The State by law makes Sunday a symbol of respect or adherence. Refraining from work or recreation in deference to the majority's religious feelings about Sunday is within every person's choice. By what authority can government compel it? . . .

These laws are sustained because, it is said, the First Amendment is concerned with religious convictions or opinion, not with conduct. But it is a strange Bill of Rights that makes it possible for the dominant religious group to bring the minority to heel because the minority, in the doing of acts which intrinsically are wholesome and not antisocial, does not defer to the majority's religious beliefs. Some have religious scruples against eating pork.

Those scruples, no matter how bizarre they might seem to some, are within the ambit of the First Amendment. . . . Is it possible that a majority of a state legislature having those religious scruples could make it criminal for the nonbeliever to sell pork? Some have religious scruples against slaughtering cattle. Could a state legislature, dominated by that group, make it criminal to run an abattoir?

The Court balances the need of the people for rest, recreation, late-sleeping, family visiting and the like against the command of the First Amendment that no one need bow to the religious beliefs of another. There is in this realm no room for balancing. I see no place for it in the constitutional scheme. A legislature of Christians can no more make minorities conform to their weekly regime than a legislature of Moslems, or a legislature of Hindus. The religious regime of every group must be respected—unless it crosses the line of criminal conduct. But no one can be forced to come to a halt before it, or refrain from doing things that would offend it. That is my reading of the Establishment Clause and the Free Exercise Clause. . . .

The State can of course require one day of rest a week: one day when every shop or factory is closed. Quite a few States make that requirement. Then the "day of rest" becomes purely and simply a health measure. But the Sunday laws operate differently. They force minorities to obey the majority's religious feelings of what is due and proper for a Christian community; they provide a coercive spur to the "weaker brethren," to those who are indifferent to the claims of a Sabbath through apathy or scruple. . . .

There is an "establishment" of religion in the constitutional sense if any practice of any religious group has the sanction of law behind it. There is an interference with the "free exercise" of religion if what in conscience one can do or omit doing is required because of the religious scruples of the community. Hence I would declare each of those laws unconstitutional as applied to the complaining parties, whether or not they are members of a sect which observes as their Sabbath a day other than Sunday.

When these laws are applied to Orthodox Jews . . . or to Sabbatarians their vice is accentuated. If the Sunday laws are constitutional, Kosher markets are on a five-day week. Thus those laws put an economic penalty on those who observe Saturday rather than Sunday as the Sabbath. For the economic pressures on these minorities, created by the fact that our communities are predominantly Sunday-minded, there is no recourse. When, however, the State uses its coercive powers—here the criminal law—to compel minorities to observe a second Sabbath, not their own, the State undertakes to aid and "prefer one religion over another"—contrary to the command of the Constitution. . . .

I dissent from applying criminal sanctions against any of these complaints since to do so implicates the States in religious matters contrary to the constitutional mandate. . . .

MR. JUSTICE STEWART dissenting [in *Braunfeld* v. *Brown*]:

Pennsylvania has passed a law which compels an Orthodox Jew to choose between his religious faith and his economic survival. That is a cruel choice. It is a choice which I think no State can constitutionally demand. For me this is not something that can be swept under the rug and forgotten in the interest of enforced Sunday togetherness. I think the impact of this law upon these appellants grossly violates their constitutional right to the free exercise of their religion.

Separate opinion of MR. JUSTICE FRANKFURTER, whom MR. JUSTICE HARLAN joins [*in all four cases*].

[*In this separate concurring opinion Justice Frankfurter sets forth in detail* the long history of Sunday legislation. The opinion is eighty-six pages long; sixteen additional pages of appendices include tables and other supporting data.]

15

Communism, National Security, and Individual Freedom

We have already seen that for more than a decade after 1930 the trend of Supreme Court decisions was toward the protection of individual freedoms. This trend, which was begun under the leadership of Chief Justice Hughes, continued, with few exceptions, under Chief Justice Stone, who presided over the Court from 1941 to 1946. Yet during the latter years of the 1930s there were rumblings that did not bode well for the future protection of individual rights. The rise of totalitarian dictatorships in Germany, Italy, and Japan, plus the continued growth of the Soviet Union, alarmed many Americans. The fears engendered by these developments resulted in numerous federal and state measures that were designed to protect the country from seditious or subversive activities. Thus, in 1938, the House Committee on Un-American Activities was set up to investigate espionage and subversion. In June 1940, Congress enacted the first peacetime sedition law since the hated Sedition Act of 1798. This was the Alien Registration Act, commonly known as the Smith Act. Shortly after its adoption, a leading scholar pointed out that the official title of the Smith Act ". . . would make us expect a statute concerned only with fingerprinting foreigners and such administrative matters. Indeed, that was the impression received from the newspapers at the time of its passage. Not until months later did I, for one, realize that *this statute contains the most* *drastic restrictions on freedom of speech ever enacted in the United States during peace.*"[1]

The Aftermath of World War II

The Smith Act provisions, which are noted in *Dennis* v. *United States* (p. 497), were adopted originally to protect the country from pro-Nazis and fascists of similar types. In practice, however, it became the major weapon for the federal prosecution of American Communist party leaders after World War II. America's participation in that war as an ally of the Soviet Union had lessened the country's prewar fears of communism. But when the war was over, apprehensions about communism and the Soviet Union flared anew to almost panic proportions. These apprehensions were increased by the knowledge that the Soviet Union would—and eventually did—possess two incredibly powerful and destructive weapons of warfare—the atom and hydrogen bombs.

The end of World War II and the beginning of the "cold war" brought many new forms of restrictions directed principally at Communists and so-called fellow-travelers. The Smith Act was enforced vigorously against the nominal leaders of the Communist party in America. By 1957, the federal government had brought indictments under the Smith Act against 145 leaders of the party, and eighty-nine convictions, some of which were later nullified by court decisions, had been secured under the act. In addition, both the states and the federal government enacted new legislation designed to help achieve national security. The most stringent of the nation's Communist control laws came into being in 1950, with the enactment of the long and involved Internal Security Act. This law, popularly known as the McCarran Act, placed many restrictions on Communists and their supporters. Among other things, Communist and pro-Communist organizations were required to register with the Justice Department; Communists were barred from federal employment and from work in any "defense facility"; the penalties for espionage were increased; Communists could not obtain passports; and the deportation of "subversives" was made easier. Later Congress enacted the uncertain and ambiguous Communist Control Act of 1954, which was designed to outlaw the Communist party. The *actual* effect of this law is still to be determined, except that it has contributed to making several provisions of the earlier McCarran Act almost totally unworkable.

These and other federal enactments have been supplemented by a wave of state legislation also designed to protect the nation against subversion and espionage. These include antianarchy or criminal syndicalism laws, sedition

[1] Zechariah Chafee, Jr., *Free Speech in the United States,* (Cambridge: Harvard University Press, 1942), p. 441. (Italics supplied.)

statutes, such as the one invalidated in *Pennsylvania* v. *Nelson* (Chapter 5), laws barring "subversive" political organizations from appearing on the ballot, and laws denying the use of public school buildings as meeting places for "subversive" groups.

Other methods were employed after World War II to control communism. Both the Senate and the House of Representatives created numerous investigatory committees that sought to track down and expose Communists and their sympathizers. Several states set up their own legislative committees to combat subversion. Loyalty and security programs designed to ferret out disloyal governmental employees and run by administrative officials were instituted by the federal government and a majority of the states. In addition, many private individuals and groups took it upon themselves to expose people who seemed to them disloyal or subversive. Such activities were undoubtedly spurred on by the fighting in Korea, which began in 1950, the spectacular charges of the late Senator McCarthy that there were many Communists in important governmental positions, and the revelation of espionage activities on the part of some Americans.

The country's preoccupation with the threat of communism evoked a veritable flood of commentaries, articles, and books on the subject. Many felt that the serious dangers to the security of the nation presented by international communism justified the repressive measures noted here. Many people today still "endorse with great sincerity steps that may conceivably strengthen national safety, even when those steps may entail some loss of freedom or occasional injustice to individuals."[2] Others, like Justice Douglas, reason as follows:

> The Communist threat inside the country has been magnified and exalted far beyond its realities. Irresponsible talk by irresponsible people has fanned the flames of fear. Accusations have been loosely made. Character assassinations have become common. Suspicion has taken the place of good will. Once we could debate with impunity along a wide range of inquiry. Once we could safely explore to the edges of a problem, challenge orthodoxy without qualms, and run the gamut of ideas in search of solutions to perplexing problems. Once we had confidence in each other. Now there is suspicion. Innocent acts become telltale marks of disloyalty. The coincidence that an idea parallels Soviet Russia's policy for a moment of time settles an aura of suspicion around a person.[3]

Many people, unable to embrace either of these points of view, were bewildered by the torrent of words, charges, and countercharges. Increasingly,

[2] Walter Gellhorn, *Individual Freedom and Governmental Restraint* (Baton Rouge: Louisiana State University, 1956), p. 16.

[3] William O. Douglas, "The Black Silence of Fear," *The New York Times Magazine* (March 23, 1952). Reprinted by American Civil Liberties Union, New York (March 1952).

many Americans have become aware that there is no simple solution to the problem of fighting communism and, at the same time, preserving individual rights.

This was the atmosphere at mid-century as the Supreme Court faced the difficult task of providing an authoritative interpretation of much of the restrictive legislation. The Court was thus again called upon to maintain the balance between liberty and authority—"perhaps the most delicate, difficult, and shifting of all balances which the Court is expected to maintain."[4]

The Vinson Court (1946–1953)

Fred M. Vinson was appointed Chief Justice by President Truman after the death of Chief Justice Stone in 1946. The new Chief Justice had been at his new post only a short time when some of the anti-Communist legislation reached the Court. The first case before the Court grew out of a provision of the Taft-Hartley Act of 1947 that required non-Communist oaths on the part of labor union officers. No union could take advantage of the act's provisions unless each of its officers filed an affidavit stating that (1) he was not a member of or affiliated with the Communist party and (2) that he did not believe in and was neither a member of nor supported any organization that believes in the violent overthrow of the government. In *American Communications Association* v. *Douds,* 339 U.S. 382 (1950), the Court held that the oath requirement did not violate the First Amendment and was therefore constitutional. Chief Justice Vinson, delivering the majority opinion, reasoned that the non-Communist oath was not intended to punish belief but rather was designed to regulate the conduct of union affairs. Congress could control union activities under its power to regulate interstate commerce in order to prevent union leaders from calling political strikes designed to interfere with the free flow of commerce and weaken the American people. Only Justice Black dissented from the basic holding of the Court, whereas Justice Douglas and two other members of the Court did not participate in the decision.

In the *Dennis* case, the Court considered the validity of the important Smith Act of 1940 for the first time. There the Court sustained the convictions of eleven top Communist party leaders under the Smith Act for conspiracy to advocate overthrow of the government by revolution and violence. But the five opinions of the *Dennis* case to be reproduced here demonstrate clearly the difficulties experienced by the Court in arriving at clear-cut decisions during this chaotic period. They reveal also the diversity of views among the justices regarding the real meaning of the clear and present danger test. Chief Justice Vinson maintained in the majority opinion that he applied the

---

[4] Robert H. Jackson, *The Supreme Court in the American System of Government* (Cambridge: Harvard University Press, 1955), p. 75.

Holmes-Brandeis clear and present danger rule. In essence, however, he applied the test of *clear and probable* danger formulated by Judge Learned Hand in the Court of Appeals or the bad tendency test of the *Gitlow* case.

In addition to the *Douds* and *Dennis* cases, the Vinson Court rendered a number of other decisions dealing with loyalty and subversion. Many of these cases were also characterized by multiple concurring and dissenting opinions that indicated a lack of unity on fundamental concepts among the members of the Court. In general, the Court upheld the measures adopted by legislative bodies against the claims of individual freedoms. The case of *Adler* v. *Board of Education*[5] (p. 517) is typical. In fact, the Vinson Court operated largely on the principle that legislative bodies should not be hampered in their efforts to stamp out subversion by a Supreme Court which was far removed from the felt needs of the American people.

> [The Vinson Court attempted] to apply the lessons of 1937 to a new and far different judicial world. The task of the Roosevelt Court was to get back in step with the country and to provide appropriate constitutional rationalization for popular economic policies. Their acceptance of the strong legislature–weak judiciary formula was, after 1941, fortified by the necessities of a global war, which had to be won by vigorous executive and legislative action, with little time for concern with legal niceties. By the time the Vinson Court came on the scene, the situation had changed. The shooting war was over, and the government's power of direction over the economy was established so firmly as to be beyond challenge. But the cold war was just beginning, and it proved harder to work out judicial relationships to a cold war than to a hot one. The Vinson Court's solution was almost entirely within the tradition of the strong legislature–weak judiciary formula which Holmes developed for the quite different purpose of controlling judicial review over state economic legislation. In fact, the Vinson Court even refused to give full faith and credit to the one doctrine Holmes proposed which did have the potentiality of strengthening judicial review, the clear and present danger test.[6]

[5] Other important cases include *Garner* v. *Board of Public Works,* 341 U.S. 716 (1951), and *Gerende* v. *Board of Supervisors,* 341 U.S. 56 (1951). In the *Garner* case, the Court upheld a Los Angeles ordinance that required all city employees to take a loyalty oath. In the *Gerende* case, the Court sustained unanimously a Maryland statute that required candidates for public office to take a loyalty oath. Individual rights were supported in a few cases. Thus, in *Wieman* v. *Updegraff,* 344 U.S. 183 (1952), a poorly drawn Oklahoma statute which required that all state officers and employees take a loyalty oath was struck down because it made simple membership in one of the listed "subversive" organizations a bar to public employment. The Court noted that, under the Oklahoma law ". . . the fact of association alone determines disloyalty and disqualification. It matters not whether association existed innocently or knowingly. Indiscriminate classification of innocent with knowing activity must fall as an assertion of arbitrary power." A decision favorable to individual freedom was rendered in *Joint Anti-Fascist Refugee Committee* v. *McGrath,* which is examined in Chapter 19.

[6] C. Herman Pritchett, *Civil Liberties and the Vinson Court* (Chicago: University of Chicago Press, 1954), pp. 239–40.

The Court and Individual Freedom After 1953

In 1953, the Supreme Court entered a new phase under Chief Justice Earl Warren, who was appointed by President Eisenhower after the death of Chief Justice Vinson. During his first year on the bench, Chief Justice Warren delivered the memorable opinions against racial segregation in the public schools that are discussed in Chapter 18. Since that time, the Court under his direction has shown a marked concern for individual freedom. In case after case, the Warren Court has established new barriers against governmental power to restrict individual freedoms; for example, in *Pennsylvania* v. *Nelson* (Chapter 5) the Court held that the states could not prosecute persons who advocate the violent overthrow of the government, because the field of anti-subversive activities had been pre-empted by the federal government. In *Cole* v. *Young,* 351 U.S. 536 (1955), the Court limited the federal employee security program to persons in "sensitive" jobs.

A series of decisions rendered during the closing months of the 1956–1957 term indicated unmistakably the new direction of the Court under Chief Justice Warren. These cases, some of which were characterized by broad, sweeping "unjudicial" language, demonstrated clearly the Court's increasing concern for the protection of individual rights. Thus, the Vinson Court, which had been almost invariably on the side of governmental authority, was "replaced by a tribunal inclined to look on claims of violation of individual rights with a far more friendly eye."[7] During 1957–1958 term, the Court's continued protection of individual rights resulted in numerous attacks upon the "liberal" justices. In addition, various proposals to curb the Court's power were introduced in Congress.

The new direction of the Court may be discerned easily by reference to two important cases. In *Watkins* v. *United States* (p. 513), while confirming the power of Congress to investigate for a valid legislative purpose that had been proclaimed in *McGrain* v. *Daugherty,* 273 U.S. 135 (1927), Chief Justice Warren went out of his way to read a sharp lecture to Congress on the abuses of its investigating function.[8] An important sequel to the *Dennis* case was the decision in *Yates* v. *United States* (p. 519). There the Court limited the application of the Smith Act of 1940.

This new trend of decisions evoked both enthusiastic approval and severe

---

[7] Bernard Schwartz, " 'Warren Court'—An Opinion," *The New York Times Magazine,* (June 30, 1957), p. 11.

[8] In the companion case of *Sweezy* v. *New Hampshire,* 354 U.S. 234 (1956), the Court placed constitutional restrictions on investigations by state legislative committees, but it did not establish any definite rules. The *Sweezy* case was practically obliterated by *Uphaus* v. *Wyman,* 360 U.S. 72 (1959), which upheld a contempt conviction of a pacifist minister for refusing to give to the Attorney General of New Hampshire the names of persons attending a "world fellowship" camp.

condemnation. Many commentators and legal scholars felt that the Court had finally come to the rescue of constitutional rights that had been abridged for too long by overzealous legislative and executive officers. Others charged that the decisions seriously weakened the internal security of the country. For example, many felt that, for all practical purposes, the *Yates* decision made convictions of Communists and dangerous subversives all but impossible, whereas the Watkins holding was thought to cripple future congressional investigations of Communist subversion. *Yates* does in fact require such strict standards of proof for conviction for "advocacy" under the Smith Act that a prosecutor in a position to prove violation of the act would also be in a position to prove criminal conspiracy or sedition punishable under other federal statutes and so would not need the act to send Communists to jail. In this sense, *Yates* deprives the Smith Act of much of its meaning. *Watkins,* in spite of its rhetoric, did not place any serious limitations on the investigating power.

The reasons for the Court's changed attitude in cases concerning individual freedom and national security is not difficult to discern. In the first place, after 1953 there was a gradual decline in the expression of frantic fears about communism: The dramatic cases involving Alger Hiss, the Rosenbergs, and others were over; the Korean fighting was ended; Americans generally became weary of continual talk about subversion; in addition, the gradual strengthening of the defenses of the Western world enabled the people and their representatives to arrive at a more reasonable estimate of the real dangers posed by domestic Communists. Secondly, the shift in attitude can be explained, in part, by changes in the personnel of the Court. On the Vinson Court, Justices Black and Douglas had usually stood alone in their attempts to curb legislative and executive encroachments on individual freedoms. But, after 1953, two of President Eisenhower's appointees often joined the two Roosevelt appointees in condemning infringements of individual rights. These were Chief Justice Warren and Justice Brennan, who replaced Justice Minton in 1956. This group could often count on a vote from at least one other justice and thereby carry the day.

Although the Court continued to defend individual rights in almost every major area, it retreated somewhat in the field of alleged subversion. In general, the Warren Court made a "tactical withdrawal" in a number of cases linked with subversion. It limited the scope and impact of the *Watkins* case in *Barenblatt* v. *United States* (p. 526), which upheld a conviction for contempt of the House Un-American Activities Committee. In two additional cases in 1961, the Court held by a vote of 5 to 4 that the refusal of a witness to tell the House Un-American Activities Committee whether he was a member of the Communist party was punishable by contempt.[9] These cases are the high-

[9] *Wilkinson* v. *United States,* 365 U.S. 399 (1961); *Braden* v. *United States,* 365 U.S. 431 (1961). However, in *Russell* v. *United States,* 369 U.S. 749 (1962), the Court set aside convictions for contempt of two congressional committees on the ground that the

water mark of the antisubversive campaign and still probably constitutionally legitimize the extremely broad use of the investigatory weapon in the area of subversion. In retrospect, however, they may be most important for their unanimous and specific holdings by the Court that the congressional investigations at issue did infringe on First Amendment rights.

Immediately thereafter, by 5 to 4 decisions, the Court upheld against First Amendment pleas the registration provisions of the McCarran Act, *Communist Party* v. *Subversive Activities Control Board,* 367 U.S. 1 (1961), and the clause of the Smith Act making criminal membership in an organization that advocates overthrow of the government by force and violence, *Scales* v. *United States* (p. 534). The *Subversive Activities Control Board* case, however, left open the question of whether the party and its members could plead self-incrimination to avoid registration, because the Communist Control Act had made membership in the party a crime, and registration is a confession of membership. Government efforts to require the party as an entity to register were thwarted when no officer of the party would step forward to register it. Then, when the government sought to force individual members to register, the Supreme Court held, in *Albertson* v. *Subversive Activities Control Board,* 382 U.S. 70 (1965), that they might refuse to do so because of the possibility of self-incrimination. Similarly, the *Scales* requirement of active, knowing membership with specific intent, like *Yates,* requires such a high level of proof that if the government can satisfy its demands, it can successfully prosecute under the normal criminal law and would not have to resort to Smith Act "membership" prosecutions.

The Court has also exerted greater control over loyalty and security programs in recent years. It has struck down the blanket prohibitions on the issuance of passports to Communists, in the process acknowledging a constitutional right to travel linked to the First and Fifth Amendments, *Aptheker* v. *Secretary of State,* 378 U.S. 500 (1964). The Court struck down another provision of the McCarran Act in *United States* v. *Robel,* 389 U.S. 258 (1967). This provision made it unlawful for any member of a "Communist-action organization" to work in a "defense facility." The Court argued that the statute failed to take into consideration the degree of the worker's committment to the illegal aims of communism and whether he was in the sort of job in which he could damage our defense efforts. Thus, the statute was not narrowly drawn to protect our defense effort without infringing on the political freedoms of government workers. Undercutting *American Communications Association* v. *Douds* (p. 492), it has declared a statute barring Communists from holding union office to be an unconstitutional bill of attainder

---

subject under inquiry was not clearly identified at the time of the defendants' refusal to answer questions. In *Deutsch* v. *United States,* 367 U.S. 456 (1961), a conviction for contempt of the House Un-American Activities Committee was set aside because answers were required to questions that were not pertinent to its inquiry.

United States v. *Brown,* 381 U.S. 437 (1965). And in a series of cases culminating in *Keyishian* v. *Board of Regents* (p. 545), which in effect overrules the *Adler* decision, the Court has struck down state loyalty oaths and employment provisions on the grounds that they were vague and/or condemned membership in general rather than only active, knowing membership with specific intent of the sort described in *Scales.*

In *Gibson* v. *Florida Investigating Committee* (p. 539), the Court has seen imposed much more serious limitations on legislative investigations that threaten political freedoms, although it has still left a broader leeway in the subversion areas than in others.

DENNIS v. UNITED STATES
341 U.S. 494; 71 Sup. Ct. 857; 95 L. Ed. 1137 (1951)

[*Dennis and ten other leaders of the Communist party were charged with violating the conspiracy provisions of the Smith Act of 1940, which are reproduced here. They were convicted in a New York district court after a sensational and hectic trial that lasted over nine months. With one exception, each of the defendants was sentenced to imprisonment for five years and to a fine of $10,000 by Judge Medina, who presided at the trial. At the conclusion of the trial, Judge Medina also imposed sentences ranging from thirty days' to six months' imprisonment on the six defense attorneys for contemptuous conduct during the trial. President Truman promoted Judge Medina to the Court of Appeals shortly after the trial.*

The convictions of the eleven Communist party leaders were affirmed by a court of appeals in an opinion by Judge Learned Hand. The defendants then sought to obtain review by the Supreme Court on all the grounds considered by the court of appeals. These included questions relating to the scope of freedom of speech, the legal composition of the jury, and the fairness of the trial. The Court granted certiorari, which was strictly limited to a review of whether Sections 2 and 3 of the Smith Act, as construed and applied, violated the First and Fifth Amendments and other provisions of the Bill of Rights.]

MR. CHIEF JUSTICE VINSON announced the judgment of the Court and an opinion in which MR. JUSTICE REED, MR. JUSTICE BURTON, and MR. JUSTICE MINTON join:

. . . Sections 2 and 3 of the Smith Act . . . provide as follows:

"Sec. 2. (a) It shall be unlawful for any person—

"(1) to knowingly or willfully advocate, abet, advise, or teach the duty, necessity, desirability, or pro-

priety of overthrowing or destroying any government in the United States by force or violence, or by the assassination of any officer of any such government;

"(2) with intent to cause the overthrow or destruction of any government in the United States, to print, publish, edit, issue, circulate, sell, distribute, or publicly display any written or printed matter advocating, advising, or teaching the duty, necessity, desirability, or propriety of overthrowing or destroying any government in the United States by force or violence;

"(3) to organize or help to organize any society, group, or assembly of persons who teach, advocate, or encourage the overthrow or destruction of any government in the United States by force, or violence; or to be or become a member of, or affiliate with, any such society, group, or assembly of persons, knowing the purposes thereof.

"(b) For the purposes of this section, the term 'government in the United States' means the Government of the United States, the government of any State, Territory, or possession of the United States, the government of the District of Columbia, or the government of any political subdivision of any of them.

"Sec. 3. It shall be unlawful for any person to attempt to commit, or to conspire to commit, any of the acts prohibited by the provisions of this title."

The indictment charged the petitioners with willfully and knowingly conspiring (1) to organize as the Communist Party of the United States of America a society, group, and assembly of persons who teach and advocate the overthrow and destruction of the Government of the United States by force and violence, and (2) knowingly and willfully to advocate and teach the duty and necessity of overthrowing and destroying the Government of the United States by force and violence. The indictment further alleged that §2 of the Smith Act proscribes these acts and that any conspiracy to take such action is a violation of §3 of the Act.

. . . Our limited grant of the writ of certiorari has removed from our consideration any question as to the sufficiency of the evidence to support the jury's determination that petitioner's are guilty of the offense charged. Whether on this record petitioners did in fact advocate the overthrow of the Government by force and violence is not before us, and we must base any discussion of this point upon the conclusions stated in the opinion of the Court of Appeals, which treated the issue in great detail. That court held that the record in this case amply supports the necessary finding of the jury that petitioners, the leaders of the Communist Party in this country, were unwilling to work within our framework of democracy, but intended to initiate a violent revolution whenever the propitious occasion appeared. Petitioners dispute the meaning to be drawn from the evidence, contending that the Marxist-Leninist doctrine they advocated taught that force and violence to achieve a Communist form of government in an existing democratic state would be necessary only because the ruling classes of that state would never permit the transformation to be accomplished peacefully, but would use force and violence to defeat any peaceful political and economic gain the Communists could achieve. But the Court of Appeals held that the record supports the following broad conclusions: By virtue of their control over the political apparatus of the Communist Political Association, petitioners were able to transform that organization into the Communist Party; that the policies of the Association were changed from peaceful cooperation with the United States and its economic and political structure to a policy which had existed before the United States and the Soviet Union were fighting a common enemy, namely, a policy which worked for the overthrow of the Government by force and violence; that the Communist Party is a highly disciplined organization, adept at infiltration into strategic positions, use of aliases, and double-meaning language; that the Party is rigidly controlled; that Communists, unlike other political parties, tolerate no dissension from the policy laid down by the guiding forces, but that the approved program is slavishly followed by the members of the Party; that the literature of the Party and the statements and activities of its leaders, petitioners here, advocate, and the general goal of the Party was, during the period in question, to achieve a successful overthrow of the existing order by force and violence.

I

It will be helpful in clarifying the issues to treat the contention that the trial judge improperly interpreted the statute by charging that the statute required an unlawful intent before the jury could convict. . . .

. . . The structure and purpose of the statute demand the inclusion of intent as an element of the crime. Congress was concerned with those who advocate and organize for the overthrow of the Government. Certainly those who recruit and combine for the purpose of advocating overthrow intend to bring about that overthrow. We hold that the statute requires as an essential element of the crime proof of the intent of those who are charged with its violation to overthrow the Government by force and violence. . . .

II

The obvious purpose of the statute is to protect existing Government, not from change by peaceable, lawful, and constitutional means, but from change by violence, revolution, and terrorism. That it is within the *power* of the Con-gress to protect the Government of the United States from armed rebellion is a proposition which requires little discussion. Whatever theoretical merit there may be to the argument that there is a "right" to rebellion against dictatorial government is without force where the existing structure of the government provides for peaceful and orderly change. We reject any principle of governmental helplessness in the face of preparation for revolution, which principle, carried to its logical conclusion, must lead to anarchy. No one could conceive that it is not within the power of Congress to prohibit acts intended to overthrow the Government by force and violence. The question with which we are concerned here is not whether Congress has such *power,* but whether the *means* which it has employed conflict with the First and Fifth Amendments to the Constitution.

One of the bases for the contention that the means which Congress has employed are invalid takes the form of an attack on the face of the statute on the grounds that by its terms it prohibits academic discussion of the merits of Marxism-Leninism, that it stifles ideas and is contrary to all concepts of a free speech and a free press. Although we do not agree that the language itself has that significance, we must bear in mind that it is the duty of the federal courts to interpret federal legislation in a manner not inconsistent with the demands of the Constitution.
. . .

The very language of the Smith Act negates the interpretation which petitioners would have us impose on that Act. It is directed at advocacy, not discussion. Thus, the trial judge properly charged the jury that they could not convict if they found that petitioners did "no more than pursue peaceful studies and discussions or teachings and advocacy in the realm of ideas." He further charged that it was not unlawful "to conduct in an American college or university a course explaining the philosophical theories set forth in the books which have been placed in evidence." Such a charge is in strict accord with the statutory language, and illustrates the meaning to be placed on those words. Congress did not intend to eradicate the free discussion of political theories, to destroy the traditional rights of Americans to discuss and evaluate ideas without fear of governmental sanction. Rather Congress was concerned with the very kind of activity in which the evidence showed these petitioners engaged.

III

But although the statute is not directed at the hypothetical cases which petitioners have conjured, its application in this case has resulted in convictions for the teaching and advocacy of the overthrow of the Government by force and violence, which, even though coupled with the intent to accomplish that overthrow, contains an element of speech. For this reason, we must pay special heed to the demands of the First Amendment marking out the boundaries of speech.

We pointed out in *Douds* . . . that the basis of the First Amendment is the hypothesis that speech can rebut speech, propaganda will answer propaganda, free debate of ideas will result in the wisest governmental policies. It is for this reason that this Court has recognized the inherent value of free discourse. An analysis of the leading cases in this Court which have involved direct limitations on speech, however, will demonstrate that both the majority of the Court and the dissenters in particular cases have recognized that this is not an unlimited, unqualified right,

but that the societal value of speech must, on occasion, be subordinated to other values and considerations.

No important case involving free speech was decided by this Court prior to *Schenck* v. *United States.* . . . Writing for a unanimous Court, Justice Holmes stated that the "question in every case is whether the words are used in such circumstances and are of such a nature as to create a clear and present danger that they will bring about the substantive evils that Congress has a right to prevent." [*The Court here discusses a number of other post-World War I cases that interpreted the "clear and present danger" test.*]

The rule we deduce from these cases is that where an offense is specified by a statute in nonspeech or nonpress terms, a conviction relying upon speech or press as evidence of violation may be sustained only when the speech or publication created a "clear and present danger" of attempting or accomplishing the prohibited crime, *e.g.,* interference with enlistment. The dissents, we repeat, in emphasizing the value of speech, were addressed to the argument of the sufficiency of the evidence.

The next important case before the Court in which free speech was the crux of the conflict was *Gitlow* v. *New York.* . . . There New York had made it a crime to advocate "the necessity or propriety of overthrowing . . . organized government by force. . . ." The evidence of violation of the statute was that the defendant had published a Manifesto attacking the Government and capitalism. The convictions were sustained, Justices Holmes and Brandeis dissenting. The majority refused to apply the "clear and present danger" test to the specific utterance. It's reasoning was as follows: The "clear and present danger" test was applied to the utterance itself in *Schenck* because the question was merely one of sufficiency of evidence under an admittedly constitutional statute. *Gitlow,* however, presented a different question. There a legislature had found that a certain kind of speech was, itself, harmful and unlawful. The constitutionality of such a state statute had to be adjudged by this Court just as it determined the constitutionality of any state statute, namely, whether the statute was "reasonable." Since it was entirely reasonable for a state to attempt to protect itself from violent overthrow, the statute was perforce reasonable. The only question remaining in the case became whether there was evidence to support the conviction, a question which gave the majority no difficulty. Justices Holmes and Brandeis refused to accept this approach, but insisted that whenever speech was the evidence of the violation, it was necessary to show that the speech created the "'clear and present danger" of the substantive evil which the legislature had the right to prevent. Justices Holmes and Brandeis, then, made no distinction between a federal statute which made certain acts unlawful, the evidence to support the conviction being speech, and a statute which made speech itself the crime. This approach was emphasized in *Whitney* v. *California* . . . , where the Court was confronted with a conviction under the California Criminal Syndicalist statute. The Court sustained the conviction, Justices Brandeis and Holmes concurring in the result. In their concurrence they repeated that even though the legislature had designated certain speech as criminal, this could not prevent the defendant from showing that there was no danger that the substantive evil would be brought about.

Although no case subsequent to *Whitney* and *Gitlow* has expressly overruled the majority opinions in those cases, there is little doubt that subsequent opinions have inclined toward the Holmes-Brandeis rationale. . . .

In this case we are squarely presented with the application of the "clear and present danger" test, and must decide what that phrase imports. We first note that many of the cases in which this Court has reversed convictions by use of this or similar tests have been based on the fact that the interest which the State was attempting to protect was itself too insubstantial to warrant restriction of speech. . . . Overthrow of the Government by force and violence is certainly a substantial enough interest for the Government to limit speech. Indeed, this is the ultimate value of any society, for if a society cannot protect its very structure from armed internal attack, it must follow that no subordinate value can be protected. If, then, this interest may be protected, the literal problem which is presented is what has been meant by the use of the phrase "clear and present danger" of the utterances bringing about the evil within the power of Congress to punish.

Obviously, the words cannot mean that before the Government may act, it must wait until the *putsch* is about to be executed, the plans have been laid and the signal is awaited. If Government is aware that a group aiming at its overthrow is attempting to indoctrinate its members and to commit them to a course whereby they will strike when the leaders feel the circumstances permit, action by the Government is required. The argument that there is no need for Government to concern itself, for Government is strong, it possesses ample powers to put down a rebellion, it may defeat the revolution with ease needs no answer. For that is not the question. Certainly an attempt to overthrow the Government by force, even though doomed from the outset because of inadequate numbers or power of the revolutionists, is a sufficient evil for Congress to prevent. The damage which such attempts create both physically and politically to a nation makes it impossible to measure the validity in terms of the probability of success, or the immediacy of a successful attempt. In the instant case the trial judge charged the jury that they could not convict unless they found that petitioners intended to overthrow the Government "as speedily as circumstances would permit." This does not mean, and could not properly mean, that they would not strike until there was certainty of success. What was meant was that the revolutionists would strike when they thought the time was ripe. We must therefore reject the contention that success or probability of success is the criterion.

The situation with which Justices Holmes and Brandeis were concerned in *Gitlow* was a comparatively isolated event, bearing little relation in their minds to any substantial threat to the safety of the community. . . . They were not confronted with any situation comparable to the instant one—the development of an apparatus designed and dedicated to the overthrow of the Government, in the context of world crisis after crisis.

Chief Judge Learned Hand, writing for the majority below, interpreted the phrase as follows: "In each case (courts) must ask whether the gravity of the 'evil,' discounted by its improbability, justifies such invasion of free speech as is necessary to avoid the danger." . . . We adopt this statement of the rule. As articulated by Chief Judge Hand, it is as succinct and inclusive as any other we might devise at this time. It takes into consideration those factors which we deem relevant,

and relates their significances. More we cannot expect from words.

Likewise, we are in accord with the court below, which affirmed the trial court's finding that the requisite danger existed. The mere fact that from the period 1945 to 1948 petitioners' activities did not result in an attempt to overthrow the Government by force and violence is of course no answer to the fact that there was a group that was ready to make the attempt. The formation by petitioners of such a highly organized conspiracy, with rigidly disciplined members subject to call when the leaders, these petitioners, felt that the time had come for action, coupled with the inflammable nature of world conditions, similar uprisings in other countries, and the touch-and-go nature of our relations with countries with whom petitioners were in the very least ideologically attuned, convince us that their convictions were justified on this score. And this analysis disposes of the contention that a conspiracy to advocate, as distinguished from the advocacy itself, cannot be constitutionally restrained, because it comprises only the preparation. It is the existence of the conspiracy which creates the danger. . . . If the ingredients of the reaction are present, we cannot bind the Government to wait until the catalyst is added.

IV

[*The Court here considers whether the trial judge was correct in not submitting to the jury the issue of the existence of clear and present danger.*]

. . . The argument that the action of the trial court is erroneous, in declaring as a matter of law that such violation shows sufficient danger to justify the punishment despite the First Amendment, rests on the theory that a jury must decide a question of the application of the First Amendment. We do not agree.

When facts are found that establish the violation of a statute, the protection against conviction afforded by the First Amendment is a matter of law. The doctrine that there must be a clear and present danger of a substantive evil that congress has a right to prevent is a judicial rule to be applied as a matter of law by the courts. The guilt is established by proof of facts. Whether the First Amendment protects the activity which constitutes the violation of the statute must depend upon a judicial determination of the scope of the First Amendment applied to the circumstances of the case. . . .

V

There remains to be discussed the question of vagueness—whether the statute as we have interpreted it is too vague, not sufficiently advising those who would speak of the limitations upon their activity. It is urged that such vagueness contravenes the First and Fifth Amendments. This argument is particularly nonpersuasive when presented by petitioners, who, the jury found intended to overthrow the Government as speedily as circumstances would permit. . . .

We agree that the standard as defined is not a neat, mathematical formulary. Like all verbalizations it is subject to criticism on the score of indefiniteness. But petitioners themselves contend that the verbalization "clear and present danger" is the proper standard. . . .

We hold that §§2(a)(1), 2(a)(3), and 3 of the Smith Act do not inherently, or as construed or applied in the instant case, violate the First Amendment and other provisions of the Bill of Rights, or the First and Fifth Amendments because of indefiniteness. Petitioners intended to overthrow the

Government of the United States as speedily as the circumstances would permit. Their conspiracy to organize the Communist Party and to teach and advocate the overthrow of the Government of the United States by force and violence created a "clear and present danger" of an attempt to overthrow the Government by force and violence. They were properly and constitutionally convicted for violation of the Smith Act. The judgments of conviction are

Affirmed.

MR. JUSTICE CLARK took no part in the consideration or decision of this case.

MR. JUSTICE FRANKFURTER, concurring in affirmance of the judgment:

. . . Few questions of comparable import have come before this Court in recent years. The appellants maintain that they have a right to advocate a political theory, so long, at least, as their advocacy does not create an immediate danger of obvious magnitude to the very existence of our present scheme of society. On the other hand, the Government asserts the right to safeguard the security of the Nation by such a measure as the Smith Act. Our judgment is thus solicited on a conflict of interests of the utmost concern to the well-being of the country. This conflict of interests cannot be resolved by a dogmatic preference for one or the other, nor by a sonorous formula which is in fact only a euphemistic disguise for an unresolved conflict. If adjudication is to be a rational process, we cannot escape a candid examination of the conflicting claims with full recognition that both are supported by weighty title-deeds.

I

. . . The language of the First Amendment is to be read not as barren words found in a dictionary but as symbols of historic experience illumined by the presuppositions of those who employed them. Not what words did Madison and Hamilton use, but what was it in their minds which they conveyed? Free speech is subject to prohibition of those abuses of expression which a civilized society may forbid. As in the case of every other provision of the Constitution that is not crystallized by the nature of its technical concepts, the fact that the First Amendment is not self-defining and self-enforcing neither impairs its usefulness nor compels its paralysis as a living instrument.

. . . The demands of free speech in a democratic society as well as the interest in national security are better served by candid and informed weighing of the competing interests, within the confines of the judicial process, than by announcing dogmas too inflexible for the non-Euclidian problems to be solved.

But how are competing interests to be assessed? Since they are not subject to quantitative ascertainment, the issue necessarily resolves itself into asking: Who is to make the adjustment?— Who is to balance the relevant factors and ascertain which interest is in the circumstances to prevail? Full responsibility for the choice cannot be given to the courts. Courts are not representative bodies. They are not designed to be a good reflex of a democratic society. Their judgment is best informed, and therefore most dependable, within narrow limits. Their essential quality is detachment, founded on independence. History teaches that the independence of the judiciary is jeopardized when courts become embroiled in the passions of the day and assume primary responsibility in choosing between competing political, economic, and social pressures.

Primary responsibility for adjusting

the interests which compete in the situation before us of necessity belongs to Congress. The nature of the power to be exercised by this Court has been delineated in decisions not charged with the emotional appeal of situations such as that now before us. We are to set aside the judgment of those whose duty it is to legislate only if there is no reasonable basis for it. . . . (W)e must scupulously observe the narrow limits of judicial authority even though self-restraint is alone set over us. Above all we must remember that this Court's power of judicial review is not "an exercise of the powers of a super-legislature. . . ."

II

. . . *First.* Free-speech cases are not an exception to the principle that we are not legislators, that direct policy-making is not our province. How best to reconcile competing interests is the business of legislatures, and the balance they strike is a judgment not to be displaced by ours, but to be respected unless outside the pale of fair judgment. . . .

Second. A survey of the relevant decision indicates that the results which we have reached are on the whole those that would ensue from careful weighing of conflicting interests. The complex issues presented by regulation of speech in public places, by picketing, and by legislation prohibiting advocacy of crime have been resolved by scrutiny of many factors besides the immenence and gravity of the evil threatened. The matter has been well summarized by a reflective student of the Court's work. "The truth is that the clear-and-present-danger test is an oversimplified judgment unless it takes account also of a number of other factors: the relative seriousness of the danger in comparison with the value of the occasion for speech or political activity; the availability of more moderate controls than those which the state has imposed; and perhaps the specific intent with which the speech or activity is launched. No matter how rapidly we utter the phrase 'clear and present danger,' or how closely we hyphenate the words, they are not a substitute for the weighing of values. They tend to convey a delusion of certitude when what is most certain is the complexity of the strands in the web of freedoms which the judge must disentangle. . . ."

Bearing in mind that Mr. Justice Holmes regarded questions under the First Amendment as questions of "proximity and degree," *Schenck* v. *United States* . . . it would be a distortion, indeed a mockery, of his reasoning to compare the "puny anonymities" . . . to which he was addressing himself in the *Abrams* case in 1919, or the publication that was "futile and too remote from possible consequences" . . . in the *Gitlow* case in 1925, with the setting of events in this case in 1950. . . .

III

. . . It is not for us to decide how we would adjust the clash of interests which this case presents were the primary responsibility for reconciling it ours. Congress has determined that the danger created by advocacy of overthrow justifies the ensuing restriction on freedom of speech. The determination was made after due deliberation, and the seriousness of the congressional purpose is attested by the volume of legislation passed to effectuate the same ends.

Can we then say that the judgment Congress exercised was denied it by the Constitution? Can we establish a constitutional doctrine which forbids the elected representatives of the people to

make this choice? Can we hold that the First Amendment deprives Congress of what it deemed necessary for the Government's protection?

To make validity of legislation depend on judicial reading of events still in the womb of time—a forecast, that is, of the outcome of forces at best appreciated only with knowledge of the topmost secrets of nations—is to charge the judiciary with duties beyond its equipment. . . .

MR. JUSTICE JACKSON, concurring:

II

. . . The "clear and present danger" test was an innovation by Mr. Justice Holmes in the *Schenck* case, reiterated and refined by him and Mr. Justice Brandeis in later cases, all arising before the era of World War II revealed the subtlety and efficacy of modernized revolutionary techniques used by totalitarian parties. In those cases, they were faced with convictions under so-called criminal syndicalism statutes aimed at anarchists but which, loosely construed, had been applied to punish socialism, pacifism, and left-wing ideologies, the charges often resting on far-fetched inferences which, if true, would establish only technical or trivial violations. They proposed "clear and present danger" as a test for the sufficiency of evidence in particular cases.

I would save it, unmodified, for application as a "rule of reason" in the kind of case for which it was devised. When the issue is criminality of a hot-headed speech on a street corner, or circulation of a few incendiary pamphlets, or parading by some zealots behind a red flag, or refusal of a handful of school children to salute our flag, it is not beyond the capacity of the judicial process to gather, comprehend, and weigh the necessary materials for decision whether it is a clear and present danger of substantive evil or a harm-less letting off of steam. It is not a prophecy, for the danger in such cases has matured by the time of trial or it was never present. The test applies and has meaning where a conviction is sought to be based on a speech or writing which does not directly or explicitly advocate a crime but to which such tendency is sought to be attributed by construction or by implication from external circumstances. The formula in such cases favors freedoms that are vital to our society, and, even if some-times applied too generously, the con-sequences cannot be grave. But its recent expansion has extended, in par-ticular to Communists, unprecedented immunities. Unless we are to hold our Government captive in a judge-made verbal trap, we must approach the problem of a well-organized, nation-wide conspiracy, such as I have de-scribed, as realistically as our prede-cessors faced the trivialities that were being prosecuted until they were checked with a rule of reason. . . .

If we must decide that this Act and its application are constituted only if we are convinced that petitioner's con-duct creates a "clear and present dan-ger" of violent overthrow, we must appraise imponderables, including inter-national and national phenomena which baffle the best-informed foreign offices and our most experienced politicians. We would have to foresee and predict the effectiveness of Communist prop-aganda, opportunities for infiltration, whether, and when, a time will come that they consider propitious for action, and whether and how fast our existing government will deteriorate. And we would have to speculate as to whether an approaching Communist *coup* would not be anticipated by a nationalistic fascist movement. No doctrine can be sound whose application requires us to

make a prophecy of that sort in the guise of a legal decision. The judicial process simply is not adequate to a trial of such far-flung issues. The answers given would reflect our own political predilections and nothing more.

The authors of the clear and present danger test never applied it to a case like this, nor would I. If applied as it is proposed here, it means that the Communist plotting is protected during its period of incubation; its preliminary stages of organization and preparation are immune from the law; the Govern-ment can move only after imminent action is manifest, when it would, of course, be too late. . . .

IV

What really is under review here is a conviction of conspiracy, after a trial for conspiracy, on an indictment charging conspiracy, brought under a statute outlawing conspiracy. With due respect to my colleagues, they seem to me to discuss anything under the sun except the law of conspiracy. One of the dissenting opinions even appears to chide me for "invoking the law of conspiracy." As that is the case before us, it may be more amazing that its reversal can be proposed without even considering the law of conspiracy. . . .

I do not suggest that Congress could punish conspiracy to advocate some-thing, the doing of which it may not punish. Advocacy or exposition of the doctrine of communal property own-ership, or any political philosophy un-associated with advocacy of its imposi-tion by force or seizure of government by unlawful means could not be reached through conspiracy prosecu-tion. But it is not forbidden to put down force or violence, it is not for-bidden to punish its teaching or ad-vocacy, and the end being punishable, there is no doubt of the power to punish conspiracy for the purpose. . . .

The law of conspiracy has been the chief means at the Government's disposal to deal with the growing problems created by such organizations. . . .

While I think there was power in Congress to enact this statute and that, as applied in this case, it cannot be held unconstitutional, I add that I have little faith in the long-range effectiveness of this conviction to stop the rise of the Communist movement. Communism will not go to jail with these Communists. No decision by this Court can forestall revolution whenever the existing government fails to command the respect and loyalty of the people and sufficient distress and discontent is allowed to grow up among the masses. Many failures by fallen governments attest that no government can long prevent revolution by outlawry. Corruption, ineptitude, inflation, oppressive taxation, militarization, injustice, and loss of leadership capable of intellectual initiative in domestic or foreign affairs are allies on which the Communists count to bring opportunity knocking to their door. Sometimes I think they may be mistaken. But the Communists are not building just for today—the rest of us might profit by their example.

MR. JUSTICE BLACK, dissenting:

. . . At the outset I want to emphasize what the crime involved in this case is, and what it is not. These petitioners were not charged with an attempt to overthrow the Government. They were not charged with overt acts of any kind designed to overthrow the Government. The charge was that they agreed to assemble and to talk and publish certain ideas at a later date. The indictment is that they conspired to organize the Communist Party and to use speech or newspapers and other publications in the future to teach and advocate the forcible overthrow of the Government. No matter how it is worded, this is a virulent form of prior censorship of speech and press, which I believe the First Amendment forbids. I would hold §3 of the Smith Act authorizing this prior restraint unconstitutional on its face and as applied.
. . .

So long as this Court exercises the power of judicial review of legislation, I cannot agree that the First Amendment permits us to sustain laws suppressing freedom of speech and press on the basis of Congress' or our own notions of mere "reasonableness." Such a doctrine waters down the First Amendment so that it amounts to little more than an admonition to Congress. The Amendment as so construed is not likely to protect any but those "safe" or orthodox views which rarely need its protection. . . .

Public opinion being what it now is, few will protest the conviction of these Communist petitioners. There is hope, however, that in calmer times, when present pressures, passions, and fears subside, this or some later Court will restore the First Amendment liberties to the high preferred place where they belong in a free society.

MR. JUSTICE DOUGLAS, dissenting:

If this were a case where those who claimed protection under the First Amendment were teaching the techniques of sabotage, the assassination of the President, the filching of documents from public files, the planting of bombs, the art of street warfare, and the like, I would have no doubts. The freedom to speak is not absolute; the teaching of methods of terror and other seditious conduct should be beyond the pale along with obscenity and immorality. This case was argued as if those were the facts. The argument imported much seditious conduct into the record, That is easy and it has popular appeal, for the activities of Communists in plotting and scheming against the free world are common knowledge. But the fact is that no such evidence was introduced at the trial. There is a statute which makes a seditious conspiracy unlawful. Petitioners, however, were not charged with a "conspiracy to overthrow" the Government. They were charged with a conspiracy to form a party and groups and assemblies of people who teach and advocate the overthrow of our Government by force or violence and with a conspiracy to advocate and teach its overthrow by force and violence. It may well be that indoctrination in the techniques of terror to destroy the Government would be indictable under either statute. But the teaching which is condemned here is of a different character.

So far as the present record is concerned, what petitioners did was to organize people to teach and themselves teach the Marxist-Leninist doctrine contained chiefly in four books: Stalin, *Foundations of Leninism* (1924); Marx and Engels, *Manifesto of the Communist Party* (1848); Lenin, *The State and Revolution* (1917); *History of the Communist Party of the Soviet Union* (B.) (1939).

Those books are to Soviet Communism what *Mein Kampf* was to Nazism. If they are understood, the ugliness of Communism is revealed, its deceit and cunning are exposed, the nature of its activities becomes apparent, and the chances of its success less likely. That is not, of course, the reason why petitioners chose these books for their classrooms. They are fervent Communists to whom these volumes are gospel. They preached the creed with the hope that some day it would be acted upon.

The opinion of the Court does not outlaw these texts nor condemn them to the fire, as the Communists do literature offensive to their creed. But if the books themselves are not outlawed, if they can lawfully remain on library shelves, by what reasoning does their use in a classroom become a crime? It would not be a crime under the Act to introduce these books to a class, though that would be teaching what the creed of violent overthrow of the Government is. The Act, as construed, requires the element of intent—that those who teach the creed believe in it. The crime then depends not on what is taught but on who the teacher is. That is to make freedom of speech turn not on *what is said,* but on the *intent* with which it is said. Once we start down that road we enter territory dangerous to the liberties of every citizen. . . .

The First Amendment provides that "Congress shall make no law . . . abridging the freedom of speech." The Constitution provides no exception. This does not mean, however, that the Nation need hold its hand until it is in such weakened condition that there is no time to protect itself from incitement to revolution. Seditious conduct can always be punished. But the command of the First Amendment is so clear that we should not allow Congress to call a halt to free speech except in the extreme case of peril from the speech itself. The First Amendment makes confidence in the common sense of our people and in their maturity of judgment the great postulate of our democracy. Its philosophy is that violence is rarely, if ever, stopped by denying civil liberties to those advocating resort to force. The First Amendment reflects the philosophy of Jefferson "that it is time enough for the rightful purposes of civil government, for its officers to interfere when principles break out into overt acts against peace and good order." The political censor has no place in our public debates. Unless and until extreme and necessitous circumstances are shown, our aim should be to keep speech unfettered and to allow the processes of law to be invoked only when the provocateurs among us move from speech to action. . . .

. . . Our faith should be that our people will never give support to these advocates of revolution, so long as we remain loyal to the purposes for which our Nation was founded.

ADLER v. BOARD OF EDUCATION
342 U.S. 485; 72 Sup. Ct. 380; 96 L. Ed. 517 (1952)

[*In 1949, the New York State Legislature passed the so-called Feinberg Law, which was designed to disqualify and remove employees and teachers in the public schools who advocated the overthrow of government by unlawful means or who were members of organizations with a like purpose. This legislation did not establish new policy; it was written to implement a 1939 civil service law that denied public employment to anyone who advocated the overthrow of the government by force and violence. The Feinberg Law required the State Board of Regents (1) to promulgate rules for the removal of ineligible public school employees; (2) to draw up a list of subversive organizations; (3) to make membership in any listed organization prima facie evidence of disqualification to hold any position in the public school system. Although no dismissals had been made under the law, Adler and others brought an action to have the statute declared unconstitutional and to enjoin its enforcement by the Board of Education of New York City. A New York State court held the Feinberg Law invalid under the due process clause of the Fourteenth Amendment. A higher court, however, reversed the judgment, and the highest state court affirmed. Adler and others then brought the case to the Supreme Court on appeal.*]

MR. JUSTICE MINTON delivered the opinion of the Court:

. . . It is first argued that the Feinberg Law and the rules promulgated thereunder constitute an abridgment of speech and assembly of persons employed or seeking employment in the public schools of the State of New York.

It is clear that such persons have the right under our law to assemble, speak, think, and believe as they will. . . . It is equally clear that they have no right to work for the State in the school system on their own terms. . . . They may work for the school system upon the reasonable terms laid down by the proper authorities of New York. If they do not choose to work on such terms, they are at liberty to retain their beliefs and associations and go elsewhere. Has the State thus deprived them of any right to free speech or assembly? We think not. Such persons are or may be denied, under the statutes in question, the privilege of working for the school system of the State of New York because first, of their advocacy of the overthrow of the government by force or violence, or secondly, by unexplained membership in an organization found by the school authorities, after notice and hearing, to teach and advocate the overthrow of the government by force or violence, and known by such persons to have such purpose.

The constitutionality of the first proposition is not questioned here. . . .

As to the second, it is rather subtly suggested that we should not follow our recent decision in *Garner* v. *Los Angeles Board of Public Works.* 341 U.S. 716. . . . We there said:

> "We think that a municipal employer is not disabled because it is an agency of the State from inquiring of its employees as to matters that may prove relevant to their fitness and suitability for the public service. Past conduct may well relate to present fitness; past loyalty may have a reasonable relationship to present and future trust. Both are commonly inquired into in determining fitness for both high and low positions in private industry and are not less relevant in public employment."

. . . We adhere to that case. A teacher works in a sensitive area in a schoolroom. There he shapes the attitude of young minds towards the society in which they live. In this, the state has a vital concern. It must preserve the integrity of the schools. That the school authorities have the right and the duty to screen the officials, teachers, and employees as to their fitness to maintain the integrity of the schools as a part of ordered society, cannot be doubted. One's associates, past and present, as well as one's conduct, may properly be considered in determining fitness and loyalty. From time immemorial, one's reputation has been determined in part by the company he keeps. In the employment of officials and teachers of the school system, the state may very properly inquire into the company they keep, and we know of no rule, constitutional or

otherwise, that prevents the state, when determining the fitness and loyalty of such persons, from considering the organizations and persons with whom they associate.

If, under the procedure set up in the New York law, a person is found to be unfit and is disqualified from employment in the public school system because of membership in a listed organization, he is not thereby denied the right of free speech and assembly. His freedom of choice between membership in the organization and employment in the school system might be limited, but not his freedom of speech or assembly, except in the remote sense that limitation is inherent in every choice. Certainly such limitation is not one the state may not make in the exercise of its police power to protect the schools from pollution and thereby to defend its own existence.

It is next argued by appellants that the provision in §3022 directing the Board of Regents to provide in rules and regulations that membership in any organization listed by the Board after notice and hearing, with provision for review in accordance with the statute, shall constitute prima-facie evidence of disqualification, denies due process, because the fact found bears no relation to the fact presumed. In other words, from the fact found that the organization was one that advocated the overthrow of government by unlawful means and that the person employed or to be employed was a member of the organization and knew of its purpose, to presume that such member is disqualified for employment is so unreasonable as to be a denial of due process of law. We do not agree.

The law of evidence is full of presumptions either of fact or law. The former are, of course, disputable, and the strength of any inference of one fact from proof of another depends upon the generality of the experience upon which it is founded. . . .

Legislation providing that proof of one fact shall constitute prima-facie evidence of the main fact in issue is but to enact a rule of evidence, and quite within the general power of government. Statutes, National and state, dealing with such methods of proof in both civil and criminal cases abound, and the decisions upholding them are numerous." *Mobile, J. & K. C. R. Co. v. Turnipseed,* 219 U.S. 35 at page 42. . . .

Membership in a listed organization found to be within the statute and known by the member to be within the statute is a legislative finding that the member by his membership supports the thing the organization stands for, namely, the overthrow of government by unlawful means. We cannot say that such a finding is contrary to fact or that "generality of experience" points to a different conclusion. Disqualification follows therefore as a reasonable presumption from such membership and support. Nor is there here a problem of procedural due process. The presumption is not conclusive but arises only in a hearing where the person against whom it may arise has full opportunity to rebut it. . . .

Where, as here, the relation between fact found and the presumption is clear and direct and is not conclusive, the requirements of due process are satisfied. . . .

It is also suggested that the use of the word "subversive" is vague and indefinite. But the word is first used in §1 of the Feinberg Law, which is the preamble to definite meaning, namely, an organization that teaches and advocates the overthrow of government by force or violence.

We find no constitutional infirmity in §12-a of the Civil Service Law of New York or in the Feinberg Law which implemented it, and the judgment is

Affirmed.

MR. JUSTICE BLACK, dissenting:

While I fully agree with the dissent of Mr. Justice Douglas, the importance of this holding prompts me to add these thoughts.

This is another of those rapidly multiplying legislative enactments which make it dangerous—this time for school teachers—to think or say anything except what a transient majority happen to approve at the moment. Basically these laws rest on the belief that government should supervise and limit the flow of ideas into the minds of men. The tendency of such governmental policy is to mold people into a common intellectual pattern. Quite a different governmental policy rests on the belief that government should leave the mind and spirit of man absolutely free. Such a governmental policy encourages varied intellectual outlooks in the belief that the best views will prevail. This policy of freedom is in my judgment embodied in the First Amendment and made applicable to the states by the Fourteenth. Because of this policy public officials cannot be constitutionally vested with powers to select the ideas people can think about, censor the public views they can express, or choose the persons or groups people can associate with. Public officials with such powers are not public servants; they are public masters.

I dissent from the Court's judgment sustaining this law which effectively penalizes school teachers for their thoughts and their associates.

MR. JUSTICE DOUGLAS, with whom MR. JUSTICE BLACK concurs, dissenting:

I have not been able to accept the recent doctrine that a citizen who enters the public service can be forced to sacrifice his civil rights. I cannot for example find in our constitutional scheme the power of a state to place its employees in the category of second-class citizens by denying them freedom of thought and expression. The Constitutional guarantees freedom of thought and expression to everyone in our society. All are entitled to it; and none needs it more than the teacher.

The public school is in most respects the cradle of our democracy. The increasing role of the public school is seized upon by proponents of the type of legislation represented by New York's Feinberg Law as proof of the importance and need for keeping the school free of "subversive influences." But that is to misconceive the effect of this type of legislation. Indeed the impact of this kind of censorship on the public school system illustrates the high purpose of the First Amendment in freeing speech and thought from censorship.

The present law proceeds on a principle repugnant to our society—guilt by association. A teacher is disqualified because of her membership in an organization found to be "subversive." The finding as to the "subversive" character of the organization is made in a proceeding to which the teacher is not a party and in which it is not clear that she may even be heard. To be sure she may have a hearing when charges of disloyalty are leveled against her. But in that hearing the finding as to the "subversive" character of the organization apparently may not be reopened in order to allow her to show the truth of the matter. The irrebuttable charge that the organization is "subversive" therefore hangs as an ominous cloud over her own hearing. The mere fact of membership in the organization raises a primi facie case of her own guilt. She may, it is said, show her

innocence. But innocence in this case turns on knowledge; and when the witch hunt is on, one who must rely on ignorance leans on a feeble reed.

The very threat of such a procedure is certain to raise havoc with academic freedom. Youthful indiscretions mistaken causes, misguided enthusiasms—all long forgotten—become the ghosts of harrowing present. Any organization committed to a liberal cause, any group organized to revolt against a hysterical trend, any committee launched to sponsor an unpopular program becomes suspect. These are the organizations into which Communists often infiltrate. Their presence infects the whole, even though the project was not conceived in sin. A teacher caught in that mesh is almost certain to stand condemned. Fearing condemnation, she will tend to shrink from any association that stirs controversy. In that manner freedom of expression will be stifled.

But that is only part of it. Once a teacher's connection with a listed organization is shown, her views become subject to scrutiny to determine whether her membership in the organization is innocent or, if she was formerly a member, whether she has bona fide abandoned her membership.

The law inevitably turns the school system into a spying project. Regular loyalty reports on the teachers must be made out. The principals become detectives; the students, the parents, the community become informers. Ears are cocked for telltale signs of disloyalty. The prejudices of the community come into play in searching out the disloyal. This is not the usual type of supervision which checks a teacher's competency; it is a system which searches for hidden meanings in a teacher's utterances.

What was the significance of the reference of the art teacher to socialism? Why was the history teacher so openly hostile to Franco Spain? Who heard overtones of revolution in the English teacher's discussion of *Grapes of Wrath*? What was behind the praise of Soviet progress in metallurgy in the chemistry class? Was it not "subversive" for the teacher to cast doubt on the wisdom of the venture in Korea?

What happens under this law is typical of what happens in a police state. Teachers are under constant surveillance; their pasts are combed for signs of disloyalty; their utterances are watched for clues to dangerous thoughts. A pall is cast over the classrooms. There can be no real academic freedom in that environment. Where suspicion fills the air and holds scholars in line for fear of their jobs, there can be no exercise of the free intellect. Supineness and dogmatism take the place of inquiry. A "party line"—as dangerous as the "party line" of the Communists—lays hold. It is the "party line" of the orthodox view, of the conventional thought, of the accepted approach. A problem can no longer be pursued with impunity to its edges. Fear stalks the classroom. The teacher is no longer a stimulant to adventurous thinking; she becomes instead a pipeline for safe and sound information. A deadening dogma takes the place of free inquiry. Instruction tends to become sterile; pursuit of knowledge is discouraged; discussion often leaves off where it should begin.

This, I think, is what happens when a censor looks over a teacher's shoulder. This system of spying and surveillance with its accompanying reports and

trials cannot go hand in hand with academic freedom. It produces standardized thought, not the pursuit of truth which the First Amendment was designed to protect. A system which directly or inevitably has that effect is alien to our system and should be struck down. Its survival is a real threat to our way of life. We need be bold and adventuresome in our thinking to survive. A school system producing students trained as robots threatens to rob a generation of the versatility that has been perhaps our greatest distinction. The Framers knew the danger of dogmatism; they also knew the strength that comes when the mind is free, when ideas may be pursued wherever they lead. We forget these teachings of the First Amendment when we sustain this law.

Of course the school systems of the country need not become cells for Communist activities; and the classrooms need not become forums for propagandizing the Marxist creed. But the guilt of the teacher should turn on overt acts. So long as she is a law-abiding citizen, so long as her performance within the public school system meets professional standards, her private life, her political philosophy, her social creed should not be the cause of reprisals against her.

[MR. JUSTICE FRANKFURTER also dissented but on different grounds. *Because the scheme (including the Feinberg Law) was still in the blueprint stage, he would decline jurisdiction to "avoid constitutional adjudications on merely abstract or speculative issues."*]

WATKINS v. UNITED STATES
354 U.S. 178, 77 Sup. Ct. 1273, 1 L. Ed. 2d 1273 (1957)

[*In 1954, John T. Watkins, a labor official, was called as a witness before a Subcommittee of the Committee on Un-American Activities of the House of Repre-*

sentatives. Before the committee, Watkins answered questions about his past activities freely and admitted cooperating with the Communist party between 1942 and 1947. However, he refused to answer questions about associates who might have been members of the Communist party in the past. Watkins explained his refusal to answer as follows: "I do not believe that such questions are relevant to the work of this committee nor do I believe that this committee has the right to undertake the public exposure of persons because of their past activities."

The committee and the House of Representatives cited Watkins for contempt. The Justice Department obtained an indictment against him after the House directed that a criminal prosecution be initiated. Watkins was found guilty in a federal district court and was fined $100 and sentenced to a year in prison. However, the sentence was suspended and Watkins was placed on probation. A court of appeals affirmed the conviction. Watkins then brought the case to the Supreme Court on certiorari.]

MR. CHIEF JUSTICE WARREN delivered the opinion of the Court:

. . . We start with several basic premises on which there is general agreement. The power of the Congress to conduct investigations is inherent in the legislative process. That power is broad. It encompasses inquiries concerning the administration of existing laws as well as proposed or possibly needed statutes. It includes surveys of defects in our social, economic, or political system for the purpose of enabling the Congress to remedy them. It comprehends probes into departments of the Federal Government to expose corruption, inefficiency, or waste. But broad as is this power of inquiry, it is not unlimited. There is no general authority to expose the private affairs of individuals without justification in terms of the functions of the Congress. This was freely conceded by the Solicitor General in his argument of this case. Nor is the Congress a law enforcement or trial agency. These are functions of the executive and judicial departments of government. No inquiry is an end in itself; it must be related to and in furtherance of a legitimate task of the Congress. Investigations conducted solely for the personal aggrandizement

of the investigators or to "punish" those investigated are indefensible.

It is unquestionably the duty of all citizens to cooperate with the Congress in its efforts to obtain the facts needed for intelligent legislative action. It is their unremitting obligation to respond to subpoenas, to respect the dignity of the Congress and its committees, and to testify fully with respect to matters within the province of proper investigation. This, of course, assumes that the constitutional rights of witnesses will be respected by the Congress as they are in a court of justice. The Bill of Rights is applicable to investigations as to all forms of governmental action. Witnesses cannot be compelled to give evidence against themseves. They cannot be subjected to unreasonable search and seizure. Nor can the First Amendment freedoms of speech, press, religion, or political belief and association be abridged. . . .

In the decade following World War II, there appeared a new kind of congressional inquiry unknown in prior periods of American history. Principally this was the result of the various investigations into the threat of subversion of the United States Government, but other subjects of congressional interest also contributed to the changed scene. This new phase of legislative inquiry involved a broad-scale intrusion into the lives and affairs of private citizens. It brought before the courts novel questions of the appropriate limits of congressional inquiry. Prior cases . . . had defined the scope of investigative power in terms of the inherent limitations of the sources of that power. In the more recent cases, the emphasis shifted to problems of accommodating the interest of the Government with the rights and privileges of individuals. The central theme was the application of the Bill of Rights as a restraint upon the assertion of governmental power in this form. . . .

. . . The theory of a committee inquiry is that the committee members are serving as the representatives of the parent assembly in collecting information for a legislative purpose. Their function is to act as the eyes and ears of the Congress in obtaining facts upon which the full legislature can act. To carry out this mission, committees and subcommittees, sometimes one Congressman, are endowed with the full power of the Congress to compel testimony. . . .

An essential premise in this situation is that the House or Senate shall have instructed the committee members on what they are to do with the power delegated to them. It is the responsibility of the Congress, in the first instance, to insure that compulsory process is used only in furtherance of a legislative purpose. That requires that the instructions to an investigating committee spell out that group's jurisdiction and purpose with sufficient particularity. Those instructions are embodied in the authorizing resolution. That document is the committee's charter. Broadly drafted and loosely worded,

however, such resolutions can leave tremendous latitude to the discretion of the investigators. The more vague the committee's charter is, the greater becomes the possibility that the committee's specific actions are not in conformity with the will of the parent House of Congress.

The authorizing resolution of the Un-American Activities Committee was adopted in 1938 when a select committee, under the chairmanship of Representative Dies, was created. Several years later, the Committee was made a standing organ of the House with the same mandate. It defines the Committee's authority as follows:

The Committee on Un-American Activities, as a whole or by subcommittee, is authorized to make from time to time investigations of (i) the extent, character, and objects of un-American propaganda activities in the United States, (ii) the diffusion within the United States of subversive and un-American propaganda that is instigated from foreign countries or of a domestic origin and attacks the principle of the form of government as guaranteed by our Constitution, and (iii) all other questions in relation thereto that would aid Congress in any necessary remedial legislation.

It would be difficult to imagine a less explicit authorizing resolution. Who can define the meaning of "un-American"? What is that single, solitary "principle of the form of government as guaranteed by our Constitution"? There is no need to dwell upon the language, however. At one time, perhaps, the resolution might have been read narrowly to confine the Committee to the subject of propaganda. The events that have transpired in the fifteen years before the interrogation of petitioner make such a construction impossible at this date.

The members of the Committee have clearly demonstrated that they did not feel themselves restricted in any way to propaganda in the narrow sense of the word. Unquestionably the Committee conceived of its task in the grand view of its name. Un-American activities were its target, no matter how or where manifested. Notwithstanding the broad purview of the Committee's experience, the House of Representatives repeatedly approved its continuation. Five times it extended the life of the special committee. Then it made the group a standing committee of the House. A year later, the Committee's charter was embodied in the Legislative Reorganization Act. On five occasions, at the beginning of sessions of Congress, it has made the authorizing resolution part of the rules of the House. On innumerable occasions, it has passed appropriation bills to allow the Committee to continue its efforts.

Combining the language of the resolution with the construction it has been given, it is evident that the preliminary control of the Committee exercised by the House of Representatives is slight or nonexistent. No one could reasonably deduce from the charter the kind of investigation that the Committee was directed to make. As a result, we are asked to engage in a process of retroactive rationalization. Looking backward from the events that transpired, we are asked to uphold the Committee's actions unless it appears that they were clearly not authorized by the charter. As a corollary to this inverse approach, the Government urges that we must view the matter hospitably to the power of the Congress—that if there is any legislative purpose which might have

been furthered by the kind of disclosure sought, the witness must be punished for withholding it. No doubt every reasonable indulgence of legality must be accorded to the actions of a coordinate branch of our Government. But such deference cannot yield to an unnecessary and unreasonable dissipation of precious constitutional freedoms.

The Government contends that the public interest at the core of the investigations of the Un-American Activities Committee is the need by the Congress to be informed of efforts to overthrow the Government by force and violence so that adequate legislative safeguards can be erected. From this core, however, the Committee can radiate outward infinitely to any topic thought to be related in some way to armed insurrection. The outer reaches of this domain are known only by the content of "un-American activities." Remoteness of subject can be aggravated by a probe for a depth of detail even farther removed from any basis of legislative action. A third dimension is added when the investigators turn their attention to the past to collect minutiae on remote topics, on the hypothesis that the past may reflect upon the present.

The consequences that flow from this situation are manifold. In the first place, a reviewing court is unable to make the kind of judgment made by the Court in *United States* v. *Rumely*. . . . The Committee is allowed, in essence, to define its own authority, to choose the direction and focus of its activities. In deciding what to do with the power that has been conferred upon them, members of the Committee may act pursuant to motives that seem to them to be the highest. Their decisions, nevertheless, can lead to ruthless exposure of private lives in order to gather data that is neither desired by the Congress nor useful to it. Yet it is impossible in this circumstance, with constitutional freedoms in jeopardy, to declare that the Committee has ranged beyond the area committed to it by its parent assembly because the boundaries are so nebulous.

More important and more fundamental than that, however, it insulates the House that has authorized the investigation from the witnesses who are subjected to the sanctions of compulsory process. There is a wide gulf between the responsibility for the use of investigative power and the actual exercise of that power. This is an especially vital consideration in assuring respect for constitutional liberties. Protected freedoms should not be placed in danger in the absence of a clear determination by the House or the Senate that a particular inquiry is justified by a specific legislative need.

It is, of course, not the function of this Court to prescribe rigid rules for the Congress to follow in drafting resolutions establishing investigating committees. That is a matter peculiarly within the realm of the legislature, and its decisions will be accepted by the courts up to the point where their own duty to enforce the constitutionally protected rights of individuals is affected. An excessively broad charter, like that of the House Un-American Activities Committee, places the courts in an untenable position if they are to strike a balance between the public need for a particular interrogation and the right of citizens to carry on their affairs free from unnecessary governmental interference. It is impossible in such a situation to ascertain whether any legislative purpose justifies the disclosures sought and, if so, the importance of that information to the Congress in furtherance of its legislative function. The reason no court can make

this critical judgment is that the House of Representatives itself has never made it. Only the legislative assembly initiating an investigation can assay the relative necessity of specific disclosures.

Absence of the qualitative consideration of petitioner's questioning by the House of Representatives aggravates a serious problem, revealed in this case, in the relationship of congressional investigating committees and the witnesses who appear before them. Plainly these communities are restricted to the missions delegated to them, i.e., to acquire certain data to be used by the House or the Senate in coping with a problem that falls within its legislative sphere. No witness can be compelled to make disclosures on matters outside that area. This is a jurisdictional concept of pertinency drawn from the nature of a congressional committee's source of authority. . . .

The problem attains proportion when viewed from the standpoint of the witness who appears before a congressional committee. He must decide at the time the questions are propounded whether or not to answer. . . . He is ". . . bound rightly to construe the statute." . . . An erroneous determination on his part, even if made in the utmost good faith, does not exculpate him if the court should later rule that the questions were pertinent to the question under inquiry.

It is obvious that a person compelled to make this choice is entitled to have knowledge of the subject to which the interrogation is deemed pertinent. That knowledge must be available with the same degree of explicitness and clarity that the Due Process Clause requires in the expression of any element of a criminal offense. The "vice of vagueness" must be avoided here as in all other crimes. There are several sources that can outline the "question under inquiry" in such a way that the rules against vagueness are satisfied. The authorizing resolution, the remarks of the chairman or members of the committee, or even the nature of the proceedings themselves might sometimes make the topic clear. This case demonstrates, however, that these sources often leave the matter in grave doubt. . . .

[W]e remain unenlightened as to the subject to which the questions asked petitioner were pertinent. Certainly, if the point is that obscure after trial and appeal, it was not adequately revealed to petitioner when he had to decide at his peril whether or not to answer. Fundamental fairness demands that no witness be compelled to make such a determination with so little guidance. Unless the subject matter has been made to appear with undisputable clarity, it is the duty of the investigative body, upon objection of the witness on grounds of pertinency, to state for the record the subject under inquiry at that time and the manner in which the propounded questions are pertinent thereto. To be meaningful, the explanation must describe what the topic under inquiry is and the connective reasoning whereby the precise questions asked relate to it.

The statement of the Committee Chairman in this case, in response to petitioner's protest, was woefully inadequate to convey sufficient information as to the pertinency of the questions to the subject under inquiry. Petitioner was thus not accorded a fair opportunity to determine whether he was within his rights in refusing to answer, and his conviction is necessarily invalid under the Due Process Clause of the Fifth Amendment.

We are mindful of the complexities of modern government and the ample scope that must be left to the Congress as the sole constitutional depository of legislative power. Equally mindful are we of the indispensable function, in the exercise of that power, of congressional investigations. The conclusions we have reached in this case will not prevent the Congress, through its committees, from obtaining any information it needs for the proper fulfillment of this role in our scheme of government. The legislature is free to determine the kinds of data that should be collected. It is only those investigations that are conducted by use of compulsory process that give rise to a need to protect the rights of individuals against illegal encroachment. That protection can be readily achieved through procedures which prevent the separation of power from responsibility and which provide the constitutional requisites of fairness for witnesses. A measure of added care on the part of the House and the Senate in authorizing the use of compulsory process and by their committees in exercising that power would suffice. That is a small price to pay if it serves to uphold the principles of limited, constitutional government without constricting the power of the Congress to inform itself.

The judgment of the Court of Appeals is reversed, and the case is remanded to the District Court with instructions to dismiss the indictment.

It is so ordered.

MR. JUSTICE BURTON and MR. JUSTICE WHITTAKER took no part in the consideration or decision of this case. [JUSTICE FRANKFURTER wrote a concurring opinion.]

MR. JUSTICE CLARK, dissenting:

As I see it the chief fault in the majority opinion is its mischievous curbing of the informing function of the Congress. While I am not versed in its procedures, my experience in the executive branch of the Government leads me to believe that the requirements laid down in the opinion for the operation of the committee system of inquiry are both unnecessary and unworkable. . . .

. . . The majority has substituted the judiciary as the grand inquisitor and supervisor of congressional investigations.

YATES v. UNITED STATES
354 U.S. 298; 77 Sup. Ct. 1064, 1 L. Ed. 2d 1356 (1957)

[*Oleta O'Connor Yates and thirteen other leaders and organizers of the Communist party on the West Coast were charged with violation of the two sections of the Smith Act of 1940, which are reproduced, in part, in the preceding* Dennis *case. As in the* Dennis *case, the fourteen leaders were charged with conspiracy to violate the Smith Act by knowingly and willfully (1) teaching and advocating the violent overthrow of the government of the United States and (2) organizing the Communist party, a society that teaches or advocates violent overthrow of the government. All fourteen leaders were convicted in a federal district court, and each was sentenced to five years' imprisonment and a fine of $10,000. The convictions were affirmed in a court of appeals. The Supreme Court then granted certiorari.*]

MR. JUSTICE HARLAN delivered the opinion of the Court:

We brought these cases here to consider certain questions arising under the Smith Act which have not heretofore been passed upon by this Court, and otherwise to review the convictions of these petitioners for conspiracy to violate that Act. Among other things, the convictions are claimed to rest upon an application of the Smith Act which is hostile to the principles upon which its constitutionality was upheld in *Dennis* v. *United States*. . . .

In the view we take of this case, it is necessary for us to consider only the following of petitioners' contentions: (1) that the term "organize" as used in the Smith Act was erroneously construed by the two lower courts; (2) that the trial court's instructions to the jury erroneously excluded from the case the issue of "incitement to action"; (3) that the evidence was so insufficient as to require this Court to direct the acquittal of these petitioners. . . . For reasons given hereafter, we concluded

that these convictions must be reversed and the case remanded to the District Court with instructions to enter judgments of acquittal as to certain of the petitioners, and to grant a new trial as to the rest. . . .

Petitioners claim that "organize" means to "establish," "found," or "bring into existence," and that in this sense the Communist Party was organized by 1945 at the latest. On this basis petitioners contend that this part of the indictment, returned in 1951, was barred by the three-year statute of limitations. The Government, on the other hand, says that "organize" connotes a continuing process which goes on throughout the life of an organization, and that, in the words of the trial court's instructions to the jury, the term includes such things as "the recruiting of new members and the forming of new units, and the regrouping or expansion of existing clubs, classes, and other units of any society, party, group or other organization." The two courts below accepted the Government's position. We think, however, that petitioners' position must prevail. . . .

The statute does not define what is meant by "organize." Dictionary definitions are of little help, for, as those offered us sufficiently show, the term is susceptible of both meanings attributed to it by the parties here. The fact that the Communist Party comprises various components and activities, in relation to which some of the petitioners bore the title of "Organizer," does not advance us towards a solution of the problem. The charge here is that petitioners conspired to organize the Communist Party, and, unless "organize" embraces the continuing concept contended for by the Government, the establishing of new units within the Party and similar activities, following the Party's initial formation in 1945, have no independent significance or vitality so far as the "organizing" charge is involved. Nor are we here concerned with the quality of petitioners' activities as such, that is, whether particular activities may properly be categorized as "organizational." Rather, the issue is whether the term "organize" as used in this statute is limited by temporal concepts. Stated most simply, the problem is to choose between two possible answers to the question: when was the Communist Party "organized"? Petitioners contend that the only natural answer to the question is the formation date—in this case, 1945. The Government would have us answer the question by saying that the Party today is still not completely "organized"; that "organizing" is a continuing process that does not end until the entity is dissolved.

The legislature of the Smith Act is no more revealing as to what Congress meant by "organize" than is the statute itself. . . .

We are thus left to determine for ourselves the meaning of this provision of the Smith Act, without any revealing guides as to the intent of Congress. In these circumstances we should follow the familiar rule that criminal statutes are to be strictly construed and give to "organize" its narrow meaning, that is, that the word refers only to acts entering into the creation of a new organization, and not to acts thereafter performed in carrying on its activities, even though such acts may loosely be termed "organizational." . . . Such indeed is the normal usage of the word "organize," and until the decisions below in this case the federal trial courts in which the question had arisen uniformly gave it that meaning. . . . We too think this statute should be read "according to the natural and obvious import of the language, without resorting to subtle and forced construction for the purpose of either limiting or extending its operation."

. . . We conclude, therefore, that since the Communist Party came into being in 1945, and the indictment was not returned until 1951, the three-year statute of limitations had run on the "organizing" charge, and required the withdrawal of that part of the indictment from the jury's consideration. . . .

II. INSTRUCTIONS TO THE JURY

Petitioners contend that the instructions to the jury were fatally defective in that the trial court refused to charge that, in order to convict, the jury must find that the advocacy which the defendants conspired to promote was of a kind calculated to "incite" persons to action for the forcible overthrow of the Government. It is argued that advocacy of forcible overthrow as mere *abstract doctrine* is within the free-speech protection of the First Amendment; that the Smith Act, consistently with that constitutional provision, must be taken as proscribing only the sort of advocacy which incites to illegal *action;* and that the trial court's charge, by permitting conviction for mere advocacy, unrelated to its tendency to produce forcible action, resulted in an unconstitutional application of the Smith Act. The Government, which at the trial also requested the court to charge in terms of "incitement," now takes the position, however, that the true constitutional dividing line is not between inciting and abstract advocacy of forcible overthrow, but rather between advocacy as such, irrespective of its inciting qualities, and the mere discussion or exposition of violent overthrow as an abstract theory. . . .

We are thus faced with the question whether the Smith Act prohibits advocacy and teaching of forcible overthrow as an abstract principle, divorced from any effort to instigate action to that end, so long as such advocacy or teaching is engaged in with evil intent. We hold that it does not.

The distinction between advocacy of abstract doctrine and advocacy directed at promoting unlawful action is one that has been consistently recognized in the opinions of this Court. . . .

We need not, however, decide the issue before us in terms of constitutional compulsion, for our first duty is to construe this statute. . . . The legislative history of the Smith Act and related bills shows beyond all question that Congress was aware of the distinction between the advocacy or teaching of abstract doctrine and the advocacy or teaching of action, and that it did not intend to disregard it. The statute was aimed at the advocacy and teaching of concrete action for the forcible overthrow of the Government, and not of principles divorced from action.

The Government's reliance on this Court's decision in *Dennis* is misplaced. The jury instructions which were refused here were given there, and were referred to by this Court as requiring "the jury to find the facts *essential* to establish the substantive crime."

. . . In failing to distinguish between advocacy of forcible overthrow as an abstract doctrine and advocacy of action to that end, the District Court appears to have been led astray by the holding in *Dennis* that advocacy of violent action to be taken at some future time was enough. It seems to have considered that, since "inciting" speech is usually thought of as calculated to induce immediate action, and since *Dennis* held advocacy of action for future overthrow sufficient, this meant that advocacy, irrespective of its tendency to generate action, is punishable, provided only that it is uttered with a specific intent to accomplish overthrow. In other words, the District Court apparently thought that *Dennis* obliterated the traditional dividing line between advocacy of abstract doctrine and advocacy of action.

This misconceives the situation confronting the Court in *Dennis* and what was held there. Although the jury's verdict, interpreted in light of the trial court's instructions, did not justify the conclusion that the defendants' advocacy was directed at, or created any danger of, immediate overthrow, it did establish that the advocacy was aimed at building up a seditious group and maintaining it in readiness for action at a propitious time. In such circumstances, said Chief Justice Vinson, the Government need not hold its hand "until the putsch is about to be executed, the plans have been laid, and the signal is awaited. If Government is aware that a group aiming at its overthrow is attempting to indoctrinate its members and commit them to a course whereby they will strike when the leaders feel the circumstances permit, action by the Government is required." . . . The essence of the *Dennis* holding was that indoctrination of a group in preparation for future violent action, as well as exhortation to immediate action, by advocacy found to be directed to "action for the accomplishment" of forcible overthrow, to violence "as a rule or principle of action," and employing "language of incitement," . . . is not constitutionally protected when the group is of sufficient size and cohesiveness, is sufficiently oriented towards action, and other circumstances are such as reasonably to justify apprehension that action will occur. This is quite a different thing from the view of the District Court here that mere doctrinal justification of forcible overthrow, is punishable *per se* under the Smith Act. That sort of advocacy, even though uttered with the hope that it may ultimately lead to violent revolution, is too remote from concrete action to be regarded as the kind of indoctrination preparatory to action which was condemned in *Dennis*. . . .

We recognize that distinctions between advocacy or teaching of abstract doctrines, with evil intent, and that which is directed to stirring people to action, are often subtle and difficult to grasp, for in a broad sense, as Mr. Justice Holmes said in his dissenting opinion in *Gitlow*, . . . "Every idea is an incitement." But the very subtlety of these distinctions required the most clear and explicit instructions with reference to them, for they concerned an issue which went to the very heart of the charges against these petitioners. The need for precise and understandable instructions on this issue is further emphasized by the equivocal character of the evidence in this record, with

which we deal in Part III of this opinion. Instances of speech that could be considered to amount to "advocacy of action" are so few and far between as to be almost completely overshadowed by the hundreds of instances in the record in which overthrow, if mentioned at all, occurs in the course of doctrinal disputation so remote from action as to be almost wholly lacking in probative value. Vague references to "revolutionary" or "militant" action of an unspecified character, which are found in the evidence, might in addition be given too great weight by the jury in the absence of more precise instructions. Particularly in light of this record, we must regard the trial court's charge in this respect as furnishing wholly inadequate guidance to the jury on this central point in the case. We cannot allow a conviction to stand on such "an equivocal direction to the jury on a basic issue." . . .

III. THE EVIDENCE

The determinations already made require a reversal of these convictions. Nevertheless, . . . we have conceived it to be our duty to scrutinize this lengthy record with care, in order to determine whether the way should be left open for a new trial of all or some of these petitioners. Such a judgment, we think, should, on the one hand, foreclose further proceedings against those of the petitioners as to whom the evidence in this record would be palpably insufficient upon a new trial, and should, on the other hand, leave the Government free to retry the other petitioners under proper legal standards, especially since it is by no means clear that certain aspects of the evidence against them could not have been clarified to the advantage of the Government had it not been under a misapprehension as to the burden cast upon it by the Smith Act. . . . [W]e have scrutinized the record to see whether there are individuals as to whom acquittal is unequivocally demanded. We do this because it is in general too hypothetical and abstract an inquiry to try to judge whether the evidence would have been inadequate had the cases been submitted under a proper charge, and had the Government realized that all its evidence must be channeled into the "advocacy" rather than the "organizing" charge. . . .

On this basis we have concluded that the evidence against petitioners Connelly, Kusnitz, Richmond, Spector, and Steinberg is so clearly insufficient that their acquittal should be ordered, but that as to petitioners Carlson, Dobbs, Fox, Healey (Mrs. Connelly), Lambert, Lima, Schneiderman, Stack, and Yates, we would not be justified in closing the way to their retrial. . . .

At the outset, in view of the conclusions reached in Part I of this opinion, we must put aside as against all petitioners the evidence relating to the "organizing" aspect of the alleged conspiracy, except in so far as it bears upon the "advocacy" charge. That, indeed, dilutes in a substantial way a large part of the evidence, for the record unmistakably indicates that the Government relied heavily on its "organizing" charge. The first is that both the Government and the trial court evidently proceeded on the theory that advocacy of abstract doctrine was enough to offend the Smith Act, whereas, as we have held, it is only advocacy of forcible action that is proscribed. The second observation is that both the record and the Government's brief in this Court make it clear that the Government's thesis was that the Communist Party, or at least the Communist Party of California, constituted the conspiratorial group, and that membership in the conspiracy could therefore be proved by showing that the individual petitioners were actively identified with the Party's affairs and thus inferentially parties to its tenets. This might have been well enough towards making out the Government's case if advocacy of the abstract doctrine of forcible overthrow satisfied the Smith Act, for we would at least have little difficulty in saying on this record that a jury could justifiably conclude that such was one of the tenets of the Communist Party; and there was no dispute as to petitioners' active identification with Party affairs. But when it comes to Party advocacy or teaching in the sense of a call to forcible action at some future time we cannot but regard this record as strikingly deficient. At best this voluminous record shows but a half dozen or so scattered incidents which, even under the loosest standards, could not be deemed to show such advocacy. Most of these were not connected with any of the petitioners, or occurred many years before the period covered by the indictment. We are unable to regard this sporadic showing as sufficient to justify viewing the Communist Party as the nexus between these petitioners and the conspiracy charged. We need scarcely say that however much one may abhor even the abstract preaching of forcible overthrow of government, or believe that forcible overthrow is the ultimate purpose to which the Communist Party is dedicated, it is upon the evidence in the record that the petitioners must be judged in this case.

We must, then, look elsewhere than to the evidence concerning the Communist Party as such for the existence of the conspiracy to advocate charged in the indictment. As to the petitioners Connelly, Kusnitz, Richmond, Spector, and Steinberg we find no adequate evidence in the record which would permit a jury to find that they were members of such a conspiracy. For all purposes relevant here, the sole evidence as to them was that they had long been members, officers, or functionaries of the Communist Party of California; and that standing alone, as Congress has enacted in §4(f) of the Internal Security Act of 1950, makes out no case against them. So far as this record shows, none of them has engaged in or been associated with any but what appear to have been wholly lawful activities, or has ever made a single remark or been present when someone else made a remark, which would tend to prove the charges against them. . . .

Moreover, apart from the inadequacy of the evidence to show, at best, more than the abstract advocacy and teaching of forcible overthrow by the Party, it is difficult to perceive how the requisite specific intent to accomplish such overthrow could be deemed proved by a showing of mere membership or the holding of office in the Communist Party. We therefore think that as to these petitioners the evidence was entirely too meagre to justify putting them to a new trial, and that their acquittal should be ordered.

As to the nine remaining petitioners, we consider that a different conclusion should be reached. . . . [W]hile the record contains evidence of little more than a general program of educational activity by the Communist Party which included advocacy of violence as a theoretical matter, we are not prepared to say, at this stage of the case, that it would be impossible for a jury . . . to find that advocacy of action was also engaged in when the group involved was thought particularly trustworthy, dedicated, and suited for violent tasks.

Nor can we say that the evidence linking these nine petitioners to that sort of advocacy, with the requisite specific intent, is so tenuous as not to justify their retrial under proper legal standards. . . . [A]ll of these nine petitioners were shown either to have made statements themselves, or apparently approved statements made in their presence, which a jury might take as some evidence of their participation with the requisite intent in a conspiracy to advocate illegal action.

As to these nine petitioners, then, we shall not order an acquittal. . . .

Since there must be a new trial, we have not found it necessary to deal with the contentions of the petitioners as to the fairness of the trial already held. The judgment of the Court of Appeals is reversed, and the case remanded to the District Court for further proceedings consistent with this opinion.

It is so ordered.

MR. JUSTICE BURTON, concurring in the result:

I agree with the result reached by the Court, and with the opinion of the Court except as to its interpretation of the term "organize" as used in the Smith Act. . . .

MR. JUSTICE BRENNAN and MR. JUSTICE WHITTAKER took no part in the consideration or decision of this case. . . .

MR. JUSTICE BLACK, with whom MR. JUSTICE DOUGLAS joins, concurring in part and dissenting in part:

I

I would reverse every one of these convictions and direct that all the defendants be acquitted. In my judgment the statutory provisions on which these prosecutions are based abridge freedom of speech, press, and assembly in violation of the First Amendment to the United States Constitution. . . .

First. I agree with Part I of the Court's opinion that deals with the statutory term, "organize," and holds that the organizing charge in the indictment was barred by the three-year statute of limitations.

Second. I also agree with the Court in so far as it holds that the trial judge erred in instructing that persons could be punished under the Smith Act for teaching and advocating forceful overthrow as an abstract principle. But on the other hand, I cannot agree that the instruction which the Court indicates it might approve is constitutionally permissible. The Court says that persons can be punished for advocating action to overthrow the Government by force and violence, where those to whom the advocacy is addressed are urged "to *do* something, now or in the future, rather than merely to *believe* in something." Under the Court's approach, defendants could still be convicted simply for agreeing to talk as distinguished from agreeing to act. I believe that the First Amendment forbids Congress to punish people for talking about public affairs, whether or not such discussion incites to action, legal or illegal. . . .

Second. I also agree with the Court that petitioners, Connelly, Kusnitz, Richmond, Spector, and Steinberg, should be ordered acquitted since there is no evidence that they have ever engaged in anything but "wholly lawful activities." But in contrast to the Court, I think the same action should also be taken as to the remaining nine defendants. The Court's opinion summarizes the strongest evidence offered against these defendants. This summary reveals a pitiful inadequacy of proof to show beyond a reasonable doubt that the defendants were guilty of conspiring to incite persons to act to overthrow the Government. . . .

. . . I cannot agree that "justice" requires this Court to send these cases back to put these defendants in jeopardy again in violation of the spirit if not the letter of the Fifth Amendment's provision against double jeopardy. . . .

In essence, petitioners were tried upon the charge that they believe in and want to foist upon this country a different and to us a despicable form of authoritarian government in which voices criticizing the existing order are summarily silenced. I fear that the present type of prosecutions are more in line with the philosophy of authoritarian government than with that expressed by our First Amendment.

Doubtlessly, dictators have to stamp out causes and beliefs which they deem subversive to their evil regimes. But governmental suppression of causes and beliefs seems to me to be the very antithesis of what our Constitution stands for. The choice expressed in the First Amendment in favor of free expression was made against a turbulent background by men such as Jefferson, Madison, and Mason—men who believed that loyalty to the provisions of this Amendment was the best way to assure a long life for this new nation and its Government. Unless there is complete freedom for expression of all ideas, whether we like them or not, concerning the way government should be run and who shall run it, I doubt if any views in the long run can be secured against the censor. The First Amendment provides the only kind of security system that can preserve a free government—one that leaves the way wide open for people to favor, discuss, advocate, or incite causes and doctrines however obnoxious and antagonistic such views may be to the rest of us. . . .

MR. JUSTICE CLARK, dissenting:

I would affirm the convictions. However, the Court has freed five of the convicted petitioners and ordered new trials for the remaining nine. As to the five, it says that the evidence is "clearly insufficient." I agree with the Court of Appeals, the District Court, and the jury that the evidence showed guilt beyond a reasonable doubt. . . .

. . . I agree with my Brother Burton that the Court has incorrectly interpreted the term "organize" as used in the Smith Act. . . .

. . . As I see it, the trial judge charged in essence all that was required under the *Dennis* opinions. . . . Apparently what disturbs the Court now is that the trial judge here did not give the *Dennis* charge although both the prosecution and the defense asked that it be given. Since he refused to grant these requests I suppose the majority feels that there must be some difference between the two charges, else the one that was given in *Dennis* would have been followed here. While there may be some distinctions between the charges, as I view them they are without material difference. I find, as the majority intimates, that the distinctions are too "subtle and difficult to grasp."

EDITOR'S NOTE. In *Brandenberg* v. *Ohio,* 89 Sup. Ct. 1827 (1969), the Supreme Court refused to draw the distinction it does in *Yates* between advocacy of abstract doctrine and advocacy of action. It struck down a state statute prohibiting "advocacy" of "criminal syndicalism" as a clear violation of freedom of speech, thus in effect reversing its decision in *Whitney* v. *California* (p. 381).

BARENBLATT v. UNITED STATES
360 U.S. 109; 79 Sup. Ct. 1081; 3 L. Ed. 2d 1115 (1959)

[*Lloyd Barenblatt, a former instructor in psychology at Vassar College, refused to tell a subcommittee of the House Un-American Activities Committee, whether or not he had been a member of the Communist party during 1947–1950 while pursuing graduate work at the University of Michigan; he also refused to reveal his current associations with the Communist party. He maintained that the subcommittee had no right to inquire into his political, religious, and personal affairs or "associational activities," arguing vehemently that the Committee had violated his constitutional rights "by abridging freedom of speech, thought, press, and association, and by conducting legislative trials of known or suspected Communists which trespassed on the exclusive power of the judiciary."*

For refusing to answer the questions, Barenblatt was placed in contempt and upon conviction in a district court was sentenced to six months in prison and fined $250. His conviction was affirmed by a unanimous court of appeals. However, the Supreme Court granted certiorari, vacated the court of appeals' judgment, and remanded the case back to that court for further consideration in the light of Watkins v. United States, *which had been recently decided. A sharply divided court of appeals reaffirmed the conviction. The Supreme Court then granted certiorari a second time.*]

MR. JUSTICE HARLAN delivered the opinion of the Court:

Once more the Court is required to resolve the conflicting constitutional claims of congressional power and of an individual's right to resist its exercise. The congressional power in question concerns the internal process of

Congress in moving within its legislative domain; it involves the utilization of its committees to secure "testimony needed to enable it efficiently to exercise a legislative function belonging to it under the Constitution." . . . The power of inquiry has been employed by Congress throughout our history, over the whole range of the national interests concerning which Congress might legislate or decide upon due investigation not to legislate; it has similarly been utilized in determining what to appropriate from the national purse, or whether to appropriate. The scope of the power of inquiry, in short, is as penetrating and far-reaching as the potential power to enact and appropriate under the Constitution.

Broad as it is, the power is not, however, without limitations. Since Congress may only investigate into those areas in which it may potentially legislate or appropriate, it cannot inquire into matters which are within the exclusive province of one or the other branch of the Government. Lacking the judicial power given to the Judiciary, it cannot inquire into matters that are exclusively the concern of the Judiciary. Neither can it supplant the Executive in what exclusively belongs to the Executive. And the Congress, in common with all branches of the Government, must exercise its powers subject to the limitations placed by the Constitution on governmental action, more particularly in the context of this case the relevant limitations of the Bill of Rights. . . .

Our function, at this point, is purely one of constitutional adjudication in the particular case and upon the particular record before us, not to pass judgment upon the general wisdom or efficacy of the activities of this Committee in a vexing and complicated field.

The precise constitutional issue confronting us is whether the Subcommittee's inquiry into petitioner's past or present membership in the Communist Party transgressed the provisions of the First Amendment, which of course reach and limit congressional investigations. . . .

The Court's past cases established sure guides to decision. Undeniably, the First Amendment in some circumstances protects an individual from being compelled to disclose his associational relationships. However, the protections of the First Amendment, unlike a proper claim of the privilege against self-incrimination under the Fifth Amendment, do not afford a witness the right to resist inquiry in all circumstances. Where First Amendment rights are asserted to bar governmental interrogation, resolution of the issue always involves a balancing by the courts of the competing private and public interests at stake in the particular circumstances shown. These principles were recognized in the *Watkins* case, where, in speaking of the First Amendment in relation to congressional inquiries, we said . . . : "It is manifest that despite the adverse effects which follow upon compelled disclosure of private matters, not all such inquiries are barred. . . . The critical element is the existence of, and the weight to be ascribed to, the interest of the Congress in demanding disclosures from an unwilling witness." . . .

The first question is whether this investigation was related to a valid legislative purpose, for Congress may not constitutionally require an individual to disclose his political relationships or other private affairs except in relation to such a purpose. . . .

That Congress has wide power to legislate in the field of Communist activity in this Country, and to conduct appropriate investigations in aid thereof, is hardly debatable. The existence of such power has never been questioned by this Court, and it is sufficient to say, without particularization, that Congress has enacted or considered in this field a wide range of legislative measures, not a few of which have stemmed from recommendations of the very Committee whose actions have been drawn in question here. In the last analysis this power rests on the right of self-preservation, "the ultimate value of any society." . . . Justification for its exercise in turn rests on the long and widely accepted view that the tenets of the Communist Party include the ultimate overthrow of the Government of the United States by force and violence, a view which has been given formal expression by the Congress.

On these premises, this Court in its constitutional adjudications has consistently refused to view the Communist Party as an ordinary political party, and has upheld federal legislation aimed at the Communist problem which in a different context would certainly have raised constitutional issues of the gravest character. . . . To suggest that because the Communist Party may also sponsor peaceable political reforms the constitutional issues before us should now be judged as if that Party were just an ordinary political party from the standpoint of national security, is to ask this Court to blind itself to world affairs which have determined the whole course of our national policy since the close of World War II. . . .

We think that investigatory power in this domain is not to be denied Congress solely because the field of education is involved. . . . Indeed we do not understand petitioner here to suggest that Congress in no circumstances may inquire into Communist activity in the field of education. Rather, his position is in effect that this particular investigation was aimed not at the revolutionary aspects but at the theoretical classroom discussion of communism.

In our opinion this position rests on a too constricted view of the nature of the investigatory process, and is not supported by a fair assessment of the record before us. An investigation of advocacy of or preparation for overthrow certainly embraces the right to identify a witness as a member of the Communist Party . . . and to inquire into the various manifestations of the Party's tenets. The strict requirements of a prosecution under the Smith Act, see *Dennis* v. *United States* . . . and *Yates* v. *United States* . . . , are not the measure of the permissible scope of a congressional investigation into "overthrow," for of necessity the investigatory process must proceed step by step. Nor can it fairly be concluded that this investigation was directed at controlling what is being taught at our universities rather than at overthrow. The statement of the Subcommittee Chairman at the opening of the investigation evinces no such intention, and so far as this record reveals nothing thereafter transpired which would justify our holding that the thrust of the investigation later changed. The record discloses considerable testimony concerning the foreign domination and revolutionary purposes and efforts of the Communist Party. That there was also testimony on the abstract philosophical level does not detract from the dominant theme of this investigation—Communist infiltration furthering the alleged ultimate purpose of overthrow. And certainly the conclusion would not be justified that the questioning of petitioner would have exceeded permissible bounds had he not shut off the Subcommittee at the threshold.

Nor can we accept the further contention that this investigation should not be deemed to have been in furtherance of a legislative purpose because the true objective of the Committee and of the Congress was purely "exposure." So long as Congress acts in pursuance of its constitutional power, the judiciary lacks authority to intervene on the basis of the motives which spurred the exercise of that power. . . . [I]n stating in the Watkins case . . . that "there is no congressional power to expose for the sake of exposure," we at the same time declined to inquire into the "motives of committee members," and recognized that their "motives alone would not vitiate an investigation which had been instituted by a House of Congress if that assembly's legislative purpose is being served." Having scrutinized this record we cannot say that the unanimous panel of the Court of Appeals which first considered this case was wrong in concluding that "the primary purposes of the inquiry were in aid of legislative processes." . . . Certainly this is not a case like *Kilbourn* v. *Thompson* . . . where "the House of Representatives not only exceeded the limit of its own authority, but assumed a power which could only be properly exercised by another branch of the government, because it was in its nature clearly judicial." . . . The constitutional legislative power of Congress in this instance is beyond question.

Finally, the record is barren of other factors which in themselves might sometimes lead to the conclusion that the individual interests at stake were not subordinate to those of the state. There is no indication in this record that the Subcommittee was attempting to pillory witnesses. Nor did petitioner's appearance as a witness follow from indiscriminate dragnet procedures, lacking in probable cause for belief that he

possessed information which might be helpful to the Subcommittee. And the relevancy of the questions put to him by the Subcommittee is not open to doubt.

We conclude that the balance between the individual and the governmental interests here at stake must be struck in favor of the latter, and that therefore the provisions of the First Amendment have not been offended.

We hold that petitioner's conviction for contempt of Congress discloses no infirmity, and that the judgment of the Court of Appeals must be

Affirmed.

MR. JUSTICE BLACK, with whom THE CHIEF JUSTICE and MR. JUSTICE DOUGLAS concur, dissenting:

The First Amendment says in no equivocal language that Congress shall pass no law abridging freedom of speech, press, assembly or petition. The activities of this Committee, authorized by Congress, do precisely that, through exposure, obloquy and public scorn. . . . The Court does not really deny this fact but relies on a combination of three reasons for permitting the infringement: (A) The notion that despite the First Amendment's command Congress can abridge speech and association if this Court decides that the governmental interest in abridging speech is greater than an individual's interest in exercising that freedom, (B) the Government's right to "preserve itself," (C) the fact that the Committee is only after Communists or suspected Communists in this investigation.

A. I do not agree that laws directly abridging First Amendment freedoms can be justified by a congressional or judicial balancing process. There are, of course, cases suggesting that a law which primarily regulates conduct but which might also indirectly affect speech can be upheld if the effect on speech is minor in relation to the need for control of the conduct. . . .

To apply the Court's balancing test under such circumstances is to read the First Amendment to say "Congress shall pass no law abridging freedom of speech, press, assembly and petition, unless Congress and the Supreme Court reach the joint conclusion that on balance the interests of the Government in stifling these freedoms is greater than the interest of the people in having them exercised." This is closely akin to the notion that neither the First Amendment nor any other provision of the Bill of Rights should be enforced unless the Court believes it is reasonable to do so. Not only does this violate the genius of our written Constitution, but it runs expressly counter to the injunction to Court and Congress made by Madison when he introduced the Bill of Rights. "If they (the first ten amendments) are incorporated into the Constitution, independent tribunals of justice will consider themselves in a peculiar manner the guardians of those rights; they will be an impenetrable bulwark against every assumption of power in the Legislative or Executive; they will be naturally led to resist every encroachment upon rights expressly stipulated for in the Constitution by the declaration of rights." Unless we return to this view of our judicial function, unless we once again accept the notion that the Bill of Rights means what it says and that this Court must enforce that meaning, I am of the opinion that our great charter of liberty will be more honored in the breach than in the observance.

But even assuming what I cannot assume, that some balancing is proper in this case, I feel that the Court after stating the test ignores it completely. At most it balances the right of the Government to preserve itself, against Barenblatt's right to refrain from revealing Communist affiliations. Such a balance, however, mistakes the factors to be weighed. In the first place, it completely leaves out the real interest in Barenblatt's silence, the interest of the people as a whole in being able to join organizations, advocate causes and make political "mistakes" without later being subjected to governmental penalties for having dared to think for themselves. It is this right, the right to err politically, which keeps us strong as a Nation. For no number of laws against communism can have as much effect as the personal conviction which comes from having heard its arguments and rejected them, or from having once accepted its tenets and later recognized their worthlessness. Instead, the obloquy which results from investigations such as this not only stifles "mistakes" but prevents all but the most courageous from hazarding any views which might at some later time become disfavored. This result, whose importance cannot be overestimated, is doubly crucial when it affects the universities, on which we must largely rely for the experimentation and development of new ideas essential to our country's welfare. It is these interests of society, rather than Barenblatt's own right to silence, which I think the Court should put on the balance against the demands of the Government, if any balancing process is to be tolerated. Instead they are not mentioned, while on the other side the demands of the government are vastly overstated and called "self-preservation." . . . Such a result reduces "balancing" to a mere play on words and is completely inconsistent with the rules this Court has previously given for applying a "balancing test," where it is proper: "(T)he courts should be astute to examine the effect of the challenged legislation. Mere legislative preferences or beliefs . . . may well support regulation directed at other personal activities, but be insufficient to justify such as diminishes the exercise of rights so vital to the maintenance of democratic institutions." . . .

B. Moreover, I cannot agree with the Court's notion that Fifth Amendment freedoms must be abridged in order to "preserve" our country. That notion rests on the unarticulated premise that this Nation's security hangs upon its power to punish people because of what they think, speak or write about, or because of those with whom they associate for political purposes. The Government, in its brief, virtually admits this position when it speaks of the "communication of unlawful ideas." I challenge this premise, and deny that ideas can be proscribed under our Constitution. I agree that despotic governments cannot exist without stifling the voice of opposition to their oppressive practices. The First Amendment means to me, however, that the only constitutional way our Government can preserve itself is to leave its people the fullest possible freedom to praise, criticize or discuss, as they see fit, all governmental policies and to suggest, if they desire, that even its most fundamental postulates are bad and should be changed; "Therein lies the security of the Republic, the very foundation of constitutional government." On that premise this land was created, and on that premise it has grown to greatness. Our Constitution assumes that the common sense of the people and their attachment to our country will enable them, after free discussion, to withstand ideas that are wrong. To say that our patriotism must be protected against false ideas by means other than these is, I think, to make a baseless charge. Unless we can rely on these qualities—if, in short,

we begin to punish speech—we cannot honestly proclaim ourselves to be a free Nation and we have lost what the Founders of this land risked their lives and their sacred honors to defend.

C. The Court implies, however, that the ordinary rules and requirements of the Constitution do not apply because the Committee is merely after Communists and they do not constitute a political party but only a criminal gang. "(T)he long and widely accepted view," the Court says, is "that the tenets of the Communist Party include the ultimate overthrow of the Government of the United States by force and violence." This justifies the investigation undertaken. By accepting this charge and allowing it to support treatment of the Communist Party and its members which would violate the Constitution if applied to other groups, the Court, in effect, declares that Party outlawed. It has been only a few years since there was a practically unanimous feeling throughout the country and in our courts that this could not be done in our free land. Of course it has always been recognized that members of the Party who, either individually or in combination, commit acts in violation of valid laws can be prosecuted. But the Party as a whole and innocent members of it could not be attained merely because it had some illegal aims and because some of its members were lawbreakers. . . .

[N]o matter how often or how quickly we repeat the claim that the Communist Party is not a political party, we cannot outlaw it, as a group, without endangering the liberty of all of us. The reason is not hard to find, for mixed among those aims of communism which are illegal are perfectly normal political and social goals. And muddled with its revolutionary tenets is a drive to achieve power through the ballot, if it can be done. These things necessarily make it a political party whatever other, illegal aims it may have. . . . Significantly until recently the Communist Party was on the ballot in many States. When that was so, many Communists undoubtedly hoped to accomplish its lawful goals through support of Communist candidates. Even now some such may still remain. To attribute to them, and to those who have left the Party, the taint of the group is to ignore both our traditions that guilt, like belief, is "personal and not a matter of mere association" and the obvious fact that "men adhering to a political party or other organization notoriously do not subscribe unqualifiedly to all of its platforms or asserted principles." . . .

The fact is that once we allow any group which has some political aims or ideas to be driven from the ballot and from the battle for men's minds because some of its members are bad and some of its tenets are illegal, no group is safe. Today we deal with Communists or suspected Communists. In 1920, instead, the New York Assembly suspended duly elected legislators on the ground that, being Socialists, they were disloyal to the country's principles. In the 1830's the Masons were hunted as outlaws and subversives, and abolitionists were considered revolutionaries of the most dangerous kind in both North and South. Earlier still, at the time of the universally unlamented alien and sedition laws. Thomas Jefferson's party was attacked and its members were derisively called "Jacobins." Fisher Ames described the party as a "French faction" guilty of "subversion" and "officered, regimented and formed to subordination." Its members, he claimed, intended to "take arms against the laws as soon as they dare." History should teach us then, that in times

of high emotional excitement minority parties and groups which advocate extremely unpopular social or governmental innovations will always be typed as criminal gangs and attempts will always be made to drive them out. It was knowledge of this fact, and of its great dangers, that caused the Founders of our land to enact the First Amendment as a guaranty that neither Congress nor the people would do anything to hinder or destroy the capacity of individuals and groups to seek converts and votes for any cause, however radical or unpalatable their principles might seem under the accepted notions of the time. Whatever the States were left free to do, the First Amendment sought to leave Congress devoid of any kind or quality of power to direct any type of national laws against the freedom of individuals to think what they please, advocate whatever policy they choose, and join with others to bring about the social, religious, political and governmental changes which seem best to them. Today's holding, in my judgment, marks another major step in the progressively increasing retreat from the safeguards of the First Amendment. . . .

Finally, I think Barenblatt's conviction violates the Constitution because the chief aim, purpose and practice of the House Un-American Activities Committee, as disclosed by its many reports, is to try witnesses and punish them because they are or have been Communists or because they refuse to admit or deny Communist affiliations. The punishment imposed is generally punishment by humiliation and public shame. There is nothing strange or novel about this kind of punishment. It is in fact one of the oldest forms of governmental punishment known to mankind; branding, the pillory, ostracism and subjection to public hatred being but a few examples of it. . . .

I do not question the Committee's patriotism and sincerity in doing all this. I merely feel that it cannot be done by Congress under our Constitution. For, even assuming that the Federal Government can compel witnesses to testify as to Communist affiliations in order to subject them to ridicule and social and economic retaliation, I cannot agree that this is a legislative function. Such publicity is clearly punishment, and the Constitution allows only one way in which people can be convicted and punished. . . . [I]f communism is to be made a crime, and Communists are to be subjected to "pains and penalties," I would still hold this conviction bad, for the crime of communism, like all others, can be punished only by court and jury after a trial with all judicial safeguards.

It is no answer to all this to suggest that legislative committees should be allowed to punish if they grant the accused some rules of courtesy or allow him counsel. For the Constitution proscribes all bills of attainder by State or Nation, not merely those which lack counsel or courtesy. It does this because the Founders believed that punishment was to serious a matter to be entrusted to any group other than an independent judiciary and a jury of twelve men acting on previously passed, unambiguous laws, with all the procedural safeguards they put in the Constitution as essential to a fair trial—safeguards which included the right to counsel, compulsory process for witnesses, specific indictments, confrontation of accusers, as well as protection against self-incrimination, double jeopardy and cruel and unusual punishment —in short, due process of law. . . . They believed this because not long before worthy men had been deprived of their liberties, and indeed their lives, through parliamentary trials without these safeguards. . . . It is the protection from arbitrary punishments through the right to a judicial trial with all these safeguards which over the years has distinguished America from lands where drum-head courts and other similar "tribunals" deprive the weak and the unorthodox of life, liberty and property without due process of law. It is this same right which is denied to Barenblatt, because the Court today fails to see what is here for all to see—that exposure and punishment is the aim of this Committee and the reason for its existence. To deny this aim is to ignore the Committee's own claims and the reports it has issued ever since it was established. I cannot believe that the nature of our judicial office requires us to be so blind, and must conclude that the Un-American Activities Committee's "identification" and "exposure of Communists and suspected Communists . . . amount to an encroachment on the judiciary which bodes ill for the liberties of the people of this land.

Ultimately all the questions in this case really boil down to one—whether we as a people will try fearfully and futilely to preserve Democracy by adopting totalitarian methods, or whether in accordance with our traditions and our Constitution we will have the confidence and courage to be free.

I would reverse this conviction.

MR. JUSTICE BRENNAN, dissenting:

I would reverse this conviction. It is sufficient that I state my complete agreement with by Brother Black that no purpose for the investigation of Barenblatt is revealed by the record except exposure purely for the sake of exposure. This is not a purpose to which Barenblatt's rights under the First Amendment can vividly be subordinated. An investigation in which the processes of lawmaking and law evaluating are submerged entirely in exposure of individual behavior—in adjudication, or a sort, through the exposure process —is outside the constitutional pale of congressional inquiry. . . .

SCALES v. UNITED STATES
367 U.S. 203; 81 Sup. Ct. 1469; 6 L. Ed. 2d 782 (1961)

[*Scales was chairman of the North and South Carolina Districts of the Communist party and in that capacity recruited new members for the party, directed a secret school where the principles of Communism were taught, and sought to strengthen the party in various other ways. In 1955, he was convicted in a federal district court for violation of the "membership clause" of the Smith Act, which makes membership in any organization that advocates the overthrow of the federal government by force a felony punishable by up to twenty years' imprisonment and a fine of $20,000. A court of appeals upheld the conviction, but the Supreme Court granted certiorari and reversed the decision when the Solicitor General agreed that the Court's intervening decision in* Jencks v. United States, 353 U.S. 657 (1956), *entitled Scales to a new trial.*

Scales was retried, convicted again, and sentenced to a six-year prison term. A Court of Appeals again affirmed, and the Supreme Court granted certiorari a second time.]

MR. JUSTICE HARLAN delivered the opinion of the Court:

. . . It will bring the constitutional issues into clearer focus to notice first the premises on which the case was submitted to the jury. The jury was instructed that in order to convict it must find that within the three-year limitations period (1) the Communist Party advocated the violent overthrow of the Government, in the sense of present "advocacy of action" to accomplish that end as soon as circumstances were propitious; and (2) petitioner was an "active" member of the Party, and not merely "a nominal, passive, inactive or purely technical" member, with knowledge of the Party's illegal advocacy and a specific intent to bring about violent overthrow "as speedily as circumstances would permit."

The constitutional attack upon the membership clause, as thus construed, is that the statute offends (1) the Fifth Amendment, in that it impermissibly imputes guilt to an individual merely on the basis of his associations and sympathies, rather than because of some concrete personal involvement in criminal conduct; and (2) the First Amendment, in that it infringes free political expression and association. . . .

FIFTH AMENDMENT

In our jurisprudence guilt is personal, and when the imposition of punishment on a status or on conduct can only be justified by reference to the relationship of that status or conduct to other concededly criminal activity (here advocacy of violent overthrow), that relationship must be sufficiently substantial to satisfy the concept of personal guilt in order to withstand attack under the Due Process Clause of the Fifth Amendment. Membership, without more, in an organization engaged in illegal advocacy, it is now said, has not heretofore been recognized by this

Court to be such a relationship. This claim stands, and we shall examine it, independently of that made under the First Amendment.

Any thought that due process puts beyond the reach of the criminal law all individual associational relationships, unless accompanied by the commission of specific acts of criminality, is dispelled by familiar concepts of the law of conspiracy and complicity. While both are commonplace in the landscape of the criminal law, they are not natural features. Rather they are particular legal concepts manifesting the more general principle that society, having the power to punish dangerous behavior, cannot be powerless against those who work to bring about that behavior. The fact that Congress has not resorted to either of these familiar concepts means only that the enquiry here must direct itself to an analysis of the relationship between the fact of membership and the underlying substantive illegal conduct, in order to determine whether that relationship is indeed too tenuous to permit its use as the basis of criminal liability. In this instance it is an organization which engages in criminal activity, and we can perceive no reason why one who actively and knowingly works in the ranks of that organization, intending to contribute to the success of those specifically illegal activities, should be any more immune from prosecution than he to whom the organization has assigned the task of carrying out the substantive criminal act. Nor should the fact that Congress has focussed here on "membership," the characteristic relationship between an individual and the type of conspiratorial quasi-political associations with the criminal aspect of whose activities Congress was concerned, of itself require the conclusion that the legislature has traveled outside the familiar and permissible bounds of criminal imputability. In truth, the specificity of the proscribed relationship is not necessarily a vice; it provides instruction and warning.

What must be met, then, is the argument that membership, even when accompanied by the elements of knowledge and specific intent, affords an insufficient quantum of participation in the organization's alleged criminal activity, that is, an insufficiently significant form of aid and encouragement to permit the imposition of criminal sanctions on that basis. It must indeed be recognized that a person who merely becomes a member of an illegal organization, by that "act" alone need be doing nothing more than signifying his assent to its purposes and activities on one hand, and providing, on the other, only the sort of moral encouragement which comes from the knowledge that others believe in what the organization is doing. It may indeed be argued that such assent and encouragement do fall short of the concrete, practical impetus given to a criminal enterprise which is lent for instance by a commitment on the part of a conspirator to act in furtherance of that enterprise. A member, as distinguished from a conspirator, may indicate his approval of a criminal enterprise by the very fact of his membership without thereby necessarily committing himself to further it by any act or course of conduct whatever.

In an area of the criminal law which this Court has indicated more than once demands its watchful scrutiny . . . these factors have weight and must be found to be overborne in a total constitutional assessment of the statute. We think, however, they are duly met when the statute is found to reach only "active" members having also a guilty knowledge and intent, and which therefore prevents a conviction on what otherwise might be regarded as merely an expression of sympathy with the alleged criminal enterprise, unaccompanied by any significant action in its support or any commitment to undertake such action.

Thus, given the construction of the membership clause already discussed, we think the factors called for in rendering members criminally responsible for the illegal advocacy of the organization fall within estabished, and therefore presumably constitutional standards of criminal imputability.

FIRST AMENDMENT

Little remains to be said concerning the claim that the statute infringes First Amendment freedoms. It was settled in *Dennis* that the advocacy with which we are here concerned is not constitutionally protected speech, and it was further estabished that a combination to promote such advocacy, albeit under the aegis of what purports to be a political party, is not such association as is protected by the First Amendment. We can discern no reason why membership, when it constitutes a purposeful form of complicity in a group engaging in this same forbidden advocacy, should receive any greater degree of protection from the guaranties of the Amendment.

If it is said that the mere existence of such an enactment tends to inhibit the exercise of constitutionally protected rights, in that it engenders an unhealthy fear that one may find himself unwittingly embroiled in criminal liability, the answer surely is that the statute provides that a defendant must be proven to have knowledge of the proscribed advocacy before he may be convicted. It is, of course, true that quasi-political parties or other groups that may embrace both legal and illegal aims differ from a technical conspiracy, which is defined by its criminal purpose, so that all-knowing association with the conspiracy is a proper subject for criminal proscription as far as First Amendment liberties are concerned. If there were a similar blanket prohibition of association with a group having both legal and illegal aims, there would indeed be a real danger that legitimate political expression or association would be impaired, but the membership clause, as here construed, does not cut deeper into the freedom of association than is necessary to deal with "the substantive evils that Congress has a right to prevent." *Schenck v. United States.* . . . The clause does not make criminal all association with an organization, which has been shown to engage in illegal advocacy. There must be clear proof that a defendant "specifically intend(s) to accomplish (the aims of the organization) by resort to violence." . . . Thus the member for whom the organization is a vehicle for the advancement of legitimate aims and policies does not fall within the ban of the statute: he lacks the requisite specific intent "to bring about the overthrow of the government as speedily as circumstances would permit." Such a person may be foolish, deluded, or perhaps merely optimistic, but he is not by this statute made a criminal.

We conclude that petitioner's constitutional challenge must be overruled. . . .

The judgment of the Court of Appeals must be

Affirmed.

MR. JUSTICE BLACK, dissenting:

. . . My reasons for dissenting from this decision are primarily those set out by Mr. Justice Brennan—that Section 4(f) of the Subversive Activities Control Act bars prosecutions under the membership clause of the Smith Act—and Mr. Justice Douglas—that the First

Amendment absolutely forbids Congress to outlaw membership in a political party or similar association merely because one of the philosophical tenets of that group is that the existing government should be overthrown by force at some distant time in the future when circumstances may permit. . . .

I think it is important to point out the manner in which this case re-emphasizes the freedom-destroying nature of the "balancing test" presently in use by the Court to justify its refusal to apply specific constitutional protections of the Bill of Rights. In some of the recent cases in which it has "balanced" away the protections of the First Amendment, the Court has suggested that it was justified in the application of this "test" because no direct abridgment in each of these cases being, in the Court's opinion, nothing more than "an incident of the informed exercise of a valid governmental function." A possible implication of that suggestion was that if the Court were confronted with what it would call a direct abridgment of speech, it would not apply the "balancing test" but would enforce the protections of the First Amendment according to its own terms. This case causes me to doubt that such an implication is justified. Petitioner is being sent to jail for the express reason that he has associated with people who have entertained unlawful ideas and said unlawful things, and that of course is a direct abridgment of his freedoms of speech and assembly—under any definition that has ever been used for that term. Nevertheless, even as to this admittedly direct abridgment, the Court relies upon its prior decisions to the effect that the Government has power to abridge speech and assembly if its interest in doing so is sufficient to outweigh the interest in protecting these First Amendment freedoms.

This, I think, demonstrates the unlimited breadth and danger of the "balancing test" as it is currently being applied by a majority of this Court. Under the "test," the question in every case in which a First Amendment right is asserted is not whether there has been an abridgment of that right, not whether the abridgment of the right was intentional on the part of the Government, and not whether there is any other way in which the Government could accomplish a lawful aim without an invasion of the constitutionally guaranteed rights of the people. It is, rather, simply whether the Government has an interest in abridging the right involved and, if so, whether that interest is of sufficient importance, in the opinion of a majority of this Court, to justify the Government's action in doing so. This doctrine, to say the very least, is capable of being used to justify almost any action Government may wish to take to suppress First Amendment freedoms.

MR. JUSTICE DOUGLAS, dissenting:

When we allow petitioner to be sentenced to prison for six years for being a "member" of the Communist Party, we make a sharp break with traditional concepts of First Amendment rights and make serious Mark Twain's light-hearted comment that "It is by the goodness of God that in our Country we have those three unspeakably precious things: freedom of speech, freedom of conscience, and the prudence never to practice either of them."

Even the Alien and Sedition Laws—shameful reminder of an early chapter in intolerance—never went so far as we go today. They were aimed at conspiracy and advocacy of insurrection and at the publication of "false, scandalous, and malicious" writing against the Government. . . . The Government then sought control over the press "in order to strike at one of the chief

sources of disaffection and sedition."
. . . There is here no charge of conspiracy, no charge of any overt act to
overthrow the Government by force
and violence, no charge of any other
criminal act. The charge is being a
"member" of the Communist Party,
"well-knowing" that it advocated the
overthrow of the Government by force
and violence, "said defendant intending
to bring about such overthrow by force
and violence as speedily as circumstances would permit." That falls far
short of a charge of conspiracy. Conspiracy rests not in intention alone but
in an agreement with one or more
others to promote an unlawful project.
. . . No charge of any kind or sort of
agreement hitherto embraced in the
concept of a conspiracy is made here.

We legalize today guilt by association,
sending a man to prison when he committed no unlawful act. . . .

The case is not saved by showing that
petitioner was an active member. None
of the activity constitutes a crime. . . .

Not one single illegal act is charged
to petitioner. That is why the essence
of the crime covered by the indictment
is merely belief—belief in the proletarian revolution, belief in Communist
creed. . . .

Nothing but beliefs are on trial in
this case. They are unpopular and to
most of us revolting. But they are nonetheless ideas or dogma or faith within
the broad framework of the First
Amendment. . . .

Belief in the principle of revolution
is deep in our traditions. The Declaration of Independence proclaims it:

"Whenever any Form of Government becomes destructive of these
ends, it is the Right of the People
to alter or abolish it, and to institute
new Government, laying its foundation on such principles and organiz-

ing its powers in such form, as to
them shall seem most likely to effect
their Safety and Happiness."

This right of revolution has been
and is a part of the fabric of our institutions. . . .

Of course, government can move
against those who take up arms against
it. Of course, the constituted authority
has the right of self-preservation. But
we deal in this prosecution of Scales
only with the legality of ideas and beliefs, not with overt acts. The Court
speaks of the prevention of "dangerous
behavior" by punishing those "who
work to bring about that behavior."
That formula returns man to the dark
days when government determined
what behavior was "dangerous" and
then policed the dissidents for tell-tale
signs of advocacy. . . .

In recent years we have been departing, I think, from the theory of
government expressed in the First
Amendment. We have too often been
"balancing" the right of speech and
association against other values in
society to see if we, the judges, feel
that a particular need is more important
than those guaranteed by the Bill of
Rights.

What we lose by majority vote today
may be reclaimed at a future time
when the fear of advocacy, dissent, and
non-conformity no longer cast a shadow over us.

MR. JUSTICE BRENNAN, with whom
THE CHIEF JUSTICE and MR. JUSTICE
DOUGLAS join, dissenting:

I think that in Section 4(f) of the
Internal Security Act Congress legislated immunity from prosecution under
the membership clause of the Smith
Act. The first sentence of Section 4(f)
is: "Neither the holding of office nor
membership in any Communist organization by any person shall constitute

per se a violation of subsection (a) or subsection (c) of this section or of any other criminal statute." The immunity granted by that sentence is not in my view restricted, as the Court holds, to mere membership, that is to membership which is nominal, passive or theoretical. The immunity also extends to

"active and purposive membership, purposive that is as to the organization's criminal ends," which is the character of membership to which the Court today restricts the application of the membership clause of the Smith Act. . . .

GIBSON v. FLORIDA LEGISLATIVE INVESTIGATION COMM.
372 U.S. 539; 83 Sup. Ct. 889; 9 L. Ed. 2d 929 (1963)

MR. JUSTICE GOLDBERG delivered the opinion of the Court:

The petitioner, then president of the Miami branch of the NAACP, was ordered to appear before the respondent Committee on November 4, 1959. . . . Prior to interrogation of any witnesses the Committee chairman read the text of the statute creating the Committee and declared that the hearings would be "concerned with the activities of various organizations which have been or are presently operating in this State in the fields of, first, race relations; second, the coercive reform of social and educational practices and mores by litigation and pressured administrative action; third, of labor; fourth, of education; fifth, and other vital phases of life in this State." The chairman also stated that the inquiry would be directed to Communists and Communist activities, including infiltration of Communists into organizations operating in the described fields.

Upon being called to the stand, the petitioner admitted that he was custodian of his organization's membership records. . . . The petitioner told the Committee that he had not brought these records with him to the hearing and announced that he would not produce them for the purpose of answering questions concerning membership in the NAACP. . . . The petitioner's

refusal to produce his organization's membership lists was based on the ground that to bring the lists to the hearing and to utilize them as the basis of his testimony would interfere with the free exercise of Fourteenth Amendment association rights of members and prospective members of the NAACP.

In accordance with Florida procedure, the petitioner was brought before a state court and, after a hearing, was adjudged in contempt. . . . The Florida Supreme Court sustained the judgment below. . . .

We are here called upon once again to resolve a conflict between individual rights of free speech and association and governmental interest in conducting legislative investigations. Prior decisions illumine the contending principles. This Court has repeatedly held that rights of association are within the ambit of the constitutional protections afforded by the First and Fourteenth Amendments. NAACP v. Alabama. . . . "It is beyond debate that freedom to engage in association for the advancement of beliefs and ideas is an inseparable aspect of the 'liberty' assured by the Due Process Clause of the Fourteenth Amendment, which embraces freedom of speech." . . . And it is equally clear that the guarantee encompasses protection of privacy of association in organizations such as that of which the petitioner is president; indeed, in both the Bates and Alabama cases, supra, this Court held NAACP membership lists of the very type here in question to be beyond the States' power of discovery in the circumstances there presented. . . . And, as declared in *NAACP* v. *Alabama*. "It is hardly a novel perception that compelled disclosure of affiliation with groups engaged in advocacy may constitute [an] . . . effective . . . restraint on freedom of association. . . . This Court has recognized the vital relationship between freedom to associate and privacy in one's associations. . . . Inviolability of privacy in group association may in many circumstances be indispensable to preservation of freedom of association, particularly where a group espouses dissident beliefs." So it is here.

At the same time, however, this Court's prior holdings demonstrate that there can be no question that the State has power adequately to inform itself—through legislative investigation, if it so desires—in order to act and protect its legitimate and vital interests. As this Court said in considering the propriety of the congressional inquiry challenged in *Watkins* v. *United States*. . . . "The power . . . to conduct investigations is inherent in the legislative process. That power is broad. It encompasses inquiries concerning the administration of existing laws as well as proposed or possibly needed statutes. It includes surveys of defects in our social, economic or political system for the purpose of enabling the Congress to remedy them." . . . It is no less obvious, however, that the legislative power to investigate, broad as it may be, is not without limit. The fact that the general scope of the inquiry is authorized and permissible does not compel the conclusion that the investigatory body is

free to inquire into or demand all forms of information. Validation of the broad subject matter under investigation does not necessarily carry with it automatic and wholesale validation of all individual questions, subpoenas, and documentary demands. . . . When, as in this case, the claim is made that particular legislative inquiries and demands infringe substantially upon First and Fourteenth Amendment associational rights of individuals, the courts are called upon to, and must, determine the permissibility of the challenged actions. . . . "[T]he delicate and difficult task falls upon the courts to weigh the circumstances and to appraise the substantiality of the reasons advanced in support of the regulation of the free enjoyment of the rights." . . . The interests here at stake are of significant magnitude, and neither their resolution nor impact is limited to, or dependent upon, the particular parties here involved. Freedom and viable government are both, for this purpose, indivisible concepts; whatever affects the rights of the parties here, affects all. . . . It is an essential prerequisite to the validity of an investigation which intrudes into the area of constitutionally protected rights of speech, press, association, and petition that the State convincingly show a substantial relation between the information sought and a subject of overriding and compelling state interest. Absent such a relation between the NAACP and conduct in which the State may have a compelling regulatory concern, the Committee has not "demonstrated so cogent an interest in obtaining and making public" the membership information sought to be obtained as to "justify the substantial abridgment of associational freedom which such disclosures will effect." *Bates* v. *Little Rock*. . . . "Where there is a significant encroachment upon personal liberty, the State may prevail only upon showing a subordinating interest which is compelling." Ibid.

Appying these principles to the facts of this case, the respondent Committee contends that the prior decisions of this Court . . . compel a result here upholding the legislative right of inquiry. In *Barenblatt, Wilkinson,* and *Braden,* however, it was a refusal to answer a question or questions concerning the witness' *own* past or present membership *in the Communist Party* which supported his conviction. It is apparent that the necessary preponderating governmental interest and, in fact, the very result in those cases were founded on the holding that the Communist Party is not an ordinary or legitimate political party, as known in this country, and that, because of its particular nature, membership therein is *itself* a permissible subject of regulation and legislative scrutiny. Assuming the correctness of the premises on which those cases were decided, no further demonstration of compelling governmental interest was deemed necessary, since the direct object of the challenged questions there was discovery of membership in the Communist Party, a matter held pertinent to a proper subject then under inquiry.

Here, however, it is not alleged Communists who are the witnesses before the Committee and it is not discovery of their membership in that party which is the object of the challenged inquiries. Rather, it is the NAACP itself which is the subject of the investigation, and it is its local president, the petitioner, who was called before the Committee and held in contempt because he refused to divulge the contents of its membership records. There is no suggestion that the Miami branch of the NAACP or the national organization with which it is affiliated was, or is, itself a subversive organization. Nor is there any indication that the activities or policies of the NAACP were either Communist dominated or influenced. . . .

Moreover, even to say, as in *Barenblatt, . . .* that it is permissible to inquire into the subject of Communist infiltration of educational or other organizations does not mean that it is permissible to demand or require from such other groups disclosure of their membership by inquiry into their records when such disclosure will seriously inhibit or impair the exercise of constitutional rights and has not itself been demonstrated to bear a crucial relation to a proper governmental interest or to be essential to fulfillment of a proper governmental purpose. The prior holdings that governmental interest in controlling subversion and the particular character of the Communist Party and its objectives outweigh the right of individual Communists to conceal party membership or affiliations by no means require the wholly different conclusion that other groups—concededly legitimate—automatically forfeit their rights to privacy of association simply because the general subject matter of the legislative inquiry is Communist subversion or infiltration. . . .

. . . We rest our result on the fact that the record in this case is insufficient to show a substantial connection between the Miami branch of the NAACP and Communist *activities* which the respondent Committee itself concedes is an essential prerequisite to demonstrating the immediate, substantial, and subordinating state interest necessary to sustain its right of inquiry into the membership lists of the association. . . .

Nothing we say here impairs or denies the existence of the underlying legislative right to investigate or legislate with respect to subversive activities by Communists or anyone else; our decision today deals only with the manner in which such power may be exercised and we hold simply that groups which themselves are neither engaged in subversive or other illegal or improper activities nor demonstrated to have any substantial connections with such activities are to be protected in their rights of free and private association. As declared in *Sweezy* v. *New Hampshire* . . . (opinion of the Chief Justice), "It is particularly important that the exercise of the power of compulsory process be carefully circumscribed when the investigative process tends to impinge upon such highly sensitive areas as freedom of speech or press, freedom of political association, and freedom of communication of ideas. . . .

To permit legislative inquiry to proceed on less than an adequate foundation would be to sanction unjustified and unwarranted intrusions into the very heart of the constitutional privilege to be secure in associations in legitimate organizations engaged in the exercise of First and Fourteenth Amendment rights; to impose a lesser standard than we here do would be inconsistent with the maintenance of those essential conditions basic to the preservation of our democracy.

The judgment below must be and is
Reversed.

MR. JUSTICE BLACK, concurring:

. . . In my view the constitutional right of association includes the privilege of any person, to associate with Communists or anti-Communists, Socialists or anti-Socialists, or, for that matter, with people of all kinds of beliefs, popular or unpopular. I have expressed these views in many other cases and I adhere to them now. Since, as I believe, the National Association for the Advancement of Colored People and its members have a constitutional right to choose their own associates, I cannot understand by what constitutional authority Florida can compel answers to questions which abridge that right. Accordingly, I would reverse here on the ground that there has been a direct abridgment of the right of association of the National Association for the Advancement of Colored People and its members. But, since the Court assumes for purposes of this case that there was no direct abridgment of First Amendment freedoms, I concur in the Court's opinion, which is based on constitutional principles laid down in *Schneider* v. *Irvington* . . . and later cases of this Court following *Schneider.*

MR. JUSTICE DOUGLAS, concurring:

I join the opinion of the Court, because it is carefully written within the framework of our current decisions. But since the matters involved touch constitutional rights and since I see the Constitution in somewhat different dimensions than are reflected in our decisions, it seems appropriate to set out my views. . . .

When the constitutional limits of lawmaking are passed, investigation is out of bounds. . . . That is to say, investigations by a legislative committee which "could result in no valid legislation on the subject" are beyond the pale. . . . In my view, government is not only powerless to legislate with respect to membership in a lawful organization; it is also precluded from probing the intimacies of spiritual and intellectual relationships in the myriad of such societies and groups that exist in this country, regardless of the legislative purpose sought to be served. "[T]he provisions of the First Amendment . . . of course reach and limit . . . investigations." *Barenblatt* v. *United States.* . . . If that is not true I see no barrier to investigation of newspapers, churches, political parties, clubs, societies, unions, and any other association for their political, economic, social, philosophical, or religious views. If, in its quest to determine whether existing laws are being enforced or new laws are needed, an investigating committee can ascertain whether known Communists or criminals are members of an organization not shown to be engaged in conduct properly subject to regulation, it is but a short and inexorable step to the conclusion that it may also probe to ascertain what effect they have had on the other members. For how much more "necessary and appropriate" this information is to the legislative purpose being pursued!

It is no answer to the conclusion that all such investigations are illegal to suggest that the committee is pursuing a lawful objective in the manner it has determined most appropriate. For, as Laurent Frantz, The First Amendment in the Balance, 71 *Yale L.J.* 1424, 1441, has so persuasively shown, "it does not follow that any objective can ever be weighed against an express limitation on the means available for its pursuit. The public interest in the suppression of crime, for example, cannot be weighed against a constitutional provision that accused persons may not be denied the right to counsel." When otherwise valid legislation is sought to be applied in an unconstitutional manner we do not sustain its application. A different test should not obtain for legislative investigations. "[A]ny constitutional limitation serves a significant function only insofar as it stands in the way of something which government thinks ought to be done. Nothing else needs to be prohibited." Frantz, supra, at 1445. . . .

There is no other course consistent with the Free Society envisioned by the First Amendment. For the views a citizen entertains, the beliefs he harbors, the utterances he makes, the ideology he embraces and the people he associates with are no concern of government. That article of faith marks indeed the main difference between the Free Society which we espouse and the dictatorships both on the Left and on the Right. . . .

Government can intervene only when belief, thought, or expression moves into the realm of action that is inimical to society. . . .

Where government is the Big Brother, privacy gives way to surveillance. But our commitment is otherwise. By the First Amendment we have staked our security on freedom to promote a multiplicity of ideas, to associate at will with kindred spirits, and to defy governmental intrusion into these precincts.

MR. JUSTICE HARLAN, whom MR. JUSTICE CLARK, MR. JUSTICE STEWART, and MR. JUSTICE WHITE join, dissenting.

The difficulties with this decision will become apparent once the case is deflated to its true size.

The essential facts are these. For several years before petitioner was convicted of this contempt, the respondent, a duly authorized Committee of the Florida Legislature, had been investigating alleged Communist "infiltration" into various organizations in Dade County, Florida, including the Miami Branch of the National Association for the Advancement of Colored People. There was no suggestion that the branch itself had engaged in any subversive or other illegal activity, but the Committee had developed information indicating that fourteen of the fifty-two present or past residents of Dade County, apparently at one time or another members of the Communist Party or connected organizations, were or had been members or had "participated in the meetings and other affairs" of this local branch of the NAACP.

Having failed to obtain from prior witnesses, other than its own investigator, any significant data as to the truth or falsity of this information, the Committee, in 1959, summoned the petitioner to testify, also requiring that he bring with him the membership records of the branch. Petitioner, a Negro clergyman, was then and for the past five years had been president of the local branch, and his custodianship of the records stands conceded.

On his appearance before the Committee petitioner was asked to consult these records himself and, after doing so, to inform the Committee which, if any, of the fifty-two individually identified persons were or had been members of the NAACP Miami Branch. He declined to do this. . . .

I

This Court rests reversal on its finding that the Committee did not have sufficient justification for including the Miami Branch of the NAACP within the ambit of its investigation—that, in the language of our cases (*Uphaus* v. *Wyman*, . . . an adequate "nexus" was lacking between the NAACP and the subject matter of the Committee's inquiry.

The Court's reasoning is difficult to grasp. I read its opinion as basically proceeding on the premise that the governmental interest in investigating Communist infiltration into admittedly nonsubversive organizations, as distinguished from investigating organizations themselves suspected of subversive activities, is not sufficient to overcome the countervailing right to freedom of association. . . . On this basis "nexus" is seemingly found lacking because it was never claimed that the NAACP Miami Branch had itself engaged in

subversive activity . . . and because none of the Committee's evidence relating to any of the fifty-two alleged Communist Party members was sufficient to attribute such activity to the local branch or to show that it was dominated, influenced, or used "by Communists." . . .

But, until today, I had never supposed that any of our decisions relating to state or federal power to investigate in the field of Communist subversion could possibly be taken as suggesting any difference in the degree of governmental investigatory interest as between Communist infiltration *of* organizations and Communist activity *by* organizations. See, e. g., *Barenblatt* v. *United States* . . . (infiltration into education); *Wilkinson* v. *United States* and *Braden* v. *United States,* . . . (infiltration into basic industries). . . .

Given the unsoundness of the basic premise underlying the Court's holding as to the absence of "nexus," this decision surely falls of its own weight. For unless "nexus" requires an investigating agency to prove in advance the very things it is trying to find out, I do not understand how it can be said that the information preliminarily developed by the Committee's investigator was not sufficient to satisfy, under any reasonable test, the requirement of "nexus."

II

I also find it difficult to see how this case really presents any serious question as to interference with freedom of association. Given the willingness of the petitioner to testify from recollection as to individual memberships in the local branch of the NAACP the germaneness of the membership records to the subject matter of the Committee's investigation, and the limited purpose for which their use was sought—as an aid to refreshing the witness' recollection, involving their divulgence only to the petitioner himself . . . —this case of course bears no resemblance whatever to *NAACP* v. *Alabama* or *Bates* v. *Little Rock*. . . . In both of those cases the State had sought general divulgence of local NAACP membership lists without any showing of a justifying state interest. In effect what we are asked to hold here is that the petitioner had a constitutional right to give only partial or inaccurate testimony, and that indeed seems to me the true effect of the Court's holding today. . . .

I would affirm.

MR. JUSTICE WHITE, dissenting:

In my view, the opinion of the Court represents a serious limitation upon the Court's previous cases dealing with this subject matter and upon the right of the legislature to investigate the Communist Party and its activities. Although one of the classic and recurring activities of the Communist Party is the infiltration and subversion of other organizations, either openly or in a clandestine manner, the Court holds that even where a legislature has evidence that a legitimate organization is under assault and even though that organization is itself sounding open and public alarm, an investigating committee is nevertheless forbidden to compel the organization or its members to reveal the fact, or not, of membership in that organization of named Communists assigned to the infiltrating task. . . .

The net effect of the Court's decision is, of course, to insulate from effective legislative inquiry and preventive legislation the time-proven skills of the Communist Party in subverting and eventually controlling legitimate organizations. Until such a group, chosen as an object of Communist Party action, has been effectively reduced to vassalage, legislative bodies may seek no information from the organization under attack by duty-bound Communists. When the job has been done and the legislative committee can prove it, it then has the hollow privilege of recording another victory for the Communist Party, which both Congress and this Court have found to be an organization under the direction of a foreign power, dedicated to the overthrow of the Government if necessary by force and violence.

I respectfully dissent.

KEYISHIAN *v.* BOARD OF REGENTS OF THE
UNIVERSITY OF THE STATE OF NEW YORK
385 U.S. 589; 87 Sup. Ct. 675; 17 L. Ed. 2d 629 (1967)

MR. JUSTICE BRENNAN delivered the opinion of the Court:

Appellants were members of the faculty of the privately owned and operated University of Buffalo, and became state employees when the University was merged in 1962 into the State University of New York, an institution of higher education owned and operated by the State of New York. As faculty members of the State University their continued employment was conditioned upon their compliance with a New York plan, formulated partly in statutes and partly in administrative regulations, which the State utilizes to prevent the appointment or retention of "subversive" persons in state employment. . . .

Appellants brought this action for declaratory and injunctive relief alleging that the state program violated the

Federal Constitution in various respects.

We considered some aspects of the constitutionality of the New York plan 15 years ago in *Adler* v. *Board of Education.* . . .

Adler was a declaratory judgment suit in which the Court held, in effect, that there was no constitutional infirmity in former §12-a or in the Feinberg Law on their faces and that they were capable of constitutional application. But the contention urged in this case that both §3021 and §105 are unconstitutionally vague was not heard or decided. Section 3021 of the Education Law was challenged in *Adler* as unconstitutionally vague, but because the challenge had not been made in the pleadings or in the proceedings in the lower courts, this Court refused to consider it. Nor was any challenge on grounds of vagueness made in *Adler* as to subsections (1) (a) and (b) of §105 of the Civil Service Law. Subsection (3) of §105 was not added until 1958. Appellants in this case timely asserted below the unconstitutionality of all these sections on grounds of vagueness and that question is now properly before us for decision. Moreover, to the extent that *Adler* sustained the provision of the Feinberg Law constituting membership in an organization advocating forceful overthrow of government a ground for disqualification, pertinent constitutional doctrines have since rejected the premises upon which that conclusion rested. *Adler* is therefore not dispositive of the constitutional issues we must decide in this case. . . .

Section 3021 requires removal for "treasonable or seditious" utterances or acts. The 1958 amendment to §105 of the Civil Service Law, now subsection 3 of that section, added such utterances or acts as a ground for removal under that law also. The same wording is used in both statutes—that "the utter-ance of any treasonable or seditious word or words or the doing of any trea-sonable or seditious act or acts" shall be ground for removal. . . . Our experience under the Sedition Act of 1798 taught us that dangers fatal to First Amendment freedoms inhere in the word "seditious." See *New York Times Co.* v. *Sullivan.* . . . The teacher cannot know the extent, if any, to which a "seditious" utterance must transcend mere statement about abstract doctrine, the extent to which it must be intended to and tend to indoctrinate or incite to action in furtherance of the defined doctrine. The crucial consideration is that no teacher can know just where the line is drawn between "seditious" and nonseditious utterances and acts.

Other provisions of §105 also have the same defect of vagueness. Subsection (1) (a) of §105 bars employment of any person who "by word of mouth or writing wilfully and deliberately advocates, advises or teaches the doctrine" of forceful overthrow of government. This provision is plainly susceptible to sweeping and improper application. It may well prohibit the employment of one who merely advocates the doctrine in the abstract without any attempt to indoctrinate others, or incite others to action in furtherance of unlawful aims. . . . And in prohibiting "advising" the "doctrine" of unlawful overthrow does the statute prohibit mere "advising" of the existence of the doctrine, or advising another to support the doctrine? Since "advocacy" of the doctrine of forceful overthrow is separately prohibited, need the person "teaching" or "advising" this doctrine himself "advocate" it? Does the teacher who informs his class about the precepts of Marxism or the Declaration of Independence violate this prohibition?

Similar uncertainty arises as to the application of subsection (1) (b) of

§105. That subsection requires the disqualification of an employee involved with the distribution of written material "containing or advocating, advising or teaching the doctrine" of forceful overthrow, and who himself "advocates, advises, teaches, or embraces the duty, necessity or propriety of adopting the doctrine contained therein." Here again, mere advocacy of abstract doctrine is apparently included. And does the prohibition of distribution of matter "containing" the doctrine bar histories of the evolution of Marxist doctrine or tracing the background of the French, American, and Russian revolutions? The additional requirement, that the person participating in distribution of the material be one who "advocates, advises, teaches, or embraces the duty, necessity or propriety of adopting the doctrine" of forceful overthrow, does not alleviate the uncertainty in the scope of the section, but exacerbates it. Like the language of §105 (1) (a), this language may reasonably be construed to cover mere expression of belief. For example, does the university librarian who recommends the reading of such materials thereby "advocate the propriety of adopting the doctrine contained therein?"

We do not have the benefit of a judicial gloss by the New York courts enlightening us as to the scope of this complicated plan. In light of the intricate administrative machinery for its enforcement, this is not surprising. The very intricacy of the plan and the uncertainty as to the scope of its proscriptions make it a highly efficient *in terrorem* mechanism. It would be a bold teacher who would not stay as far as possible from utterance or acts which might jeopardize his living by enmeshing him in this intricate machinery. The uncertainty as to the utterances and acts proscribed increases that caution in

"those who believe the written law means what it says." *Baggett* v. *Bullitt.* . . . The result must be to stifle "that free play of the spirit which all teachers ought especially to cultivate and practice. . . ." That probability is enhanced by the provisions requiring an annual review of every teacher to determine whether any utterance or act of his, inside the classroom or out, came within the sanctions of the laws. For a memorandum warns employees that under the statutes "subversive" activities may take the form of "the writing of articles, the distribution of pamphlets, the endorsement of speeches made or articles written or acts performed by others," and reminds them "that it is the primary duty of the school authorities in each school district to take positive action to eliminate from the school system any teacher in whose case there is evidence that he is guilty of subversive activity. School authorities are under obligation to proceed immediately and conclusively in every such case."

There can be no doubt of the legitimacy of New York's interest in protecting its education system from subversion. But "even though the governmental purpose be legitimate and substantial, that purpose cannot be pursued by means that broadly stifle fundamental personal liberties when the end can be more narrowly achieved." *Shelton* v. *Tucker.* . . . The principle is not inapplicable because the legislation is aimed at keeping subversives out of the teaching ranks. In *DeJonge* v. *State of Oregon* . . . the Court said:

"The greater the importance of safeguarding the community from incitements to the overthrow of our institutions by force and violence, the more imperative is the need to preserve inviolate the constitutional rights of free speech, free press and free assembly in order to maintain the opportunity for free political discussion, to the end that government may be responsive to the will of the people and that changes, if desired, may be obtained by peaceful means. Therein lies the security of the Republic, the very foundation of constitutional government."

Our Nation is deeply committed to safeguarding academic freedom, which is of transcendent value to all of us and not merely to the teachers concerned. That freedom is therefore a special concern of the First Amendment, which does not tolerate laws that cast a pall of orthodoxy over the classroom. "The vigilant protection of constitutional freedoms is nowhere more vital than in the community of American schools." *Shelton* v. *Tucker.* . . . The classroom is peculiarly the "marketplace of ideas." The Nation's future depends upon leaders trained through wide exposure to that robust exchange of ideas which discovers truth "out of a multitude of tongues, [rather] than through any kind of authoritative selection." . . . In *Sweezy* v. *State of New Hampshire,* we said:

"The essentiality of freedom in the community of American universities is almost self-evident. No one should underestimate the vital role in a democracy that is played by those who guide and train our youth. To impose any strait jacket upon the intellectual leaders in our colleges and universities would imperil the future of our Nation. No field of education is so thoroughly comprehended by man that new discoveries cannot yet be made. Particularly is that true in the social sciences, where few, if any, principles are accepted as absolutes.

Scholarship cannot flourish in an atmosphere of suspicion and distrust. Teachers and students must always remain free to inquire, to study and to evaluate, to gain new maturity and understanding; otherwise our civilization will stagnate and die."

We emphasize once again that "[p]recision of regulation must be the touchstone in an area so closely touching our most precious freedoms." *NAACP* v. *Button.* . . . "For standards of permissible statutory vagueness are strict in the area of free expression. . . . Because First Amendment freedoms need breathing space to survive, government may regulate in the area only with narrow specificity." . . . New York's complicated and intricate scheme plainly violates that standard. When one must guess what conduct or utterance may lose him his position, one necessarily will "steer far wider of the unlawful zone. . . ." *Speiser* v. *Randall.* . . . For "The threat of sanctions may deter . . . almost as potently as the actual application of sanctions." *NAACP* v. *Button.* . . . The danger of that chilling effect upon the exercise of vital First Amendment rights must be guarded against by sensitive tools which clearly inform teachers what is being sanctioned. . . .

The regulatory maze created by New York is wholly lacking in "terms susceptible of objective measurement." *Cramp* v. *Board of Public Instruction.* . . . It has the quality of "extraordinary ambiguity" found to be fatal to the oaths considered in *Cramp* and *Baggett* v. *Bullitt.* "[M]en of common intelligence must necessarily guess at its meaning and differ as to its application. . . ." *Baggett* v. *Bullitt.* . . . Vagueness of wording is aggravated by prolixity and profusion of statutes, regulations, and administrative machinery, and by manifold cross-references to interrelated enactments and rules.

We therefore hold that §3021 of the Education Law and subsections (1) (a), (1) (b) and (3) of §105 of the Civil Service Law as implemented by the machinery created pursuant to §3022 of the Education Law are unconstitutional.

Appellants have also challenged the constitutionality of the discrete provisions of subsection (1) (c) of §105 and subsection (2) of the Feinberg Law, which make Communist Party membership, as such, prima facie evidence of disqualification. . . . Subsection (2) of the Feinberg Law was, however, before the Court in *Adler* and its constitutionality was sustained. But constitutional doctrine which has emerged since that decision has rejected its major premise. That premise was that public employment, including academic employment, may be conditioned upon the surrender of constitutional rights which could not be abridged by direct government action. Teachers, the Court said in *Adler,* "may work for the school system upon the reasonable terms laid down by the proper authorities of New York. If they do not choose to work on such terms, they are at liberty to retain their beliefs and associations and go elsewhere." . . . The Court also stated that a teacher denied employment because of membership in a listed organization "is not thereby denied the right of free speech and assembly. His freedom of choice between membership in the organization and employment in the school system might be limited, but not his freedom of speech or assembly, except in the remote sense that limitation is inherent in every choice." . . .

However, the Court of Appeals for the Second Circuit correctly said in an earlier stage of this case, ". . . the theory that public employment which may be denied altogether may be subjected to any conditions, regardless of how unreasonable, has been uniformly rejected." . . . Indeed, that theory was expressly rejected in a series of decisions following *Adler.* See *Wieman* v. *Updegraff . . . Cramp* v. *Board of Public Instruction; Baggett* v. *Bullitt; Shelton* v. *Tucker; Speiser* v. *Randall.* In *Sherbert* v. *Verner,* . . . we said: "It is too late in the day to doubt that the liberties of religion and expression may be infringed by the denial of or placing of conditions upon a benefit or privilege."

We proceed then to the question of the validity of the provisions of subsection (c) of §105 and subsection (2) of §3022, barring employment to members of listed organizations. Here again constitutional doctrine has developed since *Adler.* Mere knowing membership without a specific intent to further the unlawful aims of an organization is not a constitutionally adequate basis for exclusion from such positions as those held by appellants.

In *Elfbrandt* v. *Russell,* . . . we said, "Those who join an organization but do not share its unlawful purposes and who do not participate in its unlawful activities surely pose no threat, either as citizens or as public employees." We there struck down a statutorily required oath binding the state employee not to become a member of the Communist Party with knowledge of its unlawful purpose, on threat of discharge and perjury prosecution if the oath were violated. We found that "[a]ny lingering doubt that proscription of mere knowing membership, without any showing of 'specific intent,' would run afoul of the Constitution was set at rest by our decision in *Aptheker* v. *Secretary of State.* . . . In *Aptheker* we held that Party membership, without knowledge of the Party's unlawful purposes *and* specific intent to further its unlawful aims, could not constitutionally warrant deprivation of the right to travel abroad. As we said in *Schneiderman* v. *United States* . . . "[U]nder our traditions beliefs are personal and not a matter of mere association, and . . . men in adhering to a political party or other organization notoriously do not subscribe unqualifiedly to all of its platforms or asserted principles." "A law which applies to membership without the 'specific intent' to further the illegal aims of the organization infringes unnecessarily on protected freedoms. It rests on the doctrine of 'guilt by association' which has no place here." . . . Thus mere Party membership, even with knowledge of the Party's unlawful goals, cannot suffice to justify criminal punishment, see *Scales* v. *United States* . . . ; *Yates* v. *United States;* nor may it warrant a finding of moral unfitness justifying disbarment. *Schware* v. *Board of Bar Examiners.* . . .

These limitations clearly apply to a provision, like §105(1) (c), which blankets all state employees, regardless of the "sensitivity" of their positions. But even the Feinberg Law provision, applicable primarily to activities of teachers, who have captive audiences of young minds, are subject to these limitations in favor of freedom of expression and association; the stifling effect on the academic mind from curtailing freedom of association in such manner is manifest, and has been documented in recent studies. *Elfbrandt* and *Aptheker* state the governing standard: legislation which sanctions membership unaccompanied by specific intent to further the unlawful goals of the organization or which is not active membership violates constitutional limitations.

Measured against this standard, both Civil Service Law §105(1) (c) and Education Law §3022(2) sweep overbroadly into association which may not be sanctioned. . . .

They seek to bar employment both for association which legitimately may be sanctioned and for association which may not be sanctioned consistently with First Amendment rights. Where statutes have an overbroad sweep, just as where they are vague, "the hazard of loss or substantial impairment of those precious rights may be critical," *Dombrowski* v. *Pfister,* since those covered by the statute are bound to limit their behavior to that which is unquestionably safe. As we said in *Shelton* v. *Tucker,* "The breadth of legislative abridgment must be viewed in the light of less drastic means for achieving the same basic purpose."

We therefore hold that Civil Service Law §105(1) (c) and Education Law §3022(2) are invalid insofar as they sanction mere knowing membership without any showing of specific intent to further the unlawful aims of the Communist Party of the United States or of the State of New York.

The judgment of the District Court is reversed and the case is remanded for further proceedings consistent with this opinion.

Reversed and remanded.

MR. JUSTICE CLARK, with whom MR. JUSTICE HARLAN, MR. JUSTICE STEWART and MR. JUSTICE WHITE join, dissenting.

The blunderbuss fashion in which the majority couches "its artillery of words" together with the morass of cases it cites as authority and the obscurity of their application to the question at hand makes it difficult to grasp the true thrust of its decision. At the outset, it is therefore necessary to focus on its basis.

This is a declaratory judgment action testing the *application* of the Feinberg Law to appellants. The certificate and statement once required by the Board and upon which appellants base their attack were, before the case was tried, abandoned by the Board and are no longer required to be made. Despite this fact the majority proceeds to its decision striking down New York's Feinberg Law and other of its statutes as applied to appellants on the basis of the old certificate and statement. It does not explain how the statute can be applied to appellants under procedures which have been for over two years a dead letter. The issues posed are, therefore, purely abstract and entirely speculative in character. The Court under such circumstances has in the past refused to pass upon constitutional questions. In addition, the appellants have neither exhausted their administrative remedies, nor pursued the remedy of judicial review of agency action as provided earlier by subdivision (d) of §12–a of the Civil Service Law. Finally, one of the sections stricken, §105(3), has been amended and under its terms will not become effective until September 1, 1967. (L.1965, Ch. 1030.)

I

The old certificate upon which the majority operates required all of the appellants, save Starbuck, to answer the query whether they were Communists, and if they were, whether they had communicated that fact to the President of the University. Starbuck was required to answer whether he had ever advised, taught, or been a member of a group which taught or advocated the doctrine that the Government of the United States, or any of its political subdivisions, should be overthrown by force, violence, or any unlawful means. All refused to comply. It is in this nonexistent frame of reference that the majority proceeds to act.

It is clear that the Feinberg Law, in which this Court found "no constitutional infirmity" in 1952, has been given its death blow today. Just as the majority here finds that there "can be no doubt of the legitimacy of New York's interest in protecting its education system from subversion" there can also be no doubt that "the be-all and end-all" of New York's effort is here. And regardless of its correctness neither New York nor the several States that have followed the teaching of *Adler* for some fifteen years, can ever put the pieces together again. No court has ever reached out so far to destroy so much with so little.

II

This Court has again and again, since at least 1951, approved procedures either identical or at the least similar to the ones the Court condemns today. In *Garner* v. *Board of Works of Los Angeles,* we held that a public employer was not precluded, simply because it was an agency of the State, "from inquiring of its employees as to matters that may prove relevant to their fitness and suitability for the public service." 341 U.S., at p. 720, 71 Sup. Ct. at p. 912. The oath there used practically the same language as the Starbuck statement here and the affidavit reflects the same type of inquiry as was made in the old certificate condemned here. Then in 1952, in *Adler* v. *Board of Education,* this Court passed upon the identical statute condemned here. It, too, was a declaratory judgment action—as in this case. However, there the issues were not so abstractly framed. Our late Brother Minton wrote for the Court:

"A teacher works in a sensitive area in a schoolroom. There he shapes the attitude of young minds towards the society in which they live. In this, the state has a vital concern. It must preserve the integrity of the schools. That the school authorities have the right and the duty to screen the officials, teachers, and employees as to their fitness to maintain the integrity of the schools as a part of ordered society cannot be doubted." At 493 of 342 U.S., at 385 of 72 Sup. Ct.

And again in 1958 the problem was before us in *Beilan* v. *Board of Education,* School District of Philadelphia, supra. There our late Brother Barton wrote for the Court:

"By engaging in teaching in the public schools, petitioner did not give up his right to freedom of belief, speech or association. He did, however, undertake obligations of frankness, candor and cooperation in answering inquiries made of him by his employing Board examining into his fitness to serve it as a public school teacher."

And on the same day in *Lerner* v. *Casey* . . . our Brother Harlan again upheld the severance of a public employee for his refusal to answer questions concerning his loyalty. And in the same Term my Brother Brennan himself cited Garner with approval in *Speiser* v. *Randall.* . . .

Since that time the *Adler* line of cases have been cited again and again with approval: *Shelton* v. *Tucker* . . . in which both *Adler* and *Beilan* were quoted with approval and *Garner* and *Lerner* were cited in a like manner; likewise in *Cramp* v. *Board of Public*

Instruction, . . . Adler was quoted twice with approval, and, in a related field where the employee was discharged for refusal to answer questions as to his loyalty after being ordered to do so, the Court cited with approval all of the cases which today it says have been rejected, *i.e., Garner, Adler, Beilan* and *Lerner. Nelson* v. *Los Angeles County.* . . . Later *Konigsberg* v. *State Bar* . . . likewise cited with approval both *Beilan* and *Garner.* And in our decision in In re Anastaplo (1961), . . . *Garner, Beilan* and *Lerner* were all referred to. Finally, only two Terms ago my Brother White relied upon *Cramp* which in turn quoted *Adler* with approval twice. See *Baggett* v. *Bullitt.* . . .

In view of this long list of decisions covering over fifteen years of this Court's history, in which no opinion of this Court even questioned the validity of the *Adler* line of cases, it is strange to me that the Court now finds that the "constitutional doctrine which has emerged since . . . has rejected [*Adler's*] major premise." With due respect, as I read them, our cases have done no such thing.

III

Likewise subsection (1) (3) of §105 is also inapplicable. It was derived from §23–a of the Civil Service Law. The latter provision was on the books at the time of the Feinberg Law as well as when *Adler* was decided. The Feinberg Law referred only to §12–a of the Civil Service Law, not §23–a. Section 12–a was later recodified, as subsections (1) (a) and (b) of §105 of the Civil Service Law. Section 23–a (now §105(3)) deals only with the civil divisions of the Civil Service of the State. As the Attorney General tells us, the law before us has to do with the qualifications of college level personnel not covered by Civil Service. The Attorney General also advises that no superintendent, teacher, or employee of the educational system has ever been charged with violating §105(3). The Court seems to me to be building straw men.

The majority also says that no challenge or vagueness points were passed upon in *Adler*. A careful examination of the briefs in that case casts considerable doubt on this conclusion.

IV

But even if *Adler* did not decide these questions I would be obliged to answer them in the same way. The only portion of the Feinberg Law which the majority says was not covered there and is applicable to appellants is §§105(1) (a), (1) (b) and (1) (c). These have to do with teachers who advocate, advise, or teach the doctrine of overthrow of our Government by force and violence, either orally or in writing. This was the identical conduct that was condemned in *Dennis* v. *United States,* supra. There the Court found the exact verbiage not to be unconstitutionally vague, and that finding was of course not affected by the decision of this Court in *Yates* v. *United States.* The majority makes much over the horribles that might arise from subsection (1) (b) of §105 which condemns the printing, publishing, selling, etc., of matter containing such doctrine. But the majority fails to state that this action is condemned only *when and if* the teacher also personally advocates, advises, teaches, etc., the necessity or propriety of adopting such doctrine. This places this subsection on the same footing as (1) (a). And the same is true of subsection (1) (c) where a teacher organizes, helps to organize or becomes a member of an organization which teaches or advocates such doc-

trine, for scienter would also be a necessary ingredient under our opinion in *Garner,* supra. Moreover, membership is only prima facie evidence of disqualification and could be rebutted, leaving the burden of proof on the State. Furthermore, all of these procedures are protected by an adversary hearing with full judicial review.

In the light of these considerations the strained and unbelievable suppositions that the majority poses could hardly occur. As was said in *Dennis,* supra, "we are not convinced that because there may be borderline cases" the State should be prohibited the protection it seeks. Where there is doubt as to one's intent or the nature of his activities we cannot assume that the administrative boards will not give those offended full protection. Furthermore, the courts always sit to make certain that this is done.

The majority says that the Feinberg Law is bad because it has an "overbroad sweep." I regret to say—and I do so with deference—that the majority has by its broadside swept away one of our most precious rights, namely, the right of self-preservation. Our public educational system is the genius of our democracy. The minds of our youth are developed there and the character of that development will determine the future of our land. Indeed, our very existence depends upon it. The issue here is a very narrow one. It is not freedom of speech, freedom of thought, freedom of press, freedom of assembly, or of association, even in the Communist Party. It is simply this: May the State provide that one who, after a hearing with full judicial review, is found to wilfully and deliberately advocate, advise, or teach that our Government should be overthrown by force or violence or other unlawful means; or who wilfully and deliberately prints, publishes, etc., any book or paper that so advocates *and who personally* advocates such doctrine himself; or who wilfully and deliberately becomes a member of an organization that advocates such doctrine, is prima facie disqualified from teaching in its university? My answer, in keeping with all of our cases up until today, is "Yes"!

I dissent.

16
War and the Constitution

An acute observer of the American scene has remarked that the ". . . transformation of an America nominally at peace into one of the world's two great military powers is perhaps the single greatest and most ambiguous change in America. Over the past thirty years, the armed forces have gradually become one of the most important of American social institutions."[1] The increased role of the military in American life has made the traditional distinction between military and civilian affairs less significant. Today many military leaders must do much more than simply command fighting units in battle. Instead, they must combine the qualities of soldier, statesman, and diplomat. Among other things, many of these leaders now ". . . are required to understand, to communicate with, and to evaluate the judgment of political leaders, officials of other executive agencies, and countless specialists; they must make sound judgments themselves on matters which affect a wide variety of civilian concerns. They are called upon to evaluate the motivations and capabilities of foreign nations and to estimate the effects of American action or inaction upon these nations. And above all, the new role of military leaders requires of them a heightened awareness of the principles of our democratic society."[2]

[1] D. W. Brogan, "Unnoticed Changes in America," *Harper's Magazine* (February 1957), pp. 29–30.

[2] John W. Masland and Laurence I. Radway, *Soldiers and Scholars, Military Edu-*

The framers of the Constitution could not probably have foreseen this development, which has posed new and complex problems for the preservation of individual liberties, although, of course, they were well aware of the dangers to individual freedom during periods of war or emergency. They were familiar with the struggles in England to subdue and contain the exercise of arbitrary military power. Their personal experiences with English attempts to impose various military controls over some of the colonies confirmed their deepest fears of the military. Their distrust of the military is evidenced clearly by various provisions of the Constitution that sought to subordinate military to civilian authority. Under Article II, the President, a civilian officer, was made Commander-in-Chief of the Army and Navy. Article I provided that only Congress could declare war; Congress also was given sole power to raise and support armies and to maintain a navy. A further check over the armed forces was provided by the provision that no congressional appropriation of money for military purposes "shall be for a longer term than two years." Also, under Article I, the control over the militia, or the National Guard, was divided between the state and national governments. These constitutional provisions obviously were designed not only to keep the military subordinate to civilian authority but also to divide powers over the armed forces among the President, Congress, and the states so that no one of these governmental institutions could gain sole control of the military. This was in line with the framers' basic policy of dividing authority to help prevent the establishment of despotic government.

The fact has been noted often that, in our time, the constitutional division of authority over the armed forces had paradoxical results.

> The very aspects of the Constitution which the framers and later commentators have cited as establishing civilian control are in fact those which hinder its realization: civilian control would be more easily achieved in the twentieth century if the framers had been less eager to achieve it in the eighteenth century. Objective civilian control is maximized if the military are limited in scope to professional matters and relegated to a subordinate position in a pyramid of authority culminating in a single civilian head. The military clauses of the Constitution, however, provide for almost exactly the opposite. They divide civilian responsibility for military affairs and thereby foster the direct access of the professional military authorities to the highest levels of government.[3]

Nevertheless, adjustments have been made within the constitutional framework which still make possible civilian control of the military. In addition, other factors, such as America's geographical location, which made large

---

cation and National Policy (Princeton, N.J.: Princeton University Press, 1957), p. vii. See also Fred J. Cook, "Juggernaut: The Warfare State," *The Nation,* Vol. 193 (October 28, 1961), p. 277.

[3] Samuel P. Huntington, "Civilian Control and the Constitution," *American Political Science Review,* Vol. 50 (September 1956), p. 682.

military forces unnecessary until recent years, have helped to keep the military subordinate to the civilian authorities. Today, despite the fundamental changes in the role of the military noted here, the tradition of military subordination to civil authorities is still very strong in the minds of most Americans.

From time to time, and particularly during or shortly after periods of war, conflicts between military authority and civilian rights have arisen. Many such conflicts have had to be resolved by the Supreme Court, for, as Chief Justice Hughes once wrote for a unanimous court, "what are the allowable limits of military discretion, and whether or not they have been overstepped in a particular case, are judicial questions."[4]

The Civil War Period

Not until the Civil War period did fundamental conflicts arise between the claims of military necessity and individual liberties. President Lincoln felt strongly that private constitutional rights had to be disregarded when they interfered with the winning of the war and the preservation of the Union. As a consequence, individual rights were curtailed drastically during the Civil War by the unprecedented expansion of military powers. Among other things, military officers were authorized by the President to suspend the writ of habeas corpus, martial law was instituted in a number of areas, and military tribunals were used for the trial of civilians.

The clash between civilian and military authorities during this period can be seen in the case of *Ex Parte Merryman,* 17 Fed. Cas. 9487 (1861). John Merryman, a Southern agitator of wealth and position residing in Maryland, was arrested by order of the military authorities of the area for his opposition to the Union. After his confinement in Fort McHenry, Merryman petitioned Chief Justice Taney for a writ of habeas corpus. At that time Maryland was part of the circuit over which the Chief Justice presided. Taney issued the writ, which directed the commanding general of Fort McHenry to bring Merryman before the circuit court so that the reasons for his imprisonment could be examined. The commanding general refused to comply with Taney's order and replied through a military aide that he had been authorized by the President to suspend the writ of habeas corpus. Taney thereupon ordered that the general be brought before the court, but a United States marshall was denied entrance to Fort McHenry; the general simply ignored Taney's order. Since Taney could not obtain compliance with his orders, he could do nothing but write his opinion, in which he stated that the President had no authority to suspend the writ of habeas corpus and that only Congress could suspend the writ. Taney decried the usurpation of power by military authorities and directed that a copy of the entire record of the case be sent to President Lincoln. He concluded that "it will then remain for that high officer, in fulfill-

4 *Sterling* v. *Constantin,* 287 U.S. 378 (1932).

ment of his constitutional obligation to take care that the laws be faithfully executed, to determine what measures he will take to cause the civil process of the United States to be respected and enforced." President Lincoln never *directly* answered the Chief Justice. However, Merryman was later released from Fort McHenry and turned over to civilian authorities. He was subsequently indicted for treason, but the case against him was finally dropped. "This was typical of the treatment accorded such cases by the Lincoln administration. When Merryman was no longer capable of harming the Union, Lincoln, who sought no tyranny, gladly washed his hands of the Merryman controversy. But neither the President nor the Chief Justice had a change of heart, and their differences endured."[5]

The encroachment upon civil authority by the military continued throughout the Civil War, but in only one case [*Ex Parte Vallandigham,* 1 Wall. 243 (1864)] was the system of military trials challenged in the Supreme Court, and there the Court dismissed the case, stating that it was without jurisdiction to review the proceedings of a military tribunal. The dearth of cases in the Supreme Court despite the great number of trials held before military commissions can be explained by the fact that judicial review was almost impossible to obtain during this period. "Since review by certiorari was not possible, the only way to get a case before the courts was to ask the judiciary to consider the question of the constitutionality of the President's suspension of the privilege of the writ of habeas corpus. The Supreme Court was unwilling to do this until the war was over and Lincoln was dead."[6] By that time the Court was ready to place restraints upon the exercise of military powers. This it did in *Ex Parte Milligan* (p. 563) in an opinion written by Justice Davis, who had been one of Lincoln's closest friends and most ardent supporters. The *Milligan* case stands out as one of the great landmark decisions in the cause of civil supremacy. The sweeping majority opinion of Justice Davis declared that Congress had *no* authority to establish military commissions even if it chose to do so. The concurring justices, on the other hand, were unwilling to deny, categorically, the power of Congress to establish military tribunals.

By its decision in the *Milligan* case, the Court became embroiled deeply in the conflict between President Johnson and Congress over reconstruction. The decision cast serious doubts upon the efforts of the Radical Republicans to impose military rule upon the Southern states and strengthened President Johnson's proposals for moderation. Leading Radical Republicans launched a violent attack upon the Court soon after the *Milligan* decision was rendered. In 1866, they pushed a law through Congress that reduced the number of justices from nine to seven, and when the Radical Republicans thought that

---

[5] David M. Silver, *Lincoln's Supreme Court* (Urbana: University of Illinois Press, 1957), p. 36. A thorough discussion of the *Merryman* case and the *Korematsu* case (noted subsequently) are found in Rocco J. Tresolini, *Justice and the Supreme Court* (Philadelphia: Lippincott, 1963), chaps. 1, 7.

[6] Glendon A. Schubert, Jr., *The Presidency in the Courts* (Minneapolis: University of Minnesota Press, 1957), p. 188.

the Court might hold the Reconstruction Acts invalid in a pending case, Congress enacted a statute that withdrew the Court's jurisdiction over the case. The Court acquiesced and subsequently dismissed the case on the ground that it had no jurisdiction.[7]

World War II

America's limited participation in World War I produced no significant conflicts between military and civil authority, but the unprecedented extensions of military powers during the Second World War created many new problems concerning civil-military relationships. In fact, the only two major encroachments on individual liberties during World War II resulted from military action.

Individual liberties were seriously impaired as the result of the military evacuation of some 70,000 citizens and 40,000 aliens of Japanese descent from the Pacific Coast during World War II. The details relating to the compulsory removal of these Japanese-Americans from their homes are noted subsequently in connection with *Korematsu v. United States* (p. 568), where the Supreme Court held that the evacuation program was constitutional. On the same day that the *Korematsu* case was decided, the Court held, in *Ex Parte Endo,* 323 U.S. 283 (1944), that a Japanese-American girl, whose loyalty to the United States had been clearly established, could not be held in a war relocation center. However, the Court evaded the major constitutional issue in the *Endo* case and refused to invalidate the entire internment program. The Court held simply that neither Congress nor the President had empowered the War Relocation Authority to *continue* the detention of Japanese-American citizens once their loyalty had been established. In the "calm perspective of hindsight," most postwar commentators have concluded that the military evacuation and confinement of Japanese-Americans constituted an unnecessary infringement of individual liberties.[8]

The second major instance of the military suppression of individual liberties during World War II occurred in Hawaii. Military government was established in Hawaii a few hours after the Japanese attack on Pearl Harbor on December 7, 1941. The writ of habeas corpus was suspended, and the civilian governor's powers were conferred upon the local army commander. The new military governor immediately closed all the regular civil and criminal courts and established military commissions to try civilians as well as military personnel. Sentences imposed by the new military courts were not subject to review by the regular federal courts. In 1943, civil government was partially restored by order of the President, but the writ of habeas corpus remained suspended and military courts were still authorized to try civilians for viola-

---

[7] *Ex Parte McCardle,* 7 Wall. 506 (1869).

[8] See, for example, Robert E. Cushman, "Civil Liberties in the Atomic Age," *The Annals,* Vol. 249 (January 1947), p. 54.

tions of military orders; not until October 1944, was military government in Hawaii terminated entirely. Serious objections were raised to the long-continued subordination to army control by the civil officers and inhabitants of Hawaii. They argued that military government was unnecessary in Hawaii after the battle of Midway in June 1942, because that battle had ended any danger of a Japanese invasion of the islands, Federal judges maintained that the regular civilian courts were in a position to handle effectively the cases turned over to military courts.

Not until after the war, in *Duncan* v. *Kahanamoku,* 327 U.S. 304 (1946), did the Supreme Court have an opportunity to pass on the validity of the Hawaiian military government. The Court held in the *Duncan* case that Congress had not authorized the establishment of military tribunals in Hawaii to try civilians when the civil courts were open and available. Thus, the Court ruled that the military leaders had exceeded their authority in suppressing civil government in Hawaii under the provisions of the Hawaiian Organic Act of 1900. But again, as in the *Milligan* case, judicial restraints were not placed on the military until after the war was ended.

MILITARY COMMISSIONS AND ENEMY NATIONALS

The Supreme Court was confronted with some novel questions concerning the rights of enemy nationals both during and after the war. The first case, *Ex Parte Quirin,* 317 U.S. 1 (1942), arose out of the apprehension of eight young Nazi agents who had been landed on Long Island and along the Florida coast by German submarines for sabotage purposes. Upon landing, the potential saboteurs had discarded their German uniforms and disguised themselves as civilians. They were captured by the Federal Bureau of Investigation and turned over to military authorities. President Roosevelt established a military commission to try the eight agents for violating the laws of war. Seven of the eight Nazi prisoners thereupon applied for writs of habeas corpus, contending that they were not subject to military jurisdiction because they had not been apprehended in a zone of active military operations. In July 1942, the Supreme Court convened in an extraordinary special session to hear the case. The petitions for habeas corpus were denied; the Court reasoned that the President had been authorized by both constitutional and statutory provisions to establish military commissions for the trial of enemy nationals for offenses against the laws of war. The prisoners' heavy reliance on the *Milligan* case was noted, but the Court simply remarked that the *Milligan* decision was "inapplicable to the case presented by the present record." Milligan was a citizen and resident of Indiana and had never lived in a rebellious state. As a nonbelligerent, he was not subject to the law of war. Six of the prisoners were subsequently executed, and two were imprisoned for life.

After the war, the Supreme Court was asked again to inquire into the authority of an American military commission that had condemned Japanese General Yamashita to death for war crimes. In the case of *In re Yamashita* (p. 572) the Court again sustained the jurisdiction of the military commission and held that its findings were not subject to review by the ordinary courts. In his majority opinion, Chief Justice Stone asserted that Yamashita's conviction could be reviewed only by higher military authorities and that the military commission did not need to observe the procedural rights guaranteed to an accused person by the due process clause of the Fifth Amendment when trying an enemy combatant. Justices Murphy and Rutledge dissented sharply from that holding.[9]

A somewhat different question was presented by the creation of international rather than exclusively American tribunals for the trial of war criminals. Several persons convicted of war crimes by international tribunals petitioned the Supreme Court for a review of the legality of their convictions. In *Hirota* v. *MacArthur,* 338 U.S. 197 (1948), the Court held that the "courts of the United States have no power or authority to review, to affirm, set aside, or annul the judgments and sentences imposed" by international tribunals.

Civil–Military Problems of the Postwar Period

The scope and magnitude of World War II made a return to normal peacetime conditions after the cessation of hostilities a difficult one indeed. Return to normality was made even more difficult by the efforts of the United States and the Western world to contain international communism. "In fact, since World War II no aspect of national life has assumed such overshadowing significance as has the burden of preparation for hostilities."[10] As late as 1957, more than one million Americans in the armed forces were serving in seventy-nine foreign lands. Under these circumstances, it was clear that the military was here to stay and that numerous problems involving civil-military relations would arise.

In addition to the cases presented by enemy nationals after the war, the Supreme Court was faced with important questions relating to the military trials of American civilians. In *United States* ex rel. *Toth* v. *Quarles* (p. 580), the Court ruled that a military tribunal could not constitutionally try a discharged serviceman for an offense supposedly committed while he was in the Air Force. Thus, in the *Milligan* and *Duncan* cases, the Court repulsed the effort to expand the jurisdiction of military courts to civilians.

The Court had more difficulty in trying to decide whether it should sustain the power granted to military courts to try civilian dependents of American servicemen serving abroad. Congress had made such civilian dependents sub-

---

[9] The background of the *Yamashita* case is developed fully in a readable book by an American lawyer who was a member of Yamashita's defense staff. See A. Frank Reel, *The Case of General Yamashita* (Chicago: University of Chicago Press, 1949). See also Rocco J. Tresolini, "Justice Rutledge and the *Yamashita* Case," *Social Science,* Vol. 37 (1962), p. 150.

[10] Edward Dumbauld, *The Bill of Rights and What It Means Today* (Norman: University of Oklahoma Press, 1957), p. 62.

ject to military court-martial by a section of the Uniform Code of Military Justice enacted in 1950. The statute was tested by the Supreme Court in two similar cases arising from murders committed on American military installations in foreign lands. In the first case, a Mrs. Smith killed her husband, an Army colonel, at a post in Japan. She was found guilty of murder by a general court-martial in Tokyo and sentenced to life imprisonment. The second case involved the conviction by a general court-martial in England of a Mrs. Covert for the murder of her husband, an Air Force sergeant. In *Kinsella* v. *Krueger,* 351 U.S. 470 (1956), and *Reid* v. *Covert,* 351 U.S. 487 (1956), both decided together and on the same day, the Court held that civilians accompanying members of the armed forces abroad could validly be tried by military courts. However, in each case only five members of the Court constituted the majority. Justice Frankfurter wrote a separate opinion stating that he needed more time to consider the issues. Chief Justice Warren and Justices Black and Douglas stated in their dissent that ". . . the questions raised are complex, the remedy drastic, and the consequences far-reaching upon the lives of civilians. The military is given new powers not hitherto thought consistent with our scheme of government. For these reasons, we need more time to write our dissenting views."

In the next term of the Court, the two women were granted a rehearing. In June 1957, the Court reversed its previous stand of less than twelve months and held that the two women could not be tried by military authorities.[11] In delivering the majority opinion, Justice Black noted that the founders ". . . had no intention to permit the trial of civilians in military courts, where they would be denied jury trials and other constitutional protections, merely by giving Congress the power to make rules which were 'necessary and proper' for the regulation of the 'land and naval forces.' Such a latitudinarian interpretation of these clauses would be at war with the well-established purpose of the founders to keep the military strictly within its proper sphere, subordinate to civil authority." Justice Black further asserted that ". . . there are no supportable grounds upon which to distinguish the *Toth case* from the present cases. We should not break faith with this nation's tradition of keeping military power subservient to civilian authority, a tradition which we believe is firmly embodied in the Constitution."

This still left unanswered the question whether dependents and civilians employed by the armed forces could be subject to military trial for noncapital offenses. But in three companion cases decided in 1960, the Court extended the rule by holding that Congress lacked the power to authorize military trials of any civilians for any offense.[12] In *O'Callahan* v. *Parker,* 89 Sup. Ct. 1683 (1969) the Court continued the tendency to limit more and more se-

---

[11] *Reid* v. *Covert,* 354 U.S. 1.

[12] *Kinsella* v. *United States* ex rel *Singleton,* 361 U.S. 234 (1960); *Grishom* v. *Hagan,* 361 U.S. 278 (1960); *McElroy* v. *United States* ex rel *Gringliards,* 361 U.S. 281 (1960).

verely courts-martial jurisdiction by ruling that members of the armed forces may not be tried for nonservice-connected crimes in military courts.

The postwar American policy of giving military protection to nations threatened by communism raised some important questions relating to trials of American soldiers. Since the war, the United States has negotiated status-of-forces agreements with some fifty countries where American troops are stationed. These agreements generally provide that if an offense is committed by a member of the United States armed forces against a foreign national in the performance of an official duty, American military authorities have legal jurisdiction over the offender. However, if such an offense is committed in an off-duty period, the host country may try the case in its own courts. Many members of Congress and some newspapers have condemned vigorously the practice of handing over American servicemen for trial to foreign courts where they may be convicted by legal procedures that violate the guaranties of the Bill of Rights. Some congressional leaders have pressed for legislation that would order the President to abandon the status-of-forces agreements. Others have argued that the renunciation of these agreements would jeopardize American relations with its allies and force the withdrawal of military forces from strategic world locations. The controversy reached the Supreme Court in *Wilson* v. *Girard,* 354 U.S. 524 (1957), where Girard, an American soldier who had killed a Japanese woman, was turned over to the Japanese courts for trial. In a unanimous opinion, the Court held that there are "no constitutional or statutory barriers" that prohibit surrendering American military personnel to foreign courts. "In the absence of such encroachments, the wisdom of the arrangement is exclusively for the determination of the executive and legislative branches."

EX PARTE MILLIGAN
4 Wall. 2; 18 L. Ed. 281 (1866)

[A civilian named Lambdin P. Milligan, who resided in Indiana, was a Confederate sympathizer during the Civil War. In 1864, he was arrested by order of the commanding officer of the military district of Indiana and tried before a military commission on charges of conspiracy against the United States, affording aid and comfort to the Confederacy, inciting insurrection, disloyal practices, and violation of the laws of war. Milligan was found guilty of various specifications under each charge, such as resisting the draft and conspiracy to seize arms and ammunition stored in arsenals. He was sentenced to death by hanging. In May 1865, Milligan petitioned a circuit court for a writ of habeas corpus on the ground that the military commission had no jurisdiction over him because he was a civilian resident of a state where the ordinary civil courts were still open. He also contended that the military commission's action violated his right to trial by jury as guaranteed by the Constitution.

Congress had authorized the President to suspend the writ of habeas corpus by the Act of March 3, 1863. However, that law further provided that federal courts were to discharge prisoners where a grand jury had met and adjourned without taking any action against such persons. A grand jury was empaneled by the federal circuit court in Indiana after Milligan's sentence, but it adjourned without bringing an indictment against him; therefore, the circuit court had to consider Milligan's release. The circuit court could not reach agreement on the major questions presented and so certified them to the Supreme Court for decision. After the Court's decision, Milligan was released. He subsequently won a judgment against the commanding officer of the military district and was awarded nominal damages for unlawful imprisonment.]

MR. JUSTICE DAVIS delivered the opinion of the Court:

The controlling question in the case is this: Upon the facts stated in Milligan's petition, and the exhibits filed, had the military commission mentioned in its jurisdiction, legally, to try and sentence him? Milligan, not a resident of one of the rebellious states, or a prisoner of war, but a citizen of Indiana for twenty years past, and never in the military or naval service, is, while at his home, arrested by the military power of the United States, imprisoned, and, on certain criminal charges preferred against him, tried, convicted, and sentenced to be hanged by a military commission, organized under the direction of the military commander of the military district of Indiana. Had this tribunal the *legal* power and authority to try and punish this man?

. . . The Constitution of the United States is a law for rulers and people, equally in war and in peace, and covers with the shield of its protection all classes of men, at all times, and under all circumstances. No doctrine involving more pernicious consequences was ever invented by the wit of man than that any of its provisions can be suspended during any of the great exigencies of government. Such a doctrine leads directly to anarchy or despotism, but the theory of necessity on which it is based is false; for the government, within the Constitution, has all the powers granted to it which are necessary to preserve its existence; as has been happily proved by the result of the great effort to throw off its just authority.

Have any of the rights guaranteed by the Constitution been violated in the case of Milligan? and if so, what are they?

Every trial involves the exercise of judicial power; and from what source did the military commission that tried him derive their authority? Certainly no part of the judicial power of the country was conferred on them; because the Constitution expressly vests it "in our supreme court and such inferior courts as the Congress may from time to time ordain and establish," and it is not pretended that the commission was a court ordained and established by Congress. They cannot justify on the mandate of the President; because he is controlled by law, and has his appropriate sphere of duty, which is to execute, not to make, the laws; and there is "no unwritten criminal code to which resort can be had as a source of jurisdiction."

But it is said that the jurisdiction is complete under the "laws and usages of war."

It can serve no useful purpose to inquire what those laws and usages are, whence they originated, where found and on whom they operate; they can never be applied to citizens in states which have upheld the authority of the government, and where the courts are open and their process unobstructed. This court has judicial knowledge that in Indiana the Federal authority was always unopposed, and its courts always open to hear criminal accusations and redress grievances; and no usage of war could sanction a military trial there for any offence whatever or a citizen in civil life, in nowise connected with the military service. Congress could grant no such power; and to the honor of our national legislature be it said, it has never been provoked by the state of the country even to attempt its exercise. One of the plainest constitutional provisions was, therefore, infringed when Milligan was tried by a court not ordained and established by Congress, and not composed of judges appointed during good behavior.

Why was he not delivered to the Circuit Court of Indiana to be proceeded against according to law? No reason of necessity could be urged against it; because Congress had declared penalties against the offences charged, provided for their punishment, and directed that court to hear and determine them. And soon after this military tribunal was ended, the Circuit Court met, peacefully transacted its business, and adjourned. It needed no bayonets to protect it, and required no military aid to execute its judgments. It was held in a state, eminently distinguished for patriotism, by judges commissioned during the Rebellion, who were provided with juries, upright, intelligent, and selected by a marshal appointed by the President. The government had no right to conclude that Milligan, if guilty, would not receive in that court merited punishment; for its records disclose that it was constantly engaged in the trial of similar offences, and was never interrupted in its administration of criminal justice. If it was dangerous, in the distracted condition of affairs, to leave Milligan unrestrained of his liberty, because he "conspired against the government, afforded aid and comfort to rebels, and incited the people to insurrection," the *law* said arrest him, confine him closely, render him powerless to do further mischief; and then present his case to the grand jury of the district, with proofs of his guilt, and, if indicted, try him according to the course of the common law. If this had been done, the Constitution would have been vindicated, the law of 1863 enforced, and the securities for personal liberty preserved and defended.

Another guaranty of freedom was broken when Milligan was denied a trial by jury. . . . The Sixth Amendment affirms that "in all criminal prosecutions the accused shall enjoy the right to a speedy and public trial by an impartial jury," language broad enough to embrace all persons and cases; but the Fifth, recognizing the necessity of an indictment, or presentment, before any one can be held to answer for high crimes, "*excepts* cases arising in the land or naval forces, or in the militia, when in actual service, in time of war or public danger"; and the framers of the Constitution, doubtless, meant to limit the right of trial by jury, in the Sixth Amendment, to those persons who were subject to indictment or presentment in the Fifth.

The discipline necessary to the efficiency of the army and navy required other and swifter modes of trial than are furnished by the common-law courts; and, in pursuance of the power conferred by the Constitution, Congress has declared the kinds of trial, and the manner in which they shall be conducted, for offences committed while the party is in the military or naval service. Everyone connected with these branches of the public service is amenable to the jurisdiction which Congress has created for their government, and, while thus serving, surrenders his right to be tried by the civil courts.

All other persons, citizens of states where the courts are open, if charged with crime, are guaranteed the inestimable privilege of trial by jury. This privilege is a vital principle, underlying the whole administration of criminal justice. . . .

It is claimed that martial law covers with its broad mantle the proceedings of this military commission. The proposition is this: that in a time of war the commander of an armed force (if in his opinion the exigencies of the country demand it, and of which he is to judge), has the power, within the lines of his military district, to suspend all civil rights and their remedies, and subject citizens as well as soldiers to the rule of *his will;* and in the exercise of of his lawful authority cannot be restrained, except by his superior officer or the President of the United States.

If this position is sound to the extent claimed, then when war exists, foreign or domestic, and the country is subdivided into military departments for mere convenience, the commander of one of them can, if he chooses, within his limits, on the plea of necessity, with the approval of the Executive, substitute military force for and to the exclusion of the laws, and punish all persons, as he thinks right and proper, without fixed or certain rules.

The statement of this proposition shows its importance; for, if true, republican government is a failure, and there is an end of liberty regulated by law. Martial law, established on such a basis, destroys every guaranty of the Constitution, and effectually renders the "military independent of and superior to the civil power"—the attempt to do which by the King of Great Britain was deemed by our fathers such an offence, that they assigned it to the world as one of the causes which impelled them to declare their independ-ence. Civil liberty and this kind of martial law cannot endure together; the antagonism is irreconcilable; and, in the conflict, one or the other must perish.

. . . But, it is insisted that the safety of the country in time of war demands that this broad claim for martial law shall be sustained. If this were true, it could be well said that a country preserved at the sacrifice of all the cardinal principles of liberty, is not worth the cost of preservation. Happily, it is not so.

It will be borne in mind that this is not a question of the power to proclaim martial law, when war exists in a community and the courts and civil authorities are overthrown. Nor is it a question what rule a military commander, at the head of his army, can impose on states in rebellion to cripple their resources and quell the insurrection. The jurisdiction claimed is much more extensive. The necessities of the service, during the late Rebellion, required that the loyal states should be placed within the limits of certain military districts and commanders appointed in them; and, it is urged, that this, in a military sense, constituted them the theater of military operations; and, as in this case, Indiana had been and was again threatened with invasion by the enemy, the occasion was furnished to establish martial law. The conclusion does not follow from the premises. If armies were collected in Indiana, they were to be employed in another locality, where the laws were obstructed and the national authority disputed. On *her* soil there was no hostile foot; if once invaded, that invasion was at an end, and with it all pretext for martial law. Martial law cannot arise from a *threatened* invasion. The necessity must be actual and present; the invasion real, such as effectually closes the courts and deposes the civil administration.

It is difficult to see how the *safety* of the country required martial law in Indiana. If any of her citizens were plotting treason, the power of arrest could secure them, until the government was prepared for their trial, when the courts were open and ready to try them. It was as easy to protect witnesses before a civil as a military tribunal; and as there could be no wish to convict, except on sufficient legal evidence, surely an ordained and established court was better able to judge of this than a military tribunal composed of gentlemen not trained to the profession of the law.

It follows, from what has been said on this subject, that there are occasions when martial rule can be properly applied. If, in foreign invasions or civil war, the courts are actually closed, and it is impossible to administer criminal justice according to law, *then,* in the theater of active military operations, where war really prevails, there is a necessity to furnish a substitute for the civil authority, thus overthrown, to preserve the safety of the army and society; and as no power is left but the military, it is allowed to govern by martial rule until the laws can have their free course. As necessity creates the rule, so it limits its duration; for, if this government is continued *after* the courts are reinstated, it is a gross usurpation of power. Martial rule can never exist where the courts are open, and in the proper and unobstructed exercise of their jurisdiction. It is also confined to the locality of actual war. Because, during the late Rebellion it could have been enforced in Virginia, where the national authority was overturned and the courts driven out, it does not follow that it should obtain in Indiana, where that authority was never disputed, and justice was always administered. And so in the case of a foreign invasion martial rule may become a necessity in one state, when, in another, it would be "mere lawless violence." . . .

The two remaining questions in this case must be answered in the affirmative. The suspension of the privilege of the writ of *habeas corpus* does not suspend the writ itself. The writ issues as a matter of course; and on the return made to it the court decides whether the party applying is denied the right of proceeding any further with it.

If the military trial of Milligan was contrary to law, then he was entitled, on the facts stated in his petition, to be discharged from custody by the terms of the act of Congress of March 3d, 1863. . . .

But it is insisted that Milligan was a prisoner of war, and, therefore, excluded from the privileges of the statute. It is not easy to see how he can be treated as a prisoner of war, when he lived in Indiana for the past twenty years, was arrested there, and had not been, during the late troubles, a resident of any of the states in rebellion. If in Indiana he conspired with bad men to assist the enemy, he is punishable for it in the courts of Indiana; but, when tried for the offence, he cannot plead the rights of war; for he was not engaged in legal acts of hostility against the government, and only such persons, when captured, are prisoners of war. If he cannot enjoy the immunities attaching to the character of a prisoner of war, how can he be subject to their pains and penalties? . . .

THE CHIEF JUSTICE [CHASE] delivered the following opinion:

Four members of the Court . . . unable to concur in some important particulars with the opinion which has just been read, think it their duty to make a separate statement of their views of the whole case. . . .

The opinion . . . as we understand it, asserts not only that the military commission held in Indiana was not authorized by Congress, but that it was not in the power of Congress to authorize it; from which it may be thought to follow that Congress has no power to indemnify the officers who composed the commission against liability in civil courts for acting as members of it. We cannot agree to this. . . .

We think that Congress had power, though not exercised, to authorize the military commission which was held in Indiana. . . .

MR. JUSTICE WAYNE, MR. JUSTICE SWAYNE, and MR. JUSTICE MILLER concur with me in these views.

KOREMATSU v. UNITED STATES
323 U.S. 214; 65 Sup. Ct. 193; 89 L. Ed. 194 (1945)

[*Shortly after America's entrance into World War II, the President issued an executive order that authorized the creation of military areas from which persons might be excluded in order to prevent sabotage and espionage. Military commanders were further authorized to prescribe regulations concerning the right of persons to enter, leave, or remain in these military areas. Penalties for violations of the military regulations were provided by an act of Congress. Acting under this executive and legislative authority, the commanding general of the Western Defense Command divided the entire Pacific Coast region into two military areas. Various restrictions were then imposed on certain classes of persons living in the military districts. The commanding general first imposed a curfew that applied only to aliens and persons of Japanese ancestry. In* Hirabayshi v. United States, *320 U.S. 81 (1943), the Supreme Court upheld the curfew order as a proper wartime measure.*

Later, the commanding general ordered the compulsory removal of all persons of Japanese ancestry to War Relocation Centers. Korematsu, who was one of the American citizens of Japanese ancestry subject to removal to relocation centers, refused to leave his home in California. He was convicted in a federal district court for knowingly violating the exclusion order. A circuit court of appeals affirmed the conviction. Korematsu then brought the case to the Supreme Court on a writ of certiorari.]

MR. JUSTICE BLACK delivered the opinion of the Court:

. . . In the light of the principles we announced in the *Hirabayshi* case, we are unable to conclude that it was beyond the war power of Congress and the Executive to exclude those of Japanese ancestry from the West Coast war area at the time they did. True, exclusion from the area in which one's home is located is a far greater deprivation than constant confinement to the home from 8 P.M. to 6 A.M. Nothing short of apprehension by the proper military authorities of the gravest imminent danger to the public safety can constitutionally justify either. But exclusion from a threatened area, no less than curfew, has a definite and close relationship to the prevention of espionage and sabotage. The military authorities, charged with the primary responsibility of defending our shores, concluded that curfew provided inadequate protection and ordered exclusion. They did so, as pointed out in our *Hirabayashi* opinion, in accordance with Congressional authority to the military to say who should, and who should not, remain in the threatened areas. . . .

Like curfew, exclusion of those of Japanese origin was deemed necessary because of the presence of an unascertained number of disloyal members of the group, most of whom we have no doubt were loyal to this country. It was because we could not reject the finding of the military authorities that is was impossible to bring about an immediate segregation of the disloyal from the loyal that we sustained the validity of the curfew order as applying to the whole group. In the instant case, temporary exclusion of the entire group was rested by the military on the same ground. The judgment that exclusion of the whole group was for the same reason a military imperative answers the contention that the exclusion was in the nature of group punishment based on antagonism to those of Japanese origin. That there were members of the group who retained loyalties to Japan had been confirmed by investigations made subsequent to the exclusion. Approximately 5000 American citizens of Japanese ancestry refused to swear unqualified allegiance to the United States and to renounce allegiance to the Japanese Emperor, and several thousand evacuees requested repatriation to Japan.

We uphold the exclusion order as of the time it was made and when the petitioner violated it. . . . In doing so, we are not unmindful of the hardships imposed by it upon a large group of American citizens. . . . But hardships are part of war, and war is an aggregation of hardships. All citizens alike, both in and out of uniform, feel the impact of war in greater or lesser measure. Citizenship has its responsibilities as well as its privileges, and in time of war the burden is always heavier. Compulsory exclusion of large groups of citizens from their homes, except under circumstances of direst emergency and peril, is inconsistent with our basic governmental institutions. But when under conditions of modern warfare our shores are threatened by hostile forces, the power to protect must be commensurate with the threatened danger. . . .

It is said that we are dealing here with the case of imprisonment of a citizen in a concentration camp solely because of his ancestry, without evidence or inquiry concerning his loyalty and good disposition towards the United States. Our task would be simple, our duty clear, were this a case involving the imprisonment of a loyal citizen in a concentration camp because of racial prejudice. Regardless of the true nature of the assembly and relocation centers —and we deem it unjustifiable to call them concentration camps with all the ugly connotations that term implies— we are dealing specifically with nothing but an exclusion order. To cast this case into outlines of racial prejudice, without reference to the real military dangers which were presented, merely confuses the issue. Korematsu was not excluded from the Military Area because of hostility to him or his race. He *was* excluded because we are at war with the Japanese Empire, because the properly constituted military authorities feared an invasion of our West Coast and felt constrained to take proper security measures, because they decided that the military urgency of the situation demanded that all citizens of Japanese ancestry be segregated from the West Coast temporarily, and finally, because Congress, reposing its confidence in this time of war in our military leaders—as inevitably it must—determined that they should have the power to do just this. There was evidence of disloyalty on the part of some, the military authorities considered that the need for action was great, and time was short. We can not—by availing ourselves of the calm perspective of hindsight—now say that at that time these actions were unjustified.

Affirmed.

[MR. JUSTICE FRANKFURTER wrote a concurring opinion.]

MR. JUSTICE ROBERTS:

I dissent, because I think the indisputable facts exhibit a clear violation of constitutional rights.

This is not a case of keeping people off the streets at night as was *Hirabayashi* v. *United States* . . . nor a case of temporary exclusion of a citizen from an area for his own safety or that of the community, nor a case of offering him an opportunity to go temporarily out of an area where his presence might cause danger to himself or to his fellows. On the contrary, it is the case of convicting a citizen as a punishment for not submitting to imprisonment in a concentration camp, based on his ancestry, and solely because of his ancestry, without evidence or inquiry concerning his loyalty and good disposition towards the United States. If this be a correct statement of the facts disclosed by this record, and facts of which we take judicial notice, I need hardly labor the conclusion that Constitutional rights have been violated. . . .

MR. JUSTICE MURPHY, dissenting:

This exclusion of "all persons of Japanese ancestry, both alien and non-alien," from the Pacific Coast area on a plea of military necessity in the absence of martial law ought not to be approved. Such exclusion goes over "the very brink of constitutional power" and falls into the ugly abyss of racism.

In dealing with matters relating to the prosecution and progress of a war, we must accord great respect and consideration to the judgments of the military authorities who are on the scene and who have full knowledge of the military facts. The scope of their discretion must, as a matter of necessity and common sense, be wide. And their judgments ought not to be overruled lightly by those whose training and duties ill equip them to deal intelligently with matters so vital to the physical security of the nation.

At the same time, however, it is essential that there be definite limits to military discretion, especially where martial law has not been declared. Individuals must not be left impoverished of their constitutional rights on a plea of military necessity that his neither substance nor support. Thus, like other claims conflicting with the asserted constitutional rights of the individual, the military claim must subject itself to the judicial process of having its reasonableness determined and its conflicts with other interests reconciled. "What are the allowable limits of military discretion, and whether or not they have been overstepped in a particular case, are judicial questions." . . .

The judicial test of whether the Government, on a plea of military necessity, can validly deprive an individual of any of his constitutional rights is whether the deprivation is reasonably related to a public danger that is so "immediate, imminent, and impending" as not to admit of delay and not to permit the intervention of ordinary constitutional processes to alleviate the danger. . . . Civilian Exclusion Order No. 34, banishing from a prescribed area of the Pacific Coast "all persons of Japanese ancestry, both alien and nonalien," clearly does not meet that test. Being an obvious racial discrimination, the order deprives . . . these individuals of their constitutional rights to live and work where they will, to establish a home where they choose and to move about freely. In excommunicating them without benefit of hearings, this order also deprives them of all their constitutional rights to procedural due process. Yet no reasonable relation to an "immediate, imminent, and impending" public danger is evident to support this racial restriction, which is one of the most sweeping and complete deprivations of constitutional rights in the history of this nation in the absence of martial law.

It must be conceded that the military and naval situation in the spring of 1942 was such as to generate a very real fear of invasion of the Pacific Coast, accompanied by fears of sabotage and espionage in that area. The military command was therefore justified in adopting all reasonable means necessary to combat these dangers. In adjudging the military action taken in light of the then apparent dangers, we must not erect too high or too meticulous standards; it is necessary only that the action have some reasonable relation to the removal of the dangers of invasion, sabotage, and espionage. But the exclusion, either temporarily or permanently, of all persons with Japanese blood in their veins has no such reasonable relation. And that relation is lacking because the exclusion order necessarily must rely for its reasonableness upon the assumption that *all* persons of Japanese ancestry may have a dangerous tendency to commit sabotage and espionage and to aid our Japanese enemy in other ways. It is difficult to believe that reason, logic, or experience could be marshalled in support of such an assumption.

That this forced exclusion was the result in good measure of this erroneous assumption of racial guilt rather than bona fide military necessity is evidenced by the Commanding General's Final Report on the evacuation from the Pacific Coast area. In it he refers to all individuals of Japanese descent as "subversive," as belonging to "an enemy race" whose "racial strains are undiluted," and as constituted "over 112,000 potential enemies . . . at large today" along the Pacific Coast. In support of this blanket condemnation of all persons of Japanese descent, however, no reliable evidence is cited to show that such individuals were generally disloyal, or had generally so conducted themselves in this area as to constitute a special menace to defense installations or war industries, or had otherwise by their behavior furnished reasonable ground for their exclusion as a group. . . .

The military necessity which is essential to the validity of the evacuation order . . . resolves itself into a few intimations that certain individuals actively aided the enemy, from which it is inferred that the entire group of Japanese-Americans could not be trusted to be or remain loyal to the United States. No one denies, of course, that there were some disloyal persons of Japanese descent on the Pacific Coast who did all in their power to aid their ancestral land. Similar disloyal activities have been engaged in by many persons of German, Italian, and even more pioneer stock in our country. But to infer that examples of individual disloyalty prove group disloyalty and justify discriminatory action against the entire group is to deny that under our system of law individual guilt is the sole basis for deprivation of rights. Moreover, this inference, which is at the very heart of the evaluation orders, has been used in support of the abhorrent and despicable treatment of minority groups by the dictatorial tyrannies which this nation is now pledged to destroy. To give constitutional sanction to that inference in this case, however well-intentioned may have been the military command on the

Pacific Coast, is to adopt one of the cruelest of the rationales used by our enemies to destroy the dignity of the individual and to encourage and open the door to discriminatory actions against other minority groups in the passions of tomorrow.

No adequate reason is given for the failure to treat these Japanese-Americans on an individual basis by holding investigations and hearings to separate the loyal from the disloyal, as was done in the case of persons of German and Italian ancestry. . . . It is asserted merely that the loyalties of this group "were unknown and time was of the essence." Yet nearly four months elapsed after Pearl Harbor before the first exclusion order was issued; nearly eight months went by until the last order was issued; and the last of these "subversive" persons was not actually removed until almost eleven months had elapsed. Leisure and deliberation seem to have been more of the essence than speed. . . .

I dissent, therefore, from this legalization of racism. Racial discrimination in any form and in any degree has no justifiable part whatever in our democratic way of life. It is unattractive in any setting but it is utterly revolting among a free people who have embraced the principles set forth in the Constitution of the United States. All residents of this nation are kin in some way by blood or culture to a foreign land. Yet they are primarily and necessarily a part of the new and distinct civilization of the United States. They must accordingly be treated at all times as the heirs of the American experiment and as entitled to all the rights and freedoms guaranteed by the Constitution.

[MR. JUSTICE JACKSON also wrote a dissenting opinion.]

In re YAMISHITA
327 U.S. 1; 66 Sup. Ct. 340; 90 L. Ed. 499 (1946)

[*During the final stages of World War II, General Tomoyuki Yamashita was named commander of the Japanese troops in the Philippines. Several days after his arrival in Manila, American troops invaded Leyte, and Yamashita withdrew to the mountains of northern Luzon. After his withdrawal, Manila and the rest of the Philippines suffered through one of the cruelest orgies of mass murder, rape, and pillage ever recorded in the annals of war; an estimated 30,000 people were brutally killed by the Japanese. On September 3, 1945, Yamashita came down the mountains of northern Luzon and surrendered to American forces. He was immediately imprisoned and charged with being a war criminal for permitting members of his command to commit brutal atrocities and other high crimes. An American Military Commission was named by General Douglas MacArthur to try Yamashita. On October 8, 1945, he was arraigned before the commission and pleaded "not guilty." At the arraignment, the defense was presented with a bill of particulars setting forth in detail sixty-four crimes committed by troops under Yamashita's command. Three weeks later a supplemental bill, charging him with fifty-nine more crimes, was filed. A defense motion to study the new charges was denied by the commission. On the same day, October 29, 1945, the trial began. On December 7, 1945, the military commission found Yamashita guilty and sentenced him to death by hanging. The Supreme Court of the Philippines refused to hear the case. Yamashita's counsel then filed an application with the*]

Supreme Court for leave to file a petition for writs of habeas corpus and prohibition. At the same time, his counsel filed a petition for certiorari to review the order of the Supreme Court of the Philippines denying applications for writs of habeas corpus and prohibition.

An interesting footnote to this case is that after this Supreme Court decision, President Truman refused to commute Yamashita's death penalty to life imprisonment, and Yamashita was hanged on February 23, 1946.]

MR. CHIEF JUSTICE STONE delivered the opinion of the Court:

. . . The petitions for habeas corpus set up that the detention of petitioner for the purpose of the trial was unlawful for reasons which are now urged as showing that the military commission was without lawful authority or jurisdiction to place petitioner on trial, as follows:

(a) That the military commission which tried and convicted petitioner was not lawfully created, and that no military commission to try petitioner for violations of the law of war could lawfully be convened after the cessation of hostilities between the armed forces of the United States and Japan;

(b) That the charge preferred against petitioner fails to charge him with a violation of the law of war;

(c) That the commission was without authority and jurisdiction to try and convict petitioner because the order governing the procedure of the commission permitted the admission in evidence of depositions, affidavits and hearsay and opinion evidence, and because the commission's rulings admitting such evidence were in violation of the 25th and 38th Articles of War . . . and the Geneva Convention . . . and deprive petitioner of a fair trial in violation of the due process clause of the Fifth Amendment;

(d) That the commission was without authority and jurisdiction in the premises because of the failure to give advance notice of petitioner's trial to the neutral power representing the interests of Japan as a belligerent as re-quired by Article 60 of the Geneva Convention. . . .

We . . . emphasized in Ex parte *Quirin*, as we do here, that on application for habeas corpus we are not concerned with the guilt or innocence of the petitioners. We consider here only the lawful power of the commission to try the petitioner for the offense charged. In the present case it must be recognized throughout that the military tribunals which Congress has sanctioned by the Articles of War are not courts whose rulings and judgments are made subject to review by this Court. . . . They are tribunals whose determinations are reviewable by the military authorities either as provided in the military orders constituting such tribunals or as provided by the Articles of War. Congress conferred on the courts no power "to grant writs of habeas corpus for the purpose of an inquiry into the cause of restraint of liberty." . . . The courts may inquire whether the detention complained of is within the authority of those detaining the petitioner. If the military tribunals have lawful authority to hear, decide and condemn, their action is not for the courts but for the military authorities which are alone authorized to review their decisions. . . .

It . . . appears that the order creating the commission for the trial of petitioner was authorized by military command, and was in complete conformity to the Act of Congress sanctioning the creation of such tribunals for the trial of offenses against the law of war committed by enemy combatants. And we turn to the question whether the authority to create the commission and direct the trial by military order continued after the cessation of hostilities. . . .

We cannot say that there is no authority to convene a commission after hostilities have ended to try violations of the law of war committed before their cessation, at least until peace has been officially recognized by treaty or proclamation of the political branch of the Government. In fact, in most instances the practical administration of the system of military justice under the law of war would fail if such authority were thought to end with the cessation of hostilities. For only after their cessation could the greater number of offenders and the principal ones be apprehended and subject to trial. . . .

The extent to which the power to prosecute violations of the law of war shall be exercised before peace is declared rests, not with the courts, but with the political branch of the Government, and may itself be governed by the terms of an armistice or the treaty of peace. Here, peace has not been agreed upon or proclaimed. Japan, by her acceptance of the Potsdam Declaration and her surrender, has acquiesced in the trials of those guilty of violations of the law of war. The conduct of the trial by the military commission has been authorized by the political branch of the Government, by military command, by international law and usage, and by the terms of the surrender of the Japanese government.

The Charge. Neither congressional action nor the military orders constituting the commission authorized it to place petitioner on trial unless the charge preferred against him is of a violation of the law of war. The charge, so far as now relevant, is that petitioner, between October 9, 1944, and September 2, 1945, in the Philippine Islands,

"while commander of armed forces of Japan at war with the United States of America and its allies, unlawfully disregarded and failed to discharge his duty as commander to control the operations of the members of his command, permitting them to commit brutal atrocities and other high crimes against people of the United States and of its allies and dependencies, particularly the Philippines; and he . . . thereby violated the laws of war." . . .

We do not make the laws of war but we respect them so far as they do not conflict with the commands of Congress or the Constitution. There is no contention that the present charge, thus read, is without the support of evidence, or that the commission held petitioner responsible for failing to take measures which were beyond his control or inappropriate for a commanding officer to take in the circumstances. We do not here appraise the evidence on which petitioner was convicted. We do not consider what measures, if any, petitioner took to prevent the commission, by the troops under his command, of the plain violations of the law of war detailed in the bill of particulars, or whether such measures as he may have taken were appropriate and sufficient to discharge the duty imposed on him by the law of war and to pass upon its sufficiency to establish guilt.

Obviously charges of violations of the law of war triable before a military tribunal need not be stated with the precision of a common law indictment. . . . But we conclude that the allegations of the charge, tested by any reasonable standard, adequately allege a violation of the law of war and that the commission had authority to try and decide the issue which it raised. . . .

The Proceedings Before the Commission. We cannot say that the commission, in admitting evidence to which objection is now made, violated any act of Congress, treaty or military command defining the commission's authority. For reasons already stated we hold that the commission's rulings on evidence and on the mode of conducting these proceedings against petitioner are not reviewable by the courts, but only by the reviewing military authorities. From this viewpoint it is unnecessary to consider what, in other situations, the Fifth Amendment might require, and as to that no intimation one way or the other is to be implied. Nothing we have said is to be taken as indicating any opinion on the question of the wisdom of considering such evidence, or whether the action of a military tribunal in admitting evidence, which Congress or controlling military command has directed to be excluded, may be drawn in question by petition for habeas corpus or prohibition.

Effect of Failure to Give Notice of the Trial to the Protecting Power. For reasons already stated we conclude that Article 60 of the Geneva Convention, which appears in part 3, Chapter 3, Section V, Title III of the Geneva Convention, applies only to persons who are subjected to judicial proceedings for offenses committed while prisoners of war.

It thus appears that the order convening the commission was a lawful order, that the commission was lawfully constituted, that petitioner was charged with violation of the law of war, and that the commission had authority to proceed with the trial, and in doing so did not violate any military, statutory or constitutional command. We have considered, but find it unnecessary to discuss, other contentions which we find to be without merit. We therefore conclude that the detention of petitioner for trial and his detention upon his conviction, subject to the prescribed review by the military authorities, were lawful, and that the petition for cer-tiorari, and leave to file in this Court petitions for writs of habeas corpus and prohibition should be, and they are

Denied.

MR. JUSTICE JACKSON took no part in the consideration or decision of these cases.

MR. JUSTICE MURPHY, dissenting:

The significance of the issue facing the Court today cannot be overemphasized. An American military commission has been established to try a fallen military commander of a conquered nation for an alleged war crime. The authority for such action grows out of the exercise of the power conferred upon Congress by Article I, Section 8, Cl. 10 of the Constitution to "define and punish . . . Offences against the Law of Nations. . . ." The grave issue raised by this case is whether a military commission so established and so authorized may disregard the procedural rights of an accused person as guaranteed by the Constitution, especially by the due process clause of the Fifth Amendment.

The answer is plain. The Fifth Amendment guaranty of due process of law applies to "any person" who is accused of a crime by the Federal Government or any of its agencies. No exception is made as to those who are accused of war crimes or as to those who possess the status of an enemy belligerent. Indeed, such an exception would be contrary to the whole philosophy of human rights which makes the Constitution the great living document that it is. The immutable rights of the individual, including those secured by the due process clauses of the Fifth Amendment, belong not alone to the members of those nations that excel on the battlefields or that subscribe to the democratic ideology. They belong to every person in the world, victor or vanquished, whatever may be his race, color or beliefs. They rise above any status of belligerency or outlawry. They survive any popular passion or frenzy of the moment. No court or legislature or executive, not even the mightiest army in the world, can ever destroy them. Such is the universal and indestructible nature of the rights which the due process clause of the Fifth Amendment recognizes and protects when life or liberty is threatened by virtue of the authority of the United States.

The existence of these rights, unfortunately, is not always respected. They are often trampled under by those who are motivated by hatred, aggression or fear. But in this nation individual rights are recognized and protected, at least in regard to governmental action. They cannot be ignored by any branch of the Government, even the military, except under the most extreme and urgent circumstances.

The failure of the military commission to obey the dictates of the due process requirements of the Fifth Amendment is apparent in this case. The petitioner was the commander of an army totally destroyed by the superior power of this nation. While under heavy and destructive attack by our forces, his troops committed many brutal atrocities and other high crimes. Hostilities ceased and he voluntarily surrendered. At that point he was entitled, as an individual protected by the due process clause of the Fifth Amendment, to be treated fairly and justly according to the accepted rules of law and procedure. He was also entitled to a fair trial as to any alleged crimes and to be free from charges of legally unrecognized crimes that would serve only to permit his accusers to satisfy their desires for revenge.

A military commission was appointed to try the petition for an alleged war crime. The trial was ordered to be held in territory over which the United

States has complete sovereignty. No military necessity or other emergency demanded the suspension of the safeguards of due process. Yet petitioner was rushed to trial under an improper charge, given insufficient time to prepare an adequate defense, deprived of the benefits of some of the most elementary rules of evidence and summarily sentenced to be hanged. In all this needless and unseemly haste there was no serious attempt to charge or to prove that he committed a recognized violation of the laws of war. He was not charged with personally participating in the acts of atrocity or with ordering or condoning their commission. Not even knowledge of these crimes was attributed to him. It was simply alleged that he unlawfully disregarded and failed to discharge his duty as commander to control the operations of the members of his command, permitting them to commit the acts of atrocity. The recorded annals of warfare and the established principles of international law afford not the slightest precedent for such a charge. This indictment in effect permitted the military commission to make the crime whatever it willed, dependent upon its biased view as to petitioner's duties and his disregard thereof, a practice reminiscent of that pursued in certain less respected nations in recent years.

In my opinion, such a procedure is unworthy of the traditions of our people or of the immense sacrifices that they have made to advance the common ideals of mankind. The high feelings of the moment doubtless will be satisfied. But in the sober afterglow will come the realization of the boundless and dangerous implications of the procedure sanctioned today. No one in a position of command in an army, from sergeant to general, can escape those implications. Indeed, the fate of some future President of the United

States and his chiefs of staff and military advisers may well have been sealed by this decision. But even more significant will be the hatred and ill-will growing out of the application of this unprecedented procedure. That has been the inevitable effect of every method of punishment disregarding the element of personal culpability. The effect in this instance, unfortunately, will be magnified infinitely for here we are dealing with the rights of man on an international level. To subject an enemy belligerent to an unfair trial, to charge him with an unrecognized crime, or to vent on him our retributive emotions only antagonizes the enemy nation and hinders the reconciliation necessary to a peaceful world. . . .

The determination of the extent of review of war trials calls for judicial statesmanship of the highest order. The ultimate nature and scope of the writ of habeas corpus are within the discretion of the judiciary unless validly circumscribed by Congress. Here we are confronted with a use of the writ under circumstances novel in the history of the Court. For my own part, I do not feel that we should be confined by the traditional lines of review drawn in connection with the use of the writ by ordinary criminals who have direct access to the judiciary in the first instance. Those held by the military lack any such access; consequently the judicial review available by habeas corpus must be wider than usual in order that proper standards of justice may be enforceable. . . .

[T]he charge made against the petitioner is clearly without precedent in international law or in the annals of recorded military history. This is not to say that enemy commanders may escape punishment for clear and unlawful failures to prevent atrocities. But that punishment should be based upon charges fairly drawn in light of established rules of international law and recognized concepts of justice.

But the charge in this case . . . was speedily drawn and filed but three weeks after the petitioner surrendered. The trial proceeded with great dispatch without allowing the defense time to prepare an adequate case. Petitioner's rights under the due process clause of the Fifth Amendment was grossly and openly violated without any justification. All of this was done without any thorough investigation and prosecution of those immediately responsible for the atrocities, out of which might have come some proof or indication of personal culpability on petitioner's part. Instead the loose charge was made that great numbers of atrocities had been committed and that petitioner was the commanding officer; hence he must have been guilty of disregard of duty. Under that charge the commission was free to establish whatever standard of duty on petitioner's part that it desired. By this flexible method a victorious nation may convict and execute any or all leaders of vanquished foe, depending upon the prevailing degree of vengeance and the absence of any objective judicial review.

At a time like this when emotions are understandably high it is difficult to adopt a dispassionate attitude toward a case of this nature. Yet now is precisely the time when that attitude is most essential. While peoples in other lands may not share our beliefs as to due process and the dignity of the individual, we are not free to give effect to our emotions in reckless disregard of the rights of others. We live under the Constitution, which is the embodiment of all the high hopes and aspirations of the new world. And it is applicable in both war and peace. We must act accordingly. Indeed, an uncurbed spirit of revenge and retribution, masked in formal legal procedure for purposes of dealing with a fallen enemy commander, can do more lasting harm that all of the atrocities giving rise to that spirit. The people's faith in the fairness and objectiveness of the law can be seriously undercut by that spirit. The fires of nationalism can be further kindled. And the hearts of all mankind can be embittered and filled with hatred, leaving forlorn and impoverished the noble ideal of malice toward none and charity to all. These are the reasons that lead me to dissent in these terms.

MR. JUSTICE RUTLEDGE, dissenting:

Not with ease does one find his views at odds with the Court's in a matter of this character and gravity. Only the most deeply felt convictions could force one to differ. That reason alone leads me to do so now, against strong considerations for withholding dissent.

More is at stake than General Yamashita's fate. There could be no possible sympathy for him if he is guilty of the atrocities for which his death is sought. But there can be and should be justice administered according to law. In this stage of war's aftermath it is too early for Lincoln's great spirit, best lighted in the Second Inaugural, to have wide hold for the treatment of foes. It is not too early, it is never too early, for the nation steadfastly to follow its great constitutional traditions, none older or more universally protective against unbridled power than due process of law in the trial and punishment of men, that is, of all men, whether citizens, aliens, alien enemies or enemy belligerents. It can become too late.

This long-held attachment marks the great divide between our enemies and ourselves. Theirs was a philosophy of universal force. Ours is one of universal law, albeit imperfectly made flesh of our system and so dwelling among us. Every departure weakens the tradition, whether it touches the high or the low,

the powerful or the weak, the triumphant or the conquered. If we need not or cannot be magnanimous, we can keep our own law on the plane from which it has not descended hitherto and to which the defeated foes' never rose. . . .

This trial is unprecedented in our history. Never before have we tried and convicted an enemy general for action taken during hostilities or otherwise in the course of military operations or duty. Must less have we condemned one for failing to take action. The novelty is not lessened by the trial's having taken place after hostilities ended and the enemy, including the accused, had surrendered. Moreover, so far as the time permitted for our consideration has given opportunity, I have not been able to find precedent for the proceeding in the system of any nation founded in the basic principles of our constitutional democracy, in the laws of war or in other internationally binding authority or usage. . . .

It is not in our tradition for anyone to be charged with crime which is defined after his conduct, alleged to be criminal, has taken place; or in language not sufficient to inform him of the nature of the offense or to enable him to make defense. Mass guilt we do not impute to individuals, perhaps in any case but certainly in none where the person is not charged or shown actively to have participated in or knowingly to have failed in taking action to prevent the wrongs done by others, having both the duty and the power to do so.

It is outside our basic scheme to condemn men without giving reasonable opportunity for preparing defense; in capital or other serious crimes to convict on "official documents . . . ; affidavits; . . . documents or translations thereof; diaries . . . , photographs, motion picture films, and . . .

newspapers" or on hearsay, once, twice or thrice removed, more particularly when the documentary evidence or some of it is prepared *ex parte* by the prosecuting authority and includes not only opinion but conclusions of guilt. Nor in such cases do we deny the rights of confronation of witnesses and cross-examination.

Our tradition does not allow conviction by tribunals both authorized and bound by the instrument of their creation to receive and consider evidence which is expressly excluded by Act of Congress or by treaty obligation; nor is it in accord with our basic concepts to make the tribunal, specially constituted for the particular trial, regardless of those prohibitions the sole and exclusive judge of the credibility, probative value and admissibility of whatever may be tendered as evidence.

The matter is not one merely of the character and admissibility of evidence. It goes to the very competency of the tribunal to try and punish consistently with the Constitution, the laws of the United States made in pursuance thereof, and treaties made under the nation's authority.

All these deviations from the fundamental law, and others, occurred in the course of constituting the commission, the preparation for trial and defense, the trial itself, and therefore, in effect, in the sentence imposed. Whether taken singly in some instances as departures from specific constitutional mandates or in totality as in violation of the Fifth Amendment's command that no person shall be deprived of life, liberty or property without due process of law, a trial so vitiated cannot withstand constitutional scrutiny. . . .

On this denial and the commission's invalid constitution specifically, but also more generally upon the totality of departures from constitutional norms inherent in the idea of a fair trial, I rest my judgment that the commission was without jurisdiction from the beginning to try or punish the petitioner and that, if it had acquired jurisdiction then, its power to proceed was lost in the course of what was done before and during trial.

Only on one view, in my opinion, could either of these conclusions be avoided. This would be that an enemy belligerent in petitioner's position is altogether beyond the pale of constitutional protection, regardless of the fact that hostilities had ended and he had surrendered with his country. . . .

The Court does not declare expressly that petitioner as an enemy belligerent has no constitutional rights, a ruling I could understand but not accept. Neither does it affirm that he has some, if but little, constitutional protection. Nor does the Court defend what was done. I think the effect of what it does is in substance to deny him all such safeguards. And this is the great issue in the case. . . .

The difference between the Court's view of this proceeding and my own comes down in the end to the view, on the one hand, that there is no law restrictive upon these proceedings other than whatever rules and regulations may be prescribed for their government by the executive authority or the military and, on the other hand, that the provisions of the Articles of War, of the Geneva Convention and the Fifth Amendment apply.

I cannot accept the view that anywhere in our system resides or lurks a power so unrestrained to deal with any human being through any process of trial. What military agencies or authorities may do with our enemies in battle or invasion, apart from proceedings in the nature of trial and some semblance of judicial action, is beside the point. Nor has any human being heretofore been held to be wholly beyond elementary procedural protection by the Fifth Amendment. I cannot consent to even implied departure from that great absolute.

It was a great patriot who said: "He that would make his own liberty secure must guard even his enemy from oppression; for if he violates this duty he establishes a precedent that will reach to himself."

MR. JUSTICE MURPHY joins in this opinion.

UNITED STATES ex rel. TOTH v. QUARLES
350 U.S. 11; 76 Sup. Ct. 1; 100 L. Ed. 8 (1955)

[*Robert W. Toth was honorably discharged after service with the United States Air Force in Korea. Five months after his discharge, while working in Pittsburgh, Pa., he was arrested by military authorities on a charge of murder committed while he was on active duty in Korea. He was taken summarily to Korea by the Air Force to stand trial for the murder before a court-martial under the authority of the Uniform Code of Military Justice. Toth's sister then filed for a petition of habeas corpus in a federal district court. The district court ordered that Toth be released on the ground that the Air Force had no power to remove a civilian for trial by court-martial to such a distant point as Korea without a hearing. The district court, however, did not pass on the constitutionality of Article 3(a) of the Uniform Code of Military Justice under which Toth was apprehended. A court of appeals sustained the Uniform Code, holding that Toth could be constitutionally subjected to a trial by the court-martial. The Supreme Court granted certiorari. Quarles was Secretary of the Air Force. The meaning of* ex rel *in the title of a case is explained in the* Graves *case in Chapter 10.*]

MR. JUSTICE BLACK delivered the opinion of the Court:

. . . The Government's contention is that the Act (Uniform Code of Military Justice) is a valid exercise of the power granted Congress in Article I of the Constitution "to make Rules for the Government and Regulation of the land and naval Forces," as supplemented by the Necessary and Proper Clause.

This Court has held that the Article I clause just quoted authorizes Congress to subject persons actually in the armed service to trial by court-martial for military and naval offenses. Later it was held that court-martial jurisdiction could be exerted over a dishonorably discharged soldier then a military prisoner serving a sentence imposed by a prior court-martial. It has never been intimated by this Court, however, that [under] Article I military jurisdiction could be extended to civilian ex-soldiers who had severed all relationship with the military and its institutions. To allow this extension of military authority would require an extremely broad construction of the language used in the constitutional provision relied on. For given its natural meaning, the power granted Congress "to make Rules" to regulate "the land and naval Forces" would seem to restrict court-martial jurisdiction to persons who are actually members or part of the armed forces. There is a compelling reason for construing the clause this way: any expansion of court-martial jurisdiction like that in the 1950 Act necessarily encroaches on the jurisdiction of federal courts set up under Article III of the Constitution where persons on trial are surrounded with more constitutional safeguards than in military tribunals.

Article III provides for the establishment of a court system as one of the separate but coordinate branches of the national governments. It is the primary, indeed the sole business of these courts to try cases and controversies between individuals and between individuals and the government. This includes trial of criminal cases. These courts are presided over by judges appointed for life, subject only to removal by impeachment. Their compensation cannot be diminished during their continuance in office. The provisions of Article III were designed to give judges maximum freedom from possible coercion or influence by the executive or legislative branches of the government. But the Constitution and the Amendments in the Bill of Rights show that the Founders were not satisfied with leaving determination of guilt or innocence to judges, even though wholly independent. They further provided that no person should be held to answer in those courts for capital or other infamous crimes unless on the presentment or indictment of a grand jury drawn from the body of the people. Other safeguards designed to protect defendants against oppressive governmental practices were included. One of these was considered so important to liberty of the individual that it appears in two parts of the Constitution. Article III, §2, commands that the "Trial of all Crimes, except in Cases of Impeachment, shall be by Jury; and such Trial shall be held in the State where the said Crimes shall have been committed; but when not committed within any State, the Trial shall be at such Place or Places as the Congress may by Law have directed." And the Sixth Amendment provides that "In all criminal prosecutions, the accused shall enjoy the right to a speedy and public trial, by an impartial jury of the state and district wherein the crime shall have been

committed. . . ." This right of trial by jury ranks very high in our catalogue of constitutional safeguards.

We find nothing in the history or constitutional treatment of military tribunals which entitles them to rank along with Article III courts as adjudicators of the guilt or innocence of people charged with offenses for which they can be deprived of their life, liberty, or property. Unlike courts, it is the primary business of armies and navies to fight or be ready to fight wars should the occasion arise. But trial of soldiers to maintain discipline is merely incidental to an army's primary fighting function. To the extent that those responsible for performance of this primary function are diverted from it by the necessity of trying cases, the basic fighting purpose of armies is not served. And conceding to military personnel that high degree of honesty and sense of justice which nearly all of them undoubtedly have, it still remains true that military tribunals have not been and probably never can be constituted in such way that they can have the same kind of qualifications that the Constitution has deemed essential to fair trials of civilians in federal courts. For instance, the Constitution does not provide life tenure for those performing judicial functions in military trials. They are appointed by military commanders and may be removed at will. Nor does the Constitution protect their salaries as it does judicial salaries. Strides have been made toward making courts-martial less subject to the will of the executive department which appoints, supervises, and ultimately controls them. But from the very nature of things, courts have more independence in passing on the life and liberty of people than do military tribunals.

Moreover, there is a great difference between trial by jury and trial by selected members of the military forces.

It is true that military personnel because of their training and experience may be especially competent to try soldiers for infractions of military rules. Such training is no doubt particularly important where an offense charged against a soldier is purely military, such as disobedience of an order, leaving post, etc. But whether right or wrong, the premise underlying the constitutional method for determining guilt or innocence in federal courts is that laymen are better than specialists to perform this task. This idea is inherent in the institution of trial by jury. . . .

The 1950 Act here considered deprives of jury trial and sweeps under military jurisdiction over three million persons who have become veterans since the Act became effective. That number is bound to grow from year to year; there are now more than three million men and women in uniform. These figures point up what would be the enormous scope of a holding that Congress could subject every ex-serviceman and woman in the land to trial by court-martial for any alleged offense committed while he or she had been a member of the armed forces. . . .

Fear has been expressed that if this law is not sustained discharged soldiers may escape punishment altogether for crimes they commit while in the service. But that fear is not warranted and was not shared by the Judge Advocate General of the Army, who made a strong statement against passage of the law. He asked Congress to "confer jurisdiction upon Federal courts to try any person for an offense denounced by the (military) code if he is no longer subject thereto. This would be consistent with the Fifth Amendment of the Constitution." The Judge Advocate General went on to tell Congress that "If you expressly confer jurisdiction on the federal courts to try such cases, you preserve the constitutional separation of military and civil courts, you save the military from a lot of unmerited grief, and you provide for a clean, constitutional method for disposing of such cases." It is conceded that it was wholly within the constitutional power of Congress to follow this suggestion and provide for federal district court trials of discharged soldiers accused of offenses committed while in the armed services. . . . There can be no valid argument, therefore, that civilian ex-servicemen must be tried by court-martial or not tried at all. If that is so it is only because Congress has not seen fit to subject them to trial in federal district courts.

None of the other reasons suggested by the Government are sufficient to justify a broad construction of the constitutional grant of power to Congress to regulate the armed forces. That provision itself does not empower Congress to deprive people of trials under Bill of Rights safeguards, and we are not willing to hold that power to circumvent those safeguards should be inferred through the Necessary and Proper Clause. It is impossible to think that the discipline of the Army is going to be disrupted, its morale impaired, or its orderly processes disturbed, by giving ex-servicemen the benefit of a civilian court trial when they are actually civilians. And we are not impressed by the fact that some other countries which do not have our Bill of Rights indulge in the practice of subjecting civilians who were once soldiers to trials by courts-martial instead of trials by civilian courts.

There are dangers lurking in military trials which were sought to be avoided by the Bill of Rights and Article III of our Constitution. Free countries of the world have tried to restrict military tribunals to the narrowest jurisdiction deemed absolutely essential to maintaining discipline among troops in active service. . . . But Army discipline will not be improved by court-martialing rather than trying by jury some civilian ex-soldier who has been wholly separated from the service for months, years, or perhaps decades. Consequently considerations of discipline provide no excuse for new expansion of court-martial jurisdiction at the expense of the normal and constitutionally preferable system of trial by jury.

Determining the scope of the constitutional power of Congress to authorize trial by court-martial presents another instance calling for limitation to *"the least possible power adequate to the end proposed."* We hold that Congress cannot subject civilians like Toth to trial by court-martial. They, like other civilians, are entitled to have the benefit of safeguards afforded those tried in the regular courts authorized by Article III of the Constitution.

Reversed.

[MR. JUSTICE REED, *joined by* MR. JUSTICE BURTON *and* MR. JUSTICE MINTON, *dissented on the ground that congressional power was broad enough to sustain the Uniform Code of Military Justice and that the Fifth and Sixth Amendments did not apply in "cases arising in the land or naval forces."* MR. JUSTICE BURTON, *stated an additional ground for dissenting in that Toth was not a full-fledged civilian upon his discharge. His discharge was conditional because after the 1950 act the United States reserved the right to try him by court-martial for a crime committed while he was still in the Air Force.*]

17

Race Discrimination and Equal Protection of Laws

We have seen in Chapter 11 that the wide use of the due process clause of the Fourteenth Amendment to protect private property rights pushed the equal protection clause of that Amendment into the background for many years. Also, after 1937, as the Supreme Court withdrew from attempting to make social and economic policy, it began to protect individual rights with increasing vigor. For that purpose the Court relied more and more on the equal protection clause. As a result, that clause has had a dramatic and unparalleled growth, particularly in the cause of Negro rights.

The term *equal protection of the laws* is impossible to define with any degree of precision. Nevertheless, the clause was obviously designed to guarantee the newly freed Negroes equality of treatment in the enjoyment of basic civil and political rights. Justice Miller noted in the *Slaughter House Cases* (Chapter 11) that, in the light of the historical background of the Civil War amendments, there was no difficulty in giving meaning to the equal protection clause. "The existence of laws in the States where the newly emancipated Negroes resided, which discriminated with gross injustice and hardship against them as a class, was the evil to be remedied by this clause, and by it such laws are forbidden." Despite these fine words the Court interpreted the Fourteenth Amendment very narrowly in the *Slaughter House Cases* and thereby helped to make it an ineffective instrument for the protection of Negro rights.

The Civil War was hardly over before the newly won civil and political rights of Negroes began to be curtailed by state legislation. The Radical Congress attempted to halt these efforts through the enactment of a series of civil rights acts to implement the Civil War amendments. A final serious attempt to establish civil and legal rights for Negroes was made in the Civil Rights Act of 1875. There Congress provided that all persons, regardless of race or color, were entitled to the "full and equal enjoyment of the accommodations, advantages, facilities, and privileges of inns, public conveyances on land or water, theaters and other places of public amusement." Denial of these rights to others by any person was made a federal crime punishable by fine or imprisonment. This law extended the protection of the federal government to many areas of civil rights that had traditionally been under state protection. However, with only Justice Harlan dissenting, the Supreme Court held the Civil Rights Act of 1875 unconstitutional in the *Civil Rights Cases* (p. 600). In the majority opinion, Justice Bradley reasoned that the Fourteenth Amendment only prohibited discrimination by the states. Congress could not penalize *private* persons for discriminating against Negroes. The decision in the *Civil Rights Cases* further prevented the Fourteenth Amendment from becoming an effective barrier against racial discrimination. The opinion ". . . served notice that the federal government could not lawfully protect the Negro against the discrimination which private individuals might choose to exercise against him. This was another way of saying that the system of 'white supremacy' was mainly beyond federal control."[1]

Separate but Equal Doctrine

The *Slaughter House* and *Civil Rights Cases* were decided during the period when the South was fighting bitterly to turn back the tide toward full emancipation of the Negro. By the turn of the century, the Southern states had adopted a maze of restrictions against the Negro that consigned him largely to his pre-Civil War caste status. As noted subsequently, devices such as the poll tax, the grandfather clauses, and the white primary were used to disfranchise Negroes. In addition, provisions for the rigid separation of the colored race in schools, hospitals, transportation facilities, places of amusement, and elsewhere were written into state constitutions and statutes. The segregation pattern developed in the South was formally approved by the Supreme

[1] Alfred H. Kelly and Winfred A. Harbison, *The American Constitution, Its Origins and Development* (New York: Norton, 1948), p. 491. The *Civil Rights Cases* are analyzed thoroughly in Milton R. Konvitz, *The Constitution and Civil Rights* (New York: Columbia University Press, 1946), Ch. 2.

Court in *Plessy* v. *Ferguson* (p. 605). In that case, a Louisiana statute that required railroads to provide separate but equal accommodations for white and colored races was held not to constitute a denial of the equal protection of the laws. In delivering the majority opinion, Justice Brown dismissed the contention that segregation "stamps the colored race with a badge of inferiority" with the insensitive assertion that "if this is so, it is not by reason of anything found in the act, but solely because the colored race chooses to put that construction upon it." Again only Justice Harlan dissented, in a dramatic and powerful opinion that was destined to endure.

In the years following the *Plessy* holding that separate but equal facilities were constitutional, racial segregation became a deeply intrenched way of life in the South. In case after case the separate but equal doctrine was followed but not reexamined. Actually, the doctrine had no real meaning, for the Supreme Court refused to look beyond lower court holdings to find if the segregated facilities for Negroes were in fact equal to those provided for whites. As a result, many Negro accommodations were said to be equal when it was a matter of common knowledge that they were decidedly inferior. The President's Committee on Civil Rights remarked aptly that the separate but equal doctrine ". . . is one of the outstanding myths of American history, for it is almost always true that while indeed separate, these facilities are far from equal. Throughout the segregated public institutions, Negroes have been denied an equal share of tax-supported services and facilities."[2]

Beginning in the late 1930s the Court became much stricter about the equality requirement. The first important decision was *Missouri* ex rel. *Gaines* v. *Canada,* 305 U.S. 337 (1938). In that case the state refused to admit Gaines to the Law School of the University of Missouri. There was no law school for Negroes in the state, but a Missouri statute provided for the payment of tuition charges for Negro residents of Missouri at law schools in adjacent states. Missouri argued that this provision satisfied the separate but equal requirement. The Court ruled, however, that if facilities were provided for the legal education of white students within the state, equal facilities were also to be made available in the state for Negroes desiring a law degree. Delivering the majority opinion of the Court, Chief Justice Hughes stated:

> By the operation of the laws of Missouri a privilege has been created for white law students which is denied to Negroes by reason of their race. The white resident is afforded legal education within the State; the Negro resident having the same qualifications is refused it there and must go outside the State to obtain it. That is a denial of the equality of legal right to the enjoyment of the privilege which the State has set up, and the provision for the payment of tuition fees in another State does not remove the discrimination.

[2] President's Committee, *To Secure These Rights* (Washington, D.C.: Government Printing Office, 1947), pp. 81–82. See also Rocco J. Tresolini, "John Marshall Harlan and Desegregation," *The Quarterly Review of Higher Education Among Negroes,* Vol. 30 (January 1962), p. 1.

In subsequent cases the Court continued to insist on equal facilities for Negroes. In *Sipuel* v. *University of Oklahoma,* 332 U.S. 631 (1948), the Court held that qualified Negroes must be admitted to the state law school or be provided with equal educational facilities within the state. In *McLaurin* v. *Oklahoma State Regents,* 339 U.S. 637 (1950), it ruled that Negroes may not be segregated within a university after they have been admitted to its graduate school. The Court reasoned that the equal protection clause required that Negroes receive the same treatment as other students upon admission to a state-supported graduate school.[3] On the same day the *McLaurin* decision was announced, the Court rendered its important opinion in *Sweatt* v. *Painter* (p. 609), which paved the way for the 1954 decisions on segregation in the public schools. Although the Court did not hold that segregation per se was unconstitutional in the *Sweatt* case, the decision indicated clearly that it was virtually impossible for a state to comply with the separate but equal doctrine in the area of professional and graduate education.

The stage was now set for a final assault on the *Plessy* rule, which by 1950 was under severe attack. The walls of segregation were beginning to crumble everywhere by mid-century. American Negroes had not only won many battles in the courts, but their status had been improved considerably by a variety of other factors. With the defeat of Nazi Germany and its cult of racial superiority in 1945, the doctrine of Negro inferiority was largely deprived of its intellectual justification. After the war, Negroes, who had moved north to work in defense industries, acquired the balance of power in close elections in many Northern urban centers. At the same time, increasing numbers of Negroes were voting in the Southern states. World War II and the period of prosperity that followed created new demands for manpower and brought increased employment opportunities for Negroes. The industrialization and unionization of the South after the war also created new job opportunities. The President's Committee on Civil Rights gave strong support to demands for improving conditions for Negroes and other minority groups by calling for the elimination of segregation based on race, color, creed, or national origin. In the postwar years, the armed forces all but eliminated segregation. A number of states ended segregation in the National Guard. Thus, the years after 1945 witnessed a ". . . steady amelioration of the condition of the American Negroes. Although a succession of disturbing crises has marked the way, the direction of development has been unmistakable."[4]

---

[3] In *Henderson* v. *United States,* 339 U.S. 816 (1950), the Court held that segregation of Negroes in dining cars under rules of the Interstate Commerce Commission was incompatible with equality of treatment. This decision had the effect of outlawing segregation in common carriers, but *Plessy* v. *Ferguson* was not even mentioned in the Court's decision.

[4] Oscar Handlin, "Desegregation in Perspective," *Current History,* Vol. 32 (May 1957), p. 259. The progress of the American Negro from his African origins is recorded

Segregation in Public Schools

The broadest challenge to racial discrimination came in 1952, when the Supreme Court was asked to outlaw segregation in the public schools in four states and the District of Columbia. The Court heard arguments during its 1952 term but adjourned without rendering an opinion and called for re-arguments during the next term. The Court was obviously moving cautiously, clearly aware of the full implications of any decision it might render in this explosive area. In 1952, seventeen states and the District of Columbia required segregation by law. Four other states permitted segregation by local option. More than 8,000,000 white students and more than 2,500,000 colored pupils, representing about 4 per cent of the nation's public school enrollment, were required to attend segregated schools. Obviously, the overruling of the separate but equal doctrine would bring about drastic changes in American education in many parts of the country. In addition, the death knell would be sounded for the entire pattern of segregation if the separate but equal concept could not be applied to public education.

John W. Davis, the Democratic candidate for President in 1924, headed the staff of lawyers who argued the case for the states. He relied principally on *Plessy* v. *Ferguson* in presenting his arguments for continued segregation in the public schools. He pointed out that when Congress and the states adopted the Fourteenth Amendment, there was no intention of abolishing segregation in public education. Davis further contended that under the Constitution the states were empowered to educate their children as they saw fit without interference from the federal government.

The arguments against segregation were presented by Thurgood Marshall, counsel for the NAACP. Marshall had already appeared before the Court in numerous important cases such as *Sweatt* v. *Painter* and *Shelley* v. *Kraemer* (p. 623), and had won some notable legal victories. He argued that the Fourteenth Amendment had been adopted to strike down the discriminatory legislation passed by many of the Southern states after the Civil War. Marshall urged the Court to reject completely the separate but equal doctrine. He contended that segregation stamped the Negro as an inferior and that it produced detrimental psychological effects on whites and Negroes alike.

On May 17, 1954, the Court concluded, in *Brown* v. *Board of Education* (p. 611), that "in the field of public education the doctrine of 'separate but equal' has no place." Shortly after the decision was rendered, a leading newspaper noted that ". . . it is fifty-eight years since the Supreme Court, with Justice Harlan dissenting, established the doctrine of 'separate but equal' provision for the white and Negro races on interstate carriers. It is forty-three

in John Hope Franklin, *From Slavery to Freedom* (New York: Knopf, 1956); Ch. 30 deals with the status of the Negro at mid-century.

years since John Marshall Harlan passed from this earth. Now the words he used in his lonely dissent in an 8-to-1 decision in the case of *Plessy* v. *Ferguson* in 1896 have become a part of the law of the land." The *Brown* decision ". . . dealt solely with segregation in the public schools, but there was not one word in Chief Justice Warren's opinion that was inconsistent with the earlier views of Justice Harlan. This is an instance in which the voice crying in the wilderness finally becomes the expression of a people's will and in which justice overtakes and thrusts aside a timorous expediency."[5]

The *Brown* decision was a momentous one indeed. Its impact upon many phases of American life will be felt for decades to come. That the Court was keenly aware of its heavy responsibilities in rendering a decision that cut so deeply into long-established laws and customs is indicated by the following unusual aspects of its opinion.

1. *The Court was unanimous.* Only one short, lucid opinion was written. Thus, the Court appeared united before the country and the world on a question of fundamental importance. The full weight and prestige of the Court was thrown behind its mandate. Those who might wish to thwart the decision could find little comfort in this situation.

2. *The Court postponed a decision on the application of its decision until a later date.* This was done by restoring the case to the docket for argument at the next term and inviting all interested parties to present their views as to how the decision could be carried out. One of the chief merits of this action ". . . was that it would afford a period for reflection in which sentiment in some of the most vitally affected areas might moderate. Some integration of schools could take place, and those who saw the system in operation might feel better about it."[6] In 1955, the Court ordered that the states make "a prompt and reasonable start toward full compliance" with its segregation ruling [*Brown* v. *Board of Education,* 2nd Case (p. 615)].

At the same time the *Brown* decision was handed down, the Court invalidated racial segregation in the public schools of the District of Columbia in *Bolling* v. *Sharpe* (p. 614). Because the equal protection clause of the Fourteenth Amendment cannot be applied to the federal government, the *Bolling* decision was based on the due process clause of the Fifth Amendment.

The *Brown* case did not explicitly overrule *Plessy* v. *Ferguson,* but it did indicate that segregation in areas other than public education would be difficult to maintain. Only a week after the *Brown* decision, the Court sent three racial segregation cases back to lower courts with orders that they be reexamined in the light of the *Brown* holding. The cases involved racial segregation in the amphitheater of a public park, a municipal housing project, and a city golf course. In 1955, the Court affirmed a federal circuit court ruling in *Dawson* v. *Mayor and City Council of Baltimore,* 220 F. 2d. 386, that racial segregation in public beaches and bathhouses in Baltimore was unconstitu-

---

[5] *The New York Times* (May 23, 1954), p. 10E.

[6] Luther A. Huston, "Segregation: Warren Role in Case," *The New York Times* (May 23, 1954), p. 5E.

tional. The lower court relied heavily on the *Brown* case and remarked that "it is obvious that racial segregation in recreational activities can no longer be sustained as a proper exercise of the police power of the State; for if that power cannot be invoked to sustain racial segregation in the schools . . . , it cannot be sustained with respect to public beach and bathhouse facilities." In 1956, a federal district court ruled in the case of *Browder* v. *Gayle,* 142 F.S. 707, that segregation in public buses in Alabama violated the Fourteenth Amendment. This decision was also affirmed by the Supreme Court.

REACTION TO PUBLIC-SCHOOL SEGREGATION CASES

It was inevitable that the *Public-School Segregation Cases,* which were of such vital national importance, would generate mixed reactions. Since the decisions were announced, the Court has been both highly praised and soundly denounced. In the South itself, reactions ranged all the way from open defiance of the Court to complete acceptance of its new holding. In the defiant states, a number of proposals designed to circumvent the Court's mandate have been adopted. For example, laws have been passed denying state funds to any school that admits pupils of both races. Some states have set up elaborate pupil assignment schemes that allow local school officials to maintain segregation and have enacted laws providing for the expenditure of public funds for *private segregated schools.* At the same time, a number of groups have been formed in the South to resist desegregation. These include organizations such as the National Association for the Advancement of White People, the Georgia States' Rights Council, and the White Citizens Councils found in several states. Nevertheless, one thoughtful Georgian, who has devoted much time and energy to the improvement of race relations in the South, has said:

> Despite loud public denials, leaders of the resistance movement realize that it can only be a delaying action. No one seriously believes that the Supreme Court's decisions will be reversed or that a handful of states can resist the national policy of desegregation indefinitely. And, although delay might be extended for a long time by determined efforts, the knowledge that defeat is ultimately certain should have an increasingly demoralizing effect on the movement. In sum, the Southern resistance movement is a foredoomed effort. The question is, how long can it be sustained and at what cost in human suffering and degradation?[7]

Since the Court's 1954 holdings, substantial progress has been made toward desegregation in the public schools. Segregation has been abandoned completely in the four non-Southern states—Arizona, Wyoming, Kansas, and New Mexico—where it had been permitted by local option. Immediate action was taken to desegregate public schools in the District of Columbia and in some communities in the border states of Virginia, Missouri, Delaware, and

---

[7] Harold C. Fleming, "Resistance Movements and Racial Desegregation," *Annals,* Vol. 304 (March 1956), pp. 51–52.

Maryland. Towns and villages in various other Southern states attempted to comply immediately with the Court's mandate. Oklahoma, Kentucky, Arkansas, West Virginia, Tennessee, Texas, and other states have taken important steps toward compliance. Schools have been integrated peacefully in numerous large cities. Each year finds more Negro students enrolled in integrated schools.[8]

Yet, despite these important developments, the drama of implementing the Court's historic segregation ruling has only just begun. Much still remains to be done; as noted in Chapter 3, by 1964, only 10 per cent of all Negro students were attending integrated schools. Although the proportion has risen slightly since, when calculated on some bases, both the absolute number and the proportion of minority-group children attending schools with a serious racial imbalance—that is with at least de facto segregation—has actually increased during this period as the central cities and their schools lose their white population. Many individuals in the states of the deep South—particularly in Alabama, Georgia, Louisiana, and Mississippi, where the ratio of Negroes to whites is higher than in the South as a whole—continue to resist the Court's ruling. Arrogant defiance of the law by public officials has helped bring on the terrible tragedies of Little Rock, Arkansas; Oxford, Mississippi; and Birmingham, Alabama. The difficulties encountered in enforcing the decision in the face of opposition by state authorities are revealed well by the course of events in Little Rock, set forth in *Cooper* v. *Aaron* (p. 616).

In the North, the resistance takes the less dramatic form of inertia on the part of school boards and political leaders. There is also the sometimes sincere and sometimes hypocritical concern for preserving the neighborhood school. Nevertheless, as already noted, the direction of events is unmistakable, and segregation will eventually be abolished in the United States. "There is no stopping place between the granting of a few rights and full citizenship. Once the first Negro was educated, once slavery was abolished, America made her choice. Negroes will demand and secure the same rights as other citizens. No other Americans have asked for more than this, or settled long for less."[9] It is not difficult to predict that the Court will soon be deeply embroiled in the school segregation problem in the North.

Racial Discrimination in Housing

Racial discrimination in schools and housing is closely connected, because residential segregation that forces Negroes or other groups to live in limited

[8] These statements are taken from *Southern School News,* a monthly periodical published in Nashville, Tenn., devoted entirely to school segregation problems in the South. The first issue appeared on September 3, 1954. Current legal aspects of race relations are dealt with in *Race Relations Law Reporter,* a bimonthly publication of the Vanderbilt University School of Law that first appeared in February 1956.

[9] Jack W. Peltason, *Fifty-eight Lonely Men* (New York: Harcourt, Brace and World, 1961), p. 254.

areas results in segregated schools. Only the barring of racial discrimination in housing to permit greater dispersal of populations will break down public-school segregation in many areas of the North as well as the South.

In their efforts to break out of crowded racial ghettos into unsegregated residential areas, Negroes have relied heavily on the Fourteenth Amendment. The Supreme Court early held in *Buchanan* v. *Warley,* 245 U.S. 60 (1917), that municipal residential-segregation ordinances violate the Fourteenth Amendment. Because the *Buchanan* case made it impossible to prevent Negroes from moving into white neighborhoods by law, restrictive covenants were employed widely after 1917 to effect the same purpose. Restrictive covenants are simply private agreements whereby owners of property agree not to sell or lease their property to Negroes or other groups. In *Corrigan* v. *Buckley,* 271 U.S. 323 (1926), the Court unanimously upheld the use of private restrictive covenants. The Court noted that the Fourteenth Amendment restricts only state action and not the action of private individuals. For approximately twenty years after *Corrigan* v. *Buckley* the Supreme Court refused to review subsequent restrictive-covenant cases. However, in the 1948 case of *Shelley* v. *Kraemer* (p. 623), the Court held that private restrictive covenants could not be validly enforced by the state courts because this would violate the equal protection clause of the Fourteenth Amendment.[10] At the same time the Court held, in *Hurd* v. *Hodge,* 334 U.S. 24 (1948), that the enforcement of restrictive covenants in the District of Columbia was prohibited by federal statutes.

After the *Shelley* and *Hurd* cases, attempts were made to enforce racial restrictive covenants by allowing signers of the covenant to sue those who had broken it by selling or leasing property to Negroes or other groups. But in *Barrows* v. *Jackson,* 346 U.S. 249 (1953), the Court ruled that a restrictive covenant may not be enforced by a suit for damages against a party who broke the contract. In delivering the majority opinion of the Court, Justice Minton remarked that if a state upheld such damage suits, it would be encouraging the use of restrictive covenants.

Many states have now passed various forms of open housing legislation. In *Reitman* v. *Mulkey,* 387 U.S. 369 (1967), the Supreme Court dealt with the very difficult problem of whether the state might repeal such legislation or whether repeal would itself be a form of state action in aid of discrimination In this instance it held only that the state might not insert into its constitution a provision barring future antidiscrimination statutes.

Indeed one of the most difficult problems for the Court has been drawing the line between discriminatory state action prohibited by the Fourteenth Amendment and private action that the amendment does not reach. *Shelley* v. *Kraemer* (p. 623) raises the question, as do such real judicial puzzles as

[10] The painstaking strategy of the NAACP in this case is noted in Chapter 3 and described fully in Clement E. Voste, *Caucasians Only: The Supreme Court, the NAACP, and the Restrictive Covenant Cases* (Berkeley and Los Angeles: University of California Press (1959), p. 213.

Burton v. *Wilmington Parking Authority,* 365 U.S. 715 (1961) (restaurant in municipally owned garage involves state action); *The Girard College Case,* 353 U.S. 230 (1957); and *Evans* v. *Newton,* 382 U.S. 296 (1966) (public body acting as trustees of private bequest involves state action).

In 1968, Congress passed legislation that, over a period of some years, will require the end of discrimination in the rental and sale of most federally aided housing. In the same year, the Supreme Court went even further by ruling that an obscure provision of the Civil Rights Act of 1866 prohibited private discrimination in the sale or rental of property. [*Jones* v. *Alfred H. Mayer Co.* (392 U.S. 409, 1968).]

Negro Suffrage

Although citizenship and suffrage are closely connected, they are not synonymous, for the right to vote has never been extended to all citizens. Early in our history property qualifications for voting were common; for a long time, women were not allowed to vote; and children do not have the right of franchise even though they are citizens. Neither has United States citizenship always been a requirement for voting; aliens were permitted, prior to 1926, to vote under certain conditions in some states.

The original Constitution left the regulation of suffrage almost entirely in the hands of the states. Article I (Section 2, cl. 1) provides simply that all persons who are qualified to vote for members of the most numerous house of the state legislature are eligible to vote for members of the House of Representatives. This same rule governs the election of senators, because a like provision was included in the Seventeenth Amendment. The Constitution provides also that the President and Vice-President are to be chosen by presidential electors. These electors are selected in each state "in such manner as the legislature thereof may direct." (Art. II, Section 1.) Nevertheless, the states must fix the qualifications for voting in both national and state elections within the limits set by the Fourteenth, Fifteenth, and Nineteenth Amendments. The equal protection clause of the Fourteenth Amendment prohibits the states from making unreasonable classifications or discriminations affecting the right to vote. The Fourteenth Amendment also contains a penalty clause that authorizes Congress to reduce the congressional representation of a state that has disfranchised a proportion of the adult male population. This penalty provision was designed to guarantee to the newly freed Negroes the right to vote, but it has never been enforced. The Fifteenth Amendment forbids the states to deny or abridge the right to vote because of race, color, or previous condition of servitude, while the Nineteenth Amendment prohibits discrimination because of sex.

The most important and dramatic questions regarding the right to vote have been raised by the efforts to enfranchise the Negro. The Fourteenth and Fifteenth Amendments were resisted vigorously by the Southern states, and not long after Union troops were withdrawn in 1877, Negroes were effectively disfranchised. A number of legal devices, such as poll taxes, literacy tests, and the white primary, were employed to deny Negroes the right to vote. The President's Committee on Civil Rights noted, in 1947, that in addition to the ". . . formal, legal methods of disfranchisement, there are the long-standing techniques of terror and intimidation, in the face of which great courage is required of the Negro who tries to vote. In the regions most characterized by generalized violence against Negroes, little more than 'advice' is often necessary to frighten them away from the polls. They have learned, through the years, to discover threats in mood and atmosphere."[11] Although there has been considerable loosening of suffrage restrictions since 1947, as a result of pressure from liberal forces both within and outside the South, the problem of Negro suffrage is still far from solved.

GRANDFATHER CLAUSE

As time went on, the legality of a number of the devices developed for the disfranchisement of the Negro was challenged in the Supreme Court. One of these was the interesting and novel "grandfather clause" that had been adopted in several states. In general, the various grandfather clauses permitted certain classes of individuals other than Negroes to vote without meeting certain property and literacy tests. The Oklahoma grandfather clause, for example, which was enacted as an amendment to the state constitution in 1910, required a literacy test (ability to read and write *any* section of the Oklahoma Constitution) for voting. However, it provided that the test need not be taken by persons or descendants of such persons who were entitled to vote under any form of government or who resided in a foreign nation prior to January 1, 1866. Because Negroes could not vote prior to 1866 in Oklahoma, as well as in most other states, the required literacy test was used to deny most of them the right to vote. But in the 1915 case of *Guinn* v. *United States,* 238 U.S. 347, the Supreme Court held that the Oklahoma grandfather clause violated the Fifteenth Amendment.

In 1916, Oklahoma enacted a new suffrage law that omitted the ancestral exemptions held invalid in the *Guinn* case, but which provided that all persons who had voted in the general election of 1914, when the grandfather clause was still in effect, were permanently qualified to vote without taking a literacy test. All other persons, except those given a short extension because of sickness or absence from the state, were required to register during a twelve-day period or be *permanently disfranchised.* In *Lane* v. *Wilson,* 307 U.S. 268 (1939), the Supreme Court held the statute invalid as a violation of the Fifteenth Amendment. Speaking for the Court, Justice Frankfurter pointed out that the Fifteenth Amendment ". . . nullifies sophisticated as well as simple-minded modes of discrimination. It hits onerous procedural requirements which effectively handicap exercise of the franchise by the col-

---

[11] President's Committee, *op. cit.,* p. 40.

ored race although the abstract right to vote may remain unrestricted as to race."

THE WHITE PRIMARY

For many years the most effective "legal" method for denying Negroes the right to vote was the white primary. This device simply excluded Negroes from voting in the Democratic party primary elections. For all practical purposes, this action disfranchised the colored race, because the dominance of the Democratic party in the South makes victory in a primary tantamount to election.

The white primary appeared to be legal for two major reasons. In the first place, the Constitution prohibits discrimination against the Negro by the state, but not by private individuals or organizations. Theoretically, the Democratic party ". . . acted as a purely private organization. So long as the fiction of party as private association could be maintained, all could agree on the legality of its exclusion of the Negro from the Democratic primary."[12] Secondly, it seemed, for a long time, that Congress had no control over primaries. Article I, Section 4, of the Constitution provides that Congress may make or alter the times, places, and manner of holding congressional elections. But in *Newberry* v. *United States,* 256 U.S. 232 (1921), the Supreme Court held that a primary was not an election within the meaning of that article. Consequently, Congress could not regulate primaries.

The Texas white primary law enacted in 1923, which was held void in *Nixon* v. *Herndon,* seems to have been inspired by the *Newberry* doctrine. The *Nixon* case is discussed in *Smith* v. *Allwright* (p. 633), where the Supreme Court held the Texas white primary unconstitutional after a long and tortuous process of litigation. The case of *United States* v. *Classic,* which helped pave the way for the downfall of the white primary by resolving the doubts raised by the *Newberry* case, is also discussed in *Smith* v. *Allwright.*

In a number of Southern states where the *Allwright* decision was accepted with little or no resistance, Negro participation in the political process was increased gradually. However, in some states efforts were made almost immediately to circumvent the *Allwright* holding by various ingenious methods. All of these attempts met with disaster in the federal courts.

South Carolina attempted to get around the *Allwright* decision by repealing all the state laws and constitutional provisions pertaining to party organization and primary elections, hoping that this action would make the Democatic party a private club that could continue to deny Negroes the right to vote without violating the Fourteenth and Fifteenth Amendments. A South Carolina federal district court judge held the plan void. The decision was affirmed by a federal circuit court, which noted that "no election machinery can be upheld if its purpose or effect is to deny to the Negro, on account of his race or color, any effective voice in the government of his country or the state or community wherein he lives." In *Rice* v. *Elmore,* 333 U.S. 875

---

[12] V. O. Key, Jr., *Southern Politics* (New York: Knopf, 1950), p. 621.

(1948), the Supreme Court refused to review the decision. A later attempt to reinstitute the white primary in South Carolina again met with defeat in *Baskin* v. *Brown,* 174 F. 2d 391 (1949).

Alabama's answer to the *Allwright* decision was the Boswell Amendment to the state constitution. This amendment provided that only those persons could vote who were able to "understand and explain" the Constitution of the United States to the satisfaction of local registration boards. A federal district court held that the Boswell Amendment was unconstitutional because it violated the Fifteenth Amendment. The court noted that ". . . as a rule the Boswell test of 'understand and explain' is required of Negroes while no such exaction is made of white applicants. It, thus, clearly appears that this Amendment was intended to be, and is being used for the purpose of discriminating against applicants for the franchise on the basis of race or color." The Supreme Court affirmed the district court's opinion in a *per curiam* decision without hearing argument in the case [*Schnell* v. *Davis,* 336 U.S. 933 (1949)].

Another novel attempt to offset the consequences of *Smith* v. *Allwright* was made in a Texas county where Negroes were barred from voting through the use of a preprimary primary. Negroes were excluded from the primaries of an organization known as the Jaybird Democratic Association on the ground that the group was a self-governing voluntary club. However, it was shown that, with very few exceptions, candidates endorsed by the Jaybird Association were unopposed in the regular Democratic party primaries and general elections. Every countrywide official elected to office since 1889 had first been endorsed in a Jaybird primary. With only Justice Minton dissenting, the Supreme Court relied on the *Allwright* decision in holding, in *Terry* v. *Adams,* 345 U.S. 461 (1953), that the Jaybird scheme violated the Fifteenth Amendment. The Court said that the Democratic party primary and the general election ". . . have become no more than the perfunctory ratifiers of the choice that has already been made in Jaybird elections from which Negroes have been excluded. The Jaybird primary has become an integral part, indeed the only effective part, of the elective process that determines who shall rule and govern in the country. The effect of the whole procedure is to do precisely that which the Fifteenth Amendment forbids."

The *Allwright* decision and the subsequent federal court cases noted here have destroyed the legal basis of the white primary in the South. Nevertheless, *Smith* v. *Allwright* and subsequent decisions did not prevent numerous local officials from excluding Negroes from the polls. Provisions to protect the voting rights of Negroes were included in the Civil Rights Acts of 1957, 1960, and 1964; but the strongest provisions are contained in the Voting Rights Act of 1965,[13] which is explained and upheld in *South Carolina* v. *Katzenbach* (p. 643).

[13] The key provisions of these acts may be found in Martin Shapiro (ed.), *The Constitution of the United States and Related Documents* (New York: Appleton-Century-Crofts, 1966).

Negro participation in the voting process is bound to increase in the years ahead. This prospect has been enhanced by the incisive and far-reaching case of *Gomillion* v. *Lightfoot* (p. 637), where a unanimous Court declared unconstitutional an ingenious scheme to deny Negroes the right to vote in Tuskegee, Alabama. As the first case involving a *racial* gerrymander ever considered by the Supreme Court, *Gomillion* v. *Lightfoot* serves notice that the "power of a state to determine the powers and boundaries of its internal political subdivisions is not absolute and cannot be used to defy or ignore the positive requirements of the Constitution of the United States."[14]

The Twenty-fourth Amendment has eliminated state poll tax requirements for federal elections, and the Supreme Court has struck down such taxes even for state elections as a violation of equal protection [*Harper* v. *Virginia State Board of Elections,* 383 U.S. 663 (1966).]

THE NEW CIVIL RIGHTS ACTS

The Civil Rights Acts of 1957, 1960, and 1964 contained not only voting guarantees, but provisions prohibiting discrimination in certain public accommodations and facilities, federal programs, and some areas of employment. The public accommodations portions of these acts are upheld in the *Heart of Atlanta Motel Case* (p. 639). These provisions were justified under Congress' power over interstate commerce. But, in *South Carolina* v. *Katzenbach* (p. 643), congressional legislation was given the broadest possible scope as falling under the specifically granted power in the Fifteenth Amendment, Section 2: "The Congress shall have power to enforce this article by appropriate legislation." Because the Fourteenth Amendment contains an almost identical clause, it might be argued that Congress need not rely on its commerce or other powers enumerated in Article I, but might pass laws guarding equal protection and due process directly under its Fourteenth Amendment powers.

Sex is always a little bit hard to fit into academic categories. Although it does not fall under housing, or schools, or voting, or civil rights acts, we should mention that, after avoiding the issue for many years, the Supreme Court finally struck down state miscegenation statutes in *McLaughlin* v. *Florida,* 379 U.S. 184 (1964), and *Loving* v. *Virginia,* 388 U.S. 1 (1967), probably the most aptly named case ever to reach the Court.

From the Courts to the Streets

An important turning point in the struggle for Negro rights came in 1960. Impatient with the slow pace of desegregation and with court procedures

---

[14] Jo Desha Lucas, "Dragon in the Thicket: A Perusal of *Gomillion* v. *Lightfoot*," *The Supreme Court Review* (1961), p. 243. For a readable step-by-step report on the case, see Bernard Taper, *Gomillion* v. *Lightfoot, The Tuskegee Gerrymander Case* (New York: McGraw-Hill, 1962).

generally, younger American Negroes began to press for more direct action. The struggle in the streets began in February 1960, in Greensboro, North Carolina, when four Negro college students sat down at lunch counters and demanded service. This was followed by a wave of sit-ins, kneel-ins, Freedom Rides, boycotts, and other protest demonstrations that spread throughout the country. By 1963, the Negro protest movement had exploded into the most serious social phenomena in American history. The intensity of the movement was well demonstrated by the march on Washington, D.C., in August 1963, by some 200,000 Negroes and their white allies demanding "Freedom Now." Thus, the struggle in the streets has sharply dramatized the Negroes' demands for equal rights and awakened many previously indifferent Americans to the seriousness of the situation.

Although sit-in and demonstration cases have most frequently reached the Court in the context of the Negro struggle for equal rights, they basically raise First Amendment, rather than equal protection, issues and are treated in Chapter 13.

Equal Protection and the Poor

The equal protection clause and the constitutional rights of black people have been so closely intertwined that we tend to think of the two as synonymous. Perhaps this is a good point at which to indicate that equal protection has become a key constitutional consideration in many nonracial areas. It is at the root of the apportionment cases discussed in Chapter 4 and lies behind much of the new law in the area of rights of accused persons, even though that law is usually phrased in due process terms. (See Chapter 18.) For often what the Court is arguing is that poor persons who are arrested are entitled to the same rights as rich persons.

Indeed it may well be that in the future equal protection will be as closely associated with the rights of poor persons as it currently is with the rights of black persons. In addition to the cases discussed in Chapter 18, some indication of this trend is to be seen in the Court's condemnation of the poll tax as a burden on the voting rights of poor persons, its invalidation of property qualifications for local elections [*Kramer* v. *Union Free School Dist.*, 89 S. Ct. 1886 (1969)] and its invalidation of state length of residency requirements for welfare recipients. (*Shapiro* v. *Thompson,* p. 647.) The current weight of the equal protection clause is indicated by the fact that the *Shapiro* case fits far more neatly into this chapter than into Chapter 5—"The Federal System"—where it traditionally would have been placed. *Shapiro* also suggests that the Court may eventually use the equal protection clause to eliminate length of residency requirements for voting which at one time or another have disenfranchised millions of Americans for months or years after they have moved.

The Court's concern for the poor is also to be seen in another case phrased in due process language, but backed by equal protection concerns, *Sniadach v. Family Finance Corporation,* 89 S. Ct. 1820 (1969), which declared unconstitutional state laws providing for the garnishment of debtors' wages before court judgment that the debt is actually owed.

CIVIL RIGHTS CASES
109 U.S. 3; 3 Sup. Ct. 18; 27 L. Ed. 835 (1883)

[*As noted in the introduction to this chapter, the Civil Rights Act of 1875 was designed to implement the Thirteenth and Fourteenth Amendments and thereby firmly establish the civil and legal rights of the freed Negroes. Five cases involving the Civil Rights Act of 1875 were decided together in the Civil Rights Cases. Certain persons in San Francisco, New York, and Memphis, Tennessee, were indicted for violations of the act for denying accommodations to Negroes at a hotel, admission to a theater, and admission to a ladies' car on a railway. Two of the cases went to the Supreme Court on writs of error sued out by the plaintiffs in federal circuit courts. The other three cases were certified to the Supreme Court because of a division of opinion among the lower court judges as to the constitutionality of the first and second sections of the Civil Rights Act of 1875.*]

MR. JUSTICE BRADLEY delivered the opinion of the Court:

. . . It is obvious that the primary and important question in all the cases is the constitutionality of the law: for if the law is unconstitutional none of the prosecutions can stand. . . .

The essence of the law is, not to declare broadly that all persons shall be entitled to the full and equal enjoyment of the accommodations, advantages, facilities, and privileges of inns, public conveyances, and theaters; but that such enjoyment shall not be subject to any conditions applicable only to citizens of a particular race or color, or who had been in a previous condition of servitude. . . .

Has Congress constitutional power to make such a law? Of course, no one will contend that the power to pass it was contained in the Constitution before the adoption of the last three amendments. The power is sought, first, in the Fourteenth Amendment, and the views and arguments of distinguished Senators, advanced whilst the law was under consideration, claiming authority

to pass it by virtue of that amendment, are the principal arguments adduced in favor of the power. . . .

The first section of the Fourteenth Amendment (which is the one relied on), after declaring who shall be citizens of the United States, and of the several States, is prohibitory in its character, and prohibitory upon the States. It declares that:

"No State shall make or enforce any law which shall abridge the privileges or immunities of citizens of the United States; nor shall any State deprive any person of life, liberty, or property without due process of law; nor deny to any person within its jurisdiction the equal protection of the laws."

It is State action of a particular character that is prohibited. Individual invasion of individual rights is not the subject-matter of the amendment. It has a deeper and broader scope. It nullifies and makes void all State legislation, and State action of every kind, which impairs the privileges and immunities of citizens of the United States, or which injures them in life, liberty or property without due process of law, or which denies to any of them the equal protection of the laws. It not only does this, but, in order that the national will, thus declared, may not be a mere *brutum fulmen,* the last section of the amendment invests Congress with power to enforce it by appropriate legislation. To enforce what? To enforce the prohibition. To adopt appropriate legislation for correcting the effects of such prohibited State laws and State acts, and thus to render them effectually null, void, and innocuous. This is the legislative power conferred upon Congress, and this is the whole of it. It does not invest Congress with power to legislate upon subjects which are within the domain of State legislation; but to provide modes of relief against State legislation, or State action, of the kind referred to. It does not authorize Congress to create a code of municipal law for the regulation of private rights; but to provide modes of redress against the operation of State laws, and the action of State officers executive or judicial, when these are subversive of the fundamental rights specified in the amendment. Positive rights and privileges are undoubtedly secured by the Fourteenth Amendment; but they are secured by way of prohibition against State laws and State proceedings affecting those rights and privileges, and by power given to Congress to legislate for the purpose of carrying such prohibition into effect: and such legislation must necessarily be predicated upon such supposed State laws or State proceedings, and be directed to the correction of their operation and effect. . . .

[U]ntil some State law has been passed, or some State action through its officers or agents has been taken, adverse to the rights of citizens sought to be protected by the Fourteenth Amendment, no legislation of the United States under said amendment, nor any proceeding under such legislation, can be called into activity: for the prohibitions of the amendment are against State laws and acts done under State authority. Of course, legislation may, and should be, provided in advance to meet the exigency when it arises; but it should be adapted to the mischief and wrong which the amendment was intended to provide against; and this is, State laws, or State action of some kind, adverse to the rights of the citizen secured by the amendment. Such legislation cannot properly cover the whole domain of rights appertaining to life, liberty and property, defining them and providing for their vindication. That would be to establish a code of municipal law regulative of all private rights between man and man in society. It would be to make Congress take the place of the State legislatures and to supersede them. It is absurd to affirm that, because the rights of life, liberty and property (which include all civil rights that men have), are by the amendment sought to be protected against invasion on the part of the State without due process of law, Congress may therefore provide due process of law for their vindication in every case; and that, because the denial by a State to any persons, of the equal protection of the laws, is prohibited by the amendment, therefore Congress may establish laws for their equal protection. In fine, the legislation which Congress is authorized to adopt in this behalf is not general legislation upon the rights of the citizen, but corrective legislation, that is, such as may be necessary and proper for counteracting such laws as the States may adopt or enforce, and which, by the amendment, they are prohibited from making or enforcing, or such acts and proceedings as the States may commit or take, and which, by the amendment, they are prohibited from committing or taking. It is not necessary for us to state, if we could, what legislation would be proper for Congress to adopt. It is sufficient for us to examine whether the law in question is of that character.

An inspection of the law shows that it makes no reference whatever to any supposed or apprehended violation of the Fourteenth Amendment on the part of the States. It is not predicated on any such view. It proceeds *ex directo* to declare that certain acts committed by individuals shall be deemed offences, and shall be prosecuted and punished by proceedings in the courts of the United States. It does not profess to be corrective of any constitutional wrong committed by the States; it does not make its operation to depend upon any such wrong committed. It applies equally to cases arising in States which have the justest laws respecting the personal rights of citizens, and whose authorities are ever ready to enforce such laws, as to those which arise in States that may have violated the prohibition of the amendment. In other words, it steps into the domain of local jurisprudence, and lays down rules for the conduct of individuals in society towards each other, and imposes sanctions for the enforcement of those rules, without referring in any manner to any supposed action of the State or its authorities.

If this legislation is appropriate for enforcing the prohibitions of the amendment, it is difficult to see where it is to stop. Why may not Congress with equal show of authority enact a code of laws for the enforcement and vindication of all rights of life, liberty, and property? If it is supposable that the States may deprive persons of life, liberty, and property without due process of law (and the anmendment itself does suppose this), why should not Congress proceed at once to prescribe due process of law for the protection of every one of these fundamental rights, in every possible case, as well as to prescribe equal privileges in inns, public conveyances, and theaters? The truth is, that the implication of a power to legislate in this manner is based upon the assumption that if the States are forbidden to legislate or act in a particular way on a particular subject, and power is conferred upon Congress to enforce the prohibition, this gives Congress power to legislate generally upon that subject, and not merely power to provide modes of redress against such State legislation or action. The assumption is certainly unsound. It is repugnant to the Tenth Amendment of the Constitution, which declares that powers not delegated to the United States by the Constitution, nor prohibited by it to the States, are reserved to the States respectively or to the people. . . .

In this connection it is proper to state that civil rights, such as are guaranteed by the Constitution against State aggression, cannot be impaired by the wrongful acts of individuals, unsupported by State authority in the shape of laws, customs, or judicial or executive proceedings. The wrongful act of an individual, unsupported by any such authority, is simply a private wrong, or a crime of that individual; and invasion of the rights of the injured party, it is true, whether they affect his person, his property, or his reputation; but if not sanctioned in some way by the State, or not done under State authority, his rights remain in full force, and may presumably be vindicated by resort to the laws of the State for redress. An individual cannot deprive a man of his right to vote, to hold property, to buy and sell, to sue in the courts, or to be a witness or a juror; he may, by force or fraud, interfere with the enjoyment of the right in a particular case; he may commit an assault against the person, or commit murder, or use ruffian violence at the polls, or slander the good name of a fellow citizen; but, unless protected in these wrongful acts by some shield of State law or State authority, he cannot destroy or injure the right; he will only render himself amenable to satisfaction or punishment; and amenable therefore to the laws of the State where the wrongful acts are committed. Hence, in all those cases where the Constitution seeks to protect the rights of the citizen against discriminative and unjust laws of the State by prohibiting such laws, it is not individual offences, but abrogation and denial of rights, which it denounces, and for which it clothes the Congress with power to provide a remedy. This abrogation and denial of rights, for which the States alone were or could be responsible, was the great seminal and fundamental wrong which was intended to be remedied. And the remedy to be provided must necessarily be predicated upon that wrong. It must assume that in the cases provided for, the evil or wrong actually committed rests upon some State law or State authority for its excuse and perpetration. . . .

We have discussed the question presented by the law on the assumption that a right to enjoy equal accommodation and privileges in all inns, public conveyances, and places of public amusement, is one of the essential rights of the citizen which no State can abridge or interfere with. Whether it is such a right, or not, is a different question which, in the view we have taken of the validity of the law on the ground already stated, it is not necessary to examine. . . .

But the power of Congress to adopt direct and primary, as distinguished from corrective legislation, on the subject in hand, is sought, in the second place, from the Thirteenth Amendment, which abolishes slavery. . . .

This amendment, as well as the Fourteenth, is undoubtedly self-executing without any ancillary legislation, so far as its terms are applicable to any existing state of circumstances. By its own unaided force and effect it abolished slavery, and established universal freedom. . . .

The only question under the present head, therefore, is, whether the refusal to any persons of the accommodations of an inn, or a public conveyance, or a place of public amusement, by an individual, and without any sanction or support from any State law or regulation, does inflict upon such persons any manner of servitude, or form of slavery, as those terms are understood in this country? . . .

It would be running the slavery argument into the ground to make it apply to every act of discrimination which a person may see fit to make as to the guests he will entertain, or as to the people he will take into his coach or cab or car, or admit to his concert or theater, or deal with in other matters of intercourse or business. . . .

On the whole we are of opinion, that no countenance of authority for the passage of the law in question can be found in either the Thirteenth or Fourteenth Amendment of the Constitution; and no other ground of authority for its passage being suggested, it must necessarily be declared void, at least so far as its operation in the several States is concerned. . . .

MR. JUSTICE HARLAN, dissenting:

The opinion in these cases proceeds, it seems to me, upon grounds entirely too narrow and artificial. I cannot resist the conclusion that the substance and spirit of the recent amendments of the Constitution have been sacrificed by a subtle and ingenious verbal criticism. . . .

There seems to be no substantial difference between my brethren and myself as to the purpose of Congress; for, they say that the essence of the law is, not to declare broadly that all persons shall be entitled to the full and equal enjoyment of the accommodations, advantages, facilities, and privileges of inns, public conveyances, and theaters; but that such enjoyment shall not be subject to conditions applicable only to citizens of a particular race or color, or who had been in a previous condition of servitude. The effect of the statute, the court says, is, that colored citizens whether formerly slaves or not, and citizens of other races, shall have the same accommodations and privileges in all inns, public conveyances, and places of amusement as are enjoyed by white persons; and *vice versa.*

The court adjudges, I think erroneously, that Congress is without power, under either the Thirteenth or Fourteenth Amendment, to establish such regulations and that the first and second sections of the statute are, in all their parts, unconstitutional and void. . . .

Congress has not, in these matters, entered the domain of State control and supervision. It does not . . . assume to prescribe the general conditions and limitations under which inns, public conveyances, and places of public amusement, shall be conducted or managed. It simply declares, in effect, that since the nation has established universal freedom in this country, for all time, there shall be no discrimination, based merely upon race or color, in respect of the accommodations and advantages of public conveyances, inns, and places of public amusement.

I am of the opinion that such discrimination practised by corporations and individuals in the exercise of their public or quasi-public functions is a badge of servitude the imposition of which Congress may prevent under its power, by appropriate legislation, to enforce the Thirteenth Amendment; and, consequently, without reference to its enlarged power under the Fourteenth Amendment, the act of March 1, 1875, is not, in my judgment, repugnant to the Constitution. . . .

The assumption that this amendment [the Fourteenth] consists wholly of prohibitions upon State laws and State proceedings in hostility to its provisions, is unauthorized by its language. The first clause of the first section—"All persons born or naturalized in the United States, and subject to the jurisdiction thereof, are citizens of the United States, and of the State wherein they reside"—is of a distinctly affirmative character. In its application to the colored race, previously liberated, it created and granted, citizenship of the United States, as well as citizenship of the State in which they respectively resided. It introduced all of that race, whose ancestors had been imported and sold as slaves, at once, into the political community known as the "People of the United States." They became, instantly, citizens of the United States, and of their respective States. Further, they were brought, by this supreme act of the nation, within the direct operation of that provision of the Constitution which declares that "the citizens of each State shall be entitled to all privileges and immunities of citizens in the several States." Art. 4, Section 2.

The citizenship thus acquired, by that race, in virtue of an affirmative grant from the nation, may be protected, not alone by the judicial branch of the government, but by congressional legislation of a primary direct character; this, because the power of Congress is not restricted to the enforcement of prohibitions upon State laws or State action. It is, in terms distinct and positive, to enforce "the provisions of this article" of amendment; not simply those of a prohibitive character, but the provisions—all of the provisions—affirmative and prohibitive, of the amendment. It is, therefore, a grave misconception to suppose that the fifth section of the amendment has reference exclusively to express prohibitions upon State laws or State action. If any right was created by that amendment, the grant of power, through appropriate legislation, to enforce its provisions, authorizes Congress, by means of legislation, operating throughout the entire Union, to guard, secure, and protect that right. . . .

[G]overnment has nothing to do with social, as distinguished from technically legal, rights of individuals. No government ever has brought, or ever can bring, its people into social intercourse against their wishes. Whether one person will permit or maintain social relations with another is a matter with which government has no concern. . . . The rights which Congress, by the act of 1875, endeavored to secure and protect are legal, not social rights. The right, for instance, of a colored citizen to use the accommodations of a public highway, upon the same terms as are permitted to white citizens, is no more a social right than his right, under the law, to use the public streets of a city or a town, or a turnpike road, or a public market, or a post office, or his right to sit in a public building with others, of whatever race, for the purpose of hearing the political questions of the day discussed. . . .

The supreme law of the land has decreed that no authority shall be exercised in this country upon the basis of discrimination, in respect of civil rights, against freemen and citizens because of their race, color, or previous condition of servitude. To that decree— for the due enforcement of which, by appropriate legislation, Congress has been invested with express power— every one must bow, whatever may have been, or whatever now are, his individual views as to the wisdom or policy, either of the recent changes in the fundamental law, or of the legislation which has been enacted to give them effect.

For the reasons stated I feel constrained to withhold my assent to the opinion of the Court.

PLESSY v. FERGUSON
163 U.S. 537; 16 Sup. Ct. 1138; 41 L. Ed. 256 (1896)

[*A Louisiana statute enacted in 1890 required railroads to provide "separate but equal" accommodations for white and colored passengers. A section of the statute further stipulated that train officials were to assign each passenger to "the coach or compartment used for the race to which such passenger belongs." Plessy, who was one-eighth Negro but appeared to be white, took a vacant seat in a railway coach reserved for white persons. He refused to give up his seat and was subsequently imprisoned to answer a charge of violating the statute. The Supreme Court of Louisiana held the statute valid. Plessy then brought the case to the Supreme Court on a writ of error. Ferguson was the judge of a local court in Louisiana that had ordered Plessy's imprisonment.*]

MR. JUSTICE BROWN delivered the opinion of the Court:

The constitutionality of this act is attacked upon the ground that it conflicts both with the Thirteenth Amendment of the Constitution, abolishing slavery, and the Fourteenth Amendment, which prohibits certain restrictive legislation on the part of the States.

1. That it does not conflict with the Thirteenth Amendment, which abolished slavery and involuntary servitude, except as a punishment for crime, is too clear for argument. . . .

A statute which implies merely a legal distinction between the white and colored races—a distinction which is founded in the color of the two races, and which must always exist so long as white men are distinguished from the other race by color—has no tendency to destroy the legal equality of the two races, or reestablish a state of involuntary servitude. Indeed, we do not understand that the Thirteenth Amendment is strenuously relied upon by the plaintiff in error in this connection.

2. By the Fourteenth Amendment, all persons born or naturalized in the United States, and subject to the jurisdiction thereof, are made citizens of the United States and of the State wherein they reside; and the States are forbidden from making or enforcing any law which shall abridge the privileges or immunities of citizens of the United States, or shall deprive any person of life, liberty, or property without due process of law, or deny to any person within their jurisdiction the equal protection of the laws. . . .

The object of the amendment was undoubtedly to enforce the absolute equality of the two races before the law, but in the nature of things it could not have been intended to abolish distinctions based upon color, or to enforce social, as distinguished from political equality, or a commingling of the two races upon terms unsatisfactory to either. Laws permitting, and even requiring, their separation in places where they are liable to be brought into contact do not necessarily imply the inferiority of either race to the other, and have been generally, if not universally, recognized as within the competency of the state legislatures in the exercise of their police power. The most common instance of this is connected with the establishment of separate schools for white and colored children, which has been held to be a valid exercise of the legislative power even by courts of States where the political rights of the colored race have been longest and most earnestly enforced.

. . . It is claimed by the plaintiff in error that, in any mixed community, the reputation of belonging to the dominant race, in this instance the white race, is *property,* in the same sense that a right of action, or of inheritance, is property. Conceding this to be so, for the purposes of this case, we are unable to see how this statute deprives him of, or in any way affects his right to, such property. If he be a white man and assigned to a colored coach, he may have his action for damages against the company for being deprived of his so-called property. Upon the other hand, if he be a colored man and be so assigned, he has been deprived of no property, since he is not lawfully entitled to the reputation of being a white man.

In this connection, it is also suggested by the learned counsel for the plaintiff in error that the same argument that will justify the state legislature in requiring railways to provide separate accommodations for the two races will also authorize them to require separate cars to be provided for people whose hair is of a certain color, or who are aliens, or who belong to certain nationalities, or to enact laws requiring colored people to walk upon one side of the street, and white people upon the other, or requiring white men's houses to be painted white, and colored men's black, or their vehicles or business signs to be of different colors, upon the theory that one side of the street is as good as the other, or that a house or vehicle of one color is as good as one of another color. The reply to all this is that every exercise of the police power must be reasonable, and extend only to such laws as are enacted in good faith for the promotion of the public good, and not for the annoyance or oppression of a particular class. . . .

So far, then, as a conflict with the Fourteenth Amendment is concerned, the case reduces itself to the question whether the statute of Louisiana is a reasonable regulation, and with respect to this there must necessarily be a large discretion on the part of the legislature. In determining the question of reasonableness it is at liberty to act with reference to the established usages, customs, and traditions of the people, and with a view to the promotion of their comfort, and the preservation of the public peace and good order. Gauged by this standard, we cannot say that a law which authorizes or even requires the separation of the two races in public conveyances is unreasonable, or more obnoxious to the Fourteenth Amendment than the acts of Congress requiring separate schools for colored children in the District of Columbia, the constitutionality of which does not seem to have been questioned, or the corresponding acts of state legislatures.

We consider the underlying fallacy of the plaintiff's argument to consist in the assumption that the enforced separation of the two races stamps the colored race with a badge of inferiority. If this be so, it is not by reason of anything found in the act, but solely because the colored race chooses to put that construction upon it. The argument necessarily assumes that if, as has been more than once the case, and is not unlikely to be so again, the colored race should become the dominant power in the state legislature, and should enact a law in precisely similar terms, it would thereby relegate the white race to an inferior position. We imagine that the white race, at least, would not acquiesce in this assumption. The argument also assumes that social prejudices may be overcome by legislation, and that equal rights cannot be secured to the Negro except by an enforced commingling of the two races. We cannot accept this proposition. If the two races are to meet upon terms of social equality, it must be the result of natural affinities, a mutual appreciation of each other's merits, and a voluntary consent of individuals. . . . Legislation is powerless to eradicate racial instincts or to abolish distinctions based upon physical differences, and the attempt to do so can only result in accentuating the difficulties of the present situation. If the civil and political rights of both races be equal one cannot be inferior to the other civilly or politically. If one race be inferior to the other socially, the Constitution of the United States cannot put them upon the same plane.

. . . The judgment of the court below is therefore,

Affirmed.

MR. JUSTICE HARLAN, dissenting:

. . . It was said in argument that the statute of Louisiana does not discriminate against either race, but prescribes a rule applicable alike to white and colored citizens. But this argument does not meet the difficulty. Everyone knows that the statute in question had its origin in the purpose, not so much to exclude white persons from railroad cars occupied by blacks, as to exclude colored people from coaches occupied by or assigned to white persons. Railroad corporations of Louisiana did not make discrimination among whites in the matter of accommodation for travelers. The thing to accomplish was, under the guise of giving equal accommodation for whites and blacks, to compel the latter to keep to themselves while travelling in railroad passenger coaches. No one would be so wanting in candor as to assert the contrary. The fundamental objection, therefore, to the statute is that it interferes with the personal freedom of citizens. . . . If a white man and a black man choose to occupy the same public conveyance on a public highway, it is their right to do so, and no government, proceeding alone on grounds of race, can prevent it without infringing the personal liberty of each.

. . . The white race deems itself to be the dominant race in this country. And so it is, in prestige, in achievements, in education, in wealth, and in power. So, I doubt not, it will continue to be for all time, if it remains true to its great heritage and holds fast to the principles of constitutional liberty. But in view of the Constitution, in the eye of the law, there is in this country no superior, dominant, ruling class of citizens. There is no caste here. Our Constitution is color-blind, and neither knows nor tolerates classes among citizens. In respect of civil rights, all citizens are equal before the law. The humblest is the peer of the most powerful. The law regards man as man, and takes no account of his surroundings or of his color when his civil rights as guaranteed by the supreme law of the land are involved. It is, therefore, to be regretted that this high tribunal, the final expositor of the fundamental law of the land, has reached the conclusion that it is competent for a state to regulate the enjoyment by citizens of their civil rights solely upon the basis of race.

. . . The sure guaranty of the peace and security of each race is the clear, distinct, unconditional recognition by our governments, National and State, of every right that inheres in civil freedom, and of the equality before the law of all citizens of the United States without regard to race. State enactments regulating the enjoyment of civil rights upon the basis of race, and cunningly devised to defeat legitimate results of the war, under the pretence of recognizing equality of rights, can have no other result than to render permanent peace impossible, and to keep alive a conflict of races, the continuance of which must do harm to all concerned. . . .

The arbitrary separation of citizens, on the basis of race, while they are on a public highway, is a badge of servitude wholly inconsistent with the civil freedom and the equality before the law established by the Constitution. It cannot be justified upon any legal grounds.

If evils will result from the commingling of the two races upon public highways established for the benefit of all, they will be infinitely less than those that will surely come from state legislation regulating the enjoyment of civil rights upon the basis of race. We boast of the freedom enjoyed by our people above all other peoples. But it is difficult to reconcile that boast with a state of the law which, practically, puts the brand of servitude and degradation upon a large class of our fellow-citizens, our equals before the law. The thin disguise of "equal" accommodations for passengers in railroad coaches will not mislead anyone, nor atone for the wrong this day done. . . .

I am of opinion that the statute of Louisiana is inconsistent with the personal liberty of citizens, white and black, in that State, and hostile to both the spirit and letter of the Constitution of the United States. . . .

For the reasons stated, I am constrained to withhold my assent from the opinion and judgment of the majority.

MR. JUSTICE BREWER did not hear the argument or participate in the decision of this case.

SWEATT v. PAINTER
339 U.S. 629; 70 Sup. Ct. 848; 94 L. Ed. 1114 (1950)

[*Sweatt was denied admission to the University of Texas Law School solely because he was colored, admission of Negroes to the school being prohibited by state law even though there was no law school for Negroes in Texas at the time. Sweatt brought a suit for mandamus against Painter and other school officials to compel his admission. A trial court recognized that Sweatt was denied the equal protection of the laws guaranteed by the Fourteenth Amendment because he had no opportunity for the study of law. However, the court refused to issue the mandamus; instead, the case was continued for six months to give Texas time to provide equal training facilities in law for Negroes. After the six months' period, the University revealed that a law school for Negroes would be opened within two months. The court then denied the writ of mandamus. However, Sweatt refused to enter the new law school and continued his original action for mandamus. The Texas courts denied the mandamus on the ground that substantially equal facilities were provided in the Negro law school. Sweatt then brought the case to the Supreme Court on a writ of certiorari.*]

MR. CHIEF JUSTICE VINSON delivered the opinion of the Court:

This case and *McLaurin* v. *Oklahoma State Regents* . . . present different aspects of this general question: To what extent does the Equal Protection Clause of the Fourteenth Amendment limit the power of a state to distinguish between students of different races in professional and graduate education in a state university? Broader issues have been urged for our consideration, but we adhere to the principle of deciding constitutional questions only in the context of the particular case before the Court. We have frequently reiterated that this Court will decide constitutional questions only when necessary to the disposition of the case at hand, and that such decisions will be drawn as narrowly as possible. . . .

The University of Texas Law School, from which petitioner was excluded, was staffed by a faculty of sixteen full-time and three part-time professors, some of whom are nationally recognized authorities in their field. Its student body numbered 850. The library contained over 65,000 volumes. Among the other facilities available to the students were a law review, moot-court facilities, scholarship funds, and Order of the Coif affiliation. The school's alumni occupy the most distinguished positions in the private practice of the law and in the public life of the State. It may properly be considered one of the nation's ranking law schools.

The law school for Negroes which was to have opened in February 1947, would have had no independent faculty or library. The teaching was to be carried on by four members of the University of Texas Law School faculty, who were to maintain their offices at the University of Texas while teaching at both institutions. Few of the 10,000 volumes ordered for the library had arrived; nor was there any full-time librarian. The school lacked accreditation.

Since the trial of this case, respondents report the opening of a law school at the Texas State University for Negroes. It is apparently on the road to full accreditation. It has a faculty of five full-time professors; a student body of twenty-three; a library of some 16,500 volumes serviced by a full-time staff; a practice court and legal aid association; and one alumnus who has become a member of the Texas bar.

Whether the University of Texas Law School is compared with the original or the new law school for Negroes, we cannot find substantial equality in the educational opportunities offered white and Negro law students by the State. In terms of number of the faculty, variety of courses and opportunity for specialization, size of the student body, scope of the library, availability of law review and similar activities, the University of Texas Law School is superior. What is more important, the University of Texas Law School possesses to a far greater degree those qualities which are incapable of objective measurement but which make for greatness in a law school. Such qualities, to name but a few, include reputation of the faculty, experience of the administration, position and influence of the alumni, standing in the community, traditions and prestige. It is difficult to believe that one who had a free choice between these law schools would consider the question close.

Moreover, although the law is a highly learned profession, we are well aware that it is an intensely practical one. The law school, the proving ground for legal learning and practice, cannot be effective in isolation from the individuals and institutions with which

the law interacts. Few students and no one who has practiced law would choose to study in an academic vacuum, removed from the interplay of ideas and the exchange of views with which the law is concerned. The law school to which Texas is willing to admit petitioner excludes from its student body members of the racial groups which number 85 per cent of the population of the State and include most of the lawyers, witnesses, jurors, judges, and other officials with whom petitioner will inevitably be dealing when he becomes a member of the Texas bar. With such a substantial and significant segment of society excluded, we cannot conclude that the education offered petitioner is substantially equal to that which he would receive if admitted to the University of Texas Law School.

It may be argued that excluding petitioner from that school is no different from excluding white students from the new law school. This contention overlooks realities. It is unlikely that a member of a group so decisively in the majority, attending a school with rich traditions and prestige which only a history of consistently maintained excellence could command, would claim that the opportunities afforded him for legal education were unequal to those held open to petitioner. That such a claim, if made, would be dishonored by the State, is no answer. "Equal protection of the laws is not achieved through indiscriminate imposition of inequalities."

. . . [P]etitioner may claim his full constitutional right: legal education equivalent to that offered by the State to students of other races. Such education is not available to him in a separate law school as offered by the State. We cannot, therefore, agree with respondents that the doctrine of *Plessy* v. *Ferguson* . . . requires affirmance of the judgment below. Nor need we reach petitioner's contention that *Plessy* v. *Ferguson* should be re-examined in the light of contemporary knowledge respecting the purposes of the Fourteenth Amendment and the effects of racial segregation. . . .

We hold that the Equal Protection Clause of the Fourteenth Amendment requires that petitioner be admitted to the University of Texas Law School. The judgment is reversed and the cause is remanded for proceedings not inconsistent with this opinion.

Reversed.

BROWN et al. *v.* BOARD OF EDUCATION
347 U.S. 483; 74 Sup. Ct. 693; 98 L. Ed. 591 (1954)

MR. CHIEF JUSTICE WARREN delivered the opinion of the Court:

These cases come to us from the States of Kansas, South Carolina, Virginia, and Delaware. They are premised on different facts and different local conditions, but a common legal question justifies their consideration together in this consolidated opinion.

In each of the cases, minors of the Negro race, through their legal representatives, seek the aid of the courts in obtaining admission to the public schools of their community on a non-segregated basis. In each instance, they had been denied admission to schools attended by white children under laws requiring or permitting segregation according to race. This segregation was alleged to deprive the plaintiffs of the equal protection of the laws under the Fourteenth Amendment. In each of the cases other than the Delaware case, a three-judge federal district court denied relief to the plaintiffs on the so-called "separate but equal" doctrine announced by this Court in *Plessy* v. *Ferguson*. . . .

The plaintiffs contend that segregated public schools are not "equal" and cannot be made "equal," and that hence they are deprived of the equal protection of the laws. Because of the obvious importance of the question presented, the Court took jurisdiction. Argument was heard in the 1952 Term, and reargument was heard this Term on certain questions propounded by the Court.

Reargument was largely devoted to the circumstances surrounding the adoption of the Fourteenth Amendment in 1868. It covered exhaustively consideration of the Amendment in Congress, ratification by the states, then existing practices in racial segregation, and the view of the proponents and opponents of the Amendment. This discussion and our own investigation convince us that, although these sources cast some light, it is not enough to resolve the problem with which we are faced. At best, they are inconclusive. The most avid proponents of the postwar Amendments undoubtedly intended them to remove all legal distinctions among "all persons born or naturalized in the United States." Their opponents, just as certainly, were antagonistic to both the letter and the spirit of the Amendments and wished them to have the most limited effect. What others in Congress and the state legislatures had in mind cannot be determined with any degree of certainty.

An additional reason for the inclusive nature of the Amendment's history, with respect to segregated schools, is the status of public education at that time. In the South, the movement toward free common schools, supported by general taxation, had not yet taken hold. Education of white children was largely in the hands of private groups. Education of Negroes was almost nonexistent, and practically all of the race were illiterate. In fact, any education of Negroes was forbidden by law in some states. Today, in contrast, many Negroes have achieved outstanding success in the arts and sciences as well as in the business and professional world. It is true that public education had already advanced further in the North, but the effect of the Amendment on northern states was generally ignored in the congressional debates. Even in the North, the conditions of public education did not approximate those existing today. The curriculum was usually rudimentary; ungraded schools were common in rural areas; the school term was but three months a year in many states; and compulsory school attendance was virtually unknown. As a consequence, it is not surprising that there should be so little in the history of the Fourteenth Amendment relating to its intended effect on public education.

In the first cases in this Court construing the Fourteenth Amendment, decided shortly after its adoption, the Court interpreted it as proscribing all state-imposed discriminations against the Negro race. The doctrine of "separate but equal" did not make its appearance in this Court until 1896 in the case of *Plessy* v. *Ferguson, supra,* involving not education but transportation. American courts have since labored with the doctrine for over half a century. In this Court, there have been six cases involving the "separate but equal" doctrine in the field of public education. In *Cumming* v. *County Board of Education,* 175 U.S. 528, and *Gong Lum* v. *Rice,* 275 U.S. 78, the validity of the doctrine itself was not challenged. In more recent cases,

all on the graduate-school level, inequality was found in that specific benefits enjoyed by white students were denied to Negro students of the same educational qualifications. *Missouri* ex rel. *Gaines* v. *Canada,* 305 U.S. 337; *Sipuel* v. *Oklahoma,* 332 U.S. 631; *Sweatt* v. *Painter,* 339 U.S. 629; *McLaurin* v. *Oklahoma State Regents,* 339 U.S. 637. In none of these cases was it necessary to re-examine the doctrine to grant relief to the Negro plaintiff. And in *Sweatt* v. *Painter, . . .* the Court expressly reserved decision on the question whether *Plessy* v. *Ferguson* should be held inapplicable to public education.

In the instant cases, that question is directly presented. Here, unlike *Sweatt* v. *Painter,* there are findings below that the Negro and white schools involved have been equalized, or are being equalized, with respect to buildings, curricula, qualifications and salaries of teachers, and other "tangible" factors. Our decision, therefore, cannot turn on merely a comparison of these tangible factors in the Negro and white schools involved in each of the cases. We must look instead to the effect of segregation itself on public education.

In approaching this problem, we cannot turn the clock back to 1868 when the Amendment was adopted, or even to 1896 when *Plessy* v. *Ferguson* was written. We must consider public education in the light of its full development and its present place in American life throughout the Nation. Only in this way can it be determined if segregation in public schools deprives these plaintiffs of the equal protection of the laws.

Today, education is perhaps the most important function of state and local governments. Compulsory school-attendance laws and the great expenditures for education both demonstrate our recognition of the importance of education to our democratic society. It is required in the performance of our most basic public responsibilities, even service in the armed forces. It is the very foundation of good citizenship. Today it is a principal instrument in awakening the child to cultural values, in preparing him for later professional training, and in helping him to adjust normally to his environment. In these days, it is doubtful any child may reasonably be expected to succeed in life if he is denied the opportunity of an education. Such an opportunity, where the state has undertaken to provide it, is a right must be made available to all on equal terms.

We come then to the question presented: Does segregation of children in public schools solely on the basis of race, even though the physical facilities and other "tangible" factors may be equal, deprive the children of the minority group of equal educational opportunities? We believe that it does.

In *Sweatt* v. *Painter,* . . . in finding that a segregated law school for Negroes could not provide them equal educational opportunities, this Court relied in large part on "those qualities which are incapable of objective measurement but which make for greatness in a law school." In *McLaurin* v. *Oklahoma State Regents,* . . . the Court, in requiring that a Negro admitted to a white graduate school be treated like all other students, again resorted to intangible considerations: ". . . his ability to study, to engage in discussions and exchange views with other students, and, in general, to learn his profession." Such considerations apply with added force to children in grade and high schools. To separate them from others of similar age and qualifications solely because of their race generates a feeling of inferiority as to their status in the community that may affect their hearts and minds in a

way unlikely ever to be undone. The effect of this separation on their educational opportunities was well stated by a finding in the Kansas case by a court which nevertheless felt compelled to rule against the Negro plaintiffs:

"Segregation of white and colored children in public schools has a detrimental effect upon the colored children. The impact is greater when it has the sanction of the law; for the policy of separating the races is usually interpreted as denoting the inferiority of the Negro group. A sense of inferiority affects the motivation of a child to learn. Segregation with the sanction of law, therefore, has a tendency to retard the educational and mental development of Negro children and to deprive them of some of the benefits they would receive in a racially integrated school system."

Whatever, may have been the extent of psychological knowledge at the time of *Plessy* v. *Ferguson,* this finding is amply supported by modern authority. Any language in *Plessy* v. *Ferguson* contrary to this finding is rejected.

We conclude that in the field of public education the doctrine of "separate but equal" has no place. Separate educational facilities are inherently unequal. Therefore, we hold that the plaintiffs and others similarly situated for whom the actions have been brought are, by reason of the segregation complained of, deprived of the equal protection of the laws guaranteed by the Fourteenth Amendment. This disposition makes unnecessary any discussion whether such segregation also violates the Due Process Clause of the Fourteenth Amendment.

Because these are class actions, because of the wide applicablility of this decision, and because of the great variety of local conditions, the formulation of decrees in these cases presents problems of considerable complexity. On reargument, the consideration of appropriate relief was necessarily subordinated to the primary question—the constitutionality of segregation in public education. We have now announced that such segregation is a denial of the equal protection of the laws. In order that we may have the full assistance of the parties in formulating decrees, the cases will be restored to the docket, and the parties are requested to present further argument on Questions 4 and 5 previously propounded by the Court for the reargument this Term.[1] The Attorney General of the United States is again invited to participate. The Attorneys General of the states requiring or permitting segregation in public education will also be permitted to appear as *amici curiae* [friends of the Court who give advice on matters pending before it] upon request to do so by September 15, 1954, and submission of briefs by October 1, 1954.

It is so ordered.

BOLLING et al. *v.* SHARPE
347 U.S. 497; 74 Sup. Ct. 686; 98 L. Ed. 583 (1954)

MR. CHIEF JUSTICE WARREN delivered the opinion of the Court:

This case challenges the validity of segregation in the public schools of the District of Columbia. The petitioners, minors of the Negro race, allege that such segregation deprives them of due process of law under the Fifth Amendment. They were refused admission to a public school attended by white children solely because of their race. They sought the aid of the District Court for the District of Columbia in obtaining admission. That court dismissed their complaint. We granted a writ of certiorari before judgment in the Court of Appeals because of the importance of the constitutional question presented. . . .

We have this day held that the Equal Protection Clause of the Fourteenth Amendment prohibits the states from maintaining racially segregated public schools. The legal problem in the District of Columbia is somewhat different, however. The Fifth Amendment, which

---

[1] "4. Assuming it is decided that segregation in public schools violates the Fourteenth Amendment.

"(a) would a decree necessarily follow providing that, within the limits set by normal geographic school districting, Negro children should forthwith be admitted to schools of their choice, or

"(b) may this Court, in the exercise of its equity powers, permit an effective gradual adjustment to be brought about from existing segregated systems to a system not based on color distinctions?

"5. On the assumption on which questions 4(a) and (b) are based, and assuming further that this Court will exercise its equity powers to the end described in question 4(b),

"(a) should this Court formulate detailed decrees in these cases;

"(b) if so, what specific issues should decrees reach;

"(c) should this Court appoint a special master to hear evidence with a view to recommending specific terms for such decrees;

"(d) should this Court remand to the courts of first instance with directions to frame decrees in these cases, and if so, what general directions should the decrees of this Court include and what procedures should the courts of first instance follow in arriving at the specific terms of more detailed decrees?"

is applicable in the District of Columbia, does not contain an equal protection clause as does the Fourteenth Amendment, which applies only to the states. But the concepts of equal protection and due process, both stemming from our American ideal of fairness, are not mutually exclusive. The "equal protection of the laws" is a more implicit safeguard of prohibited unfairness than "due process of law," and, therefore, we do not imply that the two are always interchangeable phrases. But, as this Court has recognized, discrimination may be so unjustifiable as to be violative of due process.

Classifications based solely upon race must be scrutinized with particular care, since they are contrary to our traditions and hence constitutionally suspect. As long ago as 1896, this Court declared the principle "that the Constitution of the United States, in its present form, forbids, so far as civil and political rights are concerned, discrimination by the General Government, or by the States, against any citizen because of his race." And in *Buchanan* v. *Warley,* 245 U.S. 60, the Court held that a statute which limited the right of a property owner to convey his property to a person of another race was, as an unreasonable discrimination, a denial of due process of law.

Although the Court has not assumed to define "liberty" with any great precision, that term is not confined to mere freedom from bodily restraint. Liberty under law extends to the full range of conduct which the individual is free to pursue, and it cannot be restricted except for a proper governmental objective. Segregation in public education is not reasonably related to any proper governmental objective, and thus it imposes on Negro children of the District of Columbia a burden that constitutes an arbitrary deprivation of their liberty in violation of the Due Process Clause.

In view of our decision that the Constitution prohibits the states from maintaining racially segregated pubic schools, it would be unthinkable that the same Constitution would impose a lesser duty on the Federal Government. We hold that racial segregation in the public schools of the District of Columbia is a denial of the due process of law guaranteed by the Fifth Amendment to the Constitution.

For the reasons set out in *Brown* v. *Board of Education,* this case will be restored to the docket for reargument on Questions 4 and 5 previously propounded by the Court. . . .

It is so ordered.

BROWN v. BOARD OF EDUCATION (Second Case)
349 U.S. 294; 75 Sup. Ct. 753; 99 L. Ed. 1083 (1955)

MR. CHIEF JUSTICE WARREN delivered the opinion of the Court:

These cases were decided on May 17, 1954. The opinions of that date, declaring the fundamental principle that racial discrimination in public education is unconstitutional, are incorporated herein by reference. All provisions of federal, state, or local law requiring or permitting such discrimination must yield to this principle. There remains for consideration the manner in which relief is to be accorded. . . .

Full implementation of these constitutional principles may require solution of varied local school problems. School authorities have the primary responsibility for elucidating, assessing, and solving these problems; courts will have to consider whether the action of school authorities constitutes good faith implementation of the governing constitutional principles. Because of their proximity to local conditions and the possible need for further hearings, the courts which originally heard these cases can best perform this judicial appraisal. Accordingly, we believe it appropriate to remand the cases to those courts.

In fashioning and effectuating the decrees, the courts will be guided by equitable principles. Traditionally, equity has been characterized by a practical flexibility in shaping its remedies and by a facility for adjusting and reconciling public and private needs. These cases call for the exercise of these traditional attributes of equity power. At stake is the personal interest of the plaintiffs in admission to public schools as soon as practicable on a nondiscriminatory basis. To effectuate this interest may call for elimination of a variety of obstacles in making the transition to school systems operated in accordance with the constitutional principles set forth in our May 17, 1954, decision. Courts of equity may properly take into account the public interest in the elimination of such obstacles in a systematic and effective manner. But it should go without saying that the vitality of these constitutional principles cannot be allowed to yield simply because of disagreement with them.

While giving weight to these public and private considerations, the courts will require that the defendants make a prompt and reasonable start toward full compliance with our May 17, 1954, ruling. Once such a start has been made, the courts may find that additional time is necessary to carry out the ruling in an effective manner. The burden rests upon the defendants to establish that such time is necessary in the public interest and is consistent with good faith compliance at the earliest practicable data. To that end, the courts may consider problems related to administration, arising from the physical condition of the school plant, the school transportation system, personnel, revision of school districts and attendance areas into compact units to achieve a system of determining admission to the public schools on a nonracial basis, and revision of local laws and regulations which may be necessary in solving the foregoing problems. They will also consider the adequacy of any plans the defendants may propose to meet these problems and to effectuate a transition to a racially nondiscriminatory school system. During this period of transition, the courts will retain jurisdiction of these cases. . . .

It is so ordered.

COOPER *v.* AARON
358 U.S. 1; 78 Sup. Ct. 1401; 3 L. Ed. 2d (1958)

[*The most dramatic clash between state and federal authorities over desegregation of the public schools occurred in Little Rock, Arkansas, in the summer of 1958. Cooper, one of the members of the school board, and others filed a petition in a federal district court seeking postponement of a desegregation plan because of extreme public hostility brought about by the actions of the Governor and the state legislature. The complex facts leading to the decision of the Supreme Court in a Special Term in August 1958, are set forth in detail in the case. Aaron was one of the Negro pupils seeking admission to the schools.*]

Opinion of the Court by THE CHIEF JUSTICE, MR. JUSTICE BLACK, MR. JUSTICE FRANKFURTER, MR. JUSTICE DOUGLAS, MR. JUSTICE BURTON, MR. JUSTICE CLARK, MR. JUSTICE HARLAN, MR. JUSTICE BRENNAN, and MR. JUSTICE WHITTAKER:

As this case reaches us it raises questions of the highest importance to the maintenance of our federal system of government. It necessarily involves a claim by the Governor and Legislature of a State that there is no duty on state officials to obey federal court orders resting on this Court's considered interpretation of the United States Constitution. Specifically it involves actions by the Governor and Legislature of Arkansas upon the premise that they are not bound by our holding in *Brown* v. *Board of Education.* . . . That holding was that the Fourteenth Amendment forbids States to use their governmental powers to bar children on racial grounds from attending schools where there is state participation through any arrangement, management, funds or property. We are urged to uphold a suspension of the Little Rock School Board's plan to do away with segregated public schools in Little Rock until state laws and efforts to upset and nullify our holding in *Brown* v. *Board of Education* have been further challenged and tested in the courts. We reject these contentions. . . .

The following are the facts and circumstances so far as necessary to show how the legal questions are presented.

On May 17, 1954, this Court decided that enforced racial segregation in the public schools of a State is a denial of the equal protection of the laws enjoined by the Fourteenth Amendment. *Brown* v. *Board of Education.* . . . The Court postponed, pending further argument, formulation of a decree to effectuate this decision. That decree was rendered May 31, 1955.

. . . In the formulation of that decree the Court recognized that good faith compliance with the principles declared in *Brown* might in some situations "call for elimination of a variety of obstacles in making the transition to school systems operated in accordance with the constitutional principles set forth in our May 17, 1954, decision." . . .

It was made plain that delay in any guise in order to deny the constitutional rights of Negro children could not be countenanced, and that only a prompt start, diligently and earnestly pursued, to eliminate racial segregation from the public schools could constitute good faith compliance. State authorities were thus bound to devote every effort toward initiating desegregation and bringing about the elimination of racial discrimination in the public school system.

On May 20, 1954, three days after the first *Brown* opinion, the Little Rock District School Board adopted, and on May 23, 1954, made public, a statement of policy entitled "Supreme Court Decision—Segregation in Public Schools." In this statement the Board recognized that

"It is our responsibility to comply with Federal Constitutional Requirements and we intend to do so when the Supreme Court of the United States outlines the method to be followed."

Thereafter the Board undertook studies of the administrative problems confronting the transition to a desegregated public school system at Little Rock. It instructed the Superintendent of Schools to prepare a plan for desegregation, and approved such a plan on May 24, 1955, seven days before the second *Brown* opinion. The plan provided for desegregation at the senior high school level (grades 10 through 12) as the first stage. Desegregation at the junior high and elementary levels was to follow. It was contemplated that desegregation at the high school level would commence in the fall of 1957, and the expectation was that complete desegregation of the school system would be accomplished by 1963. Following the adoption of this plan, the Superintendent of Schools discussed it with a large number of citizen groups in the city. As a result of these discussions, the Board reached the conclusion that "a large majority of the residents" of Little Rock were of "the belief . . . that the Plan, although objectionable in principle," from the point of view of those supporting segregated schools, "was still the best for the interests of all pupils in the District."

Upon challenge by a group of Negro plaintiffs desiring more rapid completion of the desegregation process, the District Court upheld the School Board's plan. . . .

While the School Board was thus going forward with its preparation for desegregating the Little Rock school system, other state authorities, in contrast, were actively pursuing a program designed to perpetuate in Arkansas the system of racial segregation which this Court had held violated the Fourteenth Amendment. First came, in November 1956, an amendment to the State Constitution flatly commanding the Arkansas General Assembly to oppose "in every Constitutional manner the Unconstitutional desegregation decisions of May 17, 1954, and May 31, 1955 of the United States Supreme Court." . . . Pursuant to this state constitutional command, a law relieving school children from compulsory attendance at racially mixed schools . . . and a law establishing a State Sovereignty Commission . . . were enacted by the General Assembly in February 1957.

The School Board and the Superintendent of Schools nevertheless con-

tinued with preparations to carry out the first stage of the desegregation program. Nine Negro children were scheduled for admission in September 1957 to Central High School; which has more than 2000 students. Various administrative measures, designed to assure the smooth transition of this first stage of desegregation, were undertaken.

On September 2, 1957, the day before these Negro students were to enter Central High, the school authorities were met with drastic opposing action on the part of the Governor of Arkansas who dispatched units of the Arkansas National Guard to the Central High School grounds, and placed the school "off limits" to colored students. As found by the District Court in subsequent proceedings, the Governor's action had not been requested by the school authorities, and was entirely unheralded. The findings were these:

"Up to this time (September 2), no crowds had gathered about Central High School and no acts of violence or threats of violence in connection with the carrying out of the plan had occurred. Nevertheless, out of an abundance of caution, the school authorities had frequently conferred with the Mayor and Chief of Police of Little Rock about taking appropriate steps by the Little Rock police to prevent any possible disturbances or acts of violence in connection with the attendance of the nine colored students at Central High School. The Mayor considered that the Little Rock police force could adequately cope with any incidents which might arise at the opening of school. The Mayor, the Chief of Police, and the school authorities made no request to the Governor or any representative of his for State assistance in maintaining peace and order at Central High School. Neither the Governor nor any other official of the State government consulted with the Little Rock authorities about whether the Little Rock police were prepared to cope with any incidents which might arise at the school, about any need for State assistance in maintaining peace and order, or about stationing the Arkansas National Guard at Central High School. . . ."

The Board's petition for postponement in this proceeding states: "The effect of that action (of the Governor) was to harden the core of opposition to the Plan and cause many persons who theretofore had reluctantly accepted the Plan to believe that there was some power in the State of Arkansas which, when exerted, could nullify the Federal law and permit disobedience of the decree of this (District) Court, and from that date hostility to the Plan was increased and criticism of the officials of the (School) District has become more bitter and unrestrained." The Governor's action caused the School Board to request the Negro students on September 2 not to attend the high school "until the legal dilemma was solved." The next day, September 3, 1957, the Board petitioned the District Court for instructions, and the court, after a hearing, found that the Board's request of the Negro students to stay away from the high school had been made because of the stationing of the military guards by the state authorities. The court determined that this was not a reason for departing from the approved plan, and ordered the School Board and Superintendent to proceed with it.

On the morning of the next day, September 4, 1957, the Negro children attempted to enter the high school but, as the District Court later found, units of the Arkansas National Guard "act-

ting pursuant to the Governor's order, stood shoulder to shoulder at the school grounds and thereby forcibly prevented the nine Negro students . . . from entering," as they continued to do every school day during the following three weeks. . . .

That same day, September 4, 1957, the United States Attorney for the Eastern District of Arkansas was requested by the District Court to begin an immediate investigation in order to fix responsibility for the interference with the orderly implementation of the District Court's direction to carry out the desegregation program. Three days later, September 7, the District Court denied a petition of the School Board and the Superintendent of Schools for an order temporarily suspending continuance of the program.

Upon completion of the United States Attorney's investigation, he and the Attorney General of the United States, at the District Court's request, entered the proceedings and filed a petition on behalf of the United States, as *amicus curiae,* to enjoin the Governor of Arkansas and officers of the Arkansas National Guard from further attempts to prevent obedience to the court's order. After hearings on the petition, the District Court found that the School Board's plan had been obstructed by the Governor through the use of National Guard troops, and granted a preliminary injunction on September 20, 1957, enjoining the Governor and the officers of the Guard from preventing the attendance of Negro children at Central High School, and from otherwise obstructing or interfering with the orders of the court in connection with the plan. . . . The National Guard was then withdrawn from the school.

The next school day was Monday, September 23, 1957. The Negro children entered the high school that morning under the protection of the Little

Rock Police Department and members of the Arkansas State Police. But the officers caused the children to be removed from the school during the morning because they had difficulty controlling a large and demonstrating crowd which had gathered at the high school. . . . On September 25, however, the President of the United States dispatched federal troops to Central High School and admission of the Negro students to the school was thereby effected. Regular army troops continued at the high school until November 27, 1957. They were then replaced by federalized National Guardsmen who remained throughout the balance of the school year. Eight of the Negro students remained in attendance at the school throughout the school year.

We come now to the aspect of the proceedings presently before us. On February 20, 1958, the School Board and the Superintendent of Schools filed a petition in the District Court seeking a postponement of their program for desegregation. Their position in essence was that because of extreme public hostility, which they stated had been engendered largely by the official attitudes and actions of the Governor and the Legislature, the maintenance of a sound educational program at Central High School, with the Negro students in attendance, would be impossible. The Board therefore proposed that the Negro students already admitted to the school be withdrawn and sent to segregated schools, and that all further steps to carry out the Board's desegregation program be postponed for a period later suggested by the Board to be two and one-half years.

After a hearing the District Court granted the relief requested by the Board. Among other things the court found that the past year at Central High School had been attended by conditions of "chaos, bedlam, and turmoil";

that there were "repeated incidents of more or less serious violence directed against the Negro students and their property"; that there was "tension and unrest among the school administrators, the class-room teachers, the pupils, and the latter's parents, which inevitably had an adverse effect upon the educational program"; that a school official was threatened with violence; that a "serious financial burden" had been cast on the School District; that the education of the students had suffered "and under existing conditions will continue to suffer"; that the Board would continue to need "military assistance or its equivalent"; that the local police department would not be able "to detail enough men to afford the necessary protection"; and that the situation was "intolerable."

. . . The District Court's judgment was dated June 20, 1958. The Negro respondents appealed to the Court of Appeals for the Eighth Circuit and also sought there a stay of the District Court's judgment. At the same time they filed a petition for certiorari in this Court asking us to review the District Court's judgment without awaiting the disposition of their appeal to the Court of Appeals, or of their petition to that court for a stay. That we declined to do. . . . The Court of Appeals did not act on the petition for a stay but on August 18, 1958, after convening in special session on August 4 and hearing the appeal, reversed the District Court. . . . On August 21, 1958, the Court of Appeals stayed its mandate to permit the School Board to petition this Court for certiorari. . . . The petition for certiorari, duly filed, was granted in open Court on September 11, 1958, . . . and further arguments were had, the Solicitor General again urging the correctness of the judgment of the Court of Appeals. . . .

In affirming the judgment of the

Court of Appeals which reversed the District Court we have accepted without reservation the position of the School Board, the Superintendent of Schools, and their counsel that they displayed entire good faith in the conduct of these proceedings and in dealing with the unfortunate and distressing sequence of events which has been outlined. We likewise have accepted the findings of the District Court as to the conditions at Central High School during the 1957–1958 school year, and also the findings that the educational progress of all the students, white and colored, of that school has suffered and will continue to suffer if the conditions which prevailed last year are permitted to continue.

The significance of these findings, however, is to be considered in light of the fact, indisputably revealed by the record before us, that the conditions they depict are directly traceable to the actions of legislators and executive officials of the State of Arkansas, taken in their official capacities, which reflect their own determination to resist this Court's decision in the *Brown* case and which have brought about violent resistance to that decision in Arkansas. In its petition for certiorari filed in this Court, the School Board itself describes the situation in this language: "The legislative, executive, and judicial departments of the state government opposed the desegregation of Little Rock schools by enacting laws, calling out troops, making statements vilifying federal law and federal courts, and failing to utilize state law enforcements agencies and judicial processes to maintain public peace."

One may well sympathize with the position of the Board in the face of the frustrating conditions which have confronted it, but, regardless of the Board's good faith, the actions of the other state agencies responsible for those conditions compel us to reject the Board's legal position. Had Central High School been under the direct management of the State itself, it could hardly be suggested that those immediately in charge of the school should be heard to assert their own good faith as a legal excuse for delay in implementing the constitutional rights of these respondents, when vindication of those rights was rendered difficult or impossible by the actions of other state officials. The situation here is in no different posture because the members of the School Board and the Superintendent of Schools are local officials; from the point of view of the Fourteenth Amendment, they stand in this litigation as the agents of the State.

The constitutional rights of respondents are not to be sacrificed or yielded to the violence and disorder which have followed upon the actions of the Governor and Legislature. As this Court said some forty-one years ago in a unanimous opinion in a case involving another aspect of racial segregation: "It is urged that this proposed segregation will promote the public peace by preventing race conflicts. Desirable as this is, and important as is the preservation of the public peace, this aim cannot be accomplished by laws or ordinances which deny rights created or protected by the Federal Constitution." *Buchanan* v. *Warley*, 245 U.S. 60. . . . Thus law and order are not here to be preserved by depriving the Negro children of their constitutional rights. The record before us clearly establishes that the growth of the Board's difficulties to a magnitude beyond its unaided power to control is the product of state action. Those difficulties, as counsel for the Board forthrightly conceded on the oral argument in this Court, can also be brought under control by state action.

The controlling legal principles are plain. The command of the Fourteenth Amendment is that no "State" shall deny to any person within its jurisdiction the equal protection of the laws. "A State acts by its legislative, its executive, or its judicial authorities. It can act in no other way. The constitutional provision, therefore, must mean that no agency of the State, or of the officers or agents by whom its powers are exerted, shall deny to any person within its jurisdiction the equal protection of the laws. Whoever, by virtue of public position under a State government . . . denies or takes away the equal protection of the laws, violates the constitutional inhibition; and as he acts in the name and for the State, and is clothed with the State's power, his act is that of the State. This must be so, or the constitutional prohibition has no meaning." . . . In short, the constitutional rights of children not to be discriminated against in school admission on grounds of race or color declared by this Court in the *Brown* case can neither be nullified openly and directly by state legislators or state executive or judicial officers, nor nullified indirectly by them through evasive schemes for segregation whether attempted "ingeniously or ingenuously."

. . . What has been said, in the light of the facts developed, is enough to dispose of the case. However, we should answer the premise of the actions of the Governor and Legislature that they are not bound by our holding in the *Brown* case. It is necessary only to recall some basic constitutional propositions which are settled doctrine.

Article VI of the Constitution makes the Constitution the "supreme Law of the Land." In 1803, Chief Justice Marshall, speaking for a unanimous Court, referring to the Constitution as "the fundamental and paramount law of the nation," declared in the notable case of *Marbury* v. *Madison,* 1 Cranch 137, . . . that "It is emphatically the province and duty of the judicial de-

partment to say what the law is." This decision declared the basic principle that the federal judiciary is supreme in the exposition of the law of the Constitution, and that principle has ever since been respected by this Court and the Country as a permanent and indispensable feature of our constitutional system. It follows that the interpretation of the Fourteenth Amendment enunciated by this Court in the *Brown* case is the supreme law of the land, and Art. VI of the Constitution makes it of binding effect on the States "any Thing in the Constitution or Laws of any State to the Contrary notwithstanding." Every state legislator and executive and judicial officer is solemnly committed by oath taken pursuant to Art. VI ¶3 "to support this Constitution." Chief Justice Taney, speaking for a unanimous Court in 1859, said that this requirement reflected the framers' "anxiety to preserve it [the Constitution] in full force, in all its powers, and to guard against resistance to or evasion of its authority, on the part of a State. . . ." *Ableman* v. *Booth.* . . .

No state legislator or executive or judicial officer can war against the Constitution without violating his undertaking to support it. Chief Justice Marshall spoke for a unanimous Court in saying that: "If the legislatures of the several states may, at will, annul the judgments of the courts of the United States, and destroy the rights acquired under those judgments, the constitution itself becomes a solemn mockery. . . ." *United States* v. *Peters,* 5 Cranch 115. . . . A Governor who asserts a power to nullify a federal court order is similarly restrained. If he had such power, said Chief Justice Hughes, in 1932, also for a unanimous Court, "it is manifest that the fiat of a state Governor, and not the Constitution of the United States, would be the supreme law of the land; that the restrictions of the Federal Constitution upon the exercise of state power would be but impotent phrases. . . ." *Sterling v. Constantin,* 287 U.S. 378. . . .

It is, of course, quite true that the responsibility for public education is primarily the concern of the States, but it is equally true that such responsibilities, like all other state activity, must be exercised consistently with federal constitutional requirements as they apply to state action. The Constitution created a government dedicated to equal justice under law. The Fourteenth Amendment embodied and emphasized that ideal. State support of segregated schools through any arrangement, management, funds, or property cannot be squared with the Amendment's command that no State shall deny to any person within its jurisdiction the equal protection of the laws. The right of a student not to be segregated on racial grounds in schools so maintained is indeed so fundamental and pervasive that it is embraced in the concept of due process of law. *Bolling v. Sharpe.* . . . The basic decision in *Brown* was unanimously reached by this Court only after the case had been briefed and twice argued and the issues had been given the most serious consideration. Since the first *Brown* opinion three new Justices have come to the Court. They are at one with the Justices still on the Court who participated in the basic decision as to its correctness, and that decision is now unanimously reaffirmed. The principles announced in that decision and the obedience of the States to them, according to the command of the Constitution, are indispensable for the protection of the freedoms guaranteed by our fundamental charter for all of us. Our constitutional ideal justice under law is thus made a living truth.

SHELLEY *v.* KRAEMER
334 U.S. 1; 68 Sup. Ct. 836; 92 L. Ed. 1161 (1948)

[*Two instances of private agreements known as restrictive covenants are involved in this case. These separate but similar agreements barred Negro ownership of residential property in certain areas of St. Louis and Detroit. Only the facts relating to the St. Louis case are given below, since the circumstances surrounding each case are similar.*]

MR. CHIEF JUSTICE VINSON delivered the opinion of the Court:

These cases present for our consideration questions relating to the validity of court enforcement of private agreements, generally described as restrictive covenants, which have as their purpose the exclusion of persons of designated race or color from the ownership or occupancy of real property. Basic constitutional issues of obvious importance have been raised.

The first of these cases comes to this Court on certiorari to the Supreme Court of Missouri. On February 16, 1911, thirty out of a total of thirty-nine owners of property fronting both sides of Labadie Avenue between Taylor and Cora Avenue in the city of St. Louis, signed an agreement, which was subsequently recorded, providing in part:

". . . the said property is hereby restricted to the use and occupancy for the term of Fifty (50) years from this date, so that it shall be a condition all the time and whether recited and referred to as (sic) not in subsequent conveyances and shall attach to the land as a condition precedent to the sale of the same, that hereafter no part of said property or any portion thereof shall be, for said term of Fifty years, occupied by any person not of the Caucasion race, it being intended hereby to restrict the use of said property for said period of time against the occupancy as owners or tenants of any portion of said property for resident or other purpose by people of the Negro or Mongolian Race."

. . . On August 11, 1945, pursuant to a contract for sale, petitioners Shelley, who are Negroes, for valuable consideration received from one Fitzgerald a warranty deed to the parcel in question. The trial court found that petitioners had no actual knowledge of the restrictive agreement at the time of purchase.

On October 9, 1945, respondents, as owners of other property subject to the terms of the restrictive covenant, brought suit in the Circuit Court of the city of St. Louis praying that petitioners Shelley be restrained from taking possession of the property and that judgment be entered divesting title out of petitioners Shelley and revesting title in the immediate grantor or in such other person as the court should direct. The trial court denied the requested relief on the ground that the restrictive agreement, upon which respondents based their action, had never become final and complete because it was the intention of the parties to that agreement that it was not to become effective until signed by all property owners in the district, and signatures of all the owners had never been obtained. The Supreme Court of Missouri sitting *en banc* reversed and directed the trial court to grant relief for which the respondents had prayed.

Petitioners have placed primary reliance on their contentions, first raised in the state courts, that judicial enforcement of the restrictive agreements in these cases has violated rights guaranteed to petitioners by the Fourteenth Amendment of the Federal Constitution and Acts of Congress passed pursuant to that Amendment. Specifically, petitioners urge that they have been denied the equal protection of the laws, deprived of property without due process of law, and have been denied privileges and immunities of citizens of the United States. We pass to a consideration of those issues.

I

Whether the equal protection clause of the Fourteenth Amendment inhibits judicial enforcement by state courts of restrictive covenants based on race or color is a question which this Court has not heretofore been called upon to consider. . . .

It is well, at the outset, to scrutinize the terms of the restrictive agreements involved in these cases. In the Missouri case, the covenant declares that no part of the affected property shall be "occupied by any person not of the Caucasian race, it being intended hereby to restrict the use of said property . . . against the occupancy as owners or tenants of any portion of said property for resident or other purpose by people of the Negro or Mongolian Race." Not only does the restriction seek to proscribe use and occupancy of the affected properties by members of the excluded class, but as construed by the Missouri courts, the agreement requires that title of any person who uses his property in violation of the restriction shall be divested. . . .

It cannot be doubted that among the civil rights intended to be protected from discriminatory state action by the Fourteenth Amendment are the rights to acquire, enjoy, own, and dispose of property. Equality in the enjoyment of property rights was regarded by the framers of that Amendment as an essential precondition to the realization of other basic civil rights and liberties which the Amendment was intended to guarantee. . . .

It is likewise clear that restrictions on the right of occupancy of the sort sought to be created by the private agreements in these cases could not be squared with the requirements of the Fourteenth Amendment if imposed by state statute or local ordinance. . . .

But the present cases . . . do not involve action by state legislatures or city councils. Here the particular patterns of discrimination and the areas in which the restrictions are to operate, are determined, in the first instance, by the terms of agreements among private individuals. Participation of the State consists in the enforcement of the restrictions so defined. The crucial issue with which we are here confronted is whether this distinction removes these cases from the operation of the prohibitory provisions of the Fourteenth Amendment.

Since the decision of this Court in the *Civil Rights Cases,* 109 U.S. 3 (1883), the principle has become firmly embedded in our constitutional law that the action inhibited by the first section of the Fourteenth Amendment is only such action as may fairly be said to be that of the States. That Amendment erects no shield against merely private conduct, however discriminatory or wrongful.

We conclude, therefore, that the restrictive agreements standing alone cannot be regarded as violative of any rights guaranteed to petitioners by the Fourteenth Amendment. So long as the purposes of those agreements are effectuated by voluntary adherence to their terms, it would appear clear that there

has been no action by the State and the provisions of the Amendment have not been violated. . . .

But here there was more. These are cases in which the purposes of the agreements were secured only by judicial enforcement by state courts of the restrictive terms of the agreements. The respondents urge that judicial enforcement of private agreements does not amount to state action; or, in any event, the participation of the State is so attenuated in character as not to amount to state action within the meaning of the Fourteenth Amendment. Finally, it is suggested, even if the States in these cases may be deemed to have acted in the constitutional sense, their action did not deprive petitioners of rights guaranteed by the Fourteenth Amendment. We move to a consideration of these matters.

II

That the action of state courts and judicial officers in their official capacities is to be regarded as action of the State within the meaning of the Fourteenth Amendment, is a proposition which has long been established by decisions of this Court. That principle was given expression in the earliest cases involving the construction of the terms of the Fourteenth Amendment. . . .

But the examples of state judicial action which have been held by this Court to violate the Amendment's commands are not restricted to situations in which the judicial proceedings were found in some manner to be procedurally unfair. It has been recognized that the action of state courts in enforcing a substantive common-law rule formulated by those courts, may result in the denial of rights guaranteed by the Fourteenth Amendment, even though the judicial proceedings in such cases may have been in complete accord with the most rigorous conceptions of procedural due process. . . .

The short of the matter is that from the time of the adoption of the Fourteenth Amendment until the present, it has been the consistent ruling of this Court that the action of the States to which the Amendment has reference includes action of state courts and state judicial officials. Although, in construing the terms of the Fourteenth Amendment, differences have from time to time been expressed as to whether particular types of state action may be said to offend the Amendment's prohibitory provisions, it has never been suggested that state court action is immunized from the operation of those provisions simply because the act is that of the judicial branch of the state government.

III

Against this background of judicial construction, extending over a period of some three-quarters of a century, we are called upon to consider whether enforcement by state courts of the restrictive agreements in these cases may be deemed to be the acts of those States; and, if so, whether that action has denied these petitioners the equal protection of the laws which the Amendment was intended to insure.

We have no doubt that there has been state action in these cases in the full and complete sense of the phrase. The undisputed facts disclose that petitioners were willing purchasers of properties upon which they desired to establish homes. The owners of the properties were willing sellers; and contracts of sale were accordingly consummated. It is clear that but for the active intervention of the state courts, supported by the full panoply of state power, petitioners would have been free to occupy the properties in question without restraint.

These are not cases, as has been suggested, in which the States have merely abstained from action, leaving private individuals free to impose such discriminations as they see fit. Rather, these are cases in which the States have made available to such individuals the full coercive power of government to deny to petitioners, on the grounds of race or color, the enjoyment of property rights in premises which petitioners are willing and financially able to acquire and which the grantors are willing to sell. The difference between judicial enforcement and nonenforcement of the restrictive covenants is the difference to petitioners between being denied rights of property available to other members of the community and being accorded full enjoyment of those rights on an equal footing. . . .

We hold that in granting judicial enforcement of the restrictive agreements in these cases, the States have denied petitioners the equal protection of the laws and that, therefore, the action of the state courts cannot stand. We have noted that freedom from discrimination by the States in the enjoyment of property rights was among the basic objectives sought to be effectuated by the framers of the Fourteenth Amendment. That such discrimination has occurred in these cases is clear. Because of the race or color of these petitioners they have been denied rights of ownership or occupancy enjoyed as a matter of course by other citizens of different race or color. . . .

Respondents urge, however, that since the state courts stand ready to enforce restrictive covenants excluding white persons from the ownership or occupancy of property covered by such agreements, enforcement of covenants excluding colored persons may not be deemed a denial of equal protection of the laws to the colored persons who are thereby affected. This contention does not bear scrutiny. The parties have directed our attention to no case in which a court, state or federal, has been called upon to enforce a covenant excluding members of the white majority from ownership or occupancy of real property on grounds of race or color. But there are more fundamental considerations. The rights created by the first section of the Fourteenth Amendment are, by its terms, guaranteed to the individual. The rights established are personal rights. It is, therefore, no answer to these petitioners to say that the courts may also be induced to deny white persons rights of ownership and occupancy on grounds of race or color. Equal protection of the laws is not achieved through indiscriminate imposition of inequalities. . . .

The historical context in which the Fourteenth Amendment became a part of the Constitution should not be forgotten. Whatever else the framers sought to achieve, it is clear that the matter of primary concern was the establishment of equality in the enjoyment of basic civil and political rights and the preservation of those rights from discriminatory action on the part of the States based on considerations of race or color. Seventy-five years ago this Court announced that the provisions of the Amendment are to be construed with this fundamental purpose in mind. Upon full consideration, we have concluded that in these cases the States have acted to deny petitioners the equal protection of the laws guaranteed by the Fourteenth Amendment. Having so decided, we find it unnecessary to consider whether petitioners have also been derprived of property without due process of law or denied privileges and immunities of citizens of the United States. . . .

Reversed.

MR. JUSTICE REED, MR. JUSTICE JACKSON, and MR. JUSTICE RUTLEDGE took no part in the consideration or decision of these cases.

REITMAN *v.* MULKEY
387 U.S. 369; 87 Sup. Ct. 1627; 18 L. Ed. 2d 830 (1967)

MR. JUSTICE WHITE delivered the opinion of the Court:

The question here is whether Art. I, §26 of the California Constitution denies "to any person . . . the equal protection of the laws" within the meaning of the Fourteenth Amendment of the Constitution of the United States. Section 26 of Art. I, an initiated measure submitted to the people as Proposition 14 in a statewide ballot in 1964, provides in part as follows:

"Neither the State nor any subdivision or agency thereof shall deny, limit or abridge, directly or indirectly, the right of any person, who is willing or desires to sell, lease or rent any part or all of his real property, to decline to sell, lease or rent such property to such person or persons as he, in his absolute discretion, chooses."

The real property covered by §26 is limited to residential property and contains an exception for state-owned real estate. . . .

We affirm the judgment of the California Supreme Court. We first turn to the opinion of that court, which quite properly undertook to examine the constitutionality of §26 in terms of its "immediate objective," its "ultimate impact" and its "historical context and the conditions existing prior to its enactment." . . . The Unruh Act . . on which respondents based their cases, was passed in 1959. The Hawkins Act . . . followed and prohibited discriminations in publicly assisted housing. In 1961, the legislature enacted proscriptions against restrictive covenants. Finally, in 1963, came the Rumford Fair Housing Act . . . superseding the Hawkins Act and prohibiting racial discriminations in the sale or rental of any private dwelling containing more than four units. That act was enforceable by the State Fair Employment Practice Commission.

It was against this background that Proposition 14 was enacted. Its immediate design and intent, the California court said, was "to overturn state laws that bore on the right of private sellers and lessors to discriminate," the Unruh and Rumford Acts, and "to forestall future state action that might circumscribe this right." This aim was successfully achieved: the adoption of Proposition 14 "generally nullifies both the Rumford and Unruh Acts as they apply to the housing market," and establishes "a purported constitutional right to privately discriminate on grounds which admittedly would be unavailable under the Fourteenth Amendment should state action be involved."

Second, the court conceded that the State was permitted a neutral position with respect to private racial discrimination and that the State was not bound by the Federal Constitution to forbid them. But, because a significant state involvement in private discriminations could amount to unconstitutional state action, *Burton* v. *Wilmington Parking Authority*, the court deemed it necessary to determine whether Proposition 14 invalidly involved the State in racial discriminations in the housing market. Its conclusion was that it did.

To reach this result, the state court examined certain prior decisions in this

Court in which discriminatory state action was identified. It concluded that a prohibited state involvement could be found "even where the state can be charged with only encouraging," rather than commanding discrimination. Also of particular interest to the court was Mr. Justice Stewart's concurrence in *Burton* v. *Wilmington Parking Authority* . . . where it was said that the Delaware courts had construed an existing Delaware statute as "authorizing" racial discrimination in restaurants and that the statute was therefore invalid. To the California court "[t]he instant case presents an undeniably analogous situation" wherein the State had taken affirmative action designed to make private discriminations legally possible. Section 26 was said to have changed the situation from one in which discriminatory practices were restricted "to one wherein it is encouraged, within the meaning of the cited decisions"; §26 was legislative action "which authorized private discrimination" and made the State "at least a partner in the instant act of discrimination. . . ." The court could "conceive of no other purpose for an application of section 26 aside from authorizing the perpetuation of a purported private discrimination. . . ." The judgment of the California court was that §26 unconstitutionally involves the State in racial discriminations and is therefore invalid under the Fourteenth Amendment.

There is no sound reason for rejecting this judgment. Petitioners contend that the California court has misconstrued the Fourteenth Amendment since the repeal of any statute prohibiting racial discrimination, which is constitutionally permissible, may be said to "authorize" and "encourage" discrimination because it makes legally permissible that which was formerly proscribed. But as we understand the California court, it did not posit a constitutional violation on the mere repeal of the Unruh and Rumford Acts. It did not read either our cases or the Fourteenth Amendment as establishing an automatic constitutional barrier to the repeal of an existing law prohibiting racial discriminations in housing; nor did the court rule that a State may never put in statutory form an existing policy of neutrality with respect to private discriminations. What the court below did was first to reject the notion that the State was required to have a statute prohibiting racial discriminations in housing. Second, it held the purpose and intent of §26 was to authorize private racial discriminations in the housing market, to repeal the Unruh and Rumford Acts and to create a constitutional right to discriminate on racial grounds in the sale and leasing of real property. Hence, the court dealt with §26 as though it expressly authorized and constitutionalized the private right to discriminate. Third, the court assessed the ultimate impact of §26 in the California environment and concluded that the section would encourage and significantly involve the State in private racial discrimination contrary to the Fourteenth Amendment.

The California court could very reasonably conclude that §26 would and did have wider impact than a mere repeal of existing statutes. Section 26 mentioned neither the Unruh nor Rumford Acts in so many words. Instead, it announced the constitutional right of any person to decline to sell or lease his real property to anyone to whom he did not desire to sell or lease. Unruh and Rumford were thereby *pro tanto* repealed. But the section struck more deeply and more widely. Private discriminations in housing were now not only free from Rumford and Unruh but they also enjoyed a far different status than was true before the passage of those statutes. The right to discriminate,

including the right to discriminate on racial grounds, was now embodied in the State's basic charter, immune from legislative, executive, or judicial regulation at any level of the state government. Those practicing racial discrimination need no longer rely solely on their personal choice. They could now invoke express constitutional authority, free from censure or interference of any kind from official sources. . . .

This Court has never attempted the "impossible task" of formulating an infallible test for determining whether the State "in any of its manifestations" has become significantly involved in private discriminations. "Only by sifting the facts and weighing the circumstances" on a case-to-case basis can a "nonobvious involvement of the State in private conduct be attributed its true significance." *Burton* v. *Wilmington Parking Authority*. . . . Here the California court, armed as it was with the knowledge of the facts and circumstances concerning the passage and potential impact of §26, and familiar with the milieu in which that provision would operate, has determined that the provision would involve the State in private racial discriminations to an unconstitutional degree. We accept this holding of the California court. . . .

In *Burton* v. *Wilmington Parking Authority* . . . operator-lessee of a restaurant located in a building owned by the State and otherwise operated for public purposes, refused service to Negroes. Although the State neither commanded nor expressly authorized or encouraged the discriminations, the State had "elected to place its power, property and prestige behind the admitted discrimination" and by "its inaction . . . has . . . made itself a party to the refusal of service . . . which therefore could not be considered the purely private choice of the restaurant operator. . . . Here we are dealing with a provision which does not just repeal an existing law forbidding private racial discriminations. Section 26 was intended to authorize, and does authorize, racial discrimination in the housing market. The right to discriminate is now one of the basic policies of the State. The California Supreme Court believes that the section will significantly encourage and involve the State in private discriminations. We have been presented with no persuasive considerations indicating that this judgment should be overturned.

Affirmed.

MR. JUSTICE DOUGLAS concurred.

MR. JUSTICE HARLAN, whom MR. JUSTICE BLACK, MR. JUSTICE CLARK, and MR. JUSTICE STEWART join, dissenting:

I consider that this decision, which cuts deeply into state political processes, is supported neither by anything "found" by the Supreme Court of California nor by any of our past cases decided under the Fourteenth Amendment. In my view today's holding, salutary as its result may appear at first blush, may in the long run actually serve to handicap progress in the extremely difficult field of racial concerns. I must respectfully dissent.

The facts of this case are simple and undisputed. The legislature of the State of California has in the last decade enacted a number of statutes restricting the right of private landowners to discriminate on the basis of such factors as race in the sale or rental of property. These laws aroused considerable opposition, causing certain groups to organize themselves and to take advantage of procedures embodied in the California Constitution permitting a "proposition" to be presented to the voters for a constitutional amendment. "Proposition 14" was thus put before the electorate in the 1964 election and was adopted by a vote of 4,526,460 to 2,395,747. The Amendment, Art. I,

§26, of the State Constitution, reads in relevant part as follows:

> "Neither the State nor any subdivision or agency thereof shall deny, limit or abridge, directly or indirectly, the right of any person, who is willing or desires to sell, lease or rent any part or all of his real property, to decline to sell, lease or rent such property to such person or persons as he, in his absolute discretion, chooses."

I am wholly at loss to understand how this straight-forward effectuation of a change in the California constitution can be deemed a violation of the Fourteenth Amendment, thus rendering §26 void and petitioners' refusal to rent their property to respondents, because of their race, illegal under prior state law. The Equal Protection Clause of the Fourteenth Amendment, which forbids a State to use its authority to foster discrimination based on such factors as race, . . . does not undertake to control purely personal prejudices and predilections, and individuals acting on their own are left free to discriminate on racial grounds if they are so minded, In re Civil Rights Cases. . . . By the same token, the Fourteenth Amendment does not require of States the passage of laws preventing such private discrimination, although it does not of course disable them from enacting such legislation if they wish.

In the case at hand California, acting through the initiative and referendum, has decided to remain "neutral" in the realm of private discrimination affecting the sale or rental of private residential property; in such transactions private owners are now free to act in a discriminatory manner previously forbidden to them. In short, all that has happened is that California has effected a *pro tanto* repeal of its prior statutes forbidding private discrimination. This runs no more afoul of the Fourteenth Amendment than would have California's failure to pass any such antidiscrimination statutes in the first instance. The fact that such repeal was also accompanied by a constitutional prohibition against future enactment of such laws by the California Legislature cannot well be thought to affect, from a federal constitutional standpoint, the validity of what California has done. The Fourteenth Amendment does not reach such state constitutional action any more than it does a simple legislative repeal of legislation forbidding private discrimination.

I do not think the Court's opinion really denies any of these fundamental constitutional propositions. Rather it attempts to escape them by resorting to arguments which appear to me to be entirely ill-founded.

The Court attempts to fit §26 within the coverage of the Equal Protection Clause by characterizing it as in effect an affirmative call to residents of California to discriminate. The main difficulty with this viewpoint is that it depends upon a characterization of §26 that cannot fairly be made. The provision is neutral on its face, and it is only by in effect asserting that this requirement of passive official neutrality is camouflage that the Court is able to reach its conclusion. In depicting the provision as tantamount to active state encouragement of discrimination the Court essentially relies on the fact that the California Supreme Court so concluded. It is said that the findings of the highest court of California as to the meaning and impact of the enactment are entitled to great weight. I agree, of course, that *findings of fact* by a state court should be given great weight, but this familiar proposition hardly aids the Court's holding in this case. . . .

A state enactment, particularly one that is simply permissive of private decision-making rather than coercive and one that has been adopted in this most democratic of processes, should not be struck down by the judiciary under the Equal Protection Clause without persuasive evidence of an invidious purpose or effect. The only "factual" matter relied on by the majority of the California Supreme Court was the context in which Proposition 14 was adopted, namely, that several strong antidiscrimination acts had been passed by the legislature and opposed by many of those who successfully led the movement for adoption of Proposition 14 by popular referendum. These circumstances, and these alone, the California court held, made §26 unlawful under this Court's cases interpreting the Equal Protection Clause. This, of course, is nothing but a legal conclusion as to federal constitutional law, the California Supreme Court not having relied in any way upon the State Constitution. Accepting all the suppositions under which the state court acted, I cannot see that its conclusion is entitled to any special weight in the discharge of our own responsibilities. Put in another way, I cannot transform the California court's conclusion of law into a finding of fact that the State through the adoption of §26 is actively promoting racial discrimination. It seems to me manifest that the state court decision rested entirely on what that court conceived to be the compulsion of the Fourteenth Amendment, not on any fact-finding by the state courts.

There is no question that the adoption of §26, repealing the former state antidiscrimination laws and prohibiting the enactment of such state laws in the future, constituted "state action" within the meaning of the Fourteenth Amendment. The only issue is whether this provision impermissibly deprives any person of equal protection of the laws.

As a starting point, it is clear that any statute requiring unjustified discriminatory treatment is unconstitutional. E.g., *Nixon* v. *Herndon,* 273 U.S. 536, 47 Sup. Ct. 446; *Brown* v. *Board of Education,* supra; *Peterson* v. *City of Greenville,* 373 U.S. 244, 83 Sup. Ct. 1119, 10 L. Ed. 2d 323. And it is no less clear that the Equal Protection Clause bars as well discriminatory governmental administration of a statute fair on its face. E.g., *Yick Wo* v. *Hopkins,* 118 U.S. 356, 6 Sup. Ct. 1064, 30 L. Ed. 220. This case fits within neither of these two categories: Section 26 is by its terms inoffensive, and its provisions require no affirmative governmental enforcement of any sort. A third category of equal protection cases, concededly more difficult to characterize, stands for the proposition that when governmental involvement in private discrimination reaches a level at which the State can be held responsible for the specific act of private discrimination, the strictures of the Fourteenth Amendment come into play. In dealing with this class of cases, the inquiry has been framed as whether the State has become "a joint participant in the challenged activity, which, on that account, cannot be considered to have been so 'purely private' as to fall without the scope of the Fourteenth Amendment." *Burton* v. *Wilmington Parking Authority.* . . .

Given these latter contours of the equal protection doctrine, the assessment of particular cases is often troublesome, as the Court itself acknowledges. . . . However, the present case does not seem to me even to approach those peripheral situations in which the question of state involvement gives rise to difficulties. See, e.g., *Evans* v. *Newton,* 382 U.S. 296, 86 Sup. Ct. 486, 15 L. Ed. 2d 373; *Lombard* v. *State of Louisiana,* 373 U.S. 267, 83 Sup. Ct. 1122, 10 L. Ed. 2d 338. The core of the Court's opinion is that §26 is offensive to the Fourteenth Amendment because it effectively *encourages* private discrimination. By focusing on "encouragement" the Court, I fear, is forging a slippery and unfortunate criterion by which to measure the constitutionality of a statute simply permissive in purpose and effect, and inoffensive on its face. . . .

The denial of equal protection emerges only from the conclusion reached by the Court that the implementation of a new policy of governmental neutrality, embodied in a constitutional provision and replacing a former policy of antidiscrimination, has the effect of lending encouragement to those who wish to discriminate. In the context of the actual facts of the case, this conclusion appears to me to state only a truism: people who want to discriminate but were previously forbidden to do so by state law are now left free because the State has chosen to have no law on the subject at all. Obviously whenever there is a change in the law it will have resulted from the concerted activity of those who desire the change, and its enactment will allow those supporting the legislation to pursue their private goals.

A moment of thought will reveal the far-reaching possibilities of the Court's new doctrine, which I am sure the Court does not intend. Every act of private discrimination is either forbidden by state law or permitted by it. There can be little doubt that such permissiveness—whether by express constitutional or statutory provision, or implicit in the common law—to some extent "encourages" those who wish to discriminate to do so. Under this theory "state action" in the form of laws that do nothing more than passively permit private discrimination could be said to tinge *all* private discrimination with the taint of unconstitutional state encouragement.

This type of alleged state involvement, simply evincing a refusal to involve itself at all, is of course very different from that illustrated in such cases as *Lombard, Peterson, Evans* and *Burton,* supra, where the Court found active involvement of state agencies and officials in specific acts of discrimination. It is also quite different from cases in which a state enactment could be said to have the obvious purpose of fostering discrimination. . . . I believe the state action required to bring the Fourteenth Amendment into operation must be affirmative and purposeful, actively fostering discrimination. Only in such a case is ostensibly "private" action more properly labeled "official." I do not believe that the mere enactment of §26, on the showing made here, falls within this class of cases.

I think that this decision is not only constitutionally unsound, but in its practical potentialities short-sighted. Opponents of state antidiscrimination statutes are now in a position to argue that such legislation should be defeated because, if enacted, it may be unrepealable. More fundamentally, the doctrine underlying this decision may hamper, if not preclude, attempts to deal with the delicate and troublesome problems of race relations through the legislative process. The lines that have been and must be drawn in this area, fraught as it is with human sensibilities and frailties of whatever race or creed, are difficult ones. The drawing of them requires understanding, patience, and compromise, and is best done by legislatures rather than by courts. When legislation in this field is unsuccessful there should be wide opportunities for legislative amendment, as well as for change through such processes as the popular initiative and referendum. This decision, I fear, may inhibit such flexibility. Here the electorate itself overwhelmingly wished to overrule and check its own legislature on a matter left open by the Federal Constitution. By refusing to accept the decision of the people of California, and by contriving a new and ill-defined constitutional concept to allow federal judicial interference, I think the Court has taken to itself powers and responsibilities left elsewhere by the Constitution.

I believe the Supreme Court of California misapplied the Fourteenth Amendment, and would reverse its judgment, and remand the case for further appropriate proceedings.

SMITH *v.* ALLWRIGHT
321 U.S. 649; 64 Sup. Ct. 757; 88 L. Ed. 987 (1944)

[*A Negro citizen of Texas named Smith tried to vote in the Democratic party primary election of 1940, in which candidates for state and national offices were to be chosen. Allwright, a precinct election judge, and other election officials refused to give Smith a ballot. They contended that a state Democratic party convention resolution adopted in 1932 limited membership in the party to white persons. Smith brought suit for damages against Allwright in a federal district court. He claimed that Allwright and other election officials had deprived him of his voting rights under the Constitution. The district court ruled against Smith and a court of appeals affirmed the district court's ruling on the authority of* Grovey *v.* Townsend, *which is discussed in the opinion here. Smith then brought the case to the Supreme Court on a writ of certiorari.*]

MR. JUSTICE REED delivered the opinion of the Court:

. . . The State of Texas by its Constitution and statutes provides that every person, if certain other requirements are met which are not here in issue, qualified by residence in the district or county "shall be deemed a qualified elector." . . . Primary elections for United States Senators, Congressmen, and state officers are provided for by Chapters Twelve and Thirteen of the statutes. Under these chapters, the democratic party was required to hold the primary which was the occasion of the alleged wrong to petitioner. . . . These nominations are to be made by the qualified voters of the party. . . .

Texas is free to conduct her elections and limit her electorate as she may deem wise, save only as her action may be affected by the prohibitions of the United States Constitution or in conflict with powers delegated to and exercised by the National Government. The Fourteenth Amendment forbids a State from making or enforcing any law which abridges the privileges or immunities of citizens of the United States, and the Fifteenth Amendment specifically interdicts any denial or abridgment by a State of the right of citizens to vote on account of color. Respondents appeared in the District Court and the Circuit Court of Appeals and defended on the ground that the Democratic party of Texas is a voluntary organization with members banded together for the purpose of selecting individuals of the group representing the common political beliefs as candidates in the general election. As such a voluntary organization, it was claimed, the Democratic party is free to select its own membership and limit to whites participation in the party primary. Such action, the answer asserted, does not violate the Fourteenth, Fifteenth, or Seventeenth Amendment, as officers of government cannot be chosen at primaries and the Amendments are applicable only to general elections where governmental officers are actually elected. Primaries, it is said, are political party affairs, handled by party, not governmental, officers. . . .

The right of a Negro to vote in the Texas primary has been considered heretofore by this Court. The first case was *Nixon* v. *Herndon,* 273 U.S. 536. At that time, 1924, the Texas statute . . . declared, "in no event shall a Negro be eligible to participate in a Democratic Party primary election in the State of Texas." Nixon was refused the right to vote in a Democratic primary and brought a suit for damages against the election officers. . . . It was urged to this Court that the denial of the franchise to Nixon violated his Constitutional rights under the Fourteenth and Fifteenth Amendments. Without consideration of the Fifth, this Court held that the action of Texas in denying the ballot to Negroes by statute was in violation of the equal protection clause of the Fourteenth Amendment and reversed the dismissal of the suit.

The legislature of Texas re-enacted the article but gave the State Executive Committee of a party the power to prescribe the qualifications of its members for voting or other participation. This article remains in the statutes. The State Executive Committee of the Democratic party adopted a resolution that white Democrats and none other might participate in the primaries of that party. Nixon was refused again the privilege of voting in a primary and again brought suit for damages. . . . This Court again reversed the dismissal of the suit for the reason that the Committee action was deemed to be state action and invalid as discriminatory under the Fourteenth Amendment. The test was said to be whether the Committee operated as representative of the State in the discharge of the State's authority. *Nixon* v. *Condon,* 286 U.S. 73. The question of the inherent power of a political party in Texas "without restraint by any law to determine its own membership" was left open. . . .

In *Grovey* v. *Townsend,* 295 U.S. 45, this Court had before it suit for damages for the refusal in a primary of a county clerk, a Texas officer with only public functions to perform, to furnish petitioner, a Negro, an absentee ballot. The refusal was solely on the ground of race. This case differed from *Nixon* v. *Condon.* . . . in that a state convention of the Democratic party had passed the resolution of May 24, 1932, hereinbefore quoted. It was decided that the determination by the state convention of the membership of the Democratic party made a significant change from a determination by the Executive Committee. The former was party action, voluntary in character. The latter, as had been held in the *Condon* case, was action by authority of the State. The managers of the primary election were therefore declared not to be state officials in such sense that their action was state action. A state convention of a party was said not to be an organ of the State. This Court went on to announce that to deny a vote in a primary was a mere refusal of party membership with which "the State need have no concern," . . . while for a State to deny a vote in a general election on the ground of race or color violated the Constitution. Consequently, there was found no ground for holding that the county clerk's refusal of a ballot because of racial ineligibility for party membership denied the petitioner any right under the Fourteenth or Fifteenth Amendment.

Since *Grovey* v. *Townsend* and prior to the present suit, no case from Texas involving primary elections has been before this Court. We did decide, however, *United States* v. *Classic,* 313 U.S. 299. We there held that §4 of Article I of the Constitution authorized Congress to regulate primary as well as general elections . . . "where the primary is by law made an integral part of the election machinery." . . . Consequently, in the *Classic case,* we upheld the applicability to frauds in a Louisiana primary of §§19 and 20 of the Criminal Code. Thereby corrupt acts of election officers were subjected to Congressional sanctions because that body had power to protect rights of federal suffrage secured by the Constitution in primary as in general elections. . . . This decision depended, too, on the determination that under the Louisiana statutes the primary was a part of the procedure for choice of federal officials. By this decision the doubt as to whether or not such primaries were a part of "elections" subject to federal control, which had remained unanswered since *Newberry* v. *United States* . . . was erased. . . . [Despite this statement by the Court, the *Newberry* case was generally regarded as holding that Congress could *not* regulate primaries.] The fusing by the *Classic* case of the primary and general elections into a single instrumentality for choice of officers has a definite bearing on the permissibility under the Constitution of excluding Negroes from primaries. This is not to say that the *Classic* case cuts directly into the rationale of *Grovey* v. *Townsend.* This latter case was not mentioned in the opinion. *Classic* bears upon *Grovey* v. *Townsend* not because exclusion of Negroes from primaries is any more or less state action by reason of the unitary character of the electoral process but because the recognition of the place of the primary in the electoral scheme makes clear that state delegation to a party of the power to fix the qualifications of primary elections is delegation of a state function that may make the party's action the action of the State. When *Grovey* v. *Townsend* was written, the Court looked upon the denial of a vote in a primary as a mere refusal by a party of party membership. . . . As the Louisiana statutes for holding primaries are similar to those of Texas, our ruling in *Classic* as to the unitary character of the electoral process calls for a re-examination as to whether or not the exclusion of Negroes from a Texas party primary was state action. . . .

It may now be taken as a postulate that the right to vote in such a primary for the nomination of candidates without discrimination by the State, like the right to vote in a general election, is a right secured by the Constitution. . . . By the terms of the Fifteenth Amendment that right may not be abridged by any State on account of race. Under our Constitution the great privilege of the ballot may not be denied a man by the State because of his color.

We are thus brought to an examination of the qualifications for Democratic primary electors in Texas, to determine whether state action or private action has excluded Negroes from participation. Despite Texas' decision that the exclusion is produced by private or party action. . . . federal courts must for themselves appraise the facts leading to that conclusion. It is only by the performance of this obligation that a final and uniform interpretation can be given to the Constitution, the "supreme Law of the Land."

We think that this statutory system for the selection of party nominees for inclusion on the general election ballot makes the party which is required to follow these legislative directions an agency of the State in so far as it determines the participants in a primary election. The party takes its character as a state agency from the duties imposed upon it by state statutes; the duties do not become matters of private law because they are performed by a political party. The plan of the Texas primary follows substantially that of Louisiana, with the exception that in Louisiana the State pays the cost of the primary while Texas assesses the cost against candidates. In numerous instances, the Texas statutes fix or limit the fees to be charged. Whether paid directly by the State or through state requirements, it is state action which compels. When primaries become a part of the machinery for choosing officials, state and national, as they have here, the same tests to determine the character of discrimination or abridgment should be applied to the primary as are applied to the general election. If the State requires a certain electoral procedure, prescribes a general election ballot made up of party nominees so chosen and limits the choice of the electorate in general elections for state offices, practically speaking, to those whose names appear on such a ballot, it endorses, adopts, and enforces the discrimination against Negroes practiced by a party entrusted by Texas law with the determination of the qualifications of participants in the primary. This is state action within the meaning of the Fifteenth Amendment. . . .

The United States is a constitutional democracy. Its organic law grants to all citizens a right to participate in the choice of elected officials without restriction by any State because of race. This grant to the people of the opportunity for choice is not to be nullified by a State through casting its electoral process in a form which permits a private organization to practice racial discrimination in the election. Constitutional rights would be of little value if they could be thus indirectly denied. . . .

The privilege of membership in a party may be, as this Court said in *Grovey* v. *Townsend* . . . no concern of a State. But when, as here, that privilege is also the essential qualification for voting in a primary to select nominees for a general election, the State makes the action of the party the action of the State. In reaching this conclusion we are not unmindful of the desirability of continuity of decision in constitutional questions. However, when convinced of former error, this Court has never felt constrained to follow precedent. In constitutional questions, where correction depends upon amendment and not upon legislative action, this Court throughout its history has freely exercised its power to re-examine the basis of its constitutional decisions. This has long been accepted practice, and this practice has continued to this day. This is particularly true when the decision believed erroneous is the application of a constitutional principle rather than an interpretation of the Constitution to extract the principle itself. Here we are applying, contrary to the recent decision in *Grovey* v. *Townsend*, the well-established principle of the Fifteenth Amendment, forbidding the abridgment by a State of a citizen's right to vote. *Grovey* v. *Townsend* is overruled.

Judgment reversed.

[MR. JUSTICE FRANKFURTER concurred in the result. MR. JUSTICE ROBERTS dissented.]

GOMILLION *v.* LIGHTFOOT
364 U.S. 339; 81 Sup. Ct. 125; 5 L. Ed. 2d 110 (1960)

[*Tuskegee, Alabama, is the seat of Macon County and the home of Tuskegee Institute, the famed Negro college founded by Booker T. Washington in 1881. Negroes have long outnumbered whites in Tuskegee by a margin of approximately four to one. After World War II, Negroes in Tuskegee began to register and vote in greater numbers in municipal elections, and in 1954 a Negro ran for the school board and lost by a relatively small margin. This frightened the local white leaders, who decided to press for legislation that would keep the city under white control. Accordingly, in 1957, the Alabama legislature passed, unanimously and without debate, Local Act No. 140, which redefined the boundaries of Tuskegee. The statute altered the shape of the city from a simple square to an irregular 28-sided figure resembling a "stylized sea horse." The effect was to place Tuskegee Institute and all but four or five Negro voters outside the city limits without removing a single white voter. Professor Charles G. Gomillion of Tuskegee Institute and other Negroes whose homes had been placed outside the city brought an action in a federal district court seeking a declaratory judgment that Local Act No. 140 was unconstitutional. At the same time they asked for an injunction to restrain Mayor Phil M. Lightfoot and other municipal officers from enforcing the act. The Negroes argued that enforcement of the act would deny them benefits of residence in Tuskegee in violation of the due process and equal protection clauses of the Fourteenth Amendment and also deny them the right to vote in municipal elections in violation of the Fifteenth Amendment. The district court dismissed the case, stating that it had no power to change municipal boundaries fixed by an elected legislative body, and a court of appeals affirmed, with one judge dissenting. The Supreme Court then granted certiorari.*]

MR. JUSTICE FRANKFURTER delivered the opinion of the Court:

The complaint amply alleges a claim of racial discrimination. Against this claim the respondents have never suggested, either in their belief or in oral argument, any countervailing municipal function which Act 140 is designed to serve. The respondents invoke generalities expressing the State's unrestricted power—unlimited, that is, by the United States Constitution—to establish, destroy, or reorganize by contraction or expansion its political subdivisions, to wit, cities, counties, and other local units. We freely recognize the breadth and importance of this aspect of the State's political power. To exalt this power into an absolute is to misconceive the reach and rule of this Court's decisions. . . .

[T]he Court has never acknowledged that the States have power to do as they will with municipal corporations regardless of consequences. Legislative control of municipalities, no less than other state power, lies within the scope of relevant limitations imposed by the United States Constitution. . . .

The respondents find another barrier to the trial of this case in *Colegrove* v. *Green.* . . . The decisive facts in this case, which at this stage must be taken as proved, are wholly different from the considerations found controlling in *Colegrove.*

That case involved a complaint of discriminatory apportionment of congressional districts. The appellants in *Colegrove* complained only of a dilution of the strength of their votes as a result of legislative inaction over a course of many years. The petitioners here complain that affirmative legislative action deprives them of their votes and the consequent advantages that the

ballot affords. When a legislature thus singles out a readily isolated segment of a racial minority for special discriminatory treatment, it violates the Fifteenth Amendment. In no case involving unequal weight in voting distribution that has come before the Court did the decision sanction a differentiation on racial lines whereby approval was given to unequivocal withdrawal of the vote solely from colored citizens. Apart from all else, these considerations lift this controversy out of the so-called "political" arena and into the conventional sphere of constitutional litigation.

In sum, as Mr. Justice Holmes remarked, when dealing with a related situation . . . "Of course the petition concerns political action," but "The objection that the subject matter of the suit is political is little more than a play upon words." A statute which is alleged to have worked unconstitutional deprivations of petitioners' rights is not immune to attack simply because the mechanism employed by the legislature is a redefinition of municipal boundaries. According to the allegations here made, the Alabama Legislature has not merely redrawn the Tuskegee city limits with incidental inconvenience to the petitioners; it is more accurate to say that it has deprived the petitioners of the municipal franchise and consequent rights and to that end it has incidentally changed the city's boundaries. While in form this is merely an act redefining metes and bounds, if the allegations are established, the inescapable human effect of this essay in geometry and geography is to despoil colored citizens, and only colored citizens, of their theretofore enjoyed voting rights. That was not *Colegrove* v. *Green.*

When a State exercises power wholly within the domain of state interest, it is insulated from federal judicial review. But such insulation is not carried over when state power is used as an instrument for circumventing a federally protected right. This principle has had many applications. It has long been recognized in cases which have prohibited a State from exploiting a power acknowledged to be absolute in an isolated context to justify the imposition of an "unconstitutional condition." What the Court has said in those cases is equally applicable here, viz., that "Acts generally lawful may become unlawful when done to accomplish an unlawful end . . . and a constitutional result." . . . The petitioners are entitled to prove their allegations at trial.

For these reasons, the principal conclusions of the District Court and the Court of Appeals are clearly erroneous and the decision below must be

Reversed.

MR. JUSTICE DOUGLAS, while joining the opinion of the Court, adheres to the dissents in *Colegrove* v. *Green . . .* and *South* v. *Peters,* 339 U.S. 276

MR. JUSTICE WHITTAKER, concurring:

I concur in the Court's judgment, but not in the whole of its opinion. It seems to me that the decision should be rested not on the Fifteenth Amendment, but rather on the Equal Protection Clause of the Fourteenth Amendment to the Constitution. I am doubtful that the averments of the complaint, taken for present purposes to be true, show a purpose by Act 140 to abridge petitioner's "right . . . to vote," in the Fifteenth Amendment sense. It seems to me that the "right . . . to vote" that is guaranteed by the Fifteenth Amendment is but the same right to vote as is enjoyed by all others within the same election precinct, ward or other political division. And, inasmuch as no one has the right to vote in a political division, or in a local election concerning only an area in which he does not reside, it would seem to follow that one's right to vote in Division A is not abridged by a redistricting that places his residence in Division B if he there enjoys the same voting privileges as all others in that Division, even though the redistricting was done by the State for the purpose of placing a racial group of citizens in Division B rather than A.

But it does seem clear to me that accomplishment of a State's purpose—to use the Court's phrase—of "fencing Negro citizens out of" Division A and into Division B is an unlawful segregation of races of citizens in violation of the Equal Protection Clause of the Fourteenth Amendment. . . . I would think the decision should be rested on that ground.

HEART OF ATLANTA MOTEL *v.* UNITED STATES
379 U.S. 241; 85 Sup. Ct. 348; 13 L. Ed. 2d 258 (1964)

MR. JUSTICE CLARK delivered the opinion of the Court:

This is a declaratory judgment action attacking the constitutionality of Title II of the Civil Rights Act of 1964. . . . Appellant owns and operates the Heart of Atlanta Motel which has 216 rooms available to transient guests. The motel is located on Courtland Streeet, two blocks from downtown Peachtree Street. It is readily accessible to interstate highways 75 and 85 and state highways 23 and 41. Appellant solicits patronage from outside the State of Georgia through various national advertising media, including magazines of national circulation; it maintains over 50 billboards and highway signs within the State, soliciting patronage for the motel; it accepts convention trade from outside

Georgia and approximately 75% of its registered guests are from out of State. Prior to passage of the Act the motel had followed a practice of refusing to rent rooms to Negroes, and it alleged that it intended to continue to do so. In an effort to perpetuate that policy this suit was filed.

The appellant contends that Congress in passing this Act exceeded its power to regulate commerce under Art. I, §8, cl 3, of the Constitution of the United States. . . .

This Title is divided into seven sections beginning with §201 (a) which provides that:

"All persons shall be entitled to the full and equal enjoyment of the goods, services, facilities, privileges, advantages, and accommodations of any place of public accommodation, as defined in this section, without discrimination or segregation on the ground of race, color, religion, or national origin."

There are listed in §201 (b) four classes of business establishments, each of which "serves the public" and "is a place of public accommodation" within the meaning of §201 (a) "if its operations affect commerce, or if discrimination or segregation by it is supported by State action." The covered establishments [include] "(1) any inn, hotel, motel, or other establishment which privides lodging to transient guests. . . . Section 201 (c) . . . declares that "any inn, hotel, motel, or other establishment which provides lodging to transient guests" affects commerce per se. . . .

It is admitted that the operation of the motel brings it within the provision of §201 (a) of the Act and that appellant refused to provide lodging for transient Negroes because of their race or color and that it intends to continue that policy unless restrained.

The sole question posed is, therefore, the constitutionality of the Civil Rights Act of 1964 as applied to these facts. The legislative history of the Act indicates that Congress based the Act on §5 and the Equal Protection Clause of the Fourteenth Amendment as well as its power to regulate interstate commerce under Art I, §8, cl 3 of the Constitution.

The Senate Commerce Committee made it quite clear that the fundamental object of Title II was to vindicate "the deprivation of personal dignity that surely accompanies denials of equal access to public establishments." At the same time, however, it noted that such an objective has been and could be readily achieved "by congressional action based on the commerce power of the Constitution." . . . Our study of the legislative record, made in the light of prior cases, has brought us to the conclusion that Congress possessed ample power in this regard, and we have therefore not considered the other grounds relied upon. This is not to say that the remaining authority upon which it acted was not adequate, a question upon which we do not pass, but merely that since the commerce power is sufficient for our decision here we have considered it alone. . . .

In light of our ground for decision, it might be well at the outset to discuss the Civil Rights Cases, supra, which declared provisions of the Civil Rights Act of 1875 unconstitutional. We think that decision inapposite, and without precedential value in determining the constitutionality of the present Act. Unlike Title II of the present legislation, the 1875 Act broadly proscribed discrimination in "inns, public conveyances on land or water, theaters, and other public places of amusement," without limiting the categories of affected businesses to those impinging upon interstate commerce. In contrast, the applicability of Title II is carefully limited to enterprises having a direct and substantial relation to the interstate flow of goods and people, except where state action is involved. Further, the fact that certain kinds of businesses may not in 1875 have been sufficiently involved in interstate commerce to warrant bringing them within the ambit of the commerce power is not necessarily dispositive of the same question today. Our populace had not reached its present mobility, nor were facilities, goods and services circulating as readily in interstate commerce as they are today. Although the principles which we apply today are those first formulated by Chief Justice Marshall in *Gibbons* v. *Ogden* . . . , the conditions of transportation and commerce have changed dramatically, and we must apply those principles to the present state of commerce. The sheer increase in volume of interstate traffic alone would give discriminatory practices which inhibit travel a far larger impact upon the Nation's commerce than such practices had in the economy of another day. . . .

While the Act as adopted carried no congressional findings the record of its passage through each house is replete with evidence of the burdens that discrimination by race or color places upon interstate commerce. . . . This testimony included the fact that our people have become increasingly mobile with millions of people of all races traveling from State to State; that Negroes in particular have been the subject of discrimination in transient accommodations, having to travel great distances to secure the same; that often they have been unable to obtain accommodations and have had to call upon friends to put them up overnight . . . ; and that these conditions have become so acute as to require the listing of available lodging for Negroes in a special guidebook which was itself "dramatic testimony to the difficulties" Negroes encounter in travel. . . . These exclusionary practices were found to be nationwide, the Under Secretary of Commerce testifying that there is "no question that this discrimination in the North still exists to a large degree" and in the West and Midwest as well. . . . This testimony indicated a qualitative as well as quantitive effect on interstate travel by Negroes. The former was the obvious impairment of the Negro traveler's pleasure and convenience that resulted when he continually was uncertain of finding lodging. As for the latter, there was evidence that this uncertainty stemming from racial discrimination had the effect of discouraging travel on the part of a substantial portion of the Negro community. . . . This was the conclusion not only of the Under Secretary of Commerce but also of the Administrator of the Federal Aviation who wrote the Chairman of the Senate Commerce Committee that it was his "belief that air commerce is adversely affected by the denial to a substantial segment of the traveling public of adequate and desegregated public accommodations." . . . We shall not burden this opinion with further details since the voluminous testimony presents overwhelming evidence that discrimination by hotels and motels impedes interstate travel.

The power of Congress to deal with these obstructions depends on the meaning of the Commerce Clause. Its meaning was first enunciated 140 years ago by the great Chief Justice Marshall in *Gibbons* v. *Ogden*. . . . The determinative test of the exercise of power by the Congress under the Commerce Clause is simply whether the activity sought to be regulated is "commerce which concerns more States than one" and has a real and substantial relation to the national interest. Let us now turn to this facet of the problem.

That the "intercourse" of which the Chief Justice spoke included the movement of persons through more States than one was settled as early as 1849, in the Passenger Cases . . . where Mr. Justice McLean stated: "That the transportation of passengers is a part of commerce is not now an open question." . . .

The same interest in protecting interstate commerce which led Congress to deal with segregation in interstate carriers and the white slave traffic has prompted it to extend the exercise of its power to gambling . . . to deceptive practices in the sale of products . . . to wages and hours . . . to crop control . . . .

That Congress was legislating against moral wrongs in many of these areas rendered its enactments no less valid. In framing Title II of this Act Congress was also dealing with what it considered a moral problem. But that fact does not detract from the overwhelming evidence of the disruptive effect that racial discrimination has had on commercial intercourse. It was this burden which empowered Congress to enact appropriate legislation, and, given this basis for the exercise of its power, Congress was not restricted by the fact that the particular obstruction to interstate commerce with which it was dealing was also deemed a moral and social wrong.

It is said that the operation of the motel here is of a purely local character. But, assuming this to be true, "[i]f it is interstate commerce that feels the pinch, it does not matter how local the operation which applies the squeeze." . . . As Chief Justice Stone put it in *United States* v. *Darby.*

"The power of Congress over interstate commerce is not confined to the regulation of commerce among the states. It extends to those activities intrastate which so affect interstate commerce or the exercise of the power of Congress over it as to make regulation of them appropriate means to the attainment of a legitimate end, the exercise of the granted power of Congress to regulate interstate commerce. . . ."

Thus the power of Congress to promote interstate commerce also includes the power to regulate the local incidents thereof, including local activities in both the States of origin and destination, which might have a substantial and harmful effect upon that commerce. One need only examine the evidence which we have discussed above to see that Congress may—as it has—prohibit racial discrimination by motels serving travelers, however "local" their operations may appear . . .

We, therefore, conclude that the action of the Congress in the adoption of the Act as applied here to a motel which concededly serves interstate travelers is within the power granted it by the Commerce Clause of the Constitution, as interpreted by this Court for 140 years. It may be argued that Congress could have pursued other methods to eliminate the obstructions it found in interstate commerce caused by racial discrimination. But this is a matter of policy that rests entirely with the Congress not with the courts. How obstructions in commerce may be removed—what means are to be employed—is within the sound and exclusive discretion of the Congress. It is subject only to one caveat—that the means chosen by it must be reasonably adapted to the end permitted by the Constitution. We cannot say that its choice here was not so adapted. The Constitution requires no more.

Affirmed.

JUSTICES BLACK, DOUGLAS, and GOLDBERG concurred.

SOUTH CAROLINA *v.* KATZENBACK
383 U.S. 301; 86 Sup. Ct. 803; 15 L. Ed. 2d 769 (1966)

MR. CHIEF JUSTICE WARREN delivered the opinion of the Court:

By leave of the Court, South Carolina has filed a bill of complaint, seeking a declaration that selected provisions of the Voting Rights Act of 1965 violate the Federal Constitution, and asking for an injunction against enforcement of these provisions by the Attorney General. Original jurisdiction is founded on the presence of a controversy between a State and a citizen of another State under Art III, §2, of the Constitution. . . .

The Voting Rights Act was designed by Congress to banish the blight of racial discrimination in voting, which has infected the electoral process in parts of our country for nearly a century. The Act creates stringent new remedies for voting discrimination where it persists on a pervasive scale, and in addition the statute strengthens existing remedies for pockets of voting discrimination elsewhere in the country. Congress assumed the power to prescribe these remedies from §2 of the Fifteenth Amendment, which authorizes the national legislature to effectuate by "appropriate" measures the constitutional prohibition against racial discrimination in voting. We hold that the sections of the Act which are properly before us are an appropriate means for carrying out Congress' constitutional responsibilities and are consonant with all other provisions of the Constitution. We therefore deny South Carolina's request that enforcement of these sections of the Act be enjoined.

The constitutional propriety of the Voting Rights Act of 1965 must be judged with reference to the historical experience which it reflects. Before enacting the measure, Congress explored with great care the problem of racial discrimination in voting. . . .

In recent years, Congress has repeatedly tried to cope with the problem by facilitating case-by-case litigation against voting discrimination. The Civil Rights Act of 1957 authorized the Attorney General to seek injunctions against public and private interference with the right to vote on racial grounds. Perfecting amendments in the Civil Rights Act of 1960 permitted the joinder of States as party defendants, gave the Attorney General access to local voting records, and authorized courts to register voters in areas of systematic discrimination. Title I of the Civil Rights Act of 1964 expedited the hearing of voting cases before three-judge courts and outlawed some of the tactics used to disqualify Negroes from voting in federal elections.

Despite the earnest efforts of the Justice Department and of many federal judges, these new laws have done little to cure the problem of voting discrimination. According to estimates by the Attorney General during hearings on the Act, registration of voting age Negroes in Alabama rose only from 10.2 per cent to 19.4 per cent between 1958 and 1964; in Louisiana it barely inched ahead from 31.7 per cent to 31.8 per cent between 1956 and 1965; and in Mississippi it increased only from 4.4 per cent to 6.4 per cent between 1954 and 1964. In each instance, registration of voting age whites ran roughly fifty percentage points or more ahead of Negro registration.

The previous legislation has proved ineffective for a number of reasons. Voting suits are unusually onerous to prepare, sometimes requiring as many as 6000 man-hours spent combing through registration records in preparation for trial. Litigation has been exceedingly slow, in part because of the ample opportunities for delay afforded voting officials and others involved in the proceedings. Even when favorable decisions have finally been obtained, some of the States affected have merely switched to discriminatory devices not covered by the federal decrees or have enacted difficult new tests designed to prolong the existing disparity between white and Negro registration. Alternatively, certain local officials have defied and evaded court orders or have simply closed their registration offices to freeze the voting rolls. The provision of the 1960 law authorizing registration by federal officers has had little impact on local maladministration because of its procedural complexities. . . .

The Voting Rights Act of 1965 reflects Congress' firm intention to rid the country of racial discrimination in voting. The heart of the Act is a complex scheme of stringent remedies aimed at areas where voting discrimination has been most flagrant. . . .

At the outset, we emphasize that only some of the many portions of the Act are properly before us. . . .

These provisions of the Voting Rights Act of 1965 are challenged on the fundamental ground that they exceed the powers of Congress and encroach on an area reserved to the States by the Constitution. . . .

Has Congress exercised its powers under the Fifteenth Amendment in an appropriate manner with relation to the States?

The ground rules for resolving this question are clear. The language and purpose of the Fifteenth Amendment, the prior decisions construing its several provisions, and the general doctrines of constitutional interpretation, all point to one fundamental principle. As against the reserved powers of the States, Congress may use any rational means to effectuate the constitutional prohibition of racial discrimination in voting. Cf. our rulings last Term, sustaining Title II of the Civil Rights Act of 1964, in *Heart of Atlanta Motel* v. *United States,* and *Katzenbach* v. *McClung*. . . . We turn now to a more detailed description of the standards which govern our review of the Act.

Section 1 of the Fifteenth Amendment declares that "the right of citizens of the United States to vote shall not be denied or abridged by the United States or by any State on account of race, color, or previous condition of servitude." This declaration has always been treated as self-executing and has repeatedly been construed, without further legislative specification, to invalidate state voting qualifications or procedures which are discriminatory on their face or in practice. . . . The gist of the matter is that the Fifteenth Amendment supersedes contrary exertions of state power. . . .

South Carolina contends that the cases cited above are precedents only for the authority of the judiciary to strike down state statutes and procedures—that to allow an exercise of this authority by Congress would be to rob the courts of their rightful constitutional role. On the contrary, §2 of the Fifteenth Amendment expressly declares that "Congress shall have the power to enforce this article by appropriate legislation." By adding this authorization, the Framers indicated that Congress was to be chiefly responsible for implementing the rights created in §1. . . .

Congress has repeatedly exercised these powers in the past, and its enactments have repeatedly been upheld. For recent examples, see the Civil Rights Act of 1957, which was sustained in *United States* v. *Raines,* 362 U.S. 17. . . .

The basic test to be applied in a case

involving §2 of the Fifteenth Amendment is the same as in all cases concerning the express powers of Congress with relation to the reserved powers of the States. Chief Justice Marshall laid down the classic formulation, fifty years before the Fifteenth Amendment was ratified:

"Let the end be legitimate, let it be within the scope of the constitution, and all means which are appropriate, which are plainly adapted to that end, which are not prohibited, but consist with the letter and spirit of the constitution, are constitutional." *McCulloch* v. *Maryland.* . . .

We therefore reject South Carolina's argument that Congress may appropriately do no more than to forbid violations of the Fifteenth Amendment in general terms—that the task of fashioning specific remedies or of applying them to particular localities must necessarily be left entirely to the courts. Congress is not circumscribed by any such artificial rules under §2 of the Fifteenth Amendment. In the oft-repeated words of Chief Justice Marshall, referring to another specific legislative authorization in the Constitution, "This power, like all others vested in Congress, is complete in itself, may be exercised to its utmost extent, and acknowledges no limitations, other than are prescribed in the constitution." *Gibbons* v. *Ogden.*

Congress exercised its authority under the Fifteenth Amendment in an inventive manner when it enacted the Voting Rights Act of 1965. First: The measure prescribes remedies for voting discrimination which go into effect without any need for prior adjudication. This was clearly a legitimate response to the problem, for which there is ample precedent under other constitutional provisions. . . . Congress had found that case-by-case litigation was inadequate to combat widespread and persistent discrimination in voting, because of the inordinate amount of time and energy required to overcome the obstructionist tactics invariably encountered in these lawsuits. After enduring nearly a century of systematic resistance to the Fifteenth Amendment, Congress might well decide to shift the advantage of time and inertia from the perpetrators of the evil to its victims. The question remains, of course, whether the specific remedies prescribed in the Act were an appropriate means of combating the evil, and to this question we shall presently address ourselves.

Second: The Act intentionally confines these remedies to a small number of States and political subdivisions which in most instances were familiar to Congress by name. This, too, was a permissible method of dealing with the problem. Congress had learned that substantial voting discrimination presently occurs in certain sections of the country, and it knew no way of accurately forecasting whether the evil might spread elsewhere in the future. In acceptable legislative fashion, Congress chose to limit its attention to the geographic areas where immediate action seemed necessary. . . . The doctrine of the equality of States, invoked by South Carolina, does not bar this approach, for that doctrine applies only to the terms upon which States are admitted to the Union, and not to the remedies for local evils which have subsequently appeared. . . .

We now consider the related question of whether the specific States and political subdivisions within §4 (b) of the Act were an appropriate target for the new remedies. Congress began work with reliable evidence of actual voting discrimination in a great majority of the States and political subdivisions affected by the new remedies of the Act. The formula eventually evolved to describe these areas was relevant to the problem of voting discrimination. . . . It was therefore permissible to impose the new remedies on the few remaining States and political subdivisions covered by the formula, at least in the absence of proof that they have been free of substantial voting discrimination in recent years. . . .

It is irrelevant that the coverage formula excludes certain localities which do not employ voting tests and devices but for which there is evidence of voting discrimination by other means. Congress had learned that widespread and persistent discrimination in voting during recent years has typically entailed the misuse of tests and devices, and this was the evil for which the new remedies were specifically designed. . . . Legislation need not deal with all phases of a problem in the same way, so long as the distinctions drawn have some basis in practical experience. . . . There are no States or political subdivisions exempted from coverage under §4 (b) in which the record reveals recent racial discrimination involving tests and devices. This fact confirms the rationality of the formula. . . .

We now arrive at consideration of the specific remedies prescribed by the Act for areas included within the coverage formula. South Carolina assails the temporary suspension of existing voting qualifications. . . . The record shows that in most of the States covered by the Act, including South Carolina, various tests and devices have been instituted with the purpose of disenfranchising Negroes, have been framed in such a way as to facilitate this aim, and have been administered in a discriminatory fashion for many years. Under these circumstances, the Fifteenth Amendment has clearly been violated. . . .

The Act suspends literacy tests and similar devices for a period of five years from the last occurrence of substantial voting discrimination. This was a legitimate response to the problem, for which there is ample precedent in Fifteenth Amendment cases. . . .

The Act suspends new voting regulations pending scrutiny by federal authorities to determine whether their use would violate the Fifteenth Amendment. This may have been an uncommon exercise of congressional power, as South Carolina contends, but the Court has recognized that exceptional conditions can justify legislative measures not otherwise appropriate. . . . Congress knew that some of the States covered by §4 (b) of the Act had resorted to the extraordinary stratagem of contriving new rules of various kinds for the sole purpose of perpetuating voting discrimination in the face of adverse federal decrees. Congress had reason to suppose that these States might try similar maneuvers in the future, in order to evade the remedies for voting discrimination contained in the Act itself. Under the compulsion of these unique circumstances, Congress responded in a permissibly decisive manner. . . .

The Act authorizes the appointment of federal examiners to list qualified applicants who are thereafter entitled to vote, subject to an expeditious challenge procedure. This was clearly an appropriate response to the problem, closely related to remedies authorized in the prior cases. . . . In many of the political subdivisions covered by §4(b) of the Act, voting officials have persistently employed a variety of procedural tactics to deny Negroes the franchise, often in direct defiance or evasion of federal decrees. Congress realized that merely to suspend voting rules which have been misused or are subject to misuse might leave this localized evil undisturbed. As for the briskness of the challenge procedure,

Congress knew that in some of the areas affected, challenges had been persistently employed to harass registered Negroes. It chose to forestall this abuse, at the same time providing alternative ways for removing persons listed through error or fraud. . . .

After enduring nearly a century of widespread resistance to the Fifteenth Amendment, Congress has marshalled an array of potent weapons against the evil, with authority in the Attorney General to employ them effectively. Many of the areas directly affected by this development have indicated their willingness to abide by any restraints legitimately imposed upon them. We here hold that the portions of the Voting Rights Act properly before us are a valid means for carrying out the commands of the Fifteenth Amendment. Hopefully, millions of non-white Americans will now be able to participate for the first time on an equal basis in the government under which they live. We may finally look forward to the day when truly "the right of citizens of the United States to vote shall not be denied or abridged by the United States or by any State on account of race, color, or previous condition of servitude."

The bill of complaint is dismissed.

MR. JUSTICE BLACK concurred except as to the validity of §5.

SHAPIRO v. THOMPSON
89 Sup. Ct. 1322 (1969)

[*This case involved challenges to welfare requirements in three states. Only the facts behind one of these challenges are included in the excerpt from the Court opinion provided here.*]

MR. JUSTICE BRENNAN delivered the opinion of the Court:

In No. 9, the Connecticut Welfare Department involked §17–2d of the Connecticut General Statutes to deny the application of appellee Vivian Marie Thompson for assistance under the program for Aid to Families with Dependent Children (AFDC). She was a 19-year-old unwed mother of one child and pregnant with her second child when she changed her residence in June 1966 from Dorchester, Massachusetts, to Hartford, Connecticut, to live with her mother, a Hartford resident. She moved to her own apartment in Hartford in August 1966, when her mother was no longer able to support her and her infant son. Because of her pregnancy, she was unable to work or enter a work training program. Her application for AFDC assistance, filed in August, was denied in November solely on the ground that, as required by §17–2d, she had not lived in the State for a year before her application was filed. . . .

There is no dispute that the effect of the waiting-period requirement in each case is to create two classes of needy resident families indistinguishable from each other except that one is composed of residents who have resided a year or more, and the second of residents who have resided less than a year, in the jurisdiction. On the basis of this sole difference the first class is granted and the second class is denied welfare aid upon which may depend the ability of the families to obtain the very means to subsist—food, shelter, and other necessities of life. In each case, the District Court found that appellees met the test for residence in their jurisdictions, as well as all other eligibility requirements except the requirement of residence for a full year prior to their applications. On reargument, appellees' central contention is that the statutory prohibition of benefits to residents of less than a year creates a classification which constitutes an invidious discrimination denying them equal protection of the laws. We agree. The interests which appellants assert are promoted by the classification either may not constitutionally be promoted by government or are not compelling governmental interests.

Primarily, appellants justify the waiting-period requirement as a protective device to preserve the fiscal integrity of state public assistance programs. It is asserted that people who require welfare assistance during their first year of residence in a State are likely to become continuing burdens on state welfare programs. Therefore, the argument runs, if such people can be deterred from entering the jurisdiction by denying them welfare benefits during the first year, state programs to assist long-time residents will not be impaired by a substantial influx of indigent newcomers.

There is weighty evidence that exclusion from the jurisdiction of the poor who need or may need relief was the specific objective of these provisions. In the Congress, sponsors of federal legislation to eliminate all residence requirements have been consistently opposed by representatives of state and local welfare agencies who have stressed the fears of the States that elimination of the requirements would result in a heavy influx of individuals into States providing the most generous benefits. . . .

We do not doubt that the one-year waiting period device is well suited to discourage the influx of poor families in need of assistance. An indigent who desires to migrate, resettle, find a new job, start a new life will doubtless hesitate if he knows that he must risk making the move without the possibility of falling back on state welfare assistance during his first year of residence, when his need may be most acute. But the purpose of inhibiting migration by needy persons into the State is constitutionally impermissible.

This Court long ago recognized that the nature of our Federal Union and our constitutional concepts of personal liberty unite to require that all citizens be free to travel throughout the length and breadth of our land uninhibited by statutes, rules, or regulations which unreasonably burden or restrict this movement. That proposition was early stated by Chief Justice Taney in the Passenger Cases:

> "For all the great purposes for which the Federal government was formed, we are one people, with one common country. We are all citizens of the United States; and, as members of the same community, must have the right to pass and repass through every part of it without interruption, as freely as in our own States."

We have no occasion to ascribe the source of this right to travel interstate to a particular constitutional provision. It suffices that, as Mr. Justice Stewart said for the Court in *United States* v. *Guest:*

> "The constitutional right to travel from one State to another . . . occupies a position fundamental to the concept of our Federal Union. It is a right that has been firmly established and repeatedly recognized.
>
> "[The] right finds no explicit mention in the Constitution. The reason, it has been suggested, is that a right so elementary was conceived from the beginning to be a necessary con-

comitant of the stronger Union the Constitution created. In any event, freedom to travel throughout the United States has long been recognized as a basic right under the Constitution."

Thus, the purpose of deterring the in-migration of indigents cannot serve as justification for the classification created by the one-year waiting period, since that purpose is constitutionally impermissible. If a law has "no other purpose . . . than to chill the assertion of constitutional rights by penalizing those who choose to exercise them, then it [is] patently unconstitutional." *United States* v. *Jackson.*

Alternatively, appellants argue that even if it is impermissible for a State to attempt to deter the entry of all indigents, the challenged classification may be justified as a permissible state attempt to discourage those indigents who would enter the State solely to obtain larger benefits. We observe first that none of the statutes before us is tailored to serve that objective. Rather, the class of barred newcomers is all-inclusive, lumping the great majority who come to the State for other purposes with those who come for the sole purpose of collecting higher benefits. In actual operation, therefore, the three statutes enact what in effect are nonrebuttable presumptions that every applicant for assistance in his first year of residence came to the jurisdiction solely to obtain higher benefits. Nothing whatever in any of these records supplies any basis in fact for such a presumption.

More fundamentally, a State may no more try to fence out those indigents who seek higher welfare benefits than it may try to fence out indigents generally. Implicit in any such distinction is the notion that indigents who enter a State with the hope of securing higher welfare benefits are somehow less deserving than indigents who do not take this consideration into account. But we do not perceive why a mother who is seeking to make a new life for herself and her children should be regarded as less deserving because she considers, among other factors, the level of a State's public assistance. Surely such a mother is no less deserving than a mother who moves into a particular State in order to take advantage of its better educational facilities.

Appellants argue further that the challenged classification may be sustained as an attempt to distinguish between new and old residents on the basis of the contribution they have made to the community through the payment of taxes. . . . Appellants' reasoning would logically permit the State to bar new residents from schools, parks, and libraries or deprive them of police and fire protection. Indeed it would permit the State to apportion all benefits and services according to the past tax contributions of its citizens. The Equal Protection Clause prohibits such an apportionment of state services.

We recognize that a State has a valid interest in preserving the fiscal integrity of its programs. It may legitimately attempt to limit its expenditures, whether for public assistance, public education, or any other program. But a State may not accomplish such a purpose by invidious distinctions between classes of its citizens. It could not, for example, reduce expenditures for education by barring indigent children from its schools. Similarly, in the cases before us, appellants must do more than show that denying welfare benefits to new residents saves money. The saving of welfare costs cannot be an independent ground for an invidious classification.

In sum, neither deterrence of indigents from migrating to the State nor limitation of welfare benefits to those regarded as contributing to the State is a constitutionally permissible state objective. . . .

MR. JUSTICE STEWART, concurring.

In joining the opinion of the Court, I add a word in response to the dissent of my Brother HARLAN, who, I think, has quite misapprehended what the Court's opinion says.

The Court today does *not* "pick out particular human activities, characterize them as 'fundamental,' and give them added protection . . . ." To the contrary, the Court simply recognizes, as it must, an established constitutional right, and gives to that right no less protection than the Constitution itself demands.

"The constitutional right to travel from one State to another . . . has been firmly established and repeatedly recognized." *United States* v. *Guest.* . . . This constitutional right, which, of course, includes the right of "entering and abiding in any state in the Union" . . . is *not* a mere conditional liberty subject to regulation and control under conventional due process or equal protection standards. "[T]he right to travel freely from State to State finds constitutional protection that is quite independent of the Fourteenth Amendment." *United States* v. *Guest.* . . . As we made clear in *Guest,* it is a right broadly assertable against private interference as well as governmental action. Like the right of association, *NAACP* v. *Alabama,* . . . it is a virtually unconditional personal right, guaranteed by the Constitution to us all.

It follows, as the Court says, that "the purpose of deterring the in-migration of indigents cannot serve as justification for the classification created by the one-year waiting period, since that purpose is constitutionally impermissible." And it further follows, as the Court says, that any *other* purposes

offered in support of a law that so clearly impinges upon the constitutional right of interstate travel must be shown to reflect a *compelling* governmental interest. This is necessarily true whether the impinging law be a classification statute to be tested against the Equal Protection Clause, or a state or federal regulatory law, to be tested against the Due Process Clause of the Fourteenth or Fifth Amendment. As Mr. Justice Harlan wrote for the Court more than a decade ago, "[T]o justify the deterrent effect . . . on the free exercise . . . of their constitutionally protected right . . . a 'subordinating interest of the State must be compelling.'" *NAACP* v. *Alabama.* . . .

The Court today, therefore, is not "contriving new constitutional principles." It is deciding these cases under the aegis of established constitutional law.

MR. CHIEF JUSTICE WARREN, with whom MR. JUSTICE BLACK joins, dissented.

MR. JUSTICE HARLAN, dissenting.

The Court today holds unconstitutional Connecticut, Pennsylvania, and District of Columbia statutes which restrict certain kinds of welfare benefits to persons who have lived within the jurisdiction for at least one year immediately preceding their applications. The Court has accomplished this result by an expansion of the comparatively new constitutional doctrine that some state statutes will be deemed to deny equal protection of the laws unless justified by a "compelling" governmental interest, and by holding that the Fifth Amendment's Due Process Clause imposes a similar limitation on federal enactments. Having decided that the "compelling interest" principle is applicable, the Court then finds that the governmental interests here asserted are either wholly impermissible or are not "compelling." For reasons which follow, I disagree both with the Court's result and with its reasoning. . . .

The "compelling interest" doctrine, which today is articulated more explicitly than ever before, constitutes an increasingly significant exception to the long-established rule that a statute does not deny equal protection if it is rationally related to a legitimate governmental objective. The "compelling interest" doctrine has two branches. The branch which requires that classifications based upon "suspect" criteria be supported by a compelling interest apparently had its genesis in cases involving racial classifications, which have at least since *Korematsu* v. *United States.* . . . been regarded as inherently "suspect." The criterion of "wealth" apparently was added to the list of "suspects" as an alternative justification for the rationale in *Harper* v. *Virginia Bd. of Elections* . . . in which Virginia's poll tax was struck down. The criterion of political allegiance may have been added in *Williams* v. *Rhodes.* . . . Today the list apparently has been further enlarged to include classifications based upon recent interstate movement, and perhaps those based upon the exercise of *any* constitutional right, for the Court states *ante* . . . :

> "The waiting-period provision denies welfare benefits to otherwise eligible applicants solely because they have recently moved into the jurisdiction. But in moving . . . appellees were exercising a constitutional right, and any classification which serves to penalize the exercise of that right, unless shown to be necessary to promote a *compelling* governmental interest, is unconstitutional."

I think that this branch of the "compelling interest" doctrine is sound when applied to racial classifications, for historically the Equal Protection Clause was largely a product of the desire to eradicate legal distinctions founded upon race. However, I believe that the more recent extensions have been unwise. For the reasons stated in my dissenting opinion in *Harper* v. *Virginia Bd. of Elections* . . . I do not consider wealth a "suspect" statutory criterion. And when, as in *Williams* v. *Rhodes,* and the present case, a classification is based upon the exercise of rights guaranteed against state infringement by the federal Constitution, then there is no need for any resort to the Equal Protection Clause; in such instances, this Court may properly and straightforwardly invalidate any undue burden upon those rights under the Fourteenth Amendment's Due Process Clause. . . .

The second branch of the "compelling interest" principle is even more troublesome. For it has been held that a statutory classification is subject to the "compelling interest" test if the result of the classification may be to affect a "fundamental right," regardless of the basis of the classification. This rule was fore-shadowed in *Skinner* v. *Oklahoma* . . . in which an Oklahoma statute providing for compulsory sterilization of "habitual criminals" was held subject to "strict scrutiny" mainly because it affected "one of the basic civil rights." After a long hiatus, the principle re-emerged in *Reynolds* v. *Sims* . . . in which state apportionment statutes were subjected to an unusually stringent test because "any alleged infringement of the right of citizens to vote must be carefully and meticulously scrutinized." . . . It has reappeared today in the Court's cryptic suggestion . . . that the "compelling interest" test is applicable merely because the result of the classification may be to deny the appellees "food, shelter, and other necessities of life," as well as in the Court's statement . . . that "[s]ince the classification here touches on the fundamental right of interstate movement, its constitutionality must be judged by the stricter standard of whether it promotes a *compelling* state interest."

I think this branch of the "compelling interest" doctrine particularly unfortunate and unnecessary. It is unfortunate because it creates an exception which threatens to swallow the standard equal protection rule. Virtually every state statute affects important rights. This Court has repeatedly held, for example, that the traditional equal protection standard is applicable to statutory classifications affecting such fundamental matters as the right to pursue a particular occupation, the right to receive greater or smaller wages or to work more or less hours, and the right to inherit property. Rights such as these are in principle indistinguishable from those involved here, and to extend the "compelling interest" rule to all cases in which such rights are affected would go far toward making this Court a "super-legislature." This branch of the doctrine is also unnecessary. When the right affected is one assured by the federal Constitution, any infringement can be dealt with under the Due Process Clause. But when a statute affects only matters not mentioned in the federal Constitution and is not arbitrary or irrational, I must reiterate that I know of nothing which entitles this Court to pick out particular human activities, characterize them as "fundamental," and give them added protection under an unusually stringent equal protection test.

I shall consider in the next section whether welfare residence requirements deny due process by unduly burdening the right of interstate travel. If the issue is regarded purely as one of equal protection, then for the reasons just set forth this nonracial classification should

be judged by ordinary equal protection standards. The applicable criteria are familiar and well-established. A legislative measure will be found to deny equal protection only if "it is without any reasonable basis, and therefore is purely arbitrary." . . .

For reasons hereafter set forth . . . a legislature might rationally find that the imposition of a welfare residence requirement would aid in the accomplishment of at least four valid governmental objectives. It might also find that residence requirements have advantages not shared by other methods of achieving the same goals. In light of this undeniable relation of residence requirements to valid legislative aims, it cannot be said that the requirements are "arbitrary" or "lacking in rational justification." Hence, I can find no objection to these residence requirements under the Equal Protection Clause of the Fourteenth Amendment or under the analogous standard embodied in the Due Process Clause of the Fifth Amendment.

The next issue, which I think requires fuller analysis than that deemed necessary by the Court under its equal protection rationale, is whether a one-year welfare residence requirement amounts to an undue burden upon the right of interstate travel. Four considerations are relevant: *First,* what is the constitutional source and nature of the right to travel which is relied upon? *Second,* what is the extent of the interference with that right? *Third,* what governmental interests are served by welfare residence requirements? *Fourth,* how should the balance of the competing considerations be struck? . . .

I conclude that the right to travel interstate is a "fundamental" right which, for present purposes, should be regarded as having its source in the Due Process Clause of the Fifth Amendment.

The next questions are: (1) To what extent does a one-year residence condition upon welfare eligibility interfere with this right to travel?; and (2) What are the governmental interests supporting such a condition? The consequence of the residence requirements is that persons who contemplate interstate changes of residence, and who believe that they otherwise would qualify for welfare payments, must take into account the fact that such assistance will not be available for a year after arrival. The number or proportion of persons who are actually deterred from changing residence by the existence of these provisions is unknown. If one accepts evidence put forward by the appellees, to the effect that there would be only a miniscule increase in the number of welfare applicants were existing residence requirements to be done away with, it follows that the requirements do not deter an appreciable number of persons from moving interstate.

Against this indirect impact on the right to travel must be set the interests of the States . . . in imposing residence conditions. There appear to be four such interests. First, it is evident that a primary concern of . . . the . . . Legislatures was to deny welfare benefits to persons who moved into the jurisdiction primarily in order to collect those benefits. This seems to me an entirely legitimate objective. A legislature is certainly not obliged to furnish welfare assistance to every inhabitant of the jurisdiction, and it is entirely rational to deny benefits to those who enter primarily in order to receive them, since this will make more funds available for those whom the legislature deems more worthy of subsidy.

A second possible purpose of residence requirements is the prevention of fraud. A residence requirement provides an objective and workable means of determining that an applicant intends to remain indefinitely within the jurisdiction. It therefore may aid in eliminating fraudulent collection of benefits by nonresidents and persons already receiving assistance in other States. There can be no doubt that prevention of fraud is a valid legislative goal. Third, the requirement of a fixed period of residence may help in predicting the budgetary amount which will be needed for public assistance in the future. While none of the appellant jurisdictions appears to keep data sufficient to permit the making of detailed budgetary predictions in consequence of the requirement, it is probable that in the event of a very large increase or decrease in the number of indigent newcomers the waiting period would give the legislature time to make needed adjustments in the welfare laws. Obviously, this is a proper objective. Fourth, the residence requirements conceivably may have been predicated upon a legislative desire to restrict welfare payments financed in part by state tax funds to persons who have recently made some contribution to the State's economy, through having been employed, having paid taxes, or having spent money in the State. This too would appear to be a legitimate purpose.

The next question is the decisive one: whether the governmental interests served by residence requirements outweigh the burden imposed upon the right to travel. In my view, a number of considerations militate in favor of constitutionality. First, as just shown, four separate, legitimate governmental interests are furthered by residence requirements. Second, the impact of the requirements upon the freedom of individuals to travel interstate is indirect and, according to evidence put forward by the appellees themselves, insubstantial. Third, these are not cases in which a State or States, acting alone, have attempted to interfere with the right of citizens to travel, . . . Fourth, the legislatures which enacted these statutes have been fully exposed to the arguments of the appellees as to why these residence requirements are unwise, and have rejected them. This is not, therefore, an instance in which legislatures have acted without mature deliberation.

Fifth, and of longer-range importance, the field of welfare assistance is one in which there is a widely recognized need for fresh solutions and consequently for experimentation. Invalidation of welfare residence requirements might have the unfortunate consequence of discouraging the Federal and State Governments from establishing unusually generous welfare programs in particular areas on an experimental basis, because of fears that the program would cause an influx of persons seeking higher welfare payments. Sixth and finally, a strong presumption of constitutionality attaches to statutes of the types now before us. Congressional enactments come to this Court with an extremely heavy presumption of validity. . . . A similar presumption of constitutionality attaches to state statutes, particularly when, as here, a State has acted upon a specific authorization from Congress. . . .

I conclude with the following observations. Today's decision, it seems to me, reflects to an unusual degree the current notion that this Court possesses a peculiar wisdom all its own whose capacity to lead this Nation out of its present troubles is contained only by the limits of judicial ingenuity in contriving new constitutional principles to meet each problem as it arises. For anyone who, like myself, believes that it is an essential function of this Court to maintain the constitutional division between state and federal authority and among the three branches of the Federal Government, today's decision is a step in the wrong direction. This resurgence of the expansive view of "equal protection" carries the seeds of more judicial interference with the state and federal legislative process, much more indeed than does the judicial application of "due process" according to traditional concepts. . . .

18
Criminal Procedure

The development of procedural safeguards for persons accused of crime is one of the most fascinating stories in the annals of Anglo-American law. "The long but ultimately successful struggle for procedural safeguards in criminal proceedings was an integral part of the long and ultimately successful struggle for constitutional democracy. These procedural safeguards rest upon two underlying assumptions of democracy, the integrity of the individual and government by law rather than men."[1] Today, when too many Americans look upon some of our most important procedural guaranties as mere technicalities that should be set aside or narrowed at the slightest provocation, we would do well to remember that these important rights were purchased at a very high price by many generations of men and women. "It took centuries to evolve the conception of the fair trial we have today. It was against a background poignant with memories of evil procedures that our Constitution was drawn."[2]

"It is not without significance that most of the provisions of the Bill of Rights are procedural. It is procedure that spells much of the difference between rule by law and rule by whim or caprice. Steadfast adherence to strict

[1] Leo Pfeffer, *The Liberties of an American,* (Boston: Beacon Press, 1956), p. 158. A readable account of the rights of Americans accused of crime is found in David Fellman, *The Defendant's Rights* (New York: Rinehart, 1958).

[2] William O. Douglas, *We the Judges* (Garden City, N.Y.: Doubleday, 1956), p. 379.

procedural safeguards is our main assurance that there will be equal justice under law."[3] And Justice Frankfurter has noted in an oft-quoted passage that "the history of American freedom is, in no small measure, the history of procedure."[4] We saw in Chapter 12 that Amendments Four through Eight were designed principally to afford procedural protections to persons accused of crime. In addition, remember that the original Constitution contains a few provisions relating to criminal procedure, such as those dealing with bills of attainder, ex post facto laws, and the writ of habeas corpus. Today these constitutional provisions form the basis for the protection of a person accused of crime from the time the evidence is secured and he is arrested until he is freed or punished for committing the illegal act. That present-day practices have evolved slowly over many years is made evident by simply noting the lack of procedural guaranties for persons accused of crime in early English history.[5]

The Bill of Rights and the Fourteenth Amendment

In our federal system, the administration of criminal justice is principally a function of the states. In this regard we should recall that the Fourteenth Amendment does not necessarily make *all* the procedural safeguards of the Bill of Rights applicable to the states. Justice Frankfurter noted in *Wolf* v. *Colorado,* 338 U.S. 25 (1949), that "the notion that the 'due process of law' guaranteed by the Fourteenth Amendment is shorthand for the first eight amendments of the Constitution and thereby incorporates them has been rejected by this Court again and again after impressive consideration." In *Palko* v. *Connecticut* (p. 665) Justice Cardozo undertook to draw a line between those portions of the Bill of Rights that are protected against state abridgment and those that are not so protected by classifying rights into essential and nonessential categories. Only the essential rights are protected. Thus, the states are left free to administer criminal justice without federal interference unless in so doing they offend some fundamental principle of justice.

In *Adamson* v. *California* (p. 667), the Court held, by a close 5-to-4 vote, that the due process clause does not require state courts to give accused persons the protection against self-incrimination as provided by the Fifth Amendment. In his long dissenting opinion, Justice Black argued that the Fourteenth Amendment was designed to make all the guaranties of the Bill of Rights applicable to the states. However, this view has never been openly accepted by a Court majority.

---

[3] Justice Douglas concurring in *Joint Anti-Fascist Refugee Committee* v. *McGrath,* 341 U.S. 123 (1951).

[4] *Malinski* v. *New York,* 324 U.S. 401 (1945).

[5] R. J. Tresolini, R. W. Taylor, and E. B. Barnett, "Arrest Without A Warrant: Extent and Social Implications," *Journal of Criminal Law, Criminology and Police Science,* Vol. 46 (July–August 1955), p. 187.

Since 1937, when the *Palko* case was decided, the Fourth Amendment guaranty against unreasonable searches and seizures has been added to the list of fundamental or essential rights. This was done in *Wolf* v. *Colorado,* where the Court stated that ". . . the security of one's privacy against arbitrary instrusion by the police—which is at the core of the Fourth Amendment—is basic to a free society. It is therefore implicit in 'the concept of ordered liberty' and as such enforceable against the States through the Due Process Clause. The knock at the door, whether by day or night, as a prelude to a search, without authority of law but solely on the authority of the police, did not need the commentary of recent history to be condemned as inconsistent with the conception of human rights enshrined in the history and the basic constitutional documents of English-speaking peoples. Accordingly, we have no hesitation in saying that were a State affirmatively to sanction such police incursion into privacy it would run counter to the guaranty of the Fourteenth Amendment." Despite this statement, however, the Court refused to hold that the due process clause of the Fourteenth Amendment required a state court to forbid the admission of evidence secured by unreasonable searches and seizures. However, in *Mapp* v. *Ohio* (p. 675) the Court overruled the *Wolf* case and held that a state's use of evidence secured by an unreasonable search and seizure violated due process of law. Thus, the Court took a giant step in setting standards in an important area of state criminal justice.

In *Robinson* v. *California,* 370 U.S. 660 (1962), the Eighth Amendment ban on cruel and unusual punishment was added to the list of essential rights protected by the Fourteenth Amendment. There the Court held that a state statute making it a crime for a person to "be addicted to the use of narcotics" inflicted cruel and unusual punishment under the Eighth and Fourteenth Amendments. In *Gideon* v. *Wainwright,* 372 U.S. 335 (1963), the Court added the Sixth Amendment right to counsel; in *Pointer* v. *Texas,* 380 U.S. 400 (1965), that amendment's right to confront and cross examine witnesses; in *Duncan* v. *Louisiana,* 391 U.S. 145 (1968), its right to jury trial.

In making these Bill of Rights requirements binding upon the states, the Court has continued to use the language of *Palko.* Therefore, it may be argued that technically the Court has not been "incorporating" the Bill of Rights into the due process clause of the Fourteenth Amendment, but only defining more and more rights as fundamental. Because in each instance the Court has held the states to exactly the same standards as the federal government, it makes little difference whether the language of incorporation or fundamental freedoms is used. All of the First; all of the Fourth; all of the Fifth except grand jury indictment; all of the Sixth except speedy and public trial, compulsory process, and nature and cause of accusation; and the Eighth, except excessive bail, have been declared binding on the states. It is now a fair guess that the Court will soon make all of these remaining clauses applicable except grand jury indictment. Thus, it may well be that in the end the only reason to maintain the *Palko* rule will be to avoid imposing the obsolete grand jury indictment system on the states. Indeed the Court has now over-ruled the specific holding in *Palko* itself and has found that the double jeopardy provisions of the Fifth are binding on the states. *Benton* v. *Maryland,* 89 S. Ct. 2056 (1969).

Searches and Seizures

The Fourth Amendment's prohibition against unreasonable searches and seizures is based on the ancient maxim that a man's house is his castle. This amendment was an outgrowth of the grievances of the American Colonists against the use of general search warrants, or "writs of assistance," which gave British revenue officers blanket authorization to search the houses of the Colonists for smuggled goods.

In general, the Fourth Amendment forbids police officers to search persons, houses, papers, and effects without a warrant issued by a proper judicial officer. However, there are some exceptions to this general rule: For example, as demonstrated by *United States* v. *Rabinowitz* (p. 682), a search may be made without a warrant as an incident to a lawful arrest. In addition, the Court has held that an automobile or other vehicle may be searched without a warrant if an officer has good reason to believe that an offense has been or is being committed.[6] The *Rabinowitz* and other recent decisions demonstrate clearly, however, that easy generalizations in this field are extremely dangerous, for it is difficult to formulate a precise rule that can be applied to each and every case. As a result, the law of searches and seizures is uncertain and extremely complex.[7] Currently, the Court seems to be placing great emphasis on the reasonableness of various kinds of searches in the context of the practical problems of policing a modern society. Thus, it has approved "frisks" necessary to the protection of interrogating officers but not general searches based on mere suspicion. Cf. *Terry* v. *Ohio,* 392 U.S. 1 (1968), with *Sibron* v. *New York,* 392 U.S. 40 (1968). While requiring a warrant for "administrative" searches to enforce health and safety codes, it has written far less rigorous standards of probable cause in this area than in criminal law searches. *Camara* v. *Municipal Court,* 387 U.S. 523 (1967). In criminal law, however, it has now indicated that it may closely examine whether, before issuing a warrant, the local magistrate actually has been presented with sufficient evidence to justify a finding of "probable cause" as required by the Fourth Amendment. *Spinelli* v. *United States,* 89 Sup. Ct. 584 (1969).

The Court has subsumed fingerprints, blood tests and line ups under the search and seizure provisions of the Fourth Amendment rather than the self-incrimination provisions of the Fifth. If it had treated these sources of in-

---

[6] *Carroll* v. *United States,* 267 U.S. 132 (1925).

[7] An attempt to present the issues systematically with illustrative citations may be found in Martin Shapiro (ed.), *The Supreme Court and Constitutional Rights* (Chicago: Scott, Foresman, 1967). pp. 176ff.

crimination from one's own body as self-incrimination, the state might have been forbidden to offer evidence from these sources at trial except with the accused's permission. On the other hand, it has made clear that it will enforce standards of reasonableness over searches that take the form of fingerprinting, line up identification etc. *Davis* v. *Mississippi,* 89 Sup. Ct. 1394 (1969). *Schmerber* v. *California,* 384 U.S. 757 (1966). *Foster* v. *California,* 89 Sup. Ct. 1127 (1969).

For many years the Court held to the rule that a search warrant would not issue for "mere evidence" of a crime, but only where the police could show they were seeking for contraband such as the loot from a robbery. At the same time the Court allowed officers to conduct very wide ranging searches without a search warrant in the course of making a lawful arrest. In *Warden* v. *Hayden,* 387 U.S. 294 (1967) the Court finally eliminated the mere evidence rule, making it much easier for police to obtain a warrant. But in *Chimel* v. *California* (p. 716), the Court more carefully limited the scope of police searches without a warrant.

One of the liveliest debates in the field of criminal procedure in recent years has been provoked by the increasingly wide use of wiretaps by public officials to secure convictions of persons accused of crime. In fact, wiretapping is commonly practiced by both police officers and private individuals to secure information about almost every troubled area of American life. Regardless of its form, wiretapping ". . . creates a basic American conflict. On one side are the ideals of freedom and individual privacy, on the other the arguments favoring the use of modern techniques to fight crime and to protect national security. Somewhere a line of demarcation must be drawn."[8]

The fundamental problems raised by wiretapping are best presented in the classic case of *Olmstead* v. *United States* (p. 686). In that case, a deeply divided Court held that wiretapping did not violate the unreasonable search and seizure clause of the Fourth Amendment. Particular note should be made of the dissenting opinions of Justice Holmes and Brandeis, to be reproduced here, as they state the arguments against wiretapping in eloquent terms that have not been surpassed to this day. The *Olmstead* case also reveals clearly the close relationship between unreasonable searches and seizures and the self-incrimination clause of the Fifth Amendment.

A provision inserted in the Federal Communications Act of 1934 was designed to outlaw wiretapping by federal officers. In *Nardone* v. *United States,* 302 U.S. 379 (1937), the Court held that Section 605 of the Federal Communications Act forbade wiretapping by federal officers and other persons and that evidence obtained by wiretapping was not admissible in federal courts. Nardone and his associates were subsequently tried a second time and convicted again. The wiretap evidence was not used directly in the second

---

[8] W. S. Fairfield and Charles Clift, "The Wiretappers," *The Reporter* (December 23, 1952), p. 9. This is one of the best articles on wiretapping. Part II of the article appeared in the January 6, 1953, issue of *The Reporter,* pp. 9–20. In general, see Alan F. Westin, *Privacy and Freedom* (New York: Atheneum, 1967).

trial, but much of the evidence against Nardone had been obtained from "leads" developed by wiretapping. The Court again reversed the convictions in *United States* v. *Nardone,* 308 U.S. 338 (1939). The evidence used at the second trial was termed "fruit of the poisonous tree," which was as inadmissible in court as *direct* wiretap evidence. This "fruit of the tree" doctrine is now applied to all illegal searches.

Subsequent to *Nardone,* the Court held that electronically gathered evidence was inadmissable where trespass was involved, but not otherwise. [*Silverman* v. *United States,* 365 U.S. 505 (1961); *Berger* v. *New York,* 388 U.S. 41 (1967).] One of the cases establishing the trespass doctrine, *On Lee* v. *United States,* 343 U.S. 747 (1952), raised the particularly difficult problem of the use of informers in preparing prosecutions. Not only may informers wired for sound pose a threat of unreasonable search, but their employment raises serious questions of self-incrimination and right to counsel. *Hoffa* v. *United States* (p. 711) illustrates the interconnection of these problems. *Katz* v. *United States* (p. 714) reviews and revises the Court's earlier electronic surveillance decisions.

Self-incrimination

The Fifth Amendment contains a number of provisions for the protection of persons accused of crime. One of the most important of these protections is found in the clause that "no person . . . shall be compelled in any criminal case to be a witness against himself." This concept grew out of the protests against the inquisitorial methods of English ecclesiastical courts and the Court of Star Chamber, which tortured persons accused of heresy or treason to obtain confessions. By the latter half of the seventeenth century, the privilege against self-incrimination was well established in English law and subsequently adopted in the United States. Today this right is embodied in the laws or constitutions of every state as well as in the Fifth Amendment.

Although the Fifth Amendment states that the privilege against self-incrimination applies to criminal cases alone, it may be invoked before any official body that has the power to compel testimony under oath. Thus, the protection may be invoked before a grand jury, a legislative committee, or a coroner's inquest. In recent years, the attention of the public has been dramatically focused on the privilege against self-incrimination, because it has been used frequently by witnesses before congressional committees. One writer noted, in 1953, that "hardly a day goes by, in the course of investigations into subversive activity, organized crime, political skulduggery and whatnot, but that a witness refuses to answer questions on the ground that he may incriminate himself."[9] This caused many people to question the wisdom of the privilege against self-incrimination. Much of the public hostility toward

[9] Noel T. Dowling, "I Stand on the Fifth Amendment," *The New York Times Magazine* (May 17, 1953), p. 10.

this privilege emerged while anti-Communist sentiment in the United States was at its peak in the early 1950s. As a result, many reluctant witnesses have been termed Fifth Amendment Communists and have suffered severe social and economic penalties for exercising this fundamental constitutional right. During this period, however, the self-incrimination clause also had eloquent defenders. One scholar has argued ably that "the privilege against self-incrimination is one of the great landmarks in man's struggle to make himself civilized. It is an expression of one of the fundamental decencies in the relation we have developed between government and man."[10]

The Supreme Court has sustained the right of individuals to invoke the privilege against self-incrimination before congressional committees in a number of cases. Most important, in the key case of *Malloy* v. *Hogan* (p. 692), the Court reconsidered a number of prior decisions and held that the privilege against self-incrimination is safeguarded against state action by the Fourteenth Amendment. In *Blau* v. *United States,* 340 U.S. 159 (1950), the Court ruled that a witness may refuse to answer questions before a grand jury about possible Communist connections, because he could reasonably fear that his testimony might result in a criminal prosecution under the Smith Act. A more difficult problem was presented by *Ullmann* v. *United States* (p. 723). There the Court upheld a federal immunity act that authorized congressional committees to grant immunity from criminal prosecution to witnesses who refused to testify in a proceeding involving national security. The Court has also held that where an immunity act may be applied, the witness may still exercise his privilege to refuse to answer unless he is assured against prosecution by both federal and state authorities, *Murphy* v. *Waterfront Commissioners* (p. 726).

Two weeks after the *Ullmann* case, the Court rendered another important decision in *Slochower* v. *Board of Higher Education,* 350 U.S. 551 (1956). In that case, Slochower, a professor of twenty-seven years' experience in a college (Brooklyn) operated by the city of New York, was dismissed summarily for invoking the self-incrimination clause in refusing to testify before a congressional committee about his past Communist party membership. Slochower's dismissal was based on a provision of the New York City charter that required the automatic removal of any city employee who utilized the privilege against self-incrimination in refusing to answer legally authorized questions. In a 5-to-4 opinion, the Court held that, as applied to Slochower, the municipal charter provision violated the due process clause of the Fourteenth Amendment. In the majority opinion, Justice Clark revealed clearly the Court's objection to terms, such as Fifth Amendment Communist, that imply that the assertion of the privilege against self-incrimination constitutes an admission of guilt. Justice Clark stated: "We must condemn the practice of

---

[10] Erwin N. Griswold, *The Fifth Amendment Today* (Cambridge: Harvard University Press, 1955), pp. 7–8. Dean Griswold's views have been criticized in part; see, in particular, Sidney Hook, *Common Sense and the Fifth Amendment* (New York: Criterion Books, 1957).

imputing sinister meaning to the exercise of a person's constitutional right under the Fifth Amendment. The privilege against self-incrimination would be reduced to a hollow mockery if its exercise could be taken as equivalent either to a confession of guilt or a conclusive presumption of perjury."[11] Slochower was reinstated as a faculty member after the Court's decision, but he was then suspended by the college president on new charges of "untruthfulness and perjury."

More recently the Court has held, reversing earlier decisions, that the Fifth Amendment forbids disbarment because of refusal to testify at a bar proceeding, *Spevack* v. *Klein,* 385 U.S. 511 (1967). Prosecutors are also forbidden to comment on the defendant's refusal to testify, *Griffin* v. *California,* 381 U.S. 957 (1965). The justices have decided that testimony extracted from public employees by the threat of discharge cannot be used in subsequent criminal prosecutions, nor may they be discharged because they refuse to waive their Fifth Amendment rights.

Congress has passed legislation requiring gamblers and marijuana dealers to register and pay a tax. While registering and paying such taxes would obviously be tantamount to confessing a crime. Nevertheless the Supreme Court at first upheld such provisions by focusing on their purported purpose of raising tax revenues. The Court has subsequently overturned convictions under both statutes on Fifth Amendment grounds.[11]

The Supreme Court has consistently overturned state convictions based on coerced confessions, although just what constitutes coercion has been subject to dispute.[12] The right-to-counsel cases discussed subsequently significantly extend the individual's protection against such coercion.

Right to Counsel

For many years, a corollary to the *Palko* doctrine discussed here (p. 656) was the *fair trial rule.* Even though federal courts were held to the letter of all provisions of the Bill of Rights, a state court might violate some of its provisions so long as the conduct of the trial as a whole was fundamentally fair. As the Court has held more and more provisions of the first ten amendments directly binding upon the states, the fair trial rule has dwindled. For a long time, however, its most important application was in the area of right to counsel.

The right to counsel is discussed in *Powell* v. *Alabama* (p. 699), where the Court held for the first time that counsel must be provided in capital cases in state criminal proceedings. For some time *Powell* v. *Alabama* was assumed

---

[11] *Marchetti* v. *United States,* 390 U.S. 39 (1968); *Leary* v. *United States,* 89 Sup. Ct. 1532 (1969).

[12] See *Chambers* v. *Florida,* 309 U.S. 227 (1940); *Leyra* v. *Denno,* 347 U.S. 556 (1954).

to mean that the assistance of counsel was required in *all* state criminal proceedings under the due process clause of the Fourteenth Amendment. However, in *Betts* v. *Brady,* 316 U.S. 455 (1942), the Court reasoned that the principle of the *Powell* case was limited to capital offenses alone. In the majority opinion, Justice Roberts noted that "we are unable to say that the concept of due process incorporated in the Fourteenth Amendment obligates the states, whatever may be their own views, to furnish counsel" in every criminal case. "Every court has power, if it deems proper, to appoint counsel where that course seems to be required in the interest of fairness." After *Betts* v. *Brady,* the Court held in numerous cases that counsel is required in noncapital cases only "where a person convicted in a state court has not intelligently and understandingly waived the benefit of counsel and where the circumstances show that his rights could not have been fairly protected without counsel."[13] However, in *Gideon* v. *Wainwright,* 372 U.S. 335 (1963), the Court squarely overruled *Betts* v. *Brady* and held that a state's failure to appoint counsel in a noncapital criminal case deprived the indigent defendant of due process of law under the Fourteenth Amendment In his majority opinion, Justice Black concluded that in *Betts* v. *Brady* the Court had ". . . departed from the sound wisdom upon which the Court's holding in *Powell* v. *Alabama* rested. Florida, supported by two other states, has asked that *Betts* v. *Brady* be left intact. Twenty-two states, as friends of the Court, argue that *Betts* was 'an anachronism when handed down' and that it should now be overruled. We agree."

Gideon and subsequent cases provided for free legal counsel and ancilliary services for indigents at the time of trial and appeal. A crucial question, however, was how early in the investigation and arrest process counsel must be provided. This question is closely linked with the self-incrimination area, because if counsel must be provided before trial, he may well advise his client to exercise his right to refuse to answer police questions. In *Massiah* v. *United States,* 377 U.S. 201 (1964); *Escobedo* v. *Illinois,* 378 U.S. 478 (1964); and *Miranda* v. *Arizona* (p. 704), the Court ruled that the defendant must be provided with counsel from the time of arrest and indictment and even before that time once the police investigation has focused on him as the probable culprit. Furthermore, the Court ruled that the police must, at these points in their investigation, notify the suspect as to his right to counsel and right to remain silent. Otherwise, confessions obtained by the police would be inadmissible as evidence. The Court subsequently extended this right to counsel to persons subjected to police line-ups: *United States* v. *Wade,* 388 U.S. 218 (1967); *Gilbert* v. *California,* 388 U.S. 263 (1967). However, these decisions must be compared to *Hoffa* v. *United States* (p. 711). The Supreme

---

[13] *Pennsylvania* ex rel. *Herman* v. *Claudy,* 350 U.S. 116 (1956). A complete review of the right to counsel is found in William M. Beaney, *The Right to Counsel in American Courts* (Ann Arbor: University of Michigan Press, 1955). Each of the criminal protections of the Sixth Amendment is examined in Francis H. Heller, *The Sixth Amendment of the Constitution* (Lawrence: University of Kansas Press, 1951).

Court has also made right to counsel and other Bill of Rights protections applicable to juvenile court proceedings: *In re Gault,* 387 U.S. 1 (1967).

The right to counsel decisions have given rise to high levels of political objection because of their alleged impairment of the ability of the police to extract confessions and gain convictions. As part of the "war on crime" serious efforts have been made to get some of these decisions reversed by congressional legislation. It is not clear, however, that depriving the poor and ignorant of the constitutional rights that the wealthy and knowledgeable invariably exercise—and exempting the police from obedience to and enforcement of the Constitution—is the best way to preserve the values of law in our society.

Double Jeopardy and Cruel and Unusual Punishment

Under the double jeopardy provision of the Fifth Amendment, a person who has been tried for a crime in a federal court may not be tried again for the same offense by the federal government. However, as the Court noted in *United States* v. *Lanza,* 260 U.S. 377 (1922), an act "denounced as a crime by both national and state sovereignties is an offense against the peace and dignity of both, and may be punished by each" without violation of the double jeopardy provision. Even though it has been criticized, the Lanza rule still stands. The problem was explored fully by a sharply divided Court in *Bartkus* v. *Illinois,* 359 U.S. 121 (1959), which reaffirmed the *Lanza* doctrine. The Murphy ruling (p. 726), however, bodes ill for the continuation of the two sovereignties concept that underlies *Lanza.*

The provision against cruel and unusual punishment was directed principally at the brutality of early English law. Some of the cruel and degrading punishments that the Eighth Amendment obviously bans include beheading and quartering, dragging through the streets to the place of execution, disemboweling alive, burning at the stake, mutilation by cutting off hands or ears, and the use of many barbarous forms of torture. Very few cases have arisen under the cruel and unusual punishment provision of the Eighth Amendment, but it seems likely that the Supreme Court will eventually have to deal with the question of whether capital punishment has become cruel and unusual by the third quarter of the twentieth century. In *Witherspoon* v. *Illinois,* 391 U.S. 510 (1968), the Court held that the exclusion of all those who conscientiously opposed capital punishment from juries in capital cases would invalidate death penalties in such cases. That the Court is concerned with this constitutional provision can be seen from *Trop* v. *Dulles,* discussed p. 344; *Robinson* v. *California,* 370 U.S. 660 (1962), which ruled that the state could not punish narcotics addiction as a crime; and *Powell* v. *Texas,* 392 U.S. 514 (1968), in which the justices were unable to agree on the precise line between drunkenness, which the state might punish as a crime, and alcoholism, which must be treated as a disease rather than punished as a crime.

PALKO v. CONNECTICUT
302 U.S. 319; 58 Sup. Ct. 149; 82 L. Ed. 288 (1937)

[*Palko was indicted and tried for murder in the first degree, but a jury found him guilty of second-degree murder and he was given a life sentence. However, a Connecticut statute permitted the state to appeal rulings and decisions "upon all questions of law arising on the trial of criminal cases." The state appealed, and a new trial was ordered. Palko was tried again, found guilty, and sentenced to death. The second conviction was affirmed by the highest state court. Palko then brought the case to the Supreme Court on appeal, contending that he was being placed in jeopardy twice in violation of the Fifth and Fourteenth Amendments.*]

MR. JUSTICE CARDOZO delivered the opinion of the Court:

. . . 1. The execution of the sentence will not deprive appellant of his life without the process of law assured to him by the Fourteenth Amendment of the Federal Constitution.

The argument for appellant is that whatever is forbidden by the Fifth Amendment is forbidden by the Fourteenth also. The Fifth Amendment, which is not directed to the states, but solely to the federal government, creates immunity from double jeopardy. No person shall be "subject for the same offense to be twice put in jeopardy of life or limb." The Fourteenth Amendment ordains, "nor shall any state deprive any person of life, liberty, or property, without due process of law." To retry a defendant, though under one indictment and only one, subjects him, it is said, to double jeopardy in violation of the Fifth Amendment, if the prosecution is one on behalf of the United States. From this the consequence is said to follow that there is a denial of life or liberty without due process of law, if the prosecution is one on behalf of the People of a State. . . .

We have said that in appellant's view the Fourteenth Amendment is to be taken as embodying the prohibitions of the Fifth. His thesis is even broader. Whatever would be a violation of the original Bill of Rights (Amendments 1 to 8), if done by the federal government, is now equally unlawful by force of the Fourteenth Amendment if done by a state. There is no such general rule.

The Fifth Amendment provides, among other things, that no person shall be held to answer for a capital or otherwise infamous crime unless on presentment or indictment of a grand jury. This court has held that, in prosecutions by a state, presentment or indictment by a grand jury may give way to informations at the instance of a public officer. *Hurtado* v. *California,* 110 U.S. 516. . . . The Fifth Amendment provides also that no person shall be compelled in any criminal case to be a witness against himself. This court has said that, in prosecutions by a state, the exemption will fail if the state elects to end it. *Twining* v. *New Jersey,* 211 U.S. 78. . . . The Sixth Amendment calls for a jury trial in criminal cases and the Seventh for a jury trial in civil cases at common law where the value in controversy shall exceed twenty dollars. This court has ruled that, consistently with those amendments, trial by jury may be modified by a state or abolished altogether. *Walker* v. *Sauvinet,* 92 U.S. 90. . . . *Maxwell* v. *Dow,* 176 U.S. 581.

. . . On the other hand, the due process clause of the Fourteenth Amendment may make it unlawful for a state to abridge by its statutes the freedom of speech which the First Amendment safeguards against encroachment by the Congress (*De Jonge* v. *Oregon,* 299 U.S. 353, 364, . . . *Herndon* v. *Lowry,* 301 U.S. 242, 259 . . .), or the like freedom of the press (*Grosjean* v. *American Press Co.,* 297 U.S. 233, . . . *Near* v. *Minnesota,* 283 U.S. 697, 707 . . .), or the free exercise of religion (*Hamilton* v. *University of California,* 293 U.S. 245, 262 . . .), or the right of peaceable assembly, without which speech would be unduly trammeled (*De Jonge* v. *Oregon* . . .), or the right of one accused of crime to the benefit of counsel (*Powell* v. *Alabama,* 287 U.S. 45 . . .). In these and other situations immunities that are valid as against the federal government by force of the specific pledges of particular amendments have been found to be implicit in the concept of ordered liberty, and thus, through the Fourteenth Amendment, become valid as against the states.

The line of division may seem to be wavering and broken if there is a hasty catalogue of the cases on the one side and the other. Reflection and analysis will induce a different view. There emerges the perception of a rationalizing principle which gives to discrete instances a proper order and coherence. The right to trial by jury and the immunity from prosecution except as the result of an indictment may have value and importance. Even so, they are not of the very essence of a scheme of ordered liberty. To abolish them is not to violate a "principle of justice so

rooted in the traditions and conscience of our people as to be ranked as fundamental." . . . Few would be so narrow or provincial as to maintain that a fair and enlightened system of justice would be impossible without them. What is true of jury trials and indictments is true also, as the cases show, of the immunity from compulsory self-incrimination. . . . This too might be lost, and justice still be done. Indeed, today as in the past there are students of our penal system who look upon the immunity as a mischief rather than a benefit, and who would limit its scope or destroy it altogether. No doubt there would remain the need to give protection against torture, physical or mental. . . . Justice, however, would not perish if the accused were subject to a duty to respond to orderly inquiry. The exclusion of these immunities and privileges from the privileges and immunities protected against the action of the states has not been arbitrary or casual. It has been dictated by a study and appreciation of the meaning, the essential implications, of liberty itself.

We reach a different plane of social and moral values when we pass to the privileges and immunities that have been taken over from the earlier articles of the federal Bill of Rights and brought within the Fourteenth Amendment by a process of absorption. These in their origin were effective against the federal government alone. If the Fourteenth Amendment has absorbed them, the process of absorption has had its source in the belief that neither liberty nor justice would exist if they were sacrificed. . . . This is true, for illustration, of freedom of thought and speech. Of that freedom one may say that it is the matrix, the indispensable condition, of nearly every other form of freedom. With rare aberrations, a pervasive recognition of that truth can be traced in our history, political and legal. So it has come about that the domain of liberty, withdrawn by the Fourteenth Amendment from encroachment by the states, has been enlarged by latter-day judgments to include liberty of the mind as well as liberty of action. The extension became, indeed, a logical imperative when once it was recognized, as long ago it was, that liberty is something more than exemption from physical restraint, and that even in the field of substantive rights and duties the legislative judgment, if oppressive and arbitrary, may be overridden by the courts. . . .

Our survey of the cases serves, we think, to justify the statement that the dividing line between them, if not unfaltering throughout its course, has been true for the most part to a unifying principle. On which side of the line the case made out by the appellant has appropriate location must be the next inquiry and the final one. Is that kind of double jeopardy to which the statute has subjected him a hardship so acute and shocking that our polity will not endure it? Does it violate those "fundamental principles of liberty and justice which lie at the base of all our civil and political institutions? . . . The answer surely must be "no." What the answer would have to be if the state were permitted after a trial free from error to try the accused over again or to bring another case against him, we have no occasion to consider. We deal with the statute before us and no other. The state is not attempting to wear the accused out by a multitude of cases with accumulated trials. It asks no more than this, that the case against him shall go on until there shall be a trial free from the corrosion of substantial legal error. . . . This is not cruelty at all, nor even vexation in any immoderate degree. If the trial had been infected with error adverse to the accused, there might have been review at his instance, and as often as necessary to purge the vicious taint. A reciprocal privilege, subject at all times to the discretion of the presiding judge . . . has now been granted to the state. There is here no seismic innovation. The edifice of justice stands, in its symmetry, to many, greater than before.

2. The conviction of appellant is not in derogation of any privileges or immunities that belong to him as a citizen of the United States. . . .

Affirmed.

MR. JUSTICE BUTLER dissents.

ADAMSON v. CALIFORNIA
332 U.S. 46; 67 Sup. Ct. 1672; 91 L. Ed. 1903 (1947)

[*Adamson was convicted of murder without recommendation of mercy by the jury and sentenced to death. The sentence was affirmed by the Supreme Court of California. Adamson then brought his case to the Supreme Court on appeal. He argued that a California statute that permitted the prosecutor and judge to make adverse comments to the jury upon the failure of a defendant to take the witness stand to explain or deny evidence against him was invalid under the Fifth and Fourteenth Amendments. In his trial Adamson, who had been previously convicted for burglary, larceny, and robbery, chose not to take the stand. As a result both the prosecuting attorney and the court made adverse comments. Adamson argued that this practice put him in an impossible situation. If he did testify, the previous convictions would be revealed to the jury. If he did not testify (as in his case), he would be prejudiced by the comments of the prosecutor and judge. The California procedure was not permissible in federal courts and in the overwhelming majority of state jurisdictions.*]

MR. JUSTICE REED delivered the opinion of the Court:

. . . In the first place, appellant urges that the provision of the Fifth Amendment that no person "shall be compelled in any criminal case to be a witness against himself" is a fundamental national privilege or immunity protected against state abridgment by the Fourteenth Amendment or a privilege or immunity secured, through the Fourteenth Amendment, against deprivation by state action because it is a personal right, enumerated in the federal Bill of Rights.

Secondly, appellant relies upon the due process of law clause of the Fourteenth Amendment to invalidate the provisions of the California law . . . as applied (a) because comment on failure to testify is permitted, (b) because appellant was forced to forego testimony in person because of danger of disclosure of his past convictions through cross-examination, and (c) because the presumption of innocence was infringed by the shifting of the burden of proof to appellant in permitting comment on his failure to testify.

We shall assume, but without any intention thereby of ruling upon the issue, that permission by law to the court, counsel and jury to comment upon and consider the failure of defendant "to explain or to deny by his testimony any evidence or facts in the case against him" would infringe defendant's privilege against self-incrimination under the Fifth Amendment if this were a trial in a court of the United States under a similar law. Such an assumption does not determine appellant's rights under the Fourteenth Amendment. It is settled law that the clause of the Fifth Amendment, protecting a person against being compelled to be a witness against himself, is not made effective by the Fourteenth Amendment as a protection against state action on the ground that freedom from testimonial compulsion is a right of national citizenship, or because it is a personal privilege or immunity secured by the Federal Constitution as one of the rights of man that are listed in the Bill of Rights.

The reasoning that leads to those conclusions starts with the unquestioned premise that the Bill of Rights, when adopted, was for the protection of the individual against the federal government and its provisions were inapplicable to similar actions done by the states. . . . With the adoption of the Fourteenth Amendment, it was suggested that the dual citizenship recognized by its first sentence secured for citizens federal protection for their elemental privileges and immunities of state citizenship. The *Slaughter House Cases* decided, contrary to the suggestion, that these rights, as privileges and immunities of state citizenship, remained under the sole protection of the state governments. This Court, without the expression of a contrary view upon that phase of the issues before the Court, has approved this determination. . . . The power to free defendants in state trials from self-incrimination was specifically determined to be beyond the scope of the privileges and immunities clause of the Fourteenth Amendment in *Twining* v. *New Jersey*, 211 U.S. 78. . . . "The privilege against self-incrimination may be withdrawn and the accused put upon the stand as a witness for the state." The *Twining* case likewise disposed of the contention that freedom from testimonial compulsion, being specifically granted by the Bill of Rights, is a federal privilege or immunity that is protected by the Fourteenth Amendment against state invasion. This Court held that the inclusion in the Bill of Rights of this protection against the power of the national government did not make the privilege a federal privilege or immunity secured to citizens by the Constitution against state action. . . . After declaring that state and national citizenship co-exist in the same person, the Fourteenth Amendment forbids a state from abridging the privileges and immunities of citizens of the United States. As a matter of words, this leaves a state free to abridge, within the limits of the due process clause, the privileges and immunities flowing from state citizenship. This reading of the Federal Constitution has heretofore found favor with the majority of this Court as a natural and logical interpretation. It accords with the constitutional doctrine of federalism by leaving to the states the responsibility of dealing with the privileges and immunities of their citizens except those inherent in national citizenship. It is the construction placed upon the amendment by justices whose own experience had given them contemporaneous knowledge of the purposes that led to the adoption of the Fourteenth Amendment. This construction has become embedded in our federal system as a functioning element in preserving the balance between national and state power. We reaffirm the conclusion of the *Twining* and *Palko* cases that protection against self-incrimination is not a privilege or immunity of national citizenship.

Appellant secondly contends that if the privilege against self-incrimination is not a right protected by the privileges and immunities clause of the Fourteenth Amendment against state action, this privilege, to its full scope under the Fifth Amendment, inheres in the right to a fair trial. A right to a fair trial is a right admittedly protected by the due process clause of the Fourteenth Amendment. Therefore, appellant argues, the due process clause of the Fourteenth Amendment protects his privilege against self-incrimination. The due process clause of the Fourteenth Amendment, however, does not draw all the rights of the federal Bill of Rights under its protection. That contention was made and rejected in *Palko* v. *Connecticut*. . . . It was rejected with citation of the cases excluding several of the rights, protected by the Bill of Rights, against infringement by the National Government. Nothing has been called to our attention that either the framers of the Fourteenth Amendment or the states that adopted it intended its due process clause to draw within its scope the earlier amendments to the Constitution. *Palko* held that such provisions of the Bill of Rights as were "implicit in the concept of ordered liberty" clause. But it held nothing more.

Specifically, the due process clause does not protect, by virtue of its mere existence, the accused's freedom from giving testimony by compulsion in state trials that is secured to him against federal interference by the Fifth Amendment. . . . For a state to require testimony from an accused is not necessarily a breach of a state's obligation to give a fair trial. . . .

Generally, comment on the failure of an accused to testify is forbidden in American jurisdictions. This arises from state constitutional or statutory provisions similar in character to the federal provisions. . . . California, however, is one of a few states that permit limited comment upon a defendant's failure to testify. That permission is narrow. The California law . . . authorizes comment by court and counsel upon the "failure of the defendant to explain or to deny by his testimony any evidence or facts in the case against him." This does not involve any presumption, rebuttable or irrebuttable, either of guilt or of the truth of any fact, that is offered in evidence. . . . It allows inferences to be drawn from proven facts. Because of this clause, the court can direct the jury's attention to whatever evidence there may be that a defendant could deny and the prosecution can argue as to inferences that may be drawn from the accused's failure to testify. . . . There is here no lack of power in the trial court to adjudge and no denial of a hearing. California has prescribed a method for advising the jury in the search for truth. However sound may be the legislative conclusion that an accused should not be compelled in any criminal case to be a witness against himself, we see no reason why comment should not be made upon his silence. It seems quite natural that when a defendant has opportunity to deny or explain facts and determines not to do so, the prosecution should bring out the strength of the evidence by commenting upon defendant's failure to explain or deny it. The prosecution evidence may be of facts that may be beyond the knowledge of the accused. If so, his failure to testify would have little if any weight. But the facts may be such as are necessarily in the knowledge of the accused. In that case a failure to explain would point to an inability to explain. . . .

It is true that if comment were forbidden, an accused in this situation could remain silent and avoid evidence of former crimes and comment upon his failure to testify. We are of the view, however, that a state may control such a situation in accordance with its own ideas of the most efficient administration of criminal justice. The purpose of due process is not to protect an accused against a proper conviction but against an unfair conviction. When evidence is before a jury that threatens conviction, it does not seem unfair to require him to choose between leaving the adverse evidence unexplained and subjecting himself to impeachment through disclosure of former crimes. Indeed, this is a dilemma with which any defendant may be faced. If facts, adverse to the defendant, are proven by the prosecution, there may be no way to explain them favorably to the accused except by a witness who may be vulnerable to impeachment on cross-examination. The defendant must then decide whether or not to use such a witness. The fact that the witness may also be the defendant makes the choice more difficult but a denial of due process does not emerge from the circumstances. . . .

We find no other error that gives ground for our intervention in California's administration of criminal justice.

Affirmed.

MR. JUSTICE FRANKFURTER, concurring:

Less than ten years ago, Mr. Justice Cardozo announced as settled constitutional law that while the Fifth Amendment, "which is not directed to the states, but solely to the federal government," provides that no person shall be compelled in any criminal case to be a witness against himself, the process of law assured by the Fourteenth Amendment does not require such immunity from self-incrimination: "in prosecutions by a state, the exemption will fail if the state elects to end it." *Palko* v. *Connecticut*. . . . Mr. Justice Cardozo spoke for the Court, consisting of Mr. Chief Justice Hughes, and (Justices) McReynolds, Brandeis, Sutherland, Stone, Roberts, Black. (Mr. Justice Butler dissented.) The matter no longer called for discussion; a reference to *Twining* v. *New Jersey* . . . decided thirty years before the *Palko* case, sufficed.

Decisions of this Court do not have equal intrinsic authority. The *Twining* case shows the judicial process at its best—comprehensive briefs and powerful arguments on both sides, followed by long deliberation, resulting in an opinion by Mr. Justice Moody which at once gained and has ever since retained recognition as one of the outstanding opinions in the history of the Court. After enjoying unquestioned prestige for 40 years, the *Twining* case should not now be diluted, even unwittingly, either in its judicial philosophy or in its particulars. As the surest way of keeping the *Twining* case intact, I would affirm this case on its authority. . . .

The short answer to the suggestion that the provision of the Fourteenth Amendment, which ordains "nor shall any State deprive any person of life, liberty, or property, without due process of law," was a way of saying that every State must thereafter initiate prosecutions through indictment by a grand jury, must have a trial by a jury of twelve in criminal cases, and must have trial by such a jury in common-law suits where the amount in controversy exceeds twenty dollars, is that it is a strange way of saying it. It would be extraordinarily strange for a Constitution to convey such specific commands in such a round-about and inexplicit way. After all, an amendment to the Constitution should be read in a " 'sense most obvious to the common understanding at the time of its adoption.' . . . For it was for public adoption that it was proposed." . . . Those reading the English language with the meaning which it ordinarily conveys, those conversant with the political and legal history of the concept of due process, those sensitive to the relations of the States to the central government as well as the relation of some of the provisions of the Bill of Rights to the

process of justice, would hardly recognize the Fourteenth Amendment as a cover for the various explicit provisions of the first eight Amendments. Some of these are enduring reflections of experience with human nature, while some express the restricted views of Eighteenth-Century England regarding the best methods for the ascertainment of facts. The notion that the Fourteenth Amendment was a covert way of imposing upon the States all the rules which it seemed important to Eighteenth-Century statesmen to write into the Federal Amendments, was rejected by judges who were themselves witnesses of the process by which the Fourteenth Amendment became part of the Constitution. Arguments that may now be adduced to prove that the first eight Amendments were concealed within the historic phrasing of the Fourteenth Amendment were not unknown at the time of its adoption. A surer estimate of their bearing was possible for judges at the time than distorting distance is likely to vouchsafe. Any evidence of design or purpose not contemporaneously known could hardly have influenced those who ratified the Amendment. Remarks of a particular proponent of the Amendment, no matter how influential, are not to be deemed part of the Amendment. What was submitted for ratification was his proposal, not his speech. Thus, at the time of the ratification of the Fourteenth Amendment the constitutions of nearly half of the ratifying States did not have the rigorous requirements of the Fifth Amendment for instituting criminal proceedings through a grand jury. It could hardly have occurred to these States that by ratifying the Amendment they uprooted their established methods for prosecuting crime and fastened upon themselves a new prosecutorial system.

Indeed, the suggestion that the Fourteenth Amendment incorporates the first eight Amendments as such is not unambiguously urged. Even the boldest innovator would shrink from suggesting to more than half the States that they may no longer initiate prosecutions without indictment by grand jury, or that thereafter all the States of the Union must furnish a jury of twelve for every case involving a claim above twenty dollars. There is suggested merely a selective incorporation of the first eight Amendments into the Fourteenth Amendment. Some are in and some are out, but we are left in the dark as to which are in and which are out. Nor are we given the calculus for determining which go in and which stay out. If the basis of selection is merely that those provisions of the first eight Amendments are incorporated which commend themselves to individual justices as indispensable to the dignity and happiness of a free man, we are thrown back to a merely subjective test. The protection against unreasonable search and seizure might have primacy for one judge, while trial by a jury of twelve for every claim above twenty dollars might appear to another as an ultimate need in a free society. In the history of thought "natural law" has a much longer and much better-founded meaning and justification than such subjective selection of the first eight Amendments for incorporation into the Fourteenth. If all that is meant is that due process contains within itself certain minimal standards which are "of the very essence of a scheme of ordered liberty," *Palko* v. *Connecticut* . . . putting upon this Court the duty of applying these standards from time to time, then we have merely arrived at the insight which our predecessors long ago expressed. . . . As judges charged with the delicate task of subjecting the government of a continent to the Rule of Law we must be particularly mindful that it is "a constitution we are expounding," so that it should not be imprisoned in what are merely legal forms even though they have the sanction of the Eighteenth Century.

And so, when, as in a case like the present, a conviction in a State court is here for review under a claim that a right protected by the Due Process Clause of the Fourteenth Amendment has been denied, the issue is not whether an infraction of one of the specific provisions of the first eight Amendments is disclosed by the record. The relevant question is whether the criminal proceedings which resulted in conviction deprived the accused of the due process of law to which the United States Constitution entitled him. Judicial review of that guaranty of the Fourteenth Amendment inescapably imposes upon this Court an exercise of judgment upon the whole course of the proceedings in order to ascertain whether they offend those canons of decency and fairness which express the notions of justice of English-speaking peoples even toward those charged with the most heinous offenses. These standards of justice are not authoritatively formulated anywhere as though they were prescriptions in a pharmacopoeia. But neither does the application of the Due Process Clause imply that judges are wholly at large. The judicial judgment in applying the Due Process Clause must move within the limits of accepted notions of justice and is not to be based upon the idiosyncrasies of a merely personal judgment. The fact that judges among themselves may differ whether in a particular case a trial offends accepted notions of justice is not disproof that general rather than idiosyncratic standards are applied. An important safeguard against such merely individual judgment is an alert deference to the judgment of the State court under review.

MR. JUSTICE BLACK, dissenting:

. . . This decision reasserts a constitutional theory spelled out in *Twining* v. *New Jersey* . . . that this Court is endowed by the Constitution with boundless power under "natural law" periodically to expand and contract constitutional standards to conform to the Court's conception of what at a particular time constitutes "civilized decency" and "fundamental liberty and justice." Invoking this *Twining* rule, the Court concludes that although comment upon testimony in a federal court would violate the Fifth Amendment, identical comment in a state court does not violate today's fashion in civilized decency and fundamentals and is therefore not prohibited by the Federal Constitution as amended.

The *Twining* case was the first, as it is the only, decision of this Court which has squarely held that states were free, notwithstanding the Fifth and Fourteenth Amendments, to extort evidence from one accused of crime. I agree that if *Twining* be reaffirmed, the result reached might appropriately follow. But I would not reaffirm the *Twining* decision. I think that decision and the "natural law" theory of the Constitution upon which it relies degrade the constitutional safeguards of the Bill of Rights and simultaneously appropriate for this Court a broad power which we are not authorized by the Constitution to exercise. . . .

My study of the historical events that culminated in the Fourteenth Amendment, and the expressions of those who sponsored and favored, as well as those who opposed its submission and passage, persuades me that one of the chief objects that the provisions of the Amendment's first section, separately, and as a whole, were intended to accomplish was to make the Bill of Rights applicable to the states. With full knowledge of the import of the *Barron* decision, the framers and backers of the Fourteenth Amendment proclaimed its purpose to be to overturn the constitutional rule that case had announced. This historical purpose has never received full consideration or exposition in any opinion of this Court interpreting the Amendment. . . .

In my judgment. . . . history conclusively demonstrates that the language of the first section of the Fourteenth Amendment, taken as a whole, was thought by those responsible for its submission to the people, and by those who opposed its submission, sufficiently explicit to guarantee that thereafter no state could deprive its citizens of the privileges and protections of the Bill of Rights. Whether this Court ever will, or whether it now should, in the light of past decisions, give full effect to what the Amendment was intended to accomplish is not necessarily essential to a decision here. However that may be, our prior decisions, including *Twining,* do not prevent our carrying out that purpose, at least to the extent of making applicable to the states, not a mere part, as the Court has, but the full protection of the Fifth Amendment's provision against compelling evidence from an accused to convict him of crime. And I further contend that the "natural law" formula which the Court uses to reach its conclusion in this case should be abandoned as an incongruous excrescence on our Constitution. I believe that formula to be itself a violation of our Constitution, in that it subtly conveys to courts, at the expense of legislatures, ultimate power over public policies in fields where no specific provision of the Constitution limits legislative power. And my belief seems to be in accord with the views expressed by this Court, at least for the first two decades after the Fourteenth Amendment was adopted. . . .

I cannot consider the Bill of Rights to be an outworn Eighteenth Century "strait jacket" as the *Twining* opinion did. Its provisions may be thought outdated abstractions by some. And it is true that they were designed to meet ancient evils. But they are the same kind of human evils that have emerged from century to century wherever excessive power is sought by the few at the expense of the many. In my judgment the people of no nation can lose their liberty so long as a Bill of Rights like ours survives and its basic purposes are conscientiously interpreted, enforced and respected so as to afford continuous protection against old, as well as new, devices and practices which might thwart those purposes. I fear to see the consequences of the Court's practice of substituting its own concepts of decency and fundamental justice for the language of the Bill of Rights as its point of departure in interpreting and enforcing that Bill of Rights. If the choice must be between the selective process of the *Palko* decision applying some of the Bill of Rights to the States, or the *Twining* rule applying none of them, I would choose the *Palko* selective process. But rather than accept either of these choices, I would follow what I beieve was the original purpose of the Fourteenth Amendment—to extend to all the people of the nation the complete protection of the Bill of Rights. To hold that this Court can determine what, if any, provisions of the Bill of Rights will be enforced, and if so to what degree, is to frustrate the great design of a written Constitution.

Conceding the possibility that this Court is now wise enough to improve on the Bill of Rights by substituting natural law concepts for the Bill of

Rights, I think the possibility is entirely too speculative to agree to take that course. I would therefore hold in this case that the full protection of the Fifth Amendment's proscription against compelled testimony must be afforded by California. This I would do because of reliance upon the original purpose of the Fourteenth Amendment.

It is an illusory apprehension that literal application of some or all of the provisions of the Bill of Rights to the States would unwisely increase the sum total of the powers of this Court to invalidate state legislation. The Federal Government has not been harmfully burdened by the requirement that enforcement of federal laws affecting civil liberty conform literally to the Bill of Rights. Who would advocate its repeal? It must be conceded, of course, that the natural-law-due-process formula, which the Court today reaffirms, has been interpreted to limit substantially this Court's power to prevent state violations of the individual civil liberties guaranteed by the Bill of Rights. But this formula also has been used in the past, and can be used in the future, to license this Court, in considering regulatory legislation, to roam at large in the broad expanses of policy and morals and to trespass, all too freely, on the legislative domain of the States as well as the Federal Government. . . .

MR. JUSTICE DOUGLAS joins in this opinion.

MR. JUSTICE MURPHY, with whom MR. JUSTICE RUTLEDGE concurs, dissenting:

While in substantial agreement with the views of Mr. Justice Black, I have one reservation and one addition to make.

I agree that the specific guaranties of the Bill of Rights should be carried over intact into the first section of the Fourteenth Amendment. But I am not prepared to say that the latter is entirely and necessarily limited by the

Bill of Rights. Occasions may arise where a proceeding falls so far short of conforming to fundamental standards of procedure as to warrant constitutional condemnation in terms of a lack of due process despite the absence of a specific provision in the Bill of Rights. . . .

MAPP v. OHIO
367 U.S. 643; 81 Sup. Ct. 1684; 6 L. Ed. 2d (1961)

[*Miss Dollree Mapp was convicted in Ohio of having obscene materials in her possession in violation of a state statute. After, the Ohio Supreme Court upheld the conviction, Miss Mapp brought an appeal to the Supreme Court. Additional facts are found in the opinion.*]

MR. JUSTICE CLARK delivered the opinion of the Court:

. . . On May 23, 1957, three Cleveland police officers arrived at appellant's residence in that city pursuant to information that "a person (was) hiding out in the home who was wanted for questioning in connection with a recent bombing, and that there was a large amount of policy paraphernalia being hidden in the home." Miss Mapp and her daughter by a former marriage lived on the top floor of the two-family dwelling. Upon their arrival at that house, the officers knocked on the door and demanded entrance but appellant, after telephoning her attorney, refused to admit them without a search warrant. They advised their headquarters of the situation and undertook a surveillance of the house.

The officers again sought entrance some three hours later when four or more additional officers arrived on the scene. When Miss Mapp did not come to the door immediately, at least one of the several doors to the house was forcibly opened and the policemen gained admittance. Meanwhile Miss Mapp's attorney arrived, but the officers, having secured their own entry, and continuing in their defiance of the law, would permit him neither to see Miss Mapp nor to enter the house. It appears that Miss Mapp was halfway down the stairs from the upper floor to the front door when the officers, in this highhanded manner, broke into the hall. She demanded to see the search warrant. A paper, claimed to be a warrant, was held up by one of the officers. She grabbed the "warrant" and placed it in her bosom. A struggle ensued in which the officers recovered the piece of paper and as a result of which they handcuffed appellant because she had been "belligerent" in resisting their official rescue of the "warrant" from her person. Running roughshod over appellant, a policeman "grabbed" her, "twisted (her) hand," and she "yelled (and) pleaded with him" because "it was hurting." Appellant, in handcuffs, was then forcibly taken upstairs to her bedroom where the officers searched a dresser, a chest of drawers, a closet and some suitcases. They also looked into a photo album and through personal papers belonging to the appellant. The search spread to the rest of the second floor including the child's bedroom, the living room, the kitchen and a dinette. The basement of the building and a trunk found therein were also searched. The obscene materials for possession of which she was ultimately convicted were discovered in the course of that widespread search.

At the trial no search warrant was

produced by the prosecution, nor was the failure to produce one explained or accounted for. At best, "there is, in the record, considerable doubt as to whether there ever was any warrant for the search of defendant's home." . . .

The State says that even if the search were made without authority, or otherwise unreasonably, it is not prevented from using the unconstitutionally seized evidence at trial, citing *Wolf* v. *Colorado*, . . . in which this Court did indeed hold "that in a prosecution in a State court for a State crime the Fourteenth Amendment does not forbid the admission of evidence obtained by an unreasonable search and seizure." . . .

I

Seventy-five years ago, in *Boyd* v. *United States,* 116 U.S. 616, 630 (1886), considering the Fourth and Fifth Amendments as running "almost into each other" on the facts before it, this Court held the doctrines of those Amendments

"apply to all invasions on the part of the government and its employees of the sanctity of a man's home and the privacies of life. It is not the breaking of his doors, and the rummaging of his drawers, that constitutes the essence of the offense; but it is the invasion of his indefeasible right of personal security, personal liberty and private property. . . . Breaking into a house and opening boxes and drawers are circumstances of aggravation; but any forcible and compulsory extortion of a man's own testimony or of his private papers to be used as evidence to convict him of crime or to forfeit his goods, is within the condemnation . . . [of those Amendments]. . . ."

Less than thirty years after *Boyd,* this Court, in *Weeks* v. *United States,* 232 U.S. 383 (1914), stated that

"the Fourth Amendment . . . put the courts of the United States and Federal officials, in the exercise of their power and authority, under limitations and restraints (and) . . . forever secure(d) the people, their persons, houses, papers and effects against all unreasonable searches and seizures under the guise of law . . . and the duty of giving to it force and effect is obligatory upon all entrusted under our Federal system with the enforcement of the laws. . . ."

Specifically dealing with the use of the evidence unconstitutionally seized, the Court conceded:

"If letters and private documents can thus be seized and held and used in evidence against a citizen accused of an offense, the protection of the Fourth Amendment declaring his right to be secure against such searches and seizures is of no value, and, so far as those thus placed are concerned, might as well be stricken from the Constitution. The efforts of the courts and their officials to bring the guilty to punishment, praiseworthy as they are, are not to be aided by the sacrifice of those great principles established by years of endeavor and suffering which have resulted in their embodiment in the fundamental law of the land. . . ."

Finally, the Court in that case clearly stated that use of the seized evidence involved "a denial of the constitutional rights of the accused." . . . Thus, in the year 1914, in the *Weeks* case, this Court "for the first time" held that "in a federal prosecution the Fourth Amendment barred the use of evidence secured through an illegal search and seizure." . . . This Court has ever since required of federal law officers a strict adherence to that command which this Court has held to be a clear, specific, and constitutionally required—even if judicially implied—deterrent safeguard without insistence upon which the Fourth Amendment would have been reduced to "a form of words." . . . It meant, quite simply, that "conviction by means of unlawful seizures and enforced confessions . . . should find no sanction in the judgments of the courts. . . ."

There are in the cases of this Court some passing references to the *Weeks* rule as being one of evidence. But the plain and unequivocal language of *Weeks*—and its later paraphrase in *Wolf*—to the effect that the *Weeks* rule is of constitutional origin, remains entirely undisturbed. . . .

II

In 1949, thirty-five years after *Weeks* was announced, this Court, in *Wolf* v. *Colorado, supra,* again for the first time, discussed the effect of the Fourth Amendment upon the States through the operation of the Due Process Clause of the Fourteenth Amendment. It said:

> "[W]e have no hesitation in saying that were a State affirmatively to sanction such police incursion into privacy it would run counter to the guaranty of the Fourteenth Amendment. . . ."

Nevertheless, after declaring that the "security of one's privacy against arbitrary intrusion by the police" is "implicit in the 'concept of ordered liberty' and as such enforceable against the States through the Due Process Clause," cf. *Palko* v. *Connecticut,* 302 U.S. 319 (1937), and announcing that it "stoutly adhere(d)" to the *Weeks* decision, the Court decided that the *Weeks* exclusionary rule would not then be imposed upon the States as "an essential ingredient of the right." . . .

III

Some five years after *Wolf,* in answer to a plea made here term after term that we overturn its doctrine on applicability of the *Weeks* exclusionary rule, this Court indicated that such should not be done until the States had "adequate opportunity to adapt or reject the (*Weeks*) rule. . . ."

Today we once again examine *Wolf's* constitutional documentation of the right to privacy free from unreasonable state intrusion, and, after its dozen years on our books, are led by it to close the only courtroom door remaining open to evidence secured by official lawlessness in flagrant abuse of that basic right, reserved to all persons as a specific guaranty against that very same unlawful conduct. We hold that all evidence obtained by searches and seizures in violation of the Constitution is, by that same authority, inadmissible in a state court.

IV

Since the Fourth Amendment's right of privacy has been declared enforceable against the States through the Due Process Clause of the Fourteenth, it is enforceable against them by the same sanction of exclusion as is used against the Federal Government. Were it otherwise, then just as without the *Weeks* rule the assurance against unreasonable federal searches and seizures would be "a form of words," valueless and undeserving of mention in a perpetual character of inestimable human liberties, so too, without that rule the freedom from state invasions of privacy would be so ephemeral and so neatly severed from its conceptual nexus with the freedom from all brutish means of coercing evidence as not to merit this Court's high regard as a freedom "implicit in the concept of ordered liberty." At the time that the Court held in *Wolf* that the Amendment was applicable to the States through the Due Process Clause, the cases of this Court, as we have seen, had steadfastly held that as to federal officers the Fourth Amendment included the exclusion of the evidence seized in violation of its provisions. . . . [T]he admission of the new constitutional right by *Wolf* could not consistently tolerate denial of its most important constitutional privilege, namely, the exclusion of the evidence which an accused had been forced to give by reason of the unlawful seizure. To hold otherwise is to grant the right but in reality to withhold its privilege and enjoyment. Only last year the Court itself recognized that the purpose of the exclusionary rule "is to deter—to compel respect for the constitutional guaranty in the only effectively available way—by removing the incentive to disregard it. . . ."

Indeed, we are aware of no restraint, similar to that rejected today, conditioning the enforcement of any other basic constitutional right. The right to privacy, no less important than any other right carefully and particularly reserved to the people, would stand in marked contrast to all other rights declared as "basic to a free society." . . . The Court has not hesitated to enforce as strictly against the States as it does against the Federal Government the rights of free speech and of a free press, the rights to notice and to a fair, public trial, including, as it does, the right not to be convicted by use of a coerced confession, however logically relevant it be, and without regard to its reliability. . . . We find that, as to the Federal Government, the Fourth and Fifth Amendments and, as to the States, the freedom from unconscionable invasions of privacy and the freedom from convictions based upon coerced confessions do enjoy an "intimate relation" in their perpetuation of "principles of humanity and civil liberty (secured) . . . only after years of struggle. . . ."

V

Moreover, our holding that the exclusionary rule is an essential part of both the Fourth and Fourteenth Amendments is not only the logical dictate of prior cases, but it also makes very good sense. There is no war between the Constitution and common sense. Presently, a federal prosecutor may make no use of evidence illegally seized, but a State's attorney across the street may, although he supposedly is operating under the enforceable prohibitions of the same Amendment. Thus the State, by admitting evidence unlawfully seized, serves to encourage disobedience to the Federal Constitution which it is bound to uphold. . . . In nonexclusionary States, federal officers, being human, were by it invited to and did, as our cases indicate, step across the street to the State's attorney with their unconstitutionally seized evidence. Prosecution on the basis of that evidence was then had in a state court in utter disregard of the enforceable Fourth Amendment. If the fruits of an unconstitutional search had been inadmissible in both state and federal courts, this inducement to evasion would have been sooner eliminated. . . .

Federal-state cooperation in the solution of crime under constitutional standards will be promoted, if only by recognition of their now mutual obligation to respect the same fundamental criteria in their approaches. "However much in a particular case insistence upon such rules may appear as a technicality that inures to the benefit of a guilty person, the history of the criminal law proves that tolerance of shortcut methods in law enforcement impairs its enduring effectiveness." . . . Denying shortcuts to only one of two cooperating law enforcement agencies tends naturally to breed legitimate suspicion of "working arrangements" whose results are equally tainted. . . .

The ignoble shortcut to conviction left open to the State tends to destroy the entire system of constitutional restraints on which the liberties of the people rest. Having once recognized that the right to privacy embodied in the Fourth Amendment is enforceable against the States, and that the right to be secure against rude invasions of privacy by state officers is, therefore, constitutional in origin, we can no longer permit that right to remain an empty promise. Because it is enforceable in the same manner and to like effect as other basic rights secured by the Due Process Clause, we can no longer permit it to be revocable at the whim of any police officer who, in the name of law enforcement itself, chooses to suspend its enjoyment. Our decision, founded on reason and truth, gives to the individual no more than that which the Constitution guarantees him, to the police officer no less than that to which honest law enforcement is entitled, and to the courts, that judicial integrity so necessary in the true administration of justice.

The judgment of the Supreme Court of Ohio is reversed and the case remanded for further proceedings not inconsistent with this opinion.

Reversed and remanded.

MR. JUSTICE BLACK, concurring:

. . . I am still not persuaded that the Fourth Amendment, standing alone, would be enough to bar the introduction into evidence against an accused of papers and effects seized from him in violation of its commands. For the Fourth Amendment does not itself contain any provision expressly precluding the use of such evidence, and I am extremely doubtful that such . . . a provision could properly be inferred from nothing more than the basic command against unreasonable searches and seizures. Reflection on the problem, however, in the light of cases coming before the Court since *Wolf,* has led me to conclude that when the Fourth Amendment's ban against unreasonable searches and seizures is considered together with the Fifth Amendment's ban against compelled self-incrimination, a constitutional basis emerges which not only justifies but actually requires the exclusionary rule.

The close interrelationship between the Fourth and Fifth Amendments, as they apply to this problem, has long been recognized and, indeed, was expressly made the ground for this Court's holding in *Boyd* v. *United States.* There the Court fully discussed this relationship and declared itself "unable to perceive that the seizure of a man's private books and papers to be used in evidence against him is substantially different from compelling him to be a witness against himself." It was upon this ground that Mr. Justice Rutledge largely relied in his dissenting opinion in the *Wolf* case. And, although I rejected the argument at that time, its force has, for me at least, become compelling with the more thorough understanding of the problem brought on by recent cases. In the final analysis, it seems to me that the *Boyd* doctrine, though perhaps not required by the express language of the Constitution strictly construed, is amply justified from an historical standpoint, soundly based in reason, and entirely consistent with what I regard to be the proper approach to interpretation of our Bill of Rights. . . .

The Court's opinion, in my judgment, dissipates the doubt and uncertainty in this field of constitutional law and I am persuaded, for this and other reasons stated, to depart from my prior views, to accept the *Boyd* doctrine as controlling in this state case and to join the Court's judgment and opinion which are in accordance with that constitutional doctrine.

MR. JUSTICE DOUGLAS, concurring:

. . . *Wolf* v. *Colorado* . . . was decided in 1949. The immediate result was a storm of constitutional controversy which only today finds its end. I believe that this is an appropriate case in which to put an end to the asymmetry which *Wolf* imported into the law. . . . It is an appropriate case because the facts it presents show—as would few other cases—the casual arrogance of those who have the untrammelled power to invade one's home and to seize one's person. . . .

Memorandum of MR. JUSTICE STEWART:

Agreeing fully with Part I of Mr. Justice Harlan's dissenting opinion, I express no view as to the merits of the constitutional issue which the Court today decides. I would, however, reverse the judgment in this case, because I am persuaded that the provision of Section 2905.34 of the Ohio Revised Code, upon which the petitioner's conviction was based, is, in the words of Mr. Justice Harlan, not "consistent with the rights of free thought and expression assured against state action by the Fourteenth Amendment."

MR. JUSTICE HARLAN, whom MR. JUSTICE FRANKFURTER and MR. JUSTICE WHITTAKER join, dissenting:

In overruling the *Wolf* case the Court, in my opinion, has forgotten the sense of judicial restraint which, with due regard for stare decisis, is one element that should enter into deciding whether a past decision of this Court should be overruled. Apart from that I also believe that the *Wolf* rule represents sounder Constitutional doctrine than the new rule which now replaces it.

I

From the Court's statement of the case one would gather that the central,

if not controlling, issue on this appeal is whether illegally state-seized evidence is Constitutionally admissible in a state prosecution, an issue which would of course face us with the need for re-examining *Wolf*. However, such is not the situation. For, although that question was indeed raised here and below among appellant's subordinate points, the new and pivotal issue brought to the Court by this appeal is whether §2905.34 of the Ohio Revised Code making criminal the mere knowing possession or control of obscene material, and under which appellant has been convicted, is consistent with the rights of free thought and expression assured against state action by the Fourteenth Amendment. That was the principal issue which was decided by the Ohio Supreme Court, which was tendered by appellant's Jurisdictional Statement, and which was briefed and argued in this Court.

In this posture of things, I think it fair to say that five members of this Court have simply "reached out" to overrule *Wolf*. With all respect for the views of the majority, and recognizing that stare decisis carries different weight in Constitutional adjudication than it does in nonconstitutional decision, I can perceive no justification for regarding this case as an appropriate occasion for re-examining *Wolf*.

The action of the Court finds no support in the rule that decision of Constitutional issues should be avoided wherever possible. For in overruling *Wolf* the Court, instead of passing upon the validity of Ohio's Section 2905.34, has simply chosen between two Constitutional questions. . . .

The occasion which the Court has taken here is in the context of a case where the question was briefed not at all and argued only extremely tangentially. The unwisdom of overruling *Wolf* without full-dress argument is aggravated by the circumstance that that decision is a comparatively recent one (1949) to which three members of the present majority have at one time or other expressly subscribed, one to be sure with explicit misgivings. I would think that our obligation to the States, on whom we impose this new rule, as well as the obligation of orderly adherence to our own processes would demand that we seek that aid which adequate briefing and argument lends to the determination of an important issue. It certainly has never been a postulate of judicial power that mere altered disposition, or subsequent membership on the Court, is sufficient warrant for overturning a deliberately decided rule of Constitutional law.

Thus, if the Court was bent on reconsidering *Wolf,* I think that there would soon have presented itself an appropriate opportunity in which we could have had the benefit of full briefing and argument. In any event, at the very least, the present case should have been set down for reargument, in view of the inadequate briefing and argument we have received on the *Wolf* point. To all intents and purposes the Court's present action amounts to a summary reversal of *Wolf,* without argument.

I am bound to say that what has been done is not likely to promote respect either for the Court's adjudicatory process or for the stability of its decisions. Having been unable, however, to persuade any of the majority to a different procedural course, I now turn to the merits of the present decision.

II

. . . I would not impose upon the States this federal exclusionary remedy. The reasons given by the majority for now suddenly turning its back on *Wolf* seem to me notably unconvincing. . . .

Our concern here, as it was in *Wolf,* is not with the desirability of that rule but only with the question whether the States are Constitutionally free to follow it or not as they may themselves determine, and the relevance of the disparity of views among the State on this point lies simply in the fact that the judgment involved is a debatable one. . . .

The preservation of a proper balance between state and federal responsibility in the administration of criminal justice demands patience on the part of those who might like to see things move faster among the States in this respect. Problems of criminal law enforcement vary widely from State to State. One State, in considering the totality of its legal picture, may conclude that the need for embracing the *Weeks* rule is pressing because other remedies are unavailable or inadequate to secure compliance with the substantive Constitutional principle involved. Another, though equally solicitous of Constitutional rights, may choose to pursue one purpose at a time, allowing all evidence relevant to guilt to be brought into a criminal trial, and dealing with Constitutional infractions by other means. Still another may consider the exclusionary rule too rough and ready a remedy, in that it reaches only unconstitutional intrusions which eventuate in criminal prosecution of the victims. Further, a State after experimenting with the *Weeks* rule for a time may, because of unsatisfactory experience with it, decide to revert to a nonexclusionary rule. And so on. From the standpoint of Constitutional permissibility in pointing a State in one direction or another, I do not see at all why "time has set its face against" the considerations which led Mr. Justice Cardozo, then chief judge of the New York Court of Appeals, to reject for New York in *People* v. *Defore,* 242 N.Y. 13, the *Weeks* exclusionary rule. For us the question remains, as it has always been, one of state power, not one of passing judgment on the wisdom of one state course or another. In my view this Court should continue to forbear from fettering the States with an adamant rule which may embarrass them in coping with their own peculiar problems in criminal law enforcement. . .

Our role in promulgating the *Weeks* rule and extension . . . was quite a different one than it is here. There, in implementing the Fourth Amendment, we occupied the position of a tribunal having the ultimate responsibility for developing the standards and procedures of judicial administration within the judicial system over which it presides. Here we review State procedures whose measure is to be taken not against the specific substantive commands of the Fourth Amendment but under the flexible contours of the Due Process Clause. I do not believe that the Fourteenth Amendment empowers this Court to mold state remedies effectuating the right to freedom from "arbitrary intrusion by the police" to suit its own notions of how things should be done. . . . .

A state conviction comes to us as the complete product of a sovereign judicial system. Typically a case will have been tried in a trial court, tested in some final appellate court, and will go no further. In the comparatively rare instance when a conviction is reviewed by us on due process grounds we deal then with a finished product in the creation of which we are allowed no hand, and our task, far from being one of over-all supervision, is, speaking generally, restricted to a determination of whether the prosecution was constitutionally fair. The specifics of trial procedure, which in every mature legal system will vary greatly in detail, are within the sole competence of the States. I do not see how it can be said that a trial becomes unfair simply because a State determines that evidence may be considered by the trier of fact, regardless of how it was obtained, if it is relevant to the one issue with which the trial is concerned, the guilt or innocence of the accused. Of course, a court may use its procedures as an incidental means of pursuing other ends than the correct resolution of the controversies before it. Such indeed is the *Weeks* rule, but if a State does not choose to use its courts in this way, I do not believe that this Court is empowered to impose this much-debated procedure on local courts, however efficacious we may consider the *Weeks* rule to be as a means of securing Constitutional rights. . . .

I regret that I find so unwise in principle and so inexpedient in policy a decision motivated by the high purpose of increasing respect for Constitutional rights. But in the last analysis I think this Court can increase respect for the Constitution only if it rigidly respects the limitations which the Constitution places upon it, and respects as well the principles inherent in its own processes. In the present case I think we exceed both, and that our voice becomes only a voice of power, not of reason.

UNITED STATES *v.* RABINOWITZ
339 U.S. 56; 70 Sup. Ct. 430; 94 L. Ed. 653 (1950)

[*Rabinowitz was charged with possessing and selling altered postage stamps to defraud collectors. Federal officers arrested him under a proper arrest warrant and proceeded to search the desk, safe, and file cabinets of his one-room office for more evidence, even though they did not have a search warrant. The evidence obtained (573 forged postage stamps) was used to convict Rabinowitz in a federal district court. A court of appeals reversed the conviction on the ground that the search was illegal and the evidence so obtained was inadmissible because there had been ample time to procure a search warrant. The United States then brought the case to the Supreme Court on a writ of certiorari.*]

MR. JUSTICE MINTON delivered the opinion of the Court:

. . . The question presented here is the reasonableness of a search without a search warrant of a place of business consisting of a one-room office, incident to a valid arrest. . . .

It is unreasonable searches that are prohibited by the Fourth Amendment. . . . It was recognized by the framers of the Constitution that there were reasonable searches for which no warrant was required. The right of the "people to be secure in their persons" was certainly of as much concern to the framers of the Constitution as the property of the person. Yet no one questions the right, without a search warrant, to search the person after a valid arrest. The right to search the person incident to arrest always has been recognized in this country and in England. . . . Where one had been placed in the custody of the law by valid action of officers, it was not unreasonable to search him.

Of course, a search without warrant incident to an arrest is dependent initially on a valid arrest. Here the officers had a warrant for respondent's arrest which was, as far as can be ascertained, broad enough to cover the crime of possession charged in the second count, and consequently respondent was properly arrested. Even if the warrant of arrest were not sufficient to authorize the arrest for possession of the stamps, the arrest therefore was valid because the officers had probable cause to believe that a felony was being committed in their very presence. . . .

The arrest was therefore valid in any event, and respondent's person could be lawfully searched. Could the officers search his desk, safe, and file cabinets, all within plain sight of the parties, and all located under respondent's immediate control in his one-room office open to the public?

Decisions of this Court have often recognized that there is a permissible area of search beyond the person proper. . . .

. . . In the instant case the search was not general or exploratory for whatever might be turned up. Specificity was the mark of the search and seizure here. There was probable cause to believe that respondent was conducting his business illegally. The search was for stamps over-printed illegally, which were thought upon the most reliable information to be in the possession of and concealed by respondent in the very room where he was arrested, over which room he had immediate control and in which he had been selling such stamps unlawfully. . . . In all the years of our Nation's existence, with special attention to the Prohibition Era, it seems never to have been questioned seriously that a limited search such as here conducted as incident to a lawful arrest was a reasonable search and therefore valid. It has been considered in the same pattern as search of the person after lawful arrest.

What is a reasonable search is not to be determined by any fixed formula. The Constitution does not define what are "unreasonable" searches and, regrettably, in our discipline we have no ready litmus-paper test. The recurring questions of the reasonableness of searches must find resolution in the facts and circumstances of each case. . . . Reasonableness is in the first instance for the District Court to determine. We think the District Court's conclusion that here the search and seizure were reasonable should be sustained because: (1) the search and seizure were incident to a valid arrest; (2) the place of the search was a business room to which the public, including the officers, was invited; (3) the room was small and under the immediate and complete control of respondent; (4) the search did not extend beyond the room used for unlawful purposes; (5) the possession of the forged and altered stamps was a crime, just as it is a crime to possess burglars' tools, lottery tickets, or counterfeit money.

Assuming that the officers had time to procure a search warrant, were they bound to do so? We think not, because the search was otherwise reasonable, as previously concluded. In a recent opinion, *Trupiano* v. *United States,* 334 U.S. 699, this Court first enunciated the requirement that search warrants must be procured when "practicable" in a case of search incident to arrest. . . .

A rule of thumb requiring that a search warrant always be procured whenever practicable may be appealing from the vantage point of easy administration. But we cannot agree that this requirement should be crystallized into a *sine qua non* to the reasonableness of a search. It is fallacious to judge events retrospectively and thus to determine, considering the time element alone, that there was time to procure a search warrant. Whether there was time may well be dependent upon considerations other than the ticking off of minutes or hours. The judgment of the officers as to when to close the trap on a criminal committing a crime in their presence or

who they have reasonable cause to believe is committing a felony is not determined solely upon whether there was time to procure a search warrant. Some flexibility will be accorded law officers engaged in daily battle with criminals for whose restraint criminal laws are essential.

It is appropriate to note that the Constitution does not say that the right of the people to be secure in their persons should not be violated without a search warrant if it is practicable for the officers to procure one. The mandate of the Fourth Amendment is that the people shall be secure against *unreasonable* searches. It is not disputed that there may be reasonable searches, incident to an arrest, without a search warrant. Upon acceptance of this established rule that some authority to search follows from lawfully taking the person into custody, it becomes apparent that such searches turn upon the reasonableness under all the circumstances and not upon the practicability of procuring a search warrant, for the warrant is not required. To the extent that *Trupiano* v. *United States* . . . requires a search warrant solely upon the basis of the practicability of procuring it rather than upon the reasonableness of the search after a lawful arrest, that case is overruled. The relevant test is not whether it is reasonable to procure a search warrant, but whether the search was reasonable. That criterion in turn depends upon the facts and circumstances—the total atmosphere of the case. It is a sufficient precaution that law officers must justify their conduct before courts which have always been, and must be, jealous of the individual's right of privacy within the broad sweep of the Fourth Amendment.

. . . The motion to suppress the evidence was properly denied by the District Court. The judgment of the Court of Appeals is

Reversed.

MR. JUSTICE DOUGLAS took no part in the consideration or decision of this case.

MR. JUSTICE BLACK, dissenting:

. . . In my judgment it would be wiser judicial policy to adhere to the *Trupiano* rule of evidence, at least long enough to see how it works.

That rule is based upon very strict requirements designed to narrow the occasions upon which officers can make searches and seizures without judicial warrant. Unquestionably its application will now and then permit a guilty person to escape conviction because of hasty or ill-advised action on the part of enforcement officers. But the same may be said of the requirements of the Fourth Amendment, which the exclusionary rule was fashioned to implement. The framers of the Fourth Amendment must have concluded that reasonably strict search and seizure requirements were not too costly a price to pay for protection against the dangers incident to invasion of private premises and papers by officers, some of whom might be overzealous and oppressive. . . .

I would affirm the judgment of the Court of Appeals.

MR. JUSTICE FRANKFURTER, whom MR. JUSTICE JACKSON joins, dissenting:

The clear-cut issue before us is this: in making a lawful arrest, may arresting officers search without a search warrant not merely the person under arrest or things under his immediate physical control, but the premises where the arrest is made, although there was ample time to secure such a warrant and no danger that the "papers and effects" for which a search warrant could be issued would be despoiled or destroyed?

The old saw that hard cases make bad law has its basis in experience. But petty cases are even more calculated to make bad law. The impact of a sordid little case is apt to obscure the implications of the generalization to which the case gives rise. Only thus can I account for a disregard of the history embedded in the Fourth Amendment and the great place which belongs to that Amendment in the body of our liberties as recognized and applied by unanimous decisions over a long stretch of the Court's history.

It is a fair summary of history to say that the safeguards of liberty have frequently been forged in controversies involving not very nice people. And so, while we are concerned here with a shabby defrauder, we must deal with his case in the great theme expressed by the Fourth Amendment. A disregard of the historic materials underlying the Amendment does not answer them.

. . . The test by which searches and seizures must be judged is whether conduct is consonant with the main aim of the Fourth Amendment. The main aim of the Fourth Amendment is against invasion of the right of privacy as to one's effects and papers without regard to the result of such invasion. The purpose of the Fourth Amendment was to assure that the existence of probable cause as the legal basis for making a search was to be determined by a judicial officer before arrest and not after, subject only to what is necessarily to be expected from such requirement. The exceptions cannot be enthroned into the rule. The justification for the intrusion into a man's privacy was to be determined by a magistrate uninfluenced by what may turn out to be a successful search for papers, the desire to search for which might be the very reason for the Fourth Amendment's prohibition. The framers did not regard judicial authorization as a formal requirement for a piece of paper. They deemed a man's belongings part of his personality and his life. . . .

In the case before us there is not the slightest suggestion that the arresting officers had not the time to secure a search warrant. . . .

It is most relevant that the officers had "no excuse for not getting a search warrant," . . . for that is precisely what the Fourth Amendment was directed against—that some magistrate and not the police officer should determine, if such determination is not precluded by necessity, who should be rummaging around in my room, whether it be a small room or a very large room, whether it be one room, or two rooms, or three rooms, or four rooms.

It is not as though we are asked to extend a mischievous doctrine that has been shown to hamper law enforcers. We are asked to overrule decisions based on a long course of prior unanimous decisions, drawn from history and legislative experience. In overruling *Trupiano* we overrule the underlying principle of a whole series of recent cases. . . . [T]hese cases ought not to be allowed to remain as derelicts on the stream of the law, if we overrule *Trupiano*. These are not outmoded decisions eroded by time. Even under normal circumstances, the Court ought not to overrule such a series of decisions where no mischief flowing from them has been made manifest. Respect for continuity in law, where reasons for change are wanting, alone requires adherence to *Trupiano* and the other decisions. Especially ought the Court not needlessly re-enforce the instabilities of our day by giving fair ground for the belief that Law is the expression of chance—for instance, of unexpected changes in the Court's composition and the contingencies in the choice of successors.

OLMSTEAD *v.* UNITED STATES
277 U.S. 438; 48 Sup. Ct. 564; 72 L. Ed. 944 (1928)

[*Olmstead and others were convicted in a federal district court in the state of Washington of conspiring to violate the National Prohibition Act by unlawfully possessing, transporting, and importing intoxicating liquors. The evidence revealed a conspiracy of great magnitude. Olmstead, the ringleader of the conspiracy and general manager of the business, employed more than fifty persons. He had available two seagoing vessels and other smaller craft for the transportation of liquor. A number of underground caches in and around Seattle were used by the organization for the storage of illegal liquor. The annual income from the business was estimated to be more than $2 million.*

Four federal agents obtained evidence proving the conspiracy by tapping the telephone wires of Olmstead and other defendants. These taps were made without trespassing on the property of the conspirators. A state statute of Washington adopted in 1909 made wiretapping a crime. After the convictions were sustained by a court of appeals, Olmstead and others brought the case to the Supreme Court on a writ of certiorari.]

MR. CHIEF JUSTICE TAFT delivered the opinion of the Court:

. . . The Fourth Amendment provides: "The right of the people to be secure in their persons, houses, papers, and effects, against unreasonable searches and seizures, shall not be violated, and no warrants shall issue, but upon probable cause, supported by oath or affirmation, and particularly describing the place to be searched, and the persons or things to be seized." And the Fifth: "No person . . . shall be compelled, in any criminal case, to be a witness against himself."

It will be helpful to consider the chief cases in this court which bear upon the construction of these Amendments.

. . . [P]erhaps the most important is *Weeks* v. *United States, . . .* [which involved] a conviction for using the mails to transmit coupons or tickets in a lottery enterprise. The defendant was arrested by a police officer without a warrant. After his arrest other police officers and the United States marshal went to his house, got the key from a neighbor, entered the defendant's room and searched it, and took possession of various papers and articles. Neither the marshal nor the police officers had a search warrant. The defendant filed a petition in court asking the return of all his property. The court ordered the return of everything not pertinent to the charge, but denied return of relevant evidence. After the jury was sworn, the defendant again made objection, and on introduction of the papers contended that the search without warrant was a violation of the Fourth and Fifth Amendments, and they were therefore inadmissible. This court held that such taking of papers by an official of the United States, acting under color of his office, was in violation of the constitutional rights of the defendant, and upon making seasonable application he was entitled to have them restored, and that by permitting their use upon the trial, the trial court erred.

. . . In *Silverthorne Lumber Co.* v. *United States, . . .* the defendants were arrested at their homes and detained in custody. While so detained, representatives of the government, without authority, went to the office of their company and seized all the books, papers, and documents found there. An application for return of the things was opposed by the district attorney, who produced a subpoena for certain documents relating to the charge in the indictment then on file. The court said:

"Thus the case is not that of knowledge acquired through the wrongful act of a stranger, but it must be assumed that the government planned, or at all events ratified, the whole performance."

And it held that the illegal character of the original seizure characterized the entire proceeding, and under the *Weeks* Case the seized papers must be restored. . . .

There is no room in the present case for applying the Fifth Amendment unless the Fourth Amendment was first violated. There was no evidence of compulsion to induce the defendants to talk over their many telephones. They were continually and voluntarily transacting business without knowledge of the interception. Our consideration must be confined to the Fourth Amendment.

The striking outcome of the *Weeks* Case and those which followed it was the sweeping declaration that the Fourth Amendment, although not referring to or limiting the use of evidence in court, really forbade its introduction if obtained by government officers through a violation of the Amendment. Theretofore many had supposed that under the ordinary common-law rules, if the tendered evidence was pertinent, the method of obtaining it was unimportant. This was held by the supreme judicial court of Massachusetts, in *Commonwealth* v. *Dana.* . . . There it was ruled that the only remedy open to a defendant whose rights under a state constitutional equivalent of the Fourth Amendment had been invaded was by suit and judgment for damages. . . .

But in the *Weeks* Case, and those which followed, this court decided with great emphasis, and established as the law for the Federal courts, that the protection of the Fourth Amendment would be must impaired unless it was held that not only was the official violator of the rights under the Amendment subject to action at the suit of the injured defendant, but also that the evidence thereby obtained could not be received.

The well-known historical purpose of the Fourth Amendment, directed against general warrants and writs of assistance, was to prevent the use of governmental force to search a man's house, his person, his papers, and his effects, and to prevent their seizure against his will. . . .

The Amendment itself shows that the search is to be of material things—the persons, the house, his papers, or his effects. The description of the warrant necessary to make the proceeding lawful is that it must specify the place to be searched and the person or *things* to be seized.

It is urged that the language of Mr. Justice Field in *Ex parte Jackson* . . . offers an analogy to the interpretation of the Fourth Amendment in respect of wiretapping. But the analogy fails. The Fourth Amendment may have proper application to a sealed letter in the mail because of the constitutional provision for the Post Office Department and the relations between the government and those who pay to secure protection of their sealed letters. See Revised Statutes, §§3978 to 3988, . . . whereby Congress monopolizes the carriage of letters and excludes from that business everyone else, and §3929, . . . which forbids any postmaster or other person to open any letter not addressed to himself. It is plainly within the words of the Amendment to say that the unlawful rifling by a government agent of a sealed letter is a search and seizure of the sender's papers or effects. The letter is a paper, an effect, and in the custody of a government that forbids carriage except under its protection.

The United States take no such care of telegraph or telephone messages as of mailed sealed letters. The Amendment does not forbid what was done here. There was no searching. There was no seizure. The evidence was secured by the use of the sense of hearing and that only. There was no entry of the houses or offices of the defendants.

By the invention of the telephone fifty years ago, and its application for the purpose of extending communications, one can talk with another at a far distant place.

The language of the Amendment cannot be extended and expanded to include telephone wires reaching to the whole world from the defendant's house or office. The intervening wires are not part of his house or office, any more than are the highways along which they are stretched. . . .

Congress may, of course, protect the secrecy of telephone messages by making them, when intercepted, inadmissible in evidence in Federal criminal trials, by direct legislation, and thus depart from the common law of evidence. But the courts may not adopt such a policy by attributing an enlarged and unusual meaning to the Fourth Amendment. The reasonable view is that one who installs in his house a telephone instrument with connecting wires intends to project his voice to those outside, and that the wires beyond his house and messages while passing over them are not within the protection of the Fourth Amendment. Here those who intercepted the projected voices were not in the house of either party to the conversation.

Neither the cases we have cited nor any of the many Federal decisions brought to our attention hold the Fourth Amendment to have been violated as against a defendant unless there has been an official search and seizure of his person or such a seizure of his papers or his tangible material effects or an actual physical invasion of his house "or curtilage" [courtyard] for the purpose of making a seizure.

We think, therefore, that the wiretapping here disclosed did not amount to a search or seizure within the meaning of the Fourth Amendment.

. . . But some of our number . . . have concluded that there is merit in the two-fold objection overruled in both courts below that evidence obtained through interception of telephone messages by government agents was inadmissible because the mode of obtaining it was unethical and a misdemeanor under the law of Washington. To avoid any misapprehension of our views of that objection, we shall deal with it in both of its phases. . . .

The common-law rule is that the admissibility of evidence is not affected by the illegality of the means by which it was obtained. . . .

The rule is supported by many English and American cases. . . . The *Weeks* Case announced an exception to the common-law rule by excluding all evidence in the procuring of which government officials took part, by methods forbidden by the Fourth and Fifth Amendments. Many state courts do not follow the *Weeks* Case. . . . But those who do, treat it as an exception to the general common-law rule and required by constitutional limitations. . . .

Nor can we, without the sanction of congressional enactment, subscribe to the suggestion that the courts have a discretion to exclude evidence, the admission of which is not unconstitutional, because unethically secured. This would be at variance with the common-law doctrine generally supported by author-

ity. There is no case that sustains, nor any recognized textbook that gives color to such a view. Our general experience shows that much evidence has always been receivable although not obtained by conformity to the highest ethics. The history of criminal trials shows numerous cases of prosecutions of oath-bound conspiracies for murder, robbery, and other crimes where officers of the law have disguised themselves and joined the organizations, taken the oaths, and given themselves every appearance of active members engaged in the promotion of crime for the purpose of securing evidence. Evidence secured by such means has always been received.

A standard which would forbid the reception of evidence if obtained by other than nice ethical conduct by government officials would make society suffer and give criminals greater immunity that has been known heretofore. In the absence of controlling legislation by Congress, those who realize the difficulties in bringing offenders to justice may well deem it wise that the exclusion of evidence should be confined to cases where rights under the Constitution would be violated by admitting it.

The statute of Washington . . . does not declare that evidence obtained by such interception shall be inadmissible, and by the common law, already referred to, it would not be. . . . [C]learly a statute, passed 20 years after the admission of the state into the Union, cannot affect the rules of evidence applicable in courts of the United States. . . .

Affirmed.

MR. JUSTICE HOLMES, dissenting:

. . . [T]he government ought not to use evidence obtained, and only obtainable, by a criminal act. There is no body of precedents by which we are bound, and which confines us to logical deduction from established rules. Therefore, we must consider the two objects of desire, both of which we cannot have, and make up our minds which to choose. It is desirable that criminals should be detected, and to that end that all available evidence should be used. It also is desirable that the government should not itself foster and pay for other crimes, when they are the means by which the evidence is to be obtained. If it pays its officers for having got evidence by crime I do not see why it may not as well pay them for getting it in the same way, and I can attach no importance to protestations of disapproval if it knowingly accepts and pays and announces that in future it will pay for the fruits. We have to choose, and for my part I think it a less evil that some criminals should escape than that the government should play an ignoble part.

For those who agree with me, no distinction can be taken between the government as prosecutor and the government as judge. If the existing code does not permit district attorneys to have a hand in such dirty business, it does not permit the judge to allow such iniquities to succeed. . . . And if all that I have said so far be accepted, it makes no difference that in this case wiretapping is made a crime by the law of the state, not by the law of the United States. It is true that a state cannot make rules of evidence for the courts of the United States, but the state has authority over the conduct in question, and I hardly think that the United States would appear to greater advantage when paying for an odious crime against state law than when inciting to disregard of its own. . . . I have said that we are free to choose between two principles of policy. But if we are to confine ourselves to precedent and logic, the reason for excluding evidence obtained by violating the Constitution seems to me logically to lead to excluding evidence obtained by a crime of the officers of the law.

MR. JUSTICE BRANDEIS, dissenting:

. . . The government makes no attempt to defend the methods employed by its officers. Indeed, it concedes that if wiretapping can be deemed a search and seizure within the Fourth Amendment, such wiretapping as was practised in the case at bar was an unreasonable search and seizure, and that the evidence thus obtained was inadmissible. But it relies on the language of the Amendment; and it claims that the protection given thereby cannot properly be held to include a telephone conversation. . . .

When the Fourth and Fifth Amendments were adopted, "the form that evil had theretofore taken" had been necessarily simple. Force and violence were then the only means known to man by which a government could directly effect self-incrimination. It could compel the individual to testify—a compulsion effected, if need be, by torture. It could secure possession of his papers and other articles incident to his private life—a seizure effected, if need be, by breaking and entry. Protection against such invasion of "the sanctities of a man's home and the privacies of life" was provided in the Fourth and Fifth Amendments, by specific language. . . . But "time works changes, brings into existence new conditions and purposes." Subtler and more far-reaching means of invading privacy have become available to the government. Discovery and invention have made it possible for the government, by means far more effective than stretching upon the rack, to obtain disclosure in court of what is whispered in the closet.

Moreover, "in the application of a constitution, our contemplation cannot be only of what has been, but of what may be." The progress of science in furnishing the government with means of espionage is not likely to stop with wiretapping. Ways may some day be developed by which the government, without removing papers from secret drawers, can reproduce them in court, and by which it will be enabled to expose to a jury the most intimate occurrences of the home. Advances in the psychic and related sciences may bring means of exploring unexpressed beliefs, thoughts, and emotions. . . . Can it be that the Constitution affords no protection against such invasions of individual security? . . .

Applying to the Fourth and Fifth Amendments the established rule of construction, the defendants' objections to the evidence obtained by a wiretapping must, in my opinion, be sustained. It is, of course, immaterial where the physical connection with the telephone wires leading into the defendants' premises was made. And it is also immaterial that the intrusion was in aid of law enforcement. Experience should teach us to be most on our guard to protect liberty when the government's purposes are beneficent. Men born to freedom are naturally alert to repel invasion of their liberty by evil-minded rulers. The greatest dangers to liberty lurk in insidious encroachment by men of zeal, well-meaning, but without understanding.

Independently of the constitutional question, I am of opinion that the judgment should be reversed. By the laws of Washington, wiretapping is a crime. . . . To prove its case, the government was obliged to lay bare the crimes committed by its officers on its behalf. A federal court should not permit such a prosecution to continue. . . .

Decency, security, and liberty alike demand that government officials shall be subjected to the same rules of conduct that are commands to the citizen. In a government of laws, existence of the government will be imperilled if it fails to observe the law scrupulously. Our government is the potent, the omnipresent, teacher. For good or for ill, it teaches the whole people by its example. Crime is contagious. If the government becomes a lawbreaker, it breeds contempt for law; it invites every man to become a law unto himself; it invites anarchy. To declare that in the administration of the criminal law the end justifies the means—to declare that the government may commit crimes in order to secure the conviction of a private criminal—would bring terrible retribution. Against that pernicious doctrine this court should resolutely set its face.

MR. JUSTICE BUTLER, dissenting:

. . . The question at issue depends upon a just appreciation of the facts.

Telephones are used generally for transmission of messages concerning official, social, business, and personal affairs including communications that are private and privileged—those between physician and patient, lawyer and client, parent and child, husband and wife. The contracts between telephone companies and users contemplate the private use of the facilities employed in the service. The communications belong to the parties between whom they pass. During their transmission the exclusive use of the wire belongs to the persons served by it. Wiretapping involves interference with the wire while being used. Tapping the wires and listening in by the officers literally constituted a search for evidence. As the communications passed, they were heard and taken down. . . .

. . . [T]he petitioners . . . should be given a new trial.

[MR. JUSTICE STONE also dissented.]

MALLOY v. HOGAN
378 U.S. 1; 84 Sup. Ct. 1489; 12 L. Ed. 2d 653 (1964)

MR. JUSTICE BRENNAN delivered the opinion of the Court:

In this case we are asked to reconsider prior decisions holding that the privilege against self-incrimination is not safe-guarded against state action by the Fourteenth Amendment. *Twining* v. *New Jersey, Adamson* v. *California.*

The petitioner was arrested during a gambling raid in 1959 by Hartford, Connecticut, police. He pleaded guilty to the crime of pool selling, a misdemeanor, and was sentenced to one year in jail and fined $500. The sentence was ordered to be suspended after ninety days, at which time he was to be placed on probation for two years. About sixteen months after his guilty plea, petitioner was ordered to testify before a referee appointed by the Superior Court of Hartford County to conduct an inquiry into alleged gambling and other criminal activities in the county. The petitioner was asked a number of questions related to events surrounding his arrest and conviction. He refused to answer any question "on the grounds it may tend to incriminate me." The Superior Court adjudged him in contempt, and committed him to prison until he was willing to answer the questions. Petitioner's application for a writ of habeas corpus was denied by the Superior Court, and the Connecticut Supreme Court of Errors affirmed. 150 Conn. 220, 187 A.2d 744. The latter court held that the Fifth Amendment's privilege against self-incrimination was not available to a witness in a state proceeding, that the Fourteenth Amendment extended no privilege to him, and that the petitioner had not properly invoked the privilege available under the Connecticut Constitution. . . .

The Court has not hesitated to re-examine past decisions according the Fourteenth Amendment a less central role in the preservation of basic liberties than that which was contemplated by its Framers when they added the Amendment to our constitutional scheme. Thus, although the Court as late as 1922 said that "neither the Fourteenth Amendment nor any other provision of the Constitution of the United States imposes upon the States any restrictions about 'freedom of speech' . . . ." three years later *Gitlow* v. *New York* . . . initiated a series of decisions which today hold immune from state invasion every First Amendment protection for the cherished rights of mind and spirit—the freedoms of speech, press, religion, assembly, association, and petition for redress of grievances.

Similarly, *Palko* v. *Connecticut* . . . decided in 1937, suggested that the rights secured by the Fourth Amendment were not protected against state action, citing the statement of the Court in 1914 in *Weeks* v. *United States,* that "the 4th Amendment is not directed to individual misconduct of [state] officials." In 1961, however, the Court held that in the light of later decisions, it was taken as settled that ". . . the Fourth Amendment's right of privacy has been declared enforceable against the States through the Due Process Clause of the Fourteenth. . . ." *Mapp* v. *Ohio.* . . . Again, although the Court held in 1942 that in a state prosecution for a noncapital offense, "appointment of counsel is not a fundamental right," *Betts* v. *Brady;* cf. *Powell* v. *Alabama* . . . only last Term this decision was re-examined and it was held that provision of counsel in all criminal cases was "a fundamental right, essential to a fair trial," and thus was made obligatory on the States by the Fourteenth Amendment. *Gideon* v. *Wainwright.* . . .

We hold today that the Fifth Amendment's exception from compulsory self-incrimination is also protected by the Fourteenth Amendment against abridgment by the States. Decisions of the Court since Twining and Adamson have departed from the contrary view expressed in those cases. We discuss first the decisions which forbid the use of coerced confessions in state criminal prosecutions.

Brown v. *Mississippi* . . . was the first case in which the Court held that the Due Process Clause prohibited the States from using the accused's coerced confessions against him. The Court in Brown felt impelled, in light of Twining, to say that its conclusion did not involve the privilege against self-incrimination. "Compulsion by torture to extort a confession is a different matter." . . . But this distinction was soon abandoned, and today the admissibility of a confession in a state criminal prosecution is tested by the same standard applied in federal prosecutions since 1897, when, in *Bram* v. *United States,* . . . the Court held that "[i]n criminal trials, in the courts of the United States, wherever a question arises whether a confession is incompetent because not voluntary, the issue is controlled by that portion of the Fifth Amendment to the constitution of the United States commanding that no person 'shall be compelled in any criminal case to be a witness against himself.' " . . .

The marked shift to the federal standard in state cases began with *Lisenba* v. *California,* . . . where the Court spoke of the accused's "free choice to admit, to deny, or to refuse to answer." . . . See *Ashcraft* v. *Tennessee; Malinski* v. *New York; Spano* v. *New York; Lynumn* v. *Illinois; Haynes* v. *Washing-*

ton. . . . The shift reflects recognition that the American system of criminal prosecution is accusatorial, not inquisitorial, and that the Fifth Amendment privilege is its essential mainstay. *Rogers* v. *Richmond.* . . .

Governments, state and federal, are thus constitutionally compelled to establish guilt by evidence independently and freely secured, and may not by coercion prove a charge against an accused out of his own mouth. Since the Fourteenth Amendment prohibits the States from inducing a person to confess through "sympathy falsely aroused," *Spano* v. *New York,* . . . or other like inducement far short of "compulsion by torture," *Haynes* v. *Washington,* it follows *a fortiori* that it also forbids the States to resort to imprisonment, as here, to compel him to answer questions that might incriminate him. The Fourteenth Amendment secures against state invasion the same privilege that the Fifth Amendment guarantees against federal infringement—the right of a person to remain silent unless he chooses to speak in the unfettered exercise of his own will, and to suffer no penalty, as held in *Twining,* for such silence.

This conclusion is fortified by our recent decision in *Mapp* v. *Ohio;* . . . overruling *Wolf* v. *Colorado,* . . . which had held "that in a prosecution in a State court for a State crime the Fourteenth Amendment does not forbid the admission of evidence obtained by an unreasonable search and seizure." . . . *Mapp* held that the Fifth Amendment privilege against self-incrimination implemented the Fourth Amendment in such cases, and that the two guarantees of personal security conjoined in the Fourteenth Amendment to make the exclusionary rule obligatory upon the States. We relied upon the great case of *Boyd* v. *United States,* . . .

decided in 1886, which, considering the Fourth and Fifth Amendments as running "almost into each other," . . . held that "Breaking into a house and opening boxes and drawers are circumstances of aggravation; but any forcible and compulsory extortion of a man's own testimony, or of his private papers to be used as evidence to convict him of crime, or to forfeit his goods, is within the condemnation of [those Amendments]. . . ." We said in *Mapp:*

> "We find that, as to the Federal Government the Fourth and Fifth Amendments and, as to the States, the freedom from unconscionable invasions of privacy and the freedom from convictions based upon coerced confessions do enjoy an 'intimate relation' in their perpetuation of 'principles of humanity and civil liberty [secured] . . . only after years of struggle.' . . . The philosophy of each Amendment and of each freedom is complementary to, although not dependent upon, that of the other in its sphere of influence—the very least that together they assure in either sphere is that no man is to be convicted on unconstitutional evidence." . . .

In thus returning to the *Boyd* view that the privilege is one of the "principles of a free government," . . . *Mapp* necessarily repudiated the *Twining* concept of the privilege as a mere rule of evidence "best defended not as an unchangeable principle of universal justice, but as a law proved by experience to be expedient." . . .

The State urges, however, that the availability of the federal privilege to a witness in a state inquiry is to be determined according to a less stringent standard than is applicable in a federal proceeding. We disagree. We have held that the guarantees of the First Amendment, *Gitlow* v. *New York; Cantwell*

v. *Connecticut; Louisiana ex rel. Gremillion* v. *NAACP,* . . . the prohibition of unreasonable searches and seizures of the Fourth Amendment, *Ker* v. *California,* . . . and the right to counsel guaranteed by the Sixth Amendment, *Gideon* v. *Wainwright,* are all to be enforced against the States under the Fourteenth Amendment according to the same standards that protect those personal rights against federal encroachment. . . . The Court thus has rejected the notion that the Fourteenth Amendment applies to the States only a "watered-down, subjective version of the individual guarantees of the Bill of Rights." . . . If *Cohen* v. *Hurley* . . . and *Adamson* v. *California,* suggest such an application of the privilege against self-incrimination, that suggestion cannot survive recognition of the degree to which the *Twining* view of the privilege has been eroded. What is accorded is a privilege of refusing to incriminate one's self, and the feared prosecution may be by either federal or state authorities. *Murphy* v. *Waterfront Commission.* . . . It would be incongruous to have different standards determine the validity of a claim of privilege based on the same feared prosecution, depending on whether the claim was asserted in a state or federal court. Therefore, the same standards must determine whether an accused's silence in either a federal or state proceeding is justified. . . .

It was admitted on behalf of the State at oral argument—and indeed it is obvious from the questions themselves—that the State desired to elicit from the petitioner the identity of the person who ran the pool-selling operation in connection with which he had been arrested in 1959. It was apparent that petitioner might apprehend that if this person were still engaged in unlawful activity, disclosure of his name might furnish a link in a chain of evidence sufficient to connect the petitioner with a more recent crime for which he might still be prosecuted. . . .

We conclude, therefore, that as to each of the questions, it was "evident from the implications of the question, in the setting in which it [was] asked, that a responsive answer to the question or an explanation of why it [could not] be answered might be dangerous because injurious disclosure could result," *Hoffman* v. *United States*. . . .

Reversed.

While MR. JUSTICE DOUGLAS joins the opinion of the Court, he also adheres to his concurrence in *Gideon* v. *Wainwright*. . . .

MR. JUSTICE HARLAN, whom MR. JUSTICE CLARK joins, dissenting:

. . . I can only read the Court's opinion as accepting in fact what it rejects in theory: the application to the States, via the Fourteenth Amendment, of the forms of federal criminal procedure embodied within the first eight Amendments to the Constitution. While it is true that the Court deals today with only one aspect of state criminal procedure, and rejects the wholesale "incorporation" of such federal constitutional requirements, the logical gap between the Court's premises and its novel constitutional conclusion can, I submit, be bridged only by the additional premise that the Due Process Clause of the Fourteenth Amendment is a shorthand directive to this Court to pick and choose among the provisions of the first eight Amendments and apply those chosen, freighted with their entire accompanying body of federal doctrine, to law enforcement in the States.

I accept and agree with the proposition that continuing re-examination of the constitutional conception of Fourteenth Amendment "due process" of law is required, and that development of the community's sense of justice may in time lead to expansion of the protection which due process affords. In particular in this case, I agree that principles of justice to which due process gives expression, as reflected in decisions of this Court, prohibit a State, as the Fifth Amendment prohibits the Federal Government, from imprisoning a person *solely* because he refuses to give evidence which may incriminate him under the laws of the State. I do not understand, however, how this process of re-examination, which must refer always to the guiding standard of due process of law, including, of course, reference to the particular guarantees of the Bill of Rights, can be short-circuited by the simple device of incorporating into due process, without critical examination, the whole body of law which surrounds a specific prohibition directed against the Federal Government. The consequence of such an approach to due process as it pertains to the States is inevitably disregard of all relevant differences which may exist between state and federal criminal law and its enforcement. The ultimate result is compelled uniformity, which is inconsistent with the purpose of our federal system and which is achieved either by encroachment on the States' sovereign powers or by dilution in federal law enforcement of the specific protections found in the Bill of Rights.

As recently as 1961, this Court reaffirmed that "the Fifth Amendment's privilege against self-incrimination," . . . was not applicable against the States. *Cohen* v. *Hurley*. . . . The question had been most fully explored in *Twining* v. *New Jersey*. . . . Since 1908, when *Twining* was decided, this Court has adhered to the view there expressed that "the exemption from compulsory self-incrimination in the courts of the states is not secured by any part of the Federal Constitution" . . . ; *Palko* v. *Connecticut; Adamson* v. *Cali-*

fornia; Knapp v. *Schweitzer; Cohen,* supra. Although none of these cases involved a commitment to prison for refusing to incriminate oneself under state law, and they are relevantly distinguishable from this case on that narrow ground, it is perfectly clear from them that until today it has been regarded as settled law that the Fifth Amendment privilege did not, by any process of reasoning, apply *as such* to the States.

The Court suggests that this consistent line of authority has been undermined by the concurrent development of constitutional doctrine in the areas of coerced confessions and search and seizure. That is *post facto* reasoning at best. Certainly there has been no intimation until now that *Twining* has been tacitly overruled.

It was in *Brown* v. *Mississippi* that this Court first prohibited the use of a coerced confession in a state criminal trial. The petitioners in *Brown* had been tortured until they confessed. The Court was hardly making an artificial distinction when it said:

> "[T]he question of the right of the state to withdraw the privilege against self-incrimination is not here involved. The compulsion to which the quoted statements [from Twining and Snyder, supra,] refer is that of the *processes of justice* by which the accused may be called as a witness and required to testify. *Compulsion by torture* to extort a confession is a different matter." . . . (Emphasis supplied.)

The majority is simply wrong when it asserts that this perfectly understandable distinction "was soon abandoned," . . . In none of the cases cited, . . . in which was developed the full sweep of the constitutional prohibition against the use of coerced confessions at state trials, was there anything to suggest

that the Fifth Amendment was being made applicable to state proceedings. In *Lisenba* v. *California* . . . the privilege against self-incrimination is not mentioned. The relevant question before the Court was whether "the evidence [of coercion] requires that we set aside the finding of two courts and a jury and adjudge the admission of the confessions so fundamentally unfair, so contrary to the common concept of ordered liberty as to amount to a taking of life without due process of law." . . . Finally, in *Rogers* v. *Richmond,* . . . although the Court did recognize that "ours is an accusatorial and not an inquisitorial system," . . . it is clear that the Court was concerned only with the problem of coerced confessions . . . ; the opinion includes nothing to support the Court's assertion here . . . that "the Fifth Amendment privilege is . . . [the] essential mainstay" of our system.

The coerced confession cases are relevant to the problem of this case not because they overruled Twining *sub silentio,* but rather because they applied the same standard of fundamental fairness which is applicable here. The recognition in them that federal supervision of state criminal procedures must be direcly based on the requirements of due process is entirely inconsistent with the theory here espoused by the majority. The parallel treatment of federal and state cases involving coerced confessions resulted from the fact that the same demand of due process was applicable in both; it was not the consequence of the automatic engrafting of federal law construing constitutional provisions inapplicable to the States onto the Fourteenth Amendment.

The decision in *Mapp* v. *Ohio,* . . . that evidence unconstitutionally seized . . . may not be used in a state criminal trial furnishes no "fortification" . . . for today's decision. The very passage from the Mapp opinion which the Court quotes . . . makes explicit the distinct bases of the exclusionary rule as applied in federal and state courts:

"We find that, as to the Federal Government, the Fourth and Fifth Amendments and, as to the States, the freedom from unconscionable invasions of privacy and the freedom from convictions based upon coerced confessions do enjoy an 'intimate relation' in their perpetuation of 'principles of humanity and civil liberty [secured] . . . only after years of struggle'. . . .

Although the Court discussed *Boyd* v. *United States,* . . . a federal case involving both the Fourth and Fifth Amendments, nothing in *Mapp* supports the statement . . . that the Fifth Amendment was part of the basis for extending the exclusionary rule to the States. The elaboration of *Mapp* in *Ker* v. *California* . . . did in my view make the Fourth Amendment applicable to the States through the Fourteenth; but there is nothing in it to suggest that the Fifth Amendment went along as baggage.

The previous discussion shows that this Court's decisions do not dictate the "incorporation" of the Fifth Amendment's privilege against self-incrimination into the Fourteenth Amendment. Approaching the question more broadly, it is equally plain that the line of cases exemplified by *Palko* v. *Connecticut,* . . . in which this Court has reconsidered the requirements which the Due Process Clause imposes on the States in the light of current standards, furnishes no general theoretical framework for what the Court does today. . . .

Seen in proper perspective, therefore, the fact that First Amendment protections have generally been given equal scope in the federal and state domains or that in some areas of criminal procedure the Due Process Clause demands as much of the States as the Bill of Rights demands of the Federal Government, is only tangentially relevant to the question now before us. It is toying with constitutional principles to assert that the Court has "rejected the notion that the Fourteenth Amendment applies to the states only a 'watered-down, subjective version of the individual guarantees of the Bill of Rights' " . . . . What the Court has, with the single exception of the *Ker* case, . . . consistently rejected is the notion that the Bill of Rights, as such, applies to the States in any aspect at all.

If one attends to those areas to which the Court points, . . . in which the prohibitions against the state and federal governments have moved in parallel tracks, the cases in fact reveal again that the Court's usual approach has been to ground the prohibitions against state action squarely on due process, without intermediate reliance on any of the first eight Amendments. Although more recently the Court has referred to the First Amendment to describe the protection of free expression against state infringement, earlier cases leave no doubt that such references are "shorthand" for doctrines developed by another route. In *Gitlow* v. *New York,* . . . for example, the Court said:

"For present purposes we may and do assume that freedom of speech and of the press—which are protected by the First Amendment from abridgment by Congress—are among the fundamental personal rights and 'liberties' protected by the due process clause of the Fourteenth Amendment from impairment by the States."

The coerced confession and search and seizure cases have already been considered. The former, decided always directly on grounds of fundamental fairness, furnish no support for the

Court's present views. *Ker* v. *California,* did indeed incorporate the Fourth Amendment's protection against invasions of privacy into the Due Process Clause. But that case should be regarded as the exception which proves the rule. The right to counsel in state criminal proceedings, which this Court assured in *Gideon* v. *Wainwright* . . . does not depend on the Sixth Amendment. . . .

Although *Gideon* overruled *Betts,* the constitutional approach in both cases was the same. *Gideon* was based on the Court's conclusion, contrary to that reached in *Betts,* that the appointment of counsel for an indigent criminal defendant *was* essential to the conduct of a fair trial, and was therefore part of due process. . . .

The Court's approach in the present case is in fact nothing more or less than "incorporation" in snatches. If, however, the Due Process Clause *is* something more than a reference to the Bill of Rights and protects only those rights which derive from fundamental principles, as the majority purports to believe, it is just as contrary to precedent and just as illogical to incorporate the provisions of the Bill of Rights one at a time as it is to incorporate them all at once.

The Court's undiscriminating approach to the Due Process Clause carries serious implications for the sound working of our federal system in the field of criminal law.

The Court concludes, almost without discussion, that "the same standards must determine whether an accused's silence in either a federal or state proceeding is justified," . . . About all that the Court offers in explanation of this conclusion is the observation that it would be "incongruous" if different standards governed the assertion of a privilege to remain silent in state and federal tribunals. Such "incongruity," however, is at the heart of our federal

system. The powers and responsibilities of the state and federal governments are not congruent; under our Constitution, they are not intended to be. Why should it be thought, as an *a priori* matter, that limitations on the investigative power of the States are in all respects identical with limitations on the investigative power of the Federal Government? . . .

As the Court pointed out in *Abbate* v. *United States,* . . . "the States under our federal system have the principal responsibility for defining and prosecuting crimes." The Court endangers this allocation of responsibility for the prevention of crime when it applies to the States doctrines developed in the context of federal law enforcement, without any attention to the special problems which the States as a group or particular States may face. If the power of the States to deal with local crime is unduly restricted, the likely consequence is a shift of responsibility in this area to the Federal Government, with its vastly greater resources. Such a shift, if it occurs, may in the end serve to weaken the very liberties which the Fourteenth Amendment safeguards by bringing us closer to the monolithic society which our federalism rejects. Equally dangerous to our liberties is the alternative of watering down protections against the Federal Government embodied in the Bill of Rights so as not unduly to restrict the powers of the States.

Rather than insisting, almost by rote, that the Connecticut court, in considering the petitioner's claim of privilege, was required to apply the "federal standard," the Court should have fulfilled its responsibility under the Due Process Clause by inquiring whether the proceedings below met the demands of fundamental fairness which due process embodies. Such an approach may not satisfy those who see in the

Fourteenth Amendment a set of easily applied "absolutes" which can afford a haven from unsettling doubt. It is, however, truer to the spirit which requires this Court constantly to re-examine fundamental principles and at the same time enjoins it from reading its own preferences into the Constitution. . . .

MR. JUSTICE WHITE, with whom MR. JUSTICE STEWART joins, dissenting:

The Fifth Amendment safeguards an important complex of values, but it is difficult for me to perceive how these values are served by the Court's holding that the privilege was properly invoked in this case. While purporting to apply the prevailing federal standard of incrimination—the same standard of incrimination that the Connecticut courts applied—the Court has all but stated that a witness' invocation of the privilege to any question is to be automatically, and without more, accepted. With deference, I prefer the rule permitting the judge rather than the witness to determine when an answer sought is incriminating.

The established rule has been that the witness' claim of the privilege is not final, for the privilege qualifies a citizen's general duty of disclosure only when his answers would subject him to danger from the criminal law. The privilege against self-incrimination or any other evidentiary privilege does not protect silence which is solely an expression of political protest, a desire not to inform, a fear of social obloquy or economic disadvantage or fear of prosecution for future crimes. *Smith* v. *United States*. . . . If the general duty to testify when subpoenaed is to remain and the privilege is to be retained as a protection against compelled incriminating answers, the trial judge must be permitted to make a meaningful determination of when answers tend to incriminate. . . .

POWELL v. ALABAMA
287 U.S. 45; 53 Sup. Ct. 55; 77 L. Ed. 158 (1932)

[*In 1931, Powell and six other Negroes were convicted in Alabama for the rape of two white girls. Their trial lasted one day, and they were all sentenced to death. They had been arrested, tried, and sentenced in an atmosphere of tense, hostile, excited public sentiment. Neither were they represented by counsel; the trial judge had only vaguely appointed all members of the bar to represent the defendants. The Alabama Supreme Court affirmed the convictions, with its chief justice writing a strong dissent on the grounds that the defendants had not been given a fair trial. The Supreme Court granted certiorari. The* Powell *case is the first of a series referred to as the Scottsboro cases. They are so termed because it was near the community of Scottsboro, Alabama, that the petitioners were apprehended.*]

MR. JUSTICE SUTHERLAND delivered the opinion of the Court:

. . . In this court the judgments are assailed upon the grounds that the defendants, and each of them, were denied due process of law and the equal protection of the laws, in contravention of the Fourteenth Amendment, specif-ically as follows: (1) they were not given a fair, impartial, and deliberate trial; (2) they were denied the right of counsel, with the accustomed incidents of consultation and opportunity of preparation for trial; and (3) they were tried before juries from which qualified members of their own race were systematically excluded. These questions were properly raised and saved in the courts below.

The only one of the assignments which we shall consider is the second, in respect of the denial of counsel; and it becomes unnecessary to discuss the facts of the case or the circumstances surrounding the prosecution except in so far as they reflect light upon that question. . . .

First. The record shows that immediately upon the return of the indictment defendants were arraigned and pleaded not guilty. Apparently they were not asked whether they had, or were able to employ, counsel, or wished to have counsel appointed; or whether they had friends or relatives who might assist in that regard if communicated with. That it would not have been an idle ceremony to have given the defendants reasonable opportunity to communicate with their families and endeavor to obtain counsel is demonstrated by the fact that, very soon after conviction, able counsel appeared in their behalf. This was pointed out by Chief Justice Anderson in the course of his dissenting opinion. "They were nonresidents," he said, "and had little time or opportunity to get in touch with their families and friends who were scattered throughout two other states, and time has demonstrated that they could or would have been represented by able counsel had a better opportunity been given by a reasonable delay in the trial of the cases, judging from the number and activity of counsel that appeared immediately or shortly after their conviction."

. . . It is hardly necessary to say that, the right to counsel being conceded, a defendant should be afforded a fair opportunity to secure counsel of his own choice. Not only was that not done here, but such designation of counsel as was attempted was either so indefinite or so close upon the trial as

to amount to a denial by effective and substantial aid in that regard. This will be amply demonstrated by a brief review of the record.

April 6, six days after indictment, the trials began. When the first case was called, the court inquired whether the parties were ready for trial. The state's attorney replied that he was ready to proceed. No one answered for the defendants or appeared to represent or defend them. Mr. Roddy, a Tennessee lawyer not a member of the local bar, addressed the court, saying that he had not been employed, but that people who were interested had spoken to him about the case. He was asked by the court whether he intended to appear for the defendants, and answered that he would like to appear along with counsel that the court might appoint. The record then proceeds:

"The Court: If you appear for these defendants, then I will not appoint counsel; if local counsel are willing to appear and assist you under the circumstances all right, but I will not appoint them.

"Mr. Roddy: Your Honor has appointed counsel, is that correct?

"The Court: I appointed all the members of the bar for the purpose of arraigning the defendants and then of course I anticipated them to continue to help them if no counsel appears."

. . . [U]ntil the very morning of the trial no lawyer had been named or definitely designated to represent the defendants. Prior to that time, the trial judge had "appointed all the members of the bar" for the limited "purpose of arraigning the defendants." Whether they would represent the defendants thereafter if no counsel appeared in their behalf, was a matter of speculation only, or, as the judge indicated, of mere anticipation on the part of the court. Such a designation, even if made for all purposes, would, in our opinion, have fallen far short of meeting, in any proper sense, a requirement for the appointment of counsel. How many lawyers were members of the bar does not appear; but, in the very nature of things, whether many or few, they would not, thus collectively named, have been given that clear appreciation of responsibility or impressed with that individual sense of duty which should and naturally would accompany the appointment of a selected member of the bar, specifically named and assigned.

. . . [T]his action of the trial judge in respect of appointment of counsel was little more than an expansive gesture, imposing no substantial or definite obligation upon anyone. . . . During perhaps the most critical period of the proceedings against these defendants, that is to say, from the time of their arraignment until the beginning of their trial, when consultation, thoroughgoing investigation and preparation were vitally important, the defendants did not have the aid of counsel in any real sense, although they were as much entitled to such aid during that period as at the trial itself. . . .

. . . The prompt disposition of criminal cases is to be commended and encouraged. But in reaching that result a defendant, charged with a serious crime, must not be stripped of his right to have sufficient time to advise with counsel and prepare his defense. To do that is not to proceed promptly in the calm spirit of regulated justice but to go forward with the haste of the mob. . . .

Second. The Constitution of Alabama provides that in all criminal prosecutions the accused shall enjoy the right to have the assistance of counsel; and a state statute requires the court in a capital case, where the defendant is unable to employ counsel, to appoint counsel for him. The state supreme court held that these provisions had not been infringed, and with that holding we are powerless to interfere. The question, however, which it is our duty, and within our power, to decide, is whether the denial of the assistance of counsel contravenes the due process clause of the Fourteenth Amendment to the federal Constitution.

If recognition of the right of a defendant charged with a felony to have the aid of counsel depended upon the existence of a similar right at common law as it existed in England when our Constitution was adopted, there would be great difficulty in maintaining it as necessary to due process. Originally, in England, a person charged with treason or felony was denied the aid of counsel, except in respect of legal questions which the accused himself might suggest. At the same time parties in civil cases and persons accused of misdemeanors were entitled to the full assistance of counsel. After the revolution of 1688, the rule was abolished as to treason, but was otherwise steadily adhered to until 1836, when by act of Parliament the full right was granted in respect of felonies generally. . . .

An affirmation of the right to the aid of counsel in petty offenses, and its denial in the case of crimes of the gravest character, where such aid is most needed, is so outrageous and so obviously a perversion of all sense of proportion that the rule was constantly, vigorously and sometimes passionately assailed by English statesmen and lawyers. . . .

The rule was rejected by the colonies. . . .

It . . . appears that in at least twelve of the thirteen colonies the rule of the English common law, in the respect now under consideration, had been definitely rejected and the right to counsel fully recognized in all criminal prosecutions, save that in one or two instances the right was limited to capital offenses or to the more serious crimes; and this court seems to have been of the opinion that this was true in all the colonies. . . .

. . . One test which has been applied to determine whether due process of law has been accorded in given instances is to ascertain what were the settled usages and modes of proceeding under the common and statute law of England before the Declaration of Independence, subject, however, to the qualification that they be shown not to have been unsuited to the civil and political conditions of our ancestors by having been followed in this country after it became a nation. . . . Plainly, as appears from the foregoing, this test, as thus qualified, has not been met in the present case. . . .

The Sixth Amendment, in terms, provides that in all criminal prosecutions the accused shall enjoy the right "to have the assistance of counsel for his defense." In the face of the reasoning of the *Hurtado* case, if it stood alone, it would be difficult to justify the conclusion that the right to counsel, being thus specifically granted by the Sixth Amendment, was also within the intendment of the due process of law clause. But the *Hurtado* case does not stand alone. . . .

. . . [N]otwithstanding the sweeping character of the language in the *Hurtado* case, the rule laid down is not without exceptions. The rule is an aid to construction, and in some instances may be conclusive; but it must yield to more compelling considerations whenever such considerations exist. The fact that the right involved is of such a character that it cannot be denied without violating those "fundamental principles of liberty and justice which lie at the base of all our civil and political institutions" . . . is obviously one of those compeling considerations which

must prevail in determining whether it is embraced within the due process clause of the Fourteenth Amendment, although it be specifically dealt with in another part of the federal Constitution. Evidently this court, in the later cases enumerated, regarded the rights there under consideration as of this fundamental character. That some such distinction must be observed is foreshadowed in *Twining* v. *New Jersey,* . . . where Mr. Justice Moody, speaking for the court, said that ". . . it is possible that some of the personal rights safeguarded by the first eight Amendments against National action may also be safeguarded against state action, because a denial of them would be a denial of due process of law. . . . If this is so, it is not because those rights are enumerated in the first eight Amendments, but because they are of such a nature that they are included in the conception of due process of law." While the question has never been categorically determined by this court, a consideration of the nature of the right and a review of the expressions of this and other courts, makes it clear that the right to the aid of counsel is of this fundamental character.

It never has been doubted by this court, or any other so far as we know, that notice and hearing are preliminary steps essential to the passing of an enforceable judgment, and that they, together with a legally competent tribunal having jurisdiction of the case, constitute basic elements of the constitutional requirement of due process of law. . . .

What, then, does a hearing include? Historically and in practice, in our own country at least, it has always included the right to the aid of counsel when desired and provided by the party asserting the right. The right to be heard would be, in many cases, of little avail if it did not comprehend the right to be heard by counsel. Even the intelligent and educated layman has small and sometimes no skill in the science of law. If charged with crime, he is incapable, generally, of determining for himself whether the indictment is good or bad. He is unfamiliar with the rules of evidence. Left without the aid of counsel he may be put on trial without a proper charge, and convicted upon incompetent evidence, or evidence irrelevant to the issue or otherwise inadmissible. He lacks both the skill and knowledge adequately to prepare his defense, even though he have a perfect one. He requires the guiding hand of counsel at every step in the proceedings against him. Without it, though he be not guilty, he faces the danger of conviction because he does not know how to establish his innocence. If that be true of men of intelligence, how much more true is it of the ignorant and illiterate, or those of feeble intellect. If in any case, civil or criminal, a state or federal court were arbitrarily to refuse to hear a party by counsel, employed by and appearing for him, it reasonably may not be doubted that such a refusal would be a denial of a hearing, and, therefore, of due process in the constitutional sense. . . .

In the light of the facts . . . —the ignorance and illiteracy of the defendants, their youth, the circumstances of public hostility, the imprisonment and the close surveillance of the defendants by the military forces, the fact that their friends and families were all in other states and communication with them necessarily difficult, and above all that they stood in deadly peril of their lives—we think the failure of the trial court to give them reasonable time and opportunity to secure counsel was a clear denial of due process.

But passing that, and assuming their inability, even if opportunity had been given, to employ counsel, as the trial court evidently did assume, we are of opinion that, under the circumstances just stated, the necessity of counsel was so vital and imperative that the failure of the trial court to make an effective appointment of counsel was likewise a denial of due process within the meaning of the Fourteenth Amendment. Whether this would be so in other criminal prosecutions, or under other circumstances, we need not determine. All that it is necessary now to decide, as we do decide, is that in a capital case, where the defendant is unable to employ counsel, and is incapable adequately of making his own defense because of ignorance, feeblemindedness, illiteracy, or the like, it is the duty of the court, whether requested or not, to assign counsel for him as a necessary requisite of due process of law; and that duty is not discharged by an assignment at such a time or under such circumstances as to preclude the giving of effective aid in the preparation and trial of the case. To hold otherwise would be to ignore the fundamental postulate, already adverted to, "that there are certain immutable principles of justice which inhere in the very idea of free government which no member of the Union may disregard." . . . In a case such as this, whatever may be the rule in other cases, the right to have counsel appointed, when necessary, is a logical corollary from the constitutional right to be heard by counsel. . . .

The judgments must be reversed and the causes remanded for further proceedings not inconsistent with this opinion.

Judgments reversed.

[MR. JUSTICE BUTLER, joined by MR. JUSTICE MC REYNOLDS, wrote a dissenting opinion.]

MIRANDA v. ARIZONA
384 U.S. 436; 86 Sup. Ct. 1602; 16 L. Ed. 2d 694 (1966)

[Miranda *consolidates for decision the cases of four persons convicted on the basis of confessions made after extended questioning in which they were not informed of their rights to counsel and to remain silent. The crimes of which they were found guilty included kidnapping, rape, robbery, and murder.*]

MR. CHIEF JUSTICE WARREN delivered the opinion of the Court:

The cases before us raise questions which go to the roots of our concepts of American criminal jurisprudence: the restraints society must observe consistent with the Federal Constitution in prosecuting individuals for crime. More specifically, we deal with the admissibility of statements obtained from an individual who is subjected to custodial police interrogation and the necessity for procedures which assure that the individual is accorded his privilege under the Fifth Amendment to the Constitution not to be compelled to incriminate himself. . . .

Our holding will be spelled out with some specificity in the pages which follow but briefly stated it is this: the prosecution may not use statements, whether exculpatory or inculpatory, stemming from custodial interrogation of the defendant unless it demonstrates the use of procedural safeguards effective to secure the privilege against self-incrimination. By custodial interrogation, we mean questioning initiated by law enforcement officers after a person has been taken into custody or otherwise deprived of his freedom of action in any significant way.* As for the procedural safeguards to be employed, unless other fully effective means are devised to inform accused persons of their right of silence and to assure a continuous opportunity to exercise it, the fol-

* This is what we meant in Escobedo when we spoke of an investigation which had focused on an accused.

lowing measures are required. Prior to any questioning, the person must be warned that he has a right to remain silent, that any statement he does make may be used as evidence against him, and that he has a right to the presence of an attorney, either retained or appointed. The defendant may waive effectuation of these rights, provided the waiver is made voluntarily, knowingly and intelligently. If, however, he indicates in any manner and at any stage of the process that he wishes to consult with an attorney before speaking there can be no questioning. Likewise, if the individual is alone and indicates in any manner that he does not wish to be interrogated, the police may not question him. The mere fact that he may have answered some questions or volunteered some statements on his own does not deprive him of the right to refrain from answering any further inquiries until he has consulted with an attorney and thereafter consents to be questioned.

I

The constitutional issue we decide in each of these cases is the admissibility of statements obtained from a defendant questioned while in custody and deprived of his freedom of action. In each, the defendant was questioned by police officers, detectives, or a prosecuting attorney in a room in which he was cut off from the outside world. In none of these cases was the defendant given a full and effective warning of his rights at the outset of the interrogation process. In all the cases, the questioning elicited oral admissions, and in three of them, signed statements as well which were admitted at their trials. They all thus share salient features—incommunicado interrogation of individuals in a police-dominated atmosphere, resulting in self-incriminating statements without full warnings of constitutional rights.

An understanding of the nature and setting of this in-custody interrogation is essential to our decisions today. The difficulty in depicting what transpires at such interrogations stems from the fact that in this country they have largely taken place incommunicado. From extensive factual studies undertaken in the early 1930s, including the famous Wickersham Report to Congress by a Presidential Commission, it is clear that police violence and the "third degree" flourished at that time. In a series of cases decided by this Court long after these studies, the police resorted to physical brutality—beatings, hanging, whipping—and to sustained and protracted questioning incommunicado in order to extort confessions. The 1961 Commission on Civil Rights found much evidence to indicate that "some policemen still resort to physical force to obtain confessions." . . . The use of physical brutality and violence is not, unfortunately, relegated to the past or to any part of the country. Only recently in Kings County, New York, the police brutally beat, kicked and placed lighted cigarette butts on the back of a potential witness under interrogation for the purpose of securing a statement incriminating a third party.

The examples given above are undoubtedly the exception now, but they are sufficiently widespread to be the object of concern. Unless a proper limitation upon custodial interrogation is achieved—such as these decisions will advance—there can be no assurance that practices of this nature will be eradicated in the foreseeable future. . . .

Again we stress that the modern practice of in-custody interrogation is psychologically rather than physically oriented. As we have stated before, "Since *Chambers* v. *Florida,* this Court has recognized that coercion can be mental as well as physical, and that the blood of the accused is not the only hallmark of an unconstitutional inquisition." *Blackburn* v. *Alabama.* Interrogation still takes place in privacy. Privacy results in secrecy and this in turn results in a gap in our knowledge as to what in fact goes on in the interrogation rooms. A valuable source of information about present police practices, however, may be found in various police manuals and texts which document procedures employed with success in the past, and which recommend various other effective tactics. These texts are used by law enforcement agencies themselves as guides. It should be noted that these texts professedly present the most enlightened and effective means presently used to obtain statements through custodial interrogation. By considering these texts, and other data, it is possible to describe procedures observed and noted around the country. . . .

From these representative samples of interrogation techniques, the setting prescribed by the manuals and observed in practice becomes clear. In essence, it is this: To be alone with the subject is essential to prevent distraction and to deprive him of any outside support. The aura of confidence in his guilt undermines his will to resist. He merely confirms the preconceived story the police seek to have him describe. Patience and persistence, at times relentless questioning, are employed. To obtain a confession, the interrogator must "patiently maneuver himself or his quarry into a position from which the desired object may be obtained." When normal procedures fail to produce the needed result, the police may resort to deceptive stratagems such as giving false legal advice. It is important to keep the subject off balance, for example, by trading on his insecurity about himself or his surroundings. The police then persuade, trick, or cajole him out of exercising his constitutional rights.

Even without employing brutality, the "third degree" or the specific stratagems described above, the very fact of custodial interrogation exacts a heavy toll on individual liberty and trades on the weakness of individuals. . . .

In the cases before us today, given this background, we concern ourselves primarily with this interrogation atmosphere and the evils it can bring. In No. 759, *Miranda* v. *Arizona,* the police arrested the defendant and took him to a special interrogation room where they secured a confession. In No. 760, *Vignera* v. *New York,* the defendant made oral admissions to the police after interrogation in the afternoon, and then signed an inculpatory statement upon being questioned by an assistant district attorney later the same evening. In No. 761, *Westover* v. *United States,* the defendant was handed over to the Federal Bureau of Investigation by local authorities after they had detained and interrogated him for a lengthy period, both at night and the following morning. After some two hours of questioning, the federal officers had obtained signed statements from the defendant. Lastly, in No. 584, *California* v. *Stewart,* the local police held the defendant five days in the station and interrogated him on nine separate occasions before they secured his inculpatory statement.

In these cases, we might not find the defendants' statements to have been involuntary in traditional terms. Our concern for adequate safeguards to protect precious Fifth Amendment rights is, of course, not lessened in the slightest. In each of the cases, the defendant was thrust into an unfamiliar atmosphere and run through menacing police interrogation procedures. The potentiality for compulsion is forcefully apparent for example, in *Miranda,* where the indigent Mexican defendant was a seriously disturbed individual with pronounced sexual fantasies, and in *Stewart,* in which the defendant was an indigent Los Angeles Negro who had dropped out of school in the sixth grade. To be sure, the records do not evince overt physical coercion or patented psychological ploys. The fact remains that in none of these cases did the officers undertake to afford appropriate safeguards at the outset of the interrogation to insure that the statements were truly the product of free choice.

It is obvious that such an interrogation environment is created for no purpose other than to subjugate the individual to the will of his examiner. This atmosphere carries its own badge of intimidation. To be sure, this is not physical intimidation, but it is equally destructive of human dignity. The current practice of incommunicado interrogation is at odds with one of our Nation's most cherished principles—that the individual may not be compelled to incriminate himself. Unless adequate protective devices are employed to dispel the compulsion inherent in custodial surroundings, no statement obtained from the defendant can truly be the product of his free choice.

From the foregoing, we can readily perceive an intimate connection between the privilege against self-incrimination and police custodial questioning. . . .

II

. . . As a "noble principle often transcends its origins," the privilege has come rightfully to be recognized in part as an individual's substantive right, a "right to a private enclave where he may lead a private life. That right is the hallmark of our democracy." . . . We have recently noted that the privilege against self-incrimination—the essential mainstay of our adversary system—is founded on a complex of values. . . . All these policies point to one overriding thought: the constitutional foundation underlying the privilege is the respect a government—state or federal— must accord to the dignity and integrity of its citizens. To maintain a "fair state-individual balance," to require the government "to shoulder the entire load," . . . to respect the inviolability of the human personality, our accusatory system of criminal justice demands that the government seeking to punish an individual produce the evidence against him by its own independent labors, rather than by the cruel, simple expedient of compelling it from his own mouth. . . . In sum, the privilege is fulfilled only when the person is guaranteed the right "to remain silent unless he chooses to speak in the unfettered exercise of his own will." . . .

The question in these cases is whether the privilege is fully applicable during a period of custodial interrogation. . . . We are satisfied that all the principles embodied in the privilege apply to informal compulsion exerted by law-enforcement officers during in-custody questioning. An individual swept from familiar surroundings into police custody, surrounded by antagonistic forces, and subjected to the techniques of persuasion described above cannot be otherwise than under compulsion to speak. As a practical matter, the compulsion to speak in the isolated setting of the police station may well be greater than in courts or other official investigations, where there are often impartial observers to guard against intimidation or trickery. . . .

Our decision in *Malloy* v. *Hogan,* necessitates an examination of the scope of the privilege in state cases as well. In *Malloy,* we squarely held the privilege applicable to the States, and held that the substantive standards underlying the privilege applied with full force to state court proceedings. There, as in *Murphy* v. *Waterfront Commission,* and *Griffin* v. *California,* we applied the existing Fifth Amendment standards to the case before us. Aside from the holding itself, the reasoning in *Malloy* made clear what had already become apparent—that the substantive and procedural safeguards surrounding admissibility of confessions in state cases had become exceedingly exacting, reflecting all the policies embedded in the privilege. The voluntariness doctrine in the state cases, as *Malloy* indicates, encompasses all interrogation practices which are likely to exert such pressure upon an individual as to disable him from making a free and rational choice. The implications of this proposition were elaborated in our decision in *Escobedo* v. *Illinois* decided one week after *Malloy* applied the privilege to the States.

Our holding there stressed the fact that the police had not advised the defendant of his constitutional privilege to remain silent at the outset of the interrogation and we drew attention to that fact at several points in the decision. This was no isolated factor, but an essential ingredient in our decision. The entire thrust of police interrogation there, as in all the cases today, was to put the defendant in such an emotional state as to impair his capacity for rational judgment. The abdication of the constitutional privilege—the choice on his part to speak to the police—was not made knowingly or competently because of the failure to apprise him of his rights; the compelling atmosphere of the in-custody interrogation, and not an independent decision on his part, caused the defendant to speak.

A different phase of the *Escobedo* decision was significant in its attention to the absence of counsel during the questioning. There, as in the cases today, we sought a protective device to dispel the compelling atmosphere of the interrogation. In *Escobedo,* however, the police did not relieve the defendant of the anxieties which they had created in the interrogation rooms. Rather, they denied his request for the assistance of counsel. This heightened his dilemma, and made his later statements the product of this compulsion. The denial of the defendant's request for his attorney thus undermined his ability to exercise the privilege—to remain silent if he chose or to speak without any intimidation, blatant or subtle. The presence of counsel, in all the cases before us today, would be the adequate protective device necessary to make the process of police interrogation conform to the dictates of the privilege. His presence would insure that statements made in the government-established atmosphere are not the product of compulsion.

It was in this manner that *Escobedo* explicated another facet of the pre-trial privilege, noted in many of the Court's prior decisions: the protection of rights at trial. That counsel is present when statements are taken from an individual during interrogation obviously enhances the integrity of the fact-finding processes in court. The presence of an attorney, and the warnings delivered to the individual, enable the defendant under otherwise compelling circumstances to tell his story without fear, effectively, and in a way that eliminates the evils in the interrogation process.
. . .

III

At the outset, if a person in custody is to be subjected to interrogation, he must first be informed in clear and unequivocal terms that he has the right to remain silent. For those unaware of the privilege, the warning is needed simply to make them aware of it—the threshold requirement for an intelligent decision as to its exercise. More important, such a warning is an absolute prerequisite in overcoming the inherent pressures of the interrogation atmosphere. It is not just the subnormal or woefully ignorant who succumb to an interrogator's imprecations, whether implied or expressly stated, that the interrogation will continue until a confession is obtained or that silence in the face of accusation is itself damning and will bode ill when presented to a jury. Further, the warning will show the individual that his interrogators are prepared to recognize his privilege should he choose to exercise it.

The Fifth Amendment privilege is so fundamental to our system of constitutional rule and the expedient of giving an adequate warning as to the availability of the privilege so simple, we will not pause to inquire in individual cases whether the defendant was aware of his rights without a warning being given. Assessments of the knowledge the defendant possessed, based on information as to his age, education, intelligence, or prior contact with authorities, can never be more than speculation; a warning is a clearcut fact. More important, whatever the background of the person interrogated, a warning at the time of the interrogation is indispensable to overcome its pressures and to insure that the individual knows he is free to exercise the privilege at that point in time.

The warning of the right to remain silent must be accompanied by the explanation that anything said can and will be used against the individual in court. This warning is needed in order to make him aware not only of the privilege, but also of the consequences of forgoing it. It is only through an awareness of these consequences that there can be any assurance of real understanding and intelligent exercise of the privilege. Moreover, this warning may serve to make the individual more acutely aware that he is faced with a phase of the adversary system— that he is not in the presence of persons acting solely in his interest.

The circumstances surrounding in-custody interrogation can operate very quickly to overbear the will of one merely made aware of his privilege by his interrogators. Therefore, the right to have counsel present at the interrogation is indispensable to the protection of the Fifth Amendment privilege under the system we delineate today. Our aim is to assure that the individual's right to choose between silence and speech remains unfettered throughout the interrogation process. A once-stated warning, delivered by those who will conduct the interrogation, cannot itself suffice to that end among those who most require knowledge of their rights. A mere warning given by the interrogators is not alone sufficient to accomplish that end. Prosecutors themselves claim that the admonishment of the right to remain silent without more "will benefit only the recidivist and the professional." . . . Even preliminary advice given to the accused by his own attorney can be swiftly overcome by the secret interrogation process. . . . Thus, the need for counsel to protect the Fifth Amendment privilege comprehends not merely a right to consult with counsel prior to questioning, but also to have counsel present during any questioning if the defendant so desires. . . .

An individual need not make a pre-interrogation request for a lawyer. While such request affirmatively secures his right to have one, his failure to ask for a lawyer does not constitute a waiver. No effective waiver of the right to counsel during interrogation can be recognized unless specifically made after the warnings we here delineate have been given. The accused who does not know his rights and therefore does not make a request may be the person who most needs counsel. . . .

Accordingly we hold that an individual held for interrogation must be clearly informed that he has the right to consult with a lawyer and to have the lawyer with him during interrogation under the system for protecting the privilege we delineate today. As with the warnings of the right to remain silent and that anything stated can be used in evidence against him, this warning is an absolute prerequisite to interrogation. No amount of circumstantial evidence that the person may have been aware of this right will suffice to stand in its stead. Only through such a warning is there ascertainable assurance that the accused was aware of this right.

If an individual indicates that he wishes the assistance of counsel before any interrogation occurs, the authorities cannot rationally ignore or deny his request on the basis that the individual does not have or cannot afford a retained attorney. The financial ability of the individual has no relationship to the scope of the rights involved here. The privilege against self-incrimination secured by the Constitution applies to all individuals. The need for counsel in order to protect the privilege exists for the indigent as well as the affluent. In fact, were we to limit these constitutional rights to those who can retain an attorney, our decisions today would be of little significance. The cases before us as well as the vast majority of confession cases with which we have dealt in the past involve those unable to retain counsel. While authorities are not required to relieve the accused of his poverty, they have the obligation not to take advantage of indigence in the administration of justice. Denial of counsel to the indigent at the time of interrogation while allowing an attorney to those who can afford one would be no more supportable by reason or logic than the similar situation at trial and on appeal struck down in *Gideon* v. *Wainwright*. . . .

In order fully to apprise a person interrogated of the extent of his rights under this system then, it is necessary to warn him not only that he has the right to consult with an attorney, but also that if he is indigent a lawyer will be appointed to represent him. Without this additional warning, the admonition of the right to consult with counsel would often be understood as meaning only that he can consult with a lawyer if he has one or has the funds to obtain one. The warning of a right to counsel would be hollow if not couched in terms that would convey to the indigent —the person most often subjected to interrogation—the knowledge that he too has a right to have counsel present. As with the warnings of the right to remain silent and of the general right to counsel, only by effective and express explanation to the indigent of this right can there be assurance that he was truly in a position to exercise it.

Once warnings have been given, the subsequent procedure is clear. If the individual indicates in any manner, at any time prior to or during questioning, that he wishes to remain silent, the interrogation must cease. At this point he has shown that he intends to exercise his Fifth Amendment privilege; any statement taken after the person invokes his privilege cannot be other than the product of compulsion, subtle or otherwise. Without the right to cut off questioning, the setting of in-custody interrogation operates on the individual to overcome free choice in producing a statement after the privilege has been

once invoked. If the individual states that he wants an attorney, the interrogation must cease until an attorney is present. At that time, the individual must have an opportunity to confer with the attorney and to have him present during any subsequent questioning. If the individual cannot obtain an attorney and he indicates that he wants one before speaking to police, they must respect his decision to remain silent. . . .

An express statement that the individual is willing to make a statement and does not want an attorney followed closely by a statement could constitute a waiver. But a valid waiver will not be presumed simply from the silence of the accused after warnings are given or simply from the fact that a confession was in fact eventually obtained. . . .

Whatever the testimony of the authorities as to waiver of rights by an accused, the fact of lengthy interrogation or incommunicado incarceration before a statement is made is strong evidence that the accused did not validly waive his rights. In these circumstances the fact that the individual eventually made a statement is consistent with the conclusion that the compelling influence of the interrogation finally forced him to do so. It is inconsistent with any notion of a voluntary relinquishment of the privilege. Moreover, any evidence that the accused was threatened, tricked, or cajoled into a waiver will, of course, show that the defendant did not voluntarily waive his privilege. The requirement of warnings and waiver of rights is a fundamental with respect to the Fifth Amendment privilege and not simply a preliminary ritual to existing methods of interrogation.

The warnings required and the waiver necessary in accordance with our opinion today are, in the absence of a fully effective equivalent, prerequisites to the admissibility of any statement made by a defendant. . . .

The principles announced today deal with the protection which must be given to the privilege against self-incrimination when the individual is first subjected to police interrogation while in custody at the station or otherwise deprived of his freedom of action in any way. It is at this point that our adversary system of criminal proceedings commences, distinguishing itself at the outset from the inquisitorial system recognized in some countries. Under the system of warnings we delineate today or under any other system which may be devised and found effective, the safeguards to be erected about the privilege must come into play at this point. . . .

In dealing with statements obtained through interrogation, we do not purport to find all confessions inadmissible. Confessions remain a proper element in law enforcement. Any statement given freely and voluntarily without any compelling influences is, of course, admissible in evidence. The fundamental import of the privilege while an individual is in custody is not whether he is allowed to talk to the police without the benefit of warnings and counsel, but whether he can be interrogated. There

is no requirement that police stop a person who enters a police station and states that he wishes to confess to a crime, or a person who calls the police to offer a confession or any other statement he desires to make. Volunteered statements of any kind are not barred by the Fifth Amendment and their admissibility is not affected by our holding today. . . .

Because of the nature of the problem and because of its recurrent significance in numerous cases, we have to this point discussed the relationship of the Fifth Amendment privilege to police interrogation without specific concentration on the facts of the cases before us. We turn now to these facts to consider the application to these cases of the constitutional principles discussed above. In each instance, we have concluded that statements were obtained from the defendant under circumstances that did not meet constitutional standards for protection of the privilege.

MR. JUSTICE CLARK dissented in part.

MR. JUSTICE HARLAN, whom MR. JUSTICE STEWART and MR. JUSTICE WHITE joined, dissented.

MR. JUSTICE WHITE, with whom MR. JUSTICE HARLAN and MR. JUSTICE STEWART joined, dissented.

HOFFA v. UNITED STATES
385 U.S. 293; 87 Sup. Ct. 408; 18 L. Ed. 2d 738 (1966)

MR. JUSTICE STEWART delivered the opinion of the Court:

Over a period of several weeks in the late autumn of 1962 there took place in a federal court in Nashville, Tennessee, a trial by jury in which James Hoffa was charged with violating a provision of the Taft-Hartley Act. That trial, known in the present record as the Test Fleet trial, ended with a hung jury. The petitioners now before us—James Hoffa,

Thomas Parks, Larry Campbell, and Ewing King—were tried and convicted in 1964 for endeavoring to bribe members of that jury. The convictions were affirmed by the Court of Appeals. A substantial element in the Government's proof that led to the convictions of these four petitioners was contributed by a witness named Edward Partin, who testified to several incriminating statements which he said petitioners

Hoffa and King had made in his presence during the course of the Test Fleet trial. Our grant of certiorari was limited to the single issue of whether the Government's use in this case of evidence supplied by Partin operated to invalidate these convictions. . . .

The controlling facts can be briefly stated. The Test Fleet trial, in which James Hoffa was the sole individual defendant, was in progress between October 22 and December 23, 1962, in Nashville, Tennessee. James Hoffa was president of the International Brotherhood of Teamsters. During the course of the trial he occupied a three-room suite in the Andrew Jackson Hotel in Nashville. One of his constant companions throughout the trial was the petitioner King, president of the Nashville local of the Teamsters Union. Edward Partin, a resident of Baton Rouge, Louisiana, and a local Teamsters Union official there, made repeated visits to Nashville during the period of the trial. On these visits he frequented the Hoffa hotel suite, and was continually in the company of Hoffa and his associates, including King, in and around the hotel suite, the hotel lobby, the courthouse, and elsewhere in Nashville. During this period Partin made frequent reports to a federal agent named Sheridan concerning conversations he said Hoffa and King had had with him and with each other, disclosing endeavors to bribe members of the Test Fleet jury. Partin's reports and his subsequent testimony at the petitioners' trial unquestionably contributed, directly or indirectly, to the convictions of all four of the petitioners. . . . we proceed upon the premise that Partin was a government informer from the time he first arrived in Nashville on October 22, and that the Government compensated him for his services as such. It is upon that premise that we

consider the constitutional issues presented. . . .

It is contended that only by violating the petitioner's rights under the Fourth Amendment was Partin able to hear the petitioner's incriminating statements in the hotel suite, and that Partin's testimony was therefore inadmissible under the exclusionary rule of *Weeks* v. *United States*. . . . The argument is that Partin's failure to disclose his role as a government informer vitiated the consent that the petitioner gave to Partin's repeated entries into the suite, and that by listening to the petitioner's statements Partin conducted an illegal "search" for verbal evidence.

The preliminary steps of this argument are on solid ground. A hotel room can clearly be the object of Fourth Amendment protection as much as a home or an office. . . . The Fourth Amendment can certainly be violated by guileful as well as by forcible intrusions into a constitutionally protected area. . . . And the protections of the Fourth Amendment are surely not limited to tangibles, but can extend as well to oral statements. *Silverman* v. *United States*. . . .

In the present case, however, it is evident that no interest legitimately protected by the Fourth Amendment is involved. It is obvious that the petitioner was not relying on the security of his hotel suite when he made the incriminating statements to Partin or in Partin's presence. Partin did not enter the suite by force or by stealth. He was not a surreptitious eavesdropper. Partin was in the suite by invitation, and every conversation which he heard was either directed to him or knowingly carried on in his presence. The petitioner, in a word, was not relying on the security of the hotel room; he was relying upon his misplaced confidence that Partin would not reveal his wrongdoing. . . .

Neither this Court nor any member of it has ever expressed the view that the Fourth Amendment protects a wrongdoer's misplaced belief that a person to whom he voluntarily confides his wrongdoing will not reveal it. Indeed, the Court unanimously rejected that very contention less than four years ago in *Lopez* v. *United States*. . . . In that case the petitioner had been convicted of attempted bribery of an internal revenue agent named Davis. The Court was divided with regard to the admissibility in evidence of a surreptitious electronic recording of an incriminating conversation Lopez had had in his private office with Davis. But there was no dissent to the view that testimony about the conversation by Davis himself was clearly admissible. . . .

Adhering to these views, we hold that no right protected by the Fourth Amendment was violated in the present case.

The petitioner argues that his right under the Fifth Amendment not to "be compelled in any criminal case to be a witness against himself" was violated by the admission of Partin's testimony. The claim is without merit.

There have been sharply differing views within the Court as to the ultimate reach of the Fifth Amendment right against compulsory self-incrimination. Some of those differences were aired last Term in *Miranda* v. *State of Arizona*. . . . But since at least as long ago as 1807, when Chief Justice Marshall first gave attention to the matter in the trial of Aaron Burr, all have agreed that a necessary element of compulsory self-incrimination is some kind of compulsion. Thus, in the *Miranda,* case, dealing with the Fifth Amendment's impact upon police interrogation of persons in custody, the Court predicated its decision upon the conclusion "that without proper safeguards the process of in-custody interrogation of persons suspected or accused of crime contains inherently compelling pressures which work to undermine the individual's will to resist and to compel him to speak where he would not otherwise do so freely. . . .

In the present case no claim has been or could be made that the petitioner's incriminating statements were the product of any sort of coercion, legal or factual. The petitioner's conversations with Partin and in Partin's presence were wholly voluntary. For that reason, if for no other, it is clear that no right protected by the Fifth Amendment privilege against compulsory self-incrimination was violated in this case.

The petitioner's second argument under the Sixth Amendment needs no extended discussion. That argument goes as follows: Not later than October 25, 1962, the Government had sufficient ground for taking the petitioner into custody and charging him with endeavors to tamper with the Test Fleet jury. Had the Government done so, it could not have continued to question the petitioner without observance of his Sixth Amendment right to counsel. *Massiah* v. *United States*. . . ; *Escobedo* v. *State of Illinois*. . . . Therefore, the argument concludes, evidence of statements made by the petitioner subsequent to October 25 was inadmissible, because the Government acquired that evidence only by flouting the petitioner's Sixth Amendment right to counsel.

Nothing in *Massiah,* in *Escobedo,* or in any other case that has come to our attention, even remotely suggests this novel and paradoxical constitutional doctrine, and we decline to adopt it now. There is no constitutional right to be arrested. The police are not required to guess at their peril the precise moment at which they have probable cause to arrest a suspect, risking a violation of the Fourth Amendment if they act too soon, and a violation of the Sixth Amendment if they wait too long. Law enforcement officers are under no constitutional duty to call a halt to a criminal investigation the moment they have the minimum evidence to establish probable cause, a quantum of evidence which may fall far short of the amount necessary to support a criminal conviction.

Affirmed.

MR. JUSTICE WHITE and MR. JUSTICE FORTAS took no part. MR. CHIEF JUSTICE WARREN dissented. MR. JUSTICE CLARK and MR. JUSTICE DOUGLAS would have dismissed the writ of certiorari as improvidently granted.

KATZ *v.* UNITED STATES
389 U.S. 347; 88 Sup. Ct. 507; 19 L. Ed. 2d 576 (1967)

MR. JUSTICE STEWART delivered the opinion of the Court:

The petitioner was convicted in the District Court for the Southern District of California under an eight-count indictment charging him with transmitting wagering information by telephone from Los Angeles to Miami and Boston in violation of a federal statute. At trial the Government was permitted, over the petitioner's objection, to introduce evidence of the petitioner's end of telephone conversations, overheard by FBI agents who had attached an electronic listening and recording device to the outside of the public telephone booth from which he had placed his calls. In affirming his conviction, the Court of Appeals rejected the contention that the recordings had been obtained in violation of the Fourth Amendment, because "[t]here was no physical entrance into the area occupied by, [the petitioner]." the Correct solution of Fourth Amendment problems is not necessarily promoted by incantation of the phrase "constitutionally protected area." Secondly, the Fourth Amendment cannot be translated into a general constitutional "right to privacy." That Amendment, protects individual privacy against certain kinds of governmental intrusion, but its protections go further, and often have nothing to do with privacy at all. Other provisions of the Constitution protect personal privacy from other forms of governmental invasion. But the protection of a person's *general* right to privacy—his right to be let alone by other people—is, like the protection of his property and of his very life, left largely to the law of the individual States. . . . The petitioner has strenuously argued that the booth was a "constitutionally protected area." The Government has maintained with equal vigor that it was not. But this effort to decide whether or not a given "area," viewed in the abstract, is "constitutionally protected" deflects attention from the problem presented by this case. For the Fourth Amendment protects people, not places. What a person knowingly exposes to the public, even in his own home or office, is not a subject of Fourth Amendment protection. . . . But what he seeks to preserve as private, even in an area accessible to the public, may be constitutionally protected. . . . No less than an individual in a business office, in a friend's apartment, or in a taxicab, a person in a telephone booth may rely upon the protection of the Fourth Amendment. One who occupies it, shuts the door behind him, and pays the toll that permits him to place a call, is surely entitled to assume that the words he utters into the mouthpiece will not be broadcast to the world. To read the Constitution more narrowly is to ignore the vital role that the public telephone has come to play in private communication.

The Government contends, however, that the activities of its agents in this case should not be tested by Fourth Amendment requirements, for the surveillance technique they employed involved no physical penetration of the telephone booth from which the petitioner placed his calls. It is true that the absence of such penetration was at one time thought to foreclose further Fourth Amendment inquiry, *Olmstead* v. *United States. . . ; Goldman* v. *United States,* for that Amendment was thought to limit only searches and seizures of tangible property. But "[t]he premise that property interests control the right of the Government to search and seize has been discredited." *Warden, Md. Penitentiary* v. *Hayden. . . .* Thus, although a closely divided Court supposed in *Olmstead* that surveillance without any trespass and without the seizure of any material object fell outside the ambit of the Constitution, we have since departed from the narrow view on which that decision rested. Indeed, we have expressly held that the Fourth Amendment governs not only the seizure of tangible items, but extends as well to the recording of oral statements overheard without any "technical trespass under . . . local property law." *Silverman* v. *United States. . . .* Once this much is acknowledged, and once it is recognized that the Fourth Amendment protects people— and not simply "areas—against unreasonable searches and seizures it becomes clear that the reach of that Amendment cannot turn upon the presence or absence of a physical intrusion into any given enclosure.

We conclude that the underpinnings of *Olmstead* and *Goldman* have been so eroded by our subsequent decisions that the "trespass" doctrine there enunciated can no longer be regarded as controlling. The Government's activities in electronically listening to and recording the petitioner's words violated the privacy upon which he justifiably relied while using the telephone booth and thus constituted a "search and seizure" within the meaning of the Fourth Amendment. The fact that the electronic device employed to achieve that end did not happen to penetrate the wall of the booth can have no constitutional significance. . . . It is clear that this surveillance was so narrowly circumscribed that a duly authorized magistrate, properly notified of the need for such investigation, specifically informed of the basis on which it was to proceed, and clearly apprised of the precise intrusion it would entail, could constitutionally have authorized, with appropriate safeguards, the very limited search and seizure that the Government asserts in fact took place. Only last Term we sustained the validity of such an authorization, holding that, under sufficiently "precise and discriminate circumstances," a federal court may empower government agents to employ a concealed electronic device "for the narrow and particularized purpose of ascertaining the truth of the . . . allegations" of a "detailed factual affidavit alleging the commission of a specific criminal offense." *Osborn* v. *United States. . . .* Discussing that holding, the Court, in *Berger* v. *State of New York, . . .* said that "the order authorizing the use of the electronic device" in *Osborn* "afforded similar protections to those . . . of conventional warrants authorizing the seizure of tangible evidence." Through those protections, "no greater invasion of privacy was permitted than was necessary under the circumstances." . . . Here, too, a similar judicial order could have accommodated "the legitimate needs of law enforcement" by authorizing the carefully limited use of electronic surveillance.

In the absence of such safeguards, this Court has never sustained a search upon the sole ground that officers reasonably expected to find evidence of a particular crime and voluntarily confined their activities to the least intrusive means consistent with that end. . . . The Government . . . urges the creation of a new exception to cover this case. It argues that surveillance of a telephone both should be exempted from the usual requirement of advance authorization by a magistrate upon a showing of probable cause. We cannot agree. Omission of such authorization "bypasses the safeguards provided by an objective predetermination of prob-

able cause, and substitutes instead the far less reliable procedure of an after-the-event justification for the . . . search, too likely to be subtly influenced by the familiar shortcomings of hindsight judgment." *Beck* v. *State of Ohio,* 379 U.S. 89, 96. . . . The government agents here ignored "the procedure of antecedent justification . . . that is central to the Fourth Amendment," a procedure that we hold to be a constitutional precondition of the kind of electronic surveillance involved in this case. Because the surveillance here failed to meet that condition, and because it led to the petitioner's conviction, the judgment must be reversed.

MR. JUSTICE MARSHALL took no part. JUSTICES DOUGLAS, BRENNAN, HARLAN, and WHITE concurred. MR. JUSTICE BLACK dissented.

CHIMEL *v.* CALIFORNIA
89 Sup. Ct. 2034 (1969)

MR. JUSTICE STEWART delivered the opinion of the Court:

This case raises basic questions concerning the permissible scope under the Fourth Amendment of a search incident to a lawful arrest.

The relevant facts are essentially undisputed. Late in the afternoon of September 13, 1965, three police officers arrived at the Santa Ana, California, home of the petitioner with a warrant authorizing his arrest for the burglary of a coin shop. The officers knocked on the door, identified themselves to the petitioner's wife, and asked if they might come inside. She ushered them into the house, where they waited 10 or 15 minutes until the petitioner returned home from work. When the petitioner entered the house, one of the officers handed him the arrest warrant and asked for permission to "look around." The petitioner objected, but

was advised that "on the basis of the lawful arrest," the officers would nonetheless conduct a search. No search warrant had been issued.

Accompanied by the petitioner's wife, the officers then looked through the entire three-bedroom house, including the attic, the garage, and a small workshop. In some rooms the search was relatively cursory. In the master bedroom and sewing room, however, the officers directed the petitioner's wife to open drawers and "to physically move contents of the drawers from side to side so that [they] might view any items that would have come from [the] burglary." After completing the search, they seized numerous items—primarily coins, but also several medals, tokens, and a few other objects. The entire search took between 45 minutes and an hour.

At the petitioner's subsequent state trial on two charges of burglary, the items taken from his house were admitted into evidence against him, over his objection that they had been unconstitutionally seized. . . .

Approval of a warrantless search incident to a lawful arrest seems first to have been articulated by the Court in 1914 as dictum in *Weeks* v. *United States* . . . in which the Court stated:

> "What then is the present case? Before answering that inquiry specifically, it may be well by a process of exclusion to state what it is not. It is not an assertion of the right on the part of the Government, always recognized under English and American law, to search the person of the accused when legally arrested to discover and seize the fruits or evidences of crime." . . .

That statement made no reference to any right to search the *place* where an arrest occurs, but was limited to a right to search the "person." Eleven years later the case of *Carroll* v. *United States,* brought the following embellishment of the *Weeks* statement:

> "When a man is legally arrested for an offense, whatever is found upon his person *or in his control* which it is unlawful for him to have and which may be used to prove the offense, may be seized and held as evidence in the prosecution."

Still, that assertion too was far from a claim that the "place" where one is arrested may be searched so long as the arrest is valid. Without explanation, however, the principle emerged in expanded form a few months later in *Agnello* v. *United States* . . . although still by way of dictum:

> "The right without a search warrant contemporaneously to search persons lawfully arrested while committing crime and to search the place

where the arrest is made in order to find and seize things connected with the crime as its fruits or as the means by which it was committed, as well as weapons and other things to effect an escape from custody, is not to be doubted.

And in *Marron* v. *United States* . . . two years later, the dictum of *Agnello* appeared to be the foundation of the Court's decision. In that case federal agents had secured a search warrant authorizing the seizure of liquor and certain articles used in its manufacture. When they arrived at the premises to be searched, they saw "that the place was used for retailing and drinking intoxicating liquors." . . . They proceeded to arrest the person in charge and to execute the warrant. In searching a closet for the items listed in the warrant they came across an incriminating ledger, concededly not covered by the warrant, which they also seized. The Court upheld the seizure of the ledger by holding that since the agents had made a lawful arrest, "[t]hey had a right without a warrant contemporaneously to search the place in order to find and seize the things used to carry on the criminal enterprise." . . .

That the *Marron* opinion did not mean all that it seemed to say became evident, however, a few years later in *Go-Bart Importing Co.* v. *United States,* . . . and *United States* v. *Lefkowitz.* . . . In each of those cases the opinion of the Court was written by Mr. Justice Butler, who had authored the opinion in *Marron.* In *Go-Bart,* agents had searched the office of persons whom they had lawfully arrested, and had taken several papers from a desk, a safe, and other parts of the office. The Court noted that no crime had been committed in the agent's presence, and that although the agent in charge "had an abundance of information and time to swear out a valid [search] warrant, he failed to do so." . . . In holding the search and seizure unlawful, the Court stated:

> "Plainly the case before us is essentially different from *Marron* v. *United States*. . . . There, officers executing a valid search warrant for intoxicating liquors found and arrested one Birdsall who in pursuance of a conspiracy was actually engaged in running a saloon. As an incident to the arrest they seized a ledger in a closet where the liquor or some of it was kept and some bills beside the cash register. These things were visible and accessible and in the offender's immediate custody. There was no threat of force or general search or rummaging of the place."

This limited characterization of *Marron* was reiterated in *Lefkowitz,* a case in which the Court held unlawful a search of desk drawers and a cabinent despite the fact that the search had accompanied a lawful arrest. . . .

The limiting views expressed in *Go-Bart* and *Lefkowitz* were thrown to the winds, however, in *Harris* v. *United States,* decided in 1947. In that case, officers had obtained a warrant for Harris' arrest on the basis of his alleged involvement with the cashing and interstate transportation of a forged check. He was arrested in the living room of his four-room apartment, and in an attempt to recover two canceled checks thought to have been used in effecting the forgery, the officers undertook a thorough search of the entire apartment. Inside a desk drawer they found a sealed envelope marked "George Harris, personal papers." The envelope, which was then torn open, was found to contain altered selective service documents, and those documents were used to secure Harris' conviction for violating the Selective Train-

ing and Service Act of 1940. The Court rejected Harris' Fourth Amendment claim, sustaining the search as "incident to arrest." . . .

Only a year after *Harris,* however, the pendulum swung again. In *Trupiano* v. *United States* . . . agents raided the site of an illicit distillery, saw one of several conspirators operating the still, and arrested him, contemporaneously "seiz[ing] the illicit distillery." The Court held that the arrest and others made subsequently had been valid, but that the unexplained failure of the agents to procure a search warrant—in spite of the fact that they had had more than enough time before the raid to do so—rendered the search unlawful. The opinion stated:

> "It is a cardinal rule that, in seizing goods and articles, law enforcement agents must secure and use search warrants wherever reasonably practicable. . . . This rule rests upon the desirability of having magistrates rather than police officers determine when searches and seizures are permissible and what limitations should be placed upon such activities. . . . To provide the necessary security against unreasonable intrusions upon the private lives of individuals, the framers of the Fourth Amendment required adherence to judicial processes wherever possible. And subsequent history has confirmed the wisdom of that requirement.
>
> "A search or seizure without a warrant as an incident to a lawful arrest has always been considered to be a strictly limited right. It grows out of the inherent necessities of the situation at the time of the arrest. But there must be something more in the way of necessity than merely a lawful arrest." . . .

In 1950, two years after *Trupiano,* came *United States* v. *Rabinowitz,* the decision upon which California primarily relies in the case now before us. In *Rabinowitz*, federal authorities had been informed that the defendant was dealing in stamps bearing forged overprints. On the basis of that information they secured a warrant for his arrest, which they executed at his one-room business office. At the time of the arrest, the officers "searched the desk, safe, and file cabinets in the office for about an hour and a half," . . . and seized 573 stamps with forged overprints. The stamps were admitted into evidence at the defendant's trial, and this Court affirmed his conviction, rejecting the contention that the warrantless search had been unlawful. The Court held that the search in its entirety fell within the principle giving law enforcement authorities "[t]he right 'to search the place where the arrest is made in order to find and seize things connected with the crime. . . .' " *Harris* was regarded as "ample authority" for that conclusion. . . . The opinion rejected the rule of *Trupiano* that "in seizing goods and articles, law enforcement agents must secure and use search warrants wherever reasonably practicable." The test, said the Court, "is not whether it is reasonable to procure a search warrant, but whether the search was reasonable."

Rabinowitz has come to stand for the proposition, *inter alia,* that a warrantless search "incident to a lawful arrest" may generally extend to the area that is considered to be in the "possession" or under the "control" of the person arrested. And it was on the basis of that proposition that the California courts upheld the search of the petitioner's entire house in this case. That doctrine, however, at least in the broad sense in which it was applied by the California courts in this case, can withstand neither historical nor rational analysis.

Even limited to its own facts, the *Rabinowitz* decision was, as we have seen, hardly founded on an unimpeachable line of authority. As Mr. Justice Frankfurter commented in dissent in that case, the "hint" contained in *Weeks* was, without persuasive justification, "loosely turned into dictum and finally elevated to a decision." . . . And the approach taken in cases such as *Go-Bart, Lefkowitz,* and *Trupiano* was essentially disregarded by the *Rabinowitz* Court.

Nor is the rationale by which the State seeks here to sustain the search of the petitioner's house supported by a reasoned view of the background and purpose of the Fourth Amendment. Mr. Justice Frankfurter wisely pointed out in his *Rabinowitz* dissent that the Amendment's proscription of "unreasonable searches and seizures" must be read in light of "the history that gave rise to the words"—a history of "abuses so deeply felt by the Colonies as to be one of the potent causes of the Revolution . . . ." The Amendment was in large part a reaction to the general warrants and warrantless searches that had so alienated the colonists and had helped speed the movement for independence. In the scheme of the Amendment, therefore, the requirement that "no Warrants shall issue, but upon probable cause," plays a crucial part. As the Court put it in *McDonald* v. *United States* . . . :

"We are not dealing with formalities. The presence of a search warrant serves a high function. Absent some grave emergency, the Fourth Amendment has interposed a magistrate between the citizen and the police. This was done not to shield criminals nor to make the home a safe haven for illegal activities. It was done so that an objective mind might weigh the need to invade that privacy in order to enforce the law. The right of privacy was deemed too precious to entrust to the discretion of those whose job is the detection of crime and the arrest of criminals. . . . And so the Constitution requires a magistrate to pass on the desires of the police before they violate the privacy of the home. We cannot be true to that constitutional requirement and excuse the absence of a search warrant without a showing by those who seek exemption from the constitutional mandate that the exigencies of the situation made that course imperative."

Even in the *Agnello* case the Court relied upon the rule that "[b]elief, however well founded, that an article sought is concealed in a dwelling house furnishes no justification for a search of that place without a warrant. And such searches are held unlawful notwithstanding facts unquestionably showing probable cause." Clearly, the general requirement that a search warrant be obtained is not lightly to be dispensed with, and "the burden is on those seeking [an] exemption [from the requirement] to show the need for it. . . ."

Only last Term in *Terry* v. *Ohio* . . . we emphasized that "the police must, whenever practicable, obtain advance judicial approval of searches and seizures through the warrant procedure," . . . and that "[t]he scope of [a] search must be 'strictly tied to and justified by' the circumstances which rendered its initiation permissible." . . . The search undertaken by the officer in that "stop and frisk" case was sustained under that test, because it was no more than a "protective . . . search for weapons." . . . But in a companion case, *Sibron* v. *New York* . . . we applied the same standard to another set of

facts and reached a contrary result, holding that a policeman's action in thrusting his hand into a suspect's pocket had been neither motivated by nor limited to the objective of protection. Rather, the search had been made in order to find narcotics, which were in fact found.

A similar analysis underlies the "search incident to arrest" principle, and marks its proper extent. When an arrest is made, it is reasonable for the arresting officer to search the person arrested in order to remove any weapons that the latter might seek to use in order to resist arrest or effect his escape. Otherwise, the officer's safety might well be endangered, and the arrest itself frustrated. In addition, it is entirely reasonable for the arresting officer to search for and seize any evidence on the arrestee's person in order to prevent its concealment or destruction. And the area into which an arrestee might reach in order to grab a weapon or evidentiary items must, of course, be governed by a like rule. A gun on a table or in a drawer in front of one who is arrested can be as dangerous to the arresting officer as one concealed in the clothing of the person arrested. There is ample justification, therefore, for a search of the arrestee's person and the area "within his immediate control"—construing that phrase to mean the area from within which he might gain possession of a weapon or destructible evidence.

There is no comparable justification, however, for routinely searching rooms other than that in which an arrest occurs—or, for that matter, for searching through all the desk drawers or other closed or concealed areas in that room itself. Such searches, in the absence of well-recognized exceptions, may be made only under the authority of a search warrant. The "adherence to judicial processes" mandated by the Fourth Amendment requires no less.

This is the principle that underlay our decision in *Preston* v. *United States.* . . . In that case three men had been arrested in a parked car, which had later been towed to a garage and searched by police. We held the search to have been unlawful under the Fourth Amendment, despite the contention that it had been incidental to a valid arrest. Our reasoning was straightforward:

> "The rule allowing contemporaneous searches is justified, for example, by the need to seize weapons and other things which might be used to assault an officer or effect an escape, as well as by the need to prevent the destruction of evidence of the crime—things which might easily happen where the weapon or evidence is on the accused's person or under his immediate control. But these justifications are absent where a search is remote in time or place from the arrest." . . .

The same basic principle was reflected in our opinion last Term in *Sibron.* That opinion dealt with *Peters* v. *New York* . . . as well as with Sibron's case, and *Peters* involved a search that we upheld as incident to a proper arrest. We sustained the search, however, only because its scope had been "reasonably limited" by the "need to seize weapons" and "to prevent the destruction of evidence," to which *Preston* had referred. We emphasized that the arresting officer "did not engage in an unrestrained and thoroughgoing examination of Peters and his personal effects. He seized him to cut short his flight, and he searched him primarily for weapons." . . .

It is argued in the present case that it is "reasonable" to search a man's house when he is arrested in it. But that argument is founded on little more than a subjective view regarding the acceptability of certain sorts of police conduct, and not on considerations relevant to Fourth Amendment interests. Under such an unconfined analysis, Fourth Amendment protection in this area would approach the evaporation point. It is not easy to explain why, for instance, it is less subjectively "reasonable" to search a man's house when he is arrested on his front lawn— or just down the street—than it is when he happens to be in the house at the time of arrest. As Mr. Justice Frankfurter put it:

> "To say that the search must be reasonable is to require some criterion of reason. It is no guide at all either for a jury or for district judges or the police to say that an 'unreasonable search' is forbidden—that the search must be reasonable. What is the test of reason which makes a search reasonable? The test is the reason underlying and expressed by the Fourth Amendment: the history and the experience which it embodies and the safeguards afforded by it against the evils to which it was a response." *United States* v. *Rabinowitz.* . . .

Thus, although "[t]he recurring questions of the reasonableness of searches" depend upon "the facts and circumstances—the total atmosphere of the case," (opinion of the Court), those facts and circumstances must be viewed in the light of established Fourth Amendment principles.

It would be possible, of course, to draw a line between *Rabinowitz* and *Harris* on the one hand, and this case on the other. For *Rabinowitz* involved a single room, and *Harris* a four-room apartment, while in the case before us an entire house was searched. But such a distinction would be highly artificial. The rationale that allowed the searches and seizures in *Rabinowitz* and *Harris* would allow the searches and seizures in this case. No consideration relevant to the Fourth Amendment suggests any point of rational limitation, once the search is allowed to go beyond the area from which the person arrested might obtain weapons or evidentiary items. The only reasoned distinction is one between a search of the person arrested and the area within his reach on the one hand, and more extensive searches on the other.

The petitioner correctly points out that one result of decisions such as *Rabinowitz* and *Harris* is to give law enforcement officials the opportunity to engage in searches not justified by probable cause, by the simple expedient of arranging to arrest suspects at home rather than elsewhere. We do not suggest that the petitioner is necessarily correct in his assertion that such a strategy was utilized here, but the fact remains that had he been arrested earlier in the day, at his place of employment rather than at home, no search of his house could have been made without a search warrant. In any event, even apart from the possibility of such police tactics, the general point so forcefully made by Judge Learned Hand in *United States* v. *Kirschenblatt* . . . remains:

"After arresting a man in his house, to rummage at will among his papers in search of whatever will convict him, appears to us to be indistinguishable from what might be done under a general warrant; indeed, the warrant would give more protection, for presumably it must

be issued by a magistrate. True, by hypothesis the power would not exist, if the supposed offender were not found on the premies; but it is small consolation to know that one's papers are safe only so long as one is not at home."

Rabinowitz and *Harris* have been the subject of critical commentary for many years, and have been relied upon less and less in our own decisions. It is time, for the reasons we have stated, to hold that on their own facts, and insofar as the principles they stand for are inconsistent with those that we have endorsed today, they are no longer to be followed.

Application of sound Fourth Amendment principles to the facts of this case produces a clear result. The search here went far beyond the petitioner's person and the area from within which he might have obtained either a weapon or something that could have been used as evidence against him. There was no constitutional justification, in the absence of a search warrant, for extending the search beyond that area. The scope of the search was, therefore, "unreasonable" under the Fourth and Fourteenth Amendments, and the petitioner's conviction cannot stand.

MR. JUSTICE HARLAN, concurring.

I join the Court's opinion with these remarks concerning a factor to which the Court has not alluded.

The only thing that has given me pause in voting to overrule *Harris* and *Rabinowitz* is that as a result of *Mapp* v. *Ohio* . . . and *Ker* v. *California* . . . every change in Fourth Amendment law must now be obeyed by state officials facing widely different problems of local law enforcement. We simply do not know the extent to which cities and towns across the Nation are prepared to administer the greatly expanded warrant system which will be required by today's decision; nor can we say with assurance that in each and every local situation, the warrant requirement plays an essential role in the protection of those fundamental liberties protected against state infringement by the Fourteenth Amendment.

MR. JUSTICE WHITE, with whom MR. JUSTICE BLACK joins, dissented.

ULLMANN v. UNITED STATES
350 U.S. 422; 76 Sup. Ct. 497; 100 L. Ed. 511 (1955)

[*The Immunity Act of 1954 provides that in national security cases a witness may be compelled by court order to answer all questions when immunity from criminal prosecution is granted; refusal to testify when immunity is granted is punishable as contempt of court. Ullmann, a former Treasury Department official, refused to answer a federal grand jury's questions concerning an alleged Communist spy ring despite a grant of immunity by a New York federal district court. He invoked the Fifth Amendment privilege against self-incrimination and contended that the Immunity Act of 1954 was unconstitutional. The district court upheld the statute and sentenced Ullmann to a six-month prison term for contempt; a court of appeals affirmed the judgment. Ullmann then obtained a writ of certiorari from the Supreme Court.*]

MR. JUSTICE FRANKFURTER delivered the opinion of the Court:

. . . It is relevant to define explicitly the spirit in which the Fifth Amendment's privilege against self-incrimination should be approached. This command of the Fifth Amendment ("nor shall any person . . . be compelled in any criminal case to be a witness against himself. . . .") registers an important advance in the development of our liberty—"one of the great landmarks in man's struggle to make himself civilized." Time has not shown that protection from the evils against which this safeguard was directed is needless or unwarranted. This constitutional protection must not be interpreted in a hostile or niggardly spirit. Too many, even those who should be better advised, view this privilege as a shelter for wrongdoers. They too readily assume that those who invoke it are either guilty of crime or commit perjury in claiming the privilege. Such a view does scant honor to the patriots who sponsored the Bill of Rights as a condition to acceptance of the Constitution by the ratifying States. . . .

It is in this spirit of strict, not lax, observance of the constitutional protection of the individual that we approach the claims made by petitioner in this case. The attack on the Immunity Act as violating the Fifth Amendment is not a new one. Sixty years ago this Court considered, in *Brown* v. *Walker,* 161 U.S. 591, the constitutionality of a similar Act, the Act of February 11, 1893. . . . Petitioner [Brown] appealed to this Court, urging that the 1893 immunity statute was unconstitutional.

The Court considered and rejected petitioner's arguments, holding that a statute which compelled testimony but secured the witness against a criminal prosecution which might be aided directly or indirectly by his disclosures did not violate the Fifth Amendment's privilege against self-discrimination and that the 1893 statute did provide such immunity. . . .

Petitioner (Ullmann), however, attempts to distinguish *Brown* v. *Walker.* He argues that this case is different from *Brown* v. *Walker* because the impact of the disabilities imposed by federal and state authorities and the public in general—such as loss of job, expulsion from labor unions, state registration and investigation statutes, passport eligibility, and general public opprobrium—is so oppressive that the statute does not give him true immunity. . . . But, as this Court has often held, the immunity granted need only remove those sanctions which generate the fear justifying invocation of the privilege: "The interdiction of the Fifth Amendment operates only where a witness is asked to incriminate himself— in other words, to give testimony which may possibly expose him to a criminal charge. But if the criminality has already been taken away, the Amendment ceases to apply." . . .

Petitioner further argues that the immunity is not constitutionally sufficient so long as a witness is subject to the very real possibility of state prosecution. He urges that the statute does not, and constitutionally could not, grant such immunity. . . .

Petitioner questions the constitutional power of Congress to grant immunity from state prosecution. . . . The Immunity Act is concerned with the national security. It reflects a congressional policy to increase the possibility of more complete and open disclosure by removal of fear of state prosecution. We cannot say that Congress' paramount authority in safeguarding national security does not justify the restriction it has placed on the exercise of state power for the more effective exercise of conceded federal power. . . .

We are not dealing here with one of the vague, undefinable, admonitory provisions of the Constitution whose scope is inevitably addressed to changing circumstances. The privilege against self-incrimination is a specific provision of which it is peculiarly true that "a page of history is worth a volume of logic." . . . For the history of the privilege establishes not only that it is not to be interpreted literally, but also that its sole concern is, as its name indicates, with the danger to a witness forced to give testimony leading to the infliction of "penalties affixed to the criminal acts." . . . Immunity displaces the danger. Once the reason for the privilege ceases, the privilege ceases. We reaffirm *Brown* v. *Walker.* . . .

The judgment of the Court of Appeals is

Affirmed.

[MR. JUSTICE REED concurred with the judgment except as to one brief general statement.]

MR. JUSTICE DOUGLAS, with whom MR. JUSTICE BLACK concurs, dissenting:

I would reverse the judgment of conviction. I would base the reversal on *Boyd* v. *United States,* . . . , or, in the alternative, I would overrule the five-to-four decision of *Brown* v. *Walker,* . . .

First, as to the *Boyd* case. There are numerous disabilities created by federal law that attach to a person who is a Communist. These disabilities include ineligibility for employment in the Federal Government and in defense facilities, disqualification for a passport, the risk of internment, the risk of loss of employment as a longshoreman—to mention only a few. These disabilities imposed by federal law are forfeitures within the meaning of our cases and as much protected by the Fifth Amendment as criminal prosecution itself. But there is no indication that the Immunity Act . . . grants protection against those disabilities. The majority will not say that it does. I think, indeed, that it must be read as granting only partial, not complete, immunity for the matter disclosed under compulsion. Yet . . . an immunity statute to be valid must "supply a complete protection from all the perils against which the constitutional prohibition was designed to guard. . . ."

Boyd v. *United States* . . . involved a proceeding to establish a forfeiture of goods alleged to have been fraudulently imported without payment of duties. The claimants resisted an order requiring the production of an invoice to be used against them in the forfeiture proceedings. The Court in an opinion by Mr. Justice Bradley sustained the defense of the Fifth Amendment. The Court said, "A witness, as well as a party, is protected by the law from being compelled to give evidence that tends to criminate him, or to subject his property to forfeiture." . . .

The forfeiture of property on compelled testimony is no more abhorrent than the forfeiture of rights of citizenship. Any forfeiture of rights as a result of compelled testimony is at war with the Fifth Amendment.

The Court apparently distinguishes the *Boyd* case on the ground that the forfeiture of property was a penalty affixed to a criminal act. The loss of a job and the ineligibility for a passport are also penalties affixed to a criminal act. . . . If there was a penalty suffered in the *Boyd* case, there are penalties suffered here. Both are hitched to criminal acts. And the Constitution places the property rights involved in the *Boyd* case no higher than the rights of citizenship involved here. . . .

We should apply the principle of the *Boyd* case to the present one and hold that since there is no protection in the Immunity Act against loss of rights of citizenship, the immunity granted is less than the protection afforded by the Constitution. . . .

Second, as to *Brown* v. *Walker*. The difficulty I have with that decision and with the majority of the Court in the present case is that they add an important qualification to the Fifth Amendment. The guaranty is that no person "shall be compelled in any criminal case to be a witness against himself." The majority does not enforce that guaranty as written but qualifies it; and the qualification apparently reads, "but only if criminal conviction might result." Wisely or not, the Fifth Amendment protects against the compulsory self-accusation of crime without exception or qualification. . . .

. . . The forced disclosure may open up vast new vistas for the prosecutor with leads to numerous accusations not within the purview of the question and answer. What related offenses may be disclosed by leads furnished by the confession? How remote need the offense be before the immunity ceases to protect it? How much litigation will it take to determine it? What will be the reaction of the highest court when the facts of the case reach it?

. . . [O]ne protective function of the Fifth Amendment is at once removed when the guaranty against self-incrimination is qualified in the manner it is today.

. . . [T]he privilege of silence is exchanged for a partial, undefined, vague immunity. It means that Congress has granted far less than it has taken away. . . . The guaranty against self-incrimination contained in the Fifth Amendment is not only a protection against conviction and prosecution but a safeguard of conscience and human dignity and freedom of expression as well. My view is that the Framers put it beyond the power of Congress to *compel* anyone to confess his crimes. The evil to be guarded against was partly self-accusation under legal compulsion. But that was only a part of the evil. The conscience and dignity of man were also involved. So too was his right to freedom of expression guaranteed by the First Amendment. The Framers, therefore, created the federally protected right of silence and decreed that the law could not be used to pry open one's lips and make him a witness against himself.

. . . The Fifth Amendment was designed to protect the accused against infamy as well as against prosecution. . . . Loss of office, loss of dignity, loss of face were feudal forms of punishment. Infamy was historically considered to be punishment as effective as fine and imprisonment. . . .

There is great infamy involved in the present case, apart from the loss of rights of citizenship under federal law. . . . The disclosure that a person is a Communist practically excommunicates him from society. School boards will not hire him. . . . A lawyer risks exclusion from the bar . . . ; a doctor, the revocation of his license to prac-

tice. . . . If an actor, he is on a black list. . . . And he will be able to find no employment in our society except at the lowest level, if at all. . . .

It is no answer to say that a witness who exercises his Fifth Amendment right of silence and stands mute may bring himself into disrepute. If so, that is the price he pays for exercising the right of silence granted by the Fifth Amendment. The critical point is that the Constitution places the right of silence *beyond the reach of government*. The Fifth Amendment stands between the citizen and his government. When public opinion casts a person into the outer darkness, as happens today when a person is exposed as a Communist, the government brings infamy on the head of the witness when it compels disclosure. That is precisely what the Fifth Amendment prohibits. . . .

MURPHY *v.* WATERFRONT COMMISSION OF NEW YORK HARBOR
378 U.S. 52; 84 Sup. Ct. 1594; 12 L. Ed. 2d (1964)

MR. JUSTICE GOLDBERG delivered the opinion of the Court:

We have held today that the Fifth Amendment privilege against self-incrimination must be deemed fully applicable to the States through the Fourteenth Amendment. *Malloy* v. *Hogan*. . . . This case presents a related issue: whether one jurisdiction within our federal structure may compel a witness, whom it has immunized from prosecution under its laws to give testimony which might then be used to convict him of a crime against another such jurisdiction.

Petitioners were subpoenaed to testify at a hearing conducted by the Waterfront Commission of New York Harbor concerning a work stoppage at the Hoboken, New Jersey, piers. After refusing to respond to certain questions

about the stoppage on the ground that the answers might tend to incriminate them, petitioners were granted immunity from prosecution under the laws of New Jersey and New York. Notwithstanding this grant of immunity, they still refused to respond to the questions on the ground that the answers might tend to incriminate them under *federal* law, to which the grant of immunity did not purport to extend. Petitioners were thereupon held in civil and criminal contempt of court. The New Jersey Supreme Court reversed the criminal contempt conviction on procedural grounds but . . . affirmed the civil contempt judgments on the merits. The court held that a State may constitutionally compel a witness to give testimony which might be used in a federal prosecution against him. . . .

Since a grant of immunity is valid only if it is coextensive with the scope of the privilege against self-incrimination, *Counselman* v. *Hitchcock*, 142 U.S. 547 . . . we must now decide the fundamental constitutional question of whether, absent an immunity provision, one jurisdiction in our federal structure may compel a witness to give testimony which might incriminate him under the laws of another jurisdiction. . . .

Respondent contends, . . . that we should adhere to the "established rule" that the constitutional privilege against self-incrimination does not protect a witness in one jurisdiction against being compelled to give testimony which could be used to convict him in another jurisdiction. This "rule" has three decisional facets: *United States* v. *Murdock* . . . held that the Federal Government could compel a witness to give testimony which might incriminate him under state law; *Knapp* v. *Schweitzer* . . . held that a State could compel a witness to give testimony which might incriminate him under federal law; and *Feldman* v. *United States* . . . held that testimony thus compelled by a State could be introduced into evidence in the federal courts.

Our decision today in *Malloy* v. *Hogan,* necessitates a reconsideration of this rule. Our review of the pertinent cases in this Court and of their English antecedents reveals that Murdock did not adequately consider the relevant authorities and has been significantly weakened by subsequent decisions of this Court, and, further, that the legal premises underlying Feldman and Knapp have since been rejected. . . .

In 1851, the English Court of Chancery decided *King of the Two Sicilies* v. *Willcox*, . . . a case which this Court in *United States* v. *Murdock* . . . erroneously cited as representing the settled "English rule" that a witness is not protected "against disclosing offenses in violation of the laws of another country." . . . Defendants in that case resisted discovery of information, which, they asserted, might subject them to prosecution under the laws of Sicily. In denying their claim, the Vice Chancellor said:

"The rule relied on by the defendants, is one which exists merely by virtue of our own municipal law, and must, I think, have reference, exclusively, to matters penal by that law: to matters as to which, if disclosed, the judge would be able to say, as matter of law, whether it could or could not entail penal consequences." . . .

Two reasons were given in support of this statement: (1) "The impossibility of knowing, as matter of law, to what cases the objection, when resting on the danger of incurring penal consequences in a foreign country, may extend . . . ," and (2) the fact that "in such a case, in order to make the disclosure dangerous to the party who objects, it is essential that he should first quit the protection of our laws, and wilfully go within the jurisdiction of the laws he has violated."

Within a few years, the pertinent part of *King of the Two Sicilies* was specifically overruled by the Court of Chancery Appeal in *United States of America* v. *McRae,* L.R., 3 Ch.App. 79 (1867), a case not mentioned by this Court in *United States* v. *Murdock.* . . .

[In *Hale* v. *Henkel* this Court said:] "The question has been fully considered in England, and the conclusion reached [by the courts of that country] that the only danger to be considered is one arising within the same jurisdiction and under the same sovereignty." . . . This dictum, subsequently relied on in *United States* v. *Murdock* was not well founded. . . .

Moreover, the two factors relied on by the English court in *King of the Two Sicilies* were wholly inapplicable to federal-state problems in this country. The first—"The impossibility of knowing, as matter of law, to what cases the [danger of incrimination] may extend . . . ," . . . —has no force in our country where the federal and state courts take judicial notice of each other's law. The second—that "in order to make the disclosure dangerous to the party who objects, it is essential that he should first quit the protection of our laws, and wilfully go within the jurisdiction of the laws he has violated," is equally inapplicable in our country where the witness is generally within "the jurisdiction" of the State under whose law he claims danger of incrimination, and where, if he is not, the State may demand his extradition. . . .

In 1931, the Court, decided *United States* v. *Murdock,* the case principally relied on by respondent here. . . .

This Court decided that appellee's refusal to answer rested solely on a fear of state prosecution, and then concluded, in one brief paragraph, that such a fear did not justify a refusal to answer questions put by federal officers.

The Court gave three reasons for this conclusion. The first was that: "Investigations for federal purposes may not be prevented by matters depending upon state law. Constitution, art. 6, cl. 2." . . . This argument, however, begs the critical question. No one would suggest that state law could prevent a proper federal investigation; the Court had already held that the Federal Government could, under the Supremacy Clause, grant immunity from state prosecution, and that, accordingly, state law could not prevent a proper federal investigation. The critical issue was

whether the Federal Government, *without granting immunity from state prosecution,* could compel testimony which would incriminate under state law. The Court's first "reason" was not responsive to this issue.

The second reason given by the Court was that: "The English rule of evidence against compulsory self-incrimination, on which historically that contained in the Fifth Amendment rests, does not protect witnesses against disclosing offenses in violation of the laws of another country. *King of the Two Sicilies* v. *Willcox.* . . . As has been demonstrated, . . . the English rule was the opposite from that stated in this Court's opinion: The rule did "protect witnesses against disclosing offenses in violation of the laws of another country." . . .

The third reason given by the Court in Murdock was that:

"This court has held that immunity against state prosecution is not essential to the validity of federal statutes declaring that a witness shall not be excused from giving evidence on the ground that it will incriminate him, and also that the lack of state power to give witnesses protection against federal prosecution does not defeat a state immunity statute. The principle established is that full and complete immunity against prosecution by the government compelling the witness to answer is equivalent to the protection furnished by the rule against compulsory self-incrimination. . . ."

This argument—that the rule in question had already been "established" by the past decisions of the Court—is not accurate. The first case cited by the Court—*Counselman* v. *Hitchcock*—said nothing about the problem of incrimination under the law of another sovereign. The second case—*Brown* v. *Walker*—merely held that the federal immunity statute there involved did protect against state prosecution. The third case—*Jack* v. *Kansas*—held that the Due Process Clause of the Fourteenth Amendment did not prevent a State from compelling an answer to a question which presented no "real danger of a Federal prosecution." . . . The final case—*Hale* v. *Henkel*—contained dictum in support of the rule announced which was without real authority and which had been questioned by a unanimous Court in *Vajtauer* v. *Commissioner of Immigration.* Moreover, the Court subsequently said, in no uncertain terms, that the rule announced in *Murdock* had not been previously "established" by the decisions of the Court. . . .

Thus, neither the reasoning nor the authority relied on by the Court in *United States* v. *Murdock* . . . supports its conclusion that the Fifth Amendment permits the Federal Government to compel answers to questions which might incriminate under state law.

In 1944, the Court, in *Feldman* v. *United States,* . . . was confronted with the situation where evidence compelled by a State under a grant of state immunity was "availed of by the [Federal] Government" and introduced in a federal prosecution. . . . Nevertheless, the Court, in a 4-to-3 decision, upheld this practice, but did so on the authority of a principle which is no longer accepted by this Court. The *Feldman* reasoning was essentially as follows:

"[T]he Fourth and Fifth Amendments intertwined as they are, [express] supplementing phases of the same constitutional purpose. . . ." "[O]ne of the settled principles of our Constitution has been that these Amend-

ments protect only against invasion of civil liberties by the [Federal] Government whose conduct they alone limit." . . .

"And so while evidence secured through unreasonable search and seizure by federal officials is inadmissible in a federal prosecution, *Weeks* v. *United States,* . . . incriminating documents so secured by state officials without participation by federal officials but turned over for their use are admissible in a federal prosecution. . . .

The Court concluded, therefore, by analogy to the then extant search and seizure rule, that evidence compelled by a state grant of immunity could be used by the Federal Government. But the legal foundation upon which that 4-to-3 decision rested no longer stands. Evidence illegally seized by state officials may not now be received in federal courts. In *Elkins* v. *United States,* . . . the Court held, over the dissent of the writer of the *Feldman* decision, that "evidence obtained by state officers during a search which, if conducted by federal officers, would have violated the defendant's immunity from unreasonable searches and seizures under the Fourth Amendment is inadmissible over the defendant's timely objection in a federal criminal trial." Thus, since the fundamental assumption underlying *Feldman* is no longer valid, the constitutional question there decided must now be regarded as an open one. . . .

Knapp v. *Schweitzer* involved a state contempt conviction for a witness' refusal to answer questions, under a grant of state immunity, on the ground that his answers might subject him to prosecution under federal law. Petitioner claimed that "the Fifth Amendment gives him the privilege, which he can assert against either a State or the National Government, against giving testimony that might tend to implicate him in a violation" of federal law. . . . The Court, applying the rule then in existence, denied petitioner's claim and declared that:

> "It is plain that the [Fifth Amendment] can no more be thought of as restricting action by the States than as restricting the conduct of private citizens. The sole—although deeply valuable—purpose of the Fifth Amendment privilege against self-incrimination is the security of the individual against the exertion of the power of the Federal Government to compel incriminating testimony with a view to enabling that same Government to convict a man out of his own mouth." . . .

The Court has today rejected that rule, and with it, all the earlier cases resting on that rule.

The foregoing makes it clear that there is no continuing legal vitality to, or historical justification for, the rule that one jurisdiction within our federal structure may compel a witness to give testimony which could be used to convict him of a crime in another jurisdiction.

In light of the history, policies and purposes of the privilege against self-incrimination, we now accept as correct the construction given the privilege by the English courts and by Chief Justice Marshall and Justice Holmes. See *United States* v. *Saline Bank of Virginia; Ballmann* v. *Fagin.* We reject—as unsupported by history or policy—the deviation from that construction only recently adopted by this Court in *United States* v. *Murdock,* and *Feldman* v. *United States.* We hold that the constitutional privilege against self-incrimination protects a state witness against incrimination under federal as well as

state law and a federal witness against incrimination under state as well as federal law.

We must now decide what effect this holding has on existing state immunity legislation. In *Counselman* v. *Hitchcock,* . . . this Court considered a federal statute which provided that no "evidence obtained from a party or witness by means of a judicial proceeding . . . shall be given in evidence, or in any court of the United States. . . ." Notwithstanding this statute, appellant, claiming his privilege against self-incrimination, refused to answer certain questions before a federal grand jury. The Court said "that legislation cannot abridge a constitutional privilege, and that it cannot replace or supply one, at least unless it is so broad as to have the same extent in scope and effect." . . . Applying this principle to the facts of that case, the Court upheld appellant's refusal to answer on the ground that the statute: "could not, and would not, prevent the use of his testimony to search out other testimony to be used in evidence against him or his property, in a criminal proceeding in such court, . . ." that it:

> "could not prevent the obtaining and the use of witnesses and evidence which should be attributable directly to the testimony he might give under compulsion, and on which he might be convicted, when otherwise, and if he had refused to answer, he could not possibly have been convicted. . . ."

and that it:

> "affords no protection against that use of compelled testimony which consists in gaining therefrom a knowledge of the details of a crime, and of sources of information which may supply other means of convicting the witness or party." . . .

Applying the holding of that case to our holdings today that the privilege against self-incrimination protects a state witness against federal prosecution . . . , and that "the same standards must determine whether [a witness'] silence in either a federal or state proceeding is justified," *Malloy* v. *Hogan*, . . . we hold the constitutional rule to be that a state witness may not be compelled to give testimony which may be incriminating under federal law unless the compelled testimony and its fruits cannot be used in any manner by federal officials in connection with a criminal prosecution against him. We conclude, moreover, that in order to implement this constitutional rule and accommodate the interests of the State and Federal Governments in investigating and prosecuting crime, the Federal Government must be prohibited from making any such use of compelled testimony and its fruits. This exclusionary rule, while permitting the States to secure information necessary for effective law enforcement, leaves the witness and the Federal Government in substantially the same position as if the witness had claimed his privilege in the absence of a state grant of immunity.

It follows that petitioners here may now be compelled to answer the questions propounded to them. At the time they refused to answer, however, petitioners had a reasonable fear, based on this Court's decision in *Feldman* v. *United States,* supra, that the federal authorities might use the answers against them in connection with a federal prosecution. We have now overruled *Feldman* and held that the Federal Government may make no such use of the answers. Fairness dictates that petitioners should now be afforded an opportunity, in light of this development, to answer the questions. . . . Accordingly, the judgment of the New Jersey courts ordering petitioners to answer the questions may remain undisturbed. But the judgment of contempt is vacated and the cause remanded to the New Jersey Supreme Court for proceedings not inconsistent with this opinion.

It is so ordered.

Judgment sustained in part and vacated in part and cause remanded with directions.

MR. JUSTICE BLACK, MR. JUSTICE WHITE, MR. JUSTICE STEWART, MR. JUSTICE HARLAN and MR. JUSTICE CLARK, concurred.

19
Civil Liberties and the Administrative Process

One of the most striking developments of the twentieth century in governmental affairs has been the growth in the power and prestige of administrative officers and bodies. As was noted in Chapter 6, the increased complexity of industrial America and the continued social and economic demands on government have forced Congress to delegate more and more powers to the President. At the same time, executive officers in state and local government units have also been given greater powers by their respective legislative bodies to deal with the expanding functions of government. But few of these executive officers, including the President, can carry out the new functions of government alone. In fact, as governmental functions become more specialized and complex, an increasing number of important tasks have had to be turned over to administrative officers operating under the executive branch. Thus, we now have a bewildering multiplicity of administrative boards, commissions, and bureaus at all levels of government.

The administrative process has not "come like a thief in the night." Nor did some Machiavelli "retire into a closet at night and emerge the next morning with the abdominable bureaucracy all thought up and planned out."[1] Instead,

[1] These quotations and other materials in this chapter are taken from R. J. Tresolini, "The Development of Administrative Law," *University of Pittsburgh Law Review,* Vol.

it has evolved haphazardly over a long period of time. "There can be no doubt that the instruments of administration have been established in response to the growing demands of modern government which require, above all other things, the competence and knowledge of expert administrators."[2] New administrative agencies have been "created or old ones expanded not to satisfy an abstract governmental theory, but to cope with problems of recognized public concern. It was the growth of steam navigation, rather than a predisposition toward administrative agencies, which gave rise in 1838 to 'an Act to provide for the better security of the lives of passengers on board of vessels, propelled in whole or in part by steam,' and so commenced the process of steamboat inspection which continues until the present day in the United States Coast Guard. No different in essence were the considerations that exactly a century later led to the creation of the Civil Aeronautics Authority to coordinate regulation of the air transportation industry. If human relationships within society had remained unchanged, if the Nation's territorial limitations had been unexpanded, if the arts and sciences had not progressed with the years, the machinery of government might similarly have remained undeveloped. Instead, in the span of a century and a half, new rights and duties among men have emerged, and the government has responded to demands for their adjustment, their execution, and their protection."[3]

As Congress and the states created new administrative bodies to meet the needs of a rapidly changing society, an entirely new body of public law began to develop. This administrative law[4] includes a great variety of topics, such as delegation and subdelegation of powers, methods of judicial control, liability of public officers, and administrative procedures. The great bulk of

---

12 (Spring 1951). See also Peter Woll, *American Bureaucracy* (New York: Norton, 1963), pp. 29–60.

[2] Robert M. Cooper, "Administrative Justice and the Role of Discretion," *Yale Law Journal,* Vol. 47 (February 1938), p. 600.

[3] Walter Gellhorn and Clark Byse, *Administrative Law* (Brooklyn: Foundation Press, 1954), p. 2.

[4] There has been much disagreement over the precise meaning of the term *administrative law*. Today, the following definition, given by one of the outstanding commentators in the field, is accepted generally by the majority of scholars. "Administrative law is the law concerning the powers and procedures of administrative agencies. An administrative agency is an organ of government, other than a court and other than a legislature, which affects the rights of private parties through either adjudication or rule making. Administrative law is restricted to the activities of agencies having powers of adjudication or rule making; a large portion of the law of public administration is thus excluded. It is confined to arrangements involving rights of private parties; it does not extend to internal problems affecting only the agencies and their officers and staffs." Kenneth C. Davis, *Administrative Law* (St. Paul, Minn.: West Publishing Co., 1951), pp. 1–3. See also, by the same author, *Administrative Law and Government* (St. Paul, Minn.: West Publishing Co., 1960), p. 11. Cf. Martin Shapiro, *The Supreme Court and Administrative Agencies* (New York: The Free Press, 1968), pp. 104–109 for a critique of the standard definition.

the subject matter of administrative law falls outside the scope of this book. In fact, administrative law and constitutional law are recognized as separate and distinct fields of study. But there are some topics that may appropriately be classified under both fields. For example, students in both fields need to understand the rule against delegation of legislative powers and the doctrine of separation of powers, which have been discussed in Chapters 6 and 1, respectively. In addition, the procedural requirements of the due process clauses of both the Fifth and Fourteenth Amendments are important in administrative law as well as constitutional law, for administrative proceedings must be governed by the rudimentary requirements of fair play.[5]

Most problems involving civil liberties and the administrative process arise out of the question of whether or not an administrative agency has accorded an individual procedural due process in its proceedings. "The dominant factor in the development of the procedural aspect of American administrative law has been the provision of federal and state constitutions that no person may be deprived of life, liberty, or property without 'due process of law.' (T)he ultimate legal problem is whether the procedure utilized satisfies the guarantee of due process of law."[6] The remainder of this chapter is concerned with some aspects of this important problem.

Due Process and Administrative Procedure

The rise of administrative agencies inevitably caused alarm in many quarters. Many Americans objected to growing supervision by administrative officers simply because they were attached firmly to the laissez-faire conception of government. Administrative agencies were created so rapidly that they were difficult to fit into the traditional framework of democratic government. Because they exercised powers of adjudication (quasijudicial) and rule-making (quasilegislative) as well as executive powers, they were difficult to classify as belonging to one of the traditional branches of government. Many people argued vehemently that these agencies constituted a headless fourth branch of government that violated the basic American doctrine of separation of powers. But the chief objection to administrative agencies was that they conducted their proceedings in an arbitrary and unreasonable way. It was charged that too many administrators did not afford individuals the traditional procedural safeguards available in courts of law. "The transfer of adjudicatory responsibilities from the traditional courts to the yet untraditionalized administrative agencies aroused anxious debate from the first, and the debate continues today. The methods of the new adjudicators have been praised and blamed—praised for being functional without unfairness, blamed for being

⁵ F. Trowbridge vom Baur, *Federal Administrative Law* (Chicago: Callaghan, 1942), Vol. 1, p. 273.

⁶ Gellhorn and Byse, *op. cit.,* p. 715.

incautiously careless of litigants' rights in ways that fair-minded judges would have avoided."[7]

It was soon evident that the debate engendered by the rise of administrative adjudication and rule making needed balanced and dispassionate study. In 1939, a comprehensive investigation of practices and procedures of federal administrative agencies was begun by the Attorney General's Committee on Administrative Procedure. The final report of the committee, issued in 1941, proposed that a number of procedural reforms to safeguard individual rights be instituted by federal agencies.[8] In 1946, Congress enacted the Administrative Procedure Act, which attempted to establish standards of procedure common to federal administrative agencies of all kinds. The act was "designed to protect the individual citizen from the hazards of uncertain and slipshod administrative procedures resulting in unfair and arbitrary action, while at the same time seeking to preserve the flexibility, the resourcefulness, and progressiveness of the administrative agency at its best."[9] A number of states also have enacted legislation designed to codify administrative procedures.

Of course, the courts as well as legislative bodies have played an important part in determining the procedures that must be utilized by administrative officers in proceedings affecting the personal and property rights of individuals. In fact, prior to the federal and state administrative-procedure acts, the courts had been relied on principally to control administrative proceedings. As already noted, administrative procedures must satisfy the due process requirements of the federal Constitution as interpreted ultimately by the Supreme Court. Here "it is not administrative but rather constitutional law that determines whether, and when, an administrative procedure must be in conformity with due process. This is not just a mere problem of nomenclature. It means that *administrative acts* of all kinds—regulations, individual decisions, preliminary acts, investigations, etc.—*may or may not be required to satisfy due process of law,* and that the answer to this question depends primarily on the ever-fluctuating interpretation of our Constitution."[10] Thus, the due process clauses of the Fifth and Fourteenth Amendments "are addressed very definitely, perhaps now even primarily, to acts of the administrative-executive branch of the government."[11]

---

[7] Walter Gellhorn, *Individual Freedom and Governmental Restraints* (Baton Rouge: Louisiana State University Press, 1956), p. 4.

[8] Attorney General's Committee on Administrative Procedure, *Final Report,* 77th Cong., 1st sess., Senate Document No. 8 (1941). The outstanding official study of the administrative process in particular states was made in New York. Robert M. Benjamin, "Administrative Adjudication in the State of New York," Report to Governor H. Lehman (1942).

[9] Arthur T. Vanderbilt, *The Doctrine of Separation of Powers and its Present-Day Significance* (Lincoln: University of Nebraska Press, 1953), p. 87.

[10] Reginald Parker, *Administrative Law* (Indianapolis: Bobbs-Merrill, 1952), p. 34.

[11] *Ibid.,* p. 57.

NOTICE AND HEARING

Adequate notice and a fair hearing are the principal requirements of procedural due process when private rights are being disposed of by administrative officers. Both requirements are difficult to state precisely because they vary with the circumstances of each case. Nevertheless, as the Supreme Court has stated, notice must appraise interested parties of pending administrative action and afford them an opportunity to present their objections. "The notice must be of such a nature as reasonably to convey the required information and it must afford a reasonable time for those interested to make their appearance."[12] The requirement of a fair hearing "embraces not only the right to present evidence but also a reasonable opportunity to know the claims of the opposing party and to meet them. The right to submit argument implies that opportunity; otherwise the right may be a barren one. Those who are brought into contest with the government in a quasi-judicial proceeding aimed at the control of their activities are entitled to be fairly advised of what the government proposes and to be heard upon its proposals before it issues its final command."[13]

In some instances administrative officers have been empowered to take drastic action against persons or property without affording notice and hearing. This is known as summary administrative procedure or process, because the official may act without formal proceedings of any kind. But because summary administrative powers run counter to our traditional notions of fair play, they may be exercised only in emergency situations where the health, safety, order, and morals of the community are endangered. Such powers have been conferred on revenue officers, the Attorney General, highway commissioners, health officers, and other administrators. A highway commissioner, for example, may usually remove obstructions from public highways summarily. A health officer may summarily seize and destroy food that is not fit to eat and milk from cows not tested for tuberculosis in order to protect the public. A revenue officer may seize a person's property for nonpayment of taxes on the ground that the prompt collection of tax funds is essential for the existence and preservation of government.[14]

In *Frank* v. *Maryland,* 359 U.S. 360 (1959), the Supreme Court held that administrative health and safety inspections might be made summarily without regard to constitutional guarantees against unreasonable searches. The Court overruled its *Frank* decision in *Camara* v. *Municipal Court,* 387 U.S. 523 (1967), but in the process indicated that it might apply somewhat less strict procedural requirements to the issuance of warrants for housing and business inspections than those applied to warrants requested in criminal investigations.

[12] *Mullane* v. *Central Hanover Bank and Trust Co.,* 339 U.S. 306 (1950).

[13] *Morgan* v. *United States,* 304 U.S. 1 (1937).

[14] R. J. Tresolini, "Administrative Tax Enforcement: Legal Concepts," *Temple Law Quarterly,* Vol. 27 (1953), p. 8.

In *Buck* v. *Bell* (p. 738), where the Court upheld compulsory sterilization for the first time, no question of adequate notice or hearing was involved because the Virginia statute providing such safeguards was carefully followed. *Buck* v. *Bell,* however, does demonstrate the enormous powers that may be exercised by an administrative officer acting under statutes that may well be based on false assumptions.[15] In *Skinner* v. *Oklahoma,* 316 U.S. 535 (1942), the Court invalidated a state habitual-criminal sterilization law under which persons convicted two or more times of felonies involving moral turpitude could be made sexually sterile. In declaring the statute unconstitutional under the equal protection clause of the Fourteenth Amendment, the Court failed to reconsider *Buck* v. *Bell.* However, in a concurring opinion, Justice Jackson warned that "there are limits to the extent to which a legislatively represented majority may conduct biological experiments at the expense of the dignity and personality and natural powers of a minority."

In recent years the right to a fair hearing has been at issue in a number of loyalty-security cases. Administrative officers have been given wide powers in the effort to purge Communists and fellow travelers. Among other things, they have been authorized to judge a person's loyalty or disloyalty and to draw up lists of "subversive" organizations. Some administrators have been allowed to pass judgment on such delicate matters without according individuals the traditional procedural safeguards ordinarily required by due process of law. That the exercise of such administrative powers poses important civil rights questions is demonstrated by the various opinions in the *Knauff case* (p. 740), *Joint Anti-Fascist Committee* v. *McGrath* (p. 744), and *Vitarelli* v. *Seaton* (p. 749).

BUCK *v.* BELL
274 U.S. 200; 47 Sup. Ct. 584; 71 L. Ed. 1000 (1927)

[*Because of the facts noted in the case, a special board of directors of the State Colony for Epileptics and Feeble Minded, acting under a Virginia statute, ordered that an inmate named Carrie Buck be sterilized. The decision of the special board was affirmed by a county court. The State Court of Appeals upheld the statute and affirmed the county court's holding. The case then went to the Supreme Court on a writ of error, with the plaintiff contending that the Virginia sterilization statute violated the due process and equal protecion clauses of the Fourteenth Amendment. Bell was the superintendent of the State Colony who testified before the State Court of Appeals that the sterilization law was a "blessing" for feeble-minded patients.*]

MR. JUSTICE HOLMES delivered the opinion of the Court:

Carrie Buck is a feeble-minded white woman who was committed to the State Colony. . . . She is the daughter of a feeble-minded mother in the same in-

---

[15] Walter Berns, "*Buck* v. *Bell*: Due Process of Law?" *Western Political Quarterly,* Vol. 6 (1953), p. 762. Professor Berns estimated that twenty states sterilize about 1400 persons a year.

stitution, and the mother of an illegitimate feeble-minded child. She was eighteen years old at the time of the trial of her case in the circuit court, in the latter part of 1924. An Act of Virginia approved March 20, 1924, recites that the health of the patient and the welfare of society may be promoted in certain cases by the sterilization of mental defectives, under careful safeguard, etc.; that the sterilization may be effected in males by vasectomy and in females by salpingectomy, without serious pain or substantial danger to life; that the Commonwealth is supporting in various institutions many defective persons who if now discharged would become a menace but if incapable of procreating might be discharged with safety and become self-supporting with benefit to themselves and to society; and that experience has shown that heredity plays an important part in the transmission of insanity, imbecility, etc. The statute then enacts that whenever the superintendent of certain institutions including the above-named State Colony shall be of opinion that it is for the best interests of the patients and of society that an inmate under his care should be sexually sterilized, he may have the operation performed upon any patient afflicted with hereditary forms of insanity, imbecility, etc., on complying with the very careful provisions by which the act protects the patients from possible abuse.

The superintendent first presents a petition to the special board of directors of his hospital or colony, stating the facts and the grounds for his opinion, verified by affidavit. Notice of the petition and of the time and place of the hearing in the institution is to be served upon the inmate, and also upon his guardian, and if there is no guardian the superintendent is to apply to the Circuit Court of the County to appoint one. If the inmate is a minor, notice also is to be given to his parents if any with a copy of the petition. The board is to see to it that the inmate may attend the hearings if desired by him or his guardian. The evidence is all to be reduced to writing, and after the board has made its order for or against the operation, the superintendent, or the inmate, or his guardian, may appeal to the Circuit Court of the County. The Circuit Court may consider the record of the board and the evidence before it and such other admissible evidence as may be offered, and may affirm, revise, or reverse the order of the board and enter such order as it deems just. Finally any party may apply to the Supreme Court of Appeals, which, if it grants the appeal, is to hear the case upon the record of the trial in the Circuit Court and may enter such order as it thinks the Circuit Court should have entered. There can be no doubt that so far as procedure is concerned the rights of the patient are most carefully considered, and as every step in this case was taken in scrupulous compliance with the statute and after months of observation, there is no doubt that in that respect the plaintiff in error has had due process of law.

The attack is not upon the procedure but upon the substantive law. It seems to be contended that in no circumstances could such an order be justified. It certainly is contended that the order cannot be justified upon the existing grounds. The judgment finds the facts that have been recited and that Carrie Buck "is the probable potential parent of socially inadequate offspring, likewise afflicted, that she may be sexually sterilized without detriment to her general health and that her welfare and that of society will be promoted by her sterilization," and thereupon makes the order. In view of the general declarations of the legislature and the specific findings of the court obviously we cannot say as matter of law that the grounds do not exist, and if they exist they justify the result. We have seen more than once that the public welfare may call upon the best citizens for their lives. It would be strange if it could not call upon those who already sap the strength of the State for these lesser sacrifices, often not felt to be such by those concerned, in order to prevent our being swamped with incompetence. It is better for all the world, if instead of waiting to execute degenerate offspring for crime, or to let them starve for their imbecility, society can prevent those who are manifestly unfit from continuing their kind. The principle that sustains compulsory vaccination is broad enough to cover cutting the Fallopian tubes. *Jacobson* v. *Massachusetts,* 197 U.S. 11. . . . Three generations of imbeciles are enough.

But, it is said, however it might be if this reasoning were applied generally, it fails when it is confined to the small number who are in the institutions named and is not applied to the multitudes outside. It is the usual last resort of constitutional arguments to point out shortcomings of this sort. But the answer is that the law does all that is needed when it does all that it can, indicates a policy, applies it to all within the lines, and seeks to bring within the lines all similarly situated so far and so fast as its means allow. Of course so far as the operations enable those who otherwise must be kept confined to be returned to the world, and thus open the asylum to others, the equality aimed at will be more nearly reached.

Judgment Affirmed.

MR. JUSTICE BUTLER dissents.

UNITED STATES ex rel. KNAUFF *v.* SHAUGHNESSY
338 U.S. 537; 70 Sup. Ct. 309; 94 L. Ed. 317 (1950)

[*Mrs. Ellen Knauff was the alien wife of an American citizen. When she tried to enter the United States, the Attorney General excluded her without a hearing on the basis of confidential information that her admission would be prejudicial to the country's interest. A federal district court upheld the action of the Attorney General. After a court of appeals affirmed the holding, the Supreme Court granted certiorari. Additional facts are given in the following opinion. Shaughnessy was the Acting Director of Immigration and Naturalization in the New York district. The meaning of* ex rel *in the title of the case is explained in the* Graves *case in Chapter 10.*

After the Court's decision, private bills were introduced in Congress to allow Mrs. Knauff to enter the United States. Some time later, the Attorney General ordered that Mrs. Knauff be given a hearing. The Board of Immigration Appeals ultimately decided that Mrs. Knauff was admissible, because there was no substantial evidence to indicate that she would be likely to engage in subversive activities. The Board's finding was approved by the Attorney General and Mrs. Knauff was finally allowed to enter the United States—more than three years after she was first detained on Ellis Island.]

MR. JUSTICE MINTON delivered the opinion of the Court:

. . . Petitioner was born in Germany in 1915. She left Germany and went to Czechoslovakia during the Hitler regime. There she was married and divorced. She went to England in 1939 as a refugee. Thereafter she served with the Royal Air Force efficiently and honorably from January 1, 1943, until May 30, 1946. She then secured civilian employment with the War Department of the United States in Germany. Her work was rated "very good" and "excellent." On February 28, 1948, with the permission of the Commanding General at Frankfurt, Germany, she married Kurt W. Knauff, a naturalized citizen of the United States. He is an honorably discharged United States Army veteran of World War II. He is, as he was at the time of his marriage, a civilian employee of the United States Army at Frankfurt, Germany.

On August 14, 1948, petitioner sought to enter the United States to be naturalized. On that day she was temporarily excluded from the United States and detained at Ellis Island. On October 6, 1948, the Assistant Commissioner of Immigration and Naturalization recommended that she be permanently excluded without a hearing on the ground that her admission would be prejudicial to the interests of the United States. On the same day the Attorney General adopted this recommendation and entered a final order of exclusion. . . .

. . . [P]etitioner was excluded by the Attorney General and denied a hearing. We are asked to pass upon the validity of this action. [*The Attorney General was empowered to exclude aliens under an Act of Congress of 1922, as amended in 1941.*]

At the outset we wish to point out that an alien who seeks admission to this country may not do so under any claim of right. Admission of aliens to the United States is a privilege granted by the sovereign United States Government. Such privilege is granted to an alien only upon such terms as the United States shall prescribe. It must be exer-

cised in accordance with the procedure which the United States provides. . . .

Petitioner contends that the 1941 Act and the regulations thereunder are void to the extent that they contain unconstitutional delegations of legislative power. But there is no question of inappropriate delegation of legislative power involved here. The exclusion of aliens is a fundamental act of sovereignty. The right to do so is inherent in the executive power to control the foreign affairs of the nation. . . . When Congress prescribes a procedure concerning the admissibility of aliens, it is not dealing alone with a legislative power. It is implementing an inherent executive power.

Thus the decision to admit or to exclude an alien may be lawfully placed with the President, who may in turn delegate the carrying out of this function to a responsible executive officer of the sovereign, such as the Attorney General. The action of the executive officer under such authority is final and conclusive. Whatever the rule may be concerning deportation of persons who have gained entry into the United States, it is not within the province of any court, unless expressly authorized by law, to review the determination of the political branch of the Government to exclude a given alien. . . . Normally Congress supplies the conditions of the privilege of entry into the United States. But because the power of exclusion of aliens is also inherent in the executive department of the sovereign, Congress may in broad terms authorize the executive to exercise the power, e.g., as was done here, for the best interests of the country during a time of national emergency. Executive officers may be entrusted with the duty of specifying the procedures for carrying out the congressional intent. . . .

In the particular circumstances of the instant case the Attorney General, exercising the discretion entrusted to him by Congress and the President, concluded upon the basis of confidential information that the public interest required that petitioner be denied the privilege of entry into the United States. He denied her a hearing on the matter because, in his judgment, the disclosure of the information on which he based that opinion would itself endanger the public security.

We find no substantial merit to petitioner's contention that the regulations were not "reasonable" as they were required to be by the 1941 Act. We think them reasonable in the circumstances of the period for which they were authorized, namely, the national emergency of World War II. . . .

. . . For ordinary times Congress has provided aliens with a hearing. . . . And the contention of petitioner is that she is entitled to the statutory hearing because for purposes of the War Brides Act, within which she comes, the war terminated when the President proclaimed the cessation of hostilities. She contends that the War Brides Act . . . discloses a congressional intent that special restrictions on the entry of aliens should cease to apply to war brides upon the cessation of hostilities.

The War Brides Act provides that World War II is the period from December 7, 1941, until the proclaimed termination of hostilities. This has nothing to do with the period for which the regulations here acted under were authorized. The beginning and end of the war are defined by the War Brides Act, we assume, for the purpose of ascertaining the period within which citizens must have served in the armed forces in order for their spouses and children to be entitled to the benefits of the Act. The special procedure followed in this case was authorized not only during the period of actual hostilities but during the entire war and the national emer-

gency proclaimed May 27, 1941. The national emergency has never been terminated. Indeed, a state of war still exists. . . . Thus, the authority upon which the Attorney General acted remains in force. The Act of June 21, 1941, and the President's proclamations and the regulations thereunder are still a part of the immigration laws.

The War Brides Act does not relieve petitioner of her alien status. Indeed, she sought admission in order to be naturalized and thus to overcome her alien status. The Act relieved her of certain physical, mental, and documentary requirements and of the quota provisions of the immigration laws. But she must, as the Act requires, still be "otherwise admissible under the immigration laws." In other words, aside from the enumerated relaxations of the immigration laws she must be treated as any other alien seeking admission. Under the immigration laws and regulations applicable to all aliens seeking entry into the United States during the national emergency, she was excluded by the Attorney General without a hearing. In such a case we have no authority to retry the determination of the Attorney General. . . .

There is nothing in the War Brides Act or its legislative history to indicate that it was the purpose of Congress, by partially suspending compliance with certain requirements and the quota provisions of the immigration laws, to relax the security provisions of the immigration laws. There is no indication that Congress intended to permit members or former members of the armed forces to marry and bring into the United States aliens that the President, acting through the Attorney General in the performance of his sworn duty, found should be denied entry for security reasons. As all other aliens, petitioner had to stand the test of security. This she failed to meet. We find no legal defect in the manner of petitioner's exclusion, and the judgment is

Affirmed.

MR. JUSTICE DOUGLAS and MR. JUSTICE CLARK took no part in the consideration or decision of this case.

MR. JUSTICE FRANKFURTER, dissenting:

. . . We are reminded from time to time that in enacting legislation Congress is not engaged in a scientific process which takes account of every contingency. Its laws are not to be read as though every *i* has to be dotted and every *t* crossed. The War Brides Act is legislation derived from the dominant regard which American society places upon the family. It is not to be assumed that Congress gave with a bountiful hand but allowed its bounty arbitrarily to be taken away. In framing and passing the War Brides Act, Congress was preoccupied with opening the door to wives acquired by American husbands during service in foreign lands. It opened the door on essentials—wives of American soldiers and perchance mothers of their children were not to run the gauntlet of administrative discretion in determining their physical and mental condition, and were to be deemed non-quota immigrants. Congress ought not to be made to appear to require that they incur the greater hazards of an informer's tale without any opportunity for its refutation, especially since considerations of national security, in so far as they are pertinent, can be amply protected by a hearing *in camera*. . . . An alien's opportunity of entry into the United States is of course a privilege which Congress may grant or withhold. But the crux of the problem before us is whether Congress, having extended the privilege for the benefit not of the alien but of her American husband, left wide open the opportunity ruthlessly to take away what it gave.

A regulation permitting such exclusion by the Attorney General's fiat—in the nature of things that high functionary must largely act on dossiers prepared by others—in the case of an alien claiming entry on his own account is one thing. To construe such regulation to be authorized and to apply in the case of the wife of an honorably discharged American soldier is quite another thing. Had Congress spoken explicitly we would have to bow to it. Such a substantial contradiction of the congressional beneficence which is at the heart of the War Brides Act ought not to be attributed to Congress by a process of elaborate implication. Especially is this to be avoided when to do so charges Congress with an obviously harsh purpose. . . .

MR. JUSTICE JACKSON, whom MR. JUSTICE BLACK and MR. JUSTICE FRANKFURTER join, dissenting:

I do not question the constitutional power of Congress to authorize immigration authorities to turn back from our gates any alien or class of aliens. But I do not find that Congress has authorized an abrupt and brutal exclusion of the wife of an American citizen without a hearing.

Congress held out a promise of liberalized admission to alien brides, taken unto themselves by men serving in or honorably discharged from our armed services abroad. . . . The petitioning husband is honorably discharged and remained in Germany as a civilian employee. Our military authorities abroad required their permission before marriage. The Army in Germany is not without a vigilant and security-conscious intelligence service. This woman was employed by our European Command and her record is not only without blemish, but is highly praised by her superiors. The marriage of this alien woman to this veteran was approved by the Commanding General at Frankfurt-on-Main.

Now this American citizen is told he cannot bring his wife to the United States, but he will not be told why. He must abandon his bride to live in his own country or forsake his country to live with his bride.

So he went to court and sought a writ of *habeas corpus,* which we never tire of citing to Europe as the unanswerable evidence that our free country permits no arbitrary official detention. And the Government tells the Court that not even a court can find out why the girl is excluded. But it says we must find that Congress authorized this treatment of war brides and, even if we cannot get any reasons for it, we must say it is legal; security requires it.

Security is like liberty in that many are the crimes committed in its name. The menace to the security of this country, be it great as it may, from this girl's admission is as nothing compared to the menace to free institutions inherent in procedures on this pattern. In the name of security the police state justifies its arbitrary oppressions on evidence that is secret, because security might be prejudiced if it were brought to light in hearings. The plan that evidence of guilt must be secret is abhorrent to free men, because it provides a cloak for the malevolent, the misinformed, the meddlesome, and the corrupt to play the role of informer undetected and uncorrected. . . .

Congress will have to use more explicit language than any yet cited before I will agree that it has authorized an administrative officer to break up the family of an American citizen or force him to keep his wife by becoming an exile. Likewise, it will have to be much more explicit before I can agree that it authorized a finding of serious misconduct against the wife of an American citizen without notice of charges, evidence of guilt, and a chance to meet it.

I should direct the Attorney General either to produce his evidence justifying exclusion or to admit Mrs. Knauff to the country.

JOINT ANTI-FASCIST REFUGEE COMMITTEE *v.* McGRATH
341 U.S. 123; 71 Sup. Ct. 624; 95 L. Ed. 817 (1951)

[*The Joint Anti-Fascist Refugee Committee and two other organizations (National Council of American-Soviet Friendship and International Workers Order) were among those groups that were listed as subversive by the Attorney General of the United States. The three organizations had been placed on the list without notice and hearing. The Attorney General was authorized to promulgate the list of subversive organizations under the terms of an executive order issued by President Truman in 1947. The list was used by the Loyalty Review Board in determining the disloyalty of government employees. Throughout the proceedings the three organizations maintained that they were engaged solely in charitable or insurance activities that were lawful. They contended that inclusion in the list of subversive organizations seriously impaired their work and the good will of many people. The petitioners sued McGrath, the Attorney General, to have the names of the organizations deleted from the list because of the obvious harm to their activities. A district court granted the government's motions to dismiss the complaints. A court of appeals affirmed. The Supreme Court granted certiorari.*]

MR. JUSTICE BURTON announced the judgment of the Court and delivered the following opinion, in which MR. JUSTICE DOUGLAS joins:

In each of these cases the same issue is raised by the dismissal of a complaint for its failure to state a claim upon which relief can be granted. That issue is whether, in the face of the facts alleged in the complaint . . . the Attorney General of the United States has authority to include the complaining organization in a list of organizations designated by him as Communist and furnished by him to the Loyalty Review Board of the United States Civil Service Commission. He claims to derive authority to do this from the . . . provisions in Part III, §3, of Executive Order No. 9835, issued by the President, March 21, 1947. . . .

If, upon the allegations in any of these complaints, it had appeared that the acts of the respondents, from which relief was sought, were authorized by the President under his Executive Order No. 9835, the case would have bristled with constitutional issues. On that basis the complaint would have raised questions as to the justiciability and merit of claims based on the First, Fifth, Ninth, and Tenth Amendments to the Constitution. It is our obligation, however, not to reach those issues unless the allegations before us squarely present them. . . .

The Executive Order contains no express or implied attempt to confer power on anyone to act arbitrarily or capriciously—even assuming a constitutional power to do so. The order includes in the purposes of the President's program not only the protection of the United States against disloyal employees but the "equal protection" of loyal employees against unfounded accusations of disloyalty. . . . The standards stated for refusal of and removal from employment require that "on all the evidence, reasonable grounds (shall) exist for belief that the person involved is disloyal." . . . Obviously it would be contrary to the purpose of that order to place on a list to be disseminated under the Loyalty Program any designation of an organization that was patently arbitrary and contrary to the uncontroverted material facts. The order contains the express requirement that each designation of an organization by the Attorney General on such a list shall be made only after an "appropriate . . . determination" as prescribed in Part III, §3. An "appropriate" governmental "determination" must be the result of a process of reasoning. It cannot be an arbitrary fiat contrary to the known facts. This is inherent in the meaning of "determination." It is implicit in a government of laws and not of men. Where an act of an official plainly falls outside of the scope of his authority, he does not make that act legal by doing it and then invoking the doctrine of administrative construction to cover it.

It remains, therefore, for us to decide whether, *on the face of these complaints,* the Attorney General is acting within his authority in furnishing the Loyalty Review Board with a designation of the complaining organizations either as "Communist" or as within any other classification of Part III, §3, of the order. In the National Council and International Workers Cases, the complaining organization is alleged not only to be a civic or insurance organization, apparently above reproach from the point of view of loyalty to the United States, but is also declared to be one that is not within any classification listed in Part III, §3, of the order. In the Refugee Committee Case, the negative allegations are incompatible with the inclusion of the complaining organization within any of the designated classifications. The inclusion of any of the complaining organizations in the designated list solely on the facts alleged in the respective complaints, which must be the basis for our decision here, is thereby an arbitrary and unauthorized act. In the two cases where the complaint specifically alleges the factual absence of any basis for the designation, and the respondents' motion admits that allegation, the designation is necessarily contrary to the record. The situation is comparable to one which would be created if the Attorney General, under like circumstances, were to designate the American National Red Cross as a Communist organization. Accepting as common knowledge the charitable and loyal status of that organization, there is no doubt, in the absence of any contrary claim asserted against it, the Executive Order does not authorize its inclusion by the Attorney General as a "Communist" organization or as coming within any of the other classifications named in Part III, §3, of the order.

Since we find that the conduct ascribed to the Attorney General by the complaints is patently arbitrary, the deference ordinarily due administrative construction of an administrative order is not sufficient to bring his alleged conduct within the authority conferred by Executive Order No. 9835. The doctrine of administrative construction never has been carried so far as to permit administrative discretion to run riot. If applied to this case and compounded with the assumption that the President's Order was drafted for him by his Attorney General, the conclusion would rest upon the premise that the Attorney General has attempted to delegate to himself the power to act arbitrarily. We cannot impute such an attempt to the Nation's highest law enforcement officer any more than we can to its President.

In thus emphasizing an outer limit to what can be considered an authorized designation of an organization under the order, the instant cases serve a valuable purpose. They demonstrate that the order does not authorize, much less direct, the exercise of any such absolute power as would permit the inclusion in the Attorney General's list of a designation that is patently arbitrary or contrary to fact.

When the acts of the Attorney General and of the members of the Loyalty Review Board are stripped of the Presidential authorization claimed for them by the respondents, they stand, on the face of these complaints, as unauthorized publications of admittedly unfounded designations of the complaining organizations as "Communist." Their effect is to cripple the functioning and damage the reputation of those organizations in their respective communities and in the nation. The complaints, on that basis, sufficiently charge that such acts violate each complaining organization's common-law right to be free from defamation. "A communication is defamatory if it tends so to harm the reputation of another as to lower him in the estimation of the community or to deter third persons from associating or dealing with him." . . .

These complaints do not raise the question of the personal liability of public officials for money damages caused by their *ultra vires* acts. . . . They ask only for declaratory and injunctive relief striking the names of the designated organizations from the Attorney General's published list and, as far as practicable, correcting the public records.

The respondents are not immune from such a proceeding. Only recently, this Court recognized that "the action of an officer of the sovereign (be it holding, taking, or otherwise legally affecting the plaintiff's property) can be regarded as so 'illegal' as to permit a suit for specific relief against the officer as an individual . . . if the powers, or their exercise in the particular case, are constitutionally void." . . .

The same is true here, where the acts complained of are beyond the officer's authority under the Executive Order.

Finally, the standing of the petitioners to bring these suits is clear. The touchstone to justiciability is injury to a legally protected right and the right of a bona fide charitable organization to carry on its work, free from defamatory statements of the kind discussed, is such a right.

It is unrealistic to contend that because the respondents gave no orders directly to the petitioners to change their course of conduct, relief cannot be granted against what the respondents actually did. We long have granted relief to parties whose legal rights have been violated by unlawful public action, although such action made no direct demands upon them. . . . The complaints here amply allege past and impending serious damage caused by the actions of which petitioners complain.

Nothing we have said purports to adjudicate the truth of petitioners' allegations that they are not in fact communistic. We have assumed that the designations made by the Attorney General are arbitrary because we are compelled to make that assumption by his motions to dismiss the complaints. Whether the complaining organizations are in fact communistic or whether the Attorney General possesses information from which he could reasonably find them to be so must await determination by the District Court upon remand.

For these reasons, we find it necessary to reverse the judgments of the Court of Appeals in the respective cases and to remand each case to the District Court with instructions to deny the respondents' motion that the complaint be dismissed for failure to state a claim upon which relief can be granted.

Reversed and remanded.

MR. JUSTICE CLARK took no part in the consideration or decision of any of these cases.

MR. JUSTICE BLACK, concurring:

. . . In the present climate of public opinion it appears certain that the Attorney General's much publicized findings, regardless of their truth or falsity, are the practical equivalents of confiscation and death sentences for any blacklisted organization not possessing extraordinary financial, political, or religious prestige and influence. . . .

. . . [I]n my judgment the executive has no constitutional authority, with or without a hearing, officially to prepare and publish the lists challenged by petitioners. In the first place, the system adopted effectively punishes many organizations and their members merely because of their political beliefs and utterances, and to this extent smacks of a most evil type of censorship. This cannot be reconciled with the First Amendment as I interpret it. . . . Moreover, officially prepared and proclaimed governmental blacklists possess almost every quality of bills of attainder, the use of which was from the beginning forbidden to both national and state governments. . . . It is true that the classic bill of attainder was a condemnation by the legislature following investigation by that body, . . . while in the present case the Attorney General performed the official tasks. But I cannot believe that the authors of the Constitution, who outlawed the bill of attainder, inadvertently endowed the executive with power to engage in the same tyrannical practices that had made the bill such an odious institution.

There is argument that executive power to issue these pseudo-bills of attainder can be implied from the undoubted power of the Government to hire and discharge employees and to protect itself against treasonable individuals or organizations. Our basic law, however, wisely withheld authority for resort to executive investigations, condemnations, and blacklists as a substitute for imposition of legal types of penalties by courts following trial and conviction in accordance with procedural safeguards of the Bill of Rights. . . .

MR. JUSTICE FRANKFURTER, concurring:

. . . That a hearing has been thought indispensable in so many other situations, leaving the cases of denial exceptional, does not of itself prove that it must be found essential here. But it does place upon the Attorney General the burden of showing weighty reason for departing in this instance from a rule so deeply imbedded in history and in the demands of justice. Nothing in the Loyalty Order requires him to deny organizations opportunity to present their case. The Executive Order, defining his powers, directs only that designation shall be made "after appropriate investigation and determination." This surely does not preclude an administrative procedure, however informal, which would incorporate the essentials of due process. Nothing has been presented to the Court to indicate that it will be impractical or prejudicial to a concrete public interest to disclose to organizations the nature of the case against them and to permit them to meet it if they can. . . .

. . . The Attorney General is certainly not immune from the historic requirements of fairness merely because he acts, however conscientiously, in the name of security. Nor does he obtain immunity on the ground that designation is not an "adjudication" or a "regulation" in the conventional use of those terms. Due process is not confined in its scope to the particular forms in which rights have heretofore been found to have been curtailed for want of procedural fairness. Due process is perhaps the most majestic concept in our whole constitutional system. While it contains the garnered wisdom of the past in assuring fundamental justice, it is also a living principle not confined to past instances. . . .

[MR. JUSTICE JACKSON and MR. JUSTICE DOUGLAS also wrote concurring opinions.]

MR. JUSTICE REED, with whom THE CHIEF JUSTICE [VINSON] and MR. JUSTICE MINTON join, dissenting:

. . . No objection is or could reasonably be made in the records or briefs to an examination by the Government into the loyalty of its employees. Although the Founders of this Republic rebelled against their established government of England and won our freedom, the creation of our own constitutional government endowed that new government, the United States of America, with the right and duty to protect its existence against any force that seeks its overthrow or changes in its structure by other than constitutional means. Tolerant as we are of all political efforts by argument or persuasion to change the basis of our social, economic, or political life, the line is drawn sharply and clearly at any act or incitement to act in violation of our constitutional processes. Surely the Government need not await an employee's conviction of a crime involving disloyalty before separating him from public service. Governments cannot be indifferent to manifestations of subversion. As soon as these are significant enough reasonably to cause concern as to the likelihood of action, the duty to protect the state compels the exertion of governmental power. Not to move would brand a government with a dangerous weakness of will. The determination of the time for action rests with the executive and legislative arms. An objection to consideration of an employee's sympathetic association with an admitted totalitarian, fascist, communistic, or subversive group, as bearing upon the propriety of his retention or employment as a government employee, would have no better standing. . . .

This Court, throughout the years, has maintained the protection of the First Amendment as a major safeguard to the maintenance of a free republic. This Nation has never suffered from an enforced conformity of expression or a limitation of criticism. But neither are we compelled to endure espionage and sedition. Wide as are the freedoms of the First Amendment, this Court has never hesitated to deny the individual's right to use the privileges for the overturn of law and order. Reasonable restraints for the fair protection of the Government against incitement to sedition cannot properly be said to be "undemocratic" or contrary to the guarantees of free speech. Otherwise the guarantee of civil rights would be a mockery. . . .

. . . In our judgment organizations are not affected by these designations in such a manner as to permit a court's interference or to deny due process. . . .

The Executive has authority to gather information concerning the loyalty of its employees as congressional committees have power to investigate matters of legislative interest. A public statement of legislative conclusions on information that later may be found erroneous may damage those investigated but it is not a civil judgment or a criminal conviction. Due process does not apply. Questions of propriety of political action are not for the courts. Information that an employee associates with or belongs to organizations considered communistic may be deemed by the Executive a sound reason for making inquiries into the desirability of the employment of that employee. That is not "guilt by association." It is a warning to investigate the conduct of the employee and his opportunity for harm. While we must be on guard against being moved to conclusions on the constitutionality of action, legislative or executive, by the circumstances of the moment, undoubtedly varying conditions call for differences in procedure. Due process requires appraisal in the light of conditions confronting the executive during the continuation of the challenged action. Power lies in the executive to guard the Nation from espionage, subversion, and sedition by examining into the loyalty of employees, and due process in such investigation depends upon the particular exercise of that power in particular conditions. In investigations to determine the purposes of suspected organizations, the Government should be free to proceed without notice or hearing. Petitioners will have protection when steps are taken to punish or enjoin their activities. . . .

The judgment of the Court of Appeals should be

Affirmed.

VITARELLI *v.* SEATON
359 U.S. 535; 79 Sup. Ct. 968; 3 L. Ed. 2d. 1012 (1959)

[William Vitarelli, a Quaker and conscientious objector during World War II, resided in Bucks County, Pennsylvania. In 1933, he graduated from college and entered the teaching profession. In 1949 he received his Ph.D. from Teachers College, Columbia University, and subsequently took a job with the Department of the Interior as an educational and training specialist. He was assigned to the Palau District of the Trust Territory of the Pacific Islands, held by the United

States under a United Nations trusteeship. In this post Vitarelli was responsible for organizing the school system and supervising necessary school construction.

On March 30, 1954, Secretary of the Interior Douglas McKay, Seaton's predecessor in office, suspended Vitarelli as a security risk. McKay charged that from 1941 to 1945 Vitarelli had been in "sympathetic association" with members of the Communist party and that he had concealed these associations from the government. It was also charged that Vitarelli had been a supporter of the American Labor party, said to be dominated by the Communists, and that he had subscribed to the USSR Information Bulletin. Vitarelli replied that he had never been sympathetic to the Communist party and demanded reinstatement or a hearing. The hearing was granted, and Vitarelli appeared before a security hearing board in Washington. At the hearing the Department of Interior brought in no evidence in support of its charges. No witnesses were called to testify against Vitarelli. However, the members of the security board questioned Vitarelli at length, and he and four witnesses in his behalf were extensively cross-examined. On September 10, 1954, Vitarelli was dismissed "in the interest of national security" as set forth in the letter of March 30, 1954. A "Notification of Personnel Action," dated September 21, 1954, setting forth the dismissal action, was filed with Vitarelli's records.

After failing to obtain reinstatement, Vitarelli filed suit in the federal district court for the District of Columbia seeking a judgment that his removal was illegal and a mandatory injunction that he be reinstated with back pay. On October 10, 1956, while the case was still pending, a copy of the "Notification of Personnel Action," also dated September 21, 1954, was filed in the district court by the Department of Interior. This notification was identical with the one already mentioned, except that it omitted any reference to the reasons for Vitarelli's discharge and to the authority under which it was done. The reasons for this action are noted in the case here. The district court ruled against Vitarelli, and the Court of Appeals affirmed, with one judge dissenting. Vitarelli then brought the case to the Supreme Court on a writ of certiorari.

After the decision reproduced here, Vitarelli was reinstated and he returned to the South Pacific. He also sued in the Court of Claims for back pay, legal fees, annual leave pay, and the like, and after a lengthy litigation, he recovered a substantial proportion in the sum of $21,517.42.]

MR. JUSTICE HARLAN delivered the opinion of the Court:

This case concerns the legality of petitioner's discharge as an employee of the Department of the Interior. . . .

The Secretary's letter of March 30, 1954, and notice of dismissal of September 2, 1954, both relied upon Exec. Order No. 10450 . . . the Act of August 26, 1950 . . . and Department of the Interior Order No. 2738, all relating to discharges of government employees on security or loyalty grounds, as the authority for petitioner's dismis-

sal. In *Cole* v. *Young*, 351 U.S. 536, this Court held that the statutes referred to did not apply to government employees in positions not designated as "sensitive." Respondent takes the position that since petitioner's position in government service has at no time been designated as sensitive, the effect of *Cole*, which was decided after the 1954 dismissal of petitioner, was to render also inapplicable to petitioner Department of the Interior Order No. 2738, under which the proceedings relating to petitioner's dismissal were had. It is urged that in this state of affairs petitioner, who concededly was at no time within the protection of the Civil Service Act, Veterans' Preference Act, or any other statute relating to employment rights of government employees, and who . . . could have been summarily discharged by the Secretary at any time without the giving of a reason, under no circumstances could be entitled to more than that which he has already received—namely, an "expunging" from the record of his 1954 discharge of any reference to the authority or reasons therefor.

Respondent misconceives the effect of our decision in *Cole*. It is true that the Act of August 26, 1950, and the Executive Order did not alter the power of the Secretary to discharge summarily an employee in petitioner's status, without the giving of any reason. Nor did the Department's own regulations preclude such a course. Since, however, the Secretary gratuitously decided to give a reason, and that reason was national security, he was obligated to conform to the procedural standards he had formulated in Order No. 2738 for the dismissal of employees on security grounds. . . . That Order on its face applies to all security discharges in the Department of the Interior. . . . *Cole v. Young* established that the Act of August 26, 1950, did not permit the discharge of nonsensitive employees pursuant to procedures authorized by that Act if those procedures were more summary than those to which the employee would have been entitled by virtue of any pre-existing statute or regulation. That decision cannot, however, justify non-compliance by the Secretary with regulations promulgated by him in the departmental Order, which as to petitioner afford greater procedural protections in the case of a dismissal stated to be for security reasons than in the case of dismissal with-

out any statement of reasons. Having chosen to proceed against petitioner on security grounds, the Secretary . . . was bound by the regulations which he himself had promulgated for dealing with such cases, even though without such regulations he could have discharged petitioner summarily.

Petitioner makes various contentions as to the constitutional invalidity of the procedures provided by Order No. 2738. He further urges that even assuming the validity of the governing procedures, his dismissal cannot stand because the notice of suspension and hearing given him did not comply with the Order. We find it unnecessary to reach the constitutional issues, for we think that petitioners second position is well taken and must be sustained.

Preliminarily, it should be said that departures from departmental regulations in matters of this kind involve more than mere consideration of procedural irregularities. For in proceedings of this nature, in which the ordinary rules of evidence do not apply, in which matters involving the disclosure of confidential information are withheld, and where it must be recognized that counsel is under practical constraints in the making of objections and in the tactical handling of his case which would not obtain in a cause being tried in a court of law before trained judges, scrupulous observance of departmental procedural safeguards is clearly of particular importance. In this instance an examination of the record, and of the transcript of the hearing before the departmental security board, discloses that petitioner's procedural rights under the applicable regulations were violated in at least three material respects in the proceedings which terminated in the final notice of his dismissal.

First. Section 15(a) of Order No. 2738 requires that the statement of charges served upon an employee at the time of his suspension on security grounds "shall be as specific and detailed as security considerations, including the need for protection of confidential sources of information, permit . . . and shall be subject to amendment within 30 days of issuance." Although the statement of charges furnished petitioner appears on its face to be reasonably specific, the transcript of hearing establishes that the statement, which was never amended, cannot conceivably be said in fact to be as specific and detailed as "security considerations . . . permit." For petitioner was questioned by the security officer and by the hearing board in great detail concerning his association with and knowledge of various persons and organizations nowhere mentioned in the statement of charges, and at length concerning his activities in Bucks County, Pennsylvania, and elsewhere after 1945, activities as to which the charges are also completely silent. These questions were presumably asked because they were deemed relevant to the inquiry before the board, and the very fact that they were asked and thus spread on the record is conclusive indication that "security considerations" could not have justified the omission of any statement concerning them in the charges furnished petitioner.

Second. Sections 21(a) and (e) require that hearings before security hearing boards shall be "orderly" and that "reasonable restrictions shall be imposed as to relevancy, competency, and materiality of matters considered." . . . [T]hese indispensable indicia of a meaningful hearing were not observed. It is not an over-characterization to say that as the hearing proceeded it developed into a wide-ranging inquisition into this man's educational, social, and political beliefs, encompassing even a question as to whether he was "a religious man."

Third. Section 21(c)(4) gives the employee the right "to cross-examine any witness offered in support of the charges." It is apparent from an over-all reading of the regulations that it was not contemplated that this provision should require the Department to call witnesses to testify in support of any or all of the charges, because it was expected that charges might rest on information gathered from or by "confidential informants." We think, however, that Section 21(c)(4) did contemplate the calling by the Department of any informant not properly classifiable as "confidential," if information furnished by that informant was to be used by the board in assessing an employee's status. The transcript shows that this provision was violated on at least one occasion at petitioner's hearing, for the security officer identified by name a person who had given information apparently considered detrimental to petitioner, thus negating any possible inference that that person was considered a "confidential informant" whose identity it was necessary to keep secret, and questioned petitioner at some length concerning the information supplied from this source without calling the informant and affording petitioner the right to cross-examine.

Because of the proceedings attendant upon petitioner's dismissal from government service on grounds of national security fell substantially short of the requirements of the applicable departmental regulations, we hold that such dismissal was illegal and of no effect.

Respondent urges that even if the dismissal of September 10, 1954, was invalid, petitioner is not entitled to reinstatement by reason of the fact that he was at all events validly dismissed in October 1956, when a copy of the second "Notification of Personnel Action," omitting all reference to any statute, order, or regulation relating to security discharges, was delivered to him. Granting that the Secretary could at any time after September 10, 1954, have validly dismissed petitioner without any statement of reasons, and independently of the proceedings taken against him under Order No. 2738, we cannot view the delivery of the new notification to petitioner as an exercise of that summary dismissal power. Rather, the fact that it was dated "9-21-54," contained a termination of employment date of "9-10-54," was designated as "a revision" of the 1954 notification, and was evidently filed in the District Court before its delivery to petitioner indicates that its sole purpose was an attempt to moot petitioner's suit in the District Court by an "expunging" of the grounds for the dismissal which brought Order No. 2738 into play. In these circumstances, we would not be justified in now treating the 1956 action, plainly intended by the Secretary as a grant of relief to petitioner in connection with the form of the 1954 discharge, as an exercise of the Secretary's summary removal power as of the date of its delivery to petitioner.

It follows from what we have said that petitioner is entitled to the reinstatement which he seeks, subject, of course to any lawful exercise of the Secretary's authority hereafter to dismiss him from employment in the Department of the Interior.

Reversed.

MR. JUSTICE FRANKFURTER, with whom MR. JUSTICE CLARK, MR. JUSTICE WHITTAKER, and MR. JUSTICE STEWART join, concurring in part and dissenting in part:

An executive agency must be rigorously held to the standards by which its action is to be judged. . . . Accordingly, if dismissal from employment is based on a defined procedure, even though generous beyond the requirements that bind such agency, that procedure must be scrupulously observed. . . . This judicially evolved rule of administrative law is now firmly established and, if I may add, rightly so. He that takes the procedural sword shall perish with that sword. Therefore, I unreservedly join in the Court's main conclusion, that the attempted dismissal of Vitarelli in September 1954 was abortive and of no validity because the procedure under Department of the Interior Order No. 2738 was invoked but not observed.

But when an executive agency draws on the freedom that the law vests in it, the judiciary cannot deny or curtail such freedom. The Secretary of the Interior concededly had untrammelled right to dismiss Vitarelli out of hand, since he had no protected employment rights. He could do so as freely as a private employer who is not bound by procedural restrictions of a collective bargaining contract. The Secretary was under no law-imposed or self-imposed restriction in discharging an employee in Vitarelli's position without a hearing. And so the question is, did the Secretary take action, after the abortive discharge in 1954, dismissing Vitarelli?

In October 1956 there was served upon Vitarelli a copy of a new notice of dismissal which had been inserted in the Department's personnel records in place of the first notice. Another copy was filed with the District Court in this proceeding. This second notice contained no mention of grounds of discharge. If, instead of sending this second notice to Vitarelli, the Secretary had telephoned Vitarelli to convey the contents of the second notice, he would have said: "I note that you are contesting the validity of the dismissal. I want to make this very clear to you. If I did not succeed in dismissing you before, I now dismiss you, and I dismiss you retroactively, effective September 1954."

The Court disallows this significance to the second notice of discharge because it finds controlling meaning in the suggestion of the Government that the expunging from the record of any adverse comment, and the second notice of discharge, signified a reassertion of the effectiveness of the first attempt at dismissal. And so, the Court concludes, no intention of severance from service in 1956 could legally be found since the Secretary expressed no doubt that the first dismissal had been effective. But this document of 1956 was not a mere piece of paper in a dialectic. The paper was a record of a process, a manifestation of purpose and action. The intendment of the second notice, to be sure, was to discharge Vitarelli retroactively, resting this attempted dismissal on valid authority—the summary power to dismiss without reason. Though the second notice could not pre-date the summary discharge because the Secretary rested his 1954 discharge on an unsustainable ground, and Vitarelli could not be deprived of rights accrued during two years of unlawful discharge, the prior wrongful action did not deprive the Secretary of the power in him to fire Vitarelli prospectively. And if the intent of the Secretary be manifested in fact by what he did, however that intent be expressed—here, the intent to be rid of Vitarelli—the Court should not frustrate the Secretary's rightful exercise of this power as of October 1956. . . .

This is the common sense of it: In 1956 the Secretary said to Vitarelli: "This document tells you without any ifs, ands, or buts, you have been fired right along and of course that means you are not presently employed by this Department." Since he had not been fired successfully in 1954, the Court concludes he must still be employed. I cannot join in an unreal interpretation which attributes to governmental action the empty meaning of confetti throwing.

20
Privacy

The case of *Griswold* v. *Connecticut* (p. 756) does not fit neatly into any of the traditional categories of constitutional law. Indeed, the Court experienced some difficulty in finding a specific constitutional provision on which to hang its decision. Its final position seems to be that there are some things just too intimate for government regulation. More broadly, there has been much concern in recent years about a "right to privacy" or the "right to be let alone."[1] *Griswold* may introduce such a right into constitutional law. It has been recognized in some of the states. However, another recent Supreme Court decision seems to point in the other direction. We noted *Time, Inc.* v. *Hill* (p. 760) earlier as it relates to the Court's new position on libel enunciated in *New York Times* v. *Sullivan* (p. 419). But the case actually involves a New York statute guaranteeing privacy. It, together with *Griswold,* may mean that a constitutional right to privacy may exist against government but not necessarily against other individuals or the press.

[1] See Alan F. Westin, *Privacy and Freedom* (New York: Atheneum, 1967); Morris L. Ernst and Alan U. Schwartz, *Privacy, The Right to Be Let Alone* (New York: Macmillan, 1962). The pioneering exposition is in Samuel D. Warren and Louis D. Brandeis, "The Right to Privacy," *Harvard Law Review,* Vol. 4 (1890), p. 193. Cf. Harry Kalven, "Privacy in Tort Law—Were Warren and Brandeis Wrong?" *Law and Contemporary Problems,* Vol. 31 (1966), p. 326.

The search and seizure, self-incrimination, and anonymous association cases examined earlier in this book also contribute to the notion of privacy. Part of the problem of free speech versus trespass is a concern for the individual's freedom not to be subjected to speech he does not want to hear, and to be left in the enjoyment of his peace and quiet. That interest is also reflected in Justice Douglas' dissent in *Public Utilities Commission* v. *Pollak* 343 U.S. 451 (1952). In *Martin* v. *Struthers* 319 U.S. 141 (1943), the Court struck down a local ordinance forbidding doorbell ringing by door to door solicitors because it interfered with the religious freedom of the Jehovah's Witnesses. But several of the justices expressed concern for the peace and quiet of the residents. Even in that case the Court held that the dweller could protect himself by using no trespassing signs, and it upheld similar ordinances against the challenge of purely commercial solicitors. In *Saia* v. *New York,* 334 U.S. 558 (1948), the Court struck down an ordinance directed at sound trucks because it vested too much discretion in the police chief, but the justices did indicate that statutes regulating the volume of sound emitted by such trucks might be constitutional and later upheld a statute banning "raucous" sound trucks, *Kovacs* v. *Cooper,* 336 U.S. 77 (1949).

Obviously, the scope of a right to privacy will have to be carved out step by step in the light of the real problems of modern, technologically complex, and basically urban societies, but a judicial concern for such a right will be a sign of the continuing vitality and growth of our Constitution.

GRISWOLD v. CONNECTICUT
381 U.S. 479; 85 Sup. Ct. 1678; 14 L. Ed. 2d 510 (1965)

[*Connecticut's birth control laws had been challenged twice before this case, and in each instance the Supreme Court managed to turn aside from the major issue by resting its decisions on questions of standing. Connecticut had not generally enforced its laws against individual physicians, sellers, or married couples. The main impact of the laws was to prohibit the poor from receiving the same birth control information and supplies available to the middle class. After birth control clinics were opened in spite of the statute, the state sought to enforce its laws against them. This case reached the Supreme Court.*]

MR. JUSTICE DOUGLAS delivered the opinion of the Court:

Appellant Griswold is Executive Director of the Planned Parenthood League of Connecticut. Appellant Buxton is a licensed physician and a professor at the Yale Medical School who served as Medical Director for the League at its Center in New Haven—a center open and operating from November 1 to November 10, 1961, when appellants were arrested.

They gave information, instruction, and medical advice to *married persons* as to the means of preventing conception. They examined the wife and prescribed the best contraceptive device or material for her use. . . .

The statutes whose constitutionality is involved in this appeal are §§53–32 and 54–196 of the General Statutes of Connecticut (1958 rev.). The former provides: "Any person who uses any drug, medicinal article or instrument for the purpose of preventing conception shall be fined not less than fifty dollars or imprisoned not less than sixty days nor more than one year or be both fined and imprisoned."

Section 54–196 provides: "Any person who assists, abets, counsels, causes, hires, or commands another to commit any offense may be prosecuted and punished as if he were the principal offender."

The appellants were found guilty as accessories and fined $100 each, against the claim that the accessory statute as so applied violated the Fourteenth Amendment. . . .

We think that appellants have standing to raise the constitutional rights of the married people with whom they had a professional relationship. . . . Certainly the accessory should have standing to assert that the offense which he is charged with assisting is not, or cannot constitutionally be, a crime. . . .

Coming to the merits, we are met with a wide range of questions that implicate the Due Process Clause of the Fourteenth Amendment. Overtones of some arguments suggest that *Lochner* v. *New York* should be our guide. But we decline that invitation as we did in *West Coast Hotel Co.* v. *Parrish.* . . . We do not sit as a super-legislature to determine the wisdom, need, and propriety of laws that touch economic problems, business affairs, or social conditions. This law, however, operates directly on an intimate relation of husband and wife and their physician's role in one aspect of that relation.

The association of people is not mentioned in the Constitution nor in the Bill of Rights. The right to educate a child in a school of the parents' choice —whether public or private or parochial—is also not mentioned. Nor is the right to study any particular subject or any foreign language. Yet the First Amendment has been construed to include certain of those rights.

By *Pierce* v. *Society of Sisters* the right to educate one's children as one chooses is made applicable to the States by the force of the First and Fourteenth Amendments. By *Meyer* v. *Nebraska* . . . the same dignity is given the right to study the German language in a private school. In other words, the State may not, consistently with the spirit of the First Amendment, contract the spectrum of available knowledge. The right of freedom of speech and press includes not only the right to utter or to print, but the right to distribute, the right to receive, the right to read . . . and freedom of inquiry, freedom of thought, and freedom to teach . . . — indeed the freedom of the entire university community. . . . Without those peripheral rights the specific rights would be less secure. And so we reaffirm the principle of the *Pierce* and the *Meyer* cases.

In *NAACP* v. *Alabama,* . . . we protected the "freedom to associate and privacy in one's association," noting that freedom of association was a peripheral First Amendment right. Disclosure of membership lists of a constitutionally valid association, we held, was invalid "as entailing the likelihood of a substantial restraint upon the exercise by petitioner's members of their right to freedom of association." In other words, the First Amendment has a penumbra where privacy is protected from governmental intrusion. In like context, we have protected forms of "association" that are not political in the customary sense but pertain to the social, legal, and economic benefit of the members. *NAACP* v. *Button.* . . .

In *Schware* v. *Board of Bar Examiners,* . . . we held it not permissible to bar a lawyer from practice, because he had once been a member of the Communist Party. The man's "association with that Party" was not shown to be "anything more than a political faith in a political party" and was not action of a kind proving bad moral character.

Those cases involved more than the "right of assembly—a right that extends to all irrespective of their race or ideology. . . . The right of "association," like the right of belief . . . is more than the right to attend a meeting; it includes the right to express one's attitudes or philosophies by membership in a group or by affiliation with it or by other lawful means. Association in that context is a form of expression of opinion; and while it is not expressly included in the First Amendment its existence is necessary in making the express guarantees fully meaningful.

The foregoing cases suggest that specific guarantees in the Bill of Rights have penumbras, formed by emanations from those guarantees that help give them life and substance. . . . Various guarantees create zones of privacy. The right of association contained in the penumbra of the First Amendment is one, as we have seen. The Third Amendment in its prohibition against the quartering of soldiers "in any house" in time of peace without the consent of the owner is another facet of that privacy. The Fourth Amendment explicitly affirms the "right of the people to be secure in their persons, houses, papers, and effects, against unreasonable searches and seizures." The Fifth Amendment in its Self-Incrimination Clause enables the citizen to create a zone of privacy which government may not force him to surrender to his detriment. The Ninth Amendment provides: "The enumeration in the Constitution, of certain rights, shall not be construed to deny or disparage others retained by the people."

The present case, then, concerns a relationship lying within the zone of privacy created by several fundamental constitutional guaranties. And it concerns a law which, in forbidding the *use* of contraceptives rather than regulating their manufacture or sale, seeks to achieve its goals by means having a maximum destructive impact upon the relationship. Such a law cannot stand in light of the familiar principle, so often applied by this Court, that a "governmental purpose to control or prevent activities constitutionally subject to state regulation may not be achieved by means which sweep unnecessarily broadly and thereby invade the area of protected freedoms." *NAACP* v. *Alabama.* . . . Would we allow the police to search the sacred precincts of marital bedrooms for telltale signs of the use of contraceptives? The very idea is repulsive to the notions of privacy surrounding the marriage relationship.

We deal with a right of privacy older than the Bill of Rights—older than our political parties, older than our school system. Marriage is a coming together for better or for worse, hopefully enduring, and intimate to the degree of being sacred. It is an association that promotes a way of life, not causes; a harmony in living, not political faiths; a bilateral loyalty, not commercial or social projects. Yet it is an association for as noble a purpose as any involved in our prior decisions.

Reversed.

MR. JUSTICE GOLDBERG, whom THE CHIEF JUSTICE and MR. JUSTICE BRENNAN join, concurring, said in part:

I agree with the Court that Connecticut's birth-control law unconstitutionally intrudes upon the right of marital privacy, and I join in its opinion and judgment. Although I have not accepted the view that "due process" as used in the Fourteenth Amendment incorporates all of the first eight Amendments, . . . I do agree that the concept of liberty protects those personal rights that are fundamental, and is not confined to the specific terms of the Bill of Rights. My conclusion that the concept of liberty is not so restricted and that it embraces the right of marital privacy though that right is not mentioned explicitly in the Constitution is supported both by numerous decisions of this Court, referred to in the Court's opinion, and by the language and history of the Ninth Amendment. . . .

While this Court has had little occasion to interpret the Ninth Amendment, "[i]t cannot be presumed that any clause in the constitution is intended to be without effect." *Marbury* v. *Madison.* . . . To hold that a right so basic and fundamental and so deep-rooted in our society as the right of privacy in marriage may be infringed because that right is not guaranteed in so many words by the first eight amendments to the Constitution is to ignore the Ninth Amendment and and to give it no effect whatsoever. Moreover, a judicial construction that this fundamental right is not protected by the Constitution because it is not mentioned in explicit terms by one of the first eight amendments or elsewhere in the Constitution would violate the Ninth Amendment, which specifically states that "[t]he enumeration in the Constitution, of certain rights, shall not be *construed* to deny or disparage others retained by the people." (Emphasis added.)

. . . I do not take the position of my Brother Black . . . that the entire Bill of Rights is incorporated in the Fourteenth Amendment, and I do not mean to imply that the Ninth Amendment is applied against the States by the Fourteenth. Nor do I mean to state that the Ninth Amendment constitutes an independent source of rights protected from infringement by either the States or Federal Government. Rather, the Ninth Amendment shows a belief of the Constitution's authors that fundamental rights exist that are not expressly enumerated in the first eight amendments and an intent that the list of rights included there not be deemed exhaustive. . . .

. . . In sum, the Ninth Amendment simply lends strong support to the view that the "liberty" protected by the Fifth and Fourteenth Amendments from infringement by the Federal Government or the States is not restricted to rights specifically mentioned in the first eight amendments. . . .

MR. JUSTICE HARLAN and MR. JUSTICE WHITE concurred.

MR. JUSTICE BLACK, with whom MR. JUSTICE STEWART joins, dissented:

The Court talks about a constitutional "right of privacy" as though there is some constitutional provision or provisions forbidding any law ever to be passed which might abridge the "privacy" of individuals. But there is not. There are, of course, guarantees in certain specific constitutional provisions which are designed in part to protect privacy at certain times and places with respect to certain activities. Such, for example, is the Fourth Amendment's guarantee against "unreasonable searches and seizures." But I think it belittles that Amendment to talk about it as though it protects nothing but "privacy." To treat it that way is to give it a niggardly interpretation, not the kind of liberal reading I think any Bill of Rights provision should be given. The average man would very likely not have his feelings soothed any more by having his property seized openly than by having it seized privately and by stealth. He simply wants his property left alone. And a person can be just as much, if not more, irritated, annoyed and injured by an unceremonious public arrest by a policeman as he is by a seizure in the privacy of his office or home.

One of the most effective ways of diluting or expanding a constitutionally guaranteed right is to substitute for the crucial word or words of a constitutional guarantee another word or words more or less flexible and more or less restricted in meaning. This fact is well illustrated by the use of the term "right of privacy" as a comprehensive substitute for the Fourth Amendment's guarantee against "unreasonable searches and seizures." "Privacy" is a broad, abstract and ambiguous concept which can easily be shrunken in meaning but which can also, on the other hand, easily be interpreted as a constitutional ban against many things other than searches and seizures. I have expressed the view many times that First Amendment freedoms, for example, have suffered from a failure of the courts to stick to the simple language of the First Amendment in construing it, instead of invoking multitudes of words substituted for those the Framers used. . . .

I realize that many good and able men have eloquently spoken and written, sometimes in rhapsodical strains, about the duty of this Court to keep the Constitution in tune with the times. The idea is that the Constitution must be changed from time to time and that this Court is charged with a duty to make those changes. For myself, I must with all deference reject that philosophy. The Constitution makers knew the need for change and provided for it. Amendments suggested by the people's elected representatives can be submitted to the people or their selected agents for ratification. That method of change was good for our Fathers, and being somewhat old-fashioned I must add it is good enough for me. And so, I cannot rely on the Due Process Clause or the Ninth Amendment or any mysterious and uncertain natural law concept as a reason for striking down this state law. The Due Process Clause with an "arbitrary and capricious" or "shocking to the conscience" formula was liberally used by this Court to strike down economic legislation in the early decades of this century, threatening, many people thought, the tranquility and stability of the Nation. See, e.g., *Lochner* v. *New York*. That formula, based on subjective considerations of "natural justice," is no less dangerous when used to enforce this Court's views about personal rights than those about economic rights. I had thought that we had laid that formula, as a means for striking down state legislation, to rest once and for all in cases like *West Coast Hotel Co.* v. *Parrish.*

MR. JUSTICE STEWART wrote a dissenting opinion in which MR. JUSTICE BLACK joined.

TIME, INC. *v.* HILL
385 U.S. 374; 87 Sup. Ct. 534 (1967)

[*Hill, a supermarket manager, and his family had been the victims of a kidnap-extortion plot. Some years later, in connection with the opening of a play very loosely based on their misfortune,* Life *magazine ran a picture story that conveyed a number of false impressions about the Hills' experience. Hill filed suit against* Life *under New York's privacy statute.*]

MR. JUSTICE BRENNAN delivered the opinion of the Court:

. . . Although the New York statute affords "little protection" to the "privacy" of a newsworthy person, "whether he be such by choice or involuntarily" the statute gives him a right of action when his name, picture, or portrait is the subject of a "fictitious" report or article. . . .

We hold that the constitutional protections for speech and press preclude the application of the New York statute to redress false reports of matters of public interest in the absence of proof that the defendant published the report with knowledge of its falsity or in reckless disregard of the truth.

The guarantees for speech and press are not the preserve of political expression or comment upon public affairs, essential as those are to healthy government. One need only pick up any newspaper or magazine to comprehend the vast range of published matter which exposes persons to public view, both private citizens and public officials. Exposure of the self to others in varying degrees is a concomitant of life in a civilized community. The risk of this exposure is an essential incident of life in a society which places a primary value on freedom of speech and of press. "Freedom of discussion, if it would fulfill its historic function in this nation, must embrace all issues about which information is needed or appropriate to enable the members of society to cope with the exigencies of their period." *Thornhill* v. *State of Alabama*. . . . We have no doubt that the subject of the *Life* article, the opening of a new play linked to an actual incident, is a matter of public interest. "The line between the informing and the entertaining is too elusive for the protection of . . . [freedom of the press]." *Winters* v. *People of State of New York*. . . . We create grave risk of serious impairment of the indispensable service of a free press in a free society if we saddle the press with the impossible burden of verifying to a certainty the facts associated in news articles with a person's name, picture or portrait. . . .

In this context, sanctions against either innocent or negligent misstatement would present a grave hazard of discouraging the press from exercising the constitutional guarantees. Those guarantees are not for the benefit of the press so much as for the benefit of all of us. A broadly defined freedom of the press assures the maintenance of our political system and an open society. Fear of large verdicts in damage suits for innocent or mere negligent misstatement, even fear of the expense involved in their defense, must inevitably cause publishers to "steer far wider of the unlawful zone." *New York Times Co.* v. *Sullivan*. . . . And thus "create the danger that the legitimate utterance will be penalized." *Speiser* v. *Randall*. . . .

But the constitutional guarantees can tolerate sanctions against *calculated* falsehood without significant impairment of their essential function. We held in *New York Times* that calculated falsehood enjoyed no immunity in the case of alleged defamation of a public official's official conduct. Similarly calculated falsehood should enjoy no immunity in the situation here presented us. . . .

The appellant argues that the statute should be declared unconstitutional on its face if construed by the New York courts to impose liability without proof of knowing or reckless falsity. Such a declaration would not be warranted even if it were entirely clear that this is the view of the New York courts. The New York Court of Appeals, as the *Spahn* opinion demonstrates, has been assiduous to construe the statute to avoid invasion of the constitutional protections for speech and press. We therefore confidently expect that the New York courts will apply the statute consistently with the constitutional command. Any possible difference with us as to the thrust of the constitutional command is narrowly limited in this case to the failure of the trial judge to instruct the jury that a verdict of liability could be predicated only on a finding of knowing or reckless falsity in the publication of the *Life* article.

The judgment of the Court of Appeals is set aside and the case is remanded for further proceedings not inconsistent with this opinion.

It is so ordered.

MR. JUSTICE BLACK and MR. JUSTICE DOUGLAS, concurred.

MR. JUSTICE HARLAN concurred in part and dissented in part.

MR. JUSTICE FORTAS, with whom THE CHIEF JUSTICE and MR. JUSTICE CLARK join, dissenting:

The Court's holding here is exceedingly narrow. It declines to hold that the New York "Right of Privacy" statute is unconstitutional. I agree. The Court concludes, however, that the instructions to the jury in this case were fatally defective because they failed to advise the jury that a verdict for the plaintiff could be predicated only on a finding of knowing or reckless falsity in the publication of the *Life* article. Presumably, the plaintiff is entitled to a new trial. If he can stand the emotional and financial burden, there is reason to hope that he will recover damages for the reckless and irresponsible assault upon himself and his family which this article represents. But he has litigated this case for eleven years. He should not be subjected to the burden of a new trial without significant cause. This does not exist. Perhaps the purpose of the decision here is to indicate that this Court

will place insuperable obstacles in the way of recovery by persons who are injured by reckless and heedless assaults provided they are in print, and even though they are totally divorced from fact. If so, I should think that the Court would cast its decision in constitutional terms. Short of that purpose, with which I would strongly disagree, there is no reason here to order a new trial. The instructions in this case are acceptable even within the principles today announced by the Court.

I fully agree with the views of my Brethren who have stressed the need for a generous construction of the First Amendment. I, too, believe that freedom of the press, of speech, assembly, and religion, and the freedom of petition are of the essence of our liberty and fundamental to our values. . . . I agree with the statement of my Brother Brennan, speaking for the Court in *NAACP* v. *Button*, . . . that "These freedoms are delicate and vulnerable, as well as supremely precious in our society." But I do not believe that whatever is in words, however much of an aggression it may be upon individual rights, is beyond the reach of the law, no matter how heedless of others' rights—how remote from public purpose, how reckless, irresponsible, and untrue it may be. I do not believe that the First Amendment precludes effective protection of the right of privacy—or, for that matter, an effective law of libel. I do not believe that we must or should, in deference to those whose views are absolute as to the scope of the First Amendment, be ingenious to strike down all state action, however circumspect, which penalizes the use of words as instruments of aggression and personal assault. There are great and important values in our society, none of which is greater than those reflected in the First Amendment, but which are also fundamental and entitled to this Court's careful respect and protection. Among these is the right to privacy, which has been eloquently extolled by scholars and members of this Court. Judge Cooley long ago referred to this right as "the right to be let alone." In 1890, Warren and Brandeis published their famous article "The Right to Privacy," in which they eloquently argued that the "excesses" of the press in "overstepping in every direction the obvious bounds of propriety and decency" made it essential that the law recognize a right to privacy, distinct from traditional remedies for defamation, to protect private individuals against the unjustifiable infliction of mental pain and distress. A distinct right of privacy is now recognized, either as a "common-law" right or by statute, in at least thirty-five States. Its exact scope varies in the respective jurisdictions. It is, simply stated, the right to be let alone; to live one's life as one chooses, free from assault, intrusion or invasion except as they can be justified by the clear needs of community living under a government of law. As Brandeis said in his famous dissent in *Olmsted* v. *United States, . . .* the right of privacy is "the most comprehensive of rights and the right most valued by civilized men."

This Court has repeatedly recognized this principle. As early as 1886, in *Boyd* v. *United States, . . .* this Court held that the doctrines of the Fourth and Fifth Amendments "apply to all invasions on the part of the government and its employes of the sanctity of a man's home and the privacies of life. It is not the breaking of his doors, and the rummaging of his drawers, that constitutes the essence of the offense; but it is the invasion of his indefeasible right of personal security, personal liberty and private property. . . ."

In 1949, the Court, in *Wolf* v. *People of State of Colorado, . . .* described the immunity from unreasonable search and seizure in terms of "the right of privacy."

Then, in the landmark case of *Mapp* v. *Ohio, . . .* this Court referred to "the right to privacy," no less important than any other right carefully and particularly reserved to the people," as "basic to a free society." . . . Mr. Justice Clark, speaking for the Court, referred to "the freedom from unconscionable invasions of privacy" as intimately related to the freedom from convictions based upon coerced confessions. He said that both served the cause of perpetuating "principles of humanity and civil liberty [secured] . . . only after years of struggle." . . . He said that they express "supplementing phases of the same constitutional purpose—to maintain inviolate large areas of personal privacy." . . .

In *Griswold* v. *State of Connecticut, . . .* the Court held unconstitutional a state law under which petitioners were prosecuted for giving married persons information and medical advice on the use of contraceptives. The holding was squarely based upon the right of privacy which the Court derived by implication from the specific guarantees of the Bill of Rights. Citing a number of prior cases, the Court (per Dougas, J.) held that "These cases bear witness that the right of privacy which presses for recognition here is a legitimate one." . . . As stated in the concurring opinion of Mr. Justice Goldberg, with whom The Chief Justice and Mr. Justice Brennan joined: "the right of privacy is a fundamental personal right, emanating 'from the totality of the constitutional scheme under which we live.'" . . .

Privacy, then, is a basic right. The States may, by appropriate legislation and within proper bounds, enact laws to vindicate that right. Cf. *Kovacs* v.

Cooper, . . . sustaining a local ordinance regulating the use of sound trucks; and *Breard* v. *City of Alexandria,* 341 U.S. 622 . . . (1951), sustaining a state law restricting solicitation in private homes of magazine subscriptions. Difficulty presents itself because the application of such state legislation may impinge upon conflicting rights of those accused of invading the privacy of others. But this is not automatically a fatal objection. Particularly where the right of privacy is invaded by words— by the press or in a book or pamphlet— the most careful and sensitive appraisal of the total impact of the claimed tort upon the congeries of rights is required. I have no hesitancy to say, for example, that where political personalities or issues are involved or where the event as to which the alleged invasion of privacy occurred is in itself a matter of current public interest, First Amendment values are supreme and are entitled to at least the types of protection that this Court extended in *New York Times Co.* v. *Sullivan.* . . . But I certainly concur with the Court that the greatest solicitude for the First Amendment does not compel us to deny to a State the right to provide a remedy for reckless falsity in writing and publishing an article which irresponsibly and injuriously invades the privacy of a quiet family for no purpose except dramatic interest and commercial appeal. My difficulty is that while the Court gives lip-service to this principle, its decision, which it claims to be based on erroneous instructions, discloses hesitancy to go beyond the verbal acknowledgment.

The Court today does not repeat the ringing words of so many of its members on so many occasions in exaltation of the right of privacy. Instead, it reverses a decision under the New York "Right of Privacy" statute because of the "failure of the trial judge to instruct the jury that a verdict of liability could be predicated only on a finding of knowing or reckless falsity in the publication of the Life article." In my opinion, the jury instructions, although they were not a text-book model, satisfied this standard.

The courts may not and must not permit either public or private action that censors or inhibits the press. But part of this responsibility is to preserve values and procedures which assure the ordinary citizen that the press is not above the reach of the law—that its special prerogatives, granted because of its special and vital functions, are reasonably equated with its needs in the performance of these functions. For this Court totally to immunize the press —whether forthrightly or by subtle indirection—in areas far beyond the needs of news, comment on public persons and events, discussion of public issues and the like would be no service to freedom of the press, but an invitation to public hostility to that freedom. This Court cannot and should not refuse to permit under state law the private citizen who is aggrieved by the type of assault which we have here and which is not within the specially protected core of the First Amendment to recover compensatory damages for recklessly inflicted invasion of his rights.

Accordingly, I would

Affirm.

Appendix I
Constitution of the United States of America

(Adopted September 17, 1787)
(Effective March 4, 1789)

PREAMBLE

We, the People of the United States, in Order to form a more perfect Union, establish Justice, insure domestic Tranquility, provide for the common defence, promote the general Welfare, and secure the Blessings of Liberty to ourselves and our Posterity, do ordain and establish this Constitution for the United States of America.

ARTICLE I

Section 1. All legislative Powers herein granted shall be vested in a Congress of the United States, which shall consist of a Senate and House of Representatives.

Section 2. The House of Representatives shall be composed of Members chosen every second Year by the People of the several States, and the Electors in each State shall have the Qualifications requisite for Electors of the most numerous Branch of the State Legislature.

No Person shall be a Representative who shall not have attained to the Age of twenty-five Years, and been seven Years a Citizen of the United States, and who shall not, when elected, be an Inhabitant of that State in which he shall be chosen.

Representatives and *direct Taxes shall be apportioned*[1] among the several States which may be included within this Union, according to their respective Numbers,

[1] Modified by the Sixteenth Amendment.

which shall be determined by adding to the whole Number of free Persons, including those bound to Service for a Term of Years, and excluding Indians not taxed, three-fifths of all other Persons.[2] The actual Enumeration shall be made within three Years after the first Meeting of the Congress of the United States, and within every subsequent Term of ten Years, in such Manner as they shall by Law direct. The Number of Representatives shall not exceed one for every thirty Thousand, but each State shall have at Least one Representative; *and until such enumeration shall be made, the State of New Hampshire shall be entitled to choose three, Massachusetts eight, Rhode-Island and Providence Plantations one, Connecticut five, New-York six, New Jersey four, Pennsylvania eight, Delaware one, Maryland six, Virginia ten, North Carolina five, South Carolina five, and Georgia three.*[3]

When vacancies happen in the Representation from any State, the Executive Authority thereof shall issue Writs of Election to fill such Vacancies.

The House of Representatives shall choose their Speaker and other Officers; and shall have the sole Power of Impeachment.

Section 3. The Senate of the United States shall be composed of two Senators from each State, *chosen by the Legislature thereof,*[4] for six Years; and each Senator shall have one Vote.

Immediately after they shall be assembled in Consequence of the first Election, they shall be divided as equally as may be into three Classes. The Seats of the Senators of the first Class shall be vacated at the Expiration of the second Year, of the second Class at the Expiration of the fourth Year, and of the third Class at the Expiration of the sixth Year, so that one-third may be chosen every second Year; *and if Vacancies happen by Resignation, or otherwise, during the Recess of the Legislature of any State, the Executive thereof may make temporary Appointment until the next Meeting of the Legislature, which shall then fill such Vacancies.*[5]

No Person shall be a Senator who shall not have attained to the Age of thirty Years, and been nine Years a Citizen of the United States, and who shall not, when elected, be an Inhabitant of that State for which he shall be chosen.

The Vice-President of the United States shall be President of the Senate, but shall have no Vote, unless they be equally divided.

The Senate shall choose their other Officers, and also a President pro tempore, in the Absence of the Vice-President, or when he shall exercise the Office of President of the United States.

The Senate shall have the sole Power to try all Impeachments. When sitting for that Purpose, they shall be on Oath or Affirmation. When the President of the United States is tried, the Chief Justice shall preside: And no Person shall be convicted without the Concurrence of two-thirds of the Members present.

Judgment in Cases of Impeachment shall not extend further than to removal from Office, and disqualification to hold and enjoy any Office of honor, Trust or Profit under the United States: but the Party convicted shall nevertheless be liable and subject to Indictment, Trial, Judgment and Punishment, according to Law.

Section 4. The Times, Places and Manner of holding Elections for Senators

[2] Modified by the Fourteenth Amendment.
[3] Temporary provision.
[4] Modified by the Seventeenth Amendment.
[5] *Ibid.*

and Representatives, shall be prescribed in each State by the Legislature thereof; but the Congress may at any time by Law make or alter such Regulations, except as to the Places of choosing Senators.

The Congress shall assemble at least once in every Year, and such Meeting shall be on the first Monday of December, unless they shall by Law appoint a different Day.[6]

Section 5. Each House shall be the Judge of the Elections, Returns and Qualifications of its own Members, and a Majority of each shall constitute a Quorum to do Business; but a smaller Number may adjourn from day to day, and may be authorized to compel the Attendance of absent Members, in such Manner, and under such Penalties as each House may provide.

Each House may determine the Rules of its Proceedings, punish its Members for disorderly Behaviour, and, with the Concurrence of two-thirds, expel a Member.

Each House shall keep a Journal of its Proceedings, and from time to time publish the same, excepting such Parts as may in their Judgment require Secrecy; and the Yeas and Nays of the Members of either House on any question shall, at the Desire of one-fifth of those Present, be entered on the Journal.

Neither House, during the Session of Congress, shall, without the Consent of the other, adjourn for more than three days, nor to any other Place than that in which the two Houses shall be sitting.

Section 6. The Senators and Representatives shall receive a Compensation for their Services, to be ascertained by Law, and paid out of the Treasury of the United States. They shall in all Cases, except Treason, Felony and Breach of the Peace, be privileged from Arrest during their Attendance at the Session of their respective Houses, and in going to and returning from the same; and for any Speech or Debate in either House, they shall not be questioned in any other Place.

No Senator or Representative shall, during the Time for which he was elected, be appointed to any civil Office under the Authority of the United States, which shall have been created, or the Emoluments whereof shall have been increased during such time; and no Person holding any Office under the United States, shall be a Member of either House during his Continuance in Office.

Section 7. All Bills for raising Revenue shall originate in the House of Representatives; but the Senate may propose or concur with Amendments as on other Bills.

Every Bill which shall have passed the House of Representatives and the Senate shall, before it becomes a Law, be presented to the President of the United States; if he approve, he shall sign it, but if not, he shall return it, with his Objections, to that House in which it shall have originated, who shall enter the Objections at large on their Journal, and proceed to reconsider it. If after such Reconsideration two-thirds of the House shall agree to pass the Bill, it shall be sent, together with the Objections, to the other House, by which it shall likewise be reconsidered, and if approved by two-thirds of that House, it shall become a Law. But in all such Cases the Votes of both Houses shall be determined by Yeas and Nays, and the Names of the Persons voting for and against the Bill shall be entered on the Journal of each House respectively. If any Bill shall not be returned by the President within ten Days (Sundays excepted) after it shall have been presented to him, the

[6] Modified by the Twentieth Amendment.

Same shall be a Law, in like Manner as if he had signed it, unless the Congress by their Adjournment prevent its Return, in which Case it shall not be a law.

Every Order, Resolution, or Vote to which the Concurrence of the Senate and House of Representatives may be necessary (except on a question of Adjournment) shall be presented to the President of the United States; and before the Same shall take Effect, shall be approved by him, or being disapproved by him, shall be repassed by two-thirds of the Senate and House of Representatives, according to the Rules and Limitations prescribed in the Case of a Bill.

Section 8. The Congress shall have Power: To lay and collect Taxes, Duties, Imposts and Excises, to pay the Debts and provide for the common Defence and general Welfare of the United States; but all Duties, Imposts and Excises shall be uniform throughout the United States.

To borrow Money on the credit of the United States;

To regulate Commerce with foreign Nations, and among the several States, and with the Indian Tribes;

To establish an uniform Rule of Naturalization, and uniform Laws on the subject of Bankruptcies throughout the United States;

To coin Money, regulate the Value thereof, and of foreign Coin, and fix the Standard of Weights and Measures;

To provide for the Punishment of counterfeiting the Securities and current Coin of the United States;

To establish Post Offices and post Roads;

To promote the Progress of Science and useful Arts, by securing for limited Times to Authors and Inventors the exclusive Right to their respective Writings and Discoveries;

To constitute Tribunals inferior to the Supreme Court;

To define and punish Piracies and Felonies committed on the high Seas, and Offences against the Law of Nations;

To declare War, grant Letters of Marque and Reprisal, and make Rules concerning captures on Land and Water;

To raise and support Armies, but no Appropriation of Money to the Use shall be for a longer Term than two Years;

To provide and maintain a Navy;

To make Rules for the Government and Regulation of the land and naval Forces;

To provide for calling forth the Militia to execute the Laws of the Union, suppress Insurrections and repel Invasions;

To provide for organizing, arming, and disciplining the Militia, and for governing such Part of them as may be employed in the Service of the United States, reserving to the States respectively, the Appointment of the Officers, and the Authority of training the Militia according to the discipline prescribed by Congress;

To exercise exclusive Legislation in all Cases whatsoever, over such District (not exceeding ten Miles square) as may, by Cession of particular States, and the Acceptance of Congress, become the Seat of Government of the United States, and to exercise like Authority over all Places purchased by the Consent of the Legislature of the State in which the Same shall be, for the Erection of Forts, Magazines, Arsenals, dock-Yards, and other needful Buildings;—And

To make all Laws which shall be necessary and proper for carrying into Execution the foregoing Powers, and all other Powers vested by this Constitution in the Government of the United States, or in any Department or Officer thereof.

Section 9. *The Migration or Importation of such Persons as any of the States now existing shall think proper to admit, shall not be prohibited by the Congress prior to the Year one thousand eight hundred and eight, but a Tax or duty may be imposed on such Importation, not exceeding ten dollars for each Person.*[7]

The Privilege of the Writ of Habeas Corpus shall not be suspended, unless when in Cases of Rebellion or Invasion the public Safety may require it.

No Bill of Attainder or ex post facto Law shall be passed.

No Capitation, or other direct, Tax shall be laid, unless in Proportion to the Census or Enumeration herein before directed to be taken.[8]

No Tax on Duty shall be laid on Articles exported from any State.

No Preference shall be given by any Regulation of Commerce or Revenue to the Ports of one State over those of another: nor shall Vessels bound to, or from, one State, be obliged to enter, clear, or pay Duties in another.

No Money shall be drawn from the Treasury, but in Consequence of Appropriations made by Law; and a regular Statement and Account of the Receipts and Expenditures of all public Money shall be published from time to time.

No Title of Nobility shall be granted by the United States; And no Person holding any Office of Profit or Trust under them, shall, without the Consent of the Congress, accept of any present, Emolument, Office, or Title, of any kind whatever, from any King, Prince, or foreign State.

Section 10. No State shall enter into any Treaty, Alliance, or Confederation; grant Letters of Marque and Reprisal; coin Money; emit Bills of Credit; make any Thing but gold and silver Coin a Tender in Payment of Debts; pass any Bill of Attainder, ex post facto Law, or Law impairing the Obligation of Contracts, or Grant any Title of Nobility.

No State shall, without the Consent of the Congress, lay any Imposts or Duties on Imports or Exports, except what may be absolutely necessary for executing its inspection Laws; and the net Produce of all Duties and Imposts, laid by any State on Imports or Exports, shall be for the Use of the Treasury of the United States; and all such Laws shall be subject to the Revision and Control of the Congress.

No State shall, without the Consent of Congress, lay any Duty of Tonnage, keep Troops, or Ships of War in time of Peace, enter into any Agreement or Compact with another State, or with a foreign Power, or engage in War, unless actually invaded, or in such imminent Danger as will not admit of delay.

ARTICLE II

Section 1. *The executive Power shall be vested in a President of the United States of America. He shall hold his Office during the Term of four Years, and, together with the Vice-President, chosen for the same Term, be elected, as follows:*[9]

Each State shall appoint, in such Manner as the Legislature thereof may direct, a Number of Electors, equal to the whole Number of Senators and Representatives to which the State may be entitled in the Congress: but no Senator or Represen-

[7] Temporary Provision.
[8] Modified by the Sixteenth Amendment.
[9] The number of terms is limited to two by the Twenty-second Amendment.

tative, or Person holding an Office of Trust or Profit under the United States, shall be appointed an Elector.

The Electors shall meet in their respective States, and vote by Ballot for two Persons, of whom one at least shall not be an Inhabitant of the same State with themselves. And they shall make a List of all the Persons voted for, and of the Number of Votes for each; which List they shall sign and certify, and transmit sealed to the Seat of the Government of the United States, directed to the President of the Senate. The President of the Senate shall, in the Presence of the Senate and House of Representatives, open all the Certificates, and the Votes shall then be counted. The Person having the greatest Number of Votes shall be the President, if such Number be a Majority of the whole Number of Electors appointed; and if there be more than one who have such Majority, and have an equal Number of Votes, then the House of Representatives shall immediately choose by Ballot one of them for President; and if no Person have a Majority, then from the five highest on the List the said House shall in like Manner choose the President. But in choosing the President, the Votes shall be taken by States, the Representation from each State having one Vote. A quorum for this Purpose shall consist of a Member or Members from two-thirds of the States, and a Majority of all the States shall be necessary to a Choice. In every Case, after the Choice of the President, the Person having the greatest Number of Votes of the Electors shall be the Vice-President. But if there should remain two or more who have equal Votes, the Senate shall choose from them by Ballot the Vice-President.[10]

The Congress may determine the Time of choosing the Electors, and the Day on which they shall give their Votes; which Day shall be the same throughout the United States.

No Person except a natural born Citizen, or a Citizen of the United States, at the time of the Adoption of this Constitution, shall be eligible to the Office of President; neither shall any Person be eligible to that Office who shall not have attained to the Age of thirty-five Years, and been fourteen Years a Resident within the United States.

In Case of the Removal of the President from Office, or of his Death, Resignation, or Inability to discharge the Powers and Duties of the said Office, the Same shall devolve on the Vice-President, and the Congress may by Law provide for the Case of Removal, Death, Resignation or Inability, both of the President and Vice-President, declaring what Officer shall then act as President, and such Officer shall act accordingly, until the Disability be removed, or a President shall be elected.

The President shall, at stated Times, receive for his Services, a Compensation which shall neither be increased nor diminished during the Period for which he shall have been elected, and he shall not receive within that Period any other Emolument from the United States, or any of them.

Before he enter on the Execution of his Office, he shall take the following Oath or Affirmation:—"I do solemnly swear (or affirm) that I will faithfully execute the office of President of the United States, and will, to the best of my Ability, preserve, protect and defend the Constitution of the United States."

Section 2. The President shall be Commander in Chief of the Army and Navy

---

[10] Superseded by the Twelfth Amendment, which, in turn, is modified by the Twentieth Amendment.

of the United States, and of the Militia of the several States, when called into actual Service of the United States; he may require the Opinion, in writing, of the principal Officer in each of the executive Departments, upon any Subject relating to the Duties of their respective Offices, and he shall have Power to grant Reprieves and Pardons for Offences against the United States, except in Cases of Impeachment.

He shall have Power, by and with the Advice and Consent of the Senate, to make Treaties, provided two-thirds of the Senators present concur; and he shall nominate, and by and with the Advice and Consent of the Senate, shall appoint Ambassadors, other public Ministers and Consuls, Judges of the Supreme Court, and all other Officers of the United States, whose Appointments are not herein otherwise provided for, and which shall be established by Law: but the Congress may by Law vest the Appointment of such inferior Officers, as they think proper, in the President alone, in the Courts of Law, or in the Heads of Departments.

The President shall have Power to fill up all Vacancies that may happen during the Recess of the Senate, by granting Commissions which shall expire at the End of their next Session.

Section 3. He shall from time to time give to the Congress Information of the State of the Union, and recommend to their Consideration such Measures as he shall judge necessary and expedient; he may, on extraordinary Occasions, convene both Houses, or either of them, and in Case of Disagreement between them, with Respect to the Time of Adjournment, he may adjourn them to such Time as he shall think proper; he shall receive Ambassadors and other public Ministers; he shall take Care that the Laws be faithfully executed, and shall Commission all the Officers of the United States.

Section 4. The President, Vice-President and all civil Officers of the United States, shall be removed from Office on Impeachment for, and Conviction of, Treason, Bribery, or other high Crimes and Misdemeanors.

ARTICLE III

Section 1. The judicial Power of the United States shall be vested in one Supreme Court, and in such inferior Courts as the Congress may from time to time ordain and establish. The Judges, both of the Supreme and inferior Courts, shall hold their Offices during good Behavior, and shall, at stated Times, receive for their Services, a Compensation, which shall not be diminished during their Continuance in Office.

Section 2. The judicial Power shall extend to all Cases, in Law and Equity, arising under this Constitution, the Laws of the United States, and Treaties made, or which shall be made, under their Authority;—to all Cases affecting Ambassadors, other public Ministers and Consuls;—to all Cases of admiralty and maritime Jurisdiction;—to Controversies to which the United States shall be a Party; —to Controversies between two or more States;—*between a State and Citizens of another State;*—between Citizens of different States;—between Citizens of the same State claiming Lands under Grants of different States, *and between a State, or the Citizens thereof, and foreign States, Citizens or Subjects.*[11]

In all Cases affecting Ambassadors, other public Ministers and Consuls, and those in which a State shall be Party, the Supreme Court shall have original Jur-

---

[11] Limited by the Eleventh Amendment.

isdiction. In all the other Cases before mentioned, the Supreme Court shall have appellate Jurisdiction, both as to Law and Fact, with such Exceptions, and under such Regulations as the Congress shall make.

The Trial of all Crimes, except in Cases of Impeachment, shall be by Jury; and such Trial shall be held in the State where the said Crimes shall have been committed; but when not committed within any State, the Trial shall be at such Place or Places as the Congress may by Law have directed.

Section 3. Treason against the United States, shall consist only in levying War against them, or in adhering to their Enemies, giving them Aid and Comfort. No Person shall be convicted of Treason unless on the Testimony of two Witnesses to the same overt Act, or on Confession in open Court.

The Congress shall have Power to declare the Punishment of Treason, but no Attainder of Treason shall work Corruption of Blood, or Forfeiture except during the Life of the Person attained.

ARTICLE IV

Section 1. Full Faith and Credit shall be given in each State to the public Acts, Records and judicial Proceedings of every other State. And the Congress may by general Laws prescribe the Manner in which such Acts, Records and Proceedings shall be proved, and the Effect thereof.

Section 2. The Citizens of each State shall be entitled to all Privileges and Immunities of Citizens in the several States.

A Person charged in any State with Treason, Felony, or other Crime, who shall flee from Justice, and be found in another State, shall on Demand of the executive Authority of the State from which he fled, be delivered up, to be removed to the State having Jurisdiction of the Crime.

No Person held to Service or Labour in one State, under the Laws thereof, escaping into another, shall, in Consequence of any Law or Regulation therein, be discharged from such Service or Labour, but shall be delivered up on Claim of the Party to whom such Service or Labour may be due.[12]

Section 3. New states may be admitted by the Congress into this Union; but no new States shall be formed or erected within the Jurisdiction of any other State; nor any State be formed by the Junction of two or more States, or Parts of States, without the Consent of the Legislatures of the States concerned as well as of the Congress.

The Congress shall have Power to dispose of and make all needful Rules and Regulations respecting the Territory or other Property belonging to the United States; and nothing in this Constitution shall be so construed as to Prejudice any Claims of the United States, or of any particular State.

Section 4. The United States shall guarantee to every State in this Union a Republican Form of Government, and shall protect each of them against Invasion; and on Application of the Legislature, or of the Executive (when the Legislature cannot be convened) against domestic Violence.

ARTICLE V

The Congress, whenever two-thirds of both Houses shall deem it necessary, shall propose Amendments to this Constitution, or, on the Application of the Leg-

---

[12] Superseded by the Thirteenth Amendment.

islatures of two-thirds of the several States, shall call a Convention for proposing Amendments, which, in either Case, shall be valid to all Intents and Purposes, as Part of this Constitution, when ratified by the Legislatures of three-fourths of the several States, or by Conventions in three-fourths thereof, as the one or the other Mode of Ratification may be proposed by the Congress; Provided *that no Amendment which may be made prior to the Year One thousand eight hundred and eight shall in any Manner affect the first and fourth Clauses in the Ninth Section of the first Article;*[13] and that no State, without its Consent, shall be deprived of its equal Suffrage in the Senate.

ARTICLE VI

All Debts contracted and Engagements entered into, before the Adoption of this Constitution, shall be as valid against the United States under this Constitution, as under the Confederation.

This Constitution, and the Laws of the United States which shall be made in Pursuance thereof and all Treaties made, or which shall be made, under the Authority of the United States, shall be the supreme Law of the Land; and the Judges in every State shall be bound thereby, any Thing in the Constitution or Laws of any State to the Contrary notwithstanding.

The Senators and Representatives before mentioned, and the Members of the several State Legislatures, and all executive and judicial Officers, both of the United States and of the several States, shall be bound by Oath or Affirmation, to support this Constitution; but no religious Test shall ever be required as a Qualification to any Office or public Trust under the United States.

ARTICLE VII

The Ratification of the Conventions of nine States, shall be sufficient for the Establishment of this Constitution between the States so ratifying the Same.

DONE in Convention by the Unanimous Consent of the States present the Seventeenth Day of September in the Year of our Lord one thousand seven hundred and Eighty-seven and of the Independence of the United States of America the Twelfth. In witness whereof We have hereunto subscribed our Names, Attest William Jackson
Secretary

G° Washington—Presidt.
and deputy from Virginia

New Hampshire   John Langdon
                 Nicholas Gilman

Massachusetts   Nathaniel Gorham
                 Rufus King

Connecticut   Wm. Saml. Johnson
                 Roger Sherman

New York   Alexander Hamilton

---

[13] Modified by the Twentieth Amendment.

New Jersey	{	Wil: Livingston David Brearley. Wm. Paterson. Jona: Dayton

Pennsylvania	{	B. Franklin Thomas Mifflin Robt. Morris Geo. Clymer Thos. FitzSimons Jared Ingersoll James Wilson Gouv Morris

Delaware	{	Geo: Read Gunning Bedford Jun John Dickinson Richard Bassett Jaco: Broom

Maryland	{	James McHenry Dan of St. Thos Jenifer Danl. Carroll

Virginia	{	John Blair— James Madison Jr.

North Carolina	{	Wm. Blount Richd. Dobbs Spaight. Hu Williamson

South Carolina	{	J. Rutledge Charles Cotesworth Pinckney Charles Pinckney Pierce Butler

Georgia	{	William Few Abr Baldwin

ARTICLES IN ADDITION TO, AND AMENDMENT OF, THE CONSTITUTON OF THE UNITED STATES OF AMERICA, PROPOSED BY CONGRESS, AND RATIFIED BY THE SEVERAL STATES, PURSUANT TO THE FIFTH ARTICLE OF THE ORIGINAL CONSTITUTION

AMENDMENT I

(First Ten Amendments proposed by Congress on September 25, 1789;)
(ratified and adoption certified on December 15, 1791)

Congress shall make no law respecting an establishment of religion, or prohibiting the free exercise thereof; or abridging the freedom of speech, or of the

press; or the right of the people peaceably to assemble, and to petition the Government for a redress of grievances.

AMENDMENT II

A well-regulated Militia, being necessary to the security of a free State, the right of the people to keep and bear Arms, shall not be infringed.

AMENDMENT III

No Soldier shall, in time of peace be quartered in any house, without the consent of the Owner, nor in time of war, but in a manner to be prescribed by law.

AMENDMENT IV

The right of the people to be secure in their persons, houses, papers, and effects, against unreasonable searches and seizures, shall not be violated, and no Warrants shall issue, but upon probable cause, supported by Oath or affirmation, and particularly describing the place to be searched, and the persons or things to be seized.

AMENDMENT V

No person shall be held to answer for a capital, or other infamous crime, unless on a presentment or indictment of a Grand Jury, except in cases arising in the land or naval forces, or in the Militia, when in actual service in time of War or public danger; nor shall any person be subject for the same offence to be twice put in jeopardy of life or limb; nor shall be compelled in any criminal case to be a witness against himself, nor be deprived of life, liberty, or property, without due process of law; nor shall private property be taken for public use, without just compensation.

AMENDMENT VI

In all criminal prosecutions, the accused shall enjoy the right to a speedy and public trial, by an impartial jury of the State and district wherein the crime shall have been committed, which district shall have been previously ascertained by law, and to be informed of the nature and cause of the accusation; to be confronted with the witnesses against him; to have compulsory process for obtaining witnesses in his favor, and to have the Assistance of Counsel for his defence.

AMENDMENT VII

In Suits at common law, where the value in controversy shall exceed twenty dollars, the right of trial by jury shall be preserved, and no fact tried by a jury, shall be otherwise re-examined in any Court of the United States, than according to the rules of the common law.

AMENDMENT VIII

Excessive bail shall not be required, nor excessive fines imposed, nor cruel and unusual punishments inflicted.

AMENDMENT IX

The enumeration in the Constitution, of certain rights, shall not be construed to deny or disparage others retained by the people.

AMENDMENT X

The powers not delegated to the United States by the Constitution, nor prohibited by it to the States, are reserved to the States respectively, or to the people.

AMENDMENT XI
(*January 8, 1798*)[14]

The Judicial power of the United States shall not be construed to extend to any suit in law or equity, commenced or prosecuted against one of the United States by Citizens of another State, or by Citizens or Subjects of any Foreign State.

AMENDMENT XII
(*September 25, 1804*)

The Electors shall meet in their respective states, and vote by ballot for President and Vice-President, one of whom, at least, shall not be an inhabitant of the same state with themselves; they shall name in their ballots the person voted for as President, and in distinct ballots the person voted for as Vice-President, and they shall make distinct lists of all persons voted for as President, and of all persons voted for as Vice-President, and of the number of votes for each, which lists they shall sign and certify, and transmit sealed to the seat of the government of the United States, directed to the President of the Senate;—The President of the Senate shall, in the presence of the Senate and House of Representatives, open all the certificates and the votes shall then be counted;—The person having the greatest number of votes for President, shall be the President, if such number be a majority of the whole number of Electors appointed; and if no person have such majority, then from the persons having the highest numbers not exceeding three on the list of those voted for as President, the House of Representatives shall choose immediately, by ballot, the President. But in choosing the President, the votes shall be taken by states, the representation from each state having one vote; a quorum for this purpose shall consist of a member or members from two-thirds of the states, and a majority of all the states shall be necessary to a choice. *And if the House of Representatives shall not choose a President whenever the right of choice shall devolve upon them, before the fourth day of March next following,*[15] then the Vice-President shall act as President, as in the case of the death or other constitutional disability of the President.—The person having the greatest number of votes as Vice-President, shall be the Vice-President, if such number be a majority of the whole number of Electors appointed, and if no person have a majority, then from the two highest numbers on the list, the Senate shall choose the Vice-President; a quorum for the purpose shall consist of two-thirds of the whole number of Senators, and a majority of the whole number shall be necessary to a choice. But no person constitutionally ineligible to the office of President shall be eligible to that of Vice-President of the United States.

AMENDMENT XIII
(*December 18, 1865*)

Section 1. Neither slavery nor involuntary servitude, except as a punishment for crime whereof the party shall have been duly convicted, shall exist within the United States, or any place subject to their jurisdiction.

---

[14] The dates noted under Amendments XI through XXII are dates of ratification.
[15] Modified by the Twentieth Amendment.

Section 2. Congress shall have power to enforce this article by appropriate legislation.

AMENDMENT XIV
(*July 28, 1868*)

Section 1. All persons born or naturalized in the United States, and subject to the jurisdiction thereof, are citizens of the United States and of the State wherein they reside. No State shall make or enforce any law which shall abridge the privileges or immunities of citizens of the United States; nor shall any State deprive any person of life, liberty, or property, without due process of law; nor deny to any person within its jurisdiction the equal protection of the laws.

Section 2. Representatives shall be apportioned among the several States according to their respective numbers, counting the whole number of persons in each State, excluding Indians not taxed. But when the right to vote at any election for the choice of electors for President and Vice-President of the United States, Representatives in Congress, the Executive and Judicial officers of a State, or the members of the Legislature thereof, is denied to any of the male members of such State, being twenty-one years of age, and citizens of the United States, or in any way abridged, except for participation in rebellion, or other crime, the basis of representation therein shall be reduced in the proportion which the number of such male citizens shall bear to the whole number of male citizens twenty-one years of age in such State.

Section 3. No person shall be a Senator or Representative in Congress, or elector of President and Vice-President, or hold any office, civil or military, under the United States, or under any State, who, having previously taken an oath, as a member of Congress, or as an officer of the United States, or as a member of any State legislature, or as an executive or judicial officer of any State, to support the Constitution of the United States, shall have engaged in insurrection or rebellion against the same, or given aid or comfort to the enemies thereof. But Congress may by a vote of two-thirds of each House, remove such disability.

Section 4. The validity of the public debt of the United States, authorized by law, including debts incurred for payment of pensions and bounties for services in suppressing insurrection or rebellion, shall not be questioned. But neither the United States nor any State shall assume or pay any debt or obligation incurred in aid of insurrection or rebellion against the United States, or any claim for the loss or emancipation of any slave; but all such debts, obligations and claims shall be held illegal and void.

Section 5. The Congress shall have power to enforce, by appropriate legislation, the provisions of this article.

AMENDMENT XV
(*March 30, 1870*)

Section 1. The right of citizens of the United States to vote shall not be denied or abridged by the United States or by any State on account of race, color, or previous condition of servitude.

Section 2. The Congress shall have power to enforce this article by appropriate legislation.

AMENDMENT XVI
(February 25, 1913)

The Congress shall have power to lay and collect taxes on incomes, from whatever sources derived, without apportionment among the several States, and without regard to any census or enumeration.

AMENDMENT XVII
(May 31, 1913)

The Senate of the United States shall be composed of two Senators from each State, elected by the people thereof, for six years; and each Senator shall have one vote. The electors in each State shall have the qualifications requisite for electors of the most numerous branch of the State legislatures.

When vacancies happen in the representation of any State in the Senate, the executive authority of such State shall issue writs of election to fill such vacancies: *Provided,* That the legislature of any State may empower the executive thereof to make temporary appointments until the people fill the vacancies by election as the legislature may direct.

This amendment shall not be so construed as to affect the election or term of any Senator chosen before it becomes valid as part of the Constitution.

AMENDMENT XVIII
(January 29, 1919)

Section 1. *After one year from the ratification of this article the manufacture, sale, or transportation of intoxicating liquors within, the importation thereof into, or the exportation thereof from the United States and all territory subject to the jurisdiction thereof for beverage purposes is hereby prohibited.*

Section 2. *The Congress and the several States shall have concurrent power to enforce this article by appropriate legislation.*

Section 3. *This article shall be inoperative unless it shall have been ratified as an amendment to the Constitution by the legislatures of the several States, as provided in the Constitution, within seven years from the date of the submission hereof to the States by the Congress.*[16]

AMENDMENT XIX
(August 26, 1920)

The right of citizens of the United States to vote shall not be denied or abridged by the United States or by any State on account of sex.

Congress shall have power to enforce this article by appropriate legislation.

AMENDMENT XX
(February 6, 1933)

Section 1. The terms of the President and Vice-President shall end at noon on the 20th day of January, and the terms of Senators and Representatives at noon on the 3d day of January, of the years in which such terms would have ended if this article had not been ratified; and the terms of their successors shall then begin.

Section 2. The Congress shall assemble at least once in every year, and such

[16] Repealed by the Twenty-first Amendment.

meeting shall begin at noon on the 3d of January, unless they shall by law appoint a different day.

Section 3. If, at the time fixed for the beginning of the term of the President, the President elect shall have died, the Vice-President elect shall become President. If a President shall not have been chosen before the time fixed for the beginning of his term, or if the President elect shall have failed to qualify, then the Vice-President elect shall act as President until a President shall have qualified; and the Congress may by law provide for the case wherein neither a President elect nor a Vice-President elect shall have qualified, declaring who shall then act as President, or the manner in which one who is to act shall be selected, and such person shall act accordingly until a President or Vice-President shall have qualified.

Section 4. The Congress may by law provide for the case of the death of any of the persons from whom the House of Representatives may choose a President whenever the right of choice shall have devolved upon them, and for the case of the death of any of the persons from whom the Senate may choose a Vice-President whenever the right of choice shall have devolved upon them.

Section 5. Sections 1 and 2 shall take effect on the 15th day of October following the ratification of this article.

Section 6. This article shall be inoperative unless it shall have been ratified as an amendment to the Constitution by the legislatures of three-fourths of the several States within seven years from the date of its submission.

AMENDMENT XXI[17]
(*December 5, 1933*)

Section 1. The eighteenth article of amendment to the Constitution of the United States is hereby repealed.

Section 2. The transportation or importation into any State, Territory, or Possession of the United States for delivery or use therein of intoxicating liquors, in violation of the laws thereof, is hereby prohibited.

Section 3. This article shall be inoperative unless it shall have been ratified as an amendment to the Constitution by conventions in the several States, as provided in the Constitution, within seven years from the date of the submission hereof to the States by the Congress.

AMENDMENT XXI
(*February 27, 1951*)

Section 1. No person shall be elected to the office of the President more than twice, and no person who has held the office of President, or acted as President, for more than two years of a term to which some other person was elected President shall be elected to the office of President more than once. But this Article shall not apply to any person holding the office of President when this Article was proposed by the Congress, and shall not prevent any person who may be holding the office of President, or acting as President, during the term within which this Article becomes operative from holding the office of President or acting as President during the remainder of such term.

Section 2. This article shall be inoperative unless it shall have been ratified as an amendment to the Constitution by the legislatures of three-fourths of the sev-

---

[17] This is the only amendment that has thus far been ratified by state conventions.

eral States within seven years from the date of its submission to the States by the Congress.

AMENDMENT XXIII
(*March 29, 1961*)

Section 1. The District constituting the seat of Government of the United States shall appoint in such manner as the Congress may direct:

A number of electors of President and Vice President equal to the whole number of Senators and Representatives in Congress to which the District would be entitled if it were a State, but in no event more than the least populous State; they shall be in addition to those appointed by the States, but they shall be considered, for the purposes of the election of President and Vice President, to be electors appointed by a State; and they shall meet in the District and perform such duties as provided by the twelfth article of amendment.

Section 2. The Congress shall have power to enforce this article by appropriate legislation.

AMENDMENT XXIV
(*January 23, 1964*)

The right of citizens of the United States to vote in any primary or other election for President or Vice-President, for electors for President or Vice President, or for Senator or Representative in Congress shall not be denied or abridged by the United States or any State by reason of failure to pay any poll tax or other tax.

AMENDMENT XXV
(*February 23, 1967*)

Section 1. In case of the removal of the President from office or of his death or resignation, the Vice President shall become President.

Section 2. Whenever there is a vacancy in the office of the Vice President, the President shall nominate a Vice President who shall take office upon confirmation by a majority vote of both Houses of Congress.

Section 3. Whenever the President transmits to the President pro tempore of the Senate and the Speaker of the House of Representatives his written declaration that he is unable to discharge the powers and duties of his office, and until he transmits to them a written declaration to the contrary, such powers and duties shall be discharged by the Vice President as Acting President.

Section 4. Whenever the Vice President and a majority of either the principal officers of the executive departments or of such other body as Congress may by law provide, transmit to the President pro tempore of the Senate and the Speaker of the House of Representatives their written declaration that the President is unable to discharge the powers and duties of his office, the Vice President shall immediately assume the powers and duties of the office as Acting President.

Thereafter, when the President transmits to the President pro tempore of the Senate and the Speaker of the House of Representatives his written declaration that no inability exists, he shall resume the powers and duties of his office unless the Vice President and a majority of either the principal officers of the executive department or of such other body as Congress may by law provide, transmit within four days to the President pro tempore of the Senate and the Speaker of the

House of Representatives their written declaration that the President is unable to discharge the powers and duties of his office. Thereupon Congress shall decide the issue, assembling within forty-eight hours for that purpose if not in session. If the Congress, within twenty-one days after receipt of the latter written declaration, or, if Congress is not in session, within twenty-one days after Congress is required to assemble, determines by two-thirds vote of both Houses that the President is unable to discharge the powers and duties of his office, the Vice President shall continue to discharge the same as Acting President; otherwise, the President shall resume the powers and duties of his office.

Appendix II

United States Supreme Court Justices: 1789-1969

(Capital letters indicate Chief Justices)

Name	Term of Office	Name	Term of Office
JOHN JAY	1789–1795	Thomas Todd	1807–1826
John Rutledge	1789–1791	Joseph Story	1811–1845
William Cushing	1789–1810	Gabriel Duval	1812–1835
James Wilson	1789–1798	Smith Thompson	1823–1843
John Blair	1789–1796	Robert Trimble	1826–1828
Robert H. Harrison	1789–1790	John McLean	1829–1861
James Iredell	1790–1799	Henry Baldwin	1830–1844
Thomas Johnson	1791–1793	James M. Wayne	1835–1867
William Paterson	1793–1806	ROGER B. TANEY	1836–1864
JOHN RUTLEDGE	1795[1]	Philip B. Barbour	1836–1841
Samuel Chase	1796–1811	John Catron	1837–1865
OLIVER ELLSWORTH	1796–1799	John McKinley	1837–1852
Bushrod Washington	1798–1829	Peter V. Daniel	1841–1860
Alfred Moore	1799–1804	Samuel Nelson	1845–1872
JOHN MARSHALL	1801–1835	Levi Woodbury	1845–1851
William Johnson	1804–1834	Robert C. Grier	1846–1870
Brockholst Livingston	1806–1823	Benj. R. Curtis	1851–1857

[1] John Rutledge's appointment as Chief Justice in 1795 was not confirmed by Congress.

Name	Term of Office	Name	Term of Office
John A. Campbell	1853–1861	William O. Douglas	1939–
Nathan Clifford	1858–1881	Frank Murphy	1940–1949
Noah H. Swayne	1862–1881	HARLAN F. STONE	1941–1946
Samuel F. Miller	1862–1890	James F. Byrnes	1941–1942
David Davis	1862–1877	Robert H. Jackson	1941–1954
Stephen J. Field	1863–1897	Wiley B. Rutledge	1943–1949
SALMON P. CHASE	1864–1873	Harold H. Burton	1945–1958
William Strong	1870–1880	FRED M. VINSON	1946–1953
Joseph P. Bradley	1870–1892	Tom C. Clark	1949–1967
Ward Hunt	1873–1882	Sherman Minton	1949–1956
MORRISON R. WAITE	1874–1888	EARL WARREN	1953–1969
John M. Harlan	1877–1911	John M. Harlan	1954–
William B. Woods	1881–1887	William J. Brennan	1956–
Stanley Matthews	1881–1889	Charles E. Whittaker	1957–1962
Horace Gray	1882–1902	Potter Stewart	1958–
Samuel Blatchford	1882–1893	Byron R. White	1962–
Lucius Q. C. Lamar	1888–1893	Arthur J. Goldberg	1962–1965
MELVILLE W. FULLER	1888–1910	Abe Fortas	1965–1969
David J. Brewer	1890–1910	Thurgood Marshall	1967–
Henry B. Brown	1891–1906	WARREN BURGER	1969–
George Shiras, Jr.	1892–1903		
Howell E. Jackson	1893–1895		
Edward D. White	1894–1910		
Rufus W. Peckham	1896–1909		
Joseph McKenna	1898–1925		
Oliver W. Holmes, Jr.	1902–1932		
William R. Day	1903–1922		
William H. Moody	1906–1910		
Horace H. Lurton	1910–1914		
Charles E. Hughes	1910–1916		
Willis Van Devanter	1911–1937		
Joseph R. Lamar	1911–1916		
EDWARD D. WHITE	1910–1921		
Mahlon Pitney	1912–1922		
James C. McReynolds	1914–1941		
Louis D. Brandeis	1916–1939		
John H. Clarke	1916–1922		
WILLIAM H. TAFT	1921–1930		
George Sutherland	1922–1938		
Pierce Butler	1922–1939		
Edward T. Sanford	1923–1930		
Harlan F. Stone	1925–1941		
CHARLES E. HUGHES	1930–1941		
Owen J. Roberts	1930–1945		
Benjamin N. Cardozo	1932–1938		
Hugo L. Black	1937–		
Stanley F. Reed	1938–1957		
Felix Frankfurter	1939–1962		

HUGO L. BLACK (1886–   ). President Franklin D. Roosevelt's first appointee to the Court was Hugo L. Black, an ardent New Dealer who was a Democratic senator from Alabama. The appointment stirred a storm of controversy when Black admitted he had once joined the Ku Klux Klan for political reasons. However, as evidenced by a number of his decisions, such as *Chambers* v. *Florida,* he never followed the Klan line. Opposition to Black's appointment came also from conservative Democrats and Republicans, who did not wish to see one of the most zealous Roosevelt supporters elevated to the highest tribunal.

Justice Black was born and reared in the rural area of Clay County, Alabama. He received a law degree from the University of Alabama Law School after a two-year course and was admitted to the bar in 1906. For the next twenty years he engaged in private law practice in his home state. During this period he also served as a police court judge for eighteen months and as a county prosecuting attorney for three years. In 1927, Black was elected to the United States Senate and served there until his appointment to the Court ten years later. As a senator, Black sponsored and supported many important New Deal measures, including the Fair Labor Standards Act and the TVA. He also conducted a series of major investigations into lobbying activities, ship subsidies, and trusts. In 1936, he campaigned vigorously for the reelection of President Roosevelt, and in 1937 he supported the President's court-packing plan.

Although Black joined the Court as an expert legislator with no extensive judicial experience and with little knowledge of constitutional law, incessant hard work and study have made him a strong and distinguished justice. His opinions are characterized by a simplicity of style and clarity. Justice Black's numerous opinions in this book reveal clearly that, along with Justice Douglas, he is one of the most vigorous supporters of civil rights in the history of the Court. He has failed to vote for the protection of basic civil rights in only a few instances (*Korematsu*). Although Justice Black has maintained in some cases that many problems must be resolved ultimately by legislative bodies, he would not hesitate to strike down legislative or executive action that abridges fundamental freedoms. In general, he has preached the doctrine that "government should at the same time be both all-powerful and all-weak: that over the economy it should have all the power needed to cope with the problems of each day, and that over the thought, speech and spirit of the citizen it should have no power at all." [John P. Frank, "Mr. Justice Black: A Biographical Appreciation," *Yale Law Journal,* Vol. 65 (1956), p. 461.]

Beginning in 1967 Justice Black's vote could no longer be found consistently in the liberal block. His opinions began to stress one of his old themes—that the Justices must be guided by the specific words of the Constitution—in the new context of opposing the liberal members of the Court's tendency to indiscriminately favor the underdog.

JOSEPH P. BRADLEY (1813–1892). It has been well written that "if a forcefully held judicial position, intellectual curiosity, and depth of legal knowledge are the hallmarks of judicial greatness, then Joseph P.

Bradley stands at the top in a charmed circle with Joseph Story, Oliver Wendell Holmes, and Benjamin N. Cardozo." [C. Peter Magrath, *Morrison R. Waite: The Triumph of Character* (New York: Macmillan, 1963), p. 100.] And because of his professional detachment, legal craftsmanship, and breadth of learning, Bradley's astute biographer has described him as "one of the greatest of the Justices." [Charles Fairman, "The Education of a Justice: Justice Bradley and Some of His Colleagues," *Stanford Law Review,* Vol. 1 (1949), p. 217.]

Bradley was born and raised on a farm near Albany, New York, the eldest of twelve children in a poor, but closely knit, family. As a youth Bradley shared in the heavy work of the farm, but he was primarily interested in obtaining an education. He attended rural schools four months of each year and in 1833 entered Rutgers. After graduation he read law in Newark, passed his bar examination, and began to practice law. During the next thirty years Bradley became one of the best-known lawyers in the state with a wide knowledge of railroad and corporate affairs. "Perhaps no other member down to Mr. Justice Brandeis brought to the Court so intimate a working acquaintance with the entire range of the nation's business as did Mr. Justice Bradley." (Fairman, *supra.*) First a Whig and then a Republican, Bradley was named to the Court in 1870 by President Grant. As a justice he is best remembered as a nationalist who was most influential in developing the principle of national authority over interstate commerce. Although often characterized as a "railroad lawyer," Bradley played a key role in developing the doctrine of *Munn* v. *Illinois,* which upheld the regulation of business "affected with a public interest" by state legislatures.

LOUIS D. BRANDEIS (1856–1941). Justice Frankfurter has noted that, of the ninety men who have sat on the Supreme Court, "not more than a half-dozen either created for themselves a place in the national consciousness or made an impress on the jurisprudence of the country or merely extended on the court the contribution to social thought and action they had made before coming there. All three claims can confidently be made on behalf of Mr. Justice Brandeis." [" 'Moral Grandeur' of Justice Brandeis," *The New York Times Magazine* (November 11, 1956), p. 26.] Unlike most Supreme Court justices, Brandeis was nominated to the highest tribunal in 1916 by President Wilson without any prior judicial experience and without having held any public office. Brandeis was born in Louisville, Kentucky, and received his early education in the public schools of Louisville and in Germany. In 1877, he was graduated from Harvard Law School, where he made an outstanding scholastic record. For the next forty years Brandeis engaged in a varied and extremely lucrative law practice in Boston, where he was recognized as a leader in his profession. During this period he also represented, without pay, such neglected groups as consumers and workingmen. Brandeis' nomination to the Court in 1916 aroused much protest, largely because he was generally regarded as a radical and a socialist. His nomination was opposed by seven former presidents of the American Bar Association, eminent members of the Boston bar, the president of Harvard, and important business leaders. Nevertheless, his nomination was confirmed in the Senate by a 47-to-22 vote.

Justice Brandeis was a meticulous scholar whose major opinions contain great masses of factual data. Despite his careful attention to detail, many of Brandeis' most influential opinions are written with charm and eloquence. His fine style is revealed clearly in his eloquent dissent in *Olmstead* v. *United States.* Because Justices Brandeis and Holmes voted together on so many important issues, their opinions have often been compared. In general, Brandeis and Holmes arrived at the same conclusions by different paths. Brandeis was the scientist who reasoned logically from particulars to conclusions. He was a zealous, pragmatic crusader who could not stand aloof from the conflicts of his day. Holmes, on the other hand, was the detached. Olympian philosopher of the law who "showed no dominant inclination

to shape economic forces constructively. His contributions to our liberalism are essentially negative. Holmes is the enlightened skeptic; Brandeis, the militant crusader." [Alpheus T. Mason, *Brandeis, a Free Man's Life* (New York: Viking Press, 1956), pp. 576–77.] In short, "a Brandeis sustains a new industrial or business regulation because he sees and demonstrates its utility. A Holmes sustains it in mild wondering approval, patient tolerance, magnificent disinterest." [From a book review by Karl N. Llewellyn, quoted in Samuel J. Konefsky, *The Legacy of Holmes and Brandeis* (New York: Macmillan, 1956), p. 307.] Justice Brandeis sought to shape and preserve the ideals, traditions, and institutions of liberal democracy in the industrial America of the twentieth century.

WILLIAM J. BRENNAN, JR. (1906–). When President Eisenhower named William Joseph Brennan, Jr., a Democrat, to the Supreme Court in 1956 to replace the retiring Justice Minton, many observers believed that he was a moderate middle-of-the-roader who would join neither the "liberal" or "conservative" blocs on the Court. However, it quickly became apparent during Brennan's first term that he would line up with the Court's "activist" group. Probably much to the surprise of President Eisenhower and many other Republicans, Brennan's appointment greatly strengthened the civil-libertarian bloc on the Court.

The first Roman Catholic to be appointed to the Court since Justice Murphy, who died in 1949, Brennan was born in Newark, New Jersey, the son of Irish-Catholic immigrants who had seven other children. Although the family was poor, the children were encouraged to seek an education. Brennan worked at various odd jobs to help pay for his schooling. He graduated from the University of Pennsylvania with honors in 1928, and from the Harvard Law School three years later. He returned to Newark to practice law, specializing in corporate law and management-labor problems. After army service as a colonel during World War II, he served as a judge on lower New Jersey state courts until he was appointed to the State Supreme Court by Republican Governor Driscoll. He served on that Court until he was elevated to the Supreme Court. As a state judge, Brennan was an ardent supporter of court reforms that lessened delays in the administration of justice. A long-time foe of legal narrowness, Brennan hotly defends the use of social science evidence by judges in rendering decisions. [See Francis P. McQuade and Alexander T. Kardos, "Mr. Justice Brennan and His Legal Philosophy," *Notre Dame Lawyer,* Vol. 33 (1958), pp. 321–49.]

HENRY B. BROWN (1836–1913). After the death of Justice Miller in 1890, President Harrison named Henry B. Brown to the Court. Brown was born in Massachusetts of well-to-do parents. He graduated from Yale, attended law school at both Yale and Harvard, and then settled in Michigan, where he practiced law. Brown went to the Supreme Court after fifteen years' experience as a federal district judge in Detroit. He was a competent but somewhat pompous justice who was recognized as the leading authority on admiralty and maritime law during his tenure on the Court. Justice Brown's most brilliant opinion was delivered in *Holden* v. *Hardy,* where the Utah eight-hour law for miners was sustained.

WARREN BURGER (1907–   ). Chief Justice Burger was born in St. Paul. He worked his way through the University of Minnesota and a metropolitan law school in St. Paul. In private practice in St. Paul from 1931 to 1953, he argued a number of cases before the Supreme Court. He was active in Republican politics and his switch of the Minnesota delegation pledged to Harold Stassen at the 1952 presidential convention to General Eisenhower was a key factor in Eisenhower's capture of the nomination. In 1953 Burger became Assistant Attorney General and was appointed to the Court of Appeals for the District of Columbia three years later. From his opinions and off-the-bench comments, Judge Burger gained a reputation as an outspoken critic of both the Supreme

Court's and his own court's efforts to provide more safeguards for the rights of accused persons. President Nixon had made a major campaign issue of law and order and, in a strongly implied criticism of the Supreme Court, had pledged to appoint strict constructionists. Chief Justice Burger's appointment seems to have fulfilled the promise of the Nixon campaign.

HAROLD H. BURTON (1888–1965). President Truman's first appointee to the Court was Harold H. Burton, a Republican senator from Ohio, who had served ably on Truman's special committee investigating defense production when both men were members of the Senate. Burton was born and raised in Massachusetts. He graduated from Bowdoin College and Harvard Law School and then began to practice law in Cleveland, Ohio, where he eventually settled. He taught law for a brief period, served in the Ohio legislature for a year, and was Cleveland's mayor for five years before his election to the Senate. Justice Burton is usually classified as a conservative, although he sometimes joined the liberals on important civil rights issues. This is indicated by his majority opinion in *Joint Anti-Fascist Refugee* v. *McGrath.* Burton's opinions are characterized by thoroughness and conscientious attention to technical details. Burton retired from the Court in 1958.

PIERCE BUTLER (1866–1939). Along with Justices Sutherland, Van Devanter, and McReynolds, Justice Butler is best remembered for his unbending opposition to the New Deal and the expansion of governmental powers during the 1930s. Indeed, these four justices formed a solid and powerful conservative phalanx against the experimental legislation of that period. Butler was generally regarded as the most stubborn of this group. "Tough-minded and unshakable in his convictions, he was always ready for intellectual battle. At the conference table he argued with typically Irish tenacity and force, sometimes with thrusts of wit and eloquence. Authoritarian by instinct, he brought all the power of an indefatigable and fearless personality to the support of his views." [Merlo J. Pusey,

Charles Evans Hughes (New York: Macmillan, 1951), Vol. 2, p. 670.] Pierce Butler was born of Irish immigrant parents and raised on a small farm in Minnesota. After graduation from Carleton College, he studied law for a year and was admitted to the bar. In a short time he became a highly successful railroad lawyer. Although he was a lifelong Democrat, he was nominated to the Court in 1922 by President Harding on the recommendation of Chief Justice Taft. Butler's philosophy was shaped by his life in pioneer country. His faith in laissez faire, individualism, and free competition was genuine. "These things meant the American way." (310 U.S. at vi.)

JAMES F. BYRNES (1879–   ). Byrnes has attracted considerable attention in recent years, in part because of his attacks upon his former colleagues' segregation decisions. He has argued vehemently that the Court must be curbed because it acted "politically" and "usurped power" in ending public school segregation. [His charges against the Court have been refuted ably by Professor Wallace Mendelson in *Journal of Politics* (February 1957), p. 81.] James F. Byrnes was born in Charleston, South Carolina. He was admitted to the bar after working as a court reporter and reading law on the side. He was a Democratic congressman for fourteen years and served in the Senate from 1931 to 1941. During this time he became influential in the inner circles of his party. As a senator, Byrnes was an effective and persuasive leader and a staunch supporter of President Roosevelt's policies. He was named to the Court in 1941, but resigned the following year to engage in wartime administrative work. He was appointed Secretary of State by President Truman in 1945, and is best remembered for his work while in that post. Despite his opinion in *Edwards v. California,* Byrnes usually voted against individual rights during his brief tenure on the Court.

BENJAMIN N. CARDOZO (1870–1938). The appointment to the Court of Benjamin N. Cardozo, a New York Democrat, to succeed the retired Justice Holmes in 1932, was acclaimed widely. It was recognized that Cardozo was the best-qualified jurist in the country to succeed the venerable Holmes. Cardozo's judicial career was undoubtedly one of the most illustrious in the annals of American law. He was born in New York City and took both his undergraduate and law training at Columbia University. After his admission to the bar in 1891, he practiced law and became an expert in the highly technical field of commercial law. In 1913, he was elected to the New York Supreme Court as an independent Democrat, but shortly thereafter he became a judge of the New York Court of Appeals (the highest state court), where he served until his appointment to the Supreme Court. During his last five years on the highest state court, Cardozo served as chief judge. Cardozo's impact on the New York court was very great indeed. His learning and unifying influence made that court one of the most distinguished in the land. Much of Cardozo's philosophical and scholarly approach to the law is revealed in his four short but incisive volumes: *The Nature of the Judicial Process* (New Haven: Yale University Press, 1921); *The Growth of the Law* (New Haven: Yale University Press, 1924); *The Paradoxes of Legal Science* (New York: Columbia University Press, 1928); *Law and Literature and Other Essays* (New York: Harcourt, Brace, 1931).

Cardozo ranks as one of the greatest legal philosophers in the history of the Court. "Barring only Mr. Justice Holmes, who was a seminal thinker in the law as well as vastly learned, no judge in his time was more deeply versed in the history of the common law or more resourceful in applying the living principles by which it has unfolded." [Felix Frankfurter, *Of Law and Men* (New York: Harcourt, Brace, 1956), p. 198.] Many of Cardozo's extraordinary qualities as a judge are revealed by his Supreme Court opinions. For example, his important opinion in *Steward Machine Co.* v. *Davis* indicates clearly his belief that the Constitution must serve the changing needs of the people. Cardozo was also one of the greatest literary stylists on the Court. As Attorney General

Cummings stated upon Cardozo's death, "His opinions spoke in tones of rare beauty. They might deal with things prosaic, but the language was that of a poet." Despite his accomplishments, Cardozo was a shy and sensitive man of great humility and compassion. "It was a rare good fortune that brought to such eminence a man so reserved, so unassuming, so retiring, so gracious to high and low, and so serene." [Learned Hand, "Mr. Justice Cardozo," *Columbia Law Review,* Vol. 39 (1939), p. 11.]

SALMON P. CHASE (1808–1873). Among the numerous aspirants to the chief-justiceship upon the death of Taney in 1864 was Salmon P. Chase. In fact, Chase had long awaited Taney's departure with unrestrained eagerness. After considerable delay and with some misgivings, President Lincoln named Chase to the post. The new chief justice was a New Englander by birth and ancestry. He graduated from Dartmouth College and after reading law for a short period was admitted to the bar. He began the practice of law in Ohio and became a prominent figure in the antislavery movement. Chase went to the Supreme Court after a notable political career as United States Senator from Ohio, Governor of Ohio, and Secretary of the Treasury in Lincoln's cabinet. He had an incurable ambition to be President and had sought the Republican nomination both in 1856 and 1860. He attempted, too, to replace Lincoln as the Republican nominee in 1864. Four years later he was considered for nomination to the presidency by the Democrats, for by this time he had lost the support of the Radical Republicans, who had objected vigorously to Chase's calmness, moderation, and impartiality while presiding over the impeachment trial of President Johnson. As demonstrated by *Mississippi* v. *Johnson,* the Chase Court became deeply involved in the problems of Reconstruction. It has been said that the Court's involvement with the turbulent problems of Reconstruction and Chase's own ambition for the presidency made him the least happy of our chief justices. "He would have been a greater judge and a happier man without this unsatisfied ambition; he would have left a greater reputation had he set Marshall before his mind as a model rather than Washington." [Albert B. Hart, *Salmon Portland Chase* (New York: Houghton, Mifflin, 1899), p. 362.]

TOM C. CLARK (1899–   ). The most consistent conservative in civil liberties cases on the Warren Court was Justice Clark. His dissenting opinions in such cases as *Watkins* v. *United States* and *Yates* v. *United States* indicate clearly that Clark approaches civil liberties issues from the point of view of law enforcement officials. This approach is undoubtedly rooted in his experiences as Attorney General of the United States. Clark was named to the Court by President Truman in 1949, with the support of Chief Justice Vinson. He had no judicial experience prior to his appointment; in fact, he had been a controversial political figure for a number of years. After graduation from Virginia Military Institute and the University of Texas Law School, Clark practiced law in Dallas, Texas, and became a power in Democratic party circles. He served in the Justice Department for eight years prior to his appointment as Attorney General by President Truman in 1945. He held that post until his appointment to the Court. As Attorney General, Clark was a vigorous pursuer of Communists, and many of his actions and policies were criticized severely. His more recent dissenting opinions were characterized by clarity and vigor. He retired in 1967.

BENJAMIN R. CURTIS (1809–1874). Although Justice Curtis served on the Court for only six years, he is well remembered because of his formulation of the important rule regarding the power of the state and national governments to regulate interstate commerce in *Cooley* v. *Board of Wardens.* The *Cooley* holding set the direction of adjudication under the commerce clause for years to come. Curtis was born in Massachusetts and took both his undergraduate and law training at Harvard. He eventually became a prominent Whig lawyer in Boston, and, in 1851,

President Fillmore named him to the Court. Curtis resigned from the Court after delivering a dissenting opinion in the *Dred Scott* case in 1857, because he believed that the Court's decision rested on purely political considerations. After retirement from the bench, Curtis resumed his law practice in Boston. He appeared briefly again on the public scene in 1868 as counsel to President Johnson in the impeachment proceedings.

DAVID DAVIS (1815–1886). The reputation of David Davis as a Supreme Court justice rests almost entirely on his classic opinion in the *Milligan* case. Davis was born in Maryland and graduated from Kenyon College at an early age. After studying law at Yale, he established his home in Bloomington, Illinois, and began to practice law. But Davis was an inveterate politician who soon became active in Illinois public life. In 1844, he was elected to the state legislature on the Whig ticket. Three years later he was made a member of the state constitutional convention, and in 1848 he became a state circuit judge, a post he held for fourteen years. During this period, Davis and Abraham Lincoln, who was then practicing law, became close friends. Davis took an active part in the organization of the Republican party, and in the Republican convention of 1860 he led the fight for Lincoln's nomination to the presidency. After the election, the two men remained close friends, and in 1862 Davis was elevated to the Court. But Davis' continued interest in politics made him restless on the bench. In 1872, he was nominated for President by the Labor Reform party. The same year he received strong support as a possible candidate of the Liberal Republican party. Finally, in 1877, after election as United States Senator from Illinois, Justice Davis "stepped down from the Court to renew the political activity which was his lifeblood." [David M. Silver, *Lincoln's Supreme Court* (Urbana: University of Illinois Press, 1957), p. 82.]

WILLIAM R. DAY (1849–1923). Despite his opinion in *Hammer* v. *Dagenhart,* Justice Day generally was more willing to accept social and economic legislation than many of his colleagues on the Court. This is evidenced, in part, by the fact that he joined Justice Holmes's dissent in *Lochner* v. *New York.* But Justice Day never emerged as an outstanding member of the Court. Although mentally keen and alert, frail health impaired his activities throughout his adult life. A native of Ohio, Day was educated at the University of Michigan. After his admission to the bar, he established himself as a good trial lawyer in Canton, Ohio, where he became the close friend of another strong Republican lawyer named William McKinley. Throughout his long political career, McKinley relied on Day for legal and political advice. Day served as Secretary of State when McKinley became President and later was chairman of the peace commission that negotiated the treaty with Spain that ended the Spanish-American War. In 1899, President McKinley named Day to a federal circuit court of appeals. Three years later, McKinley elevated his friend to the Supreme Court. Day resigned from the Court in 1922 because of ill health.

WILLIAM O. DOUGLAS (1898–   ). The rise of William O. Douglas to prominence constitutes one of the most fabulous rags-to-riches success stories in the annals of American law. Douglas was born in Minnesota, but when he was only five, his father, a poor Presbyterian minister, died and the family moved to Yakima, Washington. There, young Douglas took a number of odd jobs to help support his mother and the two younger children. He worked his way through Whitman College, graduating with high scholastic honors. After two years of public school teaching, Douglas proceeded to New York City, on a freight train, to enroll in Columbia Law School. He arrived in New York with only six cents, but three years later, after a number of odd jobs, he had earned his law degree. During the next three years he practiced law and taught part-time at Columbia. In 1928, Douglas went to Yale to teach law and rose rapidly as a specialist in corporate reorganization and bankruptcy. While still at Yale, he directed studies of bankruptcy for the Hoover Administration. In 1936, he moved to Washington as a member of the Securities Exchange Commission. A year later he became chairman of the commission and proved himself to be a tough administrator who could get things done. When, in 1939, President Roosevelt named him to take the seat vacated by Justice Brandeis, Douglas became, at forty, the youngest man called to the Court in over a century. In 1944, Justice Douglas was considered seriously as the vice-presidential candidate on the Democratic ticket.

On the Court, Douglas has become best known as a defender of civil liberties. The cases in this book reveal clearly that Douglas and Black have teamed together as the chief opponents of laws limiting individual rights on both the Vinson and Warren Courts. Douglas also has championed the cause of labor and opposed bigness in both business and government. He has continued to write decisions involving complex financial questions in his usually clear and incisive style. In recent years, Douglas has become well known to many people outside the legal profession through his popular books about his extensive travels in Asia.

STEPHEN J. FIELD (1816–1899). The nearly thirty-five years that Stephen J. Field served on the Court correspond almost exactly "with the growing period of the conservative ideology. [W]hen he retired, conservatism had matured both as a philosophy and as a constitutional dogma. Field did not himself contrive this conservative triumph, of course, nor can we safely impute to him much direct influence on the mind of the nation. But he did profoundly influence the character of American law, and his judicial opinions provide an excellent illustration of conservatism in transition." For it is in Field's opinions that "we find the gospel of wealth framed in absolute moral terms. The gospel is not different in its essentials from the frankly materialistic rationale of William Graham Sumner. There is the same disregard for humane values, the same worship of success, the same standard of individual merit." [Robert G. McCloskey, *American*

Conservatism in the Age of Enterprise (Cambridge: Harvard University Press, 1951), pp. 87, 124.]

Field was admirably suited for his role as spokesman of rugged American individualism and laissez faire. He came from a distinguished Connecticut family, many of whose members had become important figures in their respective fields. After graduation from Williams College, Field studied law in the office of his brother, David Dudley, who was a leading New York lawyer. He completed his law studies in another office and, after admission to the bar, practiced law in New York with his brother. In 1849, Field sailed for California to seek his fortune in the gold rush. In his newly adopted state he rose rapidly. He developed a lucrative legal practice, was elected to the California legislature, and won a seat on the California Supreme Court in 1857. Two years later he was made chief judge of the California court and quickly became its dominant figure. Although he was a Democrat, Field joined the Union party at the outbreak of the Civil War and played an important part in keeping California loyal to the Union. When President Lincoln named Field to the Court in 1863, the California jurist had already emerged as a vigorous and commanding personality, albeit with a somewhat exalted opinion of himself.

Many disparities appear in Field's Supreme Court decisions. "[T]hey reflect a shift in value premises which is characteristic not only of Field but of his age. He began his judicial career with a general bias in favor of individual rights, and for a time no difficulties appeared. Before very long, however, this value system was complicated by discordances—his own growing political ambition and a special emphasis on the sanctity of economic freedom." In the hierarchy of values that finally emerged "the property right is the transcendent value; political ambition ranks next when it is relevant; and the cause of human or civil rights is subordinate to these higher considerations." (McCloskey, *supra*, pp. 122–23.) Justice Field's mind began to fail in the early 1890s, but he was extremely reluctant to retire. It has been said that his "independence and irascibility did not abate as his mental powers waned." [Willard L. King, *Melville Weston Fuller* (New York: Macmillan, 1950), p. 222.] Finally, in 1897, Justice Field reluctantly resigned from the Court.

ABE FORTAS (1910–   ). Mr. Justice Fortas is the fifth and youngest son of a relatively poor, Orthodox Jewish cabinet-maker who immigrated from England to Memphis, Tennessee. After receiving his B.A. from Southwestern College, he attended the Yale Law School where he graduated first in his class and was editor-in-chief of the *Yale Law Journal*. He was an assistant professor of Law at Yale, teaching with Professor, later Justice, Douglas from 1933 to 1937, while commuting to Washington to fulfill important part-time legal duties in the Agricultural Adjustment Administration and the Securities and Exchange Commission. In 1937, he became a full-time legal consultant to the SEC; he became, subsequently, assistant director of its public utilities division, general counsel to the Public Works Administration, director of the Division of Power of the Department of Interior, and, at the age of thirty-two, Under Secretary of the Interior. He was an advisor to the United States delegation to the San Francisco meetings that organized the United Nations and later attended the General Assembly meetings in London, in 1946. He left his post at Interior in that year to form a law partnership with Thurman Arnold, who had also had a brilliant legal career in public service. They were later joined by Paul Porter, still another highly talented New Deal lawyer. The firm of Arnold, Fortas and Porter soon became one of the most important in Washington, specializing in representing large business firms before the regulatory commissions and in the courts. During this period, Justice Fortas also was heavily engaged in civil liberties work, defending several State Department employees and others who had fallen afoul of the Red hunts of the Fifties. He was also defense counsel in the District of Columbia case that established a more liberal legal definition of insanity as a defense in criminal prosecutions (the "Durham" rule), and was the counsel who

argued *Gideon* v. *Wainwright,* establishing the right to counsel for indigents in state criminal cases, before the Supreme Court.

In 1948, he had represented Lyndon Johnson in a crucial legal battle arising out of his first campaign for the Senate. He subsequently handled some of Mr. Johnson's legal business and became one of the President's most intimate political advisors. Justice Fortas at first refused appointment to the Court but subsequently accepted under urgings by the President.

Justice Fortas thus brought to the Court an incredible array of legal experience, both in the civil liberties and government regulation of business areas, and direct experience of the viewpoint of both government official and legal representative of private interests. He combined this with an intimate knowledge of Washington politics in both the domestic and international spheres. This close connection with the legal and political affairs of Washington, which promised to bring to the Court a high level of skill and sophistication, turned out to be the cause of great personal tragedy to the Justice and a blow to the Court's prestige. Justice Fortas did not entirely break off the professional and political connections built up over thirty-five years in the Capitol. Most other Supreme Court justices had not, including such distinguished members of the Court as Taft and Hughes, nor would we wish the justices to divorce themselves totally from the world around them. In an area in which there are no historically acknowledged standards and in which the desire for an impartial judiciary is in potential conflict with the desire for knowledgeable and professionally engaged judicial personnel, Justice Fortas' continued professional activities outside the Court created embarrassment for the Court. In 1968 the Senate refused to advance Justice Fortas to the post of Chief Justice, and in 1969, under the threat of grave public scandal and possible impeachment, he resigned from the Court.

FELIX FRANKFURTER (1882–1965). Before he took his seat on the Supreme Court, Felix Frankfurter had already established a reputation as one of the ablest students of the American constitutional system. Frankfurter was born in Vienna but came to the United States with his family when he was twelve. He graduated from the City College of New York and obtained his law degree at Harvard in 1906. After admission to the bar, Frankfurter served as an assistant United States attorney in New York City under Henry L. Stimson. When Stimson went to Washington as Secretary of War, Frankfurter went along as law officer for the Bureau of Insular Affairs. In 1914, Frankfurter became a professor at Harvard Law School, where he remained until his nomination to the Supreme Court by President Roosevelt in 1939. At Harvard, Frankfurter became widely known as a creative and vigorous teacher. During his years at the university he emerged also as a prolific writer on constitutional law, administrative law, and public affairs. He was one of the founders of the American Civil Liberties Union, an organization designed to defend the legal rights of persons whose freedoms have been abridged. He also helped found the *New Republic,* a liberal journal. In 1932, Frankfurter declined an appointment to the Massachusetts Supreme Court in order to continue teaching. In the meantime, he urged his brighter students to enter public service, and a great number of these "happy hot dogs" obtained important jobs with the New Deal. Beginning in 1932, Frankfurter himself became one of President Roosevelt's most trusted and influential advisors.

Frankfurter was regarded as one of the ablest members of the Court, but he has also been severely criticized. It has been said that "he talks too much in conference, he procrastinates in writing opinions, he lectures his brethren, he harasses the attorneys. He knows more legal history than his colleagues and seldom lets them forget it. In the heat of argument he often cannot resist satirical or self-righteous remarks that offend more than he realizes. Moreover, his personal relationships tend to fall in a master-disciple pattern that creates emotional problems when the disciples strike out on their own." [Arthur M. Schlesinger, Jr., "The Supreme Court: 1947," *Fortune,* Vol. 35 (January 1947),

p. 76.] Unlike his hero Justice Holmes, Frankfurter devoted greater attention to small points and procedural or technical matters in his decisions. This meticulous attention to detail and his insistence on individual expression led Frankfurter to write numerous concurring and dissenting opinions. One well-known authority has suggested that Frankfurter "might have served his country better by remaining at Harvard Law School and continuing there to express himself individually, instead of joining the Court and engaging in the same form of activity. On the Court, the country might have been better served by a man who was humbler as far as self-expression was concerned, even if he proved somewhat less perceptive of finer legal shadings than those so artistically presented by the distinguished ex-professor." [Carl B. Swisher, "Needed: A Rededicated Court," *The Johns Hopkins Magazine,* Vol. 14 (1953), p. 28.] Frankfurter is difficult to classify, because he has voted with both the conservative and liberal blocs on questions of civil rights. Some of Frankfurter's opinions, such as his dissent in *West Virginia State Board of Education* v. *Barnette,* can be understood only in terms of his attachment to the doctrine of judicial self-restraint. He believes that legislative bodies should be allowed a wide range of discretion and that the Court should interfere with legislative enactments only as a last resort. [A good detailed examination of Frankfurter's judicial philosophy appears in Louis L. Jaffe, "The Judicial Universe of Mr. Justice Frankfurter," *Harvard Law Review,* Vol. 62 (1949), p. 357.]

Justice Frankfurter retired from the Court in 1962, after a long illness. His judicial philosophy is well demonstrated by his last dissenting opinion in the famous case of *Baker* v. *Carr* (Chapter 4).

MELVILLE WESTON FULLER (1833–1910). A descendant of a long line of New England intellectuals, Melville Weston Fuller was born in Augusta, Maine. Largely because of a surprising family tradition, Fuller was an active Democrat throughout his life. He graduated from Bowdoin College in 1853, and after reading law and a year of study at Harvard

Law School, he began to practice in Augusta. Because of complications at home, including a broken engagement, Fuller moved to Chicago in 1856 and, after some early setbacks, developed a highly respected and lucrative law practice. He turned down several offers to serve in the federal government but finally accepted the Chief Justiceship in 1888. Fuller developed into one of the Court's most competent administrators. His success as presiding officer "lay in his character rather than in his intellect. His mental attainments inspired respect—even admiration—but not awe. Nevertheless, he was an extraordinary Chief Justice in his relations with his colleagues. They fought for his good will. The bases for this relation were his deep humility, his sense of humor and humanity, his strict impartiality, his rare capacity for friendship, and his complete freedom from rancor. He had a strong habit of command, but the poison of power never affected him." [Willard L. King, *Melville Weston Fuller: Chief Justice of the United States, 1888–1910* (New York: Macmillan, 1950), p. 336.] Under Fuller, the Court came more and more to be regarded as a "citadel of economic conservatism," interested only in preserving the property rights of the rich. Fuller's own strong laissez-faire philosophy is revealed clearly by his opinions in the *Pollock* and *Knight* cases, which resulted in angry attacks on the Court.

ARTHUR J. GOLDBERG (1908–   ). A native of Chicago, Arthur J. Goldberg was named to the Court by President Kennedy to succeed the retiring Justice Frankfurter. Goldberg was the last of eleven children born into an extremely poor but closely knit and self-reliant family. As a youth he learned to work hard for success. He helped his father, who was a fruit and vegetable peddler on Chicago's West Side. Later he worked as a delivery boy and at other odd jobs. To pay his way through the Northwestern University Law School he wrote briefs for a Chicago law firm. After graduation at the age of twenty-one, Goldberg developed into a highly successful labor lawyer. He served as general counsel for the CIO and was

one of the architects of the AFL-CIO merger agreement. A lifelong Democrat, Goldberg was one of Kennedy's early supporters and worked vigorously to generate labor support for him during the 1960 presidential campaign. After the election, he became Secretary of Labor in the Kennedy cabinet and quickly acquired a reputation for jumping into and helping to settle all sorts of labor disputes. A vigorous liberal on social and political questions, it quickly became apparent that, as a Justice, Goldberg would not subscribe to the "self-restraint" philosophy of his predecessor, Justice Frankfurter. Goldberg usually voted with the liberal bloc on the Warren Court, which believed that the Court should take a more positive role in protecting individual liberties. He resigned from the Court in 1965 and became United States ambassador to the U.N., a post he held until 1968.

HORACE GRAY (1828–1902). Like Justices Holmes and Brandeis, Horace Gray went to the Supreme Court from Boston, where he was born. Gray took both his undergraduate and law training at Harvard and, after he was admitted to the bar, served as Reporter of the Supreme Court of Massachusetts. At the early age of thirty-six, he was appointed an associate justice of that court. Nine years later he became its chief justice. Gray, a Republican, was named to the Supreme Court by President Arthur in 1881. The appointment was widely acclaimed, because Gray's work on the Massachusetts Supreme Court had stamped him as one of the outstanding jurists of his day. He emerged as perhaps the Supreme Court's outstanding legal historian. He loved legal research, and his remarkable memory enabled him to recall numerous cases at a moment's notice. He also had the ability to synthesize quickly the ideas of the other justices. His opinion in the *Wong Kim Ark* case is one of his most powerful ones.

JOHN MARSHALL HARLAN (1833–1911). Although a former slave owner, and one who had opposed abolition, Harlan later championed the rights of Negroes, particularly in his powerful dissenting opinion in *Plessy* v. *Ferguson*. Harlan's dissent in the *Plessy* case and many of his decisions in other cases were based, in part, on his conviction that common sense rather than subtle refinements should be the basis for the Court's interpretation of the Constitution.

Justice Harlan was born in Kentucky, where his father, a distinguished lawyer, was a dominant figure in Whig politics. Young Harlan graduated from Centre College in Kentucky, studied law at Transylvania University, and was admitted to the bar in 1853. His only judicial experience prior to his appointment to the Supreme Court came in 1858, when he served as a county judge for one year. During the Civil War, Harlan fought with the Union forces as commander of a regiment of Kentucky volunteers. After the war, he supported the Thirteenth Amendment and became a leading force in Republican party politics. "Harlan's conversion to Republicanism was the most significant political choice he ever made, leading as it did to his eventual appointment to the Supreme Court. Actually, it was a choice that he drifted to rather than made freely." [Alan F. Westin, "John Marshall Harlan and the Constitutional Rights of Negroes: The Transformation of a Southerner," *Yale Law Journal*, Vol. 66 (1957), pp. 654–55.] Harlan was unsuccessful as Republican candidate for governor of Kentucky in 1871 and 1875, but his vigorous campaigns revitalized and united his party. He headed the Kentucky delegation to the Republican National Convention of 1876 and led the drive that gave Hayes the nomination. The next year President Hayes named Harlan to the Court.

He quickly emerged as an aggressive and courageous justice with a mind of his own. He was a frequent and forceful dissenter. "For all his stinging rebukes to his colleagues, his distaste for judicial legislation and his occasional impatience with the judicial process, Harlan maintained an unswerving faith in the role of the Supreme Court as defender of the citizen's liberties and guardian of American constitutional ideals. That the Supreme Court of the 1950s has become the guiding force of the new reconstruction, in the spirit of

his dissents on the segregation issue, may be seen as a particularly fitting vindication of John Marshall Harlan's faith." (Westin, *supra,* p. 710.)

JOHN MARSHALL HARLAN (1899–). President Eisenhower's second appointment to the Supreme Court was Justice Harlan, the grandson of the Kentucky jurist by the same name in the preceding biographical sketch. Harlan was born in Chicago and took his undergraduate training at Princeton. After graduation from Princeton, he was a Rhodes scholar and then studied law at New York Law School. A practicing attorney for more than thirty years, he emerged as a distinguished corporation lawyer with a prominent New York City law firm. As a Republican, Harlan was not politically active, but he was supported strongly for a judicial post by former New York Governor Thomas E. Dewey and other Republican stalwarts. He was named judge of a federal court of appeals in 1954 by President Eisenhower and was serving in that post when he was elevated to the Supreme Court. As demonstrated particularly by his opinion in *Yates* v. *United States,* Harlan's decisions are well reasoned and extremely methodical. With the retirement of Justice Frankfurter in 1962, Harlan appeared to be the leader of the judicial self-restraint bloc on the Court. See in particular his dissent in *Wesberry* v. *Sanders,* Chapter 4.

OLIVER WENDELL HOLMES, JR. (1841–1935). As noted in the biographical sketch of Justice Brandeis, Oliver Wendell Holmes, Jr., was essentially a skeptical conservative who had little interest in social reform. Yet, he aligned himself with Brandeis in numerous decisions because he felt that Supreme Court justices should not write their own economic notions in the Constitution or interfere with social experimentation. "He scrupulously treated the Constitution as a broad charter of powers for the internal clashes of society, and did not construe it as though it were a code which prescribed in detail answers for the social problems of all time. Thus, the enduring contribution of Mr. Justice Holmes to American history is his constitutional philosophy. He gave it momentum by the magic with which he expressed it." [Felix Frankfurter, *Mr. Justice Holmes and the Supreme Court*, (Cambridge: Harvard University Press, 1938), p. 28.]

Holmes was well equipped to become the Court's philosopher of the law and the country's best-known and most revered justice. He was born in Boston, the son of Oliver Wendell Holmes, the distinguished physician and poet who was at the center of the literary and intellectual life of Boston. Immediately after graduating from Harvard, the future justice joined the Union army and was wounded three times. After his release from service, Holmes studied law at Harvard and was admitted to the bar in 1867. He practiced law in Boston for fifteen years. During this time Holmes also made important contributions to legal philosophy and legal history through a number of his published writings. He was appointed to the Supreme Court of Massachusetts in 1882 and served there with distinction for twenty years, the last three as chief justice. "The stream of li litigation that flowed through such an important tribunal as the Supreme Judicial Court of Massachusetts during the twenty years of his incumbency enabled Holmes to fertilize the whole vast field of law. Although questions came before him in the unpremeditated order of litigation, his Massachusetts opinions—nearly 1300—would, if appropriately brought together, constitute the most comprehensive and philosophical body of American law for any period of its history." (Frankfurter, *Of Law and Men, op. cit.*, p. 170.) Holmes was already sixty-one years old when President Theodore Roosevelt named him to the Supreme Court in 1902, but he was destined to serve there for thirty years and to make perhaps the most significant contributions to American constitutional law since John Marshall's time.

CHARLES EVANS HUGHES (1862–1948). It has been said of Charles Evans Hughes that "he was the kind of man that the American people require every generation if they are to avoid the fate that Ben Franklin feared—sinking into a despotism from an excess of democracy." [Herbert Elliston, "The Integrity of Justice Hughes," *The Atlantic* (April 1952), p. 75.] Hughes undoubtedly had one of the most distinguished public careers in American history. "Few men, in our or any other age, have packed so much and such superlative accomplishment into a single lifetime as did Charles Evans Hughes." (338 U.C. at xxiii.) Hughes, whose father was a Baptist minister, was born in Glen Falls, New York. Upon his graduation from Brown University and Columbia University School of Law, he was admitted to the bar at the early age of twenty-two. He enjoyed a "happy interlude" of teaching law at Cornell and, in 1905, gained prominence as special counsel for a state legislative committee investigating the insurance business. Hughes' fearless devotion to public duty won him the Republican nomination for governor of New York. He was elected to that office in 1906, and reelected in 1908. In 1910, he was appointed an associate justice of the Supreme Court and served on the bench until 1916, when he resigned to become the Republican presidential nominee. After his defeat by the slender margin of California's electoral vote, Hughes returned to active practice in New York City. He was named Secretary of State by President Harding in 1921, and also served in that post in the Coolidge cabinet until 1925. Three years later he was elected a judge of the Permanent Court of International Justice. He served on that tribunal until named to the chief-justiceship by President Hoover.

Hughes undoubtedly ranks as one of the great chief justices. It has been noted often that it is principally for his work as chief justice that he will become an enduring judicial figure. "He took his seat at the center of the Court with a mastery unparalleled in the history of the Court, a mastery that derived from his experience, as diversified, intense, and extensive as any man ever brought to a seat on the Court, combined with a very powerful and acute mind that would mobilize these vast resources in the conduct of the business of the Court." (Frankfurter, *Of Law and Men, op. cit.*, p. 133.) Hughes served as Chief Justice during a period of great social and political ferment. "At a time when there was a tendency to dismiss constitutionalism as being old-fashioned and to strain the balance of power on which our political system as well as our freedom rests, his judicialmindedness was a powerful restraint upon excesses. At the same time his sensitivity to the pulsing relationship between life and the law helped to save the country from economic and social atrophy. As Marshall in his day was the great expounder of the Constitution, Hughes in this century has been at once the great conservator of our political system and a tireless modernizer of outmoded judicial concepts." [Merlo J. Pusey in A. Dunham and P. B. Kurland (ed.), *Mr. Justice* (Chicago: University of Chicago Press, 1956), p. 173.]

ROBERT H. JACKSON (1892–1954). Born on a farm in Pennsylvania, Robert H. Jackson was destined to become a fighting country lawyer and to emerge as one of the most prominent figures of his day. When Jackson was five years old, he moved with his family to a small village near Jamestown, New York. He did not attend college. In referring to his legal education, Jackson once remarked that he was a "vestigial remnant of the system which permitted one to come to the bar by way of apprenticeship in a law office. Except for one term at law school [Albany Law College], I availed myself of that method of preparation which already was causing uneasiness—to which feeling I must have added, for the system was almost immediately abolished. You may be comforted to realize that I am the last relic of that method likely to find a niche on the Supreme Court." (349 U.S. at xxxi.) Jackson developed a lucrative and varied practice in Jamestown, where he served as counsel for railroad and telephone companies, the local bank, and the city itself. As a Democrat in a Republican stronghold, Jackson had little chance to become an influential political figure until Franklin D. Roosevelt became President. Then he went to Washington, in 1934, as general counsel for the Bureau of Internal Revenue. Two years later he was appointed as assistant attorney general in charge of the Tax Division of the Depart-

ment of Justice. Shortly thereafter he was placed in charge of the Department's Antitrust Division. During this period, Jackson strongly supported President Roosevelt's attempt to reorganize the judiciary. In 1938, Jackson was made Solicitor General, and two years later he became Attorney General of the United States. He was elevated to the Court in 1941. Jackson took a leave of absence from the Court for more than eighteen months in 1945 to serve as chief prosecutor for the United States in the controversial trials of Nazi war criminals in Nuremberg. He once stated that "the hard months at Nuremberg were spent in the most enduring and constructive work of my life." (349 U.S. at xl.)

Despite, or perhaps because of, his meager formal education, Jackson's opinions reveal a fine literary style and verbal brilliance. He wrote with clarity and freshness. His eloquent style is demonstrated well by his opinion in *Board of Education* v. *Barnett*. "He wrote as he talked, and he talked as he felt. The fact that his opinions were written talk made them as lively as the liveliness of his talk. Unlike what he praised in Brandeis, his style sometimes stole attention from the substance." [Felix Frankfurter, "Mr. Justice Jackson," *Harvard Law Review*, Vol. 68 (1955), p. 938.] Jackson's opinions "show a deep concern over the difficult problem of accommodating the sometimes conflicting purposes of maintaining freedom of the individual and, at the same time, a stable order of society under the reign of a rule of law. But he was generally on the side of full application of the Bill of Rights until he was convinced that the rule of law was seriously threatened." (349 U.S. at xli.)

HORACE H. LURTON (1844–1914). When he took his seat on the Court at the age of sixty-six, Justice Lurton was the oldest man ever appointed to the highest tribunal. President Taft named Lurton to the Court despite protests that he was too old and that he was a narrow conservative who was unwilling to interpret the law to meet changing conditions. A native of Kentucky, Lurton studied at the University of Chicago and took his legal training at Cumberland University in Tennessee. He fought in the Confederate Army, practiced law, and served on the Tennessee Supreme Court. In 1893, Lurton, who was nominally a Democrat, was appointed to a federal circuit court by President Cleveland. There he became a close associate and intimate friend of Taft, who was serving as presiding judge. When he became President, Taft named Lurton to fill the first vacancy on the Court. "Taft had great respect for Judge Lurton's legal talents. But it seems probable that affection born of years of association on the circuit bench was also a motivating influence." [Henry F. Pringle, *The Life and Times of William Howard Taft* (New York: Farrer & Rinehart, 1939), Vol. 1, p. 530.]

JOHN MARSHALL (1755–1835). It is generally conceded that Marshall stands without rival as our greatest Chief Justice. His enduring contributions in building the foundations of American constitutional government have been summarized in Chapter 1. More has been written about Marshall than any other justice in our history. A recent bibliography of books, articles, and pamphlets by and about Marshall covers nearly 150 printed pages. [James A. Servies, compiler, *A Bibliography of John Marshall,* (Washington, D.C.: Bicentennial Commission, 1956).] All that can be done here is to note briefly some of the high points of Marshall's life. He was born in 1755 in a frontier farm cabin in Virginia, the eldest of fifteen children. Marshall's only formal education consisted of two months of law lectures at the College of William and Mary. He served with the Virginia Minutemen and later joined Washington's Continental Army, where he served for four years. "It was during these four years of fighting and privation that Marshall received his first great object lesson in the necessity for a strong national government and in the fatal inefficiency of the state governments. So it is that the roots of *McCulloch* v. *Maryland* run back to Valley Forge and the dark and desperate days through which John Marshall passed before and after." [Albert J. Beveridge in Erwin C. Surrency

(ed.), *The Marshall Reader* (New York: Oceana Publications, 1955), p. 37.] In 1780, Marshall was admitted to the Virginia bar, and two years later he was elected to the state legislature, where he served for a number of years. As a strong supporter of the Constitution, Marshall's arguments helped to secure Virginia's ratification. After serving as an astute member of the XYZ Commission, which attempted to adjust international differences with France, Marshall was elected to the House of Representatives on the Federalist ticket. He resigned his seat in Congress to become President Adams' Secretary of State in 1800. Marshall served in that post until he was named Chief Justice in 1801. Like his army service, all of Marshall's experience in public life "carried him steadily toward that final national and conservative state of mind which we find expressed in his opinions from the bench." His opinions grew out of the great and grim events of his life, which had taught him that the "blessings of life, liberty and the pursuit of happiness can only be secured and provided by a strong, orderly national government." (Beveridge, *supra,* pp. 42, 43, 44.)

THURGOOD MARSHALL (1908–   ). The second Mr. Justice Marshall received his A.B. degree from Lincoln University in 1930 and his law degree from Howard University at the time Howard was training that generation of civil rights lawyers who have changed the face of the nation. Justice Marshall became Assistant Special Counsel to the NAACP in 1936 and was Special Counsel from 1938 to 1950. He was Director of the NAACP Legal Defense and Education Fund from 1940 to 1961. During this time he was involved in hundreds of major cases argued before the Supreme Court and lower courts. He might well claim to be the most successful advocate before the Supreme Court since Daniel Webster. He served as a judge of the Court of Appeals for the Second Circuit from 1962 to 1965 and as Solicitor General of the United States from 1965 to 1967. His appointments to the circuit and the Supreme Court were delayed in the Senate, but it was impossible to fault his professional qualifications. He has had more experience as an advocate before the bench on which he now sits than any other of the serving justices. To call him the first Negro "this" or "that" would be to belittle accomplishments of which any man could be proud at any time.

JAMES C. McREYNOLDS (1862–1946). When Justice McReynolds was appointed to the Court in 1914, he was generally regarded as a Wilsonian antitrust liberal. Upon his retirement twenty-seven years later he was the most die-hard member of the conservative group. In the intervening years the world had changed, but McReynolds remained "an enduring rock of fixed location." (334 U.S. at xix.) Born in Kentucky, the son of a plantation owner and physician, McReynolds was graduated with high honors from Vanderbilt University and the University of Virginia Law School. Until middle life he practiced law in Nashville, Tennessee, where he was known as a moral reformer. During these years he also served as a member of the law school faculty of Vanderbilt University. McReynolds ran unsuccessfully for Congress as an anti-Bryan Gold Democrat in 1896. In 1903, he became assistant attorney general under President Theodore Roosevelt in charge of antitrust prosecutions. During the next few years McReynolds' successful prosecution of many important cases won him the reputation of a vigorous trust-buster. In 1913, he became Attorney General in President Wilson's cabinet. In 1914, after a stormy career in that post, the President named him to the Supreme Court.

On the bench, McReynolds became a sincere but grim and determined exponent of rugged individualism. His legal philosophy called for "strict construction of constitutionally granted powers, vigorous defense of States' rights, and for narrow confinement of governmental interference with individual freedom of action. His literary style, characteristic of the man, was terse, direct and clear, yet capable of translating to the reader the conviction and fervor with which his views were expressed." (334 U.S. at xxii, xxiii.) Although Justice Holmes confessed a fond-

ness for McReynolds, his gruff and ill-tempered manner, as well as his petty hatreds, did not endear him to many of his brethren. Chief Justice Taft described him as a man with "a continual grouch" who "seemed to delight in making others uncomfortable." (Pringle, *op. cit.,* Vol. 2, p. 971.)

SAMUEL F. MILLER (1816–1890). Despite the fact that he went to the Supreme Court with very little legal training and without ever having held public office, Justice Miller emerged as one of the few great figures on the Court. Many writers of his day ranked Miller second only to John Marshall. Born in Kentucky, Miller received a medical degree in 1838, and practiced medicine in his native state for nearly a decade. But his keen interest in politics led him to abandon medicine in favor of the law. While still a practicing physician, Miller began to read law, and in 1847 he was admitted to the Kentucky bar. In 1850, however, Miller, who was then a Whig, moved to Iowa because his state refused to end slavery. As a bitter opponent of slavery, Miller had sought without success to bring about a gradual emancipation of the slaves in his home state. In Iowa, he became a successful practicing attorney and helped organize the Republican party. Although he was practically unknown outside of Iowa, President Lincoln named Miller to the Court in 1862. He thus became the first Supreme Court justice from west of the Mississippi River. Long considered the best of Lincoln's judicial appointments, Miller was an independent, logical thinker of keen intelligence. In general, he was a strong nationalist and defender of personal liberties. As indicated by the *Slaughter House Cases,* he also believed that the scope of judicial review should be limited so that the people and the other organs of government could assume their respective responsibilities.

SHERMAN   MINTON   (1890–1965). President Truman's last appointee to the Supreme Court was Justice Minton, who was the only member of that tribunal with extensive prior judicial experience when he retired in 1956. Minton had served previously for more than eight years as a federal court of appeals judge. A native of Indiana, Minton studied law at the University of Indiana and Yale. After his admission to the bar, he practiced law in Indiana and became active in the Democratic party. An ardent supporter of the New Deal, Minton was elected to the United States Senate in 1934 and took his seat just next to another new senator, Harry S. Truman. The two men became fast friends. Minton was defeated for reelection to the Senate in 1940, but he later became one of President Roosevelt's administrative assistants. In 1941, Roosevelt named him to a federal court of appeals. Truman promoted his old Senate colleague to the Court in 1949. Minton's opinions in this book reveal clearly that, unlike his predecessor Justice Rutledge, he gave little support to the judicial expansion and protection of civil rights. In clashes between claims of individual freedom and governmental authority, he usually voted against libertarian claims.

FRANK MURPHY (1890–1949). Born in Michigan of devout Roman Catholic parents, Justice Murphy is best remembered as a devoted defender of civil liberties. One of Murphy's warmest admirers has stated that the late justice was the embodiment of the "persistent American ideal of human justice. He consistently, and with effective prose, sought to establish or to reinforce in American law basic constitutional principles of human freedom, and basic principles of social justice." [John P. Frank, "Justice Murphy: The Goals Attempted," *Yale Law Journal*, Vol. 51 (1949), p. 26.] Both Justices Rutledge and Murphy were strong exponents of the doctrine that the First Amendment freedoms should have a preferred position in the constitutional scheme. Justice Murphy believed firmly that the protection of individual liberties was the Court's most important function. As indicated by his separate opinions in *Korematsu* v. *United States* and *In re Yamashita,* Murphy was almost invariably on

the side of the underdog. "Time and again he spoke eloquently on behalf of the constitutional and legal rights of the accused, the unpopular, and the oppressed." (340 U.S. at xii.) Murphy's attitude toward civil rights is summarized well in one of his own statements, made in a dissenting opinion in *Falbo* v. *United States,* 320 U.S. 549 (1944). There he remarked: "The law knows no finer hour than when it cuts through formal concepts and transitory emotions to protect unpopular citizens against discrimination and persecution."

Murphy took both his undergraduate and legal education at the University of Michigan. After admission to the bar, he practiced law in Detroit, saw service in World War I, worked in the Detroit office of the federal district attorney, and was elected to the Recorder's Court, a criminal court in Detroit. In 1930, he was elected mayor of Detroit, where he attracted national attention through his efforts to help the unemployed. Always a staunch Democrat, Murphy was appointed Governor General of the Philippines in 1933 by President Roosevelt. When the Islands were given commonwealth status, Murphy remained as the first High Commissioner. He returned home in 1936 to become the successful Democratic candidate for governor of Michigan. Shortly after his defeat for reelection in 1939, Murphy was appointed Attorney General of the United States. While in that office he established the Civil Rights Section in the Department of Justice to help individuals whose personal liberties had been violated. In 1940, President Roosevelt named Murphy to the Court.

RUFUS W. PECKHAM (1838–1909). A vigorous, independent, and outspoken person, Justice Peckham is best remembered for his opinion in *Lockner* v. *New York,* where he revealed clearly his strong attachment to a laissez-faire economic theory that is no longer generally accepted. Throughout his long judicial career, Peckham was a strong opponent of social and economic legislation. Born in Albany, New York, Peckham came from a family of lawyers and judges. His father was a judge of the New York Court of Appeals, the highest state court. Although Peckham had some formal college training, he never received a degree. He studied law in his father's office and was admitted to the bar in 1859. After twenty-four years of successful law practice in Albany, Peckham, a Democrat, was elected to the New York Supreme Court. In 1886, he was elected to the state court of appeals. He was serving on that tribunal when President Cleveland named him to the Supreme Court in 1895.

STANLEY F. REED (1884–   ). When he was named to the Court by President Roosevelt in 1938, Stanley F. Reed was known as a New Dealer. Upon his retirement in 1957, however, he was one of the most conservative and least venturesome members of the Court. He has been described as a "moderate progressive," a "good middle-of-the-road," and a "swing man." Born in Kentucky, Reed took his undergraduate training at Kentucky Wesleyan College and Yale. After law studies at the University of Virginia, Columbia, and the University of Paris, Reed was admitted to the bar and began to practice law in his home county. He became active in the Democratic party and, in 1912, was elected to the Kentucky legislature, where he sponsored the state's child labor and workmen's compensation laws. He continued to practice law until 1929, when he became general counsel for the Federal Farm Bureau in the Hoover administration. From 1932 to 1935 he held the same position with the Reconstruction Finance Corporation. In 1935, Reed became Solicitor General and served in that capacity until his appointment to the Court. As Solicitor General, Reed argued effectively before the Court in favor of the most important New Deal measures. His vigorous defense of New Deal legislation and his loyalty to the Roosevelt administration made him a logical choice to succeed Justice Sutherland. Despite Reed's landmark decision in *Smith* v. *Allwright,* he generally voted against the claims of individual rights. On the Vinson Court, Reed joined Justices Vinson, Burton, Clark, and Minton to form that Court's antilibertarian majority.

OWEN J. ROBERTS (1875–1955). When he retired from the Court, Justice Roberts wrote: "I have no illusions about my judicial career. But one can only do what one can. Who am I to revile the good God that he did not make me a Marshall, a Taney, a Bradley, a Holmes, a Brandeis, or a Cardozo." Justice Frankfurter has suggested that in comparing himself unfavorably with the Court's most distinguished members, Roberts underestimated his own important contributions to American constitutional law. Frankfurter has remarked that "no man ever served on the Supreme Court with more scrupulous regard for its moral demands that Mr. Justice Roberts." (Frankfurter, *Of Law and Men, op. cit.,* p. 212.) One of Roberts' most significant contributions was his opinion in *Nebbia* v. *New York*. His courageous decision in the case "was an effective blow for liberation from empty tags and meretricious assumptions. In effect, Roberts wrote the epitaph on the misconception, which had gained respect from repetition, that legislative price-fixing as such was at least presumptively unconstitutional." (Frankfurter, *supra,* p. 211.) Roberts will undoubtedly be best remembered as the "swing man" when the controversial New Deal legislation came before the Court. As the Court's "middle man," he held the balance of power between the conservative and liberal blocs.

Roberts was born and reared in Philadelphia. Both his undergraduate and law degrees were obtained from the University of Pennsylvania, where he taught law from the time he received his law degree in 1898 until 1919. He abandoned teaching to devote full time to the lucrative law practice which had developed during his years at the University. In 1924, Roberts, a Republican, became nationally known when he was appointed by President Coolidge as a special prosecutor in the Teapot Dome oil scandal. He was named to the Court in 1930 by President Hoover. After his retirement from the bench in 1945, Roberts often spoke out forthrightly on public issues and served as dean of the University of Pennsylvania Law School for four years.

WILEY B. RUTLEDGE (1894–1949).

Although he was the least known of President Roosevelt's appointees to the Court, Wiley B. Rutledge's judicial and scholarly experience made him a logical choice for the seat vacated by Justice Byrnes. Rutledge was born in Kentucky, the son of a circuit-riding Baptist minister. He attended Maryville College in Tennessee and completed his undergraduate work at the University of Wisconsin in 1914. During the next eight years Rutledge financed his legal education by teaching in a number of public schools. He obtained his law degree in 1922 at the University of Colorado. After a brief period of private practice, he began a successful career as law teacher and law school administrator, first at the University of Colorado in 1924, then, two years later, at Washington University (St. Louis) School of Law, where he served as a teacher and dean. In 1935, Rutledge became dean of the University of Iowa Law School. As a teacher and dean, Rutledge was well known for his sincere and genuine interest in students. He remained at the University of Iowa until 1939, when President Roosevelt named him to the Court of Appeals of the District of Columbia. Four years later Rutledge, a Democrat, was promoted to the Supreme Court.

Rutledge was a man of great warmth and humility who "was most widely known and is most vividly remembered for his staunch position in the protection of individual civil liberties. He was convinced that there is an irreducible number of liberties that occupy a preferred position. He insisted that the preferred position of the indispensable freedoms secured by the First Amendment gives them a sanctity and a sanction not permitting dubious intrusions." (341 U.S. at x.) But his insistence that First Amendment freedoms should occupy a preferred position did not mean that he regarded procedural rights as any less important. "There was no hierarchy of values among civil liberties

for Rutledge. They were all primary, for they were all bulwarks of human dignity. To Rutledge, the vast expansion of governmental power in social and economic matters required correspondingly greater protection of civil liberties. The impact of the massive political community on individuality must be cushioned by comprehensive safeguards of personal liberty if the promises of democratic life are to remain meaningful. Big government can remain healthy only if civil liberties are rigorously protected. To him the protection of personal liberty was the most vital responsibility of the Court." [Landon G. Rockwell, "Justice Rutledge on Civil Liberties," *Yale Law Journal,* Vol. 59 (December 1949), p. 58.] Rutledge's vigorous defense of individual freedom is best demonstrated by his eloquent dissent in the *Yamashita* case (Chapter 16).

EDWARD T. SANFORD (1865–1930).

A little-known but unusually charming and gentle man, Edward T. Sanford was born in Knoxville, Tennessee. He was graduated from the University of Tennessee and received his law degree from Harvard in 1889. A southern Republican, he returned to Knoxville to practice law and participate actively in politics. In 1908, President Theodore Roosevelt named Sanford to a federal district court, where he remained until elevated to the Supreme Court by President Harding in 1923. Although less vigorous in embracing conservatism than Justices Sutherland and Butler, Sanford usually aligned himself with the Court's conservative wing. An ardent admirer of Chief Justice Taft, Sanford often followed Taft's lead in important cases. The two men died almost simultaneously on March 8, 1930.

POTTER STEWART (1915–   ).

President Eisenhower's fifth appointee to the Court was Potter Stewart, who, at the age of forty-three, was the youngest man appointed to the Court in 105 years with the exception of Justice Douglas. Like Justice Burton, whom he replaced on the Court, Stewart was an Ohio Republican. Born in Cincinnati, Stewart's family was well known in Republican circles. His father, a lawyer, served as mayor of Cincinnati and later as a judge on the Ohio Supreme Court, Stewart graduated from Yale, spent a year in England at Cambridge University on a fellowship, and then entered Yale Law School, graduating in 1941. He practiced law for a short time in New York, saw service as a Navy lieutenant in World War II, and after another brief interlude in New York, returned to Cincinnati to practice law. He became active in local politics and was twice elected to the city council. In 1954, President Eisenhower named him to the Court of Appeals for the Sixth Circuit. On that Court Stewart quickly gained a reputation for clear, concise opinions.

When named to the Court, Stewart was described as both a liberal and a conservative. Though he prefers to disregard labels, Stewart has usually voted with the "judicial self-restraint" bloc on the Warren Court. In recent years, he has attracted considerable attention because of his dissents in the school prayer cases. Stewart's work on the Court to date seems to bear out an early appraisal made on his appointment. It was said at that time that Stewart "does not have the passion of a Black or Murphy in fashioning a new rampart. Neither does he have the feeling one senses in Harlan of puzzlement and wonder at a strange, new landscape. And, certainly, he does not smart under the disillusionment that gave overtones of tragedy to Jackson's career. The point of all this perhaps is that Stewart will bring few new values within the compass of the law. But the point is also that he can be relied on not to depreciate those values he finds already there. . . . Happily, he inherits a more spacious legal world than his predecessors. Perhaps his great task—and eventually his great achievement—will be to contribute toward making that legal world an orderly one." [J. Francis Paschal, "Mr. Justice Stewart on the Court of Appeals," *Duke Law Journal*, Vol. 1959 (1959), p. 340.]

HARLAN F. STONE (1872–1946). Although he was considered by many to be a conservative Republican, Justice Stone could not be classified either as a con-servative or a liberal. "No tag seemed to fit. Harlan Fiske Stone was a judge, a dispassionate interpreter of the law of which he was a 'well-deserving pillar.' " [Alpheus T. Mason, *Harlan Fiske Stone: Pillar of the Law* (New York: *Viking Press, 1956*), p. 809.] Born in New Hampshire and brought up in Massachusetts, Stone "always seemed the embodiment of the traditional New England virtues—frugal in habits, careful in his conduct and sturdy in his judgment." (333 U.S. at vii.) Because Stone's early interest seemed to be in farming, he enrolled in the Massachusetts Agricultural College. But he was expelled from that institution for some boisterous prank and entered Amherst College to prepare for a medical career. However, after graduation from Amherst, he taught science in a New England public school for a year and then worked his way through the School of Law at Columbia University. He was admitted to the bar in 1898, and then taught part-time at Columbia while practicing law in New York City. He subsequently gave up teaching to devote all his energies to his growing law practice, but he returned to Columbia in 1910 as dean of the Law School. He left that post in 1923, when he again decided to devote all of his time to private law practice. In 1924, President Coolidge, who had been with Stone at Amherst, named him Attorney General of the United States, A year later Coolidge elevated his former college mate to the Court. President Roosevelt named Stone Chief Justice in 1941, upon the retirement of Charles Evans Hughes.

As a highly respected member of the Court, Stone is remembered for his work as an associate justice rather than for his achievements as chief justice simply because, as presiding officer, he was unable to lead the Court as effectively as his distinguished predecessor. Like Marshall, Stone looked upon the Constitution as a broad charter of government "intended to endure for ages to come, and, consequently, to be adapted to the various crises of human affairs." He believed that the provisions of the Constitution were to be read "not with the narrow literalness of a municipal code or a penal statute, but so that its high purposes should illumine every sentence and phrase of the document and be given effect as a part of a harmonious framework of government." Stone was always faithful to "his conviction that the Constitution had not adopted any particular set of social and economic ideas, to the exclusion of others, which however wrong they seemed to him, fair-minded men yet might hold." (333 U.S. at xi, xii.) His conception of the judicial function is revealed clearly in his famous dissenting opinion in *United States* v. *Butler.*

JOSEPH STORY (1779–1845). With the exception of Marshall himself, the two outstanding figures on the Marshall Court were William Johnson and Joseph Story. Both thirty-two years old when named to the Court, they were the two youngest men ever elevated to the position of Associate Justice. But unlike Johnson, Story was a consistent supporter of Marshall's basic philosophy.

Born of a well-to-do family in Massachusetts, Story graduated from Harvard in 1798. Witty, well-bred, and hardworking, Story soon became well known as a lawyer, banker, and politician. He served several terms in the Massachusetts legislature and was elected to Congress to fill an unexpired term. In 1811, President Madison named Story to the Court against the wishes of ex-President Jefferson, who wrote that Story was a "tory and too young." Although, on paper, Story was a Republican, he had strong Federalist leanings. As Jefferson had feared and much to Madison's regret, Story's early Republican sympathies were displaced by the nationalism of the Federalist after he went on the bench. Story became one of the best-known scholars of his day, for in addition to his duties on the Court he served as Professor of Law at Harvard and wrote many commentaries on the law that were widely read. It is commonly believed that Marshall relied on Story for scholarly arguments to buttress some of his judgments. When Taney became Chief Justice in 1835, upon the death of Marshall, Story, like Daniel Webster, felt that

the Court was doomed. He thought of himself as the "last of the old race of judges" whose duty it was to preserve Marshall's conception of the Constitution. His powerful and agonizing dissent in the *Charles River Bridge* case against what he considered the Court's repudiation of the *Dartmouth College* case is an example in point. Much to his surprise, however, Story later realized that Taney did not break radically with the Marshall Court.

GEORGE SUTHERLAND (1862–1942). It is generally agreed that George Sutherland was the strongest of the four conservative justices who bitterly opposed the New Deal. Although Sutherland was devoted completely to the idea of laissez faire and opposed the expansion of governmental powers in domestic affairs, he wrote the important opinion in *United States* v. *Curtiss-Wright Corp.,* which upheld the exercise of broad presidential powers in the area of foreign relations. He also made a significant contribution to the protection of individual liberty by his opinion in *Powell* v. *Alabama.* Born in England, Sutherland was brought to America by his parents at an early age. He grew up in the pioneer community which later became the state of Utah. Sutherland's philosophy sprang from this frontier environment, "where the nineteenth century still lingered, untouched by the impact of life under conditions of modern mass production." (323 U.S. at xv.) He attended the University of Michigan Law School for one year and was admitted to the bar in 1883. For a number of years he practiced law in Utah and was active in the Republican party. It was in politics that Sutherland was destined to make his mark. He became a member of the first state legislature when Utah was admitted into the Union in 1896. He later served one term in the House of Representatives, and from 1905 to 1917 he was a member of the United States Senate. Sutherland was a delegate from Utah to the Republican National Convention on a number of occasions and was Harding's principal advisor in the campaign of 1920. He also served as president of the American Bar

Association for one year and was recognized as a leading authority on constitutional questions. President Harding named Sutherland to the Court in 1922.

Sutherland's devotion to the idea of laissez faire is best revealed by his opinion in the *Adkins* case. "He was profoundly convinced that ill-considered experimentation in government in pursuit of passing fashions in legislation, and the loose governmental control of administrative officers, would in the end prove to be the real enemies of true democracy, and a grave danger to constitutional government." (323 U.S. at xix.) Sutherland "was a heretic in two important respects. He had no faith in majority rule or in the efficacy of government. The judgment for the twentieth century is against him on both counts. Therefore, his record is for us today largely irrelevant. But his career demonstrates that even the heretic has his uses. We forget this at our peril." (Paschel, "Mr. Justice Sutherland," in *Mr. Justice, op. cit.,* p. 143.)

WILLIAM HOWARD TAFT (1857–1930). The amiable and jovial William Howard Taft was the only man in American history who was both President and Chief Justice. Born in Ohio of an illustrious family, Taft graduated from Yale University and Cincinnati Law School. Shortly after his admission to the bar, he embarked upon one of the most varied and remarkable careers in American public affairs. After serving as assistant prosecuting attorney in Hamilton County, Ohio, Taft was appointed judge of the Superior Court of Cincinnati in 1887. Three years later, President Harrison named Taft, a loyal Republican, Solicitor General of the United States. Taft served in that post until his appointment at the early age of thirty-five to a federal circuit court. He resigned his federal judgeship in 1900 to head the Philippine Commission, which was to organize and establish the new civil government of the Islands. The next year he became the Philippines' first Civil Governor. He left that post in 1904 to become President Theodore Roosevelt's Secretary of War. With the help and sup-port of Roosevelt, Taft was elected President of the United States in 1908. Later Roosevelt abandoned his protégé and ran against him in a three-cornered race in which both lost to Woodrow Wilson. After 1912, Taft taught constitutional law at Yale Law School and became president of the American Bar Association. He fulfilled a lifelong ambition when President Harding named him Chief Justice in 1921.

Taft was a conservative, property-minded justice, but he was not an extreme reactionary. He believed firmly that each branch of the national government should be allowed to exercise broad powers without interference from the others or from the state governments. As Chief Justice, Taft will long be remembered as a law reformer. Not only did he take the lead in securing the adoption of legislation designed to improve the administration of the lower federal courts, but he also was largely responsible for the Judges Bill of 1925, which gave the Court almost complete discretionary control of its own appellate business.

ROGER B. TANEY (1777–1864). In the long history of the Supreme Court no justice has been more roundly denounced and so grossly misrepresented as Roger Brooke Taney. In opposing a bill providing funds for a Taney bust in the courtroom, Charles Sumner rose on the Senate floor to proclaim that "the name of Taney is to be hooted down the page of history. Judgment is beginning now; and an emancipated country will fasten upon him the stigma which he deserves. . . . He administered justice at least wickedly, and degraded the Judiciary of the country, and degraded the age." (*Congressional Globe,* 38th. Cong., 2d. sess., p. 1012). Although this unflattering picture of Taney persisted for many years, it is now clear that Taney was a much better Chief Justice than his critics would have us believe. In fact, he is regarded today as a great Chief Justice.

Taney was born on a prosperous tobacco plantation in Calvert County, Maryland, on March 17, 1777. Both his parents were staunch Roman Catholics and descendants of some of Maryland's earliest settlers. Taney's early years were thus spent in the comfortable social environment of the Maryland landed aristocracy. After graduation from Dickinson College in Carlisle, Pennsylvania, he returned to Maryland, was admitted to the bar, and practiced law in Frederick and Baltimore for over twenty years. Though originally a staunch Federalist, Taney became an active supporter of Andrew Jackson and one of his warmest friends and most trusted advisors. As Secretary of the Treasury in the Jackson cabinet, Taney played the leading role in the Administration's spectacular battle with the Bank of the United States. Largely because of his part in that battle, the Senate refused to confirm his appointment as Associate Justice, but he later won confirmation as Chief Justice after a bitter three-month struggle along party lines.

Taney's constitutional philosophy has been outlined briefly in Chapter 1. In general, he attempted to steer a middle course between the nationalism of John Marshall and the extreme radicalism of some of the Jacksonians. With the unfortunate exception of his *Dred Scott* decision, Taney believed firmly in the principle of judicial self-restraint. Had it not been for that tragic decision, the legend that Taney was a second-rate Chief Justice would never have taken root in American history and survived for so long. Taney delivered his last great opinion in *Ex Parte Merryman* where he revealed uncommon courage in striking "the first mighty blow in federal court history on behalf of individual liberties." [See Chapter 1 of Rocco J. Tresolini, *Justice and the Supreme Court* (Philadelphia: J. B. Lippincott, 1963).]

WILLIS VAN DEVANTER (1859–1941). The first of the "nine old men" to retire from the Court, Van Devanter's laissez-faire philosophy was shaped and nurtured in an expanding pioneer community. "The Far West had been the field of his early endeavors during a period when there was still a frontier, where a man had to win his own way, and there was almost complete economic freedom, and individual initiative had its opportunity." (316 U.S.

at xxi, xxii.) The son of an Indian attorney, Van Devanter attended De Pauw University and was graduated from Cincinnati Law School in 1881. After three years of private practice in Indiana, he moved to Cheyenne, in the territory of Wyoming. There young Van Devanter rose rapidly. At the age of twenty-seven he was appointed one of the commissioners to revise the Wyoming statutes. In 1887, he became city attorney of Cheyenne, and a year later he was elected to the territorial legislature. In 1889, at the age of thirty, he became chief justice of the Supreme Court of Wyoming. He resigned that post to engage in private practice, serving for many years as counsel for the Union Pacific Railroad and leading lumber, cattle, and irrigation companies. Throughout this period he was prominent in Republican party circles. In 1896, Van Devanter was a delegate to the Republican National Convention, and the next year, President McKinley appointed him Assistant Attorney General assigned to the Interior Department. In 1903, President Roosevelt named Van Devanter to a federal circuit court; seven years later, President Taft elevated him to the Supreme Court.

Although Van Devanter did not write a large number of opinions during his long tenure on the Court, he was a skilled and competent lawyer whose decisions are lucid, thorough, and well reasoned. He played a major role in the drafting of the Judges Bill of 1925, which is noted previously in the biographical sketch of Chief Justice Taft. It has been said that Van Devanter's most notable contribution to the work of the Court was made in conference, where his wide experience, his precise knowledge, his accurate memory, and his capacity for clear elucidation of precedent and principle, contributed in a remarkable degree to the disposition of the Court's business." (316 U.S. at xi.)

FRED M. VINSON (1890–1953). When President Truman named Vinson to the chief-justiceship in 1946, the Kentucky jurist had already held important posts in all three branches of the government as congressman, judge, wartime administrator, and cabinet officer. Vinson was born in a little town in Kentucky, where his father was the local jailer. Although the family was poor, young Vinson was sent to Centre College for both his undergraduate and law training. There he made an outstanding academic record. After admission to the bar, he practiced law in his home town; he also served as city attorney. In 1923, Vinson, an active Democrat, was elected to the House of Representatives, where he served, with the exception of one term, until 1938. In Congress, Vinson emerged as a key figure on the important Ways and Means Committee and won recognition as a leading authority on tax legislation. He abandoned his legislative career in 1938 to accept a judgeship on the federal Court of Appeals of the District of Columbia, but resigned from that in turn to become Director of Economic Stabilization during World War II. He subsequently held other posts of high responsibility, culminating in his appointment as Secretary of the Treasury in President Truman's cabinet. He was serving in that office when he was named to the Supreme Court.

Although Vinson was a thoroughly capable and patient Chief Justice, he is not generally regarded as an outstanding one. He emerged neither as the intellectual leader of the Court nor as an effective compromiser. "When the benefit of every doubt has been given to Vinson, it seems clear that his success as an integrating force on the Court was quite limited." [C. Herman Pritchett, *Civil Liberties and the Vinson Court* (Chicago: University of Chicago Press, 1954), p. 231.] Despite the fact that the Vinson majority was generally antilibertarian, Vinson's opinions in such cases as *Shelley* v. *Kraemer* and *Sweatt* v. *Painter* "are landmarks in the struggle to bring to all the equal protection of the laws." (349 U.S. at xv.)

MORRISON R. WAITE (1816–1888). Justice Frankfurter has written that the "memory of Waite is so enveloped in neglect that it may seem disproportionate to find his work comparable to that of Marshall and Taney. It may be granted that he did not have the stature of either,

but to deny him significance is to allow the pedestrianism of his opinions to obstruct understanding of a great judge. History ought not to reflect contemporary misjudgment, due in no small degree to Waite's lack of the grand manner, his total want of style. But the limited appeal of his opinions is due in part to something else—to fulfillment of one of the greatest duties of a judge, the duty not to enlarge his authority. Waite preeminently belongs to the tradition of judicial self-restraint." [Felix Frankfurter, *The Commerce Clause under Marshall, Taney and Waite* (Chapel Hill: University of North Carolina Press, 1937), pp. 76, 80, 81.] It was Waite's adherence to the principal of judicial self-restraint which led him to uphold the Granger legislation in his most famous opinion—*Munn* v. *Illinois*.

Waite was born in Connecticut and graduated from Yale. After reading law in his father's office, he moved to Ohio, where he became a successful Republican lawyer. Waite served one term in the Ohio legislature, but he was virtually unknown outside his adopted state when President Grant named him Chief Justice in 1874. Never highly regarded by some of his colleagues on the bench, Waite was not considered the intellectual equal of men like Miller, Bradley, and Field. "He failed to give the Court the energetic administrative leadership it needed in a period when litigants waited while Justices doddered. But his conceptions were sound, his patience and kindness invincible, and thus possibly he proved more acceptable than any one of his brethren would have been as Chief." [Charles Fairman, *The Bacon Lectures on the Constitution of the United States, 1940–1950* (Boston: Boston University Press, 1953), p. 454.]

Waite's important contributions to American constitutional law have been recently analyzed in a significant and readable biography. [See C. Peter Magrath, *Morrison R. Waite: The Triumph of Character* (New York: Macmillan, 1963).]

EARL WARREN (1891–   ). To future generations of students, Chief Justice Warren will probably be best known as the author of the historic opinions in the

Public School Segregation Cases, which were delivered during his first year on the Court. The son of a railroad worker, Warren was born in Los Angeles and took his law degree at the University of California in 1912. After his admission to the bar, Warren practiced law for a brief period and then embarked upon a successful public career. He first served as an assistant city and county attorney. In 1925, he became district attorney of Alameda County (Oakland), where he made a notable reputation as an honest and vigorous prosecutor of lawbreakers. In 1938, Warren was elected State Attorney General, and four years later he became governor of California. Warren ran for the governorship as a Republican, but he was reelected twice with the support of Democrats as well as Republicans. He was the only man ever elected to three successive terms as California Governor. Former President Truman, who often praised Warren, once remarked that "the facts of the case are that Warren is really a Democrat, but doesn't know it." [Quoted in James Bassett, " 'Unpartisan' Chief Justice of the United States," *The New York Times Magazine* (October 11, 1953), p. 20.] In 1948, Warren was the Republican vice-presidential candidate on the ticket headed by Thomas E. Dewey.

Although his political record was impressive, Warren had no prior judicial experience when President Eisenhower named him Chief Justice in 1953. Warren's major contribution on the Court appears to have been on the administrative side. He restored unity on the Court and, as an early commentator on the Warren Court noted, by 1957 he had already displayed greater eminence as an administrator than any court head since Hughes. And it was more a great statesman than a great common-law judge that the high bench needed after Hughes' retirement." [Bernard Schwartz, " 'Warren Court'—An Opinion," *The New York Times Magazine* (June 30, 1957), p. 11.] In addition, the opinions in this book reveal clearly that, unlike the Vinson Court, the Warren Court has become increasingly concerned with the protection of individual liberties. Under Warren's leadership, the Court has been moving dramatically toward a generally libertarian position. [Irving Dillard, "Warren and the New Supreme Court," *Harper's Magazine* (December 1955), p. 59.]

The general philosophy of constitutional liberty exemplified by the libertarian wing of the Warren Court is well delineated in Edmond Cahn (ed.), *The Great Rights* (New York: Macmillan, 1963).

Chief Justice Warren retired in June 1969.

BYRON R. WHITE (1917–   ). President Kennedy's first appointee to the Court was Byron R. White, who had helped Kennedy round up Colorado delegates at the National Democratic Convention and who had led the "Citizens for Kennedy" organization during the 1960 presidential campaign. Born in Colorado, White attended the University of Colorado, where he won distinction both as a student and athlete. (He was valedictorian of his class and an All-American football player in 1938.) After graduation, he went to Oxford University for a year as a Rhodes scholar. He served in the Navy during World War II and then obtained his law degree at the Yale Law School. After serving as law clerk to Chief Justice Fred M. Vinson, White began to practice law in Denver. In 1960, he was appointed Deputy Attorney General in the Kennedy administration, where he served until named to the Court. Although a liberal Democrat, White seems to be relatively reserved in espousing an "activist" role for the Court. White is the first law clerk to be named to the Court.

CHARLES E. WHITTAKER (1901–   ). President Eisenhower's fourth appointee to the Supreme Court was Charles Evans Whittaker—the first justice ever appointed from Missouri. Brought up on a farm in Kansas, young Whittaker quit school after the ninth grade to work on his father's farm. But a burning desire to study law took him to the Kansas City School of Law (now the University of Kansas City School of Law), where he earned his law degree while working as an office boy in a law office and completing his high school studies by private tutoring. He passed the Missouri bar examination and was admitted to practice in 1923. During the next thirty years, Whittaker developed into a highly successful corporation lawyer. Although a lifelong Republican, he was never very active in partisan politics. In 1954, President Eisenhower named him a federal district judge. Two years later, Whittaker was elevated to the United States Court of Appeals, where he served until named to the Supreme Court.

Whittaker retired from the bench in 1962 because of ill health. A thorough legal craftsman, Whittaker was sometimes in agreement with the civil libertarians on the Warren Court. However, as was early predicated, he was usually found with the Frankfurter judicial self-restraint bloc. [Daniel M. Berman, "Mr. Justice Whittaker: A Preliminary Appraisal," *Missouri Law Review,* Vol. 24 (1959), pp. 1–2.] The retirement of both Justices Whittaker and Frankfurter in 1962 and the subsequent appointments of Justices White and Goldberg by President Kennedy shifted the balance within the Supreme Court toward the Warren-Black "activist" bloc.

Appendix III
Selected Readings

I. The Supreme Court, the Constitution, and Constitutional Law

Abraham, Henry J. *Freedom and the Court*. New York: Oxford University Press, 1967.
———. *The Judicial Process*. New York: Oxford University Press, 1962.
Acheson, Patricia. *The Supreme Court, America's Judicial Heritage*. New York: Dodd, Mead, 1961.
Beard, Charles A. *The Supreme Court and the Constitution*. New York: Macmillan, 1912.
Beck, David W. *Decision at Law*. New York: Dodd, Mead, 1961.
Beth, Loren P. *Politics, The Constitution and The Supreme Court*. New York: Harper & Row, 1962.
Bickel, Alexander M. *The Least Dangerous Branch, The Supreme Court at the Bar of Politics*. Indianapolis: Bobbs-Merrill, 1962.
———. *Politics and the Warren Court*. New York: Harper & Row, 1965.
Black, Charles L., Jr. *The People and the Court*. New York: Macmillan, 1960.
Cahill, Fred V., Jr. *Judicial Legislation*. New York: Ronald Press, 1952.
Cahn, Edmond. *Supreme Court and Supreme Law*. Bloomington: Indiana University Press, 1954.
Carr, Robert K. *The Supreme Court and Judicial Review*. New York: Holt, Rinehart and Winston, 1942.
Corwin, Edward S. (ed.). *The Constitution of the United States of America,*

Analysis and Interpretation. Washington, D.C., Government Printing Office, 1953.

————. *The Constitution and What It Means Today*. 11th ed. Princeton: Princeton University Press, 1954.

————. *Court Over Constitution*. Princeton: Princeton University Press, 1938.

————. *The Doctrine of Judicial Review*. Princeton: Princeton University Press, 1914.

————. *The Twilight of the Supreme Court*. New Haven: Yale University Press, 1934.

Cox, Archibald. *The Warren Court*. Cambridge: Harvard University Press, 1968.

Crosskey, William W. *Politics and the Constitution in the History of the United States*. 2 vols. Chicago: University of Chicago Press, 1953.

Curtis, Charles P. *Law As Large As Life*. New York: Simon and Schuster, 1959.

————. *Lions Under the Throne*. Boston: Houghton, Mifflin, 1947.

Danelski, David. *A Supreme Court Justice Is Appointed*. New York: Random House, 1964.

Frank, John P. *Marble Palace*. New York: Knopf, 1958.

Frankfurter, Felix. *Of Law and Men, Paper and Addresses, 1939–1956*. Philip Elman (ed.). New York: Harcourt, Brace & World, 1956.

Frankfurter, Felix, and Landis, James M. *The Business of the Supreme Court*. New York: Macmillan, 1928.

Freund, Paul A. *On Understanding the Supreme Court*. Boston: Little, Brown, 1949.

————. *The Supreme Court of the United States, Its Business, Purposes, Performance*. Cleveland and New York: World, 1961.

Haines, Charles G. *The American Doctrine of Judicial Supremacy*. 2nd. ed. Berkeley: University of California Press, 1959.

————. *The Role of the Supreme Court in American Government and Politics, 1789–1835*. Berkeley and Los Angeles: University of California Press, 1944.

Haines, Charles G., and Sherwood, Foster H. *The Role of the Supreme Court in American Government and Politics, 1835–1864*. Berkeley and Los Angeles: University of California Press, 1957.

Harris, Robert J. *The Judicial Power of the United States*. Baton Rouge: Louisiana State University Press, 1940.

Hughes, Charles E. *The Supreme Court of the United States*. New York: Columbia University Press, 1928.

Hurst, Willard. *The Growth of American Law, The Law Makers*. Boston: Little, Brown, 1950.

Hyneman, Charles S. *The Supreme Court on Trial*. New York: Atherton Press, 1963.

Jackson, Robert H. *The Struggle for Judicial Supremacy*. New York: Knopf, 1941.

————. *The Supreme Court in the American System of Government*. Cambridge: Harvard University Press, 1955.

Krislov, Samuel. *The Supreme Court and Political Freedom*. New York: The Free Press, 1968.

Kurland, Philip. *Supreme Court Review*. Chicago: University of Chicago Press. Annually.

McBain, Howard L. *The Living Constitution*. New York: Workers Education Bureau Press, 1927.

McCloskey, Robert G. *The American Supreme Court*. Chicago: University of Chicago Press, 1960.

————. *Essays in Constitutional Law*. New York: Knopf, 1957.

McCune, Wesley. *The Nine Young Men*. New York: Harper & Row, 1947.

McDonald, Forrest. *We the People: The Economic Origins of the Constitution*. Chicago: University of Chicago Press, 1958.

Magrath, C. Peter. *Yazoo*. Providence: Brown University Press, 1966.

Mason, Alpheus T. *The Supreme Court from Taft to Warren*. Baton Rouge: Louisiana State University Press, 1958.

————. *The Supreme Court, Palladium of Freedom*. Ann Arbor: University of Michigan Press, 1962.

Mendelson, Wallace. *Capitalism, Democracy and the Supreme Court*. New York: Appleton-Century-Crofts, 1960.

Miller, Arthur S. *The Supreme Court and American Capitalism*. New York: Free Press, 1968.

Murphy, Walter F. *Congress and the Court*. Chicago: University of Chicago Press, 1962.

Peltason, Jack W. *Federal Courts in the Political Process*. Garden City, N.Y.: Doubleday, 1955.

Pfeffer, Leo. *This Honorable Court: A History of the Supreme Court of the United States*. Boston: Beacon Press, 1965.

Pollak, Louis. *The Constitution and the Supreme Court: A Documentary History*. 2 vols. Cleveland: World Publishing Co., 1966.

Pritchett, C. Herman. *The Political Offender and the Warren Court*. Boston: Boston University Press, 1958.

————. *Congress versus the Supreme Court*. Minneapolis: University of Minnesota Press, 1961.

————. *The Roosevelt Court*. New York: Macmillan, 1948.

Ramaswamy, M. *The Creative Role of the Supreme Court of the United States*. Stanford: Stanford University Press, 1956.

Read, Conyers (ed.). *The Constitution Reconsidered*. New York: Columbia University Press, 1938.

Rodell, Fred. *Nine Men: A Political History of the Supreme Court from 1790–1955*. New York: Random House, 1955.

Roettinger, Ruth L. *The Supreme Court and State Police Power*. Washington, D.C.: Public Affairs Press, 1957.

Rossiter, Clinton. *1787: The Grand Convention*. New York: Macmillan, 1966.

Rosenblum, Victor G. *Law As a Political Instrument*. Garden City, N.Y.: Doubleday, 1955.

Rostow, Eugene V. *The Sovereign Prerogative: The Supreme Court and the Quest for Law*. New Haven: Yale University Press, 1962.

Rottschaefer, Henry. *The Constitution and Socio-Economic Change*. Ann Arbor: University of Michigan Law School, 1948.

Schmidhauser, John R. *The Supreme Court: Its Politics, Personalities, and Procedures*. New York: Holt, Rinehart and Winston, 1960.

Schubert, Glendon. *Judicial Policy-Making*. Chicago: Scott, Foresman, 1965.

———— *The Judicial Mind: Attitudes and Ideologies of Supreme Court Justices*. Evanston, Ill.: Northwestern University Press, 1965.

Schwartz, Bernard. *American Constitutional Law*. Cambridge, England: Cambridge University Press, 1955.

―――. *A Commentary on the Constitution of the United States*. New York: Macmillan, 1963–. Multiple vols.

―――. *The Supreme Court*. New York: Ronald Press, 1957.

Selected Essays on Constitutional Law. 4 vols. Published under the auspices of the Association of American Law Societies. Brooklyn: Foundation Press, 1938. Vol. 5, 1963.

Shapiro, Martin. *Freedom of Speech, The Supreme Court and Judicial Review*. Englewood Cliffs, N.J.: Prentice-Hall, 1966.

―――. *Law and Politics in the Supreme Court*. New York: The Free Press, 1964.

―――. *The Supreme Court and Administrative Agencies*. New York: The Free Press, 1968.

――― (ed.). *The Supreme Court and Constitutional Rights*. Chicago: Scott, Foresman, 1967.

――― (ed.). *The Supreme Court and Public Policy*. Chicago: Scott, Foresman, 1969.

Sprague, John. *Voting Patterns of the United States Supreme Court*. Indianapolis: Bobbs-Merrill, 1968.

Sutherland, Authur. *Constitutionalism In America*. New York: Blaisdell Publishing Co., 1965.

Swisher, Carl B. *The Growth of Constitutional Power in the United States*. Chicago: University of Chicago Press, 1946.

―――. *The Supreme Court in Modern Role*. New York: New York University Press, 1958.

Warren, Charles. *The Supreme Court in United States History*. Boston: Little, Brown, 1928.

Westin, Allan F. (ed.). *The Anatomy of a Constitutional Law Case*. New York: Macmillan, 1958.

―――. *An Autobiography of the Supreme Court*. New York: Macmillan, 1963.

―――. *The Supreme Court: Views from Inside*. New York: W. W. Norton, 1961.

Wright, Benjamin F. *The Growth of American Constitutional Law*. Boston: Houghton Mifflin, 1942.

II. POLITICAL AND CIVIL RIGHTS

Abernathy, Glenn. *The Right of Assembly and Association*. Columbia: South Carolina University Press, 1961.

Barth, Alan. *The Loyalty of Free Men*. New York: Viking Press, 1951.

―――. *The Price of Liberty*. New York: Viking Press, 1961.

Becker, Carl L. *Freedom and Responsibility in the American Way of Life*. New York: Knopf, 1945.

Berns, Walter. *Freedom, Virtue, and the First Amendment*. Baton Rouge: Louisiana State University Press, 1957.

Blaustein, Albert P., and Ferguson, Clarence C., Jr. *Desegregation and the Law*. New Brunswick, N.J.: Rutgers University Press, 1957.

Boles, Donald E. *The Bible, Religion and the Public Schools*. Ames: Iowa State University Press, 1961.

Bontecou, Eleanor (ed.). *Freedom in the Balance: Opinions of Judge Henry W.*

Edgerton Relating to Civil Liberties. Ithaca, N.Y.: Cornell University Press, 1960.

Brant, Irving. *The Bill of Rights.* Indianapolis: Bobbs-Merrill, 1965.

Cahn, Edmond (ed.). *The Great Rights.* New York: Macmillan, 1963.

Carr, Robert K. *Federal Protection of Civil Rights: Quest for a Sword.* Ithaca, N.Y.: Cornell University Press, 1949.

Chafee, Zechariah, Jr. *The Blessings of Liberty.* Philadelphia: J. B. Lippincott, 1956.

————. *Documents on Fundamental Human Rights.* 3 vols. Cambridge: Harvard University Press, 1951.

————. *Free Speech in the United States.* Cambridge: Harvard University Press, 1942.

————. *How Human Rights Got into the Constitution.* Boston: Boston University Press, 1952.

Chase, Harold W. *Security and Liberty, the Problem of Native Communists, 1947–1955.* Garden City, N.Y.: Doubleday, 1955.

Commager, Henry S. *Freedom, Loyalty, Dissent.* New York: Oxford University Press, 1954.

Cook, Thomas I. *Democratic Rights versus Communist Activity.* Garden City, N.Y.: Doubleday, 1954.

Corwin, Edward S. *Liberty Against Government.* Baton Rouge: Louisiana State University Press, 1948.

Cushman, Robert E. *Civil Liberties in the United States.* Ithaca, N.Y.: Cornell University Press, 1956.

Dash, Samuel, Schwartz, Richard F., Knowlton, Robert E. *The Eavesdroppers.* New Brunswick, N.J.: Rutgers University Press, 1959.

Dilliard, Irving (ed.). *The Spirit of Liberty, Papers and Addresses of Learned Hand.* 3rd ed. New York: Knopf, 1960.

Dixon, Robert G., Jr. *Democratic Representation: Reapportionment in Law and Politics.* New York: Oxford University Press, 1969.

Douglas, William O. *An Almanac of Liberty.* Garden City, N.Y.: Doubleday, 1954.

————. *A Living Bill of Rights.* Garden City, N.Y.: Doubleday, 1961.

————. *The Right of the People.* Garden City, N.Y.: Doubleday, 1957.

Dumbauld, Edward. *The Bill of Rights and What It Means Today.* Norman: University of Oklahoma Press, 1957.

Emerson, Thomas I., Haber, David, and Dorsen, Norman. Political and Civil Rights in the United States (Boston: Little, Brown, 3rd ed., 1967).

Emerson, Thomas I. *Toward a General Theory of the First Amendment.* New York: Random House, 1966.

Fellman, David. *The Constitutional Right of Association.* Chicago: University of Chicago Press, 1963.

————. *The Defendant's Rights.* New York: Holt, Rinehart and Winston, 1958.

————. *The Limits of Freedom.* New Brunswick, N.J.: Rutgers University Press, 1959.

Fraenkel, Osmond K. *Our Civil Liberties.* New York: Viking Press, 1944.

————. *The Supreme Court and Civil Liberties.* New York: Oceana, 1960.

Freund, Paul. *Religion and the Public Schools.* Cambridge: Harvard University Press, 1965.

Gellhorn, Walter. *American Rights: The Constitution in Action.* New York: Macmillan, 1960.

————. *Individual Freedom and Governmental Restraints.* Baton Rouge: Louisiana State University Press, 1956.

Grant, James A. C. *Our Common Law Constitution.* Boston: Boston University Press, 1960.

Greenberg, Jack. *Race Relations and American Law.* New York: Columbia University Press, 1959.

Hand, Learned. *The Bill of Rights.* Cambridge: Harvard University Press, 1958.

Handlin, Oscar and Mary. *The Dimensions of Liberty.* Cambridge: Harvard University Press, 1961.

Hanson, Royce. *The Political Thickett: Reapportionment and Constitutional Democracy.* Englewood Cliffs, N.J.: Prentice-Hall, 1966.

Harris, Robert J. *The Quest for Equality: The Constitution, Congress and the Supreme Court.* Baton Rouge: Louisiana State University Press, 1960.

Howe, Mark De Wolfe. *Garden and the Wilderness. Religion and Government in American Constitutional History.* Chicago: University of Chicago Press, 1965.

Hudon, Edward. *Freedom of Speech and Press in America.* Washington, D.C.: Public Affairs Press, 1963.

Humphrey, Hubert H. (ed.). *School Desegregation: Documents and Commentaries.* New York: Thomas Crowell, 1964.

Javitz, Jacob K. *Discrimination—U.S.A.* New York: Harcourt, Brace & World, 1960.

Kalven, Harry. *The Negro and the First Amendment.* Columbus: Ohio State University Press, 1965.

Kauper, Paul G. *Civil Liberties and the Constitution.* Ann Arbor: University of Michigan Press, 1962.

————. *Frontiers of Constitutional Liberty.* Ann Arbor: University of Michigan Law School, 1956.

————. *Religion and the Constitution.* Baton Rouge: Louisiana State University Press, 1964.

Konvitz, Milton R. *The Constitution and Civil Rights.* New York: Columbia University Press, 1946.

————. *Expanding Liberties.* New York: Viking Press, 1966.

————. *Fundamental Liberties of a Free People: Religion, Speech, Press, Assembly.* Ithaca, N.Y.: Cornell University Press, 1957.

Konvitz, Milton R., and Leskes, J. *A Century of Civil Rights.* New York: Columbia University Press, 1961.

Kurland, Philip B. *Religion and the Law.* Chicago: Aldine Pub. Co., 1962.

Lasswell, Harold D. *National Security and Individual Freedom.* New York: McGraw-Hill, 1950.

Levy, Leonard. *Jefferson and Civil Liberties: The Darker Side.* Cambridge: Harvard University Press, 1963.

————. *Legacy of Suppression, Freedom of Speech and Press in Early American History.* Cambridge: Harvard University Press, 1960.

Lewis, Anthony. *Gideon's Trumpet.* New York: Random House, 1964.

Longaker, Richard P. *The Presidency and Civil Liberties.* Ithaca, N.Y.: Cornell University Press, 1961.

McGrath, John J. (ed.). *Church and State in American Law*. Milwaukee: Bruce Publishing Co., 1962.

McKay, Robert. *Reapportionment: The Law and Politics of Equal Representation*. New York: Twentieth Century Fund, 1965.

Manwaring, David R. *Render Unto Caesar, the Flag-Salute Controversy*. Chicago: University of Chicago Press, 1962.

Meiklejohn, Alexander. *Free Speech and Its Relation to Self-government*. New York: Harper & Row, 1948.

———. *Political Freedom: The Constitutional Powers of the People*. New York: Harper & Row, 1960.

Mendelson, Wallace. *Discrimination, Based on the Report of the United States Commission on Civil Rights*. Englewood Cliffs, N.J.: Prentice-Hall, 1962.

Newman, Edwin S. *The Freedom Reader*. New York: Oceana, 1955.

O'Brian, John L. *National Security and Individual Freedom*. Cambridge: Harvard University Press, 1955.

Peltason, Jack W. *Fifty-Eight Lonely Men, Southern Federal Judges and School Desegregation*. New York: Harcourt, Brace & World, 1961.

Perry, Richard L. *Sources of Our Liberties*. Chicago: American Bar Foundation, 1959.

Pfeffer, Leo. *The Liberties of an American*. Boston: Beacon Press, 1956.

Pound, Roscoe. *The Development of Constitutional Guarantees of Liberty*. New Haven: Yale University Press, 1957.

President's Committee on Civil Rights. *To Secure These Rights*. Washington, D.C.: Government Printing Office, 1947.

Preston, William Jr. *Aliens and Dissenters, Federal Suppression of Radicals*. Cambridge: Harvard University Press, 1963.

Prettyman, Barrett Jr. *Death and the Supreme Court*. New York: Harcourt, Brace & World, 1961.

Pritchett, C. Herman. *Civil Liberties and the Vinson Court*. Chicago: University of Chicago Press, 1954.

———. *The Political Offender and the Warren Court*. Boston: Boston University Press, 1958.

Rankin, Robert S., and Dallmayr, Winfried R. *Freedom and Emergency Powers in the Cold War*. New York: Appleton-Century-Crofts, 1964.

Record, Wilson and Jane C. (eds.). *Little Rock, U.S.A.* San Francisco: Chandler Publishing Co., 1960.

Roche, John P. *Courts and Rights, The American Judiciary in Action*. New York: Random House, 1961.

———. *The Quest for the Dream*. New York: Macmillan, 1963.

Rutland, Robert A. *The Birth of the Bill of Rights, 1776–1791*. Chapel Hill: University of North Carolina Press, 1955.

Sowle, Claude R. *Police Power and Individual Freedom*. Chicago: Aldine Publishing Co., 1962.

Stouffer, Samuel A. *Communism, Conformity and Civil Liberties*. Garden City, N.Y.: Doubleday, 1955.

Superintendent of Documents. *The Report of the United States Commission on Civil Rights*. Washington, D.C.: Government Printing Office, 1959.

Taper, Bernard. *Gomillion v. Lightfoot, The Tuskegee Gerrymander Case*. New York: McGraw-Hill, 1962.

Tresolini, Rocco J. *Justice and the Supreme Court.* Philadelphia: J. B. Lippincott, 1963.

Vose, Clement E. *Caucasians Only: The Supreme Court, the NAACP, and the Restrictive Covenant Cases.* Berkeley: University of California Press, 1959.

Westin, Alan. *Privacy and Freedom.* New York: Atheneum, 1967.

Whipple, Leon. *Our Ancient Liberties.* New York: H. W. Wilson Co., 1927.

————. *The Story of Civil Liberty in the United States.* New York: Vanguard Press, 1927.

Williams, Edward B. *One Man's Freedom.* New York: Atheneum, 1962.

III. Judicial Biography

Beveridge, Albert J. *The Life of John Marshall.* 4 vols. Boston: Houghton Mifflin, 1919.

Bickel, Alexander M. *The Unpublished Opinion of Mr. Justice Brandeis; The Supreme Court at Work.* Cambridge: Harvard University Press, 1957.

Bowen, Catherine Drinker. *Yankee from Olympus.* Boston: Little, Brown, 1945.

Christman, Henry M. (ed.). *The Public Papers of Chief Justice Earl Warren.* New York: Simon and Schuster, 1959.

Corwin, Edward S. *John Marshall and the Constitution.* New Haven: Yale University Press, 1919.

Countryman, Vern (ed.). *Douglas of the Supreme Court: A Selection of His Opinions.* Garden City, N.Y.: Doubleday, 1959.

Dilliard, Irving (ed.). *One Man's Stand For Freedom, Mr. Justice Black and the Bill of Rights.* New York: Knopf, 1963.

Dunham, Allison, and Kurland, Philip (eds.). *Mr. Justice.* Chicago: University of Chicago Press, 1956.

Ewing, Cortez A. M. *The Judges of the Supreme Court, 1789–1937.* Minneapolis: University of Minnesota Press, 1938.

Fairman, Charles. *Mr. Justice Miller and the Supreme Court.* Cambridge: Harvard University Press, 1939.

Frank, John P. *Mr. Justice Black: The Man and His Opinions.* New York: Knopf, 1949.

————. *Justice Daniel Dissenting, A Biography of Peter V. Daniel, 1784–1860.* Cambridge: Harvard University Press, 1964.

Frankfurter, Felix. *Mr. Justice Holmes and the Supreme Court.* Cambridge: Harvard University Press, 1938.

Gerhart, Eugene C. *America's Advocate: Robert H. Jackson.* Indianapolis: Bobbs-Merrill, 1957.

Fowler V. Harper. *Justice Rutledge and the Bright Constellation.* Indianapolis: Bobbs-Merrill, 1965.

Hendel, Samuel. *Charles Evans Hughes and the Supreme Court.* New York: King's Crown Press, 1951.

Howard, J. Woodford. *Mr. Justice Murphy: A Political Biography.* Princeton: Princeton University Press, 1968.

Howe, Mark DeWolfe. *Justice Oliver Wendell Holmes, The Shaping Years, 1841–1870.* Cambridge: Harvard University Press, 1957.

————. *Justice Oliver Wendell Holmes, The Proving Years, 1870–1882.* Cambridge: Harvard University Press, 1963.

Jacobs, Clyde E. *Justice Frankfurter and Civil Liberties.* Berkeley: University of California Press, 1961.

Jones, W. Melville (ed.). *Chief Justice John Marshall, A Reappraisal.* Ithaca, N.Y.: Cornell University Press, 1956.

King, Willard L. *Melville Weston Fuller.* New York: Macmillan, 1950.

Konefsky, Samuel J. *Chief Justice Stone and the Supreme Court.* New York: Macmillan, 1945.

————. *The Legacy of Holmes and Brandeis.* New York: Macmillan, 1956.

————. *John Marshall and Alexander Hamilton, Architects of the American Constitution.* New York: Macmillan, 1964.

Lerner, Max. *The Mind and Faith of Mr. Justice Holmes.* New York: Random House, 1943.

Levy, Leonard W. *The Law of the Commonwealth and Chief Justice Shaw.* Cambridge: Harvard University Press, 1957.

Lewis, Walker. *Without Fear or Favor: A Biography of Roger Brooke Taney.* Boston: Houghton Mifflin, 1965.

McLean, Joseph E. *William Rufus Day.* Baltimore: Johns Hopkins Press, 1946.

Magrath, C. Peter. *Morrison R. Waite: The Triumph of Character.* New York: Macmillan, 1963.

Marke, Julius J. (ed.). *The Holmes Reader.* New York: Oceana, 1955.

Mason, Alpheus T. *Brandeis—A Free Man's Life.* New York: Viking Press, 1956.

————. *Harlan Fiske Stone, Pillar of the Law.* New York: Viking Press, 1956.

————. *William Howard Taft—Chief Justice.* New York: Simon and Schuster, 1965.

Mendelson, Wallace. *Justices Black and Frankfurter: Conflict in the Court.* Chicago: University of Chicago Press, 1961.

Morgan, Donald G. *Justice William Johnson, The First Dissenter.* Columbia: University of South Carolina Press, 1954.

Norris, Harold. *Mr. Justice Murphy and the Bill of Rights,* 1966.

O'Brien, William. *Justice Reed and the First Amendment: The Religious Clauses.* Washington, D.C.: Georgetown University Press, 1958.

Paschal, Joel F. *Mr. Justice Sutherland: A Man Against the State.* Princeton: Princeton University Press, 1951.

Perkins, Dexter. *Charles Evans Hughes and American Democratic Statesmanship.* Boston: Little, Brown, 1956.

Phillips, H. B. (ed.). *Felix Frankfurter Reminisces.* New York: Reynal, 1960.

Pringle, Henry F. *The Life and Times of William Howard Taft.* 2 vols. New York: Farrar and Rinehart, 1939.

Pusey, Merlo J. *Charles Evans Hughes.* 2 vols. New York: Macmillan, 1951.

Schubert, Glendon. *The Dispassionate Justice: Judicial Opinions of Robert Jackson.* Indianapolis: Bobbs-Merrill, 1969.

Schwartz, M. D., and Hogan, J. C. *Joseph Story: A Collection of Writings by and About an Eminent American Jurist.* New York: Oceana, 1959.

Swisher, Carl B. *Roger B. Taney.* New York: Macmillan, 1935.

————. *Stephen J. Field.* Washington, D.C.: The Brookings Institute, 1930.

Thomas, Helen S. *Felix Frankfurter: Scholar on the Bench.* Baltimore: Johns Hopkins Press, 1960.

Alden L. Todd. *Justice on Trial: The Case of Louis D. Brandeis.* New York: McGraw-Hill, 1964.

Umbreit, Kenneth B. *Our Eleven Chief Justices: A History of the Supreme Court in Terms of Their Personalities.* New York: Harper & Row, 1940.

Warner, H. L. *The Life of Mr. Justice Clarke: A Testimony to the Power of Liberal Dissent in America.* Cleveland: Western Reserve University Press, 1959.

Williams, Charlotte. *Hugo L. Black, A Study in the Judicial Process.* Baltimore: Johns Hopkins Press, 1950.

INDEX